Peachpit Press

D0851568

The Mac Panther Bible

Christopher Breen • Emory
Christensen • John Christopher
Michael E. Cohen • Marty Cortinas
Cheryl England • Bart Farkas
Jim Felici • Kris Fong • Dan Frakes
Maria Langer • Owen W. Linzmayer
Tara Marchand • Scholle Sawyer
McFarland • David Morgenstern
Henry Norr • Jason O'Grady
Jonathan Oski • Joanna Pearlstein
Pamela Pfiffner • John Rizzo
Steve Schwartz • Terri Stone

9TH EDITION

The Macintosh Bible, 9th Edition

Edited by Cheryl England

Peachpit Press

1249 Eighth Street
Berkeley, CA 94710
(510) 524-2178
(800) 283-9444
(510) 524-2221 (fax)

Find us on the World Wide Web at: www.peachpit.com

Peachpit Press is a division of Pearson Education

Copyright © 2004 by Peachpit Press

Editors: Cheryl England, Clifford Colby, and Nancy Peterson
Production editor: Connie Jeung-Mills
Copy editor: Elissa Rabellino
Compositor: Owen Wolfson
Margin icons: Mimi Heft
Cover illustration: Bud Peen
Cover design: Gee+Chung Design
Indexer: Rebecca Plunkett

ISBN 0-321-21349-1

9 8 7 6 5 4 3 2 1

Printed and bound in the United States of America

Contents at a Glance

"Hello, I am Macintosh. I'm glad to be out of that bag."

*—The original 128K Mac announcing itself when Steve Jobs
unveiled it at Apple Computer's annual shareholders'
meeting in Cupertino, California, on January 24, 1984*

Table of Contents

1978	1979		1981	1982
Apple begins a game-machine project, code-named Annie. Apple Chairman Mike Markkula asks Jef Raskin head it up.	Raskin proposes creating an easy-to-use computer. He becomes manager of the renamed Macintosh project. The machine will ship in September 1981 and sell for $500.	Steve Jobs and other Apple employees visit Xerox PARC.	Steve Jobs takes charge of the Macintosh project.	Apple finishes the Macintosh enclosure design; the company inscribes signatures of Macintosh team members inside the case.

1984		1985		
Apple introduces the Macintosh with the "1984" commercial.	The Macintosh 128K sells for $2,495 and includes MacWrite and MacDraw.	Apple airs the "Lemmings" commercial. Unlike "1984," it flops.	Microsoft releases Word for the Mac.	Nashoba ships its FileMaker database.

				1986
Steve Wozniak leaves Apple.	Apple rolls out the first LaserWriter printer, and Aldus unveils PageMaker. The combo heralds the desktop-publishing revolution.	Steve Jobs leaves Apple to start NeXT.	Microsoft ships Excel; it's available only for the Mac.	Apple releases the Mac Plus, the first Mac with SCSI.

1986		**1987**		
Steve Jobs purchases Pixar from Lucasfilm.	Adobe releases its first fonts for the Mac.	The desktop-publishing revolution continues. Adobe Illustrator and QuarkXPress ship.	Apple introduces the Mac II, its first expandable Mac.	Microsoft releases the first version of Windows.

Chapter 3: The Macintosh Family **165**

	1988		**1989**	
Apple announces HyperCard.	NeXT unveils its first computer: a futuristic-looking black box with an optical drive and a super-high-resolution monitor.	Claris ships its first version of FileMaker after acquiring the database from Nashoba.	Apple rolls out the Macintosh Portable. At 15.8 pounds, it weighs more than the stationary workhorse Mac IIci (13.6 pounds), which also debuts in 1989.	NeXT releases NextStep OS (12 years later, Apple will use the NeXT OS as the foundation of its own Mac OS X).

1989	**1990**	**1991**		**1992**
Microsoft ships Office 1.0 for the Mac.	Adobe Photoshop 1.0 ships.	System 7 ships.	Apple unveils the PowerBook 100. Weighing 5.1 pounds, it is Apple's first real portable.	Apple releases QuickTime. Users are wowed by the ability to embed movies in even word-processing documents.

Chapter 4: Upgrades and Memory 235

Chapter 5: Storage 259

	1993			**1994**
Windows 3.1 ships. This time Microsoft gets it right.	Apple releases AppleScript.	The Apple board makes Michael Spindler CEO, replacing John Sculley, who leaves Apple in October.	Apple rolls out the first Newton MessagePad. The much-anticipated product turns out to be clunky and problem-plagued.	Apple announces its star-crossed attempt to rewrite its operating system, code-named Copland. The modern OS will ship mid-1995, Apple says.

1994				
Apple introduces the first PowerPC systems, the Power Macs. The Power Mac 6100, 7100, and 8100 use PowerPC 601 chips running at 60–80 MHz.	System 7.5 ships.	Netscape releases the first public beta of its "network navigator."	Apple introduces its first 100 MHz PowerPC machine, the Power Mac 8100/100.	Apple announces plans to license the Mac OS to third-party hardware vendors.

	1995			
Netscape releases Navigator 1.0.	Mac OS–licensee Power Computing ships the first Mac OS–compatible clone.	Apple demonstrates Copland and says the modern OS will be available in the middle of 1996.	Apple rolls out the first PCI-based Power Mac, the Power Mac 9500, with System 7.5.2.	Apple reports a "safety problem" with the PowerBook 5300 and halts production. Within a month, Apple resumes shipping the PowerBook 5300 and cuts its price.

1995	**1996**			
Apple releases OpenDoc 1.0, the company's dazzling but little-used and short-lived scheme for building applications from software components.	The Apple board makes Gilbert F. Amelio chairman and chief executive officer of Apple, replacing Michael Spindler.	Apple loses $740 million in its second quarter. The figure marks the low point in a bruising string of bad fiscal quarters.	Apple pushes back the release of Copland to mid-1997.	Microsoft ships the first version of Internet Explorer for Macintosh.

1997

Apple cancels the first developer release of Copland and decides instead to release its MIA operating system piecemeal in upcoming releases of the Mac OS.	Apple releases its first 200 MHz system, the Power Macintosh 9500/200.	Apple says it will buy NeXT Software for $400 million. Apple gets NeXT's operating system and Steve Jobs, NeXT's chairman and CEO.	At a grinding three-hour keynote address at the January Macworld Expo in San Francisco, Apple CEO Gilbert F. Amelio unveils Rhapsody, Apple's upcoming	operating system based on NeXT and Apple technologies. Apple says Rhapsody will be released to customers within 12 months.

Part 2: Getting Productive

Chapter 9: Personal and Business Applications **421**

1997

Macromedia acquires FutureWave Software, maker of FutureSplash, and rechristens the software Flash.	Apple rolls out the PowerBook 3400.	Apple lays off 2700 employees and pulls the plug on several of its technologies, including OpenDoc.	Apple ships its first 300 MHz system, the Power Mac 6500.	The Twentieth Anniversary Macintosh is ready to ship.

| Gilbert F. Amelio, Apple's chairman of the board and CEO, and Ellen Hancock, Apple's executive vice president of technology, resign. | Apple releases Mac OS 8. Users are outraged because the new OS uses Charcoal as the default system font. | At Macworld Expo in Boston, Bill Gates pledges Microsoft's support of Apple and shows it by investing $150 million in Apple. | Apple remakes the board of directors: Mike Markkula leaves; Larry Ellison joins the board. | Apple buys the assets of clone-vendor Power Computing, effectively putting an end to Apple's short-lived Mac OS licensing plan. |

1997

Steve Jobs becomes interim Apple CEO, or iCEO.	Apple debuts its "Think Different" commercial during the TV premiere of *Toy Story,* the animation produced by Pixar, which is owned by Steve Jobs.	Apple releases Rhapsody to software developers and reiterates that the new OS will ship to customers in 1998.	Apple unveils the first PowerPC G3 Power Macs.	Apple opens the Apple Store, its online e-commerce site.

Part 3: Getting Creative

		1998		
Apple says it has added the Mac OS compatibility environment (called the Blue Box) to Rhapsody.	Macromedia releases Dreamweaver.	Claris becomes FileMaker, Inc. The new company keeps the FileMaker Pro database and hands off ClarisWorks to Apple, which renames the software suite AppleWorks.	Apple pulls the plug on Newton handheld devices.	The iMac and the redesigned, stylish PowerBook G3 are announced.

1998		**1999**		
Apple rejiggers its OS strategy and abandons its Rhapsody plans. Instead, Apple announces Mac OS X, which will ship to customers in fall 1999, Apple says.	Mac OS 8.5 ships. An Apple engineering T-shirt declares that the new version "sucks less" than Mac OS 8.	Adobe releases InDesign, in a direct challenge to industry standard QuarkXPress.	The Blue-and-White Power Mac G3s and five colors of iMacs debut.	Apple ships its first 400 MHz system, with the new Power Macs.

Apple says Mac OS X will ship early in 2000.	Mac OS 8.6 ships.	The iBook, with AirPort wireless networking, is announced.	iMovie and Mac OS 9 ship.	Apple releases the first PowerPC G4-equipped system, the Power Mac G4.

2000

Steve Jobs shows off Mac OS X at Macworld Expo in San Francisco. Tells conventioneers Mac OS X will be available as a shrink-wrapped software product in the summer.

Jobs becomes Apple CEO. The "i" is dropped from his title at last.

Apple announces its first 500 MHz system with the latest round of Power Macs.

The Power Mac G4 Cube is announced.

2001

Apple releases the first of its Titanium PowerBook G4s, as well as its first 600 MHz and 700 MHz Power Mac G4s. The products are a hit.

| Apple releases iTunes and iDVD and says that Mac OS X will ship in March. | Apple ships Mac OS X, right on schedule. | The QuickSilver Power Mac G4s ship—Apple's first 800 MHz systems. | Mac OS X 10.1 is released. | The 5 GB iPod is introduced. |

Part 4: Extending Your Reach

2002				
Mac OS X becomes the default Mac OS on all new Macs.	Flat-panel iMacs debut with a 15-inch screen. iPhoto and the 14-inch iBook also debut.	QuickTime 6 is announced. The eMac is introduced for the education market.	.Mac launches. Apple fans are surprised at the charge for the services.	Apple's first retail store opens in New York City. By the end of the year, Apple will have 50 stores.

				2003
Apple breaks its previous speed limit when it ships dual-processor 1.25 GHz and 1 GHz G4 Power Macs.	Mac OS X 10.2, nicknamed Jaguar, ships at 10:20 p.m. on Friday, August 23.	Larry Ellison, CEO of software giant Oracle and Steve Jobs' pal, resigns from Apple's board of directors.	Apple announces that starting in 2003, new Macs will be able to boot only Mac OS X, effectively sounding the death knell for Mac OS 9.	Apple announces Safari, Keynote, and iLife, as well as AirPort Extreme.

2003

Apple introduces the world's first 17-inch notebook, as well as a tiny 12-inch PowerBook.	Former vice president Al Gore joins Apple's board of directors.	The iTunes music store launches. Over 1 million songs are downloaded in the first week.	iChat AV and iSight bring videoconferencing to the masses.	The first Power Mac G5s ship, with 1.6 GHz, 1.8 GHz, and 2 GHz processors.

			2004	
Apple releases mega-huge 20 GB and 40 GB iPods.	Mac OS X 10.3, nick-named Panther, ships at 8 p.m. on Friday, October 24.	The 20-inch iMac rounds out Apple's line of con-sumer Macs.	Apple announces iLife '04, which now includes GarageBand. New Macs come with iLife; every-one else has to ante up $49.	Apple ships the iPod mini in a shimmering array of cool colors.
The G4-based iBooks ship.				

Introduction

By Cheryl England

It was just over 20 years ago that Steve Jobs and John Sculley stood up in front of Apple's shareholders in Cupertino, California, and showed off the original Macintosh. The stunning "1984" commercial had aired the previous week, but no one outside of an elite few had actually seen the product. When the Mac introduced itself to the crowd, applause shook the auditorium—and Steve Jobs proved yet again to be a showman in the grand tradition of P. T. Barnum.

Flash forward to today. After a 20-year roller-coaster ride, the Mac has proved that it is here to stay. Steve Jobs is back at the helm, Apple is still introducing innovative products and services, and the show goes on. But while the Mac retains its friendly face, its capabilities are far more complex than anyone could have imagined back in 1984. We've moved from a black-and-white world where a mouse and icons were curiosities to a world where everyone can create their own video and music and then burn it all to a DVD for friends and family to enjoy.

But most of us need some help to take advantage of all these great capabilities—that's where *The Macintosh Bible* comes in. Now in its ninth edition, the *Bible* (as the editors and authors fondly call it) is designed to give you all the information you need to use your Mac's powers to their fullest. Whether you are new to the Mac or an old hand who perhaps wants to explore a new area, the *Bible* has something for you.

You'll find that the editors and authors who contributed to this edition as well as previous editions are some of the most prominent Mac experts around. And a lot of them know each other, which is important when you're working as a team to pull together a reference work this size. (Speaking of size, the *Bible* couldn't physically get one page larger or we would have had to make a second volume!) Short of the original Macintosh 128K team, we can't imagine a greater group of people to help you learn more about your Mac.

In This Book, You'll Find Out About ...

Mac OS X 10.3 (Panther) and earlier. Because Apple has made it clear that the future is Mac OS X, we've focused the entire ninth edition of *The Macintosh Bible* on Mac OS X. We do include information on Mac OS 9, but only as it relates to the Classic environment of Mac OS X. (The Classic environment lets you run Mac OS 9 inside of Mac OS X.)

Desktop and portable Macs. We'll give you the scoop on today's Macs as well as on the Macs of yesteryear.

All the other hardware. There's a lot more to Mac hardware than just the Mac itself. We'll look at all the other hardware available, from storage options to video cards to MIDI devices and more.

Software for the home and office. We'll let you know what's available and give you helpful advice for using it, whether it's a page-layout program, a spreadsheet, or a game.

Hot topics. Digital video, photos, music, and movies—it's Apple's iLife and beyond. Plus we'll guide you through what you need to know about the Internet today, how to set up a wireless network, and even how to get started creating your own Web page using any of several different methods.

Troubleshooting tips. Unfortunately, someday something's going to go wrong with your Mac. And when it does, here's the information you'll need to know to set it all right again.

What to Look For

A glance through the ninth edition of *The Macintosh Bible* will show some differences from—and similarities to—earlier editions.

Who wrote what. We've used a group of Mac experts to create the book. Each contributor was chosen because of his or her special knowledge in a particular subject area, such as video, games, or graphics. (Turn the page to see the bios of the sharp folks who helped write and edit this edition.) At the beginning of each chapter we note who the editor and writers are for that section. You'll see the initials of the people who wrote each section in the section heading or subheading (unless, of course, the chapter has only one editor/author).

Icons to help you find specific kinds of information. You can use the icons in the margins to spot hot tips, general good-to-know information about a topic, and warnings. Here are the three types of icons you'll see:

 Hot Tip. When you see this icon, you'll find next to it a piece of advice, a bit of insight, or some sort of information that will make your computing life a little easier.

 FYI. This icon points to a bit of information that's just good to know, whether it's a bit of Mac history, trivia, or something that will increase your Mac knowledge.

 Warning. Take heed—paying attention to these icons will keep you out of trouble (well, Mac trouble, anyway).

Interviews. To celebrate the 20th anniversary of the Mac, we interviewed 20 of the key people responsible for the success of the original Macintosh. Some of these folks worked on the Macintosh team at Apple, while others developed some of the first software for the platform. We asked them what it was like to work on the Mac back then and what they think of the Mac today. We predict you'll be surprised, amused, and charmed by their answers.

About each chapter. Each editor had a free hand in determining how to approach the topics he or she was responsible for, as long as the most important things about each topic were covered. Generally, though, each chapter includes a basic introduction to the topic, pointers to products you should know about in the category, and tips and advice to make your life easier. The chapter introductions and tables of contents will give you an overview of what each editor decided to highlight.

We've included an index and glossary in the back of the book. We try to explain Macintosh terms the first time they come up, but come on—who knows what order you're going to read the chapters in, and we can't define each term each time (or the book would have to be done in two volumes!). So if you come across a term you're not familiar with, head to the glossary and index.

Finally, when we discuss a product, we include its price and company's Web address. However, Web addresses, prices, and version numbers are like San Francisco bus schedules: they change all the time. We checked everything right before we sent the book to the printer, but with all the products we talk about in this book, we are pretty sure that *something* will have changed by the time you read this.

Companion Web site. We'll provide periodic news, updates, and tips to keep this edition up-to-date. Check out www.macbible.com for *Macintosh Bible* updates.

Editors and Contributors

Christopher Breen (CB) has been writing about the Macintosh since the latter days of the Reagan administration for such magazines as *MacUser*, *MacWEEK*, and *Macworld*. Currently a contributing editor for *Macworld*, he pens the magazine's popular "Mac 911" tips and troubleshooting column. He appears each month in "Breen's Bungalow," a video tutorial included on the CD bundled with newsstand copies of *Macworld*. He's also the author of the best-selling book *Secrets of the iPod* (Peachpit Press, 2003).

Emory Christensen (EC) has been a Mac guy since 1987 when a friend brought home a Fat Mac from college. Currently a freelance copywriter, he started his career in the early 1990s at a daily newspaper where he quickly became the paper's Mac guru, moving the publication to digital layout using a bunch of Mac IIcis and Quadras. His current passion is long-distance wireless networking.

John Christopher (JC) is a data-recovery engineer at DriveSavers in Novato, California. For the past nine years he has retrieved data from drives and other storage devices that have crashed and burned (sometimes literally). Some of John's celebrated recoveries include the hard drives of writers and producers for *The Simpsons* and *Sex and the City,* band members from the group Nine Inch Nails, and others. John has also written for various publications, including *MacUser*, *Macworld*, *Tidbits*, and *MacHome Journal,* and was a contributing editor for prior editions of *The Macintosh Bible*.

Michael E. Cohen (MEC) has been doing unspeakable things with the Macintosh since the days of the Mac XL. He has produced and programmed multimedia titles for the Voyager Company and Calliope Media, and helped found the Center for Digital Humanities at the University of California, Los Angeles, where he produced esoteric multilingual instructional multimedia. He has been a contributing editor for two previous editions of *The Macintosh Bible,* and he has published numerous articles for both general and academic audiences. A pioneer in instructional-software development, he created the Homer style-analysis program, which was the only piece of software ever published by the house that published Hemingway, Fitzgerald, and Faulkner. He still owns the memory board from his Apple Lisa and remembers reading *Inside Macintosh* when it was in loose-leaf notebooks.

Clifford Colby (CC) is an executive editor at Peachpit Press and has worked at a handful of now-dead computer magazines, including *eMediaWeekly*, *MacWEEK*, *MacUser*, and *Corporate Computing*. For several years, he worked at the White House.

Marty Cortinas (MC) is a San Francisco–based editor and writer currently spending much of his time editing the Wired News Web site. He's covered the Mac professionally since 1993. During baseball season, he can be found rooting for the Giants in Section 105.

Cheryl England (CE) has been using a Mac since 1984, when she traded in WordStar for MacWrite. Since then, Cheryl has worked in senior editorial roles at *Personal Computing*, *Macworld*, and *MacUser* magazines and was the founding editor (and later publisher) for *MacAddict* magazine. She has also worked as director of marketing and PR for Canto Software and acted as editorial director for the redesign of *macHOME* magazine. In her spare time, Cheryl can be found running on the trails of the San Francisco Bay Area, walking her dogs on the beach, or scuba diving.

Bart G. Farkas (BF) is the author of more than 60 books, including *The Macintosh Bible Guide to Games* (Peachpit Press, 1995), and many computer and strategy guides for video games ranging from Warcraft III to Wing Commander. Bart lives with his wife and three children (four if you include the fuzzy one) in the icy climes of Cochrane, Alberta, Canada.

Jim Felici (JF) has been using a Mac since before there was such a thing (not officially, at least), starting back in 1983. He was a member of the start-up teams of *Macworld* and *Publish* magazines and served for years as "The Mac Advisor" for *Computer Currents*. He's written several books about electronic publishing and typography, the latest being *The Complete Manual of Typography* (Adobe Press, 2002). He now works as a freelance writer and editor from his home among the grapevines in southern France.

Kris Fong (KF), former computerphobe, was introduced to Macs in the early 1990s while recording with a band at Fantasy Studios in Berkeley, California. She wound up buying a Mac to do her own engineering and later branched out into digital photography and video editing. She won a Telly Award for music she wrote and recorded for a CNET commercial, and also won a Maggie Award for her technology writing. She has worked as an editor at *digitalFOTO*, *Digital Musician*, and *Music & Audio* magazines, and currently is senior editor at *MacAddict* magazine.

Lucian Fong (LF) is a Southern California native who has been writing creatively since the second grade. He discovered journalism in high school and eventually became the editor in chief of the school newspaper. While in college, Lucian joined the Inside Mac Games Web site as a news reporter to pass his free time. He continues to contribute to IMG as the hardware editor while he works toward completing his communications degree at California State Polytechnic University, Pomona.

Dan Frakes (DF) is an editor at MacFixIt.com and a contributing editor and columnist for *Macworld* magazine. He is the author of *Mac OS X Power Tools* (Sybex, 2004) and a contributor to *Mac OS X Disaster Relief* (Peachpit Press, 2003) and *Ted Landau's Mac OS X Help Desk* (Peachpit Press, 2004). He is also an author for TidBITS' "Take Control" series and contributes to the TidBITS electronic newsletter. He is a frequent speaker at Mac-related events and trade shows, has worked as a programmer/analyst supporting Macs at a major university, and has been a volunteer "ListMom" for some of the largest Mac mailing lists on the Internet.

Greg Kramer (GK) lives and works in Washington, D.C. He has served as an editor of Inside Mac Games and *MacSense* magazine, and has contributed to *MacAddict* and *MacHome Journal* magazines. He is the author of more than two dozen strategy guides for Prima Games and BradyGames.

Maria Langer (ML) is the author of dozens of Macintosh books and has been using a Macintosh since 1989, when her Macintosh IIcx running System 6.0.3 with MultiFinder was the hot new system. She uses her Mac for everything from writing to hosting Web sites to managing the finances of her helicopter tour business. Visit her on the Web at www.marialanger.com.

Owen W. Linzmayer (OL) is a San Francisco–based user-interface designer and freelance writer who has contributed to every major Apple II and Macintosh publication. He has also authored four Mac-related books, including *Apple Confidential 2.0: The Definitive History of the World's Most Colorful Company* (No Starch Press, 2004).

Tara Marchand (TM) works in educational technology at the University of California, San Francisco, School of Medicine, where she employs the tools and techniques described in this chapter to support and enhance the medical school curriculum. She's developed Web sites on the Mac since the mid-'90s but reluctantly uses Windows at her current job. Because she's a Virgo, Tara's happiest when her graphics and code are lean and pristine.

Scholle Sawyer McFarland (SSF) started as an editor at *MacUser* magazine way back in 1996. Currently she lives in lovely Portland, Oregon, and works remotely as a senior editor for *Macworld* magazine. She also teaches journalism at Clark College, where her students use QuarkXPress and Adobe Photoshop to spread the news.

David Morgenstern (DM) is the West Coast editor of eWEEK.com and a contributing editor for Creativepro.com. In 1986, David bought his first Mac, a modified Mac 512Ke (Fat Mac). He attended the meetings of the Berkeley Mac User Group (BMUG), which evangelized the Mac's then-unique user interface and applications. He worked the group's help desk for years and wrote a support column, before becoming chairman of the board. Later, David honed his editorial skills at *MacWEEK* and its successor, *eMediaWeekly*. He has also worked at several Silicon Valley startups in the color-calibration, high-end display, and Internet video fields.

Henry Norr (HN) has been a Mac user since 1985. He was once editor of *MacWEEK* magazine. He has also worked for the MacInTouch Web site and for the *San Francisco Chronicle*.

Jason O'Grady (JOG) got his first Macintosh in 1984 and has never looked back. He started O'Grady's PowerPage (www.powerpage.org) in 1995 as a support forum for PowerBook users; the site has since grown to become the definitive source for PowerBook information on the Web. Jason has written for *MacWEEK*, *Macworld*, *MacAddict*, and *MacPower* (Japan) magazines and was a contributing editor to the eighth edition of *The Macintosh Bible*. When he's not geeking out with new gadgets, you can find him wakeboarding or snowboarding (depending on the season) in and around eastern Pennsylvania.

Jonathan A. Oski (JO) is a manager of Network Engineering for State Street Corporation, a leading international financial services organization based in Boston, Massachusetts. He was sucked into the Steve Jobs vortex in early 1984 and has never escaped. He's been a contributing editor for the MacInTouch Web site and *MacWEEK*, and a contributor to *Macworld* and prior editions of *The Macintosh Bible*. When he's not hunkered down over his Mac, he enjoys tennis, skiing, his family, and coaching youth lacrosse.

Joanna Pearlstein (JP) is an editor at *Wired* magazine. She has written or edited articles for *The New York Times*, *Red Herring*, *LOOP* magazine (Japan), *MacWEEK*, and CNET.com. She wrote *Macworld*'s first feature article about online services (hello, GEnie and eWorld!), and as a college student she worked replacing bum logic boards of Mac SEs and Classics. Her scariest computer experience, other than a year with Windows NT, was adding RAM to a Mac Portable.

Pamela Pfiffner (PP) is the editor in chief and founder of Creativepro.com, an online resource for creative professionals. Her career in publishing encompasses print, the Web, and television. She has been editor in chief of *MacUser* and *Publish* magazines. In 1997 she launched the dynamic-media Web site of the cable television station ZDTV (now TechTV). She writes, teaches, and speaks regularly about technology and tools for designers. Her books include *Adobe Master Class: Photoshop Compositing with John Lund* (Adobe Press, 2003) and *Inside the Publishing Revolution: The Adobe Story* (Adobe Press, 2003), which was named Book of the Year by *Design, Type & Graphics* magazine.

Michael Phillips (MP) is a Mac zealot who's spent the last four years covering the Mac gaming scene. He has worked as a senior editor at the Inside Mac Games Web site, as well as being news editor at the MacGamer Web site.

John Rizzo (JR), a former staff editor for *MacUser* magazine, now writes about Mac hardware and software for CNET.com and for various Mac magazines. He also publishes MacWindows, a news and information Web site devoted to helping Mac users get along in a Windows world. His books include *Mac Toys* (John Wiley & Sons, 2004) and *Macintosh Windows Integration* (Morgan Kaufmann, 1999), and he has contributed to several previous editions of *The Macintosh Bible*. John bought his first Mac in 1984; he still has it in his garage somewhere.

Steve Schwartz (SS) is the author or coauthor of many books on popular Mac business applications, including *Microsoft Office v.X: Visual QuickStart Guide* (Peachpit Press, 2002), *Running Office 2001* (Microsoft Press, 2001), *FileMaker Pro 6 Bible* (John Wiley & Sons, 2003) and *AppleWorks 6 Bible* (IDG Books, 2000), in addition to a slew of books on games and Windows programs. Steve and his sons live in the fictional town of Lizard Spit, Arizona. To find out more about him (or to join in on the unending discussions about the miserable desert heat), visit his Web site at www.siliconwasteland.com.

Jonathan Seff (JS) is a senior associate editor at *Macworld* magazine and has been using Apple computers since the late 1980s, with the 1 MHz Apple IIe. Besides *Macworld* and Macworld.com, his articles have appeared in *Wired*, the *San Francisco Examiner,* PC World.com, *SF Weekly,* CNN.com, VH1.com, and *New City* (Chicago). He also has appeared on TechTV and CBS radio as a Mac expert.

Terri Stone (TS) is the senior how-to editor at *Macworld* magazine. She has also been an editor at *Publish* and *Mix* magazines and was a coauthor of *Web Design Studio Secrets*, 2nd Edition (IDG Books Worldwide, 2000).

Corey Tamas (CT) is a Canadian expert on games for the Macintosh. He writes for *macHOME* magazine, is full-time editor in chief of the MacGamer Web site, and can backwards rocket jump up to the Quad on Quake map DM17.

David Weiss (DW) is a writer and editor (www.davidweiss.net) living in Oakland, California, who's reviewed so many printers that he dreams in CMYK. He's worked as a senior editor at *Macworld* magazine and as the editor of *MacHome Journal*, and still contributes to both publications. His articles have also appeared in *MacAddict*, the newsletter *Step-By-Step Digital Design*, and the O'Reilly Network (www.oreillynet.com).

Jean Zambelli (JZ) began her career in the late 1980s in Boston, typesetting monographs and academic journals for Harvard University and the Massachusetts Institute of Technology. Her other monumental typography projects include converting Grolier's encyclopedias from Linotype typesetting with hot-metal printing to Mac templates with matching digital fonts. She lives in Palo Alto, California, with her husband, Mark, and two little girls, Isabel and Georgia (not necessarily named after typefaces).

Part 1

Looking at
the Mac

1

Working with Your Mac

Emory Christensen is the chapter editor and author.

David Reynolds was the chapter editor and author for the 8th edition of **The Macintosh Bible,** *from which portions of this chapter are taken.*

Welcome to the Macintosh.

Mac users fall into a few different categories: those who are new to computers altogether, those who are new to the Mac (but have used other computers), and longtime Mac devotees. New users should learn everything they need to know to get up and running, and even old hands will pick up some valuable tidbits throughout this book.

In this chapter we'll go over the basics of working with your Mac—what the various onscreen items are and how to manipulate them—and then we'll go over some tips on using the Mac OS X Finder. But first, a little orientation is in order. Without it, you may wonder why in the world anyone would design a computer to work this way. There are good reasons, and they're grounded in the history of the Macintosh.

Back in 1984, when the Macintosh first hit the scene, there was nothing else like it. While other computers required you to learn arcane text commands, the Macintosh used an easy-to-understand system of folders, files, and menus. You didn't have to be a rocket scientist to accomplish amazing things with a Mac. But that was two decades ago, and the Macintosh interface has now caught on with nearly every computer and operating-system maker out there. Now almost every computer sold   whether it's running Windows, Unix, or Macintosh—has its own graphical user interface with files, folders, and menus. When you can't beat 'em, join 'em.

Still, the Macintosh is, in our humble opinion, the best combination of hardware (the physical Macintosh) and software (the Macintosh operating system) on the market. Compared with PCs running Windows (or Unix, for that matter), the Macintosh is far more elegant, easy to use, and creatively powerful.

In This Chapter

The Big Picture

Although it comprises only a small minority of the computing world, the Macintosh has served as the inspiration for how people work with their computers—including the various flavors of Windows installed on most PCs today.

 Although the Mac is often credited as the first computer to use a mouse, windows, and menus, it's not. The idea was first conceived long before the Mac, but it was the first computer to fully realize those ideas in a commercially successful consumer computer.

The Mac has gone through a series of big changes since its introduction nearly 20 years ago—in terms of both the operating system and the hardware it runs on. Since 1984, Macintosh hardware has been based on ten different microprocessors (grouped into two major families), and the Mac operating system has been through the same number of major versions—currently standing at Mac OS X 10.3 (Panther). (The *X* is the Roman numeral 10, so the operating system's name is pronounced "Mac OS ten.")

Mac hardware went through one major transition back in the mid-1990s, with the switch from the Motorola 680x0 processor family to the PowerPC processor family. During the transition, software for the Mac hit some temporary compatibility problems—that is, it didn't work as fast or as well on newer hardware as it did on older hardware, and sometimes it didn't work at all. Once new, rewritten software came out, though, those compatibility issues went away, and the new software was able to take good advantage of the new hardware. Currently the Mac is going through a second (more minor) transition, to 64-bit processing with the PowerPC G5 processor (see Chapter 3). This time, however, there are very few compatibility problems caused by the hardware switch.

The reason this is important is that we're at the tail end of a similar big transition on the software side. The Macintosh's operating-system software has been going through a major transition since 2000. With the release of Mac OS X in 2001, the Macintosh experience changed drastically. Mac OS X was an entirely different operating system than its predecessor, Mac OS 9, and software that was written with the older version in mind had to run in a compatibility mode to work. The whole thing was like some sort of brain transplant with the catch that the new OS had to be able to think like the old one, too.

Mac OS 9 and Classic

Until recently, Macs could start up in either Mac OS 9 or Mac OS X, but the newest machines can start up only in Mac OS X; Mac OS 9 is available only in a special compatibility mode, called the *Classic environment*. So with that in mind, we'll largely refer to Mac OS X as the operating system of choice, with mentions of Mac OS 9 referring mostly to the Classic environment. To go into Classic mode, Mac OS X starts up Mac OS 9 inside itself, and it runs older software on that. Software that doesn't need the Classic mode is referred to as *Mac OS X–native* software.

Things may look and act a little different, depending on the mode your Mac is in. If every bit of software you run is a newer Mac OS X–native version, you won't see the Classic environment at all, and in fact you can remove all the Mac OS 9–compatibility software from your Mac's hard drive.

If, however, you're running a couple of older applications that were written for Mac OS 9 or earlier, you'll encounter both Mac OS 9 and Mac OS X user-interface elements (such as windows and menus). Confusing, yes, but necessary. Mac OS 9 and the Classic environment will be covered in depth in Chapter 2, but it helps to be prepared now, as we plunge into getting familiar with your Mac.

So how do you tell which mode your Mac is in? The program you're running at the moment determines this—whether it's an older Mac OS 9 program or a newer Mac OS X program. Here are a few simple characteristics:

Mac OS X mode (native). The menu bar is white with faint gray horizontal pinstripes. The Apple in the upper-left corner of the screen is blue. The windows have round red, yellow, and green buttons in the upper-left corner, and an oblong light gray button in the upper-right corner. The scrollers are blue and rounded, and the whole interface looks, as Steve Jobs once said, "lickable." Default buttons and all folders are also blue, and everything has a liquidy feel—which is why the interface is called Aqua.

Mac OS 9 mode (the Classic environment). The menu bar and everything else is a shade of gray that Apple called Platinum. The apple in the upper-left corner of the screen is the company's older logo and is composed of multicolored horizontal stripes. The windows have one box in the upper-left corner and two boxes in the upper-right corner. The scrollers are gray with squared corners.

With these elements in mind, let's dive into the basics of working with your Mac: how to make sense of the icons, pointers, menus, and windows; how to open and close documents; and what makes your Mac that special and lovable machine that it is.

The Macintosh Desktop

Whether you're running a brand-new Mac with the latest version of Mac OS X installed or you're using an older Mac with Mac OS 9 or earlier, you see the same basic thing when you start up your Mac—the famed Macintosh Desktop. Macs use the desktop metaphor to provide a familiar setting—a desk, essentially—in which Mac users can command their machines. At its heart the Macintosh Desktop works a lot like a desk in the real world. It has a space where you open folders and work with documents, as well as storage areas where you can organize your documents in folders. You can also use those storage areas to hold other devices that help you do your work, such as a calculator, a spreadsheet, or even a CD or DVD player when it's time to goof off.

While this desk metaphor is still at the heart of using a Macintosh, it's grown far beyond the confines of simply emulating file drawers and paper clip trays. These days, you can do a lot more on your Mac's Desktop than just open memos and spreadsheets. Digital video, photographs, and music all sit on the virtual desktop, ready for you to try your hand at digital wizardry. Try *that* with your solid-oak roll-top desk. (And if you're ready to get rid of it, give me a call—and a good price.)

On the Macintosh, a specialized program called the *Finder* creates the Desktop. The Finder is so named because it helps you find and work with your files—but that's not all it does. Besides maintaining a place where you can work, the Finder opens folders (showing you what's inside), launches the right program when you open a file, and lets you organize your work space by moving things around. The Finder also manages windows and can even send a few commands to the system software—for example, telling it to shut down.

 If you want the Finder to be the active application so that the Finder menus appear at the top of the Desktop, simply click the Desktop.

Anatomy of the Mac OS X Desktop

In a freshly installed version of Mac OS X, the Desktop contains some key items (which we'll go over in detail throughout this chapter). The Mac OS X Desktop has many of the same elements as the one in Mac OS 9 and earlier, such as hard-drive icons, a Trash icon, a menu bar with a clock, menus, and a pointer, but it also has a feature with no real equivalent in previous Mac OSs— the Dock. In Mac OS X the multitalented Dock hangs out at the bottom or on one side of the screen and keeps track of what programs are running. It also serves as a handy place to put shortcuts to programs, folders, and documents. You can change some system settings here, and it even serves as a resting place for minimized windows. We'll be covering the Dock in more detail later in the chapter.

Here's a closer look at some of the key elements on the Mac OS X Desktop (**Figure 1.1**):

- **Pointer**—Your virtual "hand"; it allows you to manipulate icons, menus, and windows.

- **Hard drive**—Where your documents and programs are stored.

- **Optical disc**—Signifies a CD or DVD, which can contain files, programs, movies, or music.

- **Dock**—Easy access point for programs, documents, and folders.

- **Menu bar**—A bar across the Desktop's top that contains commands (based on the active application) you can issue.

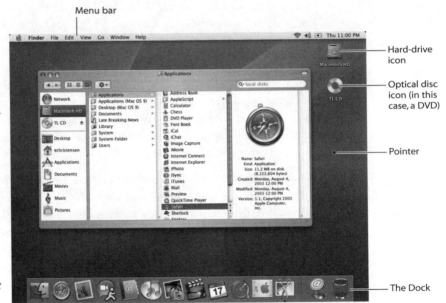

Menu bar

Hard-drive icon

Optical disc icon (in this case, a DVD)

Pointer

The Dock

Figure 1.1

The Mac OS X Desktop prominently features the Dock, the Mac's hard drive, any CDs or DVDs in the optical drive, a pointer, and a menu bar. The Desktop can also be home to icons for files, folders, aliases, clippings, or applications, if you've put them there.

Before the final edition of the first version of Mac OS X was released, the Desktop was more of a backdrop—it didn't play home to icons in the same way as it does now. As Mac OS X developed, Apple added the Mac OS 9–like ability to show hard drives, CDs, DVDs, and other icons on the Desktop.

The Mac OS 9 Desktop

The Desktop has been around since the original Macintosh. But the Mac OS 9 Desktop is different from the Mac OS X Desktop in a few ways—and its folder is even located in a different place on the hard drive.

Those used to Mac OS 9 (or able to start up in Mac OS 9) will notice some differences; the Mac OS 9 Desktop doesn't show up in Mac OS X when the Classic environment is running, although the menu bars and windows do. Here are some key ways in which the Mac OS 9 Desktop differs from that of Mac OS X:

*   The Trash is an icon on the Desktop.
*   There is no Dock.
*   The Finder's menu bar shows different menu options (this is also visible to those using the Classic environment under certain circumstances).

The Varied and Talented Pointer

The mouse pointer—usually in the shape of a small black arrow—is the little graphical doodad onscreen that connects the mouse to your Macintosh's software. When you move the mouse, the pointer moves along with it. With this powerful tool you can move files or folders around, select menu items and commands, rearrange and resize windows, and use buttons. In other words, you can pretty much do anything you *wouldn't* do by typing on a keyboard. It's known as a *pointer* mostly because you point at things with it. Of course, you can do a lot more than just point, but you get the idea.

Although the pointer (occasionally also called a *cursor*) looks like an ordinary arrow in its default stage, it is much more. Here are a few of the things you can do with the pointer:

*   Select and move icons
*   Select text, portions of a picture, or video and audio clips from a longer movie or audio file
*   Choose menu commands
*   Drag and drop text
*   Control motion in games

The pointer moves whenever you move your Mac's mouse (or run your finger over its trackpad, if you're using a PowerBook or iBook). Move the mouse left, and the pointer moves left. Move the mouse away from you, and the pointer moves up. Think of it as your virtual hand inside your Mac.

Types of Pointers

Figure 1.2

You'll probably encounter the arrow (left), spinning wait, and I-beam pointers most often.

Depending on the habitat in which the pointer finds itself, it can change its shape to suit its surroundings and tell you what you can do with it at any given moment. The pointer can take *lots* of different shapes. Besides the arrow, it can appear as an I-beam, a wristwatch, a spinning beach ball, or a swirling rainbow disc. Here's a look at the most common pointers you might encounter—they appear in Mac OS X and in Mac OS 9 (and earlier) unless otherwise indicated (**Figure 1.2**):

You may not see all the possible pointers, so unless you have a scorecard and a penchant for collecting, don't worry if a few of these look unfamiliar.

Arrow. This is the pointer in its natural form, the arrow. The arrow pointer is the one you use to select menu items, move icons, and click items in the Dock.

Hand. The hand pointer appears largely in applications running in the Classic environment or when you're running Mac OS 9 (although it can appear in Mac OS X). It provides a way of grabbing and moving the contents of a window.

Spinning pointer. The spinning pointer resembles a small black-and-white beach ball. Its job is to tell you that your Mac is busy doing something for a moment—a lot like the wristwatch (see below). It appears in the Classic environment or when you're running Mac OS 9.

Wristwatch. The wristwatch provides another way for your Mac to say "Hold on a sec—I'm busy." Usually the wristwatch will go away in short order. And even though Mac OS X is a fully multitasking system, sometimes individual programs need a little time to work things out.

I-Beam. Your pointer turns into an I-beam—a vertical line with small horizontal lines at the top and bottom and a tiny horizontal line through the middle—when it is over text that you can select or edit. Click that spot and a flashing plain vertical line (the insertion point) appears there.

Spinning wait pointer. This rainbow-colored spinning disc is the Mac OS X version of the wristwatch. It means that Mac OS X is busy and you can't work in whatever program brings it up. And occasionally it indicates that the whole system has become unresponsive. Because Mac OS X has *preemptive multitasking* (which means that Mac OS X manages how much time each application uses and is therefore more responsive to your clicks, not locking you out of using your Mac while it's thinking), you can usually move into a different program and continue working while Mac OS X works things out. You won't see this pointer if you've booted Mac OS 9, but if you're in the Classic environment, you may still see it.

Hot Spots

Pointers have a special region called a *hot spot*. This is the teeny, tiny part of the pointer where the action takes place when you click the mouse button. For example, the hot spot for the arrow is right at the tip, not at the base—which is not surprising. For the I-beam, the hot spot is located just below where the top horizontal beam meets the vertical bar, and it determines exactly where text is selected when you click and drag. This hot spot is especially noticeable when the I-beam spans two lines of text and you're trying to select text on just one line. Some pointers—such as the wristwatch, spinning wait, and spinning beach ball—don't have a hot spot (or if they do, they're not telling). That's because they're there to indicate that your Mac is busy, so clicking with them doesn't do anything.

Mouse Moves

The companion to the mouse (and the pointer) is the mouse button. With it, you perform what's known as a *click* by clicking the mouse button—nice and intuitive. Once you have the pointer located where you want it, the click is your way of performing the action.

 Despite years of multibutton mice being available on other platforms, and the fact that support for a second button and a scroll wheel is built into Mac OS X, Apple continues to ship a one-button mouse. (Windows-based PCs use the right, or second, button to call up a contextual menu.) Nice and simple, but folks who want to use a two-button mouse can purchase one and add it to their system.

Now that you know everything you'd ever care to know about pointers, it's time to dig in and start using the mouse. Aside from moving the pointer around the screen and pointing at things, you can perform six basic mouse moves:

Point. As you might think, *pointing* refers to moving the pointer to a specific item or place using the mouse.

Click. *Clicking* refers to pressing and releasing the mouse button in fairly quick succession, usually when you're pointing to something. To select an icon, for example, you click it.

Double-click. This one's easy. *Double-clicking* is clicking twice in fairly rapid succession. You double-click to perform an action, such as launching a program, selecting a word in some text, or opening a document. You can't move the mouse while double-clicking or leave too much time between clicks, or your Mac might interpret them as two single clicks. And don't worry—you can't click faster than your Mac can think.

Click and hold. This term refers to clicking and holding down the mouse button while pointing to an item onscreen. For example, you click and hold a menu item to reveal its commands, or you click and hold a Control Strip item to show what commands it contains (see the sidebar "Mac OS 9: The Control Strip," later in this chapter).

Drag. You drag by pressing and holding down the mouse button while moving the mouse. You can drag icons to move them, drag the I-beam pointer across text to select it, or drag the arrow across a series of icons to select them.

Mac OS 9 Mouse Move: Click-and-a-Half

A click-and-a-half means you start to double-click, but instead of releasing the mouse button at the end of your second click, you keep holding it to drill down through folders. The pointer then turns into a magnifying glass, and when you hold it over a hard drive, CD, or folder icon, that item will open after a short pause. You can continue by moving the pointer over a folder inside the open item—that folder will open after a pause. If you move the magnifying glass outside the currently open window, the window just opened while the pointer was hovering will close. When you release the mouse button, the last window you opened using the magnifying glass will stay open, but the others will close—assuming that you kept the magnifying glass over the last window when releasing the button. In Mac OS X, this click-and-a-half move doesn't work.

Mac OS Desktop Elements

Now that you know how to get around with the pointer, it's time to take a tour of the famed Macintosh Desktop. During this tour, you'll encounter several items. Most of these are icons—graphical representations of files, hard drives, programs, and the like. These icons let you see at a glance what you're working with. (Older operating systems used text alone to represent these items.) Unless you've been moving things about on your Mac, you'll encounter just a few icons on your Desktop—in fact, on a fresh Mac OS X installation, all you'll see is a hard-drive icon and the Dock (you can add more icons, if you like).

Figure 1.3

A file icon represents a file in the Mac OS, such as a letter, spreadsheet, or digital photo.

Files

Files are a lot like their paper counterparts in the real world. Their main job in life is to hold information. Typical files contain such things as digital photos or letters you've written. Each file has a parent program that launches when you double-click the file; you can tell what that program is by looking at the file's icon (**Figure 1.3**).

Folders

Figure 1.4
....

A folder icon represents a container in which you can put files or other folders.

Folder icons look like what they're supposed to represent—traditional file folders (only they're not manila—in Mac OS X they're blue) (**Figure 1.4**). Folders hold files, programs, and even other folders—and they provide a way to organize the items on your hard drive. To create a new folder, from the File menu choose New Folder (or for a shortcut, press ⌘ Shift N in Mac OS X, or ⌘ N in Mac OS 9 and earlier). The new folder will appear with the imaginative name "untitled folder," but you can change that to almost any name you want (see "Working with Icons," later in this chapter).

Unix Tip on Directories

Although you'd never know it, Mac OS X is based on Unix—and it is easily the most beautiful, elegant Unix variant available. Unix is a high-powered operating system that's been around for decades, and it's used for such things as running large portions of the Internet and conducting high-end scientific research. Because of that, you may occasionally hear Mac OS X folders referred to as *directories*. Folders and directories are essentially the same thing.

For example, you might refer to a file as being in the Letters folder inside the Documents folder, but in Unix speak, you'd say it's in the Letters directory inside the Documents directory. To refer to the entire path (the chain from folder to folder), you would say the file is in Documents/Letters (pronounced "documents slash letters").

Programs

Program icons come in all shapes and colors, and they're carefully crafted to let you know at a glance what programs (also known as *applications*) they represent—witness Adobe Photoshop's eye or Microsoft Word's rounded blue *W*. These icons represent a bunch of programming code that, when run on your Macintosh, lets you work with all those files you have on your hard drive. Don't worry—you don't have to know the specifics of what a program icon represents to use it (**Figure 1.5**).

Figure 1.5
....

A program icon represents an application—that is, a bunch of programming code that lets you work with files or perform a function such as searching the Web or sending an instant message to another user.

iChat

Volumes

Volume icons represent places to store files, folders, and programs. They appear on the Desktop in a column on the right side of the screen (although in Mac OS X they don't have to—you have the option of not having your hard-drive icons show up on your Desktop). Here's a list of typical volume icons (**Figure 1.6**):

Hard drives. Hard drives (or hard disks) are the volume icons you'll most commonly encounter. Although most Macs have only one hard drive, they *can* have several, producing several volume icons—one for each hard drive. You can also divide a hard drive into several volumes (or partitions), which gives that hard drive several volume icons, each representing a single storage area. This is useful only in a few specific situations, and if you're in one of those situations, you'll probably know it. Most of the time, a hard drive has a single volume associated with it.

CDs. CD icons come in several flavors, including CD-ROMs and audio CDs. They appear as disc-shaped icons on the right side of the screen. Sometimes CD-ROMs have their own custom icons, which can appear as almost anything. A CD-ROM can contain files, folders, and programs, just like a hard drive.

DVDs. Like CDs, DVDs show up on the right side of the screen, and they even share the same disclike generic icon. The difference with DVDs is that you most likely can't open them yourself unless you have the special software for playing back DVDs.

Removable volumes. Disks you can remove from your Macintosh—such as Zip disks, floppy disks, CompactFlash cards, and SmartMedia cards—appear in the right column on the Desktop, just like hard drives and CDs. Removable volumes typically have custom icons that look like the physical disks—that is, a Zip disk volume has a Zip disk icon.

iDisks and other servers. Just about every Mac ever made can connect to other Macs (and even to Windows and Unix machines) over a network. Apple's iDisk (part of Apple's .Mac package; www.mac.com) is a prime example of a volume that shows up over a network. Network volumes are displayed along the right side of the screen, just as hard drives are. And with later versions of Mac OS X, FTP servers can also appear as icons on the Desktop.

Aliases

Figure 1.7

An alias is easily identified by the right-curving arrow in the lower-left corner of the icon.

Aliases are icons that point to items on your hard drive. When you click an alias, the original file opens. Aliases are ideal when you want to get to a much-used file, folder, or program quickly but don't want to move that item. It's like having the same file in two (or more) places at once—and the neat thing is that you can open any of the aliases and work on the original file.

To find the original item to which an alias points, select the alias and choose Show Original in the File menu or press ⌘ℝ. The window containing the original item will open before your eyes—or if both the alias and the original item happen to be in the same window, the original will be selected.

Alias icons look exactly like their originating file, folder, program, or disk except for one defining feature: a little right-curving arrow in the lower-left corner of the icon (**Figure 1.7**).

Aliases in Mac OS 9

If you're running Mac OS 9, it's even easier to identify aliases, thanks to two things combined. First, the filename appears in italics; second, a little right-curving arrow appears at the bottom of the icon.

On a fresh installation of Mac OS 9 and earlier, you'll find a few aliases already on your Desktop:

- **Browse the Internet**—Opens your Web browser
- **Mail**—Opens your email program
- **QuickTime Player**—Plays music and movies
- **Sherlock 2**—Helps you find files and Web pages

Aliases and the Dock

On a fresh Mac OS X installation you won't find any aliases. Instead, you'll find several items in your Dock, which serves the same purpose in this case—offering quick access to a few often-used items. The items in your Dock work just like aliases, but because they're in the Dock, they take on a different appearance. That is, they don't have the stylish arrow.

Desktop Pictures

The last Desktop element you'll run across is the Desktop background itself—the *Desktop picture*. On your spanking-new Mac OS X installation, this picture is a nice blue image with light streaks curving across. This is not a permanent backdrop, however—you can change this picture yourself to be whatever you like. You can also have that Desktop picture change randomly on a regular basis so that you don't get bored (see Chapter 2).

The Dock

The Dock is a row of icons that appears on the bottom of the screen. It serves lots of functions, such as a quick way to get at frequently used programs and files. We'll talk more about this innovative feature in "Working with the Dock," later in this chapter.

Other Icons

The icons above represent the bulk of the icons that you'll encounter, but there are some others you may come across:

URLs. URL (Uniform Resource Locator) files store Internet addresses, such as a Web page's address or an FTP site's location. Double-click a URL file, and the appropriate Web browser (or FTP client or email client) will launch and open using that information.

Clippings. Clippings are a special kind of file created when you drag some text or a picture from a document to a Finder window or the Desktop. While you must open most files using a program, you can view and open clippings without *any* specialized program—the Finder handles them, showing you the text or image inside the clipping. Clipping icons show what kind of information is inside (such as text or picture clippings), and text clippings take their filename from the first few words in the selection, tacking the word *clipping* onto the end. A clipping looks like a ragged-edged representation of what the file is—whether that's lines of text or a teeny graphic. Mac OS X doesn't have clippings, but when you drag a bit of text or an image to the Desktop, Mac OS X creates a file that contains that text or image. In Mac OS X, though, you'll need a program to open that file.

Desktop printer. In Mac OS 9 and earlier, printers you've selected in the Chooser appear on the Desktop, and they're called *desktop printers,* logically enough. You won't automatically see them in Mac OS X, unless you look in the Mac OS 9 Desktop folder. (For more on how to create desktop printers in Mac OS X, see Chapter 6.) Desktop printers take care of printing, letting you see what files you've sent to the printer and how those print jobs are going.

The Menu Bar

The menu bar isn't really a part of the Macintosh Desktop—in a sense, it goes *over* the Desktop environment. It's a vital part of the user interface, providing a way to issue commands and giving valuable information, such as the current time or your wireless signal strength.

Menus

Menus are one of the main elements you use to tell your Mac what to do. With menus, you issue commands and give your Mac instructions. These menus are in the form of words running horizontally across the top of the screen.

Clock

At the far right of the menu bar is the system clock, and, as you would expect, the clock shows the current time and day of the week. You can change the appearance and behavior of this clock by clicking it and selecting a setting from the menu that pops up. You can select whether or not this clock appears in the System Preferences application (the icon to launch the System Preferences application is located in the Dock, provided you haven't removed it).

Menu Widgets

This is a catchall term for the rest of the icons that appear between the menu words to the left and the clock to the right. These widgets let you change some of your Mac's settings or show you some specific information about your Mac (**Figure 1.8**).

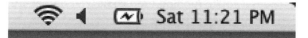

Figure 1.8

Menu widgets visible here are the AirPort signal indicator (left), the audio volume control, and the battery-level indicator.

A number of icons can appear in the widget area:

- **Battery**—On PowerBooks and iBooks this icon shows you how much power is left in your battery. It can display this in terms of percent left or time left, or with a visual indicator of how full it is.

- **Displays**—Lets you change your display's resolution and color depth, and allows you to detect newly added displays by making a single menu selection.

- **Internet connection**—Lets you change your Internet-connection settings—most useful for connecting with a modem.

- **Keyboard**—Allows you to select a keyboard and input method for one of Mac OS X's supported languages.

- **PC Card**—Gives you information about an inserted PC Card (on a PowerBook) and lets you issue basic commands, such as turning the card's power off.

- **Volume**—Controls your Mac's volume.

The menu bar can also contain icons from third-party applications, such as Netopia's Timbuktu Pro.

Mac OS 9: The Control Strip

The Control Strip, which appears in Mac OS 9, does some of what the menu-configuration icons do—it allows you to change some of your Mac's settings. Originally part of the system software created specifically for PowerBooks, the Control Strip is a little six-sided item at the bottom of your screen that floats over the Desktop as well as over any windows that happen to be near it. The Control Strip lets you change all kinds of system settings through various Control Strip modules—for example, adjusting your Mac's audio volume and the monitor's color depth and resolution or turning file sharing off or on. Many third-party developers have created their own Control Strip modules, so don't be surprised to find some non-Apple controls lurking in there. You may see this in Mac OS X under some circumstances if you're running the Classic environment.

Working with Windows

The Mac OS uses *windows* to let you look at an item's contents, whether that item is a folder, a volume, or even a file. Windows frame the contents of a folder or file, and controls nestled in that frame let you manipulate the window by changing its size, closing it, or moving its contents around to see whatever portion of it you like.

Anatomy of a Mac OS X Window

Mac OS X's windows have candylike rounded elements that appear in a variety of colors instead of the tried-and-true boxes in Mac OS 9 and earlier (**Figure 1.9**). If you're running the Classic environment on your machine (or still starting up in Mac OS 9), you'll still see these older-style windows. With Mac OS X 10.3, the windows have given up the gray-pinstriped look for a brushed-metal look.

Figure 1.9

Mac OS X 10.3 introduced brushed-metal windows— a style that's been around in Apple's QuickTime Player and Safari Web browser for a little while now.

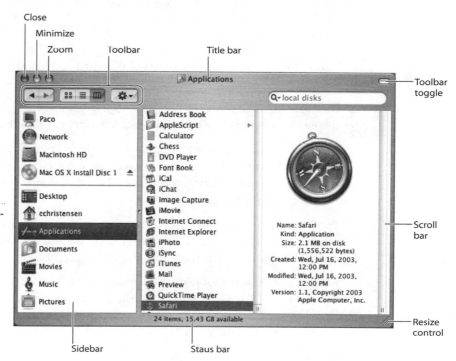

Here's a look at a Mac OS X 10.3 window:

Close button. The red button in the upper-left corner is the close button. Click it to close the window.

Minimize button. The yellow button shrinks the window and moves it to the Dock, using an impressive effect that looks like a genie going into a bottle. This is called the *genie effect,* as you might have guessed.

Zoom button. Click the green zoom button once, and the window resizes so that it's big enough to show all its contents, if possible. Click it again, and the window resumes its previous size. This behavior can be a bit confusing at first. If the window is too small to show everything, it will grow larger when you click the zoom button; if the window is larger than it needs to be to show everything, it will shrink when you click the zoom button.

Title bar. The Mac OS X window's title bar shows the name of the currently open item. You can move the window by dragging its title bar.

Sidebar. This is new with Mac OS X 10.3, and it provides quick access to commonly used destinations, such as volumes and folders. The sidebar is divided into two parts: The top part contains hard disks, such as hard drives, disk images, network volumes, or optical disks. The bottom portion is populated with the user's common destinations—Desktop, Home, Applications, Music, Movies, and Pictures. In Mac OS X 10.2 and before, many of these icons were in the window toolbar.

 To resize the sidebar, you can drag its right border to make it larger or smaller. To open or close it, double-click the sidebar's right border.

Toolbar. The toolbar is full of buttons that give you quick access to various folders and commands. It is customizable—you can change what buttons appear there. See the "Customizing the Mac OS X Window Toolbar" sidebar below for more information.

Toolbar toggle button. This button toggles the window's toolbar on and off. In Mac OS X 10.3 this button also toggles the sidebar and the status bar at the bottom on and off. It really makes windows svelte.

Status bar. This line of text at the bottom of the window (it's found below the title bar in Mac OS X 10.2 and earlier) tells you at a glance how many items are in a given folder or volume and how much space is left on the hard drive that contains the window.

Scroll bars. Every window has two of these—one horizontal and one vertical. You can use the scroll bars to move the contents of a window around if it's not big enough to show all the contents at once. (If all of a window's contents are visible, the corresponding scroll bar will be inactive.) Each scroll bar has four elements: two *scroll arrows,* the *scroller,* and the *scroll track.*

Resize control. Mac OS X windows also have a resize control in the lower-right corner that you can use to change the size of a window.

 Don't count on Mac OS X window button colors to be the same on every Mac—learn their positions as well. Mac OS X also has a Graphite color scheme that turns all of the widgets gray. Why do that? Well, certain creative professionals need a color-neutral environment to do proper design work. The widgets always appear in the same places, though.

Classic (or Mac OS 9) Windows

Although the Mac OS 9 window has been around in various forms for a long time, it hasn't changed a lot over the years. You'll find certain elements in almost every Classic window you open (**Figure 1.10**):

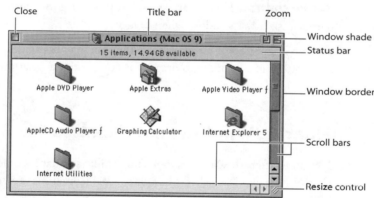

Figure 1.10

The Classic window uses the Platinum appearance, which was something special in its day. Each Finder window contains common elements.

Close box. When this small box in the top-left corner is clicked, the window closes.

Title bar. This broad horizontal border along the top provides a solid handle with which you can drag the window around. The text in the title bar reflects the name of the folder or volume you're looking at. A small icon to the left of the text shows whether the window represents a volume, a folder, the Trash, or a desktop printer. The small icon acts as a proxy icon—that is, if you drag the little icon in the title bar to a new place, you'll also move the item connected to that window.

Zoom box. This box within a box on the right side of the title bar lets you quickly resize a window. Click it once, and the window resizes so that it's big enough to show all its contents, if possible. Click it again, and the window resumes its previous size. This behavior can be a bit confusing at first. If the window is too small to show everything, it will grow larger when you click the zoom box; if the window is larger than it needs to be to show everything, it will shrink when you click the zoom box.

Window shade. The rightmost box—the one with the horizontal bar through it—is the window-shade control, and clicking it will roll up the window so that only the title bar is visible (this is known as *minimizing* a window). Click it again, and the window unrolls to its original size. (The Appearance control panel in Mac OS 9 has an option that allows double-clicking a window's title bar to trigger the window-shade effect.)

Status bar. This line of text below the title bar tells you at a glance how many items are in a given folder or volume and how much space is left on the hard drive that contains the window.

Scroll bars. Classic scroll bars work just like their counterparts in Mac OS X except that they're gray and boxy. You can use these scroll bars to move through a window if it's not big enough to show everything. Each scroll bar has four elements: two scroll arrows, the scroller, and the scroll track.

Resize control. This square area with three diagonal lines in the lower-right corner resizes the window when dragged.

Window border. You can also use the thin gray border around the left, right, and bottom of a window to drag a window to a new location—just as you would do with the title bar.

Floating Windows and Palettes

Not all Macintosh windows look and act like standard windows. There is a class of Mac window called a *floating window* (sometimes referred to as a *palette*). Floating windows often resemble regular windows (with a menu bar, close box, zoom box, and other window controls) except that all their elements are smaller (**Figure 1.11**).

Figure 1.11

A floating window often informs you of a critical event, such as your battery running out.

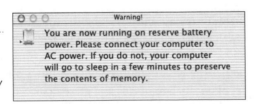

Floating windows float above all other windows (hence the name). That means you can't cover up floating windows with other windows from the same application—floating windows always end up on top. Floating windows are typically filled with buttons, text boxes, pop-up menus, and other controls—they constitute a tool palette (hence the *other* name). (Not all floating windows are tool palettes; some display chat text or a string of news headlines.) Since these windows float above other windows, the controls they contain are always accessible.

Opening and Closing Windows

Opening a Finder window is a piece of cake—just double-click a volume or folder icon and a window opens, showing you what's inside the item. You can also press ⌘N in Mac OS X. Closing a window is just as easy—click the window's close button (or press ⌘W), and the window closes. In Mac OS X, if you open a folder in an open window, the contents of that item open to fill the same window. You can use the Back and Forward buttons in the window's toolbar to go back through the windows you've opened to get there.

 If you hold down Option **while closing a window, all the open windows close. This little tidbit works in both Mac OS 9 and earlier and Mac OS X.**

Moving and Resizing Windows

To move a window, drag it by its title bar to its new location. The whole thing moves around with your mouse movements. Release the mouse button, and the window takes up residence at that point.

When dragging a Classic window or one in Mac OS 9 and earlier, a rectangular outline represents the window as you drag it. This is a holdover from many years ago when the Mac just didn't have the processing horsepower to draw the window as it moved (and redraw all the areas behind the window erased by its passing). Dragging an outline saves graphics power. In Mac OS X (and with very fast modern computers) there's no need to conserve power like that. The window moves along with the mouse pointer when dragged—no outline necessary.

To resize a window, drag the resize control in the bottom-right corner of the window. The window resizes itself as you drag, revealing or hiding contents as the borders change.

In some Mac OS X applications (and in Classic or Mac OS 9), a dotted outline forms, showing the size of the window as it will be when you release the mouse button. This, too, is a holdover from days when computing power had to be preserved in any way possible. The reason you see it in some Mac OS X applications is that those applications probably share code with older Mac OS 9 versions of the application.

Minimizing Windows

Clicking the minimize button (the yellow button on the left side of the title bar) makes the window shrink down and flow into the Dock—getting it out of the way without closing it. Once the window has assumed its place in the documents and folders area of the Dock, it stays there until you click it again, at which time it resumes its former position by expanding and flowing back to its original size. The plus side to this new minimization method is that it clears up a cluttered screen quickly—it doesn't leave behind the minimized title bar that minimizing a Classic or Mac OS 9 window does. The minus side is that you can't manipulate the windows when they're minimized, as you can in Mac OS 9.

Apple has put a lot of effort into this minimization, and it works so well with higher-powered machines that QuickTime movies will continue to play even while you're squeezing them down into a Dock-sized square.

 If you want to see the genie effect in slow motion, hold down Shift **when you click the minimize button. Great fun at parties!**

Exposé—Get to What You Need

Mac OS X 10.3 has a spiffy new feature called Exposé that provides a quick way to temporarily organize a cluttered mess of windows. Exposé shrinks down all open windows and organizes them side by side so that you can see all the open ones (**Figure 1.12**). To do this, you need to turn on Exposé in System Preferences (for more on System Preferences, see Chapter 2).

Figure 1.12

Exposé quickly displays all open windows at one time so that you can select the one you want.

Once Exposé is on, you activate it by moving your pointer to the hot corner that you selected while turning it on (you can also use a function key), and all the open windows (or just those of the currently active application, if that's how you've set things up) shrink and organize. You can then move your pointer over each open window, and that window's name will appear over the window. Click the window you want, and all the windows will return to their original positions, but the window you clicked will be up front. If you want the windows to return to their original positions without clicking one, then just move the pointer back into the hot corner again (or press the function key again), and everything will return to the way it was when you started.

Zooming Windows

The zoom box lets you quickly resize a window so that you can see all of its contents without having to scroll. A second click returns the window to its original size and shape. This can get a bit confusing. Most of the time, clicking a zoom box in a window that's too small will make it get bigger so that you can see what's inside. However, if you click a zoom box in a window that's already larger than is necessary to display all of its contents, it will actually shrink to the minimum size required. So clicking a zoom box can make a window grow or shrink, depending on its state when you click it.

Window Views

Mac OS windows let you look at their contents in several ways: as icons, as a list, or in a series of columns. In Mac OS X 10.3 (but not 10.2 or earlier), each of these views has something called the *sidebar* (inspired by iTunes), which holds volumes and a list of common locations.

By default, you see a window's contents as a series of icons you can place just about anywhere. But you can switch between any of the view modes by choosing View > as Icons, View > as List, or View > as Columns. You can also switch between view modes by clicking the appropriate View button in a Finder window toolbar. In either case, the view mode change applies only to that window.

Each mode has its advantages in particular situations, but you can use any mode you like at any time. Here's a look at them:

Icon view

This is the default view that made the Macintosh famous—a series of squarish pictures that represent files, programs, and folders. In Mac OS X these icons can be as large as 128 by 128 pixels, whereas in Mac OS 9 they were limited to 32 by 32 pixels. Mac OS X icons are beautiful compared with OS 9's (**Figure 1.13**).

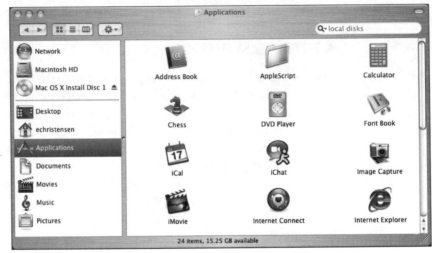

Figure 1.13

The icon view is the one that started the Mac on its way to fame. Mac OS X icons are large and colorful (or at least they can be).

List view

List view puts a window's contents into a vertical list using small icons (**Figure 1.14**). This view shows lots of information in columns, such as the sizes and the last modification dates of items, and you can sort the lists by clicking a column. You can also resize columns in a list view by dragging the edge of each column. If you don't like the order of the columns, you can drag the headers around to rearrange them. Folders appear in the list view with small triangles (called *disclosure triangles*) next to them. If you click a folder's triangle, it reveals that folder's contents in the same list without opening a new window. To reverse the sort order of a given column, click the header once to sort the contents by that column, and then click it a second time to reverse the sort order. (If the column header is blue, you only need to click it once.) This flips the window's sort order and also flips a little triangle in the column header to let you know that the sort order has changed.

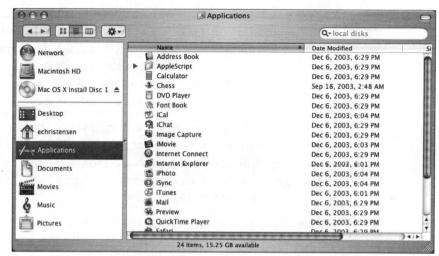

Figure 1.14

The list view is great for comparing files by different aspects—such as their sizes or modification dates.

In Mac OS 9 and earlier, a window in list view has a button in the upper-right corner resembling a small pyramid of horizontal lines. When clicked, this button reverses the window's sort order so that, for example, a list sorted by filename will read from *Z* to *A*. Clicking it again sets things right.

Column view

Mac OS X introduced the column view, which actually has its roots in another (now defunct) operating system, NextStep, which was a variant of Unix. In the column view, the window is divided into a series of columns that show the file path (the series of nested folders) leading to the selected item (**Figure 1.15**). The column series starts with the hard drive on the left and works its way through the folders you click, expanding toward the right to show you the selected item's contents.

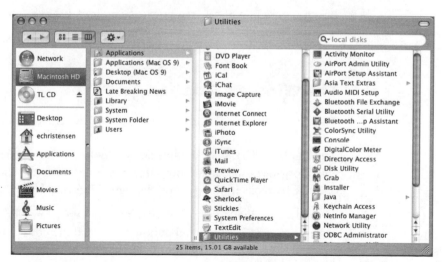

Figure 1.15

The column view is a Mac OS X invention, and it's great for quickly navigating your hard drive.

Mac OS X 10.3's column view works a little differently than previous incarnations. The columns only go as far back up the hard drive's hierarchy as the item clicked in the sidebar. For example, if you click the home icon in the sidebar and navigate a few folders deep, the columns only go back as far as the home folder. In Mac OS X 10.0–10.2, the columns go back as far as the root level of the hard drive, regardless of what was clicked.

One really cool thing about the column view is that you're never more than a couple of clicks away from any folder on your hard drive, and you don't have to keep more than one window open at a time. A second, even cooler thing is that you get a preview of selected files (such as text documents, pictures, or even movies) right in the column view.

 You can change the size of icons in the icon view in both Mac OS X and Mac OS 9. In Mac OS X, choose Show View Options from the View menu. This brings up a view-customization dialog in which you can change the size of a window's icons using a slider control. In Mac OS 9 and earlier, choose View Options from the View menu. This brings up a dialog where you can select small or large icons, and you can customize many other aspects of the window display there.

Mac OS 9—Alternative Views

Mac OS 9's Finder has its own series of views—only some of which it shares with Mac OS X. In Mac OS 9 (not Classic mode), just choose the kind of view you want to use from the View menu. Mac OS 9 has three view modes:

- **Icon**—This is the same view as in Mac OS X, except that the icons are smaller and just not as pretty.
- **List**—You guessed it. This lists the window's contents in a series of columns that you can sort to your heart's content.
- **Button**—In this simplified icon view, the contents are presented as single-click buttons.

The Window Sidebar

The sidebar has its roots in another operating system—Windows. Although it may be a difficult thought for some aficionados, not *all* good ideas originated with the Mac. That said, the sidebar also looks for its inspiration to iTunes, which organizes special locations in a pane on the left and shows the contents of those locations in the pane on the right (**Figure 1.16**).

The sidebar is divided into two sections—the top is for volumes (such as hard drives, network volumes, and optical discs), and the bottom is for commonly

Figure 1.16

The sidebar is new to Mac OS X 10.3, and it provides quick access to commonly used items.

accessed locations, such as the Applications folder and the user's home folder. In the sidebar, volumes appear and disappear as they are mounted and dismounted; you add folders to the sidebar by dragging them into it and rearrange them by moving them up and down in the list.

The sidebar can be resized by dragging its right border—the one with the small circle in it. If you want the sidebar to go away altogether, just double-click the border—the sidebar will collapse. To make it come back, double-click the left border of the Finder window, and the sidebar will roll out.

The Window Toolbar

As mentioned before, Mac OS X's Finder windows have toolbars (which you can toggle off, if you like). This toolbar contains a series of buttons (go figure) that let you quickly navigate your hard drive, search for files, and change the view (**Figure 1.17**).

Figure 1.17

The Mac OS X 10.3 toolbar contains controls to manipulate the window's contents, but you can add your own.

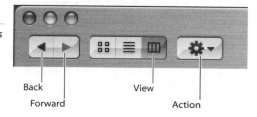

Here's a look at the default elements in the Mac OS X window toolbar:

- **Back button**—The Back button works like a Web browser Back button, in that clicking it takes you to the previous view (whatever you selected or opened).
- **Forward button**—The Forward button works the same way—it moves you forward to the *next* view.
- **View buttons**—These let you quickly toggle between icon, list, and column views.
- **Action button**—New to Mac OS X 10.3, the Action button works like a menu. Select an item in the window and click this button to get a list of commands that apply to the selected item (such as New Folder and Archive).

Mac OS X 10.3 windows have a built-in search field in the upper-right corner. Simply type a term into the field, and Mac OS X 10.3 will start searching right away for files that match the term.

Customizing the Mac OS X Window Toolbar

The buttons along the top of the window don't have to be visible. If you want to get rid of them, click the oblong toggle button on the right side of the window's title bar.

If you don't like the arrangement of buttons in your windows, you can change which buttons appear there by choosing Customize Toolbar from the View menu. This opens a dialog of all the possible buttons you can include in the toolbar. You can choose from many possible buttons, and also select whether just buttons, just their names, or both buttons and names appear in the toolbar by selecting one of these options from the Show pop-up menu (**Figure 1.18**).

Figure 1.18

Customizing the Finder window's toolbar is easy. Simply drag icons from the palette into the toolbar— into the rectangle between the buttons and the search field—and you're good to go.

Once you've made all the changes you like to the toolbar, click the Done button at the bottom to return the window to the working state (so you can't accidentally change the buttons)—along with its shiny new toolbar. If you don't like the toolbar changes you've made, you can use the default button set at the bottom of the customization dialog to return things to their original state.

You can also add folders and files to the space between the Action icon and the Search field by dragging their icons there. To open those folders and files, simply click their icons.

Working with Icons

Now that you know what the various icons on your Desktop look like, it's time to find out what you can actually *do* with them. After all, these icons—combined with your pointer—are the gateway to opening documents, arranging files, and the like.

How Hard Drives Are Organized

Before you start moving icons around, you should know a little about how Mac OS X and its special folders are organized.

Mac OS X is fairly particular about how the hard drive is organized—thanks to its Unix roots. There are lots of reasons for this, but the main one is that Mac OS X is a multiple-user system—that is, it's built to have many different people use the same machine. Mac OS X likes to have all of a user's files in the user's home folder, which is named for the user. That way, Mac OS X can protect a given user's files from other people who use the machine.

A hard drive with Mac OS X installed has a few special folders at its *root level;* this level is the first window that opens when you double-click the hard drive's icon.

- **The Applications folder** holds your Mac OS X programs.
- **The Library folder** holds files your Mac needs to run properly, such as fonts, preferences, and even Web pages your Mac can serve up.
- **The System folder** holds your Mac's system software.
- **The Users folder** holds home folders for users of your Mac, including one with your name on it as well as one titled Shared, which users can share over a network. Folders in the Users folder allow individual users to have a secure place for files, fonts, and preferences. Other users who log in to the same Mac OS X computer can't get at the items in those folders. Inside each user's folder are several other folders, which can hold documents, movies, pictures, and music. Each folder also contains a Library folder, which contains fonts, sounds, screensavers, and other system-related items specific to that user.

If you've installed Mac OS 9.2.2 with Mac OS X, you will also see several of its folders, including the System Folder, an alias to the Mac OS 9 Desktop folder, and the Applications (Mac OS 9) folder.

This hard-drive structure is important to understand, mostly because you can't just move icons anywhere you like—rather, you'll mostly be moving icons within two folders: your home folder (the one with your name on it that lives inside the Users folder) and the Applications folder (see Chapter 2).

Mac OS X also has several invisible folders at the root level of the hard drive that contain various files important to its operation. Unix pros will be familiar with these folders.

How Mac OS 9 Organizes the Hard Drive

Compared with Mac OS X, Mac OS 9 doesn't give a rat's patootie about how your hard drive is organized. In fact, it couldn't care less about where you put folders or keep your applications and documents—as long as you leave the System Folder functional.

Selecting Icons

Before you can do anything with an icon, you first have to select it. Once an icon is selected, you can apply a menu command to it, move it, or open it using the mouse. To select a single icon, you just click it—the icon will darken to show that it's selected. You have three other, often more useful, ways to select icons, especially when you want to select more than one.

Drag-select. You can drag the pointer over an area to select several icons at once. To do this, click in an area of the window or Desktop near but not on the icons you want to select, and then drag the pointer over the icons to select them. The pointer draws a rectangle—a translucent gray box in Mac OS X or a dark gray outline in Mac OS 9 and earlier—with one corner where you first pressed the mouse button and the diagonal corner connected to the pointer (**Figure 1.19**). This selects all the icons within or touching the rectangle, whether that means one icon or several hundred. If the window is too small to show all of a folder's contents, you can drag the pointer to the window's edge, which scrolls the window to reveal more of its contents.

Figure 1.19

The Mac OS X drag rectangle is a lovely shade of gray, and it leaves little doubt about what is selected.

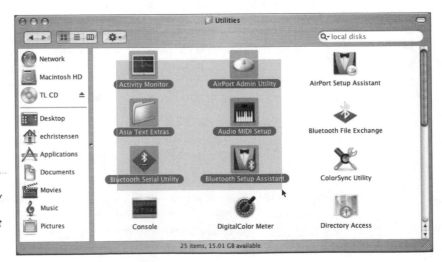

Shift-select. To select a group of icons you can't easily surround with a rectangle, in Mac OS 9 and earlier you can hold down [Shift] and then click the individual icons to select them. With [Shift] held down, every icon you click stays selected.

In Mac OS X this works a little differently. You can still use [Shift] in the manner described, but if you're viewing a window in list or column view, this method selects the first through the last icons you click. In Mac OS X, to cherry-pick only the icons you want to select, you hold down [⌘] while clicking.

Type a name. You can also select an icon by typing the first few letters of the icon's name—provided that the window containing the icon is in front. Once you have an icon selected in this manner, you can select the nearest icon in any of four directions—up, down, right, or left—by pressing the appropriate arrow key on your keyboard. You can select several icons this way by holding down [Shift] as you press the arrow key for each icon you want to select.

Moving Icons

Moving an icon (or a whole mess of icons once they're selected) is easy—just click the icon you want to move and then drag the pointer. The selected icon follows the pointer as you move it. A translucent version of the selected icon follows your pointer around, and when you release the mouse button, the icon moves to whatever location the pointer hovers over—whether that's another window or the Desktop. If you move an icon onto a folder, that icon goes inside that folder. If you drag an icon onto a different hard drive (or another volume), your Macintosh copies the file, folder, program, or even the entire volume onto that hard drive.

Opening Icons

Other than moving icons around onscreen (which, let's face it, gets boring after a while), most often what you'll do with icons is open them. To open an icon, you can click it and then select Open from the File menu or press [⌘][O]. More commonly, though, you'll open an icon by double-clicking it.

Opening an icon means different things depending on what *kind* of icon you have selected.

Volumes and folders. If you open a folder or volume icon, your Mac presents you with a window that shows all the files and folders *inside* the icon you just opened. (The same is true of the Trash, incidentally.) In Mac OS X the contents fill the same window; in Mac OS 9 a new window opens. You can change the Mac OS X behavior to mimic the Mac OS 9 new-window behavior by choosing Finder > Preferences and checking the "Always open folders in a new window" box.

Program icons. If, on the other hand, you open a program icon, your Mac starts running that program. There is a pause of a few seconds—sometimes longer—as the program goes through the process of setting things up. In Mac OS X you can go on working in other programs while one is launching; in Mac OS 9 and earlier, though, you can't do much during that pause. If you're launching a Classic application, it counts as a Mac OS X application, and you can continue to work while that application is running. We'll cover this in depth in "Launching and Quitting Applications," later in the chapter.

File icons. Opening a file icon releases a powerful one-two punch. When you open a file (or document) icon, first your Mac launches the program that created the file, and then the program reads the file you opened, making it ready for you to work on it.

Aliases. Opening an alias is the same as opening the original file from which you created the alias.

Mac OS 9 Desktop Printers

Opening a desktop printer in Mac OS 9 and earlier brings up a dialog box that shows all the items currently printing and gives you an opportunity to pause or cancel the print job—handy when you've sent that 65-page manifesto to your printer by mistake.

Renaming Icons

Unlike your parents, your Mac doesn't stick you with a set of names you have to live with. Instead, you can change the moniker attached to almost any icon to pretty much any name you like. The only limitations you face pertain to the colon and the slash—in Mac OS X you should stay away from the colon and the slash in filenames; in Mac OS 9 you can't use the colon, but the slash is okay. That's because these symbols are reserved by the Mac OS to denote pathnames—that is, the path from a hard drive through folders to a given file or folder.

AirPort Setup Assistant

Figure 1.20

The I-beam pointer is what you use to place the insertion point in text—it's also what you use to select and edit text.

To change an icon's name, click the icon to select it and then press ⟨Return⟩ or ⟨Enter⟩. The icon's name changes from white text in a black box to black text in a colored box, usually blue. At that point the icon's name is editable, and you can change it to whatever you like. You can also click the icon's name—after a short pause it becomes editable. How can you tell? Again, instead of white text on a black rectangle, you see black text on a colored rectangle. (The color of this rectangle may vary if you've done some customization; it's blue by default.) The pointer changes from the arrow to the I-beam. This lets you know that you can select and edit the text under the pointer (**Figure 1.20**).

Once the colored text is selected, you can change it by typing or by using menu commands. When you start typing, the selected text disappears and whatever you type replaces it. If you want to change only part of an icon's name, you need to select that portion of the name using the I-beam pointer. With the icon's text selected and editable, drag the pointer over the portion of text you want to change—whether it's a single letter or every bit except for a letter at one end or the other. Now, when you type, you'll replace only the selected portion of the text.

A few mouse moves can help out with shortcuts for text selection:

Click. A single click in editable text places a vertical black line (the insertion point) in the text where you click. This insertion point is where new letters will appear when you type them. If you put the insertion point to the left of any text, you'll push that text farther to the right as you type. You can also use the arrow keys to move the insertion point up or down one line (by pressing the up arrow or down arrow, respectively), or left or right one character (by pressing the left arrow or right arrow, respectively).

Double-click. A double-click when you're using the I-beam pointer selects the whole word underneath the pointer. In most programs (including the Finder), this selects only the word—it doesn't select any spaces before or after the word.

Drag. As we mentioned before, dragging involves holding down the mouse button while moving the pointer. With text, you start selecting where you first click the mouse button, and you end the selection when you release the button. You can select up, down, left, or right from your starting point.

 A triple-click when you're using the I-beam pointer selects an entire line or even an entire paragraph of text, depending on the program you're using—and this includes the Finder. A quadruple-click (yes, there is one) selects all the text.

 If you've totally messed up an icon's name while editing it and you want to return it to its previous name, select all the name's text, press ⌐Delete⌐, and then press ⌐Return⌐. Since you can't have an unnamed file, the Finder changes the icon's name back to the previous one.

 Macintosh filenames are case insensitive—that is, your Mac sees the names "My great American novel" and "mY GREat amerIcaN NOVEl" as the same. It doesn't distinguish between uppercase and lowercase letters. However, the Unix portion of Mac OS X *does* care, so if you're using Terminal—and you know who you are—you'll need to pay attention to capitalization.

Filenames in Mac OS 9 and Mac OS X

Of course, there are some differences between naming icons in Mac OS X and naming those in Mac OS 9 and earlier. Here are the basics:

Mac OS X. Icon names in Mac OS X can be very long. In fact, they can be much longer than you'd probably ever want, so you don't have to worry about running out of space. What you do have to worry about, at least a bit, is *filename extensions*. Mac OS X uses these to understand what kind of item (a folder, file, program, and so forth) a given icon is. Filename extensions, which consist of a period followed by three or four characters tacked on the end of the filename, help Mac OS X launch the correct program to handle a given file when you open it.

For example, if you create a new folder and give it the name My Poetry.jpg, Mac OS X will tell you that adding the .jpg extension to the name means the system may interpret the item as an image file, not a folder. And you might not get a warning. So be careful when you add filename extensions lest you get unexpected results, such as Preview launching when you double-click your word-processing document. **Table 1.1** gives a brief list of filename extensions you might come across.

Table 1.1 Filename Extensions

Extension	What It Means
.app	Tells Mac OS X that the item is actually an application or program. Mac OS X won't let you give an item the .app filename extension on a whim, so you can't easily turn a folder into a program—and that's a good thing. (You won't often see this extension.)
.rtf	Indicates a Rich Text Format file—these are used by word-processing programs to store text and information on how to format that text.
.pdf	Indicates an Adobe Portable Document Format file—a document that looks the same no matter what computer you view it on—Mac OS, Windows, or Unix.
.jpg or .jpeg	Indicates a JPEG image—these are commonly found in digital photos and on Web pages.
.gif	Indicates a GIF image—GIFs are also popular on Web pages.
.tif or .tiff	Indicates a TIFF image—TIFFs are used mostly in print graphics.

Mac OS 9 and earlier. Icon names in Mac OS 9 and earlier are limited to 31 characters, so although you can be somewhat descriptive, you can't write a novel underneath a folder's icon. Also, filename extensions don't mean much to this OS, so you can give an icon any extension you want—for example, you could give a word-processing document a .jpg extension—without risk of confusing your Mac, unless you take the file to a computer running Mac OS X or Windows.

Beware of using the forward slash (/) character when creating file or folder names in Mac OS X. Mac OS X's Unix underpinnings use this character to define *file paths*—basically lists of nested folders that show the folders in which a file is located, such as Macintosh HD/Users/bill/myfile.doc. Although using a slash in Mac OS X icon names won't crash your computer, it may cause some weirdness—for example, you could create new folders without meaning to—so you should avoid it. A similar problem arises when you use a colon (:) in a filename, because the colon does the same thing in Mac OS 9 that a slash does in Mac OS X, and since Mac OS X has to retain some compatibility with Mac OS 9, it also restricts the use of a colon. In Mac OS 9 and earlier, the Finder changes any colons you try to use into hyphens to avoid the problem altogether; in Mac OS X, the Finder tells you that you shouldn't use punctuation and it keeps you from making this mistake.

Getting Information About Icons

Sometimes you need to know a little more about an icon than is readily apparent from looking at it (such as what application launches when you open an icon or whether it is locked or unlocked), and the Mac has a simple tool for finding this information: the Get Info command (⌘I). We'll have more on the Get Info command below.

Using the Trash

Figure 1.21

This Trash is full— it's ready to be emptied with Finder > Empty Trash.

The Mac OS Trash is where you put files and folders you want to remove from your hard drive. In Mac OS X the Trash looks like a stainless steel wire mesh receptacle, the kind you might find by the side of a desk—that is, when it's empty. Drop an item *in* the Trash (either by dragging it onto the Trash icon or selecting it and pressing ⌘Delete), and the can appears to be full of wadded-up paper. This indicates that you have something in the Trash waiting for erasure from your hard drive (**Figure 1.21**).

Just putting an item in the Trash doesn't delete it. You have to tell your Mac specifically that you want to erase the item by emptying the Trash. To do so in Mac OS X, choose Finder > Empty Trash, and your Mac will ask if you're sure you want to permanently delete the items in the Trash. If you want to go through with it, click OK, and your Mac removes the offending items from your hard drive forever. If you've changed your mind, click Cancel, and the files remain in the Trash.

Mac OS X 10.3 has something called Secure Empty Trash, which does more than empty the Trash—it takes pains to make sure that the file is truly gone. Without a secure delete, a trashed file can sometimes be resurrected by special utility software.

If you want to empty the Trash with a keyboard command, press ⌘ Shift Delete.

 To empty the Trash in Mac OS 9 and earlier, select Special > Empty Trash.

If you've decided that you just can't live without an item you've thrown in the Trash, you can still retrieve it—that is, if you haven't yet emptied the Trash as described above. To go trash can diving and retrieve the item, open the Trash by either clicking its icon in the Dock (or double-clicking it in Mac OS 9), or selecting it and choosing Open from the File menu. The Trash pops open like any other window, and you can drag the contents wherever you like.

 Your Mac can put files back where they belong with one simple command: In Mac OS X it's Undo Move or Redo Move, found in the Edit menu; in Mac OS 9 it's Put Away, which you will find in the File menu.

Once you empty the Trash, its contents are gone forever. There's no Undo command, and there's no easy way to get those files back. A few utility programs, such as Symantec's Norton Utilities for Macintosh (www.symantec.com), can do the job with some degree of success, but even that method isn't guaranteed to work. So think before you delete.

If you're having difficulties with a stubborn file or folder that just won't delete, there is a fix. Look in the "Finder Tips" section later in the chapter for instructions.

Ejecting Disks

Desktop Macs—from the earliest models to the latest Power Mac G5—have some sort of removable media, which simply refers to a disk or volume you can unmount and remove from your computer. (*Unmounting* simply means taking a volume's icon off the Desktop.) For older Macs it's the floppy disk; for newer ones it's CDs and DVDs. You can unmount a file server, too.

In any case, the method for removing a disk from your Mac is simple, if unintuitive: drag it to the Trash. Don't worry—this won't erase the disk. Instead, it will unmount the volume and eject the disk from your computer. You can also select File > Eject. The Trash icon in Mac OS X will change to an eject-button icon when you're dragging something that can be ejected. This helps eliminate confusion.

Menus and Dialogs

Menus and dialogs are the means with which you and your Mac talk to each other. You use *menu commands* (the individual items in a menu) to tell your Macintosh what you want it to do; your Mac uses *dialogs* (called *dialog boxes* in Classic and Mac OS 9 applications) to tell you what it's doing and to ask for guidance now and then. You'll be using menus and dialogs for a fair bit of work on your Mac, so you need to become adept at using them. It's easy. The first step is working with menus.

All About Menus

The menu bar across the top of the screen is home to all of your Mac's menus; each word in the menu bar is a menu. When you click a menu, it opens downward, revealing all of its individual menu commands or items. The Finder has its own menu bar, as does almost every program you launch. These menus contain commands appropriate for the program that's running—after all, it wouldn't make much sense to have the Finder's menus (which deal mostly with folders and files and systemwide services) when you're using a word processor to write a letter. When you switch to a different program, the menus in the menu bar change to reflect the new environment.

Menus organize menu commands into related groups, and typically a menu's title describes the relationship of the commands listed under it. For example, the File menu (which almost every Mac program, including the Finder, has) lists a series of commands for dealing with files—creating a new file, opening an existing file, or printing a file (**Figure 1.22**). In Mac OS X the Quit command is in the Application menu; in Mac OS 9 and earlier, programs put the Quit command in the File menu, which doesn't make as much sense. This organizational scheme also breaks down when a program uses a menu with a generic name, such as Tools, which serves as a catchall for any menu command that one might consider a tool, from spelling checks to email-account management. Still, Mac menus are remarkably consistent across the board, and if you're looking for a particular command, the menu's name will usually lead you to it.

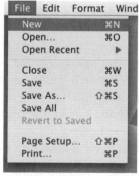

Figure 1.22

The Mac OS X File menu lists commands you can use on files in the Finder.

In a general sense, there are two kinds of menu commands: those that require you to select an item first and those that don't care whether you have anything selected. Menu commands that require a selection—whether it's an icon, some text, or part of an image—act on whatever you have selected (for example, the Finder's Make Alias command makes an alias of whatever icons you have selected). Menu commands that don't require a selection, known as *global* commands, act on the currently running program or—in the case of the Finder—on the Mac itself (for example, the Apple menu's Shut Down command, which tells your Mac to turn itself off).

When you pull down a menu (by clicking it in the menu bar), it opens to reveal all its commands. In addition to the short command phrases, you'll often see horizontal gray lines between groups of commands (in Mac OS 9, Classic, and Mac OS X 10.3 menus; in Mac OS X 10.0–10.2 you'll simply see gaps between groups of commands). These dividers organize a menu's commands into even smaller logical groups.

Finder Menus

In Mac OS X the Finder has seven menus: Finder, File, Edit, View, Go, Window, and Help (**Figure 1.23**). We'll be covering the Apple menu later, because of its unique status as a systemwide menu—it appears in all applications with menus, not just the Finder.

Figure 1.23

The Finder's menus provide all the commands you'll need to work with your Mac—that is, until you start using applications.

Here's an overview:

Finder. The Finder menu is visible only when the Finder is the active program. That's because the Finder is an application, just like others, and the Finder menu is the Application menu that's specific to the Finder application. (Each application puts up its own Application menu to the right of the blue Apple, and this menu has global commands that apply to the currently active application, such as a Quit command.) The Finder menu lets you get some information about the Finder, set the Finder's behavior by changing its preferences, and hide and show the Finder (as well as other running programs).

File. The File menu holds commands for dealing with files and folders in Mac OS X. It lets you create new folders and windows; duplicate, delete, find, and make aliases of files; and burn CDs and DVDs. And in Mac OS X 10.3 this menu reintroduces the Color Label option—which allows you to add a color to an icon. This was called the Label menu in Mac OS 9, by the way.

Edit. The Edit menu holds commands (such as cut, copy, and paste) used when editing text, pictures, video, and audio. In Mac OS X the Edit menu no longer includes the Finder's preferences as it did in Mac OS 9. It has a systemwide Undo command too, which is very cool. We'll cover the Undo command later in the chapter in "Undo Is Your Best Friend."

View. The Mac OS X View menu lists all of the possible view modes for a given window and contains options to clean up and organize windows as well as to hide and show their toolbars. The Show View Options command at the bottom of the menu opens a window called Desktop, where you can tweak the appearance of Finder windows—such as icon sizes and how icons are arranged.

Go. The Go menu connects your Mac to several locations, including your home folder, your iDisk, and your Applications folder, plus it keeps track of any folders you've recently opened. Finally, the Go menu has a command called Connect to Server that opens a connection to a file server.

Window. The Window menu in Mac OS X is a little more evolved than the one introduced in Mac OS 9.1—besides listing the currently open windows, it also contains a command to minimize a window and a command to bring all the Finder's windows to the front.

Help. This menu gives you quick access to your Macintosh help.

Mac OS 9 Finder Menus

Over the years, Apple has added to and changed several items in the menu bar. With Mac OS 9.1, Apple settled on six menu items for the Finder: File, Edit, View, Window (new in Mac OS 9.1), Special, and Help (**Figure 1.24**):

Figure 1.24

Mac OS 9's Finder menus contain some familiar items, providing commands for working with your Mac.

File. The Finder's File menu is chock-full of menu commands for working with files and folders. These commands let you create new folders, open and print documents, and find files and Web pages. The File menu also includes a cluster of commands for working with specific icons (for example, to get more information about an item, give it a label, or make a copy or alias of it).

Edit. The Edit menu is a short list of editing commands, such as Cut, Copy, Paste, and Clear. This menu is mostly for working with text and graphics in the Finder, and this work is limited primarily to icons and icon names. One curious thing: the Preferences command, nestled at the bottom of the menu, opens the Finder's Preferences window, in which you can change how the Finder behaves, otherwise known as editing the Finder's preferences.

continues on next page

Mac OS 9 Finder Menus   *continued*

View. Remember when we talked about the various views you can use in your Finder windows? This menu lets you select a view for a given window and contains some tools for cleaning up and arranging window contents. The View Options command at the bottom of this menu opens a window in which you can tweak the look of a particular window.

Window. New to Mac OS 9.1, the Window menu displays a list of all open windows (including pop-up windows); the active window has a check next to it.

Special. The Special menu is a catchall for commands that don't quite fit in any of the other menus. Besides one file-related menu item—Empty Trash—most of its commands are actually system commands, affecting your entire Macintosh, not just files and folders. The Special menu commands let you eject and erase disks, shut down and restart your Mac, and even log out of your Mac (if you have it set up to handle multiple users).

Help. Short and sweet (at least when the Finder is the active program), the Help menu is your gateway to assistance with your Mac. From the Help menu you can launch your Mac's Help Center (which contains all kinds of helpful information about the Mac OS and some of the programs installed on your Mac). This menu also lets you access balloon help—useful for finding out what a specific element or menu does.

Apple and Application Menus

Mac OS X has two menus that are worth a closer look—the Apple menu and the Application menu. These menus are present no matter what program is active. Although these menus go by the same name in both operating systems, they have different functions in each.

The Apple menu. The Apple menu is in the same place in Mac OS X as it has been in Mac OS 9 (and every version before that)—the left end of the menu bar—but instead of the old six-color version popular in the 1980s and 1990s, the Mac OS X version is glossy blue. And instead of the mélange of gadgets and widgets you'd find in Mac OS 9's Apple menu, you'll find systemwide commands in the Mac OS X version of the Apple menu—such as setting your Mac's system preferences, controlling how the Dock behaves, and shutting down your Mac. Many of the commands here are taken from the Special menu in Mac OS 9.

The Application menu. In Mac OS X the Application menu is on the left side of the menu bar, and it contains a list of commands that apply to the currently active program. In the case of the Finder, these commands can open the Finder's preferences and hide or show the Finder and other running programs (**Figure 1.25**). The Finder is probably the only program you'll run across that doesn't have a Quit command in its Application menu.

Figure 1.25

The Finder's Application menu provides commands that apply to the Finder as a program. All applications have an Application menu that has these sorts of commands.

So how do you see which programs are currently running in Mac OS X? For that you'll have to refer to the Dock. Running programs have a small upward-pointing black triangle at the bottom of their icons in the Dock.

 Mac OS X 10.3 introduces the User menu, which appears only if you've enabled Fast User Switching. This menu lets you choose from different users, switching almost instantly to the one selected.

Mac OS 9 Apple and Application Menus

Mac OS 9 also has two menus worth a closer look, and, not coincidentally, they are also the Apple menu and the Application menu. Although the names and some of the very broad functionality are the same, the specifics are different. Here's how the Mac OS 9 special menus look:

The Apple menu. In Mac OS 9 and earlier, the Apple menu is home to a potpourri of items, including small utility programs (such as the Calculator, AirPort utility software, and the Chooser) and special folders (which hold control panels, favorites, or recently opened programs). Accessing any one of these programs or folders (which act like submenus) is easy—just select it from the Apple menu. The Apple menu in Mac OS 9 and earlier is completely customizable—you can remove items and add new ones (Chapter 2 covers the specifics).

The Application menu. In Mac OS 9 and earlier, the Application menu sits on the far right side of the menu bar, and its job is to list all running programs. You can switch between programs by selecting the one you want from the menu—the currently active one has a check mark next to it. This menu also has three commands you can use to make running programs visible or to hide them, windows and all. These commands hide the currently open program, hide all other running programs, or show all hidden programs.

You can tear off the Application menu in Mac OS 9 and earlier to form a floating window (or *palette*) by clicking the Application menu and dragging the pointer off the bottom of it while the menu is open. This palette, which floats above all other windows, has buttons that allow you to select each of the currently running programs.

Selecting a Menu Item

Selecting a menu item is a simple affair. Click the menu that contains the item you want to select (such as the Edit menu), and then move the pointer down over the desired menu item. Moving the pointer over items in a menu highlights them one at a time. When the menu item you want is highlighted, click the mouse button a second time to execute the menu command.

In older versions of the Mac OS (before Mac OS 8), menus weren't sticky—that is, they didn't stay down when clicked. To select a menu item, the user had to click a menu and then keep holding down the mouse button while moving the pointer to the desired menu item, releasing the button only when the pointer was over the command. Otherwise, the menu would disappear. You can still use this method in Mac OS 9 and OS X, but it's not necessary.

The Common Menus

One of the great bits of using a Macintosh is its consistency— its windows and widgets are similar enough that you can often make things work in unfamiliar circumstances. This is true of your Mac's menus, as well.

Mac OS X

Mac OS X has a set of consistent menus that show up everywhere, and the list contains a few familiar entries: the Apple, Application, File, Edit, Window, and Help menus. The last four are similar to their counterparts in Mac OS 9.1 and 9.2.1 in that they show up in just about every program with a similar set of menu commands. However, for those who are familiar with earlier editions of the Mac OS, the Apple and Application menus have changed. The Apple menu has taken on one of the tasks that used to belong to the Special menu in Mac OS 9 and earlier—it handles system commands, such as starting up and shutting down your Mac. The Application menu no longer lists what applications are running. Instead, it takes on the name of the currently running program (such as the Finder) and provides commands appropriate to the program as a whole (such as changing its preferences, hiding or showing it, or quitting the program).

These changes to Mac OS X's menus make the menu commands a little more logical for new users. Old Mac hands may struggle with the new arrangement a bit before it becomes second nature.

Mac OS 9

In Mac OS 9 and earlier, users see five menus almost all the time: the Apple, File, Edit, Help, and Application menus. (There are exceptions to this arrangement with some programs, mostly games, but it's true in most cases.) The system software provides the Apple, Help, and Application menus, so they are almost always the same no matter what program is active. The Apple menu has a list of miscellaneous gadgets and folders available no matter what program is running. Help provides quick access to whatever help you need, such as balloon help or the Mac OS Help Center. (The Help menu changes its contents somewhat to provide help options specific to the active program, but some of its commands stay the same.)

Finally, the Application menu at the far-right end of the menu bar can have one of two looks: either a small icon showing the currently active application or an expanded version (to get this, drag the vertical bar with four tiny dots in it to the left). The Application menu shows a list of currently running programs. It also has three commands at the top that let you hide the current program, hide all programs *except* the current program, or show all programs.

The File and Edit menus, also present in almost every program, work a little differently. The system software doesn't supply these menus—instead, each program provides its own File and Edit menus, so although they may *look* the same, they're customized to meet the needs of the active program.

The Menagerie of Menu Items

You'll find lots of variations in menu items. These include whether a menu item is selectable (that is, executable), as well as special characters that indicate how menu items work. Here's a look at the variations in menu items that you'll find:

Enabled. This is the standard-issue menu item—and it's the one you'll see most. Enabled menu items are menu commands you can execute at that moment. Sometimes you can't select a menu item because it's not appropriate for the situation—for example, a Save menu item isn't enabled unless you have a file open and have made changes to it, and therefore you have something to save. Enabled menu items appear in solid black text.

Dimmed. The flip side of the enabled menu item is a dimmed menu item (or *disabled* menu item). This kind of menu item can't be selected, and thus it is grayed. (That's where the term *dimmed* comes from.) Programs sometimes disable menu items or even whole menus when you can't use them in the situation at hand—for example, you can't use the Cut command from the Edit menu when you don't have anything selected, so Cut appears in a dimmed form.

Ellipsis. An ellipsis (…) at the end of a menu item means that selecting that particular menu item brings up a dialog in which you can change some settings or tweak some controls. Usually that dialog also contains a button to cancel any changes, so in effect you get a chance to change your mind before executing the command. Menu commands *without* ellipses are executed immediately, with no intermediate dialog.

Check marks. Some menu items are called *toggle items,* because selecting them toggles an option (such as guides in a page-layout program) on or off. These menu items use a check mark to indicate whether the option is on or off. If a check mark appears next to the item, the option it represents is turned on, and selecting the item turns the option off and makes the check mark disappear. If there's no check mark, selecting the menu item turns on the option and puts a check mark next to that item.

Diamonds. Diamonds occasionally appear next to menu items that need your attention. This happens most often in the Application menu in the Classic environment (or in Mac OS 9 and earlier), when a program requests that you switch to it—perhaps a dialog box has popped up while you were working in another program. When this happens, a diamond appears to the left of the program's name.

Submenus. Sometimes a menu item encompasses too many options to fit neatly in a dialog, or too *few* to justify a dialog's existence. That's when you encounter a submenu. Submenus are indicated by right-facing triangles to the right of menu items; when you select such a menu item, another menu appears to its right. Submenus can have submenus of their own, although stacking too many menus in this fashion is considered bad form. To select an item in a submenu, click the menu that contains it and then move the pointer over the submenu item until the second menu pops up to the right. Slide the pointer horizontally until you're in the submenu, and then move it over the desired menu item. Click the mouse button a second time over that item, and you're on your way.

 If your Mac runs out of space along the right to display submenus, they'll appear on the left side of the menu, on top of whatever menu previously occupied that space—which can make for a wild mouse ride.

Scrolling menus. When there are too many items to fit in the vertical space your Mac's monitor allows (sounds crazy, but it happens, particularly with the Fonts menu), menus take on the ability to scroll so that you can see all the available selections. A scrolling menu has a gray triangle (black in Classic) at the top or bottom (or both), showing which direction has more content. Holding the pointer over a triangle makes the menu scroll in that direction—slowly, if the pointer is near the center of the menu, or quickly, if the pointer is at the menu's upper or lower edge. To select an item in a scrolling menu, click the menu, scroll through the list by holding the pointer over the appropriate triangle until you reach the desired menu item, and then click that item.

Keyboard Equivalents

You may have noticed something else in your menus that we haven't covered yet: letters and strange-looking characters to the right of some menu commands. These are called *keyboard shortcuts,* and they let you issue menu commands directly from your keyboard. Each keyboard command has a letter or number preceded by one, two, or three of four basic symbols that stand for the keys you need to hold down while pressing a particular key. These four keys—⌘, Shift, Option, and Control—are known as *modifier* keys. The most commonly used modifier for ⌘ key equivalents is the ⌘ key itself.

Most of the time, keyboard equivalents appear in menus with the ⌘ symbol and then a letter, which often stands for the command given (for example, ⌘S for Save). Sometimes, though, you'll see two or three of these symbols in a row before the letter. In this case, you have to press all those keys simultaneously before you press the letter key. For best results when using keyboard equivalents, first press and hold the modifier key or keys. With those keys held down, press the appropriate letter. Your Mac executes the command as if you had selected the menu item itself.

Common Menu Commands

Thanks to nearly two decades of attention to human interface design, the Mac has an incredibly consistent set of controls across all its programs, and this consistency goes down to the menu command level. Almost all programs— Mac OS X and Classic alike—share consistent menu items and keyboard equivalents. **Table 1.2** shows several of the most common ones.

Table 1.2 Common Menu Commands

Command	Keyboard Equivalent	What It Does
File > New	⌘N	Creates a new document. In the Finder it creates a new Finder window.
File > Open	⌘O	Opens a document or an item.
File > Close	⌘W	Closes a document or window.
File > Save	⌘S	Saves a document. (The Finder doesn't have this command.)
File > Print	⌘P	Prints the active document or Finder window.
File > Quit	⌘Q	Quits the active program. (In the Finder it logs out the current user.)
Edit > Undo	⌘Z	Undoes the last thing you did. This command is a lifesaver!
Edit > Cut	⌘X	Cuts the currently selected item and puts it on the Clipboard, removing the original item.
Edit > Copy	⌘C	Copies the currently selected item onto the Clipboard, leaving the original untouched.
Edit > Paste	⌘V	Pastes whatever is on the Clipboard into the currently active document.
Edit > Select All	⌘A	Selects everything in the currently active window.

Contextual Menus

Although we'd like to think the Macintosh side of personal computing brought up all of the good ideas, it's just not true. Occasionally Apple engineers used a couple of user-interface ideas from Windows, such as *contextual menus,* borrowed from the Windows right-click technique (in both Mac OS 9 and OS X).

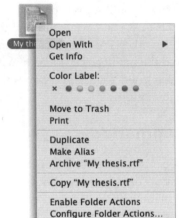

A contextual menu is a menu full of options that apply to a specific item or location. These menus make it easier to select menu commands—you don't have to dig through various menus for them (**Figure 1.26**). To invoke a contextual menu, hold down Control (which sometimes adds a little rectangular object resembling a menu to the pointer's lower-right corner) and then click the object to see a list of commands you can apply to it.

Figure 1.26

A contextual menu for a document contains commands relevant to that document—and ones that you can apply immediately, without a trip to the Finder menu bar.

For example, if you Control-click the Trash, a short menu of possible commands pops up right over it—commands such as Empty Trash. All these commands work with the Trash, and you would have to go to three different menus to find them if it weren't for contextual menus.

The Finder has built-in contextual menus, and most—but not all—Macintosh programs offer them, so you'll have to experiment by Control-clicking in your favorite programs. Don't worry if the pointer doesn't take on its familiar contextual-menu look when you press Control—some programs don't make this visual change even though they're capable of using contextual menus.

Working with the Dock

With Mac OS X Apple introduced the Dock—one of the most revolutionary features of the new operating system. The Dock, which appears at the bottom of the screen (but changes size to accommodate new icons), serves several purposes:

- Quick access to programs, files, and folders
- Status bar to show which programs are running
- Control strip to send commands to certain programs or navigate open applications
- Program switcher

We'll look at each of these functions in turn, but first let's look at what's in the Dock.

Elements of the Dock

On a fresh installation of Mac OS X the Dock comes stocked with several icons, ready for your use. Put your pointer on an icon and its name appears above it so that you don't have to guess. In Mac OS X 10.3 you'll find the following icons (**Figure 1.27**):

- **Finder**—The program that helps you work with files. It's always running, so it's always in the Dock.
- **Safari**—The brand-new Web browser from Apple.
- **Mail**—An email program from Apple.
- **iChat AV**—Apple's audio/video/text chat program, iChat.
- **Address Book**—Apple's address book for organizing your personal contact information.
- **iTunes**—Apple's own music player, which plays CDs and MP3 files.
- **iPhoto**—A digital photo organizer and editor.
- **iMovie**—Apple's video editing software.
- **iCal**—A scheduling program from Apple.
- **System Preferences**—Lets you change your Mac's settings.
- **Vertical divider**—Separates the programs from the files and folders (and the Trash).
- **Mac OS X URL**—Takes you to Apple's Mac OS X Web page.
- **Trash**—Holds files you are throwing away.

Figure 1.27

The Dock comes stocked with icon shortcuts to several of the Mac's most popular programs, including Mail, iChat AV, iMovie, and Safari.

The Trash

Figure 1.28

The Trash in Mac OS X is a retro-cool metal wire wastebasket that would do IKEA proud.

The Trash is represented by a special icon at the right end of the Dock (or at the bottom of the Dock, if you have it configured vertically). It's where you place files, folders, and programs when you want to erase them from your hard drive. You can do this by dragging the item to the Trash icon or selecting the item and then choosing File > Move to Trash or pressing ⌘Delete (**Figure 1.28**). The Trash, oddly enough, is also used as a way to eject disks (such as CDs or FireWire volumes) or disconnect from servers. To do that, drag the disk or server to the Trash, which will obligingly change its shape into an eject icon.

By the way, the Trash is always in the Dock—you can't remove it (see "Working with Icons," earlier in the chapter).

Mac OS 9: Where's the Dock?

The Dock is a Mac OS X–only feature; Mac OS 9 doesn't have such a beast. In Mac OS 9 and earlier, the Dock's functions are spread out among a couple of areas—the Control Strip and the Application menu in the upper-right corner.

In Mac OS 9 the Trash sits in the lower-right corner of the Desktop (since there is no Dock), but it does the same thing as in Mac OS X. In Mac OS 9 you can delete items by dragging them to the Trash icon or pressing ⌘Delete—the same idea as in Mac OS X. The Trash in Mac OS 9 also serves as an eject button, but unlike the Trash icon in Mac OS X, this Trash can doesn't change its shape into that of an eject icon. When you want to eject a removable disk, you drag it to the Trash.

The Finder icon

This special icon is always in the Dock, too—it represents the Finder, and it anchors the left side of the Dock (or the top, if you have it configured vertically). It provides a quick way of switching to the Finder or getting to any open window.

The divider

This small line divides the programs in the Dock from the files and folders. The programs are always on the left, while the files and folders are always on the right. The dividing line can be used to resize the Dock or change its settings, as well—as we'll demonstrate below.

Customizing the Dock

Fortunately, the Dock is somewhat malleable, or it would drive a substantial segment of the Mac-using audience bonko. You can make the Dock larger or smaller, and you can add to and remove items from it.

The System Preferences application has a section where you can easily customize the Dock's settings: in the Personal row of the System Preferences window, click the Dock icon to bring up the Dock dialog (see "Configuring the Dock's behavior" below).

Adding and removing Dock elements

Adding an icon to the Dock is as easy as dragging it there—the icons around the pointer make way for the new tenant. You can drag multiple icons into the Dock at once, adding them all. Programs go to the left of the divider; files and folders go to the right. Don't worry—you can't accidentally add icons to the wrong place.

When the Dock spans the entire width (or height) of the screen and you add an icon to it, it shrinks just a bit to make room for the new addition. It's very smart that way.

Removing an item from the Dock is similar to adding it—you just have to drag it out, and it disappears in a digital puff of smoke. No fooling! You'll even get a whoosh sound when you do so. Unfortunately, you can only drag out icons one at a time, so if you accidentally drag 140 file icons into the Dock and you want to remove them, you'll be there for a while. Better pack a lunch.

You can add as many icons as you like, and you can remove them all—except for the Finder and Trash icons. Fill the Dock with the programs, folders, and files you use the most.

Configuring the Dock's behavior

Not only can you add to and remove items from the Dock, but you can also play squadron commander and figuratively tell it when to jump and how high. Specifically, in System Preferences you set the Dock's size, whether it's visible all the time or hidden until you need it, whether it's at the bottom of the Desktop or at the side, and whether its magnification feature is on or off (**Figure 1.29**). Here's a bit about each.

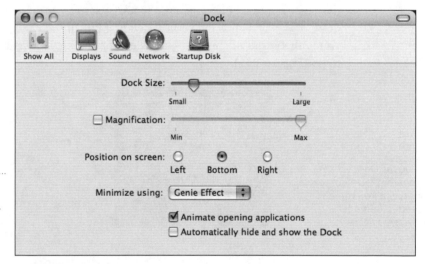

Figure 1.29

The Dock can be customized in a number of different ways via the System Preferences application.

Dock size. To change the Dock's size, simply drag the vertical dividing line up to make it larger or down to make it smaller. One tip—hold down Option while dragging the line to make the Dock "jump" to one of the native icon sizes. The theory is that since your Mac is using one of the predefined icon sizes, it doesn't have to build one on the fly, so it's a little faster. In practice, the performance boost is small at best.

Dock hiding. If Dock hiding is turned on, the Dock will slide off the Desktop until it's needed. Just position the pointer at the bottom of the Desktop (or the side if that is where you have chosen to place the Dock), and the Dock slides back into place. Then, when you move the pointer up off the Dock, it slides out of the way again.

Dock position. You can change this setting to make the Dock appear on the left or right side of the screen instead of at the bottom.

Dock magnification. With Dock magnification turned on, the icons in the Dock in the vicinity of the pointer grow larger. The result is that if you have a Dock with *lots* of icons—which are thus very small—the Magnification setting will selectively (and temporarily) make the icons larger for you (**Figure 1.30**).

Figure 1.30

With Dock Magnification turned on, the icons under your pointer grow larger—until you move the pointer away again, at which point they return to their normal size.

We've already looked at how to change the Dock's size—just drag the Dock's vertical dividing line up to make it larger or down to make it smaller. To change the other settings, either open the Dock pane in System Preferences or hold down (Control) and click the vertical dividing line in the Dock. This will present you with a menu of choices—just select the setting you want, and you're good to go (**Figure 1.31**).

Figure 1.31

Changing the Dock's settings is easy from the Dock's contextual settings menu. You can also change these settings (and more) using System Preferences.

What the Dock Can Do for You

The Dock is your friend. Even if it seems like a strange beast to longtime Mac users, at least it's a *friendly* beast. It can give you quick access to often-used programs, tell you what's running on your Mac, and even let you issue commands to certain running applications. Here's a quick look:

Icon repository. The Dock holds icons of all sorts for easy access. To open the item that an icon represents, just click it—this is the same as double-clicking the icon in a Finder window. This works for application, file, and folder icons, and it even works for the Trash icon on the right side.

Application status. The Dock can give you some feedback on what your applications are doing. Specifically, the Dock tells you that an application is running by putting a small black triangle below its icon. It indicates that an application is launching by repeatedly bouncing the application's icon until the application has finished launching. It also tells you that an application needs your attention by causing that application's icon to pop up periodically. Be a sport—click it.

Figure 1.32

The Dock can serve as a remote control for applications, allowing you to issue commands to them.

Issuing commands from the Dock. You can use the Dock to issue commands to files, folders, and applications in the Dock. For files, this is limited to the Show In Finder command, which opens a Finder window that contains the real item. The Dock can also show you a list of a folder's contents in the form of a menu, and you can select an item from that menu to open it. Finally, you can send a few commands to running applications, such as Quit (or Force Quit), open one of the application's open windows, or show the application's icon in the Finder. A few applications show a whole host of commands, such as Play, Shuffle, and Repeat One for Apple's iTunes. To get at these commands, simply click and hold an icon, and after a brief delay the command list will pop up (**Figure 1.32**).

Program switcher. Finally, the Dock acts as a program switcher, allowing you to bring a running application to the front. To do this, simply click its icon in the Dock, and that application—with all its menus—comes forward.

Dialogs

Now that you've learned how to tell your Mac what to do with menu commands and double-clicks, it's time to learn how to listen to some feedback from your Mac. The primary way this happens is through dialogs, which serve a couple of purposes: to notify you of some event you may not know about (such as a program crashing in the background), and to solicit more information so that your Mac can complete a task (such as printing a document).

Dialogs come in two major flavors: *modal* and *modeless*—and, thankfully, in Mac OS X, modal dialogs are all but nonexistent. Modal dialogs put your Mac (or an application) in a specific mode, and they don't go away until you deal with them—by either dismissing them or providing the information they ask for. You can't get away from a modal dialog until you fulfill its needs. A modeless dialog is a friendlier dialog (some might call it a pushover) that won't stop you from working on other things—it waits patiently in the background for you to get around to it, if you ever do. Most dialogs—especially in Mac OS X—are of the modeless variety. That's because modern operating systems strive not to come to a total halt for a single event, such as your Mac's asking you how many copies of your party invitation it should print.

Anatomy of a Dialog

Dialogs range from the dead simple to the hideously complicated, depending on what they're designed to do. A dialog can contain anything from a few words of text (such as "Your AppleTalk network is now available") to an array of controls (such as pop-up menus, text boxes, buttons, check boxes, and so on), arranged to help you finish a complicated task such as printing a document (**Figure 1.33**).

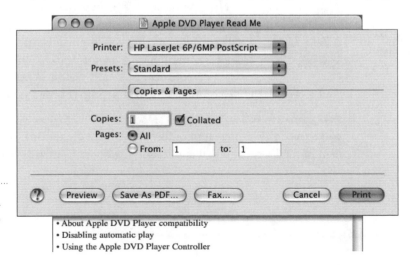

Figure 1.33

The Print dialog contains a number of options that can help you get the prints you want.

Here's a look at some of the items you might encounter inside a dialog:

Static text. This is plain-vanilla text that sits inside a dialog. It's there to pass along a message from your Macintosh to you—such as the text "You're now running on reserve power."

Text-entry box. If your Macintosh needs some information from you (such as the name or size of a font), you'll often respond in a text-entry field, typically a rectangle in which you type the information your Mac needs.

List boxes. A list box provides a place to show a list of items you can select, such as filenames in an Open dialog. List boxes resemble a Finder window in list-view mode. Mac OS X list boxes often use column views rather than the old list view, by the way.

Buttons. These items look and work like their real-world counterparts on machines. You click a button to make something happen. Usually labels on the button itself (say, Print or Cancel) indicate what will happen.

Radio buttons. Radio buttons let you select a single item from a list of choices by clicking the button next to the choice you want. Clicking another button in the list deselects the first one and selects the new one. Radio buttons take their name from the mechanical buttons on car radios. When you pushed one to tune in a favorite radio station, the previously pushed button would pop out because you could only tune in one radio station at a time.

Check boxes. Check boxes let you choose one or more items from a list of choices by clicking the check boxes next to the ones you want. When you do so, a checkmark appears in each selected box. You can choose as many check boxes in a group as you like.

Pop-up menus. Pop-up menus, like radio buttons, let you choose a single option from a list. You'll see pop-up menus instead of radio buttons in cases where the list of options is long (more than three or four). That's because pop-up menus take up a lot less space than a list of radio buttons—only one menu choice at a time has to be visible.

Tabs. These hang out at the tops of some dialogs, providing access to more than one set of controls. They work like the physical tabs found in reference books (dictionaries, for example), which let you quickly locate a new section in the book. In a dialog, tabs group closely related controls in the same pane, and they often appear in dialogs where you set preferences.

Types of Dialogs

Dialogs are difficult to categorize. They come in all shapes and sizes, from a screen-filling, show-stopping print dialog to a polite little floating window telling you that your AppleTalk network has gone down, to a little speech bubble coming from Microsoft Office's animated Assistant. That doesn't mean we can't try. Here are some of the common dialogs you'll encounter.

Settings dialogs

These dialogs allow you to change settings in response to a menu command, and they pop up when you select a menu item with an ellipsis after it. This ellipsis indicates that the menu command will bring up a dialog, because the menu command is too complex or has too many options for a simple menu command to handle (**Figure 1.34**). Selecting such a menu item brings up a dialog full of controls, which you tweak to customize the menu command you just issued. After you've finished fiddling with the controls in a dialog, you typically have two ways to make it go away: by clicking the OK button or clicking the Cancel button, both of which are at the bottom of the box (some dialogs may offer more or different buttons). Clicking OK accepts all the settings in the dialog and then executes the menu command that brought it up in the first place, using your settings. Clicking Cancel cancels the menu command altogether, and none of the settings you've changed take effect.

Figure 1.34

A menu item with an ellipsis leads to a dialog—count on it.

Queries

These dialogs often appear when your Mac needs a quick answer to a simple question, such as "Do you want to save changes to this document before closing?" To allow you to respond, the dialogs present a few buttons, typically two or three, each with a different response, such as Save, Don't Save, and Cancel (**Figure 1.35**).

Figure 1.35

Queries offer a quick group of choices—a quick answer to a quick question.

Open and Save dialogs

One basic dialog style is important in dealing with files, whether you're opening a file or saving one. This style refers to Open or Save dialog boxes, and it has two variations: one for opening a file and one for saving a file. The reason they're so similar is that they're flip sides of the same function—navigating through your hard drive when you want to open or save a file. These are two different dialogs, but they're so similar in form and function that we grouped them together.

First, let's tackle the Open dialog.

There are several variations on the basic Open dialog, but they all share a few characteristics—even the Mac OS X and Classic versions (**Figure 1.36**).

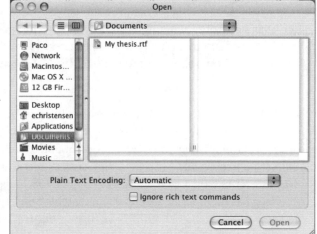

Figure 1.36

Using the Open dialog is a basic way to find the file you want to open. With Mac OS X 10.3, the Open dialog also includes the sidebar—and it looks a lot like a Finder window.

 Although the Open dialog can vary a great deal, the variations do share some common characteristics, such as displaying a list of files and providing a way of canceling or opening a given file.

Open and Cancel buttons. These are the two basic Open dialog controls. The Open button opens the file selected in the list field. The Cancel button closes the Open dialog *without* opening a file. The Open button is the default, which means that pressing Return or Enter is the same as clicking Open.

Browser view. This is the largest part of an Open dialog. In it you'll see a column view similar to that of a Finder window in column-view mode. When opening a file, you'll see two kinds of items in this list field—black (or active) folders and files, and disabled files and applications (which are grayed out in the list). The reason? You can open folders here, as well as files the program is capable of reading. However, you can't open the wrong kinds of files—for example, graphic files in a word-processing program—or other applications. In a Classic application or Mac OS 9, the browser view is actually a list field, which shows your current location as a list of files.

From menu. This pop-up menu shows you which folder the Open dialog is currently looking into. When you click the Folder pop-up menu, one of two things happens, depending on whether you're using a Mac OS X–native application or one in Mac OS 9 (or Classic). In Mac OS X, clicking the From pop-up menu shows the current folder, a list of Favorite Places (also folders), and a list of Recent Places (recently visited folders), along with other items. (Note, however, that not all applications call these From or Folder menus.) If you're using a Classic application (or Mac OS 9) and earlier, this menu is called the Folder menu, and clicking it shows a list of all the folders enclosing the current folder, all the way to the Desktop. If you want to move up one or more levels in the folder list, just select the target folder, and the Open dialog looks inside *that* folder.

Other controls. Depending on the program you're using, your Open dialog may offer other controls, including the ability to see a preview version of files you select and a pop-up menu that can filter out certain files (for example, in a graphics program you might want to see only JPEG-format graphics).

Now, let's tackle the Save dialog box.

The Save dialog also has common characteristics in all its versions. The first time you save a document, you're presented with a Save dialog—after that (in most applications), when you save that document, you don't see the Save dialog unless you choose File > Save As. In Classic applications the Save dialog box functions a lot like the Open dialog box. In Mac OS X applications, though, the Save dialog has incorporated some changes, which we'll go over shortly. Here are some of the elements of the Save dialog (**Figure 1.37**).

Figure 1.37

Similar to an Open dialog, the Save dialog provides a way of finding a place to save a document and then saving it. In Mac OS X 10.3, this dialog has a sidebar as well, and looks a lot like a Finder window.

Save and Cancel buttons. These are the two basic controls in any Save dialog. The Save button saves your file, and the Cancel button closes the Save window *without* saving the file. When you save a file, it goes in the folder you're currently viewing in the browser view (or list field, in a Classic application), using the name you've typed in the filename field. The Save button is the default button, which means that pressing Return or Enter has the same effect as clicking the Save button.

Browser view. This is also the largest single feature of a Save dialog. In it you'll see a list of everything in the current folder that the Save dialog is pointing to. Usually this is one of a few default locations: the folder where the program lives, your Documents folder, or the last folder in which you saved or opened a file. Some programs let you customize this default location. This browser field shows your current location in a series of columns going all the way back to the hard drive. When saving a file, you'll see two kinds of items in this browser view: black (active) volumes and folders, and grayed-out (disabled) file and application icons. The reason for this is simple: you can open folders in the Save dialog, but you can't open applications or files there.

In Mac OS X you open and close the browser view by clicking the triangle button to the right of the Where pop-up menu. This expanded window also usually features two new buttons—New Folder and Add to Favorites—that let you create a new folder or add the current location to your Favorite Places list, respectively (see below). A Mac OS X Open dialog contains the same elements but doesn't share the Save dialog's compressed form.

In a Classic application the browser view is replaced by a list view. When you select a folder in the list field, the Save button changes to read Open. Clicking this button now (or double-clicking a folder) opens the selected folder, revealing all *its* contents in the list field.

Filename field. To give a file a name, type it in this field (which is probably called Save As. When you first open a Save dialog, you'll probably find some text already in this field (something imaginative, such as "Untitled document"). You can (and probably should) replace it with a name of your own (that is, unless you *meant* to title your great American novel "Untitled"). By default, the name in this field is selected when the dialog first appears, so you can just start typing your new filename without having to select the text first.

Where pop-up menu. This pop-up menu, which is not always labeled, is almost identical to the one in the Open dialog. It provides a menu of common and convenient locations where you might want to save a document, including folders you've frequented recently—it's a good alternative to using the browser view. In Mac OS 9 and earlier it's called the Folder pop-up menu, and it shows a list of the nested folders containing the current folder, going all the way to the Desktop.

New Folder button. Click New Folder and your Mac creates a new folder in the current location shown in the Save dialog. After you click the button, a small dialog pops up, asking you to give the new folder a name. Do so and click the Create button. Your Mac creates a new folder in that location, and then the Save dialog puts your file there. This little button saves a lot of time by not forcing you to exit the program just to create a new folder.

Add to Favorites button. This button allows you to add an alias of the currently visible folder in the Save dialog to your Mac OS X Favorites folder. This is handy for adding often-used locations to your Favorites folder.

Classic Open/Save Dialog Box Styles

Besides Open and Save flavors, the Open/Save dialog box comes in a couple of variations, depending on the age of the program in question as well as the operating system you're using.

Old-style dialog boxes. Open/Save dialog boxes found in older Mac applications are simple affairs, with basic controls for finding locations and files. They're found only in programs written for Mac OS 9 and earlier—you won't find an old-style dialog box in a program written with Mac OS X in mind.

Navigation Services Open/Save dialog box. Some Mac OS 9 applications use Navigation Services. These dialog boxes—which are nonmodal and contain a number of new controls—are much more powerful than their simple cousins. Besides containing the basic controls for getting around your hard drive, these Open/Save dialog boxes have a title bar, can be moved around like other Mac windows, and have a resize control at the bottom. Their list fields show both file-names and the last modification dates for those files, and you can sort the window by name *or* date by clicking the appropriate column. Clicking the Sort icon (it looks like four horizontal lines forming a pyramid) reverses the current sort order. Three buttons appear at the top of each Open/Save dialog box: Shortcuts, which lets you select a volume from the list; Favorites, which shows you items in your Favorites folder; and the Recent Items pop-up menu, which shows you a list of items you've opened recently. Finally, each Navigation Services–based Open/Save dialog box has a Help button (a circle with a question mark in it) that lets you get help with one click.

Mac OS X emphasizes the difference between Open and Save dialogs a little more than Mac OS 9 and earlier, but the two are still closely related. In its simplest form, a Save dialog in Mac OS X drops down like a sheet from the top of the window of the file that's being saved. The benefit here is that you can move on and work in another document in the same application—even without completing the Save. You also know which document you're saving if you happen to get distracted.

We'll go over how to open and save files in the next section, "Beyond the Desktop."

Alerts

Alerts are specialized dialogs in which your Mac provides some vital bit of information, such as telling you that a program has crashed or a network has become available. Alerts don't pop up in response to a menu command you've selected; rather, they reflect your Mac's internal state of affairs. You might see a few types of alerts, but they all serve the same function: to provide you with some vital bit of information. They often consist of an icon that tells you how serious the issue is, some text that explains the issue, and a button or two (or three) that allows you to take some action.

In Mac OS X, alerts come in two styles: one that requires a response and one that notifies you of an event but doesn't require a response. The response-required type tells you that something has occurred, and it wants you to let it know that you've received this information, such as when an application unexpectedly quits (**Figure 1.38**).

Figure 1.38

An alert may tell you something very serious—such as that your FireWire drive has stopped responding.

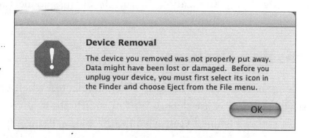

The less demanding cousin serves to tell you of an immediate condition, and it doesn't wait for a response, such as when your PowerBook battery is almost dead and you're running on reserve power.

Early Alert Types

Before Mac OS 9 came on the scene, alerts occurred in three flavors: Stop, Caution, and Note. A Stop alert, which showed a red stop sign next to some text, came up to alert you of a problem so big that your Mac couldn't complete an action. You dismissed Stop alerts by clicking the OK button at the bottom. A Caution alert, which showed a yellow caution triangle, popped up to tell you that something undesirable might happen if you continued, and it gave you the option of continuing or canceling the action. A Note alert, with a Note icon (usually a face with some bubble text), came up to tell you about a minor error or other situation that wouldn't wreak havoc if left alone. Most Note alerts had a single OK button at the bottom that dismissed them, although a few had two or more buttons offering you a choice of actions to take.

You may see different sorts of alerts when running Classic or Mac OS 9, but they often contain the same elements—an icon, some text, and a couple of buttons. One typical alert is a *notification* alert—a small floating window with a gray border, a yellow background, and black text. This sort of alert pops up in the upper-right corner of the Desktop.

Notifications are reserved for times when your Mac (or some other program running in the background) has something to tell you—just like an old-style alert. For example, when a previously unavailable AppleTalk network comes back online, your Mac may send you a notification; a shareware program may use one to remind you to pay up.

Notifications can also tell you that another program needs your attention—for example, when the Finder has noticed a program crash or when your email program has received new messages. (When a background program asks for attention like this, a diamond appears next to that program's name in the Classic or Mac OS 9 Application menu.) To dismiss an alert in a floating window, simply click its close box.

Dismissing Dialogs

Most dialogs have a default button, which is selected when you press Return or Enter. In Mac OS X the default button is difficult to miss—it pulses blue (or gray, if you've changed your Mac OS X color scheme); in Classic (or Mac OS 9 and earlier), the default button is the one with the thick border around it. The default button can be the OK button, Cancel button, or another button altogether, depending on what button would be picked most of the time.

Beyond the Desktop

If the Macintosh consisted of just the Finder and the Desktop, it would amount to a very expensive and moderately amusing diversion, but one that would wear thin quickly. Fortunately, the Desktop and the Finder are just the start of things when it comes to using your Mac. They let you run programs, which is how you make *real* use of your Mac by sending email, editing video, browsing the Web, writing short stories or papers, doing your taxes, manipulating photos, and so on. The list of possibilities is nearly endless.

Applications and Documents

Other than volumes (such as hard drives and CDs) and folders, you'll encounter two common kinds of items while using your Macintosh: *applications* and *documents*. Applications (also known as *programs*) are the active force behind all those wonderful things your Mac is capable of—they make things happen on your Mac.

Your Mac comes with several programs already installed on its hard drive that let you view Web pages, write text documents, watch movie clips, listen to music, and check your email. These programs are just the tip of the iceberg—thousands more applications cover just about everything you can imagine when it comes to using your Mac. Companies and individuals other than Apple create most of these programs and sell them in software packages you can buy at your local Mac-friendly computer store or from online or mail-order vendors, although Apple has increasingly gotten into the business of writing its own applications.

Documents are the passive counterpart to applications—they are where you store information created using an application. You use applications on your Mac to create and change documents. Also commonly known as *files,* documents are where your Mac stores data of a specific kind, such as a digital photograph of your dog, that term paper you wrote last fall, or a QuickTime movie trailer of an upcoming blockbuster.

Not all programs create and edit documents. In games, you fire up a program just to play around, whether that means a rousing round of solitaire or a deathmatch in Unreal Tournament 2003. Most of the time, though, programs have the ability to open and save documents of some sort—even games. This also applies to Web browsers, such as Safari. At first glance, you might think they don't do anything but browse the Web. However, what a Web browser actually *does* when it shows a Web page is open a special file (called an *HTML file*) that's sitting on another computer somewhere else on the globe, through your network connection. A browser operates via your modem and telephone line—or if you're one of the lucky folks with high-speed Internet access, your cable modem or DSL connection.

Commercial Software, Shareware, and Freeware—Paying for Software

There are lots of ways to differentiate the thousands of programs available for the Mac. One very useful way for those of us on a budget is to consider how those programs are sold—whether they are commercial products, shareware programs, or free applications.

Commercial programs. These are typically sold in computer stores or via mail-order catalogs, and they're almost always the most powerful programs in their categories. You pay for all that power, though—commercial programs are typically the most expensive in their categories as well. Commercial software is most often created by software companies (such as Adobe, Microsoft, and Macromedia) that employ lots of programmers to do the job—hence the high cost.

Shareware programs. Usually smaller in scale and ambition than their commercial counterparts, shareware programs are most often the creations of individuals or small groups who know how to write Macintosh programs. You can usually download shareware from the Internet or copy it from a CD or DVD and use it before you have to pay any money at all. Then, if you like the software (or find it useful), you can pay for it (**Figure 1.39**).

Figure 1.39

Using it for more than 90 days? Pay up—it's about time!

It typically costs much less to register shareware than to purchase commercial software, but you face a couple of trade-offs. First of all, shareware is almost never as powerful as a commercial program in the same category. Second, shareware typically focuses on a specific task, not a general mode of working. For example, a shareware program might be great for creating text-only documents, but a commercial program might do that *and* let you lay out a newsletter, complete with multiple fonts and pictures. You often get what you pay for, but if you need a program for a specific task, shareware is a great way to go. (If you use shareware, don't be a cheapskate—pay the shareware fee.)

Freeware programs. These are generally programs that an individual (or a small group) writes and then gives away. Sometimes people release freeware as an act of kindness, as when a programmer recognizes the need for some bit of software, writes it, and makes it available for free. Other times, freeware forms part of a company's larger strategy, as in the case of Apple's digital-hub applications: iTunes, iMovie, iDVD, iPhoto, and GarageBand. These applications come with every new Mac; iTunes can also be downloaded for free from Apple's Web site (except for iDVD, which is too flamin' big to download). Some freeware programs released by software companies fall in the category of player programs, used to play movies, music, and live Internet broadcasts; others, such as Safari and Microsoft Internet Explorer, are Web browsers.

Launching and Quitting Applications

To use a program, you'll first need to launch—or open—it. There are a few ways to do this:

- Double-click the application icon in a window or on the Desktop.

- Click the application icon in the Dock.

- Select the application icon, and choose Open from the File menu or press ⌘O.

- Open a document created in the application.

These approaches work whether you're using Mac OS X or Mac OS 9 and earlier, and they have the same basic result: your Mac starts running the selected program.

When you launch a program in Mac OS X, its icon zooms out in all directions (in Mac OS X 10.2 and earlier, it's just a rectangle that zooms out, not the icon). Once this happens, the application initializes (by building menus and creating structures in memory) and then puts its menu bar across the top. While a program is launching in Mac OS X, its icon appears in the Dock, bouncing up and down like a rubber ball on concrete. When the program has finished launching, a small black triangle appears under or next to the icon in the Dock to indicate that the application is active.

 Program icons may appear in the Dock even if those programs aren't running. That's because the Dock serves as a placeholder for icons of all types— programs, documents, and folders. If you've already put a program's icon in the Dock for easy access, it will start bouncing up and down immediately when clicked (or when you otherwise launch the program).

In Mac OS 9 and earlier, when a program launches, the first thing you'll see is a rectangle that zooms out in all directions from the application's icon, and then the name of the program you just launched will appear in the menu bar. During this time, the freshly launched program initializes. Once that's done, the program's name shows up in the Application menu, its menus appear in the menu bar, and any windows the program uses—including palettes or blank document windows—pop up. While a program is busy launching in Mac OS 9, you can't do anything else with your Mac—you have to wait for initialization to complete.

If you launch a Mac OS 9 program in Mac OS X, it launches Apple's Classic environment, which starts up a version of Mac OS 9 within Mac OS X. Once that's done, the program launches as it would as if you were running Mac OS 9.

There's one other way to launch a program, and that's by opening a document. When you open a document (by double-clicking it, by selecting it and choosing Open from the File menu, or by pressing ⌘O), this signals your Mac to open the program that created the document (or at any rate, one that *can* open the document). Once that program is running, it opens the document in a new window so that you can view it, print it, or work on it. You can also open a document by clicking its icon in the Dock, if the icon is there.

 Sometimes when you double-click a document, your Mac will get confused about which program it should launch. In that case, you'll get a dialog displaying a list of programs that might be able to open the document. Just choose the one you need.

Finally, you can open a document by dragging it onto the icon of a program that can open it (for example, dragging an image document onto Preview, a program for viewing pictures and PDFs). This method, called *drag and drop,* launches the program, which in turn opens the document. This way you can choose which program opens a given document.

Once you've launched a program and have finished working with it, you should probably *quit* it. Quitting programs frees up memory and processor power and guards against crashes (at least when working in Mac OS 9 and earlier; Mac OS X manages its resources differently, so quitting isn't quite so important, although it is still recommended). To quit a program you're no longer using, select Quit under the File menu in Mac OS 9 or the Application menu in Mac OS X, or press ⌘Q, which sends a quit command to the currently active program (the one whose menus appear in the menu bar). The program stops running, freeing up any memory or other resources on your Mac that it may be using. If you have any unsaved documents open (or you've made changes to those documents since you last saved), the program asks if you want to save the changes before quitting.

Classic, Carbon, and Cocoa

The two Macintosh operating systems in widespread use—Mac OS 9 and earlier and Mac OS X—have given rise to three flavors of applications that run on one or both operating systems. These application types are called Classic, Carbon, and Cocoa, and you should know a few things about each kind of program—there are some differences in how they work.

Classic. A Classic application is a program written to run in Mac OS 9 and earlier only—although almost all Classic programs will run in Mac OS X. When running in Mac OS 9 and earlier, Classic applications run normally; when running in Mac OS X, Classic applications have to run in the Classic environment. Classic programs running in Mac OS X don't have Mac OS X's new features, such as its rounded buttons and stylish windows, or the crash protection and responsiveness that other application types—such as Carbon and Cocoa—have.

continues on next page

Classic, Carbon, and Cocoa *continued*

Carbon. A Carbon application is a Classic application that has been modified to run in Mac OS X and take advantage of its new user interface, crash protection, and responsiveness. The beauty of Carbon applications (also called *Carbonized* applications) is that they run in Mac OS 9 just fine. Carbon applications offer the best of both worlds. GraphicConverter is one such application.

Cocoa. A Cocoa application (yes, the name is a bit goofy) is an application written for Mac OS X only. While it benefits from Mac OS X's new user interface, crash protection, and improved responsiveness, a Cocoa application can't run at all in Mac OS 9 and earlier. More and more programs are written as Cocoa applications as developers take advantage of new technologies. Apple's own Mail program is a Cocoa application.

We'll be talking more about Classic, Carbon, and Cocoa programs, as well as the Classic environment, in Chapter 2. We'll also look at how to tell the difference between Classic applications and the newer Carbon and Cocoa applications.

Mac OS 9 Feature: The Launcher

Mac OS 9 and earlier has a simple way to help you open programs, files, and even folders—the Launcher, a small program that keeps a single window open. This window, which looks like a standard Finder window, holds a series of buttons with icons taken from documents, folders, and applications on your hard drive. Click a button in a Launcher window, and the program, document, or folder represented by that icon opens. It takes only a single click to launch a program from the Launcher, as opposed to the double-click required to open a standard application icon. That's because the items in a Launcher window are actually buttons, not icons.

You can add your own buttons to the Launcher so that it offers access to the applications, folders, and documents you use most. To add a button to the Launcher, drag an item to the open Launcher window. A button with the item's name and icon appears in the window; the original item stays put, so you aren't actually moving it with this little drag operation. The Launcher window arranges items in alphabetical order.

To remove a button from the Launcher, drag it *by its name* to the Trash. The button will disappear from the window. If you try to drag the item out of the window by grabbing the button itself, you'll be disappointed—the button won't drag. If you drag the button elsewhere (that is, not to the Trash), an alias to the original item will appear where you release the mouse button, but the Launcher button will disappear from the Launcher window.

The Launcher doesn't appear by default on your Mac— you have to turn it on. To do so, open the General Controls control panel (Apple menu > Control Panels > General Controls), and check the box next to "Show Launcher at system startup." The next time you start up your Mac, the Launcher window will appear.

Moving Between Applications

Since the early 1990s, Macs have had the ability to run more than one program at a time. Usually programs are thought of as running in layers—that is, the program you're actively using is the one *in front,* and all other programs run *behind* that program (or *in the background*). Mac OS X's interleaved windowing scheme has changed this a bit, since windows belonging to different applications can intermix (see "Window layering" below). When you have more than one program running at once (and the Finder does count as a program), you need a way to switch between running programs. Fortunately, your Mac provides several:

The Dock. In Mac OS X all running programs have an icon in the Dock (complete with a small black triangle at the bottom), and you can switch between running programs by clicking the appropriate application's icon in the Dock, which brings it to the front. Note that if you click the icon of a program that is *not* running, you'll launch that program.

Pressing ⌘Tab. Both Mac OS X and Mac OS 9 (and earlier) have the ability to cycle through open programs using a key combination—⌘Tab. This brings the next program to the front, moving the currently active one to the background. Mac OS X selects the next program depending on its placement in the Dock, going from left to right. It highlights the next running program in the Dock and lets you repeatedly press ⌘Tab to get to another running program without switching to the ones between. In Mac OS 9 and earlier the next program is determined alphabetically. ⌘Shift Tab moves you backward through your open programs.

Double-clicking the open program's icon. When you double-click a program's icon, your Mac opens that program. If the program is already open, it becomes the active program. Choosing Open from the File menu or pressing ⌘O with the program's icon selected does the same thing.

Clicking a program's window. If you click a window in the background, the program that opened that window moves to the foreground, and the window becomes active. In Mac OS X only the clicked window comes forward; in a Classic program all the program's windows come forward.

The Application menu. When running a Classic application (or in Mac OS 9 and earlier), all running programs are listed in the Application menu at the right end of the menu bar. The currently active application (the one that's in front) has a check mark to the left of its name when you pull down the menu. To switch to a different program, select its name from the Application menu.

In any case, a program you've concealed using the Hide command in the Application menu becomes visible again when you make it active.

Some specialized utility programs—called *background applications*—always run in the background; you can't ever bring them to the front. A couple of examples are Login (a small program in Mac OS 9 that keeps track of who is currently logged in to your Mac) and Application Switcher (another tiny program that handles switching between programs).

Window layering

Most applications are able to display several windows simultaneously. How these windows are layered when several applications are running is a bit tricky. Mac OS 9 applications, whether running in Mac OS 9 or as Classic applications, group all their windows together. That is, when you bring a Mac OS 9 application to the front by clicking one of its windows, *all* its windows move above all other applications' windows—there's no mixing.

In Mac OS X, however, window mixing is allowed. That is, a group of Finder windows, Word document windows, and Safari windows can mix together, and clicking a Finder window brings that window (and the Finder) to the front—but the rest of the windows stay put.

If you're an old Mac OS hand, you can simulate the grouped-window behavior by switching applications using the Dock—clicking the application's icon in the Dock or using ⌘Tab to switch to the application. All the newly activated application's windows come forward.

Creating Documents

If you want to create an entirely *new* document, first you have to launch the program that you want to use to create the document. Once it's open, select New from the File menu (⌘N in most programs). This tells the program to create a new blank document. Some programs open a dialog when you create a new document, asking for a few specifics before creating it. For example, a graphics program might ask for the dimensions of your new document, while a video editing program might ask what kind of video camera you'll be using.

Opening Documents

Opening programs is a fine pastime for a Sunday afternoon when there's nothing but golf on, but sooner or later you'll want to do more than that. You'll probably want to start working with documents so that you can write reports, balance budgets, play with digital photos, and edit movies, you slacker. Just about everything else besides documents on your Mac—the operating system, the programs, and the folders—exists so that you can do this sort of thing: create, view, and change documents of all kinds.

Before you can work with a document, you must first open a program that can read it—whether or not that program created the document in question. Once the program is running, you can use it to open the document. Fortunately, your Mac takes care of much of this for you, so you don't have to first open a program and then journey all the way back to the Finder to open the document (although you can go about it that way if you want). Here's a look at the myriad ways to open documents using the Mac:

Double-clicking. The most basic—and efficient—way to open a document is to double-click it. This first opens the program that created the file and then opens the document itself. Selecting the icon and choosing Open from the File menu (or pressing ⌘O) does the same thing.

Drag and drop. You can also open a document by dragging it on top of a program's icon, whether that icon is in a window, in the Dock, or on the Desktop. (Remember that the program has to be able to open a file of that type.) If the program can handle the file, its icon darkens. When you release the mouse button, the program launches and then opens the document you dropped on it.

Opening files from inside the program. You can also open a document from within a program by first launching the program and then selecting Open from the File menu (or pressing ⌘O). The Open command, along with its keyboard equivalent, appears in the File menu of just about every Mac program ever written. When you use the Open command from within a program, an Open dialog pops up. You can use the controls in this dialog to navigate through the folders on your hard drive and find the document.

The other method is to select the file and choose File > Get Info. The Get Info window opens, displaying several options, one of which is "Open with." Click the triangle (called a *disclosure triangle*) next to "Open with" to reveal a menu that allows you to choose the application to use when opening the file. This change, however, is permanent—that is, the document will always be opened by the new application.

Choosing the Application to Open the File

Mac OS X allows you to easily choose which application will open a file when it's double-clicked—for example, if you'd rather use Adobe Acrobat instead of Preview to open PDFs. There are a couple of ways to go about this: by using a contextual menu or by changing the application in the Get Info window (see the "Get Info" section, later in the chapter).

To use the contextual-menu method, [Control]-click the file you want to open, and select the Open With menu, which displays a list of applications that can open the selected file (**Figure 1.40**). If the application you want to use isn't listed, select Other, and a dialog pops up, allowing you to locate and choose an application. Once selected, the document opens in the application you chose, but the next time you open it, it will open with the original application.

Figure 1.40

The Open With menu allows you to open a file with the application of your choosing.

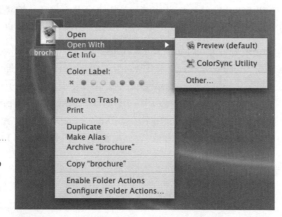

Saving Documents

When you have a changed document (either a brand-new document or an existing one you've altered), you can save the changes you've made onto your hard drive so that the next time you open the document, the changes are reflected.

 Most but not all applications require you to actively save a document—that is, to issue a Save command. A few applications, such as FileMaker Pro, automatically issue a Save command when you make changes.

If the document is new (that is, you've never saved it onto your hard drive), select Save from the File menu (or press [⌘][S]). This brings up the Save dialog. If you're working with a document that already exists on your hard drive, saving changes is easy. All you have to do is select Save from the File menu (or press [⌘][S]), and your Mac saves the file without opening the Save dialog.

Sometimes, though, you'll *want* to see that Save dialog again—particularly when you want to save a copy of the file with a new name. That's when it's time to take advantage of the Save As command. Located in the File menu, the Save As command opens a Save dialog as if you'd never saved the file before. In it, you can give the file a new name or save it in a different location. Afterward you'll be working with the new copy—the Save As command closes the original without saving any changes you made to it since the last save.

Closing Documents

Most of the time, closing a document is a lot like closing a Finder window. You can go about it in three ways: click the close box in the upper-left corner (or upper-right corner, if it's a Classic window), select Close from the File menu, or press ⌘W (the keyboard equivalent of the Close command).

One of two things happens when you close a document. If you haven't made any changes to it since you opened it, the document's window just closes—no muss, no fuss. If you've made *any* changes to the file, sometimes even as subtle as adding a space character to a word-processing document, the program asks if you want to save them and most likely gives you three choices in the form of buttons: Save, Don't Save, and Cancel (**Figure 1.41**).

Figure 1.41

Three choices—easy. This dialog keeps you from losing work.

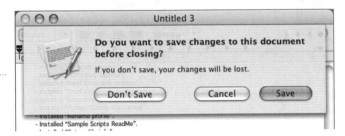

If you choose Don't Save, the document closes and any changes you've made evaporate into nothing. If you choose Save, the changes are saved on your hard drive—and if this is a new document, your Mac presents you with the Save dialog so that you can enter a name and select a location. If you choose Cancel, the dialog disappears and you end up back in your unsaved document. (By the way, the same sequence of events happens when you *quit* a program—before it quits, all its open windows close, and if a document has unsaved changes, the program asks if you want to save them.)

There's one important concept you should know: closing all of a program's windows does *not* quit the program. This can pose a bit of a problem, especially if you happen to be running Mac OS 9. When you switch from one program without any open windows to another program, it's easy to forget that the first program is running—and even without any windows open, it's still taking up system resources unnecessarily. This is much more of a problem in Mac OS 9 and earlier than in Mac OS X (because Mac OS X is much better at managing system resources), but it's still a good idea in Mac OS X to quit any programs you're not using. In Mac OS X you can identify currently running programs by the upward-pointing triangles that appear below their icons in the Dock; in Mac OS 9 you can see a list of running programs by clicking the Application menu in the upper-right corner.

Finding Files

Given the sizes of today's hard drives and the tens of thousands of files that live on modern Macs, it shouldn't be too surprising that you might need help finding a file. Fortunately, your Mac has a built-in way to help you with this.

With the Finder active, select File > Find or press ⌘F. This brings up the Find dialog, which allows you to search your hard drive (**Figure 1.42**). This simple dialog asks where to look and what to look for, and also includes a Search button.

Figure 1.42

Mac OS X's built-in Find function lets you quickly find what you're looking for.

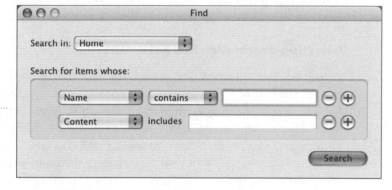

At the top of this dialog is the "Search in" pop-up menu, where you select a location to search in; choices include "Everywhere," "Local disks," "Home," and "Specific places."

- **Everywhere**—This searches on all available volumes.
- **Local disks**—This searches only disks connected directly to your Mac (network volumes aren't searched).
- **Home**—This searches the current user's home directory.
- **Specific places**—This lets you select specific drives and folders to search, helping you narrow your search.

After you've selected where you'll search, you need to tell your Mac what you want to search for. That's what the "Search for items whose" field is for. By default, this field searches for filenames that contain some text that you type in, but you can modify the filename search and add or remove criteria, such as the file's content, the date it was modified, and even its visibility.

Older versions of Mac OS X (10.1 and earlier as well as Mac OS 9) rely on a program called Sherlock to do the searching. Sherlock not only searches your hard drive for files, but it also searches the Internet for Web pages, products to buy, news, and that sort of thing. Later versions of Mac OS X still have Sherlock, but it only searches the Internet.

 You can also add a Find field to your Finder window's toolbar in Mac OS X prior to 10.3, which lets you search the current directory's contents for the filename that you type in the field.

Moving Information Between Documents

Open documents are not worlds unto themselves. In fact, you can move information from one document to another, even if they weren't created in the same program. For example, you can create a graphic in a drawing program and move it to a word-processing document, even though the two documents serve different purposes and are created by different applications. Your Mac gives you three main ways to go about this: cut, copy, and paste; drag and drop; and importing. (You can also use these commands to move stuff around in the same document.)

Selecting information in a document

Before you start moving things around inside and between documents, you have to tell your Mac exactly what you want to move by selecting it. You make a selection with the pointer. In practice, this is just like selecting icons or text in the Finder, and you can use the same techniques—usually, dragging the pointer over the area you want—to select a region of text or a specific area in a graphics document. Often your Mac changes the pointer so that you can select whatever's underneath, but sometimes (especially when you're using a graphics program) you have to select the right pointer from a tool palette to make a selection. Here's a glimpse of a few different selections you can make:

Text selection. When you're working with text, you're working with the I-beam pointer, which lets you select text by dragging over the letters, words, or lines you want. You can also double-click a word to select it (which most often doesn't select spaces to either side, though this varies from program to program), and in some programs you can triple-click to select an entire line or paragraph.

Image selection. When you're working with an image using a graphics program, you can select a portion of the image by dragging the pointer over the area you want. This draws a selection rectangle starting where you first click the mouse button and ending where you release it. If you're using a higher-end image-editing program (such as Adobe Photoshop or the shareware program GraphicConverter) to open the image, you'll probably have your choice of selection pointers (also known as *tools*) for selecting circles, rounded rectangles, polygons, or even free-form shapes.

Sound or movie selection. When you're working with real-time media (mostly video or sound files) in QuickTime, you can select a portion of the file by holding down [Shift] and dragging in the timeline above the play controls. If you're using a video- or audio-editing program, you'll probably need to use a special tool to select a section of the file.

Once you've made a selection, you're ready to start moving—either within the same document or between documents.

Cut, Copy, and Paste

These three basic commands have been around since the Mac first came on the scene, and they appear in the Edit menu of almost every Mac program ever written. With them you can cut or copy something you've selected in one document and then paste that selection in another. The Mac OS has a feature called the *Clipboard* that holds your selection while it's in transition. You can think of the Clipboard as a temporary holding place for whatever you cut or copy—some text, a picture, a movie clip, or a snippet of music. Putting something new on the Clipboard erases what was previously there, and when you shut down your Mac, the contents of the Clipboard go away. You use Cut and Copy to put something *on* the Clipboard; you use Paste to move the contents of the Clipboard into the active document.

Cut. Use the Cut command (Edit > Cut, or [⌘][X] in almost every program) when you want to move a selected item from one place to another. The Cut command cuts whatever you have selected (whether that's a paragraph of text or part of a digital photograph) out of the document and puts that data on the Clipboard. It's a lot like cutting an item out of a newspaper or magazine and putting it on a clipboard so that you can carry it somewhere else for another use.

Copy. The Copy command (Edit > Copy, or [⌘][C] in almost every program) is best used when you want to put a copy of a selected item in another place. The Copy command places a copy of whatever you have selected (text, graphics, video, audio—you name it) on the Clipboard, leaving the original selection intact.

Paste. The Paste command is the flip side of Cut and Copy. It pastes the contents of the Clipboard into the currently active document. If the document has an insertion point, the item you're pasting in appears to the left of the insertion point, and everything to the right of the insertion point gets pushed to the right. If you're working with an image and you have an area selected, the item you're pasting should appear in that area. If you don't have anything selected, the application chooses where the selection appears, but you can move it where you like.

You can use the Paste command as many times in a row as you like without erasing the contents of the Clipboard. This makes short work of writing "I will not talk in class" 500 times! Just copy the phrase, put the pointer where you want it, paste the selection 500 times, and you're done. (Or if you really want to speed it up, paste ten copies, select those ten, copy them to the Clipboard, and then paste those ten copies 49 times—and you're all done.)

Sometimes you'll find the Paste command grayed out, even though you know you copied *something* to the Clipboard. This often means that the program into which you're trying to paste doesn't know how to handle the kind of data you've got on the Clipboard. For example, this can happen if you try to paste text into an open image document. Sometimes you can get around this limitation if the program has an appropriate tool for the data. If your aforementioned graphics program has a text tool and you use that to create a text box on top of the image, you should then be able to paste text into that box.

 Several shareware utilities can give your Mac more than one Clipboard so that you can copy multiple items without erasing the Clipboard's contents. Check out Chaotic Software's **Clipboard Manager** ($20; www.chaoticsoftware.com/ ProductPages/ClipboardManager.html), Script Software's **CopyPaste-X** ($30; www.scriptsoftware.com), and Northern SoftWorks' **ClipDoubler Pro** ($14.95; www.northernsoftworks.com/clipdoublerpro.html).

Drag and drop

Mac programs offer another way of moving information around in the same document (or between documents). It's called *drag and drop,* and it works just as the name implies. With drag and drop, you simply drag a selection to a new location (whether that's inside the same document or in a different document) and drop it there. If you're dragging the selection to a different document, your Mac makes a copy of the selection in the receiving document—which can be another document created by the same program or even one created by a different program. All that's required is two open windows and some item you've selected to drag between them.

Not all programs support drag and drop, but most that have been updated in the last few years do. To test whether a specific program supports it, select some text or part of an image, then click and hold in the middle of the selection. Drag the pointer over to the Desktop and release the mouse button. If a new clipping file appears on the Desktop where you released the mouse button, your program supports drag and drop. If you want to move data between documents with this method, *both* programs have to support drag and drop, and the receiving document has to be able to understand the kind of data you're dragging onto it. Otherwise, your dragged material bounces back and nothing happens.

Importing information

There is one other way to get information from one document into another: by importing that document. It's like opening a document inside another. Unfortunately, there are a couple of caveats. First, you can't use the import function to move a portion of a file from one place to another in the same document; second, you can't import just a portion of a document into another—it's all or nothing, baby.

A couple of other things: the application has to support file importing, and it has to be able to import the kind of file you're trying to import. For example, a page-layout program might be able to import text and image files.

Still, Import is an immensely useful tool. To use it in a typical situation, you open the document you want to use as a container for the imported document and then select the Import command from wherever it is in the particular application you're using. The application asks you to locate the file to import, and once you've found it, you can import it. The entire contents of the imported file are placed in the document at the insertion point, if there is one.

Undo Is Your Best Friend

One of the first things every Mac user should learn is that the Undo command is your friend. Undo (accessible in most Mac programs via Undo from the Edit menu or by pressing ⌘Z) does what its name implies—it *undoes* your last action. This can be especially useful if you've accidentally erased everything in a 50,000-word document. A simple ⌘Z will undo the deletion, restoring things to the way they were. Some programs undo only the very last thing you did, so if you accidentally erase everything in a document and then type *Oops,* you can undo only your typing of the word. The lesson: don't do *anything* after you've made a horrendous mistake. Select Undo from the Edit menu right away to see if that fixes things.

Some programs have a multiple-undo feature, which lets you step backward in time by selecting Undo over and over again. With each Undo command you issue, your program undoes one more action; in some cases you can go back hundreds of steps.

A few programs, including SimpleText and the Finder in Mac OS 9 and earlier, have a disabled Undo command in the Edit menu. (Mac OS X, however, *does* have a version of Undo.) That's because these programs haven't implemented Undo, even though it shows up in the menu, and pressing ⌘Z won't do any good. You've been warned.

The lesson: when in trouble, use ⌘Z.

Other Application Features

These days, many programs have tools you won't find in the Finder: *tool palettes, control palettes,* and *button bars.* (Button bars have made it into Mac OS X Finder windows, but that's a pretty recent thing.)

Tool palettes are floating windows containing several different tools—essentially different pointers—that you can use on an open document. (For example, a graphics program might have a tool palette containing an airbrush, a paint bucket, a pen, a pencil, and an eraser.) To use a tool, select it in the palette, and then either click inside an open document with it or drag the tool around in an open document—the technique varies depending on the tool you're using. For example, you might click with a text tool to place an insertion point, but you might drag with a paintbrush tool to paint inside a document.

Like tool palettes, control palettes are small floating windows, but instead of different pointer tools, they contain a selection of settings for controlling what happens in a document. For example, a control palette for a word-processing program might have controls that let you select a font, a font size, text alignment (such as left-aligned or centered text), and text styles (such as bold or italic).

Finally, button bars hang out above or to the left of a program's main windows, and they're typically attached to the edges of the screen—although you can move some of them around wherever you like. Button bars typically provide one-click access to menu commands. For example, many button bars have cut, copy, and paste buttons with the same functions as those menu commands. Some people find clicking buttons easier than selecting menu commands.

Mac OS X Services

Mac OS X offers something called Services as a choice in the Application menu. Think of Services this way—if you could take menu commands out of an application and make them available at any time, whether or not that application was open, that would be a Service.

The problem with Services is that they work only with some Mac OS X applications. Remember the discussion in the "Classic, Carbon, and Cocoa" sidebar earlier in the chapter? Well, Services only work with Cocoa applications—Classic and Carbon applications can't use them. Even though the Services menu item shows up when using a Classic or Carbon application, everything in it is grayed out. Not so for Cocoa applications.

The items in the Services submenu change, depending on the programs you have installed on your Mac. For example, if you install Safari on a Mac that doesn't come with it, you may notice that a new item titled Open URL in Safari is now available under this menu.

To use a Service, have a Cocoa application (such as Mail or Safari) open in the foreground, and select an item in the application's open window. Then, select Services from the Application menu, and choose the service you want to use.

 The Services menu is a good way to find out if an application is a Carbon or Cocoa application. Open the application, select something in its open window, and open the Services submenu. If the items are enabled, the application is a Cocoa application. If not, it's Carbon.

Finder Tips

As you start working your way around the Finder, you'll learn various shortcuts and tips for how to do things more easily and quickly. To accelerate that process and make you a superuser right away, we've compiled some of the best Mac OS Finder tips for your perusal.

Common Commands

You should get familiar with a few Finder commands if you want to convince others of your Macintosh guru status—or if you just want to work more efficiently.

Power button. Pressing the power button on your Mac's keyboard brings up a dialog with four choices: Restart, Sleep, Cancel, and Shut Down. (If you press this button on the front of a desktop Mac, it may automatically put your Mac to sleep instead.) Shut Down is the default choice, so if you press Return or Enter, your Mac shuts down—it's the same thing as choosing Shut Down from the Special menu, and it only takes two quick presses on your keyboard or Mac.

 If you hold down the power button for 5 seconds, your Mac will restart itself—without going through the shut-down process first. This is only to be used if your Mac has frozen beyond all recovery, and your only other choice is to pull the power cord.

Select All. To select every item in the currently active Finder window, choose Select All from the Edit menu (or press ⌘A). This trick is especially handy when you have a couple hundred files you'd like to move from one place to another and you don't relish the thought of dragging your pointer that far. This trick also works well in many applications, so give it a try.

New Folder. Odds are you'll outgrow the basic folder structure on your hard drive pretty quickly, and you'll want to create new folders. To do so, open the window where you want the new folder to appear and select New Folder from the File menu (⌘Shift N in Mac OS X; ⌘N in Mac OS 9 and earlier). When you issue this command, a freshly minted folder appears with its name selected and ready to edit. Just type the name you want to give the folder and then press ⟨Return⟩ or ⟨Enter⟩ to make it stick.

Move to Trash. To move something to the Trash without dragging it there, select the item in question and select Move to Trash from the File menu (or press ⌘⟨Delete⟩).

Make Alias. When you select an item or items in the Finder and select Make Alias from the File menu (⌘⟨L⟩ in Mac OS X; ⌘⟨M⟩ in Mac OS 9 and earlier), your Mac makes an alias of the selected icon in the same window and tacks the word *alias* onto the end. In Mac OS 9, the icon's name is also in italic text.

Show Original. This command is available only when you've selected an alias in the Finder. Select Show Original from the File menu (or press ⌘⟨R⟩), and your Mac opens the folder that contains the original item and selects that item so that there's no mistaking the alias's origin.

Cancel. Pressing ⌘⟨.⟩ (period) cancels most actions already in progress.

Put Away. This command is for Mac OS 9 and earlier. When you've just moved an item to a new folder, you can send it back to its previous location by choosing Put Away from the File menu (or pressing ⌘⟨Y⟩). This makes the Finder move the item back to the folder where it came from, and that includes moving items out of the Trash. (Mac OS X does, however, have an equivalent in its Undo command, which can undo moving an item to a different location.)

Get Help. You can call up Macintosh Help while you're in the Finder by pressing ⌘⟨?⟩ (⌘⟨/⟩ also works in Mac OS 9, because the forward slash (/) and the question mark (?) are located on the same key.)

Force Quit. At times in every Mac user's life, programs may crash or freeze, and it can happen more often than you'd like. Sometimes a program just stops responding, even though you can still move the mouse, and sometimes *everything* (pointer included) freezes. If this happens, you can try *force-quitting* the program by pressing ⌘⟨Option⟩⟨Esc⟩ (**Figure 1.43**). This brings up the Force Quit Applications dialog.

Figure 1.43

The Force Quit dialog shows you a list of running applications, from which you can choose the one to make go away.

In Mac OS X you can select Apple menu > Force Quit to bring up the Force Quit Applications dialog.

In Mac OS X the Force Quit Applications dialog shows *all* running programs on your Mac, including a few background programs you might not even know about, and it has one button at the bottom labeled Force Quit (if you select the Finder, you see a Relaunch button). Select the troublesome program and click this button. Your Mac will give you a chance to back out, noting that you might lose any unsaved changes in the program you're force-quitting. Click Force Quit again and the rebel program goes down (or Cancel if you want to back out). In Mac OS X there's no need to restart your Mac, thanks to its advanced crash protection.

 You can also force-quit an application in Mac OS X by Control-clicking its icon in the Dock and selecting Force Quit from the pop-up menu.

In Mac OS 9 and earlier this dialog offers two choices: Cancel and Force Quit. Clicking Cancel returns your Mac to its previous state (which is great if you pressed this key combination by accident), and clicking Force Quit forces the troublesome program to go away. When you force-quit a program in Mac OS 9 and earlier, you should restart your Mac as soon as possible because it may now be unstable. But if you had to force-quit a program in the first place, your Mac isn't in the most stable state, anyway. We'll cover crashes and trouble-shooting techniques in much more detail in Chapter 8.

Soft restart. Then there are the times when your Mac crashes so hard that you can't do anything. It's time for a soft restart. To execute this, press ⌘ Control-Power button. Your Mac *immediately* restarts, and anything you were working on is gone—it's somewhat similar to pressing and holding the restart button on your CPU, if it has one.

Do not use this command unless you have no other choice. You won't get a chance to change your mind, and your Mac will take much longer to restart, because it has to check its disk structure for any errors that might have occurred due to the quick restart. Again, there'll be more on dealing with crashes in Chapter 8.

Modified Clicks and Drags

When you're using the Finder, you may notice that the pointer sometimes takes on a little extra icon, depending on what keys you're holding down while you click or drag. These modified pointers tell you that instead of a plain-vanilla click or drag, you're actually going to issue one of four com-mands—copy an item, make an alias, open a contextual menu, or grab the contents of an open window to move them (this last one's a bit tricky). These are *modified drags,* and they serve as shortcuts for Finder menu commands. Here's a bit about each:

Figure 1.44

The plus sign next to the pointer indicates that the file will be copied when it's dropped.

Copy. If you hold down (Option) while dragging a file, the pointer acquires a little plus sign (+) in the lower-right corner (**Figure 1.44**). When you release the mouse button, the Finder makes a copy of the dragged item in the location where the pointer is when you release the mouse button.

Make an alias. Hold down ⌘ and (Option) while dragging an item, and a small right-curving arrow appears in the pointer's lower-right corner. When you release the mouse button, the Finder creates an alias—or pointer—to the original file in the location where you let go.

Open a contextual menu. Hold down (Control) (without clicking anywhere), and a small rectangle appears in the pointer's lower-right corner. This means that if you click an item (or even the Desktop), you'll open a contextual menu with choices specific to that item (see "Contextual Menus," earlier in the chapter).

Navigation by Keyboard

Believe it or not, you can navigate through your Mac, opening folders and launching programs, without ever leaving the comfort of your keyboard. Here are a couple of tricks you'll need:

Typing names. If you start typing an item's name, the Finder will do its best to match an icon in the currently active window (or on the Desktop) to the name you're typing. The Finder makes a selection after you enter the first few characters, picking the first item in alphabetical order that matches the characters you've typed. Once an item is selected, you can use other Finder commands on it (such as Open or Move to Trash).

Arrow keys. These let you select an icon to the left, right, above, or below the currently selected icon, depending on which arrow key you press.

Mac OS 9: Modified Arrow Keys

If you hold down ⌘ and press ↑, the Finder opens the selected item, whether it's a folder, file, or icon. It's the equivalent of selecting Open from the File menu or pressing ⌘O. Holding down (Option) while using this shortcut closes the window that contained the item you're opening. For example, when you open the hard drive and then hold down (Option) while opening the Documents folder, the hard-drive window will close and the Documents folder will open.

Get Info

The Get Info command is your key to understanding all about an item on your hard drive. It tells you how big the item is, where it's located, and when it was modified, among other things. To find out more about an item on your Mac, select it and choose File > Get Info (or press ⌘I) to open the Get Info window, and then choose General Information. The Get Info window changes its contents slightly, depending on whether you've selected a file, a folder, an application, or a volume (**Figure 1.45**).

The Show Info Interlude

In Mac OS X 10.0 and 10.1, the Get Info command was renamed the Show Info command, and it worked a bit differently, although the way you invoked it was the same.

With the Show Info window, you could have only one Info window open at a time in Mac OS X, and it changed its contents to reflect whatever you had selected in the Finder. Select something new, and it changed to match. The Show Info window also had a pop-up menu at the top that let you change how items were shared over a network; this menu contained different items depending on the kind of icon selected. For example, if you selected a document, you could choose a program to open it; if you selected an application, you could turn on different languages for the program to use.

Here's what you can expect to see in a Get Info window for each basic item type:

Documents. The document's name, which application created it, how big it is, where it's located, when it was created, and when it was last modified. It also contains a Stationery Pad check box, which we'll cover in "Tips for Working with Files," later in the chapter.

Folders. The folder's name, its size (in Mac OS 9 it also shows how many items are inside the folder), where the folder is located, when it was created, and when it was last modified.

Applications. The application's name, its size, where it's located, when it was created and last modified, and its version. This last piece of information can be useful if you don't know exactly which version of a program you have on your hard drive, or if you have multiple versions on your hard drive.

Volumes. The volume's format, how much information it's capable of holding, how much space is available, how much is already in use, the number of items on the volume, the volume's location (including some details about its physical interface to your Mac), when the volume was created, and when it was last modified.

The Get Info windows for files, folders, and applications (basically anything you can throw in the Trash) also include a Locked check box, which we'll cover in "Tips for Working with Files," below.

Mac OS X Get Info windows have a series of sections below this chunk of information, with a little gray disclosure triangle to the left of each section. Click a triangle and its section opens to reveal more information and controls. The four basic types of Get Info windows have the following elements in common:

Name & Extension. This is simply the item's name and extension (if any). You can edit the item's name here by typing a new one.

Preview. This shows a preview of the file's contents in some cases, such as with a graphic or text file. With other items, such as an Excel file, hard drive, or application, it shows a full-size version of the icon.

Ownership & Permissions. This indicates who can manipulate an item, and it's divided into three parts: who owns it, what group it belongs to, and what others who don't own it or belong to the group can do with it. We'll discuss these permissions—and how they relate to Unix permissions—below.

Comments. This is a convenient place to write comments about a particular file, such as where an item was downloaded from or who last modified it.

Some Get Info items are unique to an individual item—here's a look at some of the ones you'll see, depending on what is selected:

Content index. This section appears with volumes and folders, and it allows you to find out whether and when your Mac has indexed a given item (indexing allows for quick searching for the contents of a specific file). This section also includes two buttons—Index Now and Delete Index—that allow you to force your Mac to begin indexing the item or delete the index for a given item, respectively. Why would you want to delete an index? Because it can take up significant hard-drive space.

Languages. This section, showing Mac OS X's multilingual nature, appears with applications, and it allows you to choose the languages in which the program can operate. You can also add or remove languages.

Open with. This section appears only with documents. As we discussed earlier, you can choose which application opens a given document, and you do that here. When you expand the "Open with" section, you're presented with a pop-up list of applications that can open the document, and a Change All button. Choose an application from the pop-up list, and if you want *all* documents of that type to open with that application, click the Change All button.

Mac OS 9 Get Info Elements

In Mac OS 9, Get Info windows have a few common elements, including a pop-up menu that lets you select a label for the item, a field for comments (if you want to jot down a few notes about what's in an item), and a Show pop-up menu. This last feature lets you set who can see the item over a network via file sharing, as well as the amount of memory a program gets when you launch it. We'll cover these details in later chapters.

Permissions

File permissions are a basic part of a multiuser operating system, like Mac OS X or Unix. These permissions, which apply to anything on your hard drive (not just files), determine who can read or change items, which is critical for making sure that no one's messing with your stuff.

Brace yourself—we're about to take the plunge into discussing Unix and Mac OS X. We promise that you won't need NoDoz, though.

Mac OS X permissions

Mac OS X permissions are somewhat similar to Unix permissions, for those of you familiar with them, but they're not the same. In Mac OS X, permissions are organized into three groups of users: the item's owner, the group associated with the file, and others who aren't part of the first or second. You can then set the access level for each of these groups by choosing from the Access pop-up menu. Mac OS X 10.3 has the additional perk of showing you what you can do in a pop-up menu above the others (**Figure 1.46**).

Figure 1.46

This section allows you to set the permissions of the selected item. In Mac OS X 10.3 you can also see what you can do with a given item, and you can change that, too.

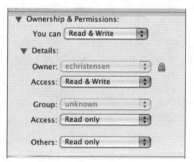

Here's more about each:

Owner. This is who owns a given item. Typical owners include you or one of the other users of that particular Mac—if it's you, the word *(Me)* appears to the right of the name. This name is the short name that you provided when you created the account, and it's the Unix short name. You'll also notice that there are others in this list, such as mysql, nobody, sshd, and system. These are users of a sort—they're users set up by the operating system to do specific tasks. For example, mysql is set up to do certain operations in the SQL database in Mac OS X.

Group. This represents the group of users on that particular Mac. Typical groups include admin, mysql, nobody, staff, and wheel, among others. Like items in the Owner field, many of the groups are created by the system for its own purposes. Users are members of the Staff group, and you'll note the word *(Me)* to the right of the word *Staff.*

Others. This group is everyone else who isn't the file's owner or a member of the group associated with the file.

As we said before, you can set access for each of these groups by selecting an option from the Access pop-up menu below that group. Options include "Read & Write," "Read only," and "No Access."

- **Read & Write**—This setting allows the user or group to open the file or folder and make changes to it.
- **Read only**—This setting allows the user or group to open the file or folder, but changes are not allowed.
- **No Access**—This setting means that the user or group isn't allowed to manipulate the file at all.

To change a file's permissions, select the item and choose File > Get Info (or press ⌘I). Then click the disclosure triangle to the left of the Ownership & Permissions section. (In Mac OS X 10.3 you'll also have to click the Details disclosure triangle.) Click the lock icon to the right to unlock the permissions section, and select the new permissions for the Owner, Group, or Others groups; you can also change the Owner and Group.

One situation in which you may want to change file permissions is when you run into the dreaded undeletable-file problem. You try to delete a file and your Mac won't do it, saying something about not having inadequate permissions to do the job. If that's the case, you can change the file's permissions to solve the problem (see the sidebar "How to Delete a Stubborn File," below).

 Be very careful when changing file permissions—changing permissions on some files can even keep your system from working properly. If you aren't sure, don't change permissions.

Unix permissions

Mac OS X permissions are closely related to Unix permissions, which are another way of accomplishing the same goal—keeping the wrong people from manipulating your stuff. There are some important differences, though. Unix permissions are set using the Terminal application, which provides a command-line interface for your Mac. Also, while Unix permissions set the file's ownership (Owner, Group, and Others) and whether the file is readable and writable, they also set whether a file is executable—that is, whether it can run as a program or not.

Unless you work with Unix on your Mac (whether you're doing Web-site work or are installing a Unix program), you probably won't ever have to worry about the Unix side of permissions.

Tips for Working with Files

When you spend some time working with the files on your hard drive, you'll develop your own techniques for doing things quickly. Even so, here are a few tools to help you on your way.

Locking and unlocking files

If you want to protect an important file or program from changes, you can lock that document so that no one can rename or change it when it's open and so that it's harder to delete from your hard drive. To lock a file or application, select it and then choose File > Get Info (or in Mac OS X 10.0 or 10.1 choose File > Show Info) or press ⌘I. This brings up the Get Info window. (In Mac OS 9 select File > Get Info > General Information.) Check the Locked check box at the bottom and close the window. The item's icon now sports a little lock in the lower-left corner, and users won't be able to change the item's name or alter the item (although they can still open it), nor can they delete the file without first unlocking it. The aim of this is to keep you from accidentally deleting an important document—not to provide solid security. That's because it's easy to unlock an item. To do so, open its Get Info or Show Info window, and uncheck the Locked check box in the lower-left corner.

Trashing locked icons

Occasionally you'll throw away a locked item you really *do* want to get rid of, or, worse yet, you'll throw away a passel of locked files, and when you try to empty the Trash, your Mac will tell you it can't delete the locked files. To get around this, hold down Option and select Empty Trash from the Application menu (or, in Mac OS 9 and earlier, from the Special menu). Your Mac will obediently erase everything in the Trash without asking any questions. Be careful, though, because with Option held down, your Mac won't ask if you're really sure you want to throw everything away. If this doesn't work—and sometimes it won't—you may have to unlock the file manually.

How to Delete a Stubborn File

Sometimes you'll throw a file away and try to delete it, only to discover that you can't. The Finder tells you something to the effect that you don't have enough privileges to do so. That's where our lecture on file permissions comes in handy. To change a file's permissions, open the Trash and select the reluctant file. Choose File > Get Info and open the Ownership & Permissions section. In this section, click the lock icon to the right (if it's locked—if it's open, don't bother) and change the Owner pop-up menu to your name with the word *(Me)*. Set the access to Read & Write. Change the Group pop-up menu to staff (Me) and change the access to Read & Write. Finally, change the Others pop-up menu to Read & Write. This is overkill, but it should make the file easy to delete. Go ahead and close the Get Info window, and then try to empty the Trash—it should work just fine.

Archiving a file

Mac OS X 10.3 has the ability to archive a file or folder. This compresses the item as a Zip file, which takes up less space than the original—great for long-term storage and sending over the Internet. To compress a file or folder, select it in the Finder and then choose File > Archive. The Finder compresses the item. If it's a file, the compressed item will have the file's name with a .zip file extension; if it's a folder, the compressed item will be given the name Archive.zip.

Creating stationery

The Mac provides special documents called *stationery,* which act conceptually like pads of paper with preprinted designs. When you open stationery, it's like ripping the top sheet off. You still have the pad for later use, but you can work with the sheet you just ripped off, and you don't have to go through the trouble of adding items that are used every time, such as a logo or address. Opening a stationery document opens a copy of the document, complete with all of that document's contents—text, pictures, and the like. For example, stationery is useful for items such as letterhead, which has your name, address, and company logo on it but is otherwise blank. Opening your letterhead stationery opens a copy of the letterhead document, leaving the original untouched, ready for the next time you need to write a letter.

You can make stationery out of any document by selecting its icon and choosing File > Get Info (⌘I) in Mac OS X or File > Get Info > General Information in Mac OS 9 and earlier. Check the Stationery Pad check box and then close the window. The document's icon should now look like a pad of paper instead of a single sheet. When you open that document, you'll get an untitled document with the same content as the stationery document. To turn stationery into a regular document, open its Get Info window and uncheck the Stationery Pad check box.

Assigning a label

Mac OS X 10.3 and Mac OS 9 and earlier have the ability to assign a label color to a selected item; this allows you to mark the file for easier organization. In Mac OS X 10.3 you can assign a label by selecting File and then choosing a color label icon below the Color Label menu item—you have eight choices; in Mac OS 9 and earlier, select File > Label and then choose a color label from the list.

Mac OS 9 File Tips

Here are a couple of tips that will help you get the most out of working with files when using Mac OS 9.

Turning off the Trash warning. In Mac OS 9 and earlier, if you don't want your Mac to ask if you're sure you want to delete items in the Trash when you choose Empty Trash, you can turn off this warning by selecting the Trash icon and choosing File > Get Info > General Information (or pressing ⌘I). In the Trash's Get Info window, uncheck the check box next to "Warn before emptying." (In Mac OS X choose Preferences from the Finder menu to bring up the Finder Preferences window. Uncheck the box next to "Show warning before emptying the Trash" near the bottom of the window.) Now, when you empty the Trash, its contents just go away. This also means that you don't get a warning, so be sure you want to get rid of the Trash's contents before you select the Empty Trash command. You can't undo it.

Encrypting an item. In Mac OS 9, if you want to protect an item from prying eyes, you can do so by selecting the item (this doesn't encrypt a folder full of items, by the way) and then choosing Encrypt from the File menu. Your Mac asks for a password and encrypts the item. If you want to open an encrypted item, you'll first have to type in the password. It's important not to forget your password—if you do, there's no way to unencrypt your file. Encrypting an item also makes it smaller, so if you're dying for a little hard-drive space, you can encrypt a few items you don't use on a regular basis.

Tips for Working with Windows

We've shown you the basics of working with your Mac's windows, but now it's time to pick up a few advanced techniques. You'll save lots of time and keystrokes if you learn these few simple tricks.

Cleaning up a window's contents

After a short time, you might find that a window in icon or button view might start looking a little, well, disheveled. After all, it's hard for humans to move items around with machinelike orderliness. You can fix your messy windows with a quick menu command: View > Clean Up. This makes your Mac square up all the icons in the currently active window according to a grid, making order out of chaos. The problem with this command is that it sometimes doesn't arrange icons sensibly. To make up for that, use View's Arrange submenu in Mac OS 9 and earlier, which offers you the choice of arranging by name, date, label, size, or kind. In Mac OS X go to View > Show View Options to choose how to arrange the icons.

Customizing window views

If you want to *really* keep your windows looking their best, open the View Options window, which lets you set the currently active window's appearance— the size of icons, how they're arranged (and whether they snap to an invisible grid), and which columns to include in a list view. To open the View Options window, choose View > Show View Options (or select View > View Options in Mac OS 9 and earlier). The keyboard equivalent in either case is ⌘J.

Finding the path to a window

You can take a look at the folder path (the list of folders in which the currently open window is nested) by ⌘-clicking the window's title bar. This creates a pop-up menu showing each folder that lies between the current window and the root level (the hard drive in Mac OS X or the Desktop in Mac OS 9), and you can open any of these intermediate folders by selecting it from the menu. Some programs, such as Microsoft Word and Internet Explorer, also support this trick—very handy.

Closing a window when you open something in it

If you hold down Option while double-clicking an item, that window closes when the item opens. It's a convenient way to keep your Desktop tidy when drilling down through a series of folders. This is especially convenient when you have the preferences set to open a new window each time an item is opened.

Hiding an application

If you want to hide the currently active application without going to the Application menu, you can do so by holding down Option and clicking another program's window (or clicking the Desktop). The currently active application disappears, and the program for the item you clicked becomes active.

Dragging an inactive window

To drag a window that's behind another window without bringing it to the front, hold down ⌘ and drag the window by its title bar. When you release the mouse button, the window stays behind the other windows.

Using characters to sort files in list view

Although your Mac does a fair job of sorting items alphabetically in list view, sometimes you want just one file or folder to show up in a different place—say, at the top or bottom of the list. You can achieve this by adding a character to the beginning of a file's name. To get a file to bubble up to the top of an alphabetically sorted list, put a space at the beginning of its name, or put a bullet in front of its name (press Option 8 to get a bullet). You can also use numbers in front of filenames to arrange files in the desired order (**Figure 1.47**).

Figure 1.47

Adding a space to the filename can change a file's place in the sort order, as can adding a bullet or number.

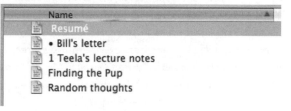

Interview: Bill Atkinson

Among the engineers responsible for developing the Mac, perhaps none played a more important role than Bill Atkinson. Atkinson abandoned graduate studies in neuroscience at the University of Washington to join Apple in 1978. After some early work on the Apple II, he became the lead software developer for the Lisa group. Atkinson designed the machine's user interface, which provided the foundation for the Mac interface, and wrote much of the low-level software behind it, including LisaGraf, the package of powerful graphics routines that later became the Mac's QuickDraw.

For me, it's always been about empowering creative people.

—Bill Atkinson, on his role as the creator of the Mac interface

To early Mac users he was probably best known as the author of MacPaint, the black-and-white bitmapped graphics program that, along with MacWrite, was included with every early Mac. Atkinson went on to create another sensation with HyperCard, a software package that made it easy even for users with no programming experience to create slick interactive applications. In 1990 he left Apple to cofound General Magic, a much-hyped effort to create an operating system and graphical interface for handheld "personal communicators." When General Magic shut down in 1992, Atkinson devoted himself to nature photography and now displays and sells his work in galleries and on his Web site (www.billatkinson.com). —Henry Norr

Given all that you have done, what do you think was your most important contribution to the Mac?

I feel my major role at Apple was creating tools to empower creative people. I made tools, like MacPaint, that didn't tell you what to draw but made it much easier for you to do that drawing. Or HyperCard, which didn't tell you what kind of custom software to make but let you make your own little HyperCard stacks that did the things you wanted to do. For me, it's always been about empowering creative people. And what's wonderful now, the perfect payback, is that I'm a heavy user of Macs—my own personal creativity is greatly amplified by the tools on the Mac. I didn't have to write Photoshop, and I use it every single day.

Are you all Mac?

Oh, I have got a couple of PCs on the network, just for testing and compatibility stuff, but I have about 14 Macs in the house, plus a G5 on order. I've got about five computers I use all the time, from my laptop to my OS 9 computer, my OS X computer, the computer that runs the drum scanner, and the one that runs the spectrophotometer and photo studio stuff. And then my wife's got a couple, and my kids have a couple.

What do you think about Mac OS X?

I love it. It's been painful switching over, but it's been worth it. The user interface is clearly better; the reliability is better; the performance is better.

Did you think the Mac would take over the world?

My hope was that what we were doing would sort of become a standard way of doing things until people improved on it and made it better. In any kind of a user-interface situation, what you want is for the best way to prevail. You don't want all this stuff about "I was there first!" to get in the way of that, because really the whole purpose of any kind of intellectual property is for the benefit of the public in the long run.

What would you have done differently with the Mac?

I would have licensed it to all comers, and designed it in such a way that Apple still kept the standard, so it didn't diverge into 50 different ones. Then everyone would have benefited from the work we did.

Do you resent Microsoft's dominance?

It's business! They're very good businesspeople. I wish Apple were a little more astute at business. I remember a point where Compaq came to Apple and said, "We want to make Macs." And Apple was afraid to let them—afraid they'd lose control and maybe the standard would get all bastardized. Maybe Apple would even have been unable to compete. So Apple said, "No, you can't make them," so Compaq went away and made Windows machines.

I still see the Windows interface as kind of lumpy and awkward, but better than it used to be, and I think over time the user interfaces are moving closer together. I'd like to see them be essentially identical, because it's awkward for people to switch back and forth.

Do you still use HyperCard?

Oh, I use HyperCard all the time. I look at my computer screen now, and HyperCard's up with my address book. I use it for custom kinds of programming. When I needed to choose the quality of JPEGs for my Web site, first I had each of the images converted into JPEGs in Photoshop at 12 different qualities. Then I made a HyperCard stack that has one card per image, with a graph on it of the quality settings versus the file size. In a second window it shows that JPEG at 200 percent. So now as I make the arrow keys go up and down, it goes to more and less quality, so I can very quickly find the optimum settings for each of my 715 images.

Tell us about what you're doing now.

I'm a nature photographer, and I use the tools of color management and digital printing to make really beautiful nature photographs that I sell in galleries. I do intimate landscapes and flower portraits, and the latest thing I'm doing are these mineral abstracts, where I take rocks and slice them with a diamond saw and polish them with a lap polisher and then photograph the details. What I get are images that to me look more like paintings than either photographs or rocks. They are abstract, and they have wonderful, very evocative shapes and colors—they're kind of like colored Rorschach tests.

continues on next page

How do you distribute your images?

They're doing very well selling at the galleries, and they're all online! But you don't have to buy them—you can go look at them. I also want to reach a much wider group of people, and so I'm creating a book called *Within the Stone: Nature's Abstract Rock Art,* which will be published by Brown Trout Publishing [in July 2004]. In order to print it, I'm faced with the limitations of a CMYK offset press. The first try, less than half of the images that I want to use would print to my satisfaction. So I've been working with a printer in Tokyo to make a dramatic increase in the quality of CMYK printing.

Ah, so you're back in the technology after all!

[He laughs.] Well, it's always a right-brain, left-brain thing. You use technology to support vision, and if you can't get your hands around the technology, then you're limited by what's right in front of you. The ICC profiles that I made for the Epson [Stylus Pro] 7600 and 9600 are now the gold standard—they bring a level of quality to that printer that wasn't possible before.

You wrote those profiles?

Yeah, I spent 1200 hours, measured over half a million spectral samples, in order to figure out how to get the highest-quality profiles.

Are you getting any money back for that?

I could sell them for a thousand bucks a pop and do pretty well, but because I put so much work into them, I wanted that to be leveraged by as many artists as possible. And so I put them up at the Epson Web site [http://prographics.epson.com] for free download, basically sharing my tools with other artists. My reward, instead of being a financial reward, is a reward in contributing to the art community.

2

System Software

Emory Christensen is the chapter editor and author.

David Reynolds was the chapter editor and author for the 8th edition of **The Macintosh Bible,** *from which portions of this chapter are taken.*

Although your Macintosh's hardware is well designed and its various components work together very efficiently, it's the system software running on your Mac that makes it distinct. Until recently, Apple offered two versions of Macintosh system software: Mac OS 9 and Mac OS X. Mac OS 9.2.2 was the last of the original line of Macintosh operating-system software, which has a lineage going all the way back to 1984. Mac OS 9.2.2 was exceptionally mature—and exceptionally vulnerable to certain kinds of crashes. Mac OS X, on the other hand, is a brand-new operating system that has its roots in Unix, not in the original Mac OS, and is much more stable than Mac OS 9.

Using a technology called the *Classic environment,* Mac OS X can run Mac OS 9 and earlier applications. These programs run inside a copy of Mac OS 9 that runs *inside* Mac OS X. Yes, it's conceptually a little complicated, but fortunately it all works almost transparently.

Here are a few tasks your system software handles:

- It starts up your Mac and it lets your Mac's hardware components (its memory, hard drive, processor, and so on) talk to each other.

- It draws windows, menus, and other items on the screen, and it handles requests you make using the keyboard or mouse.

- It handles requests from running programs (for memory or processor time).

- It does pretty much everything else that makes your Mac run.

In This Chapter

The Macintosh Operating System

Every personal computer ever made has some sort of *operating system* at its heart. An operating system (often abbreviated as OS) is a highly specialized program that tells the computer's hardware components how to behave and how to talk to each other. It also takes care of the *user interface*—the part of the software that handles interaction with the computer's users. This latter part of the system software gets all the attention, mainly because it's the most visible. Operating systems go much deeper than their user interfaces, though.

Under your Mac's serene surface area of windows and icons is a labyrinth of programming code that keeps busy by moving data between the hard drive, the memory, the processor, and the display, all the while keeping track of what programs are running, which windows are open, and what network connections it needs to maintain. Add to *that* keeping track of every key press and mouse click, among other things, and you start to understand why operating systems get so big and complex. Fortunately, you don't have to become too intimately acquainted with the inner workings of your Mac's operating system, but it's a good idea to understand the basics of how it all works. That way, when you run into a problem or need to do some tweaking beyond moving a few folders around, you're more likely to have the knowledge required to take care of things yourself.

System Software

The Macintosh operating system (Mac OS), often referred to as the Mac's *system software,* is what really makes a Macintosh a Macintosh. In fact, you can run other operating systems (such as Linux) on your Macintosh and never install the Mac OS at all, although that would seem, well, wrong.

In Mac OS X, the system software (and all its miscellaneous support files) is spread throughout thousands of files in a couple of special folders—System and Library, which we'll talk about later. These support files include (but aren't limited to) fonts, sounds, and pictures.

At its heart, Mac OS X has a core system (called Mach) that handles memory, hard-drive connections, and other really low-level stuff. On top of that is a flavor of Unix that provides capabilities such as graphics and networking, and on top of *that* is the Finder, which handles the interface between you and your Mac.

 There are several invisible folders that are part of Mac OS X as well—they're actually part of the BSD Unix foundation that Mac OS X is based on. Unless you're a real Unix aficionado, you'll never encounter these folders.

In Mac OS 9 and earlier, the system software consists of the System file (the core of the Mac OS), the Finder, and lots of add-ons, such as fonts and extensions, that enhance what your Mac can do. The problem is that because of the way Mac OS 9 and earlier systems were designed, these add-ons can really interfere with how your Mac works.

Mac OS 9 is a monolithic operating system, and Mac OS X is a modular one. Think of the differences between the two operating systems this way: You have two public service departments. One has the police, fire, parking and traffic, and water and sewer departments housed together in one big room with one door, with the dispatcher shouting orders in the room, hoping to get the right personnel to the right places. Problems arise when the traffic officers are all shuffling out and the firefighters need to use the door—they crash. This is Mac OS 9.

In Mac OS X, these various departments each have their own offices (and doors), with a central dispatcher coordinating the actions of all. The police can't interfere with the firefighters since they occupy different offices, and the dispatcher is able to send targeted messages to the various departments so that they know what to do and the other departments don't have to bother listening in. This is Mac OS X.

Version Numbers

The Mac OS has been around for 20 years now, and it's grown and changed a lot since its inception. Software—system software included—uses *version numbers* to keep track of what came first. It's like naming your children after yourself—you have Charles, Charles the second, Charles the third, and so on. If Charles were software, the naming would go like this: Charles (or Charles 1.0), Charles 2.0, Charles 3.0, and so on. The Mac OS is now at version 10 (and then some)—and that's a *long* time by system-software standards.

The first number (the one before the decimal) is the main version number. Changes to that number indicate huge changes to the software and the addition of major new features. A change to the first number *after* the decimal (say, from 5.0 to 5.1) usually indicates a few new features and some bug fixes—you're likely to find the software a little more useful and stable, but it probably won't boast a slew of new capabilities. Finally, a change to a second number, after another decimal (say, from 9.0.3 to 9.0.4), indicates some bug fixes but no new features. Of course, these rules aren't hard and fast, and some companies ignore them entirely to represent a year, not a version number, as when Windows 3.1 went to Windows 95. And not all program version numbers have a second decimal place.

History of the Mac OS

The Mac OS falls into six major groups according to its version-number scheme. This grouping says a lot about Apple's history.

System 1 to 6.0.8 (1984–91). This is the first set of releases, back when the system software was simply known as the System, followed by a number. The original series of Mac operating systems lasted from 1984 to 1991 and demanded little from the hardware that ran it, compared with today's operating systems. The entire operating system could fit comfortably on a floppy disk (in fact, it often had to), and it required less than 1 MB of RAM to run.

System 7 to 7.5 (1991–97). Released in 1991, System 7 brought multitasking (the ability to run more than one program at a time) to the Macintosh. With System 7's new abilities came a new need for power: System 7 required what was for the time a whopping 4 MB of RAM to work well—that was four times what its predecessor used. Apple made some tweaks to System 7 over the years, but no major changes hit the operating system through version 7.5.3, released in 1996. That's because Apple engineers were concentrating on the next Mac operating system, code-named Copland, which was never released. After years of development that drained resources from System 7, it was clear that Copland was in trouble. In late 1996, Apple announced that it had purchased NeXT, a computer company founded by Steve Jobs (who had cofounded Apple in 1976), and that NeXT's operating system, OpenStep (formerly named NextStep) would become the basis for the next OS.

Mac OS 7.6 (1997). In 1997, Apple released Mac OS 7.6 as part of its plan to clean up the neglected operating system. Mac OS 7.6 represented a name change—from System to Mac OS—as well as the start of regularly scheduled system-software updates. With version 7.6, the Mac OS had grown considerably since its debut in 1984—it could no longer fit on a floppy disk, and it needed 16 MB of RAM to operate well. By this time, Apple had also announced the impending release of its next-generation operating system, based on recently acquired technology from NeXT, with the code name Rhapsody. Apple promised more updates to the now-venerable Mac OS before Rhapsody's release.

Mac OS 8 to 8.6 (1997–99). With the release of Mac OS 8 in 1998, parts of the ill-fated Copland project saw the light of day in release form as Apple engineers salvaged parts of Copland by grafting them onto the original Mac OS. These parts included the ability to make multiple file copies simultaneously and a simplified installer. Mac OS 8 was the biggest thing to happen to the Macintosh system software since the introduction of System 7 in 1991. Mac OS 8 was also the first operating system that required a PowerPC chip—stranding all Macs built before 1994 (and a few built after that) at Mac OS 7.6. Mac OS 8.6 shipped in 1999 (with Mac OS 8.1, 8.5, and 8.5.1 in between), and while this series of releases added modern niceties such as indexed file searches for speedy file finding, much of those improvements centered on under-the-hood tweaks for speed and stability. In the meantime, the Rhapsody project, renamed Mac OS X, promised to cure the ills of the now-aging Mac OS while still letting users run their old programs on their Macs.

Mac OS 9 to 9.1 (1999–2001). By the time Mac OS 9 hit the scene in late 1999, the original Mac OS had seemingly undergone as much refinement as was possible. Remarkably stable and capable, Mac OS 9 still relies on the technology of the original 1984 release. Mac OS 9 set the stage for its successor, Mac OS X, by including such features as support for multiple users (a way of letting several people use the same Mac at different times without messing up each other's work spaces).

Mac OS X (2001–present). Mac OS X is the first totally new Macintosh operating system since the original in 1984. Although it took nearly ten years (Apple started the Copland project in the early 1990s), Apple engineers managed to marry the brute strength of Unix (on which NextStep was also based) with the best parts of the traditional Mac OS to produce Mac OS X. This powerhouse of an operating system can act as a Web and file server while it helps you send email, listen to MP3 music files, and create DVDs.

 Over the years, the system requirements for the Mac OS have grown from a measly 400 Kbyte floppy disk and 128 Kbytes of RAM for the original Mac OS to 1 GB of hard-drive space and at least 128 MB of RAM for Mac OS X 10.3 (Panther)—that's more than 2000 times the hard-drive space and 1000 times the memory needed for the first Mac OS.

The Flavors

Given all this history, it shouldn't be surprising that the Mac OS comes in a couple of flavors. These days, Apple's focus is entirely on Mac OS X. Almost all Macs sold currently boot *only* Mac OS X—Mac OS 9 won't start up these machines. Still, Mac OS 9 is worth talking about for two reasons: millions of Mac users still boot and use Mac OS 9 on a daily basis, and Mac OS 9 lives on in the form of the Classic environment in Mac OS X. Here are descriptions of the three current versions of the Mac OS:

- **Mac OS X**—Mac OS X is Apple's flagship operating system—it's what comes preinstalled on almost every single new Mac sold (Xserve, Apple's server hardware, which uses Mac OS X Server, is the notable exception). Mac OS X is meant for everyday use by Mac owners of all stripes.

- **Mac OS X Server**—This variant of Mac OS X software takes tremendous advantage of the operating system's Unix roots to work as a server— serving up files, Web sites, video and audio, and the like. Although it *can* be used by an everyday Mac user to do everyday work, it's really meant to be used on a Mac that's sitting in a closet somewhere, pushing bits through a network.

- **Mac OS 9 (Classic)**—This is the end point of the venerable original Mac OS line. It lives on as the Classic environment in Mac OS X.

Booting Mac OS 9 vs. Running Classic

Throughout this book, you'll see numerous references to running Classic and to booting Mac OS 9. These terms can get confusing. Here's a quick look at what they mean:

Booting Mac OS 9—This means starting your Mac using Mac OS 9. In this case, from the moment you press the power button on your Mac, it starts up using Mac OS 9, and Mac OS X doesn't enter the picture. Not all Macs allow you to do this.

Running Classic—This is Mac OS X's way of allowing older programs written for Mac OS 9 and earlier to run. When you run Classic, you first start up Mac OS X, and then you start the Classic environment from the Classic icon in System Preferences. This actually runs Mac OS 9 within Mac OS X, as if Mac OS 9 were another program. Once Classic starts up, programs that weren't created with Mac OS X in mind can still run in Mac OS X, by taking advantage of Classic.

How Mac OS X Differs from Mac OS 9 and Earlier

Although Mac OS 9 and Mac OS X can run some of the same software, and they look somewhat similar on the surface, the two are entirely different operating systems that share very little in their inner workings. However, as we've mentioned, Mac OS X hosts Mac OS 9 in the Classic environment, letting you run programs for both Mac OS X and Mac OS 9 without restarting your Macintosh. We'll be covering that in detail in "The Classic Environment," later in this chapter.

Here are some of the important differences between Mac OS X and Mac OS 9.

Underpinnings

Mac OS 9 (and the versions of the Mac OS leading up to it) is largely a *monolithic* operating system, which means it's difficult to separate into parts or layers. With programming code and concepts that date back to 1984 and even earlier, Mac OS 9 is its own animal and has little in common with other operating systems at its most basic level. This structure (or architecture) is one of the reasons why Mac OS 9 seems so long in the tooth from a technical standpoint. Programs can access your Mac's hardware directly (generally a bad thing, because it can cause crashes), and the system doesn't have many built-in mechanisms to keep one program from stomping all over another program's memory; both of these faults lead to crashes. To add new capabilities to Mac OS 9 (such as OpenGL for handling graphics and QuickTime for handling video and audio), engineers mostly had to use extensions and shared libraries, which brought their own set of problems.

Mac OS X, on the other hand, has well-defined parts that give it some serious power. At its heart, Mac OS X is built on the Mach kernel, an itty-bitty operating system in its own right. The Mach kernel is the only part of the operating system that works directly with hardware, managing the operation of hard drives, memory, video cards, and the like. It's this separation that makes Mac OS X so stable—Mach knows how to handle all the hardware, and all other programs have to ask Mach to do things with that hardware. This way, programs aren't sneaking around behind Mach's back, making hardware demands Mach doesn't know about—a situation that can result in a crash, as often happens in Mac OS 9 and earlier.

On top of the Mach kernel sits a version of BSD (short for Berkeley Software Distribution) Unix, a Unix flavor that's popular in education and as a server operating system—it runs a *lot* of Web servers. Several new technologies (graphics and networking, largely) are built into Mac OS X at a fairly low level, giving your Mac amazing power without adding a single crash-inducing, memory-swilling Mac OS 9–style extension to the mix. Finally, on top of all this is the user interface, with its rounded buttons, translucent menus, and gorgeous drop shadows.

 Like Mac OS 9, Mac OS X can be extended in a number of ways either by users or developers. Both users and developers can add new System Preferences panes (which are similar to Mac OS 9 control panels) in Mac OS X, and developers can add kernel extensions (which you will probably never have to deal with). The reason these aren't as dangerous as their Mac OS 9 counterparts is that Mac OS X System Preferences aren't allowed to modify the operating system at a low level, and although kernel extensions are, they are usually carefully written to avoid any trouble.

Graphics

The Mac OS has always been known for its graphics capabilities. After all, the desktop-publishing revolution of 1985 catapulted the Mac to the top design-tool position, where it remains strong today. Over the years Apple added new graphics capabilities to the Mac (such as QuickTime, OpenGL, and ColorSync), largely via extensions. At its core, Mac OS 9 still uses a program called QuickDraw to handle graphics, and QuickDraw came on the scene in 1984 with the original Mac.

Mac OS X, on the other hand, has all-new graphics capabilities, using Adobe's Portable Document Format (PDF) as the basis for two-dimensional graphics and OpenGL for three-dimensional graphics. Along with that sits the latest version of QuickTime, the über-media format that can play back almost any audio or video file, including MP3 audio, MPEG video, and even interactive Macromedia Flash files. All this means that Mac OS X can do amazing graphics tricks, and graphic designers, gamers, and video producers alike will find this system very powerful. To tie all its graphics panache together, Apple engineers created Quartz (which is now Quartz Extreme), which lets all these graphics capabilities work seamlessly. For example, it allows you to drag a translucent, miniaturized QuickTime movie over an active OpenGL animation, and while the movie plays without missing a beat, you can see the animation showing through. Now *that's* power. Add to this the ability to save files as PDF documents, and you have an unmatched graphics powerhouse.

Memory use

Of all the ways in which Mac OS 9 and Mac OS X differ, memory use is at the top of the list. When a program launches in Mac OS 9, it gets a fixed slice of the available memory. Programs have a default amount assigned by the programmer, but this amount is just a best guess—it's often not enough, especially when you're working with graphics, sound, or video programs. When a program doesn't get enough memory, it may crash more often. If a memory conflict occurs, you can set how much memory each program receives, but this often requires a lot of tweaking. Mac OS 9 and earlier has a version of virtual memory (hard-drive space that acts like RAM), but again you have to set how much hard-drive space to use as virtual memory in the Memory control panel. You can turn off virtual memory in Mac OS 9, but then your programs generally take up more RAM.

In Mac OS X, on the other hand, the operating system handles all memory needs for programs, using virtual memory (which is always on and grows and shrinks to meet memory needs) to keep things running smoothly. Mac OS X users never have to adjust the memory use of any Carbon or Cocoa program (programs updated or specifically written to run on Mac OS X), and if one application needs more memory, Mac OS X is smart enough to take it from programs that aren't using their share. (Because programs in the Classic environment are still running under a version of Mac OS 9, which runs inside Mac OS X, they may require the user to adjust their memory use—even though the memory ultimately comes from Mac OS X.)

Responsiveness

Both Mac OS X and Mac OS 9 and earlier can perform more than one task at a time—for example, running a word processor, a photo editor, and an email program, all while downloading files from the Internet. They go about this in different ways, though. Mac OS 9 uses *cooperative multitasking,* in which the active application gets to say how much of your computer's resources it wants to use, while all the other running programs must make do with what's left over. This means that a single program can hog your Mac, preventing you from doing the simplest things (such as pulling down menus) while it's working— bad news if that program takes a few minutes or hours to complete a task.

Mac OS X approaches the problem of sharing a single Mac among several programs with *preemptive multitasking.* Instead of relying on the programs to divvy up available time on your Mac's CPU, the system software schedules each task, leaving some room for basic jobs like switching between programs, moving the pointer, and using menus. The result is that Mac OS X feels more responsive than Mac OS 9 when several programs are vying for your Mac's attention, and you'll never have to deal with a rogue program taking over your entire system again.

Crash protection

Because the Macintosh operating system was designed to run just one program at a time, it didn't have any built-in mechanisms to keep a bug in one program from running roughshod over the memory that another program was using. This wasn't a problem until the early 1990s, when System 7 gave every Mac the ability to run more than one program at a time. Despite ten years of work on the problem, Mac OS 9.2.2 still can't prevent one running program from corrupting another's memory space, and that includes the system software. This weakness can—and does—lead to some spectacular crashes.

Mac OS X *can* prevent one program from taking down another program—or the entire system. Through a feature called *protected memory,* Mac OS X separates the memory used by the operating system and by each running program. If a program tries to write over another program's memory, Mac OS X shuts the first program down, leaving the rest of the system untouched. You don't even have to restart your Mac!

Installing the Operating System

When you first bought your Mac, it came with the most recent version of the operating system at that time. The problem with this cozy arrangement is that while you're happily using your Mac, Apple is happily writing new operating-system software, complete with shiny new features and bug fixes. So, at some point, you'll probably want to install a new version of the operating system. That, of course, is the cheerier scenario. There are also times when things may go quite wrong with your Mac, and the only solution is to reinstall your operating system.

Installing a new operating system may be the Mac equivalent of a personality transplant, but the prospect isn't nearly as daunting as it sounds. After all, Apple *intended* your Mac to undergo an occasional personality overhaul in the form of an operating-system upgrade, and its engineers have made installation pretty easy. Also, if your current installation has gone bad and you just *can't* set it right using any other troubleshooting method, reinstalling your Mac's operating system may be your last hope (see Chapter 8 for more on when to reinstall the Mac OS).

 It's always a good idea to keep a copy of your system software and any updates you have performed in case you do need to reinstall the Mac OS some day.

Installing Mac OS X

After years of all-nighters and gallons of Mountain Dew, Apple's engineers have come up with an easy-to-use, easy-to-install version of Unix—an accomplishment for which we should laud them. Installing Mac OS X is surprisingly easy given its size and scope (**Figure 2.1**).

Figure 2.1

This is where it all begins. Click Restart, and you're on your way to installing Mac OS X.

Installing Mac OS X on Nonqualified Macs

With the help of some specialized utilities, it's possible to install Mac OS X on older Macs that are not officially supported by Mac OS X. This includes a good deal of the Power Mac line as well as certain Mac clone models. Although it's possible, it's probably not wise, unless you're really into tinkering with your machine. That's because Mac OS X—especially newer versions—isn't written with older machines in mind, and it may not support everything, such as starting up from FireWire hard drives or using a machine's L2 and L3 caches, which boost your Mac's processor speed.

Getting ready

To get started installing Mac OS X, insert the Mac OS X installation disc. When it mounts, it should pop open a window that says, "Welcome to Mac OS X." Inside that window a couple of documents talk about Mac OS X, and several folders contain the same documents in several other languages. One of these folders has some utilities that can erase your hard drive and set the startup disk, if you like.

But you'll most likely be interested in the Install Mac OS X icon at the top of the window. Double-click this icon to start the installation process. When you do, the installer puts up a window with some text and a single button, labeled Restart. Clicking this button restarts your Mac from the Mac OS X CD and begins the installation process—but first you'll have to enter your administrator password, if you're installing on a machine that's already running Mac OS X. You can also start up from the Mac OS X CD by putting it in your CD drive and starting up with ⓒ held down.

 You can also get a list of *all* available startup disks by holding down Option when you start your Mac. You can choose the Mac OS X install disc icon from the icons that pop up.

Starting the Mac OS X installation process

Once your Mac has restarted from the Mac OS X CD, you'll see the Apple logo and a spinning circle made up of color-changing rectangles. This is your indication that your Mac is starting up into Mac OS X for the first time.

Once your Mac finishes getting its act together, it will start up into the Mac OS X Installer. The first window you face in the Installer is the language-selection window, in which you'll start working through your installation.

 If you change your mind and want to go back a step, you can always click the Go Back button in the installer.

Select a language. In the first Installer window, you have your choice of 15 languages to use. Choose one and click Continue.

Introduction. This is simply a welcome screen, in which Apple sends its warmest wishes and tells you how to cancel the installation, if you so choose. In this screen you'll notice a series of bulleted items on the left that show your progress. They read:

- Introduction
- Read Me
- License
- Select Destination
- Installation Type
- Installing
- Finish Up

These items mark the major portions of the installation process. Click Continue to move on. (If for some reason you *don't* want to proceed, choose Installer >

Quit and then click the Startup Disk option when it comes up to let your Mac know which disk it should now use to start up.)

Read Me. Although it may look a little boring, you really should take the time to read through this document—it *does* contain important information that you may need to know during or after your installation, and it might save your bacon during installation. Once you've read it, click Continue.

License. Before installing Apple's software on your hard drive, you should at least glance at the Mac OS license agreement, a scintillating bit of legalese likely to put you to sleep and containing such words as *subsidiary* and *nuclear facilities*. Click Continue and you'll see a no-nonsense dialog where your options are Agree or Disagree. Click Agree to continue to the actual installation pane; click Disagree to drop the whole matter and cancel installation.

Select Destination. The Installer looks for any available hard drives on which to install Mac OS X and lists them in this pane. Click the desired hard-drive icon to select it. When you do, the Mac OS X 10.3 Installer checks to see what version of the Mac OS (if any) is installed. After collecting the information, it tells you how much space you need to finish the installation. This pane also contains an Options button in the lower-left corner. Click it to bring up a list of three installation options:

- **Upgrade Mac OS X**—This option is the default selection. It does a simple installation, upgrading any previous version of Mac OS X or Mac OS 9 and earlier to Mac OS X 10.3. User settings and documents are left alone.

- **Archive and Install**—This option is the equivalent of the Clean Install in Mac OS 9 (see the sidebar "Installing Mac OS 9/the Classic Environment," later in this chapter). It moves the existing Mac OS X system software to a folder named Previous System and then installs a brand-new copy of Mac OS X. The files in the Previous System folder are there only so that you can recover specific items—you can't start up from the Previous System folder.

  If you check the box next to Preserve Users and Network Settings, the installation will leave the existing user accounts and network settings alone, importing them into the new copy of the system software.

- **Erase and Install**—This option erases the hard drive completely and then installs a brand-new copy of Mac OS X on top of that. Use this option only if there's nothing on the hard drive you want or need.

 If you use this option, *only* Mac OS X will be installed; you won't have access to the Classic environment for running Mac OS 9 applications. To get access to the Classic environment, you'll need to do a separate Mac OS 9 installation.

This option also lets you choose the format for your hard disk: Mac OS Extended (Journaled) or Unix File System. Mac OS Extended is the default. Unless you *know* you want Unix File System as your hard-disk format, leave this as Mac OS Extended.

Choose one of these installation options and click Continue.

Installation Type. By default, the Installer does an easy installation, which installs everything Apple thinks Mac OS X needs to run properly. Most folks should go with the easy installation—it has everything that most users will want. If your installation of Mac OS X came on multiple discs, the Installer will list the CDs you'll need to complete the installation.

If you want to customize your Mac OS X installation, click Customize at the bottom. This presents you with the Custom Install pane, in which you can choose which parts of the operating system to install by checking or unchecking their boxes. Here are your options:

- **Essential System Software**—You can't uncheck this option. This is the system software required to start up your Mac.

- **BSD Subsystem**—This installs BSD 4.4 command-line utilities, and its presence enables such cool things as Rendezvous, Internet Sharing, and SSH. Leave this checked—it provides a number of utilities you might need someday.

- **Additional Applications**—Installs applications such as iTunes, iPhoto, iCal, and iSync. This is checked by default; leave it checked. You can also check (or uncheck) individual applications.

- **Printer Drivers**—Installs printer drivers for lots of different printers from Canon, Epson, Hewlett-Packard, and Lexmark, as well as Gimp-Print drivers (these are Unix printer drivers). You can choose to install the whole group or select only certain drivers.

- **Additional Speech Voices**—Installs more voices for Mac OS X's speech technology. Although this is not checked by default, it's worth checking. It takes up only 50 MB of disk space, and you never know when you might want some variety in your Mac's speech.

- **Fonts**—By default, this installs additional Asian fonts (Japanese, Chinese, and Korean), and you can check the box next to Fonts for Additional Languages to install Arabic, Hebrew, Thai, Cyrillic, Devanagari, Gujarati, Punjabi, Armenian, Cherokee, and Inuktitut. Leave this checked if you will need to work with these languages.

- **Language Translations**—Provides additional languages for Mac OS X. It's checked by default; unless you *know* you won't need any of these languages, leave this checked. Alternatively, you can choose only the languages you want.

- **X11**—This is the X11 windowing system for Mac OS X—of interest only if you plan on running certain Unix applications. Most users can leave this unchecked.

Installing. Now the Installer goes to work. First it checks the installation disk, and then it starts copying software from the CD and moving things around on the hard drive. This process can take anywhere from a few minutes to half an hour, depending on your CD-drive speed, your Mac's processor speed, and how many options you have chosen to install. The Installer keeps you apprised of how long the process will take, but don't take the installer at its word until the final stages—the number can vary wildly. This is another good time for a snack or a trip to the restroom. You may have to swap CDs during the installation (depending on which components you chose to install), so check in occasionally to see how things are going.

Finish Up. Once the Installer has completed its job, it lets you know that it's done, and it tells you to click Quit to finish installing. It also automatically quits after 30 seconds, giving you a countdown. After that, your Mac does some of its own mojo, and moves from the Installer to the Setup Assistant. That's it! You've installed Mac OS X. Now you just have to go through the setup.

Setting up Mac OS X

You're not done yet, though. The next step is to fill out a set of forms that Mac OS X will use to create a user account, set up Internet access, and make other basic tweaks to your Mac's settings. During this process, you'll also be asked to register Mac OS X with Apple. This registration information gets sent to Apple the next time you connect to the Internet. Here's a quick look at the process:

Welcome. In a beautiful blue movie, Apple welcomes you to Mac OS X and asks what country you live in, giving you a short list of common choices and the option to see the entire long list. Select your country and click Continue.

Personalize your settings. The next step in your setup is to choose a keyboard layout. These layouts are listed by country, and there are a lot of them; fortunately, the setup program presents a short list of the most common ones with the option to show all, if yours isn't present. Once you've selected your keyboard, click Continue.

Set up your Apple ID. Setup Assistant now makes its debut and asks you to set up your Apple ID. This is the ID and password you use to access Apple's services, such as the Apple Support Web site, the iTunes Music Store, and the Apple Store. If you have a .Mac membership, your Apple ID is your member name.

You have three options here: enter your existing Apple ID, create a new Apple ID, or don't create a new Apple ID. Make your choice by clicking the appropriate radio button, and then click Continue.

Registration information. Setup Assistant now asks for your name, address, phone number, email address, and company or school. Most of this information is *not* optional, and you can't proceed without entering it. If you try, Setup Assistant uses a red icon to mark the mandatory fields you didn't fill in. After you provide this information, click Continue. You can also click the Privacy button to read Apple's privacy policy, indicating what the company will and will not do with this information.

A few more questions. The next pane asks how you plan to use your Mac and what your occupation is. You have to answer these two questions from pop-up menus or you can't proceed with your setup. The pane also asks permission for Apple and other companies to contact you with news and information about related products—this *is* optional. Once you've entered your answers, click Continue. The final registration pane tells you that your registration information will be sent to Apple the next time you connect to the Internet. Click Continue.

Create your account. Again, Setup Assistant asks you to enter your name, as well as a short name (or Unix-style nickname) that you can use when entering a user name and password. The Installer fills in these two bits of information based on the information you entered previously. You can either accept the supplied short name or change it. This short name shows up, for example, when you install software. You need to enter a password and a hint, which Mac OS X uses to create an account for you—every installation has at least one account. You also have the opportunity to select an icon for yourself from those preinstalled—this icon shows up in the Login window under certain circumstances. You can change this icon later in the Accounts pane in System Preferences. Click Continue.

 Mac OS X account passwords are case sensitive, so be sure that your Caps Lock key is off when you type your password.

Get Internet ready. In this pane, you can tell Mac OS X about your Internet connection. You have four choices: activate a free trial EarthLink account, redeem a special EarthLink offer, use your existing Internet service, or skip Internet setup altogether. Click the radio button next to your choice, and then click Continue.

If you've chosen one of the two options that make EarthLink your provider, you're asked for your credit card, billing information, and, if applicable, your special promotion code.

If you've chosen to use your existing Internet service provider, Mac OS X asks how you connect to the Internet—via modem, cable modem, DSL modem, an Ethernet LAN, or an AirPort wireless LAN. Depending on which of these you select, the next couple panes will walk you through the specific settings for your ISP; you'll need to get that information from your service provider. Click Continue in each pane to move on to the next setting.

If you choose to skip Internet setup altogether, Setup Assistant notes that Mac OS X takes great advantage of the Internet and you should reconsider. Click Continue to move on.

Get .Mac. Once you've picked your ISP, Apple gives you the opportunity to sign up for a .Mac account; if you already have one, you can enter your information here. You have three choices: create a trial account, use an existing .Mac account, or set up a .Mac account later. If you choose to create a .Mac trial account, this account name will be used as your Apple ID. Click Continue.

You're ready to connect. Now that you've completed your Internet setup, Mac OS X connects to Apple's servers and sends in your registration information. If you cancel this process before it finishes, Mac OS X won't send your information, but you can continue to set up your Mac. (It will send the information the next time you connect to the Internet.)

Set up Mail. In the final round of questions, Mac OS X asks whether you'd like to use a mac.com email address or set up another address for your email information. If you choose to set up another account, Setup Assistant asks for your email address, incoming mail server, account ID, email password, and outgoing mail server. (You can get information on your incoming and outgoing mail server from your ISP.) This step is optional, by the way. Click Continue to move on.

Select a time zone. The next question's an easy one—you're asked to select a time zone on a nifty map.

Set the date and time. Getting down to the minutiae, this pane asks you to set the current date and time for your Mac. Odds are, it'll be entered correctly already.

Congratulations! When you move on from setting the date and time, the next thing you see is your Mac OS X Desktop. Your Mac automatically checks for new updates, and if there are any, it recommends that you download and install them (for more on this process, see "Updating Your System Software," later in the chapter).

Installing Mac OS 9/the Classic Environment

Some of you may still need to install Mac OS 9. For example, if you are installing Mac OS X on a brand-new hard drive where there is currently no operating system, you will only get Mac OS X; you won't be able to run applications in Classic because Mac OS X does not install Mac OS 9 for you. For some folks that may be fine, but others may still need access to Mac OS 9 applications and thus will need to install Mac OS 9.

The process of installing Mac OS 9 is similar to the process of installing Mac OS X. As with Mac OS X, use the CD with the system-software Installer on it as the startup volume. After restarting from the system-software CD, click the Installer icon to begin. The first screen you see when installing (aside from the splash screen that briefly pops up) is a welcome that gives you an overview of the installation process. When you click Continue, the Installer starts its work. As with Mac OS X, the Installer pretty much guides you through the process. Here's a brief summary of what happens:

Destination disk. First, in the Select Destination screen you choose the destination disk from a pop-up menu with a list of hard drives on which you can install Mac OS 9 (**Figure 2.2**). If you click Options at the bottom of this screen, you can perform a clean install. Unlike a regular install, a clean install starts from scratch, creating a brand-new System Folder with all-new components (you may need to do a clean install if Mac OS 9 is causing you problems; see Chapter 8 for more on when you would need to do this). It gives the existing System Folder the name Previous System Folder so that you don't lose everything you had in that folder. The tricky part about clean installs is that you have to merge the folders, moving items such as preferences, browser bookmarks, and fonts from your old System Folder to the new one. Because of this daunting task of sifting through hundreds of files, clean installs are typically a last resort. Clicking Select takes you to the next couple of screens, which are chock-full of nutritious information.

continues on next page

Figure 2.2

Select the hard drive on which you want to install Mac OS 9 from the Destination Disk menu.

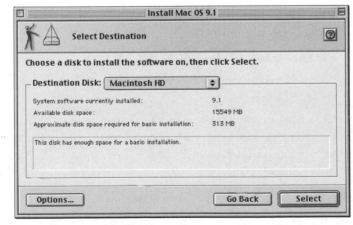

Installing Mac OS 9/the Classic Environment   *continued*

Documentation. The next couple of screens contain some documentation you should read. The Before You Install message is a bit daunting, but it may contain a tidbit that will save your Mac's life—and save *you* from pulling out your hair when things go wrong. You can save or print this document for later perusal. The other document is Apple's license agreement. You'll be asked if you agree or disagree with the legal information here. Click Agree to continue to the actual installation screen; click Disagree to drop the whole matter and cancel installation.

Installation time. Finally! You're now presented with the Install Software screen. If you click the Start button, the Installer will begin an Easy Install (one that includes all the default components). Click the Customize button, and the Custom Installation and Removal screen appears, in which you can select just the components you want to install on your hard drive. While this allows some truly magnificent customization, it also means you'll have to wade through a slew of check boxes and pop-up menus, plus you'll have to know enough about the Mac OS to select all the items you need. Finally, if you click Options, you can tell the Installer whether it should update the hard-disk drivers (you'll almost always want to do this) and whether you want it to create a text file that logs installation progress.

Once you've clicked Start and the actual installation process has begun, your Mac takes anywhere from 10 to 30 minutes (typically closer to 10) to install Mac OS 9 on your hard drive. After the installation is done, you can restart the Mac using your new system software. Make sure you've selected the disk with the newly installed system software in the Startup Disk control panel. This ensures that your Mac uses the correct disk when it starts up.

Setup Assistant. After you finish installing Mac OS 9 and restart your Mac, Setup Assistant greets you. This utility was designed to ask you some questions about how you'll use your Mac and then change settings in several control panels based on your answers. But since you'll have already created these system settings through Mac OS X, you don't need to bother with this step.

Updating Your System Software

These days, with more and more people having high-speed Internet access, updating system software is much easier than it was in the dark days of the mid-'90s. And, fortunately, Mac OS X has a built-in mechanism it uses to look for system-software updates (as well as some updates for other Apple-developed software, such as QuickTime, iPhoto, and Safari). This mechanism can find the updates, download them, and install them—all with just a couple of clicks. There are two ways to update your Apple software, one of which uses Apple's built-in mechanism and one of which requires manual labor. You can either use Apple's built-in Software Update software, or manually download and install the software update. If you have a dial-up connection, you may be in for a long, long download—some of these updates can be as big as 100 MB or more. Occasionally, Apple releases a CD with an update that you can buy from the company for around $20.

Software Update

Software Update is the built-in version checker that comes as part of Mac OS X. It's set to automatically contact Apple's servers and compare your currently installed software with the latest versions on Apple's servers. This check looks at your system software as well as other Apple-developed applications installed on your Mac, such as iTunes and iMovie. And if it finds an update, it lets you know, giving you the option of downloading the software and installing it for you.

This process is triggered two ways: either automatically according to a schedule, or manually by clicking a button in a section of System Preferences. The automatic check is pretty self-explanatory—your Mac simply does the check at a predetermined time. (You need to be connected to the Internet at that predetermined time, however, in order for Software Update to work.) You might do the manual check if an update has come out and you want to grab it before the automatic check happens or if you have not been connected to the Internet during a scheduled check. Here's how to do a manual check.

In Mac OS X 10.3, you can do a manual check in one of two ways. The easiest by far is to make sure you are connected to the Internet and then select Apple menu > Software Update. Software Update automatically begins checking for updates.

The other way to do a manual check in Mac OS X 10.3—and the *only* way to do it in Mac OS X 10.2 and earlier—is to launch System Preferences (see "System Preferences," later in this chapter). This special application lets you set a large number of your Mac's settings. Once System Preferences is open, click the Software Update icon in the System section to bring up the Software Update pane.

In Mac OS X 10.3 you will see a couple of choices, denoted by tabs—Update Software and Installed Updates (**Figure 2.3**). If the Update Software tab is not already selected, click it. The set of controls under the Update Software tab includes a "Check for updates" check box that lets you choose whether to have Mac OS X automatically check for updates and a pop-up menu that lets you set how often it will check. At the bottom is the Check Now button; click it to have Mac OS X check for new software updates right away. (Remember, you'll need to be connected to the Internet for Software Update to work.) The other tab, Installed Updates, displays a log of the updates you've already installed via Software Update, showing when those updates took place.

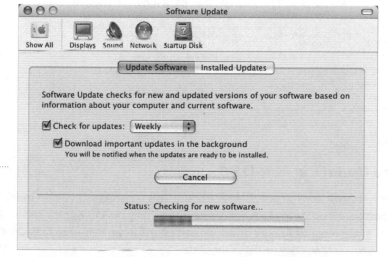

Figure 2.3

When triggered, Software Update talks to Apple's servers to see if there is any new software available.

In Mac OS X 10.2 and earlier you have the same functionality as in Mac OS X 10.3, but the interface is slightly different. For example, instead of two tabs, there is only one window with two buttons at the bottom, one for checking for updates immediately (Update Now) and one for showing the update log (Show Log).

Regardless of whether the update was initiated automatically or manually, Mac OS X says howdedoo to Apple's servers and politely requests a list of all new updates. If there are any new software updates, a list of them pops up in the Software Update pane. Software Update displays the name of the update, its version number, and its size.

From this list (**Figure 2.4**) you can choose the updates you want to install, and Software Update will do the dirty work, letting you know whether a restart is required.

Figure 2.4

Software Update gives you a slew of information about the current updates available on Apple's Web site. You can pick which ones you want to install.

Software Update in Mac OS 9

Mac OS 9 has its own version of Software Update. This control panel works in much the same fashion as Software Update in Mac OS X—by automatically polling Apple's servers for any updates to Mac OS 9. Since most of Apple's development efforts have shifted to Mac OS X, however, you won't see too many Mac OS 9 updates these days.

If you try to run the Mac OS 9 Software Update using Classic, Mac OS X politely lets you know that you can't do that—run the Mac OS X version instead.

Manual Update

Software Update isn't the only way to update your Mac OS X software. You can also download the installers from Apple's support site (www.info.apple.com) and then run them from your hard drive. When you run the Installer, you'll need to authenticate (provide your user name and password) to prove that you're allowed to do the update, select the hard drive on which you want to install, and then go ahead with the installation. Some updates will ask you to restart your Mac after completing an update, which you can defer until you're ready.

There are a couple of advantages to doing it this way. First, once you have the installer downloaded, you don't need a network connection to do the installation.

Second, you can rerun the updater later without a network connection, which can be a useful troubleshooting technique (or it may come in handy if you need to update more than one Mac).

Inside the System Software

As we've mentioned before, every computer has a special set of software that provides the intelligence behind the machine, and the Mac is no different. This system software makes your Mac run—without it, you may as well not even plug in your Mac. Although the transition to Mac OS X is largely complete (from Apple's perspective, at least), there are still two sets of system software you should know about: Mac OS X and Mac OS 9. Here's an inside look at each—and at how your hard drive is organized when using each.

Disk Structures

Before we jump right into talking about the system software, it's important to understand how Mac OS 9 and Mac OS X impose order on the hard drive. Each does it differently, and these differences can be a little challenging to get used to.

Mac OS X disk structure

Mac OS X, thanks to its Unix roots and its secure, multiuser nature, imposes a fairly rigid structure of folders on your Mac's hard drive—at least rigid by Mac OS 9 standards. The days of "put it anywhere" are gone with Mac OS X. This is because Mac OS X is particular about separating what belongs to the system software from what belongs to the computer's users, as well as keeping each user's stuff separate and secure.

A good example of this new focus on separation is the OS's handling of fonts. Mac OS X needs certain fonts to run properly—to create text in menus and windows, for example. These fonts belong to the system and are available to all users at all times. Individual users, on the other hand, have the option of installing fonts that are available only to them and not to any other user of the same computer. And that's why a clean installation of Mac OS X has these folders at the top level of the hard drive:

- **Applications**—Holds the applications installed on your Mac. They don't *have* to live here, but if they do, they'll be available to all users. You can put your applications elsewhere, if you like.

- **Documents**—If you have Mac OS 9 installed, you may also have a Documents folder at the root level of your hard drive. This Documents folder is a holdover from Mac OS 9, and you probably won't use it to store your documents (although you can).

- **Library**—Contains files that are used by multiple users of your Mac, such as help files, fonts that are available for all users, and systemwide preference panes.

- **System**—Holds files that Mac OS X needs to run properly, including the Finder and the Dock applications. Strangely, all these files are shoved into a folder titled Library that lives in the System folder. This is *not* the same as the Library folder at the top level of the hard drive.

- **Users**—Contains folders for each user with an account. These folders, in turn, hold files that belong to individual users, including documents, movies, music, fonts, preferences, and so on.

- **System Folder**—If you have Mac OS 9 installed, then you'll have a System Folder here, which contains the software you'll need to run Classic and boot Mac OS 9 (for more on the Mac OS 9 System Folder see "The Mac OS 9 (Classic) System Folder," later in the chapter).

In Mac OS X you can't just do anything you like with these folders. That's because you don't *own* these folders—the system does. You'll find that if you try to rename one of these folders by selecting it and pressing (Return), it's no go—the filename isn't editable. (The Documents folder and System Folder are the exceptions.)

It's not all a Big Brother control grab here—there is an upside. Applications go in one place, documents go in another, and system modifications go in still another place. It enforces order, so that it's easier to keep your hard drive organized.

 If you try to move one of these special folders (except for Users) to the Trash, you'll be asked for a password, and then the folder will dutifully be put in the Trash. If you do this with the System folder, your Mac will be instantly crippled, and the fix—moving the System folder back out of the Trash to the root level of the hard drive—is complicated. Don't do it—not even to see if it works.

It helps if you think of Mac OS X as a user of your computer—which, in some ways, it is. It uses your hardware to run applications, render windows, and reveal menus. And like any other user, Mac OS X owns certain folders, which include Applications, Library, System, and Users. In fact, if you open the Ownership & Permissions section of the Get Info window for any of these items, you'll see that "system" is listed as the item's owner—not you. If you're the administrator for the Mac, you're part of the group that has read and write permissions, though, so you can add and remove items from these folders. For more on permissions, see "Permissions" in Chapter 1.

 If you have a Mac that can boot Mac OS 9 and you want to delete these folders (or any protected Mac OS X folders), just boot Mac OS 9 and toss 'em in the Trash. This is possible because Mac OS 9 doesn't understand Unix permissions. Of course, your Mac won't start up using Mac OS X any longer, and you'll have to reinstall Mac OS X in order to use it.

Mac OS 9 disk structure

Mac OS 9 is much looser and freer about its disk structure. A fresh installation of Mac OS 9 has three folders:

- **Applications (Mac OS 9)**—Holds the applications installed on your Mac. Usually reserved for Mac OS 9 applications.
- **Documents**—Holds your documents (go figure).
- **System Folder**—Contains the files that Mac OS 9 needs to run.

These folders are just suggested locations—you don't have to keep your applications in your Applications (Mac OS 9) folder, and you don't have to keep your documents in the Documents folder. In fact, you can delete both of these folders if you like. The only one that's necessary to a computer running Mac OS 9 is the System Folder. And Mac OS 9 makes no effort to keep you from moving or using almost any file anywhere on the hard drive. We'll go into this in more detail in "The Classic Environment," later in this chapter.

Best of Both Worlds

If you have Mac OS 9 and Mac OS X installed on the same Mac, you *may* see the following additional folders:

- **Applications (Mac OS 9)**—A folder for your Mac OS 9 applications (your Classic applications when using Mac OS X).
- **Desktop (Mac OS 9)**—An alias to your Mac OS 9 Desktop folder, which is different from a user's Mac OS X Desktop Folder.

And you'll see a document titled Late Breaking News, which contains the latest information about Mac OS 9.

The Mac OS X System Folder

The Mac OS X system software is fundamentally different from that of earlier versions of the Mac OS, and that difference ranges from its plumbing to its user interface. It's actually a melding of three operating systems: OpenStep (a product of Steve Jobs' previous company, NeXT), BSD Unix (a powerful flavor of Unix), and the Mac OS. This hybrid makes Mac OS X a powerful beast, but it also introduces a few quirks and some dark magic necessary to make the whole mélange work together properly.

Unlike Mac OS 9, Mac OS X doesn't put all its system software components in a single blue folder. Instead, it places many invisible files and folders in various places on your hard drive—you'll probably never need to see or do anything with these—along with a bunch of folders you *can* see and manipulate.

The System folder in Mac OS X contains items the operating system needs to work properly. Most often, you probably won't need to add items to or delete items from the System folder—in fact, Mac OS X makes it somewhat difficult to do so, in cases. When you open the System folder, you'll find the Library folder. It contains shared resources that your Mac's system software can use. Although nearly 50 folders nest in the /System/Library folder, only a few are of real interest (that is, they contain things you might want to manipulate or that may appeal to your inner geek).

CoreServices. This folder holds many of the items you use all the time when you use Mac OS X, including BootX (which lets you select whether to start up in Mac OS 9—if your Mac can do so—or Mac OS X), the Dock program, the Mac OS X System and Finder files, Help Viewer, and the Software Update engine. While you may only want to look at some of these files for curiosity's sake, others may be useful. For example, you can run Software Update by launching the application from this folder, or you can add items to your Mac menu bar by double-clicking an item in the Menu Extras folder. Do be careful, though—you are mucking about in the system's realm here.

Fonts. This folder holds fonts that the system uses—not those you use in your day-to-day computing. There are other folders you use to host additional fonts—we'll cover those in more detail in "The Library Folder" and "The Users Folder," below.

PreferencePanes. This folder contains System Preferences files, such as Dock, Mouse, and QuickTime preferences. These items show up in your System Preferences window, but you can neither add nor remove items to or from this folder.

Screen Savers. Modules for the Mac OS X screensaver live in this folder. If you want to add a screen saver, you should do it elsewhere, however—in your /Users/Library folder. We'll cover that in "The Users Folder," below.

Sounds. System beeps reside in this folder—they're simple AIFF files. You can add sounds here, but you'll be asked to authenticate first. If you do so, those sounds will be available via your Sounds System Preferences pane. Again, you'd probably be better off adding sounds to the Library folder in your Users folder—that way, they'll show up for you in System Preferences, and you won't have to muck with the system's special folders.

StartupItems. This folder contains many of the system services that run in the background, such as Apache, Cron, and SSH—mostly Unix services. You probably should not mess with this folder, unless you *really* know what you're doing. It's still pretty interesting to browse through, though, if you happen to be a bit on the geeky side.

As mentioned above, you're better off not adding to these folders unless you're a Mac OS X power user. There are other places where you can add fonts, preference panes, screensavers, and so on. You're going to sense a trend when we delve into the /System/Library folder and the Library folder that lives inside the Users folder: each has a similar set of folders inside, providing resources for the various users of the computer.

 Unix aficionados may want to delve into the User Template folder—it provides a template for new user accounts when those are created. Unix pros will be happy about this—the template makes it easier to create custom user accounts. Others probably won't ever need to deal with this.

The Applications Folder

This special folder holds your Mac OS X applications. You don't *have* to put them here; it's just a convenient holding place, and you'll find that it's where Apple has put its applications.

Applications in this folder are accessible to all users of the computer—if the application shows up here, it's fair game for anyone who can log in to your Mac. If, however, you have an application that you want to keep to yourself—that no one else should use—do this:

1. Create a folder in your home folder. You access your home folder from the Users folder or from the sidebar in a Finder window (for more on your home folder see "The Users Folder," below).

2. Name this new folder Applications or whatever you like; you'll notice that Mac OS X gives it the nifty Application folder icon (the one with a graphic drawing of an *A*).

3. Move (or install) the application that you want to keep private into your new applications folder.

The Library Folder

At the top, or root, level of the hard drive you'll find the Library folder. This Library folder contains resources that all users have access to, such as fonts you can use in a word-processing document or screensaver modules that anyone can use.

 Although there are a few folders within your Library folder that you might want to add something to, it's become increasingly unnecessary—almost everything you'd want to add to these folders comes with an installer that does the job for you.

Confusingly enough, this Library folder is not the /System/Library folder. However, this root-level Library folder contains some items similar to those in the /System/Library folder. For the lowdown on Library folders, see "What About All Those Library Folders?" below.

A couple of noteworthy items that live in this Library folder are the Receipts folder, which contains installation information about programs that have been installed on your Mac, and the User Pictures folder, which contains the icons you use to identify yourself in the login screen. This Library folder also contains the WebServer folder, which contains the file that the Apache Web server serves up as a Web site to other folks who may connect to your Mac using a Web browser.

Here are the folders you might want to modify. Items you add to them will be available to all users.

- **Desktop Pictures**—The Desktop pictures that come with your Mac live here, and you can add your own (or remove the existing ones) by adding them to or deleting them from this folder.

- **Fonts**—You can provide fonts for all users by adding them to this folder.

- **PreferencePanes**—You can add preference panes (items that show up in your System Preferences) by dropping their files in here. Installers often take care of this for you.

- **QuickTime**—You can add QuickTime codecs (such as DivX) by dropping them in this folder. Most of the time, an installer will take care of it for you (such as with Toast Video CD Support).

- **WebServer**—If you'd like to take advantage of Mac OS X's built-in Apache Web server, then this is where you'll find the Web server's root folder and its CGI folder.

You probably won't need to touch (and probably shouldn't touch, unless you have a compelling, specific reason) any of the rest of the folders.

What About All Those Library Folders?

If you've done much browsing through your hard drive, you've probably noticed several folders titled Library in places like the root level of your hard drive, the System folder, and your home folder. So what is the deal?

All those Library folders serve a similar purpose—they provide resources (such as fonts and sounds) to the various users (and this includes the operating system as a user).

continues on next page

What About All Those Library Folders?   *continued*

Here are the three flavors of the Library folder (**Figure 2.5**):

*   **Library**—This Library folder provides resources for all users of the Macintosh. It lives at the top level of the hard drive.

*   **System Library**—This Library folder is inside the System folder. It provides resources for the system software.

*   **User Library**—These Library folders live inside each user's home folder, and they provide resources for each user. A user's Library folder is restricted to that user—other users can't access the resources there.

So, to add fonts, sounds, and other things that only you can use, add them to the Library folder in your home folder. To add them for all users, put them in the Library folder at the top level of the hard drive.

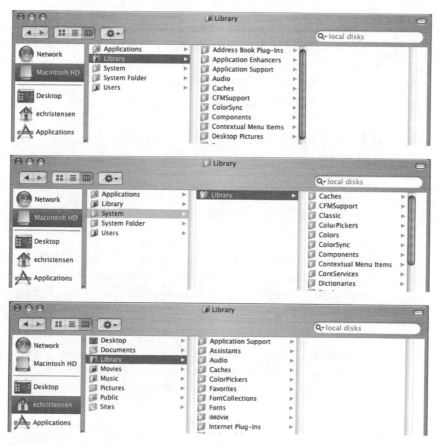

Figure 2.5

The Library, System Library, and user Library folders (top to bottom, respectively) all contain resources for users (but you have to consider the system software a kind of user).

The Users Folder

This folder contains a special folder for each user account you've set up in Mac OS X. Each user's folder is protected so that other users can't access it (**Figure 2.6**). These folders are known as *home folders*.

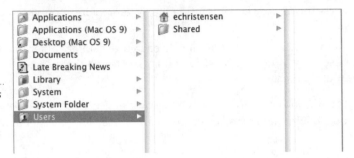

Figure 2.6

This installation has only one home folder, indicated by the little house icon in the Users folder.

The home folder is a special folder created inside the Users folder, and it's given the short name you entered when installing Mac OS X. This folder is also created when you set up a user account. Each user's home folder contains a special set of eight folders (**Figure 2.7**):

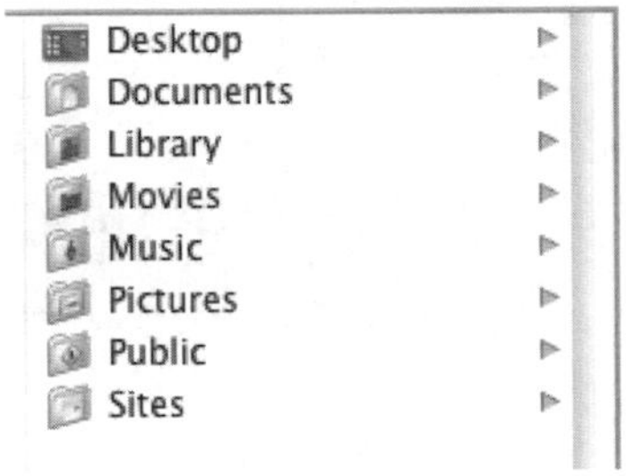

Figure 2.7

Every user's home folder has eight special folders to help organize documents of various kinds.

Desktop. Through the strange magic of Mac OS X, the Desktop folder contains the items that appear on a user's Desktop. If you add an item to the Desktop folder, it appears on your Desktop, and vice versa. Remove an item from your Desktop folder, and it disappears from your Desktop. Anything you drag to your Desktop is reflected here as well.

Documents. This is a handy folder for all your documents. There are other places you *can* store your documents, such as anywhere within your home folder, but this folder provides some structure since it is clearly labeled Documents.

Library. This folder contains your personal fonts, sounds, screensaver modules, mailboxes, browser plug-ins, preferences, and other such items. You probably won't dig into this folder much, if at all. Here are the folders you may want to touch:

- **Fonts**—Drop new fonts into this folder to make them available just to you.

- **Mail**—You won't add anything to this folder, but you should back it up to ensure that the email in Mail is backed up, since your email is stored here.

- **Preferences**—Put Preference panes that you'd like to install for your use only into this folder. Some installers will do this for you.

- **Safari**—Although you probably won't put anything in this folder, you can back it up to preserve your Safari bookmarks.

- **Screen Savers**—Drop new screensaver modules in this folder to use them, if an installer doesn't do it for you.

- **Sounds**—New alert sounds can be dropped into this folder, and they'll be available for your account.

You probably won't have a reason to go into the other folders, but feel free to browse.

Movies. Got a movie? Drop it in here. iMovie will, if you tell it to.

Music. This is the perfect folder for your MP3s. iTunes stores its music libraries here.

Pictures. Digital photos go here. iPhoto stores its picture libraries here, too.

Public. Any user on your Mac can open the Public folder, unlike the other folders in your home folder (**Figure 2.8**).

Figure 2.8

The Public folder provides an easy way to share files between users on the same Mac. Each includes a drop box where others can drop files— but they don't have privileges to get the files back.

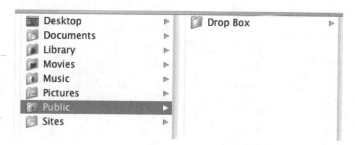

Sites. If you turn on Mac OS X's built-in Web server, it can serve up the Web sites located in this folder, if someone connects to your Mac using a Web browser.

System Preferences

Mac OS X doesn't have extensions and control panels in the same sense as Mac OS 9 does, which makes it much more stable. Mac OS X *does* have something similar to control panels, called *system settings.* System Preferences—which you can access from the Apple menu, the Applications folder, or the Dock—lets you change how your Mac behaves. This window has three main parts: the Show All button, the shelf, and a content area that shows controls in specific groups.

 If you find Max OS X's preferences too limiting, check out Tinker Tool (free; www.bresink.com/osx/tinkertool.htm), which lets you activate hidden features in Mac OS X. You can change the animations produced by the Finder, change default icons, add new settings to font smoothing, and more.

When clicked, the Show All button, in the upper-left corner, shows more than 20 icons in the content area—the number varies a bit (**Figure 2.9**). These icons represent the various groups of controls, and they often correspond to control panels in Mac OS 9 and earlier, such as Energy Saver, Keyboard, and QuickTime. The System Preferences window is divided into four groups: Personal, Hardware, Internet & Network, and System.

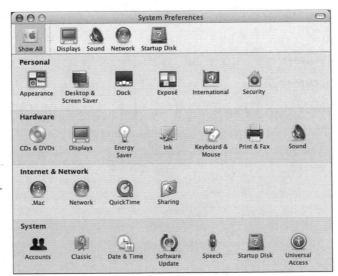

Figure 2.9

System Preferences gives you the opportunity to customize your Mac's appearance and behavior. Click an icon to reveal the settings for that item.

 If these categories don't work for you, you can always rearrange them alphabetically. To do so, choose View > Organize Alphabetically.

To change your Mac's settings, open System Preferences by selecting Apple menu > System Preferences. Then click the icon for the settings you want to change. The System Preferences window automatically changes size and shape to accommodate the specific controls.

The System Preferences window has a toolbar that runs across the top of the window, which serves as a shelf for preferences that you frequently use. By default, it contains four icons: Displays, Sound, Network, and Startup Disk. You can add items to this shelf by dragging them from the main window—the items that are already there will move to make room. You can also remove items from the shelf by dragging them off. If you need to see the entire list of preferences, just click the Show All icon in the upper-left corner.

Here's what each of the preference panes does, by category. Note that the descriptions here are for Mac OS X 10.3. You'll find much of the same functionality in Mac OS X 10.2 and earlier, but the panes are arranged differently. For example, Mac OS X 10.2 has a General pane, which has been renamed Appearance in Mac OS X 10.3. Not all of the differences between Mac OS X 10.3 and Mac OS X 10.2 are noted below, but you can still use the descriptions as a general guide.

Personal

The Personal category contains settings that apply to the ways you like to use your Mac. These settings can be different for different users.

Appearance. The Appearance pane lets you set your Mac's color theme (Blue or Graphite), the highlight color for selected text and lists, how scroll bars behave, how many items show up in the Recent Items section of the Apple menu, and how font smoothing behaves. In Mac OS X 10.2 this pane is named General.

Desktop & Screen Saver. This pane lets you set your Desktop pattern using the images that come with the system or those you have in another folder. You can set whether the pictures change periodically here. You can also use this preference pane to set which screensaver Mac OS X uses and how long it waits before starting the screensaver. In Mac OS X 10.2 the Desktop and Screen Saver panes are separate and offer slightly different functionality.

Dock. Here you can set the Dock's size, magnification, and position on the screen, as well as whether the Dock automatically hides. You can also set whether application icons bounce in the Dock when opening and how windows minimize when they are pulled into the Dock.

Exposé. This is where you control how Exposé, Apple's fancy new window-management tool, behaves. You can set which screen corners trigger Exposé, which function keys produce the desired Exposé effect, and which mouse buttons trigger Exposé.

International. This pane lets you set your preferred languages; your date, time, and currency formats; and what keyboard layouts appear in the Input menu.

Security. This pane, new to Mac OS X 10.3, allows you to turn on a new item called FileVault. FileVault encrypts your home folder on the fly so that if your computer falls into the wrong hands, the files are encrypted and unavailable to any no-goodniks. When you first set up your master password and turn on FileVault, you'll be forced to log out of your Mac while it encrypts the home folder. You can also set other security settings, such as whether a password is required to wake your Mac from sleep, whether automatic login is disabled, whether secure system preferences are locked or unlocked, and whether your Mac will log you out automatically after a period of inactivity.

 FileVault encrypts your files using your login password. If you forget your log-in password and you don't have the master password, your data will be lost forever.

Hardware

The Hardware category contains settings that allow you to control the behavior of your Mac's hardware.

CDs & DVDs. New to Mac OS X 10.3, this pane lets you set what action your Mac takes when you insert a CD or DVD, such as opening a certain application or running a script—or even taking no action at all (**Figure 2.10**).

Figure 2.10

In Mac OS X 10.3 you can tell your Mac what to do when you insert a CD or DVD.

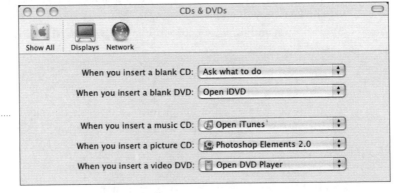

Displays. This allows you to choose your monitor's resolution, brightness, and color depth. If you have more than one monitor, you can arrange them all here. You can also set whether or not the Monitors icon appears in the menu bar.

Energy Saver. In this pane you adjust the sleep settings for your Mac components (the system, display, and hard drive). You can also schedule your Mac to start up and shut down at a certain time each day.

Ink. This pane lets you control all aspects of Mac OS X's built-in handwriting-recognition system. You can set whether handwriting recognition is on or off, what language you use, your handwriting style, special gestures, and a list of uncommon words that you frequently use—which helps speed things along. This pane doesn't show up unless you have a tablet plugged into your Mac.

Keyboard & Mouse. This pane contains three tabs: Keyboard, Mouse (or Trackpad, if you're using a laptop, and both Mouse and Trackpad if you have a mouse plugged into your laptop), and Keyboard Shortcuts. These sections allow you to set your key repeat rate and delay until repeat; mouse-tracking, scrolling, and double-click speed; trackpad tracking and double-click speed, as well as whether the trackpad can be used to click and drag; and keyboard shortcuts for such things as screen shots, universal access, Dock shortcuts, keyboard navigation, and application keyboard shortcuts.

Print & Fax. New to Mac OS X 10.3, this pane lets you set up and share printers, change how the Print dialog behaves, and choose whether your Mac can receive and send faxes and where those faxes are saved.

Sound. This pane contains a nice set of volume controls that let you set system volume and balance as well as alert volume. You can also choose your system alert here, and set audio output and input options.

Internet & Network

This category contains network-related settings.

.Mac. If you have a .Mac account, you can enter your .Mac account information here and set Mac OS X's access to your iDisk.

Network. This big pane lets you make your networking settings, including those for TCP/IP, PPP, proxy, and modem. You can also create multiple locations and configurations for Ethernet, modem, and AirPort connections. You can even create several configurations to use on a single port, for easy switching. Mac OS X 10.3 provides an "Assist me" button that walks you through making your network settings.

QuickTime. This information-rich pane is home to five groups of settings, including those related to your QuickTime Plug-in, your connection speed, whether QuickTime updates automatically via the Internet, which music synthesizer to use, and any media keys you may have. (Media keys let you use restricted media, such as watching a pay-per-view video.)

Sharing. This pane lets you turn on Mac OS X's sharing services, such as personal file sharing, Windows sharing, FTP, remote login, personal Web sharing, and several others. You can also use this pane to configure Mac OS X's built-in firewall, as well as to set up your Mac to share an existing Internet connection.

System

This set of preference panes lets you control how your Mac handles various operating-system functions.

Accounts. This pane lets you set account information for your (and other) accounts; alter user pictures (these are used when logging in, as the default picture in iChat, and as the picture on your My Card entry in Address Book); change your FileVault settings for users' accounts; and choose which items start up automatically when a given user logs in. You can also set which account automatically logs in and how the login dialog appears.

Classic. The Classic pane features three tabbed areas that let you choose which Mac OS 9 System Folder to use with Classic; start, restart, or force-quit the Classic environment (more on this in "The Classic Environment," later in the chapter); and view how Classic applications are using memory.

Date & Time. In this pane you set the current date, time, and time zone, plus you can control whether your Mac sets its own clock using a network time server and how the clock in the menu bar behaves. You can even have your Mac announce the time at given intervals.

Software Update. This contains a schedule of when Software Update checks with Apple's server for updates. You can also peek at Software Update's log to see what the application has been up to—what updates it's installed and when.

Speech. This controls your Mac's speech-recognition capabilities and the voice your Mac uses when it talks to you. You can also turn on (or off) Talking Alerts and choose whether your Mac reads selected text or announces when an application needs your help.

Startup Disk. In this pane you can choose which operating system on which disk to use when you start up your Mac.

Universal Access. This pane lets you adjust the use of the keyboard and mouse if you have difficulty using the standard mouse and keyboard settings.

 If you have a third-party driver installed (such as for a keyboard or an 802.11b PC Card), it may show up in the Universal Access pane. You can use items here just as you would the other, standard items.

Beyond the System

Mac OS X has an impressive array of applications and technologies that go along with the basic operating system. These include automation and programming software, the famous digital-hub applications, media technologies, a way to access the Unix underside of Mac OS X, and a host of other useful widgets and gadgets.

AppleScript

First released in 1993, AppleScript (found in the Applications folder) is a quirky but powerful automation utility that lets you give your Mac a list of tasks to perform. AppleScript is powerful enough to be considered a programming language, but it's simple enough that mere mortals who don't relish the thought of learning how to program can still use it. AppleScript is a standard part of every recent Mac OS version in the last several years.

Besides providing a list of tasks for the Finder, such as hiding or showing all Finder windows, AppleScript can tell many other applications what to do, and it can even make two programs that understand AppleScript work together. For example, you could use AppleScript to build a Web page in BBEdit and then email that content using Microsoft Entourage. That's powerful stuff! In addition, AppleScript has the ability to include logic (or decision making), which renders it much more powerful than a simple macro language. This decision-making ability allows you to write scripts that compare values and do different things depending on the results. As a real programming language, AppleScript can do things you might do with BASIC or C, such as create a program that watches a folder and batch-changes the names of any files dropped there.

Of course, there's one caveat: to use AppleScript on programs, those programs must understand AppleScript. Otherwise they can't use AppleScript at all. There are three levels of AppleScript comprehension when it comes to applications: scriptable, recordable, and attachable.

 Providing a complete description of AppleScript is beyond the scope of this book. If you're serious about writing AppleScripts, there are several Web resources; you can find a list on Apple's AppleScript Resources page (www.apple.com/applescript/resources).

Scriptable applications. This is the most basic level of AppleScript compatibility. A scriptable application might understand only the most basic of commands (such as open and close); on the other hand, it might comprehend hundreds of commands, covering every single one of AppleScript's features.

The only way to tell for sure is to take a look at its AppleScript dictionary (see "Using a Dictionary," later in this chapter). The majority of programs that work with AppleScript are scriptable.

Recordable applications. Recordable applications allow you to record a series of actions and turn them into an AppleScript by letting you take an I'll-show-you-what-to-do approach. Because it's harder to make a program recordable than it is to make it scriptable, there are fewer of these types of applications. By default, a recordable application is also scriptable.

Attachable applications. This is the rarest category of AppleScript-capable programs. Attachable applications let you add AppleScripts to their menus, making the scripts part of the program. Very few programs are attachable; Entourage is one.

AppleScript in Mac OS 9 and Mac OS X

AppleScript works about the same way in Mac OS 9 as it does in Mac OS X. Each OS has a set of AppleScript commands that it understands, and each creates scripts in a program called Script Editor.

Mac OS X 10.3 contains three additional items that make your scripting life easier: Install Script Menu, Remove Script Menu, and Folder Actions Setup, which are all found in the /Applications/AppleScript folder.

Install Script Menu puts a script icon called the Script Menu in your menu bar. This icon gives you access to a bevy of useful AppleScripts (as well as Perl and Shell scripts) from the menu bar (**Figure 2.11**). Perl and Shell scripts are somewhat similar to AppleScripts, and Mac OS X can use them thanks to its Unix heritage.

 To obtain Script Menu for earlier versions of Mac OS X, go to Apple's AppleScript in Mac OS X page (www.apple.com/applescript/ script_menu) and download Script Menu. Then drag the Scriptmenu.menu file up to the right side of your menu bar.

The third item, Folder Actions Setup, is a tool to help you attach AppleScripts to Finder folders. These scripts are activated when the folders change—such as when an item is added to them either by you or automatically by a program. For example, you might use a Folder Action Script to process graphics files

Figure 2.11

If you choose Install Script Menu in AppleScript, the program adds an icon to your menu bar from which you can access any number of handy scripts. To get rid of the icon in your menu bar, simply choose Remove Script Menu.

that are dropped into a given folder. Folder Actions Setup helps you manage these scripts.

Creating an AppleScript

You have two ways to create an AppleScript: writing it or recording it. Both of these methods involve using Script Editor (which you'll find in the Applications folder in Mac OS X or in the Apple Extras folder in Mac OS 9 and earlier). To create an AppleScript, start by launching Script Editor. Script Editor is a simple affair, with only a few controls: a place to describe the script, four control buttons (Record, Stop, Run, and Compile), and a text area in which you can write AppleScripts (**Figure 2.12**).

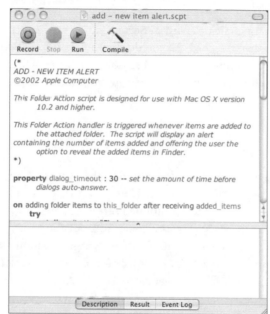

Although it may not look like much, this window can be used to write some pretty impressive applets.

Writing an AppleScript. Most of the time, you'll create an AppleScript by writing it in the Script Editor window. A simple AppleScript might look like this:

```
tell application "Finder"
    activate
    select folder "Applications" of startup disk
    open selection
end tell
```

This script tells the Finder to select and open the folder titled Applications at the root level of whatever disk starts up the Mac on which the script is running. As you write your script, you can test it by clicking Run or stop a running script by clicking Stop.

Besides giving applications a laundry list of instructions to carry out, scripts can also put up dialogs that gather information from you, making AppleScript a useful way to write *applets*. An applet is a program that's smaller in scope than a full-blown application—thus the name.

Recording an AppleScript. The second, and easier, way to create an AppleScript is to record it rather than write it. Of course, this requires that you use a recordable application, so don't hold your breath—there are very few of these. One great exception is the Finder in Mac OS 9—in fact it's the most popular recordable and scriptable application around. When Apple introduced Mac OS X, the company made the Finder scriptable but not recordable. In the latest version of Mac OS X, 10.3, Apple has made the Finder recordable as well as scriptable.

To record a script, click Record in Script Editor and then run through the actions you want to record. As you do this, a list of AppleScript commands appears in Script Editor. When you're done recording, click Stop in Script Editor. You've just created an AppleScript without writing a line of scripting code. Recording an AppleScript and looking it over is a great way to learn how one works.

Saving a script

Once you have a script recorded, you'll probably want to save it, which brings you face-to-face with a few choices (**Figure 2.13**). You can save an AppleScript in one of three formats: text, compiled script, or application, and these scripts can work across Mac OS X and Classic. You can also save scripts as stationery or as regular documents. You might save a script as stationery if you'll want to use it as a common starting point for a number of scripts without having to retype or import it over and over.

Figure 2.13

Script Editor in Mac OS X 10.3 lets you save your scripts in several formats; the ones you'll be most interested in are Script, Application, and Text.

Text. Saving an AppleScript as text simply saves the text in the Script Editor window. You won't be able to run the script without first opening it in Script Editor. Save your script as text if you want to share it with other script writers or if you want to work on it later.

Compiled script. You still have to run a compiled script using Script Editor, but Script Editor has already checked it out to make sure that everything works and that its instructions have been converted into a form your Mac can understand. Save your script as a compiled script if you want to run it and still go back and edit it later.

Application. When you save a script as an application, it will run as a stand-alone program. Combine this with the power of the professional-level development environment AppleScript Studio (see "AppleScript Studio," below), and you can create some pretty amazing applications. Save a script as an application if you want something you can double-click to use and don't need to make any more changes to the script.

You can also save an AppleScript as a run-only script so that others can't open your script to make changes to it. To do this, choose Save As from the File menu. This brings up a Save dialog in which you can choose to have the script saved as run only (as well as set other parameters).

Running a script

As with creating an AppleScript, you have two ways to run a script. Which method you choose depends on how you've saved the script. If it's text or a compiled script (or if you've never saved it), you'll have to run it by opening it in Script Editor and clicking Run (or choose Run from the Control menu or press ⌘R). If you've saved the script as an applet (either for Classic or Mac OS X), just double-click it to run it.

Using a dictionary

Although engineers have tried to make AppleScript easy to use, you'll probably need to look at a program's AppleScript dictionary to find out what commands it can understand. You have a couple of ways to do so. You can drop the program's icon on the Script Editor icon, which opens the command dictionary. Alternatively, you can open Script Editor and choose Open Dictionary from the File menu; this brings up an Open dialog. Navigate to the application in question. When you open the application, it presents its AppleScript dictionary to you (**Figure 2.14**).

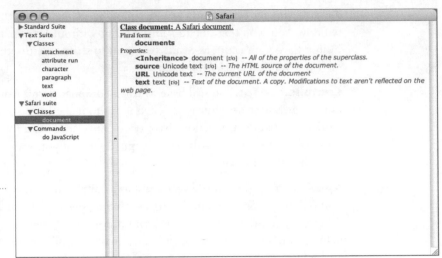

AppleScript Studio

AppleScript Studio is a relatively new programming environment that lets you build honest-to-goodness applications using AppleScript, complete with windows, check boxes, sliders, buttons, and tabs. AppleScript Studio is a professional-level development environment with all the bells and whistles, such as step-by-step debugging, interface design, and script-writing environments.

You can download AppleScript Studio from Apple's Web site at www.apple.com/applescript/studio, or you can purchase a CD from Apple. (The CD also includes Apple's new Xcode developer tools, so it's a bargain at $20.) Either way, if you're serious about writing AppleScripts, you'll need to take a look at AppleScript Studio.

The iApps and the Digital Hub

When the computer industry took a nosedive at the turn of the century, Steve Jobs declared that the industry was not dead—it was merely changing shape. Thus the vision of the digital hub was born.

This digital-hub idea put the Mac squarely at the center of the new set of digital-media devices—MP3 music players, digital video cameras, digital cameras, DVD players, and the like. With great hardware and a set of best-of-class applications (referred to as the iApps), Apple positioned the Mac as the machine that connects all those devices and allows the user to move seamlessly between them. Users can edit their own movies and digital photos, create their own DVDs, listen to the best music with the best software (and hardware) available, and more—all from one device, their Macintosh.

There are five key iApps that make up the cornerstones of the software side of the digital hub: iMovie, iTunes, iDVD, iPhoto, and GarageBand.

iMovie. One of the original digital-hub applications, iMovie provides an easy, powerful way to edit movies. iMovie's simple interface, extensive library of effects, and powerful integration with digital video camcorders make it a fantastic tool for editing video. With iMovie, you can quickly create your own home videos, editing those 17 hours of videotape of your family vacation down to the 20 minutes that are really, really good (**Figure 2.15**).

Figure 2.15

iMovie provides the power to make great videos without being too complicated.

iTunes. iTunes is Apple's answer to the MP3 music revolution. With iTunes, you can convert your music CDs into MP3 files, play audiobooks, load music into your iPod (if you're lucky enough to have one), listen to online radio stations, share your music collection with a few other Macs, and purchase (and play) music from Apple's online music store. It's all built into iTunes.

iPhoto. iPhoto is an easy-to-use digital-photo-management program. With it, you can easily download pictures from your digital camera; arrange them into albums; do basic photo editing; and create slide shows, Web pages, and even prints and books.

iDVD. Not too many years ago, creating a DVD took a great deal of very expensive equipment and some serious arcane knowledge. With iDVD, creating a DVD is as easy as drag and click. iDVD requires a Mac with a built-in SuperDrive (an optical drive that can burn DVDs).

GarageBand. With GarageBand you can now turn your Mac into a digital recording studio. You can use Apple's pre-recorded riffs or record your own and more.

All of the iApps come bundled with new Macs. If you have an older Mac, you'll need to purchase all five in an iLife bundle from Apple for $49. Only iTunes is available as a free download from Apple's Web site (www.apple.com).

The best thing about these five applications is how they work together. For example, when you're working in iDVD, you have access to the iTunes music library for sound tracks, the iPhoto picture library for slide shows, and iMovie for the video portion of your project.

QuickTime

QuickTime is one of Apple's biggest success stories. Since its introduction in the early 1990s as a way to watch video on your Macintosh, QuickTime has grown to encompass just about every kind of media available—whether audio, video, or still images. QuickTime is unsurpassed in the number of file formats it can handle, and it makes those capabilities available to all kinds of programs, which rely on QuickTime for the heavy lifting. QuickTime is available for both Macs and Windows-based PCs, and it can play streaming video and audio from the Web as well as play movies and music located on your hard drive. QuickTime is built into Mac OS X; Mac OS 9 and earlier enables QuickTime through a group of extensions.

 For all things QuickTime-related, visit Apple's QuickTime Web site (www.apple.com/quicktime). This Web site has killer movie trailers, QuickTime downloads, and resources for those creating QuickTime content or embedding it in Web pages.

QuickTime Player

QuickTime Player (found in your Applications folder) is a program that handles all *dynamic media*—files that change over time, such as sound files, movies, and Flash animations. It consists of a window with a content area for viewing the file; a timeline showing where you are in the currently playing file; a volume slider; five playback controls (start of file, rewind, play and pause, fast forward, and end of file); and a TV button that shows a group of digital-media channels (**Figure 2.16**). If you launch the latest version of QuickTime Player by double-clicking the icon, it attempts to connect to the Internet and load the Hot Picks movie, which gives you a preview of all kinds of QuickTime content. For more on what you can do with QuickTime, see Chapter 17.

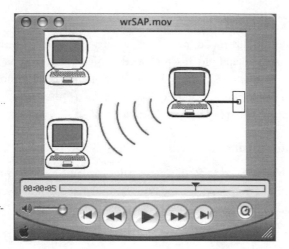

Figure 2.16

It's amazing what QuickTime movies lurk on your hard drive; this one shows how AirPort Internet sharing works. It also shows the QuickTime interface—sleek, classy, and easy to use.

Standard vs. Pro versions

QuickTime comes in two versions—standard and Pro. The standard version lets you play back QuickTime-based content, and it's the version that comes preinstalled with Mac OS X. The Pro version, on the other hand, lets you unlock QuickTime's editing capabilities. With it you can save, edit, and translate movie and sound files, and you can even add special effects. QuickTime Pro goes for $29.95, but it is well worth the upgrade price.

To upgrade, you can visit Apple's QuickTime page (www.apple.com/quicktime). Alternatively, in Mac OS X, open the QuickTime System Preferences pane and click the Registration button; in Mac OS 9, open the QuickTime Settings control panel and choose Registration from the pop-up menu at the top. With either one, click the Register Online button. This opens your Web browser and points it to Apple's QuickTime purchase page.

Installing QuickTime

Mac OS X comes with QuickTime preinstalled. If for some reason you need to reinstall it (or you need to update it), go to www.apple.com/quicktime and download the Installer. Unlike most other software installers, it's a network installer—that is, it connects to the Internet, downloads the files it needs, and installs those, ensuring that you get the latest version. During this process you can choose the minimum installation, for playing back some media files; the standard installation, which covers most bases; or the custom installation, which lets you choose what components you want to install—or you can install every single QuickTime file. Remember, the more you install, the longer the files take to download.

Updating QuickTime

QuickTime can download *codecs* (bits of software used to compress and decompress audio and video—the word comes from *compress/decompress*) on the fly. If you try to play a movie that QuickTime doesn't understand, it'll connect to Apple's servers and look for a codec (QuickTime calls this an *update*) that lets you play back the movie.

QuickTime settings

The QuickTime System Preferences pane contains a ton of settings, arranged into five tabbed areas: Plug-In, Connection, Music, Media Keys, and Update (**Figure 2.17**).

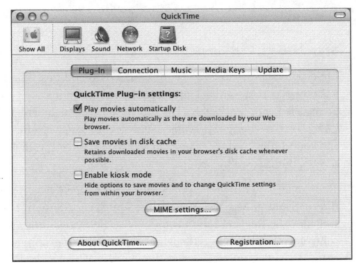

Figure 2.17

QuickTime comes complete with its own System Preferences pane, in which you can control its behavior.

Plug-In. These settings let you change how the QuickTime Plug-in behaves: whether movies play automatically in a Web browser as they're downloaded; whether movies are saved in the browser's disk cache when possible; and whether the QuickTime movie controls are visible in a browser window. You can also select the MIME types that you want QuickTime to handle here. MIME (Multipurpose Internet Mail Extensions) allows you to send email attachments, such as pictures, sounds, and other documents. If your MIME types aren't set properly, email attachments (and certain Web-based content) won't work properly (**Figure 2.18**).

 If you're looking for help on MIME, visit www.faqs.org/faqs/mail/mime-faq/ mime0 or http://hunnysoft.com/mime.

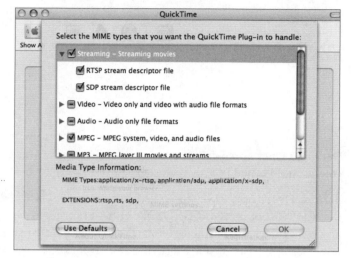

Figure 2.18

QuickTime lets you set which MIME types it can handle, such as real-time streaming.

Connection. Here you set your Internet connection speed; choose a transport setup; and enable (or disable) Instant-On technology, which allows you to play streaming-media files immediately.

Music. This option lets you select a music synthesizer from a list, if you have more than one installed on your hard drive.

Media Keys. If you have access to private media files, your keys to those files are stored here.

Update. Use this screen to tell your Mac whether to automatically check for updates to the QuickTime software when you run QuickTime. You can allow it to update the QuickTime software or install new third-party QuickTime software.

Terminal

Terminal is a special application included with Mac OS X that lets you access the operating system's Unix underpinnings. When you launch Terminal, you'll be presented with perhaps the most nondescript application window of any in Mac OS X. In it you'll see three lines of text: one to indicate the last time you logged in; a welcome message (which says "Welcome to Darwin" and provides a clue about Mac OS X's foundation); and a third line that has some text between brackets, followed by your user name, a dollar sign (or a percentage symbol if you are using Mac OS X 10.2 or earlier), and a blinking cursor (**Figure 2.19**). You daring souls who wonder about Terminal can launch it and quit it without fear—you won't hurt anything unless you start typing Unix commands.

Figure 2.19

The simple Terminal window has the power to destroy the data on your Mac's hard drive—but its powers are mostly for good.

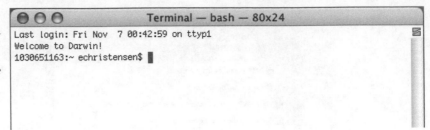

```
 ● ● ●              Terminal — bash — 80x24
Last login: Fri Nov  7 00:42:59 on ttyp1
Welcome to Darwin!
1030651163:~ echristensen$ ▌
```

 Darwin is what Apple calls the Unix underpinnings of Mac OS X. Darwin itself can run Intel-based PCs, by the way.

Terminal is the Mac OS X command-line interface. It's also the window into the true Unix portion of Mac OS X. With Terminal you can do strange and powerful things, all with lines of text. You can also do terrible things if you're not careful, such as erasing every single file from your hard drive with a single command—that's no joke!

Although you need to be wary of Terminal's power, you don't need to be afraid of it. With some caution and good judgment, you can use Terminal for forces of good. We'll ease you in with a few basic commands.

 The Mac's single greatest claim to fame is that it moved the computing world from the command-line interface to the graphical user interface—you know, menus, folders, and the like. As it turns out, a command-line interface has its place, too—and now it's in Mac OS X.

Simple Terminal commands

So you've decided to take the plunge and work with Terminal. Good. It can be a rewarding path. To learn a few simple Terminal commands, first fire up Terminal (it's in /Applications/Utilities). Once it's open, you'll see the first two lines of status text, and then a third line of text with your user name and a prompt. This third line is your command line—you're ready to drive. We'll run through three commands: pwd, ls, and cd. With these three commands you'll be able to navigate your hard drive.

pwd. The first command we'll tackle is pwd. It simply tells you your *present working directory,* or what folder Terminal is pointing to. (When you first launch Terminal, it points to your home directory.)

To use pwd, type pwd and press [Return]. This lays out a path to the current directory right there in the Terminal window. It should read /Users/yourloginname if you haven't changed the directory.

 If you want to clear the Terminal window, type clear and press [Return]. This clears all the text from the screen and puts up a new prompt at the top of the window.

ls. This command stands for "list," and it lists files in the present working directory. To use it, type 1s and press (Return). Terminal prints a list of all files and folders (or directories) in the current directory. It's a simple list, and if you haven't changed the present working directory, it should show all the folders in your home directory (**Figure 2.20**). It may vary if you've added anything to that level of the home directory.

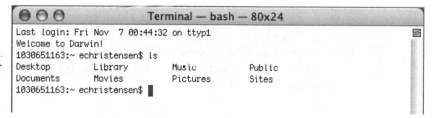

Figure 2.20

This is what's in your home directory, from a Unix point of view.

You can add one or more *flags* to the command (and to many Terminal commands), which make 1s work differently. For example, say you want to know more about the items in a directory. You can type 1s -1 in Terminal and press (Return). The -1 after the 1s command is the long-form flag, and it makes the command return a detailed list of the current directory's contents (**Figure 2.21**).

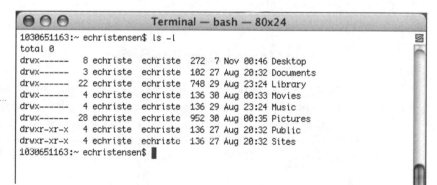

Figure 2.21

The long listing shows you important details about the files and folders in the current directory.

This list includes the file and directory names, as well as a whole slew of other bits of information. Each line now contains a list of permissions, the directory or file's owner, the directory or file's group, its size, when it was modified, and its name. This information can be very handy if you're having some funky permissions problems.

Another variation is to add the -a flag to the 1s command. Try this by typing 1s -a and pressing (Return). You'll get a much larger list that includes the folders in your home directory, as well as a bunch of other items, most (or all) of which begin with a period—items such as .Trash and .DS_Store. These are invisible files in the directory revealed by the -a flag, which shows all items in a directory, invisible or not.

You can combine these flags to do a long listing of all items in a directory by typing ls -la, by the way.

cd. You use the cd command to change directories in Terminal. To change to the Music directory, for example, type cd Music and press (Return). You're now in the Music directory. How do you know? The text between the brackets in your prompt now has ~/Music in it. The tilde stands for your user name, and the /Music means that your present working directory is in the Music folder inside your home folder. To prove it, type pwd to see.

 You can automatically complete a directory or filename when using cd (or other Unix commands) by typing the first few characters of the item and then pressing (Tab). Terminal will fill in the text for you.

Of course, this works well for going deeper into a directory, but what about going back *up* a directory? That's where the cd .. command comes in. Yes, it's just cd followed by a space and two periods, but it'll move you to the previous directory. To try it, type cd .. and press (Return). You should be taken back to your home folder.

If you're really into learning Unix and Terminal, there are a ton of Web-based resources and books you can read. The good news is that any Unix or Linux Terminal tutorial will apply to Mac OS X's Terminal.

Other Useful Applications

Mac OS X ships with a handful of small and tremendously useful programs that you can use to send and receive email, open pictures, connect to the Internet, browse the Web, maintain a list of addresses—all kinds of things. We've talked about a few select applications above—here's a bit about most of the rest.

Application programs

These days Apple is going back to its roots, when Apple-developed programs such as MacWrite (a word processor) and MacPaint (a paint program) were preinstalled on your Mac. Now the company preinstalls a batch of applications that make your Mac immediately useful. Here's a list of the current ones as of late 2003.

Address Book. This program stores names, addresses, phone numbers, and email addresses. It coordinates with your email program so that when you're writing an email message, Address Book entries appear automatically. Address Book also connects to iSync and your .Mac account, if you have one.

Calculator. This simple utility lets you add, subtract, multiply, and divide—as you might expect (**Figure 2.22**).

Chess. Your Mac can play chess with you through this program, and it's a pretty good opponent!

DVD Player. This program lets you play DVD movies on your Mac. It's especially handy if you happen to have a PowerBook or iBook and a long plane ride.

Font Book. Font freaks will spend a *whole* lot of time playing with this application. It lets you preview the fonts on your Mac, getting samples, changing sizes, and generally managing your fonts.

Figure 2.22

The Calculator in Mac OS X 10.3 looks, acts, and feels like the real thing.

iCal. This is Apple's very own scheduling application.

iChat. Apple's chat application works with both .Mac and AOL Instant Messenger accounts. iChat AV, which was built with Mac OS X 10.3 in mind, also provides video and audio chat.

Image Capture. This utility downloads pictures from a digital camera to your hard drive.

Internet Connect. This program lets you set the way your modem or AirPort card connects to the Internet; you can enter a phone number, user name, and password.

Microsoft Internet Explorer. The popular Web browser is included in a Mac OS X–native version.

iSync. iSync keeps your critical information (such as contacts) synchronized between your Mac, your PDA, and your .Mac account (if you have one).

Mail. Apple's nifty and flexible email client lets you send and receive email from several accounts, and it handles spam like no one's business.

Preview. This opens and displays still images, such as JPEG, TIFF, and PDF files.

QuickTime Player. This program plays QuickTime-supported video and sound files—which includes most files.

Safari. This is Apple's own Web browser, built with speed and compatibility in mind.

Sherlock. The Mac OS X–native version of the powerful search utility helps you find files and information on the World Wide Web.

Stickies. These digital sticky notes let you make your Mac's Desktop as messy as your real one!

System Preferences. This application lets you set the appearance and behavior of various elements of Mac OS X.

TextEdit. A basic text editor, TextEdit lets you write documents using all of your operating system's fonts. It also includes basic formatting controls (such as for bold and centered text), and you can even check your spelling.

Utilities

Mac OS X ships with a folder full of utilities (/Applications/Utilities) that let you manage and configure your Mac OS X installation. Here's a quick look at some of them:

Activity Monitor. Known as Process Viewer in Mac OS X 10.2 and earlier, this program lists all running programs in a window. Mac OS X relies on a lot of background programs to do its work, so you may be surprised at how many programs appear when you launch this. It provides some pretty interesting information about the inner workings of your Mac OS X programs. You can use Activity Monitor to see if one program is hogging your Mac's processor, and you can use it to watch network activity and memory use—very nice for troubleshooting.

AirPort Admin Utility. This program lets you change your AirPort Base Station's settings.

Asia Text Extras. This folder contains a few utilities to help in work with Asian-language texts.

Audio MIDI Setup. New with Mac OS X 10.3, this program lets you set the way your Mac works with its audio input and output, and with any attached MIDI music devices.

Bluetooth File Exchange and Bluetooth Serial Utility. These two programs let you work with any Bluetooth hardware that your Mac might connect to. Bluetooth is a type of wireless networking protocol used to connect peripherals to a computer.

ColorSync Utility. For publishing pros, the ColorSync Utility lets you set and view installed ColorSync profiles, which define how a particular piece of hardware handles color. It also lets you repair damaged profiles.

Console. This program pulls up a Unix Console window—useful for viewing activity and logs on your Mac.

DigitalColor Meter. This simple utility lets you take the color reading of any pixel under the pointer.

Directory Access. You can use this utility to configure various directory services available on your Mac, such as Active Directory, AppleTalk, and Rendezvous.

Disk Utility. Combining Drive Setup and Disk First Aid, Disk Utility lets you verify and repair disks, as well as format them.

Grab. This utility allows you to take screen shots in Mac OS X. You can still use the good old ⌘ Shift 3 key combination, too.

Installer. This installs Mac OS X application packages.

Java. This folder contains a few utilities for launching and running Java applets. You may come across a stand-alone Java program that you can use with these utilities.

Keychain Access. Use this utility to edit keychains, which are specialized files that store passwords.

NetInfo Manager. A heavy-duty utility for manipulating NetInfo domains, it enables root access, for you Unix folks. If you're not working with NetInfo or don't need to enable root access, you can (and should) safely ignore this.

Network Utility. This underrated utility lets you look at all of your network interfaces, including AirPort and Ethernet connections. It's very useful for diagnosing network problems and for other odd tasks, such as locating information on domain names or specific email addresses.

ODBC Administrator. This program lets you connect to and administer ODBC database data sources. ODBC (short for Open Data Base Connectivity) is a way of moving data into or out of a corporate database.

Print Center and Printer Setup Utility. These utilities let you search for available printers and then connect your Mac to them. Oddly, the Print Center icon is an alias that launches the Printer Setup Utility. (In Mac OS X 10.2, Print Center is the only game in town.)

StuffIt Expander. This is a Mac OS X–native version of the popular file decompression utility by Aladdin Systems.

System Profiler. When launched, it tells you tons about your Mac, including what processor is inside and how much memory is installed (**Figure 2.23**).

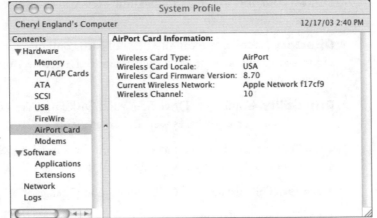

Figure 2.23

System Profiler gives you lots of information about your Mac—sometimes more than you need to know.

Terminal. This application opens up a Unix command-line window, which lets you use Unix commands directly in Mac OS X.

The Classic Environment

When Apple was developing the first version of Mac OS X, the company realized that most people would want to run their old (Mac OS 9 and earlier) software—especially early on in Mac OS X's life. That's because when Mac OS X was first introduced, not too many companies had written or rewritten their programs to run specifically on it. Now that software companies are producing more and more Mac OS X–native versions, this is becoming less of an issue. Still, you may have a program or two that requires Mac OS 9, either because a Mac OS X–native version is not available or because you have not yet upgraded to the Mac OS X version. For those of you, there's the Classic environment.

The Classic environment is actually a clever engineering feat that lets you run your older programs unmodified in Mac OS X—as long as those programs don't use hardware directly (as hard-drive utilities and certain games do). Giving programs access to hardware without going through Mac OS X would make the operating system prone to crashes. Despite this restriction, Classic works surprisingly well, running almost every program written in the last ten years—and in some cases even older programs.

How Classic Works

Apple implements this amazing compatibility by running Mac OS 9 in a *virtual machine*. This means that Mac OS X creates a kind of software Macintosh inside its own memory and then runs Mac OS 9 on that virtual machine. When you launch a program written for Mac OS 9 or earlier and not rewritten for Mac OS X, Mac OS X actually starts up a copy of Mac OS 9 and then runs that program inside the virtual operating system. Mac OS 9 and earlier program icons show up in the Dock alongside those for Mac OS X programs. Classic application windows appear right next to Mac OS X windows, and you can switch between Classic and Mac OS X programs just by clicking their windows or their icons in the Dock.

When a Classic application first launches, a window pops up with a progress bar that represents Mac OS 9 starting up inside Mac OS X (**Figure 2.24**). Click the little disclosure triangle in this window to see the Mac OS 9 startup screen and extensions as they load. This process takes about as long as starting up Mac OS 9 on a real-world Mac—anywhere from 30 seconds to a few minutes. Once this process is done, the Classic program launches as it would in Mac OS 9 (**Figure 2.25**). The Classic environment needs to start up only once—when it's open, all Classic programs run in this virtual environment, and they launch in about the same amount of time as they would take in a real-world Mac OS 9 environment (Classic programs also *run* almost as fast in the Classic environment as they do in Mac OS 9, by the way).

Figure 2.24

When Classic is starting, it's actually booting Mac OS 9— and you can watch the progress in the Classic startup window.

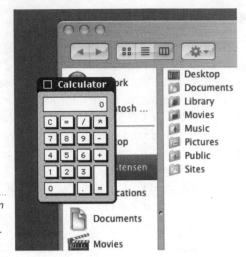

Figure 2.25

That's right—the Calculator from Mac OS 9 is running side by side with a Mac OS X 10.3 Finder window, thanks to Classic.

Although Classic programs can run in Mac OS X, they don't benefit from any of Mac OS X's nifty advantages, such as the spiffy user interface or crash pro-

tection. Instead, Classic programs use the old set of windows and scroll bars as well as the old-style menu bar, along with the Application menu and clock. And this also means that one misbehaving Classic program can take down every single Classic program currently running. Fortunately, this is limited to the Classic layer—at worst, you'll have to use the Classic pane in System Preferences to restart your Classic environment. (No more trips to the coffee shop while you're starting up a crashed Mac!)

 If you have problems running a particular application in the Classic environment, try booting Mac OS 9 (if your Mac will let you) and running the application there.

Classic applications also have the old-style Apple menu, complete with its set of control panels and the like (**Figure 2.26**). You can use these control panels to tweak some of what happens in Classic programs, but don't count on them to change everything. For example, the

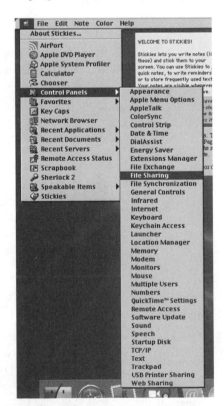

Figure 2.26

Look familiar? Classic applications still have access to the old-style Apple menu and all its features.

Appearance control panel can change how scroll bars appear in Classic programs, but it won't let you change your Desktop picture—Mac OS X handles that.

It's pretty easy to tell whether you're working with a Classic program or a Mac OS X–native program. If you see Mac OS 9–style windows, menus, and scroll bars, the program is a Classic application. If you're looking at rounded buttons and widgets, you're using a Mac OS X–native program.

Configuring Classic

Mac OS X contains a few tools, which you'll find in the Classic pane of System Preferences, for working with Classic. To configure Classic, launch System Preferences and click the Classic icon. The Classic pane has three tabs: Start/Stop, Advanced, and Memory/Versions (**Figure 2.27**).

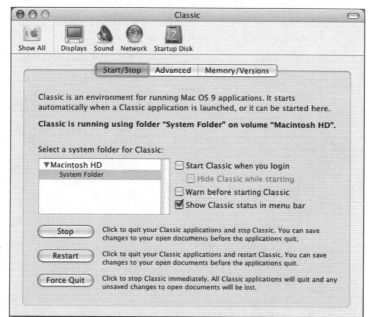

Figure 2.27

The Classic pane lets you perform all kinds of tasks to exercise some control over Classic.

Start/Stop contains some simple controls that let you choose which Mac OS 9 System Folder runs Classic applications; this System Folder doesn't have to live on the same disk as your Mac OS X system software. This tab contains a check box that lets you set whether the Classic environment launches when you start up your Mac. You can also set whether Mac OS X warns you before launching Classic, and whether the Classic status icon shows up in the menu bar. This widget lets you see Classic's status at a glance, as well as restart and shut down Classic, or open the Classic preferences.

The bottom of this window contains three buttons that let you start and stop Classic, restart Classic (which quits all Classic programs and relaunches the Classic environment), and force-quit the Classic environment—something you might have to do if it locks up.

The Advanced tab holds a few tools that let you troubleshoot Classic and control how it works with the operating system (**Figure 2.28**). At the top of the tab is a menu that lets you restart Classic with extensions off, with Extensions Manager open during startup (if you're having trouble with an extension), or with a certain key combination held down (such as a key that disables a specific extension). In the center of the tab is a slider that can put Classic to sleep if it's inactive for a specified period of time. This improves performance in Mac OS X programs, but it can take some time for Classic programs to wake up if the Classic environment goes to sleep. If you plan to use a lot of older programs that can't run natively in Mac OS X, move this slider all the way over to Never. Finally, at the bottom of the tab is the Rebuild Desktop button, which rebuilds the Classic Desktop so that the correct icons are displayed and the correct program launches when you double-click a document. You can rebuild the Desktop without starting the Classic environment.

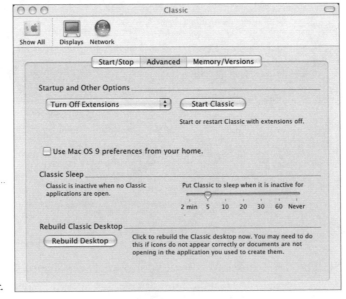

Figure 2.28

The Advanced tab of the Classic pane of System Preferences gives you some nifty options for troubleshooting and customizing Classic.

Finally, the Memory/Versions tab shows all running Classic processes, revealing their names and how much memory they're using from the chunk allotted to them. In this list you can also see which Classic applications are running in the background.

In its thoughtfulness, Apple provided a way for developers to get their programs ready to run natively on Mac OS X without rewriting them from the ground up. This technology is Carbon, and a Mac OS 9 and earlier program tweaked to run natively in Mac OS X is described as *Carbonized*. The beauty of Carbonized programs is that they can also run unmodified in Mac OS 9 or later using the Carbon Library (or CarbonLib). For example, AppleWorks 6 is one of the first Carbonized programs, and it can run unmodified in both Mac OS 9 and Mac OS X.

Switching Between Mac OS 9 and Mac OS X

For those of you who have Macs that can boot both Mac OS 9 and Mac OS X (and that should be several million of you), switching back and forth between the two operating systems is fairly painless. In both cases it involves using the Startup Disk software built into the OS. Here's how to boot either operating system.

Booting into Mac OS 9 from Mac OS X. If you're running Mac OS X and you want to boot Mac OS 9, open System Preferences and click the Startup Disk icon. This loads a list of disks that contain valid system software. In the Startup disk pane simply click the one you want and click the Restart button (or close the pane, saving changes, and restart later). Next time you boot, you'll start up in Mac OS 9.

Booting into Mac OS X from Mac OS 9. If you're running Mac OS 9 and you want to boot Mac OS X, it's a similar process. Select Apple menu > Control Panels > Startup Disk, which opens the Startup Disk control panel. This panel lists all eligible startup disks, including those with both Mac OS 9 and Mac OS X installed on them. Choose the disk you want to start up from, and then close the control panel. Next time you restart your Mac, it'll boot Mac OS X.

Using Option. Newer Macs let you select a startup volume before you've started up your Mac by pressing the power button and then holding down [Option]. Your Mac scans the available hard drives for valid system software and then presents you with a series of icons representing the startup volumes. You also see two arrows onscreen—a circular arrow that scans for valid startup drives and a right-pointing arrow that tells your Mac to continue starting up. Click the volume icon you want to use, and then click the right-facing arrow. Your Mac will now start up using the volume you selected.

The Mac OS 9 (Classic) System Folder

The System Folder used to run Classic is a stock installation of Mac OS 9.1 or later with a few resources that Mac OS X adds to it. Some Macs will let you boot Mac OS 9 (meaning that you can start up your Mac using only Mac OS 9; Mac OS X will never show up), while other Macs allow you to run it only from the Classic environment within Mac OS X. Either way, if you plan to use Classic, you still need to know about it.

 When you change settings in Classic, the changes affect *only* Classic—they do not affect the rest of Mac OS X.

 When we mention that a particular feature works in Classic, that also means it works when you boot Mac OS 9. We'll note specifically if a feature works only in one environment or the other.

The System and Finder files

There are two special files inside your Mac OS 9 System Folder named System and Finder. The System file is fairly meaty (in Mac OS 9.2.2, it weighs in at 13.6 MB), and it contains most of the information your Mac (or Classic) needs to start up and run properly. And, as in Mac OS X, the Finder is your interface with your Mac. It's responsible for creating icons, and for moving files around on the hard drive when you drag them to different places. It also launches programs when you double-click them and links double-clicked documents to the appropriate programs. The Finder is the public face of your Mac's system software. The Mac OS 9 Finder doesn't run in the Classic environment in the old familiar way (but it does need to be present for Classic to run)—that's because the Mac OS X Finder is already doing the job.

System Folder

Figure 2.29

A blessed folder in Mac OS 9 is one that contains a valid System file and Finder—and sports a jaunty Mac happy face.

Together, the System file and the Finder run Classic, and their presence in a folder makes it a special folder—*blessed,* in Apple jargon (**Figure 2.29**). You can run Mac OS 9 from a blessed folder, whether that's by booting into it at startup or running it in the Classic environment. Here's a look inside that special System Folder.

The System file. Despite its placid appearance, the System file contains hundreds of resources your Mac needs to run properly—everything from icons to text strings you might see in an error message, to the Application menu. The System is a *suitcase* file—that is, you can open it and put stuff inside it, just as if it were a real suitcase. You can open the System file only if you boot Mac OS 9; if you're using Mac OS X and Classic, you can't open this file. In the old days (say, in System 7.0), if you wanted to add a sound or a font to your Mac, you opened the System file and dropped it in. Fonts have moved out into their own room—a Fonts folder inside the System Folder—but the System file still houses your system sounds and keyboard layouts. (System sounds are the beeps your Mac makes to alert you that it needs your attention; keyboard layouts let you change your Mac keyboard layout from the standard QWERTY to Dvorak or any number of other layouts for other languages, such as German, Italian, or Japanese.)

The Finder file. The other special denizen of the System Folder is the Finder. Unlike the System file, the Finder can't be opened or modified even when you've booted into Mac OS 9, except by technically minded folks using special software. As we've said before, the Finder is responsible for your Mac's user interface. It draws windows, moves files, displays icons, launches applications—it handles the basics. In Classic, though, these tasks are handled by the Mac OS X Finder, so *this* Finder stands by, largely unused. Of course, if you've actually booted Mac OS 9, you'll be using this Finder.

Special files

Besides the System file and the Finder, the System Folder contains a handful of special files that provide services or otherwise make your Mac experience a great one. Here are a few you will encounter:

Clipboard. The Clipboard file is where Mac OS 9 stores data that you cut or copy using Cut or Copy from the Edit menu. If you want to know what the Clipboard currently holds, double-click the Clipboard file and a window will open, showing you its contents (this works only for Mac OS 9—you can't open this file in Mac OS X).

Mac OS ROM. Older Macs had a special set of chips called the Mac OS ROM, which contained basic instructions on how a Mac should start up and run. Newer Mac models (starting with the iMac) keep most of these instructions in the Mac OS ROM file in your System Folder. The Mac OS ROM file needs to be present for Classic or Mac OS 9 to work, but you can't modify it.

Panels. The Panels file provides an alternative to the Finder. That's right— your Mac doesn't absolutely *have* to have the Finder in order to function correctly. The Panels interface is a simple Finder, with program and file buttons arranged in neat panels. You can't open Panels—it's strictly for the system's use. This file works properly only when you've booted Mac OS 9; in Classic, the Mac OS X Finder takes precedence.

Scrapbook File. The Scrapbook File is a holding place for snippets of text, movie clips, sound files, or pictures you've come across and would like to keep for a while. To put something in the Scrapbook, select the item and copy it to the Clipboard (choose Cut or Copy from the Edit menu). Then choose Scrapbook from the Apple menu to open the Scrapbook window. Choose Edit > Paste to paste the item you put on the Clipboard in the Scrapbook window. You can use your Scrapbook items by scrolling to the one you want, copying it to the

Clipboard, and then pasting it where you want. This works both when you've booted Mac OS 9 and when using Classic.

System Resources. After years of development, the System file was packed so full of resources that Apple reached the limit for resources in a single file. So engineers created the System Resources file to hold some of those additional resources. You can't open System Resources—only the OS uses it. The System Resources file needs to be present for Classic or Mac OS 9 to work, but you can't modify it.

Special folders

The System Folder is also home to several special folders containing hundreds of files that your Mac needs to go about its business, such as fonts, Desktop pictures, and items that launch when your Mac starts up.

Appearance. The Appearance folder is where your Mac stores all the files it needs to present a pretty face. Specifically, this folder stores your Desktop pictures, as well as theme files and sound sets. *Theme files* govern the color and shape of Classic windows, buttons, and controls. Apple Platinum is the only appearance theme that comes with a Macintosh—the Mac is capable of using other themes, but they are exceedingly difficult to find, and they'll affect only the Classic environment, so you may want to skip the exercise altogether. *Sound sets* provide a sound track for your Mac by assigning sounds to button presses, menu choices, opening and closing of windows, and so on. The sound sets affect your Mac only if you've booted Mac OS 9—they don't affect Classic in Mac OS X. The Appearance themes will change how Classic windows look.

Apple Menu Items. Any items you place in the Apple Menu Items folder show up in the Apple menu—this is an incredibly powerful and customizable feature—but only in the Apple menu that appears when you're running Classic or you've booted Mac OS 9. You can put programs, files, folders, and even aliases to other items in here. If you put a folder in the Apple Menu Items folder, it appears as a hierarchical menu in the Apple menu, showing off its contents for all the world to see.

Application Support. When you install programs, they sometimes put items they need in this folder. It's just a convenient storage place that programs use—you probably won't ever need to open it. This folder is used only when you're running Classic applications or you've booted Mac OS 9.

ColorSync Profiles. The Mac's color-management software, ColorSync, makes sure that graphics professionals get the colors they expect in every aspect of their work—on the monitor and from the printer. ColorSync saves profiles that show how an individual piece of hardware handles color. Mac OS X's version of ColorSync is the active utility, but if you're running a Mac OS 9 application that uses ColorSync, it may still use the Mac OS 9 ColorSync files.

Contextual Menu Items. The files in this folder add items to your Mac's contextual-menu capabilities. These contextual menus are confined to Classic or when you've booted Mac OS 9.

Control Panels. The Control Panels folder contains a special set of files called *control panels,* which you can use to change settings on your Macintosh. You can tweak a *lot* of settings here; a standard Mac OS 9.2.2 installation includes more than 30 control panels, which let you set up your AppleTalk network, change your Desktop picture, control how quickly your mouse moves the pointer, and even share a USB printer over a network. When you launch a control panel by choosing it from the Control Panels submenu (or double-clicking it in the Control Panels window), that panel puts up a small window full of settings that you can change. When you close the window, the changes are saved and the control panel quits.

Again, these settings are confined to Classic and Mac OS 9, and some of them—such as network settings—shouldn't be changed. Others either can't be used or don't work the way you might expect. That's because the idea behind control panels is that they let you change how your Mac operates— and that's something Mac OS X handles.

Control Strip Modules. This folder holds items that show up in your Mac's Control Strip, which is a slender bar that graces the bottom of your Mac's Desktop in Mac OS 9. These modules offer an easy way to change your Mac's settings; they contain a subset of the controls you'll find in certain control panels. Although they contain fewer settings than the corresponding control panels, they're easier to access. A standard Mac OS 9.2.2 installation has tons of Control Strip modules, which let you turn AppleTalk on or off, choose a different printer, control audio CD playback, change monitor resolution, and so on. The Control Strip doesn't show up in Mac OS X, even under Classic. It does appear when you boot Mac OS 9, however.

Extensions. The Extensions folder holds all your Mac's extensions—you'll become intimate with these if you ever have to do Mac OS 9 troubleshooting (**Figure 2.30**). Extensions are special files that add new capabilities to Mac OS 9 (or Classic), and they must be in this folder to load properly. Not all extensions work in Classic. (For more on these, see the sidebar "Extensions," below.)

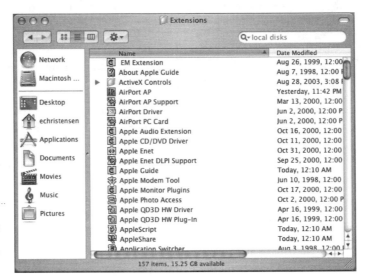

Figure 2.30

If you've used Mac OS 9 or earlier, then this folder should look pretty familiar to you.

Favorites. This underused folder contains a quick way to get at folders, files, URLs, and applications. Items put in the Favorites folder (whether they're the real thing or just aliases) appear in the Favorites submenu in the Apple menu (but only in the Classic Apple menu or when you've booted Mac OS 9), as well as next to the Favorites button in the Open or Save dialog box, if the program in question can use them. For example, the Favorites button in Microsoft Word's Open dialog box shows you those documents Word can open, as well as any folders its Open dialog box can point to. To open an item in your Favorites folder, choose Favorites from the Apple menu and select the item.

Fonts. The Fonts folder holds all the fonts available to your Classic applications. To add a font in Mac OS 9 and earlier, drag it to the closed System Folder and your Mac puts the font in the Fonts folder; or you can drag new fonts directly to this folder. To remove a font, simply drag it out of this folder to a new location. Any Classic program running at the time you add fonts can't use them until you quit and relaunch it. To remove fonts, you'll have to quit all the programs so that only the Finder is running, and then move the fonts you no longer want out of the Fonts folder.

Help. This folder holds help files for Classic applications. When you go to the Help menu and choose a topic, these files provide information about your Mac and the software installed on it. Mac help files are mostly plain HTML files that you can read with a Web browser, if you're so inclined, but there's no need to do so, as the built-in Help Viewer program pops up automatically when you open a topic from the Help menu.

Internet Plug-Ins. The Internet Plug-Ins folder holds plug-ins for Internet programs that give your Web browser new capabilities. Each browser also maintains its own plug-ins folder, so it's unlikely that you'll find anything other than the QuickTime Plug-in here—and that's for Classic Internet applications.

Internet Search Sites. This folder contains Sherlock plug-ins, which enable the Classic version of Sherlock to scour the Internet for whatever you request. You can add new Sherlock plug-ins by putting them in this folder, but they work only in Classic or when you've booted Mac OS 9. In Mac OS X, the Mac OS X version of Sherlock takes over.

Language & Region Support. The items in this folder let Classic work well with multiple languages, such as Chinese, Finnish, Japanese, and Swedish.

Launcher Items. Items you put in the Launcher Items folder (including aliases to other items) show up in the Launcher, which is a floating palette that contains buttons representing applications, files, folders, and disks.

Preferences. The Preferences folder is where Classic programs store specialized *preference* files, which contain both default and customized settings for a given program. It's not uncommon for the Preferences folder on a Mac you've been using for a while to have hundreds of items in it.

PrintMonitor Documents. When you print a document, your Mac creates a file that represents this print job and puts it in the PrintMonitor Documents folder. The program that handles background printing in Classic is called PrintMonitor, and it looks to this folder for any waiting print jobs. You probably won't ever need to open this folder, unless you're having some difficulty with a print job.

Scripting Additions. This folder holds scripting additions files, which give AppleScript more power. Mac OS 9 has several scripting additions by default, and you can add more of your own by putting them in this folder, but they only affect Classic AppleScripts.

Scripts. The Scripts folder is a convenient place to store Classic AppleScripts, and if you drop an AppleScript on the System Folder, it'll go here. By default, this folder contains a Folder Action Scripts folder, which holds a group of AppleScripts you can attach to a folder. These scripts run when the folder to which they're attached changes. (See "AppleScript," earlier in this chapter.)

Servers. This folder holds aliases to servers that open whenever Classic starts up or when you boot Mac OS 9. You can remove these autoconnecting servers by removing their aliases from this folder; you can delete them if you're sure you no longer need them, or you can move the aliases to another location, where you can double-click them to open the servers they represent.

Startup Items. Any items in this folder (including aliases) open when Classic starts up. For example, if you always launch a particular program when you start up Classic, put its alias here and your Mac will launch it for you whenever Classic launches or when you boot Mac OS 9.

Text Encodings. This folder contains items that help your Mac convert one type of text (say, English) into another (say, Hebrew). They're necessary in order for Classic to work properly.

Extensions

Extensions are special files that extend your Mac's abilities—hence the name. A typical extension might let your Mac talk to a new hardware peripheral, add the ability to listen to a new music file format, or even change the way your Mac's menus look. At startup, your Mac loads those it finds in the Extensions folder. Extensions still modify how Classic and Mac OS 9 behaves, but they don't have any effect on Mac OS X. Not all extensions work in Classic, by the way.

Extensions are different from applications in that they're *global*, whereas applications generally aren't. That means that extensions change your whole Classic experience, no matter what program you're using. Applications, on the other hand, have an impact only when they're active. And although extensions resemble control panels (they both load bits of code into the Mac OS at startup), control panels let you easily change their settings; extensions might rely on a sibling in the control panel to do that work for them. Many extensions don't allow you to change their settings at all. You can generally tell which files are extensions because of their icons, which look like interlocking puzzle pieces.

Types of extensions. You'll find a couple of types of items in your Extensions folder: extensions and libraries. Extensions are active bits of code that load when your Mac starts up, and libraries are passive bits of code that other programs go to when they need to do certain things. For example, the QuickTime extension modifies your Mac so that it can play music and videos with ease, and DrawSprocketLib provides a way for other programs to draw onscreen. Libraries just need to be present in the background—they don't have to load during startup.

continues on next page

Extensions   continued

Extension memory use. If your Mac can boot Mac OS 9, this will concern you. When extensions load while your Mac is starting up, they take up some of your Mac's memory. Although a single extension may take less than a few hundred kilobytes, by the time you've loaded 30 or so extensions, you've added several megabytes to the amount of memory your Mac needs for system software—sometimes as much as 15 or 20 MB. If your Mac doesn't have a lot of memory, you might experiment with disabling some extensions by moving them into the Extensions (Disabled) folder to free up some memory.

Problems that extensions can cause. Extensions are powerful things, even in Classic—they essentially replace little bits of the operating system with their own programming code. For example, an extension might replace the part of the Mac OS responsible for drawing windows with its own code, so that your Mac can draw windows with a pink stripe through the title bar. This can cause some serious problems. First, if the programmer hasn't done the job just right, the extension might not do what it's supposed to, resulting in a crash. Second, another extension might try to modify the same bit of the system software or expect to encounter unmodified code. Known as an *extension conflict,* this is one of the leading causes of Mac crashes. (By the way, Mac OS X doesn't use extensions in this fashion, which is one reason why it's so darned stable.)

How extensions load. When your Mac starts up either with Mac OS 9 or in the Classic environment, it first goes through a series of tests and then finds a hard drive with system software on it, from which it starts loading the system software. This is what's happening when you see the splash screen in Mac OS 9 and earlier. Next, your Mac looks inside the Extensions folder and starts loading the extensions it finds there. It loads these items alphabetically, which means you can change the order in which extensions load by altering their names. Put a space in front of an extension's name and it will load early; put a z (or a bullet) in front of an extension's name and it will load near the end. The reason you might want to change an extension's load order is that certain extensions crash unless they load first—or last. Unfortunately, it's a game of trial and error to figure out the correct order.

A few items load before items in the Extensions folder (such as MacsBug or enabler software for processor upgrade cards). These early startup items also load alphabetically, but they do so before regular extensions. So if you find an extension that loads before any of the others even though its name comes up later alphabetically, this is probably why. The reason why some extensions are set to load early is that order matters—and if they load at the wrong time, crashes can result.

Interview: Andy Hertzfeld

Although he left the Apple payroll just weeks after the launch of the Macintosh in 1984, Andy Hertzfeld remains one of the most celebrated of all Mac programmers. To software developers he is remembered as the lead author of the original Macintosh User Interface Toolbox, the built-in software routines that helped ensure the elegance and consistency of Mac applications. A series of nifty hacks he produced later—including Switcher, the utility that first made it possible to run multiple programs simultaneously on the Mac, and the software for ThunderScan, the first low-cost scanner for the Mac—made him a hero among users, too.

> To understand Apple, you have to understand Steve. To understand Steve, you have to understand that the business motivation is important but secondary. The prize is artistic.
>
> —*Andy Hertzfeld, on the Mac's importance to Apple as a business*

In recent years Hertzfeld has become an advocate of open-source software. Along with several other Mac pioneers, he worked at Eazel, a now-defunct startup dedicated to producing software to make Linux easier to use. Today he works with the Open Source Applications Foundation (www.osafoundation.org), an organization set up to "create open-source application software of uncompromising quality." Specifically, Hertzfeld and the foundation are developing an open-source application for managing email, appointments, contacts, and tasks that will run on the Mac and Linux, as well as on Windows. —Henry Norr

When did you start at Apple, and when did you begin working on the Mac?

I went to work at Apple in August 1979. I was 26. I dropped out of graduate school to go to Apple. I was in a doctoral program [in computer science] at the University of California, Berkeley, but in my second year of grad school I bought an Apple II, and that was, like, infinitely more interesting than grad school.

My first project at Apple was doing the software for the first Apple-branded printer, called the SilenType. Then I did a variety of system stuff for the Apple II and III, until I switched to the Mac in February 1981. Steve [Jobs] had just taken over the Mac project. So I had an encounter with Steve, a sort of very brief interview. Once he decided he wanted me on the Mac project, he came over to my desk and told me the good news.

I said, "Well, great, just give me one day to finish up what I'm doing on the Apple II." He said, "No, that stinks, you're wasting your time working on the Apple II." I said, "Come on, please, just give me a couple of hours." And he said "No!" and he unplugged my Apple II—pulled it right out of the wall—lifted it up, and started carrying it away. And so the only choice I had was to trail behind him.

What was your role in the Mac group?

I was the main author of the User Interface Toolbox, but before that I was the main author of the underlying I/O [input/output] system. The first work to do was making sure the hardware worked as it was specced to work—writing tests for the hardware and then breathing life into the various peripherals—you know, getting the mouse going, the keyboard going, the serial ports going, all of that. I spent the first couple of months just working on that stuff…

In May 1981 the very first thing that looked like the Macintosh GUI was on the Mac. What our job really was—my job in particular—was essentially taking what Bill Atkinson did for the Lisa and transplanting it to work on a machine with one-eighth the memory. The Mac had a faster processor, but it had much fewer resources in other respects.

Did you think that Mac was a historic project?

Yes, no doubt about it. We had Steve, who would just hammer that in every day. He felt that, and he made sure we felt that.

I thought it would be essentially the Apple II of the next ten years. I thought it would open the computer market to ten times as many people as had been able to take advantage of a personal computer previously. Maybe 100 times, because we were making computers radi-cally easier to use, just changing the ground rules completely, and we knew that would have a huge effect. Now, we weren't thinking of Microsoft, and that it would reach most people by copying everything from the Mac.

Were you thinking about what the project would do for Apple as a business?

Absolutely. But you know, to understand Apple, you have to understand Steve. To understand Steve, you have to understand that the business motivation is important but secondary—that's not the prize. The prize is artistic—he has artistic values. The prize is to do the greatest thing that's ever been done. The prize is to live up to the potential that's before you. You know, it's aesthetic more than it is financial, and I do believe that was the main motivation of the Macintosh.

What do you think of Mac OS X?

It's OK. Overall, in usability, in the things I care about most, I wouldn't say it's better than Windows XP, and I think that's very sad. In terms of living up to what it could be, it gets low marks. In terms of just the bad standards that we all live under, it's pretty good.

Want to elaborate on what you think should be better?

The root of the problem comes right from Steve, and it essentially is a very superficial view of usability. Appearance is more important than usability, everywhere.

Such as?

Here's one place where just a gratuitous visual thing hurts usability: the way the top of the scroller looks in the default setting. Even when the scroller is all the way to the very top, the rounded top edge doesn't look like it's all the way to the top—there's about a 10-pixel gap.

continues on next page

It's just horrible. It's showing you that it's not at the very top when it is. Oooh, it just makes me cringe. The software is full of stuff like that—I can go on and on.

Do you think Apple could survive as a business if it went open source?

Yeah, I think the ice is starting to break, although I think it's a good couple of years yet before you really see it in a big way. But when that happens, there's a historic opportunity for Apple in there somewhere, if they play it right.

And what would that look like?

That would be trying to become the mainstream user experience on the desktop computer, by giving up control over certain pieces.

That would have to mean making it run on Intel-based PCs?

That's certainly part of it. It's unbelievable, really, that Apple still hasn't done that. It has to do with Steve, though. I truly believe Apple wouldn't even be here today if he hadn't come back, but Steve can't make a transition to open source because he's too much of a control freak.

So your vision would involve making the entire Mac OS open source?

No, not necessarily, but it would be to find a few key pieces to get adopted as the consensus standard. They have a good chance to be able to. I really believe that the Microsoft hegemony is going to dissipate—you can see that coming, because of all kinds of different forces. And so what replaces it?

The user interface would surely be Apple's greatest opportunity, because it's their great strength. What if Apple could specify the mainstream user interface that 80 percent of the PCs are on? You would think that would create enormous opportunities. Now, creating the right business model is a complex issue, and I don't pretend to know all the answers, but I know the right direction.

3

The Macintosh Family

Cheryl England is the chapter editor.

Christopher Breen (CB), David Morgenstern (DM), and Jason O'Grady (JOG) are the chapter coauthors. Clifford Colby (CC) also contributed to this chapter.

Sharon Zardetto Aker (SA), Mike Breeden (MB), and Daniel Drew Turner (DT) contributed to earlier editions of **The Macintosh Bible,** *from which portions of this chapter are taken.*

At first, choosing which Mac to buy was a snap: in 1984 you paid $2,495 for the original Macintosh, and Apple threw MacWrite and MacPaint in with the deal. Your big decision: did you want an Apple carrying case for $99?

Ten years later, your choices were more varied—and bewildering. For example, just in the Performa line, at one time or another you could pick from (or wade through) the Performa 520, the Performa 5320CD, the Performa 630CD DOS Compatible, the Performa 6218CD, the Performa 6360, and 50-something other Performa models. To make sense of any of it, you had to know about processor speeds, whether you wanted PCI or NuBus slots, how fast the CD-ROM drive could read data, and a dozen other speeds and specifications.

Flash forward to today. The Mac is 20 years old. You've got more choices than you did with the original Mac (which is a good thing) but not as many as you did 10 years ago (which is also a good thing). Now Apple has trimmed down its product line to form a simple grid: there are desktop Macs for consumers, desktop Macs for professionals, portable Macs for consumers, and portable Macs for professionals. Still, the lines can be blurred in this simple grid, so you'll need to know about removable-storage options, connectors, networking options, video, and, of course, processor speeds. This chapter will get you going on what all that hardware inside your Mac does and help you sort through the machines in Apple's product line—both now and in the past.

In This Chapter

Inside the Macintosh (DM)

Before we start examining the various Macintosh models, we would do well to briefly look at the personal computer in general. In other words, what are the common elements found in any computer, whether it's housed in a desktop model, notebook, or even personal digital assistant?

All computers require a *central processing unit* (or *CPU*) that runs the machine's instructions and data; an amount of *random-access memory* (or *RAM*) to hold the data during manipulation; a program to start up the device; a means of displaying the data to the user; one or more storage devices; and perhaps one or more *input-output* (or *I/O*) interfaces that can send and receive instructions. (Of course, we can't forget software: the operating system and applications that transform the hardware from an expensive doorstop to a productivity tool. We cover the essential system software components in Chapters 1 and 2.)

Understanding the CPU (DM/SA)

The central processing unit is a type of *integrated circuit (IC),* or chip, which is a little silicon wafer with microscopic circuits etched into it. In a computer you don't see or touch the actual chips, since they're encased in plastic or ceramic blocks with metal connectors protruding from them. A computer uses many other kinds of chips as well, such as RAM, graphics, and I/O.

The CPU, which is also referred to as a *microprocessor* or just a *processor,* processes instructions. The processor handles and routes millions, and now even billions, of instructions every second. Of course, it's all submicroscopic, so we never directly witness this miracle of computing. The performance of this component is so vital that some people say "CPU" when they mean a whole computer. Apple focuses much of its branding on the CPU, by naming its Power Macintosh line after the generation of PowerPC chip used in the box—these days we are up to generation 5, or G5.

Information marches through a processor chip—as well as all the other components on a computer logic board (the board that holds the processor and the other major components)—to the beat of an oscillator, usually a quartz crystal, which vibrates in response to an electric current. The pulses are so rapid that they're measured in megahertz (MHz)—millions of cycles per second; or gigahertz (GHz)—billions of cycles. This *clock* determines the speed of your processor: a 500 MHz clock beats 500 million times a second. Components can operate at different speeds, although the speeds are usually some multiple of the base clock timing.

You'll see the prefix *giga-* in hardware specifications, such as gigabit, giga-byte, gigahertz, and gigaflop. The prefix stands for a billion, or 10^9, and comes from the Greek *gigas* ("gigantic"). The list continues after gigabyte with terabyte, petabyte, exabyte, zettabyte, and yottabyte, which is a 1 followed by *23* zeros.

Common sense suggests that to compare computers, all one has to do is check the processor clock rates. Most computer users believe this to be true. Unfortunately, and despite its common use in almost all marketing materials, clock speed is no real measure of the actual performance of a particular computer or even of competing computers using the same processor.

Too many other variables can affect real-world performance: how well a processor can crunch different types of data, like streaming media or large sets of records, the relative speeds and architectures of the other components housed on and off the logic board, and even how fast data can be moved between those components. As Intel keeps boosting the clock speed of the Pentium architecture (with a technology demo heading past 5 GHz), Apple and manufacturers of Intel-compatible CPUs such as Advanced Micro Devices (AMD) have referred to this long-held folk wisdom among users as "The Megahertz Myth." However, with both AMD and Apple having introduced fast 64-bit processors (which use wider, and thus faster, 64-bit data paths)—the Opteron and G5, respectively—companies are starting to put this marketing theme in the background.

Memory and RAM Caches (DM)

RAM provides working space for applications and instructions, and it's used in several important places. Principally it's found in a series of caches for frequent use, and it provides the primary system RAM, which is placed on the logic board (frequently in upgradeable slots). There's also a separate piece of memory in the graphics subsystem, which is used to drive the display.

A *memory cache* is an area of memory set aside for data that the processor will need imminently and frequently. Cache memory is closely connected to the processor and uses a faster route than the system RAM. Computers can have more than one memory cache—in fact, most have a couple. The caches on a given Mac are determined by the processor and model; years ago, some Mac models were differentiated by their cache architecture.

The three levels of cache memory are the following:

- **Level 1** (L1), which is a small piece of memory on the processor itself that holds the latest information
- **Level 2** (L2), which is a larger cache that may be incorporated in the chip itself
- **Level 3** (L3), which is always physically separate from the processor chip and usually runs at a slower speed

After checking the L1 cache for needed information, the processor next looks at the L2 cache and subsequently the L3 cache—anything to avoid having to request data from the main system memory, which offers the slowest memory access—except for recalling something that's been *paged* to the hard drive with virtual memory. But that's a different story (see Chapter 4 for more on virtual memory). In some older Macs the L2 cache was separate, like today's L3 cache, and occasionally upgradeable.

For example, the PowerPC G5 processor integrates a small 64 Kbyte Level 1 cache and a 512 Kbyte Level 2 cache into the processor chip itself, working at full speed—meaning that it transfers data back and forth between the caches and the processor at the processor's clock rate. This is called an *on-chip,* or *internal,* cache. However, the first Power Macs based on the G5 didn't come with a Level 3 cache, unlike the previous PowerPC G4 models that came with a 2 MB *backside,* or Level 3, cache, running at a quarter of the processor speed. This "missing" L3 cache in the original Power Mac G5s was a bit of a surprise to longtime Mac watchers. The G5 processor is so fast and its memory bus runs so quickly that Apple determined that the new Power Mac doesn't need the extra cache to boost performance. In the future, no doubt, one will be added when the cost and performance benefits warrant it. The Mac's primary system memory is located on the logic board and uses one or more industry-standard, *dual inline memory module (DIMM)* expansion slots. Each module is a small circuit board that holds an array of memory chips. Although the modules comply with a standard specification, they are not necessarily interchangeable between Mac models, and some cost more than others. Thus, the modules for a PowerBook are smaller (and more expensive) than those used in a desktop machine.

Even similar Mac models, however, can have problems when exchanging modules or even when using different-speed DIMMs in the same Mac. For example, the Power Mac G5 comes in two versions: the entry-level model's logic board has four memory slots, and the higher-end models have eight slots (really these are pairs of slots—two and four pairs, respectively). Each slot can hold a 184-pin *double-data-rate synchronous dynamic RAM (DDR SDRAM)* DIMM; as of this writing the Power Mac G5s can support 128, 256, and 512 MB modules, and 1 and 2 GB modules (when the latter come on the market). However, the models use different-speed DIMMS—either 333 MHz PC2700-compliant or 400 MHz PC3200-compliant parts. More confusingly, some RAM from earlier Power Mac G4 models will work in *some* of the Power Mac G5s—such as the PC2700-compliant modules in the later PowerPC G4s—but the 168-pin non-DDR modules from the earlier range of G4 models won't work. (To learn much more about RAM, see Chapter 4.)

For more technical details on memory, including what kind of RAM your Mac needs, you can do one of several things: go to Apple's support site (www.info.apple.com) and search for your model name and the term *memory specifications;* refer to the Memory Questions section of Accelerate Your Mac's FAQ (www.xlr8yourmac.com); check MacFixIt (www.macfixit.com); or look up your model at MemoryX (www.memoryx.net/apple.html).

Starting Up Your Mac (DM)

After you press its power button, a computer runs a set of instructions. These instructions are usually stored in *ROM (read-only memory).* This type of small, memory-based instruction package is called *firmware.* The small program checks the computer's hardware, runs diagnostic routines on memory and other hardware elements, and sets values that will be needed by programs, the operating system, and hardware. It also loads *drivers,* which are special small, low-level programs for hardware devices connected to the machine. In the Windows/Intel world this startup ROM is known as the *BIOS,* or Basic Input and Output System. The Mac ROM uses Open Firmware, the IEEE 1275-1994 standard, to regulate the startup procedure.

A primary function of Open Firmware is to determine which operating system will start up your Mac. After initializing the system, the Open Firmware code searches the various volumes and drives connected to the Mac and finds the correct system folder identified in the Startup Disk pane in System Preferences. On some models this can be either Mac OS X or Mac OS 9.

 The transition from one operating system to another can be a moving target, especially for users of Mac OS 9.2.2. Until January 2003, Mac users could choose between booting Mac OS X or Mac OS 9.2.2, a feature called *dual-boot.* At that time, with the release of the Power Mac G4 Mirrored Drive Doors version, the capability was nixed—for a while. In the fall, with the release of the Power Mac G5, which will never boot Mac OS 9, Apple reversed its policy and again sold dual-boot G4s. Where there's a market, there's a way.

In the distant past, the Mac ROM held all the code necessary to start up the computer, as well as the Mac ToolBox, a collection of small software pieces that were available for Mac programs to use (see the sidebar "Why the Mac ToolBox?" below). This was a novel approach to programming. Following the introduction of the iMac, the ROM has conformed to Apple's NewWorld Architecture. This scheme focused the ROM on the low-level startup process—under this plan, the new name for the Mac ROM is the Boot ROM.

The higher-level ToolBox items were moved to a file called the ToolBox ROM Image, which is located on the primary hard drive. When a Classic Mac OS 9 application wants a ToolBox item, it's loaded into the main system RAM and works just like the old versions stored in the ROM. Unlike the architecture for Mac OS 9 and earlier, Mac OS X is based on Unix. Its system and services are loaded after being invoked by the Open Firmware boot command.

Mac OS X's Classic environment lets Mac OS 9 applications run on a Mac OS X system. A variety of other user-related system settings required by your Mac are stored in the *parameter RAM* (or *PRAM*), a small memory chip located on the logic board. There's also an Extended PRAM, but it's really all the same thing. (For more on PRAM see Chapter 8.)

Why the Mac ToolBox? (DM)

Back in 1983, when the Mac was invented, RAM was terribly expensive. Placing a set of shared high-level routines on a relatively less-expensive ROM was more efficient for Mac programs and the Mac OS, and it saved everyone money. That's hard to imagine nowadays, when a 512 MB module costs well under $100. However, in 1986 a 512 KB (yes, kilobyte) memory upgrade was $1,000. Ouch, indeed. The Mac ROM in a Power Mac G5 is 1 MB.

A Bus Runs Through It: Graphics/Video and I/O (DM/DT)

Although the processor is critical to your Mac's performance, there's much more to a logic board than the CPU. A *data bus* connects the processor to other subsystems that provide display and graphics, I/O (input/output) connectors for storage and networking, and other devices for expanding the computer's capabilities. There's no way that the main processor could control all the functions of the computer; instead, each subsystem has its own set of integrated circuits.

When bits and bytes flow through the various components of your Mac, they do so through one or more data buses. Just as a wider pipe allows a greater flow of water, a wider bus can make for faster data transmission; however, at other times a faster, smaller pipe can also move data efficiently. One factor for overall system performance (some think it's the most important) is the avoidance of bottlenecks; computers don't like to wait for data. Even a small slowdown of data moving through one part of the logic board can create a chain reaction in other parts.

Current Power Mac G5s use a wide range of data-bus technologies to connect components: a 64-bit high-speed, bidirectional bus connects the processor and its memory controller; a 128-bit bus connects the processor to the RAM slots; and HyperTransport, an intelligent bus, routes traffic from I/O devices and expansion slots to their destinations. The bus branches out to connect with the different subsystems at different speeds and widths; the G5 data paths include 8-, 16-, 32-, and 64-bit buses.

Here are the common subsystems and I/O ports found on today's Macs:

Video

To handle the image on the screen, all computers use a graphics subsystem, usually with its own memory and integrated circuits. The video circuitry can be found on a removable card in a dedicated slot or simply integrated on the logic board. It often accelerates display performance by independently processing 2D and 3D graphics routines.

If your Mac uses a video card, then that card connects to the logic board through the Advanced Graphics Port (AGP), an industry standard for video. Different versions of the standard are designated with an *x;* the Power Mac G5 has an AGP8x; earlier Power Mac models have 4x or 2x connectors.

Depending on its capabilities, the video subsystem can also support more than one display. Today's desktop Macs offer two types of external ports for video: the DVI-I (DVI with support for analog VGA displays) and a proprietary connector, called the Apple Display Connector (ADC).

Expansion slots

Most computers offer one or more ways to expand their hardware capabilities, usually through some industry-standard card interface. Mac and Windows desktop machines have several *PCI (Peripheral Component Interconnect)* slots, and portables often provide a *PC Card* interface. The Power Mac G5 introduced a PCI-X controller, which is the 64-bit next-generation version of the PCI standard and is common on high-performance Windows desktops and servers.

Depending on the model, the Mac PCI-X slots can run at 133 MHz or 100 MHz, much faster than the previous 33 MHz of the standard PCI connectors. The new PCI-X slots support older 3.3-volt cards but not 5-volt keyed or signaling cards.

Apple documentation warns that for the Power Mac G5, it is critical to shut down the computer and remove the power cable before removing or installing PCI or PCI-X cards. The logic board has a red LED to warn users that power is present, even if the computer is asleep.

 PCI-SIG (www.pcisig.com/home) has more information than you ever wanted to know about PCI technology.

Storage I/O

Most computers use a separate subsystem to handle I/O devices inside and outside of the case. The latest Mac I/O controller, called K2, supports internal and external storage, FireWire, digital and analog audio interfaces, modems, and networking.

The Power Mac G5 uses a wide range of storage standards, including the *Serial AT Attachment (SATA)* interface for hard drives and the *Ultra DMA/100 ATA* interface for an internal optical drive.

SATA offers many benefits over the traditional parallel ATA or IDE interface. It uses less power, has a thinner cable, supports hot-plugging so that devices are recognized immediately after being plugged in, and provides theoretical data-transfer speeds of up to 150 MBps. Its point-to-point architecture removes the master-slave limitations of the older standard.

USB

Intel spearheaded the development of *Universal Serial Bus (USB)* to encompass separate interfaces needed for the keyboard and mouse as well as for serial and parallel devices. Now it's used for a wide variety of external devices, such as digital cameras, printers, scanners, and MP3 players. Version 2.0 of the standard supports speeds of up to 480 Mbps, which is drastically higher than the older version 1.1's data-throughput rate of 12 Mbps.

FireWire

Apple invented FireWire in the early 1990s. Its standard name is IEEE 1394, but Sony and its partners call it iLink. There are now two versions of FireWire: FireWire 400, which runs at 400 Mbps; and a double-speed version, FireWire 800, which runs at 800 Mbps. The goal for FireWire was to improve upon the flavors of the venerable SCSI interface for digital video cameras and players, scanners, and storage devices. FireWire can connect as many as 62 devices, and it allows users to plug and unplug devices without shutting down (USB also has this *hot-swapping* capability). (For more on USB, FireWire, and SCSI, see Chapter 5.)

 In fall 2003, Apple released a warning about reliability issues with FireWire 800 hard drives. The problem may require installing a firmware update on your external FireWire drive or a software update or both. Check with your hard-drive vendor about the requirements for your particular drive.

Digital audio

Another first for the Mac platform with the Power Mac G5 is support for the *S/PDIF (Sony/Philips Digital Interface Format)* standard. The physical interface is a pair of 7.5 mm digital optical Toslink connectors for input and output. S/PDIF is used on a wide range of professional MIDI equipment and other digital peripherals that take advantage of digital audio, such as home theater systems. The port can synchronize data streams to either an internal or an external clock, letting users better match up video and audio during editing.

Networking

Many computers support networks with an add-on card or integrated interface. Most Macs come standard with an Ethernet port; the latest models offer a single interface supporting the Gigabit Ethernet standard. In addition, all recent Macs support either 802.11b or 802.11g wireless networking, branded by Apple as AirPort and AirPort Extreme, respectively. (The rest of the world calls it *Wi-Fi.*)

The plain AirPort provides a top speed of 11 Mbps, while the newer AirPort Extreme standard provides theoretical speeds as high as 54 Mbps. The Power Mac G5 comes with an external white antenna shaped like a T that's easy to install and remove, as technicians on campuses have discovered. Some third-party antennas can be mounted on a wall, which may prevent theft.

 For more information on 802.11 see the Wi-Fi Alliance site (www.wi-fi.org).

Recent Macs also include support for Bluetooth, a popular wireless standard that's a replacement for infrared. Named after a Danish king, Harald "Bluetooth" Blatland, the Bluetooth 2.4 GHz wireless specification is now widely found in a range of devices, from phones to keyboards and PDAs to printers. It offers a range of up to 30 feet and communicates at speeds as high as 720 Kbps. Apple integrated support for the standard starting with the Power Mac G4 series (desktop Macs require an optional external antenna), and Apple's latest wireless mouse and keyboard use Bluetooth.

 Why did Bluetooth take its name from a Danish king? King Blatland united the Danes and the Norwegians; Bluetooth, a wireless technology, unites electronic devices without cables.

 For more information on the standard, see the Official Bluetooth Site (www.bluetooth.com) and Apple's Bluetooth page (www.apple.com/bluetooth).

The Ages of the Desktop Macintosh (DM)

The easiest way to assess Macintosh design is by processor. However, it's also the most likely to lead you astray, because much of the time, differences in machine performance are a result of cache architecture, expansion ports, and graphics capabilities. Nevertheless, here, going from newest to oldest, are the four major processor ages of desktop Macintosh:

- **New Age Mac**—Machines with the PowerPC G5 processor
- **Modern Macs**—The machines compatible with Mac OS X, spanning the Power Mac G3 (Blue and White) and Power Mac G4 series (as well as a couple of strays)
- **RISC Pioneers**—Macs that used the first generations of the PowerPC processor
- **The Golden Age**—Machines that ran a Motorola 680x0 processor (starting with the original Mac)

Aside from the industrial design that we appreciate, modern Mac desktop computers are very different on the inside from their forebears. In earlier times, Apple favored mostly homegrown technologies for internal architectures and for connecting to peripherals and networks. Today, Macs rely on industry-standard parts and connectors. For example, the familiar USB ports and PCI slots replaced proprietary and pricey Apple buses. This approach has reduced the expense of development and manufacturing, as well as provided a larger market for upgrades and peripherals, because PC vendors can now offer their devices on the Mac side often just by writing a Mac driver.

When compared with those in ordinary Intel-based PCs, Apple logic boards do still have a number of proprietary parts. For example, the Power Mac G5—with its new processor, memory architecture, and system bus—requires custom logic such as the U3 PCI bridge and memory controller chip, and the K2 I/O controller. Still, even here Apple is working with outsiders; for example, HyperTransport technology is also used in PC logic boards based on Advanced Micro Devices' 64-bit processors. A similar machine in the past might have had an Apple-derived, proprietary memory bus, expansion-slot architecture, and even storage interface.

In addition, Apple has reduced the number of logic boards used in its line of Macs. In the past, each machine had its own design team, making things difficult (and expensive) on the compatibility front for Apple's own system-software team as well as for third-party developers. Now, Apple follows Steve Jobs' grid of professional and home markets, trying when possible to use one logic-board design for professional desktop models, another for iMacs, and another for PowerBooks and iBooks.

The New Age: The Power Mac G5 Series (DM)

The introduction of the Power Mac G5 series in the summer of 2003 represents one of the most important hardware milestones in Apple's history (**Figure 3.1**). For the first time in a very long while, Apple's professional-level computer can truly be described as a workstation-class machine, incorporating 64-bit processing; a new, faster frontside- and system-bus architecture; and support for the latest PCI-X expansion bus.

Photo courtesy of Apple Computer

Figure 3.1

Apple's Power Mac G5 provides workstation-class performance.

The 64-bit capability of the new PowerPC G5 processor on which the Power Mac G5s are based lets the processor work with larger data sets at a time and lets it use more system memory. However, developers will need to tune their applications to take advantage of this difference. Still, all current 32-bit Mac OS X applications can benefit from the new processor's greater speed and longer data pipelines. (Pipelines allow a processor to execute several instructions, or different parts of an instruction, at the same time. A longer pipeline helps a processor run at a higher frequency.)

Another important technology introduced in the Power Mac G5 is its advanced frontside bus, which shuffles data between the processor, the memory controller, and the PCI bridge chip. The Power Mac G5 frontside bus offers two 32-bit channels, one in and one out, running at 800 MHz, 900 MHz, or 1 GHz, depending on the model. On a dual-processor model, there are two such bidirectional buses. This overcomes a significant bottleneck found in the previous generation of machines. In the Power Mac G4, which provides a single 64-bit frontside connection to the processor, data can flow in only one direction at a time. Though the G4's channel is twice as wide as that in the new Power Mac G5s, all the data in the channel must be cleared before data can move in the opposite direction.

Open the side panel of the Power Mac G5 and another new feature becomes evident: a complex cooling system. The plastic panel divides the interior of the enclosure into zones, each with its own set of fans (nine in all) and temperature sensor (**Figure 3.2**). When the Mac senses high temperature and power consumption in one or more zones, the fans engage, each with a different rate and only while it's needed.

Figure 3.2

The Power Mac G5 is divided into zones, each of which has its own set of cooling fans.

Photo courtesy of Apple Computer

 Your Power Mac G5's sophisticated power and cooling management system may not operate this way when running another operating system, such as one of the flavors of Linux available for the machine. So don't worry if the fans just stay on all the time.

There are three versions of the Power Mac G5 at this writing in early 2004:

Power Mac G5/1.6 GHz. The logic board of this entry-level model (starting at $1,799) has four DIMM slots for memory (supporting up to 4 GB) and three standard 33 MHz 64-bit PCI slots. Its frontside bus operates at 800 MHz.

Power Mac G5/1.8 GHz. The logic board of this midrange model (starting at $2,499) comes with two processors and dual frontside buses, operating at 900 MHz each. It provides eight DIMM slots for memory (supporting up to 8 GB). It has three PCI-X slots, one running at 133 MHz and two at 100 MHz.

Power Mac G5/Dual 2 GHz. The logic board of this top-end model (starting at $2,999) comes with two processors and dual frontside buses, operating at 1 GHz each. It provides eight DIMM slots for memory (supporting up to 8 GB) and three PCI-X slots, one running at 133 MHz and two at 100 MHz. Its frontside bus operates at 1 GHz.

All three of these Macs come with a SuperDrive and a slew of ports: one FireWire 800 port, two FireWire 400 ports, and three USB 2.0 ports. There are both ADC and DVI connectors, and the included nVidia GeForce FX 5200 Ultra video card supports digital resolutions of up to 1920 by 1200 pixels. Inside there is an extra bay for an additional hard drive and one for an additional optical drive. And, of course, there's Gigabit Ethernet, AirPort Extreme readiness, and a Bluetooth option.

Meanwhile, Apple's series-branding scheme, fully developed with the Power Mac G4, continues to cause confusion. The company designates a series of machines with a single name without differentiating between models with varying enclosures, processors, logic-board architectures, and support for peripherals. It's the user community that has come up with the designators.

Determining which model is which can be difficult at times, as is discovering the technical details. You can get some answers by checking the readout in System Profiler (which you'll find in the /Applications/Utilities folder). In addition, the documentation on Apple's Specifications page (www.info.apple.com/support/ applespec.html) often provides answers; however, this documentation can suffer from amnesia about the exact version of the PowerPC processor used in a model. This isn't much of a problem with the Power Mac G5—yet. The excellent EveryMac.com offers this information at www.everymac.com/systems/apple.

The Power Mac G4 Series (DM)

The Power Mac G4 series brought several important technologies to the platform: the PowerPC G4 processor, the revival of multiprocessing, and the AGP. The PowerPC G4 also incorporated what Apple calls Velocity Engine and Motorola calls AltiVec. Whatever the moniker, it's a special vector-execution unit that lets the processor subdivide a task and work on each part simultaneously. Applications like 3D graphics, image and video processing, and audio encoding use vector data and can benefit from this parallel engine and some of its multimedia-specific routines. Some tasks can run as much as ten times faster on a PowerPC G4 than a PowerPC G3 at the same speed.

The first models of the Power Mac G4 came with the PowerPC 7400 processor. Later models graduated to the PowerPC 7410 and then in 2001 to the PowerPC 7450, a version with higher speeds, longer pipelines, and a 256 Kbyte on-chip cache.

In addition, the PowerPC G4 returned symmetric multiprocessing—the use of two processors instead of just one—to the Mac. (Several 1990s Macs came equipped with dual processors, but that capability was set aside with the arrival of the PowerPC G3 processor, which Apple used in the first of the modern Macs.) Just as some applications can be accelerated with AltiVec, others can be tuned to take advantage of two CPUs.

The Power Mac G4 series also switched video connections from PCI to AGP. AGP improves the Mac's performance for 3D graphics capabilities, such as textures, alpha buffers, and z-buffers.

Here's the Power Mac G4 series, in reverse order of introduction:

Power Mac G4 (Mirrored Drive Doors). As of early 2004 this is the only Power Mac G4 that Apple ships, and it starts at a low $1,299 (**Figure 3.3**). It introduced a logic board based on the Xserve, Apple's server technology. The front bezels of the enclosure are mirrored with a silver plastic. Some models don't support booting Mac OS 9.2.2. It includes a 1.25 GHz G4 processor, a 167 MHz system bus, and 1 MB of L3 cache. There's a Combo drive, an 80 GB hard drive, two FireWire 400 ports, two USB ports, and ADC and DVI connectors, as well as three 33 MHz PCI slots, three additional internal hard-drive bays, and one additional optical-drive bay. Like the Power Mac G5s, it also has Gigabit Ethernet and comes AirPort Extreme ready. (See the sidebar "Wind Tunnels 'R' Us," below.)

Photo courtesy of Apple Computer

Figure 3.3

It's easy to see why the current Power Mac G4 sports the "Mirrored Drive Doors" moniker.

Power Mac G4 (QuickSilver). "QuickSilver" refers to the slight changes in the enclosure's front bezel.

Power Mac G4 (Digital Audio). This model introduced a digital-audio port.

Power Mac G4 (Gigabit Ethernet). This model introduced a speedy 10/100/1000Base-T Ethernet port.

Power Mac G4 (AGP Graphics). This model introduced the AGP card slot.

Power Mac G4 (PCI Graphics). These were the lower-end models. You can distinguish these from the Power Mac G4 with AGP graphics because on these machines the microphone and sound-output ports on the rear panel are placed sideways.

Several versions were also sold as servers, one with Mac OS X Server software.

G4 Cubed (DM)

One of the most controversial models in many years, the Power Mac G4 Cube debuted in July 2000. The system featured a PowerPC G4 processor and AGP graphics in a striking 8-inch enclosure, about a quarter of the size of most desktop computers. It was marketed with Apple's equally high-style flat-panel displays. Some pundits complained about PCI expansion slots stripped from the Cube's logic board, and still others yelped about its cost. Although more than 100,000 Cubes were sold, Apple had expected them to do better. Steve Jobs told financial analysts in early 2001 that the Cube had been accepted by the market. "The disappointment to us was the market wasn't as big as we thought," he said.

The Arrival of the PowerPC G3 (DM)

The landing of the PowerPC G3 processor on the Mac was vitally important to the company and to users. It provided a big step forward in performance from the first generations of PowerPC Macs; the G3 was more than 30 percent faster than the speediest chip of the preceding generation, the PowerPC 604e. The PowerPC G3, so named for the third generation of the line, was also much smaller and used less power.

The first three models to use the PowerPC G3 processor—the Desktop, the Mini Tower, and the large, tooth-shaped All-In-One version—were similar in design to previous machines. Today they are known as the Beige G3 models.

With the 1999 introduction of the Power Macintosh G3 (Blue and White), the shape of modern Macs became evident. The enclosure was colorful and provided easy access to the interior. But the most important changes were inside. The new model offered a much different set of interfaces than before.

First, Apple offered FireWire as a replacement for SCSI, a connector that had been standard on the platform since 1986. Today it's easy to see the advantages of FireWire for video and storage, and a whole market has grown up around it. But at that time, few FireWire peripherals were available. The move away from SCSI alarmed users who had a heavy investment in SCSI.

In addition, Apple replaced serial, printer, and Apple Desktop Bus (ADB) interfaces with USB. Of course, many users had serial modems and printers and even older LocalTalk networking.

Table 3.1 PowerPC G3, G4, and G5 Macs

Model	Processor	Chip Speed (MHz)	PCI Slots	FireWire [1]	USB [2]	Ethernet	Intro.
Power Mac G5	G5	1.6 GHz/1.8 GHz/ 1.8 GHz dual/ 2 GHz dual	3	2	3	10/100/1000	8/03
Power Mac G4 (Mirrored Drive Doors 2003)	G4	867 dual/ 1GHz dual/ 1.25 GHz dual	4	2	–	10/100/1000	6/03
Power Mac G4 (FW 800)	G4	1 GHz/ 1.25 GHz dual/ 1.42 GHz dual	4	2	–	10/100/1000	2/03
Power Mac G4 (Mirrored Drive Doors)	G4	867 dual/ 1 GHz dual/ 1.25 GHz dual	4	2	–	10/100/1000	8/02
Power Mac G4 (QuickSilver 2002)	G4	800/933/ 1GHz dual	4	2	–	10/100/1000	2/02
Power Mac G4 (QuickSilver)	G4	733/800 dual/ 867	4	2	–	10/100/1000	7/01
Power Mac G4 (Digital Audio)	G4	466/533 dual/ 667/733	4	2	–	10/100/1000	1/01
Power Mac G4 Cube	G4	450/500	-	2	–	10/100	7/00
Power Mac G4 (Gigabit Ethernet)	G4	400/450 dual/ 500 dual	3	2	–	10/100/1000	7/00
Power Mac G4 (AGP Graphics)	G4	350/400/450/500	3	3	–	10/100	9/99
Power Mac G4 (PCI Graphics)	G4	350/400	4	3	–	10/100	9/99
Power Mac G3 (Blue and White)	G3	350/400/450	4	2	–	10/100	1/99
Power Mac G3 All-In-One	G3	233/266	3	–	–	10	4/98
Power Mac G3 Desktop	G3	266/300	3	–	–	10	11/97
Power Mac G3 Mini Tower	G3	266/300	3	–	–	10	11/97

1. The Power Mac G5 and the Power Mac G4 (FW 800) also have one FireWire 800 port.

2. The Power Mac G5 also has three USB 2.0 ports.

Wind Tunnels "R" Us (DM)

The Power Mac G4 Mirrored Drive Doors model is often called "Wind Tunnel." Some of the power supplies in the models were very noisy, and the fans were also loud. A community of users, including those on G4noise.com, created such a ruckus that Apple finally offered a replacement program for them, which ran from February through June of 2003. When purchasing a used model in this line, check to see if the upgrade was applied. Third-party replacement power supplies are also available. There's a firmware update that reduced the high-speed fan cycling under Mac OS 9.2.2 (http://docs.info.apple.com/article.html?artnum=120186).

One-Time Wonder (DM)

In spring 1997, before the introduction of the Power Mac G3 models, Apple released a special-edition Mac to commemorate the company's founding 20 years earlier. The Twentieth Anniversary Macintosh had a bold design, incorporating a 12.1-inch flat-panel screen, a television tuner, stereo speakers, and a CD-ROM drive. Its power supply was separate and contained the subwoofer. Its custom components were expensive, but potential purchasers considered it underpowered, given its $7,500 price tag.

The Golden Age and Pioneer Power Macs (DM/SA)

For those Mac users who missed the original Macintosh in action, it's difficult to understand the impact it had on the public following its 1984 release. *Electrifying* comes close to the mark. The lightweight, all-in-one box had a tiny black-and-white screen, but it showed fonts and pictures. Instead of entering commands, users could physically interact with its interface via a mouse. It was simply amazing.

For the first decade of its life, the Macintosh platform was based on the Motorola 680x0 family of processors. The chip was so named because it had 68,000 transistors etched on it. The PowerBook 190 was the last model to be manufactured with a Motorola 680x0-series processor. Here's a list of the CPUs:

- The 68000 was used for the first Macs. The PowerBook 100 used a special low-power version, the 68HC000.
- The 68020 handled 32-bit chunks internally and had a 256 byte instruction cache.
- The 68030 added a 256 byte data cache, and its two 32-bit data paths could handle twice the information traffic. It also featured a paged memory management unit (PMMU), needed for virtual memory.
- The 68040 had larger instruction and data caches as well as a built-in math coprocessor. The 68LC040 was a low-cost version without the math functions.

The earliest Macs were all based on a closed, semiportable design with an integrated handle and were passively cooled. The original Mac—later dubbed the 128K—was launched with the famous "1984" Super Bowl ad. The Macintosh 128K aimed to be the first computing appliance, a relatively low-cost and accessible computer. The $2,495 Mac 128K was a wild success. Although its 128 Kbytes of memory was generous at the time, it still wasn't enough to meet the demands of a graphical interface. Even a simple file copy would require users to spend many minutes swapping 400 Kbyte floppy disks in and out of the drive. Later that year, Apple released the Mac 512K, also called the Fat Mac.

In 1986, Apple offered the Macintosh Plus, the first real update to the platform. It addressed the primary shortcomings: slots for RAM upgrades and a SCSI port, the first use of the interface on any desktop computer.

One stroke of genius on the early Macs was AppleTalk, the networking protocol built into every Mac. When combined with the PostScript-capable LaserWriter, the small Mac Plus suddenly became a digital-publishing workstation out of the box.

A year later Apple offered the Macintosh SE (code-named Aladdin), the first Mac to feature an internal hard drive and a cooling fan as well as an Apple Desktop Bus connector. Unlike the simple dedicated cables used on earlier Macs and PCs, ADB was a standard bus that could be used by a variety of devices, much as USB is today. The SE also featured the Mac's first upgrade slot, called the Processor Direct Slot.

Apple in 1989 also updated its all-in-one line with the faster 68030 processor. The computer's small monochrome screen required scant overhead, when compared with the Mac II series and its larger displays. The result was a screaming little box that became a favorite among AppleTalk network managers.

Opening the Closed Box (DM/DT)

It wasn't until 1987, however, that Apple finally created an "open" Mac—the Mac II—that you could open up and add cards or other upgrade components to. Running a 68020 processor, the desktop model offered color graphics, an internal hard drive, and a set of six expansion slots using NuBus, an advanced connector technology. Like today's PCI, Apple's NuBus was self-arbitrating, meaning that it registered the cards automatically with the Mac at startup time. The upgrade slots on DOS machines required users to adjust tiny DIP switches and jumpers when adding an expansion card. The connector was also sturdy and secure, something PCI could still learn.

A series of Mac II models followed:

IIx. The IIx introduced the 68030 processor and included a floating point unit; it also was the first to use 1.4 MB floppy drives.

IIcx. The smaller IIcx (1989) was a slightly faster version of the IIx but with only three NuBus slots.

IIci. The IIci (1989) ran at 25 MHz instead of its predecessors' 16 MHz. This model was well built and a favorite of Mac fanatics, with its built-in video circuitry and a slot to expand the cache memory. It was a workhorse known for its longevity.

IIsi. The IIsi (1990) offered affordable performance with a single NuBus slot and a low-profile "pizza box" case. It featured a sound-input port and came with a microphone.

IIfx. The IIfx (1990) was the fastest of the lot—Steve Jobs claimed it was "wicked fast."

IIvx. The IIvx (1992) came with an internal CD-ROM drive.

IIvi. The IIvi (1992) followed in the footsteps of the IIci.

A Macintosh by Any Other Name (DM)

In 1990 and 1991, Apple decided to rebrand its desktop lines, based on market segment, processor, and channel. Apple aimed certain lines at certain markets—such as education, SOHO (small office/home office), and enterprise—and then confined the distribution of each brand to its own channel. The result was a complicated sales picture.

The Macintosh Quadra series was based on the 68040 chip (*quad* = 4, get it?); the Macintosh Centris was a line of middle-of-the-road systems; and Macintosh LCs were low cost, aimed primarily at the education market. The company also revived the all-in-one form factor with several Macintosh Classic models and even a Color Classic.

In 1992, Apple expanded this structure with the Macintosh Performa, a new brand aimed at consumers and sold at mass-market retailers such as Sears. The models came bundled with a variety of software, similar to today's iMac. The hardware, however, was identical to that in other lines, albeit with some slight variations in memory, hard-disk size, or cache. The Performa naming scheme, which tried to inform customers of processor, speed, and extras, grew complicated for retailers and users alike.

Table 3.2 Name Game: Differentiating the Performa Siblings

Performa	Alternate
200	Classic
250	Color Classic
275	Color Classic II
400	LC II
405/410/430	LC II (with modem and larger hard drive)
450	LC III
460/466/467	LC III+
475/476	LC 475/Quadra 605
520	LC 520
550/560	LC 550
575/577/578	LC 575
580CD/588CD	LC 580
600/600CD	IIvx (but with no cache card and FPU)
630	LC 630

In 1993, Apple offered the Macintosh TV, a machine aimed at college students. Using the Mac LC 530 case and integrating a TV tuner, the model had a black case instead of the usual platinum. Unfortunately, this Mac was a flop.

Apple phased out these brands over time, especially as the company shifted its machines to the PowerPC processor and away from the 68040. The Performa had the most staying power, but Apple finally retired the Performa brand in 1997. It used the Power Mac name for all desktop machines until it introduced the iMac in 1998.

Today, Apple uses four brands for its computers—Power Macintosh, iMac, PowerBook, and iBook—and each corresponds to a market segment. The big difference is that Apple manufactures usually four (sometimes five) logic boards for its models, rather than the dozen or so that it tried to mix and match among brands in the past.

Table 3.3 Original 680x0 Macs

Quadra/Centris	Processor	Chip Speed (MHz)	Slots	Introduced
Quadra 950	68040	33	5	5/92
Quadra 900	68040	25	5	10/91
Quadra 840AV	68040	40	3	7/93
Quadra 800	68040	33	3	2/93
Quadra 700	68040	25	2	10/91
Quadra 660AV	68040	25	1	10/93
Centris 660AV	68040	25	1	7/93
Quadra 650	68040	33	3	10/93
Centris 650	68040	25	3	2/93
Quadra 630	68040	33	-	7/94
Quadra 610 DOS Compatible	68040	25	-	2/94
Quadra 610	68040/68LC040	25	1	10/93
Centris 610	68LC040	20	1	2/93
Quadra 605	68LC040	25	-	10/93

Performa	Processor	Chip Speed (MHz)	Slots	Introduced
640CD DOS Compatible	68LC040	66	-	5/95
638CD	68LC040	66	-	7/94
637CD	68LC040	66	-	7/94
636/636CD	68LC040	66	-	7/94
635CD	68LC040	66	-	7/94
631CD	68LC040	66	-	7/95
630/630CD	68LC040	66	-	7/94
600/600CD	68030	32	3	9/92
580CD	68LC040	66	-	5/95
578	68LC040	66	-	2/94
577	68LC040	66	-	2/94
575	68LC040	66	-	2/94
560	68030	33	-	1/94
550	68030	33	-	10/93

continues on next page

Original 680x0 Macs *continued*

Performa	Processor	Chip Speed (MHz)	Slots	Introduced
476	68LC040	50	-	10/93
475	68LC040	50	-	10/93
467	68030	33	-	10/93
466	68030	33	-	10/93
460	68030	33	-	10/93
450	68030	25	-	4/93
430	68030	16	-	4/93
410	68030	16	-	10/93
405	68030	16	-	4/93
400	68030	16	-	9/92
250	68030	16	-	2/93
200	68030	16	-	9/92

LC	Processor	Chip Speed (MHz)	Slots	Introduced
LC 630 DOS Compatible	68LC040	66	-	4/95
LC 630	68LC040	66	-	7/94
LC 580	68LC040	66	-	4/95
LC 575	68LC040	66	-	2/94
LC 550	68030	33	-	2/94
LC 520	68030	25	-	6/93
LC 475	68LC040	50	-	10/93
LC III+	68030	33	-	10/93
LC III	68030	25	-	2/93
LC II	68030	16	-	3/92
LC	68020	16	-	10/90
Macintosh TV	68030	32	-	10/93

continues on next page

Original 680x0 Macs   continued

II	Processor	Chip Speed (MHz)	Slots	Introduced
IIvx	68030	32	3	10/92
IIvi	68030	16	3	10/92
IIsi	68030	20	1	10/90
IIfx	68030	40	6	3/90
IIci	68030	25	3	9/89
IIcx	68030	16	3	3/89
IIx	68030	16	6	9/88
II	68020	16	6	3/87

All-in-One	Processor	Chip Speed (MHz)	Slots	Introduced
Color Classic	68030	16	-	2/93
Classic II	68030	16	-	10/91
Classic	68000	8	-	10/90
SE/30	68030	16	-	1/89
SE	68000	8	-	3/87
Plus	68000	8	-	1/86
512Ke	68000	8	-	4/86
512K	68000	8	-	9/84
128K	68000	8	-	1/84

PowerPC Pioneers (DM)

For the first decade of its existence, the Mac platform ran processors using *CISC (complex instruction set computing*—technology still used today for most processors in the world). In 1994, Apple changed tack and based its computers on the PowerPC chip, which instead uses a *RISC (reduced instruction set computer)* architecture. According to theory, RISC is inherently more efficient than CISC, because each additional instruction set makes the chip bigger, more complicated, and, hence, slower. Apple, IBM, and Motorola formed an alliance, called AIM, to engineer and manufacture the chip.

In addition to pure speed, the PowerPC offered other technologies that could benefit the Mac platform. First, some versions could handle multiprocessing, a performance-boosting technology that appeals to Mac users in the scientific and video fields. Second, the alliance produced flavors of the processor for mobile computing, letting Mac notebooks perform faster than comparable-speed Intel versions. And Apple would benefit from economies in production, since the alliance believed that the PowerPC would be used widely in computers and servers running the Windows and Unix operating systems, as well as Mac clones.

Here's a list of the first PowerPC generations:

601. The first-generation processor used in Apple transition models.

603/603e. Designed to be inexpensive and energy-efficient, the 603 processor was used in PowerBooks and low-end desktop Macs. This and the 604 processor are the G2 processors.

604/604e. Bigger and faster than the 603, the 604 sported larger caches and multiprocessor capabilities.

Early PowerPC-based Macs also brought the PCI bus to the Mac platform, and Apple incorporated faster flavors of SCSI. The combination of performance, expandability, and options for integrated A/V technology helped maintain the Mac platform in the important markets for multimedia and print-content creation and for scientific data analysis. Some popular A/V configurations were offered with S-Video and RCA video input/output connectors.

Here's a rundown of the first generation of the Power Mac models:

4400. Based on the Tanzania logic-board design originated for AIM licensing, the model used a desktop case and many industry-standard parts to lower production costs.

5200/5260. A 603-based CPU with an elegant all-in-one enclosure. The similar 5300 used a 603e processor.

5400/5500. Also an all-in-one box, the 5400 changed to the Alchemy logic board; the 5500 used the Gazelle board.

6100/6200/6300. These used a low-profile desktop enclosure similar to the Centris 610's. Also known as the Performa 6xxx series and Work Group Server 6xxx.

6400. It used a minitower enclosure and an SRS 3D surround-sound system with integrated subwoofer.

6500. Based on the Gazelle board, the line used a tower case with an integrated Zip drive.

7100/7200/7220/7300. With a high-profile desktop case, the 7100 was based on the BHA logic board; the 7200 used the Catalyst board; and the 7220 used the Tanzania design. The 7300 graduated to the TNT architecture used on the 7500.

7500/7600. With a case similar to that of the other 7xxx models, these models used the high-performance TNT board design. The 7500 came with a 601 CPU.

8100/8115/8200/8500/8515/8600. Encased in a tower enclosure, the 8100/80 was based on the Cold Fusion logic-board design. The 8200 used the Catalyst architecture, and the 8500 and 8600 stepped up to a board code-named Nitro.

9500/9600. The 9500 offered six PCI slots in a tall tower case. The later 9600 and 8600 used a larger tower chassis, called K2 (for the Chogori mountain peak), which provided a hinged side-panel door holding the fan and easy access to the board and seven storage bays.

Table 3.4 PowerPC Macs

Performa	Processor	Chip Speed (MHz)	L2 Cache	PCI Slots	NuBus	Introduced
6400	603e	180/200	Opt/256 KB	2	-	8/96
6360	603e	160	Opt	1	-	10/96
6320CD	603e	120	256 KB	-	-	4/96
6300CD	603e	100	256 KB	-	-	10/95
6290CD	603e	100	256 KB	-	-	1/96
6230CD	603	75	256 KB	-	-	7/95
6220CD	603	75	256 KB	-	-	7/95
6218CD	603	75	256 KB	-	-	7/95
6216CD	603	75	256 KB	-	-	7/95
6214CD	603	75	256 KB	-	-	8/95
6210CD	603	75	256 KB	-	-	10/95
6205CD	603	75	256 KB	-	-	8/95
6200CD	603	75	256 KB	-	-	7/95
6118CD	601	60	Opt	-	1	11/94
6117CD	601	60	Opt	-	1	11/94
6116CD	601	60	Opt	-	1	7/95
6115CD	601	60	Opt	-	1	11/94
6112CD	601	60	Opt	-	1	11/94
6110CD	601	60	Opt	-	1	11/94
5400CD	603e	120	Opt	1	-	4/96
5300CD	603e	100	256 KB	-	-	10/95
5260	603e	120	Opt	-	-	10/96
5260CD	603e	100	Opt	-	-	4/96

continues on next page

Table 3.4 PowerPC Macs

Performa	Processor	Chip Speed (MHz)	L2 Cache	PCI Slots	NuBus	Introduced
5215CD	603	75	256 KB	-	-	7/95
5200CD	603	75	256 KB	-	-	7/95

Power Mac	Processor	Chip Speed (MHz)	L2 Cache	PCI Slots	NuBus	Introduced
9600	604e	200/200 Dual/ 233/300/350	512 KB/1 MB	6	-	2/97
9500	604e	200/180 Dual/	512 KB	6	-	8/96
9500	604	120/132/150	512 KB	6	-	5/95
8600	604e	200/250/300	256 KB/1 MB	3	-	2/97
8500	604	120/132/150/180	256 KB	-	3	8/95
8100	601	80/100/110	256 KB	-	3	3/94
7600	604	120/132	256 KB	3	-	4/96
7500	601	100	Opt	3	-	8/95
7300	604e	180/200	256 KB	3	-	2/97
7200	601	75/90/120	Opt	3	-	3/96
7100	601	66/80	Opt/256 KB	-	3	3/94
6500	603e	225/250/275/300	256 KB/512 KB	2	-	2/97
6400	603e	200	256 KB	2	-	10/96
6100	601	60/66	Opt/256 KB	-	1	3/94
5500	603e	225/250	256 KB	1	-	2/97
5400	603e	120/180/200	Opt/256 KB	1	-	4/95
5300	603e	100	256 KB	-	-	8/95
5260	603e	100/120	Opt/256 KB	-	-	8/96
5200	603	75	256 KB	-	-	8/95
4400	603e	200	256 KB	2	-	2/97
4400	603e	160	Opt	3	-	11/96
Twentieth Anniversary Mac	603e	250	256 KB	1	-	6/97

The iMac: Back in Fashion (CB)

The original Bondi Blue iMac—the cute-as-a-bug Macintosh phenom—is credited with single-handedly saving Apple's bacon in 1998. And little wonder. Apple iCEO Steve Jobs (the *i* in Jobs' title was jokingly added by Apple employees and stood for "interim") had recently returned to an Apple that more closely resembled its cookie-cutter-PC competitors than the innovative dynamo of the mid-1980s. At the time of the Second Coming of Steve in 1997, Apple's products were more expensive and less powerful than Mac-compatible models manufactured by the likes of Power Computing, Umax, and Motorola. Apple was dabbling in everything from handheld computers to TV-console systems to online services, and its market share—thanks to a Microsoft operating system that "borrowed" substantially from the Mac OS—was eroding at an alarming rate. In short, Apple was in deep distress.

When Jobs pulled the cover off the iMac in May 1998, it marked more than the unveiling of a new, inexpensive computer. It signaled the return of innovation at Apple and the beginning of a new design philosophy that valued form as much as function.

Despite the concerns of many industry pundits that the iMac's nonexpandable all-in-one design was a step backward, the iMac sold in record numbers—not only ensuring that Apple would live to fight another day but also demonstrating that Steve Jobs still had the Midas touch.

Look and Feel

At first blush, the obvious difference between the iMac and its predecessors was the playful design. No previous computer—Mac or PC—was so approachable, so much fun to use, and still so functional. The iMac's friendly appearance paid off in significant sales to new computer users—seniors and students in particular. Apple also benefited from more than a little free advertising when iMacs popped up in countless TV programs, were featured in national newsmagazines, and adorned the showrooms of trendy furniture outlets.

Thanks to the iMac, for the first time in a long time, it was cool to own a Mac.

But the iMac was far more than an indication that Apple was interested in making unique-looking computers. It was also a pronouncement that Apple intended to break from the past and spearhead (or at least embrace) the latest technical innovations.

There's No Future in the Past

Once people got over the initial shock of seeing such an unusual computer, the first question that came to mind was, "Where's the floppy drive?" Yes, unlike every other Mac since the beginning of time, the iMac lacked a slot for floppy disks. Horror of horrors!

Apple's response: "Get over it. The floppy's dead."

Our reply: "But we've got a bunch of important Microsoft Word documents on floppies, and we'd really love to use them on our spiffy new iMacs!"

Apple's rejoinder: "Oh, very well. If you need to use floppy disks, you can add an external floppy drive via the iMac's built-in USB port."

Our riposte: "Oh, OK, we'll just add a floppy drive to the … *WHAT?!* What the heck is a USB port?"

And then we opened the little side door on the iMac, looked at the ports in residence, turned the iMac around and around to be sure we weren't missing something, and returned to the side door with a look of dumb dismay.

Floppy drive—gone. Modem (GeoPort) port—gone. Printer port—gone. ADB port—gone.

In their place we found two USB (Universal Serial Bus) ports, an Ethernet connector, a sound-input port, a sound-output port, a modem connector, a couple of tiny holes for accessing the reset and interrupt buttons, and something called the *mezzanine port* (see the sidebar "The Mezzanine Port," below); on the front of the iMac were two headphone jacks, a CD-ROM drive, and an IrDA (infrared) port (**Figure 3.4**).

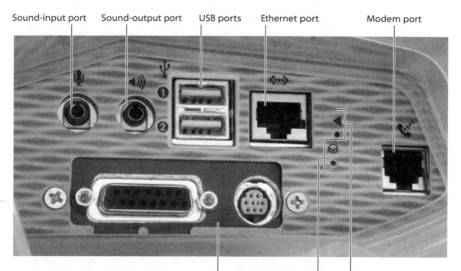

Sound-input port   Sound-output port   USB ports   Ethernet port   Modem port

Mezzanine port (with Griffin   Interrupt button   Reset button
Technology's iPort adapter)

Figure 3.4

The ports of the first iMac, including the enigmatic mezzanine port.

The Mezzanine Port

The first Bondi Blue iMacs (Revs. A and B) included the mysterious mezzanine port—a rectangular port that was visible (if you removed the blue metal plate) on the right side of the iMac. Typically tight-lipped, Apple never bothered to explain the purpose of this port; all it would say was that the port was "for internal purposes only." Developers were warned in no uncertain terms that this was an unsupported port—if any of them developed a product for it, they were on their own.

A couple of intrepid developers forged ahead anyway. Griffin Technology produced something called an iPort that fit in the mezzanine slot. This capable card provided a serial port as well as a 15-pin video-output port that allowed you to run a second monitor at resolutions greater than the three available on the iMac.

Micro Conversions also produced a card for the mezzanine port—the Game Wizard, a video gaming card that carried a then-state-of-the-art 3dfx Voodoo2 processor. Considering the lackluster gaming performance of the ATI graphics chip included with the iMac, the Game Wizard was a godsend for gamers.

The mezzanine port met its maker with the release of the five fruit-colored iMacs in early 1999. While Griffin had a broad enough product base to bear the loss, Micro Conversions regrettably did not—the company disappeared a few months later.

Looking Forward

Apple was prepared for users' concerns about legacy peripheral devices and their skepticism about this new USB port. During the iMac's unveiling, Jobs announced that a handful of USB devices—floppy drives, input devices, and adapters that would allow you to use many of your old peripherals—would be available when the iMac was released. And many were. Imation's SuperDisk (www.imation.com) allowed you to read 1.44 MB floppy disks as well as higher-density 120 MB disks; several alternative mice and keyboards arrived on the scene; and a host of adapters—USB to serial, USB to ADB, even USB to SCSI—appeared in short order. In addition, USB-native devices such as printers and scanners began to pop up—some in eye-catching colors that matched the iMac. And although Apple's pronouncement of the floppy's demise inconvenienced some software developers, most had been distributing software on CDs for quite some time.

Suddenly the loss of the floppy drive didn't seem so bad.

The iMac Reborn

Flash forward four years to 2002. The *i* preceding "CEO" had vanished from Steve Jobs' title; Apple had introduced numerous desktop and laptop Macs that featured innovative technologies and dynamic designs; flat-panel LCD displays had replaced Apple's CRT monitors; and the iMac looked decidedly dated—despite revisions that introduced new colors, faster processors, higher-capacity hard drives, and CD burners, as well as an education-oriented version called the eMac (see the sidebar "The Education Mac," below). It was time for a new iMac.

To Apple's chagrin, that iMac was revealed the night before its intended introduction when *Time* magazine's Canadian Web site posted a story—complete with pictures—that described the new iMac and how it came into being. Despite the leak, the new iMac was enthusiastically received when Jobs officially unwrapped it during his keynote presentation at January 2002's Macworld Expo in San Francisco.

From the outside, the new iMac had little in common with its predecessor. Gone was the CRT monitor; a 15-inch flat-panel display hung from a hinged metal arm that sprouted from a heavy white dome base. The front of that base was unmarred by the presence of any ports—Apple placed the power button as well as ports for USB 1.1, FireWire 400, video out, a modem, 10/100Base-T Ethernet, Pro speakers, headphones, and power on the back of the dome. Even the media-drive slot was barely in evidence: its outer door was contoured to be unnoticeable when closed.

The iMac bore significant differences on the inside as well. It now included the PowerPC G4 processor rather than the less-powerful G3 processor used in previous iMac models. This was also the first iMac to offer a SuperDrive—available on the most expensive iMac, it was capable of playing and recording DVDs as well as CDs. With these features, the iMac was no longer just the machine you might purchase for your parents or children, but a computer that could easily fit into a professional environment.

The Education Mac

In April 2002, Apple introduced an iMac-like computer designed specifically for schools—the eMac (**Figure 3.5**). The "education Mac" featured the kind of power, connectivity options, and robust case design that schools required: a 700 MHz PowerPC G4 processor, 128 MB of SDRAM, a 40 GB hard drive, a 24x CD-RW drive, a 17-inch flat CRT display, FireWire and USB ports, 10/100Base-T Ethernet, a 56K V.90 modem, and AirPort wireless compatibility, combined with a "childproof" case that offered sturdy features such as rugged stereo grills that couldn't be popped off.

Originally priced at $999, the eMac quickly changed its status from an education-only computer after Apple was bombarded with requests from consumers who, like schools, sought an inexpensive Macintosh powered by a G4 processor. Apple altered the eMac's pricing and configuration with its release to the general public. Consumers could have the same eMac that was sold to schools for $1,099 or opt for a model with a Combo drive for an additional $100.

continues on next page

The Education Mac *continued*

These eMacs shipped with a software bundle similar to what one would find on an iMac: AppleWorks, Intuit's Quicken, the World Book Encyclopedia, a few games, and Mac OS 9 and Mac OS X, with accompanying Apple applications, such as iMovie, iPhoto, and iTunes. These eMacs could boot either Mac OS X or Mac OS 9.

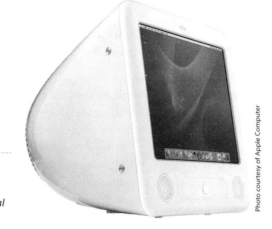

Figure 3.5

The eMac that Apple sells today sports the same look as the original iMac.

Photo courtesy of Apple Computer

Apple then revved the eMac, offering models priced between $799 and $1,299. The differences between the two lay in processor speed, amount of included RAM, hard-drive capacity, and type of media drive. The least expensive model included an 800 MHz PowerPC G4 processor, 128 MB of RAM, a 40 GB hard drive, and a CD-ROM drive. The midrange model offered a 1 GHz G4 processor, 128 MB of RAM, a 60 GB hard drive, and a Combo drive. And the high-end eMac included a 1 GHz G4 processor, 256 MB of RAM, an 80 GB hard drive, and a 4x SuperDrive. All three included a more-powerful graphics chip (the ATI Radeon 7500). These eMacs shipped with Mac OS 9 and Mac OS X, but only the CD-ROM and Combo drive models could boot Mac OS 9. The SuperDrive-equipped eMac had to be started in Mac OS X, so you could only run Mac OS 9 in the Classic environment.

In October 2003, Apple tweaked the eMac line slightly, offering the two models available today. The $799 eMac carries a 1 GHz G4 processor, 128 MB of RAM, a 40 GB hard drive, a Combo drive, and the ATI graphics card and connectors found in the previous $799 eMac. The top-of-the-line eMac is now priced at $1,099 and includes the same 1 GHz G4 processor, 256 MB of RAM, 80 GB hard drive, and SuperDrive as its $1,299 predecessor. The latest eMacs ship with Mac OS 9 and Mac OS X, as well as Apple's iLife creative suite bundle (which includes iMovie, iPhoto, iTunes, GarageBand, and iDVD for eMacs with a SuperDrive). These Macs boot only Mac OS X.

continues on next page

The Education Mac *continued*

Though priced to move and configured with nearly everything a school or home might need, the eMac has an uneven track record. Early models were plagued with video problems, and Apple's discussion boards continue to cite problems with eMacs' waking from sleep.

Table 3.5 eMacs

Model	Processor	Chip Speed (MHz)	FireWire 400	USB	Introduced
eMac 1 GHz G4	G4	1 GHz	2	5	10/03
eMac (ATI Graphics)	G4	800/1 GHz	2	5	5/03
eMac	G4	700	2	5	4/02

Which Old iMac Is Which?

Between the "old," original iMacs (those that used a CRT monitor) and the "new" iMacs (those with a dome-shaped base and LCD display) Apple revised the original iMac multiple times before it released the flat-panel iMacs. (We'll get to the latest generation of iMacs in "Today's iMac," below.)

The first two revisions (called Rev. A and Rev. B) featured a Bondi Blue case. The Rev. B iMac differed little from the original iMac, but it had a more-powerful graphics chipset (the ATI Rage Pro) with more video RAM. Both of these models included the mezzanine and IrDA ports.

January 5, 1999, saw the release of the Rev. C iMacs—a new line of iMacs in five new colors—Strawberry (pink), Blueberry (blue), Grape (purple), Lime (green), and Tangerine (orange). Due to this fruity naming scheme, the world never saw a yellow iMac—I mean, honestly, would Apple dare call one of its iMacs a Lemon?

These first colorful models were slightly faster than the Bondi Blue models—offering a PowerPC G3 processor that, at 266 MHz, was 33 MHz faster than its predecessor—and had a hard drive with 2 GB of additional space and a slightly spiffier ATI graphics card. Mostly, however, the five new flavors of iMacs were noteworthy because of what they lacked rather than what they included. With this generation of iMacs, the mezzanine and IrDA ports were now *portis non gratis* (**Figure 3.6**).

Neither port was particularly missed. Most vendors took heed of Apple's warning not to develop for the mezzanine port, so except for employees of Griffin Technology and Micro Conversions (see the sidebar "The Mezzanine Port," above), few folks mourned its departure. More might have missed the iMac's IrDA port if it hadn't been an inappropriate port to include in the first place. After all, how many iMac owners had also dropped several thousand dollars on an IrDA-bearing PowerBook? And why would Palm owners bother hot-syncing their PDAs via IrDA when using a USB cradle was so much easier and faster?

Sound-input port   FireWire ports   Modem port   USB ports   Ethernet port

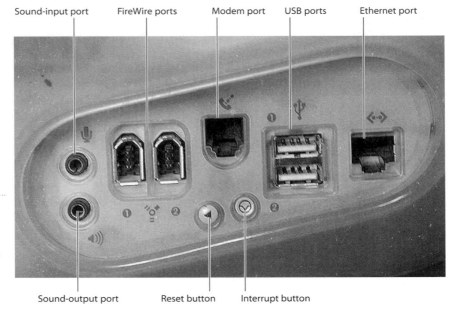

Figure 3.6

The CD-ROM slot-loading iMacs added FireWire ports and dropped the mezzanine and IrDA ports.

Sound-output port   Reset button   Interrupt button

Released in the summer of 1999, the Rev. D iMacs came in the same fruit flavors as the Rev. C models. The only difference here was the inclusion of a faster processor (a 333 MHz G3).

 It's possible to swap out the hard drive in your old iMac for a higher-capacity drive, but there's a catch on Rev. A–D iMacs. These iMacs won't start up unless the Mac OS is contained on a volume no larger than 8 GB, and if that volume is a partition on a larger hard drive, the Mac OS must be installed on the first partition. Therefore, if you purchase a higher-capacity hard drive, you must partition that drive with either Mac OS 9's Drive Setup or Mac OS X's Disk Utility, make the first partition 8 GB or smaller, and install the Mac OS on that first partition.

The Rev. E iMac was issued in October 1999 and was the first to include a slot-loading media drive (meaning that you mounted CDs by inserting them into a slot rather than placing them in a tray). With 64 MB of RAM, it carried more base RAM than its predecessors. It was also a tiny bit faster, with its 350 MHz G3 processor, and included a faster graphics chip (the ATI Rage 128). Most important, it was the first iMac priced under $1,000 (OK, at $999 it was *juuuuuuust* under $1,000). Color these iMacs either Blueberry or Strawberry.

When Apple introduced the Rev. E iMac, it also released the first generation of the iMac DV (Digital Video). This iMac included a 400 MHz G3 processor and a 10 GB hard drive, and it was the first iMac to include a FireWire port, AirPort wireless connectivity, a video-out port (which supported video mirroring only), and a DVD player. The Special Edition of this iMac came in a Graphite (transparent gray) case and included 128 MB of RAM and a 13 GB hard drive.

And then, quite frankly, all hell broke loose. Apple released a slew of iMacs over the next couple of years that included faster processors, more RAM, higher-capacity hard drives, and a collection of new colors and patterns—including Sage, Ruby, Snow, Indigo, and, to the dismay of many, Flower Power and Blue Dalmatian. These patterned iMacs were noteworthy not only for their questionable color schemes, but also because they were the first iMacs to include CD-RW (compact disc rewritable) drives—devices that allow you to record your own CDs.

After the Flower Power and Blue Dalmatian iMacs were greeted with a disparaging "Yecch," Apple abandoned such flights of fancy and returned to single-color models, eventually issuing the last generation of CRT iMac models—in Indigo, Snow, and Graphite—in summer 2001. These iMacs included a G3 processor running between 500 MHz and 700 MHz, a CD-RW drive, FireWire, USB 1.1, 10/100Base-T Ethernet, a 56K V.90 internal modem, an ATI Rage Ultra video card with 16 MB of video RAM, VGA video mirroring, and an AirPort slot.

Today's iMac

Since its release, Apple has enhanced the flat-panel iMac a couple of times, bumping up processor speed, RAM, and hard-drive capacities. A more-noticeable enhancement was the release of an iMac with a 17-inch display and another with a 20-inch display. While the iMac's 20-inch display offers the same wide-screen dimensions as Apple's stand-alone 20-inch Cinema Display (1680 by 1050 pixels), the iMac's 17-inch display differs in dimensions from Apple's standalone 17-inch Studio Display. Where the Studio Display's screen is close to being square, the 17-inch iMac's display is noticeably wider than taller—with a native resolution of 1440 by 900 pixels (versus 1280 by 1024 pixels offered by the 17-inch Studio Display). Although this means that the iMac's viewing area is less roomy than that of the Studio Display by 14,720 pixels, its width makes it a desirable display for watching wide-screen DVDs.

In late summer 2003, Apple updated the iMac to include support for such technologies as USB 2.0 (a faster implementation of the Universal Serial Bus), AirPort Extreme (the faster 54 Mbps 802.11g wireless networking standard), and Bluetooth (a short-range wireless standard). Oddly, Apple chose to not include support for FireWire 800. As we go to press in early 2004, Apple offers three models of the iMac (**Figure 3.7**).

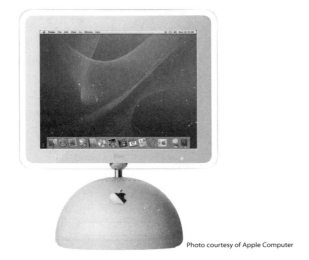

Photo courtesy of Apple Computer

Figure 3.7

Apple's latest iMacs sport a small base and your choice of a 15-, 17-, or 20-inch LCD.

The $1,299 iMac includes a 15-inch LCD, a 1 GHz G4 processor, a Combo drive (for reading CDs and DVDs and burning CD-Rs and CD-RWs), an nVidia GeForce4 MX video chipset with 32 MB of video RAM, 256 MB of DDR333 SDRAM, an 80 GB hard drive, 10/100Base-T Ethernet, three USB 2.0 ports, two FireWire 400 ports, a 56K V.92 internal modem, Apple Pro Speakers, and optional AirPort Extreme and Bluetooth.

The $1,799 iMac is similarly configured except for the substitution of a 17-inch LCD, a 1.25 GHz G4 processor, a SuperDrive (for reading and recording DVDs), and an nVidia GeForce FX 5200 Ultra chipset with 64 MB of video RAM. AirPort Extreme and Bluetooth are optional on this iMac as well.

The $2,199 iMac is configured exactly like the $1,799 iMac described above, except that it has a 20-inch LCD.

OK, sharp-eyed readers see one other option offered by the online Apple Store: the $2,448 17-inch iMac with SuperDrive. This iMac includes all the add-ons: 1 GB of RAM ($400), a 160 GB hard drive ($100), an AirPort Extreme card ($99), and a Bluetooth adapter ($50). All these upgrades—except the additional RAM—are priced competitively.

Rounding up $400 to maximize the RAM in these iMacs is the most painless way to go about it. The iMac includes two RAM slots. You can easily get to one of them by removing the iMac's bottom plate. The other is buried within the bowels of the iMac and should be accessed only by a qualified technician. Regrettably, Apple sells these iMacs with 256 MB of RAM in the hard-to-get-at slot, making it next to impossible for you maximize the RAM without paying Apple or a qualified technician to do the job.

In addition to the iLife applications that accompany all new Macs (iTunes, iMovie, iPhoto, GarageBand, and, when the iMac comes with a SuperDrive, iDVD), the latest iMac also includes Safari, iCal, AppleWorks, Quicken Deluxe, the World Book Encyclopedia, and Sound Studio (an audio editing application); Tony Hawk's Pro Skater 4, Deimos Rising, and Mac OS X Chess; and a batch of other, smaller utilities, such as iSync and iChat.

Table 3.6 iMacs

Flat-Panel iMac	Processor	Chip Speed (MHz)	FireWire 400	USB	USB 2.0	Colors	Intro.
iMac (USB 2.0)	G4	1 GHz/1.25 GHz	2	2	3		9/03
iMac (17-inch 1 GHz)	G4	800/1 GHz	2	5	-		2/03
iMac (17-inch) Flat Panel	G4	700/800	2	5	-		7/02
iMac (Flat-Panel)	G4	700/800	2	5	-		1/02

Original iMac	Processor	Chip Speed (MHz)	FireWire 400	USB	USB 2.0	Colors	Intro.
iMac (Summer 2000)	G3	500/600/700	2	2	-	Graphite, Indigo, Snow	7/01
iMac (Early 2001)	G3	400/500/600	2	2	-	Blue Dalmatian, Flower Power, Graphite, Indigo	2/01
iMac (Summer 2000)	G3	350/400/450/500	2	2	-	Graphite, Indigo, Ruby, Sage, Snow	7/00
iMac/iMac DV (Slot Loading CD-ROM)	G3	350/400	2	2	-	Blueberry, Grape, Graphite, Lime, Strawberry, Tangerine	10/99
iMac 333 MHz	G3	333	-	2	-	Blueberry, Grape, Lime, Strawberry, Tangerine	4/99
iMac 266 MHz	G3	266	-	2	-	Blueberry, Grape, Lime, Strawberry, Tangerine	1/99
iMac 233 MHz	G3	233	-	2	-	Bondi Blue	9/98

Year of the PowerBook (JOG)

Steve Jobs christened 2003 "The Year of the Laptop"—and he was right. Laptop computer sales have surpassed those of desktop computers. According to a survey by market research firm The NPD Group, notebook computers accounted for more than 54 percent of the nearly $500 million in retail computer sales in May 2003, which was up from a paltry 25 percent in January 2000. Keep in mind that the laptop sales figures are for the entire industry, so that means they include Windows notebooks, but even Apple's own numbers show the same trend toward smaller computers. In Apple's first quarter of 2004, the company sold 195,000 PowerBooks and 201,000 iBooks.

This trend toward notebook computers is bound to continue as the technology advances and the prices drop. PowerBooks today contain many of the high-end features found in desktop computers: 17-inch displays, DVD burners, and built-in 802.11g wireless networking and Bluetooth. In fact, the second generation of aluminum-enclosed PowerBooks is reigniting the passion that began with the announcement of the original Titanium PowerBooks only two years ago.

There are many exciting things ahead for mobile technologists. Apple's announcement of the G5 (fifth-generation) processor in June 2003 has PowerBook users salivating for that kind of processor muscle in a portable enclosure. Also on the horizon are some exciting advancements that will creep into PowerBooks in the future:

- Zinc-air and fuel cell batteries continue to advance, promising over 40 hours of run time and half the weight of today's lithium-ion (LiIon) batteries.
- LCDs are getting thinner, brighter, and more prevalent; there is even talk about "roll-up" LCDs.
- HyperSonic Sound (HSS), by American Technology Corp., is like a laser for sound. Laptop speakers could "beam" music directly to the person in front of the screen without anyone else hearing it.

Perhaps the most versatile Macintoshes in the Apple lineup, the PowerBook and its smaller sidekick, the iBook, have become tools coveted by everyone from students to creative types to CEOs. And you can't blame them. After all, who *wouldn't* want a portable Macintosh?

Even if you don't travel often, you may want to consider insurance for your PowerBook or iBook. The AppleCare Protection Plan (www.apple.com/support/products) is economical ($349 for three years for the PowerBook; $249 for three years for the iBook), especially when you compare it with the cost of any PowerBook repair, but it does not cover theft or accidental damage that occurs when you drop your computer. Some homeowners' policies cover computers outside the home, but always check with your insurance agent before taking a chance. SafeWare (www.safeware.com) sells insurance especially designed for computers and even offers policies that cover theft and accidental damage.

Mini Mac

A PowerBook is just a smaller Macintosh with basically the same components: a CPU, a monitor, a keyboard, memory, a hard drive, and an optical drive. The major difference between a desktop Mac and a PowerBook is that the latter miniaturizes everything to fit inside a smaller enclosure—and this adds a premium to the price.

Previously, this price gap was as much as 300 percent—I paid almost $6,000 for my PowerBook 5300ce/117 in 1996—but Apple has since realized that prices had to be more in line with those of PC notebooks to remain competitive. Today you can buy an iBook or PowerBook for as little as $1,100 or $1,600, respectively—about the same as the equivalent Sony Vaio notebook. That kind of price for an Apple laptop was unthinkable just a few years ago.

Displays

The most expensive part of a PowerBook or an iBook is the display. Today's TFT (thin film transistor) color active-matrix displays can cost as much as the rest of the computer's parts put together. The original Mac Portable shipped with a simple 1-bit (non-backlit) black-and-white display. A backlit model, which you could use in the dark, soon followed.

Apple introduced the first color PowerBook, the 165c, in 1993. Unfortunately, it came with a passive-matrix screen. If you haven't had the displeasure of working with such a display, imagine a screen on which images are practically unviewable unless you look at them straight on. In addition, the pointer would often disappear while you were moving the mouse because the screen could not redraw fast enough (critics dubbed this flaw *submarining*). For early adopters and Mac diehards, though, the PowerBook 165c was the only color laptop option available.

A scant four months later Apple released the first PowerBook with an active-matrix display, the PowerBook 180c. Although it represented an evolutionary upgrade for the product line, users hailed its bright, crisp display as revolutionary. TFT active-matrix displays are much brighter and sharper than their passive cousins, with better color depth and wider viewing angles. Today, all PowerBooks and most PC notebooks ship with active-matrix displays.

 If you are buying a used PowerBook, avoid models with passive-matrix displays. Passive displays, also called *dual-scan* or *DSTN (Double-Layer Supertwist Nematic),* are much cheaper than active-matrix models, but if you spend the extra money, you'll thank yourself later for making a worthwhile investment.

Apple broke new ground with the display in the Titanium PowerBook G4. The machine's 15.2-inch TFT active-matrix display was the best ever in a PowerBook, and its massive 1152-by-768-pixel resolution was 128 pixels wider than the PowerBook G3s'. The wider display is perfect for editing an HTML document and previewing it in an adjacent browser window, crunching numbers in a large spreadsheet, or even keeping two word-processing documents open side by side. Those who spend a lot of time in palette-happy graphics applications like Adobe Photoshop will love this display, as the palettes tend to take over valuable screen space.

Emphasizing exactly how important display real estate is on a PowerBook, Apple surprised the marketplace with another first for any notebook—a 17-inch screen. The 17-inch PowerBook (my current ride) has to be seen to be believed. The massive 1440-by-900-pixel display is expansive and a thing of beauty. Even Dell and HP and were caught on their heels by that one. PC vendors have begun to catch on to the larger-display trend, but once again Apple deserves a lot of credit for innovation in the computer marketplace as a whole.

Input Devices

Another defining attribute of a PowerBook or an iBook is its keyboard, which is smaller than one for a desktop system. Keeping a laptop as small and light as possible requires tradeoffs. Sure, it would be nice to have access to an Apple extended keyboard with a full numeric keypad, but it just isn't practical in coach class on an airplane.

PowerBook and iBook keyboards will seem flimsy to experienced touch typists because they don't have much key travel (up-and-down movement of keys) or feedback (the audible click that a key makes when depressed) compared with a desktop keyboard. If you are using a PowerBook as your main computer, you may want to purchase an external USB keyboard for use at the office or at home.

Many PowerBook and iBook keyboards leave faint marks on the display, but don't panic! The marks are only visible with the backlighting turned off, and you can easily remove the marks by gently buffing them out with an ultra-microfiber cloth. I clean my PowerBook screen with a Laptop ScreensavRz cloth from RadTech ($13.95–$17.95; www.radtech.us). When I'm finished cleaning the screen, I simply lay the cloth on top of the keyboard so that it protects the display when the PowerBook is closed.

Similarly, PowerBooks and iBooks do not come with a mouse. Instead, they have a trackpad that you use to move the pointer. As you move your finger across the trackpad, the pointer follows. Once you get used to it, a trackpad can be as efficient as a mouse. Still, some people may prefer using a mouse as desk space allows.

Batteries

The other defining attribute of a portable computer is that it has its own power supply and, unlike a desktop system, doesn't require access to electrical outlets other than to recharge the battery. The venerable rechargeable battery is an indispensable commodity for mobile technology. Although it's improving technologically, the battery remains the weakest link in the mobile-computer system. Running out of power reduces your computer to an expensive paperweight.

Battery technology has made great strides in the past several years. The new lithium-ion (LiIon) batteries in the PowerBook G4 are specified to last as long as 5 hours, though 3 to 4 hours is more realistic in everyday use. Within the next few years, expect battery run time to increase to as much as 30–40 hours with the advent of new technology such as zinc-air and fuel cell batteries and more-efficient processors and memory.

Battery life is so crucial for some users, especially those who often travel by airplane, that it may be the single most important reason to upgrade to the newest PowerBook model. By the same token, take care when considering the purchase of a used PowerBook. Older models often suffer from weak battery life (5 to 30 minutes), so you could end up with a PowerBook that requires a constant AC connection.

Types of batteries

The original PowerBook 100 used lead-acid batteries, like the ones in cars, but these were not efficient for their weight. Apple switched to nickel-cadmium (NiCad) batteries starting with the PowerBook 140 and stayed with this technology for the rest of the 100 series because it yielded a run time almost double that of lead-acid batteries at the same weight.

Both lead-acid and NiCad batteries suffer from the memory effect, a condition that occurs when you partly charge a battery several times consecutively. The battery develops a chemical memory of the charge level and will not allow charging past that point, resulting in run times of less than 20 minutes.

 If your PowerBook suffers from the memory effect described above, allow the battery to discharge completely and then charge it until the battery monitor indicates a full charge. Repeat this process three times and see if the battery functions normally. If it does not, replace the battery.

Another type of battery, the nickel-metal hydride (NiMH) cell, includes a small microchip with an energy-monitoring module circuit that detects the battery's capacity and tells the computer when it requires charging. As NiMH battery technology improved over the years, Apple released updated cells: Type I is the original, and Types II and III are its successors.

The PowerBook Duo 210, the PowerBook 500 series, the PowerBook 190 and 5300 models, and the PowerBook 1400 use NiMH batteries. Some third-party vendors sell NiMH cells for the PowerBook 3400, but the superior LiIon cells provide more-reliable power via intelligent charging circuitry inside the battery itself. The PowerBook 500 series were the first to ship with a smart battery.

(Apple's Knowledge Base article 16168 in its Tech Info Library [www.info.apple.com/kbnum/n16168] identifies the AC adapters and battery types and gives recharger information for all PowerBooks and iBooks.)

Current PowerBooks and iBooks ship with the latest LiIon batteries—these are among the most efficient batteries on the market today, with an excellent power-to-weight ratio. LiIon batteries typically last 2 to 4 hours and can recharge in about half their run time (1 to 2 hours). They're also lighter than their predecessors, and—like NiMH cells—they allow recharging at any point during their life cycle. Lithium polymer batteries, which are half the weight and have all the power of lithium-ion batteries, are shipping in cameras and cell phones today; expect these to show up in PowerBooks and iBooks soon.

 Battery Reset 2.0 (www.info.apple.com/kbnum/n60655) addresses a situation that may occur with some PowerBook G3 Series and iBook computers, in which the battery doesn't show up in the Control Strip in Mac OS 9, or a red X appears over the battery icon in the menu bar.

 iBook (FireWire) Battery Update 1.0 (www.info.apple.com/kbnum/n88052) addresses an issue with battery charging in some FireWire-equipped iBook computers, in which the battery doesn't recharge after a long period of inactivity.

Expansion Bays

Expansion bays are slots in PowerBooks that allow you to extend the feature set of your machine easily by swapping out media devices, such as floppy drives, SuperDrives, magneto-optical drives, CD and DVD drives, and batteries. Expansion bays add a new level of hardware customization not available in early PowerBooks.

Expansion bays debuted with the dual-battery bays in the PowerBook 500 series, released in May 1994. The revolutionary dual-bay design meant that you could use your PowerBook for an extended run time and even change a battery without putting the machine to sleep. By far the most popular expansion-bay device for the PowerBook 500 series was the card cage, a small battery-shaped enclosure that contained two PC Card slots.

The 190- and 5300-series PowerBooks also featured an expansion bay, filled with a floppy drive from Apple, but its different size and shape made previous expansion-bay devices incompatible. The PowerBook 1400 featured expansion bays as well but placed them on the front of the machine—again frustrating consumers with a different form factor that didn't accept earlier devices.

The PowerBook 3400, and subsequently the original PowerBook G3, shipped with an expansion bay, but it rarely held anything other than a factory-installed floppy or CD-ROM drive. The PowerBook 3400 had the same expansion bay as the PowerBook 5300/190-series, allowing them to share devices.

The trend continued with the PowerBook G3 series—but this time Apple heeded customer complaints about compatibility, or at least attempted to listen. The PowerBook G3 series released in 1998 (code-named Wall Street) and its successor (Wall Street II or PDQ) had the same expansion-bay dimensions and thus could share devices.

When Apple revised the PowerBook G3s in 1999, it made the form factor significantly thinner, necessitating another change to expansion-bay architecture. You can easily identify these newer, thinner PowerBook G3s (code-named Lombard and Pismo) by their bronze-colored keyboards. These models can share expansion-bay devices with each other but not with earlier PowerBook G3s that have black keyboards. Still confused? The Apple Knowledge Base article "PowerBook: Proper Method for Exchanging Expansion Bay Modules" should shed additional light (www.info.apple.com/kbnum/n45055).

PowerBook Upgrades

If you are like me, you will eventually own several PowerBooks and will have a small entourage of family and friends carrying around your old models. The best way to upgrade is to buy a new model and sell the old one to a friend. That way you have a new machine with a new warranty—the problem is, this is also the most expensive option.

In the unlikely event that you can't find someone among your family or friends who will buy your PowerBook or iBook, you can easily sell it on any number of Web sites, but I recommend that you first check with Macintosh user groups in your area. To find a user group near you, go to the Apple User Groups page on Apple's Web site (www.apple.com/usergroups/locator).

 To find the value of an old PowerBook or iBook, surf over to eBay (www.ebay.com) and do an advanced search for your model. Be sure to check the option "Completed Items only." The results give you recent selling prices of similar models, so you'll have a pretty healthy barometer of what people are willing to pay for your machine. Keep in mind that eBay is at the low end of the pricing spectrum because of the huge amount of competition and that you can usually get more by selling locally.

If you don't want to bother with selling your old PowerBook or iBook, consider donating it to a charity. Check local directories for charities in your area and ask if they are looking for computer donations. Web sites like Share Technology (http://sharetechnology.org) allow you to search their computer-donation database, which lists requests from schools, nonprofit organizations, and people with disabilities. Schools and registered charities can provide receipts for tax purposes.

Memory and storage

With most PowerBooks, as with most computers, RAM and hard drives are the most commonly purchased upgrades because they pack the most bang for the buck. My rule of thumb is to figure out the maximum amount of RAM I think I'll ever need—and then *double* the number. And I opt for the largest hard drive I can afford. Memory and storage prices have never been lower, and you won't regret an investment in them.

Processor upgrades

The other way to upgrade a PowerBook is to switch out the processor for a faster one. You can accomplish this only on PowerBooks that have the processor on a daughtercard (this means the CPU is on a separate card that you can remove from the main motherboard). CPU-upgradeable PowerBook models include the PowerBook 500 and 1400 series, the 2400, and the G3 series.

PowerBook 500 series. Because the PowerBook 500 ships with a 68040 processor, you're probably best off selling the PowerBook and getting a new one. If you cannot afford a new one, Newer Technology's 167 MHz PowerPC upgrade is worth a look. Unfortunately, the Newer Technology PowerPC upgrade is no longer being manufactured; in fact, not many accessories are made for the wonderful PowerBook 500 anymore. To find upgrades, you will have to go through used-equipment channels, such as auction Web sites or the PowerPage message boards (www.powerpage.org).

PowerBook 1400 series. Although this model is much newer than the PowerBook 500, the same rule applies: consider carefully before spending any money on this machine. It lacks USB and FireWire connections and will not run Mac OS X—you're probably better off selling it and buying a used PowerBook G3. If that doesn't discourage you, check out Sonnet Technologies' **Crescendo PB/G3** upgrade card ($299.95; www.sonnettech.com), which replaces the original 117, 133, or 166 MHz PowerPC 603e processor with a PowerPC G3 processor running at 333 or 466 MHz with 1 MB of backside cache. An additional advantage of the Crescendo PB/G3 is that the low-power copper IBM PowerPC G3 processor in it can extend the PowerBook 1400's battery life by 30 percent.

PowerBook 2400c. The PowerBook 2400c has cult status in Japan. Originally developed under the code name Comet, the PowerBook 2400c was the closest thing to an Apple subnotebook since the PowerBook 100; the 12-inch PowerBook G4 has since supplanted it as the most coveted compact PowerBook. The PowerBook 2400c originally shipped with a 180 MHz PowerPC 603e processor; a subsequent model shipped with a 240 MHz CPU, but only in Japan. Newer Technology manufactured a 240 MHz G3 upgrade card for the PowerBook 2400c. Interware (also known as Vimage), a Japanese firm, manufactured the Booster 400 MHz G3 upgrade for the PowerBook 2400c; this upgrade shipped with 1 MB of backside cache for around $1,400. Again, the best place to find such cards is on the used market.

PowerBook G3. You can upgrade the processors on all PowerBook G3s, with the exception of the original model (which carried the Kanga code name and has a 250 MHz G3 in the PowerBook 3400 enclosure). You might not want to upgrade the latest PowerBook G3s (Lombard and Pismo) because they already have reasonably fast processors in them. But if you do decide to upgrade, Newer Technology offers the **Newer Tech NuPowr Pismo G4/500 MHz** ($289.99; www.newertech.com), which has a 500 MHz G4 processor and includes 1 MB of backside cache. PowerLogix offers the **BlueChip G3 900** ($349; www.powerlogix.com) for Pismo; it includes a G3 processor running at 900 MHz and 512K of backside cache.

If you own a 233, 250, 266, 292, or 300 MHz PowerBook G3 (denoted by Family No. M4753, which you can find by flipping your PowerBook over and looking at the bottom label), you will probably be more motivated to upgrade due to the slower processor speeds in these PowerBooks. Sonnet Technologies offers the **Crescendo/WS G3** and **G4** ($249.95 and $349.95, respectively; www.sonnettech.com). The Crescendo/WS G3 includes a 500 MHz G3 processor, and the Crescendo/WS G4 includes—surprise!—a 500 MHz G4 processor. Both upgrades include 1 MB of backside cache.

Travel Survival Tips

If you own a PowerBook, you probably like to travel (or at least roam around your home or apartment). PowerBook ownership implies that you're independent, mobile, and always on the move. That may not *always* be the case—but let's face it, you are much more likely to take a PowerBook on a trip to Las Vegas than to lug along any desktop machine.

That said, follow a few rules of the road when you're preparing for a trip—they'll save you a lot of hassle while you're traveling. First, do not overpack. Some people have the tendency to bring the kitchen sink on a weekender to the Jersey shore and then don't end up so much as breaking the safety seal on the PowerBook bag throughout the whole trip. Be realistic and know your limitations. Are you really going to work on that project or balance your accounts on the flight? Or is the DVD *Old School* more likely?

 Back up all your data before you go on any trip. For extra piece of mind, drop a copy of your important presentation (or report or résumé or whatever) on an FTP server or an Apple iDisk before you depart—that way, you should be able to access your important data even in the worst possible scenario. Traveling is risky, and anything can and will happen—your computer can get lost, stolen, or damaged easily while you are on the road. Replacing your PowerBook or iBook is simple, but replacing your data is not. You have been warned.

What to bring

If you expect to need all of your electronic devices, having the right batteries, cables, and AC adapters is paramount—forget one and you may be out of luck. The well-stocked PowerBook bag should contain these items:

AC adapter. The AC adapter is easily the most overlooked accessory for mobile technologists. Rather than disconnecting your power supply, invest in a portable AC adapter from MadsonLine (www.madsonline.com) or MacResQ (www.macresq.com). These AC adapters (about $75) are smaller and lighter than the usual power supply, and you can keep one permanently located in your bag, thus avoiding the horror of arriving at a meeting with no juice.

You should also consider bringing a cigarette-lighter adapter and/or an airline EmPower adapter (which plugs into a new form of electrical outlet found in business-class seats on almost 40 airlines), depending on your method of transportation. MCE Tech (www.mcetech.com) offers cigarette-lighter adapters for around $25, and MadsonLine offers EmPower adapters for around $30.

A bootable system CD/DVD. Make sure that you have a current bootable CD or DVD and that it starts up your specific PowerBook. Keep it in a safe place. Newer PowerBook G4s ship with the system software, Apple Hardware Test, and the Software Install and Restore images on a single DVD, replacing up to five CD-ROMs. Be careful, though—these DVDs cannot be used to boot any machine that only has a CD-ROM drive.

Cables. Here are the cables you'll want to pack:

- **Two RJ-11 (telephone) cables and an RJ-11 coupler.** Why *two* RJ-11 cables? Although a 6-foot cable is sufficient for most locations, you will probably need a 12- to 25-foot cable in your hotel room. You don't want to be chained to the desk when you could be surfing the Web while watching *Monday Night Football* in bed. The coupler is useful for times when you need both cables or when the phone line is hardwired to the wall.

- **RJ-45 (Ethernet) and crossover cables.** Most PowerBooks support Ethernet, which provides a great way to share files with someone else quickly. Bring both cables if you have a PowerBook G3 or earlier; PowerBook G4 and iBook Dual USB users need only a regular (or "straight") Ethernet cable because those machines will automatically sense whether they are connected to another machine or to a hub.

- **FireWire (1394) cables.** You should always bring a 6-pin-to-6-pin (standard) FireWire cable if your machine has a FireWire port. A FireWire cable can be used to connect two Macs for file transfers that are much faster than Ethernet—400 Mbps versus 10 or 100 Mbps (depending on the speed of your network).

 For blazing-fast instant networking, bypass the Sharing pane in System Preferences and instead use Target Disk Mode. It's much easier than setting up a new user and privileges: simply connect two FireWire Macs and restart one of them while holding down ⊤. The Mac that you are restarting becomes a FireWire hard drive mounted on the desktop of the other Mac.

A mouse. A mouse will increase your efficiency if you plan to work for an extended period of time. Most optical mice will work on any available surface—even your pants leg!

 Avoid infrared and Bluetooth mice when traveling. They too easily get powered on when something in your bag accidentally presses one of the buttons. I can't tell you how many times I have found myself unexpectedly out of battery life because of an infrared mouse that was accidentally triggered.

Earphones or headphones. Nothing is worse for your fellow travelers than having to listen to every ping and boing your computer makes—not to mention your blaring Audioslave MP3s. Do everyone a favor and bring a pair of earphones. If you are traveling with a loved one, bring a second pair of earphones and a ⅛-inch headphone splitter so that you can both watch a DVD (or listen to iTunes) together.

The **Boostaroo** ($29.95; www.boostaroo.com) is a nice addition to your bag if you travel with a buddy. In addition to splitting your audio output into three so that you can plug in three sets of headphones, it also provides a 40 percent increase in volume.

Tools. Pack miniature Torx 8 and Torx 10 screwdrivers, a Phillips-head screwdriver, and a small pocketknife in your checked luggage. You can often mitigate PowerBook accidents that happen while you're traveling—for example, spilling a soda on your keyboard—by taking the keyboard and battery out, wiping them off, and letting the machine dry open and upside-down overnight.

If you are flying, pack as much of your electronics as possible in your checked luggage—you probably don't need your hot-sync cradle and a bunch of wall-warts in your carry-on bag.

Power Management

The most important aspect of traveling with a PowerBook is proper power management. Bring enough batteries to last the duration of your flight, and about 50 percent extra for unexpected delays and cancellations. To figure out how many batteries you need, first determine the length of your flight. Most domestic flights in the lower 48 states are 1 to 5 hours (not counting connections and layovers). This means you should carry one or two LiIon batteries if you want to stay productive during a coast-to-coast flight from, say, Philadelphia to Seattle.

Keep in mind that although a direct flight may take 5 or more hours, a third of that time might be spent boarding, taxiing, taking off, and landing. Add to that a meal service and possibly a nap, and you may have only 2 to 3 hours of actual PowerBook use.

Make sure all your batteries are fully charged before you depart, and remember that batteries charge fastest when your PowerBook is shut down, second fastest when it is asleep, and slowest when it is in use.

To maximize your battery's run time, dim the backlighting on your PowerBook's or iBook's LCD—set it just one notch above completely off. This will increase your run time by about 10 to 15 percent and is a perfectly comfortable level for use, especially on a dark plane.

You can dramatically improve your battery's run time by using the Energy Saver pane in System Preferences in Mac OS X (**Figure 3.8**).

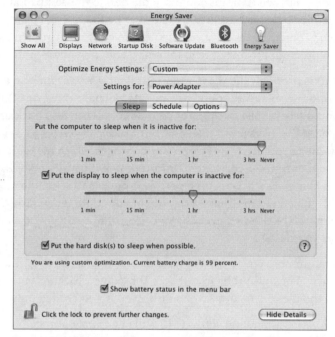

Figure 3.8

The Energy Saver pane in System Preferences lets you create custom settings that you can use when your PowerBook is connected to AC power or running off the battery, depending on your needs.

The Sleep tab allows you to set the time when your PowerBook or iBook will go to sleep, dim the display, and spin down the hard drive. You can also adjust these settings based on whether you are connected to AC power or running off the battery. When using the battery, I usually set my PowerBook to general sleep in 5 minutes, display to sleep in 2 minutes, and the hard-drive to sleep whenever possible. When it's connected to AC power, I set all three options to Never.

The best feature in the Energy Saver pane is the Optimize Energy Settings pop-up menu: instead of always tweaking individual power settings, I rely on the default settings for Highest Performance and Longest Battery Life. Most times when traveling, I use my PowerBook for word processing and email—not exactly reaching the limits but productive nonetheless. If you don't need to push pixels in Photoshop or edit that film you shot over the weekend, you can extend your run time by selecting Longest Battery Life, which drops the speed of your processor.

File Synchronization

With a desktop system, connecting additional external hard drives is an easy solution if your internal hard drive is full. But you won't want to do that with your laptop. (You do want it to be portable, don't you? It won't be if you have to lug around an external hard drive.)

You have two ways to store files offline: *archiving,* which means you move the files to the destination disk and then *delete* them from your hard drive; and *backing up,* which means you move the files to the destination disk and then *keep* the files on your hard drive. You'll use the first if you create a lot of data, don't need constant access to it, and do need to conserve hard-drive space; the second is a precautionary measure to minimize your downtime in the event of data loss.

 This is probably the most important tip in *The Macintosh Bible*: if you have not done so already, purchase an external hard drive, or CD-R or DVD-R drive, and make regular backups of your data. You can also back up to another Mac, if you have more than one, but a dedicated storage device is better because you don't use it for other purposes, which makes it less likely to crash or become corrupted. Unfortunately, it usually takes a major data loss (as in a hard-drive crash) to persuade people to schedule regular backups. Don't be a victim—make a backup of your data today. (See Chapter 5 for more on backing up and Chapter 8 for what to do if—heaven help you—you do lose data.)

The simplest way to back up your data is to drag and drop it to an external hard drive. The only problem is that in subsequent backups you have to replace all the files on the destination disk, even if you created only one new file.

File-synchronization software is available from a number of third-party developers. It lets you specify pairs of documents, folders, or disks and synchronize them, saving the most recently modified versions of your files in both places (newer versions write over older ones). Tri-Edre's **Tri-Backup** ($49; www.tri-edre.com) is my favorite file-synchronization program because it features automatic backup (**Figure 3.9**).

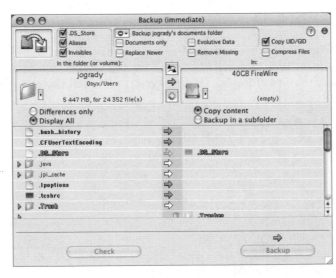

Figure 3.9

Tri-Backup will automatically back up your files and will also let you synchronize files stored in two different locations.

With Tri-Backup, you can create as many different actions as needed. For example, you can set Tri-Backup to back up your entire disk every week and a special folder every day, synchronize your customer file twice a day, and so on. It does its magic by comparing the modified dates of both files and only copying a file if it has a newer modified date than the file on the destination disk. It can also copy files in both directions—this is called *synchronizing*—as you would do with a PDA and your Mac.

Early PowerBook Models

The PowerBook began life as an entirely different machine, the Mac Portable—a large, clunky, and somewhat non-Macintosh machine that couldn't be further from a modern-era PowerBook. But Apple's first portable is an important part of Apple history: it allowed the company to get a product out to market and helped Apple learn from its mistakes. Amazingly, Apple's next portable, the first real PowerBook (the PowerBook 100), was a complete departure from the Mac Luggable, as the Mac Portable was not-so-endearingly nicknamed. The PowerBook 100 was light, had a small footprint, and is still considered by some to be the best PowerBook of all time.

The Mac Portable

Apple released the Mac Portable, the first portable Macintosh and the grandparent of them all, on September 20, 1989, for $6,500 (or around $7,300 with a hard drive). At 15.8 pounds, the original Mac Portable wasn't much smaller or lighter than a desktop Mac, but it did run on a battery. Some unique features of the Mac Portable included support for dual floppy drives or one floppy and one 3.5-inch hard drive, a lead-acid battery with a life of 5 to 10 hours, and a cool keyboard with a swappable trackball and numeric keypad. Today, Mac Portables are collector's items.

The PowerBook 100, 140, 170

Realizing the errors of its ways, Apple went back to the drawing board to create a truly portable Mac. This time the company came back with a really cool model—the PowerBook. Apple launched the PowerBook 100, 140, and 170 models with much fanfare in October 1991. The PowerBook 100—the first genuinely portable Mac—was also the first Apple hardware to bear the PowerBook moniker. Lexicon Branding, in Sausalito, California, came up with the term "PowerBook" for Apple; Sony manufactured the first model, the PowerBook 100.

The PowerBook 100 had the same relatively slow processor (a 16 MHz Motorola 68000) as the Mac Portable's but was the first and, as of early 2004, the only PowerBook to have an instant-on feature that allowed you to open the machine and begin using it almost immediately. PowerBooks running Mac OS 9 and earlier have to wake from sleep—a process that can take anywhere from 30 seconds to a couple of minutes, depending on your model and configuration. This is less than beneficial when inspiration strikes. The good news is that PowerBooks wake from sleep in less than 1 second in Mac OS X.

Following the PowerBook 100 were the PowerBook 140, which used a 16 MHz 68030 processor, and the PowerBook 170, which used a 25 MHz 68030 processor. The PowerBook 100 and 140 had black-and-white passive-matrix screens, and the PowerBook 170 had a black-and-white active-matrix screen.

In the years to come, Apple continued to enhance the line and release other 68030-based PowerBooks: the 145, 145b, 150, 160, 165, 165c, 180, and 180c. True to Apple style, prices remained about the same (with the exception of color models, which cost more) with each new model, but Apple added features with each revision.

The PowerBook Duo

The PowerBook Duo was one of Apple's most innovative ideas in mobile computing. It stripped the PowerBook down to the bare essentials: keyboard, monitor, trackball, and only the basic ports (power, ADB, and modem). The idea was to strip away any excess weight not absolutely required for productivity and deliver a machine thinner and lighter than any of the PowerBooks before it.

Sure, video out and networking are nice, but at the time Apple didn't consider them essential requirements—and besides, you could add the missing pieces by strapping on a dock that met your needs. The market agreed, and the PowerBook Duo was a success. The PowerBook Duo series ranged in weight from 4.2 pounds for the minimalist black-and-white PowerBook Duo 210, 230, 250, and 280 to 4.8 pounds for the color PowerBook Duo 270c and 280c, released in 1993 and 1994, respectively.

The PowerBook 500 Series

In 1994, Apple released the first 68040-based PowerBooks, the PowerBook 520, 520c, 540, and 540c, all of which used Motorola's 68LC040 processor. The PowerBook 500 series had a radically different case design and introduced an input device still used in modern laptops (yes, even some Intel-based notebooks)—the trackpad. This device allowed the pointer to follow the movement of your finger on a special pad.

The PowerBook 5300

In September 1995 Apple started a new chapter in PowerBook history: it announced the PowerBook 5300, the first PowerBook based on Motorola's PowerPC processor. However, quality problems plagued the PowerBook 5300 (and the PowerBook 190 series)—motherboard issues, breaking plastics around the lower LCD bezel, and defective AC connectors. The model faced a handicap even before it was shipping in quantity, following reports that a prototype's LiIon battery caught fire in Apple's labs. Motherboard problems with the PowerBook 5300 and the PowerBook 190 series prompted Apple to institute a repair-extension program that extended the warranty period for these machines.

The PowerBook 1400

The PowerBook 1400 series was an evolutionary step for Apple, building on the PowerBook 5300's strengths and repairing its weaknesses. The PowerBook 1400 holds the distinction of being the first notebook computer to ship with a built-in CD-ROM drive. The PowerBook 1400 also shipped with a unique changeable "book cover" that allowed users to switch the standard black cover for a clear cover and insert colored panels underneath it for a new personality. You even got several colorful sample inserts and a template for creating your own designs on any printer.

The PowerBook 2400

Codesigned with IBM Japan, the PowerBook 2400c was Apple's first small PowerBook since the PowerBook Duo series. At 4.4 pounds, the PowerBook 2400 fell just outside the technical specifications for a subnotebook (it had to weigh less than 4 pounds), but many still consider it one. Designed only for the United States and Japanese markets, the PowerBook 2400c is not covered by warranty in other countries.

The PowerBook 2400c shipped with a reduced-size keyboard, which featured the first inverted-T arrow-key configuration, now standard on all PowerBooks. The PowerBook 2400 lacked a built-in floppy or CD-ROM drive, but customers didn't seem to mind, especially in Japan, where it became highly popular.

The PowerBook 3400

Code-named Hooper, the PowerBook 3400c was a full-size PowerBook that featured a PowerPC 603e processor running at 180, 200, or 240 MHz, making it the fastest portable in the world. Apple based the PowerBook 3400 on a new PCI motherboard and used its industrial design as the form factor for the original PowerBook G3.

The PowerBook 3400 was unique because it featured a domed lid that housed two additional speakers, for a total of four. The PowerBook 3400 also accepted expansion-bay devices from the older PowerBook 5300/190 models and was the first PowerBook to take advantage of the faster 1 MB IrDA infrared standard.

Table 3.7 Mac Portables Prior to the G3 Series

PowerPC Models	Processor	Speed (MHz)	Display Type	Colors	Weight (lbs.)	Introduced
5300ce/117	603e	117	active	color	6.2	8/95
5300cs/100	603e	100	passive	color	6.2	8/95
5300c/100	603e	100	active	color	6.2	8/95
5300/100	603e	100	passive	grays	5.9	8/95
3400c	603e	180/200/240	active	color	7.2	2/97
2400c	603e	180/240	active	color	4.4	5/97
1400cs	603e	117/133/166	passive	color	6.7	10/96
1400c	603e	117/133/166	active	color	6.6	10/96

680x0 Models	Processor	Speed (MHz)	Display Type	Colors	Weight (lbs.)	Introduced
540c	68LC040	66	active	color	7.3	5/94
540	68LC040	66	active	grays	7.1	5/94
520c	68LC040	50	passive	color	6.4	5/94
520	68LC040	50	passive	grays	6.3	5/94
190cs	68LC040	66	passive	color	6.3	8/95
190	68LC040	66	passive	grays	6	8/95
180c	68030	33	active	color	7.1	6/93
180	68030	33	active	grays	6.8	10/92
170	68030	25	active	B&W	6.8	10/91
165c	68030	33	passive	color	7	2/93
165	68030	33	passive	grays	6.8	8/93
160	68030	25	passive	grays	6.8	10/92
150	68030	33	passive	grays	5.8	7/94
145B	68030	25	passive	B&W	6.8	6/93
145	68030	25	passive	B&W	6.8	8/92
140	68030	16	passive	B&W	6.8	10/91
100	68000	16	passive	B&W	5.1	10/91
Portable	68000	16	active	B&W	15.8	9/89

continues on next page

Table 3.7 Mac Portables Prior to the G3 Series *continued*

Duo Models	Processor	Speed (MHz)	Display Type	Colors	Weight (lbs.)	Introduced
Duo 2300c	603e	100	active	color	4.8	8/95
Duo 280c	68LC040	66	active	color	4.8	5/94
Duo 280	68LC040	66	active	grays	4.2	5/94
Duo 270c	68030	33	active	color	4.8	10/93
Duo 250	68030	33	active	grays	4.2	10/93
Duo 230	68030	33	passive	grays	4.2	10/92
Duo 210	68030	25	passive	grays	4.2	10/92

The PowerBook G3

The release of the original PowerBook G3 in 1997 changed everything and opened a new chapter in mobile computing for Apple. Building on the successes of previous "world's fastest" notebooks, the first PowerBook G3 introduced a new level of price and performance in a portable that even the most vehement PowerBook detractors could not ignore. Finally, true desktop power had migrated to the laptop.

PowerBooks were long the mainstay of senior executives immune from corporate budget limitations. In addition to offering greater speeds, this generation of PowerBooks—the G3s—cost significantly less than their predecessors. At last, Apple's coveted portables were within reach of average consumers.

The PowerBook G3 (Kanga)

Apple introduced the PowerBook G3 in the fall of 1997 as a logical extension of its wildly popular line of desktop Power Mac G3s. Packed in the same enclosure as the PowerBook 3400, the PowerBook G3 marked the first time Apple had squeezed so much horsepower into such a small package. At this machine's heart was the zippy 250 MHz PowerPC 750 (G3) processor with a 512K backside cache running at a fast 100 MHz.

The PowerBook G3 signified a revolution for Apple: for the first time, the PowerBook line was on par with its desktop counterparts. No longer a slower cousin, it had evolved into the desktop's speedy little sibling in the top bunk.

The PowerBook G3 Series 1998 (Main Street, Wall Street, PDQ)

Apple announced the PowerBook G3 series in May 1998 (at the same time as the iMac debut), calling it—you guessed it—the PowerBook G3 Series (see the sidebar "A PowerBook by Any Other Name? A Good Idea!" below, for more on Apple's disastrous PowerBook G3 naming conventions).

The PowerBook G3 Series I models, aka Main Street (233 MHz) and Wall Street (250 and 292 MHz), featured a new style of enclosure and were the first PowerBooks that offered numerous build-to-order options. You could pick from a 233, 250, or 292 MHz PowerPC G3 CPU and a 12.1-inch passive-matrix, 13.3-inch TFT active-matrix, or 14.1-inch TFT active-matrix display at a price range of $2,500 to $6,000.

In summer 1998 Apple revved the PowerBook G3 series to 233, 266, and 300 MHz under the code name PDQ, which stands for Pretty Damned Quick. Now *that's* what I call a name!

The PowerBook G3 Series 1999 (101, Lombard, Bronze)

In May 1999 Apple released yet another PowerBook G3 series, running at 333 and 400 MHz and code-named 101, Lombard, or Bronze, after its beautiful translucent mocha-colored keyboard. The new PowerBook G3 looked similar to the model it replaced, but closer inspection revealed that it was 20 percent thinner and almost 2 pounds lighter. In addition, this new PowerBook G3 featured a pair of stacked USB ports—a PowerBook first, which essentially killed ADB ports in the line.

The PowerBook 2000 (102, Pismo, FireWire)

Apple announced the last professional PowerBook G3 in February 2000 at Macworld Expo Tokyo. The new model shipped with the same form factor as the previous PowerBook G3, but it ran at either 400 or 500 MHz, and Apple replaced the long-in-the-tooth HDI-30 SCSI port with two 400 Mbps FireWire ports. Additionally, the system featured a new Unified Motherboard Architecture (UMA) that ran at a sizzling 100 MHz (up from 66 MHz).

The new motherboard also included an AirPort wireless networking slot under the keyboard, an AGP-based ATI Rage 128 graphics chip set, and a 6x DVD-ROM drive. The PowerBook G3 with FireWire came in two configurations: one with a 400 MHz G3 processor, 64 MB of RAM, and a 6 GB hard drive for $2,499; and one with a 500 MHz G3 processor, 128 MB of RAM, and a 12 GB hard drive for $3,499.

A PowerBook by Any Other Name? A Good Idea!

Although most commercial products have unique names—mostly to differentiate the newest model from the one it replaced—PowerBooks work a little differently. Since 1997, Apple has more or less called them all PowerBook G3s and, recently, PowerBook G4s, leaving consumers and tech-support reps alike confused.

In the early and middle 1990s, Apple incremented product names by a few digits to differentiate models—a widely criticized move (it's hard to tell what a Performa 5430 is, for example), but it usually allowed you to tell which model was newer. When Steve Jobs returned to Apple in 1997, he streamlined the number of product offerings, which was a good thing. He may have taken the process too far with the PowerBook line, however. The issues got so confusing that Apple had to create a Knowledge Base article (http://docs.info.apple.com/article.html?artnum=24604) to help people identify which model they had.

The original PowerBook G3 had one of the best code names around—Kanga. Apple called the PowerBook G3 Series Wall Street and PDQ (for Pretty Damned Quick) in the labs; it called the next model 101 or Lombard, for the names of the overall project and the logic board, respectively. Wall Street and Lombard are much friendlier names than PowerBook G3 Series/300, and I wish Apple had considered a similar naming convention for its PowerBooks.

Table 3.8 PowerBook G3

Model	Speed (MHz)	Code Name	Introduced	Family	Feature
PowerBook G3 (FireWire)	400/500	102, Pismo	2/00	M7572	FireWire, USB
PowerBook G3 (Bronze Keyboard)	333/400	101, Lombard, Bronze	5/99	M5343	USB only
PowerBook G3 Series	233/266/300	PDQ	9/98	M4753	Speed bump
PowerBook G3 Series	233/250/292	Wall Street	5/98	M4753	Thin form factor
PowerBook G3	250	Kanga	10/97	M3553	G3 processor

The PowerBook G4

The PowerBook G4 (code-named Mercury) set the entire computing world on its ear in January 2001 when Apple announced it at Macworld Expo in San Francisco. The newest PowerBook was a speed demon because of its 400 or 500 MHz PowerPC 7410 (G4) processor, and it was also a total design departure for Apple, ushering in a new generation of portable Macs.

Previous PowerBooks were solid, curvy, and functional, but they always contained compromises. Whether it was size, weight, performance, or battery life, users always found something to complain about in their PowerBooks. The PowerBook G4 threw all those complaints out the window.

The PowerBook G4 came wrapped in a spectacular enclosure that was an incredibly slim 1 inch thick and weighed a paltry 5.3 pounds. The new machine was thinner than even the smallest Sony portable, giving Apple major bragging rights in the marketplace. Another outstanding feature was the PowerBook G4's beautiful 15.2-inch (1152-by-768-pixel) wide-screen display. On top of all this, it came in an exquisite enclosure crafted of titanium, which—as Steve Jobs pointed out—is stronger than steel and lighter than aluminum. You'll frequently hear these PowerBooks referred to as TiBooks.

 Original TiBooks with 400 or 500 MHz processors only shipped with CD-ROM, CD/RW, or Combo drives. If you wanted DVD-burning capabilities, you had to upgrade to a newer model. Well, no more. MacResQ's PowerBookResQ ($299; www.macresq.com) is a SuperDrive upgrade that can be installed in any Titanium PowerBook G4.

Nothing Is Flawless

The original PowerBook G4, while breaking ground in industrial design, wasn't without its flaws. Most notorious was its ridiculously poor AirPort wireless networking performance. Apple placed the TiBook's antenna in the lower part of the enclosure, thus limiting range. When you combine the low placement with the shielding provided in the Titanium enclosure, the TiBook's AirPort performance is easily the worst of all Macs'—it has almost half the range of the less-expensive iBook. At Apple's Worldwide Developers Conference (WWDC) in May 2002, attendees coined the phrase "PowerBook Wave" for Titanium owners seen standing up during conference sessions waving their PowerBooks in the air in an attempt to get a good AirPort signal from the provided base stations.

Paint chipping was another problem with PowerBook G4s because Apple painted the titanium enclosures with a silver paint. The right wrist rest area of the top case (just above the optical drive) is extremely susceptible to chipping because it is a high-traffic area. Corners and edges are also vulnerable to chips, and most TiBooks develop several chips after as little as 6 to 12 months of use. Don't sweat this too much—it just adds character!

Some users also experienced problems with their PowerBook G4s' latches breaking off. The TiBook latch was designed to auto-drop when the PowerBook is closed via a unique magnet mechanism, but because of their small size the latches are fragile and easily broken if you close the lid off-angle or too roughly.

 The slot-loading optical drives found in all PowerBook G4s don't accept small or nonstandard-shaped CDs, like the widely available 160 MB mini CD-R discs and 50 MB business-card CD media. Apple mentions this in the manual, but many users get these specialty CDs jammed in their drives—requiring a $500 (!) repair.

Early PowerBook G4 optical drives are prone to failure because of their slim form factor. They'll even whine if your right hand places too much pressure on the wrist rest while the optical drive is in use. Some hinges in first-generation machines were a little brittle, and because of the way they were designed, early displays required a total replacement for even the smallest repair.

Problems also surfaced with the FireWire controller chip on the motherboard. Connecting a malfunctioning FireWire device or using a questionable cable could blow out the FireWire port pretty easily—the result is a costly motherboard replacement.

Another thing to keep in mind if you are considering acquiring an original PowerBook G4 is that its VGA output will work only with an analog monitor; you can't connect it to any of Apple's ADC flat-panel displays without an expensive adapter. Worse, when the PowerBook is opened, the Apple logo on the lid is upside-down! This was a result of focus-group testing where users couldn't figure out how to release the latch without looking at the Apple logo going up and down. Veterans already know that the latch is on the *other* side of the PowerBook.

PowerBook G4 (Gigabit Ethernet)

Nine months after the announcement of the groundbreaking PowerBook G4 (Titanium), Apple released its first in a series of speed bumps to the wildly successful portable lineup. The first such upgrade was given the name "Gigabit Ethernet" because it had the distinction of being the first PowerBook to feature 1000Base-T (Gigabit) Ethernet networking on board. Previous PowerBooks topped out at 100Base-T, which is (theoretically, anyway) ten times slower. Other improvements in the PowerBook G4 (Gigabit Ethernet) were faster processor speeds (550 and 667 MHz) and faster bus speeds (100 and 133 MHz, respectively).

PowerBook G4 (DVI)

April 29, 2002, a paltry six months after the announcement of the Gigabit Ethernet PowerBooks, Apple revved the PowerBook G4 line to include DVI (Digital Visual Interface). This made the PowerBook G4 the first PowerBook that was able to drive an Apple ADC digital flat-screen monitor. I always found it ironic that Apple's high-end PowerBooks couldn't connect to the company's flat-panel displays. Silly, really.

Processor speed was also bumped to 667 and 800 MHz, and the new DVI interface and 32 MB ATI Mobility Radeon 7500 graphics card allowed this PowerBook to display a higher screen resolution of 1280 by 854 pixels, compared with the previous model's 1152 by 768.

PowerBook G4 (867 MHz and 1 GHz)

Six months later Apple did something rare—it updated the PowerBook G4 *again*. Previous PowerBook lines—such as the G3 Series—were updated about every nine months. This new and faster upgrade cycle was a boon for new buyers, but others worried about the rapid depreciation of such a high-ticket item.

This time around, Apple bumped up the processor speed to 867 MHz and 1 GHz. It added a Level 3 cache, a DVD-burning SuperDrive (on the 1 GHz model only), and a 32 or 64 MB (again, on the 1 GHz model) ATI Mobility Radeon 9000 graphics processor for video. The 1 GHz model's blazing processor and SuperDrive truly made it a compelling upgrade, judging by the number of older PowerBook G4s suddenly available for sale on eBay.

PowerBook G4 (12-, 15-, and 17-Inch)

On January 7, 2003, Apple again turned the portable computing world on its ear by announcing at Macworld Expo in San Francisco the smallest and largest PowerBooks ever—the PowerBook 12- and 17-inch models. The newest PowerBooks were more than evolutionary—they were revolutionary. Apple not only changed the form factor but also completely rebuilt the PowerBook from the ground up. The PowerBooks before these were mostly differentiated by clock speed, video card, and optical drive; the 12- and 17-inch PowerBooks were entirely new products. Apple revved the 15-inch Titanium PowerBook to match its new siblings in the fall of 2003 (**Figure 3.10**).

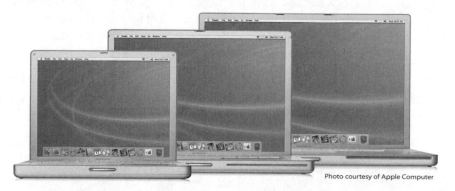

Figure 3.10

Apple's classy family of PowerBooks, circa 2004, offered users a choice of three screen sizes—12, 15, or 17 inches.

Photo courtesy of Apple Computer

For example, all PowerBooks since then include built-in Bluetooth (previously available only as an external USB dongle (a separate hardware piece) and support for ultra-cool AirPort Extreme (802.11g) wireless networking. (Some models include AirPort Extreme cards; others offer AirPort Extreme only as an option.) Once again, Apple is a true pioneer in mobility.

To address the AirPort range problems uncovered in the original Titanium PowerBook design, Apple switched to an aluminum alloy for the new enclosures and moved the antennas to the bezel around the screen. Aluminum has the added benefit of an unpainted finish, thus eliminating the paint-chipping problems of yore. The only downside I have found to the aluminum enclosure is that it dents more easily than titanium. I already have two dents in aluminum machines from bonking them lightly against my desk; I'm certain that would not have happened to my Titanium PowerBook.

PowerBook G4 (12-Inch)

The sleek new 12-inch PowerBook G4 weighs a mere 4.6 pounds and costs as little as $1,599 but packs in a lot of functionality. All models include a 1 GHz G4 processor and 512K of backside cache. You can get either a 40 or 80 GB hard drive, and you can opt for a Combo drive (which can read CDs and

DVDs and burn CDs, but cannot burn DVDs) or a SuperDrive (which both reads and records DVDs). The screen (which is really 12.1 inches) offers a wide-screen display resolution of 1024 by 768. New in this small PowerBook is the nVidia GeForce FX Go5200 graphics processor, which marks a departure from Apple's long-standing partnership with ATI on all PowerBook video chipsets.

The 12-inch PowerBook includes a 10/100Base-T Ethernet port, one FireWire 400 port, and two USB 2.0 ports. There's also a mini-DVI port; and Apple thoughtfully includes an adapter for connecting DVI-equipped flat-panel displays and another adapter for connecting VGA displays to the mini-DVI port. (Adapters for connecting S-Video and composite video monitors are optional.)

While the 12-inch PowerBook ships with an AirPort Extreme card slot, it does not include a PC Card slot. This is an issue only for professional digital photographers who rely on PC Card adapters to download large photos from CompactFlash (CF) cards.

Most consumers will find a lot to love in this ultracompact PowerBook. If your work centers on the graphic arts or video or music editing, however, then you'll probably be better off checking out a desktop Power Mac or the 15- or 17-inch PowerBooks.

PowerBook G4 (17-Inch)

The PowerBook G4 17-inch is the first notebook computer in the world to ship with a 17-inch screen. It is the same TFT active-matrix panel that ships attached to the arm on the iMac 17-inch. The gorgeous display features a whopping 1440-by-900-pixel resolution in a wide-screen format that was just made for watching movies on DVD. The wide LCD contains 1.3 million pixels and offers the same viewing area as a 19-inch CRT monitor. The machine is so wide (yet only 1 inch thick) that some users have nicknamed it "Lunch Tray" and "Aircraft Carrier." The wide screen is perfect for all your multiple-palette applications and easily displays your email program side by side with a full-length browser window, for instance.

You'll find that this PowerBook ups the ante in almost all other areas as well. For example, not only is there a FireWire 400 port, but there's also a second, faster FireWire 800 port, two USB 2.0 ports, a 10/100/1000Base-T Ethernet port, and a PC Card slot. The PowerPC G4 processor runs at a blazing 1.33 GHz, and you can max out this machine's RAM to 2 GB. An AirPort Extreme card is included, as is Bluetooth. Of course, all models include a SuperDrive.

Video support is also top-notch. The 17-inch PowerBook includes the ATI Mobility Radeon 9600 graphics processor and 64 MB of video RAM to power that large screen. There are both standard DVI and S-Video output ports; adapters are included for VGA and composite video output.

And, of course, Apple couldn't produce a top-of-the-line PowerBook without including a futuristic touch—in this case, an ambient lighting system that automagically illuminates the keyboard and dims the display when room lighting dims. This is extremely cool for us night owls who like to type in the dark and aren't touch typists.

The 17-inch PowerBook G4 packs all this into a 1-inch-thick case (**Figure 3.11**)—even the 12-inch PowerBook G4 is thicker, at 1.18 inches. In short, the 17-inch PowerBook is a marvel. If you want an extremely powerful, fully equipped Mac that you can take with you, then this could be your machine.

Figure 3.11

The very powerful 17-inch PowerBook G4 is only 1 inch thick.

Photo courtesy of Apple Computer

PowerBook G4 (15-inch)

The all-new 15-inch aluminum PowerBook replaced the old workhorse—the original PowerBook Titanium 15-inch—in September 2003.

The 15-incher was the last machine to get bumped to Apple's new aluminum-alloy enclosure, completing the migration to an all-aluminum PowerBook lineup. The PowerBook 15-inch ships as either a Combo drive 1 GHz G4–equipped model ($1,999) or a SuperDrive 1.25 GHz G4–equipped model ($2,599). It, too, includes such niceties as built-in 10/100/1000Base-T Ethernet, Bluetooth, a PC Card slot, an AirPort Extreme slot, FireWire 400 and 800 ports as well as USB ports, and an ambient-lighting-enabled keyboard. The screen sports resolutions up to 1280 by 854.

Having used all three PowerBook models, I prefer to use the 15-inch PowerBook these days. I find the size and industrial design of the 15-inch aluminum PowerBook to be perfect for my current needs. The 17-inch model feels a little large and bulky when used off-desktop. Being a mobile person, I spend at least half of my PowerBook time using it on my lap, on the couch, and in bed, and the 17-inch model feels a little big in those situations. For air travel, the midsize 15-inch PowerBook is also best, especially if you want to use it while the person in front of you has the seat reclined.

Table 3.9 PowerBook G4

Aluminum Models	Speed (MHz)	FireWire 400	FireWire 800	USB	USB 2.0	Introduced
PowerBook G4 (12-inch DVI)	1 GHz	1	-	-	2	9/03
PowerBook G4 (15-inch FW 800)	1 GHz/1.25 GHz	1	1	-	2	9/03
PowerBook G4 (17-inch 1.33 GHz)	1.33 GHz	1	1	-	2	9/03
PowerBook G4 (12-inch)	867	1	-	2	-	1/03
PowerBook G4 (17-inch)	1 GHz	1	1	2	-	1/03

Titanium Models	Speed (MHz)	FireWire 400	FireWire 800	USB	USB 2.0	Introduced
PowerBook G4 (1 GHz/867 MHz)	867/1 GHz	1	-	2	-	11/02
PowerBook G4 (DVI)	667/800	1	-	2	-	4/02
PowerBook G4 (Gigabit Ethernet)	550/667	1	-	2	-	10/01
PowerBook G4 (Titanium)	400/500	1	-	2	-	1/01

The iBook

The iBook, announced in July 1999 at Macworld Expo in New York, was Apple's first real foray into the consumer portable market. It may have been the most anticipated Apple portable in history, after the PowerBook G4 (Titanium).

The iBook filled the empty consumer-portable quadrant in Steve Jobs' two-by-two product matrix. The iBook sat directly under the wildly successful iMac in the matrix—the Apple doesn't fall far from the tree. A completely new class of notebook, the iBook brought the power of the G3 processor to the masses in an attractive, portable, and inexpensive package.

Borrowing design cues from the iMac, the iBook attempted to appeal to everyone from students to computer novices to early adopters (or die-hard users) who had to have every new Apple model. The original iBook came in two colors—Blueberry and Tangerine—and its rounded case included a handle. It soon earned the nickname "Clamshell." The iBook offered several technical innovations as well—AGP graphics, AirPort wireless networking, and a 6-hour LiIon battery.

To achieve the desired price point, however, Apple had to make some compromises: the iBook lacked a PC Card slot, IrDA, video out, audio in, and high-speed connectivity (either through SCSI or FireWire). Even then, early iBooks were priced at a premium that was out of the reach of many customers. The company switched gears and brought prices down to $2,500 for the entry-level model—a major step in the right direction. But $2,500 (and even the eventual $1,800 price of that model) was too much for the average student. Enter the iBook at $1,599 ($900 less than the least expensive PowerBook)—who *wouldn't* want one?

However, even the first-generation iBook had its detractors. Some early critics found it too big and heavy for students or small children and considered the screen too small at 12.1 inches and 800 by 600 resolution—all valid points, as the iBook was larger than the professional PowerBook G3. Adding fuel to the fire, some PC-oriented journalists characterized it as girlish, saying it looked like a purse or makeup compact.

With the iBook SE (for Special Edition), announced in February 2000, Apple bumped the base RAM from 32 to 64 MB and increased the hard drive's size from 3.2 to 6 GB. This iBook lost the handle and came in a less-girly Graphite color.

The second-generation iBook arrived in September 2000 and came in two flavors—regular and extra crispy … that is, regular and yet another Special Edition. The new iBook added a new, faster 366 MHz PowerPC 750CX (aka the G3e) processor that featured an on-chip Level 2 cache running at the same speed as the processor. It also shipped with a FireWire port and video output and came in two new colors: Indigo and Key Lime. The SE version included a DVD-ROM drive and a 466 MHz processor, and came in Graphite and Key Lime.

The iBook (Dual USB)

Apple changed everything again in May 2001 with the announcement of the iBook (Dual USB). The new iBook amazed customers and silenced the critics with a totally redesigned enclosure—a chip off the block of the amazing PowerBook G4. Significantly smaller and lighter (4.9 versus 6.6 pounds), it looked nothing like the previous iBook. The new iBook was square and compact and had an elegant white case, as opposed to the round, curvy, colorful original design (**Figure 3.12**). The 500 MHz iBook also added innovations like two USB ports and even an audio input port.

Photo courtesy of Apple Computer

Figure 3.12

Today's iBook looks nothing like the original.

iBook (Late 2001 and 2002)

Since the Dual USB iBook was introduced with its radical new design, Apple has continually released models with faster speeds, better storage, and higher-end features such as FireWire ports and a Combo drive. The first of these upgrades happened in October 2001 when Apple announced a speed bump to the iBook (Dual USB). The processor speed on all but the lowest-end configuration was increased to 600 MHz, and the bus speed was increased to 100 MHz. Installed RAM on the entry-level configuration was increased to 128 MB, and hard drives were increased to 15 GB in most configurations.

The iBook was available in four configurations, each with a different optical drive: The $1,299 CD-ROM model ran at 500 MHz, the $1,499 model came with a DVD-ROM, the $1,599 CD/RW model was only available as a Built-To-Order (BTO) option at the Apple Store, and a special $1,699 "Combo" (DVD-ROM/CD-RW) model was available with a larger 20 GB hard drive. They all sported the ATI Rage Mobility (2x AGP) graphics processor under the hood.

In January 2002 Apple released a 14.1-inch iBook offering customers a choice of 12.1- or 14.1-inch displays. You got the same resolution of 1024 by 768 on either one, but the 14.1-inch display was noticeably easier to view at the highest resolution.

The processor in the iBook introduced in May 2002 was upgraded to 700 MHz (600 MHz for the low-end model, but all were 100 MHz faster than the previous models). All models also had their VRAM increased to 16 MB. The 600 MHz CD-ROM model sold for $1,199, the 700 MHz Combo drive model with a 12.1-inch display was $1,499, and the 700 MHz model with a 14.1-inch display was $1,799.

The 700 MHz models shipped with a 24x CD-ROM drive, 16 MB of VRAM, and a 20 GB hard drive. The 14.1-inch model shipped with 256 MB of RAM. The 800 MHz configurations shipped with 32 MB of VRAM, a 30 GB hard drive, and a Combo drive. All of these iBooks shipped with an ATI Mobility Radeon 7500 (2x AGP) video subsystem.

iBook (Early 2003)

Announced in April 2003, the iBook (Early 2003) is a 100 MHz speed bump from the previous iBook series. The 800 MHz CD-ROM model sold for $999 and included a 30 GB hard drive. A model with a 900 MHz processor and a Combo drive sold for $1,299, and the 14.1-inch 900 MHz configuration with Combo drive sold for $1,499.

iBook G4

The iBook G4, announced in October 2003, was a complete surprise and a total departure from the iBooks' processor lineage. It was always assumed that the iBook was to be powered by the G3 processor and that the faster G4 processor was reserved for the more-expensive PowerBook—part of Apple's professional line. Well no more. Apple's announcement of the desktop PowerMac G5 has reshaped the Mac OS landscape quite dramatically.

Apple took the iBook line to new heights by upgrading that machine's CPU to the much-faster PowerPC G4 processor, the same one found in the company's more-expensive PowerBook models. Apple launched the new G4 iBooks with an 800 MHz PowerPC G4 processor and a slot-loading Combo drive, but otherwise they were largely the same as the previous iteration. The iBook G4 12-inch model costs $1,099, and the 14-inch version is $1,299 and $1,449, making them Apple's least expensive G4 notebooks ever.

Table 3.10 What's Your iBook?

Model	Processor	Speed (MHz)	FireWire 400	USB	USB 2.0	Introduced
iBook G4	G4	800/933/1 GHz	1	-	2	10/03
iBook (Early 2003)	G3	800/900	1	2	-	4/03
iBook (Opaque 16 VRAM), (32 VRAM), (14.1 LCD 32 VRAM)	G3	700/800	1	2	-	11/02
iBook (16 VRAM)	G3	600/700	1	2	-	5/02
iBook (14.1 LCD)	G3	500/600	1	2	-	1/02
iBook (Late 2001)	G3	500	1	2	-	10/01
iBook (Dual USB)	G3	500	1	2	-	5/01
iBook (FireWire)	G3	366/466	1	1	-	9/00
iBook	G3	300/366	-	1	-	9/99

Interview: Bruce Horn

Bruce Horn was the original developer of the Finder, probably the Mac's most distinctive element. In that capacity, he contributed several of the key technologies that made the classic Mac Desktop work, including the concept of resources, the type and creator system for files and applications, and the Dialog Manager, which produced the Mac's user-friendly dialog boxes. Horn grew up in Palo Alto, California, and while still in high school he began working at Xerox's Palo Alto Research Center (PARC), where countless innovations that were central to the Mac and modern computing were forged. Today, Horn is cofounder and CTO of Marketocracy (www.marketocracy.com), an online mutual fund company. He is also developing a Mac OS X information-management application code-named iFile (www.ingenuitysoftware.com).
—Henry Norr

> *If the Mac ever disappears, I'll just give up on computing completely, because Windows has this grating feel, and I don't really like to use it.*
>
> *—Bruce Horn, on his current use of the Macintosh*

When did you start working at Apple?

I started in October or November of '81, right after Stanford. I was 22.

Did you go right into the Mac team?

Yeah. I knew Larry Tesler from Xerox PARC. So when I finished Stanford, I went to Larry [who had moved to Apple], and I said, "I'm looking around for something interesting to do." He showed me the Lisa, then the Mac, and I met Steve and all the Mac people. They were all amazing—great people—but I actually decided to go work at a different company. I decided that on a Friday, and Friday night Steve called me and said, "So what do you think of Apple?" I said, "Well, actually, I've already accepted another job." And he started going nuts—he said, "What do you mean? You get down here Saturday morning—we're going to talk some more about this. Wah, wah, wah" [he laughs]. He basically browbeat me into coming back in.

So when you started at Apple, you jumped right into the Mac OS?

Yeah. Andy Hertzfeld basically said, "I think you should work on this thing called the Finder."

Were you working on it alone?

Toward the end of the Finder, about six months before we shipped, Steve Capps came in, and we sequestered ourselves in a separate room and worked night and day and got the thing out. If he hadn't come in, there's just no way [the software would have gotten done on time], because team programming is so much better.

Was Andy Hertzfeld also involved with the Finder?

Every once in a while, in my sources [code files] I'd see a note from Andy that he'd changed a line or something, but no, Andy wasn't really a Finder guy. He was the guru. Andy was pretty much the spiritual center of the Mac group—he and of course Steve [Jobs].

But Andy, I think more than anybody, was the guy who said computing should be really fun, and the Mac should have a personality. I remember him saying that when you delete a column in a spreadsheet, it should explode or poof in a puff of smoke or something. He just had so much personality—Andy's personality kind of pervaded the whole thing.

What were your expectations about how the Mac would do?

We kind of didn't really think about that. I think we all felt that we were making something that we wanted personally and that we thought was great, and we kind of figured that if we liked it, a lot of people would like it. I thought it would sell like crazy. Now, Steve wanted to sell it for $1,495, but as you know, that didn't happen. If we'd sold it for $1,495, the world would be a different place.

What was the single most important innovation in the Mac?

That's so hard to say. I think the whole thing was a package of the uniform graphical user interface that was simple enough that you could understand it and say, "Gosh, well, if it works this way in this program, it should work this way in another program," and have that by and large be true.

If you had had the power to change one thing, what would it be?

The price, first of all. And I guess the other thing would be not to have invited [Microsoft's Bill] Gates in.

Were you suspicious of Bill Gates at the time?

No, just in hindsight. In hindsight I just remember him coming in, and Andy [Hertzfeld] was giving him this demo, and my experience of him was not positive. He didn't seem to really want to help us, and he'd be very arrogant. Given he had our machines to reverse-engineer and our documentation to clone Windows from, it was clearly not a good thing for him to come in.

You left Apple pretty quickly after the Mac shipped. Was the reality already falling short of the expectation?

No, I just felt I'd done what I could do at Apple, and I wanted to do some other things. Part of it is that I'd worked 20 hours a day for two and a half years, and I was pretty tired. But I was totally thrilled with the Mac. I loved it—I wanted to have a trailer full of them and drive around and give them to friends.

So has Apple moved in the directions you want?

I would say the current direction of the Finder is nothing like where I would take it—that's why I have my own project [Ingenuity Software]. And I'm using Panther—it's even worse. Steve says, "Oh, it's more user-oriented." I talked to him in 1999 and said, "You know, the way the Finder is going [in Mac OS X, then in prerelease form] is not a good direction.

continues on next page

It has to be really user-oriented, it has to be oriented to what people are trying to do and not get in their way." Because at that time I was kind of upset that the top level of the disk wasn't yours anymore, and I said, "God, look at all the stuff you have to slog through before you get a place where you can put things." And not only that, it's telling you where to put things.

I basically said, "You know, all of a sudden it's changed from the user being in charge to the computer being in charge." Now the computer is telling you what you can and can't do, and I find that that's a major departure from what makes the Mac a Mac. And they're still departing in that way, which is kind of too bad. iPhoto, for example: when you say, "Hey, manage my pictures," it sucks them into this folder hierarchy that I can't understand. I think that's very non-Mac.

But you still use a Mac?

Oh, yeah, I still use a Mac.

Do you use a Windows-based PC, too?

No, I don't use Windows. If the Mac ever disappears, I'll just give up on computing completely, because Windows kind of has this grating feel, for me, and I don't really like to use it.

But Apple does seem to be continuing to improve the Mac OS X user experience.

I'll tell you what: the best user-interface thing I've seen in the last five years from Apple is Exposé. That works brilliantly.

4

Upgrades and Memory

Owen W. Linzmayer is the chapter editor and author.

Mike Breeden contributed to earlier editions of **The Macintosh Bible,** *from which portions of this chapter are taken.*

This chapter covers the types of upgrades available for your Macintosh, from faster processors to more memory. The focus is on practical, useful information, and technical details are discussed only when they help to clarify distinctions between confusing terms or are necessary to assist in buying decisions.

All upgrades are either feature additions or performance enhancements. Feature additions add new capabilities to your Mac. For example, to use an iPod, your Mac needs a FireWire port, which also allows you to use a whole slew of additional peripherals. Performance enhancements, on the other hand, don't allow your Mac to do anything different; they just help it work much faster. Enhancements include CPU upgrades, speedier hard drives, and additional memory. Since adding memory to your Mac is such a common but sometimes perplexing task, it is discussed separately in the second part of this chapter.

In This Chapter

Upgrades

Upgrades are a great way to extend the useful life of your Mac. Although it's impossible to cover all of the many upgrades available, we'll examine the most popular types. For more information, we point you to Web sites to help you wade through the various choices.

CPU Upgrades

The CPU (central processing unit) is the engine, or data pump, for your Mac and plays a primary role in how fast programs run. No other component upgrade is going to provide the same sort of dramatic boost to your Mac's overall performance as installing a faster CPU. Processor upgrades also tend to be the most expensive, but they're often worth every penny. Before you decide to invest in a pricey CPU upgrade, keep in mind that sometimes it's more economical to buy a new computer instead. New models not only have faster processors, but they also have faster system buses, faster memory, faster and larger hard drives, more powerful graphics capabilities, and new expansion ports.

Unfortunately, not all Macs have upgradeable CPUs. Most portable and consumer models (such as iMacs) have their CPUs soldered on the motherboard, although in some cases specialized CPU upgrades can work around this limitation. CPU upgrades are readily available for most Power Mac G3 and G4 models (the current top-of-the-line Power Mac G5 is too new and too fast for upgrades to make economic sense, but as time passes, don't be surprised to see CPU upgrades for these models, too). For the most part, upgrading a CPU is pretty much a simple operation that can be performed by even the most technophobic user.

Typically, upgrades from Sonnet Technologies (www.sonnettech.com) are plug and play (nonadjustable), whereas those from PowerLogix (www.powerlogix.com) and XLR8 (www.xlr8.com) have switch settings that allow you to change the card's speed. The adjustable cards usually ship with a default setting that should work fine, but you can change settings if you want to experiment with higher speeds. Not all settings are reliable, and *overclocking* (running the CPU at higher-than-rated speeds) may lead to data corruption or premature failure of the processor.

Verify that the CPU upgrade you are considering is compatible with your Mac model. The vendor's product pages should list compatible Macs for each of its CPU upgrades. The documentation includes important hardware and software installation notes you should read.

Types of CPU upgrades

The type of CPU upgrade you can install depends on the expansion capabilities of your Mac model.

CPU card models. The easiest types of CPU upgrades to install are those that replace the CPU daughtercards in many older Macs that have *PCI (Peripheral Component Interconnect)* slots. All you have to do is open your Mac's case, remove the existing CPU daughtercard, and insert the new card in the empty slot.

ZIF models. Most of the modern Power Mac G3 and G4 models have the CPU on a small circuit board called a *ZIF (zero insertion force)* module, which allows you to upgrade easily by replacing the existing processor with a faster model.

 If you're buying a ZIF CPU module that doesn't have a name brand such as Formac, Metabox, Newer Technology, PowerLogix, Sonnet, or XLR8, chances are it is an OEM (original equipment manufacturer) model and thus will not include speed adjustments on the module. (The same is true of the ZIF CPU modules that shipped in G3 Macs.) These modules rely on the motherboard's jumper settings to determine their operating speeds. Some of these vendors include information on how to do this in their manuals; others do not. Be sure to check with the vendor to see if it can provide help with jumper settings.

PCI models. Some vendors have figured out ways to install faster processors in the PCI expansion slots of older Macs. Sonnet Technologies (www.sonnettech.com) offers some consumer-level upgrades.

PDS models. Vintage Macs with NuBus expansion slots often have a *PDS (processor direct slot),* which vendors have used to upgrade the CPU. Many vendors of PDS upgrade cards are no longer in business, but Sonnet Technologies still offers a wide selection, and used PDS cards are often available on eBay.

PCI Cards

Apple used to equip its Macs—from the Mac II through the Power Mac 6100, 7100, and 8100 series—with 10 MHz NuBus slots for expansion, but now it has embraced industry-standard PCI slots. Early PCI slots ran at 33 MHz with a 32-bit wide interface, allowing 132 MBps rates (actual rates vary depending on the motherboard controller and other factors). With the Power Mac G3 (Blue and White) in 1999, Apple began to include faster PCI slots, which are compatible with higher-performance 64-bit cards. The Power Mac G3 (Blue and White) and Power Mac G4 PCI models also included one 32-bit, 66 MHz PCI slot, used for the graphics card. Later Power Mac G4 desktop systems replaced this 66 MHz PCI slot with an *AGP (Accelerated Graphics Port)* slot for the graphics card.

The beauty of the switch from NuBus to PCI is that now Mac users have a much wider choice of expansion cards because it's a simple matter for vendors to make their Windows products compatible with Macs, too. No matter what type of feature you want to add to your Mac, there's probably a PCI card that'll do what you want. Although we can't possibly cover every type of PCI card, here are some of the major examples:

FireWire and USB ports. You can add FireWire (Apple's name for the IEEE 1394 standard) and USB (Universal Serial Bus) capability to your PCI-based Mac with cards available from sources such as FirewireDirect (www.firewiredirect.com), FireWire Depot (www.fwdepot.com), Keyspan (www.keyspan.com), and Orange Micro (www.orangemicro.com). You'll find cards with FireWire 400 and 800 ports, as well as cards with USB 1.1 and 2.0 ports, and there are even cards that mix various combinations of all four port types, so be sure to shop around for the right one for your needs. Armed with these new ports, your Mac should be able to connect to a wide array of peripherals, including external hard drives, digital cameras, video cameras, scanners, and printers.

 Many PCI FireWire cards sold for Windows computers also work in Macs. If the box notes that the card is OHCI-compliant, it should work in Macs using Apple's FireWire drivers. (Mac OS 8.6 or later is required for FireWire support.)

Networking. Macs prior to the Blue and White series of G3s have at best a 10Base-T (10 Mbps) Ethernet interface for networking. However, more-recent models have 10/100Base-T (100 Mbps) and even Gigabit Ethernet built in. If you want your older Mac to talk to these at top speed, you can add a faster Ethernet port via PCI. Furthermore, if you want to access an AirPort wireless network from your desktop Mac, there are also PCI cards for that. Check with Adaptec (www.adaptec.com), Asanté (www.asante.com), Macsense (www.macsense.com), or Proxim (www.proxim.com).

ATA/IDE controllers. Most pre-G3-series Macs don't have an onboard ATA/IDE controller (there are exceptions, such as some Performa models and some clones) for running a fast hard drive. ACARD Technology (www.acard.com) and Sonnet Technologies (www.sonnettech.com) offer Mac-compatible PCI IDE controllers with dual ATA/66 (66.6 MBps maximum) ports that allow you to connect as many as four IDE hard drives either internally (if there's enough space inside your Mac) or externally. Both ACARD and Sonnet also offer an IDE RAID card that makes multiple ATA/IDE drives appear as a single drive without requiring RAID software. One problem you'll often encounter when you install PCI ATA/IDE controllers in pre-G3 Macs is stuttering audio during playback from the IDE drive. (For more on ATA and IDE see Chapter 5.)

SCSI controllers. Many high-performance *SCSI (Small Computer System Interface,* pronounced "scuzzy") controllers are available. These cards offer much higher clock rates and wider data paths to the hard drive than the standard SCSI ports found in older Macs. Adaptec (www.adaptec.com), ATTO Technology (www.attotech.com), and Initio (www.initio.com) are the best-known manufacturers of high-performance PCI SCSI controllers for the Macintosh. Ultra SCSI (40 MBps), Ultra2 SCSI (80 MBps), and Ultra 160 (160 MBps) models are available for both internal and external drives. Keep in mind that the actual drives you're using with these cards are the limiting factor, as no single drive currently available can sustain the transfer rates of the fastest SCSI controllers. Connecting a fast PCI SCSI card to the drive that shipped in an older Mac won't get you anywhere, since those drives had lower performance than the original onboard SCSI interface's limits. (For more on SCSI see Chapter 5.)

Audio/MIDI interfaces. Since the onboard audio capability of Macs is rather limited, PCI cards are the logical choice for adding better sound support, such as surround sound or enhanced bass, as well as support for MIDI devices. M-Audio (www.m-audio.com) has a variety of consumer and professional audio products worth investigating. (For more on audio, see Chapters 7 and 17.)

Video-capture cards. PCI video-capture cards are available in several price ranges and offer advanced features such as a variety of input options for different video sources, including S-Video, composite video, and component video. Some of these cards also include the ability to import (capture) analog video from devices such as video tape decks and camcorders. The best-known manufacturers are Aurora Video Systems (www.auroravideosys.com) and Media 100 (www.media100.com).

Graphics cards. Faster and more-capable graphics cards are available from many manufacturers. Modern graphics cards from ATI Technologies (www.ati.com) and others offer 3D hardware acceleration, higher resolutions, and other features, such as *DVI (Digital Video Interface),* which is for connecting to digital flat-panel LCD monitors. Furthermore, you can add as many displays to your Mac as you have video sources, so you can have a multiple-monitor Mac just by adding video cards. Within the limits of your Mac's CPU and other system components, these cards offer faster drawing of screen content, along with improved 3D and game performance.

PCI graphics cards come in 33 MHz and 66 MHz versions. If your Mac has a 66 MHz PCI slot, you'll want to use a 66 MHz card for top performance. However, you may be able to use a slower card in the faster slot but you won't see any performance increase. Likewise, you can usually insert a 66 MHz card into a 33 MHz slot, and the card will automatically downclock to the slower speed.

PC Cards

PowerBooks are built to be as small and light as possible, so portability trumps expandability in notebooks. However, PowerBooks still have a wide range of upgrades available in the form of *PCMCIA (Personal Computer Memory Card International Association)* devices. So called PC Card devices are the size of a credit card and can be used to add faster Ethernet, wireless networking capability, FireWire/USB ports, enhanced video support, and other features.

PC Cards come in 16-bit and 32-bit (CardBus) versions, in three different sizes, referred to as Type I, II, and III, with the larger numbers indicating greater thickness. A 16-bit PC Card can be used in a 32-bit slot, but a 32-bit CardBus device can't be used in a 16-bit slot. Likewise, thinner PC Cards will work in slots designed for thicker devices, but you can't cram a thick PC Card into a smaller slot. As a result, make sure whatever PC Card you are buying is compatible with the PC Card slot on your particular PowerBook.

AGP Cards

Intel originally developed AGP as an expansion slot to replace PCI for use with high-performance graphics cards. Unlike PCI, AGP is a dedicated interface that does not share bandwidth with other cards or slots. AGP has a direct path to main system memory and is a higher-performance interface that has become the standard for onboard graphics in new PowerBooks, iBooks, and iMacs, as well as standard for upgrade cards for Power Macs.

The Macs with AGP graphics released in 1999 and 2000 use a 2x AGP interface (this has a 66 MHz clock speed but triggers on both the rising and the falling edge of the clock pulse, for an effective 133 MHz rate). The Power Mac G4 models released in 2001 were the first Macs with an even faster 4x AGP slot. If you have a 1999 Power Mac G4 system and wonder whether it's a PCI or an AGP model, look at the graphics card's connector on the motherboard. PCI connectors are white; AGP connectors are brown. (A PCI card cannot fit into an AGP slot and vice versa, as the connectors are different.) Finally, the Power Mac G5 introduced in the summer of 2003 contains an even-faster 8x AGP slot. When shopping for AGP video cards, but sure to get one that matches the speed of your Mac's AGP slot.

Storage

The variety of storage-related upgrades available for the Mac is bewildering. Not only can you get larger drives if you need more storage space, but you can also buy faster drives if you find that reading and writing to your existing drive has become annoyingly slow (a pronounced problem when burning DVDs on first-generation DVD drives that could write data only at 1x speeds).

Hard drives (both SCSI and ATA/IDE) have continued to get larger, faster, and more affordable (prices now average less than $1 per gigabyte for internal IDE drives). Dozens of vendors also offer FireWire and USB hard drives (both AC-powered and portable), CD/DVD recorders, and removable-media drives. If your Mac didn't ship with USB or FireWire and you have an available PCI slot, you can buy a card to add these interfaces. The same holds true for IDE and SCSI—upgrade cards can add faster IDE or SCSI capability to almost any PCI-slot Mac.

 If you're replacing your Mac's internal ATA/IDE hard drive, you don't have to relegate it to the trash heap. Instead, you can install the disk mechanism in an inexpensive case that sports USB and/or FireWire ports, allowing you to use the drive as an external device. The Macally PHR-250cc FireWire/USB 2.0 enclosure ($59; www.macally.com) is one example of an external case, but there are literally dozens available from various manufacturers and online retailers.

Memory

RAM (random-access memory) is one of the primary factors affecting system performance, and it's usually the first thing you should upgrade unless your Mac shipped with a large amount of it. There's never been a better time to buy memory. Due to record low prices, more memory for your Mac is the best bang for the buck that you can buy.

Second only to a CPU upgrade, adding RAM is the most universally beneficial upgrade for your Mac, as it is a core component used by every application. RAM allows your Mac to comfortably run multiple programs simultaneously, increasing your productivity by eliminating the time wasted launching and quitting applications. Also, because having adequate RAM eliminates the need for virtual memory (see "Virtual memory," later in this chapter) to access the hard drive, performance increases, too. Furthermore, an abundance of memory helps reduce crashes and lockups, greatly increasing stability and reducing support costs.

The Types of Memory

Computer memory comes in all sorts of configurations and packages, and to get the most out of your Mac, it helps to understand the different types of memory and how they are used. For everything in your Mac to work properly, you must make sure you are referring to and using the appropriate kind of memory. Here's a listing of the types of memory in your Macintosh, with basic descriptions of their function and purpose.

DRAM

Most references to memory pertain to the *DRAM (dynamic RAM)* used by your programs and the Mac's operating system. Therefore, whenever you see the term *RAM* used in this chapter, we're referring to DRAM—the memory modules that you can install in your Mac. It's called *random access* because individual pieces (locations) of RAM can be read or changed directly. It is *volatile,* which means that it retains its contents only while power is on (or while the computer is in sleep mode). If you forget to save your documents before shutting down the computer or if a power outage occurs, the contents in RAM are gone, so any unsaved changes to open data files will be lost.

 With the current cost of a *UPS (uninterruptible power supply)* relatively low, we recommend that you buy one for protection from power outages, line surges, and lightning strikes. APC (www.apc.com), for example, makes several models starting as low as $60.

How do I determine which type of RAM my Mac uses? The type and size of compatible memory varies by Mac model, as explained in "Upgrading Your Mac's Memory," later in this chapter.

How do I determine how much RAM my Mac has? To see how much memory is installed in your Mac, choose About This Mac (**Figure 4.1**) from the Apple menu (choose About This Computer in Mac OS 9 and earlier).

Figure 4.1

About This Mac in Mac OS X tells you how much and what type of RAM you have installed in your Mac—1 GB in this case.

How do I make the most of the RAM I have? If you use Classic mode in Mac OS X or you are still using Mac OS 9, there are a number of techniques you can use to get the most out of your existing memory. (Because Mac OS X handles memory differently than Mac OS 9 or Classic, there's no need for memory management techniques.) Under Classic or Mac OS 9, first you should minimize the amount of RAM the operating system is using. Control panels and extensions consume memory and waste processor power, so use the Extensions Manager control panel to disable unnecessary options. Also, open the System Folder and trash any printer drivers and fonts that you don't need. (You can always reinstall them later from the System CD if you need them.) Finally, in Mac OS 9 and earlier, open the Memory control panel and click the "Default setting" radio button for the Disk Cache.

 If you're confused about what all those extensions in your System Folder are for, or you need a little help managing them, you might want try Extension Overload ($29 single user; www.extensionoverload.com). This shareware program includes descriptions of almost 6000 extensions, control panels, and Control Strip modules.

Another way to make the most of your memory in Classic mode and Mac OS 9 or earlier is to manually allocate memory to applications. In the Finder, select a program's icon (not an alias of it) and then choose Get Info from the File menu. In the Get Info window, choose Memory from the Show pop-up menu (**Figure 4.2**). Make sure the Preferred Size field is set to at least the size suggested in the Suggested Size field, but don't go overboard. If an application is slow or problematic, increase its Preferred Size setting in 1024K increments until it performs better.

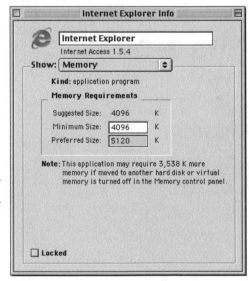

Figure 4.2

In the Classic environment and in Mac OS 9 or earlier, the Get Info window allows you to change a program's memory allocation.

How much RAM do I need? That depends on the types and number of applications you want to run simultaneously, but as a practical matter, buy as much as you can afford. Most vintage Macs can be maxed out for very little money, and all but the highest-end modern Macs can be pumped up to capacity for less than a few hundred dollars.

Cache memory

Since the advent of personal computers, CPUs have outpaced memory technology in operating speeds. High-speed memory, called *cache,* is used between the CPU and main system memory to minimize the time the CPU waits when reading or writing data. Cache memory allows the CPU to run faster and more efficiently without the speed of main memory creating a bottleneck. A cache stores data and instructions that the CPU is working on at the time or is predicted to need (a technique called *branch prediction,* in which the CPU prefetches data or code into the cache based on educated guesses of what will be needed next). Having code or data in the cache allows the programs to execute more quickly than if it had to be fetched from main memory. Cache is also used to store data written from the CPU to avoid waiting on much slower main memory. In general, the larger the cache the better, since a large cache can hold more program code and data for high-speed access by the CPU. If the CPU can't find the data it needs in the cache, it has to wait for it to be fetched from main memory (called *wait states*).

Cache memory is referred to by *levels,* generally denoting how close the cache memory is to the CPU. For instance, Level 1 cache (often called *L1 cache*) is normally a part of the CPU chip itself and is very high speed. Level 2 (*L2*) caches used to be external to the CPU, although most Power Macs now have on-chip L2 caches, and some higher-end G4 and G5 models also have a Level 3 (or *L3*) cache, external to the processor. If you have an older Mac that has an L2 cache slot, fill it with as large a cache module as you can afford to maximize performance. But with modern Macs, you don't have the option of increasing the size of the caches, so you needn't give them much thought, other than to gain an understanding of why the lack of a cache on a particular Mac model may explain why its real-world performance lags that of a similar model with a cache.

 If you're upgrading the CPU of a pre-G3 (PowerPC 604/603/601 CPU) series Power Mac with a PowerPC G3 or G4 CPU upgrade card, it's usually best to remove the L2 cache module on the logic board (motherboard), if one is present. Often the faster bus speeds or different timing of the CPU upgrade card can cause problems with the original system's L2 cache module. Some Power Macs have soldered-in L2 cache that you cannot remove. However, the soldered-in cache is usually not a problem for most CPU upgrades.

The Mac OS 9 Disk Cache

The different levels of CPU caches should not be confused with the Disk Cache feature of the Memory control panel in Mac OS 9 and earlier (**Figure 4.3**). This feature enhances read/write performance by storing data from your hard disk in RAM for faster access. While you can use the "Custom setting" radio button to change the size of the Disk Cache, it's recommended that you keep it on the Default setting instead.

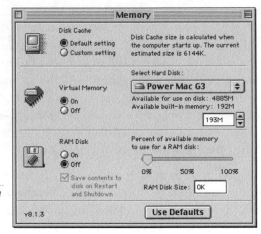

Figure 4.3

Mac OS 9's Memory control panel lets you manipulate Disk Cache settings.

Virtual memory

Virtual memory, as the name implies, is not actually RAM at all. It's the term for assigning part of the hard drive's disk space for use as if it were physical RAM. In Mac OS 9 and earlier, turning on Virtual Memory in the Memory control panel is a useful way to instantly boost the amount of usable memory. Apple recommends setting Virtual Memory to 1 MB more than the amount of physical memory present in the Mac and leaving it on all the time. However, virtual memory sometimes noticeably degrades performance—such as causing stuttering in audio, dropped frames in video, and delays for disk access when switching between open applications—because accessing data on a hard drive is much slower than reading the same data from real memory. If you have plenty of real memory and your programs aren't exhibiting any signs of RAM starvation such as those mentioned above, leave virtual memory turned off. The good news for Mac OS X users is that you needn't concern yourself with virtual memory at all. The operating system uses this feature at a low level, but there are no user-configurable options, as everything is handled transparently—and very efficiently, we might add.

Video RAM

Often called *VRAM* for short, *video RAM* is memory dedicated for use by the graphics card or onboard graphics chip. (If your Mac doesn't have a graphics card installed, it has a graphics chip on the motherboard—called *onboard video*.) The graphics chip uses VRAM to store the contents of the monitor's screen images. The amount of memory required primarily depends on the resolution and number of colors set in the Display pane of System Preferences in Mac OS X (**Figure 4.4**) and the Monitors control panel in Mac OS 9 and earlier. The more VRAM your Mac has, the better, as it allows for more colors at greater resolutions. Three-dimensional software and games also use additional amounts for buffering, texture storage, and display-page flipping (holding a second screen already calculated in VRAM to allow rapid changing of the display for animation, for instance).

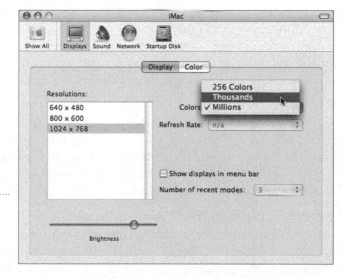

Figure 4.4

Higher resolutions and more colors require greater amounts of video memory.

In all but rare cases you cannot increase the amount of VRAM on graphics cards, which typically include anywhere from 8 MB to 64 MB of VRAM. On the other hand, early Power Mac models with onboard video have VRAM slots on the motherboard that can be upgraded. Check prices, however—you may be able to add more performance and functionality by adding a graphics card than by upgrading the onboard VRAM. Adding VRAM won't add 3D graphics acceleration to the onboard-video chip or make it faster; it will only allow your computer to run higher resolutions and color depths. If you have a second monitor, connecting it to the graphics card will allow you to run dual displays (using the onboard video for one monitor and the graphics card for the other). The Mac OS can treat both monitors as one wide Desktop area (a great boon to productivity), or it can mirror the output of one display on the other (useful for presentations).

Related Links

For reviews and performance tests of Macintosh graphics cards, and related articles, see Accelerate Your Mac! (www.xlr8yourmac.com/video.html). If you have a PCI or AGP slot model, you can see how your Mac may perform with a new graphics card by searching the systems and video-card performance database at http://forums.xlr8yourmac.com/fpsdb.

PRAM

Your Mac stores settings for such system elements as the startup disk, AppleTalk, and the time zone in a special type of memory called *NVRAM (nonvolatile RAM)*. NVRAM chips are used to store settings in the *PRAM (Parameter RAM)* on the Mac. (Don't confuse PRAM, the name for the area where your system settings are stored, with NVRAM, which is a chip type used.) This small amount of memory has its contents preserved, even when the computer power is off, by means of the logic-board battery. The battery is typically a nickel-cadmium (NiCad) or lithium-ion (Li-Ion) type good for five years or more. If you ever notice that your Mac doesn't retain settings such as the date when powered off, it's time to replace this battery. Apple dealers and electronics stores such as Radio Shack usually carry replacements.

The PRAM is where certain system settings are stored for access whenever you start your Mac. The precise settings stored in PRAM depend on the version of the operating system, your Mac model, and devices attached to your Mac, but they include settings for such things as Startup Disk, time zone, DVD region, speaker volume, time and date, and so on.

Clearing, or zapping, the PRAM. Sometimes you may want to reset the PRAM contents when you're troubleshooting a problem to make sure that no corrupted settings are stored there. (This technique can also help if you have problems after replacing a graphics card, for instance.) The common term for this is *zapping the PRAM*. To do this, restart the Mac while holding down ⌘ Option P R. You must press this key combination before the gray screen appears. For best results, hold down the keys until you hear the Mac's startup chime repeat. This will clear the startup-disk selection, so you may see a flashing question mark, but after some delay the system disk will be found and the Mac will start up. Remember to reset System Preferences to your preferred settings.

Another way to clear the PRAM settings is to use the logic-board reset button (called the CUDA on pre-G3 Macs). This is also recommended when upgrading older Macs with a different type of CPU card, such as a PowerPC G3 or G4 upgrade, or in extreme troubleshooting cases in which zapping the PRAM does not fully clear contents. (The instruction manual for the CPU upgrade usually shows the location of the reset button, which is often near the CPU card slot.) In some severe cases, removing the logic-board battery overnight is another way to clear the NVRAM/PRAM contents.

ROM

When a computer is powered on, the main memory of the system contains no data or code. To allow the system to start up (or *boot*), access the hard drive for loading the operating system, and perform other low-level system functions, instructions are permanently stored in memory called *ROM (read-only memory),* or *firmware.* (On PCs this is often called the BIOS—"basic input/output system.") It's called read-only memory because it cannot be written to or modified, since erasing or changing this basic low-level code and instructions could render the system inoperable. The Blue and White Power Mac G3 and later Macs can have the ROM updated with special Apple system software (and button-press sequences) to allow firmware updates that address bugs and increase performance or to provide for things like future OS support.

The system's boot ROM is not to be confused with the Mac OS ROM file present in the System folder in Mac OS X and the System Folder in Mac OS 8 and higher. Without the boot ROM, the computer would not be able to access the higher-level Mac OS ROM file stored on the hard drive, which includes more of the system functions used by the Mac than are in the boot ROM. (On modern Macs, Apple's System Profiler—found in the Apple menu in Mac OS 9 and earlier and in /Applications/Utilities in Mac OS X—lists your firmware version, Mac OS ROM file version, and boot ROM version if available.) This information could be helpful to a Mac technician in troubleshooting.

Upgrading Your Mac's Memory

Macs through the years have used various types and sizes of RAM. Here's a technical rundown of the types of memory modules used in Macs, through the early-2004 models.

SDRAM specifications

The most common—and therefore the least expensive—type of memory used in personal computers today is *SDRAM (synchronous dynamic RAM).* All Mac-compatible SDRAM modules must be 3.3-volt, unbuffered, 8-byte, non-parity (parity requires the use of an extra bit as an error check), non-ECC (Error Correcting Code memory is often used in non-Mac servers or workstations). While that may seem pretty complex, the fact is that Macs use the same type of memory most common in the Windows world. You can safely ignore all that technical mumbo jumbo and focus instead on the more important distinction between the two major flavors of SDRAM: SDR *(single data rate)* and DDR *(double data rate).*

- **SDR** (single data rate) SDRAM is typically just called "SDRAM" because it arrived on the scene before there was a need to differentiate it from DDR SDRAM. This type of memory transfers data only at the beginning of the clock cycle, thus making it slower than DDR SDRAM.

- **DDR** (double data rate) SDRAM is typically called "DDR memory." It provides higher throughput because it transfers data on both the rising and falling edges of each clock cycle, rather than just at the beginning of the clock cycle like SDR memory. Suffice it to say, DDR is faster than SDR, but you don't have the option of choosing one over the other. You must use whatever type your Mac requires.

When buying either type of memory, all you need to specify are speed, form factor, and size (see below for more on each of these considerations). The first two attributes are determined by what your Mac model requires. If you're not sure what you need, check the technical specifications in the user guide that came with your computer or consult a knowledgeable memory vendor. Once you know the specific kind of memory you must buy, it's just a matter of how much you want to install.

Speed. Both types of SDRAM are sold using a shorthand name that refers to their speed. SDR memory is available in PC66, PC100, and PC133 flavors, which are designed for computers with 66, 100, and 133 MHz system buses (that's not the same thing as the speed of the CPU), respectively. But the naming conventions for DDR memory are a little trickier. DDR memory is commonly available in PC2100, PC2700, and PC3200 flavors. Whereas the numbers in SDR names refer to the bus speeds for which they were designed, these numbers refer to the total bandwidth of the DDR memory. For example, PC2100 has a bandwidth of 2.1 GB per second. Things are complicated by the fact that sometimes PC2100, PC2700, and PC3200 are also called DDR266, DDR333, and DDR400, respectively, and in these names the numbers refer to twice the system bus speed. As system bus speeds increase in the future, expect new flavors of memory to be introduced to keep pace.

With some exceptions, you can use faster memory than is required by your Mac (for example, you can use PC133 memory in a Mac that needs only PC100 or PC66 provided that the form factor is the same), but you won't see any speed improvement. The only benefit is that when you ultimately buy a new Mac down the road, you may be able to transfer some of this faster memory to the new computer.

To a lesser extent, a memory module's speed is also determined by its *CAS (column address strobe)* latency. SDRAM is often described by a three-digit number (such as 3-3-3 or 2-2-2); the first digit indicates the delay in clock cycles necessary to switch between the module's banks of memory, with lower numbers indicating greater speed. This CAS latency is sometimes abbreviated as a CL rating of 3 or 2. Apple's System Profiler (found in /Applications/ Utilities) displays only the CL shorthand for some Macs and the detailed three-digit numbers for other Macs (**Figure 4.5**). No Macs require any particular latency, so you are free to mix and match modules with different latencies, although sometimes this may limit all modules to the latency of the slowest module. The real-world performance difference between the slowest (CL3) and the fastest (CL2) memory is usually imperceptible, but if you demand maximum efficiency, insist on the latter if the price is about the same.

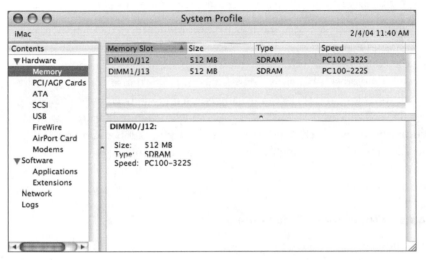

Figure 4.5

Apple's System Profiler gives you information about your Mac's memory slots as well as the size, type, and speed of any memory you have installed. This Mac has two DIMM slots, each of which has a 512 MB SDRAM module installed. Speeds of the two modules are rated at a 100 MHz bus speed (PC100), although the first module has a slightly slower latency time, as noted by the "322S" designator.

Form factor. Vintage Macs used memory that came on *SIMMs (single inline memory modules),* but these days Mac memory is divided into two main form factors: *DIMMs (dual inline memory modules)* and *SO-DIMMs (Small Outline Dual Inline Memory Modules).* DIMMs are used primarily on desktop Macs, whereas the physically smaller SO-DIMMs are used mostly in portable Macs and the compact iMacs. Some Macs have both kinds of slots due to internal space design, and there are even some models, such as the early PowerBook G3 and iMac models, in which Apple insists that you use only special "low-profile" SO-DIMMs. SO-DIMMs are usually more expensive than DIMMs of the same size, which means that you can expect to pay more for 1 GB of iBook memory than for 1 GB of Power Mac memory.

All SDR memory (PC66, PC100, and PC133) has 168 *pins* (connectors) in DIMM format and 144 pins in SO-DIMM format, whereas DDR memory (PC2100, PC2700, and PC3200) has 184 pins in DIMM format and 200 pins in SO-DIMM format. Nobody expects you to be able to count all those pins; modules have notches along their connector edges that prevent you from forcing the wrong size module into a slot or inserting it in the wrong direction.

Size. The all-important attribute for a memory module is how much data it can hold, typically expressed in megabytes or gigabytes. Larger modules typically cost more than smaller ones, but if your Mac has only a few memory slots, it's usually best to fill them with the largest modules you can afford.

Keep in mind that each Mac model's maximum memory cited by Apple is based upon the highest capacity memory modules commonly available at the time the computer was introduced. However, higher-density memory modules are often released subsequently (TransIntl.com [www.transintl.com] specializes in such modules), and these can usually be used to safely go beyond Apple's official specifications. Rather than repeat Apple's sometimes artificially low memory limits, we've chosen instead to publish the number and types of slots each model uses. Using this information in consultation with a vendor knowledgeable in the latest advances in memory technology, you can determine the actual maximum for your Mac.

Memory for modern Mac models

The following pages contain information pertaining to all the modern Macs, defined roughly as models released since the millennium. The memory configurations of the hundreds of earlier Mac models are too numerous and varied to cover individually here. If you have a vintage Mac and are curious about its memory specifications, there are several great resources available for free online. Apple's Memory Guide can be downloaded as a PDF file by searching for "memory guide" under the Support tab on Apple's Web site or by going to http://docs.info.apple.com/article.html?artnum=20025. Another useful RAM-compatibility guide for older Macs is Newer Technology's GURU application (search the Web for current availability). Both of these are good references, but they are no longer updated as is Mactracker (www.mactracker.ca), which lists all sorts of technical specifications for every Macintosh-compatible computer ever created.

 You can find specifications for all Macs by clicking Specifications on the Support tab of the Apple Web site.

Power Mac G5. The 1.6 GHz Power Mac G5 introduced in August 2003 came standard with 256 MB, which can be expanded through its four PC2700 DIMM slots. All the other Power Mac G5 models released in 2003 shipped standard with 512 MB and can hold a maximum of 8 GB in their eight PC3200 DIMM slots, although doing so would cost over $2,000 at the memory prices prevailing at press time.

Power Mac G4 (FireWire 800). The Power Mac G4 models introduced in January 2003 were the first to sport FireWire 800 ports, and all have four DIMM slots. The single-processor 1 GHz model uses PC2100 modules, whereas the dual 1.25 GHz and dual 1.42 GHz models use PC2700 modules.

Power Mac G4 (Mirrored Drive Doors). Introduced in August 2002, Mirrored Drive Doors versions of the Power Mac G4 (with speeds of 867 MHz to 1.25 GHz) have four PC2100 DIMM slots.

Power Mac G4 (Digital Audio and QuickSilver). Both the Digital Audio and QuickSilver versions of the Power Mac G4 have three PC133 DIMM slots.

Power Mac G4 (AGP Graphics). In fall 1999, Apple released its first systems with an AGP graphics-card slot. In summer 2000 it made Gigabit Ethernet standard, replacing the 10/100-Mbps Ethernet of the original models. You can tell if your Power Mac G4 is a Gigabit model by the small silver heat sink on the networking chip on the motherboard. These systems have four PC100 DIMM slots.

Power Mac G4 Cube. The cool, compact Cube has three PC100 DIMM slots.

Power Mac G4 (PCI Graphics). This system, introduced in September 1999, has four PC100 DIMM slots. These models cannot fully address memory chips denser than 128 Mb. As such, 256 MB modules can be used only if constructed out of sixteen 128 Mb chips, and no 512 MB modules are compatible.

 If you're unsure if your Power Mac G4 is the PCI or AGP model, look at the graphics-card slot (the slot closest to the middle of the motherboard). If the connector on the motherboard for the graphics card is white, the computer is a PCI Graphics box. If it's brown, it's an AGP Graphics model.

Power Mac G3 (Blue and White). The Blue and White Power Mac G3 has four PC100 DIMM slots. These models cannot fully address memory chips denser than 128 Mb. As such, 256 MB modules can be used only if constructed out of sixteen 128 Mb chips, and no 512 MB modules are compatible.

Power Mac G3 Desktop, Mini Tower, and All-In-One (commonly called the Beige Power Mac G3s). These were the first SDRAM-based Macs, and they have three PC66 DIMM slots (the G3 Desktop can't accept any DIMM with a height greater than 1.15 inches). These models cannot fully address memory chips denser than 128 Mb. As such, 256 MB modules can be used only if constructed out of sixteen 128 Mb chips, and no 512 MB modules are compatible.

PowerBook G4 (15 to 17 inches). All the aluminum-clad PowerBook G4 models with 15- and 17-inch screens have two PC2700 SO-DIMM slots.

PowerBook G4 (12 inch). The two aluminum-clad PowerBook G4 models with 12-inch screens come with 256 MB on the motherboard and one PC2100 SO-DIMM slot.

PowerBook G4 (Titanium). All of the titanium-clad PowerBook G4 models released prior to 2003 have two PC133 SO-DIMM slots under the keyboard. The top slot is very easy to access, and the bottom slot requires only a little more effort to reach. When buying memory for these models, insist on modules with a maximum height of 1.5 inches.

PowerBook G3 (FireWire). The FireWire model PowerBook, rolled out in February 2000, was the first Mac portable to use PC100 SO-DIMMs in its two slots (one under and one on top of the CPU module).

PowerBook G3 series (1998–1999). These models all have two SO-DIMM slots (one under and one on top of the CPU module). The bottom slot requires low-profile 1.25-inch modules, whereas the top slot can use 2-inch modules. While you can go to the trouble of finding slower memory to match the bus speed of each particular model, use PC100 modules instead for simplicity's sake. These models cannot fully address memory chips denser than 128 Mb. As such, 256 MB modules can be used only if constructed out of sixteen 128 Mb chips, and no 512 MB modules are compatible.

PowerBook G3 first model (aka 3500/Kanga). Unlike the later PowerBook G3s, this model uses a nonstandard memory design. There is 32 MB of RAM on the motherboard plus one RAM expansion slot that can be filled with a 128 MB module to achieve the total maximum RAM of 160 MB.

iBook G4. Apple finally upgraded the iBook line to the PowerPC G4 in October 2003. All three G4 models come standard with 128 MB soldered on the motherboard and another 128 MB PC2100 module in the single SO-DIMM slot, which can be replaced with a larger module.

iBook G3. All G3-based iBooks have some memory soldered on the motherboard (anywhere from 32 MB to 256 MB), with one SO-DIMM expansion slot that can accept PC100 modules, although all models released prior to 2002 can use slower PC66 memory if that's all that is available.

Flat-panel iMacs (1 GHz to 1.25 GHz). These flat-panel iMacs come from the factory with an empty SO-DIMM slot (easily accessible by removing the iMac's metal base) and a replaceable memory module installed in the DIMM slot (accessible by separating the iMac's plastic base from the half dome). The specifications for the 1 GHz 17-inch flat-panel iMac introduced in February 2003 call for PC2100 modules; however, you can also use the PC2700 modules required by the iMacs with USB 2.0 ports, introduced in late 2003.

Flat-panel iMacs (700 MHz to 800 MHz). The 15-inch flat-panel iMacs introduced in January 2002 as well as the 17-inch model released in August 2002 use PC133 memory. Each comes from the factory with one empty SO-DIMM slot and a replaceable memory module installed in the internal DIMM slot.

iMacs (350 MHz to 700 MHz). These iMacs have two PC100 DIMM slots, which are easily accessible without disassembly, unlike earlier iMac models.

iMacs (233 MHz to 333 MHz). The motherboard of the original iMac series is similar to that of the PowerBook G3 series, with two PC66 SO-DIMM slots. The bottom slot supports low-profile 1.25-inch modules only, whereas the top slot supports up to 2-inch memory modules.

eMacs. All eMacs have two DIMM slots that can accept PC133 modules, although the 700 MHz and 800 MHz models with nVidia GeForce2 MX graphics processors can use slower PC100 memory if that's all that is available.

Memory-Buying Tips

There are just a few things to keep in mind when buying memory for your Mac:

Reputation. Memory is a commodity product, and as such, there are many dealers from which to choose. However, due to the Mac's relatively small market share, not all vendors are as well versed with the Mac's particular needs as they are with Windows'. Therefore, it's best to patronize dealers with a good reputation and a history of serving the Mac market. To find a Mac-friendly dealer, you'll need to ask around in online forums or at your local user groups. Also, look for dealers that specifically mention Macs in their ads or on their Web sites. There are tons of Windows PC commodity vendors out there that have memory that'll work in a Mac, but they don't generally offer the best advice for Mac owners.

Compatibility. Always verify that the memory you are buying will work with your specific Mac model. Armed with the information in this chapter, you should be able to accurately determine the type of memory you need for your Macintosh. However, if you have any doubts, only buy from a dealer that guarantees their memory will work with your Mac and doesn't charge a restocking fee if they make a mistake.

Pricing. Always compare the total *delivered* cost, which includes the price of the memory plus installation or shipping and handling fees. Buying online can save you a bundle over catalog and retail-store prices, but beware of deals that seem too good to be true.

Warranty. Buy memory only from a dealer that offers a lifetime warranty. There are plenty to choose from, and their prices are typically competitive with those of the crowd that offer short or nonexistent warranties.

Name-brand vs. generic RAM. Everything else being equal, buying memory from a major manufacturer such as Crucial (www.crucial.com) or Kingston (www.kingston.com) may provide additional peace of mind. However, components used in generic memory modules are usually just as good as anything that carries a brand name.

Used memory. For older Macs in particular, you may be able to get a great deal by buying used memory on eBay. Most individuals selling used memory on eBay won't offer lifetime warranties, but they should be willing to guarantee the memory against being dead on arrival, which is usually sufficient if the memory was pulled from a working computer. Although there are commercial utilities that purport to test memory, they may be overkill. Usually it's obvious if your Mac is suffering from bad memory. Either the Mac will fail to start properly after installing the new modules, or its behavior will become noticeably less stable (crashing, hanging, slowing down, and/or presenting error notices). (For more on problems resulting from bad memory, see Chapter 8.)

Precautions for Handling Memory

Vendors like to point out that memory modules, like all electronic components, are extremely sensitive to static electricity. The levels of static electricity that can be generated in the typical home are sufficient to destroy or shorten the life of a memory module, and you don't even have to feel the spark for the damage to be done. For all their supposed fragility, in reality, memory modules are pretty robust as long as you exercise a modicum of common sense.

Most vendors ship memory in antistatic bags. Leave the memory in this protective plastic until you're ready to install it in your Mac. When memory modules are removed from the antistatic bag, treat them with care like photographs, only handling their edges, and never touching the metal contacts on the module or the pins on the memory chips. For maximum protection, wear an inexpensive antistatic wrist strap, available from computer and electronics-supply stores, and always discharge yourself by touching a grounded metal part of the Mac's chassis (such as the power-supply housing) before touching, inserting, or removing any parts inside the computer. See your owner's manual or the Apple guides referred to in this chapter for other precautions. If you're not comfortable with installing RAM yourself, a local dealer can do this for a nominal fee (anything over $50 is excessive).

Interview: Larry Tesler

Before joining Apple in 1980, Larry Tesler worked at Xerox's legendary Palo Alto Research Center (PARC), where many of the key features of modern computing—including graphical user interfaces, object-oriented programming, Ethernet networking, and laser printing—were first developed. Among his contributions there was the development of a word-processing program called Gypsy, which introduced the concepts of cut and paste.

If I had to choose three great innovations the Mac brought to the market, they would be 3.5-inch diskettes, networking built into every Mac, and plug-and-play peripherals.

—*Larry Tesler, on the Mac's contributions*

At Apple, Tesler's first assignments were managing the design of the user interface and the development of applications for the Lisa, a business computer Apple introduced in 1983. Slow and expensive ($9,995!), the machine was not a commercial success, but it was the first Apple system with a GUI—in fact, the Mac interface was a direct descendent of the Lisa's. Tesler was promoted to director of advanced development at Apple in 1986 and to vice president of advanced technology a year later. From 1990 to 1993 he worked on the Newton, Apple's failed handheld computing device. In 1993 he became Apple's chief scientist and began working on some of the company's first Internet-related projects. —Henry Norr

When did you move to the Mac from the Lisa?

Before the launch of the 128K Mac, I was friendly with the Mac software team. The Lisa Applications Group that I managed shared code with them when we could. I visited the Mac team every week or two to socialize and discuss our projects. When the Lisa and Mac divisions merged in 1984, I began my shift to the Mac.

[While working on the Lisa project,] I managed the development of the first commercialized object-oriented application framework, the Lisa Toolkit. When the Lisa was discontinued in 1985, we retargeted the Lisa Toolkit to the Mac and renamed it MacApp. MacApp became the foundation of Adobe Photoshop and many other Mac applications. MacApp also proved that object-oriented frameworks were a viable way to develop mass-market applications.

What were your expectations for the Mac when it was released in 1984?

I knew it would be tough for the Mac to displace the IBM PC and MS-DOS, but I wasn't willing to concede without a fight. I knew that all mass-market computers had to move to a GUI. And I knew that it would be hard for companies with operating systems not designed for a GUI to match the Mac's ease of use.

continues on next page

Did you imagine that the Mac would still be around 20 years later?

I expected a derivative of the Mac to be around—something more like the Lisa, with multiple applications running at once, in a protected multitasking operating system. It took a while, but that is what happened.

From the perspective of someone who was deeply involved with the Lisa, what was really innovative about the Mac, aside from the price?

Many of the innovations people think about in the Mac were in the Lisa. The original Mac and most Macs since have combined even greater software simplicity than the Lisa with outstanding hardware—beautiful, high-quality product design at a modest price. If I had to choose three great innovations the Mac brought to the market, they would be the Sony 3.5-inch diskettes; networking built into every Mac from 1985 on; and plug-and-play peripherals. Of those, the greatest and most durable advantage has been plug and play. The competition still has not gotten it right.

If you had it to do over again, how would you have made the original Mac different?

I would have taken the painful hit in cost to give it 256K of RAM instead of 128K. The extra RAM would have allowed the OS to run in protected mode. The reliability advantage over MS-DOS and Windows might have helped Apple's market share considerably. I would also have given it a second built-in diskette drive, or at least made that an option.

How would you sum up your experience at Apple?

During my 17 years at Apple, I made some pretty good calls, like MacApp, QuickTime, and AppleScript. I made some pretty bad calls during the Lisa and Newton projects. I always appreciated that I was allowed the freedom to take risks.

What have you been doing since you left Apple?

I cofounded and ran Stagecast Software. Their game-programming product is used in most computer camps and in many schools. In October 2001, I joined Amazon.com as a technical vice president. I currently manage a group called Shopping Experience.

Do you ever feel the urge to go back to Apple?

Now that they are back in the applications business, I am glad to see that they are making themselves independent of some software companies that used to have them at their mercy. With that change of strategy, I suppose my skills and interests could be relevant again. But it is hard for me to imagine a job as stimulating as what I do for Amazon. The Amazon risk-taking culture suits my personality. And there is nothing that gives a usability person immediate customer feedback like a Web site frequented by millions of people.

What computer(s) do you use now?

I still prefer the Mac. I use a beautiful G4 Cube to run Quicken and iMovie. For almost everything else, I rely upon an aging PowerBook G4 with a cracked case. I take it with me everywhere. I hope it holds up until the PowerBook G5 appears.

5

Storage

John Christopher (JC) is the chapter editor and author.

If you're like most computer users, you aren't much more interested in computer storage than in bookcases. After all, hard disks don't seem to actually do much—they just provide a place to store the files you've created and collected.

In reality, nothing is more critical to the performance and reliability of your Mac than your storage devices. If your hard disk is slow, you'll be staring at the screen, watching the spinning beach ball and twiddling your thumbs when you should be working or having fun. If your hard disk crashes, you could lose hours or years of your work, and if you haven't taken the necessary precautions, you may never get those files back. Problems like these can make you rue the day you ever heard about the Mac's great benefits and time-saving abilities.

No one can guarantee that you'll never have such hassles, but in this chapter we aim to improve your odds by providing background information and tips to help you understand how storage devices work, know what to look for when purchasing a new hard drive, and manage your devices effectively to avoid the worst.

In This Chapter
. . . .

Hard Disks

Hard disks are truly precision instruments that rely on principles of aerodynamics, electricity, and magnetism to operate. What follows are the gruesome anatomical details of hard-disk innards. While the following descriptions may seem somewhat technical, they will help you understand exactly what is happening as you use your Mac, and they'll prepare you for our "Hard-Disk Buyer's Guide," later in this chapter.

Hard-Disk Anatomy

The numerous moving parts inside a hard disk work together for the sole purpose of reading and writing data. The main components—the platters, spindle, and actuator assembly—are contained inside a sealed housing to protect them from dust and other airborne contaminants (**Figure 5.1**).

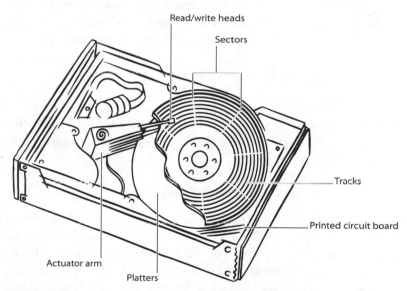

Figure 5.1

Inside a hard-disk mechanism, the platters are stacked on a spindle that spins rapidly as the read/write heads, attached to the actuator arm, move back and forth.

Platters. The word *platter* might conjure up thoughts of serving a Thanksgiving feast. When it comes to your hard disk, the platter serves up your data. Platters are flat and circular, manufactured from a durable material such as aluminum or magnesium alloys. The term *hard disk* alludes to the rigid material used in the platter itself. Every hard disk contains at least one platter; modern high-capacity drives usually have more than one. A magnetic material coats both sides of a platter, allowing it to function as a receptacle for your data.

Spindle. At the heart of the hard-disk assembly is a spindle, on which the platters are stacked like old-fashioned phonograph records. A built-in high-speed motor rotates the platters at a constant rate—typically 7200 revolutions per minute (rpm). Many new hard disks spin even faster—some disks spin as fast as 15,000 rpm.

Actuator. The actuator includes a flexible arm that extends the diameter of the platter and moves rapidly across it at a speed greater than 60 miles per hour. Sets of read-write heads are mounted at the end of the arm, one head for each side of the platter. These miniature heads read and write your data.

This is how it all works together. When you switch on your Mac, electrical current spins up the spindle motor. When the motor reaches the correct speed, the actuator arm unlocks and air pressure pushes the heads up above the platters, allowing them to ride on a cushion of air. The heads' flying height is less than the width of a human hair.

The read-write heads store your data by giving bits of the magnetic coating a positive or negative magnetic charge, corresponding to the 1s and 0s of digital data; they read the data by checking to see what the charges are.

 Is it a hard disk or a hard drive? Does your Macintosh have a hard drive or a hard disk? You may wonder what the difference is. In fact, these terms mean the same thing—you can use them interchangeably.

Logically Speaking

Beyond the physical characteristics of hard disks are their logical attributes—the features that make a hard disk usable with a Macintosh computer. Next we'll describe some technical details on the creation of a Mac hard disk and how it affects your data.

Formatting and initializing disks

Every type of storage media used with a Mac must be formatted to set up the file system (see "File systems," below) and keep track of stored data; this process is sometimes called *initialization*. Most hard disks and other storage media these days are preformatted to work automatically with your Mac. If your storage media has not been set up to work with your Mac, then you can use a special disk utility known as a *hard-disk formatter* to carry out the task.

Apple's Disk Utility program, included with Mac OS X (it's in the /Applications/ Utilities folder), can handle formatting tasks for all brands of hard disks as well as removable media like CDs and DVDs (**Figure 5.2**). When you erase your drive, Disk Utility creates a new directory—essentially a table of contents for it. The formatting process may also include some other options, such as setting up multiple partitions and zeroing out all sectors (overwriting all the files on the entire disk for security purposes).

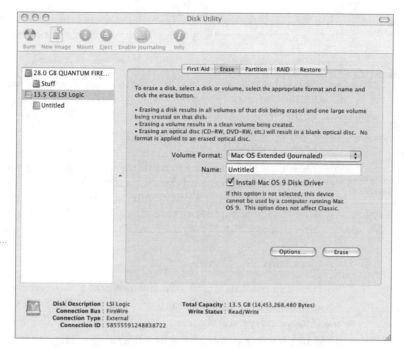

Figure 5.2

Disk Utility is included with Mac OS X and can be used for all sorts of hard-disk tasks, such as formatting and repair.

 If you're still running Mac OS 9 or earlier, you may need to use a universal hard-disk formatter that works with just about every kind of drive. The best of the crop are FWB Software's **Hard Disk Toolkit** ($84.95; www.fwb.com) and CharisMac Engineering's **Anubis Utility** ($89.95; www.charismac.com). These programs have features that let you control every aspect of hard-disk performance and security.

Partitioning—the logical divide

Partitioning means dividing a single physical disk into two or more logical volumes—individual sections that the Mac regards as completely separate hard disks. It used to be that if you wanted to squeeze every iota of performance you could possibly get from your hard disk, you could reduce its access time by creating partitions. Also, partitions were handy in cases where multiple people used a Mac, since each partition could be password protected. These days the benefits of partitioning are becoming fewer, thanks to faster hard drives and Mac OS X's multiple user profiles, which can be used to control access to files.

It seems that one remaining benefit of partitioning is for Adobe Photoshop users. Specifically, you may be aware of Photoshop's *scratch-disk setting*, which allocates logical space on your hard disk to store data temporarily. If you create a separate partition dedicated to Photoshop, some scratch-disk operations might speed up because your temporary data will not become fragmented.

At the burner

hypnotizing chickens

ashtray floors

Figure 5.3

Partitions look and act like independent hard disks, but they're not. Don't use them to back up your data.

This is a real benefit if you work with very large image files. Beyond that, there is simply no need to partition your hard drive under Mac OS X.

Here are a couple of things to consider before partitioning your hard disk:

- **You'll have to reformat to create or increase the size of partitions.** Some hard-disk formatters allow you to increase the size of a lone partition as long as you have free space on your drive. However, in most cases you will probably have to reformat the entire hard disk to adjust sizes. Don't forget to back up first!

- **Don't use partitions for backing up!** As we mentioned at the beginning of this chapter, hard disks are mechanical devices that can fail without warning. Do not use a partition to back up your critical files (**Figure 5.3**). Invest in a backup device (see "Back Up, Back Up, Back Up!" later in this chapter).

File systems

To store data efficiently, your Mac must rely on a filing system. Just as you would organize folders in a real-world file cabinet, your Mac has its own method of tracking your files and folders, called *HFS (Hierarchical File System).* HFS uses a treelike hierarchy to keep track of stored files. Here are the different flavors of HFS as well as a few other filing systems.

Mac OS Standard (HFS). In the early days of the Mac, HFS was an efficient method for file management. As hard disks grew in capacity and the number of files stored on them expanded, HFS eventually needed an overhaul. Its main problem lay in the *allocation blocks,* the smallest units the Mac uses for storing a file. HFS required that all data stored on a hard disk be spread out over a set number of blocks—65,536 of them, to be exact. This method was fine for 10 or 20 MB drives, but as drives increased in capacity, the structure of HFS created a real problem because it forced small files to use large blocks of space.

Mac OS Extended (HFS+). Introduced in Mac OS 8.1, Mac OS Extended (sometimes called HFS+ or HFS Plus) allowed many more allocation blocks per disk. It had a limit of 4.2 billion blocks, with the smallest possible block size being 4 Kbytes. So, for example, a 1 GB hard disk formatted under HFS would have allocation blocks of 17 Kbytes; under HFS+ the allocation blocks shrink to a much smaller 4 Kbytes. HFS+ makes much better use of the space on your hard disk, especially if the disk is larger than 1 GB. This is now the default format for hard disks in new Macs.

UFS. Beginning with Mac OS X, Apple added UFS (Unix File System). The original Unix, developed in 1969 by AT&T, was created to support multiple users in a multitasking environment. Apple built Mac OS X on a Unix foundation. When you install Mac OS X, you can choose to erase your hard disk and create either UFS or HFS+ volumes. Realistically, you probably want to avoid formatting your hard disk as UFS. There have been a few problems identified with UFS-formatted drives. Specifically, a UFS-formatted hard disk will not appear on the Mac OS 9 Desktop if you boot Mac OS 9. Also, a UFS-formatted hard disk may not function with the first-generation Apple AirPort Base Station.

MS-DOS (Microsoft Disk Operating System). DOS was designed for use on PCs, not Macs. However, over the years, to encourage cross-platform compatibility Macs inherited the ability to read and write data on storage media formatted for PCs. You should opt to use the DOS format only when you are sharing data with PCs that are running any version of the Microsoft Windows operating system, and only on removable media such as Iomega Zip disks, USB flash memory drives, or floppy disks.

Hard-Disk Buyer's Guide

Let's face it—your hard disk is full. How do we know? Well, if you're like us, you've probably built up a massive collection of MP3s and digitally edited a cinematic masterpiece of your vacation in Hawaii, and now you don't have enough space to install the latest version of Quicken. Even if you don't fall into that category, in general you need more disk space to do more things. But should you buy an internal hard disk to replace the shrinking one you currently own, or simply add an external hard disk and use them both? What sort of connector should your hard disk have? Buying a new hard disk can be confusing, but sit tight as we help you make an informed decision.

The Eternal Question: Internal or External?

One question that is likely to cross your mind when you're ready to upgrade your hard drive is whether to buy an internal or an external drive. Internal drives are installed inside your Mac, while external drives come in an external enclosure and plug into your Mac's USB or FireWire port.

 Apple doesn't manufacture hard disks. As is the case with many other components, Apple buys drives from all the major vendors—Western Digital, Seagate, Toshiba, IBM, and others—and puts an Apple label on them before installing them inside your Mac. So if you decide to replace your internal hard drive tomorrow, rest assured that whatever brand of drive mechanism you choose, it is likely to be fully Mac-compatible.

Internal drives

Sometimes known as hard-disk mechanisms, internal drives are self-contained units—that is to say, they come equipped with everything they need to function (see the sidebar "What's Inside," below). They connect and communicate with your Mac using an ATA interface (see "What's an Interface?" below).

On the upside, internal drives cost about $70–$100 less than their external counterparts and require no extra space on your desk. If you have a Power Mac with an extra drive bay, you simply open the case and plug in the new drive (with all these models you even get to keep your old drive). Also, if you own a portable such as a PowerBook or iBook, then storing all your working data on one internal hard drive keeps your portable, well, portable.

But on the downside, unless you have a Power Mac with an empty hard-drive internal expansion bay, you'll have to completely replace the old hard drive and somehow transfer your files and other data to your new drive (for example, by copying them to CDs). This may prove to be challenging if you own an iMac, PowerBook, or iBook model that doesn't lend itself easily to hard-drive expandability.

You'll also end up having to deal with your old hard disk by either throwing it out, giving it away, or selling it. Finally, you could end up paying as much, if not more, than the cost difference between an external drive and an internal one to have a technician transfer your data and install the drive for you.

Unless you own a PowerMac with extra drive bays, or you want a highly portable PowerBook, or your Mac's original drive has kicked the bucket, you should stick with an external hard drive.

External drives

An external drive houses the hard-disk mechanism in a box known as an *enclosure.* The enclosure contains a power supply and the electronic circuitry to run the drive, and some include a fan to keep everything cool. You can purchase an external hard drive to connect to your Mac's USB or FireWire port.

External drives offer some real advantages over internal models. Specifically, you can transport the drive and your data easily. Adding an external drive is much easier than installing an internal one, no matter which Mac model you own. Also, when you graduate to a new Mac, you won't have to remove the old drive or worry about transferring your data from it—just unplug it and go.

Probably the biggest disadvantage of adding an external drive is for PowerBook and iBook users. If you add an external drive to store additional working data (as opposed to using it as a backup or archival device), then your portable becomes much harder to take with you.

For most other Macs, however, external drives offer more flexibility and are a lot easier to configure and use (even if they do use up some desk space sitting next to your Mac).

What's Inside

Are you curious about your Mac's internal hard drive? One way to find out about it is to use System Profiler, which is included with Mac OS X in the /Applications/Utilities folder. It provides detailed information about your Mac, its components, and your installed software.

To get technical information about your hard disk, launch System Profiler. In the Contents column, click the triangle to the left of Hardware. You'll see a list of items. Click ATA, SCSI, USB, and FireWire to see if your Mac has any hard drives attached to those interfaces. Note that your Mac's internal hard drive is usually an ATA device (**Figure 5.4**).

Figure 5.4

System Profiler reveals detailed information about the devices connected to your Mac. Here it is showing that this Mac has an internal 30 GB (28 GB when formatted) hard disk connected to the ATA interface.

What's an Interface?

The term *interface* refers to the method by which peripherals connect to your Macintosh. In this case we're talking exclusively about storage devices, so the applicable interfaces are *FireWire, USB, SCSI,* and *ATA.* Two of the most popular interfaces for connecting external hard drives these days are FireWire and USB 2.0. The long-time favorite, SCSI, has waned in popularity, however. For internal hard drives, ATA is the interface of choice. Here's more about each interface.

FireWire 400 and 800

FireWire is a high-speed serial interface featured on all current Macs. Created by Apple, the standard is now developed by an IEEE-recognized association. The most frequently found flavor is FireWire 400, or 1394a, which runs at 400 Mbps. A double-speed version, 1394b, was introduced in 2003 and is more commonly known as FireWire 800. High-end Power Macs like the Power Mac G4 (FW 800) and the Power Mac G5 models feature FireWire 800 ports.

These speed figures are of course only *potential* transfer rates; in reality, as with any interface, the physical device can be the limiting factor. FireWire is often compared to SCSI, which was the original external expansion connector for Macs, starting with the Mac Plus. One huge advantage FireWire has over SCSI is that with FireWire, you don't have to deal with any device IDs or termination settings. Like USB, FireWire allows you to connect and disconnect devices with the power on and without requiring a restart. (For drives, however, make sure you drag their icons to the Trash or use the Put Away command before disconnecting them.) FireWire is also a popular interface for DVD recorders and can even be used to network Macs and PCs together.

FireWire 400 can daisy-chain 62 devices using cable lengths as long as 14 feet. Hubs and repeaters can provide even more connections and an extended range. With the introduction of FireWire 800 drives, the connector situation is more complicated. FireWire 800 uses a different connector, which is similar in appearance to the older, six-pin (U-shaped) plug. While the FireWire 800 connector is compatible with older cables, it requires an adapter, which may decrease speeds for other drives on the chain. Some drives address this problem by supplying both 400 Mb and 800 Mb connectors. Check your equipment carefully to see if you need an adapter—a six-pin-to-six-pin cable is common for hard drives and DVD recorders.

USB 1.1 and 2.0

USB (for *Universal Serial Bus*) was developed in the mid-1990s by a consortium of computer companies, primarily Intel, to provide a common connector for peripherals. USB 1.1 has a maximum interface rate of 12 Mbps, so it is best used for devices that don't require a high-speed connection, such as keyboards, mice, graphics tablets, game controllers, and lower-speed CD-ROM recorders. With the introduction of the Power Mac G5, Apple added USB 2.0 to the Macintosh platform, and it's now a standard feature. This interface runs 40 times as fast as the original specification, at a theoretical speed of 480 Mbps, which challenges the performance of FireWire 400 products. Many hard disks and DVD drives on the market offer a USB 2.0 interface.

Theoretically, you can connect as many as 127 devices at once, but in reality that's not practical. You can buy a hub to provide more ports if you use a lot of USB devices and don't like switching cable connections.

 If you're not sure what kind of drive you should buy, consider a hybrid drive that combines USB and FireWire. These days you can purchase a single external hard drive that features a USB port and a FireWire port. This is the ultimate in convenience if you have multiple Macs and move your data around a lot.

SCSI

In 1986, when Apple built SCSI (for *Small Computer Systems Interface* and pronounced "skuzzy") into the Macintosh Plus, it was a revelation in connectivity. SCSI was the first easy way to connect multiple devices such as hard drives, scanners, and printers to a computer. However, as peripherals became faster and more plentiful, SCSI aged less than gracefully. Since 1999 Apple has been abandoning the familiar SCSI DB-25 connector. In its place are USB and FireWire connectors for external devices and ATA for internal drives.

You can still purchase internal and external SCSI drives today, but you'll need a third-party SCSI card, such as those from Adaptec (www.adaptec.com), installed inside a PCI slot in a Power Mac to make it work. You'll also need to take care in configuring the ID number of a SCSI device and follow the rules of termination. In a nutshell, here's what you need to know:

Each SCSI device must have a unique SCSI ID between 0 and 6. Most external drives provide a push button to set the ID. On an internal SCSI drive, you configure the ID by setting tiny rice-grain-size jumpers in a particular on/off pattern. Consult the drive documentation to configure an internal drive.

For external drives, you must use a small square hardware device called a SCSI terminator to stop the electrical data signal when it gets to the end of the SCSI chain, thus preventing it from reflecting back and causing data errors. The rules of the termination call for the first and last devices on a SCSI bus to be terminated.

SCSI also has restrictive cable rules. The faster the type of SCSI, the shorter the allowed cable lengths. SCSI I, the type of SCSI built into early Macs, transfers data at a maximum of 5 MBps and allows as much as 18 feet of cable. However, the more-modern Ultra SCSI—which supports 20 MBps— allows a total cable length of just 3 feet.

The latest version of SCSI, called Ultra 320 SCSI, has a top speed of 320 MBps, which is faster than USB 2.0 or FireWire 800. However, these drives are mostly attached to servers instead of personal computers. Although there's an Ultra 640 SCSI on the drawing board, many vendors in the storage industry are moving to a new serialized version of the standard, called Serial-Attached SCSI (SAS).

ATA

The ATA interface (sometimes called *IDE*) is used to connect your internal drive inside your Mac. Various incarnations of ATA exist. Apple includes Ultra ATA/100 in its G4 systems. G5 Macs have shifted gears into something called Serial ATA, capable of moving data at 150 MBps.

The Rest of the Details

There are other factors to consider when you purchase a new hard drive. You might ask yourself some questions like these: How large a drive should I buy? If I choose an internal drive, will it fit inside my Mac? What's the fastest hard drive made, and do I really need it? These questions can be a bit tricky, but we'll take you down the right path.

Capacity

Once you've decided on whether to buy an internal or an external hard drive, you should next think about *capacity*—the amount of storage space you need for current data and free space you require for future expansion. First and foremost, purchase the largest-capacity drive you can afford, especially if you work with graphics, video, or sound files. Buying a hard drive with more space than you currently need is a good idea, since your requirements (like your data) are ever expanding.

When looking at the capacity of a new hard drive, keep in mind that some areas of the disk contain directories and other data, so you never get to use the drive's advertised capacity. It's not uncommon to lose roughly 5 percent of the total capacity of a formatted drive. For example, an 80 GB drive formats out to less than 75 GB.

Sizes and shapes

When installing a new internal hard drive, be aware of its physical dimensions. Most modern hard disks are 3.5-inch low-profile models and are only 1 inch high; you'll find these inside almost every desktop Mac, from the ancient Mac SE/30 to the Power Mac G5s. PowerBooks and iBooks contain 2.5-inch drives.

You won't need to worry about installing the 3.5-inch drives in your Mac. But the 2.5-inch models for PowerBooks and iBooks have different heights. Some of these drives are thinner and smaller to fit into tight spaces. Check with your friendly Mac technician or service provider to ensure the proper fit of a new drive.

External drives come in all sizes and shapes, including ultra-small keychain-style hard drives (see the sidebar "It's USB and It's on a Key!" below). You can opt for larger (and sometimes less-expensive) models if you aren't picky about looks. Alternately, you can find sleek external drives, such as LaCie's compact **PocketDrive,** in 40 to 80 GB capacities ($219–$399; www.lacie.com). The device's small size means that you can take it on the road with your PowerBook as well as keep it at home with your Power Mac. Either way, you won't need to mess with an external power adapter when using it with FireWire—this baby gets the power it needs right from the FireWire port.

It's USB and It's on a Key!

These days, most hard-drive manufacturers are busy pushing the high-capacity limit into the upper atmosphere, but a few have focused on creating what could be the next big thing in storage. What they came up with is a line of Pez-dispenser-size drives. They function exactly like typical hard drives but have no moving parts inside, and they operate using flash memory technology to keep your data—similar to the way digital cameras store images. Known as *USB keychain drives* or *flash memory drives,* these devices plug directly into your Mac's USB port, mount an icon on your Desktop, and act like any other storage device.

What makes these devices so appealing is their size. They fit on your keychain! Currently available in up to 1 GB capacities, they are the ultimate backup devices for PowerBook and iBook owners when they're on the road. Check out the DiskonKey drives, made by M-Systems (www.diskonkey.com), and FlashHopper, from SmartDisk (www.smartdisk.com).

Drive performance

You want the fastest hard drive you can get, right? Well, before you cough up the extra dollars to get a high-performance drive, take a few milliseconds and think about your needs. Do you use your Mac strictly for business purposes, like creating spreadsheets, sending email, and word processing? Or are you the creative type that dives into projects with programs like Photoshop, iDVD, or Final Cut Pro? If you're closer to the latter, then you really do need speed. Otherwise, it's OK to go the economy route and save a few bucks.

If you care about maximum speed, pay attention to several variables and weigh them according to your type of Mac and what you plan to do with it.

Average seek time and average access time. The simplest variables are the *average seek time* and *average access time,* both of which are measured in milliseconds (ms). The average seek time is how long it takes the heads to move to the desired track; nowadays it can be anywhere from 3 to 12 ms, depending on the type of drive interface. The average access time is the sum of that figure plus an additional, smaller amount (normally about 2 to 3 ms) for *latency,* the average wait for the desired sector to come around under the heads once they get to the right track.

Throughput or transfer rate. *Data-transfer rate* is a measure of how fast a drive can deliver data to the Mac once it gets to the data it's seeking. The transfer rate is counted in megabytes per second (MBps) or sometimes, just to confuse things, megabits per second (Mbps).

Spindle speed. In the last few years, drive manufacturers have been delivering drives that spin at 7200, 10,000, or even 15,000 rpm. The faster the disks are spinning, the faster the drive should read the data it's after. You'll notice the difference mainly with big files.

Warranty

The length of time a drive remains under warranty is an extremely important consideration. Expect a warranty period of at least one year for most drives and as long as five years for some. Should the drive mechanism or any components inside an external case fail (such as the power supply or fan), the vendor will typically replace the drive at no charge. It will not, however, cover the cost to recover or re-create any data lost as a result of a drive failure, so back up your hard drive *religiously.*

Backup Devices and Removable Storage

We hadn't even invented computers when Murphy's Law (anything that can go wrong will go wrong) became popular. Nevertheless, it rings doubly true in the case of computer technology. Always be prepared for the worst to happen, and *protect your data.*

To avoid running smack into disaster, follow this simple rule of thumb: whenever you use your Macintosh, back up your critical data. This is especially urgent if you rely on your computer for business purposes. The time involved in backing up seems minuscule when you consider the hours of frustration and effort that re-inputting or re-creating the data would involve.

Back Up, Back Up, Back Up!

Hard disks are mechanical devices that can operate only for a certain amount of time before they break down. There is no reliable early-warning system when a hard disk fails, so to protect yourself from losing everything you've ever created, you've got to back up. Backing up creates a copy of your critical files on a completely separate storage device or media. That means your data resides somewhere else in addition to your hard disk.

What to back up. Once you commit to performing backups, you need to decide what you will back up. Your ultimate goal is to be able to restore your data effortlessly in the event of a hard-drive crash so that you can get on with your work. You can focus selectively on your most important files, or you can pick the safest route, which is to back up the entire drive—applications, operating system, and all. Of course this method requires a larger-capacity backup device, but it can prove to be the most convenient.

Tailor backups to your needs. Your basic backup can be as simple as copying a handful of critical files to a CD or other storage device. But that won't take care of the rest of your data and other information, such as preferences and settings, email, and Internet bookmarks or favorites. You can always reinstall applications and the system software from their CDs, but you could miss an awful lot if you simply grab a few essential files. For example, think about all the programs you may have downloaded from the Internet and for which you don't have installation CDs, or all the updates you've grabbed from Apple for your system software. You should invest in a backup device and software if you can afford them—that will make your backup tasks easier and more efficient.

Use multiple media. Another adage—"Don't put all your eggs into one basket"—holds a lot of truth when it comes to backing up. Don't put your data on just one CD, DVD, hard drive, or whatever. After all, what if your backup disk gets mangled, stolen, or destroyed? Whenever possible, you'll want multiple copies of your important data.

Configure and schedule. The first time you connect your backup device, you'll need to take it out for a spin. Hook it up, peruse the manual, and get acquainted with it. Run some test backups to ensure that things are working properly.

The same goes for your backup software. Learn how to schedule backups so that they won't interrupt your workflow. A good time is right after you stop work. Do you leave your office at 5 p.m. every day? Set up your backup to run automatically at 5:15 p.m. All you have to do is configure the program and make sure that the media is available and your Mac is left on.

If your backup software has a verification option, check to see that it's turned on. That way, the software will check every file it has backed up against the original to make sure the copy is accurate. This can double the time required to complete a backup, but it's worth it.

Store your backups offsite. OK, so you've been good about backing up, but there is one thing you may not have thought of: the destruction or theft of your computer and all the data it holds. For this reason, always keep a backup someplace outside your office. When you leave at day's end, take a backup with you. If you work at home, store a backup in a fireproof safe.

Check your backups. Your backups need occasional checkups. Don't back up religiously for months, only to discover that the backup device never transferred a single file to your media. Restore a few critical files and make sure they work. You should check your backups every month or so.

Archive old data and applications. You make backups of active files so that you can get right back to work if something happens to the originals. But you may want to keep another kind of backup, too: an *archival* backup of inactive files you want to keep—just not on your hard drive, though, where they take up too much room.

When you archive your old data and applications, make multiple copies. Keep a copy in your office for convenience, another at home, and perhaps one more in a safe-deposit box at a bank or elsewhere.

 Remember that newer versions of applications and newer hardware may not be able to read or open older files. Most applications can open documents only one or two versions back. When you upgrade to newer versions of the parent application, resave old documents in an updated format and then re-archive them as necessary.

Backup Software

The backup process doesn't have to be tedious and time-consuming. A few companies publish software that simplifies the entire backup process by automating when, what, and where you back up.

- Dantz Development (www.dantz.com) specializes in backup software—that's all the company does, and it does the job well. For years many tape drives have bundled its **Retrospect Desktop Backup** ($129). But Retrospect isn't just for tape—it supports all kinds of devices, including backing up to hard drives, CDs, and DVDs (**Figure 5.5**). For multiple users on a network, you'll need **Retrospect Workgroup Backup** ($499), which supports as many as 20 users.

Figure 5.5

Dantz's Retrospect Desktop Backup is the most full-featured backup program for the Mac.

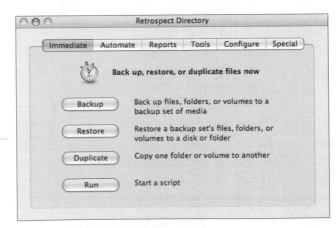

- When Apple introduced its .Mac service ($99.95 annually; www.mac.com), it included its own backup software utility, which allows members to back up over the Internet. Aptly named **Backup**, the program features a list of predefined file types, such as AppleWorks and Microsoft Excel, allowing for virtually effortless backups to your .Mac iDisk, CDs, or DVDs.

- Intego's **Personal Backup** ($59.95; www.intego.com) and Prosoft Engineering's **Data Backup** ($49; www.prosofteng.com) work in similar ways (both are in version X), providing a simplified user interface and scheduled backup operations (**Figure 5.6**). They also support all types of removable media and hard disks. Both companies offer downloadable demo versions of their products, so you can try before you buy.

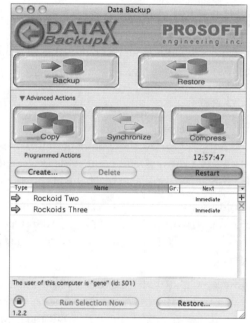

Figure 5.6

Prosoft Engineering's Data Backup offers a simplified interface but also has advanced options for power users.

Choosing Backup Storage

Once a quiet corner of the computer industry, the removable-storage market is now changing at a breakneck pace. Over the past several years, some brands familiar to the Mac market departed the scene or were supplanted by new technologies. Instead of facing a desktop littered with floppies and Iomega Zip disks, today's Mac user can choose from a growing stack of external storage technologies, including writable and rewritable CDs and DVDs, a new class of portable hard drives, and USB flash memory drives.

In addition, most Macs now come with built-in storage devices such as writable CD and DVD drives. These devices work great for backup routines and save you the expense of purchasing an additional storage device. If you don't know what you've got already, use System Profiler to check out what's under your Mac's hood.

 Almost all removable media are susceptible to heat damage, especially writable CD and DVD media. You're better off storing archive discs and backup sets in a safe designed specifically for data; safes designed for paper records or money won't do the job. Sentry Group (www.sentrysafe.com) offers several models of media vaults and claims its boxes will keep removable media cool in a fire, withstanding temperatures of 1700 degrees F. for half an hour. That's about the temperature of my car's interior after a day in a Silicon Valley parking lot.

Removable-Storage Technologies

You have a lot of choices when it comes to removable media. Here are the finer points of each type.

CD, CD-R, and CD-RW

Designed more than 20 years ago as a consumer-targeted audio format, the shiny 120 mm, 700 MB CD is now the dominant digital-media format. All computers ship with some form of CD-compatible drive, and many desktops and laptops come with a rewritable CD mechanism.

A single CD can hold roughly 700 MB of data or 80 minutes of digitized audio. CD drives come in four flavors: *CD-ROM (compact disc read-only memory), CD-R (compact disc recordable), CD-DA (compact disc digital audio),* and *CD-RW (compact disc rewritable).*

More common now are CD-RW drives, which can use special rewritable media as well as burn CD-R discs. The reusable media are more expensive, perhaps $1 each, versus less than 50 cents for CD-R media. Figuring out the performance factor of CD-RW drives can be confusing. Usually, vendors cryptically express the speed in a set of three numbers separated by *x*s, as in 52x|32x|52x. The numbers correspond to recording, rewriting, and reading speeds, respectively. The meaning of the *x* comes from prehistory; it's based on the first CD-ROM players, which had a data-transfer rate of 150 KBps. So a 52x drive is supposedly 52 times faster than that prototypical player.

External CD-RW drives now come in a wide variety of sizes, colors, and interfaces, including FireWire, USB, or both. Some of the low-power models draw their power directly from the FireWire bus.

Toasting Your Own CDs and DVDs

When you invest in an external DVD-R or CD-RW drive, you get some CD/DVD-creation software along with it. Roxio's Toast software (www.roxio.com) comes bundled with many drives. You can also upgrade to **Toast Titanium** ($99.95), which includes some nice extras that let you create low-cost Video CDs playable on most DVD players, as well as print custom labels and cases for your new discs.

Charismac Engineering's **Discribe** ($69.95; www.charismac.com) allows you to write discs in a couple of clicks. The company offers a free demo of the program on its Web site, and if you own a competing product, you can upgrade for as little as $39.95.

NewTech Infosystems' **Dragon Burn** ($49.95; www.ntius.com) has a plethora of features, including the ability to burn multiple discs simultaneously if you have more than one CD or DVD drive (**Figure 5.7**).

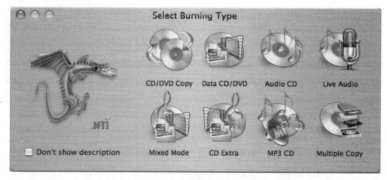

Figure 5.7

With just one click, NTI's Dragon Burn lets you choose the type of disc-creation task you're after.

In addition, both Apple's iTunes and iPhoto programs let you burn your music and photos to CDs or DVDs. For burning data to discs from the Desktop, simply load a blank CD or DVD into your drive so that it mounts on the Desktop. Then drag your selected files to the mounted disc to copy them. Finally, drag the mounted disc icon toward the Trash, which magically changes to the Burn Disc icon. A window appears and prompts you to burn the disc.

 Time for spring cleaning: When a CD-R or CD-RW disc suddenly becomes unreadable, the culprit might not be the media. Dust sometimes builds up on the drive's lens, which is used to focus the laser on the disc; you can easily remove the dust with a CD-cleaning kit, available at any office-supply store.

DVD drives

Exciting news occurred in early 2001 when Apple added a SuperDrive to the high-end Power Mac G4. Now standard equipment in many Macs, the SuperDrive is capable of writing data to a wide range of discs, such as CD-R, CD-RW, DVD-R, and DVD-RW.

The formats of each of the aforementioned types of DVDs differ in some ways, but they break down like this:

DVD-R (digital video disc–recordable). DVD-R is a recordable DVD that can store up to 4.7 GB of data, including files, music, or video. You can write to a DVD-R disc just one time. When you use these in conjunction with Apple's iDVD program, you can create videos that can be played back on most home DVD players.

DVD-RW (digital video disc–rewritable). These discs work exactly like the DVD-R type, but you can reuse them over and over again up to 1000 times! (At least in theory, anyway.) They are excellent for backing up your data, as well as for creating videos.

DVD-RAM (digital video disc–random-access memory). DVD-RAM is an early precursor of DVD-RW technology. Apple installed some DVD-RAM drives into early G3 and G4 models. Equally capable of handling 4.7 GB of data, DVD-RAM discs are currently used in some home DVD/DVD-RAM video recorders, such as those made by Pioneer. They are mostly incompatible with the SuperDrive. However, as new Macs and DVD drives are introduced, DVD-RAM compatibility may eventually make its way back to the Mac.

DVD media

It's easy to get confused when you go shopping for DVD media and see one box with the term *DVD-R* and another with *DVD+R*. While these disc formats are quite similar, the +R type offers some benefits when you use it for producing video.

For instance, DVD+RW offers direct editing on disc—meaning that you can edit video on the DVD instead of editing on your hard disk and then burning the video to the DVD. DVD+RW also offers multisession writing, whereby you can write a file to a portion of the disc and then write another file to another portion of the disc later, as well as other unique recording features. As you might have guessed, DVD+RW discs can be rewritten (hence the *RW* for *rewritable*). Newer Apple SuperDrives are now capable of using this newer format, but you should review the manual that came with your Mac before making a purchase.

Tape drives

When backing up files, Mac owners have traditionally avoided tape in favor of other types of devices. And it's no wonder, because tape backups are expensive (around $1,000). In fact, unless you regularly work with vast amounts of data (let's say over 80 or 120 GB), you should stick with cheaper technology, such as external hard drives, CDs, and DVDs.

But if your data collection is ever growing, consider a tape drive, especially for professional digital video and audio projects. The primary tape technologies currently offered in the Mac market are *AIT1* and *AIT2 (Advanced Intelligent Tape)*. AIT1 drives are capable of handling up to 90 GB of compressed data on a single tape! AIT2 pushes the envelope even further by allowing up to 130 GB of compressed data on a single tape. LaCie (www.lacie.com) offers its AIT Libraries drives with a combination USB and FireWire interface.

Digital film and beyond

Odds are pretty good that if you own a digital camera, you may already have a CompactFlash, SmartMedia, Sony Memory Stick, or other kind of memory card. These tiny solid-state storage cards can store your camera's images and so much more when coupled with a PDA (personal digital assistant), such as a Palm device.

Although you may initially consider only memory-card formats for these applications, vendors have also developed rotating memory drives—little hard disks. Some have capacities and price points appropriate for casual backup. Most of this type of storage requires a reader or dock to connect with your computer.

Hitachi offers the **Microdrive** ($499; www.hgst.com) in a 4 GB capacity. Formerly offered by IBM, the disks fit into devices that have a CompactFlash slot.

Interview: Susan Kare

Susan Kare's artwork has probably commanded more eyeball time from more people than the work of any other artist in history. Hired at Apple in 1982 with the title "Macintosh artist," she developed the icons and bitmapped fonts that lent the original Mac much of its charm. She went on to design the icons and buttons for Windows 3.0, the first popular version of the Microsoft operating system, plus the cards used in the version of Solitaire that Microsoft included with Windows—a game that has kept PC-laptop-toting execs entertained on long flights ever since. In addition, she created the icons for Steve Jobs' NextStep operating system and for OS/2, IBM's failed alternative to Windows.

Steve Jobs thought that city names were fine, but that they ought to be "world-class" cities.

—Susan Kare, on naming the fonts for the original Mac

Kare holds a B.A., summa cum laude, from Mount Holyoke College and M.A. and Ph.D. degrees in fine arts from New York University. At her Web site (www.kare.com) you can see samples of her work, purchase fonts she has designed (including fonts consisting of tiny food and animal images), and even order T-shirts and housewares decorated with some her best-known icons.

A statement on her site describes her design philosophy: "With the icon and font work [at Apple], I hoped to help counter the stereotypical image of computers as cold and intimidating. My work has continued to be motivated by respect for, and empathy with, users of software. I believe that good icons are more akin to road signs rather than illustrations, and ideally should present an idea in a clear, concise, and memorable way. I try to optimize for clarity and simplicity even as palette and resolution options have increased. … I hope the cumulative effect makes the process of interacting with machines— the way people "see" the software—more gratifying." —Henry Norr

How did you come to work on the Mac?

I had finished a Ph.D. in sculpture and art history, and moved to California to work at the de Young Museum [in San Francisco]. Thanks to my friend from high school near Philadelphia, Andy Hertzfeld, I had the chance to work at Apple, starting in the fall of 1982. I was originally hired part-time to design pixel fonts and icons for the Macintosh; there ended up being plenty of projects, so I worked full time.

What was your title?

Macintosh artist.

Did you do all the fonts and icons for the original Mac, or just some of them?

I did all the icons—I was the only bitmap person—and I did all the fonts except for the italic script, Venice, which Bill Atkinson did. I also did the control panel [the original Mac had only one], art for the Scrapbook, illustrations for the manuals, art for the advertising, etc. And I did the icons and patterns for MacPaint, and app icons for MacDraw, MacProject, and MacWrite.

The fonts I designed at Apple in 1983—New York, Geneva, Chicago, San Francisco (originally Ransom), Monaco, etc.—were specifically designed for the screen. Most were named after Philadelphia suburbs—Paoli, Rosemont, Ardmore, and Harriton, Andy Hertzfeld's and my high school. Steve Jobs thought that city names were fine, but that they ought to be "world-class" cities, so we ultimately renamed them.

When did you leave Apple?

I left to be the tenth employee at NeXT in 1987. I founded my design business, Susan Kare LLP, in 1989. I've subsequently worked on many user-interface and font projects, and designed thousands of icons for hundreds of clients.

What was your role in Windows?

For Windows 3.0 I did all the icons, buttons, and the fronts and backs for the cards for Solitaire. I didn't do the fonts.

Did you anticipate at the time that virtually all personal computers would move to a graphical user interface?

We were busy working on the project at hand. Its ultimate influence wasn't something I thought about. The Mac's success exceeded our expectations in some ways: there were only 256 numbers available for fonts.

In hindsight, if you had had the power to change the original Mac, how would you have made it different?

This is irrational, but no floppy disk swapping. And licensing for the Mac OS.

What computers do you use now?

I have a Macintosh desktop machine and an IBM ThinkPad. I have three sons; they are all comfortable on Macs and PCs, but my oldest son uses an iMac.

How do you think the Mac OS stacks up against Windows today?

I mostly use email, the Internet, Photoshop, and Illustrator, so it's easy to switch between the platforms. It's a bit disappointing to me that the icon-creation guidelines for each focus chiefly on appearance and not on meaning, metaphor, and economy of expression.

Any urge to go back to Apple?

I love working on devices with limited screen real estate, and Apple makes some of those!

Did you work on the Newton or the iPod?

No, although the iPod uses Chicago.

6

Printing

Jim Felici (JF) is the chapter editor.
Jon Seff (JS) and David Weiss (DW) are the chapter coauthors.

Printing represents reality. When a tree in Ohio topples onto a power line and blacks out half the country, you can still read your printed pages and admire your printed travel photos. Compared with the solidity of the printed page, all the singing, dancing magic on your Mac's screen seems, well, ephemeral, fragile, temporary. The books I've written are still accessible on my bookshelf, long after my Mac decided it could no longer read the 400K floppies they were backed up on.

In Mac OS X the translation of what's on your screen into a faithful reproduction on paper is still complex. It requires software (applications, operating systems, drivers, image processors), hardware, and—heaven help us all—wires. There's a lot that can go wrong. This chapter is dedicated to making sure that it all goes right.

In This Chapter

. . . .

PostScript and WYSIWYG (JS)

You probably take it for granted that when you tell your Mac to print a page of text or graphics, what you get on paper is the same as what you were just looking at onscreen. This seemingly simple process, described by the geeky acronym *WYSIWYG* (which is pronounced "wiz-ee-wig" and stands for "what you see is what you get"), helped spark the beginnings of desktop publishing. And since the Macintosh was one of the first wide-scale commercial venues for WYSIWYG, it's not hard to understand how the Mac earned its place in the desktop-publishing world. (WYSIWYG has also taken on meaning for Web designers. Instead of hand-coding entire sites with markup languages such as HTML, people now use programs like Macromedia Dreamweaver or Adobe GoLive to see what will appear on the Web while they are creating it, and then tweak the code as needed.)

 "What you see is what you get" originated as a catchphrase of Flip Wilson's cross-dressing character Geraldine from the late-'60s–early-'70s TV show *Rowan and Martin's Laugh-In.* It was first applied to computers in the 1980s.

For most of the Mac's two-decade lifetime, the technology Apple used to achieve this simple-sounding magic was QuickDraw, which provided a platform-wide format for displaying text and graphics on a monitor and outputting to printers. QuickDraw worked very well, especially at the beginning, when the resolution of Apple's monitors and its first printers was the same: 72 dots per inch (dpi).

As printing became more complicated, changes had to be made, and eventually Apple decided to abandon QuickDraw when making the transition to Mac OS X. Apple's new underlying technology is named Quartz. Since Quartz is based on Adobe's *Portable Document Format (PDF)* drawing model—which itself comes from Adobe's *PostScript page-description language (PDL)*— what gets displayed onscreen is again very close to what you get in your printed output.

A PDL like PostScript is a language that explains how to form the type and graphics on a page. This same description can be used to convey information to your Mac's screen or your Mac's printer. It is written to be *device-independent.* A PostScript interpreter, in turn, deciphers this page description and expresses it such a way that the page can be displayed on a specific device. Mac OS X has a software-based interpreter for your Mac's screen, but a PostScript printer generally contain a hardware-based interpreter—in effect, a small computer—to process images for print.

PostScript treats text and artwork the same way: as graphics composed of lines and curves. Because the same data used to create screen images is also sent from your Mac to any PostScript printer—the printer itself does most of the data processing—a page should look the same, regardless of the printer brand or model. Note that most (but not all) laser printers use PostScript, while most inkjet printers do not.

Before sending that information to your printer, your Mac first converts it to the proper format. Because this step needs to take place, you can actually "print" a document to a PostScript file (identifiable by its .ps filename extension) or to a PDF file, instead of printing it to paper (see "Printing to Disk: PDF and PostScript," later in the chapter). You can then take that file to your local Kinko's or any other copy shop and print it out. Once a file is in PostScript or PDF format, it's independent of the program—Microsoft Word or Excel, QuarkXPress, whatever—that created it. This independence from the originating application is what makes these files highly portable.

Dots

The tech world is full of wonderfully vague jargon, but when it comes to what you see on your monitor and on paper, the word is simple: *drawing*. However, your Mac and printer obviously don't reach out, grab a pencil, and start doodling or writing a letter. Although both you and your programs may conceive of your drawings as being composed of lines and curves, the computer drawings you see onscreen and on paper are made up of lots of tiny dots (onscreen they are also known as *pixels*, short for "picture elements"). Just as images you see on your monitor are drawn at 72–100 dpi, so a printer draws images on paper with rows and rows of small dots.

In the first dot-based printers, the small number of dots per inch made for blocky results (remember those old dot-matrix printers that used paper with pull-off, perforated tabs?), and you could forget about color. Today's printers start at 300 dpi and climb all the way up to more than 5000 dpi (**Figure 6.1**). Although the top numbers may be a bit phony (see "DPI," later in the chapter), the point is that printers can lay down an amazing number of dots per inch—and the more dots per inch, the less the eye can tell that they are there at all, instead of an actual drawn image.

Figure 6.1

All printer output is made up of dots—the smaller the dots, the smoother the image. The letters at the left show 12-point type imaged at 75 dpi, as on an old dot-matrix printer. The samples to the right are the same text at 150 dpi, 300 dpi, and 600 dpi.

In addition to the number of dots per inch, another important factor in the quality of a printed image is the size of those dots. Inkjet printers measure dot size in *picoliters*—that is, millionths of a millionth of a liter. The smaller the dot, the better (at least in theory). Epson claims that its inkjet printers have the smallest dots of all brands of printers, at 3 picoliters.

Bitmaps

If you've ever downloaded a graphic from the Web or used an image-editing application such as Adobe Photoshop, you've probably encountered *bitmaps* (sometimes spelled *bit maps*) and heard the term bandied about in various contexts. What does it mean?

Put simply, a bitmap is a representation of a graphic image using rows and columns of dots (GIF, JPEG, and TIFF are examples of graphics formats that use bitmaps). A bitmap defines the display space (the monitor coordinates) and color for each pixel, and that information about—or the *value* of—each of those dots is stored in a series of binary digits, or *bits*. A bit, in turn, is the basic unit of digital information, representing an on/off or yes/no statement. A monochrome (black-and-white) image needs only 1 bit to describe a pixel, since each pixel is either on or off (a state represented by a 1 or a 0). Eight bits per pixel can describe 256 colors or shades of gray (256 being 2 raised to the eighth power). Computer monitors today support 16.7 million colors (24 bits of data per pixel) or 4.2 billion colors (32 bits), depending on how much video memory they have.

 Since the human eye can distinguish only a few million colors, both 24- and 32-bit color are known as *true color.*

Using dots to describe all kinds of images is known as the *raster graphics* method of image display (*raster* just means an image is made of rows of dots). When you view a bitmapped image at its intended resolution, it looks fine—clear and smooth. But if you've ever tried to zoom in on a digital photo on your monitor, you know that the bigger things get, the worse they look. This is because the screen can display only the amount of information present in an image file—the bits present in the bitmapped image—so blowing it up just enlarges the grid of dots that make it up. *Vector graphics*, on the other hand, are composed of lines, which scale beautifully (see "Raster Image Processing and RIPS," below, as well as Chapter 13 for more information on raster and vector graphics).

What Happens When You Press Command-P (JS)

Telling your Mac to print a document may require only a simple keyboard shortcut on your part, but the process of getting something you see on the screen to a piece of paper is a fascinating journey. To begin with, there's the software you need to make it all happen.

Drivers and PPDs

When you attach a piece of hardware to your Mac—whether it's a scanner, printer, audio interface, or trackball—the computer needs to be able to "talk" to the device. In order to do that, your Mac needs a special piece of software, called a *driver*, that allows the device to understand commands and information sent to it from the Mac. Mac OS X's universal PostScript driver provides basic support for most PostScript printers. But there's another important piece of software for PostScript printing, known as a *PostScript Printer Description,* or *PPD*. This is a file that describes to the printer driver what a particular PostScript printer can do—that is, its printing resolution, the sizes of paper it can handle, and more (see "PPDs," later in the chapter).

When it comes to inkjets and other non-PostScript printers, Mac OS X includes many drivers for popular printers from Lexmark, Epson, Canon, and Hewlett-Packard. If you didn't install them with Mac OS X (to save space, perhaps), you can add them later without having to reinstall the entire Mac OS. Insert Disc 2 of the Mac OS X installation CDs (or the single DVD, if your system shipped with a DVD-ROM version), open the Packages folder, find the appropriate installer package (CanonPrinterDrivers.pkg or HewlettPackardPrinterDrivers.pkg, for example), and double-click the package. (Note that you don't need to boot from the CD as you would when installing the entire Mac OS.) You'll be asked to authenticate the installer with your user password and then choose the hard drive on which you want the drivers installed.

If the CDs don't have the right driver, you'll probably find it on the CD that came with your printer or on the company's Web site. It's always a good idea to check the company's Web site for an updated version, anyway, since a newer version may be available.

Some printers don't yet—and may never—have Mac OS X drivers. If you have such a printer, try Gimp-Print. This series of free drivers supports more than 500 models (even many printers classified as "Windows only"). Starting with Mac OS X 10.3 (Panther), Apple includes Gimp-Print drivers as part of the printer-driver installation option. You may also want to get ESP Ghostscript, an open-source PostScript interpreter; you can find it and information about Gimp-Print at http://gimp-print.sourceforge.net.

Printer drivers in Mac OS X 10.3 are located in the /Library/Printers folder, and they're now nicely categorized by printer vendor (**Figure 6.2**).

Figure 6.2

Mac OS X 10.3 organizes your printer drivers in individual folders by vendor.

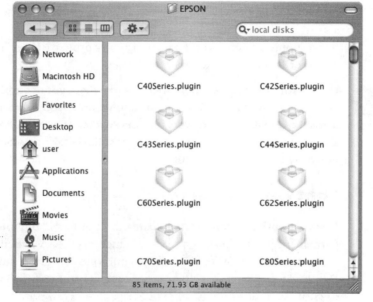

If you plan to print something in Mac OS 9, or even from the Classic environment from within Mac OS X, you'll need to have a Mac OS 9 version of the driver installed in the Extensions folder of the Mac OS 9 System Folder. Some driver installers run in Classic, but others may require you to boot Mac OS 9 (a potential problem if you've got one of the Power Mac G4 models that can't do this).

Raster Image Processing and RIPs

Most programs create type and line-based artwork as *vector graphics*. That is, these images are described as lines and curves that can be scaled to any size. Unlike bitmaps, they are *resolution-independent*—they can be scaled to any size without distortion or loss of clarity. Since almost every printer works by laying down dots, vectors need to be converted into bitmaps before they can be printed.

Drawing applications such as Adobe Illustrator and Macromedia Freehand and Flash use vectors, whereas paint and photo applications such as Adobe Photoshop use bitmaps. Images produced by drawing applications need to be converted into bitmaps before being printed, whereas images produced by paint applications can be printed without the extra conversion step.

A *raster image processor* (or *RIP*) is hardware or software that converts your programs' page descriptions (the descriptions of how text and graphics should be formed on a page) into raster (bitmap) graphics so that a printer can lay down the right dots in the right places on a page. For some printers, such as inkjets, the printer driver handles this conversion. Some PostScript printers have RIPs built into them, however. Higher-end PostScript printers used by professionals often have a separate piece of hardware that sits between the printer and the computer. There are even software-only printer RIPs. The Mac itself uses a kind of RIP to generate its screen images.

 Unless you are involved in high-end work where your comps need to be as close to perfect as possible, you probably don't need to worry about having a PostScript RIP. Printer drivers for non-PostScript printers have gotten so accurate and powerful that they will most likely take care of the work you'd normally count on from a RIP.

Font Downloading

PostScript printers come with a standard set of fonts built into them, stored permanently in the printer's read-only memory (ROM). Being equipped with such a *core set* of fonts serves two purposes. First, it ensures that every PostScript document has a base set of fonts it can use—if you use these fonts to create your documents, any PostScript printer can print them. Second, having fonts built in speeds up the printing process. These core fonts include at least four members each of the Helvetica, Times Roman, and Courier typeface families, plus the Symbol font. Some printers include many more.

But when you want to print a QuarkXPress document, for example, that uses fonts other than these, the fonts need to be sent, or *downloaded*, from the Mac to the printer. This is where the printer's RAM comes into play.

As your Mac prepares to print, it sends the necessary font descriptions to be stored temporarily on the printer. These are erased from RAM once the job is finished printing. This transfer—called *automatic downloading*—can slow down printing (font files can be big, not to mention numerous), especially if your computer is connected to a printer via a slow connection. But the process is automatic, which means that you don't need to think about it.

If you're going to be using some fonts repeatedly, however, you can add them to your printer's memory in such a way that they will stay there until you shut off the printer. This is called *manual downloading*. When you manually download fonts, you pay the transfer-time penalty only once; after that, your printing is much faster because your printer is using fonts that are *on board*. PostScript printers come with a font-downloading utility to take care of this.

If you use a certain group of fonts all the time, it is more efficient to add them to the printer's memory on a long-term basis. Most PostScript printers have additional ROM, and some have optional hard drives, for this purpose. The same utility used for manual downloading will do these tasks as well.

Flavors of PostScript

PostScript was developed and released by Adobe in the mid-1980s, and like so many firsts (world wars, *Rocky* movies, and so on), it needed no suffix until the next version appeared. About seven years later PostScript Level 2 came on the scene, and it was faster and more reliable than the original. Then, in 1998, the current version, PostScript 3, arrived with higher quality, support for 4096 levels of gray (12 bits per pixel), and better PDF output, among other things.

Many people enjoy the aforementioned benefits of PostScript but don't revel in paying the additional costs for PostScript printers, part of which is attributable to Adobe's licensing fees. For that reason, PostScript clones emerged. A PostScript clone is software that conforms to the PostScript standard and impersonates it to varying degrees of success. These days, almost all desktop PostScript printers use Adobe PostScript; PostScript clones are found mostly in the high-end, high-resolution imagesetters used by professional printers and publishers.

Choosing a Printer (JS)

At the most basic level, printers can be divided into two categories: PostScript and non-PostScript. PostScript is the de facto standard for desktop publishing, but most inkjet printers, as well as some laser printers, do not support PostScript. Why should you care? Well, as mentioned earlier, the nice thing about a standard and widespread page-description language such as PostScript is that a file in the PostScript language can be read and output more or less identically by any printer with a PostScript interpreter. Your results are more predictable. If your work eventually involves PostScript output, it's a good idea to use PostScript every step of the way.

If all you want to do is print photographs, basic text documents, Web pages, and the like from your home computer, having a PostScript printer isn't all that important. In fact, for some things, such as printing photographs, a PostScript printer can actually reduce the quality of your output. And a PostScript printer can be expensive—more than twice the cost of an inkjet printer. Here are all the things you need to know about choosing the perfect printer.

Specifications

When buying a printer, you're assaulted by all sorts of numbers meant to impress you and persuade you that one manufacturer's products are better or more advanced than another's. Of course this is nothing new, and there's a very common word for it: marketing. The key to knowing what type of printer you need for a particular function is to understand what the numbers mean, why you should care about them, and how they translate into something that can help you.

DPI

An important factor in accurate printing is the resolution of the printer—that is, the number of dots per inch (dpi) it creates. In theory, the higher the number the better—and you'd better believe that those who market printers to the public are well aware of that. The result is that resolution claims are not always what they seem.

The true resolution of a printer is the number of dots it can lay down side by side, both vertically and horizontally. It used to be that a printer with a resolution of 300 dots per inch (that's 300 dots vertically and 300 dots horizontally, or 90,000 dots per square inch) was considered pretty darned good—and in most cases it is.

Often you'll see printer resolutions specified using two numbers, such as 600 by 300 dpi, but that resolution is not accurate. When you see two different numbers specified for the resolution, it means that the manufacturer is trying to make a printer with (in this example) 300-dpi imaging look as if it is laying down twice as many dots side by side in one direction. In truth, what the printer is really doing is overlapping dots. The overlapping does cause the image to appear smoother, with the individual dots being harder to discern, but the dots themselves are no smaller, as you would expect them to be at higher resolutions. Printer dots are essentially round, not oblong, so the only way a printer can have different resolutions vertically and horizontally is to overlap them.

Many inkjet printers offer resolutions with numbers as high as 5760 by 1440, which may sound too good to be true. And it is: 5760 is four times 1440, so you can judge the degree of overlapping going on. You will hear these very high numbers referred to as *optimized resolutions* or *interpolated resolutions*.

 You can get slightly better results from printers with optimized resolutions, but keep in mind that the lower number denotes the printer's true resolution.

Speed

When it comes to how fast a printer can do its thing—that is, print—the key term is *pages per minute* (ppm). Monochrome laser printers are the fastest desktop printers, spitting out 15–45 pages per minute. With color printers, both laser and inkjet, the numbers are a bit more complicated. Printing a page with color requires that more information, and more ink or toner, has to be laid down on the page. Therefore, with color printers you'll always see two numbers—the higher one for black and white, and the lower one for color.

Inkjet printers typically can print 10–20 ppm in black and white, and 5–10 ppm in color. Color laser printers can manage 20–25 ppm in black and white, and 5–20 ppm in color (**Figure 6.3**). Keep in mind that these are theoretical maximums, often representing the speed at which the printer's rollers can push blank paper. What's on the page also makes a big difference, with graphics printing slower than text.

Figure 6.3

The HP Color LaserJet 3700 printer can print high-quality color documents at speeds up to 16 ppm.

Photo courtesy of HP

 You shouldn't necessarily expect to get the kinds of speeds a printer manufacturer tells you a printer can achieve. Consider speed claims relatively, not as real-life measures.

Memory

Just like your Mac itself, a printer has memory—RAM (random access memory)—inside of it. Known as a *memory buffer*, this high-speed, solid-state memory temporarily stores bits of code to allow your Mac's processor to function most efficiently. The idea is to keep a backlog of information at the ready in the printer so that it can print continuously, without having to start and stop as the print data arrives in dribs and drabs from your Mac.

In addition, your Mac has its own temporary storage for print jobs in the works, where jobs are held in queue and handed off to the printer in sequence. In the printing world, this process is known as *spooling*, with your Mac sending data to the printer's buffer so that the printer can work at its own pace. This process takes place in the background, so your Mac is free to do other things.

Like other buffers (or *caches*), a printer's memory is measured either in kilobytes (KB) or megabytes (MB), 1 MB comprising either 1000 or 1024 KB, depending on whom you ask. Memory numbers for inkjet printers are the least likely specification to be touted in the promotional materials and on the box. In fact, I challenge you to find how much memory most inkjets have; if the number is listed at all, it is usually buried at the end of a laundry list of other specifications. Most inkjets have small buffers of between 32 KB and 64 KB—enough to hold the image data for only a segment of a printed page—while inkjet photo printers have as much as 256 KB.

Memory becomes a much bigger selling point with laser printers, however. If you can't easily find out how much RAM a laser printer has, there's something rotten in the state of Denmark. Laser printers need more RAM than inkjet printers because they typically build a bitmap of the entire page before they begin to print it. And a 300-dpi black-and-white bitmapped image of a letter-size page weighs in at about 8 MB.

Monochrome laser printers usually come with a minimum of 8 MB of RAM, and they may have 16 MB or 32 MB standard. Color laser printers need more RAM to function efficiently, so they usually come with a minimum of 32 MB, and they might come equipped with 64 MB or 128 MB. Unlike inkjets, laser printers are often upgradeable, meaning that you can increase the amount of RAM as you would with your Mac. Where upgrades are possible, maximum amounts of RAM can range from a low of 32 MB all the way up to 512 MB.

In laser printers more memory is useful for several reasons. First, it gives you more room to store fonts (if there are too many fonts in a document, a printer can run out of memory or print with errors). Second, it allows your printer to start processing another page's image while it's printing the current one. It's all about speed.

Types of Printers

Specifications aside, there are many different types of printers out there. Some are meant for printing the occasional document at home, some for printing your digital photos, and some for proofing pages to be professionally printed. Yet others are for printing thousands of pages a month in an office environment, and still others are for creating the films and plates for high-quality offset printing.

When deciding what kind of printer to buy, an important consideration is the cost per page. A page from a cheap printer may cost far more to print than one from an expensive model. How much of a difference this ultimately makes depends, of course, on how many pages you print.

Black-and-white laser printers

As you may have guessed from the name, a laser printer uses a laser as part of the printing process. It works in much the same way as a copy machine. Once your Mac has sent a page to the printer, a laser there produces ("draws") an image of the page on a selenium-coated drum using electrical charges. When the laser has finished, the drum rolls through a powdered ink called *toner*, which sticks to the charged image on the drum. This ink is transferred to the paper using a combination of heat and pressure. The charge is then removed from the drum, and the next page is printed in the same way.

Laser printers can be much larger and more expensive than inkjet printers. For example, laser printers range in cost from $200 for a personal printer to around $2,500 for a networkable laser printer with more memory, more (and larger) paper trays, and other additional features. But any real cost analysis of a printer must include what is referred to as *consumables*: ink and paper. Laser toner cartridges are somewhat expensive (ranging from $50 to $200, depending on your printer model and how many prints the cartridge is designed to provide), but they'll last for thousands of pages without having to be changed, as opposed to short-lived inkjet cartridges. And, also unlike inkjet printers, laser printers can typically use standard copier paper, which is very cost-effective, especially if you buy it in bulk.

A laser printer is an ideal choice for home and business users who mostly want to print pages filled with black-and-white (or grayscale) text and graphics. Laser printers are much faster and much quieter than inkjets, which makes them more suited to a business environment. And because laser printers can easily be attached to a network, they are also a great solution for homes and businesses that want to have just one printer, shared by all the computers.

Color laser printers

A color laser printer works in the same way as a black-and-white laser printer, with the obvious improvement being color printing. In addition to black, color laser printers use cyan, magenta, and yellow toner cartridges; this makes for CMYK four-color processing similar to the kind used in commercial printing. Both types of laser printers are good at producing high-quality text and graphics. Also like monochrome laser printers, color laser printers can easily be networked.

Color laser printers cost more than monochrome laser printers, ranging from $700 to $7,000, depending on features. Color toner costs slightly more, and you need to buy separate cartridges for each color. Color lasers print a tad more slowly, as well. Still, color laser printers are a good option for businesses that need to do some color proofing or that need to print small quantities of color pages, such as presentations. And with the low end of the range at around $700, color lasers are even viable for home users.

Inkjet printers

Although black-and-white laser printers are still widespread, and companies continue to come out with new models, the demand for black-and-white inkjet printers has, shall we say, dried up. For several years, the only inkjet printers on the market have been color. Generally, inkjet printers fall into two categories: non-photo printers, which can still print photos but are designed for more general use; and photo printers, which are designed specifically to print photos but can also print other types of general color documents.

Unlike laser printers, inkjets use liquid inks. The heart of an inkjet printer is the print head assembly. When you print a page, a stepper motor moves the print head—which has more than 100 nozzles for spraying drops of ink—and its attached ink cartridges across the page in steps. Using a *piezoelectric* technology, crystals in each nozzle vibrate when they receive electrical charges, causing ink drops to be sprayed accurately on the paper.

Inkjet printers are very inexpensive, with general-use models ranging between $50 and $150. In fact, they've gotten so inexpensive that they are often given away free when you buy a new Mac from a catalog or online reseller. (Be sure to read the fine print, however, to make sure that any rebates you receive on a printer are applicable for the exact model of Mac you are purchasing.) As you might expect, the more expensive printers are faster, have higher resolutions, and are often smaller and quieter.

Standard inkjet photo printers range in price from $75 to $250; the more-expensive models offer higher-end options such as borderless printing, inks with longer life expectancies, and media readers that are built-in so that you don't even need your Mac to print your digital images. Specialized inkjet photo printers, which are used for color prepress proofing, cost more ($400–$700) but have even more features. For example, **Canon's i9100** ($499.99; www.usa.canon.com) prints extra-wide 13-by-19-inch borderless photos and uses six colors of ink. Epson's more-expensive **Stylus Photo 2200** ($699; www.epson.com) also makes extra-wide 13-inch borderless photos; plus it offers both USB and FireWire connections, uses seven ink colors, and even supports both matte and glossy black inks (**Figure 6.4**). (Glossy inks are better for photos; matte inks provide better coverage and quality on regular paper.)

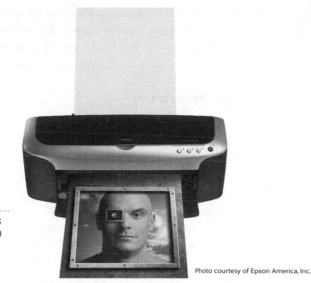

Figure 6.4

Specialized inkjet photo printers like the Epson Stylus Photo 2200 offer high-end features such as the ability to print extra-wide 13-inch borderless photos.

Photo courtesy of Epson America, Inc.

Again, however, the true cost of an inkjet printer lies in the consumables. Manufacturers claim that ink cartridges will last for several hundred pages, but those numbers are usually based on economy modes (that is, reduced resolution) and pages with little ink coverage. Some printers have individual cartridges for each color—typically four, but sometimes six (two cyans and two magentas) or seven (same as six but with two blacks)—which means that you can replace colors as they are used up. However, other printers have only two separate cartridges—one for black, one for color—making you replace all colors at once, which is wasteful.

 For larger photo reproductions, it may be cheaper to have your photos processed traditionally than to print them on your inkjet printer, as they use so much ink.

Paper is another consideration. For best results when printing photos on either general-use or photo inkjet printers, for example, it is important to use the photo paper specifically designed for your printer. Because of the large amount of ink used to print a photograph, standard paper can curl up and inks can bleed because the paper is so absorbent. Photo paper is thick and glossy, and the ink sits on it better, giving you output that looks more like a real photograph. However, it can cost $1 or more per sheet.

If you are buying an inkjet printer mainly to print your digital photos and want the best possible quality and photo-specific features, then a photo-specific inkjet printer is the way to go. But if you want to use an inkjet for a variety of purposes, such as printing letters, school reports, presentations, and photographs, then a general-purpose inkjet will do the job nicely. Either way, most home users will find inkjets to be fun general-purpose printers.

Bubble-jet printers, such as those from Canon and Hewlett-Packard, are basically the same as inkjets, but they use a slightly different printing method, known as *thermal bubble*. Bubble-jet printers use heat to vaporize ink, creating bubbles that push ink out from hundreds of tiny nozzles onto the paper.

High-end color printers

There are several other kinds of printers you aren't as likely to use at home. *Dye-sublimation* (also known as *dye-sub*) printers use a long roll of transparent colored film embedded with solid CMYK dyes. The print head heats up over the film and vaporizes the dyes one at a time, which permeate the glossy paper before solidifying. Because of the way the dye is fused to the paper, the dots' edges are softened, and therefore the result looks more like solid, unscreened printing—ideal for printing photographs (but not very good for printing text or line art). Also, dye-sublimation prints won't fade easily over time. Several photo-printing dye-sub printers are now available in the $300–$400 range.

 Thermal wax and thermal autochrome printers are similar to dye-sublimation printers, only they use a different method of printing. Thermal wax printers use a ribbon with bands of CMYK colored wax and a print head with heated pins. The pins melt the wax, which sticks to the paper and then hardens. Thermal autochrome printers use colored paper; the print head applies different amounts of heat to the paper to activate each colored layer one at a time.

Imagesetters

On the super-high end are imagesetters. It's safe to say that you won't be buying one of these, but if you send something to a service bureau or prepress house, it'll be using one. Basically, an imagesetter uses a laser and a PostScript RIP to expose photographic film (either paper or transparency) or printing plates to be used in four-color offset printing. Imagesetter resolutions can go up to 4000 dpi and beyond. They come in all shapes and sizes, and cost from $5,000 up to more than $60,000.

Connecting Your Printer (DW)

Macs are sociable machines and can speak with a variety of printers using several languages across numerous kinds of networks, but the most common methods that Macs use to converse with printers are USB and Ethernet. USB (Universal Serial Bus) is almost exclusively used for dedicated, direct connections (one Mac, one printer), while Ethernet is mostly used for shared, or networked, connections, which allow more than one Mac to use the same printer. That said, if you use the right software, some USB printers *can* be shared; likewise, Ethernet-capable printers don't necessarily *need* to be shared.

Connecting a Printer Directly to Your Mac

Today, all Macs offer USB connections, with their signature rectangular jack. If you are going to connect just one Mac directly to one printer, you'll most likely use USB. However, you can also directly connect a printer to a Mac using FireWire or by going through a USB hub that sits between your Mac and your printer. (A USB hub works like an electrical power strip: you can use it to connect many USB devices to your Mac.)

Connecting a printer to your Mac via USB (or FireWire or a hub) is very straightforward. To connect a printer using USB, you install the printer's driver software on your Mac, load up the printer with ink and paper (or toner and paper, if it's a laser printer), and run a USB cable from the printer to your Mac. (In the case of a hub, you would run a cable from your Mac to the hub.) Some printers require you to restart your Mac. There's only one catch: USB cables are almost never included when you buy a printer, and these things are not cheap. (I had to pay about $15 for my last one.)

 Don't buy a 3-foot USB cable just to save a couple of bucks! One of these days you're bound to rearrange your furniture, and you'll wish you'd gotten at least an 8-foot cord.

After you install the printer's driver software, set up the printer, and connect the USB cable, the printer's name should be listed in the Printer pop-up menu at the top of the Print dialog, which appears when you tell your Mac to print by pressing ⌘P, selecting Print from the File menu, or clicking the Print icon in your application. If it's not, you may need to use Printer Setup Utility to add the printer (see "Printer Setup Utility," below.) This is plug and play at its simplest.

Connecting a Printer over Ethernet

All Macs have Ethernet capability, but the same can't be said of printers. Many laser printers have Ethernet built in. You can add Ethernet to most laser printers and some inkjets for a premium not to be sneezed at ($200–$400). Many inexpensive inkjets, though, are simply incapable of doing their work over Ethernet. They're considered personal printers and are not meant to be shared.

If your printer has an Ethernet connector, then you simply plug it into an Ethernet-based network, or directly into the Ethernet port on your Mac; no hub or additional networking gear is required. But since Ethernet is set up for networking, there's more involved than just plugging in a cable from your printer to your Ethernet network. You'll also have to use some sort of networking language (or *protocol*) when you print using Ethernet, and Mac OS X offers several options, which we'll discuss in "Printer Setup Utility," below.

Printer Setup Utility (DW)

Figure 6.5

This is the icon for Printer Setup Utility, which in Mac OS X 10.3 takes the place of Print Center in Mac OS X 10.2 and earlier.

In Mac OS X 10.3, Printer Setup Utility (**Figure 6.5**) is where you choose which printer to use (if you have access to more than one), add printers to the list of those available to you, and even adjust or clean your printer. You can find Printer Setup Utility in the /Applications/Utilities folder.

Printer Setup Utility (**Figure 6.6**) replaces Print Center from Mac OS X 10.2. However, unlike Print Center, Printer Setup Utility doesn't also monitor print jobs when they're in progress. In Mac OS X 10.3, the operating system itself performs that function. Each time you set up a printer using Printer Setup Utility, Mac OS X 10.3 creates a Proxy Printer file (a file that identifies your particular printer) and stores it in your home directory (~/Library/Printers). Whenever you print, an icon representing your printer appears in the Dock, and it indicates the status of your print jobs. For more information about monitoring print progress, see "Managing Print Jobs," later in this chapter.

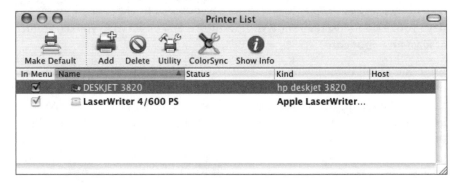

Figure 6.6

Printer Setup Utility lets you add, delete, configure, and get information on printers. Here you can also choose which will be your default printer—the one that your Mac assumes you want to use all the time.

 In Mac OS 9 terms, Printer Setup Utility has the printer-oriented functions of the Chooser.

In a networked office, several Macs and several printers might be scattered about in different rooms. If you'd like to print to that snazzy color laser in the art department but you don't see it listed in Printer Setup Utility, follow these steps.

Adding Printers

If you have only one printer that is connected directly to your Mac, you can pretty much avoid this process unless your printer does not automatically show up in your Printer list in the Print dialog or unless you accidentally delete your printer from the Printer list. In either case, you may want to follow these steps. And in the case of networked printers, you'll need to know a bit about the process of adding printers.

To add a networked printer:

1. Start Printer Setup Utility, which you can do in one of three main ways:

   Open the /Applications/Utilities folder and double-click Printer Setup Utility.

   or

   Open System Preferences by clicking its icon in the Dock or selecting it from the Apple menu, and click the Print & Fax icon; in the Print & Fax pane click the Printing tab, and click the Set Up Printers button.

   or

   Print any document by pressing ⌘P or choosing Print from the File menu, and choose Edit Printer List from the Printer menu.

2. Printer Setup Utility opens. Click the Add icon. At the top of the dialog that appears you'll see a menu listing several types of connections (**Figure 6.7**):

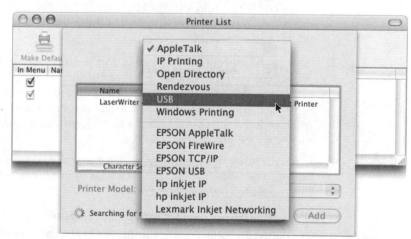

Figure 6.7

You can add many different kinds of networked printers using Printer Setup Utility. Here, you can select the way in which a particular printer is connected to your Mac.

 When you open Printer Setup Utility, the dialog that appears is called **Printer List.**

AppleTalk. This is the most common method for connecting laser printers across a network. Select AppleTalk, and any available AppleTalk printers appear. If you're working in a large office, you may see several AppleTalk zones (such as "Marketing" or "Art Department") listed in a menu; if so, toggle through the zones until the printer you're looking for appears.

IP Printing. IP works a little differently from the other methods; printers don't announce themselves over IP, as they do over AppleTalk. To connect with a printer over IP, whether the printer's in another building or sitting right there on your desk, you need to know the printer's IP address. (Some printers display this on their LCD display panel; often, though, you'll have to get this information from your printer's manual or your network administrator.) Select IP Printing and enter the printer's IP address, and the printer will then appear in the Printer list.

Open Directory. Using Open Directory, you'll see a list of printers that are specifically registered as Directory Services to be used with your computer. You'll use Open Directory printers only if you are on a large network. Just choose Open Directory from the pop-up menu to see a list of printers that are available, and select any you'd like to use.

Rendezvous. Introduced in Mac OS X 10.2, Rendezvous is a networking protocol that allows devices to find each other easily. Select Rendezvous, which will cruise the network looking for printers; choose any Rendezvous printers you want to use from the list.

USB. Pick USB and your Mac will search for all printers connected via USB cables, including directly connected printers and networked USB printers.

Windows Printing. As the name implies, you can choose Windows Printing to scan the network for any networked Windows printers.

"Brand name" printing protocols. In addition to the above methods, you might also see a list of connection methods with names like "Epson AppleTalk," "HP Inkjet IP," or "Lexmark Inkjet Networking." With these methods you can connect to specific printers using AppleTalk, USB, or other standard protocols.

3. Choose the appropriate connection method, depending on the type of printer you're trying to add. If you're not sure what type of printer you're looking for, but you know its name, flip from one menu item to the next until you find it; this could take a little time, depending on how fast your machine is, because your Mac has to perform a new search for printers each time you change the menu.

4. Click the name of the printer you want to add, and then click the Add button. The next time you tell your Mac to print, you'll be able to choose this printer from the Printer list.

 If you select "Share my printers with other computers" in the Print & Fax preferences pane, your printers will automatically appear in Printer Setup Utility and will be available to all users on the network. Printer Setup Utility's Host column will be filled in with the name of the Mac that's doing the sharing.

Deleting Printers

To delete a printer, select its name in Printer Setup Utility and click the Delete icon. Only do this if you're tired of seeing some old printer up there that you never use. Otherwise, having extra printers in this list does absolutely no harm. Also, be careful not to delete a printer when you actually want to delete a print job.

If you want to stop a document from printing, don't delete your printer from the Printer List! Instead, click the Cancel button in the Print status dialog if your Mac is still sending the document to the printer or press ⌘.. You can also click the printer icon in the Dock, and in the dialog that appears click the Stop Jobs icon, or select the name of the print job and click the Delete or Hold icon.

The Default Printer

If you have more than one printer listed in Printer Setup Utility, the printer you added first is considered the *default* printer. This is the one your Mac assumes you want to use when you tell it to print. If you want a different printer to play this role, select that printer's name and click the Make Default icon in the upper left. The name of the printer now appears in bold. There can be only one default printer at a time.

To temporarily print to a different printer, don't use Printer Setup Utility to change the default; there's a much more graceful way:

After you tell your Mac to print a document (by pressing ⌘P or choosing Print from the File menu) and the Print dialog appears, go to the Printer menu at the top of the dialog and choose the printer you'd like to use. This affects only the current print job, and your default printer remains your Mac's first choice.

Getting Info on a Particular Printer

To get information about a printer, highlight its name in Printer Setup Utility and click the Show Info icon (or press ⌘I). The Printer Info window (**Figure 6.8**) has three panes.

Figure 6.8

Click Show Info in Printer Setup Utility to learn a bit about your printer. For inkjets you'll see driver version information, which could come in handy if you run into trouble.

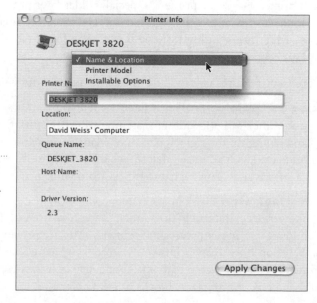

Name & Location. The Printer Name field shows, as you might expect, the printer's name. You can change this to something more personal, if you'd like. The Location field shows the computer that the printer is connected to, or its local zone if the printer is on a network. Oddly, this field can also be changed. But to avoid confusion, you probably shouldn't mess with it.

Printer Model. For non-PostScript printers, such as your average inkjet, the printer's name will be listed in a grayed-out menu, meaning that you can't change anything here. For PostScript printers, such as higher-end laser printers, you can use the Printer Model menu to switch PostScript Printer Descriptions (PPDs), which provide your Mac with a list of your printer's capabilities. You might want to switch PPDs if, for example, you don't have the exact PPD for your printer and want to experiment with PPDs for similar models. (For more on this, see "PPDs," later in the chapter.) The list of PPDs is organized by manufacturer; if you click a manufacturer name, you'll see a list of printer models in the box below.

Installable Options. For many lower-end printers this pane will be blank, but fancier printers will allow you to select different amounts of RAM, tell the computer that double-sided printing *(duplexing)* is possible, and apply other options.

Using a Printer's Utilities

To make basic changes to your printer, select its name in Printer Setup Utility and click the Utility icon. (In Mac OS X 10.2, this is called the Configure button.) What you see when you click this icon depends on which printer you're configuring, because printer manufacturers provide a separate module for each printer. For some printers, especially older laser printers used over a network, the Utility icon will be grayed out, and therefore unavailable. That's because such printers' utility software was written long before Printer Setup Utility was conceived.

Here are some features you might come across in a Utility window:

Printing a sample page. This is handy when you want to easily show off what your printer can do, without searching your hard disk for the perfect image and calling up the right application. Many manufacturers let you click a single button to print an image that shows the printer in its best possible light. This is a good way to gauge what to expect from your printer.

Ink-level indicator. Many inkjet printers will show you graphic images of your ink cartridges, indicating how much ink you've used up (**Figure 6.9**). Keep in mind that in many cases the printer's software is using *estimated* ink levels, based on how many prints you've made, and assuming about one quarter of the page being covered with ink. Your actual mileage may vary, especially if you're fond of printing large blocks of solid colors.

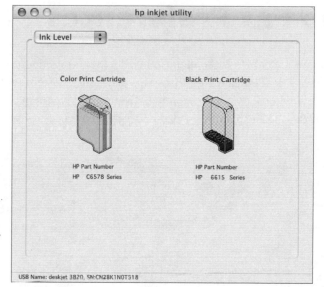

Figure 6.9

The Ink Level pane of the HP Inkjet Utility lets you know approximately when it is time for a new cartridge.

Test pages. Your printer may allow you to print one or more test pages, showing lines, color bars, or letters. If your prints have glitches, these test pages help you figure out if the problem lies in your software or in the printer itself.

Cleaning. Periodically, inkjet print heads need to be cleaned, and you'll know that day has arrived when you see white streaks running through your images. Many inkjets will let you initiate cleaning simply by clicking a single button in the Utility's Cleaning pane. It takes about 2 minutes to clean your inkjet's print heads.

Calibrating. For inkjets, the color and black print heads need to be perfectly aligned, and after several months of printing, or after changing one or both cartridges, this alignment can slip. Many printers allow you to print out a pattern from the Utility window, and you can calibrate the print heads by looking at the image and making selections in the pane based on what you see.

Company contact info. Many manufacturers also provide buttons in the Utility window that take you to tech support or registration sections of the company's Web site.

ColorSync

When you click the ColorSync icon in Printer Setup Utility, it opens the ColorSync utility, which lives in the /Applications/Utilities folder. ColorSync is a system for controlling the color consistency between monitors, scanners, and, of course, printers. Using ColorSync, you can change the profile that your printer uses to mix colors.

Print and Fax Preferences

With Mac OS X 10.3, Apple introduced a System Preferences pane called Print & Fax (**Figure 6.10**). To see this pane, click System Preferences in the Dock or choose System Preferences from the Apple menu, and then click Print & Fax. The pane is divided between preferences for printing and preferences for faxing.

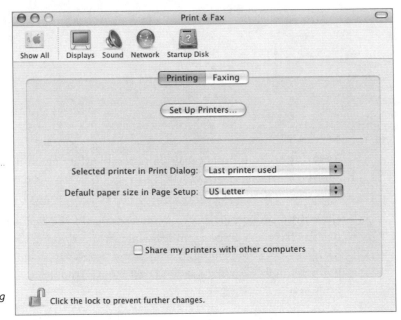

Figure 6.10

Mac OS X 10.3's new Print & Fax preferences pane gives you an easy way to control printing options and introduces a new feature—faxing—into the core of the operating system.

Printing Preferences

Most likely, you'll spend the majority of your printing setup time using Printer Setup Utility or tweaking detailed settings in an application's Page Setup dialog. Still, there are several printing preferences that can save you time for your most common printing chores.

Set Up Printers. This button calls up Printer Setup Utility, which was introduced with Mac OS X 10.3. The ins and outs of Printer Setup Utility are described in "Printer Setup Utility," above.

Selected printer in Print Dialog. The printer you choose from this menu will become the default printer in the Print dialog—that is, the printer that your Mac assumes you want to use when you issue the Print command. If you don't select a specific printer from this menu but instead choose "Last printer used," your Mac will remember which printer it used the last time and use that one as the default in the Print dialog. Using the preferences pane to pick a default printer overrides any default printers that you selected using Printer Setup Utility.

The last option you can choose from this menu is Edit Printer List, which calls up Printer Setup Utility.

Default paper size in Page Setup. Page Setup is where you prepare your pages for printing, including choosing to shrink or enlarge your print and selecting the paper you'd like to print on (see "Using Page Setup," later in the chapter). From this menu, you can choose the paper size that Page Setup will assume by default: letter size (8½ by 11 inches), legal size (8½ by 14 inches), or a variety of other standard sizes, including envelopes.

Share my printers with other computers. When this option is checked, other computers in your network will be able to connect to these printers by selecting them in Printer Setup Utility.

Faxing Preferences

It's important to remember that a fax is not a normal text file. It's an image of a page, a kind of digital photostat. This means that fax files are (a) big, like black-and-white photo files, and (b) not editable. If you want to reuse the text in a fax file, you have to use optical character recognition (OCR) software to translate the image of the text into live, editable text.

The options in the Faxing preferences are pretty straightforward (**Figure 6.11**).

Figure 6.11

Using the Faxing tab of the Print & Fax preferences pane, you can set up your Mac and printer to behave like a virtual fax machine.

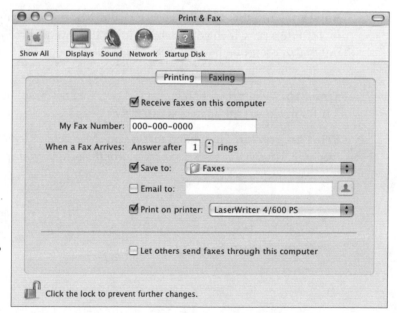

Receive faxes on this computer. This is the most important option in the Faxing preferences. Click this to enable fax receiving, but keep a few things in mind:

- You need a modem to send or receive faxes. Most Macs have modems, but some don't, usually because the previous owner removed it.

- It's best to have a dedicated phone line for faxing; otherwise you can't use the modem or your phone when you're faxing.

- If you do use the same phone line for faxes that you use for voice, only turn this option on when you've spoken with the person who is sending the fax, and you know a fax is on its way. If you leave this option on all the time, your Mac will try to answer all your voice calls as well.

 The very best setup for handling all your communication needs is to have a dedicated phone line for faxing and a separate DSL or cable connection for accessing the Internet. Then you can leave "Receive faxes on this computer" on at all times.

My Fax Number. Enter either your telephone number (if you're using just one line) or your dedicated fax number.

When a Fax Arrives. Here you choose the number of rings your Mac will wait before picking up a fax.

 If you use your Mac fax line for your phone as well, set the number of rings before the fax picks up so that incoming fax calls are answered before the answering machine picks up.

Save to. When this option is checked, your Mac will save any received faxes in TIFF format, which you can open using Preview, the free image-viewing utility that comes with Mac OS X. Using the menu to the right, you can specify where you'd like to store those faxes.

Email to. When this option is checked, received faxes will be emailed—in TIFF format—to the address you specify.

Print on printer. This option makes your Mac behave most like a fax machine. Received faxes will emerge from the printer you specify here.

PPDs (DW)

First, a bit of background. In Mac OS 9, printer drivers (the software that tells your printer what and how to print) appeared as icons in the Chooser; Macs shipped with a variety of drivers that would quickly crowd the Chooser. To save space and to cut down on the confusion of having too many drivers, Apple and Adobe Systems created a single driver that would address all PostScript printers in Mac OS 9. So how did the driver distinguish between one printer and another, each with its slightly different features? It did so with the help of PostScript Printer Description files, or PPDs. Each PostScript printer has its own PPD, but you can use a generic PPD to address just about any PostScript printer. Also, you can use a different printer's PPD, and you'll still be able to print, since you're using the same driver. If you don't have the printer's specific PPD installed, however, any of the printer's fancier features, such as double sided printing, will be unavailable.

In Mac OS X 10.3, printer drivers keep a low profile in Printer Setup Utility. They don't have their own icons, and they don't prominently announce their names or version numbers. They run, but more or less in the background, letting Mac OS X provide the interface. However, PostScript printers in Mac OS X still need PPDs in order to access those fancy features.

Mac OS X ships with many PPDs, and they're stored in the /Library/Printers folder. To find specific PPDs, follow this path: PPDs/Contents/Resources/ en.lproj. The "en" in en.lproj stands for English. If you'd like your printer to communicate with you using a different language, simply choose another PPD from inside the folder with your preferred language folder.

Installing PPDs

If your Mac doesn't have a PPD for your particular printer, check the manufacturer's Web site. If you still can't find what you're looking for, try Adobe's PostScript printer drivers Web page (www.adobe.com/support/downloads/ product.jsp?product=pdrv&platform=mac); it offers a cornucopia of free PPDs, organized by vendor.

To install a PPD, just place it in the en.lproj folder (/Library/Printers/PPDs/ Contents/Resources/en.lproj). You may notice that the PPD files are all compressed, and have the .gz extension. Don't worry about that; the Mac OS can use them even if they're compressed, and if you place uncompressed files in this folder, they will work as well.

PPDs are text files, so the same file will work for both Mac OS 9 and Mac OS X, but one PPD can't be used in both Mac OS X and the Classic environment simultaneously. You'll need to place a copy in the System Folder for Mac OS 9 as well as a copy in the /Library/Printers folder for Mac OS X.

To switch between different PPDs for the same printer—for example, if you don't have the printer's specific PPD, you might want to experiment with a PPD for a similar printer—highlight the printer's name in Printer Setup Utility and select Show Info from the Printers menu (or press ⌘Ⓘ). Select Printer Model from the pop-up menu at the top, and use the second menu to display a list of PPDs organized by manufacturer (**Figure 6.12**).

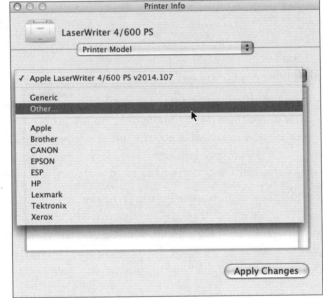

Figure 6.12

Select Show Info from within Printer Setup Utility to find out which PPD you have installed for your printer, and swap another for it, if you like.

When you use this menu to select PPDs, you're pulling them from the collection that Apple loaded onto your system plus any that you have added. To use a PPD that's stored in another spot on your disk (such as one you recently downloaded), choose Other and then browse to select the file. To use a one-size-fits-all PPD, choose Generic.

Printing Your Files (DW)

Most applications assume that if you're going to print something, you're going to use letter-size paper (8½ by 11 inches), with the page oriented vertically, and that you want the printed document to be the same size as the file in your Mac. Those are fair assumptions, but if you have a different type of page in mind, the place to inform your Mac is the Page Setup dialog, which you'll find in your application's File menu.

 Changes you make in the Page Setup dialog affect only the document you're currently working on. However, there's one notable exception to this rule: most changes made in a Web browser's Page Setup dialog affect all browser windows and remain in effect until you quit the browser.

Using Page Setup

The Page Setup dialog has four panes, and you switch from one to another using the Settings pop-up menu (**Figure 6.13**). A fifth selection, Save As Default, lets you save any changes you make as the default settings in each of the panes. Here's a bit about each of the panes.

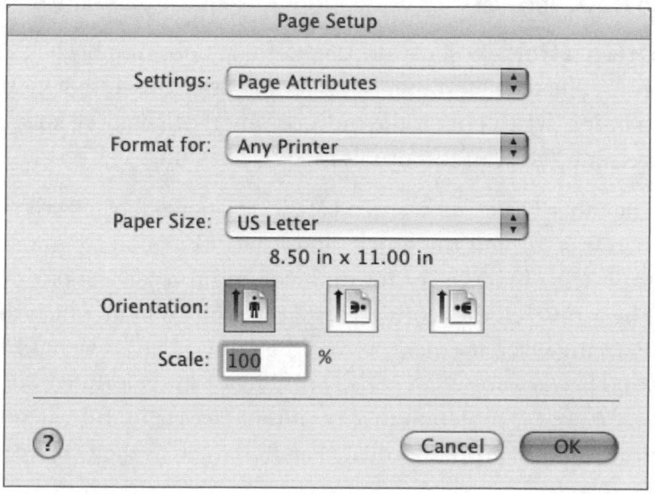

Figure 6.13

In the Page Setup dialog you decide on the basic options for your document, such as paper size, printing orientation, and image size.

> **Page Setup**
>
> Settings: [Page Attributes ▾]
>
> Format for: [Any Printer ▾]
>
> Paper Size: [US Letter ▾]
> 8.50 in x 11.00 in
>
> Orientation: [↑☺] [↑▣] [↑◃]
>
> Scale: [100] %
>
> (?)   (Cancel) (OK)

Page Attributes

This is the main pane of Page Setup; from here you can choose paper size, page orientation, and page scale (that is, the degree to which you want to enlarge or shrink your image).

Format for. This pop-up menu lets you pick any printer that you have available and also lets you access any special formats the printer offers. For example, if you're lucky enough to have a wide-format printer, which can print on tabloid-size paper (11 by 17 inches), then choosing this type of printer in the "Format for" menu adds 11 by 17 as a paper-size choice in the Paper Size menu.

If you choose Edit Printer List from the "Format for" menu, your Mac opens up Printer Setup Utility, where you can add, delete, or get information (such as name and location) about available printers.

You can also choose Any Printer from the "Format for" menu. If you do, the Paper Size pop-up menu shows a more-limited list of standard paper sizes.

Paper Size. This pop-up menu shows a list of common paper sizes that your printer is capable of handling. You can narrow or expand your choices using the "Format for" menu. In the list, you may see one or more custom paper sizes, such as US Letter (8½ by 11 inches) and US Legal (8½ by 14 inches), and several standard envelope sizes. For information about adding or removing custom paper sizes from this list, see "Custom Paper Size," below.

 You may wonder what the difference is between US Letter and US Letter Small, since they both measure 8½ by 11 inches. US Letter tells the printer to use as much of the paper as it possibly can, whereas US Letter Small tells the printer to leave one-half inch of nonprintable area around the edge of the paper.

Orientation. To set your page's orientation, simply click one of the three icons. The first icon represents *portrait* orientation, in which the page is taller than it is wide. This is the most common orientation, so most applications are set up to print in portrait mode by default.

The other two icons represent *landscape* orientations, in which the page is wider than it is tall. You might use landscape orientation for graphics projects such as posters or menus, or for multicolumn spreadsheet or database printouts. The arrows on the icons represent the direction in which the document will be facing when it emerges from the printer: left or right. Whichever direction you choose, you won't see any difference in the printed document; the ability to choose the direction that a printout faces is useful when you want your printed pages properly collated and oriented as they emerge from the printer.

Scale. Select a value less than 100% to shrink the printed image or greater than 100% to enlarge it. Shrinking or enlarging an image won't affect the original file or its size, just the printed size, so it's a handy way to create a large version of a small image for a presentation, for example, or to shrink a large graphic to fit on one page. Type and line art usually scale gracefully, but bitmapped images may lose clarity or detail when enlarged. Scaling usually slows down printing.

Custom Paper Size

In the Custom Paper Size pane of the Page Setup dialog (**Figure 6.14**), you can create new paper sizes that will appear as choices in the Paper Size menu of Page Setup's Page Attributes pane.

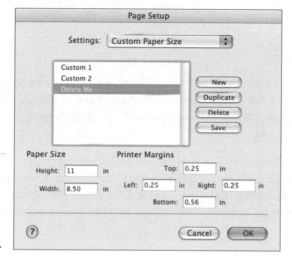

Figure 6.14

Page Setup's Custom Paper Size pane is the place to go if you're designing your document for a specific, non-standard paper size.

To create a custom paper size:

1. Click the New button, and a new paper size appears in the Custom Paper Size pane, bearing the name Untitled. Change this name to whatever you'd like.

2. Under Paper Size, the fields for Height and Width show the most common dimensions for the printer you're currently using. Change these to whatever you'd like.

3. Under Printer Margins, the fields for Top, Bottom, Left, and Right show the most common margins for your printer. Most laser printers will show .25 all around, but full-bleed printers (ones that let you print right to the edge of the paper) will show 0. Anything outside of the printer's margins will not print.

 If you set printer margins here, remember that you can almost always set a wider margin in your document. You can't however, set a narrower margin (that is, you can't print something closer to the edge of the paper) than the printer margin will allow. For this reason, it's best to set a very narrow (small) printer margin. A quarter inch is always a safe bet, unless you know that your printer can handle *full-bleed* printing (edge to edge), in which case you can enter zero.

4. Click Save.

5. To create a new custom paper size based on an old one, click the old one to highlight it and then click Duplicate. A copy of the new custom paper size is added to the list, with the word *copy* appended to the name. You can rename this anything you like.

6. To use your new custom paper size, change Page Setup's Settings menu back to Page Attributes, and select your new custom paper size from the Paper Size pop-up menu. Custom paper sizes appear at the bottom of the list and are separated from standard paper sizes by a thin line.

7. To delete a custom paper size, go back to the Custom Paper Size pane, select the size you want to delete, and then click Delete.

Printing at the Margins

Often, you can print more on a page than the manufacturer of your printer says you can. My Apple LaserWriter 4/600 (a slow but dependable workhorse released in the early '90s) says that it needs one-quarter inch on the left and right margins, but it can actually print up to one-sixteenth inch from the left side of the page.

To test your printer's true limitations, create a document (using any word processor) with a 0 margin for all sides of the page: top, bottom, left, and right. Then create three lines of repeating numbers across the top (01234567890123 ...) and three lines across the bottom, and print it out. You'll see where the characters are cut off, and this represents your printer's true limitations.

Application-specific settings

Page Setup's Settings menu might also give you an option that bears the name of whatever application you're currently using. Each application puts different options into these panes. Here are a few of the kinds of options you're likely to find:

Custom page options. Generally, custom page options perform much the same function as the Custom Paper Size setting. To avoid confusion and possible errors, it's best to control custom paper sizes from the Custom Paper Size pane of Page Setup. You can leave application-specific custom page options unchanged, and any changes you make using the Custom Paper Size setting will still go into effect.

Separations. Desktop-publishing applications such as QuarkXPress and Adobe InDesign give you the option of printing each main color (cyan, magenta, yellow, and black) on a separate sheet. This is used when preparing documents for service bureaus (see "Preparing Files for Remote Output," later in this chapter).

Resolution. When a laser printer is your default printer, some applications give you the option of printing at a lower resolution in order to save toner. If the default printer is an inkjet, the option to change resolution may be unavailable, but you can always change the print quality (using a scale with levels like Good, Better, and Best) in the Print dialog.

Summary

This option in the Page Setup's Settings menu simply shows—in one window—all of the Page Setup settings (**Figure 6.15**). You can scroll through it, but that's about it; you can't select any of the text, and, ironically, you can't even print it.

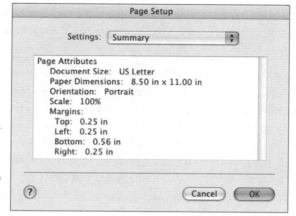

Figure 6.15

Page Setup's Summary screen shows you all of your print settings in a single panel. Just don't try to print it!

The Print Dialog

When you choose Print from an application's File menu, click the Print icon in the application's toolbar, or press ⌘P, your pages don't immediately start emerging from the printer, as your Mac needs a little more information from you before it can tell the printer what to do. So when you issue the Print command, you're greeted by the Print dialog (**Figure 6.16**).

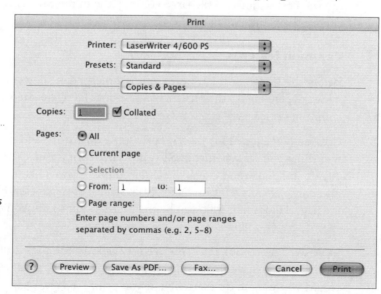

Figure 6.16

From Mac OS X's Print dialog you can change the number of copies you want to print, choose which pages to print, or simply click Print if you're ready to roll. In Mac OS X 10.3, you can even send a fax from here.

The Print dialog looks a little different for every printer you use. Printers that share the same driver, such as many PostScript laser printers, have identical Print dialogs, and inkjets that are very similar might also have identical Print dialogs, differing only in the printer's name displayed.

Standard features

All Print dialogs have a couple of standard features, regardless of the printing technology your printer uses, what company made it, or how it's connected to your Mac.

Printer. At the top of every Print dialog is the same Printer pop-up menu with the same list of available printers as that in Printer Setup Utility and the Page Setup dialog. The Printer menu shows the default printer—the one that's set up as your Mac's first main printer—but you can select a different printer from the menu just for this one time. If you don't see the printer you want listed, but you know it's there because your buddy just used it and you share the same network, choose Edit Printer List from the Printer menu. Printer Setup Utility will open, and you can use it to add printers.

Presets. This is a wonderful time-saving feature. After you've made all the changes you want in the Print dialog, but before you click the Print button, select Save As from the Presets pop-up menu and then give your settings a name. Thereafter, that name will appear in the Presets menu, and the next time you choose it from the menu, everything will be set up just as it was when you saved it. This way, when you want, for example, to print quick, low-resolution thumbnails on the laser printer, just select Quick 'n' Dirty (or whatever you want to call it) from the Presets menu. When you're ready to use the best settings on the six-color inkjet with the expensive paper, just choose the Grand Finale settings.

Common features

Below the Printer and Presets menus is a menu that shows slightly different items, depending on the printer you're using. Here are a few of the more-common options:

Copies & Pages. This pane is fairly self-explanatory, and most likely it's the first thing you see when you tell your Mac to print. Enter the number of copies you'd like; and check the Collated box if you'd like the pages collated into complete sets (if it isn't already checked), or uncheck it if you want all the page 1s together, followed by the page 2s, and so on. You can opt to print specific pages, a range of pages, or all the pages.

Layout. The Layout pane (**Figure 6.17**) allows you to print two small pages instead of one normal-size one, or even up to 16 very small pages. Now why would you want to do that? Well, if you print *2-up* (two per page), most of the time you can still read the pages, and it saves paper and toner or ink when you're printing long documents or many drafts. Or sometimes you might want to see a basic layout of all your pages.

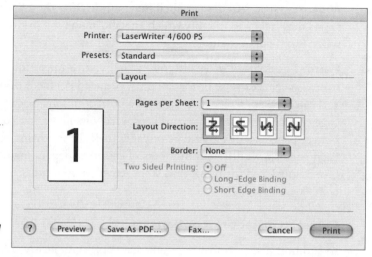

Figure 6.17

From the Layout pane of the Print dialog you can choose to print multiple pages on a single sheet and decide how those page images should be arranged.

Output Options. When you check the box next to Save as File, your document won't be printed on paper; instead it will be printed to a file. This means that all the pictures in your file will be drawn, and all the type will be rendered, but in an electronic form. (For more information on this topic, see "Printing to Disk," later in this chapter.) If you have a PostScript printer selected, PostScript will be one of the options listed in the Format pop-up menu; otherwise, the only option will be PDF. PDF files can be opened by Adobe Reader, Mac OS X's Preview, and other applications, whereas PostScript files can be opened only by PostScript printer utilities or raster image processor (RIP) software, which is specifically created for reading PostScript files. In either case, your file can be printed without the application used to create it.

Summary. As with the Page Setup dialog, Summary displays a list of all your settings, which you can view but not change. (If you click Print, you won't print the Summary, but instead you'll print your document.)

Common PostScript print options

The menu options we've listed here vary from printer to printer, but since many PostScript printers use the same driver, many have the same options. In addition to the standard ones listed above, you'll most likely see these:

Error Handling. In the event of a PostScript error (a particularly annoying event, since it prevents your document from printing), you can choose to get either a detailed report on the error or just the simple phrase "A PostScript

Error Has Occurred." For more information on PostScript errors, see "Troubleshooting," later in this chapter.

 When selecting PostScript Error Handling, opt for the detailed report. It may not always help, but then again it just might. "Offending Command" messages may help you identify which specific image the printer was processing when it ran out of memory.

Paper Feed. From this pane you can tell your printer either to pull paper from a specific cassette or to wait until you feed it a piece of paper manually. You can even opt to have the first page print from one place and the following pages to print from another; this is especially handy if, say, you want to print a cover page on a different type of paper than the following pages. The Paper Feed pane shows different numbers of cassettes, depending on your printer. Use manual feed for heavy card stock, envelopes, or other kinds of paper that won't work with cassettes.

Common inkjet print options

In addition to the standard options that come with nearly all Print dialogs, many inkjet drivers offer these or similar options:

Paper Type/Quality. This is a very important pane for inkjets. All inkjet printers let you select from a variety of paper types. It's important to match the paper as closely as possible; don't tell the printer to expect photo paper when you've got regular copier-quality paper in the printer. Otherwise, your vacation photo from the Bahamas will come out looking like a Rorschach test.

All inkjets allow you to print at a few different quality settings. As you go up on the quality scale, your printer uses more ink (because higher quality means more information—and more dots—on the page), and your pages take longer to print. Some inkjets also allow you to select different color profiles from the Print dialog, and this changes the way your printer mixes colors.

Printer Driver Information. Some inkjets also provide a pane that lists the name and version of the driver you're using. There isn't much you can do with this information, but it might come in handy if something goes awry with the printer and you need to make a call to the manufacturer's technical-support line.

Standard buttons

Along the bottom of the Print dialog you'll see a standard set of buttons. Here's what they do:

Question mark. As always, this button calls up the Help utility that pertains to whatever dialog you found it in.

Preview. This opens Preview, an application that can open and view PDFs, TIFFs, and other graphics files. Here, the application turns your document into a PDF so that you can see onscreen how it's likely to appear when printed. For more information on creating PDFs, see "Printing to Disk," below.

Save As PDF. This "prints" your file to disk in PDF format (see "Printing to Disk," below).

Fax. New to Mac OS X 10.3, this option lets you send any document as a fax. Enter the fax number, note any cover-page information you'd like to add, and click the Fax button (**Figure 6.18**).

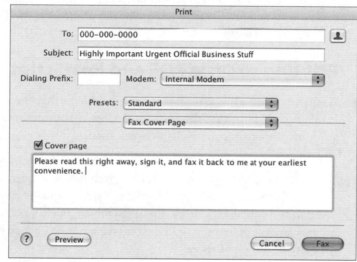

Figure 6.18

Mac OS X 10.3's fax dialog lets you fax any document you have on your Mac and specify separate fax cover-sheet information as well.

Cancel. Closes the Print dialog, thereby canceling the Print command and ignoring any changes you've made in the Print dialog.

Print. Need I say more?

Printing to Disk (DW)

Printing, as we said at the beginning of this chapter, involves translating bits of computer code into bits of visible black or colored dots on a physical page. But printing doesn't always involve putting marks on paper; it's also possible to print to a digital file—a process called *printing to disk*. If this sounds to you like the Save As command, where you save a copy of a file in a different file format, you're right—it is. But a file that's been printed to disk has a few special characteristics:

Platform-independent. You can open files that have been printed to disk on many computers, regardless of which operating system that computer is running. You can also print these files on paper even if you don't have the application used to create them.

Stable. That is, all the elements of the file, including the appearance of type, the shades of colors, the textures of graphics, and so on, look exactly the same when viewed on any computer. You never need to worry, for example, whether your intended recipients have the proper fonts installed on their computers.

Set in stone. Files that have been printed to disk can't be directly edited or changed in any way. Sure, you can often copy some of the information and paste it into another file for editing, but the printed file itself can't be edited without special tools.

Printing to Disk: PDF and PostScript

When you print a file to disk, you have two file format choices: PDF and PostScript. Although Adobe Systems pioneered both of these formats, there are some important differences between them.

PDF files are by far the most commonly used. All you need to open, view, and print these files is a copy of Adobe's free Adobe Reader, which you can download at www.adobe.com. Since there are versions of Adobe Reader for every flavor of Mac, Windows, Linux, Symbian, Pocket PC, Palm, and many other operating systems, any PDF you create can be opened by the vast majority of computer users.

PostScript uses a system of mathematical formulas, rather than dots, to describe objects on a page, and it does so in such a way that a PostScript shape will always be printed at the highest resolution (number of dots per inch) that a printer can handle. But PostScript files aren't really meant for use by the average Joe. Instead they're meant for *printers* (the machines) and *printers* (the professionals who run those machines). A few applications can open and view PostScript files, such as some PostScript printer utilities and RIP software. In general, however, applications that work with PostScript files are designed to send such files to printers (the machines) rather than to users for viewing.

 If you need to view a PostScript file but don't have an application that can open it directly, you can always use Preview to convert it to a PDF and view it that way.

PostScript files are quite *verbose,* and the language they're written in is very detailed, so they tend to take up much more disk space than PDF files. The PDF format, by comparison, has been designed to be more compact, reducing repeating elements, for example, to shorthand expressions rather than spelling them out every time they appear. PDF files are also *normalized*, which means that odd PostScript locutions that some applications may use (the equivalent of a bad foreign accent) are standardized for more-reliable output.

If you want to print to a device-independent file that most people can easily read and print, go PDF. If you want to create a file to be professionally printed, ask your printer (the person) what he or she prefers. Many will request a PostScript file, but depending on the job, some will prefer PDF (precisely because it's been normalized); in either case you'll see no difference in the printed file.

PDF

Printing to a PDF file is ridiculously easy in Mac OS X 10.2 and later. There are three ways to do it, even though the results are exactly the same. Here's a rundown on the three methods:

- **Save As PDF.** From the Print dialog, simply click Save As PDF, name your file, choose where to save it, and click Save. All the fonts used in the document will be included in the PDF file, and all images will appear in the same resolution at which they were created.

- **Save as File.** From the Print dialog, choose Output Options from the third pop-up menu, check the Save as File box, choose PDF from the Format pop-up menu, and click Save (**Figure 6.19**). Once again, name your file and choose where to save it.

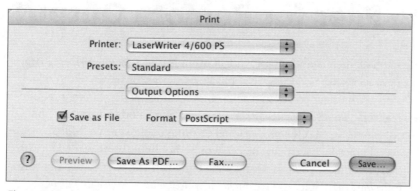

Figure 6.19

If you want to print to a digital file instead of a piece of paper, open the Print dialog and either click the Save As PDF button or select Output Options from the third pop-up menu, check the Save as File box, and select PostScript or PDF from the Format menu.

- **Preview.** From the Print dialog, click the Preview button. You'll then see your document onscreen. Choose Save As from the File menu, name your file, and choose where to save it.

By default, Preview shows you an approximation of what you would see if you printed your file using the printer selected at the top of the Print dialog; hence the name Preview. That's why the Soft Proof box at the bottom of the Preview screen is checked by default. So, for example, if your selected printer is a monochrome laser printer and your file is in color, Preview will display your file in grayscale. However, if you do a Save As while Soft Proof is checked, the resulting digital file will look exactly like the original no matter what type of printer you have.

PostScript

Printing to a PostScript file is also ridiculously easy in Mac OS X 10.2 and later. In the Print dialog, choose Output Options from the third pop-up menu, check the Save as File box, choose PostScript from the Format pop-up menu, and click the Save button. Give your PostScript file a name, choose where to save it, and you're done.

 To see PostScript listed as an option in the Format menu, you must have a PostScript printer selected as the default. If you don't have an actual PostScript printer, you can add a virtual one: using Printer Setup Utility, add an IP printer with the printer address "localhost" (without quotes).

Preparing Files for Remote Output

People hand off their work to professional printers when they're printing large numbers of copies, they need special binding services, or they need to match colors with near-perfect precision. Each printing company has different requirements regarding PostScript files, PDF files, and files in other formats. The subject of preparing files for professional printing could very well fill an entire book several times heavier than the one you're holding. But if you take your work to professionals, you can save yourself anguish and money by adhering to the following principle: *Ask them what they need, and then give it to them.*

Every printer is a little bit different, and most of them truly want you to be happy with your proof, or trial print. If you have to do ten proofs to get something you like, you'll probably go somewhere else next time (and the printer may not be wild about seeing you again, either). That said, there are a few requirements that most printers share, and the more you know about the process, the better you'll fare when you get that first proof. The following are a few basic principles to keep in mind.

Turn In the Right Kind of PDF

In most cases, your printer will not want to use a PDF created using Save As PDF from the Print dialog. Files created this way are fine for the Web, but since they embed the document's fonts in each individual file, they may take up far more disk space than they need to and, therefore, take more time to print. Also, professional printers like to (and need to) have precise control over fonts. So they don't like it when two versions of one font (the version stored in the file and the version stored in the printer) are fighting over the same file.

So what's a graphic designer to do? Both QuarkXPress 6 and Adobe InDesign 2.0 offer sophisticated PDF-export capabilities, giving you control over font embedding, image compression, and other features. But the safest and best bet for the pro, in terms of creating a PDF, is to use Adobe Acrobat Distiller, an application bundled into **Acrobat 6.0 Professional** ($449; www.adobe.com) that's specifically geared toward preparing files for professional output. Here are a few tips for using Acrobat Distiller:

1. Acrobat Distiller can embed all fonts in a document, or just a subset of them. So check with your printer to see what he or she prefers. Subsets take up less space—they embed only the characters from a font that are actually used in the document.

2. When creating your final PDF for printing, experiment with various compression schemes for each of your graphic types to see what gives you the best compression without sacrificing image quality. Acrobat 6 offers compression using JPEG2000, which has a reputation for providing excellent compression with very high quality.

3. Use the Separations Preview feature to check for trapping—the way in which adjoining blocks of colors line up when printed. For example, poorly trapped text on a background color will show cracks where the color of the paper peeks through. Using the Separations Preview, you can find such problems before seeing your first proof and make necessary changes.

4. Use the Loupe tool to zoom around your document and check for precise alignment and other details that usually don't show up until the first proof.

5. Use the program's built-in preflighting tools to anticipate any problems (and fix them). Printers will love you for doing this.

6. When the file is compete, run the Audit Space Usage command to alert you to places where you can trim unnecessary fat.

Switch to CMYK

Professional printers don't care about RGB, a color model designed for monitors, scanners, and cameras that blends red, green, and blue light to create a spectrum of colors. Professional printers speak the language of CMYK, a color model that creates a spectrum of colors using cyan, magenta, yellow, and black inks. So convert all your files to CMYK using your image-editing or page-layout application. If you have some RGB images that, for whatever reason, you can't convert, some printers require you to identify those files beforehand.

Turn In Well-Prepared Page-Layout Files

Here are a few tips for preparing files using QuarkXPress or Adobe InDesign, the two most popular desktop-publishing packages:

- Use the Collect for Output feature. Both applications are savvy enough to recognize all the supporting files that most professional printers need when it comes to imaging digital files—including fonts—and they put everything into one simple folder that you can hand off to the printer.

- Proof your file using a color swatch. Pantone makes a series of these, and they're extremely useful because the color you see on the screen is going to be very different from that in your printed output.

- Use filename extensions. Yes, most service bureaus use Macs, but a good percentage of them use complex systems that might misinterpret a file if it doesn't have a visible extension.

Managing Print Jobs (DW)

Figure 6.20

When you tell your Mac to print, a printer icon such as this one appears in the Dock.

Seconds after you click the Print button in the Print dialog, you should see a small progress bar counting off the pages of your document, followed by the sound of your printer's motor revving up. (If it's a long document with lots of images, it might take quite a few more seconds.) You may also notice that a tiny icon of your printer appears in the Dock, with a page icon alongside it (**Figure 6.20**). Once a print is in progress, clicking this icon brings up a dialog that gives you a few options for monitoring, stopping, or otherwise controlling your print jobs (**Figure 6.21**). Select the print job that you want to affect to activate the following options:

Change the priority. For any job that has yet to be printed, you can assign a higher priority, to bump it ahead in the line by clicking the Status column heading.

Hold/resume a job. Click the Hold icon to keep a document from printing temporarily, and click the Resume icon to continue where it left off.

Delete a job. If you just discovered a typo but you already clicked Print, just delete the job.

Stop/Start Jobs. Click the Stop Jobs icon to stop the printer from printing anything and everything. When a printer has been stopped in this manner, you'll see an exclamation mark alongside its name in the Print dialog. If you try to print to a printer that's been stopped, you'll get an error message. This message will tell you that you can reverse the Stop command to have all printing continue, or add the current print job to the queue. To manually tell the printer to continue to do its job, just click the Start Jobs icon.

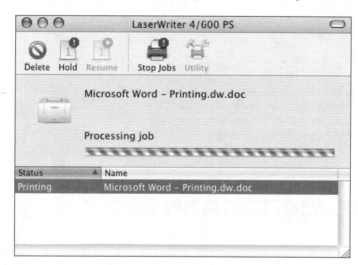

Figure 6.21

When a document is being printed, you can click the printer's icon in the Dock to open a dialog where you can delete, pause, or resume jobs, or switch the priority of jobs lined up in the queue waiting to be printed.

 After you issue the Print command and the printer's Dock icon shows that it has received the job, you can close the file or even quit the program; the printer has everything it needs to print the document.

If the printer is having a problem, such as a software error or a lack of paper, a dialog appears telling you what the printer needs. If the printer icon in the Dock shows a red stop sign and exclamation mark, it means that all current printing has been stopped (**Figure 6.22**).

Figure 6.22

When the printer icon in your Dock looks like this, it means that printing has been temporarily stopped.

Creating a Desktop Printer

If you're familiar with Mac OS 9, then you're no stranger to the concept of desktop printers. They disappeared in the early versions of Mac OS X, but they've returned in Mac OS X 10.3. Desktop printers are icons that sit on the Desktop (or anywhere else you like) and represent printers that you have available (**Figure 6.23**). If you drag a document onto a desktop printer, the appropriate application opens and the Print dialog appears. To create a desktop printer in Mac OS X 10.3, do the following:

1. Highlight the name of a printer in Printer Setup Utility.
2. Choose Create Desktop Printer from the Printers menu.
3. Tell your Mac what you'd like to name your desktop printer and where you'd like to put it.
4. Click Save.

Figure 6.23

With Mac OS X 10.3, you can create desktop printers that have icons like these. Notice the tiny arrows: desktop printers in Mac OS X 10.3 are actually aliases of the printer icons that appear in the Dock when a print is in progress.

Printer Maintenance (DW)

Printers respond better and last longer when they're well maintained. So at the very minimum it's good to keep them as free of dust as possible by covering them up when you're not using them. And because printers contain a number of delicately synchronized parts, it's especially important to keep them clean; you certainly don't want to store your printer by the kitchen stove within range of a splattering pot of spaghetti sauce. Beyond those obvious considerations, here are a few other ways to keep your printer in tip-top shape:

Use the manufacturer's ink or toner. You might be enticed into buying generic ink cartridges rather than your printer manufacturer's brand, or you might even experiment with kits that help you inject ink into used cartridges. The problem with both of these strategies is that should you encounter any kind of printer malfunction, your warranty will be voided. And ink kits tend to be messy and usually more trouble than they're worth. The last thing you want in an inkjet is ink mess.

Laser printers are a bit more forgiving, and they tend to last much longer than inkjets. I've had my Apple LaserWriter 4/600 for about nine years, and I've used various kinds of toner cartridges in it, including refurbished ones.

Use the manufacturer's paper. Some manufacturers claim that their printers can use regular copier-quality bond paper. This is actually a very welcome ability, because the other printers—the ones that say they can only print on Brand X paper—usually really mean it. With a few printers, I've experimented with regular paper even though the manufacturer has specified a particular paper, and the prints looked awful.

Feed thick card stock manually. When using thick card stock, feed it through the printer manually rather than putting it in the cassette. Some papers, such as the Avery label kits, claim to be "Jam Free," and I've never had any trouble putting this type of paper in the cassette.

Clean the ink heads. Every so often, you might notice that your inkjet printouts have gaps or missing letters. This usually means that one of the print heads is clogged. Most inkjets provide a software clean-up command, which is usually found in the pane that comes up when you click the Utility icon in Printer Setup Utility.

Troubleshooting (JS, DW)

After you click that Print button in the Print dialog, your work is done and it's time to kick back and enjoy the fruits of your labor. Your Mac will send your file to the printer, merrily counting off the pages in a progress bar, and your printer's motor should hum as the pages emerge. But sometimes you click the Print button only to be greeted with Trouble. Your Mac displays an error message. Or, worse, your Mac behaves as though everything is fine while your printer just sits there and does nothing. Or your file prints, but it looks completely different than it does onscreen.

Because printing involves many elements—the file, your Mac and its software, the cables, your printer and its media—many things can go wrong. Fortunately, these problems fall into a few basic categories. We'll look at the most common kinds of problems and offer some advice to get your Mac and printer back on speaking terms.

Your Mac Complains

There are many reasons why a Mac might give you an error message rather than simply passing off the file to the printer. These messages differ, depending on which operating system you're using. In Mac OS 9, error messages appear as dialog boxes. In Mac OS X, the printer icon in the Dock bounces, and you see a yellow exclamation mark icon next to it. Problems that bring up error messages tend to be fairly common and easily resolved.

The Print button is gray

If the Print button in the Print dialog is gray, clicking it will have no effect. You should also notice that at the top of the dialog, the selection in the Printer menu says No Printer Selected. Actually, this message is slightly misleading. What it really means is that Printer Setup Utility doesn't have a single printer in its list. This could be because you haven't added any yet, or because you've deleted the printer or printers that were previously in this list. In either case, what you need to do is add a printer. For details on how to do this, see "Adding Printers," earlier in this chapter.

Opening Printer Connection Failed

This one sounds ominous, but most likely the printer simply isn't turned on, warmed up, or plugged in. If it's a USB printer and it is turned on, warmed up, and plugged in, but you still get this message, try unplugging the USB cord from the printer and plugging it in again. If you're using a USB hub, unplug the USB cord from the Mac and plug it in again. Another thing to try is turning the printer off and on again. Some laser printers take a long time to warm up, so you might check to see whether or not it's fully "awake." Many say "Ready" or something to that effect. Finally, check all cable connections. One loose cable, and the line between your Mac and the printer will be broken. If you're on a network, troubleshooting this issue will be more difficult, but it's the same idea. See if others are having the problem, too, as a way to narrow it down.

PostScript errors

These are particularly nasty, because they're intermittent and often cryptic. But here are a few tips for dealing with them:

- Get detailed information. In the Print dialog, under Error Handling, choose the option "Print detailed report." You may not be able to glean anything from the information, but then again you may. Note that you won't see this option in the Print dialog if you do not have a PostScript printer.

- If your QuarkXPress file uses many fonts, try selecting the option "Include unlimited downloadable fonts" in the Page Setup dialog. This slows down printing, but it will prevent fonts from overloading available printer memory by forcing your Mac to download them one at a time and then deleting each to make room for the next one.

- Conserve memory. Often PostScript errors are due to a lack of memory in your Mac. Try quitting unused applications and closing unnecessary windows.

- Restart the printer. This refreshes the printer's memory, freeing it to better take on new tasks.

- Copy everything from one file and put it into a new file. Believe it or not, this sometimes does the trick, particularly when you're working with

PostScript-heavy applications like QuarkXPress and Adobe InDesign. Using File > Save As to save your document with a new name often does the same thing.

- Sometimes you'll get PostScript errors while printing pages from the Web, particularly if the Web page is a long document with lots of interactive elements. One thing you can try is to uncheck any options you may be using for "shrinking the image to fit on the page" (or however your particular browser puts it), and then set your browser's preferences to use a smaller type size, or set the scale in Page Setup to 85% (I've found that this works best). You can also try saving the page as a PDF before printing it. If worse comes to worst, copy all the text, paste it into a word-processor file, strip out all the formatting, and print it that way.

- If you get frequent PostScript errors and you have a PostScript printer, consider upgrading its memory. It wouldn't hurt to upgrade your Mac's memory too, since for non-PostScript printing it's doing the lion's share of the page-image processing.

"Printing of jobs for this printer is stopped"

When you stop a job in the middle of printing, you may also notice that there's a stop sign with an exclamation point on the printer icon in the Dock, and there's a tiny version of this icon alongside the printer's name in the Print dialog. To continue printing, click the printer icon on the Dock to bring up your printer's status dialog. Select the name of the stalled print job and click the Start Jobs icon. Your document should print and the Stop icon should disappear.

The Printer Misbehaves

What if your Mac seems fine, but the printer isn't working correctly? Here are a few of the common things that can cause your printer to hiccup.

Nothing happens

That is, you've told your Mac to print, and it's done its part, but the printer just sits there doing nothing. In all likelihood, your document is being sent to a different printer, so check all your settings and make sure it's going to the right place.

Slooooowwww printing

Large files take a while to print, and many factors determine exactly how long. Operating-system version, amount of RAM, and kind and speed of your Mac's processor all play a role in printing speed. To remedy this situation, see if there's anything you can do to cut down on file size. Do you have any large images with resolutions of 2400 dpi? Reduce these to 600, tops, even though your printer says it can print in thousands of dots per inch. Are you using a thousand fonts? You may be a creative soul, but you'll need as much patience as you have passion, because processing fonts takes time. If you're printing a document containing bitmapped graphics, using the Scale command in the Print dialog will slow down printing—recalculating the positions of all those bits takes time.

Wrong typefaces or jagged type

If your beautifully designed document with fancy type comes out looking as though it were produced on a typewriter, with boring, plain-looking 10- or 12-point text, most likely you're getting Courier instead of the typefaces you're after. Courier is the font that laser printers use when they don't have the font you need. Check your font setup. Is the font stored in the proper location? If you're using a font-management program, is the font activated? If the file printed fine yesterday but uses Courier today, it's probably a memory problem; restart the printer to clear its memory banks.

If some of the type looks jagged on a PostScript printer, most likely you're missing the corresponding PostScript printer font for your screen font (for more about fonts, see Chapter 15).

Jagged output

If your document contains EPS (Encapsulated PostScript) images, most of the time they'll look fine, even on a non-PostScript printer, because printer drivers are getting sophisticated enough to translate line information such as PostScript into relatively well-placed dots on a page. However, if you stretch the image or distort its shape in any way, a non-PostScript printer might render the image very poorly. In this case, the only solution is to use your graphics application to change the format from EPS to JPEG, TIFF, or Photoshop.

Faded output

When your printed pages start looking as faded as worn-out blue jeans, it's time for some maintenance. Most likely, your inkjet printer is spitting up the last bits of ink or your laser printer is starving for toner. In both cases, the simple solution is to replace the offending consumables. One good trick to remember: when a laser printer is producing weak printouts or the printer complains that the toner is low and refuses to print at all, remove the toner cartridge, hold it firmly with both hands, and rock it sharply but gently from side to side several times. Now replace it and try printing again. By shifting around the remaining toner, you should be able to get some more life out of your seemingly washed-up cartridge—giving you at least enough time to buy a replacement, if nothing else. Also, laser printers allow you to set the print density—that is, the amount of toner being used. You may just need to pump it up a bit.

Unfortunately, this won't work with inkjet cartridges, but there is a way you can save some money. You don't throw out your car when it needs gas or chuck your coffee mug when you're out of java—you refill them. The same is possible for many inkjet cartridges. For about the price of replacing a series of cartridges, you can buy refill kits that can refill your cartridges half a dozen times or more. A quick Web search (or reading some of your daily spam) will provide you with lots of sources.

 Using refilled cartridges may void your printer's warranty. This is a strategy best reserved for older, out-of-warranty printers. In addition, refill kits can be messy to use, so take special care if you go this route.

If you still have sufficient ink, the problem could be that the ink-spraying nozzles have become clogged like cholesterol-choked arteries and aren't up to the task. In that case, consider an option that printer manufacturers include just for this purpose: head cleaning. Running this function forces the printer to do the equivalent of shooting a spitball through each nozzle, clearing them out. Although this process can be quite useful, it can also be quite wasteful—the extra ink forced through the nozzles has to come from somewhere, and that somewhere is your ink tanks. It's best to keep this as a last resort.

Splotchy, sketchy, or skewed output

What if your prints aren't faded, but they are uneven? Of course, this could be caused by low ink or toner as well, but there can be other reasons. You could have paper-feeding issues, or you may be using the wrong kind of paper altogether for your printer. With laser printers, it's possible that the insides are dirty. There are cleaning paper sheets that you can run through your laser printer to collect toner residue and dust. Or you can clean the roller with a soft cloth and some isopropyl alcohol. Before you open up a laser printer, let it cool down for a while—the insides of these things get extremely hot.

Miscellaneous Problems

Some problems can't be pinned down to either the Mac or the printer right away. Often these problems are related more to software issues than to hardware issues. Here are a few common things that can happen and some ways to deal with them.

Bad or wrong color

When you print something—whether it's a digital photo you took during the family vacation to Italy last summer or a flyer you're printing up to make color copies of at a local print shop—you expect it to look pretty similar to whatever you see on your monitor. But alas, this isn't always the case. With an inkjet printer there are a few physical things that could be causing the discrepancy between the printed page and the image you see onscreen. The print head assembly may have collected dirt or other junk from previous printings. Or you could be low or out of a particular color. Because your inkjet uses a four-color (CMYK) process, a missing or weak component color will throw the whole balance off.

The larger, and probably more common, problem is that your monitor and printer don't see eye to eye on how colors are supposed to look. Mac OS X includes the ColorSync utility for choosing a printer's ICC (International Color Consortium) color profile; this can help tell your Mac and monitor about a printer's abilities. For the best possible output, you'll need to calibrate your monitor for your output device using a somewhat expensive hardware calibrator.

Freaking out

Technology is supposed to make our lives easier, but sometimes strange things happen for no good (apparent) reason. For example, you may send a document to the printer, and a light flashes, informing you that the printer is processing something, but it never actually prints anything. Or various lights do various things that don't look entirely kosher. Take a deep breath, resist the urge to kill, and simply turn the printer off and back on. This will clear the memory buffer and usually get things back in business. If that doesn't work, restart your Mac. The next thing to try is reinstalling the printer's driver or downloading a new one from the manufacturer's Web site (drivers can get broken—the official term is *corrupted*—after repeated uses). If you're still having problems, make sure the cable that connects the printer to your Mac (assuming it's directly connected and not on a network) is secure and hasn't been gnawed through by mice (the vermin, not the input devices).

The default printer doesn't stick

First, check your Print & Fax preferences, and make sure that "Last printer used" is not chosen in the "Selected printer in Print Dialog" pop-up menu, because the Print & Fax preferences will override any changes you make in Printer Setup Utility.

If you've already set up a printer using Print Center (Mac OS X 10.2) or Printer Setup Utility (Mac OS X 10.3), and each time you try to print, Mac OS X tells you that no printers are set up, there are a few things to try (and they can help with a variety of Mac OS X problems). First, do something called *zapping the PRAM*. By holding down ⌘ Option P R while restarting your Mac (and waiting until it goes through three cycles of chimes), you will clear the parameter RAM. The PRAM holds information needed for startup and keeping track of some settings, and zapping it resets it to factory settings (meaning that you'll have to reset your date and time settings, among others).

The other thing to try is repairing disk permissions on your startup disk. Open Disk Utility (in the /Applications/Utilities folder) and click the First Aid tab. Then select your disk and click Repair Disk Permissions.

Interview: Jef Raskin

As every Apple history buff knows, the man who initiated the Macintosh project and gave it its name was not Steve Jobs but Jef Raskin. Already an experienced system designer—he began building computers for scientific research in 1959, when he was just 16—he joined Apple in 1978 and began work in 1980 on what he envisioned as an "information appliance." After Jobs took command of the project in 1982, Raskin was forced out of it and soon left the company. Just how much influence his ideas had on the final product has been the source of endless debate, but he continues to call himself "creator of Apple's Macintosh" (www.jefraskin.com).

After leaving Apple, Raskin started a company called Information Appliance Inc., where he developed an Apple IIe add-on called the SwyftCard and a stand-alone system that was marketed, briefly, as the Canon Cat. Since 1989 he has been an independent consultant and writer, concentrating primarily on "making computers more usable and their interfaces efficient as well as pleasant." He's the author of a treatise called The Humane Interface *(Addison-Wesley, 2000) and is currently working on a software project called THE (The Humane Environment). —Henry Norr*

> *Jobs made a gutsy move in making music available on a per-song basis; we need an equally gutsy move in usability.*
>
> —Jef Raskin, on the state of the Mac interface today

Talk about your years at Apple and how the Mac program got started.

I started working with Jobs and Woz in 1976, first meeting them in the now-legendary garage. I wrote some of the early manuals and later became Apple's 31st full-time employee in January 1978. First I was manager of publications and new product review, then manager of applications software. Starting in 1980 I was manager of advanced systems [as the Macintosh project was known originally].

I was thinking about a Mac-like product before I came to Apple. At Apple, I never joined the Mac team: other people joined me to form the Mac team. At first, I was the Mac team, writing the proposal and doing the initial design. I also named the project Macintosh. I started writing *The Book of Macintosh* in 1978, so for me the Mac is a quarter century old.

From the first, I conferred with my long-term friend Brian Howard [employee number 32, and still at Apple]. At first this was unofficial, and done on our own time. The initial crew, once the project was approved officially, consisted of four people. I was the project leader.

When the Mac was released in 1984, did you expect that it would still be around today?

No, but I expected that its ideas would influence the way computers would be used. I believed that if Apple did not have a product like the Mac, the company was dead in the water.

continues on next page

I realize that each of us sees history from our own narrow perspective, with ourselves as the leading player, but I am convinced that if I had not started the Macintosh project, and if I had not kept it going—sometimes secretly—in spite of Jobs' disapproval, we would not have had an Apple Computer, Inc., today. Jobs thought the Lisa was the product that Apple needed.

Obviously, there are many others without whose solo contributions Apple would have failed, but I think I can safely number myself among those.

Did you anticipate that nearly all personal computers would move to a graphical interface?

Yes. I had thought that long before Apple. I wrote about it in 1967. For those who say that Apple's ideas are just derivative from the great work done at Xerox PARC: note that PARC opened in 1972, well after I had published my view that computers should be designed to be compatible with humans as their first aim, and that it was necessary for them to be graphics-based, not character-based.

What computer do you use now?

I use a number of computers. On my desk is a G4 tower with two large displays. In my travel bag is the smallest-footprint iBook. My house is wired for Ethernet, and wireless fills in where the cables don't reach. My wife uses an iBook identical to mine. We have a few other Macs floating around, including the Millionth Mac, that was awarded to me for having created the Mac project, and some elderly Macs that are not much use now. I also have Apple II S/N 0002 and my old Apple I. I have two PCs, each of which is tied to a numerically controlled machine tool. They have to be PCs because the makers of the tools didn't provide Mac software.

What do you think about Mac OS X?

I'm glad that Apple went to Unix. That's a plus from the programming point of view. I am horrified that they did not make the thing fundamentally easier to use, although they have some nice built-in apps. But Apple has kept the same old desktop/applications/icons-style interface that we started with. This ignores nearly all that has been learned about human-computer interaction in the quarter century since the design was started.

Do you like Windows any better?

To my disgust, I find that I can move between the Apple and the Windows machines pretty easily. Apple is still better, but where there used to be a day-and-night difference, they're now just an eye blink apart. Sure, it's nice to not have to relearn things to move from one to the other, but it also means that there is little differentiation between the products, and therefore little reason to fight the mainstream. Usability-wise, Windows gives you 80 to 90 percent of what you get in a Mac. That's deplorable. Apple needs to move ahead. Jobs made a gutsy move in making music available on a per-song basis; we need an equally gutsy move in usability.

Do you have any urge to go back to Apple?

Yes; I would love to give Apple an interface that is light-years ahead of what the competition is even thinking about. But Apple seems to be in a pretty-box, faster-processor groove, having forgotten what made the Mac a win in the first place.

7

Peripherals

Kris Fong is the chapter editor and author.

When it comes to our Macs, we like to think outside the box. After all, what sits beyond the Mac's enclosure is just as important as what lurks inside. While a keyboard and mouse are vital, there are plenty of other peripherals that can add functionality, control, and fun to your computer. And just because Apple wraps up its own keyboard and mouse all nice and spiffy with your purchase doesn't mean you have to stick it out with these, either.

In this chapter we cover many common peripherals that can enhance your Mac experience and make projects easier to tackle. Whether you're considering a digital camera, can't stand using your PowerBook's trackpad, want a way to record your band's next CD, or want to do nothing but play video games and watch TV, there are peripherals that'll satisfy each of the above. While we can help guide you toward choosing the right device, be aware that other oddball gadgets we don't mention—like USB fans, DJ controllers, lights, and microscopes—exist for those who seek them.

In This Chapter

Port Authority: Know Your Connections

You learned as a kid that square pegs don't fit in round holes; the same applies to plugging peripherals into your Mac. While it's a given that you should seek out devices that match the types of ports on your Mac, you can also add ports that your Mac lacks, by way of upgrade cards and adapters.

Before you start buying toys for your Mac, get to know its connection capabilities first. The more knowledgeable you are about each port type's transfer capabilities and limits, the easier it will be for you to choose products that fit your needs—whether that be speed (you might want to consider adding a SCSI card), budget concerns (if speed is of no concern, USB devices are cheaper than FireWire devices), or appearances (you might prefer a spiffy new LCD display on your desk rather than a bulky CRT monitor). Macs built in the last four years (from the Blue-and-White G3 on) all sport FireWire and USB (Universal Serial Bus) connectors. Macs older than the original Bondi Blue iMac (which has USB but no FireWire) generally have SCSI, serial, and ADB connectors. And if you want to clear some of the spaghetti mess of wires, you can add Bluetooth wireless technology. Here's a closer look at these connection types.

FireWire

When you need speed, FireWire (**Figure 7.1**) is the answer (hold your tongues, you SCSI fanatics—we'll get to you in a moment). You'll find FireWire mainly in multimedia devices such as digital video cameras and external media drives where fast transfer speeds are vital.

Figure 7.1

You'll find FireWire 400 (left) and the newer FireWire 800 (right) mostly on media drives, burners, and digital video cameras—devices that benefit from super-speedy transfer rates.

FireWire is Apple's implementation of IEEE 1394, an Apple-invented peripheral standard that bridges consumer electronics devices with computers and the standard implementation allows data-transfer rates of up to 400 megabits per second (Mbps). Unlike SCSI connections of the past (ID conflicts or termination troubles, anyone?), FireWire doesn't require any futzing to make things work.

FireWire is both cross-platform and hot-swappable, meaning that you don't have to shut down your Mac every time you plug in or pull out a device, and it allows you to chain up to 63 devices together. It also provides bus power—up to 45 watts—so that connected devices can draw power without an AC adapter. You'll find support for FireWire in peripherals where transfer speed is crucial, such as digital video cameras, external hard drives, printers, scanners, DVD and CD burners, the iPod, pro digital cameras, audio interfaces, and other gadgets.

But there's more.

Apple introduced FireWire 800 in its PowerBook and G4 lineups in January 2003. This up-and-coming technology based on IEEE 1394b boasts transfer rates up to 800 Mbps over a cable distance up to 100 meters (FireWire 400 maxes out at 4.5 meters). It's also backward compatible with older FireWire devices, though your oldies can't take advantage of the faster speed and you may need an adapter to make the connection.

Because of its infancy, FireWire 800 peripherals were slim pickings as of press time—just a few storage devices from LaCie (www.lacie.com), Mac Power (www.macpower.com), and EZQuest (www.ezq.com) were available. But we expect many digital video, pro audio, and storage manufacturers to decorate store shelves with FireWire 800 product in the future.

USB

If FireWire is liquid lightning, USB (**Figure 7.2**) is Heinz ketchup. For those of you who've had the excruciating experience of transferring 5 gigs' worth of music files from your Mac to any MP3 player other than the iPod, you know what we mean.

Figure 7.2

USB is the most common connection type for Mac peripherals. Current Macs with USB 2.0 feature ports that are identical to the older USB 1.1, which allows backwards compatibility.

Don't get us wrong; USB is no also-ran—it happens to be the most popular, multiplatform peripheral standard today, and can shuttle data much faster than serial or ADB. While FireWire capitalizes on gadgets that thrive on speed, USB satisfies all other peripherals, including keyboards, mice, printers, scanners, game controllers, MP3 players, consumer digital cameras, and speakers. The technology allows data transfers of up to 12 Mbps, provides power on its bus, is hot-swappable, and supports up to 127 simultaneous device connections (with the help of an army of USB hubs—and a large credit line).

USB 2.0 was unleashed in 2000 to little Mac fanfare. Why? Apple at the time resisted adding USB 2.0 to its Mac lineup, but that didn't stop third-party vendors from developing USB 2.0 upgrade cards to give Mac users that luxury (see "Hubs, Adapters, and Upgrade Cards" later in this chapter). After all, plenty of peripheral manufacturers were already cranking out USB 2.0 devices for PC punks. But in June 2003, Steve Jobs unveiled the new Power Mac G5s—with USB 2.0.

With transfer speeds of up to 480 Mbps, USB 2.0 is faster than FireWire 400 but no match for FireWire 800, though the focus for this new standard isn't the audio-video arena, which FireWire has cornered. It's mainly a speed bump to advance the next crop of USB devices and is also backward compatible to support current USB 1.1 peripherals. Many USB 2.0 peripherals, such as external hard drives, CD and DVD burners, and scanners, already support the Mac platform; and now that Apple has decided to run with the technology, you can expect to see this field grow.

Bluetooth

A world without wires—that's the mantra that Bluetooth's development team kept psyching us up with for years. The technology works by using radio frequencies in the 2.4 GHz range to deliver information. It's been in development since 1997, but earlier products mainly revolved around mobile phones.

In 2002, Apple and Microsoft adopted the standard to integrate into their operating systems. Manufacturers started making Bluetooth PCI cards and USB dongles so that peripherals would be able to talk to the computer hardware. D-Link (www.dlink.com) came out with a Bluetooth USB dongle for Macs back in October 2002, giving any USB-equipped Mac running Mac OS X 10.2 or later wireless capabilities (**Figure 7.3**). In January 2003, Apple integrated Bluetooth into its new product line. No longer were wires needed to transfer data from a Mac to any supported Bluetooth-enabled device, and vice versa. But Bluetooth peripherals for the Mac remain sparse. There isn't much beyond a few cell phones, printers, mice, and PDAs.

Figure 7.3

D-Link's Bluetooth adapter plugs into any USB port and provides instant wireless capability to any Bluetooth-enabled device.

Photo courtesy of D-Link

Bluetooth is still a fairly new technology, and manufacturers are giving the standard strong support; but it remains to be seen what new types of products will support the Mac OS.

SCSI

SCSI wuzzy was a bear. No kidding! If there was one connectivity standard that could strike fear into the hearts of the technology-challenged, it was SCSI (**Figure 7.4**). SCSI (pronounced "skuzzy") stands for Small Computer System Interface and is probably the most aggravating of all connectivity standards for any technophobe. Connecting SCSI devices requires assigning each a unique SCSI ID number and setting a terminator; if you fail to set things properly, the device might not be recognized by your Mac.

Figure 7.4

Though FireWire replaced SCSI connections in modern Macs, many audio and video professionals today still rely on SCSI drives for their sheer speed.

The standard first appeared on the Mac Plus in 1986 and had a bus speed of 1.5 megabytes per second. Over the years SCSI greatly improved, going from a transfer speed of 5 MBps with SCSI-1 up to 320 MBps (much faster than FireWire) with Ultra320 SCSI. Its evolution also sprouted crops of sales-pitchy names like Ultra SCSI, Fast Wide SCSI, Ultra2 SCSI, Wide Ultra SCSI, and other amalgamations.

During its heyday, plenty of SCSI peripherals flooded the market—hard drives, removable-media drives, printers, and scanners. Today most peripheral vendors, with the exception of storage-drive manufacturers, have dropped SCSI support in favor of USB or FireWire.

Although Apple abandoned outboard SCSI in 1999 in favor of FireWire, you can still have your SCSI if you want it by way of a PCI upgrade card. Many loyalists remain—primarily those in the multimedia, pro audio, and video production fields, where large projects demand exceptionally fast transfer rates and mondo storage mediums. If you know how to deal with its temperament, SCSI is still the way to go if you *really* need incredible speed (and most of us *really don't*).

Serial and ADB

If you're relatively new to the Mac, meaning you bought your first Mac within the last five years, you missed out on Apple's old connection stalwarts: serial and ADB (**Figure 7.5**). Serial was used mainly to connect modems, printers, and other devices to a Mac. ADB was used to connect Macs to mice, keyboards, game controllers, and other input devices.

Serial had been featured on every Mac starting with the original Macintosh 128k in 1984 (remember Apple's "1984" commercial?). The last time we saw a serial port on a Mac, the Mac was colored beige (or black, if you count the PowerBook G3). ADB had its debut with the Macintosh SE and Macintosh II in March 1987, and it remained until mid-1999. ADB managed to hang on with the Blue and White Power Mac G3 in January 1999 (the machine offered one ADB port along with USB and FireWire) before disappearing into oblivion.

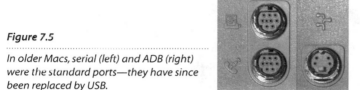

Figure 7.5

In older Macs, serial (left) and ADB (right) were the standard ports—they have since been replaced by USB.

You'd be hard-pressed to find many serial or ADB peripherals right now, but if you've got an old Mac, eBay's a pretty good place to start.

Hubs, Adapters, and Upgrade Cards

There are a gazillion and one gadgets and gizmos you can buy and hook up to your Mac (time to give up that expensive Starbucks habit). But unless Apple designs some 50-port atrocity in the future, your Mac comes with just a handful of ports to connect peripherals. Thankfully, you can expand what you have by adding hubs, adapters, and upgrade cards.

Hubs

A hub turns one port into many (kind of like a power strip), allowing you to connect a bunch of devices simultaneously to one port instead of swapping gadgets between shared ports. Hubs come in different flavors, including USB, FireWire, serial, and Ethernet (see Chapter 20 for more on Ethernet hubs), and in various sizes—from two-port hubs on up. You can also string multiple hubs together to accommodate your ever-growing peripheral collection.

If you need USB, the Belkin **USB 4-Port Hub for Mac** ($39.95; www.belkin.com) and **Keyspan 4-Port USB Hub** ($39; www.keyspan.com) are two dependable, good-looking hubs to consider. For FireWire, the Iogear **GFH600** six-port FireWire hub ($99.95; www.iogear.com) and Belkin **6-Port FireWire Hub** ($99.95) both offer plenty of ports packed inside stylish casings. But if you really want the "monster" of all hubs, Charismac's **FireWire Dino** ($69.95; www.charismac.com), a Godzilla-like creature with movable limbs and embedded with a four-port FireWire hub, is one cool beast (**Figure 7.6**).

Figure 7.6

Hubs let you connect a slew of devices to just one of your Mac's ports. Charismac's FireWire Dino is just one example of these cool beasties; it lets you hook up three FireWire devices to your Mac.

Adapters

If you have an older peripheral that supports an ADB, SCSI, or serial connection but have a newer USB and FireWire Mac, an adapter will let you bridge the two. Adapters are basically devices that feature different types of connection plugs on opposing ends. With them, you can turn ports that your Mac has into ports that your Mac doesn't have. And if your modern Mac lacks PCI or CardBus slots, which is the case with an iMac or iBook, adapters offer the only solution for bringing older devices into your current fold.

For example, you can use a USB-to-serial adapter to hook up an old serial printer or PalmPilot to your Mac's USB port. Or you can use a USB-to-ADB adapter to connect an older graphics tablet or gamepad to your current machine. If serial is what you need, the **Keyspan USA-28X** ($79; www.keyspan.com) is one of the most popular adapters, offering two serial ports via USB. For ADB hook-ups, Griffin Technology's **iMate** ($39; www.griffintechnology.com) works superbly. If you want to connect a SCSI device, you can get a FireWire-to-SCSI adapter, such as the Belkin **FireWire/SCSI Adapter** ($89.95; www.belkin.com) or 2nd Wave **FireWire to SCSI Adapter** ($99; www.2ndwave.com).

Though adapters are often employed to allow the use of older peripherals, they can also bring your Mac up to speed with the latest technology. You can add wireless capability to your Mac with a Bluetooth adapter, which allows you to sync your Mac with a Bluetooth-enabled peripheral, such as a cell phone or PDA, without physically connecting them with a cable. The D-Link **DBT-120 Wireless USB Bluetooth Adapter** ($49; www.dlink.com), a popular model, adds Bluetooth via USB.

Upgrade cards

If you have a slew of older peripherals, have an older PCI- or CardBus-supporting Mac that lacks USB and/or FireWire, or want to equip a newer Mac with different ports, an upgrade card is the way to go.

You'll find products that provide USB, FireWire, both USB and FireWire, FireWire 800, USB 2.0, SCSI, or serial ports on a single PCI card for desktop machines or PC Card for PowerBooks. Adaptec (www.adaptec.com) is the leader when it comes to adding a SCSI card to your system. For everything else, Sonnet (www.sonnettech.com), Iogear (www.iogear.com), Orange Micro (www.orangemicro.com), Belkin (www.belkin.com), and Keyspan (www.keyspan.com) are the top manufacturers for various upgrade cards and CardBus adapters.

Take Control: Input Devices

Macs can't read minds. That's why they rely on input devices—including keyboards, mice, trackballs, trackpads, joysticks, and graphics tablets—to tell them what to do. Whether you're looking for a device that can offer better control for your tasks at hand, or you simply want to replace your current mouse or keyboard, here's a look at the types of input devices available and a few things to consider before you plunk down the plastic.

Keyboards

Though they function pretty much the same, all keyboards are not created equal. If you're not happy with the keyboard that came with your Mac, you can simply replace it. USB keyboards are the current Mac standard, and there are plenty to choose from, given that USB is a cross-platform technology. If you have an older ADB Mac, you won't find many choices—Macally (www.macally.com), Adesso (www.adesso.com), and Datadesk Technologies (www.data-desk.com) still carry various models, but most manufacturers have abandoned ADB.

Features

If you do a good amount of number crunching, a numeric keypad is a must. It comes standard on most full-size keyboards, so don't be swayed by cute, compact designs without a keypad. However, if you can't help yourself, you can get a standalone USB numeric keypad from Macally, Kensington (www.kensington.com), or Adesso . If desk space is at a minimum, look for a board with a small footprint, or consider a keyboard with a built-in trackball or trackpad. Don't like being tethered to your Mac? Consider a wireless keyboard such as Macally's **RFKey** ($69) or the Logitech **Cordless Elite Duo** ($99.95; www.logitech.com), which provide wireless connections via USB.

If you have more specific interests, Macally's **iMediaKey** ($49) and Adesso's **MediaNet Pro** ($59.99) feature programmable hot keys for CD control, email, the Web, and more. Microsoft put out the shortcut-laden **Microsoft Office Keyboard** ($44.95; www.microsoft.com) if you're a slave to Word and Excel. And if you're a total klutz, the **Crywolf CoolMac Keyboard** ($50.96; www.coolmacstuff.com) can withstand coffee and soda spills (or any other liquid you tend to throw down) and can be rolled up for compact travel, thanks to its über-flexible design.

Comfort

Comfort comes into play if you and your keyboard spend long sessions together. If you're not mindful of your typing posture, you can develop discomfort in your arms and wrists, which can lead to a more serious injury. Before you buy a keyboard, take the keys out for a test drive and make sure that you feel no stress in your fingers and wrists as you type.

If you're prone to injury or want to avoid repetitive stress problems, an ergonomic keyboard may be beneficial. These types of keyboards can take a little time getting used to, but they may reduce the chance of injury by getting you to place your palms and wrists in a more natural position.

Adesso makes a few wrist-friendly models, including the **Tru-Form 3D Ergo Keyboard** ($99), which features a split-keyboard, contoured layout and built-in palm rests. Kinesis, which specializes in ergonomic products, offers unique keyboards, including the **Evolution Desktop Keyboard** ($269; www.kinesis-ergo.com), a keyboard split in two so that you can place its parts up to 20 inches apart (you'll need to buy a PS2-to-USB adapter to plug it into your Mac).

Mice, Trackballs, and Trackpads

What's more important than a mouse when it comes to operating your Mac? Without it, you wouldn't be able to control the pointer to launch apps, drag and drop files, click Web links, edit photos, or launch viruses (just kidding). But if your original one-button Apple mouse seems a bit anemic or you can't stand trackpadding across your iBook or PowerBook screen, get something else.

Mice

Just like keyboards, mice come in all shapes and sizes. The current crop requires USB (**Figure 7.7**), though you can still find ADB mice. And just as when choosing a keyboard, the more time you spend with mouse in hand, the more weight you should give its comfort level.

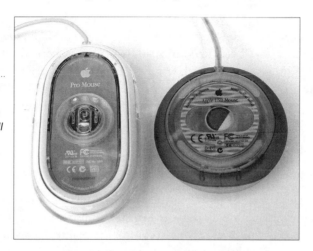

Figure 7.7

An optical mouse, such as Apple's Pro Mouse, shown belly up (left), won't go all wiggy on you since its tracking mechanism can't clog up like Apple's old roller-ball mouse puck's (right). Both mice require USB connections.

Historically, Apple has been fond of simplicity—thus its one-button mouse. With Mac OS X, Apple added native support for two-button critters, and peripheral makers responded with varying designs. While you can access all that is to be had with a one-button mouse, a mouse with two or more buttons can make some tasks go faster. For example, a two-button mouse allows you to access contextual-menu items with a simple right-button click. Multiple-button mice allow you to program buttons to launch items or perform other functions, such as pasting form letters into documents or printing.

Mice still come in the old roller-ball variety (the mouse uses a small rubber ball to track movements, which requires a mousepad and regular cleaning to keep it running smoothly), but the rage these days is for optically sensitive ones (the mouse uses a clog-free optical sensor to track movement). Apple currently ships its desktop Macs with the optical **Apple Pro Mouse** ($59).

Other common features for mice include a finger scroll wheel, which lets you scroll up and down Web and document pages, and wireless support. Mice also vary wildly in size, shape, and color—anything from the cool blue, droid-looking **Kensington Iridio** ($29.99; www.kensington.com), a two-button optical mouse with a scroll wheel, to the lipstick case–shaped Atek **Super Mini Optical Mouse** ($49.95; www.atek.com), a miniature two-button oddity.

Trackballs

If a roller-ball mouse went belly-up, you'd have a trackball—in theory, anyway. These devices work similarly to old-school mice in that they use a ball to control your Mac's pointer, but with a trackball you use your hand or fingers to control the ball directly.

Like mice, trackballs vary, offering programmable buttons, scroll wheels, and wireless capability. Kensington makes some of the most popular models, including the bear paw–like **Turbo Mouse Pro** ($144.95 corded, $179.95 cordless; www.kensington.com), which features a large ball and plenty of programmable buttons. If you need a little more precision, Logitech's **TrackMan Wheel** ($29.95 corded, $49.95 cordless; www.logitech.com) features a small, optically sensed ball designed for thumb control, plus programmable buttons and a scroll wheel.

Trackpads

Apple uses trackpads (also known as *touchpads*) on its PowerBook and iBook, but some desktop users opt for trackpads because they're compact. These touch-sensitive pads allow you to control the pointer by sliding your finger across the pad, and they feature a button or two at the bottom for clicking, though you can also "click" by tapping on the pad.

Some keyboards, such as the **Adesso Tru-Form Ergo Contoured Keyboard with Glidepoint Touchpad** ($99; www.adesso.com), feature a built-in trackpad for those who want two in one. If you want just a pad, Cirque Corp. makes a few, such as the **Cirque Easy Cat Touchpad** ($44.95 USB, $39.95 serial; www.cirque.com).

Graphics Tablets

Using a mouse, trackball, or trackpad to do something as simple as draw a circle can be difficult; these devices are hard to control with any precision. That's why graphics tablets are the saving grace of many artists, designers, photo retouchers, and anyone else who prefers the familiarity of holding a pen to pushing pixels with a mouse.

With a graphics tablet, you use a cordless pen (which looks and feels like any ordinary pen but contains no ink) and draw on a digital tablet, which is sensitive to both the pen's proximity and pressure, to control your Mac's pointer. Unlike a trackpad, which requires a few finger slides across the pad to move the pointer from one side of the screen to the other, with a graphics tablet, when you move the pen across the tablet, the pointer on your monitor follows in the exact same manner. That's because the active surface area of the tablet is mapped to the area of your Mac's monitor screen, regardless of the tablet size.

Graphics tablets are also pressure sensitive—the harder you press, the thicker, darker, and more opaque the line when you use it with a graphics application that supports pressure sensitivity. But a graphics tablet can also replace your mouse in your day-to-day tasks. For some, using a pen to control the Mac is more comfortable than using a mouse.

Wacom is the leader for these types of devices with good reason—its tablets offer more precise control than those from any other manufacturer. If you're a graphic designer or artist, the Wacom **Intuos2** line of tablets (from $199.99 for a 4-by-5 tablet to $749.99 for a 12-by-18 tablet; www.wacom.com) all come with shortcut buttons, 1024 levels of pen and eraser-tip sensitivity, and a cordless mouse. For occasional use, the **Wacom Graphire2** ($99.95) offers a 4-by-5 tablet, 512 levels of pressure sensitivity, and a cordless mouse.

Displays and Monitors

Their function is simple—to provide visual feedback for everything you do on your Mac—but the differences among monitors are more complex. Take LCD displays and CRT monitors, for instance (**Figure 7.8**). CRT (cathode ray tube) monitors have been around for decades and are the norm across all computer platforms. They're similar to your TV in that the images displayed onscreen are made up of tiny pixels comprising red, blue, and/or green lights (RGB color).

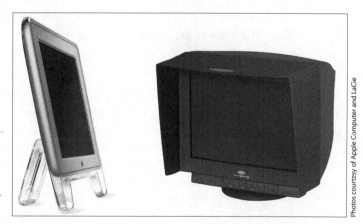

Figure 7.8

LCD displays, such as Apple's Studio Display (left), conserve desk space, but CRT monitors, such as LaCie's electronblue (right), offer better color accuracy and brightness.

Photos courtesy of Apple Computer and LaCie

Though they had a slow start, LCD (liquid crystal display) displays are all the rage today. These displays have a screen made up of liquid crystals that are sandwiched between two thin polarized panels. One of the polarized panels contains a "sheet" of pixels, which are arranged on a matrix of columns and rows. Images are created when an electrical charge allows light to pass through the liquid crystals and onto the pixel matrix. The color of each pixel is determined by the voltage of the electrical charge.

Both types of monitors display images at a resolution of 72 pixels per inch (ppi). The bigger the monitor, however, the more space it has to house pixels and the more pixels a monitor can display, the greater its resolution will be. For example, a 17-inch monitor displays fewer pixels than a 20-inch monitor. Thus the 20-inch monitor will have higher resolutions.

LCD vs. CRT

When LCDs first arrived, they used a passive matrix system (a simple grid that feeds a charge from a circuit to a pixel), which tended to provide poor contrast, dim screens, and terrible viewing angles, and they carried high price tags, but they took up a lot less desktop space than any bloated CRT. Today's offerings, which mostly use active matrix technology (the grids house the electronics that supply the charge) with thin film transistors (TFT), provide much better performance at a smaller price, though they're still pricier than CRTs. Then again, you could save some money in the long run—LCDs are more energy efficient than CRTs.

LCDs' non-flickering displays also help prevent eyestrain—a pitfall of some CRTs. CRTs redraw images line by line many times a second to display them on the screen. This frequent redrawing is known as the *refresh rate* and is measured in hertz (Hz). If a monitor has a refresh rate of 60 Hz, it redraws every pixel on the screen 60 times a second, but at this slow rate it also displays a noticeable flicker. To avoid headaches, get a CRT with a high refresh rate (75 Hz and up).

CRTs have their advantages: they're cheaper, have brighter and sharper displays, display more image detail, and are generally more color accurate—a very important factor if you work in a color-critical profession, such as advertising or catalog production. Still, for most people, monitor preferences are subjective. The best thing to do is narrow the field to a few choices (decide on CRT or LCD, a size, and a price) and then get an eyeful of each contender in a store display to see how they measure up.

Which Display Works Best for What

You may be drooling over Apple's Cinema Display, but if you work in a graphics-intensive field where color needs to be spot-on, an LCD display isn't the way to go, due to its viewing angle and color-accuracy discrepancies. Stick with CRT monitors that have a 19-inch or larger screen (you'll benefit from the extra size when viewing high-resolution images) and good color accuracy, such as LaCie's **electronblue IV** ($379, $799; www.lacie.com), a superb flat-screen CRT that comes in 19- and 22-inch models, and Sony's **Artisan Color Reference System** ($1,799.99; www.sony.com), a 21-inch flat-screen Trinitron CRT that ships with a color-calibration package to ensure accuracy.

For everyone else, size only matters if your work dictates it. While 17-inchers are standard desktop accoutrements these days, larger monitors provide more screen real estate, allowing you to view a larger area of a big file, have multiple windows open without feeling claustrophobic, work more efficiently with display-hogging applications, and view videos and DVDs in cinematic glory.

If you're looking to regain some desk space and want an LCD display, Apple's **17-inch Studio Display** ($699; www.apple.com) and the 17-inch **Sharp LL-T17D3** ($499; www.sharpsystems.com) both provide good brightness and detail. If you don't mind the bulk and prefer the clarity of a CRT (and the lower cost), NEC's 17-inch **MultiSync FE770** ($159.99; www.necmitsubishi.com) and ViewSonic's 17-inch **Optiquest Q71** ($169.99; www.viewsonic.com) both offer great display quality on the cheap.

If you work in a graphics profession that doesn't require absolute color matching or you work with large spreadsheets, a 19-inch or larger LCD or CRT allows a better view of big files. If you're a gamer—especially if you tend to play darker games like shooters and dungeon crawls—you'll find that a CRT brings out more detail and displays brighter graphics; a 17-inch monitor is all you need. LCDs tend to have problems keeping up with fast-action video, so if you're a couch potato, CRTs are still your best bet for DVD watching. If you use your Mac only to email, surf the Web, or word process, anything above 17 inches is overkill.

If you work with audio or video applications, you might be better served with two 17-inch or larger monitors rather than one big monitor. Two monitors provide more screen space in which to spread out software-editing windows, allowing you to view your work and access all necessary controls instead of having to close or overlap windows to get to what you need. If you work frequently with digital photos, text documents, or page layouts, you'll want to check out the LCDs that feature a pivoting display, which allows you to rotate the screen 90 degrees into portrait view. This lets you see documents in their full, natural state without having to scroll as much.

Communication Devices

Some say that you should never mix business with pleasure—these folks obviously don't own Macs. While Apple has been marketing the Mac as a moviemaking, music-playing, photo-sharing box of fun, it's a great machine for getting down to business, too.

Apple's iCal and Address Book applications (part of Mac OS X) make it easy to manage hectic schedules and mountains of contacts, but what about when you're away from your Mac? Thankfully, PDAs (personal digital assistants) and mobile phones can be synchronized to your Mac, allowing you to have all your iCal appointments and Address Book info at your fingertips.

Personal Digital Assistants (PDAs)

Carrying around a Day-Timer is so 1990s, but lugging around a PowerBook or iBook isn't always the most convenient way to conduct business on the go, either. If you need interactivity with your day-to-day schedule, a PDA can help keep your affairs in order.

These small handheld computer devices run a different operating system than the Mac OS—either Palm OS or Pocket PC. Each OS features its own set of applications that allow you to schedule, email, play games, compose text documents, connect to the Internet, maintain your contact list, and more. Some even allow you to listen to MP3s, take pictures, and make phone calls.

All PDAs feature an LCD touchscreen display (either color or grayscale) that does double duty as a monitor and input device (you use a cordless stylus to select items and enter info), and a few buttons for scrolling or accessing applications quickly. You can sync a PDA to your Mac via USB to share and back up information.

If napkins, hotel notepads, and business cards are cluttering up your briefcase or purse, a PDA can simplify and organize your connections. Here are a few things to consider when shopping.

Operating system

We said earlier that you have two choices—Palm OS or Pocket PC—but it's not that simple. The Palm OS and all its applications (called *conduits*) sync flawlessly with your Mac and are easy to use. Apple's iCal, Address Book, and iSync work with Palm devices, too. PDAs from Palm (www.palm.com) and Handspring (www.handspring.com) feature the Palm OS.

Pocket PC devices generally offer better screen resolutions, faster processors, and a lite version of Microsoft Office. But the operating system is rooted in Windows, and PDAs that support this OS aren't Mac compatible out of the box. However, you can use Information Appliance Associates' **PocketMac Pro** ($69.95; www.pocketmac.net) to translate data between a Pocket PC device and your Mac. PDAs from Hewlett-Packard and Compaq (which is now owned by HP; www.hp.com), Casio (www.casio.com), and Toshiba (www.toshiba.com) use the Pocket PC OS.

Display

Color or grayscale? Your first thought is probably color, but color comes at a price. If you don't plan on carrying around photos, playing games, or looking at anything that benefits from added hue, you don't really need to pay extra to get color.

Memory

All PDAs come with some amount of internal memory to store your data and files—anywhere from 2 MB to 64 MB. However, you can add extra storage and, thus, content to most handhelds with an expansion card, which is essentially flash memory—(usually in the form of SD (Secure Digital) or MMC (MultiMedia Card technology).

Features

What do you need or want in a PDA? All come with some form of scheduling, email, to-do list, Web, and note-taking software, and some feature a built-in camera, mini-keyboard, navigational joystick, wireless capability, or phone. And just like Macs, some PDAs allow you to connect peripherals, such as a full-size keyboard, camera, or battery charger, or add features and content, such as an MP3 player or audiobooks, via an expansion card.

Palm has a PDA for every type of user. The no-frills **Zire** ($99) is a 2 MB monochrome-screen PDA that features basic applications for general use. The **Zire 71** ($299) gives you color, 16 MB of storage, a built-in camera, and multimedia capabilities. And the **Tungsten C** ($499) offers color, 64 MB of storage, a built-in mini-keyboard, and a 400 MHz processor for power users.

Handspring's **Treo 270** ($399) is both a phone and a Palm-based organizer; it features a built-in mini-keyboard, color, and 16 MB of storage. Hewlett-Packard's **iPAQ h1945** ($299.99) is a Pocket PC device that features color, 32 MB of storage, Bluetooth, and a voice recorder. Casio's **Cassiopeia E-200** ($480) is also Pocket PC and features color, 32 MB of storage, and an MP3 and video player, and supports SD/MMC and CompactFlash.

Mobile Phones

Cell phones are fairly new to the Mac family of peripherals, but now that we've got Bluetooth in our corner, we can only hope that this genre continues to grow. With a Bluetooth-enabled cell phone, you can use Apple's iSync to sync Address Book and iCal information between it and any Bluetooth-enabled Mac with a simple click of the mouse.

Figure 7.9

A Bluetooth-enabled phone, like this Sony Ericsson T68 is, can be synced to your Mac's Address Book and iCal schedule, turning it into a lite PDA.

Currently, only a handful of Bluetooth-enabled GSM/GPRS (a newer digital cellular phone technology) phones are available—mostly from Sony Ericsson and Nokia. The **Sony Ericsson T68is** ($149.99; www.sonyericsson.com) is one of the most popular Bluetooth-enabled phones (**Figure 7.9**). If you want picture-snapping capability, the **Nokia 3650** ($299.99; www.nokia.com) lets you take photos and download them to your Mac wirelessly.

See No Evil: Graphics and Multimedia Peripherals

As a creativity tool, the Mac dominates the graphics industry. So it should come as no surprise that you'll find more graphics and multimedia peripherals for your Mac than any other type of device. Whether you're a creative visionary, you're visually inspired, or you want some entertainment, there is a device for you. Here are some pointers on everything from scanners to digital cameras. (If you're looking for the printer aisle, refer back to Chapter 6, where they're covered in detail.)

Scanners

Scanners could be considered the polar opposite of printers. While printers produce tangible copies of digital content, scanners take the tangible and digitize it. With a scanner, you can create digital images from print photos, paintings, scrap material, newspaper and magazine clippings, film negatives and slides, your face, or anything else that can be laid across a scanner bed. Most scanners these days offer one-touch scanning, USB 1.1/2.0 and/or FireWire connections, and adapters for scanning slides, film negatives, and transparencies.

The Mac OS X dilemma

While scanners are popular, Mac OS X put a kink in their path by excluding scanners that don't have Mac OS X drivers from the Aqua world. Due to problems with establishing a Mac OS X TWAIN standard (the technology that allows a scanner to capture an image), driver software trickled out slooowly or not at all. Most folks just stuck it out with the same scanner in Mac OS 9, or they've been using Hamrick Software's **VueScan** ($59.95; www.hamrick.com), a third-party scanner driver that makes most scanners work in Mac OS X.

Scanners are beginning to show some signs of life again. Umax, Epson, Canon, and Hewlett-Packard have recently released scanners that play in Mac OS X (though some require Adobe Photoshop or Photoshop Elements for native Mac OS X compatibility), but beyond the Mac OS X christening, scanners really haven't changed.

Color depth and resolution

If you want good color accuracy, look for a scanner with a high *color depth*—the number of colors that a scanner can capture (measured in bits). One-bit color is black-and-white; 8-bit is 256 colors; 24-bit is 16.7 million colors. Shoot for 32-bit color or higher for the most accuracy.

If you're scanning prints, magazine clippings, documents, and the like, a scanner with a 1200-dpi (dots per inch) resolution is all you need. Resolution consists of a width and length measurement that's measured in dpi. For example, a scanner with a resolution of 1200 by 2400 dpi can scan an image 1200 dpi across the width of the scanner bed and 2400 dpi across its length (the width measurement is what you should concern yourself with). If you're scanning small items like slides and film negatives, look for a higher resolution, which enables more enlargement.

For instance, if you want to scan a 4-by-6-inch print and make a reprint using a printer, you could scan the print at 300 dpi and then print the image out at 300 dpi to keep the same 4-by-6 size. But if you want to blow up the image to print an 8 by 12, you'll need to scan the photo at 600 dpi and then print at 300 dpi to get the enlargement. Likewise, if you scan a 1-by-1.5-inch slide and want an 8-by-12 print, you'll need to scan at 2400 dpi to have enough image resolution if you print the resulting image at 300 dpi. In other words, the smaller the item you want to scan, the higher the resolution you should use.

 Always choose a scanner based on its stated optical resolution. Many scanners offer higher—but inferior—resolutions by way of interpolation, meaning that the scanner generates extra pixels by an artificial means. Always look at the optical resolution as a scanner's true scanning capability.

Mac OS X choices

If you want a Mac OS X scanner, the new **Epson Perfection 3170 Photo** ($199; www.epson.com) is a USB 2.0 scanner that offers true optical 3200-by-6400 resolution and 48-bit color, and features a cool one-touch button that automatically removes dust or fixes color. Canon's **CanoScan LiDE 50** ($99.99; www.canon.com) is a super-slim scanner that features 1200-by-2400 resolution via USB 2.0, 48-bit color, and a handy-dandy expansion lid for scanning bulkier items. The **HP ScanJet 5500c** ($249.99; www.hp.com) offers 2400-by-2400-dpi resolution, 48-bit color, an automatic photo feeder (for 3-by-5 and 4-by-6 prints), and a detachable adapter for negatives and slides.

Digital Still Cameras

Digital cameras are one of the most popular peripherals (**Figure 7.10**). Unlike traditional film cameras, digital cameras can be connected to your Mac, allowing you to instantly view snapshots without having to kill an entire roll of film or spend time getting your pictures developed. Instead of capturing images on film, digital cameras record images on a CCD (charge-coupled device)—an image sensor that turns light information into a digital signal to create a picture.

Figure 7.10

Digital cameras basically come in three flavors— consumer point-and-shoot (left), prosumer (middle), and professional SLR (right)—and show up on your Mac Desktop as a mounted volume when connected.

Going digital can make the casual snapper a better photographer by taking away the expense of buying film and developing it, and allowing the freedom to experiment. Here's a closer look at some key camera features.

Focus on features

When shopping for a digital camera, you'll run across a vast array of features for each model. Not all features, however, are created equal. Here are the ones we think it is most important for you to pay attention to when deciding which camera to purchase.

Resolution. When people talk about digital cameras, *megapixel* is the buzz-word. A camera's resolution is determined by the size of its CCD chip, which is measured in megapixels (1 million pixels). The more megapixels a chip has, the higher the image resolution it can capture. For example, a 3.2-megapixel camera might have a resolution of 2048 by 1536 pixels—enough to print an 8-by-10-inch photo-quality print, while a 5-megapixel, 2560-by-1920-ppi (pixels per inch) resolution camera allows you to produce a 9-by-12 print.

Aperture and shutter controls. Photos are created from light hitting a camera's CCD. The amount of light and the length of exposure time are controlled by the camera's aperture and shutter, respectively. Think of the aperture as your eye's iris; it opens up to let in more light in low-light situations and constricts to decrease the amount of bright light flooding in. The shutter is like your eyelid; opening it for a length of time exposes your retina to light, while closing it stops the exposure.

To get a good image exposure, you need to balance an aperture size (measured in f-stops) with the right shutter speed, or vice versa. While all digital cameras offer an auto-exposure mode (many also include presets) to handle these settings for you, a camera with manual shooting modes can make you a better and more creative photographer. For example, setting a large aperture can create an artistic composition with a sharply focused subject against a blurred background. Setting a slow shutter speed allows the camera to capture motion trails from moving objects.

Media-card support. Most cameras feature some type of removable media, such as CompactFlash, SmartMedia, MultiMedia Card (MMC), Secure Digital (SD), IBM Microdrive, Memory Stick, or xD-Picture Card, depending on the camera manufacturer.

CompactFlash is the most widely used digital camera media. SmartMedia is on its way out; replacing it are the tiny MMC and SD cards. The IBM Microdrive, which is actually a CompactFlash-size hard drive, is mostly supported by pro-level cameras. Memory Sticks are proprietary to Sony devices. xD-Picture Cards are mostly found in Olympus products.

Different cards come in varying sizes (from 4 MB up to 4 GB), but most manufacturers package their cameras with the smallest-capacity media card that the camera can tolerate—in other words, if you set a camera at its highest resolution setting, expect to snap about one or two pics max, though you can snap a lot more if you shoot lower-resolution JPEGs. Needless to say, expect to buy a bigger card at some point.

Physical size. Digital cameras vary greatly in size—some point-and-shoots are as small as an Altoids tin, while SLR (single-lens reflex) cameras can be huge and hulky. But don't judge a camera by its size; even some of the tiniest cameras can pack a 5-megapixel CCD and full manual controls into their dinky frames. However, if you've got big paws, handle a few models before you buy. Always make sure that you can comfortably grip the camera without accidentally engaging its controls.

Zoom options. Zoom lenses allow you to capture a close-up of a subject from a distance. A 3x optical zoom (meaning it provides three times the magnification of the subject) is standard on most digital cameras, though some sport 4x and even 10x optical zooms. Optical zoom uses glass elements in the lens to magnify images. Cameras with optical zooms also feature a digital zoom, but don't be fooled. While optical zoom is a true lens-based zoom, digital zoom takes the highest optical magnification and enlarges the image using pixel interpolation to create the illusion of zooming in closer. The result: blurry or pixilated images. Always judge a camera's zoom capability by its optical zoom only.

White balance. How do you keep whites from looking blue, green, or orange? The answer isn't in a box of Tide—it's in your camera. A camera's white-balance settings allow you to compensate for a light source's color cast. Cloudy skies typically cast a bluish hue. Fluorescent lights cast a green pallor, and tungsten lights (household lightbulbs) cast an orangey glow.

Most cameras feature an auto white balance and several presets that counteract different light-source hues. The gem is a custom white balance, which allows you to set the white balance according to your current light for the best accuracy. Some cameras also offer settings to offset the camera's flash.

Movie capability. Many digital cameras offer a movie mode, which allows you to shoot short video clips. They're no replacement for video cameras; the quality, in general, isn't that great and recording times vary from a maximum of 15 seconds to 3 minutes continuously. Others let you shoot until you fill up your memory card. Most only capture video at 15 frames per second (fps) with 320-by-240 resolution, though some can do 640 by 480. If video is an important feature to you, compare camera specs before you buy.

Lens support. Point-and-shoot cameras feature a built-in zoom lens—you can't remove it. Most SLRs feature interchangeable lenses, which allow you to alter what the camera sees. If you have lenses for a 35 mm camera, you might not have to give them up when you switch to digital. Some Nikon and Canon lenses for nondigital cameras are compatible with Nikon and Canon digital SLRs. Check the manufacturer's Web site to see if your lenses are compatible with any digital cameras.

Some point-and-shoots support additional lenses via an adapter ring if the built-in one doesn't satisfy all your needs. You won't find any long zoom lenses in the bunch, but there are wide-angle, teleconverter, fish-eye, and macro lenses to be had. Nikon, Olympus, and Canon offer various lens accessories for some of their digital models.

Camera types

Go to any store that stocks electronics and you'll see a glut of digital cameras muscling for your attention, each with its own dizzying array of features. This can make choosing a camera seem overwhelming, but it doesn't have to be. Just decide which of the three camera types—consumer point-and-shoot, prosumer, and professional SLR—you most relate to, assess all the features that matter to you, and go from there.

Consumer point-and-shoots. These general-purpose USB cameras feature automatic everything (focusing, exposure, and so on)—just press a button and get a good photo. If you have zero desire to fiddle with aperture or shutter controls, this is the camera type for you.

Most consumer point-and-shoots fall under $500; are compact in size; capture images in JPEG format; feature movie and macro modes, a fixed LCD screen, and user-selectable scene modes (such as portrait, landscape, sports, and so on) and white balance modes; and generally have a 2- to 3.2-megapixel CCD. Some offer limited manual controls—don't expect the full range that you find in prosumer cameras.

The Nikon **Coolpix 3200** ($299; www.nikon.com) is a 3.2-megapixel compact camera that consistently captures great pics on SD media without having to think, and features auto and user-selectable controls and a movie mode. If you want higher resolution, Canon's SD card–supporting **PowerShot S400 Digital Elph** ($499; www.powershot.com) packs a 4-megapixel CCD, movie mode, and a rechargeable battery into a camera the size of a deck of cards. For über-portability, the **Minolta DiMAGE Xt** ($399; www.minolta.com) is a tiny square camera that packs a 3.2-megapixel CCD into a supermodel-thin frame.

Prosumer. These full-featured cameras offer everything that the consumer models have but also provide a range of manual aperture, shutter, and focusing controls; continuous shooting modes; more flash modes; better exposure metering; TIFF and sometimes RAW (the pure image directly from the CCD without any in-camera image processing) capture; image levels controls (which allow you to edit the exposure); and other user settings. If you know your way around manual controls (or want to learn) but don't want the bulk of an SLR, prosumer point-and-shoots offer most of the bells and whistles of pro cameras at a fraction of the cost and size.

Most prosumer cameras fall into the $500 to $1,000 range and have a 3.1- to 5-megapixel CCD. They're generally a little bigger than the consumer types and feature better lenses. They also come equipped with features that lend themselves to creative photography, such as long bulb exposures, selective focusing, and a good range of aperture sizes and shutter speeds. Many also feature a hot shoe for attaching an external flash and an adjustable LCD screen that can be tilted or even swiveled out so that you can shoot from any angle.

If image quality is important, the Olympus **C-5060 Wide Zoom** ($699; www.olympus.com) is an excellent performer: it can capture RAW and TIFF formats; it features a 5.1-megapixel CCD and a swivel-out LCD; and it supports xD-Picture Card, CompactFlash, and IBM Microdrive media. The 5.1-megapixel Nikon **Coolpix 5400** ($799.95; www.nikon.com) offers a wide-angle lens equivalent to 28 mm and a 4x optical zoom, an ultra-macro mode, and a swing-out, swivel LCD so that you can take pictures of yourself.

Professional SLRs. If you're a photographer by trade or hobby and know your way around lenses and manual controls, a pro SLR is for you. These types of cameras offer every feature imaginable and are capable of producing clean images, but be prepared to pay for the advanced technology—they can range from $1,000 on up, with most falling in the $2,000 to $5,000 range.

Most pro-level SLRs pack a 5- or 6-megapixel CCD and support RAW and TIFF capture for squeaky-clean, noise-free images, though they feature JPEG options, too. They also feature true through-the-lens (TTL) viewfinders, real manual focusing control, large memory buffers for continuous shooting, level histogram displays and controls (these allow you to view an image's tonal depth and make changes), FireWire or USB 2.0 ports for fast connections, faster capture and processing speeds, and everything else under the kitchen sink to perfect your images. Many of these types of cameras are sold as bodies only (though not all), and they're fairly large; you'll need to shell out extra for lenses—and possibly card media, too.

Olympus is setting new standards with its 5-megapixel **E-1** ($2,199; www.olympus.com), the first digital camera and digital lens combo to use the new 4/3 (four-thirds) system. This digital SLR technology (developed jointly by Olympus and Kodak) enables all 4/3 digital lenses to work with any 4/3 camera, allowing photographers to mix and match products from different manu-facturers. If you've got Canon EF lenses, Canon's affordable **Digital Rebel** ($899 body only, $999 with lens; www.canon.com) is a great 6.3-megapixel camera that uses a CMOS sensor instead of a CCD (CMOS consumes much less power than a CCD) and produces stunning noise-free images.

Digital Video Cameras

If you're looking to be the next Steven Soderbergh, George Lucas, or Spike Lee, a digital video (DV) camera (aka *camcorder*) will get you one-tenth of the way there—the rest involves talent, talent, talent (a little money and luck wouldn't hurt, either). DV cameras are much like analog video cameras except that the imagery is captured onto digital tape, which offers image and sound quality far superior to video's, and it won't degrade no matter how many times you copy it. Not only that, but DV cameras feature FireWire, which allows you to bring footage directly into any FireWire-capable Mac for editing.

Camera characteristics

If you're in the market to buy, here are some important features to note.

Format. There are five basic types of DV camera formats: Mini DV, Digital8, DVD, DVCAM, and DVCPRO. Mini DV cameras, which record onto Mini DV tape, have the most common format of the bunch for both consumer and professional cameras. Sony makes Digital8 cameras, which record footage digitally onto Digital8 or Hi8 tapes and allow you to digitize old 8 mm and Hi8 analog formats. DVD cameras are new; they record onto mini DVD-RAM or DVD-R discs. Both DVCAM and DVCPRO are professional formats—you won't find them at your local Good Guys.

CCD. As with digital cameras, the bigger the CCD, the better the image quality. However, most DV cameras have CCDs that are under 1 megapixel—usually between 300,000 and 700,000 pixels (TV viewing requires only a 640-by-480-pixel resolution, or about 307,200 pixels). Some manufacturers, such as Canon and Sony, are beginning to stock DV cameras with 1-megapixel (1 million pixels) CCDs.

Some cameras feature a progressive-scan CCD, which is capable of capturing images in a full frame instead of in a half frame (aka *a field*) like a typical CCD (during playback, fields are interlaced to present the image at full frame). Progressive-scan CCDs eliminate frame flicker (what you see when you pause interlaced video) and are mostly found in cameras that offer digital still capabilities and in higher-end models. Higher-end and pro cameras use a 3-CCD system, which produces better clarity, detail, and color.

Exposure controls. A DV camera uses the aperture and shutter to create its images just like a digital camera, except that these two factors control the exposure in every frame of video (see the "Aperture and shutter controls" section of "Digital Still Cameras," earlier in this chapter).

All cameras feature an auto-exposure mode, which selects a proper aperture size and shutter speed for you, but if you want to obtain the best video quality for your lighting situation, manual controls will do wonders—if you know how to use them. Some cameras offer exposure modes for specific situations (like sand/snow, sports, and backlight compensation), allowing you to easily dial up a preprogrammed setting in a pinch.

Lux rating. A camera's lux rating indicates the range in which the camera can capture footage under low-light conditions; the smaller the number, the better the camera is at seeing images in dim light. In general, a lux rating of 1 lux indicates that a camera will be able to capture a subject lit by a candle 1 yard away. A higher lux rating means that the camera will require more light to get the same exposure. Some cameras feature an infrared system (like Sony's NightShot) that allows you to shoot in total darkness (0 lux).

Image stabilization. An invaluable feature. Most of us don't have a steady-cam to keep our cameras stable when we're shooting on the move. Nor do we want to lug around a tripod everywhere we go. With image stabilization, the camera helps eliminate any herky-jerkiness caused by a jittery hand or other erratic movement you make while shooting.

Audio. All DV cameras can capture sound at CD quality (16-bit, 44.1 kHz stereo), but you'll get better sound if you use an external mic. Although all cameras feature a built-in stereo microphone, it picks up all ambient noise in any given location, which can be detrimental if you're shooting in a noisy or windy area. Look for a camera with a mic input to get the best possible audio.

Zoom lens. DV cameras feature longer zoom lenses than those of digital still cameras; a 10x optical zoom is the average, which means that you can magnify a subject by up to 10 times. Don't go fawning over some camera that touts a 440x digital zoom; as we said with regard to digital cameras, measure a zoom lens's worth by its optical zoom—not its digital zoom, which magnifies pixels to simulate a longer zoom.

Interchangeable-lens capability. Some prosumer DV cameras and all professional ones allow lens interchangeability. This provides more shooting and framing options, such as wide angles and super zooms, but it also adds expense. All consumer DV cameras are outfitted with a built-in zoom lens only.

Consumer vs. prosumer

Like digital cameras, DV cameras come in consumer, prosumer, and professional models. However, unless you're a big-time moviemaker, professional DV cameras (which are big and bulky and can cost more than $100,000—yes, that's five zeros) are out of most people's leagues. Therefore, let's focus on consumer and prosumer DV cameras.

Consumer cameras are small in size and highly portable (some even fit in a coat pocket) and feature noninterchangeable zoom lenses. These cameras generally cost $700 to $2,000; most fall in the sub-$1,000 range. Many consumer DV cameras also allow you to take digital stills, though the image resolution is generally low (1 megapixel or less). The Panasonic **PV-GS70** ($999.95; www.panasonic.com) packs a three-CCD system into a small Mini DV camera and lets you snap pics on an SD card (it also sports USB for photo downloads). If you want real portability, the Sony **DCR-TRV22** ($699.99; www.sony.com) fits in a purse or coat pocket and features NightShot, which allows you to shoot in the dimmest light or even complete darkness.

Prosumer cameras are bigger and use three CCDs to capture higher-quality images. These cameras generally cost $2,000 to $5,000. Some filmmakers prefer these cameras for shooting movies instead of professional-grade models (like

Soderbergh with *Full Frontal* and Lee with *Bamboozled*—Lucas used a pro camera to film *Star Wars: Episode II*). The **Canon XL1S** ($4,499; www.canondv.com) is the most popular camera in this league; it uses a three-CCD system, shoots on Mini DV, and features interchangeable lenses. The Sony **DSRPD150** ($3,940) is also a popular camera; it shoots both DVCAM and DV formats, uses a three-CCD system, and can snap still images, too.

Web Cams

Before reality TV, there was the Web cam. These inexpensive, no-frills cameras feature a fixed lens, capture images on a CCD (newer cams) or CMOS sensor (older cams), and sport either a FireWire or USB connection. They allow users to videoconference with others and stream real-time video content on a Web site. But in the last three or four years, these devices have grown stale in the Mac market.

That may change.

Apple recently released iChat AV—a visual chat program that lets you see and hear your fellow chatter—and its companion, the **iSight** ($149; www.apple.com), a FireWire Web cam that sports a large, f/2.8 aperture for brighter images in low light and a built-in mic. With iChat AV and any FireWire DV or Web camera, users can "call" each other without incurring any long-distance charges over a modem, or any charges over a broadband line.

Though videoconferencing programs have been available for the Mac for some time, Apple's foray into videoconferencing software and hardware may boost the technology's popularity again. If you're not keen on plunking down the money for an iSight, consider Orange Micro's **iBot** ($99; www.orangemicro.com) or ADS Tech's **Pyro 1394 WebCam** ($89; www.adstech.com), two cute, eyeball-style FireWire Web cams. If you'd rather bypass iChat AV and check out your USB options, Logitech (www.logitech.com) makes some nice USB Web cams.

TV Tuners

Technology is all about convergence, so why not TVs and computers? With a TV tuner device you can watch your favorite channels on your Mac. These devices connect to your Mac via USB and rely on an antenna or cable connection to bring TV reception to your Mac's Desktop. But don't chuck your TV just yet; the image quality on these types of devices is inferior. Still, if you've gotta have *Oprah* on while you're at work, a tuner can keep you from having to lug your TV to the office.

While older PCI card–based tuners mostly gave you just a television signal, TV-tuner peripherals go one step further, allowing you to record programs to your hard drive—kind of like using a digital VCR or TiVo. El Gato's **EyeTV** ($199; www.elgato.com) and Eskape Labs' **MyTV** ($134.99; www.eskapelabs.com) both feature a cable-ready TV tuner and TV recording capability in a compact USB device (**Figure 7.11**).

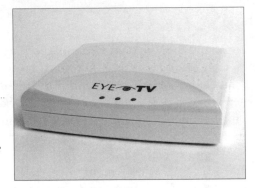

Figure 7.11

TV tuners like El Gato's EyeTV let you watch and record your favorite TV shows right on your Mac.

Video Digitizers

If you've got old videocassettes or an analog video camcorder, you're not excluded from desktop digital video editing. A video digitizer allows you to bring your old analog video into your Mac. These USB or FireWire devices typically feature stereo RCA audio inputs and a video input for connecting a camcorder or VHS machine, as well as analog-to-digital converters inside the box to digitize footage.

However, most of these devices won't allow you to import footage into iMovie for editing, though some ship with editing software (you can also use QuickTime Pro to convert footage into an iMovie-compatible DV clip). XLR8's **InterView 2.2 USB** ($74; www.xlr8.com) is a bare-bones, inexpensive product for digitizing analog video over USB and comes with video editing software. Formac's **Studio DV** ($199; www.formac.com) connects via FireWire and allows you to capture and digitize any analog source, and convert digital video back to analog.

Hear No Evil: Audio Input Peripherals

Plug a microphone or stereo directly into your Mac's audio input and you'll get good CD-quality (16-bit, 44.1 kHz) audio on your Mac. Plug an audio interface peripheral into your Mac and you can get a cleaner audio signal than with a direct connection. Why? Audio input peripherals package their analog-to-digital (A/D) and digital-to-analog (D/A) circuitry inside the device, allowing an audio signal to bypass your Mac's internal A/D converters and keep away from any processor and drive noise. Some even offer better sampling rates.

When it comes to recording sound, Macs rule. Go to any professional recording studio and chances are you'll find a Mac running the show. Many musicians, both professional and amateur, also use Macs as a part of their MIDI synthesizer setup. You can even use your Mac to digitize your old vinyl record or cassette-tape collection, overdub audio in iMovie, or record voice memos.

Whether you're a musician, need a way to get audio into your Mac, or simply want better quality inputs, here are the devices that'll keep things sounding sweet.

Consumer Audio Input Devices

Most Macs have a ⅛-inch audio input for connecting microphones, home stereos, and other sound devices. But for those that don't (such as iBooks, Titanium PowerBooks, and some G4 Power Macs), you can add an audio input via USB.

If you're interested in hooking up your stereo to your Mac, you need a device that offers a stereo line input, such as the **Griffin iMic** ($39.99; www.griffintechnology.com)—a great, inexpensive gadget that features a ⅛-inch stereo input and comes with a ⅛-inch miniplug-to-stereo RCA adapter for home-stereo hookups via USB. Griffin's USB **PowerWave** ($99.99) not only features mic and line support, a miniplug input, and RCA inputs and outputs, but it also offers a 15-watts-per-channel amplifier.

Pro Audio Interfaces

If you're a musician who's serious about your craft, you've got a wealth of toys to choose from at every price imaginable, depending on the type of music gear you want to connect to your Mac. With the right device, you can tether professional microphones, guitars and basses, MIDI gear, recording consoles, ADAT recording systems, and more to your Mac, and get higher-quality audio.

MIDI interfaces

If you're strictly a MIDI musician (no real guitars, drums, vocals, and such), look for MIDI interfaces. If you have only one MIDI device, Edirol's **UM-1S USB MIDI Interface** ($45; www.edirol.com) offers a MIDI input and output via USB that can send and receive up to 16 channels of MIDI data. If you're a MIDI gearhead, M-Audio's **USB MIDISport 4x4** ($199.95; www.m-audio.net) features four MIDI ins and outs that can send and receive up to 64 MIDI channels.

Audio interfaces

If you're a real player (an instrument player, that is), you'll need a pro audio interface—a hardware box that contains an assortment of analog inputs and outputs (I/O), MIDI ports, digital optical ports, and more. These devices connect to Macs via FireWire or USB and allow your Mac to record at a higher sound quality than a direct connection alone; most can sample up to 24-bit/96 kHz audio.

Most interfaces feature ¼-inch TRS (Tip, Ring, Sleeve) inputs and outputs for connecting outboard audio effects and instruments, and MIDI I/O. If you have professional microphones, look for boxes that feature XLR inputs. If you're a one-man or one-woman band with real instruments and no MIDI gear, Digidesign's **Mbox** ($495; www.digidesign.com) provides two combo XLR/TRS ¼-inch inputs plus S/PDIF I/O in a compact USB device. If you need to connect more gear, the **MOTU Audio 828mkII** ($895; www.motu.com) offers 24-bit/96 kHz audio, eight TRS ins and outs, two XLR/TRS combo inputs, ADAT optical, and S/PDIF via a FireWire single-space rack.

If you need analog audio inputs and outputs as well as MIDI connections, M-Audio's compact **FireWire 410** ($499.95; www.m-audio.net) supports up to 24-bit/96 kHz audio and features two XLR/TRS combo inputs, 1x1 MIDI, and digital I/O with S/PDIF. Need more inputs? The Digidesign **Digi 002 Rack** ($1,295) supports up to 24-bit/96 kHz audio and crams in eight TRS I/Os, four XLR ins, 1x2 MIDI, ADAT optical/two-channel S/PDIF, and more in a FireWire double-space rack.

MIDI Controllers

If you don't have the money or the know-how to include every type of instrument you want in your recordings, a MIDI controller will help you tap into a world of virtual instruments and modulated sounds. These devices, which are similar to piano keyboards, connect to your Mac via USB, but they don't contain any built-in sounds.

To get sound, you can connect a MIDI keyboard or other MIDI sound module to a controller and tap into its sounds, or install virtual-synthesizer or instrument software on your Mac and map these sounds to the controller's keys. This allows you to play and record sounds from a variety of sources (hardware and software) all at the same time from one keyboard. A cheaper solution: the Mac OS comes equipped with an entire bank of built-in, realistic sounds called QuickTime Musical Instruments—and they're free. These "instruments" can be mapped to the keys of any MIDI controller, allowing you to play and record a full range of drums, piano, bass, synths, strings, brass, and more.

If you need to play only melody lines and small chordal passages, and you'll trigger drum loops or other software samples, you don't need a large keyboard. M-Audio's **Ozone** ($299; www.m-audio.net) is a 25-key controller that not only supports MIDI, but also features support for pro audio connections. (**Figure 7.12**). If you're a keyboardist or want to map lots of sounds on one keyboard, get a bigger board, such as Edirol's 49-key **PCR-50** MIDI keyboard controller ($295; www.edirol.coms), which includes a bevy of knobs, faders, and buttons, and an expression pedal for shaping sounds.

Figure 7.12

MIDI controllers such as the Ozone, from M-Audio, connect to your Mac via USB and let you tap into a world of virtual instruments.

Speak No Evil: Sound-Producing Peripherals

Listening to sound emanating directly from your Mac's speaker (or speakers on a 'Book) is about as enjoyable as listening to Muzak over the telephone—it sounds flat. Luckily, you have plenty of options to make your listening sessions a lot more enjoyable. Speakers will give you better sound, a multichannel sound device gives you surround-sound options, and an MP3 player allows you to take your Mac-housed music collection to go.

Speakers

If you listen to music, watch DVDs, or play games, good speakers are an integral part of the experience. Those who tell you that all computer speakers sound like hyenas on helium haven't had the pleasure of hearing real speakers. Today's computer speakers sound better, look better, are available in multiple-speaker setups, and aren't made just by computer-peripheral manufacturers anymore. Along with stalwarts such as Altec Lansing, Labtec, and Logitech, you'll find offerings from Harmon Kardon, JBL, Bose, Klipsch, Yamaha, and Cambridge SoundWorks. (Also see Chapter 18 for additional speaker recommendations.)

Unless you buy a sound card or a multichannel audio peripheral to support multiple speaker connections, you'll need to stick with stereo speakers that connect to your Mac's audio output via a ⅛-inch stereo miniplug or USB. However, you can get better sound from a 2.1 speaker system, which has two channels (left and right) plus one subwoofer (thus the 2.1 moniker). You'll pay a bit more for a 2.1 system, but it is definitely worth it if you appreciate sound. Look for powered speakers, which offer better sound and louder volume than nonpowered speakers. The **Monsoon Planar Media 9** ($99.99; www.monsoonpower.com) is a superb-sounding 2.1 system that features two flat-panel speakers and a meaty subwoofer. If you prefer good sound coming from a PacMan-ghost-looking set of speakers, the **JBL Creature** ($129.95; www.harman-multimedia.com) offers 2.1 audio in a cute package.

If you frequently watch DVDs or play games on your Mac, and you have an audio card or multichannel device to support the sound, a 4.1 or 5.1 speaker system will improve the experience. The Altec Lansing **251** ($99.95; www.altecmm.com) is a 5.1 speaker system that's great for gaming and has a nice price. If you'd rather be a passive participant, **Cambridge SoundWorks DTT3500 DeskTop Theater 5.1** ($199.99; www.hifi.com) is great for movies and music on your Mac.

Multichannel Sound Devices

As an alternative to plain old stereo (two-channel sound, left and right front speakers), some peripherals allow you to get 5.1 (six-channel sound—left and right front, center, left and right sides, and a subwoofer) and even 7.1 (eight-channel sound—left and right rear added) surround sound out of your Mac. With a DVD-ROM drive, your Mac can become part of your home theater setup. If you like music and games, a multichannel audio device allows you to immerse yourself in sound. If you're an audio engineer, you can mix your tracks into surround sound.

M-Audio's **Sonica** ($89.95; www.m-audio.net) connects a surround-sound receiver to your Mac's USB port; supports Dolby Digital 5.1, Dolby Pro

Logic, and DTS sound; upgrades your Mac's audio output to 24-bit/96 kHz audio; features S/PDIF optical and analog outs; and slips easily into a shirt pocket. The **Sonica Theater** ($119.95) offers the same features as its little brother but doesn't require a receiver connection to connect speakers (it houses all necessary outputs). It supports up to 7.1 surround sound and offers SRS Circle Surround II for surround-sound music enjoyment and EAX (and others) for gaming (**Figure 7.13**).

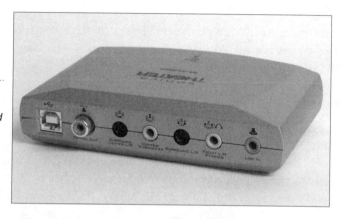

Figure 7.13

Want that theater experience on your Mac? Then you need a multichannel sound device such as Sonica's Theater to get awesome surround sound from it.

MP3 Players

Shouldering a hulking boom box down the street isn't a good look for anyone taking his or her tunes to go. If you want true portability without the hassle of schlepping a stack of CDs, MP3 players allow you to pack song files from a couple of albums—or a couple hundred albums—on a discreet device. Just connect the player to your Mac, load MP3 files onto the device, and you're good to go. Today's MP3 players store files in one of two flavors: flash memory or a hard drive. Here's a look at each.

Flash memory players

Flash memory players are generally smaller and cheaper than their hard-drive counterparts. These USB devices generally supply some amount of internal memory (usually between 32 and 128 MB) to store files, plus a media-card slot to hold more via removable media (CompactFlash, SmartMedia, or MMC/SD card, depending on the model). Most have a small LCD screen to display song info. Some offer voice-recording and FM-tuner support.

The biggest benefits of flash players are that the music won't skip when you're bouncing around, since they contain no moving parts, and they tend to be on the tiny side, making them great exercise companions. But because their storage capacities are dependent on your media-card stash (and dictated by your budget), you may wind up shelling out a wad o' cash if you want to archive a lot of songs.

Creative Labs' **Nomad IIc** ($99.99, $169.99; www.americas.creative.com) does triple duty as an MP3 player, flash drive, and voice recorder, and features 64 or 128 MB of internal memory that can be expanded via its SmartMedia card support. If you want small, the **MPIO FL100** ($149.99; www.mpio.com) features 128 MB of internal memory, SD/MMC support, an FM tuner, and recording capabilities in a Zippo lighter–size player.

Hard-drive players

Hard-drive-based MP3 players are bigger than flash players but are still compact. These players can hold a vast amount of music —anywhere from 4 GB up to 60 GB, depending on the player—and do double duty as external hard drives. Due to the nature of hard disks (they spin), these players are more fragile, though most feature skip protection to compensate for any frolicking you do.

One important thing to look at when considering this type of player is its connection type; some devices feature FireWire, some feature USB 2.0, and others have USB 1.1. Stick with FireWire or USB 2.0 (if your Mac supports it), as these will give you speedy transfer rates—after all, do you really want to spend time transferring your 20 GB MP3 collection over USB 1.1?

Apple's **iPod** ($299, $399, $499; www.apple.com) is the most popular player of this breed and comes in three capacities (15 GB, 20 GB, and 40 GB). It features a FireWire connection, supports MP3 and AAC files, syncs with Mac OS X's Address Book and iCal to function as a mini PDA, and is small enough to stash easily in a coat pocket (**Figure 7.14**). If you want to go even smaller, Apple's **iPod Mini** ($249) packs a 4 GB hard drive into Easter egg–colored enclosures. Also good is the Archos **Jukebox Recorder 20** ($289.95; www.archos.com), a 20 GB USB 2.0 player that allows you to record sound from a connected mic or stereo device.

Figure 7.14

Apple's iPod is the coolest MP3 player around due to looks and features. You'll often find it mentioned in "my favorite things" lists compiled by ordinary folks as well as the hippest people on the planet.

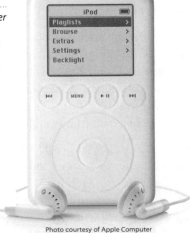

Photo courtesy of Apple Computer

Interview: Guy Kawasaki

Guy Kawasaki joined Apple in September 1983 as a "software evangelist"—part of a small team assigned to persuade developers to write programs for the Macintosh. He was recruited for the job by Mike Boich, a college classmate at Stanford University, who had launched the evangelism program at Apple. In fact, Kawasaki jokes, his job initially meant "carrying Mike Boich's bags as we circled the country spreading the word to software developers."

> *In 20 years, the Mac better not be around, and Windows shouldn't be, either. We'd better have the next leap before 20 years.*
>
> *—Guy Kawasaki, on the future of the Mac*

Kawasaki went on to lead Apple's software product-management activities, which included both working with outside developers and managing the Apple-labeled Mac software (MacPaint, MacWrite, and so on). In 1987 he quit to form ACIUS (now 4D, Inc.) and publish 4th Dimension, a groundbreaking database package for the Macintosh. Two years later he left ACIUS to, in his words, "write and speak and pursue my bliss." He became a columnist (first at MacUser, then at Macworld), lecturer, and author of Mac-inspired business-advice books (among them The Macintosh Way, Rules for Revolutionaries, and How to Drive Your Competition Crazy). He also launched Fog City Software, a small software-development company best known for creating what became Claris Emailer.

In 1995 he began a second stint at Apple, with the title Apple Fellow. In this capacity he became the Mac's most prominent and outspoken public champion, cheering on the faithful, heaping scorn on critics, and generally trying to fill the charisma void left by then-CEO Gil Amelio.

Kawasaki left Apple again in 1997, and in 1998 he launched Garage.com—now Garage Technology Ventures—a venture-capital investment bank and matchmaking service for emerging technology companies. He sells his speeches and presentations, at prices ranging from 10 to 99 cents each, at http://bitpass.garage.com/speeches.shtml. —Henry Norr

When the Mac came out in 1984, what kind of impact did you think it would have on Apple and on the rest of the computer industry?

I expected nothing short of worldwide domination—110 percent market share. There was no doubt in my mind it would influence the rest of the computer industry. The only thing I got wrong is that we couldn't monetize this influence. Today, 20 years later, I still haven't come to grips with this. Apple didn't profit by this impact, and most people ended up buying an imitation.

Why do you think this happened?

It's easy to say it's because we didn't license the operating system, but it would have taken a lot of courage and insight to go from making $750 per computer to $20 per [OS] license. It's not clear that Wall Street would have approved of such a decision at the time. And clearly, as Palm has shown, licensing is not necessarily a magic bullet. God has a sense of humor and wanted to see how people would react to using Windows.

continues on next page

Any urge to go back to Apple?

I have the urge, every once in while, to go 125 mph on [Interstate] 280, too. But I've learned to suppress such urges because they could both cause my premature death.

What's your current computer?

PowerBook 12-incher. I travel a lot and need something small, since Apple didn't buy me a Gulfstream as a going-away gift.

What changes would you most like to see in Apple's products?

I'd sure like longer battery life. I don't know who is rating the batteries, but I only get 90 minutes or so of use.

Anything else?

Streaming music from iTunes. I'd like iTunes to stream music by genre; then, when I hear something I like, I can click and buy the track with one click.

"Traveling AirPort"—that is, a small AirPort I can set up to access the Internet from anywhere in my hotel room.

Good feet on the PowerBooks. The rubber things come off in a month. The Apple Store told me they'd need the computer a week to replace them.

A line of bumps or a grip strip on the bottom of the PowerBooks, so that when you grab them out of a bag, your fingers can grip something.

As you can see, my desires are mere nits. I am, for the most part, quite happy with my Apple stuff. This is a sign of old age—I can no longer think outside of the box. That's why I do what I do today: find revolutionaries to invest in, not be one myself.

What's been the greatest disappointment in your Macintosh experience?

This one's easy: going into an Apple Store and not being recognized by the staff. Of course, to be fair, most of the staff are young enough to be my children.

What changes would you most like to see in the Mac OS?

Stop corrupting files; boot faster; buy VersionTracker and integrate it into Software Update.

Do you think the Mac will be around in another 20 years?

It better not be, and Windows shouldn't be around by then, either. We'd better have the next leap before 20 years.

8

Prevention and Troubleshooting

Dan Frakes is the chapter editor and author.

John Christopher and Ted Landau edited earlier editions of **The Macintosh Bible,** *from which portions of this chapter are taken.*

The Mac OS and its accompanying hardware are beautiful things—when they work. And the truth is that most of the time they do work, and work well. However, like any high-performance machine, your Mac needs preventive maintenance to keep running smoothly; even then, things may occasionally go wrong. This chapter walks you through the things you need to do to keep your Mac chugging along, and what to do when it isn't.

We start with steps you can take to avoid many problems in the first place. We then discuss the types of problems you're likely to have and how to approach fixing them. After that, we list some of the specific issues that you're most likely to encounter, along with quick fixes for each. Finally, we provide you with a bunch o' resources to use when the contents of this chapter aren't quite enough.

The problem with troubleshooting tips is that most users don't read them until they're having problems, so pay close attention to the word *prevention* in the chapter title. At the very least, read the first section now; the best way to avoid problems is preventive maintenance!

In This Chapter

Prevention: Keeping Your Mac Happy

The best way to avoid problems—or, at the very least, to minimize the damage if you do experience problems—is to use a healthy dose of good ol' prevention. Prevention falls into two categories: taking precautions and doing routine maintenance.

Taking Precautions

There are a few things you can do *right now* that will make troubleshooting easier should a problem arise, and in the worst-case scenario they'll help you survive a loss of data.

Create a "troubleshooting" user

In Chapter 2 you read about user accounts in Mac OS X. If you're the only user of your Mac, you may have skimmed over that section, thinking you had no use for multiple user accounts. If so, go back and read it now, because I recommend that you create an extra account just for troubleshooting purposes. Name it "troubleshooting" or something similar, give it administrative privileges, and then leave it alone—don't use it unless you have problems. As I'll discuss later in this chapter, one of the first things you need to do when you experience a problem in Mac OS X is to isolate the problem, and having an extra account will help you do just that. (Don't worry if that doesn't make a lot of sense right now; I'll cover it in detail later.)

Back up your data—now!

If you ask a group of computer users if backing up their data is important, most will say that it is. But if you ask that same group how many actually back up their own data regularly, you'll probably discover a prime example of "Do as I say, not as I do"—most people simply don't back up their data, or don't do it regularly. People forget, or don't do it just because seems like a hassle. But trust me on this: the first time you lose important data, you'll realize what a hassle truly is.

If you haven't backed up your important data, or if you don't back up regularly, place your favorite bookmark here and go to Chapter 5 for the scoop on why, when, and how to back up.

As an aside, in addition to regularly backing up your data, you should also be sure to regularly *check* your backups. Backing up won't do you much good if you later discover that your critical data is damaged or that the backup program or device failed. To avoid the future shock of a failed backup, restore a few critical files from your backup and then open and view them to make sure they remain intact. However, do be careful if you are restoring files from a backup to the hard disk where your current data resides. You could potentially overwrite more recent versions of your files with older data you have backed up.

Protect your software investments

In addition to protecting your data, you should also take steps to protect your software and hardware. Not just the software already installed on your Mac, but the original discs on which that software was provided. Your Mac OS X installer CDs, Adobe Photoshop CD, Microsoft Office CD—all the CDs that would cost you hundreds or even thousands of dollars to replace in the event of a fire—should be stored in an alternate location, such as a relative's house or a safe-deposit box. This may seem inconvenient when you need to reinstall software, but you have a right to make a copy of your own software CDs for backup purposes—keep these copies near your computer instead.

Consider insurance

If your hardware and data are important to you, you should also consider insuring them with a policy specifically tailored for computers. Many homeowners' policies have special riders you can buy that cover computer hardware and accessories. In addition, specialized insurance companies like Safeware (www.safeware.com) provide policies that cover *only* computers and related items, and even cover accidental damage and installed software.

Routine Maintenance

Once you've taken the above precautions, the most important thing you can do to keep your Mac running smoothly is to perform regular, routine maintenance. The tasks listed below don't take much time, and they'll save you a lot of headaches in the long run. In the description of each, I've included my personal recommendation for how often that task should be performed. If you have trouble remembering to do such tasks, set up a repeating event in your calendar program to remind you.

Keep your drives healthy with disk utilities

Just as the table of contents in a book references pages and chapters, each hard drive or other volume connected to your Mac has its own directory structure that keeps track of the locations of files and programs stored on that device. These directories can be damaged (or *corrupted*) if you shut down your Macintosh improperly, if your Mac crashes, or even if an application freezes. Luckily, the chances of major directory damage seem to be much lower under

Mac OS X than under previous versions of the Mac OS; however, just as a library's catalog of books gets out of sync as books are moved around, left on tables, and placed on the wrong shelves, your drives' directories can develop minor glitches during regular use. The best way to fix these minor problems, and to avoid major ones, is to use a *disk utility* that cleans up and/or repairs volume directories.

See "Disk Utility Diversity" below for a list of some of the most popular utilities.

Frequency: Once a month, or after a major system crash or other problem.

Disk Utility Diversity

A plethora of disk utilities exists to prevent, and fix, problems that might otherwise deal a knock-out punch to your Mac. All disk utility programs are capable of repairing minor directory damage, while a few include features to prevent such damage from occurring in the first place.

Since you can't repair directory damage on the drive you started up from, most utilities come on a bootable CD. You start up from that CD by placing it in your CD/DVD drive and then starting up while holding down [C]— be patient; your Mac generally takes a long time to start up this way—and then you run the utility from the CD to repair your drive. (To use Mac OS X's Disk Utility to repair your drive, start up from the Mac OS X Installer CD.)

 Before using *any* disk-repair utility on your Mac, make sure that it's *officially* compatible with the version of Mac OS X you're running. Disk-repair utilities can fix a lot of problems, but because they work with such important parts of your hard drive, they can also cause serious problems if you're using an incompatible version. Check the vendor's Web site to find the latest version and compatibility information.

Disk Utility. Mac OS X's built-in utility (/Applications/Utilities/Disk Utility) is actually quite powerful—it's able to fix most minor directory corruption, and many users get by without ever having to use another utility. To use it to fix drive problems under Mac OS X 10.3 (Panther), select the volume or drive you want to repair on the left, click the First Aid tab, and then click the Repair Disk button. (In Mac OS X 10.2—Jaguar—you have to select the First Aid tab, first and then select the volume to repair.) If you get a message that repairs were made, you should run the Repair Disk function again until you get the message that the drive is OK. (Disk Utility also includes functionality to format and partition hard drives, and to repair disk permissions, which is discussed in "Repair permissions" and "Startup Problems," later in this chapter.)

Disk Utility is your first line of defense when it comes to repairing directory damage. Other, third-party utility software may fix problems that Disk Utility doesn't, but Disk Utility is Apple's "official" solution, so use it first. That being said, there are good reasons to own and use third-party utilities.

continues on next page

Disk Utility Diversity　*continued*

DiskWarrior. Alsoft's DiskWarrior ($79.95; www.alsoft.com) (**Figure 8.1**) does one thing but does it exceptionally well. Like Apple's Disk Utility, DiskWarrior focuses on volume directories; however, instead of fixing them, it painstakingly rebuilds them from scratch, ensuring that you have the most complete and error-free directories possible. This process often allows DiskWarrior to recover "lost" data that no other utility can find. In addition, by optimizing the replacement directories it creates, DiskWarrior improves drive performance and prevents minor damage from becoming major damage. After creating a new directory, DiskWarrior even lets you compare the new one with the existing one before replacing it, to make sure you want to go ahead with the repair. (OK, DiskWarrior does two things; it also monitors your hard drive's hardware, like TechTool Pro, below, to watch for potential hardware problems.)

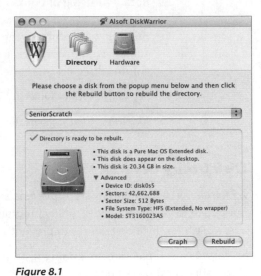

Figure 8.1

DiskWarrior can rebuild even severely damaged disk directories.

Norton Utilities. The granddaddy of disk utilities—it's been popular since before Mac OS X was a twinkle in Steve Jobs' eye—Symantec's Norton Utilities ($99.95; www.symantec.com) is a collection of programs designed to help your Mac out of a jam as well as improve its performance. The jewel of Norton Utilities has always been Disk Doctor, which, like Apple's Disk Utility, repairs directory damage, but it does much more: it scans your disk looking for bad sectors, fixes incorrect creation and modification dates, and identifies damaged files that could contribute to future crashes. Norton Utilities also includes a number of other useful tools: UnErase (which helps you rescue data from a damaged drive), Volume Recover (which helps you recover an entire volume), Speed Disk (for disk optimization, discussed later in this chapter), FileSaver (which keeps track of drive contents to help UnErase and Volume Recover do their jobs), and Wipe Info (to securely delete data from your drive).

TechTool Pro. Micromat's TechTool Pro ($97.98; www.micromat.com) contains more bells and whistles than just about any other piece of Macintosh utility software. Although it certainly qualifies as a disk utility, its feature set extends far beyond that of similar programs. In addition to mending damaged directories, TechTool Pro optimizes drives, recovers data, and even allows you to create an emergency partition on your hard drive that you can use to start up from in case you can't start up in Mac OS X. But what really sets TechTool Pro apart from other utilities is its hardware testing. It checks your Mac's hardware and peripherals for problems, and watches your hard drive for telltale signs of future problems. Whether you're dealing with a suspect modem or a malfunctioning keyboard, TechTool Pro can test almost every hardware component inside your Mac. (Note that Micromat also sells a utility called **Drive 10** ($69.95); however, TechTool Pro incorporates all of Drive 10's features and offers so many more that it's worth it to spend the extra moola and get TechTool Pro.)

continues on next page

Disk Utility Diversity *continued*

All of these utilities are excellent; however, if I had to recommend one, it would probably be DiskWarrior; most users can get by with the combination of Apple's Disk Utility and Alsoft's DiskWarrior. For an excellent comparison of Mac OS X disk utilities, check out the TidBITS article "Shootout at the Disk Repair Corral" (http://db.tidbits.com/getbits.acgi?tbart=07451).

fsck: Disk Utility's Command-Line Counterpart

In the sidebar "Disk Utility Diversity," I mentioned that most disk utilities cannot be run from the startup volume; you need to start up from another volume or from a CD to run them. However, there is one exception: the combination of *fsck* and *single-user mode*. Disk Utility's Repair Disk functionality actually uses a Unix utility called fsck to do its thing. Mac OS X has a special startup option called *single-user mode* that lets you run Unix commands. Combine the two, and you get a convenient way to run Disk Utility when you don't have your Mac OS X Install CD (or when you just want to run it quickly—it's much faster to boot into single-user mode and run fsck than to start up from a CD and run Disk Utility).

Note that if you're running Mac OS X 10.3, there is some debate over whether or not fsck is necessary. Apple claims that the *journaling* system Mac OS X 10.3 uses to reduce disk problems renders fsck unnecessary. However, some people claim that it can still be useful in circumstances where your drive is having serious problems. If all else fails, it can't hurt to give it a try.

Here's how to run fsck:

1. Restart your Mac.
2. Immediately press and hold down ⌘S; eventually you'll see a black screen with white text (you can stop holding the keys at this point).
3. When you see a prompt (a white square cursor, indicating that you can type), enter /sbin/fsck -yf and press Return. This starts fsck and tells it to check, and repair, your boot volume. (If you're running Mac OS X 10.2 or earlier and have resorted to running fsck, instead type /sbin/fsck -y.)
4. If you see a message that says "FILE SYSTEM WAS MODIFIED," this means that problems were found and fixed. If so, type the command in step 3 again—you want to make sure that the fixes didn't uncover other problems.
5. Continue running fsck until you see the message "The volume *volumename* appears to be OK." This means that all problems were fixed.
6. Type exit and press Return. Your Mac will start up normally.

If you keep getting the "FILE SYSTEM WAS MODIFIED" message, no matter how many times you run fsck, it means that your drive has problems too serious for Disk Utility or fsck to repair. It's time to get a third-party utility like Alsoft's DiskWarrior.

Repair permissions

Every file and folder in Mac OS X has a set of permissions that dictate who can do what with it. It's OK (and sometimes necessary) to change these permissions for user-level files, but changing them for system-level files (files outside of user home directories) can have unfortunate consequences. You can always change things back, but what if you don't remember the original permissions?

In addition, permissions can just, well, change. Sometimes the cause is a software installer or Mac OS X update; sometimes there is no apparent reason. (It's one of those mysteries of Mac OS X.) But the effect is the same: incorrect permissions.

Incorrect permissions on system-level files and folders can have significant consequences: printing problems, applications that refuse to launch, and even an inability to start up your Mac properly. So making sure that your system-level files have the correct permissions is an important part of good routine maintenance.

You can repair permissions using Apple's Disk Utility (/Applications/Utilities/Disk Utility). Launch Disk Utility, and click the First Aid button. Select your Mac OS X startup volume from the list on the left, and then click the Repair Disk Permissions button. The process takes a few minutes, but you can work away while Disk Utility does its thing. You also have the option to stop the repair at any time by clicking the Stop Permission Repair button (**Figure 8.2**). Note that you should run Repair Disk Permissions while booted from the volume being repaired, not from the Mac OS X Installer CD.

Frequency: Once every week or two, and after Mac OS X system updates.

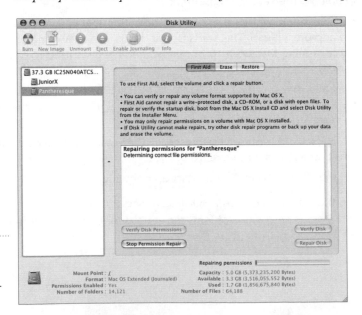

Figure 8.2

Disk Utility allows you to repair the permissions on Mac OS X's system-level files.

Run the Unix scripts

Most Mac users are probably reading that heading and saying, "What Unix scripts?!" Fear not—you don't have to know, or even use, any Unix to perform these maintenance tasks. However, you might find a bit of background information on the topic useful.

As a Unix-based operating system, Mac OS X relies on a few Unix scripts to keep things tidy. These scripts (called the *daily, weekly,* and *monthly scripts*) perform a number of under-the-hood tasks, such as updating and backing up Unix databases used by Mac OS X, mopping up system logs, and cleaning out temporary files. Making sure that these tasks occur regularly frees up disk space and helps Mac OS X do its thing.

In an ideal world these scripts would run by themselves; in fact, they're scheduled to do just that—at 3:15 a.m. every morning (the daily script), 4:15 a.m. Saturdays (the weekly script), and 5:30 a.m. on the first of each month (the monthly script). Why has Apple chosen to have these scripts run at such inconvenient times? The answer has to do with Mac OS X's Unix roots—Apple didn't make the decision—and isn't that important; what *is* important is that if your Mac isn't on and awake at those times, the scripts won't run.

A Unix geek could reschedule the scripts to run at decent times, but the average Mac user should get a utility such as the freeware **MacJanitor,** by Brian Hill (http://personalpages.tds.net/~brian_hill/macjanitor.html). Launch MacJanitor and click the padlock button to unlock it (you'll be asked to provide your admin-level user name and password) (**Figure 8.3**). Then click the appropriate button (Daily, Weekly, Monthly) to run that script (or click the All Tasks button to run all three sequentially). You can view the log generated by each script in the lower part of the window. (Alternatively, the shareware utility **Macaroni** [$7.99; www.atomicbird.com] will automatically run the scripts for you on startup.)

Frequency: Ideally, daily, weekly, and monthly, respectively. However, most users can get by running the daily and weekly scripts weekly and biweekly, respectively.

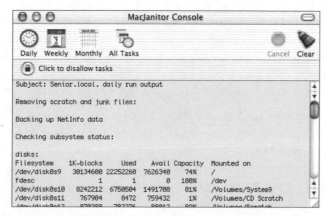

Figure 8.3

MacJanitor lets you run Mac OS X's Unix cleanup scripts on your command—no Unix knowledge required.

Keep space free on your hard drive

As a Unix-based operating system, Mac OS X uses the hard drive to temporarily store data and code (using what are called *swap* files) in order to manage memory efficiently. In addition, some applications store temporary—or *scratch*—files on the hard drive as you work with data and content. As a result, even if you think you have quite a bit of empty hard-drive space, in reality you may have much less ... or none at all! When this happens, you'll often notice a significant decrease in performance, or even system error messages stating that there is no free space on your hard drive. You may be prevented from saving changes to a document you're working on. In the worst-case scenario, the computer itself may simply grind to a halt, forcing you to restart (and losing any unsaved changes).

Needless to say, you want to avoid such situations. You can do so by making sure that your hard drive has a significant amount of free space available. (You can see how much space you have by selecting your hard drive in the Finder and then selecting File > Get Info; the amount next to Available is the free space.) I generally recommend a minimum of 3 GB (3000 MB) of free space, or three times your installed RAM, whichever is larger. If you use applications such as Adobe Photoshop, iMovie, or iDVD and work with extremely large files, you should increase that amount by the size of the largest files you use. If you have an older Mac with a small hard drive, this may mean buying a larger hard drive (4 GB, or even 6 GB, hard drives are pretty small by Mac OS X standards).

How do you free up space? Consider deleting applications you never use and files you rarely or never access. If you want to keep a copy of some of these files around, consider burning them to a CD or DVD.

Frequency: Check the free space on your startup volume once a week, unless you frequently create large files or your drive is getting full; then keep an eye out more often.

Update your software

Keeping the software on your hard disk up-to-date is more important than you might think. Mac OS X itself is updated regularly with new features, bug fixes, and security patches. In addition, new versions of applications (from both Apple and third-party vendors) are regularly released; these new versions often provide additional or improved functionality, but they often also provide better compatibility with Mac OS X, so it's important to stay on top of them.

As discussed in Chapter 2, Mac OS X provides its own Software Update system, which allows you to make sure you've always got the latest and greatest versions of Mac OS X and Apple's own applications. In addition, you can check Apple's Recent Software Downloads page (http://docs.info.apple.com/article.html?artnum=75150). Ensuring that you have the newest versions of third-party software is another matter.

If you regularly read the major Mac news Web sites, you'll catch a lot of updates in the daily news. However, to be sure you don't miss anything, you can check one of the major Mac software-update Web sites, VersionTracker (www.versiontracker.com/macosx) or MacUpdate (www.macupdate.com), both of which provide up-to-the-minute listings of the latest version of each software title available for Mac OS X.

If manual searching isn't your thing, several companies provide applications and services similar to Apple's Software Update, except that they search your hard drive for third-party software and then notify you when updates to any titles are available. The most popular is the commercial program **VersionTracker Pro** ($49.95; www.techtracker.com/products/vtpro), which uses VersionTracker's listings to keep track of updates (**Figure 8.4**). It can even be set up to send you an email when a particular product is updated.

Frequency: Weekly or biweekly.

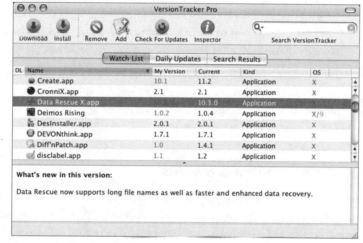

Figure 8.4

VersionTracker Pro tells you which software on your computer is up-to-date and which has a newer version available.

Invest in an antivirus package

If you've been even half-conscious over the past few years, you've heard about all the horrible computer viruses running rampant. Of course, if you've been using a Mac during that time, you probably didn't experience any of these viruses yourself. That's partly because the Mac platform is a smaller target, but mostly it's because the Mac OS is just plain harder to infect and hack than Windows. We Mac users don't have to worry nearly as much about viruses as our Windows-using friends.

That being said, you can bet that eventually a few people *will* decide that it would be fun to write a Mac virus, and that at least one of them will be successful. In addition, although OS-based viruses aren't a major threat to the Mac right now, cross-platform *macro* viruses—which infect Microsoft Word and Excel documents—are fairly widespread. Finally, even though most Windows viruses can't infect your Mac, many of them are spread via email, so your Mac can be a carrier if you accidentally forward an email that contains a virus to a Windows-using friend. For all these reasons, it's not such a bad idea to invest in an antivirus utility. The four major products available for Mac OS X are (in alphabetical order):

- **McAfee Virex for Macintosh,** by Network Associates ($35.03, also available free to subscribers of Apple's .Mac service; www.networkassociates.com/ us/products/mcafee/antivirus/desktop/virex.htm)

- **Norton AntiVirus for Macintosh,** by Symantec ($69.95; www.symantec.com)

- **Sophos Anti-Virus,** by Sophos (prices vary—the product is geared toward business and corporate users; www.sophos.com)

- **VirusBarrier,** by Intego ($59.95; www.intego.com/virusbarrier/home.html)

All these programs are capable of scanning your hard disk for viruses and inoculating it against new viruses. The products are also fairly similar in terms of features, offering one-click downloads of antivirus updates as well as protection against infected files delivered via the Internet.

Frequency: Once you've installed the software, it does its thing for you. However, you should make sure that your virus software's virus definition files, which keep track of all known viruses, are up-to-date by checking for new definitions every week or two. (All these packages have a mechanism for checking for new virus definitions.)

A Bug Is a Bug, and a Virus Is a Virus

To be crystal clear, here's the difference between a virus and a bug: A bug occurs when a programmer makes a mistake while creating the software product. This in turn may cause the program to crash when used. A virus is a malicious program typically created for the purpose of destroying data, frustrating users, and providing its creator with some twisted sense of gratification.

Defragment your hard disk—but only in some cases

As you save, copy, and duplicate files, Mac OS X places them in the first available block of *contiguous* hard-drive space—wherever it can find a space big enough to fit the file in question. When you delete files, spaces open up. However, since the new space and new files don't always fit perfectly, your hard drive gets a bit cluttered, with files all over the drive's physical surfaces and smaller empty spaces in between. This is called *disk fragmentation*.

In addition, sometimes the disk fragmentation gets so bad that when you try to save a large file to the drive, there are no single contiguous spaces large enough to hold the file. In such a case, Mac OS X splits the file into smaller sections and saves those to available spaces on the drive. This is called *file fragmentation*.

In theory, both types of fragmentation can affect the performance of your drive— the more your hard drive's heads have to skip around the physical disk surface(s) to find data, the slower the drive will perform. As a result, *defragmentation* (the reassembly of files into contiguous blocks) and *optimization* (moving often-used files closer together) software have long been popular maintenance utilities. And, in fact, under Mac OS 9 and earlier, defragmenting and/or optimizing your hard drive often provided significant performance gains.

However, with the advent of Mac OS X, there has been a lot of debate over the continued need for these utilities. The Mac's file system, HFS+ (Hierarchical File System Plus), has always been pretty good about avoiding file fragmentation. In addition, Mac OS X handles both file and disk fragmentation better than previous versions of the Mac OS. I personally have only defragmented my main Mac OS X startup volume once over the past three years of running Mac OS X (and when I did, I didn't notice any significant improvement in performance).

Because of this, I no longer recommend regular defragmentation/optimization for most users. The exceptions are hard drives used for video or audio work— situations where huge contiguous blocks of free space are needed in order to store and work with extremely large files. In these cases, defragmenting your drive can make a difference. (However, I would instead recommend buying a second hard drive and using it *only* for your video or audio files.)

If you decide that defragmenting and/or optimizing is for you, there are a few popular utilities that can do the job:

- MicroMat **Drive 10** ($69.95; www.micromat.com) (defragmentation)
- MicroMat **TechTool Pro 4** ($97.98) (defragmentation)
- Norton **Speed Disk** (www.symantec.com) (part of Norton Utilities; defragmentation/optimization)
- Alsoft **PlusOptimizer** ($29.95; www.alsoft.com) (defragmentation; only works on Macs that can start up in Mac OS 9)

Frequency: Once every few months, if that, unless you're frequently working with video or audio files.

Troubleshooting Techniques

Later in this chapter, I'll talk about some specific, common problems you're most likely to encounter as you use your Mac. However, because many problems won't appear in that list, the best thing I can do is to provide you with some helpful troubleshooting tips and guidelines. You don't need to be an expert to fix problems that might occur with your Mac; often, just knowing what to look for will help you find solutions. In this section I'll show you the questions to ask and the steps to take in isolating and, hopefully, fixing most Mac problems.

I've divided this part of the chapter into several sections. First I talk about some tools to have on hand in case of problems. Then I present some general troubleshooting tips that apply to pretty much any kind of problem. Finally, I discuss specific procedures you should use based on the type of problem you're having—hardware, application, file, login, system, startup, and so on. In general, you should troubleshoot problems in the order presented here. (In other words, check for obvious hardware problems first; then consider if the problem could be caused by an application, or by a bad file, or by a particular account, and so on.)

Troubleshooters' Toolbox

The key to fixing problems that pop up is making sure you have the right tools handy. Your toolbox doesn't have to be big—you only need a few items for most fixes:

- The Mac OS X Install CD that came with your Mac or that you used to install Mac OS X if you bought it separately. In addition to containing the operating-system installer—important if, in the worst-case scenario, you need to reinstall Mac OS X—it also contains Disk Utility, discussed earlier in the chapter. It may also contain Apple's official Hardware Test software.

- The CD provided with any third-party disk utilities, such as Alsoft's DiskWarrior or Micromat's TechTool Pro; this CD usually allows you to start up from the CD to run the utility on the startup volume. (See the sidebar "Disk Utility Diversity," earlier in the chapter.)

- A paper clip. Yes, you really should have one handy. You'll find the paper clip an invaluable tool for forcing your Mac to restart when other methods fail, and for removing CDs, removable cartridges, or floppy disks that get stuck in their drives, as described in "Force-Restarting Your Mac During a Crash or Freeze" and "Can't eject a CD or other removable disk," later in this chapter.

Also, as you read through this chapter, make note of any utilities you might like to have handy the next time you get in a bind. If a problem doesn't affect your entire system, you can usually get by with just keeping these utilities on your hard drive. However, in the case of major problems, you'll want to have them on a CD you can start up from (see the sidebar "Create Your Own Bootable Mac OS X Utility CD").

Create Your Own Bootable Mac OS X Utility CD

The Mac OS X Install CD includes Disk Utility, and a third-party utility like DiskWarrior or Norton Utilities most likely comes on a bootable CD. However, this means that to use more than one, you need to restart several times (once for each CD). In addition, there may be other utilities that you want to use while troubleshooting that aren't on these CDs.

Another problem with the bootable CDs provided with many disk utilities is that as new Mac models are released, they often require newer versions of the Mac OS—meaning that utility CDs sometimes no longer boot the newest hardware. The solution to these problems is to make your *own* bootable CD that contains all of your favorite utilities. Apple has purposely made doing so difficult (to prevent people from pirating Mac OS X); however, the third-party freeware utility **BootCD,** from CharlesSoft (www.charlessoft.com), provides a convenient solution. It creates a bootable CD based on the version of Mac OS X installed on your Mac and allows you to add your favorite utilities and applications so that they're available when you start up from the CD.

The instructions for creating such a CD are too long to include here, so be sure to read the documentation that comes with BootCD for the scoop.

The Basics First

You can't get past square one without applying some of the fundamentals of effective troubleshooting. Here are a few tips you should keep in mind no matter what the problem.

What went wrong?

Whenever something appears to have gone wrong while you're working on your Mac, stop and review the following steps:

- Take notes! Jot down exactly what happened, describing the problem in as much detail as possible, including what you were doing at the time. This will help you get a clearer picture of what is going on and will provide you with a written record of the details—useful if you need to describe the problem to someone else (or even if you just decide to give up for now and try to fix it the next day).

- Answer the following questions: What has changed since the last time you used the system without problems? What software did you recently install? What hardware did you recently install or connect?

- If you're having trouble fixing a problem, take a break. Besides giving you a chance to relax, taking a break can let you get a fresh perspective on a frustrating problem.

Check the obvious

Before you do any further troubleshooting, start here. Although these suggestions may seem obvious, you'd be surprised how often they solve the problem. (I once spent 3 hours trying to fix a startup issue, only to find out that the cause was a loose keyboard connection!) Only after you have answered yes to each of these questions should you proceed to the next section.

- Is everything plugged in? Believe it or not, this is the most common reason that a hardware component doesn't work. Do yourself a favor and make sure that all your cables are securely attached and snug in their sockets. This includes the keyboard and mouse. (Don't just look—make sure that connections are snug. Sometimes a cable that looks secure is ready to fall out.)

- If you have external peripherals—monitors, external drives, scanners, and so on—you also need to confirm that each is properly attached *and* getting power. Is each one plugged in (that is, getting electricity) and switched on? Check for power lights and other indicator lights; if they're not glowing, double-check the connections and power.

Hardware (and Hardware-Related) Problems

Hardware problems are both the most obvious and the least obvious issues you can experience. Sometimes a particular piece of hardware just stops working. Other times a defective hardware device contributes to problems in your Mac that seem to be completely unrelated.

First steps

If you're having trouble with a particular hardware device, run through these steps first:

- Make sure the device is officially compatible with Mac OS X and your particular Mac (check the box or the manufacturer's Web site).

- If the device requires software drivers, check the manufacturer's Web site to make sure that you have the latest version of those drivers. If not, download and install them, and see if the problem goes away.

- If the device just doesn't seem to work, launch System Profiler (/Applications/Utilities/System Profiler, called Apple System Profiler in Mac OS X 10.2 and earlier) and check the appropriate connection type to make sure that your Mac is recognizing the device as being attached (**Figure 8.5**). If not, double-check your connections.

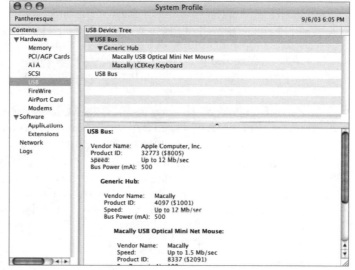

Figure 8.5

System Profiler (Apple System Profiler in Mac OS X 10.2 and earlier) lets you confirm that your Mac recognizes connected hardware.

SCSI effects

If you're using any external SCSI devices, ask yourself these questions (if they don't make sense, read the sections in Chapter 5 dedicated to SCSI):

- Are the SCSI devices properly terminated?
- Does each SCSI device have its own separate address?

Miscellaneous problems

Even if you're having problems that appear to be unrelated to hardware, before you move on to the sections that follow, try disconnecting all nonessential, unrelated hardware (such as scanners, keyboards, and mice) and see if the problem disappears. If it does, chances are one of the hardware items you've disconnected is contributing to the problem; to find the culprit, reconnect the devices one at a time until the problem reappears. Also, try swapping your keyboard and mouse with ones from another Mac; if the problem disappears, it's possible that your keyboard or mouse (or both) has bitten the dust. Sometimes even a loose AirPort card can cause problems, so check for that, as well.

Bad RAM and old batteries

Two hardware-related issues that can be the cause of problems, but are often overlooked, are bad RAM and old logic board batteries:

- **Bad RAM.** Bad (defective) RAM has been known to cause such varied issues as system instability, application crashing, and even an inability to install software (or Mac OS updates or the entire OS). If you've recently added RAM *(memory)* to your Mac and are now experiencing odd behavior, the problem could be defective RAM. Shut down your computer, remove the additional RAM, and restart. If the problem is gone, chances are your RAM was the culprit. If so, contact the vendor that sold you the RAM to get a replacement.

   (Even if you haven't recently installed RAM, it's possible that bad RAM is causing problems, so keep it in the back of your mind as something to try later if nothing else seems to solve your current problem.)

   Note that most recent Macs come with a Hardware Diagnostics or Hardware Test CD that allows you to test RAM. If there is a problem with your RAM, the Diagnostics CD will often detect it. However, it's not perfect—sometimes RAM that "passes" the Diagnostics CD can still cause problems. So I generally just recommend temporarily removing extra RAM as a foolproof test.

- **Bad logic board battery.** Many Macs, especially desktop Macs and older PowerBooks, have a small battery on the logic board that provides the computer with just enough power to store a few system-level settings (such as the date and time and the startup disk) in memory, even when the computer is turned off. Like all batteries, eventually these lose their juice (luckily, they usually last three to five years). If you have an older Mac that starts having problems starting up, retaining monitor settings, and/or keeping the date and time, you should consider swapping out your current logic board battery with a new one. Radio Shack sells batteries for many Macs; most authorized Apple Service Providers can also find the right one for you.

The Mac won't start up

If your computer refuses to start up, try the following hardware-related diagnostics:

- Unplug every peripheral, including the keyboard and mouse, and then try to start up your Mac. If it works, then one of your peripherals was most likely to blame. Shut down your Mac, plug in the keyboard, and then start up again. If *that* works, shut down the Mac, plug in the mouse, and then start up. And so on ... when the Mac no longer starts up, chances are the last thing you plugged in was the cause.

- If the above procedures don't find the problem, try starting up using the Hardware Diagnostics CD mentioned above. (To do so, start up the computer, put in the CD, and then power down the computer. Then start up the computer holding down © until you see the startup screen.) The Hardware Diagnostics CD tests the various parts of your Mac—RAM, logic board, video card, hard drive, and so on—and lets you know if any of them are exhibiting problems. If the Diagnostics CD finds a problem, it's usually time to take your Mac in for repair.

- If your Mac appears to start up but shows a blinking question mark, a screen full of garbled text, or a screen that tells you that you need to restart your computer, chances are the problem is software-related. See "Startup Problems," later in this chapter.

Application Problems

The most common problems you're likely to experience are issues with specific applications. Your Mac as a whole works fine, but a particular application just doesn't want to behave. Here are some steps to take with a misbehavin' application.

- Make sure that you have the latest version of the offending application and that the version is compatible with Mac OS X (and, specifically, the version of Mac OS X installed on your Mac). Check the vendor's Web site to be sure.

- If an application is acting oddly—certain features don't work, windows or menus look weird, or it just isn't working the way it's supposed to—often simply quitting the application and launching it again will bring things back to normal.

- If an application has crashed or quit unexpectedly, you can simply try to launch it again. Most of the time an application crash is an isolated event, and you can get right back to work. (In Mac OS 9 and earlier you would often need to restart your Mac before launching the application again.)

- If an application has frozen—it's completely unresponsive—you may have to force the application to quit. (After force-quitting an application, you'll often find that you can simply relaunch it and resume working.) You can do this in one of four ways:

  1. Press ⌘ Option Esc, which brings up the Force Quit Applications dialog (**Figure 8.6**). Select the stubborn app, and then click the Force Quit button (you'll be asked if you're sure you want to quit it).

Figure 8.6

The Force Quit Applications dialog allows you to force a stuck, or frozen, application to quit.

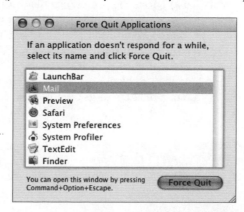

2. If you're trying to quit the application in front (the active application), press ⌘ Shift Option Esc, which will quit it immediately without your having to open the Force Quit Applications dialog.

3. Control-click (or right-click, if you have a multi-button mouse) the offending application's icon in the Dock; the resulting menu will include a Quit item. Press Option, and Quit will change to Force Quit. Select this item from the menu to force the application to quit (**Figure 8.7**).

4. Open the Activity Monitor utility, located in /Applications/Utilities (called Process Viewer in Mac OS X 10.2 and earlier). Select the offending application and then choose Process > Quit (you'll be asked if you want to force the application to quit).

Figure 8.7

You can force-quit any application from the Dock menu by holding down Option *while clicking the application's icon.*

• If the offending application is a Classic application, you can force-quit it using the first procedure above. However, be aware that this will often cause the entire Classic environment and all other Classic applications to quit, as well.

• If you relaunch an application and it still doesn't operate properly, first try working with a different document (assuming it's a document-centric application such as Microsoft Word or TextEdit). If another document works fine, it may be that the problematic document has somehow become damaged (or *corrupted*). If that's the case, try to copy as much data as possible from the bad document to a new one, and then delete the old one. (See "File Problems," below.)

• If the problem isn't with a specific document, there's a good chance that the application's preference file has somehow become corrupt. Quit the application and then locate its preference file. Most preference files are located in /Users/*username*/Library/Preferences (where *username* is your Mac OS X user name) and include the application's name in the filename; a few are located in /Library/Preferences. (If the preference file isn't in one of those locations, contact the application's developer to find out where it is.) Move the preference file to the Desktop and then relaunch the application; if the problem is gone, your old preference file is most likely to blame, so you can place it in the Trash for deletion. (Note that you'll lose any custom settings; however, if the problem is fixed, that's probably a decent trade-off.) If the problem still exists, the preference file probably wasn't to blame, so you should quit the application and move the preference file back to its original position, replacing the new one that was created.

- If the problem *still* exists after you've tried all of the above steps, you're basically left with four likely causes. The first is that the application itself has become corrupted or damaged; the solution is to reinstall it. The second is that your hard drive is having problems; you should run one of the disk utilities discussed earlier in the chapter to verify and, if necessary, repair your drive. The third possibility is that you've found a bug (a problem) with the application that is beyond your control; check out the sidebar "Don't Forget Tech Support." Finally, the issue could be a problem with your user account or with Mac OS X as a whole. I talk about these issues later in the chapter under "Account/Login Problems," "System Problems," and "When to Reinstall."

Don't Forget Tech Support

Sometimes an application problem is just that: a problem with an application. Maybe it's a bug, or maybe it's simply an incompatibility with other software or with the version of the Mac OS you have installed. Strangely, many computer users forget that most software developers offer some kind of technical support for their products. If you're confident that the problem is application-related, and you've tried the various application troubleshooting procedures in this chapter to no avail, consider contacting the application's developer. Contact information can generally be found in the application's About box; in the application's Help menu; in the Read Me file or documentation that came with the application; or in the developer's Web site.

Before you contact a developer for tech support, however, make sure you're prepared. Write down the following information: the version number of the product in question (which you can get from the application's About box, or by using the Finder's Get Info command on the application); the version of the Mac OS installed on your computer (available from Apple menu > About This Mac); your Mac's tech specs (model, processor speed, amount of RAM—all available from System Profiler); and finally, the complete details of the problem (exactly what happens, when and how it happens, what you've done to try to fix the problem, and so on). In addition, the developer may ask you for a Mac OS X *crash log*. These logs are created automatically by Mac OS X 10.3 when an application crashes, and are located in /Library/Logs and ~/Library/Logs (inside your home directory) with the name of the application included in the filename. (Note that in Mac OS X 10.2 and earlier you need to enable crash logging by launching /Applications/Utilities/Console, opening the Preferences dialog, and checking the "Enable crash reporting" box.) Having this information handy will better help the developer help you.

File Problems

Sometimes you'll encounter files that won't open at all, or that open but don't function properly (for example, a Word document that has garbled text, a picture that displays only "noise," or an email database that is missing messages or has dates that are clearly incorrect). If the application used to open that file (this includes the Finder, by the way) works fine with other files, chances are the problem is not with the application or the Mac OS but with the file itself. When that happens, try these techniques:

- If you try to open a file but you get an error message saying that you "don't have permission" or that the file has "incorrect privileges" (or a similar error), the problem is just that: incorrect permissions. Every file in Mac OS X has a set of permissions that determines which users can access that file and what they can do to it. Assuming that the file isn't a system-level file—which has its permissions set restrictively for a reason—you can use the Finder's Get Info command to change the file's permissions so that you can open it and edit it. Select the file in the Finder, choose File > Get Info, and then expand the Ownership & Permissions section (**Figure 8.8**). (If you're using Mac OS X 10.3 or later, you'll then have to expand the Details section.) Change the Owner to your own user name (your user name may have "(Me)" next to it), and make sure that Access for Owner is Read & Write. (You may need to click the padlock icon to unlock it in order to change these values.)

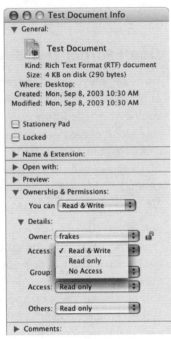

Figure 8.8

Use the Ownership & Permissions section of a file's Get Info window to change who can open and edit it.

 Apple has an entire Knowledge Base article dedicated to troubleshooting permissions issues, available at http://docs.info.apple.com/article.html?artnum=106712.

- If a file keeps opening in the wrong application, or Mac OS X claims that it can't find the right application, you'll want to read the tips on such problems in "Common Problems and Solutions," later in the chapter.

- If the problem still exists after you follow the above steps, the problem could be that the file itself is damaged. You should run one of the disk utilities discussed earlier in the chapter to verify and, if necessary, repair your drive.

Force-Restarting Your Mac During a Crash or Freeze

Sometimes a problem—whether caused by a misbehaving application, a bad file, an issue with a particular account, or a problem with the system itself—is so bad that it completely incapacitates your Mac. The pointer is frozen, or it moves but you can't do anything. Or perhaps you see the "spinning wheel of death" (the rainbow colored disc that just sits there, spinning and spinning and spinning). You can't even use the Force Quit Applications dialog to quit the frozen application(s) and get things working normally again (possibly because it's the Mac OS itself that has frozen).

In these cases, sometimes your only option is to force your Mac to shut down or restart. This is called a *hard shutdown* or *hard restart* and is something you want to do only as a last resort, because none of the helpful cleanup tasks that your Mac normally does when it restarts or shuts down—saving unsaved data, writing disk caches, writing changes to system preference files, and so on—are done. It's like suddenly pulling the rug out from under the OS—it's not ready for the event and falls down flat.

How to force-restart or force–shut down your Mac depends on which Mac you have:

- Most Macs will force-restart if you simultaneously press ⌘Control and the power button. If that fails, try one of the following procedures.

- On most recent Macs, holding down the power button for a few seconds should force the Mac to shut down.

- For many desktop Macs and many PowerBooks and iBooks, pressing Control and the power button will shut the computer down.

- For first-generation iMacs (Bondi Blue) and early PowerBooks, locate the Reset button and use your trusty straightened paper clip to press it. On iMacs, it's located next to the power cable. Press the Reset button with the paper clip to force a restart. (You can also use a ballpoint pen in a pinch.)

- For Power Mac G4s and Blue and White Power Mac G3s, use the Reset button, located on the front panel of the Macintosh and marked with a triangle symbol, to force a restart.

- For PowerBook G3 models that don't have a reset button, pressing Function-Shift⌘ and the power button should force a restart.

- If all else fails, gently unplug the power cord from your Mac, being careful not to jar or move the computer. (For PowerBooks, remove the battery first, and then unplug the power cord.)

If you had to force–shut down instead of force-restart, wait until you hear the computer go completely silent (meaning that the hard drive and fans have completely stopped) before you start it up again (using the power button on the Mac or the keyboard). Note that it's generally a good idea to run a disk utility (such as fsck at startup, explained earlier in this chapter) after forcing your Mac to restart or shut down.

Account/Login Problems

Over the life of your Mac, there are going to be times when it appears to start up fine, and you can log in to your account, but you experience general problems that can't be isolated to a single application or file (or to hardware). When this happens, the first thing you need to do is determine whether the problem is caused by an issue with your personal user account or by a problem with Mac OS X in general. This is actually much easier than you might think; in fact, if you followed my recommendation earlier in the chapter to create a "troubleshooting" user account, you already have the tools you need to find and fix the problem. (If you didn't create such a user, go do it right now.) Follow these steps:

1. If your normal user account is set to automatically log in (you never see the Mac OS X login window and never need to enter your account password at startup), you need to turn this feature off for testing purposes. Open the Accounts pane of System Preferences. Under Mac OS X 10.3, click the Login Options button on the left, and then uncheck the box next to "Automatically log in as." Under Mac OS X 10.2, click the Users tab and then uncheck the box next to "Log in automatically as *username*."

2. Log out of your account (Apple Menu > Log Out).

3. Log in to your troubleshooting account.

4. See if the problem is gone. Try doing the things that caused the problem before. (You were paying attention to that, right?) If the problem didn't have a clear cause-and-effect sequence, just work in the troubleshooting account for a while and see if the problem occurs.

This test basically removes *all* of your normal account files—preferences, Login Items, and so on—from the equation.

If the problem occurs even in your troubleshooting account, it's likely that it's being caused by something at the system level; see the "System Problems" section, later in the chapter.

If the problem disappears when you're using your troubleshooting account, it means that one or more of those files in your normal user account is most likely the cause, and it's time to figure out which one(s). Use these steps:

1. Log in to your normal user account again; however, after entering your name and password in the Login window, hold down ⟨Shift⟩ as you log in. Hold it down until Mac OS X is ready for you to work (in other words, until you can use the Finder). (This procedure disables any Login/Startup Items that were set to automatically launch when you log in.) Now use your account for a while and see if the problem occurs. If the problem is gone, most likely one of your Login/Startup Items was to blame; skip the next few steps and proceed to "Isolating Login/Startup Item problems," below. If the problem still occurs, proceed to step 2.

2. If step 1 didn't solve the problem, the most likely cause resides some-where in your home Library folder (located at /Users/*username*/Library, or ~/Library for short). The most likely cause is a bad preference file, so we're going to test for that first. Move the folder ~/Library/Preferences onto your Desktop; then log out and log in again. Is the problem gone? If so, one of the files in the Preferences folder is the culprit; proceed to "Isolating bad preference files," below. If the problem still occurs, move your Preferences folder back to its original location and then proceed to step 3.

3. If the problem still occurs after steps 1 and 2, there's a good chance that the cause of the problem resides somewhere *else* in your ~/Library folder (apart from the Preferences folder). Move the folder ~/Library onto your Desktop, and then log out and log in again. If the problem is gone, one of the files inside your Library folder is the culprit; proceed to "Isolating problematic Library folder items," below. If the problem still occurs, move your Library folder back to its original location and then proceed to step 4.

4. If none of the above steps (or their associated sections below) isolated the problem, you may want to look for further assistance, such as through one of the resources listed at the end of this chapter.

Isolating Login/Startup Item problems

If holding down [Shift] during login (*not* during startup; for that procedure see "System Problems" and "Startup Problems," later in this chapter) solved your problems, the cause is almost certainly one of your Login Items. Login Items—listed in the Startup Items tab of the Accounts pane of System Preferences under Mac OS X 10.3, or the Login Items pane of System Preferences in Mac OS X 10.2—are applications, utilities, and files that are automatically opened when you log in to your account. Each user has his or her own Login Items. (Even though Mac OS X 10.3 calls them Startup Items, they're called Login Items in Mac OS X 10.2, and for clarity's sake I'm going to continue to call them Login Items since they load at login.)

In order to figure out which Login Item is the culprit, use the following procedure:

1. Make a copy of the file ~/Library/Preferences/loginwindow.plist and move it to the Desktop. (Remember that ~/Library means the Library folder inside your personal user folder.) This file keeps track of which items are chosen as Login Items. You'll use this copy at the end of this exercise.

2. In System Preferences, remove the first item listed in your Login Items by selecting it and then clicking Remove (in Mac OS X 10.2) or the minus sign (in Mac OS X 10.3). Log out and then log in again.

3. Is the problem gone? If so, you've found the culprit. If not, repeat step 2 with the next Login Item, and so on. Remove Login Items one by one, logging out and back in each time, until you find the item that was caus-ing the problem.

4. Once you've found the offending Login Item, you probably want to restore all the ones that *weren't* causing problems, right? Open ~/Library/Preferences and delete the loginwindow.plist file. (You've been editing this copy in steps 1 through 3.) Then move the backup copy you made earlier from the Desktop to the Preferences folder, and log out. (This restores your original Login Item preferences.)

5. Log in again, holding down Shift (as before, to prevent any Login Items from loading). Open System Preferences and go to your Login Items. You'll notice that the list is back to its original composition. Find the offending item and remove it.

6. Log out and then log back in. This time, all your "safe" Login Items will load, but the offending one has been permanently removed.

Isolating bad preference files

If you've used the procedure at the beginning of this section to determine that your problem is due to something in your own Preferences folder, the next step is to figure out which file is the culprit. This can be a tedious process, especially if you have a lot of preference files.

Basically, you want to move a few preference files to the Desktop, log out and back in, and then see if the problem occurs. If it doesn't, one of the files you moved is the cause. If it does reoccur, those files are innocent bystanders—move them back to the Preferences folder, move a few others to the Desktop, and then log out and back in. Lather, rinse, repeat until the problem is gone, indicating that one of the files you moved to the Desktop is the cause. (Repeat this process with those files, one file at a time, until you isolate the single guilty file.) Delete the problem file and get on with your computing life.

 Before you start this procedure, I recommend viewing the Preferences folder in List view and then clicking the Date Modified column to sort the files inside by date. Preference-file damage generally occurs during a change to the file, so start by testing those files that have a modified date around the time you started experiencing problems.

Isolating problematic Library folder items

If you're sure the problem you're experiencing is with your own account, but the procedures above indicate that the cause is not a Login Item or a bad preference file, you're basically down to the contents of your personal Library folder. Unfortunately, this means that finding the particular file or files causing the bad behavior is going to be a bit of a hassle, because the procedure is simply a bigger version of the one for finding a bad preference file described above. First you need to remove one folder at a time, logging out and then logging back in, until you find the folder containing the offending file. Once you've identified the problem folder, you then need to replace that folder (put it back in ~/Library) and remove files *within* that folder one at a time, logging out and back in, until you find the file causing the problems. Not a lot of fun, but sometimes that's what it takes. That being said, here are a couple of folders you should pay special attention to:

- **Caches**—The cache files located inside this folder are used by Mac OS X on a regular basis; as such, they're more prone to corruption than many other files. However, they are re-created automatically if you throw them away, so it won't hurt to delete them to see if that fixes things. Many times, emptying this folder and then logging out and back in will solve a problem.

- **Fonts**—Font conflicts and corrupt font files can cause many different problems. I talk about font problems briefly later in this chapter (see "Font Problems").

What's a Kernel Panic?

Sometimes you'll be using your Mac when all of a sudden a gray screen will appear that contains text in many different languages. The ones you can read tell you that you need to restart your Mac! This, my friend, is the dreaded *kernel panic*. (If you're using a version of Mac OS X prior to Mac OS X 10.2, a kernel panic will instead turn your entire screen black and fill it with indecipherable white text. At least the newer one looks nicer.) When this happens, your only option is to restart your computer. You're going to lose any unsaved work; there's nothing you can do about it.

Luckily, kernel panics are fairly rare, and most of the time they're isolated incidents—once you restart, the problem is gone. However, the solutions for chronic problems are often found using the same procedures outlined in this chapter for finding the causes of other problems. The most common causes of kernel panics are hardware problems and corrupt or out-of-date hardware drivers—especially those provided via kernel extensions. You should first ensure that you have the latest version of Mac OS X installed, and then test for hardware or driver problems. Use the procedures in "Hardware (and Hardware-Related) Problems," earlier in this chapter, to check your hardware. To isolate a problematic kernel extension, use the procedures described in "Startup Problems," below.

One other tool that can be useful when experiencing kernel panics is the kernel panic log that Mac OS X sometimes creates when such a problem occurs. When you fall victim to a kernel panic, after restarting, check the folder /Library/Logs. If you see a file called panic.log, open it and see if it contains any useful information about what was going on at the instant the kernel panic occurred. Sometimes you'll see the name of the file that caused the operating system to hiccup.

Note that sometimes kernel panics occur because Mac OS X system files are missing. Maybe you accidentally threw important system-level files away, or maybe one of them became so corrupt that the OS could no longer use it. In these cases, the only solution may be to reinstall Mac OS X. (See "When to Reinstall," later in this chapter.)

System Problems

If you're experiencing general problems that affect *all* accounts on your Mac—in other words, you weren't able to isolate them to a single user account—it's a good bet that the problem is with the Mac OS itself (or at least a system-level add-on or utility that has been installed). If this is the case, try the following procedures, preferably in this order, until the problem is gone:

- Run a disk-repair utility as described earlier in the chapter; often systemwide problems are symptoms of underlying hard-drive issues.

- Delete the contents of /Library/Caches and restart. As with user-level cache files, these system-level cache files can become corrupt and lead to systemwide problems.

- Download Northern Softworks' shareware utility **Panther Cache Cleaner** ($7.95; www.northernsoftworks.com)—despite its name, it also works with older versions of Mac OS X. From the Caches tab, first run the Light Cleaning option and then restart; if the problems don't go away, try the Deep Cleaning option. These procedures delete a number of cache files, temporary files, and nonvital Finder and system settings files, any one of which can cause problems if it gets damaged.

- Restart your Mac, but hold down Shift until you get to the login screen—this is called a *safe boot*. First your Mac checks the startup drive for damage and attempts to fix any damage it finds (it's actually using fsck, discussed earlier in the chapter); then Mac OS X boots with only essential, Apple-provided kernel extensions and startup items active. If the problem still occurs, move on to the next procedure. If the problem is gone, skip to the sidebar "Following Up a Successful Safe Boot," below.

- Use the procedure described in "Isolating bad preference files," earlier in this chapter, except with the *main* Preferences folder located at /Library/Preferences (instead of your own user-level Preferences folder). These preferences affect all user accounts; like any other preference files they can become corrupt, which can affect the OS as a whole.

- Restart your Mac, holding down ⌘ Option P R until you hear a second startup chime. This "zaps" (clears out) the *PRAM* (parameter RAM), which stores a number of low-level system settings, such as the date and time and the startup disk. If the PRAM gets corrupted, weird things can happen. You'll probably lose a few system settings by zapping the PRAM, but if it fixes the problems you're experiencing, it's worth it.

- Restart your Mac, holding down ⌘ Option O F. This brings up a scary-looking gray screen with some text—you've just entered what is called Open Firmware. Be careful what you type here, because you're interacting *directly* with your Mac's hardware. Type reset-nvram and press Return. Then type reset-all and press Return. Your computer should restart; if it doesn't, type mac-boot and press Return. This procedure resets your Mac's *NVRAM* (nonvolatile RAM), which is similar to PRAM. Many users find that resetting NVRAM solves odd system issues.

Unfortunately, if all of the above procedures fail, you may end up having to reinstall Mac OS X (see "When to Reinstall," later in the chapter).

Following Up a Successful Safe Boot

If your system problem went away after a *safe boot*, this means that the problem was caused either by disk damage or by a bad startup item or kernel extension. To figure out which, restart normally. If the problem is still gone, disk damage was the culprit, and the safe boot repaired the damage—you're set!

If the problem resumes when you restart normally, chances are that you have a bad startup item or kernel extension. Do another safe boot; the problem should again go away. If you have any third-party items in /Library/StartupItems, move them out of the StartupItems folder (you can place them on the Desktop for now) and then restart normally. If the problem is gone, one of those startup items is the culprit. Contact the developer of the startup item about getting an updated or compatible version. (If this doesn't solve the problem, you can move the items back into the/Library/StartupItems/ folder.)

If a startup item isn't the problem, a kernel extension—located in /System/Library/Extensions—is probably responsible. Figuring out which one is the guilty party is much like the procedure for figuring out which preference file is bad (described in "Isolating bad preference files," earlier in the chapter); the extra hurdle here is that most kernel extensions have their permissions set to be off-limits to users. In order to remove one from the Extensions folder, you need to use the Finder's Get Info window to change the owner to yourself. Just be sure that if you move a kernel extension *back* into the Extensions folder, you change the permissions back exactly as they were before.

One tip I can give you: before laboriously moving kernel extensions in and out, one at a time, restarting each time, stop and think about software you installed (including hardware drivers) just before you started experiencing problems. If one of those software packages installed a kernel extension, there's a good chance it's the cause of your trouble.

Startup Problems

Although startup problems are far less common in Mac OS X than they are in Mac OS 9 and earlier (at least in my experience), they can still happen. You may see one of a number of startup symptoms, such as a plain blue screen, a blank gray screen, a kernel panic (described in "What's a Kernel Panic?" earlier in this chapter), a flashing question mark, a screen full of text, odd startup chimes, or (if you're running older versions of Mac OS X) a broken folder icon. Here are some general steps to take if you experience a stalled startup.

1. One of the most common causes of startup issues is hardware: bad hardware peripherals, bad cables, or bad RAM. If your Mac is having trouble starting up, first check for hardware issues, as described earlier in this chapter under "Hardware (and Hardware-Related) Problems." Be sure

to check all RAM, and if you have peripherals, especially SCSI and USB peripherals, be sure to disconnect them to see if they're preventing startup.

2. If all is well on the hardware front, it's time to check your hard drive. Run a disk utility or fsck, as described earlier in this chapter (in the sidebars "Disk Utility Diversity" and "fsck: Disk Utility's Command-Line Counterpart"). If you can then start up normally, the problem was disk corruption.

3. If your hardware and hard drive are OK, the problem is probably software- or settings-related. The most general—and generally most effective— procedure you can use to verify this is called a *safe boot*, which is a special startup mode that first checks your drive for damage and then loads a bare-bones version of Mac OS X, with all nonessential and third-party drivers, kernel extensions, and startup items disabled (see the previous section, "System Problems").

    To perform a safe boot, shut down your Mac and then start up while holding down Shift. Keep Shift pressed down until the words "Safe Boot" appear on the screen. If your Mac starts up successfully, restart normally. If startup proceeds normally, safe boot's drive-repair mode fixed some problem with your hard drive and you're good to go. If the startup problem returns, your hard drive is fine, and the problem is most likely with a startup item or kernel extension. Check out the sidebar "Following Up a Successful Safe Boot," above, for instructions on how to isolate a bad startup item or kernel extension.

 Kernel extensions are drivers that interact with Mac OS X at a very low level and therefore can cause some nasty problems if they conflict with anything. Third-party startup items, located in /Library/StartupItems, are services that launch at startup, before you even get to the LogIn window.

Special startup problems

The above procedures apply to all startup problems. However, there are a few startup issues that may require specific troubleshooting techniques in addition to the steps recommended above.

A flashing question mark appears. If you see a flashing question mark, your Mac cannot find a startup volume that has a copy of the Mac OS installed. Sometimes if you wait a few seconds, the flashing question mark will disappear and your Mac will start up normally; other times it stays there and your Mac never starts up. In either case, there are a couple of possible reasons for this behavior—besides disk corruption, which you already tested for—and they are listed below with their solutions. Try them in order; if the first doesn't fix things, proceed to the second.

1. Your Mac doesn't have a startup disk selected. Start up or restart your Mac, holding down Option. This should bring up the Startup Manager— a blue screen with a gray button for each connected volume with a valid OS. Click your hard drive's icon, and then click the right arrow to continue startup. If you're able to successfully boot into Mac OS X using this

procedure, launch System Preferences, select the Startup Disk pane, and then make sure your hard drive is selected as the preferred startup disk. If you can't start up into Mac OS X, and [Option] at startup isn't working, start up from the Mac OS X Install CD (or DVD, if applicable) by inserting the disc and restarting, and then holding down [C] until you see the Installer screen. From the Installer menu, choose Startup Disk, and then use the Startup Disk utility that appears to select the appropriate hard drive containing Mac OS X. Quit out of the Startup Disk Utility, and then quit the Installer to restart.

2. Your Mac's PRAM, which remembers your startup-disk preferences, is corrupt. To reset it, shut down your Mac, and then start it up again while holding down [⌘][Option][P][R]. Keep holding down these keys until you hear the startup chime two or three times, and then release them. If the problem was bad PRAM, you Mac should start up normally.

Figure 8.9

If you see this symbol at startup, you have a startup problem!

The screen is gray and has a "prohibitory" sign. If you see a gray screen with a sign like that shown in **Figure 8.9** (a circle with a line through it), or with an icon that looks like a broken folder, it means that you do not have a valid or complete copy of Mac OS X installed (or at least your Mac doesn't think you do). A few different possible causes—besides disk corruption and hardware, which you already tested for—are listed below, along with solutions for each:

1. Your Mac's NVRAM settings have become corrupted. Follow the procedure for resetting NVRAM under "System Problems," above.

2. The permissions settings for one or more system-level files are incorrect or corrupt. Start up from your Mac OS X Install CD, launch Disk Utility from the Installer menu, and then run the Repair Disk Permissions function. If this allows your Mac to start up normally, be sure to run Repair Disk Permissions again when started up from the hard drive, using the copy of Disk Utility on the hard drive.

3. The version of Mac OS X installed on your computer is too old to start up your computer. Perhaps you transferred a copy of Mac OS X from an older Mac to your current Mac? If this is the cause of the problem, you need to install a newer version of Mac OS X that is compatible with your computer.

4. The copy of Mac OS X installed on your Mac is missing key components. This can happen if you've started up in Mac OS 9 and thrown away certain files (including several that are invisible in Mac OS X but visible in Mac OS 9). For example, if any of the following files or folders, normally located at the root level of your hard drive, are missing, Mac OS X will not load: Applications, automount, Library, mach_kernel, System, Users. If you've thrown away any of these files or folders and cannot restore them, you'll need to reinstall Mac OS X.

A blue screen appears at startup. If you see a blue screen at startup and the general procedures for solving startup problems don't identify the culprit, the cause may be a bad font in a Mac OS 9 System Folder installed on your hard drive (used either for the Classic environment or for starting up into Mac OS 9).

Start up in safe boot mode and then drag the Fonts folder from the Mac OS 9 System Folder to the Desktop. Restart normally; if the problem is gone, a bad font is the offending file.

Nothing helps. If you've tried everything in this section and you still can't get your Mac to start up at all, even from the Install CD or a disk utility CD, it's probably time to take it to an Authorized Service Provider to see if there is a hardware problem.

Font Problems

Under Mac OS 9 and earlier, fonts were the bane of many a user's existence. Luckily, Mac OS X is much less sensitive to font problems; however, that's not to say they don't happen. And, unfortunately, identifying a font problem is often more difficult than fixing one.

Font problems generally manifest as odd application or document behavior (jagged or odd font displays); applications unexpectedly quitting or refusing to launch; and even problems starting up your Mac. What makes font problems so difficult to diagnose is that problems caused by fonts can also be caused by other things (as discussed in previous sections of this chapter). So checking for font issues—corrupt or damaged fonts, conflicting font IDs, or multiple versions of the same font—is usually done as a last resort when the usual fixes don't actually fix. For more information on how to diagnose and fix font problems, check out Chapter 15.

Network/Internet Problems

Below are a few general tips for figuring out problems with network or Internet connectivity. Unfortunately, space limitations prevent me from providing a comprehensive discussion of network and Internet issues. If you're having trouble connecting to the Internet or a network, the first thing you should do is read Chapters 19 and 20 to make sure you have everything set up correctly and to try some of the troubleshooting tips covered there. If you want more information, be sure to check out the additional troubleshooting resources listed at the end of this chapter.

- Check all your network connections (cables, wires, DSL or cable modem power cables, and so on). Double-check!

- If you're experiencing Internet problems in a particular application, try using a different Internet application. For example, if you're having trouble using Safari, try using Microsoft Internet Explorer. If Internet Explorer works, the problem is with Safari, not your Internet connection. Likewise, if you're having trouble receiving email, try using a different email client or a shareware utility like **POPmonitor** ($25; www.vechtwijk.nl/dev/popmonitor/index.html) to connect to your email account. If you're successful, the problem is with your primary email client or your settings, not your Internet connection.

- If you can't use any Internet-related applications and you've checked all connections and settings, it's possible that your ISP is having problems and there's nothing you can do but wait for them to fix things. Many ISPs have a special phone number you can call for status reports on Internet problems. (If you're sure the problem is with your ISP, you can also call your ISP's technical support line to report the problem; chances are they already know about it, but you never know!)

Printing Problems

Below are a few general tips for dealing with printing problems. As with the previous section, space limitations prevent me from providing a comprehensive discussion of printing problems and solutions. If you're having trouble printing, I recommend first reviewing Chapter 6, to make sure you have everything set up correctly and to try some of the setup and troubleshooting tips described. If you want more information, be sure to check out the additional troubleshooting resources listed at the end of this chapter.

- Make sure the printer is connected properly. Double-check!

- Make sure you have the latest drivers for your printer; check the vendor's Web site for more information on drivers and compatibility.

- Try printing from another application. If the printing problems affect only a single application, chances are it's a problem with that application rather than the printer.

- Apple has provided an excellent set of documents on troubleshooting printing at Mac OS X: Troubleshooting Printing Issues (http://docs.info. apple.com/article.html?artnum=106714) and—for Mac OS X 10.2—Mac OS X: Troubleshooting Print Center (http://docs.info.apple.com/ article.html?artnum=25385).

- Many common printing problems can be solved using the shareware utility **Print Center Repair** for Mac OS X 10.1–10.2 ($15; www.fixamac.net/ software/pcr) or **Printer Setup Repair** for Mac OS X 10.3 ($15; www.fixamac.net/software/psr/index.html). Be sure to read the manual before using it.

- If you're using Mac OS X 10.2.x and the problem you're experiencing is related to a printer that isn't officially supported by Mac OS X, you may be able to add support for that printer via the free **Gimp-Print** printer drivers. These drivers, available from http://gimp-print.sourceforge.net/ MacOSX.php3, provide support for hundreds of additional printers. Just be sure to read the accompanying documentation that details installation and setup. (The Gimp-Print printer drivers are already installed by default with Mac OS X 10.3.)

Disk Problems

In many of the previous sections I've recommended using a disk utility to check for and, if necessary, repair drive and volume damage. I covered the use of major Mac OS X disk utilities previously in this chapter (see the sidebar "Disk Utility Diversity") as a form of preventive maintenance. However, most people are more familiar with disk utilities as a way to *fix* problems that have already occurred. The process is identical—start up from the utility CD and run the utility on your hard drive.

When to Reinstall

Unfortunately, there are times when none of the above solutions will work (nor will any of the solutions described in the next section), because the operating system itself has become damaged and unusable. These situations are rare, but when they happen, the only solution is to reinstall Mac OS X. Luckily Mac OS X 10.2 and later includes an installation option called Archive and Install that keeps all your user accounts, data, and installed applications, and just installs a new copy of the operating system. You lose some settings and third-party add-ons, but you gain a brand-spankin'-new (and hopefully problem-free) copy of Mac OS X.

Data Recovery—the Last Resort

I hope you never, ever have to read this section of the chapter. It means that not only have you not been able to solve the problems that ail your Mac, but you've also lost data in the process and didn't have a backup. I'll save you the lectures about backing up since you're probably already feeling pretty lousy at this point—you just want to know how to get your data back.

If you can access the hard drive or removable disc in question, there are several options you can try. **Data Rescue X,** from Prosoft Engineering ($89; www.prosofteng.net), is often able to retrieve data from a hard drive, assuming that the drive still works. Data Rescue X does this by analyzing the entire drive and scavenging the actual file data.

Besides Data Rescue X, several of the utilities mentioned earlier in the chapter (see the sidebar "Disk Utility Diversity") provide file-recovery functionality. If the problem is simply a damaged directory, the excellent DiskWarrior can often create a new directory that allows you to access data. In addition, if you previously installed Norton Utilities or TechTool Pro, they may be able to salvage data using directory information they automatically saved at various intervals. However, if they weren't installed before you had problems, chances are you're better off with Data Rescue X or DiskWarrior.

What if these tools don't work for you, you've tried everything and everyone else (including the resources listed at the end of this chapter), and you *absolutely* need to recover data from a damaged or broken hard drive or removable disk? Assuming you don't have a backup, *data recovery services* are most likely your last resort. **DriveSavers** (www.drivesavers.com) and **Ontrack Data International** (www.ontrack.com) are the leaders in this industry, with DriveSavers being a longtime Mac-focused data savior. By combining proprietary software with years of experience, these companies are capable of coaxing lost data from hard disks and other types of media when no one else can. They have successfully recovered data from Macs destroyed in floods, fires, and other disasters. I've personally suffered a misfortune that required the services of DriveSavers, and they came through with flying colors, recovering vital data that otherwise would have been lost.

Before using a service of this kind, take a step back and evaluate your data loss objectively. Consider the amount of time and money necessary to re-create the data. Ask yourself some important questions: Is it more cost-effective to hire temporary personnel to input the missing data? Do printed copies of the material exist? How quickly is the data needed? Data recovery tends to be very expensive, but sometimes it's cheaper than the alternative, and in certain cases your critical data is worth almost any price. On the other hand, it's sometimes cheaper to just redo the work.

Common Problems and Solutions

The previous section suggested a number of general procedures you should use when you encounter various types of problems. However, some problems are so common that it's possible to provide you with specific solutions. I've listed a number of them here. Hopefully, if you have a problem with Mac OS X, it will be one of these issues, and you'll be back at full steam in no time.

The Mac won't shut down

If you've instructed your Mac to shut down—by selecting Shut Down from the Apple menu, or by pressing the power button and then clicking Shut Down—and it doesn't, the problem is usually an application that refuses to quit, thus preventing shutdown. Sometimes the issue is as simple as an application that has an open document with unsaved changes; chances are it's sitting there waiting for you to tell it whether or not to save changes before quitting. After you do so, you can issue the Shut Down command again and it will proceed normally.

However, sometimes the issue is that an application has frozen and is not responding, thus preventing shutdown. The solution in this situation is to use the procedures described in "Application Problems," earlier in the chapter, to force-quit the problematic application. If it's not obvious which application is preventing shutdown, open the Activity Monitor utility in Mac OS X 10.3 and change the Show pop-up menu to My Processes. Any process shown in red type with "(Hung)" next to its name is frozen. Select it and click Quit Process to force it to quit. You should then be able to shut down your Mac normally.

If you have Mac OS X 10.3's Fast User Switching feature enabled (an option found in the Accounts pane of System Preferences), and another user is currently logged in, when you try to shut down you'll get an error message that states this. If you're an administrative user, you can provide your user name and password to force shutdown to occur. However, keep in mind that this basically force-quits any applications being used in the other user's account, so if the user has left any documents open with unsaved changes, those changes will be lost.

If nothing else works, and you simply can't get your Mac to shut down, your last resort may be to simply hold the power button down for a few seconds, forcing it to shut down ungracefully. In the worst-case scenario, you may have to pull the power cord (on a PowerBook or iBook you'll also have to remove the battery). If you do this, you should probably run a disk utility on your hard drive the next time you start up, since shutting down in this manner often causes minor (or even major) drive problems.

Files open in the wrong application

Sometimes you double-click a document, expecting it to open in a particular application, but instead it opens in a completely different one. (This seems to happen most frequently in Mac OS X with PDF and graphics files.) There are several solutions to this dilemma, both temporary and permanent. If you're not concerned with "permanently" fixing the problem, you can immediately open the file in your preferred application in one of the following ways:

- Drag the file onto the icon of the application with which you want to open it (either in the Finder or, if applicable, in the Dock). Assuming that the application can work with the file, it will open within that application.

- Control-click (or right-click, if you have a multibutton mouse) the file's icon in the Finder. In the contextual menu that appears, choose the Open With item, and then choose the appropriate application from the Open With submenu that appears. If the desired application isn't listed, choose Other (at the bottom of the submenu) and then navigate to the application.

- Launch the desired application (or switch to it if it's already open), and then use the application's Open command (usually found in the File menu); navigate to the file in the Open dialog to open it from within that application.

The above procedures will allow you to open the problem file in the desired application *this time*. The next time you double-click the file, it will revert to its previous "bad" behavior. If you want to *permanently* change the application used to open the file, you need to change the application assigned to that file. To do so, follow these steps:

1. Select the file in the Finder.

2. Choose File > Get Info.

3. Expand the "Open with" section of the Info window by clicking the small triangle on the left.

4. Click the application pop-up menu and choose the desired application (**Figure 8.10**).

5. (Optional) If you want to change the behavior of *all* documents like the current one (for example, all PDF files if the current file is a PDF file), click the Change All button in the Info window.

6. Close the Info window.

The next time you double-click the file, it will open in your preferred application.

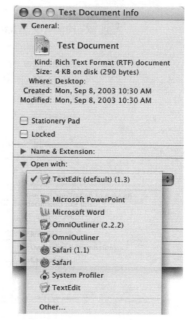

Figure 8.10

You can permanently change the application that opens a particular file by using the Get Info window's "Open with" section.

Mac OS X can't find the application needed to open a file

If Mac OS X claims that you can't open a file because the necessary application can't be found, but you know that you have an application that can open the file, you have several options. If the error message includes a Choose Application button, you can simply click that button and then find the correct application. If not, you can use any of the methods described in the previous item, "Files open in the wrong application," to open the file in a particular application (including the procedure described to permanently associate the file with an application).

Files won't delete

One of the most common problems that users experience in Mac OS X is when files won't delete. Sometimes this is a good thing—Mac OS X tries to prevent you from deleting important files that it needs to function. However, sometimes you *really* want to delete a particular file, and know it's not important to the OS, but can't. Here are a few tips for doing so, in the order in which you should try them.

This problem is less common in Mac OS X 10.3 than in earlier versions of Mac OS X, because OS X 10.3 added a feature that brings up an authentication dialog when you attempt to delete a file that the OS thinks you shouldn't. After you provide your admin-level user name and password, the file will be deleted. (If it's a system-level file, you'll be asked if you're sure you want to do this.) Nevertheless, the issue isn't completely solved—there are still times when you'll have trouble deleting a file.

- Make sure it isn't a system file or other important file. In general, unless you know what you're doing, you shouldn't delete anything outside of the Users and Applications folders (and only delete things inside the Applications folder if you really want to get rid of an application or a related file). The one exception is the /Library folder—you don't want to go around deleting files in there if you can help it, but if you've installed a system add-on and later want to remove it, or if you're troubleshooting a problem and you've found that it's caused by a file in /Library, it's usually OK to delete it.

- Is the file "in use"? If you get an error message saying that a file can't be deleted because it is "in use," this is because it's either (a) an application that is still running, or (b) a file that is being used by an application or by Mac OS X itself. If it's the former, quit the application and then move the file to the Trash or empty the Trash. If it's the latter, close the file (if it's a document open in an application) or, if it's being used by the system and you can't figure out how to get Mac OS X to "let it go," log out and then back in, or restart. You should now be able to delete the file.

- Unlock the file. Select the file in the Finder and choose File > Get Info. If the Locked box is checked, uncheck it. Then try to delete the file.

- Give yourself permission. If you don't have Read & Write access to a file, or to its enclosing folder, you won't be able to delete it. Assuming you really want to delete a file for which you don't have such privileges, use the technique described in "File Problems" to change the file's permissions (or, if that doesn't work, those of its enclosing folder) so that you have such access.

- Check the filename and volume name. Certain characters can cause problems in Mac OS X if they're used in file, folder, or volume names. For example, if a file or folder name contains a slash (forward or back), or a trademark or copyright symbol, you may not be able to delete the file or folder (or files within such a folder). If a volume has a "bullet" or trademark symbol in its name, you may not be able to delete files from that volume. The solution is to rename the file, folder, or volume without the offending symbol.

- Use a third-party utility. If all else fails, many third-party utilities allow you to delete a file that you just can't seem to delete otherwise. My favorite such utilities are the following shareware and freeware programs: Gideon Softworks' **FileXaminer** ($10; www.gideonsoftworks.com), SkyTag Software's **File Buddy** ($37.50; www.skytag.com), Rainer Brockerhoff's **XRay** ($10; www.brockerhoff.net/xray), and **BatChmod** (free; www.macchampion.com/arbysoft). The first two applications allow you to delete files immediately (no need to move them to the Trash); FileXaminer even allows you to do so from Finder contextual menus. The latter two applications simply force the Trash to empty, including all troublesome files. (You'll most likely need to enter your admin-level user name and password for all of them to do their thing.)

- Use the Terminal application. You can also delete troublesome files using Terminal. However, this can be *very* dangerous if you're not careful. Because of this danger, the fact that it would take up a lot of space to explain how to do so, and the fact that the other solutions listed here should work just as effectively, I'm going to leave it at that.

If you're having ongoing problems deleting files, the problem is most likely a more general issue with your hard drive. Try one of the following:

- **Repair permissions.** Sometimes you *should* be able to delete certain files, but because of corrupted permissions, you can't. If the above suggestions fail, try running Disk Utility's Repair Disk Permissions feature, as described in "Repair permissions," earlier in this chapter, and see if you can then delete the file.

- **Run a disk utility.** The inability to delete a file is occasionally caused by disk corruption. If you repeatedly have such problems, be sure to check your hard drive for damage using one of the disk utilities described in the sidebar "Disk Utility Diversity," earlier in this chapter.

File and folder icons can't be moved in the Finder, or files and folders have generic icons

If you find that icons can no longer be moved in the Finder, or files and folders appear in the Finder with generic icons, the cause is usually one or more corrupt cache or preference files in various locations around your hard drive. The donationware **Dragster,** from If Then Software (www.ifthensoft.com), deletes the most likely culprits and then restarts your computer, hopefully fixing the problem. Note that Dragster offers a number of options when you launch it (**Figure 8.11**); I recommend simply going with the default settings and clicking Start. After Dragster does its thing, your Mac will restart.

Figure 8.11

Dragster can often fix problems with generic icons or a frozen Finder.

Donationware is somewhat akin to shareware. With shareware, the software's author "requires" you to pay a small fee if you try the software and decide to keep it. With donationware, the author only requests that you make a donation (of a specified or unspecified amount) if you find the software useful.

Missing or duplicate System Preferences panes

In the System Preferences application, sometimes the display of panes goes a bit wonky. You may see two of the same pane, or a pane that you know should be visible—the Accounts pane, for example—doesn't show up at all. When this happens, take the following steps:

1. Quit System Preferences.
2. Delete the file ~/Library/Caches/com.apple.preferencepanes.cache.
3. Relaunch System Preferences; the various panes should appear normally.

Keychain problems

In Mac OS X, your *keychain* stores your secure information, such as passwords and encrypted notes. You're probably most familiar with the keychain from the times when you're asked if you want to add a password to it or if you want to allow an application to access data from it. Normally it works great, but if you start experiencing odd behavior—an application repeatedly asking you for access, even though you've already indicated, several times, that it should always have access, or Mac OS X itself asking you for access (it should have access automatically at login)—the problem may be a damaged keychain file.

Fortunately, in Mac OS X 10.3 Apple provides the ability to repair damaged keychain files from within the Keychain Access Utility (/Applications/Utilities/Keychain Access)—select Window > Keychain First Aid. If you are running Mac OS X 10.2 or earlier, Apple provides a separate Keychain First Aid utility for repairing damaged keychain files. For more information, see http://docs.info.apple.com/article.html?artnum=107234).

Can't eject a CD or other removable disk

Have you ever had a CD or DVD (or any other type of removable disk) that you couldn't get out of your Mac, no matter how hard you pressed the eject key? It happens to the best of us. Luckily there is a plethora of possible solutions to this problem:

- Try the usual methods several times: press the eject key (if your keyboard has one); drag the CD or DVD or other type of disk to the Trash icon in the Dock; select the volume in the Finder and press ⌘E or choose File > Eject.

- Open the folder /System/Library/CoreServices/Menu Extras, and double-click Eject.menu. This adds an eject icon to the menu bar that allows you to eject CDs and DVDs.

- Use the Eject command in iTunes, DVD Player, or Disk Utility. Even if you weren't using one of those apps, sometimes launching one of them will let you eject a CD or DVD.

- Open Terminal, type df, and press (Return). Find the pesky volume that won't eject (look at the "Mounted on" column), and then note its device name (the part after /dev/ on the left). Then type hdiutil eject *devicename* and press (Return) (for example, hdiutil eject disk1).

- Restart your Mac and press the eject button on the front of the drive—CD, DVD, Zip, or whatever—assuming that it's accessible.

- Restart your Mac, holding down the mouse button at startup until the item ejects.

- Restart your Mac, holding down (Option) until a blue screen with all bootable drives appears. Pressing (E) should eject the CD or DVD. (To continue startup, select your normal startup volume and click the right arrow button.)

- Restart your Mac, holding down (⌘)(Option)(O)(F) until you see the Open Firmware screen (mentioned in "System Problems," earlier in the chapter). Type eject cd and press (Return)—which should eject the CD or DVD—and then type mac-boot and press (Return) to resume startup.

If none of these procedures work, you may have a damaged or defective drive (or possibly just a jammed CD). In order to force the disk out, straighten out that paper clip we mentioned at the beginning of the chapter and then find the *manual eject* hole—usually located just below or beside the slot where the tray ejects or the slot into which you insert a disk. Insert the straightened end of the paper clip into the hole until you feel some resistance. Push in gently—keeping the paper clip straight—until your rebellious disk pops out.

PowerBook/iBook battery will not charge, or AC adapter is not recognized

One of the most common problems with portable Macs—PowerBooks and iBooks—is corruption of the Power Management Unit (PMU) settings. When this happens, your PowerBook or iBook may no longer charge its battery, may not recognize the AC adapter as being connected, may not sleep or wake from sleep, or may not even turn on. If you're experiencing any of these symptoms, you should reset the PMU settings to see if that solves the problem. Unfortunately, the process for resetting the PMU differs for each model of PowerBook and iBook, so instead of listing every procedure here, which would take a few pages, I'm going to refer you to Apple's own Knowledge Base article on the subject, PowerBook and iBook: Resetting Power Management Unit (PMU) (http://docs.info.apple.com/article.html?artnum=14449), which lists the different models and the procedure to use for each.

Troubleshooting Resources

If after reading this chapter you're still having problems (or you just can't get enough troubleshooting information and are aching for more), there are plenty of places to go to further your quest.

Use the Built-In Mac OS Help

There you are with your elbows on the table and your head in your hands, staring glumly at the Desktop. Right there under your nose—actually, under the Help menu—is the Help Center, which even lets you get help on the Help system itself. Once you've opened the Help Viewer, clicking the Help Center button displays a list of topics—you can click one to browse information about that specific topic (**Figure 8.12**). Many Help topics even provide guided tutorials—you can find information about many application or OS problems, or discover tips and tricks about applications and Mac OS X itself. Don't ignore the useful Search field at the top of the main Help Viewer window; often a carefully worded search will elicit the answer you're looking for immediately. And check out Apple's Mac Help Web page, which provides more information about Mac Help (www.info.apple.com/support/help/machelp).

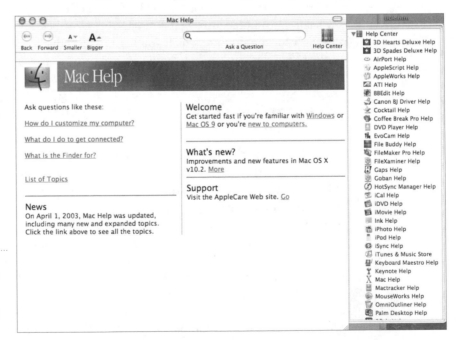

Figure 8.12

You say you need help? Choose from the main help topics, or type a question and press Return.

Take Advantage of the Knowledge Base

Apple documents many known problems (and even a few bugs) in its mammoth AppleCare Knowledge Base (http://kbase.info.apple.com). You can browse Knowledge Base articles by topic or product, or you can use the search function to search for articles by keywords. The Expert Search option lets you refine your search if the initial one provides too many results.

Even more convenient, you can use Mac OS X's Sherlock application to search the Knowledge Base directory. Just click the AppleCare button, enter a search term, and click the search button (**Figure 8.13**). The results are listed by relevance; clicking a result downloads the article and displays it in the lower pane of the Sherlock window—you don't even have to open your Web browser.

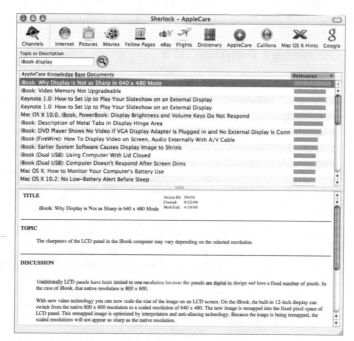

Figure 8.13

You can use Sherlock to search Apple's AppleCare Knowledge Base without ever opening your Web browser.

Visit Apple's Discussions Area

If you believe that two heads are better than one, you'll really appreciate Apple's online Discussions area. As part of the Support section of Apple's Web site, the Discussions area features a free-flowing interchange of ideas between Mac users and Apple staff. When you post a message, the resolution to your problem may come from a user like you who has experienced the same situation, or from one of Apple's qualified technicians. Either way, hopefully you'll get a response that will do the trick. To visit the Discussions area, go to http://discussions.info.apple.com. Note that you need to set up an Apple ID before you can enter this part of the Web site.

Get Help from Apple

When you purchase a new Mac, you get 90 days of free telephone technical support. That means that you can call Apple as many times as you want during the first three months you own your Mac and get help at no charge. Take advantage of this service, because after the 90-day period you're going to have to shell out $49 per incident unless you've purchased an AppleCare Protection Plan (see "Consider AppleCare," below). The good news is that it's pretty unlikely you'll need to contact Apple beyond the initial 90 days unless something goes drastically wrong with your Mac's hardware. If it does, your hardware warranty lasts for an entire year. (Note that if you call Apple after the initial 90 days but before the one-year warranty expires, and your problem turns out to be hardware-related, you won't be charged for the phone call.) In the United States, you can reach Apple support at 800/APL-CARE (800/275-2273).

Consider AppleCare

The AppleCare Protection Plan extends your Mac's warranty (including phone support) an additional two years and gives you the extra cushion of support you need whenever something goes "bump in the Mac." It covers almost any kind of situation you might experience, from basic installation questions to the replacement of any and all parts that make up your Macintosh. The plan also includes a CD containing a few troubleshooting and diagnostic utilities. (Note that Apple calls AppleCare a "three-year" plan—it includes the first year of warranty in those three years.)

You can purchase AppleCare at any time before your initial one-year warranty expires. At the time of this writing, the AppleCare Protection Plan runs from $169 (for iMacs and eMacs) to $349 (for PowerBooks). You can get the latest pricing and other information at www.apple.com/support/products/proplan.html.

Surf the Web

In addition to Apple's own Web-based discussion forums and support site, the Web offers a veritable cornucopia of self-help opportunities. In many ways, it offers some real advantages over telephone support—you don't have to remain on indefinite hold and you won't get disconnected during a call transfer, for starters. You can also print Web pages and save them for future use. Finally, you can benefit from the combined experiences—in both problems and solutions—of millions of Mac users around the world.

The granddaddy of all troubleshooting Mac Web sites is MacFixIt (www.macfixit.com). MacFixIt was founded by former *Macintosh Bible* contributor Ted Landau and is currently edited by Dan Frakes, the editor and author of this chapter. The site provides daily updates of the latest troubleshooting news, feature articles on troubleshooting topics, and a vast, searchable database of troubleshooting information. The first two are open to everyone; the database, however, is only open to subscribers of MacFixIt's "Pro" service, which, at $24.95 per year, is half the price of a single call to Apple!

Another helpful source of information is Randy Singer's Mac OS X troubleshooting pages (www.macattorney.com/panther.html, for Mac OS X 10.3, and www.macattorney.com/tutorial.html, for Mac OS X 10.2), which attempt to address some of the most common problems that users experience. (Randy is also a past contributor to *The Macintosh Bible*.)

If you're having trouble with a specific application, the MacInTouch site (www.macintouch.com) features "User Reports" that include feedback from users, and even developers, on specific topics and applications.

Finally, there are many forums where users can communicate with each other, such as those on *Macworld* magazine's Web site (www.macworld.com).

Even if you aren't troubleshooting your Mac, visiting some of these sites daily will keep you so up-to-date that your Mac-loving friends will worship you as a guru!

Read a Troubleshooting Book

A good Mac book can provide both general info and specific answers. When it comes to troubleshooting books, the former can help you become a better troubleshooter; the latter can often help you find a quick answer to a puzzling predicament.

The gold standard in Mac OS X troubleshooting books is *Ted Landau's Mac OS X Help Desk,* Third Edition (2003), and its predecessor, *Mac OS X Disaster Relief*, Updated Edition (2002), both by Ted Landau (published by Peachpit Press; chapter editor Dan Frakes is a contributor to both). Whereas this chapter provides you with a handful of pages of troubleshooting help, *Mac OS X Help Desk* gives you almost 700 pages of background information, troubleshooting techniques, and quick fixes.

Another book—available only electronically, in PDF format—is *Troubleshooting Mac OS X,* by Gregory Swain, an official Helper in the Apple Discussions forums. It contains approximately 300 pages of troubleshooting tips and costs $15. You can get more information at the X Lab Web site (www.thexlab.com).

Join/Ask a Macintosh User Group

Macintosh User Groups (or MUGs, for short) have long been a place for like-minded Mac users to gather. Most groups hold monthly meetings to demonstrate new products, discuss topics of interest, and even give away prizes of hardware and software. MUGs are also excellent sources for help when your Mac is misbehaving. The combined knowledge of the diverse membership will often provide the solution to your problem.

To find a MUG in your area, go to the Apple User Groups page of the Apple Web site (www.apple.com/usergroups). With hundreds of these groups in the United States to choose from, you're likely to find one wherever you are.

Hire a Macintosh Consultant

If figuring out what's wrong with your Mac—and fixing it—aren't the kinds of things you want to spend your time on, you might consider hiring someone else to do the dirty work. For an hourly fee you can hire an expert to come to your home or office and attend to these tasks while you focus your energies on other things, like your business's day-to-day operations or your toddler's first steps.

Finding a qualified Macintosh consultant used to be a challenge, but Apple has made it easier via the Apple Consultants Network. Simply go to the Network's page on the Apple Web site (http://consultants.apple.com) and then click the "Find a Consultant" link.

Visit an Apple Authorized Service Provider

If you've given up on fixing your Mac yourself, and a consultant isn't an option, it's time to turn to an Apple Authorized Service Provider. I emphasize *authorized* because if your Mac is under warranty, taking it to a vendor that isn't authorized can void your warranty.

A good place to start is the store where you purchased your Mac, as most have a service department capable of ordering Apple parts. If you bought your Mac through an Internet or mail-order company, you can still get service through any Apple Authorized Service Provider or Apple reseller. You can find the closest one by visiting the Resource Locator page on Apple's Web site (http://buy.apple.com) and clicking the "Find a Service Provider near you" link. (If your Mac is so ill that you don't have access to the Internet, you can fall back on the telephone directory; just make sure that the shop you choose is Apple Authorized.)

Interview: Heidi Roizen

In an industry dominated by men, Heidi Roizen was one of the first and eventually one of the most prominent Mac software developers. T/Maker, the company she cofounded in 1983, originally made its mark in the Mac world with a pioneering line of clip-art disks. In 1986 the company published the Mac version of a midrange word processor called WriteNow, and the program's speed, simplicity, elegance, and low cost quickly made it a favorite among discerning Mac users put off by Microsoft Word.

> *The Mac just made so much sense. I thought it was the way computers ought to be.*
>
> *—Heidi Roizen, on her first impression of the Mac*

Roizen served as president of the Software Publishers Association from 1988 to 1990. In 1994 she sold T/Maker, though she stayed on as CEO until early 1996. When Gil Amelio became Apple's chief executive officer that year, Roizen joined his executive team as vice president of worldwide developer relations, charged with trying to improve the company's then-troubled relations with third-party developers.

After leaving Apple the following year, she served on the boards of several companies, including Great Plains Software (later acquired by Microsoft) and Jean-Louis Gassée's Be, Inc., and began a new career as a venture capitalist. Today she is a managing director of Mobius Venture Capital, a technology fund with $2.5 billion under management, and a member of the board of directors of the National Venture Capital Association. —Henry Norr

When did you first see the Mac?

I had started a CP/M software company called T/Maker with my brother Peter in 1982. [CP/M, the grandfather of MS-DOS, was an operating system with a command-line interface that was common on personal computers before the emergence of the IBM PC and the Mac.] In August of 1983, shortly after I got out of business school, a former classmate of mine, Alain Rossmann, called me to tell me about his role at Apple evangelizing a new computer. He invited me down to meet with Guy Kawasaki and see what they were up to. I went to the building on, I think, Bandley Drive and went into a little room next to the lobby. Guy had bought me a Togo's sandwich, a cup of coffee, and had a Mac there.

How did you react to the machine?

I was just blown away. Of course, it reminded me of the Lisa, only a cuter, friendlier form factor. Relative to the usability of the CP/M user interface, which I had been using since 1979, the Mac just made so much more sense. I thought it was the way computers ought to be.

Did you decide immediately to develop software for the Mac?

Guy and company were pitching us about porting our spreadsheet/integrated software [a CP/M application also called T/Maker] to the Mac, but it just didn't make sense for us to do so, as our product was very character-based and would not have translated well.

continues on next page

However, he gave us a Mac around November to have in our office for a week, just to play with it. I noticed that everyone gravitated towards MacPaint, but not everyone had the talent to create something. They would all use the canned images that came with the program—the robot, the fish, and so on—to show it off. Then one person in our office, with some talent, drew a picture of Chuck Yeager *[The Right Stuff]* and left it on the screen. We were blown away by it. That night I started thinking, people would be buying Macs and creating documents but would not have the talent to illustrate them themselves. I had been production manager at *The Stanford Daily* as an undergrad, and went on to be the editor of the company newspaper at Tandem [another computer company located in Cupertino, California] before going to business school, so I was well acquainted with the use of clip art. So I thought, why not do electronic clip art?

We went from the idea to product in seven weeks. There were no scanners, no tablets; we had to do all the art with artists sitting at Macs, drawing with mice, at 72 dpi. Some of the more tech members of the community thought it was pretty cheesy to sell "software" that wasn't code, but I thought it was a cool idea. We called it ClickArt. I think we were the fifth product to ship for the Mac.

How did it do?

It sold well. We ultimately created an entire line out of it, and the last year I was at the helm, 1995, it was a $15 million business for us. So I think we did OK!

But we bet on the low-cost Macintosh being released in 1989. Unfortunately, that was not a wise bet, as it was late and also not so low-cost. So that did hurt us. On the other hand, it was much cheaper to stand out as a big Mac company than a Windows company since it was just a smaller world, the customers were easier to locate, there were fewer magazines to advertise in, etc. So I do believe that positioning ourselves as a Mac company gave us a better chance at prospering, particularly during the late '80s, though ultimately we had to support both Mac and Windows in order to expand the market for our products.

You worked at Apple for a while. What was that like?

A wild ride and very interesting, sort of a *Mr. Smith Goes to Washington* experience. But I discovered that I did not like the corporate environment, and the rigors of the job were keeping me away from my kids, aged 1 and 3 at the time, so I left.

What computer do you use now?

I have six Macs at home and one PC at work. I still love my Macs—the user interface is still clearly superior, and the media features are terrific. I do wish they were easier to maintain vis-à-vis networking. Both kids, now 8 and 10, use iMacs.

What do you think about the platform's future?

I think the personal computer in general will morph into a central command for communications, home control, media, etc. So the Mac as we know it may not look the same, but many of the principles and features on which it has achieved success will clearly show in the lineage.

Part 2

Getting Productive

9

Personal and Business Applications

Steve Schwartz is the chapter editor and author.

We love our Macs for all the fun things they can help us do—like movie editing, digital photography, graphics and design, and game playing. But when it comes down to it, we also need our Macs to help us get work done or manage our schedules. Fortunately, there are lots of programs that meet these needs and more.

The applications discussed in this chapter are broadly classified as *business software.* These programs are designed to help you handle important business functions, manage your time and appointments, or deal decisively with business data. Even if you aren't a businessperson, you shouldn't skip this chapter; home users and students will also find many of these programs useful. For example, there are programs to manage your finances and taxes, and programs that can create outlines for your presentations or papers. Here's a sampling of some of the best personal and business applications available for the Mac.

In This Chapter

. . . .

Integrated Software

If you're looking for one set of programs that does it all, *integrated software* is the answer. These programs combine many of the basic software tools that people use every day. Depending on the integrated suite you choose, you'll get a collection of interrelated programs, such as a word processor, a spreadsheet, a database, an email and newsgroup client, drawing tools, and a presentation program.

When I wrote about integrated software in the last edition of *The Macintosh Bible,* only two serious contenders were in the category: Microsoft Office and ClarisWorks (now known as AppleWorks). Nothing has changed. If you want integrated software for your Mac, you *still* have the same two choices. Both products, however, are mature, widely available, and widely used.

So which one should you choose? Because of its high price and advanced capabilities, Microsoft Office v. X for Mac may be more than many home and small-business users need. For a fraction of the price, AppleWorks 6 provides the basic tools that many users require. But if you need to ensure compatibility with others (whether they're across a network, on Windows, or around the country) and require more-advanced tools for creating and formatting documents, Microsoft Office may be the better choice.

Microsoft Office

Microsoft Office has long set the standard for business software on Macs and PCs. In buying this suite of primary applications, many users have found that they needed little else to meet their general computing needs in corporate America. By design, files for the different applications can be opened and edited with either the Mac or Windows version of Office. And any current version of Office on either platform is still file-compatible with versions going back to Office 97.

Like the previous Mac version (Office 2001), **Microsoft Office v. X for Mac** ($399 Standard Edition; $499 Professional Edition; www.microsoft.com/mac) includes **Word X** (word processing), **Excel X** (spreadsheet), **PowerPoint X** (presentations), and **Entourage X** (email client, newsgroup reader, and personal information manager). And, as in previous editions, drawing and painting features are also included in several of the applications. (Internet Explorer, Microsoft's Web browser, is included with new Macs; it can also be downloaded for free from Microsoft's Web site at www.microsoft.com/mac.) But for the first time, Office is a Mac OS X application.

The difference between the Standard and Professional versions of Microsoft Office v. X is that the latter includes Virtual PC for Mac and the Windows XP Professional operating system, enabling you to run Windows programs on your Mac.

The Office applications are all stand-alone programs. Not only do they launch and run separately from each other, but also there is no requirement that you use the entire suite. Rather than adopt Internet Explorer as your browser or PowerPoint for creating presentations, you may prefer using Apple's Safari and Keynote, for example. Other than having become a Mac OS X–native application, Office v. X doesn't contain a lot of spectacular new features. Here are some of the highlights:

- You can base new documents on any Office document you've recently worked on—effectively turning all your documents into templates.

- Entourage sports a new interface, making it easier to quickly switch from one activity to another.

- When an Entourage calendar event occurs, a notification dialog appears on the Desktop (**Figure 9.1**)—even when Office isn't running! You can tell Entourage how far in advance you want to be notified of an upcoming event.

Figure 9.1

Microsoft Entourage notifies you of upcoming appointments at time intervals you specify—and it even does so when Entourage is not running.

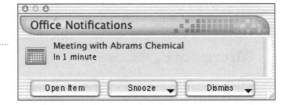

- Pictures and movies can be inserted directly into HTML-formatted email messages in Entourage, rather than sent as attachments.

- You can *finally* clear the contents of the recently used address list in Entourage.

- Word supports noncontiguous text selections, enabling you to apply the same formatting to text that's scattered throughout a document. For instance, you might select all the main headings and apply a new style to them. Word can now read AppleWorks 6 documents, too.

- A PowerPoint presentation can now be saved as a PowerPoint Package, storing all necessary files in one folder. This greatly simplifies transferring a presentation to another user or computer.

- PowerPoint now offers true transparency support so that you can layer objects on slides and create elegant effects.

 If you're upgrading to Microsoft Office v. X, you don't have to remove your old version of Office. Leaving it installed will enable you to work in Office on those occasions when you need to boot Mac OS 9.

AppleWorks

If you're on a budget or don't want or need all the whiz-bang features of Microsoft Office, Apple Computer's **AppleWorks** ($79; www.apple.com/appleworks) is for you. Long a favorite of teachers, students, small-business owners, and home users, AppleWorks (now in version 6.2) can readily meet your basic word-processing, spreadsheet, graphics, and presentation needs. If sharing Microsoft Office files is an issue, fear not: AppleWorks lets you open and edit Word and Excel files and then save them back into Word and Excel formats that Microsoft Office users can open.

AppleWorks 6 includes applications (referred to as *environments*) for word processing, spreadsheets, drawing, painting, and presentations. The Communications environment from earlier versions has disappeared but will be missed by few; it was useful only for connecting to other computers or bulletin board systems, not the Internet. Unlike the Microsoft Office applications, the AppleWorks environments really *are* integrated. When you need to create a document in a different environment, you never leave AppleWorks; you just switch environments within the program. You can embed different types of documents within almost any AppleWorks document. For example, when writing a memo in the word-processing environment, you can embed separate frames that include a spreadsheet table or a scanned picture. When you click inside any of the embedded frames, AppleWorks displays a set of menus and tools appropriate for working within that environment. Slick.

Among the other notable features introduced in AppleWorks 6.2:

* AppleWorks 6 was designed to run under Mac OS X. But it still runs fine under Mac OS 8.1 and higher, too.

* The tabbed Starting Points window serves as AppleWorks' new interface for creating documents, selecting templates, and accessing Web content (**Figure 9.2**). Other interface changes include the Clippings window (replacing the older Libraries palette), for organizing clip art, and the enhanced Tools window (adding support for tables).

Figure 9.2

You can create new documents, base a document on a template, open recently used documents, or summon helpful assistants from AppleWorks' tabbed Starting Points window.

- AppleWorks 6 takes advantage of an Internet connection. When you want to add a graphic image to a document, for example, you can download clip art from Apple's Web site by entering a search string in AppleWorks' Clippings window. After the results appear, you can download any images you want by either dragging them into a document or double-clicking them.

- The *autosave* feature lets you instruct AppleWorks to automatically save copies of your open documents at regular intervals, reducing the likelihood that you'll lose data if your Mac crashes.

- Mail merge can merge database data to a single file, to multiple files, or directly to the printer.

- The improved spreadsheet environment lets you create formulas that reference cells in *other* worksheets; simplifies the formula-creation process by allowing you to choose functions from the Insert Function dialog; and automatically adds closing parentheses to formulas if you forget to type them.

- Rather than create tables using a spreadsheet frame, you can use the new table feature. Simply go to the Tools palette, click the Table icon, and then just click and drag the cursor within any open AppleWorks document to create a table. Click where you want the upper-left corner to be and then drag the cursor; as you drag, the table and its cells appear. (Note that once you save a document in the Painting environment, any tables that document contains will be changed to bitmapped graphics, which you can't edit.)

The Upgrade Dilemma

Whether you're a manager, a small-business owner, or a home user, upgrading your software can incur significant expense. How do you know when you need to upgrade? Here are some considerations:

- *Is the program a tool of your trade?* If you make your living using a particular application—whether it's a desktop-publishing, image-editing, database, or statistics program—it's important to stay current. Your clients, employers, and industry associates will expect it.

- *Are the new features compelling?* When a mature program is upgraded for the umpteenth time, the changes may simply consist of a prettier interface, for instance. Unless the changes will improve your productivity, the older version may suffice.

- *Is compatibility an issue?* When some programs are updated, their file format changes. If you have many employees using a previous version of the program, you may have to upgrade everyone to ensure that files can be exchanged among users. The same consideration applies if you routinely share files with others, such as colleagues or people in other branches of your company. Similarly, some programs may need to be updated in order to work with the latest version of the Mac OS.

- *What's the average time between updates?* When you decide that it's time to upgrade, get a feel for the software's release schedule. If you wait until it's close to the end of a version's life cycle (often 12–18 months), your new upgrade will quickly be outdated. You may want to wait a little longer; you'll probably be rewarded by being able to upgrade to the *next* version.

Outliners

Do you remember outlining from high school or college? In addition to preparing term papers, outliner software can help you organize presentations and projects of almost any type. If you're tired of making do with Word's so-so outlining capabilities, either of the following "built for Mac OS X" outliners can do the job.

NoteBook

NoteBook ($49.95; www.circusponies.com), by Circus Ponies Software, is a wonderfully complete, feature-packed, fun-to-use application for outlining or collecting your thoughts. NoteBook, now in version 1.2, has all the common features of outlining applications that you may have previously used. You can rearrange, promote, or demote items (called *cells*) by dragging them, choosing menu commands, or using keyboard shortcuts. You can assign formatting styles to the outline levels and apply an optional numbering scheme, such as 1, 2, 3 or I, II, III.

NoteBook uses the metaphor of an actual notebook, complete with tabs and page numbers. Each NoteBook (or project file) can contain multiple outlines, and you can have multiple NoteBooks for your various projects. Individual cells in outlines can link to other pages in your NoteBooks. Here's where NoteBook differs from the rest of the outlining pack:

- You can specify any of several attractive backgrounds for a NoteBook, such as a ruled pad, a legal pad (**Figure 9.3**), graph paper, or ledger paper.

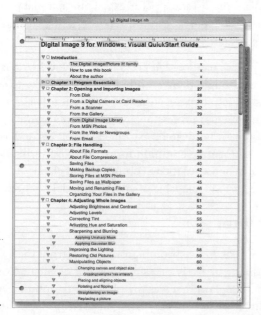

Figure 9.3

While hardly essential, cool backgrounds like this legal pad make NoteBook fun to use.

- A NoteBook can contain multiple outlines.

- In addition to formatted text, cells can contain playable QuickTime movies, as well as clickable Web URLs, email addresses, and links to other documents on your computer. (Adding document links to an outline provides a simple way to open and view related material, regardless of the Mac OS X application in which it was created.)

- You can use the Voice Annotation command to record audio comments for cells.

- Using the Media Capture feature, you can directly import images from a USB-connected digital camera or scanner.

- To make cells or selected text stand out, you can apply a color highlight to them. You can also set a cell to be an *action item* (preceding it with a check box to show whether the item has been completed), as well as assign keywords and icons to cells, which is handy for finding important information quickly.

- NoteBook automatically creates a table of contents and a dozen types of indexes for each file. Some of the more useful indexes are the Text Index (which automatically lists every important word in the NoteBook) and the Internet Addresses Index (which shows all URLs and email addresses in the NoteBook). To go directly to any page or cell, you just click its entry in the table of contents or index.

- If you have other applications that support Mac OS X Services, you can insert selected material directly from their documents into the current NoteBook. For example, text from an open Mail message can be added as a new cell simply by selecting the appropriate Service (for more on Mac OS X Services, see Chapter 1).

Features new in NoteBook 1.2 include the ability to export a NoteBook as a set of Web pages, the ability to add a cover page with optional password protection and encryption, and support for multiple sort criteria, such as an alphabetical sort by action-item status *and* the first word of each cell.

This modestly priced, feature-rich program is easy to love. As good as it is in this early version, though, there *are* other features I'd like to see. First, while the HTML-based Help bypasses Mac OS X's tediously slow Help system and is attractively laid out and professionally written, it's skimpy. Since this is the only documentation, it needs to be expanded—a lot! Second, one or more floating toolbars for performing common formatting and similar actions would be a blessing. Third, a contextual menu command for deleting the current page would eliminate a trip to the table of contents to delete the page's entry.

OmniOutliner

OmniOutliner ($29.95; www.omnigroup.com), from the Omni Group, approaches outlining in a way that's reminiscent of Attain Corp.'s In Control, the now-defunct program that was my old favorite outliner. At a minimum, every outline line has two parts, appearing in two separate columns: the normal outline element and comments (**Figure 9.4**). If you like, you can add more columns to any outline. (Columns serve the same function as fields in a database.) For instance, when outlining a book's table of contents, I might add columns for Page Count, Submission Date, Edits Received, and so on. The additional columns let you go far beyond simple outlining capabilities, serving as a project management tool, for example.

Figure 9.4

OmniOutliner has a clean, professional look. The toolbar provides ready access to the most common commands.

Each column must be defined as a particular *data type*. While most columns will be Text or Rich Text, other options include Checkbox, Date, Duration, Pop-up List, and Number. Columns can also have calculation capabilities (called *summaries*). When a number column is summed, for instance, the number displayed for each parent item is the total of the children items. However, there is no option to display a grand total for the column, limiting the usefulness of this feature. So, for example, you might add up the duration for each parent item, but you wouldn't be able to add up the duration of all the parent items, which would total the duration for the entire project.

OmniOutliner has many features that make it a pleasure to use and extend its outlining capabilities. For instance, a toolbar of common commands is displayed above the outline. You can use the ever-present Info palette (patterned after Word's Formatting Palette; see Figure 9.4) to assign row, column, and overall formatting, such as column text alignment, background colors, and row prefix text (1, 2, 3; i, ii, iii; and the like). Although OmniOutliner doesn't offer different outliner "looks" as NoteBook does, you can set a variety of color options, such as using separate column-background and gutter colors or showing alternating rows in different colors. And in addition to being able to choose an optional numbering sequence for any level, you can also specify numbering prefix and/or suffix text. For a chapter outline, instead of simply designating the chapters with the numbers 1–20, You can label them Chapter 1, Chapter 2, and so on.

There's a lot to recommend in OmniOutliner. In fact, the only real problem I've had is an occasional difficulty using drag and drop to rearrange topics. Dragged topics don't always end up where I expect or at the desired indent level. However, the accuracy of such actions seems to have improved in version 2.2.6. OmniOutliner is an excellent choice—and an obvious one—for outlines that require multiple columns, such as those created to track projects, for example.

Business Graphs and Charts

Lengthy text passages aren't always the best way to present business information, especially when data is involved. A carefully crafted, attractive graph or chart is easier to interpret than text and is less likely to be ignored. As you'll see with the programs listed below, the selection of charts and graphs available for use can be almost overwhelming at first. But once you get the hang of using them correctly for displaying and analyzing data, you'll find charts and graphs indispensable.

DeltaGraph

Red Rock Software's **DeltaGraph** ($299; www.redrocksw.com) is the gold standard of cross-platform graphing programs. You can create 84 types of graphs, including 2D, 3D, double-axis, and overlays. Version 5, which was released in spring 2003, offers 11 new graph types, such as Volume Open High Low Close (for stocks), Intensity Scatter, and Floating Stacked Bar and Column (for data analysis). DeltaGraph can import data in Excel or text-delimited formats, and it can import most types of graphic files. It can export graphs in common graphic formats such as PICT, JPEG, and QuickTime. Unfortunately, DeltaGraph 5 cannot export graphs in TIFF format. In addition to exporting charts, you can also display them as a slide show from within DeltaGraph—a fantastic feature for creating presentations.

You work with your data in four *views*: Data (for entering and editing data), Chart (for displaying and modifying graphs and charts), Sorter (for organizing pages and slides), and Outliner (for viewing a presentation's structure and creating text charts). You can apply stored layouts to charts to give them a consistent appearance—as you might do for slides or the pages of a company's annual report, for example (**Figure 9.5**). To make this easy, DeltaGraph provides 60 layout sets for your use, each with a dozen slide styles. Also included is the Formula Builder dialog, which you can use to compute data transformations and generate simple statistics.

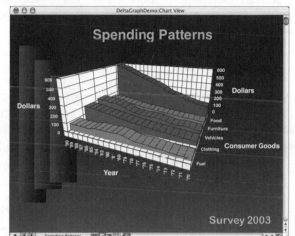

Figure 9.5

The ability to churn out gorgeous graphs on professionally designed layouts makes DeltaGraph a winning choice for business users.

 The purposes of the toolbar icons aren't exactly obvious. To learn the meaning of any toolbar icon by just resting the pointer over it for a moment, you'll need to enable tool tips. To do this, go to DeltaGraph > Preferences and click the Tool Tips check box on the General tab.

Chartsmith

You can use Blacksmith's **Chartsmith** ($129; www.blacksmith.com) to create impressive business and scientific charts. To standardize your charts (as you might want to do for a presentation or just to put forth a consistent image for your company), you can save any chart as a reusable template. However, since premade templates aren't included, creating truly gorgeous charts depends on your own design skills. While I can easily create very presentable charts in Chartsmith, stunning is out of my reach (**Figure 9.6**).

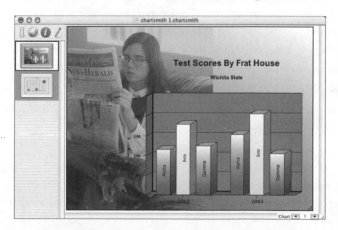

Figure 9.6

You can reduce the opacity of a photo to create an interesting background for a Chartsmith chart.

For small data sets, you can enter information manually by typing it. To bring in existing data, you can use copy and paste or Mac OS X Services, or you can import it from an ASCII text or Excel .xls file. Context-sensitive Inspectors (floating palettes that change to reflect options for whatever you are doing at the moment) can be used to modify any selected chart component. You can drag and drop images onto special chart areas, such as the background, a rectangle or circle that you've drawn, and series elements (such as a single bar in a bar chart).

 If you want to see how a particular chart element (for example, the background, the grid, or a series element, such as a bar in a bar chart or a slice in a pie chart) will look with a different color, you can use Chartsmith's color-preview feature to find out. Just select a color from the Colors palette, hold down Option**, and drag the selected color over the chart element whose color you want to change.**

If you're also a Keynote user, you'll be delighted to learn that any Chartsmith chart can be exported as a Keynote slide. PowerPoint users will need to save the chart as a graphic and add it to a PowerPoint slide just as they would any other graphic. Chartsmith, now in version 1.2.4, can export charts to most popular graphic formats, and it can also create TIFF or PDF files if you drag the chart image to the Desktop.

OmniGraffle Professional

Unlike the previous two programs, **OmniGraffle Professional** ($119.95; www.omnigroup.com) isn't for charting data; it's for charting *things*. You can use it to make flowcharts, organizational charts, decision trees, and so on.

You can't help but be impressed by the depth of OmniGraffle, now in version 3. There are *20* Inspectors (formerly referred to as *palettes*)—each with multiple sections—that you can use to add and modify shapes, lines, text, and images. If you have difficulty doing something, it's more likely due to the program's cluttered interface than to your inexperience or a missing feature or option. The wealth of capabilities can be that overwhelming. As a result, until you become proficient, expect to spend lots of time hunting for the correct Inspector when you need to make a change to a chart. (Don't expect a lot of help from the manual; it's more of a tutorial than a complete rundown of features.)

 You can manage the clutter of Inspectors by linking them together. Simply drag an Inspector to the bottom of another, and they'll lock on to one another in a nice, neat stack. Click a member of the stack to bring it into full view again.

Noteworthy features include the rubber stamp tool (for duplicating a graphic object), stencils (predesigned or personally created shapes, such as flowchart symbols or furniture icons), multiple export options (including PDF, HTML, and several graphic formats), presentation mode (displays a full-screen interactive version of your chart, as shown in **Figure 9.7**), and the option to attach an *action* to an object so that when you click the object, one of several actions occurs: you jump to another spot in the document, a URL opens in your browser, an addressed email message appears, or an AppleScript runs.

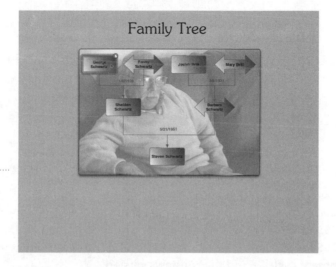

Figure 9.7

You can turn any OmniGraffle chart into an interactive presentation by displaying it in full-screen mode.

 If you don't need all the whiz-bang features of OmniGraffle Professional (such as the ability to import and export Visio 1001 XML files, create multipage documents, and display charts in a Presentation Mode slide show), you may find that the core product—OmniGraffle ($69.95)—will do the job for you.

Statistics

Although *statistics programs* are specialized applications not meant for novices, many businesses make heavy use of them to analyze sales data and project trends, examine customer demographics, perform market research, and do data mining. The Mac market for these types of programs is tiny when compared with the Windows market, but there is no shortage of heavy-duty statistical packages for the Mac. What follows are reviews of my two favorite Macintosh statistics applications: SPSS and JMP. For information on Stata (another popular statistics program), visit the company's Web site at www.stata.com.

SPSS

SPSS Base 11 ($1,249; www.spss.com), by SPSS, is the first Mac OS X version of this popular statistics package. Although many new features and enhancements have been added, the main thrust of version 11 was to bring it on par with SPSS 11 for Windows. Unfortunately, while it is still one of the most capable, complete, easy-to-use statistics packages for the Mac or Windows, version 11 is considerably slower than version 10.

Table 9.1 compares the times it took the two versions to perform some common tasks on a 400 MHz Power Mac G4 (AGP Graphics) with 700 MB of RAM.

Table 9.1 Speed Differences Between SPSS 10 and 11

	SPSS 10 (Time in secs.)	SPSS 11 (Time in secs.)
Launch SPSS	24	44
Load data set (474 cases, ten variables)	3	7
Calculate frequencies for three variables	4	7
Create static bar graph (one category variable)	5	34
Change the bar color in the static graph	1	16
Create interactive bar graph	6	8

 SPSS 11 for the Mac is mostly on par with SPSS 11 for Windows. However, SPSS for Windows is now up to version 12. The Mac product remains a development cycle behind the Windows version.

Kiss the manuals goodbye

On opening SPSS, the first thing you'll notice is just how small the package has become. Instead of containing a weighty stack of manuals, SPSS 11 comes with only a 150-page Brief Guide containing a series of tutorials to help you learn the basics. SPSS's excellent manuals have been folded into the Help system—although you can buy the manuals for SPSS 11 for Windows, which should be useful since the products are so similar. If you're already an SPSS maven, the Help system may suffice. If you're a first-time user, however, learning the ins and outs of such a complex program by reading help screens and running tutorials is definitely the hard way.

New and improved

Like previous Mac versions, SPSS 11 shows little of its mainframe, batch-oriented roots. All procedures are performed in a decidedly Mac-like fashion. You choose analyses and graphs from menus, set dialog options, and select options from toolbars to change the output formatting. Many users will never see SPSS's underlying command language, but it's there if you need it. For example, if there's a complex analysis you need to run repeatedly, you can save the automatically generated command language and run it later on a new or revised data set. While SPSS's built-in scripting isn't available in SPSS 11, advanced users can perform many of the same functions using AppleScript.

SPSS 11 provides several useful improvements in data-sharing capabilities. Data files from SPSS 10 are compatible with those of version 11 and are automatically converted when first opened. Data, syntax, and output files from SPSS 11 for Windows can now all be opened in the Mac version. Using Mac OS X's Services > Mail > Send File command, you can easily email output files to others. And if your organization or department springs for the new SmartViewer Web Server ($25,000), SPSS statistical reports and graphs can be published to the Web or an intranet, where they can be viewed and modified by anyone with the appropriate permissions using a Web browser.

Other welcome changes include updates to the Database Wizard and Text Wizard (making it easier to read and recode data from other sources), improvements to the Categorical Regression and Principal Components analyses, and the ability to calculate arithmetic and percentage differences between variables or categories of a grouping variable in OLAP cubes (data-exploration tools).

Stats in the slow lane

Rather than update the existing Macintosh code from version 10, SPSS ported the code from SPSS 11 for Windows to the Mac. Windows modules that have yet to be ported include Maps, Exact Tests, and Tables. Perhaps due to the fact that this *is* a ported product, many operations vary from slightly slower to agonizingly slow when compared with SPSS 10 running under Mac OS 9. The exception is in creating and modifying interactive graphs, which are still quite snappy and responsive (**Figure 9.8**).

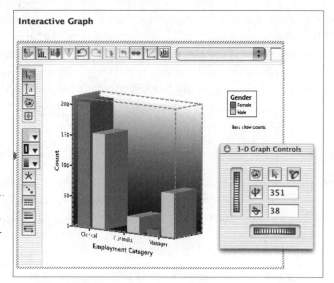

Figure 9.8

You can quickly customize most elements of an interactive SPSS graph by choosing options from the toolbars.

In general, the program feels sluggish. Although lengthy operations are noted by the spinning wait pointer, it can sometimes take as long as 10 seconds for this rainbow-colored ball to appear—leaving you with the impression that your mouse click or command choice wasn't acknowledged.

 The biggest performance hits occur when creating or modifying static graphs as part of a statistical procedure. You can avoid a lot of foot tapping by creating interactive graphs instead.

The most compelling reasons for moving up to SPSS 11 are its new Mac OS X support, improved compatibility with the Windows version of SPSS, the ability to share output using Mac OS X's email services and the new SmartViewer Web Server, and the handful of new or improved analyses.

If you're new to SPSS and already a Mac OS X convert, the purchase decision is a no-brainer. Like its predecessor, SPSS 11 is a capable, flexible, easy-to-use program. On the other hand, if you already have SPSS 10, you might want to wait until SPSS 11 (or the next version) gets a much-needed speed bump. When compared with the zippy version 10, SPSS 11 drags its feet.

 The $1,249 price tag is for SPSS Base 11 only. Additional statistical modules (Advanced Models, Category, Conjoint, Missing Value Analysis, Regression Models, Tables, and Trends) can be purchased for $599 to $799 each.

JMP

JMP ($995; www.jmp.com), the popular all-in-one cross-platform statistics package from the SAS Institute, continues to expand its feature set in version 5.1 by providing new statistics (discriminant analysis, partial least squares analysis, neural networking, Ishikawa charts, and recursive partitioning), shape-drawing tools for embellishing reports, and speed improvements when performing cluster analyses or computing formulas across table rows. Although difficult to learn, JMP remains an excellent choice for statisticians and researchers who perform exploratory analyses.

Working with JMP

You enter or import your data into a spreadsheet-style grid in which columns are variables and rows are observations or cases. Any column can be classified as an independent or dependent variable, numeric weight, frequency (setting the number of repetitions for each observation), or a row state (indicating whether the associated row should be hidden, labeled, or colored, for example).

In a traditional research project, many of the specific analyses to be performed are decided during the design phase. JMP, on the other hand, encourages interactive analysis. Depending on what you see in the initial analyses, you can easily request additional statistics, modify graph display options, and so on.

For example, you might begin a JMP analysis by generating frequencies, summary statistics (mean, median, and so on), and bar charts. If you click a bar, JMP automatically selects those observations in all other displayed charts and in the data table—making it simple to work with subsets and to see how the data interrelates (**Figure 9.9**). When working with two-dimensional or three-dimensional spinning plots, you can select *outliers* (statistically unusual data points) for separate analysis, or you can hide them to see how the statistics are affected. To generate additional statistics or change the display options for a plot (or any plot element), you can choose commands from pop-up menus on the plot or ⌘-click the plot to bring up contextual menus. JMP's highly graphical approach and the ease with which you can change options make it an ideal tool for exploratory analyses.

Figure 9.9

JMP excels at helping you work with subsets of data. Here, just click the Single bar in the center graph to view the sex and age breakdowns (the darkened areas) of only the single people.

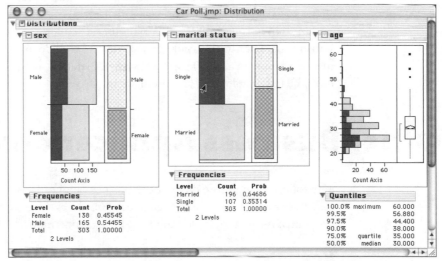

You can choose menu commands or click buttons in the tabbed JMP Starter window to initiate analyses (called *platforms*) and graphs. The results from each analysis automatically open in a separate window. JMP can even help design your experiments or trials via its DOE (Design of Experiments) dialogs. And if you want to be able to easily repeat an analysis, compute a specialized statistic, or create a custom graph, you can use JMP's scripting language. Scripts can be created in two ways: manually by typing the commands into a text file, or by using or modifying the scripts that JMP automatically generates (when you run an analysis, JMP automatically creates a text script that represents the commands needed to rerun exactly the same analysis; you can then edit it to use different options or apply it to a different data set). After completing any analysis, you can opt to display or save the generated script.

JMP journaling

Each time you perform a new type of analysis (univariate, bivariate, or multivariate), JMP displays the results in a new window. To include a results window (or selected parts of it) in a report, you can copy the graphs and statistics into a *journal* (a scrolling report window). Statistics and plots in a journal do not have a live connection with the original analyses, so you can freely change the formatting of the elements. Journals can be saved as rich text format or HTML files.

JMP 5 is a complex application with an impressive feature set that is well-suited for manufacturing research, financial services, and proponents of Six Sigma (a management philosophy based on eliminating mistakes and reducing waste). It's also worth considering by those in nonmanufacturing professions, such as the social sciences. Note, however, that many of the statistics and analysis options will be unfamiliar to those in other disciplines, as well as to novice statisticians. Luckily, the available statistics are well documented in JMP's manuals (more than 1500 pages of written material), interactive tutorials, hundreds of sample files, and online help.

Other Business Applications

The following are some noteworthy business applications that aren't quite as easy to categorize because of their special purposes. Like so many current Mac programs, most of the following have little competition.

Keynote

Hey! Here's a program with a *printed* manual! What *will* they think of next? **Keynote** ($99; www.apple.com/keynote) is Apple's answer to PowerPoint, Microsoft's presentation application.

To create a presentation, you can select any of a dozen *themes* (**Figure 9.10**). Each theme provides eight different master slide layouts on which you can base new slides. Three of the layouts include decorative picture placeholders that serve as image frames. If you aren't satisfied with the small number of included themes or want different backgrounds for the masters, you're free to create your own.

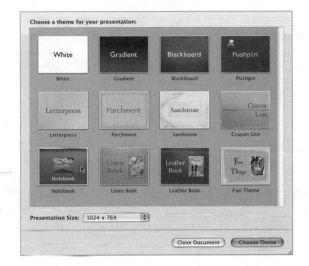

Figure 9.10

When creating a new Keynote presentation, you can base it on one of these attractive themes.

 If your design skills aren't up to the task of creating new themes or masters, a small group of graphics professionals will be happy to sell you some. From Keynote's Help menu choose Keynote on the Web. The program will take you to a page in the Keynote section of Apple's Web site where you can find new themes.

As with PowerPoint, you can add material to a slide by typing over text placeholders, drawing shapes, and placing, pasting, or using drag and drop to insert pictures from your hard drive. Floating Inspector windows let you change the settings for any selected object or text. In addition to the usual modification options, you can set the opacity/transparency of any placed item to create artistic slide elements that blend with nearby objects or the background. To make it easy to precisely place objects and text, crosshair guidelines automatically appear as you move the items. The guidelines show whenever the current object is center-aligned with any nearby object or text block—or when a picture is perfectly centered within a frame, for example.

You can also use Keynote's table and chart features to present data in an attractive, informative manner. However, getting data into a table can be a chore. You can paste data into any single cell, but there's no way to import, paste, or drag and drop existing data into *multiple* cells. (You can create a chart in Excel and then import it into a Keynote slide, however.) Keynote provides eight types of charts from which you can choose, including line, bar, column, pie, and area.

You can set animation options within each slide (enabling bullet points to appear one-by-one, for example), as well as specify between-slide transition effects. Version 1.1.1 of Keynote includes several dramatic new effects, such as Cube, which displays each slide as another face on a rotating cube. You can also add a sound file to any slide, such as narration or an MP3, but the sound can play only while its slide is onscreen.

If several sides in a row use the same transition, you don't have to apply it to each one separately. To simultaneously set an effect for multiple slides, select the slide range in the Navigator pane by Shift**-clicking and then pick the transition effect you want to use.**

In addition to creating presentations in Keynote, you can import existing PowerPoint and AppleWorks presentations. Finished presentations can be exported to QuickTime (as a movie), PDF (one slide per page), or PowerPoint. However, there is currently no option to export to HTML, which would enable your presentation to be viewed in a browser.

While Keynote is fun to use and has many excellent features to recommend it, it may take another release or two before it can be considered a worthy PowerPoint replacement. Keynote needs improved data-import capabilities and more of everything: themes, master slides per theme, transition effects, and chart types.

A free update to Keynote 1.1.1 can be obtained from Apple's Web site via Software Update, a Mac OS X System Preferences pane.

Quicken

Unless you're new to computing, you've heard of Intuit's **Quicken** ($59.95; www.intuit.com). On both the Mac and PC, the name Quicken is synonymous with financial management for the home and small-business user. I can't even remember how many years I've been using it to track my own business and personal expenses. (I even wrote a book about one version.)

Like the previous versions (and there's a new one every year), Quicken 2004 lets you track your checking, savings, money market, and credit card accounts, as well as the items in your investment portfolio. When you make transactions in these accounts, you then enter the data into Quicken—either manually or by downloading it from your financial institution. (More than 1000 financial institutions can provide Quicken-compatible data.)

If you want to use Quicken to track credit card purchases or banking activities, you should know that the level of support varies widely among financial institutions. Some—such as Discover—let you retrieve transactions as they occur; others only allow you to download monthly statements, and still others provide no online support. To check for supported institutions, choose Online > Financial Institutions from within Quicken or visit http://dwww.intuit.com/ personal/quicken/filist_index.cfm.

As you enter data, Quicken memorizes your most common transactions and lets you reuse the information in subsequent ones with the same payee. If Quicken notices that a transaction recurs on a regular basis (such as a mortgage payment), it offers to create a *scheduled transaction*—automatically recording it each month or simply reminding you when the payment is due. You can use

Quicken 2004 to add these transactions as calendar events in Apple's iCal (see "iCal," below), so you'll always know when they're due.

When your statements arrive, Quicken makes it a snap to reconcile the accounts. And by assigning a category to each transaction (such as Telephone or Social Security), you can use Quicken's extensive reporting and graphing capabilities to get a handle on your spending patterns, create a budget, or prepare for tax time. You can create about two dozen reports and graphs, as well as customize them to show selected dates, expense types, and so on. At any time, you can open the Quicken Insights window to get a quick overview of your current financial situation—and optionally print it to impress potential spouses (**Figure 9.11**).

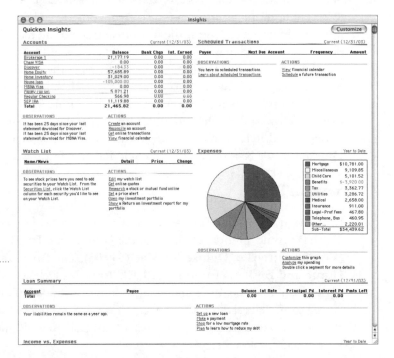

Figure 9.11

You can open the Quicken Insights window to get a quick summary of your financial situation.

Over the years, Intuit has enhanced Quicken to track many other types of financial information. You can track outstanding loans and use the portfolio features to record, update, and follow stocks and mutual funds. Quicken 2004 offers 25 new investment indicators to help you analyze your holdings, and you can download related news and articles. Quicken 2004 also includes an Emergency Records Organizer, a separate application that helps you keep

track of the details and location of critical data, such as doctors' names and numbers, rental property information, insurance policies, safe-deposit box numbers, credit cards, and birth certificates.

Quicken provides a variety of financial calculators and planners, enabling you to determine whether conditions are right to refinance your mortgage or whether you're carrying sufficient life insurance, for instance. It also includes a retirement planner and planning calculators for loans and college expenses.

Quicken 2004 makes excellent use of the Internet. You can download a daily update of the values of your investments, research securities, and pay bills electronically (if you've registered for online banking with your bank). You can also export your portfolio to the Web, letting you examine it from anywhere you have Internet access.

The only negative thing I can say about Quicken is that it's become something of an octopus application. It's evolved from being an excellent checkbook minder to becoming all things financial. The constant drive to add features has expanded Quicken in ways that have made it confusing and more than the average user needs or wants. Every new command you choose opens yet another window—and they never go away unless you manually close them. Although I love using Quicken to enter my checks and perform the monthly reconciliation, whenever I try to do anything else, I have a hard time finding the menu command or clicking the right button. I invariably end up somewhere related but wrong, and then have to open Help or the PDF manual. Sometimes I think Quicken would be more useful if I could hide the features I seldom use.

TurboTax

In short, Intuit's **TurboTax** (www.intuit.com) is *the* tax program for the Mac. TurboTax comes in three versions for the Mac: **TurboTax Basic for Mac** ($39.95), **TurboTax Deluxe for Mac** ($49.95), and **TurboTax Premier Home and Business for Mac** ($79.95). TurboTax Deluxe offers more tax advice than TurboTax Basic and includes a free download of one state module (state tax modules sell for $29.95 each). TurboTax Premier Home and Business also includes a free download of one state module and is geared toward self-employed taxpayers.

TurboTax can import filing information from last year's TurboTax or as well as import data from Quicken or any financial software that can create TXF files. Of course, if your tax data isn't in an appropriate format, you can enter it manually. Doing so for a personal return or a sole proprietorship isn't really that time-consuming. And TurboTax can import W-2 and 1099 information from participating employers and financial institutions, such as T. Rowe Price.

After you gather up the year's tax data and papers, you can do your taxes by answering questions in an interview format or by entering numbers directly into onscreen tax forms, or you can combine the two approaches. Most users will want to stick with the EasyStep interview, in which you answer questions, check check boxes, and enter tax data as it's requested. As you enter each piece of information, you can see it appear in the correct lines of the actual IRS forms (shown in the bottom half of the window). TurboTax continuously calculates your tax and displays it in the upper-right corner of the window. It's fun watching how your tax liability changes as you progress through the interview. Since the program remembers where you stopped the interview, there's no need to complete your taxes in one session; you can always pick up where you left off. When you're done, you can print federal and state forms—as well as any worksheets—on any inkjet or laser printer. If you're in a rush to receive a refund, you can take advantage of the program's electronic-filing capability (for a small fee).

iCal

It's not often that you can get a commercial-quality application for nothing, but that's the case with Apple's **iCal** (free; www.apple.com/ical). It's a superb calendar-based scheduling program. You can use it to keep track of business and personal appointments, recurring events (such as birthdays and mortgage payments), and your to-do list. iCal rivals and, in some respects, surpasses the major calendar applications available for the Mac, such as Entourage and **Now Up-To-Date & Contact** ($159.90; www.poweronsoftware.com). The first big difference you'll notice about iCal, now in version 1.5.1, is that you aren't restricted to just a single set of calendar events. You can create separate sets of events (called *calendars*) for work, home, school, family members, coworkers, or specific projects, for example. Each calendar is color-coded so that its events can be immediately distinguished from those of other calendars. You can display all calendars simultaneously (**Figure 9.12**) or select just the one(s) you want to see at the moment.

Figure 9.12

Events in iCal are color-coded by type (in this example, home, business, and holidays) so that you can instantly distinguish the different types.

You can set a reminder (called an *alarm*) for any event or to-do item; iCal doesn't need to be running at the time that the alarm is triggered. (Note, however, that alarms have inexplicably *stopped* working for me in the last few weeks.) An alarm can be presented in a dialog (with or without a sound effect) or sent as email to your default address, or it can cause a file to be opened (such as a word-processing document that you need to read or edit). You can also schedule repeating events that recur daily, weekly, monthly, yearly, or on a custom schedule, such as every third Thursday of the month.

If you want to share a calendar with others, you can publish it to a .Mac account or to any Web site that's powered by a WebDAV server. There are also a variety of public calendars to which you can subscribe, enabling you to view a schedule of upcoming sporting events or TV shows on the Fox network, for example. iCal's smart search feature shows matches as you type the search string, so you can quickly locate any event based on its description or the names of the people involved in it.

Bottom line: Even if you're already using another calendar program, I strongly encourage you to give iCal a try. It's a pleasure to use and is likely to become one of your favorite programs. Besides, you can't beat the price.

Mariner Calc

Remember when there was competition in the software market—when there were multiple word processors, browsers, and other business applications from which to choose? Well, you still have some variety of choices, but you have to hunt for them. Mariner Software provides some alternatives. Rather than go head to head with Microsoft, Mariner pitches **Mariner Calc** ($79.95; www.marinersoftware.com), now in version 5.2.2, as a smaller, faster, and less feature-rich program for people who need a spreadsheet program but don't want the complexity of Excel. In fact, other than the lack of support for macros, you probably won't notice any major omissions.

Data entry and editing can be done in the cell editor at the top of the window or within the active cell. You can create worksheets with multiple layers; add charts, shapes, arrows, and other objects to dress up your worksheet; use 140 built-in functions in formulas; and format cells in all the traditional ways.

Mariner Calc's multiple toolbars are one of its most compelling features. Rather than make them context-sensitive as is commonly done, you switch from one toolbar to another by clicking a toolbar button. If you don't see the command you want, just click until it appears. You can customize the toolbars by adding, deleting, or moving buttons, as well as by specifying that a particular toolbar should be displayed when editing cell data.

Rather than stick with the normal column letters, you can optionally *name* any column head (**Figure 9.13**). The "floating precision" cell format is another novel feature. When applied to a cell that holds numeric data, the data is formatted as necessary to make it fit within the cell. You can also add a custom prefix or suffix to data, and optionally apply a dozen or so table styles to a cell range. However, each table style can be applied only to certain types of data. A column of dates, for instance, may end up displaying as serial numbers.

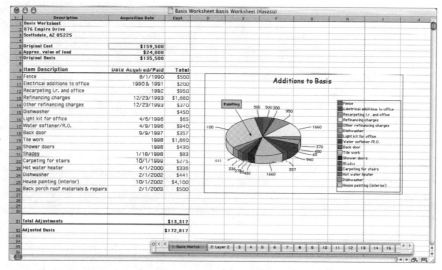

Figure 9.13

If you want to make it easy to identify worksheet columns, you don't have to waste a row for it in Mariner Calc. Just assign the names to the columns themselves.

Mariner Calc includes both Mac OS X and Mac OS 9 compatibility, support for split panes, the ability to import Excel worksheets, up to nine levels of undo, spelling checking, and user-designed date and time formats. The manuals, however, could use a thorough edit. They aren't well organized or well written, contain errors, and are really only helpful as an introduction. The Help information, on the other hand, is a bit more complete and useful.

Business Card Composer

Business Card Composer ($39.95; www.belightsoft.com), from BeLight Software, is one of those business applications that are both fun and useful. Think of Business Card Composer as desktop publishing for business cards.

You can design cards from scratch or use one of the attractive templates. The program works in conjunction with Apple's Address Book, taking field data—name, company, phone numbers, and so on—from any chosen contact card (yours or an employee's, for example).

Cards can include any combination of graphic backgrounds, geometric designs, artwork from the provided clip-art collection, or your own images, as well as frames, lines, and rectangles (**Figure 9.14**). Graphics can be further embellished by changing their opacity/transparency and by applying any of the included masks.

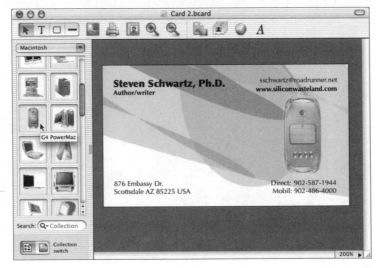

Figure 9.14

Using Business Card Composer to create eye-catching business cards is child's play.

With few exceptions (for example, the documentation and Help should be rewritten to avoid the occasional lapse into tortured English), Business Card Composer is supremely easy and fun to use. Whenever you select an object or text string, the appropriate Properties palettes are automatically displayed, enabling you to change the color, line thickness, font settings, and so on. When you drag an object to a new location, alignment guides appear whenever the object aligns with an edge of any other object.

Version 2.0 adds the ability to do a Google search for images on the Web, have your cards professionally printed ($38 for 100 four-color cards), specify custom paper sizes (to accommodate nonstandard business cards, badges, and labels), and reuse a card for multiple people.

Books

Do you remember *freeware*—software that you could download and use for free? Although freeware hasn't disappeared, it's unusual to find many useful business programs that are being given away. **Books** (free; http://books.aetherial.net) is one such rare find. Written by Chris Karr, Books is a Mac OS X application for keeping track of the books in your business or personal library.

A number of business and personal shareware applications cover a wide range of specialized needs. You can find programs for tracking eBay listings, creating forms, budgeting, calculating mortgages, and much more. Check out VersionTracker (www.versiontracker.com) for these applications.

Books, now in version 1.2, is an example of a dedicated database. It provides a large (but fixed) set of fields into which you can type information about the books you own (**Figure 9.15**). You can assign a rating to each book, enter comments and keywords, and perform searches based on the contents of any combination of fields. Several fields, such as Publisher and Genre, keep track of your entries and then present them in pop-up lists, enabling you to pick the correct entry for subsequent books. The Gift From and Recommended fields present contact names from your Address Book. (They're just starting points. You can enter other names, as needed.)

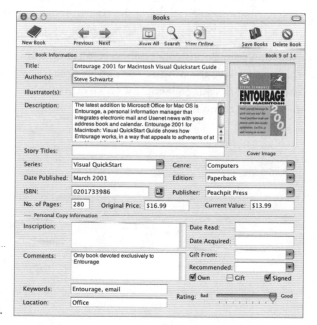

Figure 9.15

Books provides plenty of fields to handle your most important book-related information.

Books' neatest feature is that it uses Amazon.com Web Services to auto-fill key information. All you have to do is type a book's ISBN number and click a button, and—if the book is known to Amazon.com—its data is downloaded into the record. If the book is still current (newer than six or seven years old), an image of its cover may also be saved as part of the record. If you want to see the complete listing for a book, click the View Online button to launch your browser and display the book's Amazon.com page.

Book listings from Amazon.com frequently contain errors. Although the listing information is supplied by publishers, it often comes well in advance of the book's release. Thus, it's not unusual for the page count, the price, or even the author's name to be wrong. For example, on one of my books, the technical editor is listed as the author, followed by my name spelled three different ways and two sets of pseudonyms. Moral: when a listing is correct, you'll avoid a lot of typing. But you shouldn't assume that it's right.

Other useful features include the ability to display your entire collection as a list, the option of exporting the collection as a set of HTML pages or as XML, and a spelling checker.

If you don't already have a means of cataloging and tracking the locations of your books, there's no reason *not* to give Books a try. It's easy and fun to use, and it lets Amazon.com do some of the data-entry work for you. It would be nice if it were customizable (allowing the user to rename, repurpose, or eliminate some of the fields), but it's hard to complain about something that's free!

When exporting your Books collection to HTML, begin by creating a new, empty folder to receive the output. The export procedure creates a separate file for each record in your collection. If you export to the Desktop or to a folder that already contains files, you'll be sorry!

Interview: Floyd Kvamme

Floyd Kvamme's tenure at Apple was relatively brief, but it came at a crucial time: he was appointed executive vice president of sales and marketing in 1982, as the Mac was in gestation, and held that position until just after the machine was launched in January 1984. Kvamme began his career in the semiconductor industry. Immediately before joining Apple he was president of National Semiconductor's National Advanced Systems subsidiary, which made mainframe computer systems. When he left Apple, it was to become a partner at Kleiner Perkins Caufield & Byers, one of Silicon Valley's oldest, largest, and most celebrated venture capital firms. Still a partner emeritus there, he's now on the board of directors at more than a half dozen tech startups. Kvamme is a member of the advisory board at Santa Clara University's Markkula Center for Applied Ethics (named after Mike Markkula, Apple's first investor and first chairman), and since 2001 he has been cochair of the President's Council of Advisors on Science and Technology. —Henry Norr

> *I never looked at it as adult supervision, because I found the people at Apple absolutely inspiring.*
>
> —Floyd Kvamme, on being, at 45, the "old" guy at Apple

I've heard it said that you were one of the people who tried to provide adult supervision at Apple.

You know, it was an interesting experience for me, because when we started National [Semiconductor in 1967], I was clearly the kid. I was in my 20s. When I became general manager of semiconductor operations, I was, I think, 32—33, maybe. So I was always the young guy. In 1982, I was 45. So I moved from being the young guy to being the old guy overnight. And I never looked at it as adult supervision, because I found the people at Apple absolutely inspiring. It really is part of what motivated me to get into venture capital, to back young people doing exciting new things, because if you think about it, we were in our 20s when we started the semiconductor industry; people in their 20s started the personal computer businesses; people in their 20s started the software business; and this last decade people in their 20s started the Internet businesses. People in their 20s can do amazing things.

The famous "1984" ad for the Mac was made when you were in charge of sales and marketing, but a lot of the company's senior management didn't want to run it. Were you in favor of it?

Oh, absolutely. That's the closest I've ever come to insubordination in my life. We made two ads in the summer of '83. We made the "1984" ad, and we made an ad titled "Alone Again" for the Lisa. They were both done by Ridley Scott, and they both were the same dark kind of a genre. We started to run the "Alone Again" ad promoting the Lisa. The idea of the ad was that it was alone again; it was in a whole new category by itself. Unfortunately, some people thought it meant you'll be alone if you buy this. I was responsible for it, but it bombed—it was terrible. So it put a pall in some people's minds over the "1984" ad.

continues on next page

But at our sales meeting in Hawaii [in October 1983] we showed the "1984" ad, and the sales force went ballistic. They loved it. I think the ads were already in the can by the time Bill [Campbell] arrived [at Apple as vice president of marketing], but Bill saw the reaction of the sales force also, and he and I wanted to run that ad.

Our [original] idea was to run the ad across all the college football games on January 1. But by that time the Lisa had been so unsuccessful that we couldn't afford that, and we had to cut our budget. So we went to the notion of the Super Bowl, and we bought 2 minutes on the Super Bowl, for 900 grand a minute, as I recall. The board [of directors] saw the ad in the December meeting, and with the background of the "Alone Again" ad failing, they voted against running it. So we were directed to sell the time.

We immediately sold a half-minute, so we had a minute and a half left to sell. The Friday before Super Bowl, Campbell and I were sitting in my office, and [a colleague] popped in and said they had an offer for our last minute—I don't remember what happened to the last 30 seconds, somehow we got rid of that. Campbell and I decided we hadn't heard anything [he laughs]. So we ran the ad anyway, and of course it just went over like gangbusters.

But then you got all kinds of news coverage…

There was all kinds of news coverage, and stations clamoring to get tapes so that they could run the ad without our even paying. It ran, in a number of markets, a number of times as a news story.

That was quite a coup.

It was a coup. It was an unusual decision, because we absolutely were directed to do something else. But it would have been a huge letdown to the sales force not to have done that, because they loved it. But again I respect the decision of the board guys. We were short of money—$900,000 is a lot of money—and if you thought it was going to be as unsuccessful as "Alone Again" was, I could see [being wary].

The other thing that everybody feared was that the advertising world was going to overdo emphasis on 1984, that there would be a lot of ads with the same theme. But we got super lucky—I don't know of another 1984-based ad. Nobody did it. Sometimes it's better to be lucky than smart, right?

The aesthetics remain a big part of the Mac's appeal, wouldn't you say?

That's Steve. Steve has a feel for product and for product design—he's a genius at it. And he realizes the value of getting it right. Just before the Mac was ready to ship, I got a call from a guy in the distribution center, which my organization ran. Steve had just been over there, and had rejected all of the packing crates because they weren't the right white! People were going nuts! But the point is, he was right—he realized those boxes were going to sit within the store, and rather than have crappy-looking boxes, he looked at the product as a whole product. There was a scramble, and somehow we got the right white. The notion of "do it right"—that was his kind of motto, and he's good at it.

10

Word Processing

Marty Cortinas is the chapter editor and author.

You're ready to put that Underwood typewriter in the closet, and you're determined that your next letter to Mom will slide out of your Mac's printer. Sure, you could use Stickies to write her a note. But what you'll really want, to produce that letter, is a program called a *word processor*.

A word processor can help you craft the letter, from setting the margins to checking your spelling to picking a flowery font that Mom is sure to love. Even better, today's word processors offer much more than simple letter-writing capabilities. You can add graphics to your text and even do basic page layout with a word-processing program. You can create tables of contents and indexes. You can automate tasks and customize the program's interface and dictionary. Just try to do all that quickly and easily with your old Underwood!

In this chapter I'll give you an overview of exactly what a word processor can do for you—and what it can't. In addition, I'll discuss the word-processing programs available, giving you an overview of each one's strengths and weaknesses. (And yes, believe it or not, there are more word processors for the Mac than just Microsoft Word.) I'll even go over some of the add-ons, such as spelling and grammar checkers, which can help you in your writing life. So what are you waiting for? Let's get started!

In This Chapter

Getting Started

Defining exactly what a word processor is can be tricky. So many applications can perform a variety of tasks that it's difficult to draw boundaries. For example, the spelling-check and formatting options in many email and page-layout programs make them viable options when you need to do some writing in a pinch.

For the purposes of this chapter, if a program has extensive tools for manipulating words, it's a word processor. The distinction lies in the program's being able to change what is written, rather than being able to change how the written material looks. If the program's main function deals with something else—such as sending email or producing page layouts—it is not a word processor. So, by this logic, Microsoft Word, Nisus Writer Express, Mariner Write, and AppleWorks qualify. Adobe Acrobat, QuarkXPress, and Macromedia Dreamweaver do not.

Choosing a Word Processor

If you don't have a word processor, your first question probably will be, Which one should I get? But in reality, what you should ask yourself first is, What do I want to do with my word processor? That's because what you want to do will lead you to find the appropriate word processor.

For example, if you are just going to do some simple tasks, such as writing letters, creating flyers, or crafting essays, you can stick to a simple, inexpensive word processor. AppleWorks would probably be fine.

If you need to do heavy-duty editing and create things like indexes, outlines, or bibliographies, a program such as Word or Mariner Write is the correct call. If you need to collaborate with others, especially if they are working on different platforms, you'll probably end up with Word.

The bottom line is that word processors are not created equal. Unless you have a lot of disposable income, you must define your needs before you pick a word processor.

Working with Text

With a typewriter, you type and the words pretty much stay where they are on the page. Word-processing programs are a lot more flexible; you can easily move, alter, insert, or delete text.

Inserting Text

Before you can process words, you have to get them into the Mac. Let's forget about preexisting text, such as that file your boss just gave you, and start from scratch. You create and name a new document and are greeted by white space. Now what? Well, you type.

Notice that everything you type is entered at the insertion point, which is represented by a vertical flashing bar. In fact, everything you do happens at the insertion point. Selections start there, and paste operations happen there. Typing and deleting are based at the insertion point. To move the insertion point, you can click with the mouse somewhere else in your document or use the arrow keys.

 If you want to move the insertion point below the end of your text, down to where all that inviting white space is, you might have to add some paragraph marks or returns to get there. Although a large enough window will show space beyond the end-of-file marker, the program doesn't recognize it as such—there's no there there. (If you want to get metaphysical, there is an infinite amount of white space after the end, but the window only shows part of it.) So to put some text farther down, you'll have to push down the end-of-file marker with line feeds of some sort.

In addition to typing text into your document, you can import other documents into it using the commands in your word processor. Or you can use cut and paste to swipe text from another source. In any case, you're still going to have to master the basics of the insertion point and selecting text.

Selecting Text

If you wish to perform an action on a piece of text, such as deleting it, copying it, or styling it, you must first select it. You can select text by clicking and then dragging across it (**Figure 10.1**). If the selection you want runs for several lines, you don't need to move the pointer over every single word—just click at the beginning and drag to the end of the selection via the shortest route. You can even select backward. When you release the mouse button, all text between the starting point and the ending point will be selected. If you didn't quite select what you wanted, you can hold down (Shift) and click or use the arrow keys to modify your selection.

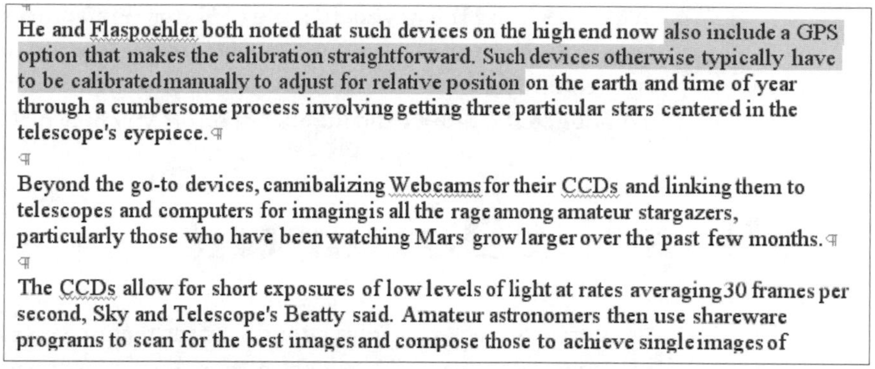

He and Flaspoehler both noted that such devices on the high end now also include a GPS option that makes the calibration straightforward. Such devices otherwise typically have to be calibrated manually to adjust for relative position on the earth and time of year through a cumbersome process involving getting three particular stars centered in the telescope's eyepiece. ¶

¶

Beyond the go-to devices, cannibalizing Webcams for their CCDs and linking them to telescopes and computers for imaging is all the rage among amateur stargazers, particularly those who have been watching Mars grow larger over the past few months. ¶

¶

The CCDs allow for short exposures of low levels of light at rates averaging 30 frames per second, Sky and Telescope's Beatty said. Amateur astronomers then use shareware programs to scan for the best images and compose those to achieve single images of

Figure 10.1

The highlighted text has been selected. Any actions you perform now will be applied only to the selected text

You have other ways to select text, depending on the application you're using. For the most part, double-clicking will select one whole word. Microsoft Word, for example, will also let you select a whole sentence by ⌘-clicking or let you select columns of text using (Option)-drag. Nisus Writer Express and Word both do a neat trick that Nisus Writer Express calls *noncontiguous selection* and Word X calls *multi-selection*—in both cases the feature lets you select unconnected blocks of text. Consult the help files of the application you're using for any specialized selecting.

To deselect text, simply click outside the selected text. If you use an arrow key, you will instantly move to the beginning or end of the selection, which will then be deselected.

 If you find that you can't quite get the selection exactly the way you want it, this may be because the program insists on "helping" by selecting only entire words. Dig into the program's preferences to turn off this feature. In Word X, for example, go to Word > Preferences, and in the Edit pane, make sure the box next to "When selecting, automatically select entire word" isn't checked.

Now that you have text selected, what can you do with it? You can style it— that is, change its appearance through the use of fonts and the like. You can copy it. You can cut it. Depending on your purposes, you can cut text in two ways. If your intention is to cut the selection to move it somewhere else, you'll want to use ⌘X. This removes the selected text and places it in the Clipboard; ⌘V pastes it wherever you want. (These are not specifically features of word processors but are commands you can use in any Mac program.) If your goal is to delete the offending selection forever, just start typing or press (Return) or (Delete). The words you type will take the place of the selection, which won't move to the Clipboard. (If you accidentally delete something in this way and you wanted to save it, don't despair. Most applications nowadays have an undo feature, usually ⌘Z. In fact, many have multiple levels of undo, so you can go back several steps to redo a misstep.)

In Mac OS X, use the Keyboard pane of System Preferences to set the Key Repeat Rate and the Delay Until Repeat; use the General pane to pick a highlight color. Both of these settings will help you customize your text-editing experience and reduce the number of errors you may make in typing.

Styling the Document

Word processing is not only about the words themselves, but also about how they look on the page. There's formatting, line breaks, margins, graphics, and more to consider.

Formatting

Formatting means setting the fonts, point sizes, and styles (such as bold or italic) of selected characters. When you format an entire paragraph, you can also set other parameters, such as margins, indents, the amount of space before and after a paragraph, leading (the amount of space between lines of text), and tabs.

For example, as I type the draft of this chapter, I am using regular 10-point Palatino with a left indent of 1 inch, single-line spacing, 6 points of space before each paragraph, and widow and orphan control (options that help prevent single words or single lines from being placed awkwardly). That's what Word tells me in its Style dialog, at least (**Figure 10.2**).

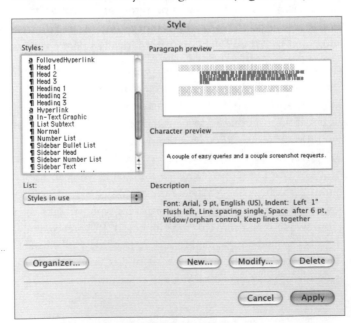

Figure 10.2

The Style dialog shows the different formatting options you can apply to your paragraphs.

You should think of formatting as what is done to characters once they are in the document. When you type in a document, the program records them as they are entered and then changes their appearance as you apply format changes. This can give weird results if you don't understand the logic. For example, let's say I type some goofy word with a capital in the middle of it, like AppleWorks. If I then apply the all-caps format, I get APPLEWORKS. However, typing AppleWorks and then applying the all-caps format is *not* the same thing as simply typing APPLEWORKS, because deep in the Mac's reptilian brain, it knows that in the first case only the *A* and the *W* are capped. So if I then undo the all-caps formatting of the two all-capped (but different) words, I get two different results: the first word reverts to upper- and lowercase, while the second remains all uppercased.

You can also layer styles—that is, apply one style on top of another. For example, you can apply an all-caps format to a selection and then also opt to make the selection boldfaced and italic. (For more on this, see "Text Styles and Templates," below.)

 Mac OS X features *font smoothing,* which is another term for *anti-aliasing.* Smoothing blurs the edges of letters to make them look less jagged. This works especially well at larger point sizes, but to sensitive eyes it is annoying at the smaller sizes. In Mac OS X you can set the font-smoothing style (for example, light or strong), and also opt to turn off font smoothing for specified small font sizes, in the General pane of System Preferences. Some Mac OS X applications—such as the OmniWeb browser from the Omni Group— also give you the option to forgo font smoothing.

Special Characters

Most word processors allow the writer to be specific about how words and punctuation behave in a document through the use of special characters. The most common of these are those little horizontal lines between words: hyphens and dashes. You can use two types of dashes (en and em), but most people won't be concerned about the distinction between the two.

The hyphen, on the other hand, is a versatile animal in the word processor. It not only serves its usual purpose when you use it in your writing, but it also can be used to control how a word breaks at the end of a line of text. Depending on how your paragraphs are formatted, when you get to the end of a line, the program will either drop the entire word down to the next line or try to hyphenate it. You can control where the word breaks by inserting an optional hyphen, also known as a *soft hyphen*. A soft hyphen won't show up in a word unless it's needed at the end of a line. Many programs allow you to use the soft hyphen in front of a word to prevent it from being hyphenated at all. A relative is the *nonbreaking hyphen*. This hyphen is used in a word that is hyphenated already—it simply tells the program not to break the hyphenated word over two lines. The *nonbreaking space,* on the other hand, goes between two words that you want to keep together on the same line. Consult the documentation of your chosen word processor to access these options, which are usually invoked using a keyboard combination.

 Speaking of keyboard combinations, there is a pitfall to watch out for if you use the Dvorak keyboard layout. The Mac OS is flexible when it comes to alternative keyboard layouts, and it even includes an option to use the Dvorak layout with QWERTY ⌘-key combinations. In theory, this is helpful to those folks who are learning Dvorak but have years of experience typing ⌘Q to exit a program. But in practice, the feature is hit-or-miss, depending on what program you're using. Word seems to decide at random what keyboard layout to use, while Microsoft Excel handles the hybrid flawlessly. My advice: no half measures. Go full-on Dvorak or stick to QWERTY.

Line breaks: Why should you care?

If you start writing with your word processor right out of the box, you might wonder what all this talk of line breaks is about. After all, you've been typing all this time and you've never seen the computer add a hyphen to any of your words. The reason is that the default justification of paragraphs is *ragged right,* which means that every line starts in the same place on the left but varies on the right, depending on how many characters are in the line, and each line ends with a whole word. If you change the justification to *flush right,* the lines will end at the same vertical point on the right but vary on the left. If you change the setting to *justified,* both sides of your paragraphs will line up. To accomplish this, the Mac adjusts the amount of white space between words so that each line starts and ends at the same vertical point. When the white-space trick doesn't quite work, a word at the end of the line has to be hyphenated. The program will usually make an educated guess about the best place to break a word, but it's often a bad guess. Using special characters such as the soft hyphen can help the program make the right decisions.

Text Styles and Templates

Word processors make it easy for you to change the way words look. You can select individual words and change their appearance, and you can define a way that certain types of documents (such as business letters) look. The tools that allow you to do this are text styles and templates.

Styles

A *style* is a set of parameters, such as point size, font, font style, text alignment, and line spacing, that you can apply in one quick step. Usually you apply a style to entire paragraphs or to selected text. An example of where you would use styles is a small newsletter. You could have one style for the body text and another for headlines. One of the great advantages of styles is that many word processors allow you to change the look of a style and apply those changes globally in one step. So if you are writing the Great American Novel and your editors decide that they prefer 14-point Courier to 12-point Times, you don't have to scroll through your document paragraph by paragraph to make the change. Simply edit the appropriate style and update it.

Templates

A template is a blueprint for documents, and it usually contains information about menus, toolbars, palettes, shortcuts, formatting, layout, and styles. For example, most word processors come with a collection of templates for business letters, brochures, presentations, and the like.

Templates are handy tools, especially when you are working with other users. With templates, you can make sure that everyone is working on the same page. In the making of this book, for example, the writers were given a template to ensure that everyone was using the same fonts for the text, captions, and headlines. Instead of telling everyone the specific parameters for each item, the book's editors distributed a template containing all that information.

Take care with templates. When dealing with templates, it is important to make sure that you are using them, not modifying them. In Word X, for example, if a coworker gives you a template for a business letter, you should not just open it and start typing. If you do this, you will be modifying the template, which is not what you want to do. Store the template in the appropriate folder in your Templates folder (yes, folders within folders—it never ends); it will show up in the Project Gallery, where you'll be able to create a new document based on the template. You can also attach the template to an existing document, which gives you access to all the styles in the template (**Figure 10.3**).

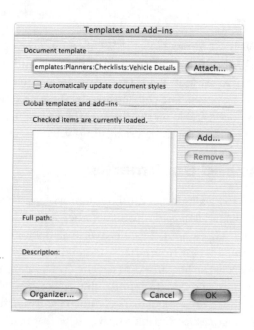

Figure 10. 3

In Microsoft Word you can attach a template to an existing document.

Graphics

If you're doing more than simple writing, you'll probably need to include some pictures with your work. Thankfully, most word processors handle basic graphics easily, although you won't get the versatility of a program made especially for the task, such as QuarkXPress. You can easily insert graphics and modify how they behave with text. For example, you can arrange for the text to wrap around your graphic or even have the graphic sit below or above the text.

Views

To use graphics effectively, you must be comfortable with switching between various views in your word processor. In Word, for example, most folks usually work in the Normal view, but graphics aren't visible there. Page Layout view shows how your work will look when it is output.

Image formats

Many word processors come with clip art that can be plopped into your document. You can also include your own pictures. Keep in mind how your work is going to be output, however. While JPEG and GIF images are popular because of their relatively small file sizes, especially for images that will go on the Web, they are not always the best option for other documents. If you plan to print your work, a better option is a TIFF or similar high-resolution format. Just be aware that TIFF files can be enormous in relation to a text-only word-processing document.

HTML

Speaking of the Web, word processors today often offer the option to save your documents in HTML format, the language of the Web. Although this seems like a good idea, try to avoid it. Word processors are not made to create Web content, and it often shows. The code created by these programs is usually bloated, which is not desirable on the Internet. However, if you need a Web page in a pinch, it works. (For more on creating Web content, see Chapter 16.)

Hyperlinks and Bookmarks

In Word, you have to be a little careful about terminology. For example, there's the case of *hyperlinks* and *bookmarks*. In some other applications, a bookmark is an Internet address. That's not the case in Word; a bookmark is a location in a document that you name for future reference, and it works much like a real, physical bookmark. You use bookmarks to navigate to a location, mark page ranges, create cross-references, and do other similar things. For example, you can select some text and use the Insert > Bookmark command to name the selection. Now you can use the Bookmark command to navigate to that named bookmark. It is important to realize that the bookmarks allow you to move only within one document. A hyperlink is *hot* text (or even an image) that takes you to another location when you click it. For example, a hyperlink can point to a Web site, an email address, another Office document, or somewhere else in the current document.

Structure and Organization

Jack Kerouac wrote *On the Road* without paragraphs or punctuation on a 120-foot strip of Teletype paper. (His editor must have loved him.) You and I probably can't get away with that, and we must have some structure to our documents. Fortunately, we have tools that Kerouac and his typewriter did not. Word processors make it easy to add footnotes, headers, tables of contents, and many other organizational features.

Tables of Contents and Indexes

Another advantage of modern word processors over old-fashioned typing is that they give you the ability to quickly create accurate tables of contents and indexes. You go about creating these in slightly different ways, but both are fairly painless.

Tables of contents

Tables of contents are usually derived from the hierarchy set up by the use of styled headings (**Figure 10.4**). In Word, you can also create a table of contents from any outline you may have created for the document. Generally, you pick a menu option, fiddle with the settings, and bingo—you've got a table of contents.

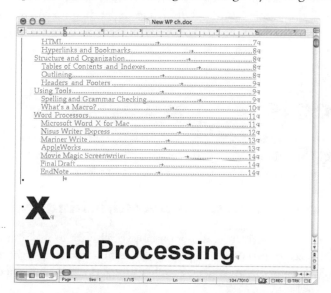

Figure 10.4

This table of contents was derived from the headings of this chapter.

Indexes

These are a little trickier, as they are more comprehensive. First, you need to decide what is worth listing in an index. When you decide that a word or term is worth indexing, you mark it in a special manner. After you've done this for the entire work, you can generate an index. It's a bit of work but still much quicker than compiling an index by hand. Not all word processors have indexing features; you have been warned.

Outlining

Outlining allows you to see the structure of your document, as long as you have been using styles to define different parts of it. In Word, for example, the Outline view lets you collapse text under topics and subtopics and assign different levels to each section. You can also generate a numbered list outlining your document.

Currently, only Word provides powerful outlining tools as part of its base package.

Headers and Footers

Headers and footers are pieces of text that appear at the top and bottom of each page of a printed document. For example, they might include a title, page number, and date. Most programs go beyond that simple functionality, however, and allow the use of multiple variables to produce dynamic headers and footers. For example, if you were creating a member directory for a local organization, you could include headers that show the first and last entries of each page, like those found in dictionaries or phone books. You can also create a unique header and footer for the first page or for different sections of a document. You can set up the headers so that they change depending on whether the page number is odd or even. Basically, if you can think of a use for headers and footers, you can accomplish it.

Using Tools

Word processing is not just typing and formatting. There are tools to cut down on errors and to make repetitive tasks less taxing.

Spelling and Grammar Checking

Once you've written your document, you'll want to make sure that you don't embarrass yourself by misspelling something, and that's where the spelling checker comes in. As much as spelling checkers can do, it is important to remember what they can't do: spell. A spelling checker simply compares the words in a document with its dictionary; if a word isn't in the dictionary, it is flagged. Most spelling checkers these days will suggest a replacement for the unknown word or phrase. For example, Word suggests that "Marty Cortinas" should be "merry courtesan." As you can see, the efficiency of the spelling checker is directly influenced by the quality of the dictionary.

 You can edit most dictionaries. Take advantage of this to add your name, names of friends or businesses, or any other proper names you use a lot.

Another shortcoming of spelling checkers is that an incorrect spelling can be a correct spelling for another word, and the checker won't catch it. If you are talking about Bambi's mom, you may write, "She's a dear," when you meant "She's a deer." Both are "right," but one is wrong in the context. The spelling checker won't catch it, so you must maintain your vigilance even though the word processor has "checked" your spelling. Another problem is when the dictionary has a flat-out wrong entry. This can be doubly vexing when the misspelling is close to a commonly used word. I can't stress enough that a spelling checker is just a tool, not a solution.

Most word-processing programs and many other programs that handle text, such as desktop-publishing programs, have spelling checkers built in. Naturally, the result is that fewer and fewer stand-alone spelling checkers are available. For most folks that's OK, but there are a few hardy souls out there who would rather keep track of one dictionary than a half dozen. Instead of relying on several individual dictionaries in various stages of customization, you can use a stand-alone spelling checker that lets you work with just one dictionary. If you type your name in Nisus Writer and OK it in your spelling checker, you won't have Word flagging your name as wrong.

 If you use a stand-alone spelling checker, deactivate the spelling checker functions in your main applications or else you'll have a redundancy problem.

Most stand-alone spelling checkers for Mac OS X are freeware or shareware options. Dig deep enough and you can probably find one that suits your special needs. For a start, you might look at Rainmaker Research's **Spell Catcher X** ($39.95; www.rainmakerinc.com). It can autocorrect commonly misspelled words, and it has dictionaries and thesauruses for nine languages. One final word of advice: Don't try to find these types of utilities via the Apple Web site, as they are lumped in with all sorts of unrelated utilities—more than 200 general utilities, as a matter of fact. Your best course of action is to do a Web search and then download and try the ones that look promising.

Grammar checking is a little more sophisticated, and today's grammar checkers do an amazing job, considering the technical hurdles. However, I find that grammar checkers are more trouble than they're worth because often the suggestions can be confusing or downright wrong (**Figure 10.5**). If you have problems with grammar, however, they can be quite helpful, although it still pays to keep a close eye on them—they're not always right. If you need a grammar checker because your word processor does not include one or because you are not happy with the one it *does* have, check out Linguisoft's **Grammarian Pro X** ($39.95; www.linguisoft.com). Aside from its grammar-correction features, it can also serve as a spelling checker, so it's sort of a two-for-one.

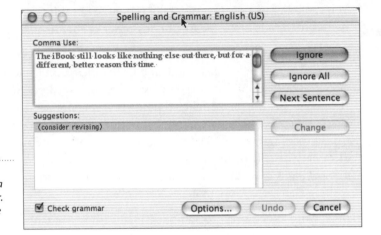

Figure 10.5

Here's a typical suggestion from a grammar checker. Uh, thanks for the "help."

What's a Macro?

A macro is a stored set of instructions you can use to perform a task automatically. Macros are particularly useful for performing repetitive tasks. For example, if you routinely insert a table of specific proportions into your documents, you can save a lot of work by making a macro for it. In Word, you can use the macro recorder to copy the steps you take and then assign a shortcut key or menu command to trigger the steps. So instead of your going to the trouble of pulling down the Insert menu, choosing Index and Tables, and fiddling with the settings in the dialog, the macro lets you simply press a shortcut key to create a table.

Although you can "record" a macro, there are limits to what a macro can contain. Figure that if you can perform an operation using only the keyboard and menu selections, you can make it into a macro. The minute the mouse enters the picture, a macro is pretty much out of the question. Still, within those limits, much can be done; you are limited mainly by your imagination and your macro-designing skill. And macros don't just have to be serious labor-saving devices. I've seen amusing "personality tests" that are actually macros. These macros present a series of questions, which you answer, and then the macro produces an analysis of your personality based on your answers.

Macro viruses

Macros are powerful time-savers, but that power comes at a cost, at least in Microsoft Word. Word's macro capabilities tap into Visual Basic, a programming language. Although that allows macros to perform all sorts of neat tricks, it also opens the door for the evil that is the macro virus.

A macro virus lives among the macros in a document or template, and it is usually designed to be triggered whenever the affected document is opened. It can then find its way to your global template and infect every file you open. As an added feature, this infection ability is cross-platform, so the virus can move from Windows to Mac to Windows again. Soon your coworkers will refer to you as Typhoid Mary.

There are two ways to prevent this. One is to purchase a commercial antivirus package, such as Symantec's **Norton AntiVirus** ($49.95; www.symantec.com). The other is to have Word disable macros in any suspect document. Actually, Word can't tell what is suspect and what is not. Once you activate the macro-virus protection in Word's General preferences, the program will simply alert you that a document has macros and give you the option to disable them. If the document is from a trusted source, go ahead and run them. If you're not sure, turn them off.

Word Processors

So you're ready to write. Now what do you do? Unless you're perfectly happy with Stickies, you'll have to get a word processor. Although there aren't a ton of them available, you do have some choices to make. The focus here is on products available for Mac OS X. If you're still running Mac OS 9 or earlier, pick up an earlier edition of *The Macintosh Bible* for suggestions or visit Jag's House (www.jagshouse.com/classicsoftware.html) on the Web. Also consider this a select sampling of the word-processor market: it aims to show off the best available, but some gems may be overlooked.

Microsoft Word

Microsoft Word X for Mac, by Microsoft Corp. (www.microsoft.com), is the 800-pound gorilla of the word-processing world. The latest version is available by itself ($229, upgrade $109) or as part of the Office v. X suite ($399, upgrade $299), which also includes Microsoft Excel, Entourage, and PowerPoint. In many cases, when people talk about word processing, they are talking about Word. Naturally, this has its good points and its bad points.

Cons

The main disadvantage is that for many businesses and almost any collaborative projects, you don't have a choice of word processors. It's Word or nothing. For many years, Word was merely tolerated in the Mac community. It didn't help matters that the program came from the same company that produced Windows, the rival personal-computing platform (or "the enemy," as some people call Microsoft). Each new version of Word seemed to drift further and further away from what users considered the Mac experience. The nadir came in the early 1990s with the release of Word 6 for the Mac, which was not only overburdened with toolbars and buttons but was a pig of an application. It demanded a lot of RAM to run and took seemingly forever to start up. Word 6 was so reviled that many conspiracy theorists pointed to it as a sort of Trojan horse, sent by Microsoft to undermine the Macintosh.

OK, so Word 6 was bad. (So bad, in fact, that the company I worked for at the time refused to "upgrade" and stuck with the old, reliable Word 5.1.) But a funny thing happened in 1997. Steve Jobs had come back to Apple, and that summer he kicked up quite a ruckus by marking the clone market for death and creating an alliance with Microsoft.

Pros

You can argue all you want about whether making peace with Microsoft was a good move by Jobs, but you can't argue that Word for the Mac is a much better product now. Microsoft not only has put together a fine Macintosh team, but it also has let the team members loose. Before the Apple deal, the feature sets in Word and the other Office products were already converging, with the result that the products were looking and acting more and more like Windows programs, even on the Mac. If there were any cool new features, you could be sure they would be available for Windows months if not years before Mac users got a taste. Nowadays, Microsoft's Mac products are more faithful to the Mac aesthetic, and many of the cool new features start life on the Mac.

So that's good. Another good thing is that the current versions of Word, on both the Mac and Windows sides, share file formats. That makes Word the perfect vehicle for trading files across platforms. No good deed goes unpunished, though, so that cross-platform capability has the drawback of allowing the nefarious among us to distribute macro viruses that much more easily.

If you're a single user who doesn't do a lot of work with others, or someone who only needs a word processor every once in a while, Word is probably too much—like using a bulldozer instead of a spoon. However, if you're in business, you don't have a choice: it's Word.

Making Word less helpful

Microsoft Word includes several tools to make your work go more smoothly. Unfortunately, almost all of them are enabled when you first start up the program, and this can be more of a detriment than a benefit. You may find yourself typing some simple notes to yourself, when the Office Assistant will burst in and announce, "It looks like you are writing a letter. Would you like help?" Aside from the creepiness you may feel from having the computer "watch" what you're doing, this intrusion can often be just a waste of time because no, you don't want any help, and you have to make the assistant go away.

Other times, Word may not even ask but will go ahead and format what you're typing in a manner it believes is correct. Now it's a double waste of time because you have to go back and fix what Word did. So how do you keep Word on a leash?

The top of most folks' Word hit lists has a space reserved for the Office Assistant, the little animated computer named Max (**Figure 10.6**). Max can be helpful by offering context-sensitive tips, but unless you are completely new to Word, he becomes a bother rather quickly. He's easily silenced; just uncheck the Use the Office Assistant command in the Help menu.

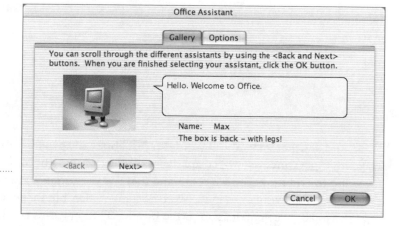

Figure 10.6

It's Max the Office Assistant. Friend or foe?

More pernicious is Word's habit of automatically formatting certain words or paragraphs. For instance, if you write something that appears to be an Internet link, whether it's a URL or an email address, Word will make it into a live hyperlink. Getting Word to stop doing this is a little more involved than it should be, but easy enough to fix.

Open the AutoCorrect dialog from the Tools menu and you'll find four tabs: AutoCorrect, AutoFormat As You Type, AutoText, and AutoFormat. Somewhere deep in the bowels of the Microsoft programming hutch there is a coder who can explain why there are two AutoFormat tabs. I cannot. But I can tell you that to fix many of the annoying automatic functions in Word, you must make changes on both tabs.

Let's take the Internet link as an example. If you choose the AutoFormat tab and uncheck the "Internet paths with hyperlinks" option under Replace, you might think Word won't insert hyperlinks anymore. You'd be wrong. Move to the AutoFormat As You Type tab, and you'll find the same option under "Replace as you type" (**Figure 10.7**). Uncheck that box as well, and you'll banish automatic hyperlinks forever. The moral of the story is that you often have to look in more than one place to change Word's behavior.

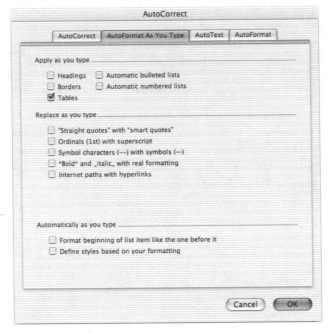

Figure 10. 7

Here's the AutoFormat As You Type tab. Note the AutoFormat tab on the far right. Often, changes you make here will also need to be made there.

 And another thing about Word—or just about any program that supports multiple windows—if you are dense like me, you may become frustrated trying to find the keyboard command that lets you toggle between Word document windows. It's not in the Word documentation, but there's a good reason. It's a global command supported by Mac OS X: ⌘~. This command lets you toggle between the open document windows in any given application—for example, between all open Word documents or all open PDF documents.

Nisus Writer Express

Nisus Writer Express ($59.95, upgrade $39.95; www.nisus.com) is a bit of a cipher. In its previous, pre–Mac OS X incarnations, Nisus Writer was the only viable professional alternative to Microsoft Word, and it built a small but dedicated following, thanks to several distinctive features, like GREP (Global Regular Expression Program) searching and noncontiguous selections (**Figure 10.8**). If you are curious about GREP searching, just know that it's a powerful but arcane way to find text. For example, the search "\(yak.*\)*\." will find "yak yak yak," "yakkety yak yak," and "yakkety-yak; yak," among other things. On second thought, maybe you're better off not knowing.

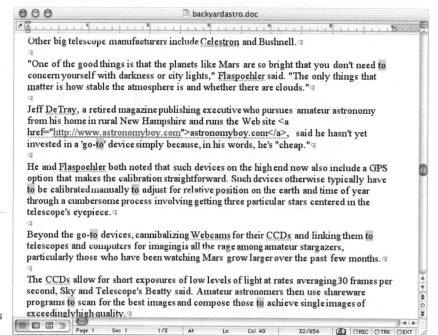

Noncontiguous selections let you have blocks of selected text that are not adjacent to one another. In this example, we have selected all instances of the word to.

So what is noncontiguous selection? In traditional text-handling applications, the text you select has a discrete beginning and end, and anything between is selected. In other words, there is only one block of selected text. Nisus Writer Express (and now other programs, including Word) lets you have more than one block of selected text not adjacent to one another. For example, you can do a search for all occurrences of the word *the* in your document, and Nisus Writer will select them all. You can then do anything to this non-contiguous selection that you could do to a regular selection, such as bolding or changing fonts.

Then along came Mac OS X, and the folks at Nisus were faced with a decision: rewrite Nisus Writer or not? Creating new code for old standbys like Nisus Writer is no small task, so a sort of compromise was struck. Nisus merged with Okito, the makers of a little Mac OS X–native word processor called Okito Composer. Building on Composer, Nisus came up with Nisus Writer Express.

As the name implies, Nisus Writer Express is a slimmer version of the original. But while the feature set isn't as deep as the classic Nisus Writer, there still is powerful GREP searching, the ability to create Perl scripts, a customizable interface, and support for reading and writing Microsoft Word files.

If you ever doubted the dominance of Microsoft Word in this market, just take a look at the feature sets of other word processors. Most go out of their way to point out any kind of compatibility with the Word file format.

The good news is that there now is a Nisus word processor for Mac OS X. The bad news is that not everyone is happy. Many longtime users aren't migrating to it because much of their hard customization work, particularly macros, would go to waste. Others are wary because it is truly a 1.0 release, with all the attendant instabilities you might expect.

In any case, Nisus Writer Express is one of the few viable alternatives to Word out there. So if you just can't deal with Microsoft, take Nisus Writer Express for a spin.

Mariner Write

Mariner Write ($79.95; www.marinersoftware.com) is another case of the little guy taking on big, bad Microsoft. It's a full-function word processor that can—you guessed it—read (but not write) Word files. That's not its only attribute, though. It has the usual array of features, like headers and footers, a spelling checker, and WYSIWYG font menus, but its real cool feature is that it uses very little memory—as little as 2 MB of RAM. Word uses several times more than that. While Mac OS X handles memory much better than the old-school operating system, it's nice to have a little breathing room.

AppleWorks

The word-processor portion of Apple Computer's **AppleWorks** is worth a quick mention here; it is covered in depth in Chapter 9. If you need simple word processing at a small price, it's hard to go wrong with AppleWorks—plus you get spreadsheet, database, painting, drawing, and presentation modules ($79; www.apple.com/appleworks).

Movie Magic Screenwriter

Although a mainstay like Microsoft Word can handle most of your writing needs, it doesn't necessarily cover all of them. The product line from Screenplay Systems (www.screenplay.com) is a perfect example of filling a niche.

Presentation of the material in a script for television or the movies demands a lot of attention to detail. There are conventions for handling scene headings, action, camera angles, character names, dialogue, transitions, and a host of other elements. **Movie Magic Screenwriter 4.6** ($249) takes care of all that formatting for you.

Screenplay Systems has a host of related products for the budding or professional creative writer, such as **Dramatica Pro** ($269), which aids you in story development. However, Screenwriter is currently the only one of the company's products that works in Mac OS X-native mode. (The others do, however, run in the Classic environment under Mac OS X.) Check the company's Web site for more information on the other products.

Final Draft

Final Draft ($199.95; www.finaldraft.com) and the companion **Final Draft AV** ($179) make up another scriptwriting package ($299.95 bundled). Final Draft is designed to help write movies, TV shows, plays, and even commercials. It's full of clever ideas, including a text-to-speech feature that lets you assign different voices to characters for playback on your Mac. (I'm sure that Bruce, one of the voices included on the Mac, is a terrible actor, though.) Its most compelling feature is probably that it is fully cross-platform, supporting different flavors of Mac operating systems as well as the entire Windows family.

EndNote

EndNote, from ISI ResearchSoft ($299.95; www.endnote.com), is a stand-alone program for creating bibliographies. It allows you to search online bibliographic databases, organize references, and consequently produce a bibliography. The program comes with more than 200 predefined connection files for online databases to make it easier to get up and searching.

EndNote can insert figures or tables directly into Microsoft Word files, and it can create bibliographies from any program that can produce RTF files. Other recent additions include Palm compatibility and XML exporting.

Interview: Debi Coleman

An English-literature major in college, Debi Coleman went on to business school at Stanford, then to work at Hewlett-Packard. She moved to Apple as controller of the Mac group in 1981. In 1984 she was put in charge of the ultramodern, highly automated factory in Fremont, California, that Apple had built to manufacture the Mac. Later she served stints as chief financial officer and as vice president of information systems and technology for the company.

> *I'm still very loyal to the Mac, and I think it's a wonderful product, but it was incredible, the amount of work that went into it and the personal toll it took on people.*
>
> —*Debi Coleman, on developing the original Mac*

After leaving Apple in 1992, she went to work at Tektronix, a world leader in test and measurement equipment, and then went on to become CEO of one of its spin-offs, a circuit-board manufacturer named Merix. She is currently managing partner of SmartForest Ventures, a venture-capital firm based in Portland, Oregon. She also works with several women's organizations and serves on the boards of a number of technology companies, including Applied Materials and Synopsy. —Henry Norr

What was your first job at Apple?

Well, they called me a controller. Sounds powerful, but it's fairly misleading. What I didn't realize was that the group Steve Jobs managed wasn't even officially funded [she laughs]. There was this little tiny budget under this little tiny group called the Special Task Force. We were a little bit of a skunkworks group. It was a group that Jef Raskin had started to make this information appliance, which became the Macintosh. I was actually interviewing for the controllership of the Lisa division, which was a real division, but when Steve heard I was interviewing with them, he decided he would steal me into his pet project.

When did you start planning the Fremont factory?

The factory was planned very early on—almost along with the product. Steve of course wanted it to be state-of-the-art, with Japanese automation—all that sort of thing.

Was the goal to drive costs down?

Well, ultimately, when you take a strategy like that, it does drive the cost down, and it also drives quality up, but those were the results—the effect rather than the cause. The cause was Steve wanting to do something flashy and brilliant and very high-tech. And I'll be honest with you, I fell it for it lock, stock, and barrel. When he talked about the product and wanting to change the way people worked and communicated from their very desktop, that was an extension of the original Apple vision from the Apple II. This time he wanted to make it intuitive and make it easy to use for people. But what really won me over was his vision for the manufacturing. I was really enamored of electronics manufacturing at the time, and I wanted to get into it.

Was the factory appreciably in advance of what anybody else was doing?

Oh, absolutely. Unbelievably so.

In the use of robotics?

Robotics and a lot of other things. We were trying all kinds of things at once to get high-volume, highest-quality-possible production. We studied the Toyota factory, where the suppliers deliver things on the hour to the line. You have to realize that at the time there was no such thing as [a factory that could produce] a thousand computers a day. Not the IBM PC, not the Apple II, not anything. And Steve of course always thinks big, and he wanted this electronic product to come out every few seconds off a factory line.

Did it really work that well?

At first the yields at the factory weren't even 10 percent [she laughs]. Everything went wrong, and we didn't know what. That was when I came in, In May [1984], to run manufacturing operations. The very first thing, I sat down with all the engineers. We had tons of brilliant engineers. They had identified 80 to 100 problems, but nobody had sat down and said "Well, if we solve this one, it'll bring our yield from 10 percent to 30 percent." Nobody had prioritized it. So one of the first things I did was sit down with everybody who knew a heck of a lot more than I did—all I knew was decision-making. We went through the list, and we came up with the three or four things that if we solved them, we would make real progress. We got incredibly better, we celebrated all the successes, and we built on them.

So by the end of the first year it was a success, not just in terms of PR but also from a hard-nosed business point of view?

Yeah, it really was. From 1984 to 1987, it clearly was the best single-board, high-volume computer manufacturing in the world. Once, a group of executives came in on a tour, the American Electronics Association or something like that. We had an online, real-time quality-control process that was running the factory statistics, so whenever you walked through the factory, you would see how many units were being built; how many passed and failed. This was about a year after we started, and the cumulative first-half yield was about 95 percent. We had five go/no-go test points, and you had to have test results of, like, 99.5 percent or better for each test point. I remember the hard work it was to get to that point. But these people accused us of lying—[they said] it was all fake data that we put up on the monitors. They said it was impossible to do.

It's sometimes said that the factory never got up to the capacity it was designed for.

Oh no, it actually got up to double the capacity it was designed for. The first few months it didn't—that's true—the first summer it didn't. But you never saw people work so hard in your whole life. The Macintosh operations team routinely worked 14-hour days for the first year after the launch.

continues on next page

Did you think the Mac was going to change the world?

Boy, I'm in a minority. What you just described is how the way most of the team felt, but I thought the toll on people was too high. There were several women who started out as what we call "admins" but went on to take bigger roles. I remember asking them once what it felt like to be part of the Mac team and work so hard for those years—1982, '83, '84. They all thought it was absolutely worth it, and that they had been part of a team that changed the world. I think in any objective way I was the one who got the most fame and fortune out of it, but I was the only one who wasn't convinced it was worth it.

I say that sitting in front of an iMac today [she laughs]. I'm still very loyal, and I think it's a wonderful product, but it was incredible, the amount of work that went into it and the personal toll it took on people.

Burnout? Conflict?

Oh, tons of conflict—you can't be around Steve Jobs without a lot of conflict. There were always fights. But everybody shared the same values and goals, so he always kept everybody together.

Have you always used Macs?

Absolutely. It's funny—even though this Mac on my desk looks so different from the original, I still think the design principles and what it stands for is the same. It's huggable, it's fun, it's easy to use, and I identify with it personally. It's not that same beige blob that I used to hug, but it's kind of like the Corvette—I think the Corvette stayed true as one of those great American products.

Do you use Windows at all? Are you familiar with Windows?

No, I wouldn't last a second, not a second. I won't even go near it—it's like the evil empire.

11

Databases

Steve Schwartz is the chapter editor and author.

If you're still keeping track of important names and addresses, critical sales data, stacks of recipes, or a mountain of CDs using a word processor or spreadsheet (or even a paper-based system), you're a prime candidate for a *database program*. Database programs offer far more flexibility in managing information than do word processors or spreadsheets. And they are certainly a huge improvement over paper-based methods of organizing information.

In this chapter, you'll learn how databases organize information. We'll also give you a rundown of the most popular software available, so that you can decide which program is right for you. Finally, scattered throughout the chapter you'll find tips for getting the most from your database program.

In This Chapter

What Is a Database Program?

Generically speaking, a *database* organizes information by dividing it into small, discrete pieces called *fields.* An address book might consist of name, address, and phone number fields; a checkbook might include check number, payee, description, and amount fields. A computer can use these fields to sift quickly through huge amounts of data—to help you find a particular name or check number or to arrange a client list by zip code, for example.

A database arranges fields into *records.* A record consists of the complete collection of fields for one person, item, or entity in the database. For example, in an address book database, each person or company has a separate record. Thus, when you want to enter address information for Sarah Johnson, you create a new record for her and fill in the name, address, and phone number fields with her information. Later, if you need to know Sarah's phone number or mailing address, you simply search for and display her record. All of Sarah's address data is collected in one place—her record.

The address book and checkbook mentioned above are both *databases.* You create, view, and manipulate databases with a database program, such as FileMaker Pro, 4D's 4th Dimension, or ProVUE's Panorama (see "Choosing a Database Program," later in this chapter). The tricky part is that many people use the term *database* when speaking about both the files and the programs. To make things easy for you, we'll refer to the files as *databases* and the programs as *database programs.*

You can use any of the programs discussed in this chapter to create custom databases, in which you can organize and present your information in any way you like. Some examples of homegrown databases are recipe files and CD catalogs, but you can also create contact managers, checkbook registers, and bookkeeping databases. If you'd rather just concentrate on entering data— leaving the design work to others—you'll be pleased to learn that many database programs include a variety of *templates* (preformatted databases that you can immediately put to use in your home or business).

 Some stand-alone programs are actually single-purpose database programs, usually marketed as personal information managers. If your needs are fairly limited in scope, these programs can save you time, effort, and money compared with a full-fledged database program. Similarly, if what you're looking for is a basic contact manager, Mac OS X's Address Book or your current email program (such as Microsoft Entourage or Outlook Express, or Qualcomm's Eudora) may suffice.

What a Database Program Can Do

Word processors and spreadsheets can also hold information such as names and addresses, recipes, and the contents of your CD collection. So why would you want to use a database program to organize that information? The answer lies in the way a database stores information. It stores the information for each item as a discrete piece of data (that is, a *field*)—for example, a first name, check number, or recipe ingredient. This data segmentation allows the database program to access and manipulate the information quickly and easily, which in turn allows you to consult individual parts of your data, sort it in a specific order, and then output portions of it (or the whole thing).

You can view information stored in a database in many ways—selected, sorted, and presented according to your current needs. For example, suppose you have a list of names and addresses. A database enables you to sort the list by last name to create a printed phone directory. Later you can sort by zip code to print labels for a bulk mailing. You can also quickly select the portions of your data with which you want to work—for example, all clients in the Northeast or just those who haven't placed an order in the last six months. These tasks would be much more difficult to accomplish with a list stored in a simple text document.

You'll generally perform two types of work with a database program: designing databases, and entering and viewing the information.

Database-Design Basics

When you create your own database, it is up to you to decide how to divide up the information, enter it, and display or output it. If you use a little fore-thought and planning, you'll make it easier for yourself and others to enter and utilize the information.

Defining fields

The fields in a database divide the information into smaller, discrete pieces so that the program can sift through the data more efficiently. You should create a field for each important piece of information that differs in some way from the *other* information you want to record.

One example is a Last Name field. In an address database, all records will have a Last Name field, clearly distinguishable from the other information fields in the record (Address, Zip Code, Telephone Number, and so on). Another example might be a Meal Type field in a recipe database. Each recipe will be of a certain type, such as Dessert, Main Course, or Appetizer. The Meal Type information clearly differs from that in the other fields, such as Ingredients, Directions, Prep Time, and Cooking Time.

You specify the kind of information acceptable in a field by assigning a *type* to that field. Most programs provide half a dozen or more field types, such as Text, Numeric, and Date. You might also want to specify default data for some fields (for example, today's date in a Last Modified field) and validation criteria (such as allowing only numbers from 1 to 12 for a Month field).

In addition to list-style databases (such as address books), you can perform simple and complex computations with your database program. You could create a Total field that sums items on an invoice, for example. Using the program's built-in functions, you could even instruct the database to make decisions based on the data entered for each record. An IF function, for instance, could tell the database to assign one of two sales commission amounts to a record based on the size of the sale, the customer's average purchases, or the salesperson's seniority.

Specifying relationships

Depending on the type of data you're collecting, some databases (as explained in the sidebar "Flat-File vs. Relational Databases" below) are best designed using multiple files or tables. These are known as a *relational databases*. Rather than reenter certain data for each new record, it can simply be drawn from a related file or table, as needed. To relate two files or tables, you define *key fields*; normally, these are fields that contain unique, unduplicated data, such as a numeric ID, a Social Security number, or a part number, for example. Within the main database or table this field is often called the *primary key*. The matching field in the second database or table is the *foreign key*. By placing the field in both databases (or tables) and then specifying a relationship between the two fields, you can draw the correct data from the second database or table into the first (**Figure 11.1**).

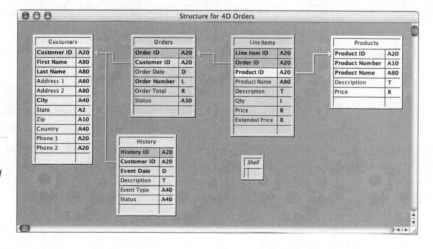

Figure 11.1

In 4th Dimension, relationships are graphically created by dragging lines between matching fields in the data tables.

As an example, suppose you've created a petty-cash-voucher database that you'll use to record employee cash disbursements. A second, related database or table can store all the employee-specific data, such as name, title, and department. Both databases (or tables) will contain an Employee ID field in which they'll be related. When the person responsible for the database needs to enter a new cash disbursement, he or she creates a new record and enters the employee's ID number in the appropriate field on the form. Doing so causes the matching employee information (name, title, and department) to be drawn from the related database or table and instantly displayed on the voucher form. You can also set up the relationship so that if you bring up a record with the employee-specific data, you can also see that person's cash disbursement history.

Flat-File vs. Relational Databases

Half a dozen years ago, two types of database programs existed: flat-file and relational. Today, almost all database programs are fully relational, allowing you to create flat-file or relational databases as your needs dictate.

Suppose you have an invoicing database. To cause each client's name and address to appear on an invoice, the database must either contain fields for this information or link to another database that stores client addresses.

In a flat-file database program, you include all the necessary fields in a single database. Thus, the address information would be an integral part of the invoicing database. A relational database can make a link (based on a key field such as a client ID) to information in a client database that stores the address data. Whenever you look at or print an invoice, the program consults the client file and displays the latest address information for that client ID.

Note that different database programs use different approaches when it comes to creating and designating relationships. In FileMaker Pro, relationships are created between different databases. Each database is a separate file on disk. In 4th Dimension and other more traditional relational programs, all data is stored in a single file but is divided into data tables within that file.

The primary advantage of a flat-file database is ease of learning. The advantages of relational databases include speed and avoiding data duplication. Instead of copying or retyping address information into every database that requires it, you can place it all in a separate database and then simply refer to it. Understanding how relationships work, when to use them, and how to define them, however, can be difficult.

Creating layouts and forms

The second step in creating your own database is designing layouts or forms (the term used varies from one program to the next). You can create different layouts for different purposes: entering data, viewing lists onscreen, creating mailing labels, displaying or printing various reports, and so on (**Figure 11.2**). You'll have to decide which fields to put in each layout and where to place them. Usually you'll place field labels next to the fields so that you can remember what information they contain.

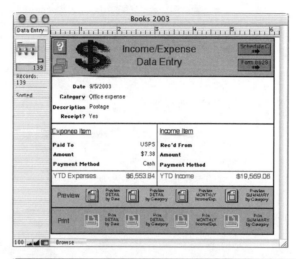

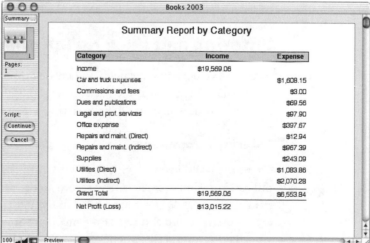

Figure 11.2

Different layouts for different purposes... Here are two layouts from a FileMaker Pro bookkeeping database: one for data entry (above) and another for displaying a report (below). This database actually has ten layouts for displaying a splash screen, performing data entry, previewing and printing reports, and displaying help information.

In current database programs (such as the three discussed in "Choosing a Database Program," later in this chapter), creating layout is like using a graphics program. The process involves dragging elements around the screen, changing their size, drawing lines, aligning objects, and adding graphics for buttons and logos.

The final important step in form creation is to format the various elements (**Figure 11.3**). You can specify different fonts, sizes, and styles for the fields and field labels. And you aren't stuck with displaying a drab text box for every field; fields that are meant to present a set of choices can be formatted as radio buttons, check boxes, or pop-up lists, for example. Buttons on the form must also be associated with the commands that they'll perform when you click them, such as displaying a different form, deleting the current record, or generating a complex report.

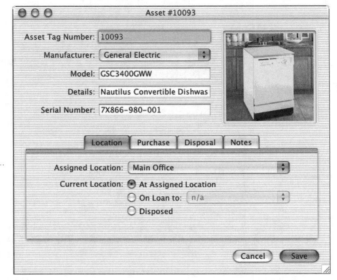

Figure 11.3

This gorgeous 4th Dimension data entry form features pop-up lists, radio buttons, pictures, and a tabbed interface—with a classy Mac OS X look.

Entering and Viewing Information

After you've defined your fields and created the layouts, you can begin to enter data, search or sort the database, and output your data in any desired format. This is where you'll really start to see the power of a database.

Entering information

Of all the tasks involved with databases, this is by far the easiest—and the dullest. You simply create a new record and start typing, tabbing from one field to the next. When you've filled in the information for one record, you create a new record and repeat the process. Some database programs save your data automatically whenever you create a new record, make changes to a layout, or modify the database structure, just as many accounting programs do to avoid potential data loss. Others require that you periodically issue a save command.

Most database programs also allow you to import existing information from word processors, spreadsheets, and other databases so that you can avoid retyping old data. The original information must be divided into fields (usually that means it's *tab- or comma-delimited*—tabs or commas separate the fields) and records (generally by ending each record with a return) so the database knows where to put each piece of information.

Sorting

All databases allow you to set the order of records according to your specified criteria. For example, you can sort an address database by last name or zip code (or by both), or sort a recipe database by ingredients, preparation time, or category. In addition to using any criterion or a combination of criteria, you can usually sort in ascending or descending order. Sorting is not permanent; you're free to change the sort order as your needs change. For instance, you might want to sort invoice records by invoice number. However, in a sales report based on those records, you might want to sort by date and—within each date—by sales amount or salesperson.

Searching and selecting records

Searching lets you instantly find and/or select records containing certain information. For example, you can locate a client that has a particular ID code or Social Security number, or you can find all the recipes that contain salmon and heavy cream. Searching yields all the records that satisfy all or part of the given criteria, depending on the logical operators you use. For instance, if you're looking for a client whose first name you've long forgotten, you could search for all people with *Anderson* in the Last Name field. To make it even easier to identify the correct person, you might search for all Andersons whose City field contains *San Jose*.

Previewing and printing data

The simplest way to output data is to show it onscreen (called *previewing* in many programs). For example, you can examine an individual record or preview a multipage report. Database programs are especially useful because they allow you to print your data in almost any way you can imagine. Some of the things you can create are mailing labels, directories, monthly summaries, form letters, and fax templates.

Summary reports are one of the more powerful database features. In this type of report you can list a catalog of baseball cards by card type and then by year, for example, and have the database calculate the value of each year's collection.

Using macros or scripts

Most database programs let you create macros or scripts to speed up and automate your work (**Figure 11.4**). To generate monthly mailing labels, you might normally search for all active clients, sort them by zip code and last name, and then print them using a layout or form called Mailing Labels. Alternatively, you could create a macro or script named Print Monthly Mailing to perform all those steps automatically. The next time you needed to print mailing labels, you would just run the script.

Figure 11.4

In 4th Dimension, creating scripts (called methods) requires you to master a programming language. But with this added complexity comes a great deal of flexibility and power.

Many Macintosh database programs are also scriptable using AppleScript, a component of the Mac system software. With AppleScript you can create multistep procedures within the database program, as well as script actions that involve multiple programs. For example, you might design a script that takes summary data from one of your databases, exports it to Microsoft Excel, and then graphs the data.

Choosing a Database Program

In the following sections, we examine three of the leading database programs for Mac OS X—FileMaker Pro, Panorama, and 4th Dimension—to help you decide which one is best for you. Each varies in ease of use, feature set, and how it works.

FileMaker Pro

Like most other database programs, **FileMaker Pro,** from FileMaker, Inc. ($299; www.filemaker.com), started out as a flat-file database program. Over the past several releases, the company has enhanced FileMaker to fully support relational databases, provide connectivity tools for linking to non-FileMaker databases, enable users to publish and interact with databases on the Web or an intranet, and simplify sharing databases across a workgroup.

FileMaker has long been the preferred database program of Macintosh owners, and its market share attests to this. Of all major Macintosh and Windows databases, FileMaker is one of the simplest to learn and use, and it doesn't sacrifice much power to accomplish this. While FileMaker has always made it supremely easy for users to design beautiful and highly functional databases, recent versions have added very little that enhances it for designers. The thrust of revisions has been to target corporate users by providing additional workgroup, Web publishing, and security features.

Here are the highlights of changes introduced in FileMaker Pro 6:

- New templates include Photo Catalog, Product Catalog, Student Emergency Card, and Contact Management. Many of the older templates have been updated.

- Finds are now extensible. That is, the initial Find is still based on all records in the database—essentially starting from scratch each time. However, subsequent Finds can work from the current found set—either by adding more records to it (extend) or by removing records from it (constrain). You could already do this by performing an AND search or an OR search, but this new approach is more natural when exploring your data.

- A word-processing-style Find/Replace command has been added, allowing you to search for and optionally replace data within a given record, across all records (or all records in the current found set), or within a given layout.

- In Browse mode you can now easily perform a single-field sort. Just (Control)-click in the field on which you want to sort and choose one of three sort commands from the contextual menu that appears (**Figure 11.5**).

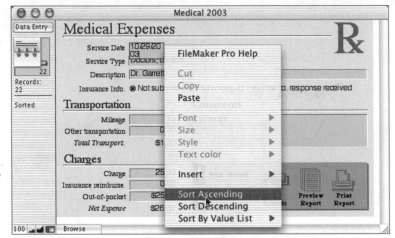

Figure 11.5

Single-field sorts are a snap in FileMaker Pro 6 and no longer require a trip to the menu bar.

- Taking another tip from Microsoft Word, FileMaker Pro 6 includes a new Format Painter tool for quickly duplicating object and text formatting in a layout. For instance, after painstakingly formatting a data field in Layout mode, you can select the field, choose the Format Painter tool, and then click any other field to which you want to apply the identical formatting.

- You can now create complex custom dialogs for your scripts that prompt for data from up to three fields (**Figure 11.6**).

Figure 11.6

Using the Show Custom Dialog script step, you can prompt the user for data from up to three fields. In this example, the data is used as input for a Find request. The resulting report will consist only of records that correspond to the entered date.

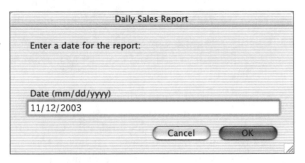

- Importing options have been expanded in FileMaker Pro 6. On a Mac running Mac OS X, you can directly import images from a connected digital camera or memory card. On a Mac *or* a PC you can import an entire folder of image or text files.

- XML data can now be imported and exported. During export, you can apply an XSLT style sheet to transform the XML results into a different XML or non-XML format for display in another application.

While most users are familiar with FileMaker Pro, they may not be aware that FileMaker Pro is actually a *family* of software products. Its members include the following:

- **FileMaker Pro** ($299) is a cross-platform program for designing databases and performing data entry in any FileMaker database. FileMaker Pro also allows small networked workgroups (of as many as ten people) to share databases. Using the provided Web Companion plug-in, you can host databases on the Web or on a company intranet (ten guests in any 12-hour period).

- **FileMaker Server** ($999) is the program you need if your workgroup contains more than ten people or if more than that number need to connect to a database simultaneously. FileMaker Server can serve any combination of FileMaker Pro 5.0, 5.5, and 6.0 databases.

- **FileMaker Pro Unlimited** ($999) serves a function similar to FileMaker Server but is for hosting FileMaker databases on the Web or on an intranet. FileMaker Pro 6 Unlimited removes the ten-guest limit, enables the new features of FileMaker Pro 6 to be incorporated into Web-published databases, and improves the security of CDML format files used in custom Web publishing solutions.

- **FileMaker Developer** ($499), now in version 6, provides tools that enable you to create stand-alone databases for either the Mac or PC (referred to as *run-time applications*). You can also document your databases using the Database Design Report and identify problems in complex scripts with the Script Debugger. If you intend to create databases that you wish to sell or to use widely in your company, you should consider FileMaker Developer.

- **FileMaker Mobile** ($49) enables you to view, edit, delete, and add data to a FileMaker Pro database using any Palm PDA (personal digital assistant) or Palm-compatible device. FileMaker Mobile includes the Palm and conduit software required to load your databases onto a Palm handheld; view, create, and edit records on the Palm; and synchronize changes between the Palm and desktop databases. Version 2.1 adds Pocket PC support, as well as support for data input with a bar code scanner.

FileMaker Server. Contrary to what you might think, FileMaker Server is *not* a shareable network version of FileMaker Pro. If you install Server, you still need a separate copy of FileMaker Pro for each user in the workgroup. FileMaker Server has one function: it *serves* shared FileMaker databases to people on the network. For instance, the members of your sales department might all require access to a database that shows the company's current inventory or all customer invoices.

Although FileMaker Pro 6 does have built-in networking, this feature is designed only for small workgroups. Sharing a database that's installed on your Mac can have a major impact on your computer's performance. Server, however, gets around these limitations, as well as the ten-user limit imposed by FileMaker Pro's built-in networking. First, because the shared databases reside on a computer you've chosen to use as a file server, you don't have to worry about a performance hit to your Mac. Second, Server can handle 250 simultaneous guests and can host as many as 125 open databases at the same time. Finally, sharing databases with Server is much faster than it is with FileMaker Pro. The network administrator can monitor Server's performance remotely from any copy of FileMaker Pro on the network. FileMaker Server can also automate database backup.

FileMaker Server provides support for Linux, Mac OS X and Mac OS 9, and Windows 2000. It also includes LDAP (Lightweight Directory Access Protocol) support, optional guest authentication by a Windows domain controller, and automatic distribution of plug-in updates.

FileMaker Pro Unlimited. This isn't the greatest name for a product, since it tells you little about its function. Essentially, FileMaker Pro Unlimited is FileMaker Server for Web-published FileMaker databases. As mentioned previously, when you use FileMaker Pro to publish a database on the Web or on an intranet, only ten users can access the database in any 12-hour period. If additional users attempt access, they're locked out. While this may work for small workgroups and infrequently accessed databases, it's woefully insufficient for most published databases. FileMaker Pro Unlimited is intended for large workgroups and Web sites; it doesn't impose a limit on the number of simultaneous Web guests or visitors. For improved performance, FileMaker Pro 6 Unlimited can also connect to the following Web servers: Mac OS X Server 10.1 and Apache Web Server 1.3.23/24, Windows 2000 Server and Microsoft IIS 5.0, and Red Hat Linux 7.1 and Apache Web Server 1.3.19.

FileMaker Developer. Don't let the name confuse you. You don't *need* FileMaker Developer to develop databases for yourself or your company or to sell them to others. But does it help? Absolutely! FileMaker Developer 6 includes standard copies of FileMaker Pro 6 for Macintosh and Windows, as well as tools that simplify the development process. The biggie for most developers is the ability to create *stand-alone databases*—ones that Mac or Windows users who don't own FileMaker Pro can run. If you're designing databases you intend to sell, this expands your potential market to virtually every computer user. Other important, useful features in Developer 6 include a script debugger, a tool for examining and documenting a database's structure, and the ability to create applications that run in kiosk mode.

FileMaker Pro tips

Of the literally thousands of tips and tricks we could pass along to you, here are just a few we've found valuable. We've even included a tip on where to go to get more tips!

- If you need to share one of your FileMaker 6 databases with a Windows user, append .fp5 to the filename (as in FaxForm.fp5). This three-character extension tells Windows that the file is a FileMaker Pro 5, 5.5, or 6.0

database. Without an extension in the filename, Windows won't have the vaguest notion that it's a FileMaker file.

- FileMaker automatically saves your work as you go along. (You've probably noticed there isn't a save command—that's why.) Before making changes to the database's structure or design, as well as before performing any function that might harm the integrity of your data (such as a mass deletion or import of records), it's a good practice to make a backup of the database. From the Finder, [Control]-click the database icon and choose Duplicate, or [Option]-drag it to another folder. You can also accomplish this from within FileMaker Pro by choosing File > Save a Copy As.

- FileMaker Pro instantly switches back to the Pointer tool as soon as you finish using most of the layout-mode tools. You can use the same tool indefinitely by double-clicking its icon in the tool palette. Or if you want to lock tools with a single click, check the box next to "Always lock layout tools" on the Layout tab of the Application Preferences dialog. (To reach the dialog box, choose FileMaker Pro > Preferences > Application.)

- FileMaker Pro supports both *lookups* and *relationships.* How do you decide which one to use? When triggered, a lookup performs a one-time copy of data from a second file. A relation, on the other hand, *displays* the related data rather than actually copying it; what you see automatically changes to reflect the most current data. If you want FileMaker to look up data once and then leave it unchanged (say, when you're recording an item amount for an invoice), use a lookup. If you want data to change as necessary (for example, always displaying a customer's current phone number rather than the one that was initially available when you created the record), use a relation.

- In addition to the common one-to-one and one-to-many relationships between databases, you can also create a *self join* (a relationship between a single database and itself). For example, in the database shown in **Figure 11.7,** a relationship was defined between the Sales Person field and itself. The related fields in the portal for Listing ID, Price, and Footage, show every open listing for the current salesperson, regardless of the record that's displayed. Pretty cool, huh?

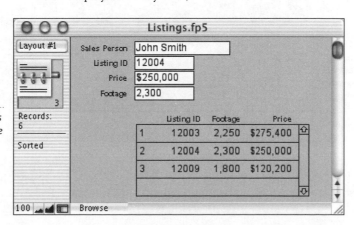

Figure 11.7

Using a self join, this real estate database can display all the current salesperson's active listings in a portal at the bottom of the record.

- If it's been a while since you updated FileMaker Pro, it's important to know that value lists are no longer field-specific, as they were in FileMaker Pro 3. Value lists are created and maintained via the File > Define Value Lists command. You can associate a single value list with as many fields as you like. For instance, if you've created a questionnaire database, you can create one value list containing Yes and No as choices, and then associate it with every yes-or-no question. (Note that you can also reuse value lists from other FileMaker databases.)

- To publish your databases on the Web using the Web Companion plug-in that is included with FileMaker Pro 6, you must have a static *IP address,* one that never changes. Whenever you connect to the Internet, your ISP (Internet service provider) assigns an IP address that identifies your computer. Unfortunately, every time most users reconnect to the Internet, their ISP assigns them a new IP address from the available pool. People connect to your FileMaker databases by typing your IP address, found in the Network pane of System Preferences in Mac OS X, into the browser. If your address is constantly changing, they'll have a hard time connecting. Contact your ISP to determine if you can get a static IP address. (Note that the IP addresses for some broadband accounts—cable or DSL—may change so seldom that they can be treated as though they're static.)

- You can test a Web-destined database on your own Mac without an active Internet connection. After you've performed the steps to publish the database, launch your Web browser, type `http://localhost/` in the browser's Address field, and click the database's name to view and interact with it as you would over the Web (**Figure 11.8**).

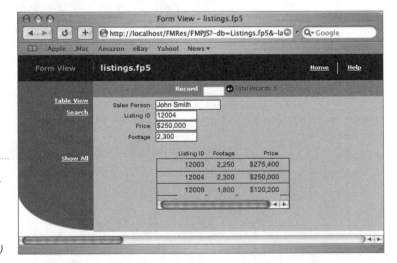

Figure 11.8

Viewed in a browser, a FileMaker Pro 6 database looks remarkably like the original. (It's sometimes necessary to tweak the layout a little, though, to correct display problems.)

- Can't find the capability you need within FileMaker Pro? Plug-ins (add-on utilities that give FileMaker Pro new capabilities) may provide the answer to your programming conundrum. Check out Troi Automatisering (www.troi.com), for example, for a selection of powerful plug-ins.

- Following a crash or power failure, FileMaker often reports that the database open at the time wasn't closed properly. While the data can generally be recovered without difficulty, a more insidious problem—and an unapparent one at that—can occur. The *structure* of the database may be damaged, resulting in serious problems down the line. As a preventive measure, smart developers routinely save one or more empty, pristine copies of every mission-critical database. Use the Save a Copy As command to create a clone (a copy of the database without any records). Should you ever experience or even suspect database damage, you can export the data from the current database and then import it into a copy of the clone.

- If you need some help with a tricky FileMaker Pro concept or scripting problem, consider subscribing to the free FileMaker Pro Talk mailing list sponsored by Blue World (maker of Lasso, the professional software tools for designing and serving data-driven Web sites). Many of the sharpest FileMaker developers routinely follow this list, and they're often willing to lend a hand. Visit www.blueworld.com/blueworld/lists for the sign-up info. Unless you want to be flooded with dozens of individual email messages per day, sign up in Digest mode. This is a very popular mailing list.

- FileMaker, Inc., has recently begun marketing ready-to-use business databases for managing donations, meetings, business tasks, and employee recruiting. Visit the FileMaker Store at http://store.filemaker.com to check out these new offerings.

Panorama

ProVUE Development's **Panorama** ($299; www.provue.com) is a cross-platform, programmable relational-database program. Both Macs and PCs can access Panorama databases over a mixed-platform network.

Speed—one of Panorama's most-touted features—continues to be a selling point. While most database programs are disk based (reading from the disk as they require more data, as well as automatically saving new data and changes to disk), Panorama is *RAM based*; that is, the computer's memory holds all data until you perform a manual save.

Panorama has many features that distinguish it from the competition. For example, you can turn on *clairvoyance* for any field. When you begin typing into a field, Panorama checks all previously entered data for that field and tries to finish typing for you. If you enter San F in a City field, Panorama might complete it as "San Francisco." You can also specify that clairvoyance display data from a field in another database. Clairvoyance is extraordinarily useful; I've wished for years that other database programs would offer it.

Another particularly useful feature is Panorama's ability to perform a "sounds like" search. If you don't know the exact spelling of a bit of data (such as a name), you can ask Panorama to find all matches that sound phonetically like what you've typed. These kinds of thoughtful features abound in the program. For example, not only does Panorama recognize almost every conceivable format for entered dates (such as 12/5/03 or Dec 5, 2003), but it also lets you enter today, Wednesday (to indicate a day in the week that's just passed), or next Tuesday. Panorama then substitutes the correct date for you.

If you have a lot of important databases that you use regularly, keeping them organized and handy can really be a production. In Panorama, you can store them all in the Favorite Databases Wizard. Panorama V includes dozens of wizards, each designed to perform a special function, such as displaying a calculator, calendar, or ASCII chart; altering the appearance or size of the current database window; simultaneously searching all fields for a text string, rather than just searching a single field; or displaying the Panorama Handbook in PDF form.

It's always been simple to script repetitive actions in Panorama. In fact, you can create many scripts (called *macros*) by simply turning on the Recorder and recording your actions. If a macro doesn't do precisely what you want, you can view its steps (automatically transformed into text) and edit them. For example, if you want to re-sort a database by a different field after viewing a report, you can copy a sort step from the current macro, paste it in as the final step, and then just substitute the correct field name.

In addition to now being Mac OS X-native, Panorama V includes the following new features:

- The new Live Clairvoyance Wizard (**Figure 11.9**) searches all or selected fields of all records as you type a search string, displaying all potential matching records. To go to a found record, you just double-click its entry in the Live Clairvoyance Wizard.

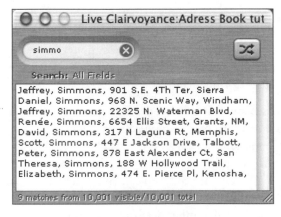

Figure 11.9

Using an iTunes-style search box, Panorama quickly identifies records that match the search string you're typing.

- Using the Speech Wizard, you can have Panorama read data or scripts to you.

- You can use the new Hotkey Manager Wizard to assign keyboard shortcuts to database actions, such as opening a favorite wizard or displaying the current contents of the Clipboard.

- The URL Wizard scans all fields in the current record for Web and email addresses, and then lists them in a separate window. Double-clicking any of the found addresses will open the Web page in your browser or address a message in your email program, as appropriate.

- The new Programming Reference Wizard provides online help with Panorama formulas and programs.

- Panorama V now fully supports drag and drop: within the program, into other applications, and from other applications.

Panorama V is an excellent program and a good choice for business users. Like any capable and flexible application, it does have a learning curve. However, Panorama comes with extensive PDF documentation: an 1800-plus-page manual, tutorials, a function reference guide, and a 50 MB getting-started QuickTime video. The program's only significant drawbacks:

- Some common activities are performed in nonstandard ways. For instance, to open multiple views of a database, you must press (Option) while choosing a form from the View menu.

- Panorama has an unusual interface and a confusing menu structure. Tool icons don't have pop-up screen identifiers. Instead, you must click each icon to see a description of what it does. There are no Window or Help menus. And rather than being grouped in hierarchical/pop-out submenus, subordinate commands are either all listed as primary commands or indented as one might do in an outline. For example, the Sort menu lists five separate Sort commands and four Group commands.

- Data forms are completely customizable and very easy to figure out, but not quite as attractive as those of FileMaker Pro or 4th Dimension (**Figure 11.10**).

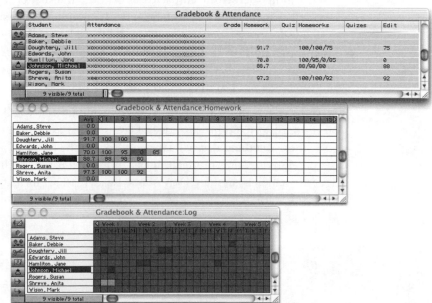

Figure 11.10

Forms in Panorama V are more attractive than they were in previous versions, and they still retain their ease of use, but they aren't as elegant as those in FileMaker Pro.

If only one person in your company will be developing databases (the others are designated as *users*), you just need to buy one full copy of Panorama V for the developer. Everyone else can use Panorama Direct ($130) to access the databases and perform data-entry tasks.

4th Dimension

4D's **4th Dimension Standard Edition** ($349; www.4D.com)—called 4D for short—is a fast, powerful, cross-platform, programmable relational-database program. Unlike the other database programs discussed in this chapter, 4D targets developers more than end users. Sure, you can use 4D to create flat-file or relational databases for your own use or for members of a small workgroup, but if that's all you have in mind, a simpler program may do the job. (I think of 4D as a cross between FileMaker Pro and Microsoft Office Access for Windows. While you can create stunning forms with capabilities that go beyond those of FileMaker Pro, it can take hard work and programming to reach that point.)

 If you're already a FileMaker Pro aficionado and are considering either switching to 4D or using it as an additional tool, visit www.4d.com/support and search for FileMaker for an excellent explanation of the similarities and differences between these two development environments.

As with FileMaker Pro, 4D is actually a family of products. 4th Dimension 2003 Standard Edition includes **4D, 4D Runtime** (which enables you to create databases that run as stand-alone applications), and basic utilities. Like FileMaker Pro, Standard Edition also has built-in Web publishing capabilities. Users can interact with your databases over the Internet or on their company intranets using any current Web browser. If you intend to distribute your 4D databases to a wider audience, you should consider **4th Dimension 2003 Developer Edition** ($799). It includes the Standard Edition plus a variety of advanced plug-ins that let you add spreadsheet, word-processing, drawing, and other advanced capabilities to your databases.

As is the case with many programs, when you buy 4D, you'll need to stock up on printer paper and ink cartridges, because as far as printed documentation goes, there's nothing that will take you beyond the installation process. Even the previous version's printed Quickstart manual has been eliminated. All documentation is on the CD in Adobe Reader (PDF) format. You can download additional PDF documents, as well as several very useful tutorials from 4D's Web site.

You use 4D to create single-user databases. If people need to share your 4D databases, you can buy **4D Server** ($899), which allows your single-user databases to function as multiuser ones. 4D Server can operate on a Mac, Windows, or mixed-platform network.

4D's plug-in support extends its connectivity options. For example, a 4D database can serve as a front end for any ODBC-compliant database such as Oracle Database, enabling you to execute SQL queries and extract data from non-4D databases. (*SQL,* or *Structured Query Language,* is an English-like language that you use to specify search criteria for identifying a record subset. You might, for example, wish to locate only those records of clients from Minneapolis.) Other database programs can do the opposite—pulling data from 4D tables. 4D also has extensive Internet functionality. You can publish secure databases on the Web (via SSL), as well as send and receive email or connect to an FTP server from within a 4D database.

While FileMaker Pro provides separate modes for performing different activities (Browse, Layout, Find, and Preview), 4D provides only two essential modes. The Design mode is used for creating forms, writing *methods* (the term that 4D uses for scripts), customizing menus, and otherwise preparing a database to receive data, as shown in **Figure 11.11**. The User mode is for entering data, viewing reports, and interacting with the database in all other ways.

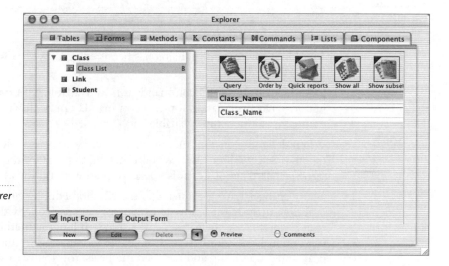

Figure 11.11

You use the Explorer window to view, create, and edit components of a 4D database.

New features introduced in 4D 2003 include the following:

* There is file compatibility with versions 6.7.x and higher. When you open a database in 4D 2003 that was created with one of these earlier versions, it's automatically converted to a 2003 database. Conversely, 2003 databases can be opened in 4D 6.8.x *without* conversion.

* You can create new databases based on templates (**Figure 11.12**).

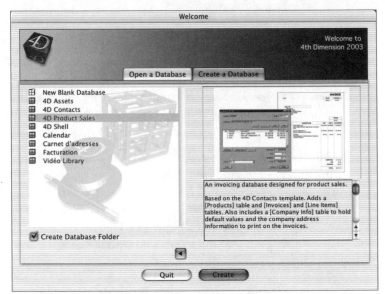

Figure 11.12

When launching 4D or issuing the File > Open Database command, you can optionally create a new, ready-to-use database based on a template.

* The Database Properties dialog has been replaced by an 18-section Properties dialog.

* Documentation for 4D commands is now available within the Explorer window. Documentation for new commands can be downloaded automatically, as it becomes available and is needed.

* When designing custom menus, you can now associate a standard action (such as Select All or Quit) without having to program the action. (These same standard actions can also be associated with buttons.)

* Many changes have been made to the Method editor. Some of the important ones include the ability to expand or collapse code within loops (to enable you to "see the forest for the trees" in lengthy methods), displaying optional line numbers, customizable indentation settings, support for drag and drop within and between methods, the ability to share methods via importing and exporting, and the inclusion of macro commands within methods.

* As you type a method, 4D now uses "type ahead" to try to complete the function that you're about to type. Up to 20 levels of undo and redo are now offered. And the maximum method size has been increased from the previous 32K limit to a whopping 2 GB!

- Support has been added for importing and exporting data in XML format.

- The functionality of the separate 4D Compiler has been incorporated within 4th Dimension. As a result, you can now compile databases without leaving 4D.

- The new Application Builder handles the finalization and deployment of your 4D databases on the various supported operating systems.

- You can publish *Web services* (sets of functions that perform useful services such as providing stock quotes or package tracking via the Internet) and then call them from within any of your 4D databases.

 For detailed information on the changes introduced in 4th Dimension 2003, download the lengthy 4th Dimension Upgrade Guide (2003.1) from the 4D Product Documentation page (www.4d.com/support/documentation.html).

Database Tips and Techniques

Regardless of which program you use, you'll find the following tips helpful for designing and working with databases. We've broken the tips into two categories: General Tips and Design Tips.

General Tips

- If you're still in the process of choosing a database program, don't buy more program than you need or can handle. Because of their complexity and advanced feature sets, some database programs are meant for corporate developers; others are more appropriate for end users and casual developers. (If all you really need is a way to maintain ordered lists, for example, you may find that Excel or another spreadsheet program will suffice.)

- Because database programs are complex, it's not unusual for any major release to go through one or more minor updates. Whether you've just purchased a database program or have been using it for a year or more, you should check the company's Web site periodically for downloadable updates. (Minor updates are generally free.)

- When people buy a database program, they often have a specific need in mind—not an overwhelming desire to conquer a complex application. If this describes you, before buying a database program, check the Internet for ready-made solutions to your problem. You may find a commercial or shareware program that does the trick. Or you may discover a free or inexpensive template that you can use with a particular database program, making your buying decision that much simpler. (Note that database programs often include free templates. One of them may be exactly what you need!)

- When sorting on multiple fields, specify sort fields in order of their importance, with the most important one first. All others are treated as tiebreakers. For example, when sorting business contact data, you might specify Company as the first sort field, followed by Last Name and First Name (**Figure 11.13**).

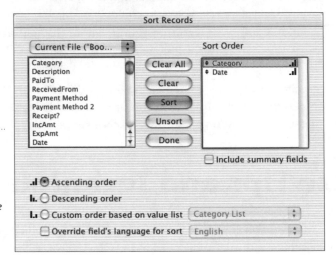

Figure 11.13

These sort instructions will first sort the database by expense category and then—within each category—the individual records will be arranged by date.

- It's critical that you understand what actions can be undone in your database program. For example, record deletions in FileMaker Pro are permanent and cannot be undone. Changes in Panorama, on the other hand, are saved only when you choose File > Save. And you can restore the most recently saved version of any Panorama database by choosing File > Revert to Saved.

Design Tips

- Not every database needs or merits the extra work required to create custom data-entry forms. If the default form will do the trick (and the database won't be staring you in the face every day), your job is done. On the other hand, if you (or others) will be using a given database regularly, some extra design work will pay off. Think carefully about how best to organize the fields, set a custom tab order, specify field-validation criteria, make every layout easy on the eyes, and add buttons for common commands (such as creating/deleting records and generating reports).

- Databases differ from standard paper-based files (which serve as the basis for many business, home, and education databases) in that it's more efficient to break database fields into as many discrete components as possible than to combine them into a single field. For example, than defining a single Name field (as you might do with a paper form), you usually should create separate fields for Salutation (Mr., Ms., Mrs., Dr.), First Name, Middle Initial, Last Name, and Suffix (M.D., Ph.D., Jr.). Doing so ensures that the information will be entered in a consistent form.

It also enables you to reuse the data in ways that would be clumsy if you only had a single Name field. For instance, you could start a form letter with

```
Dear <<Honorific>> <<Last Name>>,
```

This would result in "Dear Ms. Andrews," appearing in the letter rather than "Dear Ms. Marcia J. Andrews," for instance.

- If your database program allows you to make multiple layouts, resist the temptation to jam everything in your database into a single layout. For instance, it usually makes sense to create separate layouts for data entry and for each type of report you'll generate. Data entry forms are generally great for recording data but a poor choice for printed reports. Who wants to see a single record printed on each page? If you create a separate report layout, you can exclude data you don't need to see, display summary information (such as totals and record counts), and organize the data in useful ways (grouping sales figures by employee or division, for example).

- If your database is so complex that it requires more than a couple of layouts, consider adding a main menu layout that lets you choose what to do next. At its simplest, it might contain buttons for data entry, reports, and help information. A more complex menu system could incorporate several submenus, enabling you to select specific types of reports, for example.

- Unless your database is extremely simple, you should take advantage of the program's documentation features. (A couple of years from now, do you really want to have to examine code to figure out how a complex procedure or report works?) For example, you can use available features to add comments to your scripts and macros, create dialogs or pop-up menus that explain data-entry requirements for important fields, or create a separate help database that users can open by clicking a button in your database.

- If a database requires that you enter the same information in multiple records—for instance, customer address information in an invoice database—it pays to think relational. By keeping the repeating data in a separate related file, you can avoid retyping it.

- When working with images in a database (such as employee pictures), it's best to store only a reference to each image's location on disk rather than the actual picture. Unless you have massive amounts of hard-disk space to spare, including pasted or imported images in a database will quickly make it *immense!*

- Similarly, unless you're displaying full-size pictures in a database, you may want to use a program like Adobe Photoshop to make a copy of each image in the correct size. Why force the database program or system software routines to resize each image and take the accompanying performance hit whenever a new image has to be displayed?

Interview: Bill Campbell

Bill Campbell's background was unusual for a high-tech executive: he had been head football coach at Columbia University from 1974 to 1979. But Campbell played a central role in Apple's marketing efforts in the early years of the Mac: in 1983 he was hired as vice president of marketing, and just after the Mac launch in January 1984 he was also put in charge of sales. In September 1984 he was promoted again, this time to executive vice president, in charge not only of marketing and sales, but also of distribution, service, and support.

> *There isn't a thing out there today that hasn't been influenced by Apple's graphics approach, user interface, and visual-communication capability.*
>
> —Bill Campbell, on the Mac's place in history

In 1987, when Apple started Claris Corp., a subsidiary charged with developing an applications software business, Campbell became its CEO. In 1990 he left Claris to become CEO of Go Corp., a much-hyped but ultimately unsuccessful pioneer in pen-based computing. From 1994 to 1998 he was CEO of financial-software maker Intuit, where he's now chairman of the board. Since 1997 he's also been a member of Apple's board of directors. In addition, he's a board member at Marc Andreessen's Opsware, a director of the National Football Foundation and Hall of Fame, and a trustee of Columbia University. —Henry Norr

How did you go from head football coach at Columbia to Apple?

I was largely unsuccessful as coach at Columbia. I got them out of their long losing streaks and got three and four wins, but never really was successful. I was discouraged at that point, and before my last year told them I was going to step out of coaching. One of the firms I interviewed with was Pepsi, where John Sculley was the CEO. [Pepsi offered Campbell a job, but he turned it down in favor of one with the advertising firm of J. Walter Thompson, where he worked on marketing for Kraft and then for Kodak. Kodak then hired him, and he eventually served as general manager of consumer products in Europe.]

John Sculley kept in touch with me. One day I got this call from him asking me if I was interested in coming to Apple. I was totally stunned. I hadn't been in Europe that long, and I thought, "No, I'm gonna stay here at this."

What persuaded you to change your mind?

Sculley kept after me, so I agreed to meet him during a trip to the U.S. I flew to San Francisco. An hour out I went into the rest room and changed into a blue suit since I was going to this corporate interview [laughs]. Sculley met me at the airport, and he's there in a T-shirt and jeans. How little did I know about Silicon Valley culture.

I got a chance to see Steve, meet Mike Murray and a lot of the development people, and then I saw the Macintosh. Of course, you know at that point you're just blown away by what you'd seen. So I went there right at the end of April 1983.

Did you have any experience with high tech?

I was an Apple II guy. Kodak was so in the dark in those days, they used to give you those big old printouts from the mainframe. I'd have to translate this stuff into market data so I could figure out where the g— d— film products were being sold. It used to drive me nuts.

So I started plugging that stuff into VisiCalc [a spreadsheet program for the Apple II]. I would carry the Apple II home, with a big old 5 MB Pro File drive, and then back to work. That was the extent of my use of computers up to then. But I guess I was one of the few that had done even that.

Do you think Apple made a mistake in setting the price too high for the original Mac?

There was a lot—a lot—of discussion about that. You know, Sculley was a marketing guy. What he wanted to do was have the higher price so that he could use that money to fuel the marketing programs. Steve was on the lower end of it, at least at the beginning. So what we did was compromise on $1,000 for higher ed and $2,495 for consumer purchases. It wasn't a contentious thing—it was pretty amicable when it was recognized that the money was going to be plowed back in to create that 100-day awareness and make the Macintosh what it became—a marvel of the industry at that time.

Did you think the Mac was going to change the world?

Oh, I totally did. Absolutely. And in fact, I was somewhat surprised that we weren't able to continue the early momentum. To me it was a blowaway. Look, Lisa had an enormous number of flaws. It was a good shot across the bow, but the integrated applications, without any third-party development, made it brain-dead right from the very beginning. At least with the Macintosh, we had the prominent third-party developers behind us—we had Gates [Microsoft] and Mitch Kapor [Lotus] onstage at our sales meeting. Of course, the fact that that software didn't get into the marketplace quickly, initially, was a problem.

Did you think it was going to be a major challenger to the IBM PC in the business market?

Oh, no question. Go back to the Apple II days, and all of Steve's vision about ubiquity [of computers in the future]. I call it "the democratization of the personal computer." If you really believed in ubiquity, you were thinking that ease of use was going to be the greatest hurdle to overcome, not functionality. And with the Mac you had both—no-compromise functionality, but also just a breakthrough in ease of use, accessibility—and you thought you had a home run.

But the reality turned out to be more complicated.

You know, in a gross sense today, 20 years later, you look at it and say there were some missed opportunities. The fact that it's in a less-than-5-percent market share position is disappointing. But if you think about its impact on the industry—look, there isn't a thing that's out there today that hasn't been influenced by Apple's graphics approach, user interface, and visual-communication capability. Today, under Steve, people continue to think about us as an innovator. Unfortunately, we've been unable to capitalize on those innovations and win the bulk of the market share, but we continue to set those standards.

continues on next page

What would you have done differently to make things turn out better?

We should have gotten multiple models out in a timely fashion—you know, high end, low end, those kinds of things. And it was a long time before we were able to get an open Mac—the Mac II—and lower-cost Macs. Those are the things that hurt.

A lot of people think that Apple's big mistake was not licensing the Mac OS. You don't?

I'm the only one. I don't know anybody else that will go there. I just keep thinking that, had we been able to satisfy our constituencies with appropriate models—and "appropriate" means right product with the right price, with the right software—the licensing issue would have gone away.

Do you still use a Mac?

I sure do!

Have you used one all the way through, or …

I go through periods of, you know, corporate acceptance problems inside companies, but on my desk at work now I have both a PC and a Mac. At home, I probably have seven computers in the house, and we've got an AirPort network. My wife is an avid user, as is my daughter and my son—all Mac users. They don't get a vote [he laughs].

12

Spreadsheets

Maria Langer (ML) is the chapter editor and author.

Sharon Zardetto Aker (SA), Christian Boyce (CB), Elizabeth Castro (EC), Dennis Cohen (DC), and Eve Gordon (EG) contributed to earlier editions of **The Macintosh Bible,** *from which portions of this chapter are taken.*

The first breakthrough software package for the personal computer, VisiCalc, was a spreadsheet program. It became wildly successful and made people realize that perhaps there was money in selling software. Another spreadsheet program—Microsoft Excel—made people finally take the Macintosh seriously as a computer that could perform fast business calculations, and not just think of it as a "toy" useful only for creating pictures in MacDraw or MacPaint.

Thirty years later, spreadsheets have grown up quite a bit. Used for more than just addition and subtraction, spreadsheets now let you solve complex financial-analysis problems, create 3D graphs, and generate monthly reports. We'll tell you just what you can expect from today's spreadsheets, get you started with some spreadsheet basics, and give you a collection of tips you can use with your spreadsheet software package.

In This Chapter

What Is a Spreadsheet?

Imagine an accountant's worksheet filled with columns and rows of numbers. Now put that worksheet inside a computer, add the ability to change inputted and calculated values instantly, and throw in a few extras—such as built-in formulas, charting capabilities, and database sorting. What you'll have when you're finished is a spreadsheet.

Spreadsheets Explained (ML)

A spreadsheet software package is like a word processor, but for numbers. You use a spreadsheet to organize, calculate, and present numerical information neatly. The resulting document is usually a spreadsheet—often called a *work-sheet*—but can also be a chart or a list.

Like a paper worksheet, an electronic worksheet is laid out in a grid. *Rows,* labeled with numbers, and *columns,* labeled with letters, intersect at *cells.* Each cell has an *address* or *reference* that consists of the column letter and the row number. So you'd find cell C16 at the intersection of column C and row 16.

To use a spreadsheet you enter *values* and *formulas* into cells. A value can be text, a number, a date, or a time. It's often called a *constant value* because it won't change unless you change it. A formula is a calculation that you want the spreadsheet to perform for you. You begin a formula with an equals sign (=) and follow it with a combination of values, cell references, operators, and functions; more on those later.

The beauty of a spreadsheet is that if properly constructed, it can calculate the results of complex formulas in less time than it takes to bat an eye. And if you change any of the values referenced by a formula, the results change instantly. It sure beats being an accountant with pencil-stained fingers and a ten-key calculator.

Real-World Spreadsheets

The best way to see what spreadsheet software is all about is to look at some real-life examples. With spreadsheets like the ones described on the next few pages, you can calculate totals and averages, create a loan amortization table, perform what-if analyses, manage and report data, and create charts. This is just a small sampling of what's possible; with a little imagination and practice, you'll soon be taking spreadsheets to their limits.

Simple calculations (CB). Here's a simple little AppleWorks spreadsheet that does some straightforward mathematics (**Figure 12.1**). When you enter expense information, the spreadsheet calculates totals and averages for each category, such as Dining or Telephone, and totals for each month. It does this by using formulas in the Totals and Averages cells that refer to values entered in the categories.

Figure 12.1

This simple AppleWorks spreadsheet calculates totals and averages for the numbers entered into the light gray cells.

	First Quarter Expenses.cwk (SS)					
A1						
	A	B	C	D	E	F
1		January	February	March	Totals	Averages
2	Dining	$631	$400	$650	$1,681	$560
3	Hotels	395	442	574	1,411	470
4	Car Rentals	606	547	973	2,126	709
5	Airfare	240	128	585	953	318
6	Telephone	983	135	938	2,056	685
7	Postage	515	525	550	1,590	530
8	Totals	$3,370	$2,177	$4,270	$9,817	$3,272
9						
10						

Complex calculations (EG/ML). Not every formula you write or spreadsheet you create will be simple. By combining simple formulas with advanced functions (predefined formulas with specific uses), you can create more-complex spreadsheet models, such as a loan amortization table (**Figure 12.2**). Using good spreadsheet design, the Excel spreadsheet in the figure includes an input, or *assumption*, area where you enter the amounts you already know: the amount or principal of the loan, the interest rate, and the loan term. The monthly payment is calculated based on Excel's built-in PMT (payment) function.

Figure 12.2

You can build a loan amortization table by combining simple and complex formulas, taking advantage of Excel's built-in financial functions.

	A	B	C	D
1	Car Loan Payments			
2	Loan Amount			$20,000.00
3	Annual Interest Rate			3.75%
4	Number of Years			4
5	Monthly Payment			$449.35
6	Pmt #	Interest	Principal	Balance
7	0			$20,000.00
8	1	$62.50	$386.85	$19,613.15
9	2	$61.29	$388.06	$19,225.10
10	3	$60.08	$389.27	$18,835.83
11	4	$58.86	$390.49	$18,445.34
12	5	$57.64	$391.71	$18,053.63
13	6	$56.42	$392.93	$17,660.71
14	7	$55.19	$394.16	$17,266.55
15	8	$53.96	$395.39	$16,871.16
16	9	$52.72	$396.63	$16,474.54
17	10	$51.48	$397.87	$16,076.67
18	11	$50.24	$399.11	$15,677.56
19	12	$48.99	$400.36	$15,277.20
20	13	$47.74	$401.61	$14,875.60

What-if analysis (EG/ML). Probably the most powerful feature of a spreadsheet is its ability to recalculate results quickly when you make changes to referenced values. This is known as a *what-if analysis* because by changing a value, you're asking, "What happens if this number changes?"

Based on the previous loan amortization table, what if you borrow less money, change the loan term, or find a better interest rate? It's easy to see how these changes will affect the monthly payment. Just change the information in the appropriate cell and—presto!—the spreadsheet reflects your change.

Database management (DC/ML). Spreadsheets are also useful for simple database functions. By setting up columns for different categories, or *fields,* of information and rows for the data, or *records,* you can organize, sort, summarize, and otherwise analyze data. Here's an example that shows the inventory for a store (**Figure 12.3**).

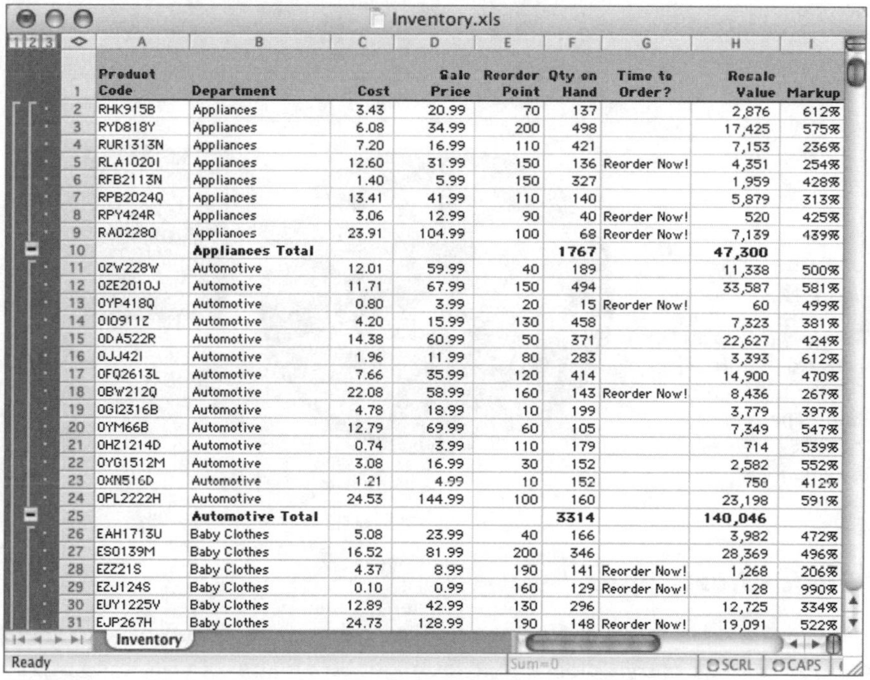

Figure 12.3

This Excel worksheet contains an inventory database with a wealth of information for various products. By using database features like sorting and subtotaling, you can quickly analyze the information.

	Product Code	Department	Cost	Sale Price	Reorder Point	Qty on Hand	Time to Order?	Resale Value	Markup
2	RHK915B	Appliances	3.43	20.99	70	137		2,876	612%
3	RYD818Y	Appliances	6.08	34.99	200	498		17,425	575%
4	RUR1313N	Appliances	7.20	16.99	110	421		7,153	236%
5	RLA1020I	Appliances	12.60	31.99	150	136	Reorder Now!	4,351	254%
6	RFB2113N	Appliances	1.40	5.99	150	327		1,959	428%
7	RPB2024Q	Appliances	13.41	41.99	110	140		5,879	313%
8	RPY424R	Appliances	3.06	12.99	90	40	Reorder Now!	520	425%
9	RA02280	Appliances	23.91	104.99	100	68	Reorder Now!	7,139	439%
10		**Appliances Total**				**1767**		**47,300**	
11	0ZW228W	Automotive	12.01	59.99	40	189		11,338	500%
12	0ZE2010J	Automotive	11.71	67.99	150	494		33,587	581%
13	0YP418Q	Automotive	0.80	3.99	20	15	Reorder Now!	60	499%
14	0I0911Z	Automotive	4.20	15.99	130	458		7,323	381%
15	0DA522R	Automotive	14.38	60.99	50	371		22,627	424%
16	0JJ42I	Automotive	1.96	11.99	80	283		3,393	612%
17	0FQ2613L	Automotive	7.66	35.99	120	414		14,900	470%
18	0BW212Q	Automotive	22.08	58.99	160	143	Reorder Now!	8,436	267%
19	0GI2316B	Automotive	4.78	18.99	10	199		3,779	397%
20	0YM66B	Automotive	12.79	69.99	60	105		7,349	547%
21	0HZ1214D	Automotive	0.74	3.99	110	179		714	539%
22	0YG1512M	Automotive	3.08	16.99	30	152		2,582	552%
23	0XN516D	Automotive	1.21	4.99	10	152		750	412%
24	0PL2222H	Automotive	24.53	144.99	100	160		23,198	591%
25		**Automotive Total**				**3314**		**140,046**	
26	EAH1713U	Baby Clothes	5.08	23.99	40	166		3,982	472%
27	ES0139M	Baby Clothes	16.52	81.99	200	346		28,369	496%
28	EZZ21S	Baby Clothes	4.37	8.99	190	141	Reorder Now!	1,268	206%
29	EZJ124S	Baby Clothes	0.10	0.99	160	129	Reorder Now!	128	990%
30	EUY1225V	Baby Clothes	12.89	42.99	130	296		12,725	334%
31	EJP267H	Baby Clothes	24.73	128.99	190	148	Reorder Now!	19,091	522%

Inventory.xls

Inventory

Ready — Sum=0 — SCRL CAPS

Charting (CB). A picture is worth a thousand words, and when the picture stands in for numbers, it's probably worth even more. You can use the charting features of spreadsheet software to make sense of a mystifying bunch of numbers. The column chart (**Figure 12.4**) and pie chart (**Figure 12.5**) are two examples of graphic displays of a spreadsheet's results.

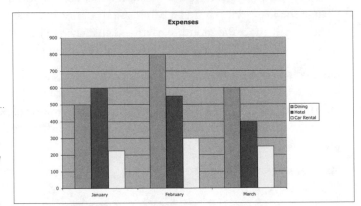

Figure 12.4

The column chart quickly tells you which expenses are greatest. Try getting information like that quickly from raw numbers!

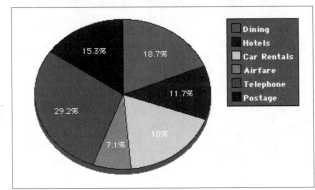

Figure 12.5

The pie chart makes it easy to see that Telephone is more than 29 percent of the total expenses for January.

Basic Chart Types (SA/ML)

With the wide range of chart types and styles that spreadsheets have to offer, you may find it tempting to go crazy. Colors and styles might be a matter of taste, but keep in mind that certain types of charts are best used for certain types of data. Here are the four basics:

- A *line chart* shows how something changes over time, with multiple lines charting multiple items.
- A *bar or column chart* is useful for comparing differing items, either with no time component or with the same time component.
- A *pie chart* shows how various components make up a whole—it shows the components in relation to each other and to the whole but gives no indication of how large the whole actually is.
- A *stacked bar chart* resembles a pie chart somewhat in that both show you the relationship of the parts to the whole, but stacked bars also let you compare different wholes and see the overall size or numbers of each.

Spreadsheet Software (ML)

If you're shopping for spreadsheet software, you won't have many choices to consider. Over the past 20 or so years, spreadsheet packages have been disappearing, like members of an endangered species. Only two well-established options are left, so let's take a look at them. (There is a third, much less well known option, with Mariner Software's **Mariner Calc** [$79.95; www.marinersoftware.com]. For more on this program see Chapter 9.)

Microsoft Excel

Microsoft Excel (www.microsoft.com/mac) is undoubtedly the most feature-packed spreadsheet package ever created. It goes beyond the basics of spreadsheets and charts by offering hundreds of built-in functions, extensive database features, drawing tools, a wide range of formatting capabilities, and a comprehensive macro language. (A *macro* is a program that stores a series of commands you can later use as a single command to automate complex or repetitive tasks.) The power of Excel goes beyond *what* it can do to *how* it does it. This well-thought-out package includes many features that make data entry easier or more accurate. Its dialogs are well organized and easy to use and understand (with a few exceptions not worth detailing here). Excel provides extensive online help with hypertext links, making it easy to navigate from topic to topic and find the information you need. Surprisingly, its heavy feature load does not affect its performance.

Although some people think I'm partial to Excel because I've written seven books about it, that's not true. I can objectively look at Excel and its alternatives and tell you that Excel is the best and most powerful spreadsheet package around. But is it for everyone? Of course not! The vast majority of folks who use their Macs at home or school don't need even half of Excel's bells and whistles. But if you're in corporate finance, science, or other industries where heavy-duty number crunching and presentation are musts, I doubt that you'll find a better spreadsheet program for your needs than Excel.

In case you're wondering what Excel costs in terms of dollars, disk space, and RAM, hold on to your hat. You'll pay about $229 for **Microsoft Excel X** (for Mac OS X 10.1 or higher), which will take up at least 196 MB of hard-disk space and 128 MB of RAM. (If you use Microsoft Word for word processing, you can save money by purchasing **Microsoft Office X** [$399], which contains both programs plus PowerPoint and Entourage.) But serious number crunchers will find Excel worth the price. If you haven't upgraded to Mac OS X yet, Microsoft has you covered. Microsoft Office 2001 works on Mac OS 8.1 to 9.2.2 with 160 MB of hard-disk space and 32 MB of RAM. The feature set and interface for Excel X and Excel 2001 are very similar, so you won't miss out on much.

AppleWorks

AppleWorks ($79; www.apple.com), now in version 6, is an integrated software package that includes word-processing, spreadsheet, database, drawing, painting, and presentation modules. A "do-it-all" package, AppleWorks handles spreadsheet functions well, but not as well as a specialist like Excel. Still, for most home and school users and small-business owners, the spreadsheet module of AppleWorks has everything needed to get the job done, including built-in functions, extensive formatting capabilities, and linked charting. Because it's an integrated package, you can insert word-processing and other types of documents right on your spreadsheet without additional software.

One of the most attractive features of AppleWorks is its $79 price tag. Remember—that's for the entire package, not just the spreadsheet module. Seems like quite a bargain, doesn't it? It requires a Mac with 24 MB of RAM and at least 40 MB of hard-disk space. Versions are available for Mac OS X and Mac OS 8.1 to 9.2.2. (See Chapter 9 for more on AppleWorks).

Using Spreadsheets (ML/CB)

Ready to try your hand at creating a spreadsheet? It's not difficult, but there are a few tricks to learn. Read this section and you'll soon be using spreadsheets with style and verve—at least to the point where you can impress your friends and pets.

Spreadsheet Basics

Let's start with a few basics you'll use whenever you create a spreadsheet.

Moving around

You can't put anything into a cell until you *activate* it. You can tell that a cell is activated by looking at its border: an activated cell's border is thick or colored. You can activate a cell in two ways:

- Position the pointer (which looks like a fat plus sign [+]) over a cell and click once. You have to click—just moving the pointer over a cell does not activate it.
- Use a key to move to a cell. Here are the most commonly used keystrokes:

This key …	selects this cell
→ or Tab	The cell to the right of the current cell
← or Shift Tab	The cell to the left of the current cell
↓ or Return	The cell below the current cell
↑ or Shift Return	The cell above the current cell

Cell references

When you select or activate a cell, the spreadsheet program reports the active cell's reference in the *formula bar* (Excel) or *entry bar* (AppleWorks), at the upper left of the Desktop just below the application's toolbars. (If the formula bar isn't visible in Excel, choose View > Formula Bar.) As mentioned earlier, the cell reference consists of the letter (or letters) of the cell's column and the number of the cell's row. (There are alternative ways to describe cell locations, such as using numbers for both rows and columns, but nobody uses them because they're confusing.) Although you can select more than one cell simultaneously by dragging through several cells at once, only one cell is active at a time. Remember, the active cell is the one with the border; it's the one where whatever you type will appear.

Cell ranges (SA/ML)

A group of cells constitutes a *range.* You refer to a range by the addresses of the cells at its beginning and end, separated by a colon (Excel) or a pair of periods (AppleWorks). For example, *A1:A5* describes the first five cells in the first column in Excel, and *A1..E5* is a five-by-five-cell grid in the upper-left corner of an AppleWorks spreadsheet.

Kinds of entries

There are two kinds of entries: those you type in *(values)* and those that compute values *(formulas)*.

Entering values

Activate the cell into which you want to put a value, type what you want to appear in the cell, and then do one of the following:

*   Press ⌐Return⌐ to enter the value and activate the next cell down.
*   Press ⌐Enter⌐ to enter the value and leave the same cell active.
*   Press ⌐Tab⌐ to enter the value and activate the next cell to the right.
*   Click the checkmark button near the top of the window in the *formula bar* (Excel) or *entry bar* (AppleWorks). That's the Enter button, and it works the same way as pressing ⌐Enter⌐, entering the value and leaving the cell active.

 If you make a mistake while entering a value (or a formula, for that matter), you can start over by clicking the X button in the formula bar (Excel) or entry bar (AppleWorks). That's the Cancel button. If you prefer keyboard shortcuts, pressing ⌐Esc⌐ does the same thing.

Editing entries

You can change the contents of a cell in two ways:

*   Activate the cell and type something different into it.
*   Activate the cell, click in the formula/entry bar where the cell's contents appear, and use standard word-processing techniques to edit what's there.

No matter how you edit an entry, don't forget to press Return or Enter or click the Enter button.

Creating formulas

Just putting numbers and words into neat rows and columns is fine, but spreadsheets are built to compute. You can tell your spreadsheet to add two cells, calculate sales tax, or figure out what day of the week it will be 100 days from now. In fact, you can do just about anything that involves math—and some things that don't. But to do these fancy things, you must know how to create formulas.

 You must remember one thing to enter a formula successfully: all formulas start with an equals sign—no exceptions!

To enter a formula, select the cell where you want the formula's results displayed, type an equals sign, type the formula, and complete the formula by pressing Return or Enter or clicking the Enter button. Here's an example. Let's say you have a number in cell A1 and another number in cell A2. You want to add them and put the answer in cell A3. Select cell A3, type =A1+A2 (no spaces!), and press Return; the result appears in cell A3.

You do have other ways to enter the parts of formulas. For example, you can enter a cell reference in a formula by clicking the cell: to write the above formula by clicking, just click in cell A3, type an equals sign, click in cell A1, press +, click in cell A2, and click the Enter button. The answer appears in cell A3.

A well-constructed spreadsheet includes cell references in its formulas whenever possible, to make modifications easier. Here's another example: you can write formulas that include the percentage rate as a constant within the formula, like this: =B2*15% (**Figures 12.6** and **12.7**). But it's a lot more convenient to write formulas that reference a cell containing the percentage rate, like this: =B4*C1.

 Using cell references in formulas is especially handy for preventing typing errors—the less you type, the less chance you have of making mistakes!

Figure 12.6

To change the commission rate in this spreadsheet, you would have to edit the contents of the formulas in cells C2 through C6. That's five changes! And if you forgot to make a change, the spreadsheet would produce incorrect results.

◇	A	B	C
1		Sales Amount	Commission
2	Alan	5342.00	801.30
3	Becky	7943.00	1191.45
4	Charles	4823.00	723.45
5	Dean	8297.00	1244.55
6	Eric	4351.00	652.65

Figure 12.7

In this spreadsheet, you'd only have to change the contents of cell C1 to recalculate all commissions in column C correctly. So you're making one change that's impossible to miss. Which method would you prefer?

◇	A	B	C
1	Commission Rate:		15%
2			
3		Sales Amount	Commission
4	Alan	5342.00	801.30
5	Becky	7943.00	1191.45
6	Charles	4823.00	723.45
7	Dean	8297.00	1244.55
8	Eric	4351.00	652.65

 To select a range of cells, you can simply drag with the pointer instead of clicking in each cell individually.

As you may have noticed, the plus sign appears by default if you click a cell without first specifying an operator. What you may also notice is that if you forget to complete the formula by pressing Return or Enter or clicking the Enter button, any cell you click in is added to the formula in the formula bar/entry bar. That's why it's important to complete each entry properly before continuing to other cells.

$2 + 3 + 5 * 10 = ?$ (EG/ML)

The answer is 55. Why? Well, in spreadsheets, mathematical operations don't happen in their order of appearance, but rather they occur in a specific order. In the example above, the spreadsheet multiplies 5 by 10 first and then adds 2 and 3 to get 55. Here's the order in which operations happen:

Parentheses	( )
Exponents	^
Multiplication	*
Division	/
Addition	+
Subtraction	-

To force an operation to occur first, put it in parentheses. In the example above, if you wanted to add 3 and 5 first, you would use the formula 2+(3+5)*10. The spreadsheet would first add 3 and 5 to get 8, then multiply that by 10, and then add 2, with the result of 82. See what a difference a couple of parentheses can make?

Those Darned Error Messages (EC/ML)

When you write a formula incorrectly, the spreadsheet program usually tells you by displaying an error message in a dialog or within the cell. Here's a table of some of Excel's error messages—other spreadsheet programs offer similarly vague expressions.

Error Message	What It Means
#DIV/0!	Your formula is trying to divide by zero, which is a no-no.
#N/A	One of the referenced values is not available.
#NAME?	You've used an unrecognizable cell or range name. If you didn't mean to use a cell or range name, you've probably spelled a function name incorrectly.
#NUM!	Your formula uses a number incorrectly.
#REF!	Your formula references an invalid cell. This can happen if you delete cells after writing the formula.
#VALUE!	Your formula uses an incorrect argument or operator. Check for extra or missing commas and parentheses and for proper function names.

Beyond the Basics

So far, we've given you enough information to get you started with just about any spreadsheet program. Here are a few additional techniques and concepts to consider as you hone your spreadsheet skills.

Functions (CB)

Remember high school math? No? Fortunately, the people who make spreadsheet software do remember, and they've loaded their programs with handy calculations called *functions*. A function in a formula generally takes the form of =*SUM(B1:B5)* where the operators are in parentheses after the function. Here are some of my favorites. You've seen a few of them in action earlier in this chapter.

- **SUM** sums (adds) a bunch of numbers. It's especially handy for totaling a column or a row.

- **AVERAGE** calculates the average of a range of cells. As with most functions, it's a lot easier to use the function than to calculate averages yourself.

- **MAX** looks at a range of cells and returns the largest value. You could do this by looking at the cells yourself, but the MAX function is faster, and it never makes mistakes.

- **MIN** determines which cell in a range is the smallest.

- **IF**—my favorite—gives you supreme power and flexibility. It evaluates a condition (such as "Is B10 greater than 5000?") and performs a calculation (or returns a result) based on whether the condition is met (true) or not met (false). Creative use of this function can add intelligence to your spreadsheets.

- **PROPER** changes the first character of text to a capital letter.

- **SIN**—as in *sine,* not "Thou shalt not"—is trigonometry, the high school math subject you understood either completely or not at all. Fortunately, spreadsheets excel (hey, a spreadsheet pun!) at trigonometry. If you have an angle, the sine is a function away. **COS** gives you cosines, and **TAN** produces tangents.

- **WEEKDAY** returns the day of the week on which a certain date falls. The answer you'll get is a number from 1 to 7 representing the day of the week. (The actual result depends on the settings in the Date & Time System Preferences pane in Mac OS X or control panel in Mac OS 9 and earlier.)

- **SQRT**—that's *square root,* not *squirt*—it calculates square roots.

- **PMT** figures out how much the periodic payments will be when you borrow a certain amount of money at a certain rate of interest for a certain length of time.

Copying formulas (ML)

You can create a spreadsheet like the expense summary or loan amortization tables shown earlier without entering each formula down the columns. How? By copying similar formulas. The spreadsheet software changes cell references as necessary so that the copied formulas are correct. Of course, this technique has its limitations (see the sidebar "Absolute References," below), so check the formulas you copy to make sure they're correct.

Absolute References (EG)

You can use two kinds of references in your formulas: *relative* (as in *D5*) or *absolute* (as in *D5*). The only time the kind of reference matters is when you copy a formula. A relative reference changes relative to where you paste it. (For example, if a formula sums the four cells immediately above it, when the formula is copied to a new location, the pasted-in formula will sum the four cells immediately above its new location.) An absolute reference always refers to the same cell no matter where you paste it. This is probably the most complex concept you'll encounter in dealing with spreadsheets, but once you master it, it can help you quickly create error-free spreadsheets.

Formatting (ML)

Of course, all spreadsheet software offers the ability to format your spreadsheets and charts with fonts, colors, styles, borders—you name it. The spreadsheets shown throughout this chapter offer good examples of clean formatting. With a little creativity, you can make a spreadsheet look like a million bucks—even if it's reporting a loss.

Printing (ML)

When you print a spreadsheet, what emerges from your printer depends on several factors:

- **Did you specify a print area?** A print area is the rectangular selection of cells that will print. If you don't specify a print area, most software will print the entire spreadsheet, inserting page breaks wherever necessary to get it all on paper.

- **Did you insert manual page breaks?** You can specify where you want one page to end and the next to begin, to eliminate page-break surprises.

- **Did you set page orientation, margins, or scale?** By fiddling around with these page-setup options, you can squeeze a relatively large spreadsheet onto standard-size paper—or magnify spreadsheet cells for use in a presentation.

- **Did you set print titles?** If your spreadsheet is lengthy, you may want to print row or column headings as titles on each page. You must tell the spreadsheet software which columns or rows to use as titles.

These options vary from one spreadsheet package to another. Explore the Page Setup and Print dialogs of your spreadsheet software to see how their settings affect your printouts. (For more on printing, see Chapter 6.)

Tips (ML/EC/CB/SA/EG/DC)

Because there's more than one spreadsheet package out there, we've done our best to come up with a few generic tips you can use with either Excel or AppleWorks. We've also rounded up some application-specific tips that will come in handy for the application you use.

General Spreadsheet Tips

No matter which spreadsheet program you are using—Excel or AppleWorks—these tips are sure to come in handy.

Use arrow keys to change the active cell, but use the scroll bars to change the portion of the spreadsheet being viewed. Although you can use the scroll bars to change your view of a spreadsheet, using them does not change the active cell.

Pay attention to the pointer. Spreadsheets change the pointer to provide visual clues about things you can do.

- The pointer appears as a white cross (or fat plus sign) when it's in the spreadsheet area: click to select a cell, drag to select multiple cells, or click to add a cell to a formula if the formula bar/entry bar is active.

- The pointer appears as a black arrow when it is on a column letter or a row number: click to select the entire column or row.

- The pointer appears as an I-beam pointer when it's in the formula bar/entry bar: click to edit the contents of the formula or entry bar at the spot where the I-beam sits.

- The pointer appears as a thick black crossbar with arrows when it's between column or row headings: drag to change the width of the column or height of the row.

- The pointer appears as a standard arrow pointer when you move it out of the spreadsheet window: use it to pull down a menu, scroll with a scroll bar, move or resize a window, or switch to another open window or application.

Turn a formula into a text value. If you're having trouble entering a formula correctly and your spreadsheet keeps beeping at you each time you try to move to another cell, delete the equals sign from the beginning of the formula and press Return. The spreadsheet accepts what remains as mere text, allowing you to move on to other things. Later (when you're older and wiser), you can come back to fix the formula. Why not just delete the formula and start from scratch later? Because often you'll get close to getting a formula right—to throw it all away is to waste the time and effort you've already put into it.

Use Shift-click to select a range of cells. Select the first cell of a range and then hold down Shift and click in the last cell of the range, or use the arrow keys to extend the selection.

Select all cells with your pointer. Click in the empty box at the top-left corner of the worksheet window (to the left of column A and above row 1). This selects every cell in the spreadsheet. (Pressing ⌘A also selects every cell in the spreadsheet.)

Understand the difference between relative and absolute references. You indicate that all or part of a cell reference is absolute by putting a dollar sign ($) before it. To remember what that symbol means in a cell reference, think of the word *always*. So, for example, you can think of D5 as *always D, always 5*—or *always D5*. (See the sidebar "Absolute References," above.)

Make a column the best width. To make a column just wide enough to display the longest item in the column, double-click the line to the right of the column letter in the column-heading area. The pointer will look like a black crossbar with arrows.

When You Enter Too Much ... (CB/ML/DC)

For long entries, the cell width determines what appears in the cell.

- If a number (or date or time) doesn't fit into a cell, the cell's contents appear as a series of number signs (#####) or in that ever-popular scientific notation.

- If you type more text than can fit in the cell and nothing is in the cell to its right, the text overflows to the right so that you can see all of it. Even if text appears to overflow into other cells, that text is still contained in only one cell.

- If you type more text than can fit in the cell and something is already entered into the cell to its right, the text appears truncated in the cell in which you entered it. This doesn't mean the text is cut off—it isn't. It just doesn't show onscreen.

In most cases you can properly display lengthy numbers or text by making the column wider. Just drag the right boundary of the column heading at the top of the column.

Another way you can make lengthy text fit in a cell is to turn on the *word wrap* feature for that cell so that the text wraps within the cell. Both Excel and AppleWorks offer this feature. In Excel go to Format > Cells; in the resulting dialog click the Alignment tab and choose the "Wrap text" option. In AppleWorks simply choose Format > Alignment > Wrap.

Use drawing tools to annotate spreadsheets and charts. You can draw attention to spreadsheet results by drawing circles and arrows right on the spreadsheet.

Use contextual menus. Hold down Control and click a selection. A pop-up menu appears, listing commands you can use on the selection.

Transpose rows and columns. You organized your spreadsheet with months in columns and categories in rows, but now you've decided that you really want categories in columns and months in rows. What do you do? Transpose them. Select the cells you want to transpose and copy them by pressing ⌘C. Then choose the Paste Special command from the Edit menu and click the Transpose check box. Click OK to transpose the rows and columns.

Split the screen so that headings stay put when you scroll. At the very top of the vertical scroll bar, you'll see a blue oval with a thin black line through it (Excel) or a small thin bar (AppleWorks); this is called a *split box*. Drag the split box down as far as you wish to split the screen (as you start to drag the split box, you'll see a line, called a *split line,* going across the spreadsheet). Now you can scroll either the top or the bottom half of the window. Horizontal splitting works the same way—look for the split box at the right of the horizontal scroll bar.

Hide columns or rows. Hiding a column or row is a good way to get something out of your way temporarily. To hide a column or row, set its column width or row height to 0. (You can access the column width dialog from the Format menu in both Excel and AppleWorks). It disappears! Your only clue to the fact that there are hidden rows or columns in the spreadsheet is the missing letters or numbers in the headers. Displaying a hidden column or row is a little trickier—you can't easily select a column or row if you can't see it. One way to display a hidden column or row is to use the Go To or Go to Cell command to select a single cell in the column or row and then set the column width or row height to something other than 0.

Excel Tips

Excel is a powerful spreadsheet program, full of great features and functions. Here are just a few of our favorite tips for making the most efficient use of it.

Edit directly in the cell. If you want to change the contents of a cell without having to use the formula bar, double-click the cell.

Make noncontiguous selections. You can select cells or blocks of cells that aren't next to each other (for example, to apply formatting). Select the first cell or block and then hold down ⌘ while you select subsequent cells.

Move a selection block. If you've selected a block of five cells in a row to apply some formatting and then want to select another five cells two rows down to apply some more formatting, don't reach for the mouse. Instead, move the selection block (but not the data): Option Tab moves the block to the right, Shift Option Tab moves it to the left, and Shift Option Return and Option Return move it up and down, respectively.

Select referenced cells. If the current cell has a formula in it, you can select all the cells to which the formula directly refers by pressing ⌘ [. Press ⌘ Shift [to select *all* cells to which the formula refers, even indirectly.

Move cells with drag and drop. You can drag a cell or a range of cells by its border to move it to a new position. (The hand cursor indicates that you can move the cell or range.) Hold down Shift while dragging to insert a cell or range of cells between other cells. Hold down Option while dragging to copy a cell or range of cells to the new location (the hand cursor includes a plus sign to indicate that you are making a copy).

Name cells. You can also give cells or ranges custom names, which make it easier to write formulas and use the Go To command.

Enter the current time or date quickly. To enter the current date in an Excel cell, press ⌘ -. To enter the current time, press ⌘ ;.

Use AutoFill to enter data into adjacent cells. Enter a value or formula in the first cell, press Enter to complete the entry, and then drag the *fill handle* (the little box in the bottom-right corner of the cell) to extend a box around the other cells you want to contain the same value or formula. If the original cell contains a day, month, or other component of a familiar series, Excel completes the series for you.

Use AutoSum to add columns or rows. Select the cell at the bottom of a column or the right side of a row you want to total. Then double-click the AutoSum button, the one with the sigma (Σ) on it. Excel guesses which cells you want to total and writes a formula complete with the SUM function and references to the cells. You can use this feature in a variety of ways—even to total more than one column or row at a time. Be sure to check for accuracy the formula that Excel creates, however. For example, if the column you want to total contains empty cells, Excel may total only the last completely filled grouping of cells instead of the whole column.

Use Natural Language Formulas. This Excel feature enables you to write formulas using column and row headings to refer to cells. For example, in this little spreadsheet, the formulas in cells B9, C9, and D9 are =*SUM(FY02)*, =*SUM(FY03)*, and =*SUM(FY04)*, respectively (**Figure 12.8**). Neat, huh?

Figure 12.8

Natural Language Formulas make it possible to write formulas without using cryptic cell references. For example, in this spreadsheet the formula in cell B9 is =SUM(FY02).

◇	A	B	C	D
1	**Flying M Air Sales**			
2	(in thousands)			
3		FY02	FY03	FY04
4	Alan	$17	$2	$95
5	Becky	29	88	76
6	Charles	97	15	51
7	Dean	8	4	31
8	Eric	70	97	67
9	Totals	$221	$206	$320

Use the Formula Palette to write formulas using functions. The Formula Palette not only provides online help in understanding functions, but it also takes you every step of the way through the creation of a formula with one or more functions. To access the Formula Palette, use the Insert menu's Function command, and then use the Paste Function dialog to paste in the function you want to use. The Formula Palette appears, to help you complete the formula.

Change relative references to absolute references with a keystroke. If you've already entered a cell reference in a formula and want to change the reference type, select the cell reference and press ⌘T until Excel places the absolute reference dollar sign wherever you want it.

Float a toolbar. Position the pointer anywhere on a toolbar other than on a button and drag the toolbar down from the top of the screen. You'll get a floating toolbar that you can put anywhere you like. Drag it back to dock it again.

Tear-off toolbar menus. If a toolbar button's pop-up menu has a *move handle*—a double border along its top or side edge—you can tear the menu off the toolbar. Display the menu, and then click the move handle to turn the menu into a floating palette with its own tiny title bar.

Rename sheets. You can change the name of a worksheet in an Excel workbook file by double-clicking the sheet tab for the sheet, entering a new name, and pressing (Return).

Move or copy sheets by dragging. You can change the order of sheets in a workbook by simply dragging tabs to new positions. You can copy a worksheet by holding down (Option) as you drag the tab. You can move (or copy) a sheet to another workbook by dragging (or (Option)-dragging) its tab from one workbook file to another.

Experiment with the macro feature. This feature enables you to perform repetitive tasks quickly or create custom functions. To get started, let Excel's macro recorder write the macro for you. This is a nice—although limited— use of macros that can familiarize you with the macro language. To access the macro feature go to Tools > Macro.

Apply basic formatting from the keyboard. You can apply all the basic number-formatting options to a cell by using keyboard commands:

General	(Control)(Shift)(~)	Exponential	(Control)(Shift)(^)
Currency	(Control)(Shift)($)	Date	(Control)(Shift)(#)
Percentage	(Control)(Shift)(%)	Time	(Control)(Shift)(@)

Use the Format Painter. A cell's format includes text formatting (font, size, and style), alignment (left or centered), and number formats (dollar signs and the number of decimals). You can use the Format Painter to copy formatting and apply it to other cells. Start by selecting the cell that contains the formatting you want to copy. Click the Format Painter button in the Standard toolbar (it looks like a paintbrush). Then select the cells to which you want to apply the formatting. To apply formatting to multiple cell selections, double-click the Format Painter button; press (Esc) when you want to stop painting.

Copy a selection as a graphic. You can copy a selected section of the spreadsheet to the Clipboard as a PICT graphic (which will include gridlines and row and column headings) and then paste it into any program as a graphic. Just make your selection, hold down (Shift), and choose Copy Picture from the Edit menu.

Apply conditional formatting. Suppose you want all values over a certain amount to appear in green or bold or with a yellow background? Use the Conditional Formatting dialog (which you access via the Format menu) to define the conditions and related formatting (**Figure 12.9**). Excel does the rest based on spreadsheet contents.

Figure 12.9

The Conditional Formatting dialog makes it easy to set up the conditions under which to apply formatting.

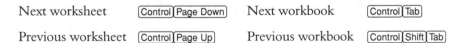

Use the Range Finder feature. While you're editing a formula that refers to one or more cell ranges, the range names are color-coded in the formula bar to match Range Finder frames around the ranges in the spreadsheet. (These frames appear automatically when you start to edit the formula.) To change a range in the formula, grab the appropriate Range Finder handle and drag to surround more or fewer cells—the formula changes to reference the new range. This works with charts, too; when a chart series is selected, adjustable Range Finder frames appear around associated spreadsheet ranges. Just drag the frame's handle to change the chart.

Switch worksheets—or workbooks—without using the mouse. Use these shortcuts instead:

Next worksheet	`Control` `Page Down`	Next workbook	`Control` `Tab`
Previous worksheet	`Control` `Page Up`	Previous workbook	`Control` `Shift` `Tab`

Select multiple worksheets. You can select more than one worksheet at a time to perform certain global operations, such as deleting the worksheets, running a spelling check, or turning off all the gridlines. Start by clicking the tab of the first worksheet to include in the selection. Then:

* To select multiple contiguous worksheets, hold down `Shift` and click the tab of the last worksheet. This selects all worksheets in between.
* To select noncontiguous worksheets, hold down `⌘` and click their tabs.
* To select all worksheets, hold down `Control`, click any worksheet tab, and choose Select All Sheets from the contextual menu that appears.

Enter the same data in the same cells of multiple worksheets. First select the tabs of the worksheets in which you want to enter the data. Then enter the data in the top worksheet. It appears in all selected worksheets.

AppleWorks Tips

While AppleWorks isn't quite as full-featured as Excel, it offers most of the functions an average user will need. Here are our top tips.

Put some life in your spreadsheets. Select a range of cells to color, and then choose Show Accents from the Window menu to add background colors, patterns, and other formatting (**Figure 12.10**). If you just need to change your text color, pick a color for selected cells with the Text Color command under the Format menu.

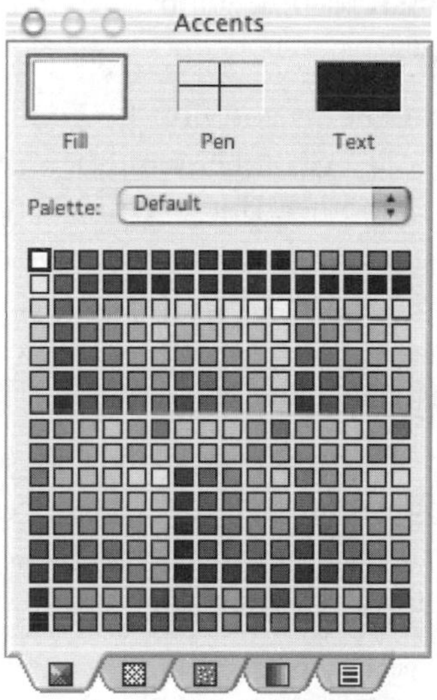

Figure 12.10

The Accents palette offers a variety of colorful formatting options for cell backgrounds and lines.

Customize the button bar. Use options in the Customize Button Bar dialog to specify which buttons appear on the button bar and in what order they appear. To access this dialog, select Preferences from the AppleWorks menu and then select Button Bar.

Zoom out to see more of your work at once. Click the zoom-out control (the small-mountains button at the bottom left of a spreadsheet window) to zoom out; click the zoom-in control (the big-mountains button) to zoom in. The number in the bottom-left corner displays your current magnification level. Click it and hold the mouse button down, and you'll get a pop-up menu that lets you zoom as far as you want in a single move.

Select all data with your mouse. Hold down (Option) while clicking in the empty box at the intersection of the column and row headings. This selects everything from cell A1 to the farthest cell containing data. (Holding down (Option) also changes the Edit menu's Select All command to Select All Data.)

Use the Fill Special command to type stuff for you. Need to enter a series of months into adjacent cells? Click in a cell that contains the first month of the series, and drag to the right or down as far as you want to go. Then choose Fill Special from the Calculate menu. This works for all kinds of series.

Auto-enter absolute references. If you're clicking or dragging in cells to enter their names into a formula, you can make the references absolute by holding down (⌘)(Option) while clicking or dragging in the cells.

Copy-and-paste formatting. Select a cell with formatting you want to copy to other cells. Then choose Copy Format from the Edit menu. Now select the cells to which you want to copy the formatting, and choose Apply Format from the Edit menu. This copies the formatting of the first cell to the other cells. It's much easier than choosing formatting options by hand.

Use the Lock Title Position command to keep column or row titles in sight. This prevents column or row titles from scrolling out of the window and ensures that column or row titles print on each page. It's also a handy way to identify a range of cells. To use this feature, select the column or row you want to lock and then choose Lock Title Position from the Options menu.

 You can only lock either row or column headings, not both. Also, when selecting the headers to lock, be aware that AppleWorks locks your selected row or column as well as any preceding rows or columns.

Set the arrow-key action. If your pointer is in the entry bar, then pressing the arrow keys moves you around in the entry bar for editing cell contents. Similarly, if the pointer is in the cell area of the spreadsheet, pressing the arrow keys moves you from one cell to another. But you can change that so that pressing the arrow keys always moves you from one cell to another no matter where the pointer is located. To do so, choose General from the Preferences submenu in the AppleWorks menu and click Always Selects Another Cell. (While you're in there, you can change the action of the Enter key, too.)

Reverse the arrow-key action. Whichever way you've set the preferences for the arrow keys, pressing Option reverses it temporarily. So, if an arrow key normally lets you edit in the entry bar, pressing an arrow key while holding down Option will let you move from cell to cell, and vice versa.

Activate the entry bar. If you're working from the keyboard and have selected a cell, don't click in the entry bar to activate it so that you can edit the cell contents. Instead, press Option↓ to put the insertion point at the end of the entry bar or Option↑ to put the insertion point at the beginning of the entry bar.

Move a selection without dragging and dropping. You can move a selected cell or a block of cells by holding down ⌘Option while clicking where you want the selection moved. As with a drag-and-drop move, this doesn't change any of the cell references in formulas you may be moving.

Use AutoSum to add columns or rows. Select the range of cells you want to total, as well as the empty cell where you want the total to appear. Then double-click the AutoSum button (the one with the sigma [Σ] on it). AppleWorks writes a formula with the SUM function and references to the cells.

Reverse the axes in a chart. When your chart's axes are reversed—the x-axis is where you want the y-axis and vice versa—you can switch them. Choose Options > Make Chart and then go to the General pane to make the switch.

Interview: Mike Murray, Part 1

Originally employed at Apple as a summer intern in 1980 while he was pursuing an M.B.A. degree at Stanford, Mike Murray returned to the company in early 1982 to help plan the marketing for the Mac. Soon promoted to director of marketing, he worked closely with Steve Jobs in devising the hugely successful publicity campaign that accompanied the platform's launch.

> *In a very short period of time in January of 1984, we were able to create tremendous momentum around this little funny-looking box.*
>
> *—Mike Murray, on the marketing impact of the original Mac*

In 1985, however, Murray was caught in the crossfire as relations between Jobs and John Sculley, then Apple's president and CEO, deteriorated. After Jobs was forced out, Murray left the company to work for a manufacturer of Unix-based business systems. In 1989 he moved to Microsoft to run a networking software group and went on to become vice president of human resources and administration. He retired from Microsoft in 1989 and now devotes himself primarily to his family foundation and its chief project, a nonprofit called Unitus. —Henry Norr

Were you the first marketing person on the Mac team?

When I got there, a really good guy named Barry Cash, who's now a venture capitalist in Texas, had been hired as a consultant to put together the original marketing for the Macintosh. But he left, and Steve appointed me acting marketing director until they could find a "good person" to run that area. That was the memo that went out—you know, "We're going to put Mike in here until we can find a good person" [he laughs]. I was going to be the acting marketing director, so I decided to act like a marketing director.

Did you eventually get the "acting" removed from your title?

I did. I kept acting like one forever …

Did you work closely with Steve Jobs?

Steve was my boss. I worked directly with Steve while I was on the Mac team, and we worked many, many hours very, very closely together on the advertising, positioning, packaging, pricing, promotional strategy, training the sales force, everything that had to do with the imagery, as well as some very hard blocking and tackling behind the scenes that you do in marketing in the high-tech industry.

We invented what today is called "event marketing," which is using very large events to introduce your products to garner a lot of public awareness, news, PR, and so forth. We did the 1984 Super Bowl advertising; we had blockbuster advertising in *Newsweek*, where we purchased all the ads in one particular issue—every single ad was a Macintosh-related ad in the entire magazine. And we created *Macworld* magazine. It was intentionally not published by Apple, but we underwrote it to make sure the magazine survived to create the image that this was going to be a very successful product.

continues on next page

We also invented the concept of software evangelism. Today, Microsoft and other companies [use that term] as if that's been around forever and ever, but it was a brand-new idea that you'd take your product and go out and convince the software community that they needed to write software for it without paying them. We never paid anybody to write any software for the Mac.

Before the launch, was it general knowledge in the industry that Apple was doing the Mac?

I think it was general knowledge, but there wasn't much hope given for it because the Lisa was so horrible—it was overpriced, it underperformed, there was no software for it—it just didn't work. In October of 1983, I think it was, *BusinessWeek* had a cover story on the personal-computer industry, and the cover said, "And the winner is … IBM." They were saying IBM was the de facto owner of the PC industry, and everyone else might as well just go home now. And three months later we were planning on introducing the Macintosh, so there was anti-momentum.

Do you have any nostalgia for those days?

No, I don't think so. But when you try to find analogs in business history, where a truly innovative product was brought to market, and so many things had to go right…. In the technology sector you've got to have software, you had to energize this whole third-party software community, you had to have dealers ready to go, you had to have spare parts, you had to have a marketing engine that could convince people that this was a product worth looking at, the product had to work, it had to be manufactured, we had to build this factory, and you're talking about a team where the average age was probably 27, 28. So [there were] a lot of things that would say, "They can't do this." That's what's fun for me, when I think back on it: how did this thing succeed—just saying, "Wow, that was just a real treat, being part of that whole project."

Can you talk about why the "1984" ad almost didn't run?

Because we were going to be spending a million and half dollars, whatever, to run this ad on the Super Bowl, it had to be approved by the board of directors. There was a board meeting, and Steve and I were very enthused about the commercial, as was the ad agency. He had me bring a videotape of the ad into a board meeting and show it to the board. And when they finished seeing this commercial, one of the board members had his head down on this big table, and he was kind of pounding his fist, and I thought that meant this was the greatest ad he'd ever seen, that he just loved it. In fact it was just the opposite—[he said] it was the worst commercial he'd ever seen, and he couldn't believe that we'd wasted the company's money doing this.

To a person in the room, they said, "You're not allowed to run this ad. What were you guys ever thinking of? Sell the time, and if you can't do that, run some Apple II ad." It was a huge, huge, huge defeat, and we were upset too because we thought they didn't understand what we were trying to communicate with this product; nor did they understand the necessity to do something very bold and aggressive in order to get people's attention.

You ended up running the ad anyway. It got—still gets—huge critical acclaim, but how well did it work as a marketing tool?

The ad ended up doing just what we wanted it to do. The goal was to turn the ad into news itself. This was all based on a little news clipping that Steve had found months and months before, when George Lucas was coming out with the original *Star Wars* movie. Lucas had cooked up this idea that if he could do a whole bunch of stuff before the movie came out, so that the day it came out, there'd be this huge noise about it, followed up with T-shirts and television shows about it, and toys in toy stores, it would create additional momentum all by itself. People would think, "Wow, this must be a big deal. We'd better go see this movie."

So Steve came to me and said, "This is what we need to do with the Macintosh." We took that idea, and we said, "Let's turn the introduction of the Macintosh into news—not just public relations, but literal news." And if we could get the three major networks—ABC, CBS, NBC—to broadcast this on their nightly news, then it would move beyond the realm of PR. If Tom Brokaw and if Peter Jennings were saying, "An exciting new product has been announced, and we want you to take a look at it," that'd be a thousand times better than anything we could say, because those guys are trusted. And if *The Wall Street Journal* and *The New York Times* and *Time* magazine and *Newsweek* and *BusinessWeek* would say the same thing, then we'd done it—it'd be real, and people would be saying, "This must be the truth."

Did it work?

We accomplished everything. It was on the nightly news, and the commercial was shown over and over again. They'd show this commercial, and people would say, "Whoa, this is great—look at this. What's it mean?" And then *Newsweek, Time, BusinessWeek, Fortune, Forbes*—the launch of the Macintosh was on the cover of all five of those magazines, which had never been done before. And it was on the front page of *The New York Times* and *The Wall Street Journal*. So in a very short period of time in January of 1984, we were able to create tremendous momentum around this little funny-looking box with just a few software packages, and that gave lifeblood to a product that for all other reasons might not have survived. As innovative as it was, which was extraordinary, it might not have made it if we couldn't have created enough noise out there. Luckily, we were operating in a very, very large market—you know, there were 250 million people in America, so you don't need a whole lot of them to go out and pay in those days $2,500 for this cool little product.

continues on page 572

Part 3

Getting Creative

13

Graphics

Pamela Pfiffner and Scholle Sawyer McFarland are the chapter editors and authors.

Even if you've grown up with a paintbrush (or camera) in hand, making the leap to digital artwork is not always painless. Here the subtlety of paints, film, and pencils gives way to the science of pixels (little electronic dots).

Luckily, it's a lot easier to learn how to handle your graphics applications than it was to learn how to draw in the first place. Once you master new terminology and tools, you'll find that computer graphics offer a lot of time-saving advantages over manual methods. Even better, you'll soon discover that computer graphics can also open up new paths for your creative potential.

In This Chapter

Welcome to Computer Graphics

Going digital brings big benefits. Just think—you don't have to empty a trash can filled with crumpled first tries anymore. You can make unlimited copies of your photos and other artwork to print, email, or incorporate into another project. You can go back to an earlier version of your drawing and try a different technique, and then compare the two versions. Before you dive in, though, it helps to understand some concepts.

Bitmaps vs. Vectors

The first thing you need to know about computer graphics is that they come in two flavors—*bitmap* and *vector*. Bitmapped graphics (aka *raster* graphics) consist of tiny dots, each filled with a single color or just black or white. When combined, the little dots, or pixels, make up the picture you see on your Mac's display. (The picture is, in fact, a *bit map*—the value of each pixel is stored in one or more bits of computer memory.)

Although the image is made up of little bits, most programs let you select and manipulate the entire form, resizing and reshaping it to your taste. Programs that make bitmapped graphics are called *paint* programs, because they work rather like real-world painting. With regular painting, you use your brush to cover up the parts of the picture you want to change. In a paint program, you have features such as the Eraser tool, which you can use to remove unwanted portions of your artwork or photographs. (Say bye-bye to those power lines in your scenic landscape!) You can create bitmapped illustrations with great subtlety of color and texture, but they have a serious shortcoming. Because each pixel is a fixed size, if you enlarge the illustration, the quality gets worse. The edges become jaggy, details get fuzzy—and the greater the size, the more blatant the effect.

MacPaint—an Apple-developed application that was included with the original Macintosh—kicked off the creation of bitmap graphics on the Mac, and now the paint component of AppleWorks incorporates an expanded version of its basic feature set. Some other programs that work with bitmaps are Adobe Photoshop and Photoshop Elements, as well as Corel Painter and ACD Systems' Canvas.

A vector graphic (aka *object-oriented* graphic), on the other hand, is made up of a mathematical formula that defines all the shapes, or *curves,* in the image. This means that vector graphics are more flexible than bitmapped graphics. Since they aren't translated into bitmaps until the last moment, after all sizes and resolutions have been specified, they can be output on any device at any size without becoming fuzzy. Whether you want your vector graphic to fit on the head of a pin or the side of a bus, the formula is the same; the image resizes perfectly.

Vector graphics usually take up less storage space than bitmapped graphics. A vector graphic stays the same size regardless of the resolution at which you print it. The size of a bitmapped graphic changes depending on the number of pixels it contains. Large color photos and other full-color pictures (which are typically saved as bitmap graphics) can occupy many megabytes of storage space.

The vector format is usually used for line drawings, illustrations, and CAD (computer-assisted design). Programs that create and manipulate vector graphics are called *draw* programs. Vector graphics made their debut back in 1986 in an Apple-developed program called MacDraw. As with MacPaint, AppleWorks incorporates and enhances MacDraw's capabilities. For professional illustration, however, computer-based artists use programs such as Adobe Illustrator and Macromedia FreeHand, sometimes Canvas, and (often if they're converts from the Windows platform) Corel's CorelDRAW. (Note, however, that Corel will not be producing a Mac version for the next release of CorelDRAW, which is sold as the CorelDRAW Graphics Suite 12. The company will continue to support CorelDRAW 11 for the Macintosh for the foreseeable future.)

 Graphics programs such as FreeHand and Illustrator are sometimes called *PostScript illustration* **programs. The files they make use the PostScript language and can print to a PostScript device (usually a laser printer) at the maximum possible resolution.**

PDF Under the Hood

Starting with Mac OS X, Apple embraced a technology based on Adobe's Portable Document Format (PDF), a vector-based imaging technique. In addition to providing sharp display with built-in anti-aliasing (sometimes called *edge, text,* or *font smoothing*), this technology allows you to drag objects around the screen in real time. As a result, you can see the actual objects rather than just an outline. Creating a PDF is *very* easy—in fact, that's exactly what you do when you take a screen shot using the shortcuts ⌘Shift 3 (to capture the entire screen) or ⌘Shift 4 (to capture part of the screen). You can also create PDF files directly from the Print dialog in Mac OS X.

Graphics File Formats

As soon as you try to save a graphics file, you're faced with a confusing array of options. JPEG, GIF, TIFF—what's up with this alphabet soup? There are as many graphics file formats as there are ways to use graphics. But don't despair; it's easy to get the hang of what to use when. (For a quick cheat sheet, check out **Table 13.1,** below.)

Here's a list of the formats you'll encounter most often. You'll notice a Windows-based one in the mix, since chances are you'll come across it before long. Note that each format's *filename extension* is listed in parentheses. It's helpful to know these whether you're sending something to a Windows user or to your printer (the person, not your trusty Epson). To avoid problems, make sure your file has the right filename extension.

 Just because you may not *see* filename extensions in your filenames doesn't mean they're not there. Mac OS X uses extensions, but since Mac users aren't accustomed to such things, it often hides them. To learn your file's extension, click the file in the Finder and press ⌘I or choose Get Info from the Finder's File menu. In the dialog that appears, click the disclosure triangle for Name & Extension to see the file's complete name, extension, and all.

BMP (.bmp). This standard Windows bitmapped file format is created when the print-screen feature in Windows is used to capture the image onscreen. Most Mac graphics programs (even AppleWorks) can read and export BMP files.

GIF (.gif). GIF (short for "graphics interchange format") is a standard format for Web-based graphics. The name is pronounced with either a soft G (as in "jiffy") or a hard G (as in "gopher"). (Believe it or not, the debate over the pronunciation dominates entire Web pages. See "The GIF Pronunciation Page," www.olsenhome.com/gif.) Since bandwidth is scarce on the Web, the GIF format saves bytes by using no more than 256 colors. The fewer the colors, the smaller the file. The subtlety of high-end graphics is lost in the translation, but at least people don't have to wait half an hour for a single graphic to download! The GIF format works best if your image is composed primarily of big areas of flat color—in other words, if it's not a photograph. GIF is also the best choice if the graphic includes text that must be readable, you want the image to appear to float on the page (the GIF format supports transparency), or you want to the image to be a simple animation.

EPS (.eps). This composite file format (also known as Encapsulated PostScript) stores both PostScript data and information for screen display. As with any PostScript file, EPS files can be scale to any size, up or down, and printed at the highest resolution your printer can support—that is, if you have a desktop printer with PostScript capability. If not, all you see is the jaggy, low-resolution image. EPS files are frequently used in page-layout programs, such as Adobe InDesign and QuarkXPress.

JPEG (.jpg). This compressed image format's name is an abbreviation for Joint Photographic Experts Group and is pronounced "jay-peg." As you might guess, you use this format for photographs—especially when you're saving them for the Web or need to send them by email. (It's also useful for drawings with a lot of subtle color shifts.) In most programs you can choose from several levels of JPEG compression. The highest-quality setting produces images almost indistinguishable from the original, but they take up a lot of disk storage space. The lowest-quality settings create images with poor quality but small file sizes. Creating good Web graphics is a balancing act. Take note: JPEG compression makes text look awful. If text must be legible, then you should save the image as a GIF. JPEG 2000 is a newer variant of this file format.

PDF (.pdf). The PDF (Portable Document Format) file type was developed by Adobe Systems. PDF files capture complex formatting information from a variety of desktop-publishing applications (or from any application, for that matter). This makes it possible to send documents and have them appear on the recipient's monitor or printer the same way as they would on yours. To view a file in PDF format, you can use Adobe Reader, a free application distributed by Adobe Systems, or Mac OS X's built-in Preview application. You may not think of PDF as a graphics format per se, but it's now the standard format for Mac OS X screen captures; you can use the keyboard shortcuts ⌘Shift3 (to capture the entire screen) or ⌘Shift4 (to capture part of the screen).

 Want to send a carbon copy of a complex document to someone? It's easy to create a PDF in Mac OS X—no special software is required. Just choose File > Print (or press ⌘P) and click the Save As PDF button.

PICT (.pct). This is the standard classic Mac image format, and it has the added ability to store both bitmap and vector attributes in the same file. Most Mac OS 9 and earlier programs save in this format. It's also the standard format for Mac OS 9 screen captures (although some programs let you save those in other formats).

PSD (.psd). You'll run into Photoshop's internal format for graphics files if you use Adobe Photoshop or Photoshop Elements. PSD files (the name stands for "*Photoshop document*") can include all sorts of goodies, such as layers and editable text. If you want to change your image in the future, it's helpful to keep a PSD file around, but to use the image elsewhere—on the Web or in your page-layout program—it's usually necessary to save it in another format. (The exception is Adobe InDesign, which lets you place PSD files in your layouts.)

TIFF (.tif). This bitmapped image format (its name is short for "tagged image file format") is prominent in the publishing industry. A TIFF file may include black-and-white, grayscale, and color illustrations and photos. TIFFs offer extremely high image quality, and file sizes can grow incredibly large. A big color photo, for example, may consume many megabytes of storage space. Both Macs and Windows-based computers can handle the format, but it's not as common on the Windows platform. If you're using Mac OS X's Grab application (Applications > Utilities > Grab) to take pictures of your screen, it saves them in this format.

Table 13.1   The Right Format for the Job

If you want to ...	... then use this file format
Send photos via email	JPEG
Post photos on your Web site	JPEG
Post photos that aren't bound by a box on your Web site	GIF
Post logos, banners, or simple animations on your Web site	GIF
Include line-art illustrations in your page layout	EPS
Include photos in your page layout	TIFF
Send a non-editable image to someone	PDF
Save a Photoshop image so that you can change it later	PSD
Send a bitmapped image to a Windows user	BMP
Create Flash animations for the Web	SWF

Conversion Experience

Most of us have run into a funky file at one time or another: a client sends you a logo, for example, and a weird mess of gobbledygook appears in your in-box instead. Learning filename extensions helps a lot—you'll at least have a clue about what you're dealing with. Once you know what format the file is in, you may find that you need to convert it to another format so that you can use it. However, if you don't have a high-powered program such as Photoshop at your disposal, or if you also want to convert a whole mess of graphics files quickly, sometimes you can use a little extra help.

GraphicConverter, Lemke Software ($35 shareware; www.lemkesoft.de). Thorsten Lemke's versatile shareware program can open files in about 175 file formats. It also offers batch-processing capabilities and can handle basic image-editing chores, such as scaling and color correction.

DeBabelizer Pro, Equilibrium ($449.99; www.equilibrium.com). This program is a whole lot pricier than GraphicConverter, but it can automate some 300 image-editing commands, optimize graphics files for the best combination of quality versus image size (perfect for Web-based art), and translate files in more than 100 file formats. The company also offers the more limited $99.95 **DeBabelizer LE,** which doesn't include batch-processing or optimization features. However, at this writing, DeBabelizer LE hadn't been updated for Mac OS X.

Graphics Applications for All

If you recently bought a new Mac, you already have at least one program—iPhoto—that lets you perform many graphics tasks. If iPhoto isn't enough, then AppleWorks is a mere download away. Both AppleWorks and iPhoto include basic tools for creating and editing images and drawings. But if you want to go further, you'll need to look beyond the Apple logo.

The standard-bearer for graphics applications is Adobe Systems, the company that along with Apple started the desktop-publishing revolution 20 years ago. Long known for its professional applications Photoshop and Illustrator, Adobe has recently introduced products aimed at the consumer market. Photoshop Elements contains much of the capability of its high-end sibling, at a fraction of the cost.

But while Adobe may be the dominant player in graphics, it is by no means the only one, as Macromedia, Corel, and a slew of smaller companies can attest. Applications such as Macromedia FreeHand and Corel Painter have strong followings as well.

In this section we'll provide an overview of the main players. Let's start with the programs that tax your wallet the least—AppleWorks, iPhoto, Photoshop Elements, and a couple of oft-overlooked products—and work up to the heavy hitters.

 If you don't know which program is right for you, check for a demo version on the company's Web site. Many companies offer 15- or 30-day download-able versions of applications so that you can try before you buy. Some demo programs won't let you save or print files, while others simply stop working after a certain amount of time, so by no means use demo software for a critical project! If you like it, then you can pay for the full version.

Low-Cost Graphics Gems

Professional graphic artists traditionally ignore inexpensive applications. After all, the more expensive the program, the better it is, right? That may have been true in the past, but today products such as iPhoto and Photoshop Elements are powerful enough to accomplish many graphics tasks formerly in the purview of high-end applications. (In fact, Pamela, one of this chapter's authors, spends a great deal of time with professional software but prefers using Photoshop Elements when preparing graphics for her Web site.) If you want a quick and easy way to produce graphics for relatively simple projects, like a newsletter or a personal Web page, then one of the following applications will do the trick. Best of all, they're inexpensive—or even free.

Adobe Photoshop Elements. Adobe Photoshop is the big daddy of graphics applications, but its little brother is no slouch, either. **Photoshop Elements** ($99; www.adobe.com) is actually a pared-down version of Photoshop, so you get many of the more expensive product's features at a fraction of the price. (Indeed, some features first appeared in Photoshop Elements *before* making the leap to Photoshop!) But whereas Photoshop targets professional designers and artists who produce magazines, newspapers, books, and the like, Photoshop Elements has its sights set on photography enthusiasts. You can buy Photoshop Elements on its own, but chances are, if you bought a low-cost scanner or digital camera in the last few years, Photoshop Elements came with it. (If your scanner dates back to the 1990s, it probably came with either Adobe Photoshop LE [Light Edition] or Adobe PhotoDeluxe. Photoshop Elements has replaced both of those now-defunct products.) Photoshop Elements (on version 2 as of this writing) runs on Mac OS 9.1 or higher and Mac OS X.

Photoshop Elements includes such user-friendly features as Quick Fix (**Figure 13.1**). Use this tool to quickly correct flaws common to images imported from digital cameras, such as color, contrast, and brightness problems, as well as red-eye; and you can also use it to straighten and rotate scanned photos. The Hints palette guides you through the program, and the Recipe palette gives you step-by-step procedures for creating common effects such as deckled edges and drop shadows. As with Photoshop, you can apply special-effect filters and brushes to artwork for artistic-looking results like those found in mosaics or Impressionist paintings.

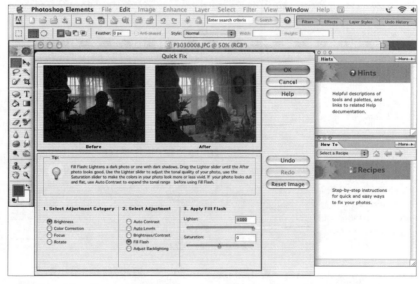

Figure 13.1

Photoshop Elements' Quick Fix feature helps you restore scenes otherwise destined for the digital trash can, such as this badly lit photo.

Photoshop Elements even has a Layers palette that makes it easier to construct image composites or collages (perfect for putting your ex-husband's head on a rat's body). Another feature lets you stitch a sequence of individual photographs into a seamless panorama. Should you feel like tackling more advanced image adjustments, you'll find geeky items such as Histograms, Levels, and Curves tucked in Photoshop Elements' menus, although unlike the similar features in Photoshop, these apply only to RGB images.

Photoshop Elements is incredibly versatile, but it does have some limitations. For example, you can't save images in CMYK format for four-color printing. You can, on the other hand, save files in the PDF format, which is the foundation of Mac OS X graphics and is a compact way to move images across networks or through email. If you take a lot of digital photos, produce graphics for the World Wide Web, or just want to experiment with image editing, you can't go wrong with Photoshop Elements.

AppleWorks. As its name suggests, **AppleWorks** (free with iMacs and iBooks, $79 otherwise; www.apple.com/appleworks), formerly ClarisWorks, is a low-cost, one-size-fits-all application that has word-processing, spreadsheet, database, and presentation components (**Figure 13.2**). But since it comes with 30 templates, 50 fonts, and 100 pieces of clip art (and access to tens of thousands more via the Internet), it also offers just about everything you need to create simple graphic and page-layout projects. AppleWorks (on version 6 as of this writing) has both draw and paint features. (See Chapter 9 for more on AppleWorks' other capabilities.)

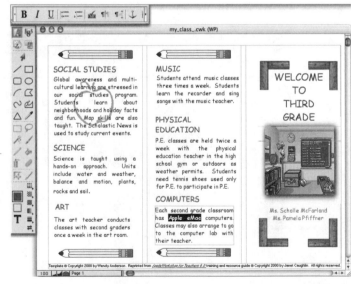

Figure 13.2

AppleWorks' all-in-one approach to graphics lets you design a page layout, write text, create drawings, and add clip art, like the pencils that serve as border elements here. It lets you use graphic touches like the grayed-out apple in the background.

With AppleWorks' paint tools you can create bitmap graphics from scratch or import images from a digital camera and apply special effects to them. In addition to the clip art that comes on the CD, nearly 25,000 more pieces of art and 150 project templates located on an Apple server are available to you over the Internet.

Because it uses QuickTime as its image translator, AppleWorks lets you work with a wide variety of image formats, including EPS for drawings, JPEG and GIF for the Web, TIFF and Photoshop for print graphics, and many more.

As might be expected from a consumer-friendly application, AppleWorks definitely errs on the side of quantity over quality, so it lacks the sophistication to produce high-quality output. If you want your kids to look smart in school or if you print only on inkjet devices, you'll be fine. High-end CMYK output? Forget about it. On the plus side, AppleWorks does run under System 8.1 and higher, although you'll have access to more cool features if you use Mac OS X.

iPhoto. This application from Apple (free with new Macs or $49 for the iLife bundle) works with your digital camera to produce the raw materials that constitute most of today's graphics—digital photographs. Plug your camera's USB or FireWire cable into the corresponding port on your Mac, and **iPhoto** automatically downloads your photos and adds them to your image library. Once you open images in iPhoto, you can rotate, crop, and scale them for inclusion in digital photo albums, Web sites, and personal printed projects such as calendars or cards (**Figure 13.3**). iPhoto is not an image editor per se, but it does let you organize your photos and perform simple adjustments, such as removing red-eye caused by flash, adjusting color and contrast, and retouching blemished areas. iPhoto is excellent for organizing images into easily accessible collections. It's clearly not as high-powered as an industrial-strength image cataloger like **Canto Cumulus** ($69.95; www.canto.com) or **Extensis Portfolio** ($199.95; www.extensis.com), and its image-editing capabilities aren't as robust as those of Photoshop Elements, but it's so easy to use that photographers of all levels use it regularly to bring their digital images into the Mac. If you don't have iPhoto, you can purchase the entire iLife package, which includes iPhoto, iMovie, iTunes, iDVD, and GarageBand, on CDs or DVDs for $49 from the Apple Web site.

Figure 13.3

Once you select a photo and click the Edit button, iPhoto's tools are at your service. Here we've clicked and dragged to select the part of the image we want to keep. When we click the Crop button in the lower left of the window, the grayed-out parts of the image will be discarded.

Graphics Programs for Older Macs

Graphics applications and the files they produce eat RAM and fast processors for breakfast. But if you can't let go of your old Mac IIci and System 7, don't despair. The following two applications run on older operating systems with minimal RAM and slower processors:

- **Color It**—This inexpensive image editor from MicroFrontier ($49.95; www.microfrontier.com) requires as little as 3 MB of RAM to operate, so it can run on 68020-processor Macs under System 7. **Color It** is not yet available for Mac OS X, however. Like more powerful programs, it has the ability to use third-party plug-ins, create CMYK print separations, and open files in the Photoshop format. (The program can save files in Photoshop 2.5 and lower.) Color It offers many of the tools you need to doctor imported images, such as the Magic Wand, Airbrush, and Clone Stamp, while the usual arsenal of color-correction features helps you spruce up photos. You can create graphics with 24 different brush shapes and fill them with linear or radial gradients. Color It also produces complex graphics, including those containing clipping paths (a *clipping path* is a special layer that contains the outline of the subject) for print layouts and image maps for Web pages.

- **PhotoFix**—You can also skirt high RAM requirements with Microspot's **PhotoFix** ($53.10; www.microspot.com), which needs just 5 MB of RAM. PhotoFix sports features comparable to those of other low-end image editors, including tools for adjusting color, contrast, and brightness (but no support for CMYK printing). Two features distinguish PhotoFix. First, its Quit Special option closes out your current file and loads the most recent image. That option, coupled with an Automatic Save function, gives you more insurance during system crashes and protection from making regrettable image edits. The second feature worth noting is PhotoFix's ability to import your digital camera's EXIF data, which includes such helpful information as camera type, ISO, and lens focal length. This feature has only recently been added to Photoshop, so PhotoFix certainly holds its own here. By the way, PhotoFix comes in a Mac OS X version, too.

If you're serious about graphics, though, get a faster Mac and Mac OS X.

Programs for the Pros

These big guns have the most features, power, and capabilities—at a correspondingly high price. The applications covered here—Photoshop, Illustrator, Painter, Canvas, and FreeHand—each cost hundreds of dollars. Further complicating matters is a movement toward selling these programs as parts of larger suites of tools, which means your final tally could be $1,000 or more. We'll talk more about the suites in "Suite mania," later in this chapter.

Professional illustration applications

As we said earlier, graphics applications are either drawing (vector) programs or painting (bitmap, or raster) programs—and some applications combine aspects of both. The foundation of vector programs is the *Bézier curve,* which describes curves and arcs according to a mathematical formula. The principal tool is a pen, with which you draw line segments and define angles and end points along the way. To the uninitiated, working with a Bézier-based program can be unnerving. Lines seem to appear out of nowhere, and curves have minds of their own. But once mastered, the Pen-tool-and-Bézier-curve combination is a flexible and powerful way to create complex, precision graphics.

The three programs most used by illustration professionals are Illustrator, Canvas, and FreeHand. Illustrator and FreeHand are the leaders of this group, but Canvas has its fans, too. These drawing programs all have many of the same features, such as the ability to create, read, and save files in many formats, and to print in the four process ink colors necessary for professional output on a printing press. Yet although their forte is creating smooth vector drawings, the line between these applications and their bitmap brethren is thin indeed. To varying degrees, the illustration programs described here also let you work with raster files and make graphics for the Internet.

Adobe Illustrator. Apple's MacDraw may have been the first drawing program for the Macintosh, but **Adobe Illustrator** ($499; www.adobe.com) is the one that put Mac graphics on the map. It harnessed the power of Adobe's PostScript language to create smooth, crisp lines that could be scaled to any size while retaining their integrity. The latest version, Illustrator CS, is really the 11th major edition of the product—the CS suffix comes from "Creative Suite" (see "Suite mania," later in this chapter, for more)—so its feature set is mature and stable. As a result, Adobe has been bolstering it with features normally found in other applications.

For example, Illustrator lifts some tools from Photoshop, such as the Magic Wand tool for selecting similar colors and the Liquify brush for distorting graphics into fun-house-mirror shapes. Illustrator also shares with Photoshop an ability to create transparent drawings and text, giving you endless possibilities for sophisticated translucent graphics. You can apply various Photoshop-like styles and effects to Illustrator artwork. And because the two programs are designed to work well together, Photoshop bitmaps can even be imported into Illustrator for use as drawing templates, and more.

Illustrator also borrows some of Photoshop's Web capabilities—such as saving illustrations in the ubiquitous bitmapped Web graphic formats GIF and JPEG— but it adds support for the vector standard SVG (Scalable Vector Graphics) and Macromedia's Flash (SWF) format, often used for Web-based animation. Among other Web-based features is the ability to create buttons for a Web site with live drop shadows and shapes; you can create text for the shadow or shape, and the text grows or shrinks in size depending on its content.

Illustrator not only includes many of the paint features found in Photoshop, but it also incorporates the text-handling capabilities of Adobe's page-layout program, InDesign CS. Illustrator has long been used as an ersatz page-layout program for single-page ads and posters that combine text and graphics. (To this day, the program can't create multipage documents, but FreeHand can.) Until the release of InDesign 2.0, Illustrator also provided the best method for adding charts and tables to layouts. With Illustrator CS, however, Adobe has beefed up the application's text-handling capabilities even more. For example, you can now create, save, and apply character and paragraph styles to text just as you would in a page-layout program (**Figure 13.4**). And like InDesign, Illustrator also supports the OpenType font format, a type technology that includes thousands of special characters (see Chapter 16 for more on font formats). Make no bones about it, though: Illustrator is not set up for creating long, multipage documents. That remains the purview of programs like InDesign and QuarkXPress.

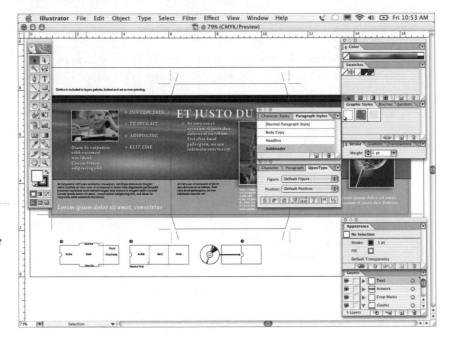

Figure 13.4

The text-handling tools in Illustrator CS—which include style sheets and OpenType support—are now on a par with those in page-layout programs.

Despite the addition of paint and page-layout features, Illustrator is still undeniably, irrefutably a drawing program. Version 10 of the program added features like Envelope Distortion, which allows you to enclose Illustrator drawings or type in an invisible container that can be warped or distorted as a unit while its content remains independently editable. Illustrator CS upped the ante with new drawing features like the Scribble Effect, a means of giving lines a carefree, hand-drawn look. This latest version of Illustrator—which is for Mac OS X 10.2 and higher only—also incorporates another dimension: the ability to make true three-dimensional graphics and to wrap each surface with a texture or image (**Figure 13.5**). But as always, no matter how many other features are piled on, the heart of Illustrator is its ability to create crisp, smooth drawings that effortlessly make the leap from postage stamp to billboard without skipping a Bézier.

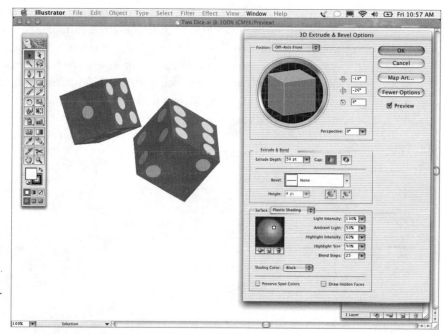

Figure 13.5

One of the newer features in Illustrator CS is the ability to create 3D objects.

The First Professional Graphics Application

John Warnock, cofounder of Adobe Systems, developed Illustrator as a paean to his wife, a graphic artist. When the product shipped in 1987, Adobe included a videotaped tour in the package—much as Apple had included a cassette tape tour in the first Macintosh box. In the video, Warnock himself demonstrated how to use Illustrator. He was the only person who could show how to use the Pen tool.

Illustrator made shockwaves in the art and design community, but the reaction initially wasn't positive. Many designers and illustrators refused to believe that software made by engineers and a "toy" computer called the Macintosh could possibly create anything that compared to traditional pens, ink, and French curves. That perception soon changed. Today Illustrator is used worldwide to create advertising, posters, magazine covers, and, yes, even art.

ACD Systems' Canvas. Canvas (www.acdsystems.com) has always prided itself on its ability to do anything: drawing, painting, page layout, Web design—you name it. The program's original developer, Deneba, even marketed Canvas as the most versatile of graphics programs, and for a long time, that's how the program distinguished itself. But just as you wouldn't want to assemble a bicycle with a Swiss army knife even though it has a screwdriver, many illustrators in the creative field viewed Canvas's additional features as distracting. Subsequently Deneba (and now ACD Systems) repositioned Canvas to meet the needs of its core audience—technical illustrators. To that end Canvas now comes in three editions: **Canvas 9 Professional Edition** ($349.95);

Canvas 9 GIS Mapping Edition ($599.95); and **Canvas 9 Scientific Imaging Edition** ($599.95). Unless you're a cartographer or an engineer, you'll want the Professional Edition (for Mac OS X 10.2 or higher only). Canvas 9 Professional Edition picks up where previous versions of Canvas left off, but it adds features specific to technical illustration (**Figure 13.6**). For example, you can create documents up to 2000 miles square, zoom in increments of 0.0001 percent, and define up to 2 billion control points per polygon or Bézier curve. That's overkill for most users, but such precision is critical for scientific drawing.

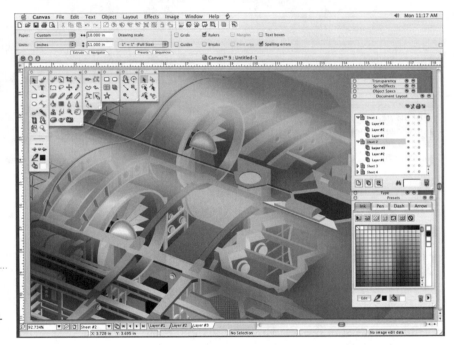

Figure 13.6

Canvas has long been known for its precision—a sure-fire draw for technical illustrators.

But even with its new slant on technical illustration, Canvas still has plenty of features for graphic designers. It now supports more color-rich 16-bit graphics files. ACD Systems has added time-savers like one-step cropping and scaling, which reduces mouse trips to the menu bar. SmartLines and Smooth Polygons help less-skilled users create good-looking drawings with less frustration. You can create multiple-page documents in Canvas, and a new tabbed interface at the bottom of the document window lets you navigate through not only pages but layers as well. The list of file types supported reads like a veritable encyclopedia of formats.

Because it is laden with features, Canvas has borne the criticism of buckling under the weight of too many palettes and options. As a remedy, the program now sports both a Smart Toolbox and a Properties Bar to help increase your efficiency. In other graphics applications, accessing hidden tools means first selecting the current tool, then clicking a tiny triangle to expose the other tools.

Canvas's Smart Toolbox instantly reveals related tools when you click the current tool so that you can quickly see what options are available. The Properties Bar gives you immediate feedback about active objects and tools. This feature is similar to the Control palette or Options bar found in other applications, but Canvas's implementation has one benefit: clicking the pasteboard shows the document's global properties, such as paper size and units of measurement.

Is Canvas right for you? Its all-in-one approach may be just the ticket if you want many of the bells and whistles found in separate products but don't see the need for all the dedicated programs. If you produce professional graphics for output, though, check with your printer to make sure it accepts Canvas-generated files.

Macromedia FreeHand. For years, FreeHand has competed neck-and-neck with Illustrator, but recently the two have diverged in terms of target audience. Macromedia (which acquired the program from its developer, Altsys, which had regained it from its original distributor, Aldus) increasingly positions **FreeHand** ($399; www.macromedia.com) as an adjunct to its Web development tools Dreamweaver and Flash. However, that bit of marketing spin doesn't mean that FreeHand shouldn't be used for making print illustrations (**Figure 13.7**). Indeed, FreeHand has a loyal following among print illustrators, and devout users proclaim FreeHand's superiority over its rival.

Figure 13.7

FreeHand MX has a full complement of tools for creating illustrations that can be used in print, but its close integration with Flash also makes it a good choice for designing Web pages.

In fact, FreeHand and Illustrator are evenly matched. As in any good contest between equal adversaries, each leapfrogs the other only to watch it catch up during the next revision cycle. Even the product names are testament to the intense competition. After FreeHand 10, Macromedia changed its naming strategy from numbers to the moniker FreeHand MX. This year Adobe skipped from Illustrator 10 to Illustrator CS (see the sidebar "What's in a Name?" later in the chapter for more on this silliness).

FreeHand's most immediate advantage over Illustrator has always been its wider range of text-handling tools—style sheets, paragraph controls, and so on—although the new type controls in Illustrator CS dull that edge. But where FreeHand still reigns supreme is in its ability to create multiple-page documents. You create additional pages in your document in much the same fashion as you would in a page-layout program; you can even make master pages to streamline not only print layouts but also Flash-animation backgrounds.

Although both programs allow you to create graphics for the Web, FreeHand has the lead here. It's more tightly integrated with Macromedia's market-leading Web development tools Dreamweaver and Flash (Adobe's concession to export Flash SWF files from Illustrator notwithstanding). When you're working in FreeHand, you can launch Flash or Fireworks to edit drawings destined for the Web, or you can create print layouts in FreeHand for your Flash animations. If you create a lot of graphics for the Web, this seamless back and forth will prove invaluable.

In other respects, you'll find more similarities than differences between these two powerful applications. Both now have live effects that let you endlessly apply changes to a graphic without altering its underlying shape, so trying different effects is easy. Both have live previews for fast onscreen feedback of object edits. Both let you apply multiple attributes to a single object by nesting operations, so you can make highly sophisticated drawings in a more streamlined fashion. And the list goes on.

So what's the bottom line? It's a matter of preference. Entrenched users of FreeHand will continue to work with it. If you're just looking to get into professional illustration, then consider what types of images you want to produce. If you lean toward Web design, FreeHand is the way to go. If print is your cup of tea, FreeHand can certainly do the job, but you'll want to factor in your choice of page-layout and image-editing software as well. If you use Adobe InDesign and Photoshop, you'll probably lean toward Illustrator. If you use QuarkXPress, then it's pretty much a toss-up between FreeHand and Illustrator.

The Oldest Mac OS X Graphics App

Straddling the line between low and high end is a graphics application that came to the Mac from Mac OS X's roots in the NextStep operating system (see Chapter 2). Stone Design's **Create** ($149; www.stone.com) is similar to AppleWorks but puts more emphasis on graphic design. It offers drawing, page-layout, and Web-page authoring features all in one package. One of Create's special touches is its ability to animate transformations. For example, you can quickly create a spinning graphic for your Web page. On the page-layout front, you'll also find document-level layers, which act as master pages and let you add graphics and type to several pages at once.

Depending on what features you need, Create (now in version 11.2) could be an inexpensive answer to your graphic-design needs. Download a 30-day demonstration version to try it out.

Professional image-editing applications

If the truth be told, there is only one professional image-editing application: Photoshop. It is so popular and so entrenched that its name is often used as a verb (much to the dismay of Adobe's legal eagles and trademark police). It's even appeared on *Friends* and in *Saturday Night Live* skits. Over the years contenders have tried to wrest the crown from Photoshop's head, only to fall on their swords. In our humble opinion the only real alternative to Photoshop as an image editor is one of the lower-cost applications (like Photoshop Elements) discussed in "Low-Cost Graphics Gems," earlier in this chapter.

But if your interest lies not just in fixing photos but also in creating original graphics, then you'll want to take a look at Corel Painter, a truly marvelous program that inspires the artist in all of us.

Adobe Photoshop. **Adobe Photoshop** ($649; www.adobe.com) is many things to many people. To the graphic artist it's a paint program. To the photographer it's a photo-retouching program. To the print-shop owner it's a prepress program. To the film producer it's a special-effects generator. To the Web designer it's a Web graphics program. The amazing thing is that Photoshop is big and full-featured enough to embrace all these different users. Recent advances in Photoshop—what would have been version 8 but is now called Photoshop CS—have mainly addressed the interests of photographers. Given the stampede toward digital cameras, that's hardly surprising. But don't forget that at its core, Photoshop is a raster-based paint tool (with a few vector drawing tools thrown in).

Among the recent photo-savvy features appearing in Photoshop is the ability to import digital camera files in their native format, dubbed Raw. This means that Photoshop will honor the image's color and detail as captured by the camera itself without meddling during the importation process. The image's EXIF data—information about camera type, ISO, and so on—translates intact as well. For professional photographers, these details are critical. Adobe has also added features to Photoshop to assist in browsing, organizing, and giving keywords to images, which is a boon to anyone who would rather sort images visually than decipher the arcane naming conventions of most digital cameras.

Once you've brought your image, scanned or from a digital camera, into Photoshop, the fun begins. You can choose to make your image look as realistic as possible through a deep array of color-adjustment controls, or you can opt to make it look as unrealistic as possible using a wide variety of filters and special effects.

To accomplish the former, Adobe has added new tools to its arsenal of Curves, Levels, Histograms, Channels, and other color-correction controls. The new Color Match feature lets you adjust the color in an image simply by sampling a color you like from another image and then applying it to the first image. Shadows/Highlights controls perform similar magic on under- or overexposed photos (**Figure 13.8**).

Figure 13.8

Photoshop lets you automatically compensate for over- and underexposed images with new Shadows/Highlights controls.

If making an artistic statement is your preference, then you can access dozens of special effects—for example, to turn an ordinary photo into a pointillist masterpiece. You can also combine several images by selecting pieces of one and grafting them onto another using Photoshop's layer and masking tools. A recent addition with Photoshop CS is the concept of Layer Comps, which lets you experiment with layer combinations, allowing you to try out variations without making each layer visible one at a time.

Photoshop also works hand in glove with Illustrator. You can easily import Illustrator files into Photoshop, ending up with an interesting hybrid of vector and raster graphics in one file. Photoshop has borrowed a few features from its vector cousin as well, including a Pen tool for making pinpoint selections and, more recently, the ability to place text on curved path.

For a few releases now, Adobe has bundled ImageReady along with Photoshop. ImageReady lets you prepare Photoshop graphics for the Web—making JavaScript buttons and animated GIFs, for example. In addition to saving files as JPEGs or GIFs with transparency, Photoshop can now export files in the Flash (SWF) format.

We could go on and on about Photoshop—indeed, thousands of Photoshop books have done just that (a search for Photoshop within the Books category on Amazon.com yielded 2227 results). Suffice it to say that Photoshop provides all the things you need to retouch and enhance photos, giving you the equivalent of a darkroom on your Mac. If you work with images on a daily basis, you need Photoshop.

Corel Painter. Not an image-editing application per se, **Corel Painter** ($299; www.corel.com) is often described as a natural-media paint program (**Figure 13.9**). What does that mean exactly? Painter sports a mind-blowing variety of brushes that simulate media used by traditional artists—oils, pastels, charcoals, watercolors, crayons, and more. Each of these can be adjusted according to variables such as pressure, angle, paint amount, and paper texture, giving you literally thousands of permutations. The result can be simply stunning, especially when used in conjunction with an input device, such as a pressure-sensitive tablet, that mimics the artist's natural drawing motion.

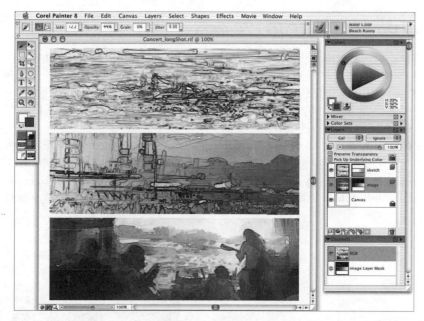

Figure 13.9

Like a traditional artist's palette and equipment, the tools in Corel Painter simulate real-life brushes, papers, and effects.

Because Painter uses the metaphors and methods of traditional art, it can be a little intimidating. That's especially true if you're the kind of person who likes to feel perfectly in control. If, on the other hand, you can let your hair down and go with the flow, you'll find Painter a delight. That doesn't mean Painter is an undisciplined rogue of an application; we merely suggest that you jump in and start experimenting. Don't know what a Smeary Bristle Spray brush will look like on Corrugated Paper with a Grainy Blender variant? Go on and give it a try.

Corel Painter 8—the current, Mac OS X–native version as of this writing—shows considerable improvement over earlier releases, particularly in the area of interface design. The program's palettes and menus have been cleaned up, making it easier to work with the more than 400 new brushes added in this release alone. If the present brush options aren't enough, you can also design your own brush by modifying its stroke or combining several brushes into one. As in traditional painting, you can use the Mixer palette to blend colors interactively so that you can see immediately if adding a little more red, for example, will yield the color you want.

This amazing program (which for years was packaged in a real paint can) is often considered an adjunct to, not a replacement for, Photoshop. And for good reason: the two applications work extremely well together. Painter not only opens Photoshop files with all their layers intact, but it also saves files in the Photoshop format with all their layers intact. Additionally, Painter accepts Photoshop-compatible plug-ins (see the sidebar "Soup Up Your Graphics Program"). Many artists start with an image in Photoshop, bring it into Painter to apply creative flair, and then send it back out to Photoshop for production. Together they're a one-two graphics punch.

Soup Up Your Graphics Program

The big graphics applications offer an amazing array of features, but you don't have to stop there. Add-on programs, usually called *plug-ins* or *filters,* allow you to add new features or enhance existing ones. You can find a wide assortment of plug-ins for Photoshop, Photoshop Elements, Illustrator, and FreeHand at the PowerXChange Web site (www.powerxchange.com). Here's a sampling of Photoshop plug-ins available for Mac OS X:

- **Eye Candy 4000,** Alien Skin Software ($169; www.alienskin.com). This program contains 23 filters that help you create such effects as shadows, glows, fire, smoke, and chrome.

- **Image Doctor,** Alien Skin Software ($129). These image-correction filters help you remove unwanted details and blemishes, as well as repair other image ills (**Figure 13.10**).

continues on next page

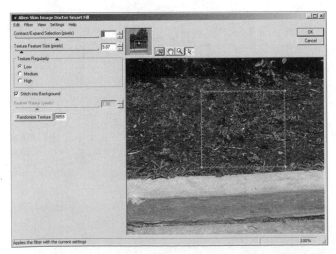

Figure 13.10

Alien Skin makes a number of plug-ins that extend the functionality of Photoshop, such as Image Doctor, which fixes image flaws.

Soup Up Your Graphics Program   continued

- **Mask Pro,** Extensis ($199.95; www.extensis.com). This Photoshop plug-in makes it easier to create a mask, or object you use to conceal parts of artwork.

- **PhotoFrame,** Extensis ($199.95). Frame your image with one of 2000 included frames or create a custom one.

- **PhotoTools,** Extensis ($149.95). This plug-in adds special effects, such as shadows, seamless textures, and custom bevels.

- **RedEyePro,** Andromeda Software ($39; www.andromeda.com). This one-trick pony lets you banish red-eye from your Photoshop images.

- **Splat!,** Alien Skin Software ($99). Create frames, special edges, borders, mosaics, and more with this plug-in.

- **VariFocus Filter,** Andromeda Software ($47). This plug-in lets you bring objects in and out of focus to create special effects.

- **Xenofex 2,** Alien Skin Software ($129). The 14 special effects in this plug-in let you change your images into jigsaw puzzles or mosaics, or create lightning, clouds, and distortions.

Suite mania

While the professional products we've described thus far are all sold as individual applications, the trend recently has been to sell programs as part of an integrated suite. Unlike a collection in which individual products are sold together in the same package, a suite signifies that the applications are designed to work together, making it easy to create a file that moves between various applications. Generally, all the applications install from a single disc or set of discs that share the same serial and registration numbers. Sound familiar? Yes, this is a lot like what Microsoft does with its Office applications.

What accounts for this trend? One factor is that companies think they can add more value to existing products by integrating them with sibling software. This creates a codependency—if you have one, you need the other. Second, as applications mature (and remember that Illustrator has been around for 16 years), it's more difficult to add new and innovative features to them. As a result, customers stop buying every upgrade, which eats into the corporate bottom line. But bundling a top-selling program like Photoshop with a newer entrant like InDesign boosts sales of the former while piquing interest in the latter.

Adobe Creative Suite. Released in late 2003, the Adobe Creative Suite (www.adobe.com) brings together Adobe's top creative applications under one umbrella. The suite is available in two flavors: **Adobe CS Standard** ($999) contains Photoshop CS; Illustrator CS; InDesign CS, Adobe's second-generation page-layout application; and Version Cue. **Adobe CS Premium** ($1,299) includes those four programs as well as the Web-page design application GoLive CS and the high-end PDF program Acrobat Professional.

For years Adobe products have been migrating toward a consistent user interface with the same technological underpinnings. In other words, tools, palettes, graphics, and text behave the same across applications. The Creative Suite underscores the strategy that once you learn one Adobe application, you feel at home in any Adobe application.

A few features act as the linchpins of CS interactivity: Version Cue, a means of tracking and updating files as they move between programs (**Figure 13.11**); and PDF, the file format that has become the lingua franca of Adobe applications, and indeed of some third-party software as well.

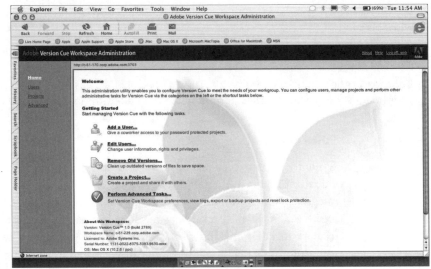

Figure 13.11

The glue that holds the Adobe Creative Suite together is Version Cue, a file-management system that tracks files across applications.

It's too early to tell if Adobe Creative Suite will take off. Some long-standing Adobe users have balked at the price of the suite and instead are opting to buy the products as individual applications, as they have done in the past.

Macromedia Studio. **Macromedia Studio MX 2004** ($899; www.macromedia.com) is geared toward Web designers. It includes the Internet tools Dreamweaver MX 2004, Fireworks MX 2004, Flash MX 2004, FreeHand MX, and ColdFusion MX 6.1 Developer Edition. A second version, **Studio MX 2004 with Flash Professional** ($999), which includes—surprise!—the more advanced Flash MX Professional 2004, is also available. Each application is so rich and deep that we can't go into them all. If Web design is your main interest, then you'll want to page over to Chapter 16 to read about them. One thing is clear: Macromedia is as dominant in Web applications as Adobe is in graphics (**Figure 13.12**).

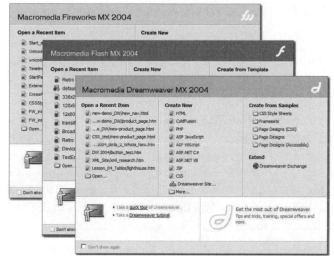

Figure 13.12

*Macromedia Studio
MX 2004 integrates
Macromedia's Web
applications with
FreeHand MX.*

In Studio MX 2004, Macromedia deepens the connection between its applications by allowing you to drag and drop Flash elements into your Web page and then edit them right within Dreamweaver. You can also use round-trip functionality to manage graphics between Dreamweaver and Fireworks.

Interestingly, even though the other applications in the suite have been updated for MX 2004, FreeHand MX was not. Macromedia says it's because FreeHand is on a different development cycle.

What's in a Name?

It used to be so easy, the predictable progression of version numbers from one software update to another. We understood the numbers game: if a program went up a whole number, big changes were afoot. A ".5" release meant marginal changes. Now with the advent of suites, companies are playing with naming conventions to convey a new attitude. Many applications have dropped numbers altogether and turned to letters instead. Perhaps it's to undercut our very reliance on numbers as a measure of whether or not to purchase an upgrade. Perhaps a clever marketing person conducted a focus group. Whatever the reason, Adobe's products now bear the CS moniker to show that they're part of the new Creative Suite. Macromedia's products picked up the nonsensical MX tag last year (Macromedia even admits on its Web site that "MX" does not stand for anything). For its next version, "2004" was added ("MXX" and "MZ" apparently didn't make the cut). Ironically, many people still refer to the alphabetized versions by their would-be numerical name, so Photoshop CS is Photoshop 8.

Software by any other name would smell as suite.

The Page-Layout Alternative

We mentioned earlier that applications increasingly borrow features and technologies from each other: Illustrator has InDesign's type controls, Photoshop has Illustrator's drawing tools. For the past few years, page-layout tools have gained drawing tools, too.

Both Quark's **QuarkXPress 6** ($1,045; www.quark.com) and Adobe's **InDesign CS** ($699; www.adobe.com) include tools for drawing graphic shapes like ellipses, starbursts, and rhomboids. The Pen tools in both applications let you draw free-form shapes much as you do in a Bézier drawing program. You can also make text follow the shape of a path, as you do in dedicated graphics applications. You can apply gradient fills to objects, modify stroke widths, and more.

Thanks to its close kinship with Illustrator and Photoshop, InDesign goes even further, providing drop shadows, feathered edges, transparent effects, and other graphics goodies (**Figure 13.13**). Its toolbox contains a pencil, an eyedropper, and various ways to transform the shapes and sizes of graphics.

Figure 13.13

The decorative lines and boxes in this page layout were created right in InDesign CS. Even with so many graphics features available in page-layout programs, there are still good reasons to purchase a stand-alone graphics program.

Given that both QuarkXPress and InDesign seem to be morphing into graphics applications, the question arises: If you compose pages, is dedicated graphics software really necessary? The answer depends on the kind of work you do. If you mostly flow text and graphics that other people give you, or if your graphics consist of relatively straightforward items—basic boxes, simple schematics, and so on—then probably not. But some things are just better done in a dedicated application, like creating detailed drawings and refining large color images. Dedicated graphics programs let you adjust nuanced graphics.

There's one more reason to use a dedicated graphics program: When you draw a complicated graphic in a page layout, it becomes part of the page itself;

it's not a separate file you can edit and then place in another page or file. If your layout application should crash (heaven forbid!), you may lose the graphic along with everything else. Moreover, a separate file such as a logo can be used in multiple documents and updated across applications accordingly. Keeping valuable graphics separate seems like a good practice to us.

Stock Graphics to the Rescue

Of course you need the right graphics software, but once you have it, where are you going to get the graphics? In the old days of traditional typesetting, artists used to buy books filled with artwork, better known as *clip art,* that they could copy or alter to suit their purposes. If you needed a picture of a tomato for your farmers' market ad, for example, you'd look in the book for vegetables. You didn't have to go pick the perfect one and draw or photograph it yourself.

Stock graphics—both photographs and artwork—can still serve as useful shortcuts. Whether we're looking for something for work or for home, many of us don't have the time, money, or talent to draw every bit of artwork we need. And when it comes to photography, there are a lot of things you just *can't* shoot yourself: Earth from space, the rings of Saturn, or (depending on your budget) the Great Wall of China.

Graphics in a jiffy

Today we don't turn to books; instead we go to the Web. Almost anything you can imagine is instantly available online. Better yet, when you go to one of the stock image sites, you can search vast databases using keywords. Type in specific terms, such as "dinner party," or even an abstract concept, such as "fun." The site displays small versions *(thumbnails)* of any images that match. If you like what you find, you can register with the site and save selections to look at later. Most online photo and clip-art providers let you download free, low-quality versions of images *(comps)* to try out in your designs.

Once you find the images you want, you can usually buy them at the resolution you need right from the provider's Web site. (The higher the resolution, the more expensive the image. For more on what resolution you need, see the sidebar "The Right Resolution for the Job," below.) However, stock images are also available in themed CD compilations. For example, at the Getty Images Web site (www.gettyimages.com) you can buy individual photos of schnauzers, Hungarian vizslas, and guinea pigs off the Photodisc Animal Attraction CD. Prices range from $55 to $350 a pop, depending on what resolution you need. But if you *regularly* need pictures of animals, it's probably less expensive to buy the whole CD with 120 photos for $400. (For a list of stock image companies, see **Table 13.2,** below.)

Table 13.2 Where the Graphics Are: An Online Sampler

Company	Web Address
Artbeats	www.artbeats.com
Corbis	www.corbis.com
EyeWire	www.eyewire.com
Getty Images	www.gettyimages.com
Havana Street	www.havanastreet.com
Veer	www.veer.com

 If you're interested in images just for your Web site, yard sale flyer, or holiday cards, don't be intimidated by those prices. Many sites have "personal use" collections for nonpros where you can pick up low-resolution photos that cost less than $10 each. Also, if you need more images, a bargain clip-art collection may fit the bill. We'll get to those in "Clip-art collections," below.

Royalty-free vs. rights-managed

When you buy stock imagery, you're paying not only for the image, but also for a license that gives you the right to use it—much like buying software. Depending on how you plan to use it, you'll buy stock imagery that's either *royalty-free* or *rights-managed*.

What does that mean? Simply put, 99 percent of the time most folks need royalty-free images. These are purchased for a flat price. You can use them in almost any sort of project for an unlimited amount of time. You can include them in personal projects or in something you create for a client. Royalty-free doesn't mean rule-free, however. Typically, you can't resell the image *itself*, for example on a poster or T-shirt. Instead, it should be integrated with other images and remade into your own creation. Also, you can't share the media on more than a certain number of computers. (The stock imagery company's license will tell you how many.)

Rights-managed images are more expensive *and* more restricted. This is the province of pros who need photos taken by famous photographers. Prices depend on a number of variables, including how you want to use the image, the length of time you'll need it, and whether royalty payments will go to the photographer, model, or anyone else.

Picking the right pictures

When you're browsing for images, keep a few things in mind:

Get the right format. If you're going to use the material for a printed document, choose vector EPS for drawings and TIFF for photos. JPEG will suffice for the latter, but the loss of quality may be noticeable in some collections. For Web art, GIF and JPEG do the trick.

Look for layers and clipping paths. One thing stock imagery suffers from is a lack of originality. However, some sources give you a head start toward customization. Many photographs show people and objects against white backgrounds and include a clipping path that contains an outline of the subject in the photo. This makes it easy to place the image against the background of your choice. For instance, a collie could quickly conquer Mount Everest or perch atop the Eiffel Tower.

Value the vectors. Similarly, if you need illustrations instead of photos, look for vector artwork. You'll be able to go to town on these in your draw program, changing and rearranging lines to suit your fancy.

Don't forget freebies. Before you drop your hard-earned cash, make sure to look at the images you already have. Many programs, including AppleWorks, Photoshop, and Office, come with free images. There might be one in there that does the trick.

 Once upon a time, there used to be many small companies that created stock imagery. Now two big guys—Getty Images and Corbis—dominate the field. Make sure to dig down in their Web sites to find the goodies. One of our favorite collections is Art Parts, available through EyeWire (part of Getty Images). Check it out at www.eyewire.com/products/clipart/artparts/index.htm.

Clip-art collections

Some companies offer bargain collections of images that may fit your needs. Quality varies a lot, so make sure to look through samples on the company Web site or on the box at the store. Here are two worth checking out:

Hemera's **The Big Box of Art 800,000 for Macintosh** ($129.99; www.hemera.com) includes 800,000 images on eight DVDs. Best of all, the images come in several varieties and include vector illustrations and photo objects with clipping paths. You can also purchase a smaller collection with 215,000 images for $69.99.

Nova Development's **Art Explosion 750,000** ($199.95; www.novadevelopment .com) packs 750,000 images in 48 CDs and a two-volume image catalog that spans 1,800 pages. This package offers a reasonable mixture of illustrations in a handful of formats—vector art, TIFF, JPEG, Web graphics, animations, fonts, and more.

The Right Resolution for the Job

If your image isn't saved in the right resolution, it doesn't matter how much you tweak it—it's not going to look good. So what *is* the right resolution? The answer depends on where you're using the image and how much editing you need to do.

For one thing, it's usually better to scan at a higher resolution than you'll eventually need. This gives you wiggle room by allowing for pixels lost during editing. It also lets you enlarge the image without making it grainy. Don't go crazy, though. The higher the resolution, the bigger your files will be.

To make life easier, here are some basic guidelines for your *completed* graphics in pixels per inch (ppi). Take them with a grain of salt:

- Web or onscreen graphics: 72 ppi.
- Graphics printed on a desktop printer: 150–300 ppi, depending on the printer's maximum resolution.
- Digital photographs sent to a photo service: most recommend sending the maximum resolution your camera supports—check your service's site for details.
- Graphics printed professionally: whatever your printer recommends, or 300 ppi.

Tips and Techniques

Now that you've got the basics, it's time to dive in! Here are some tips and tricks for using graphics applications. We've focused on the programs you might already have—AppleWorks and iPhoto—because they ship free with many Macs. But to whet your appetite, we've also included tips for Photoshop, the professional standard for image editing.

Get Creative with AppleWorks

Before you open your wallet, take a look in your Applications folder. You might already have the software you need to whip up some flyers, create covers for your CD and DVD projects, or express your inner Picasso. AppleWorks comes free with the iMac and iBook. If you don't have it, it's inexpensive enough that even if you never exploit all its capabilities, you might find it handy to have around.

AppleWorks is at version 6.2.9 at this writing. Download the free updater from www.apple.com/appleworks/update if you have version 6.

In this section we cover some handy ways to get the most out of AppleWorks' graphics capabilities. You'll find it easy to apply many of these methods to other graphics-related programs that work in essentially the same way.

Free Web Extras

AppleWorks includes many clip-art images and ready-made designs (templates) on the CD. But don't miss all the other stuff available from the Apple Web site! You can access it from within AppleWorks if you have an active Internet connection.

To get your hands on more clip art, select File > Show Clippings (or press ⌘2). Make sure you have an active Internet connection, and select the Search Web Content option located below the Search field. Now you can pore through Apple's large *free* collection of clip art for whatever you need. These aren't the most sophisticated drawings, but they may suit your purposes.

To find loads of useful resources for teachers, open the Starting Points palette by selecting File > Show Starting Points. Next, click the Web tab at the bottom of the palette and click the Templates button. One link takes you to school-related templates, such as a Great Job Postcard, Stickers for Kids, and a Class Newsletter layout. Another includes templates from the Apple Learning Interchange organized by subject, such as Social Studies and Math (available directly from http://ali.apple.com/ali_appleworks/templates.shtml).

Off to a good start

You've launched the program. Now what do you do? First things first: let's get a handle on how to do basic tasks.

The modes. AppleWorks splits up its many functions by making you choose a document type when you start. The program's default document type is word processing, so don't press ⌘N (for new document) if you want to make an illustration; instead use the Starting Points palette.

Select Painting if you want to work on a photograph or illustration. The painting environment gives you some extra tools. Among these are the Magic Wand for selecting complex shapes, plus a Paintbrush, Paint Bucket, Spray Can, and Pencil. Select Drawing if you want to create a drawing *or* integrate different document types—such as paintings and spreadsheets—into a design.

 Lost your bearings? AppleWorks puts a two-letter cue in the window title bar to help you remember what kind of document you're in (DR for drawing, PT for painting, WP for word processing, SS for spreadsheet, DB for database, and PR for presentation).

Frame your content. If you've made a drawing document, bring in other content by creating the appropriate *frame* for it. For example, add text by clicking the Text tool at the top of the Tool palette. (If you don't see that palette, go to Window > Show Tools.) You draw a box of the appropriate size using the Text tool and then type your text in that box. Similarly, create a painting frame by clicking the Paint tool in the Tool palette.

Make a duplicate. You've made the perfect circle, but you wish you had two. Don't try to make another from scratch—create a duplicate. Select the item you want to duplicate, hold down ⟨Option⟩ and then drag the item. Voilà! Two copies.

Fast Eyedropper access. The Eyedropper tool lets you copy the attributes of a selected item, such as its color or—if it's a drawing—even its outlines and fills. Access the Eyedropper by pressing ⟨Tab⟩, regardless of which tool you are using. Press ⟨Tab⟩ again to switch back to the tool you were using before.

Polygon shortcuts. Use the Polygon tool to create multisided shapes. When you hold down ⟨Shift⟩, you can constrain (or hold) a shape to exact 45-degree angles. Just click your starting point and then double-click to end the shape.

Keep it straight. To paint or draw a straight line, hold down ⟨Shift⟩ while drawing the line.

Get to work

Here are some tips that can help you be more efficient when using AppleWorks' drawing and painting tools.

Perfect your shapes. This is a standard feature available in most drawing programs that helps ensure precision. Just hold down ⟨Shift⟩ when you draw an object to constrain it to exact angles, squares, or circles. For example, a rough oval becomes a perfect circle and a rectangle becomes a square.

 If you hold down ⟨Shift⟩ **while moving one or more objects, you'll restrict the movement to an exact horizontal or vertical line or to a 45-degree angle.**

Mind the corners. If you create a drawing with the Rectangle or Rounded-Rectangle tool, double-click the shape and a dialog appears. Here you can set the radius of the corners and whether to round the object's sides.

Position your illustration precisely. This tip works whether you're in a drawing or a painting document. If you want to place an object precisely, use the Autogrid feature. It creates a set of automatic alignment points where the items you drop snap into place. To activate the feature, go to the Options menu and select Turn Autogrid On. To set your grid to a specific size (in a Painting document only), choose Grid Size from the Options menu. Pick a grid increment that lets you accurately position the elements of your illustration.

Although the Autogrid feature helps you refine the positions of elements, it also prevents free movement. If you don't want a specific element to snap into a fixed location, return to the Options menu and choose Turn Autogrid Off. Activate Autogrid again via the same steps for those elements you do want to snap into place.

Select paint images. Paint documents don't have corners and handles to help you when you want to change an object's shape. Here's how to change an object's shape in a paint document:

1. If the object is rectangular, click the Selection Rectangle tool in the lower half of the Tool palette. The pointer changes to a crosshair.

2. Drag the crosshair pointer to the start of the area you wish to select, and then drag to cover the area.

3. Now go to the Transform menu and choose your option. For example, if you want to make the object bigger, choose Resize. Corners will appear on your selection box. Pull these to make the object wider or taller.

To select an irregular image, use the Lasso tool. You can select several painted items and bypass the blank space between them by double-clicking the Lasso tool.

Make custom colors. Looking to replicate your school colors? It's easy to blend your own special shades. Here's how:

1. Open the Accents palette (Window > Show Accents) and double-click any color you want to edit.

2. You'll see a list that contains color-configuration options. For the most part, just moving a slider will change colors. Choose a color-configuration option from the following:

   CMYK Picker lets you select a color based on a four-color model. Cyan, magenta, yellow, and black (K) are the four inks used by most printers.

   Crayon Picker gives you a choice of 60 colors from a screen that looks like a box of crayons.

   HLS Picker presents a color wheel that lets you adjust three color settings—one for Hue Angle, another for Saturation, and a third for Lightness.

   HTML Picker is designed for Web pages. The sliders let you choose from the standard range of Web colors. (What's a Web color? The extremely short answer is that it's a color that will appear the same whether you're looking at a Mac or PC monitor.)

   RGB Picker creates colors the same way your monitor does—by combining the three primary colors: red, green, and blue.

3. Once you've found a color you like, click OK. The selected color appears in the color palette, ready for you to use in your document.

If you want to save a custom color (or a pattern) for use in other documents, follow these steps:

1. Once you've selected your new color or pattern, click the pop-up menu in the Accents palette and select Save As.

2. Give your color a descriptive name so that you can identify it later.

3. Click Save. From here on, you can choose your custom color from the Palette pop-up menu in the Accents palette and use it in any of your AppleWorks illustrations.

AppleWorks Time-Saver: Master Pages

Making a newsletter? AppleWorks has one important feature in common with page-layout programs: the ability to create a master page containing items that appear in all other pages of your document. On the master page you can place items—such as page numbers or images—that you want to appear on all pages. Here's how:

1. Create a drawing document.

2. From the Options menu choose Edit Master Page.

3. Use your drawing or text tools to create the objects you want to appear on all pages in your document.

4. Once the master page is ready, return to the Options menu and choose Edit Master Page again to return to your normal page. From here on, the master-page elements will appear on all the pages in this document.

 If you don't want a master-page element to appear on a specific page of your document, cover it up with a rectangle or other object that's the same color as the page background.

Perfect Your Shots with iPhoto

Digital photography has been one of the biggest things to hit home computing in the past few years. Steve Jobs is no dummy; he made sure the Mac was ready to ride the wave. Apple's iPhoto comes free on all new Macs and is also available as part of Apple's $49 iLife package.

iPhoto makes it easy to download photos off your digital camera, but that's not all it can do. It also includes basic tools for making your shots look better—from fixing Aunt Ida's red eyes to making your boss look less washed-out.

Touch-up tricks

You've hooked up your camera, iPhoto has launched, and your photos have downloaded. Now comes the fun part—making them look good! Here's how to do basic touch-up tasks using iPhoto's built-in tools.

Rotate. Are some of your photos on their sides? No problem. Use the Rotate tool—which is right above the Crop button—to set them straight. First, select a photo in iPhoto and click the Edit tab to enlarge the image. Now click the Rotate button until your photo's orientation is correct. With each click the image turns 90 degrees. If you'd rather an object turn in the opposite direction, go to iPhoto > Preferences and change the Rotate option.

 Can't tell what tool is what? In almost all Mac programs you can find out by pausing your pointer over a tool. Wait a second and a little yellow box (called a *tool tip*) appears with its name.

Crop. There's no need to include extraneous stuff in your photos. Use the Crop tool to focus in on what's important. Go into Edit mode by clicking the Edit tab. Next, click and drag the crosshair pointer over the part of the image you want to preserve. The unselected part of the image will be grayed out— that's the part that will be discarded. To adjust your selection, first let go of the mouse. Now the pointer changes to a little hand. Click and drag the selection area to wherever you please. Once you're satisfied, click the Crop button in the lower-left corner of the iPhoto window. Experiment with cropping— it's one of the easiest ways to improve your photos.

 If you know your photos need to be a certain size—for instance, you plan to order 4-by-6-inch prints—iPhoto can help. Choose a preset crop size from the Constrain pop-up menu in the lower-left corner of the iPhoto window *before* dragging to enclose the area you want.

One-click enhance. If your image is too bright or dim, you could fiddle with the Brightness and Contrast sliders, but first try using the Enhance option. Select the photo and click the Edit button. Click the Enhance button at the bottom of the Edit window to automatically correct most contrast problems. Keep clicking the Enhance button until you like what you see.

Red-eye begone. No, the Devil has not possessed your family, friends, or dog. That red dot in their eyes is the result of your camera's flash reflecting off the blood vessels inside their eyes. (Yuck!) To reduce red-eye, select the photo and click the Edit button. Choose None from the Constrain pop-up menu to make sure that your selection area will be free-form. Then place the crosshair pointer at the corner of an eye and click and drag to include both eyes. Finally, click the Red-Eye button at the bottom of the screen. If you get a strange result, try correcting one eye at a time.

The adolescent's friend. Cheaper than a trip to the dermatologist, iPhoto's Retouch wand can make blemishes (or the stray hair that flew in front of your lens) disappear. Select the photo and click the Edit button. Click the Retouch button at the bottom of the screen, and place the crosshair pointer over the blemish. Click and drag to blend the area into the picture.

Get back to black and white. If you're going for that old-timey look (or don't have a color printer), don't miss the chance to change color photos to black and white or, as of version 4, sepia. Simply select the photo and click the Edit button. Click and drag to select the entire photo, and then click the B&W or Sepia button; or—if you're feeling adventurous—select only a particular *area* of the photo and then click the button you desire.

Love your edits. Hate what you've done? Choose Undo from the Edit menu (or press ⌘Z) to take back the last edit, or choose File > Revert to Original to get back to where you began. Better yet, duplicate your file before you start by selecting the image and choosing File > Duplicate (or press ⌘D).

Automatic albums. The newest version of iPhoto lets you create albums automatically. For example, you can create an album that includes every photo with the keyword "Dog" or every photo you took between January 1 and March 1, 2004. Whenever you import a new image that fits the criterion, it's added to the album. To make a Smart Album, choose File > New Smart Album. Give it a name in the "Smart Album name" field. Finally, select your criterion from the pop-up menus.

Online Photo Services

You don't need a fancy photo printer and reams of glossy paper to get the most out of your digital camera. When you send files to an online photo service, you'll get prints back in the mail—just as if you'd sent off a roll of film. Some services will mail copies to your family and friends. Most will put your images on greeting cards, mugs, T-shirts, and more. (You can even make a full-color book and get prints through iPhoto itself!) Here are some of our favorite online photo services:

- **Club Photo** (www.clubphoto.com)
- **Kodak Picture Center Online** (http://picturecenter.Kodak.com)
- **PhotoAccess** (www.photoaccess.com)
- **Shutterfly** (www.shutterfly.com)
- **Snapfish** (www.snapfish.com)

Take the Next Step with Photoshop Elements

Once you've got the hang of iPhoto, you may long for more control over your digital photos and other images. For instance, you might want to cut out *(mask)* part of one image and place it in another, or apply a fancy effect to your photo to make a psychedelic album cover.

What's next? You don't have to spend $649 for Photoshop if you're not going to do professional printing. Instead, we recommend Photoshop Elements. It lets you do almost everything Photoshop does except the high-level stuff that pros do to prepare images to go to press. It's also *a lot* easier to use.

Tips and Tricks for Photoshop

Photoshop is a monster program, and the path to greatness in Photoshop can be paved with frustration. That's why magazine articles, Web sites, and indeed entire books are devoted to Photoshop tips and tricks alone. We recommend the following Web sites for Photoshop how-tos and tips: Adobe Studio (www. studio.adobe.com), the National Association of Photoshop Professionals (www.planetphotoshop.com), and Creativepro.com (www.creativepro.com). In the meantime, here are some basic tips (some of these work with Photoshop Elements as well).

Using different screen modes. Photoshop gives you three different ways to configure your screen when working. You can access these three modes at the bottom of the Toolbox (**Figure 13.14**). The first—Standard Screen Mode—is most similar to that of other applications. The Photoshop Toolbar is present, and the Mac Desktop is visible behind the document window. The second—Full Screen Mode with Menu Bar—surrounds the document window with a gray work area so that the Mac Desktop is not visible. The Mac menu bar is also visible here. The third—Full Screen Mode—also places the document against a gray background but shows only Photoshop menus and palettes. Which one you use is a matter of personal preference, but most Photoshop pros use Full Screen Mode with Menu Bar. That way, if they accidentally click outside the document window, they stay in Photoshop instead of being dumped into the Finder.

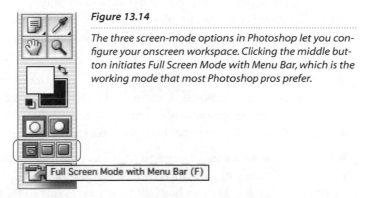

Figure 13.14

The three screen-mode options in Photoshop let you configure your onscreen workspace. Clicking the middle button initiates Full Screen Mode with Menu Bar, which is the working mode that most Photoshop pros prefer.

Accessing contextual menus. Instead of mousing up to the menu bar to access Photoshop or Photoshop Elements functions, use contextual menus. The next time you go to use a tool, hold down (Control). A tiny menu icon shows up next to the pointer. When you click, a floating menu pops up showing functions and options pertaining to that tool. It's a fast, efficient way to work.

Seeing tool alternatives and palette menus. If you see a tiny triangle (called a *disclosure triangle*) next to a tool or on a palette in Photoshop or Photoshop Elements, click it. The triangle indicates that there are alternatives available. For example, clicking the disclosure triangle on the rectangular Marquee tool brings up a menu that exposes Elliptical, Single Row, and Single Column Marquee tools. You can then select and use one of those tools. Palette menus show additional controls, some of which are the same as those found in the menu bar, while others can be found *only* in the palette menus. The Layers palette menu, for instance, reveals controls for creating or deleting layers, flattening multiple layers into a single layer, and so on.

Using the Option key. A fast way to access hidden tools in Photoshop or Photoshop Elements is to hold down Option while clicking the tool. Each click shows one of the alternate tools available. Continue clicking to cycle through all the available tools.

Setting tool options. Some tools also have special features you can set in the Options bar that appears at the top of the Photoshop or Photoshop Elements window. For example, the Brush tool options let you change brush size and opacity, among other features. A quick way to see if a tool has any options is to double-click it. The Options bar reflects the choices accordingly.

Getting rid of palettes. Heavy-duty graphics programs such as Photoshop can fill your screen with a plethora of palettes—and soon you find you can barely see the image you're working on. You can easily dismiss any individual palette by clicking its close box, but if you want to dismiss all the palettes and the toolbar, just press Tab. Another press of Tab, and you get them back. This is a boon for any Mac user stuck with a small monitor (or any owner of an iMac or Apple laptop).

Zooming in and out. As with any application, the trick to working quickly is to know the right keyboard shortcuts. Using keyboard modifiers with the Zoom tool is an indispensable shortcut in Photoshop. With the Zoom tool active, hold down Shift to zoom in; hold down Option to zoom out.

Navigating with ease. Photoshop's Navigator palette provides a great way to get your bearings in your document. When you open the palette, a document proxy appears. The red box indicates the area that's visible onscreen. Drag the box to another part of the proxy, and the file window updates to show that area (**Figure 13.15**). Want to increase the magnification of the file quickly? Use the zoom slider at the bottom of the Navigator palette.

Combining different-size images. It's fun to combine two images into one with Photoshop. But what happens if the images are not the same size? In either Photoshop or Photoshop Elements, copy the image or layer that you want to resize, and then press ⌘T to activate the Free Transform control. A bounding box appears. Click a corner point and drag to make the copied image larger or smaller. Holding down Shift while dragging maintains image proportions.

Exporting transparent images. An assistant or wizard offers a great way to simplify a complex process. In its Help menu, Photoshop has an assistant called Export Transparent Image, which lets you select and then export illustrations that contain transparent regions. For example, you can remove an unnecessary background so that just an image's silhouette appears. Once you call up the Export Transparent Image assistant, follow the instructions and you'll make simple work of a formerly difficult task. You just pick the steps that apply to your particular needs, and the assistant guides you through the process. If your image already includes a transparent region, the assistant deletes it, or you can designate an area of the image to be made transparent. Then you export it in the proper format for print or the Web.

Save for Web. One of the features of Photoshop (and Photoshop Elements) that we use most often is Save For Web, in the File menu. If you routinely prepare files for an online service, then get used to using this command instead of Save As to convert to GIF or JPEG. That's because Save For Web automatically applies the compression and optimization you'll need for Web graphics, resulting in the creation of much smaller files more quickly. The programs even show you the difference between the original file and its Web-optimized version (**Figure 13.16**). Plus you can see how long the file will take to download on a modem.

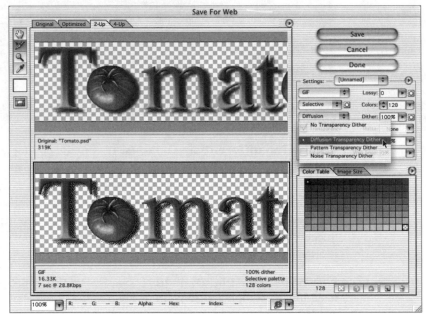

Figure 13.16

Save For Web automatically compresses and optimizes files for the Web. You can set parameters for how much compression and what kind of dithering should be applied.

Finding images with the File browser. If you have a lot of images on your hard disk but can't remember which ones you named what, then the File Browser is for you. In both Photoshop and Photoshop Elements, you can scan the contents of folders visually from within the program. Open the File Browser and navigate to a folder on your hard disk. All the images readable by Photoshop appear as thumbnails in the File Browser window. Click an image and the window reveals information about it—filename, date created, image dimension, file size, and more (**Figure 13.17**). If you take a lot of pictures with a digital camera, this feature is a real time-saver.

Figure 13.17

Photoshop's File Browser lets you select images visually. The File Browser also shows information about the file type, size, and more. Since most digital cameras use non-intuitive naming conventions, the File Browser is great for sifting through photos.

Revving up your system. Photoshop is a hungry beast. It likes lots of RAM and a fast processor. If you find stuff slowing down in either Photoshop or Photoshop Elements, try changing your *scratch disk* (you do this in Preferences, accessible from the Photoshop menu). Photoshop uses a scratch disk to squeeze more performance from your system. It uses a hard disk as virtual RAM. For best results, don't use your start-up disk as your scratch disk (you can designate as many as four scratch disks), and make sure that whatever disk you do use has plenty of space on it. Another trick is to occasionally purge your system (Edit > Purge). Cleansing your Clipboard and History file frees up memory.

Experimenting with the Option key. Option provides a great way to exploit secret features of Photoshop and Photoshop Elements. For example, you can use the Eyedropper tool to fix your artwork's foreground color. But if you hold down Option, the Eyedropper affects the background color instead. When you hold down Option O while dragging an object, you make a copy (this works the same way in AppleWorks). Experiment with Option to see what other treasures it will reveal.

Getting another view of your artwork. If you're lucky enough to have a large display (or, even luckier, the gorgeous wide-screen Apple Cinema Display), this technique can give you a different perspective on your project. In Photoshop, choose New Window from the Window menu to bring up a second window showing the same document. You can establish separate zoom settings for each window and click between them to check your changes quickly at various views. This trick also works with a multiple-monitor setup.

Interview: Mike Murray, Part 2   *continued from page 527*

Why did you decide to give university students such a discount?

That was another plan. We realized that if we could create a next generation of kids who would use Macintoshes in college, in a very short period of time, four or five years later, that's what they'd want in business. We pulled that idea from what Apple had been able to do in the K–12 market. It's hard to [imagine], the time has gone by so quickly, but people were not using personal computers in colleges in 1984. This was a very bold new idea.

Steve's strengths sometimes become his weaknesses. That's the thing with a very strong leader.

> *—Mike Murray, on the good and bad points of the original Mac*

We did a little research and realized that the most prestigious colleges in America don't like being left behind. So we cooked up an idea. We hired a woman to tell us a little about the college marketplace, and the word *consortium* kept coming up—colleges like to join consortiums. "Fine," I said, "we're creating the Apple University Consortium …"

So then what happened?

There was a guy who'd been working in the marketing group for the Lisa product named Dan'l Lewin, and he was a really neat guy—good salesman. He'd been a sales guy for Sony consumer products, and he just knew how to do sales. So we brought him over to our group and said, "Dan'l, we want you to create the Apple University Consortium, and here's what it is. We want ten universities to each agree to purchase 1000 Macintoshes each, at $1,000 per Macintosh, which was like our manufacturing cost. And they have to agree contractually before January 24, so that on January 24, the day we publicly introduce the Macintosh, we can say that these ten major universities in America have all standardized on the Macintosh and have agreed that this is the product for their students." That would be huge, because you're talking about Harvard, Stanford, University of Michigan, University of Texas, and you kind of cover the whole country, and you create this feeling that "Wow, these are the smartest people in America, and if they've decided that this—and look, they're $1,000 each!"

Dan'l hit the road and came back with 12 colleges instead of 10. It was an extraordinary success. And the day after this got announced as part of the Macintosh introduction, the phone started ringing off the hook from colleges all across America saying, "We want the same deal." So, on the fly, we said "Sorry, that consortium is closed—it's just those 12 colleges in the consortium," because that's what we'd guaranteed the 12. But we created the "Apple College (Something) Program" in the hallway, while we had someone on hold. And that was something like you had to buy 500 (Macs) at $1,500, and the computers started just flying out of the factory for that reason. It was really pretty funny.

Within a few months, though, sales had slumped pretty badly. Do you think the retail price ($2,495) was the main problem?

The real killer wasn't the price point, the real killer was the lack of software. Even innovators are going to say, "Whoa, I'd love to buy the product, but what can you do with it?" You can paint a picture, you can write a memo, and there's a spreadsheet, but beyond that you couldn't do much with it. The product had no hard-disk drive—Steve was adamant that we were never going to put a hard-disk drive in the Mac, ever.

Why?

He was religiously opposed to it, because it didn't meet the pristine design of what this thing was supposed to be. And in those days the product had no plans of ever having a color display—didn't need it. Black and white was what people wanted.

That was Steve's thinking, but did everybody agree?

No, not at all. Nor did our marketing research ever suggest that that was correct. But you know Steve's strengths sometimes become his weaknesses. That's the thing with a very strong leader. The product never, ever would have gotten done without him. He was so fixated and convinced about what the original Mac could be and that everyone would want one, he didn't want to tamper with the recipe at all.

How long did you stay at Apple?

I stayed until the end of 1985. Prior to that, the war had started between Sculley and Jobs, and for a while I quit working for Steve and was working directly for Sculley, but that didn't work out, either.

Was that your decision, to switch?

Yes, because I'd gotten to the point where I thought Steve was asking us to create marketing messages around products that weren't there and solutions we didn't have …

What happened then?

It became an untenable situation, but Sculley didn't want me to leave the company, so I had a kind of big-time marketing-strategy job working for him. But then right after that happened, those two guys started warring with each other, and things just kind of had a train wreck, and Steve got fired. I was too closely aligned with him, so the Apple II group that ended up running the company couldn't trust me, I guess—I don't know, because no one would even ever talk to me; and even though I had a big job in the company, I stopped being invited to meetings, people wouldn't come into my office, I was persona non grata. It was really distressing—you know, you're 29, 30 years old, and you're going, "What's going on here?" But it was very high emotions, and Steve got kicked out, so I left.

I didn't want to leave Apple, and I couldn't believe it—I loved that company. I was very excited about what they represented, in terms of the democratization of technology.

continues on next page

Did you see that as the central significance of the Mac?

Well, a bunch of us in the Mac group were pretty idealistic about what we thought the role of technology could be. We saw technology as not just a bunch of bits and bytes, but as something that would allow students, housewives, businesspeople, people in the United States, people in faraway places, to be more productive, to be more creative, to be able to communicate better with each other, to be able to get their jobs done—to improve the quality of their lives, essentially. We could open up the door to millions of people who up till now had been locked out of using these types of products because they were so difficult to use. That was a very exciting idea—that you could be working on a highly innovative, fun product if you liked technology, but at the same time bringing great benefit to many people who would be using it. And that was fundamentally sound, and I still subscribe to that. And Apple, more than any company that I was ever aware of, endorsed that and got into that as well, so there was a lot of goodness behind that.

Now you are president of the Crystal Springs Foundation. What's that all about?

The foundation is really a private thing that my wife and I use to fund things that we care a great deal about. Where I spend most of my time is with one of those projects. It's an organization called Unitus that I'm a cofounder of and serve as chairman of. Unitus provides support to poor women in developing countries through microcredit lending. These women get loans of $100, and they use these loans to run their tiny little one-person businesses and then to turn around and increase their income for their families, so they can have more food on the table, they can buy medicine for their children, they can make sure their kids get educated, and they can ratchet themselves incrementally up the economic ladder, and get out of abject poverty. And moreover, their kids can get educated and not have to have the life that their parents have had. We also sponsor an inner-city kids program in Seattle for some of the most vulnerable at-risk kids in our community up here.

Ever think about going back to Apple?

No. No, never. It's just a great chapter, but it's long ago. I look back with very fond memories. You know, it was very hard work, and there were good days and bad days, but it was just a remarkable period for a lot of people.

14

Page Layout

Terri Stone (TS) is the chapter editor.

Kathleen Tinkel (KT) and Phil Gaskill (PG) contributed to earlier editions of The Macintosh Bible, *from which portions of this chapter are taken.*

Putting letters and images on a page—a process now known as *page layout*—is as old as printing, but it has gotten a lot easier over time.

In the Middle Ages, printers carved images and bold letters in blocks of wood that they painted and then stamped on vellum or paper to create a page. If they made a mistake, they had to sand out the image, mortise in a plug of fresh wood, and start again.

At the dawn of the Renaissance, Johannes Gutenberg laid out pages by assembling pieces of movable metal type—but first he had to engrave punches and hand-cast all the type.

By the end of the 19th century, typesetting-machine operators could set type from a keyboard (not a smoothly clicking one like ours, but still an improvement over picking up thousands of little bits of metal type and arranging them backward in a chase). They also remelted type metal, which was much easier and much less time-consuming than putting small pieces of type back in cases so that it could be reset. When photo-offset lithography began to take over printing after World War II, graphic designers pasted typeset galleys on art boards, ready for the printer's process camera. (Reprinting was as easy and cheap as reusing negatives.)

Today we flow digital text and images onto a Mac's virtual pages and never need to get our hands dirty. Desktop-publishing software is so easy to use that we may be tempted to take its power for granted. Page-layout programs make it simple to edit and format text, arrange text on the page, add rules and other graphic elements, import scanned photos and line art, and specify color and output settings for printing on your desktop inkjet or laser printer, or on a commercial offset press. In this chapter we talk about page layout and the programs available for doing it on the Mac.

In This Chapter

Page Layout and Desktop Publishing (TS/KT)

Thanks to modern technology, any Mac user with a yen to communicate can sit at the computer and arrange pages of type, digitized photos, graphics, and other elements. A few mouse clicks let you reproduce your pages faithfully, printing a few copies on an in-house desktop inkjet or laser printer or printing hundreds or thousands of copies by sending files to an outside service for output on such high-end equipment as imagesetters, computer-to-plate systems, or high-capacity direct digital printers.

What makes this miracle possible is page-layout software—programs designed for setting type and for mixing text and images freely on the page. There are six of these programs for Mac OS X; among them, Quark's QuarkXPress and Adobe's InDesign are the top contenders for creative professionals these days.

 Page-layout programs are also the best tools for creating customized, top-quality PDF files to send to print shops and service bureaus. PDF files preserve the design and format of a document.

Some optimists try to use a word-processing program such as Microsoft Word to lay out publications for printing. That's really the hard way, however, as you can see in the "Word for Page Layout?" sidebar, later in the chapter. A page-layout program is the right tool for the job. It saves time, gives you more control over the pages, and produces better-quality type.

What Is Page Layout?

Unlike word processors, with their riverlike approach to text, page-layout programs deal with objects: blocks (or frames) of text; imported bitmap and vector graphics; and rules, circles, rectangles, and polygons drawn in the program. This emphasis on the page as a whole rather than only the text is a fundamental difference. You begin by specifying the size and shape of your finished page (the trim size), which may not be the same as the standard paper sizes supported by your printer. You set explicit margins, columns, and other boundaries to order the pages. And you have both WYSIWYG and numeric control over type and typography, the placement of elements on the page, and the elements' sizes and appearance when printed.

Here are a few of the essential functions that all page-layout programs support:

Document. Allows publications of any useful size, from miniature books and business cards up through banners, signs, and other large formats, with a single page or many that can be printed on one or both sides. Provides space for images or color to bleed (print beyond the trim lines) and for crop marks and other printer markings. Provides a working view that shows trim lines (printable area), margins, and text columns, and the gutters between them. Shows pages as you intend them to be read, with spreads shown as facing pages with a useful range of zoom-in ratios for detailed work. Provides master pages for control of repeating elements and variations of the basic layout.

Graphics. Accepts standard formats of graphic files (at least EPS, TIFF, and JPEG, as well as others from both major platforms). Has the ability to crop, resize, and rotate imported images and has some sort of mask or clipping-path function. Includes drawing tools for rules, circles, rectangles, and polygons, with control over line weights and ability to fill these objects with color and assign color separately to outlines. Supports all industry-standard color spaces: CMYK (for commercial printing), RGB (for film recorders, some inkjets, and conversion to and from Web pages), and more.

Text. Provides word-processing functions, including a spelling checker and search-and-replace tools that work with text content and type attributes. Supports import of plain ASCII text as well as common word-processor formats (Word, primarily) from both Mac and Windows, retaining user-selected formatting that can include styles. Filters text and replaces double hyphens and typewriter (or straight) quotation marks and apostrophes with typographic characters (em dashes and curly quotes, respectively).

Pages. Lets you set up columns and flow type automatically from column to column and page to page. Has rulers, nonprinting grids and guides, and numeric controls for all elements on the page, with access through keyboard shortcuts as well as menus or palettes. Capable of creating newsletter-like documents, with stories starting on one page and jumping to other pages. Allows text to flow controllably around images, sidebars, callout text, and other elements. Supports folios (automatic page numbering) and running heads and feet.

Typography. Gives you control of hyphenation and all aspects of the spacing of type—between words and characters (including automatic and manual kerning) and between lines and paragraphs. Supports paragraph styles.

Technical control. Lets you control output specs for a wide range of devices: specify screen resolutions, transfer functions, color specs, and other output functions and print separations or composite pages to PostScript and non-PostScript printers (inkjets, for example), as well as to high-resolution equipment at output services. The software will also *preflight* (or check for output quality of) files and gather all needed files, including fonts, for remote output.

Word for Page Layout? (TS/PG)

Some people, cowed by the complexity of programs dedicated to page layout, try to use Microsoft Word in their place. But can Word really play with the big boys? In a word (pardon the play on, er, words), the answer is a resounding no.

Word's main problem is that it's merely a word processor—a sort of souped-up text editor. It thinks of text as a river that flows smoothly along and gets broken up into pages at print time. Because of this, it's difficult to accomplish the common desktop-publishing task of starting a story on page 1 and then jumping it to the back of the book. To be fair, it's not impossible. You can create blank pages with Word's page-break commands and then come back and "float" graphics and text boxes (yes, Word does have text boxes, of a sort) on those empty pages, making sure they're not anchored to the text stream that contains the page breaks. It's not even a huge hassle, really; it's just dumb that you have to do it this way.

Word can import graphics. It can crop and resize them, and you can even apply basic drop shadows and perform primitive color adjustments. If you want graphics that can be freely positioned (as opposed to graphics that are anchored to, or in line with, text), you must muck about in the Format Picture dialog.

You'll probably want to place an image at a precise spot on a page. Good luck. Word's positioning capabilities are minimal. There are no guides. Let me say that again: there are *no* guides; if you want a guide to help you align objects, draw a rule. You won't be able to have objects snap to this "guide," of course. And don't forget to delete the rule before printing.

The worst problem is that Word does a lousy job of setting type. There is limited support for manual tweaking of hyphenation and kerning, but the controls are too coarse.

Bottom line: Word is a limited and clumsy page-layout tool that produces lousy-looking pages.

Surveying the Field (TS/KT)

If you regularly produce work destined for commercial printing, you probably use one of the top two high-end programs: Quark's **QuarkXPress** ($1,045; www.quark.com), or Adobe's **InDesign** ($699; www.adobe.com). But you do have other options.

 If you curse Adobe for having kicked PageMaker to the curb, investigate the company's Adobe PageMaker Plug-in Pack ($49; www.adobe.com). It adds several features to InDesign CS that were previously PageMaker exclusives. For example, you'll get PageMaker's toolbar, keyboard shortcuts, and page-imposition capabilities. You can also automatically style text with bullets and numbered lists. Data Merge is part of the plug-in pack, as are scores of templates.

Graphic artists with the demanding job of creating supermarket ads, flyers, coupons, and other detailed pieces on a short timetable should look at MultiAd Creator (see "Other Possibilities," later in this chapter).

But maybe you don't intend to make page layout your life's work. In that case, a less full-featured (some would say less-bloated) program like the following might be perfect for you: Grasshopper LLC's PageStream and PageStream Professional; Diwan Software Limited's venerable Mac program Ready,Set,Go!; and ACD Systems' Canvas Professional Edition (see "Other Possibilities," later in this chapter).

The layout, typesetting, and output functions in these three are more than serviceable. Their drawbacks: They have fewer users on the Mac and among graphic designers and others who specialize in page layout. Except for Canvas, the programs tend to have fewer exotic bells and whistles. You won't find articles detailing tips and tricks in *Macworld* or other magazines. And many output services won't know what to do with files from these programs, which means that instead of supplying application files as you can with QuarkXPress or InDesign, you'll have to create print files—PostScript or Acrobat PDF—when you send your job.

 If you need to create manuals, textbooks, or other long technical works, then you should consider Adobe FrameMaker ($799; www.adobe.com). Unfortunately, FrameMaker is available only for Mac OS 9 and Adobe has no plans to make a Mac OS X version. So for the long term, FrameMaker is not a good option on the Mac; but for now, if you are still running Mac OS 9, FrameMaker provides features that other Macintosh page-layout programs do not.

The Top Two: QuarkXPress and Adobe InDesign (TS/PG/KT)

QuarkXPress and InDesign share many capabilities, but each has a distinctive working style, and each has its strengths and weaknesses.

General Approach

First came PageMaker, then QuarkXPress, and finally InDesign. Although these programs evolved in part by copying features from each other, the remaining two have unique advantages and disadvantages, and both retain their own feel and working style. Here's how the two compare in major feature areas.

Align and distribute. QuarkXPress and InDesign let you specify the size of gutters between objects.

Bézier drawing tools. InDesign and QuarkXPress both have a handy subset of the functions found in standalone vector drawing programs such as Adobe Illustrator, Macromedia FreeHand, and ACD Systems Canvas. Still, for all but the simplest work, you'll probably also need one of the vector drawing programs as well.

Extensibility. Historically, QuarkXPress has been the extensibility winner. Quark originated the notion of third-party *plug-ins,* or *extensions* (which it calls XTensions), and QuarkXPress has the largest selection. Some are amazing in what they do (and can even cost more than QuarkXPress); others perform only one task and are inexpensive or free. However, many XTension developers declined to release QuarkXPress 5 versions of their applications. The Mac OS X–only nature of QuarkXPress 6 caused even more XTension developers to delay updating their software or to pull out of the market entirely since professional users are often slow to update their page-layout software, waiting instead for bugs in the programs to be discovered and fixed.

InDesign got a late start, but the pace is picking up. Look for plug-ins from the same companies that develop for QuarkXPress, and from relative newcomers, such as Woodwing Software (www.woodwing.com), which was the first company to release plug-ins for InDesign and is still the most prolific plug-in developer for InDesign.

Eyedropper tool. Borrowed from graphics programs, InDesign's tools include an eyedropper tool that can pick up not only colors (and other fill and stroke attributes) but also text attributes and then apply those attributes to other text. QuarkXPress does not have an eyedropper tool.

Frames. QuarkXPress is still resolutely based on frames—you draw a text or picture box and then fill it with text or a graphic. InDesign is also frame-based but is more casual about it—what you put into a frame determines whether it is a text or image box, and you can import text or graphics and it will automatically create the frame for you.

Group. Both programs let you group two or more objects.

Initial default settings. InDesign has the best settings right out of the box, possibly because being newer, it has less legacy rubbish to sustain. But software engineers and marketing experts set the defaults, and every user needs to review—and revise—all the settable functions after installing a new version of one of these programs (and periodically thereafter).

A few defaults are positively dangerous, such as QuarkXPress's hyphenation-and-justification (H&J) settings. (See the "Fixing the Dreadful Defaults" section, later in the chapter.)

Layers. Both InDesign and QuarkXPress support *layers,* which are handy for creating customized variants of a brochure or other documents. Items on layers can be handled together, and a layer may be hidden or revealed at print time.

Layout adjustment. InDesign (but not QuarkXPress) has this sometimes-handy (but disastrous if misused) function, which gives you the option to have elements rearranged automatically when page dimensions are revised, either on a regular page or by making changes to master-page templates.

Lock. InDesign lets you lock the size and position of an object—nothing can be changed unless you first unlock it. QuarkXPress's lock function prevents accidental moves with the mouse but will let you move a locked item by using the Measurements palette or the Modify dialog.

Long-document support. InDesign and QuarkXPress ship with book, indexing, and automatic table-of-contents functions. The book function not only assembles individual files (chapters) in one print operation, automatically repaginating in response to revisions, but also lets you index and create a table of contents across the whole book.

Master pages. Both programs have master pages, a sort of template that helps keep even a large document consistent without a lot of repetition.

InDesign's override option lets you decide whether master-page items should be locked or editable on the regular pages. Elements from QuarkXPress's master pages can all be edited on the regular pages. Only InDesign lets you base one master page on another—changes made to the parent ripple down through the child templates.

Moving and scaling. Both programs provide for precise numeric positioning and resizing of objects.

InDesign has an extremely useful "proxy"—a schematic diagram in the control palette that lets you select a point (corner, side, or center) to be used as the location from which transformations will occur. The object remains fixed at the selected point when you enlarge/reduce, rotate, or otherwise shift the object.

Packaging/preflighting. Both programs package (assemble) document files, fonts, and graphics necessary for output. InDesign checks files before packaging them for output. If it finds problems with a document, it gives you a detailed preflight report listing the potential errors and their locations.

Projects. In version 6, QuarkXPress introduced the concept of *projects*. One QuarkXPress document, now called a project, can hold several related jobs. For example, you can place designs for a company's business cards, letterhead, brochures, and Web site in one QuarkXPress project. Each piece is in a separate *layout space* within that project. Layout spaces, also new to QuarkXPress 6, are accessible via tabs at the bottom of the project window. You set application preferences, style sheets, colors, and H&Js across the project. Each layout space can have its own page dimensions, margins, orientation, number of pages, and kerning, tracking, and trapping values.

There are no projects or layout spaces in InDesign.

Screen display. InDesign offers several high-quality options for how the program shows imported graphics onscreen. The default setting is an adequate compromise between faster page previews and higher-quality display. You can also choose to display graphics at higher and lower resolutions.

Although QuarkXPress 6 made much-needed improvements in this area, there's room for more. The only way to enable the program's Full Resolution Preview and EPS Preview XTensions is to register your copy after installation. Registration is a complicated process, and even if you do register your copy of QuarkXPress 6, the preview modes you get do not equal those of InDesign.

Search and replace. Both programs search on text, styles, and some type attributes (the particulars vary by program).

InDesign can search on several paragraph attributes that QuarkXPress cannot, including paragraph indent, paragraph spacing, drop caps, composer version, and "keep" format settings, such as lines you've elected to keep together to avoid bad line breaks.

Sections. InDesign and QuarkXPress support this feature, which lets you have front matter with one series of page numbers (lowercase roman numerals, for example) and then begin the main series of page numbers with an Arabic number 1.

Spreads. QuarkXPress and InDesign both allow spreads of more than two pages. InDesign has a nifty function that prevents designated spreads from being split apart when changes are made to the pagination. There's nothing like it in QuarkXPress.

Step and repeat. InDesign and QuarkXPress both have a Step and Repeat command you can use to quickly create columns or rows of duplicates.

Story editor. You can edit text manually on layout pages in both programs, but InDesign allows you to use search-and-replace, spelling-checker, and other global functions in a special plain-text story-editor view. This is usually a time-saver; you can make changes to multiple stories and the software moves quickly without having to deal with laid-out pages. But when you want to see the effect of a change, it's a nuisance. QuarkXPress does not have a built-in plain-text editor—you edit text in layout view, which allows you to observe the effects of changes while you work but may also slow down the process as revisions ripple through the text.

Text and Typography

There's more to typography than placing text on the page and letting it flow. The two programs have their own approaches to setting type. (For more on fonts see Chapter 15.)

Automatic character substitution. InDesign and QuarkXPress both replace *fi* and *fl* with the appropriate ligatures. If a small-caps or expert font is open, InDesign also swaps small-caps and old-style figures. InDesign supports the extended OpenType character set and makes other automatic substitutions if such a font is available.

Built-in kern pair editor. QuarkXPress lets you adjust kerning in live text and have the changes applied globally to that font in the document. The actual font remains unchanged.

Composition methods. InDesign alone has a multiline composer, which evaluates a user-specified number of lines and number of alternatives when determining how to control hyphenation and spacing in justified type. QuarkXPress uses a single-line composer, which is also an option in InDesign.

Drop caps. Both QuarkXPress and InDesign permit more than one character in their automatic drop caps.

Hyphenation controls. QuarkXPress and InDesign let you specify minimum word length and number of characters before and after the hyphen. Both programs also have user-editable hyphenation dictionaries. QuarkXPress hyphenation is primarily based on a set of algorithms, while InDesign defaults to a dictionary. QuarkXPress uses a separate spelling dictionary; InDesign uses one dictionary for both spelling and hyphenation. QuarkXPress sometimes breaks a word at other than a syllable and is prone to breaking contractions before the *n't*.

Justification. InDesign is unusual in that it lets you select a justified paragraph alignment with the last line centered or flush right rather than flush left (useful for academic abstracts and ornamental typography).

Kerning. Both applications support automatic pair kerning, based on metrics defined in fonts.

InDesign offers optical kerning, which ignores the font's kern pairs and adjusts spacing based on the way the characters look and fit. In uneducated hands this function can be dangerous, but is useful for fonts that are badly spaced to begin with. The feature is integrated with the program and can be included in style sheets.

Optical alignment. InDesign offers the option of optical alignment, which allows punctuation marks and sprawling letters (*A* and *W,* for example) to protrude slightly into the gutter. Used with discretion, this technique can make the margin look straighter; used carelessly, it can create columns of type that appear to have random whiskers down the side.

Styles. Both programs have paragraph and character styles. InDesign also supports nested styles—that is, a paragraph style can encompass several different character styles.

Synchronize text. Only QuarkXPress has the ability to synchronize boiler-plate text. Within one project, you can designate one or more master text boxes. Any change you make to the text of a master is reflected in the child text boxes. Formatting is unique to each text box, not synchronized by the master.

Text wrap. Both programs allow you to set how text flows around intrusions. You can also invert wraps so that text flows around the interior of an element.

Vertical justification. Both QuarkXPress and InDesign support it.

Color

Both programs support most industry-standard color libraries. QuarkXPress includes its own Quark CMS (Color Management System), which claims to support Apple's ColorSync Utility. InDesign supports several color-management options.

Mac OS X 10.3 and Color Quandaries (TS)

If you're disappointed in the colors of your printed jobs, you may need to spend time and money on complicated color-management tools. But first go to /Applications/Utilities and open ColorSync Utility.

From here you can customize color profiles for Apple displays; replace profiles for printers, scanners, and digital cameras; and see a device's color gamut.

Many a designer has been surprised to discover how little the gamut of a monitor overlaps the gamut of even the best printer. To visually compare the gamuts of two or more devices, click the Profiles button and then click the first profile you want to view. A graph appears, showing that profile's color gamut. Click the triangle in the upper-left corner of the graph and then select "Hold for comparison" from the pop-up menu. Choose a second color profile and again select "Hold for comparison." Now if you click the first profile again, the two profiles' color gamuts will be shown overlapping. Note that the gamut is a 3D object you can rotate by dragging its corners.

Production Features

The craft of layout has always included responsibility for some aspects of print production, but today's page-layout software is also the primary production tool.

Adobe Illustrator/Photoshop file import. In InDesign, you can place native files from these two programs, even retaining the layers of the originals. This eliminates the need to create and track EPS and TIFF files. It's one of the ways Adobe helps its various products work together. For QuarkXPress, you'll need a third-party extension, such as Techno Design's **Photoshop Import XT** ($69; www.techno-design.com).

Automation. Both programs support tags (ASCII codes that are interpreted by QuarkXPress or InDesign when text is imported). InDesign can read QuarkXPress tags as well as its own. InDesign and QuarkXPress are AppleScriptable.

Data merge. The only way to get data-merge functionality in one of the top two applications is to buy the PageMaker Plug-in Pack for InDesign. Data merge is not available for QuarkXPress.

HTML export. InDesign does not let you export files to HTML—instead, it forces you to save all document elements as a package for another Adobe application, GoLive. QuarkXPress can export a single text story as HTML, but if you want to convert an entire page or layout space (including text and graphics) to the Web, you also have to bring along the page geometry—that is, the layout of the page. The only way to avoid that is to use a third-party extension.

PDF export. InDesign creates its own PDF files, including documents that conform to the PDF/X subset of the PDF standard (see the sidebar "PDF Output Options," below).

 PDF/X is a subset of the PDF standard. It is defined by a strict set of rules such as requiring all images to be in CMYK format and all fonts to be embedded. The rules were designed to save service bureaus time and money.

Separations Preview. InDesign's Separations Preview palette provides detailed information on spot and process plates, overprinting, knockouts, ink aliasing, and ink limits. QuarkXPress doesn't offer this functionality.

PDF Output Options (TS)

PDF output has become an increasingly important part of the print production process. There are three basic ways to export a PDF from InDesign and QuarkXPress.

Mac OS X. The 2D graphics in Mac OS X have a PDF foundation, so it's easy to generate PDFs from documents in almost any application. In InDesign and QuarkXPress select File > Print. In the Print dialog go to the Printer pop-up menu and choose Adobe PDF. Now just click the Print button, and you're done!

But like so many things in life, easy doesn't always equal best. Though the resulting PDF will do for comps, it probably won't pass muster at a service bureau or print shop. You'll have to resort to lengthier methods when you need a PDF for professional printing.

Page-layout applications. In InDesign, go to File > Export. In the resulting dialog, choose Adobe PDF from the Formats pop-up menu. Click Save; in the dialog that follows, you can choose from a slew of options, including Acrobat version compatibility, image and font compression, color profile, and security settings.

In QuarkXPress, go to File > Export > Layout as PDF. In the Export as PDF dialog, click the Options button; this brings up the PDF Export Options dialog, where you can specify image compression, font subsetting, registration and bleed details, and a few other settings. Beware that Quark doesn't support PDF/X, any security features, or versions 1.4 and 1.5 of the PDF standard.

QuarkXPress and Distiller. When you need more power or flexibility than QuarkXPress's Export tool offers, you can bring in Adobe's Distiller program. Part of Acrobat Professional, Distiller gives you extensive control over the transformation of PostScript files into PDF documents. To generate a PostScript file from QuarkXPress, choose File > Print; in the Print dialog that opens, click the Printer button; in the following Print dialog select Output Options from the third pop-up menu, check Save as File, and choose PostScript from the Format pop-up menu.

Making Your Decision

While there are certainly differences between QuarkXPress and InDesign, their core print-publishing features are quite similar. Choosing between the two is easy only if you must have a function supported in only one of these programs.

QuarkXPress is still the de facto standard among designers at ad agencies, publishing houses, commercial print shops, and output services. Knowing how to use QuarkXPress makes it easier to get a job with one of these companies or to work as a freelancer for them. The myriad users also offer peer support in online venues, magazine articles, and the workaday world.

However, InDesign is catching up. It exports PDF and PDF/X files that any shop can print, and its interface shares many elements with the commonly used Illustrator and Photoshop.

Your best bet, should you be able to afford the time and monetary investment, is to learn both programs. However, that may not be realistic, in which case economics will probably make the decision for you. If you want to work for companies in which QuarkXPress is established, go with QuarkXPress. If you're in an environment where you can choose your own page-layout program—and especially if fine typography is important to you and your clients—consider InDesign.

Other Possibilities (KT/TS)

We're always interested in software of exceptional value, a category that includes these three page-layout programs: Canvas, Ready,Set,Go!, and PageStream. It's not merely that they cost less than QuarkXPress and InDesign but that they are all capable of producing commercial-caliber work. Despite their capabilities, you don't usually see collections of "tips and tricks" articles for them, and you may have to coax your printer or service bureau to accept files from these programs (or supply it with Acrobat PDF or PostScript print files) for output.

We're also always interested in software that offers specialized features. You can produce almost any sort of publication with any of the standard page-layout programs. The ability to handle business cards, brochures, signs, simple packaging, magazines, books, and whatever else you may need to throw at them in the course of a day's work is what makes programs such as QuarkXPress and InDesign useful. But if your work revolves around creating advertisements, then you may be able to save time and get better results with MultiAd Creator.

Canvas Professional Edition

ACD Systems' **Canvas Professional Edition** ($349.99; www.acdsystems.com), now in version 9, has been around in one form or another since the Mac's early years, but it still can't seem to get any respect outside of a few niche markets, such as technical illustration. It's a capable Bézier drawing program whose essential features compare favorably with those in Illustrator and FreeHand. It's a useful bitmap editor; though not the equal of Photoshop, it has sufficient image-editing, retouching, color-correcting, and painting tools to suffice for most print (and Web) production work. More interesting for desktop publishers, the program also includes a respectable set of page-layout features that make Canvas, while not in the QuarkXPress and InDesign class, usable for booklet, brochure, newsletter, ad, and letterhead work.

Canvas lets you type or paste text into predrawn columns, as in a frame-based layout program, but you can also type in a drawn object, on a vector path, or directly on the page. The program allows you to apply unusual effects to type-set text (to extrude the letters or apply a drop shadow, or both, for example). Canvas doesn't distinguish page-layout documents from any others; you can add a text frame (with one or multiple columns, including columns of varying width) to any page and add pages (specifying whether they are one- or two-sided and whether they should appear as spreads). It supports master pages, layers, grids and guides, and other page-layout essentials.

This program is almost unbelievably feature-laden. See for yourself: you can download a 15-day demo version at www.acdsystems.com and decide if the program is worth $350 to you. (For more on Canvas, see Chapter 13.)

Ready,Set,Go!

Although it runs in Mac OS X, don't expect a polished Aqua interface in Diwan Software Limited's **Ready,Set,Go!** ($175; www.diwan.com). This veteran application, now in version 7.6, is spartan and more than a little old-fashioned. If you're accustomed to the way QuarkXPress or InDesign handles features such as color, the differences in Ready,Set,Go! may frustrate you. There isn't even a help menu (though the program comes with an HTML user guide).

However, Ready,Set,Go! does have the essentials of page layout and typesetting. If your projects are relatively simple, it is easier to fine-tune their layouts in Ready,Set,Go! than in, for example, Microsoft Word or AppleWorks. And, as with PageStream, you can export PDF files from Ready,Set,Go! and send them to a print shop.

Ready,Set,Go! also has a few surprises. One of these is Ready Script, a complex macro language well suited for automating tasks. The program's user guide explains how to generate Ready Script from word processors and put it to work in Ready,Set,Go! You can download a fully functioning demo at www.diwan.com.

PageStream

Grasshopper LLC's **PageStream** ($99, $149 Professional; www.grasshopper-llc.com) is essentially frame-based (like QuarkXPress), but it also allows for free-form text blocks. These blocks cannot be linked, however, and if you change their height or width, the text within the block is rescaled to fit.

In addition to a complete set of standard text-formatting functions, PageStream also has some fairly advanced features, including an eyedropper tool (like InDesign's) that copies and pastes attributes for text as well as graphic elements, and a kern pair editor similar to the one in QuarkXPress (changes to a text pair apply to all instances of that pair in the document). It creates numbered and bulleted lists (and lets you define the font and character to use as the bullet). Its output functions include object-level trapping and simple imposition, as well as a Collect for Output function, which places the layout file and graphics in a folder for sending to the printer.

The program exports Acrobat PDF files using its own software (although graphic-rich documents may still require Acrobat Distiller). It also exports HTML-encoded text and imports HTML as well. Indexing is built in, as is generation of tables of contents and lists of figures. It has many organizational tools, including sections.

The programmer himself offers technical support via email.

MultiAd Creator

We've noted in the past several editions of *The Macintosh Bible* that MultiAd's **MultiAd Creator** ($99 Desktop, $750 Professional; www.creatorsoftware.com) was a well-kept secret, and as far as computer and design venues are concerned, that's still true. MultiAd Creator is marketed directly to ad-making pros and advertising businesspeople as part of a comprehensive package of services that includes content development, clip-art subscriptions, placement services, and direct-mail printing and management. MultiAd has been supplying advertising producers for years—it didn't spring up in recent times as a software company.

The program comes in two versions: Desktop and Professional. Both run in Mac OS 9 and Mac OS X. The low-priced MultiAd Desktop is aimed at people who aren't professional designers. MultiAd Professional contains high-end features, such as a magic-wand masking tool and support for Pantone colors and OPI comments.

Although MultiAd Creator now supports multiple pages, it still doesn't attempt to compete with QuarkXPress and InDesign. You would probably find it especially frustrating to use for most other sorts of work, especially long documents. Its typography can be superb, but it seems designed to allow for (and require a certain amount of) manual tweaking. And even though the standard layout programs have added many of MultiAd Creator's essential functions—drawing tools and clipping paths, for example—they don't compete with it, either. MultiAd Creator's strength is its focus on ad production. It ships with hundreds of ornamental borders, including all the standard dashed-line borders essential for coupons. It creates starbursts and other vector graphics at the click of a mouse, as you'd expect. It provides for good control over all aspects of color, including trapping; lets you easily define a mask (clipping path) affecting one or several objects; and has special features that automate the creation of coupons.

If you think MultiAd Creator might be useful for you but are hesitant to spend money without firsthand experience, MultiAd offers downloadable demos of both versions at www.creatorsoftware.com.

Real Estate Rewards (TS)

Today's page-layout programs take up a *lot* of screen real estate. Regain a bit of breathing space with Mac OS X 10.3 (Panther).

Mac OS X 10.3 includes a great feature called Exposé, which may become your best friend. Press `F9` and Exposé resizes open windows so that you can see them all in one glance. Some windows may be tiny, but very visible filenames appear when you mouse over windows. Once you find the window you want, click it or press `F9` again.

Say you're in InDesign, working on a company's business card, and you need to compare it with the company's brochure and letterhead. How do you do so quickly when those file windows are buried beneath windows for iTunes, the local weather Web site, and a letter to your mom? Just click the business card file and press `F10` to dim everything but open InDesign documents. Oops—you remember that the letterhead is in Illustrator. Then press `Tab` to cycle through windows of other applications.

To reveal the disks, files, and folders on your Desktop, press F11 to make all open windows fly to the edges of your screen.

If you're not fond of using the function keys, you can still benefit from Exposé. To activate it when you move your pointer into a corner of your screen, go to the Exposé pane of System Preferences and choose which corner you want to correspond to which action. If you have a multibutton mouse, this preferences pane is also the place to set a button so that it corresponds to an Exposé action.

Fixing the Dreadful Defaults (TS/PG/KT)

The first thing you should do after installing any of these layout programs is change the worst of the initial default settings.

To change default settings, launch the program but do not open or create a document. (Changes made with a document open will apply to that file only, which is useful for customizing settings for particular jobs.) As soon as you have finished making changes, quit, and the changes will be written to the appropriate preferences files.

Then make a backup copy of the new defaults file. Find the file (locations for InDesign and QuarkXPress follow), duplicate it, and save the copy. The next time you need to reinstall, you can simply replace the new, out-of-the-box preferences file with your backup defaults copy.

- **InDesign**—Replace two files—InDesign Defaults and InDesign SavedData. To get there in Mac OS X, use the following path: ~Library/Preferences/Adobe InDesign/Version 3.0.

- **QuarkXPress**—The defaults file is named XPress Preferences.prf. In Mac OS X, use the path ~Library/Preferences/Quark/QuarkXPress 6.0.

Here are some of the defaults we routinely change in current versions of these two programs. Some settings are merely annoying, but a few are downright dangerous.

InDesign CS

InDesign has the fewest settings that need changing, and none of them are of the terribly stupid variety. However, we do change these:

Preferences

General. These are essentially fine. You may want to choose Absolute Numbering from the Page Numbering pop-up menu. Tool Tips are useful until you've learned the program, at which point they become very annoying.

Text. The Superscript, Subscript, and Small Cap default percentages are fine until you need to use them—then you're likely to need to adjust them for a particular font. Under Type Options, leave the defaults for Use Typographer's Quotes and Automatically Use Correct Optical Size checked—you'll always want them turned on for print work.

Composition. Keeping the Substituted Fonts option checked is important especially when opening PageMaker or QuarkXPress files that may include styled italics or bold type instead of the named italic, bold, or bold-italic fonts. We also suggest turning on H&J Violations, as it warns you if your settings are making too many spacing problems that InDesign cannot resolve.

Units & Increments. We prefer using a page-based ruler origin (choose Page from the Origin pop-up menu) just because most page elements are measured on the page (even if they are viewed on the whole spread). Experienced designers and typesetters make sure to choose Picas in both the Horizontal and Vertical Ruler Units pop-up menu, unless you need to measure column inches (usually for newspaper work). The keyboard increments are up to you; the default values are fine.

Grids. Retain the setting for Grids in Back; the others are a matter of personal preference.

Dictionary. Turn on the Recompose All Stories When Modified option and retain the other settings.

Story Editor Display. The defaults are good starting places, though you may want to change the text display font to reflect personal preference; for example, we prefer Matthew Carter's Verdana for onscreen reading.

Display Performance. Change the Adjust View Settings to High Quality if you find that EPS and other placed graphics are hard to see clearly. If you really dislike anti-aliased type, you can turn that off.

Keyboard Shortcuts (from the Edit menu). If you're coming to InDesign for the first time from QuarkXPress, choose the Shortcuts for QuarkXPress 4.0 from the Set pop-up menu. Customize the commands in the menus according to your own preferences, assigning keystrokes to the commands you use the most.

Text Frame Options (from the Object menu). Set the columns for each job; if you'll be creating many two- or three-column text boxes, for example, change this setting so that you won't have to modify each box individually. You may prefer to choose Leading rather than the default Ascent from the First Baseline Offset pop-up menu.

Paragraph palette

To open the Paragraph palette, choose Paragraph from the Type menu. To access the default options below, click the triangle in the upper-right corner of the Paragraph tab and you'll get a fly-out menu with these options and more listed.

Adobe Paragraph Composer. Make sure this option is checked, instead of Adobe Single-line Composer—unless you have a very slow Mac or you just don't care about precision typography.

Justification. The default values are perfectly acceptable but will often need adjustment for particular fonts. You can widen the ranges if InDesign is having trouble composing text (Word Spacing to 75/100/175 and Letter Spacing to –2/0/2; the numbers indicate minimum, desired, and maximum spacing, respectively). If you like to experiment with type sizes, setting Auto Leading to 100% is convenient.

Hyphenation. Change "Words with at Least" to 6. The other default settings are OK (though you may want to reduce the Hyphenation Zone to 1 or 1p6).

QuarkXPress 6

Over the years QuarkXPress has come to set the standard for page-layout programs. It's not that the QuarkXPress way is necessarily best, but hordes of designers and output specialists have adapted to it, so any different behavior seems nonstandard.

Preferences

When you open QuarkXPress, go to the QuarkXPress menu and then select Preferences to open the Preferences pane. On the left side of that pane is a list of preferences, divided into three areas: Application, Project, and Print Layout. Check the Drag and Drop Text box to turn it on.

Application: XTensions Manager. Under Show XTensions Manager at Startup, click the Always radio button.

Print Layout: General. As a matter of convenience, in the Guides section select In Front. Always set Auto Picture Import to Verify unless you really know what you're doing.

Print Layout: Measurements. Most designers and typographers want picas as the measurement units.

Print Layout: Paragraph. Unless you know what you're doing, uncheck the Maintain Leading box (you can always turn it on when you need it).

Print Layout: Character. Check the Ligatures and Standard Em Space boxes.

Now we get to one of the foolish settings you absolutely, positively must fix:

Print Layout: Tools. Click the Text Box icon (the first icon in the top row), click the Modify button, and in the Modify dialog choose the Runaround tab. Choose Item from the Type pop-up menu. It's usually convenient to set the defaults for Item to zero. This lets you insert into a column a text or picture box of the same width, which can come in handy when you need to insert a picture box in the text stream.

H&Js (from the Edit menu). In the H&Js dialog click Edit to bring up the Edit Hyphenation & Justification dialog. In the Justification Method section change the Space settings for Min., Opt., and Max. to 80%, 100%, and 150% (or the last could be 133% for classically tight word spacing); and change the settings for Char to –2%/0%/2% (or 0/0/0 for the classical settings). The program's initial defaults are so bad that we're mentioning them twice. With this change you will have undone the single most nonsensical default value in QuarkXPress. (See the "Improving the H&Js" sidebar, below, for the rest of the diatribe.) It's also a good idea to set the Flush Zone to 6 and to uncheck the Single Word Justify box.

After clicking OK, duplicate the Standard H&J (click the Duplicate button); back in the Edit Hyphenation & Justification dialog type No hyphenation in the Name field, uncheck the Auto Hyphenation box, change all the Space values to 100%, and make sure that all the Char values are 0%. Use this H&J for ragged—flush left, centered, or flush right—text. Base all other H&Js on one of these.

Kerning Table Edit (from the Utilities menu). Some fonts, even some from Adobe, have problematic kern pairs. If you use a font frequently and don't mind grappling with a poor interface, you can make changes to its kern pairs so that they will apply in new QuarkXPress documents. Just edit the kern pairs with no document open: in the Kerning Table Edit dialog select a font and click Edit; this brings up the Kerning Values dialog for that font, where you can edit the kern pairs. The changes are not recorded in the font, so they will apply only to QuarkXPress documents. Kerning edits can be exported and imported into existing QuarkXPress documents as well.

Tracking Edit (from the Utilities menu). QuarkXPress's tracking function is a little-known secret; most users just select a bunch of text and use keyboard shortcuts to modify spacing on the fly. However, the program does provide a track for each font, and it's always on as long as automatic pair-kerning is on. The default settings are zero, however, which means that no tracking changes are applied. Tracking is a powerful tool when you need to use a font designed for text (10- to 12-point size range) in a headline: the track can be set to automatically tighten the letterspacing as the type size increases, to ameliorate that weak and sloppy look that otherwise occurs. To use this, choose a font, click Edit, and edit the track in the Tracking Values dialog for that font. Smaller point sizes need very little positive tracking, text sizes need no change at all, and larger sizes need negative tracking. You make these changes by moving points on a line graph. The result should be a straight line, or close to it, but at a slight angle, moving from small positive values at, say, 6 or 8 point, through zero at 10 or 11 to larger negative values at 24 or larger sizes. (You'll have to experiment.) If you do this with no document open, the tracking will affect the font in all new documents.

Improving the H&Js (PG/KT)

All the page-layout programs ship with H&Js (hyphenation and justification settings) that cause more problems—in the form of typesetting that ranges from bad to mediocre—than they solve. If you care about the way type looks on your pages, you'll always have to do some manual tweaking, but we think the programs should try to minimize the need for much of this tedious work.

Background

Every font has a space character (sometimes referred to as a *spaceband* for historical reasons) that was designed with a specific width. The width is not the same in all fonts—designing the space is a critical aspect of designing the font as it relates to the fit of letters and words overall. Thus the word-spacing values discussed later in this sidebar refer to the width of a character in the font, expressed as a percentage.

continues on next page

Improving the H&Js continued

The letterspacing values are a bit more complicated. There is normally no space between letters—the bounding box (a PostScript term; it more or less replicates the block on which the old metal characters sat) of one letter fits snugly against the next. Digital type has an advantage over metal—we can move these boxes around and even overlap them without having to saw or file away metal as in the old days. But we still need something to measure. When we refer to character spacing or letterspacing, we are applying a percentage of some other unit to the fit. In most programs this unit is the word space; in QuarkXPress the unit is the zero character. The normal letter space is thus 0% (no adjustment).

In classical typography, all justification adjustments were made to word spacing, and none to letter fit. You can see why: the printer would have had to insert bits of spacing metal between some pieces of type and cut away metal from others. It was simply not done. Since the 1970s, when type became nonphysical (photo images, later digital data), it has been fashionable at times to set letters tightly, especially in advertising work. Against this one can only argue for good taste (and relatively natural spacing).

Here are the initial settings and two sets of enhancements, Phil's and Kathleen's. Phil's are much more practical; Kathleen's assume some manual tweaking (especially to get rid of consecutive hyphens) to make the text work out.

Canvas

To make your Canvas projects look as good as possible, change the word and letter spacing defaults and the hyphenation settings.

	SPACING SETTINGS (%)		
	Original	Phil's	Kathleen's
Word	100, 100, 150	80, 100, 150	80, 100, 133
Letter*	100, 100, 150	95, 100, 110	100, 100, 100

	HYPHENATION		
	Original	Phil's	Kathleen's
Minimum word	6	5	5
Characters before	3	2	2
Characters after	2	3	3
Consecutive	3	2	6

*It appears that Canvas bases its letterspacing adjustments on the em.

continues on next page

Improving the H&Js   *continued*

InDesign

InDesign comes the closest to shipping with a perfectly workable set of default values. We would be happier working with these values than with the default values that come with any other of these applications.

InDesign has a sophisticated feature—the paragraph composer, a text-composition routine that examines more than one line at a time. Using InDesign's single-line composer (thus basing composition on each line as if it were alone on the page) can create ugly stripes of loose and tight lines, which calls for a lot of manual tweaking if you care about typography.

	SPACING SETTINGS (%)		
	Original	Phil's	Kathleen's
Word	80, 100, 133	80, 100, 150	80, 100, 133
Letter*	0, 0, 0	–2, 0, 2	0, 0, 0
	HYPHENATION		
	Original	Phil's	Kathleen's
Minimum word	8	4	4
Characters before	3	2	2
Characters after	3	3	3
Consecutive	2	2	6
	COMPOSER		
	Original	Phil's	Kathleen's
Number of lines	5	10	12
Number of alternatives	5	10	12

*Letterspace adjustments are a percentage of word space in the font.

continues on next page

Improving the H&Js   *continued*

PageStream

This program hides its word- and character-spacing settings in the Preferences > Tracking dialog.

	SPACING SETTINGS (%)		
	Original	Phil's	Kathleen's
Word	80, 100, 133	80, 100, 150	80, 100, 133
*Letter**	–10, 0, 20	–5, 0, 10	0, 0, 0

	HYPHENATION		
	Original	Phil's	Kathleen's
Minimum word	6	5	5
Characters before	3	2	2
Characters after	2	3	3
Consecutive	3	2	6

*Letterspace adjustments are a percentage of the em.

QuarkXPress

QuarkXPress has the strangest set of default values of any of these programs. Once you've fixed them, QuarkXPress sets acceptable type.

That 110% value for Optimum word spacing is a very, very, very bad value. It means that QuarkXPress normally uses a word space that's 10% wider than the font designer intended. What ego! What chutzpah! What wrongheadedness! What a slap in the face to font designers!

	SPACING SETTINGS (%)		
	Original	Phil's	Kathleen's
Word	85, 110, 250	80, 100, 150	80, 100, 133
Letter*	0, 0, 4,	–2, 0, 2,	0, 0, 0

	HYPHENATION		
	Original	Phil's	Kathleen's
Minimum word	6	5	5
Characters before	3	2	2
Characters after	2	3	3
Consecutive	No limit	2	No limit

*Letterspace adjustments are a percentage of the en.

Interview: Dan Kottke

After Steve Jobs and Steve Wozniak, Dan Kottke was Apple's first employee. He had been a buddy of Jobs' at Reed College, and though Kottke had virtually no background in electronics, Jobs invited him in 1976 to help out in the legendary garage where Apple was born. He apparently learned fast, because he quickly became a top technician for the company. Kottke left Apple in August 1984 and went on to consulting and engineering jobs at a variety of Silicon Valley companies. He also picked up a law degree and became a fathers' rights activist. Unfortunately, however, he'd been out of work for a year and a half at the time of this interview.
—Henry Norr

> *Originally, the Mac was supposed to ship in '82, but things kept changing. It was always for good reasons, though—it was a very innovative product.*
>
> *—Dan Kottke, on shipping the first Mac*

How did you come to be Apple's first employee?

I knew Steve in college—we were good buddies—and we went to India together. In the summer of 1976 he invited me out to work on the Apple I, in the garage. I was actually the only person who really worked in the garage and got paid for it. If you've seen *Pirates of Silicon Valley*, I'm the Dan in the movie.

Had you studied computer science in college?

No, I did not have any background in electronics or computer science. I was a music major, but I wasn't a musician, either. I really just had a liberal arts degree—I studied philosophy and literature.

And from that you were able to go right into hardware engineering?

Well, it's a cautionary tale, actually. Neither Woz nor Jobs had degrees, and I'm a bright lad and a quick study, so I thought, you know, I can pick this stuff up. But it didn't work out well for me at Apple, because I wasn't an engineer until I joined the Mac project at the end of 1980, which was after Apple had gone public, and consequently I didn't have stock options.

What were you doing between '77 and '80?

I was a technician. The month I got my college degree, in '77, I came back to Apple full time, as employee number 12, and very quickly became the chief technician. I got to build all the prototypes of all the Apple II boards, and then I became the technician on the Apple III. Then, let's see, November of '80 is when Apple went public, and it was January '81 when the Mac project was officially getting ramped up, and I was the sixth person on the team.

At the Apple I stage I really was extremely green. I didn't know how anything worked, really. I had had basic transistor theory—that was about it. And, you know, Steve is not the kind of guy who really takes time to explain things to people. [He laughs.] It was very frustrating to me, and I kept thinking, "Well, I'll learn this, I'll learn this." What I didn't understand was that Jobs and Woz had been doing electronics for years, and it took me years to catch up.

continues on next page

What was your role once you moved to the Mac?

Me and a guy named Brian Howard built all the prototypes. I think I may well have built the first prototypes using the 68000 [the then-high-powered Motorola processor that Jobs put in the Mac]. The design kept changing, and I was always the one who brought the new boards to life every time there was a major design revision. I saved one of all of them, and I have a set. There's like 12 of them. [Pictures are at www.digibarn.com/stories/dankottke/index.htm.]

That's partly why the product slipped many times. Originally, you know, it was supposed to be shipping in '82, but things kept changing. It was always for good reasons, though—it was a very innovative product.

When the Mac came out, it was criticized for being underpowered. Did you feel that way?

It was underpowered in terms of user perception, because it was fairly slow; but booting off a floppy, of course it's going to be slow. Once it was running, it wasn't particularly slow. The criticism, if any, was that the 68000 wasn't a fit for the cost of the basic box—it was too big, too expensive for a home computer, because it was a workstation processor at that point.

Was it Steve who insisted on the 68000?

I don't know, but Steve Jobs definitely gets the credit for holding the line on that, despite the cost. If Steve didn't feel like someone was giving him a really good deal, he would just say, "We're not buying anything from them!"

Did he follow through?

In fact, that happened with National [Semiconductor] back in 1981, the first year of the Mac project. My initial part of the design was the detached keyboard, which was a single-chip computer. We were using a microcontroller from National, and we actually got the thing all designed and working, and it was very cool. Then one day we had an engineering meeting with the National sales rep, and they hemmed and hawed and said, "Well, you know, we can only deliver 5000 a month." And Steve blew his top, just completely, because we were projecting ten times that volume. Steve called up Charlie Sporck [then National's CEO] and read him the riot act. That was the end of any parts that we were ever going to buy from National.

What kind of computer do you use now?

I use both a Mac and a PC. I had to start using the PC the last five years, when I was at Vertical Networks.

What do you do now?

I'm a telecom engineer now, but Vertical Networks laid me off a year and a half ago, and I'm still looking for work. It's a bad depression. I have hundreds and hundreds of engineering contacts, and you know, I am just amazed—I never ever thought I would see a situation like this where I couldn't find something to work on.

15

Fonts

Jim Felici is the chapter editor and coauthor.

Jean Zambelli is the chapter coauthor.

With Mac OS X, the Mac's font handling has finally come of age. The Mac operating system now treats all fonts—PostScript, TrueType, OpenType—as equals, so you don't need Adobe Type Manager to see smooth versions of PostScript type onscreen. Also, font-management savvy is built right into Mac OS X—you can activate and deactivate whole sets of fonts at the click of a mouse, look inside fonts to see *all* the characters lurking in there (far more than before), and unleash more typographic power than ever before on the Mac. Mac fonts may be easier to use now, but there's still a lot to know about them, simply because they're involved in just about everything you and your programs do on your Mac. Your first step to becoming a Mac font expert starts on the next page.

In This Chapter

About Fonts and Typefaces (JF)

The words *font* and *typeface* are often used interchangeably, but they're actually quite different things.

A font is a computer file (sometimes more than one) that describes how type should look on the screen or on a printed page. It consists of a collection of drawings of characters, numerals, symbols, punctuation marks, and assorted other linguistic and decorative gewgaws. These drawings can be scaled so that one font can create type in any size.

As technology has advanced, fonts have grown increasingly complicated (see "Font Formats," later in this chapter), and they're now more than just a collection of characters: they're programs in their own right that also tell those characters how to act in different situations.

A typeface, in contrast, is artwork—a set of characters that share a common design. There are tens of thousands of typefaces out there, each giving the alphabet a somewhat (sometimes wildly) different appearance. When you look at a page, you see type set in a typeface. That type was generated by a font of the same name.

When you look at a page, then, you can say, "What typeface is that?" or "What font was used to set that type?" But you can't say, "What font is that?" because you're not looking at a font; the font is back in the computer (**Figure 15.1**).

Figure 15.1

A typeface (left) is a set of characters that share a set of design motifs, such as in Adobe Garamond Semibold Italic. A font, by contrast, is a computer file that is nothing much to look at, apart from its icon (right). The font is the vehicle that carries the typeface.

Adobe Garamond Semibold Italic

What's in a Name?

Not all fonts are created equal. Vendors usually design their own typefaces, and the fonts they create are all unique. The names of fonts, though, are often not trademarked, so there's nothing to keep ten different font vendors from selling ten different versions of Bodoni, Baskerville, or Garamond. So Linotype Bodoni is not the same as Monotype Bodoni, and both are different from ITC Bodoni.

It's also possible to have two identically named fonts from the same vendor show up in two different font formats (see "Font Formats," later in this chapter). Both will look the same in a font menu, and you won't be able to tell one from the other.

When you're specifying a font for a colleague, client, or service bureau, you have to specify the vendor's name as well to make sure the person you're working with gets the full picture.

There are industry-wide conventions these days for how fonts should be named. These names reflect a font's format and parentage. Nevertheless, some older fonts—as well as fonts with public-domain names such as Bodoni and Garamond—have names that make their vendor and formats unclear.

So to be perfectly clear for both yourself and those who share your files, it's important to be precise about the names and identities of the fonts you use. Otherwise, documents may not look right to your clients or coworkers, and font conflicts may confuse your Mac, causing various oddities.

How Fonts Work

On the Mac, every character you type is represented on the screen by a typeface. If you don't actively select a typeface to use, your application chooses one by default. If you don't like the default choice, you can change it by selecting another font (**Figure 15.2**). That font will generate text set in the typeface you prefer. You cannot, however, choose the fonts that Mac OS X uses for its screen displays, menus, and dialogs.

Figure 15.2

Many programs (here, Safari) allow you to choose the default font.

Application programs—your word processor, for example—generally don't do much in the way of handling type. This is a service provided mainly by the Mac system. By centralizing type-handling in this way, the Mac can guarantee that your fonts will work the same way in all your programs. Desktop-publishing programs are an important exception since they need to take typographic aesthetics far beyond what the Mac OS can do.

What Happens When You Type

Before you type a single character, your application makes a note of which font you've chosen to use, and it asks the Mac operating system to provide it with the font information it needs. As you type, the system notes each of your keystrokes and reaches into the font to recover the image of the character you requested. It then scales this to the size you requested and displays the character on the screen as a bitmapped image, drawn in the same pixels that your monitor uses to display everything. When you print, this same array of characters is bitmapped again, but at a much higher resolution.

For every character you type, the system is also reading from the font's *metrics* information, noting how wide each character is and handing this information to your program. As you type a line, your program is adding up all those widths and comparing the total with the line length (column width) you've specified. At the same time, your program may be making spacing adjustments between certain characters, and these adjustments are calculated in, too. When there's no more room on the line, your program ends that line and begins a new one.

It's important to remember that this isn't a visual system—it's all numeric. Your Mac doesn't "see" when a line of type is full, but rather it comes to that decision based on a counting process. As we'll see later, that counting process can become quite complicated.

It's also important to realize that everything in your text has a font associated with it. Even blank spaces, such as those between words, have a font attributed to them (**Figure 15.3**). When you're creating documents, then, it's easy to end up having it call for fonts that aren't apparently being used (a Times Roman word space looks pretty much like a Helvetica word space). You won't know that your document is calling for a font that isn't apparently being used unless you try to open or print the document on a system that lacks that font.

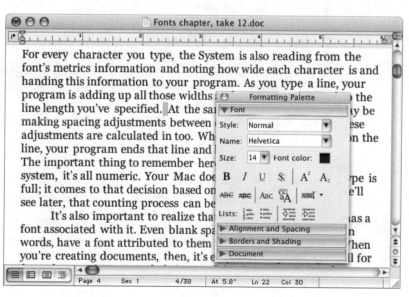

Figure 15.3

Every bit of text has typographic characteristics—even a word space, as shown here. Amid all that text set in Georgia there lurks a single word space formatted in Helvetica. When it comes time to print, you'll need all the fonts used to format a document—even when that formatting is invisible.

How the Mac OS Finds Your Fonts (JF)

The Mac OS can find your fonts only if they're stored—*installed*—in one of a few designated folders. All these folders are conveniently named Fonts. In OS versions before Mac OS X 10.3 (Panther), when the system finds fonts in one or more of these folders, it lists them by name in your programs' font menus. Starting in Mac OS X 10.3, installed fonts are first listed in the Mac's new font-management program, Font Book. In Font Book (located in the Applications folder) you have the power to make only selected fonts available to your applications, a process called *enabling* and *disabling* them, or (depending on the Mac Help file you're reading) turning them *on* or *off* (see "Installing and Enabling Fonts," below). The most common of the Fonts folders is inside the Library folder at the root level of your hard disk (**Figure 15.4**). Everyone who uses your Mac can use the fonts stored in this folder. If you have system administrator privileges (which you will if it's your own personal machine), you can add, remove, or modify fonts in this folder.

Figure 15.4

The fonts stored in the /Library/Fonts folder (shown here) are available to everyone who uses your Mac.

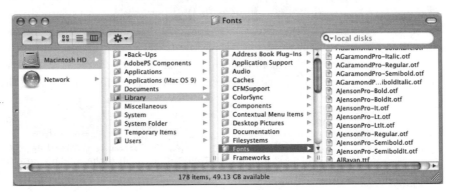

If you share your Mac with other users, and you each have your own account, you can store fonts for your private use inside the /Users/*username*/Library/Fonts folder (or ~/Library/Fonts, for short).

Fonts can also be stored in shared volumes on servers that your Mac is connected to. Their home is the /Network/Library/Fonts folder, and they're under the control of the network administrator.

The Mac OS keeps its own fonts—the ones it uses for the Mac interface and the *core set* it uses for compatibility with other systems—in the /System/Library/Fonts folder. Don't mess with these! Don't add any fonts to this folder, and by all means don't take any out. In fact, forget that I even mentioned it.

Fonts in the Classic Environment

You can also store fonts in the /System/Fonts folder in the Mac Classic environment. These fonts will be available to all the applications you run, both those in Classic mode and those running under Mac OS X. This is a one-way street, though, and programs running in Classic mode will not be able to use any fonts installed in Mac OS X Fonts folders, either on your Mac or on any other file servers.

If you install fonts that have identical names (but are not identical fonts) in both Mac OS X and the Classic environment, you can use Font Book to remove the duplicate fonts (see "Weeding out duplicate fonts with Font Book," later in this chapter). You won't suffer any font conflicts, but Mac OS X will opt to use the fonts installed in any of its Fonts folders over those installed in the Classic environment. In addition, you should know that fonts installed in the Classic environment are available to anyone using the Mac in Classic mode, and anyone can add fonts to Classic's System Folder.

Installing and Enabling Fonts

Before Mac OS X 10.3, to use a font, all you had to do was *install* it, which meant putting it in a folder where the operating system expected to find it. To uninstall it, you dragged it somewhere else. In Mac OS X 10.3, with Font Book you have the added option of enabling or disabling installed fonts—that is, making them available or unavailable to your programs—simply by selecting them from a list. No dragging is involved.

In Mac OS X 10.3, you can still install fonts by dragging them into the Fonts folder of your choice. Or you can use Font Book to install them, through its File > Add Fonts command. Here you select the fonts you want to install and click the appropriate radio button to add them to the Fonts folder of your choice. Selecting "for me only" puts them in your ~/Library/Fonts folder; "for all users of this computer" puts them in the /Library/Fonts folder; and "for Classic Mac OS" puts them in the /System Folder/Fonts folder.

 You can choose only one of the three installation options with Font Book. Choosing "for me only" puts the fonts in a Mac OS X Fonts folder, which is out of reach for applications running in the Classic environment. Choosing "for all users of this computer" makes fonts available to all Mac OS X users but not to Classic users. Choosing "for Classic Mac OS" makes the fonts available to everyone, no matter which version of the OS they are running.

When Font Book installs a font, it is automatically enabled, available for use. In the "Font Book: A Built-In Font Manager" section, later in this chapter, you will learn more about enabling and disabling fonts, and about how you can manage your font library to keep font menus manageable and make your typesetting more efficient.

Newly installed fonts may not become available for use with your programs immediately. Some programs that are running when you install a font have to be shut down and relaunched before they'll include newly installed fonts in their Fonts menus. Microsoft Word is one such program. (These programs take an inventory of available fonts only when they start up.) Other programs, which offer *dynamic font updating,* make those fonts available immediately. TextEdit is an example of the latter. In general, native Mac OS X applications (those written from the ground up for Mac OS X, so-called Cocoa applications) have dynamic font updating. Applications updated for Carbon (which work with Mac OS X but don't take full advantage of all that Mac OS X offers) usually don't.

Font Formats (JF)

Like any other computer technology, fonts evolve. Fortunately, this evolution happens slowly—no one wants to have to buy another entire font library every time a better one comes along.

Today there are three major font formats available for the Mac: PostScript Type 1 (the original scalable Mac font), TrueType (its eventual competitor), and OpenType (a fusion of the other two, marking the end of the "font wars").

Mac OS X handles all three equally well, and you can mix them in a single document without fear. This is great progress over earlier versions of the Mac OS.

PostScript Type 1

The first popular high-quality font format for desktop computers was PostScript Type 1, from Adobe Systems. It had a capacity of 256 characters and keyboard commands, and it featured scalable character outlines, so a single font could create type in any size. (The 256 characters and commands that a PostScript font contains can be numbered using a single byte of computer data, so PostScript fonts are referred to as *single-byte* fonts.)

When PostScript fonts first appeared, though, no operating system could reproduce their outline characters properly onscreen. Makers of PostScript fonts had to include sets of special hand-drawn bitmapped fonts—*screen fonts*—in four or five sizes to create the accurate screen previews that users wanted. The fonts used for printing were separate files. Screen fonts were stored in a special kind of folder called a *suitcase.*

A typical PostScript Type 1 font, then, consists of two parts: a printer font (often with a hard-to-understand name, such as UniBolCon) and a folder of screen fonts (usually with a more comprehensible name, such as Univers Bold Condensed), as shown in **Figure 15.5**.

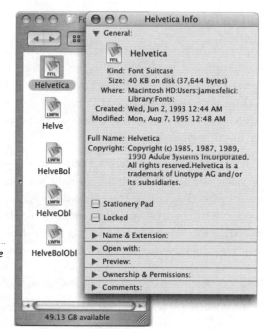

Figure 15.5

A suitcase of screen fonts used by the operating system complements the four outline fonts (with hard-to-follow names). Now that Mac OS X uses the same icon for all font files, it's hard to tell them apart.

As with its predecessors, Mac OS X still needs to have PostScript Type 1 screen fonts installed, mainly because important font-metrics information is contained there. If the screen fonts aren't installed, the font they represent will not appear in any application's Font menu or in the Font panel. (The Font panel appears only in applications that support it. See "Using the Font Panel," later in this chapter.) If you have the screen fonts installed but not the printer font, you may see a certain typeface onscreen, but when you print, you'll see a substitute typeface.

About Adobe Type Manager

Before Mac OS X, the Mac OS could scale a PostScript font's bitmaps to other sizes for screen display, but the results were horrific. So Adobe introduced Adobe Type Manager (ATM), a piece of software that worked with the operating system and could create smoothly scaled versions of a font's characters at any size. ATM used the outlines in the printer fonts to create this type, but the Mac system still needed the screen fonts before it could serve type to an application program.

Mac OS X doesn't need ATM anymore, because it uses a version of PostScript itself to create all screen images, including type. Mac OS X's Classic environment, though, still uses the original Mac technology for its screen display—called QuickDraw—so if you want smooth screen type when using PostScript fonts in the Classic environment, you'll still need ATM.

TrueType

For years, Apple chafed at its reliance on a non-Apple technology (that is, PostScript) for the success of its font strategy, so it worked with Microsoft to create a new, better font format, which it called TrueType. Ironically, the Mac community—content with its PostScript fonts—never embraced TrueType, but Microsoft used it to make Windows a powerful competitor to the Mac in the desktop-publishing market.

A TrueType font can contain several font files—usually other *font family* members, such as bold, italic, and bold italic versions—and even screen fonts in some cases. (While TrueType fonts don't require separate screen fonts, some vendors may opt to include them for sizes and designs that Mac OS X's TrueType rasterizer might not render well.) Because TrueType fonts can contain several font files, they are also packaged in folders called suitcases (**Figure 15.6**).

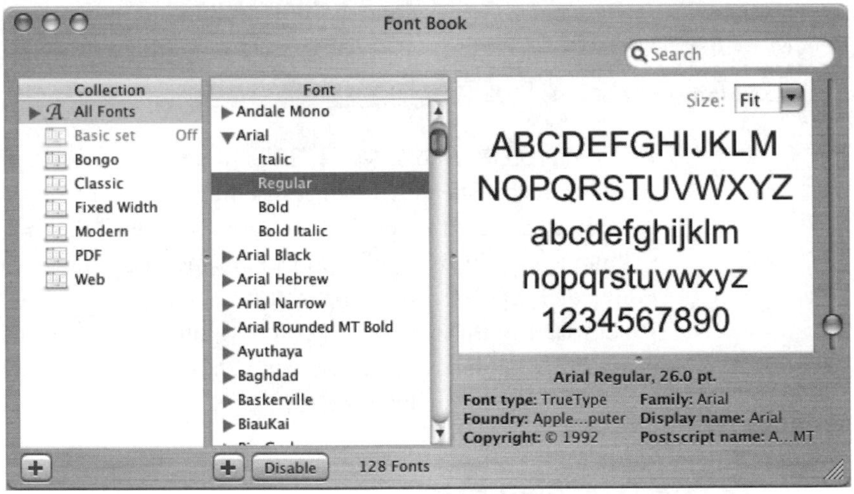

Figure 15.6

Although Arial is represented by only a single icon in the Fonts folder, it is actually four fonts in one. Arial is a TrueType font, which means that its icon represents a suitcase that can hold more than one font.

TrueType fonts are *double-byte* fonts, which means that it takes 2 bytes of computer data to enumerate all the characters they can contain: up to nearly 65,000 of them. No TrueType fonts are this big, but they have the room to accommodate in one font all the characters you would need to set type in several different language scripts in addition to the Latin alphabet used in English.

TrueType also introduced the idea that fonts could provide other services, for example offering alternate forms of characters. A single *character*—say, a capital *A*—can contain many alternate forms. Each of these forms is called a *glyph* (**Figure 15.7**). In Arabic, for instance, many characters can be represented by alternate glyphs—forms that have different shapes when used in different contexts. In English, many characters—capital letters, numerals, fractions— can also have alternate forms. Most of the fonts that come with Mac OS X are TrueType fonts.

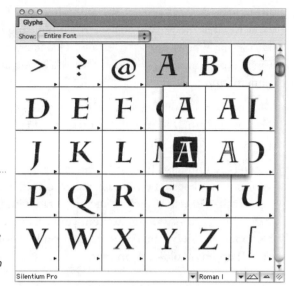

Figure 15.7

Adobe InDesign has a powerful built-in tool for searching all the glyphs in a font and copying them into your pages. The little triangles in each character window indicate that each of these characters has alternative glyphs, which pop up in their own window.

TrueType fonts, dfonts, and Mac OS X

Mac OS X, though, has introduced a new variety of TrueType font, which bears the filename extension .dfont. All the System fonts installed with Mac OS X are TrueType dfonts.

This is a concession to Unix, the operating-system technology that underlies Mac OS X. Before Mac OS X, all Mac fonts were structured like Mac files, with two *forks,* one for data (content, in short) and one for additional information called *resources.* Unix doesn't work this way, so dfonts are TrueType fonts whose resources have been packed into the data fork of the file.

Huh? Fortunately, this will probably never make a difference to you, as Mac OS X still handles older TrueType fonts (the forked ones) as it did in Mac OS 9 and previous versions of the operating system. Apart from this new way of packaging the System fonts, nothing has changed, and everything works the way it did.

OpenType

OpenType fonts were developed collaboratively by Adobe Systems and Microsoft.

OpenType is a modified and expanded kind of TrueType font that can store either TrueType or PostScript font data. (Apple's technical documentation refers to the latter as "Macintosh PostScript Type 1 enabled SFNT font suitcases." Yikes.) It's an ingenious system that allows font vendors to use whichever kind of character outlines they prefer (Adobe obviously prefers PostScript), with operating systems and application programs working equally well no matter what. OpenType's main advantage is its large character set, which should mean good-bye to "expert sets" and "alternate" fonts—auxiliary fonts for typefaces that have too many characters for old, single-byte font formats such as PostScript Type 1. These "overflow" characters can now be built into a single OpenType font along with their everyday companion letters, numbers, and punctuation marks.

One of the additional charms of OpenType is that a single font file can work on any platform. No more Mac versions of fonts and Windows versions of fonts—one file fits all.

OpenType fonts also have an expanded range of *layout features,* which help applications choose the right character in certain situations. For example, by performing an action such as clicking a radio button or selecting a check box in an OpenType-savvy application, you can automatically have lining numerals (ones that sit on the baseline and are all the same height, such as 1, 2, 3, and 4) appear as old-style numerals (1, 2, 3, and 4).

OpenType fonts and Mac OS X

Staring with Mac OS X 10.3, the Mac supports many of OpenType fonts' character-switching tricks. You can, for example, opt to have a program automatically insert ligatures (twinned characters, such as *fi* and *fl*) where appropriate, and you can switch uppercase numerals to old-style numerals and substitute small capitals for full-size ones. You manage these switches in the Font panel (see "High-end typography with the Font panel," later in the chapter).

For applications that weren't written specifically for Mac OS X (*Carbonized* applications) the Mac serves up OpenType fonts in the familiar old way, as it does with PostScript and TrueType fonts. In fact, using OpenType fonts in Mac OS X is indistinguishable from using any other kind of font unless you are using any of the switching tricks mentioned above.

Recognizing a Font's Format

Gone are the days when you could recognize a Mac font by its icon. In Mac OS X, all fonts—including screen-font suitcases—have the same icon. (You might ask why Apple persists in calling these things "suitcases" if they don't even have an appropriate icon to go along with the name. Well, don't ask.)

 Mac OS X's jargon is confusing here. TrueType fonts and TrueType dfonts are stored in suitcases. So are PostScript screen fonts. But OpenType fonts, which may be technically indistinguishable from TrueType fonts, are referred to by Apple as *font files.* **Ditto for PostScript fonts.**

Fortunately, Apple has added wee legends to the font icons, and if you have good eyes, you can often see what the icons represent (**Figure 15.8**). Unfortunately, the legends are not consistent and not always helpful. Here are the legends:

AJensonPro–
SemiboldIt.otf   AlBayan.ttf

AmeriBTMedItaA   Arial Rounded Bold

Figure 15.8

If your font icons are large enough (64 by 64 pixels in this case), you can read the tiny legends that indicate the nature of each font file: OTF, TTF, LWFN, FFIL, and DFONT.

Apple Chancery.dfont

- OTF is an OpenType font.
- TTF is a TrueType font.
- LWFN is a PostScript font (or LaserWriter font, to make some sense of the initials).
- FFIL is a screen-font suitcase, such as a PostScript screen font, or possibly an older TrueType font (also stored in a suitcase).
- DFONT is a dfont TrueType font.

In a Fonts folder, the easiest way to recognize the format of a font file is by its filename extension:

- .otf denotes an OpenType font.
- .ttf denotes a TrueType font.
- .ttc denotes a TrueType font collection (several fonts—usually family members, such as regular, italic, bold, and bold italic—packed into a single file, er, suitcase).
- .dfont denotes a dfont TrueType font.

Fonts with no filename extension may either be pre–Mac OS X TrueType fonts (from the days when filename extensions were considered un-Mac) or PostScript fonts. In this latter category are both printer fonts (the ones that contain the scalable character outlines) and suitcases of screen fonts. The best way to tell a PostScript printer font from a suitcase with a similar name is by using Get Info (File > Get Info). As for a TrueType font, the Get Info window may not overtly identify its format (calling it simply a "font suitcase"), but the manufacturer's description you find there may be more explicit.

The surest—but slowest—way to discover a font's format is to use Font Book. It's slow because you can learn about only one font at a time, but the information Font Book reveals is detailed and precise. In Font Book's Preview menu, make sure that Show Font Info is turned on. This shaves a slice off the bottom of the preview window, but in that space you'll see intimate details about the font and who made it.

Problems with Duplicate Fonts

Even when the Mac had only a single Fonts folder, there was a chance that you could have two fonts with the same name installed at the same time. Now that Mac OS X has several Fonts folders to choose from, this possible confusion is multiplied. Duplicate names can happen when two vendors use the same name for their otherwise unique fonts or when a single vendor releases the same typeface in more than one font format.

To scan for duplicate fonts, use Font Book. Duplicates are indicated in the Font Book Font list by a bullet (**Figure 15.9**). To solve the problem, select Resolve Duplicates from the Edit menu (for more on this see "Weeding out duplicate fonts with Font Book," later in this chapter).

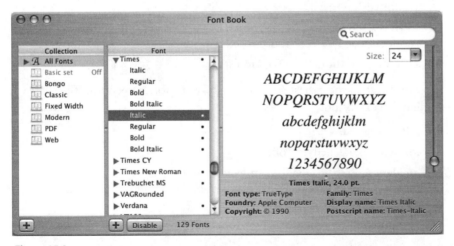

Figure 15.9

Font Book flags duplicate fonts (or those with duplicate names) with a bullet (•). Before letting Font Book decide how to resolve this conflict, look into the identity of the apparent duplicates. Here, one set of Times fonts is made up of dfonts, but the others are TrueType fonts, and you may prefer to keep one kind or the other. Use the Disable button to turn off the ones you don't want.

What's in a Font? (JF)

Who knows?! Once upon a time, in the era of single-byte fonts, nearly all text fonts contained the same things—that is, they had the same standard *character set.* Even when TrueType fonts came along, with their potentially vast character sets, fonts generally stayed small, consisting mainly of Latin characters (with enough accented ones to set most, but not all, European languages), numerals, punctuation, and a handful of mathematical and special symbols.

OpenType threatens to break this wide open, introducing fonts with large, unpredictable character sets and a variety of possible layout features. When buying OpenType fonts, it's important that you know what you're getting, because the minimum definition of an OpenType font is "a TrueType font with a digital signature" (this signature being an antipiracy device that Microsoft intends to impose on all Windows software someday). Such a font could contain 60,000 characters or 6.

Adobe, for its part, has converted its entire library to the OpenType format, but the character set doesn't look that different from the one in the old PostScript Type 1 fonts (**Figure 15.10**).

Likewise, an OpenType font may offer no layout features and function exactly like an "old-fashioned" font, except that it can work on either the Mac or Windows.

a	b	c	d	e	f	g	h	i	j	k	l	m
n	o	p	q	r	s	t	u	v	w	x	y	z
A	B	C	D	E	F	G	H	I	J	K	L	M
N	O	P	Q	R	S	T	U	V	W	X	Y	Z
1	2	3	4	5	6	7	8	9	0	?	¿	@
!	¡	#	$	¢	¥	£	€	%	‰	^	&	*
+	±	÷	=	-	–	—	(	)	[	]	{	}
_	;	:	'	"	\	|	,	.	<	>	/	¦
~	™	ƒ	¶	•	ª	º	®	†	‘	’	“	”
ß	©	·	°	¬	…	‹	›	«	»	˘	⁄	¤
ﬁ	ﬂ	‡	˚	·	‚	„	œ	Œ	æ	Æ	ı	§
¸	˛	¯	`	´	¨	ˆ	ˇ	˜	˝	˙	ç	ø
å	à	è	ì	ò	ù	á	é	í	ó	ú	ä	ë
ï	ö	ü	ÿ	â	ê	î	ô	û	ñ	ã	õ	Ç
Ø	À	È	Ì	Ò	Ù	Á	É	Í	Ó	Ú	Ä	Ë
Ï	Ö	Ü	Ÿ	Â	Ê	Î	Ô	Û	Å	Ñ	Ã	Õ
Ð	ð	Þ	þ	Š	š	Ý	ý	Ž	ž	¼	½	¾
1	2	3	−	×	∫	√	∞	≈	≠	≤	≥	◊
µ	∏	π	Ω	∑	∆	∂	ℓ	℮				

Figure 15.10

Although an OpenType font can contain tens of thousands of characters, most contain far fewer. The character set shown here is the standard for fonts in the Adobe Font Library that were converted from PostScript format. Adobe's Pro fonts are much more complex.

Under the Hood: the Old (Mac Roman) and the New (Unicode)

Computers—even clever ones like the Mac—don't know one character from another. When you type an *A* on your keyboard, your Mac doesn't say, "Aha! The master wants an *A*." In fact, your Mac says, "Aha! The master wants character number 65." It then runs off to the font you're using and displays character number 65, which is usually an *A*.

This system of assigning numbers to characters is called *encoding*. Encodings are important because different computer systems use different encodings, and Mac OS X uses a different one (Unicode) from that used by Mac OS 9 and earlier (Mac Roman).

Pretty much all encodings agree on the meanings of numbers 0 through 127, which represent the American Standard Code for Information Interchange (known as ASCII, pronounced *ass-key*). But above 127, definitions diverge. For example, before Mac OS X, number 165 was a bullet (•) on a Mac but a yen sign (¥) on a Windows PC (which used an encoding scheme called Win ANSI).

Mac OS X and new versions of Windows (NT, XP, 2000) have calmed the confusion (theoretically, at least) by settling on a new, international standard—Unicode—as the basis of their new font encodings. The two platforms now agree on the ID numbers of more than 100,000 characters from around the world. The ultimate implications of this are huge and global, but in the short term it should help eliminate weird character substitutions in files that travel from Mac to PC or vice versa. That is, of course, as soon as all Mac and PC applications sign on to Unicode as well.

How to Get the Characters You Want (JF)

Hold on to your hat. Getting at characters other than the ones printed on your keyboard's keys has always required some work (and a good memory for some odd keystroke combinations), but with Mac OS X things have become quite a bit more complicated. This is not just an arbitrary new finger dance, though—it's a path to a whole new world of typographic possibilities.

The adventure starts at the Input menu (**Figure 15.11**).

Figure 15.11

The Input menu allows you to change keyboard layouts for various languages and font encodings, as well as giving you access to the all-important Character Palette.

The Input Menu: Open Sez Me

The Input menu has two functions. First, it allows you to switch your keyboard layout, which defines which characters you get when you strike particular keys. If your keyboard had an electronic display on each key, switching keyboard layouts would cause different characters to appear on different keys. The familiar QWERTY of an American keyboard, for example, would appear as AZERTY when you chose a French keyboard layout or QWERTZ if you opted for German.

Second, the Input menu (via the Character Palette) allows you to switch between font encodings—mainly between Mac Roman and Unicode.

 Unless you have some good reason to choose a Unicode keyboard layout, stick with one labeled Roman, such as the one named U.S. (You'll find the labels in the third column of the Input menu). This leaves you with the old familiar Mac methods of getting at a font's characters.

Perhaps the most striking thing about the Input menu is that when you first start using Mac OS X, it's probably not even on your screen. It's up to you to make it appear. Sound dumb? You bet.

To make the Input menu appear for the first time, open System Preferences and click International among the Personal settings. In the first pane click the Input Menu tab, and then in the Input Menu pane just check the box at the lower left marked "Show input menu in menu bar." If you're using Mac OS X 10.2 or earlier, click the Input Menu tab. Next you'll need to change something in this pane (such as checking an additional option) before the Input menu icon will appear in the menu bar.

In Mac OS X 10.3, the Input menu icon appears at the right end of the menu bar, by the date and time, sound, and modem-connection icons (if you have those options turned on). In earlier Mac OS X versions, it appears to the right of the main menu titles. The Input menu icon is usually a flag reflecting the language of the keyboard layout you've chosen.

Customizing the Input menu

In the System Preferences/International/Input Menu pane, you can control what will appear in the Input menu. If you're an English speaker (actually, an English typist), the most useful keyboard layouts to select (by checking their boxes) are U.S., U.S. Extended, and Unicode Hex Input. If you create text in other languages, scroll down the list and check off the languages you want to work in. Two other crucial options to select are Character Palette and Keyboard Viewer, which are discussed below. Once you've made your choices, close the dialog and you'll find your choices listed as options in the Input menu (which you display by clicking the flag icon in the menu bar).

In Mac OS X 10.3, to change the options available from within the Input Menu, select Open International, which whisks you to the appropriate System Preferences pane. In earlier Mac OS X versions, select Customize Menu from the Input menu.

The Character Palette

The Character Palette allows you to see a large selection of characters and to copy into your documents the ones you need (**Figure 15.12**). It does this in a most peculiar way, though, which takes some getting used to. In fact, it's so byzantine that you'll come to suspect it was designed by infiltrators from the Windows development team.

You can open the Character Palette through the Input menu or—in applications that have been rewritten for Mac OS X—through the Edit > Special Characters menu.

Continuing with the "find me if you can" theme inaugurated by the Input menu, you should first open up the Character Palette to its maximum view. To do this, first click the capsule-shaped button at the top right of the palette, which makes the View menu appear. Then click the disclosure triangles next to Character Info and Font Variations at the lower left. In Mac OS X 10.2 and earlier, just click that solitary triangle on the left-hand side to reveal the rest of the window.

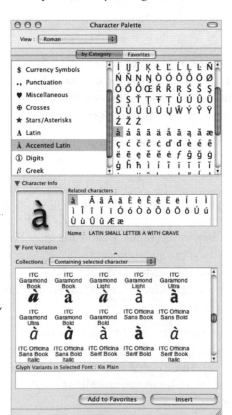

Figure 15.12

The Character Palette is a complex bit of business, but most of the time you'll be using it simply to find accented characters, symbols, and dingbats. Once you've found them, copy them to the Favorites section so that you can access them quickly next time.

The Character Palette can show you the characters in a particular font, but it takes some effort. (This is more easily done in Font Book, but there you can only look at them, not copy them.) In Mac OS X 10.3, select Glyph from the View menu at the top. Then click the Glyph Catalog tab. (In Mac OS X 10.2 and earlier, select All from the View menu and then click the Glyph Catalog tab.) Next, from the Font menu select the font you want to examine, and from the pop-up menu to its right choose which family member you're after (such as bold or italic). You can then scroll down through the character window to peruse what's available.

The default view in the Character Palette, selected from the View pop-up menu at the top of the palette, is Roman. In this view, the Character Palette shows you a generic collection of characters that are divided into categories, such as Math, Arrows, Latin, and the ever-popular Miscellaneous. These characters represent a selection—but not all—of those accounted for by Unicode's character ID numbering scheme. You can also opt for Unicode in the View menu, which gives you a longer but somewhat more comprehensible list of categories and a larger range of characters to choose from.

To locate the character you want in either of these views, you laboriously search through the many categories, and having found it, you click it. It appears in an enlarged view in a character pane in the Character Info section of the palette.

Getting the character you want into your document

Once you've found the character you're after, you have three ways of getting it into your document, where it will appear at the insertion point (the spot with the blinking vertical bar). Two of these methods add the character using the font currently in use in your text. The third method, which is new to Mac OS X 10.3, allows you to add a character from another font.

To add a character from the current font, you can either double-click the character in the character-array pane at the upper right or single-click it and click the Insert button at the bottom of the palette. Then click the Add to Favorites button so that you don't have to go through this nonsense again. Your Favorites list consists of any and all characters you've found once and would like to find more easily in the future. To get to your collection of Favorites, click the Favorites tab above the character-array pane.

To add a character from a font other than the one currently in use in your document, first click the character you want by selecting Glyph from the View menu, and then select a font on the Glyph Catalog pane. From the Collections pop-up menu, select "Containing selected character," if it's not already selected. This causes the pane below it to display your chosen character in every typeface available to your Mac. You can scroll through this pane to find the font you're after. Click once on the sample character representing the font of your choice.

Now place the insertion point where you want to insert the character and click the character-preview pane in the Character Info section of the palette. The character is pasted at the insertion point.

 This technique works only if you have just changed the position of your pointer. If you're typing along in, say, Times, and you pause to select a character from another font, this copying technique will simply add the character in Times, which is the font in use at the insertion point.

If the Character Palette refuses to insert the character you want, it's because either (a) that character doesn't exist in the font you're using in your document or (b) you've chosen a character that requires Unicode support lacking in your application. Look for a tiny warning along the bottom of the Character Palette that says, "The current application does not support this Unicode-only character."

 The Character Palette does not show directly which characters are in a given font. (For that, there's Font Book.) Instead, it shows all the common Unicode characters that might be found in a font. (You'll notice that when you select different fonts in the Character Palette, the character array never changes). This approach lets you select a character and then figure out which of your fonts contain it. If you need that Polish l-slash, you can select it and have the Character Palette show you all the installed fonts that contain it.

Advanced Character Palette techniques

For a more complete view of all the characters that a Unicode-based font may contain, select the Unicode option (in Mac OS X 10.2 and earlier, select All) from the View menu in the Character Palette and then select the Unicode Blocks or Unicode Table tab. Selecting Unicode Blocks gives you many more categories of characters to wade through, but their labels are more specific, and you have more characters to choose from.

Here characters are called *glyphs,* because in Unicode terms the word *character* refers to an abstract form of a letter—say the numeral 4—and a glyph is a visual representation—perhaps one of many—of that character. As far as Unicode is concerned, the glyph for a lining four (4) and that for an old-style four (4) are both representations of the same character. This may sound needlessly complicated, but it actually makes life easier if a four is always a four regardless of what it looks like. Before Unicode, an old-style four that appeared in a document on a computer without the appropriate font wouldn't even be recognizable as a number.

Alternate glyphs for a particular character (if they exist) appear at the bottom of the palette in the Glyph Variants in Selected Font section. Cleverly, Apple has designed this pane to be too small to display some fonts' characters (notably those of Zapfino). The window cannot be resized. Yet.

The "Related characters" pane appears to be there mainly to cloud your mind. The relationships between some of these characters and the character you've chosen may be apparent. But don't count on it.

The deep end: using Unicode ID numbers

Application programs that strictly support Unicode—such as TextEdit—enable you to access any Unicode-font character by typing its ID number. To see a character's Unicode number in Mac OS X 10.3, go to the Character Palette and select Unicode (in Mac OS X 10.2 and earlier select All) from the View pop-up menu. Then click the Unicode Table tab. Now you see all the glyphs in the font of your choice, along with their Unicode numbers.

Well, sort of. The labels on the left indicate the Unicode numbers of the first column of characters on the left. The ID numbers of the characters to their right each increment by one, as indicated by the labels across the top of the table (**Figure 15.13**).

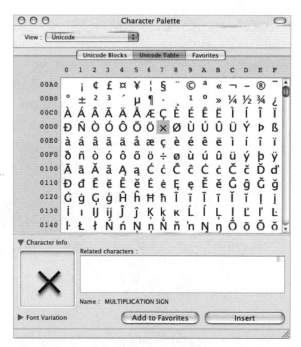

Figure 15.13

The Unicode Table option in the Character Palette shows you the Unicode numbers for individual characters. The number in the left-hand scale represents the Unicode ID number for the first character in that row. The ID numbers of characters ranging to the right increment by one, as shown in the scale running above the window. The number for the multiplication sign shown here, then, is 00D7. Why couldn't the palette just spell that out somewhere? Don't ask.

To use this number (which is expressed in *hexadecimal notation*—hence the combination of numerals and letters), first go to the Input menu and switch your keyboard layout to Unicode Hex Input. Then hold down Option while typing the four-character Unicode ID number. When you've typed the fourth character, the glyph you seek appears onscreen at the insertion point. (Note that if Unicode Hex Input is grayed out in the Input menu, then your application does not support hexadecimal notation.)

For offbeat Unicode characters that you'll need often, make a list of their ID numbers, as typing them will probably be faster than running off to your Favorites in the Character Palette.

The Heartbreak of Hexadecimal

Unicode may provide a standard numbering scheme for Mac and PC fonts, but the numbering system itself is not what you're used to. Instead of being a base-10 system like everyday numbers (using the ten digits 0 through 9), hexadecimal uses a base-16 system, which uses the digits 0 through 9 plus the letters A through F. This allows a single character to represent the numbers zero through 15 like so: 0, 1, 2, 3, 4, 5, 6, 7, 8, 9, A, B, C, D, E, F.

Yeah, yikes. In hexadecimal notation, 10 actually means 16, and 1A means 26. Worse yet, Unicode ID numbers always have four digits, often beginning with one or more zeros. This is because Unicode-based fonts are double-byte fonts, and 2 bytes contain 16 bits. Each bit can be numbered with a single character, which—believe it or not—makes it easier for programmers to handle.

Fortunately, no one expects you to be able to count in hexadecimal, but when you're working with Unicode-based fonts in the Character Palette, you'll see that the ID number for a particular character may be something like 00E7. You can use this number to access the characters you want, as explained in "The deep end: using Unicode ID numbers," above.

The trouble with Unicode and the Symbol and Dingbats fonts

By and large, life with Unicode feels pretty much the same as life with Mac Roman. You type an *A,* you get an *A.* You press Option G, you get a copyright symbol (©). That's because Mac Roman uses most of the same character ID numbers that Unicode uses. In cases where they're not the same, your application (with the help of the Mac OS) maps characters so that they appear under the old familiar keystrokes used by Mac OS 9 and earlier.

But the characters of two popular fonts—Symbol and ITC Zapf Dingbats—have Unicode numbers that are wildly different from what Mac Roman uses, and some Unicode-based applications may have trouble getting at them. When you're using TextEdit, for example, you can't simply switch to Dingbats and press Shift = to get a little hand with a pointing finger (☞).

In these cases—and to take advantage of both Unicode and Mac Roman fonts—you have to use the Input menu.

Good-bye Key Caps, Hello Keyboard Viewer

Key Caps was a feature of the Mac OS forever. Until Mac OS X 10.3, that is, where it's been replaced by the very similar Keyboard Viewer (**Figure 15.14**). You open Keyboard Viewer by selecting it in the Input menu. If it's not there, you can add it in the System Preferences/Personal/International pane (see "Customizing the Input menu" earlier in this chapter).

Figure 15.14

Keyboard Viewer works much like the old Mac Key Caps. Holding down ⎇Shift⎇ *and/or* ⎇Option⎇ *on your physical keyboard while clicking a key in Keyboard Viewer causes the utility to show what characters you would get by pressing a key on your keyboard along with those keystroke modifiers. Clicking keys in Keystroke Viewer causes those characters to be inserted into your document at the insertion point.*

Keyboard Viewer is a utility program (creepily called a *menulet*, as you can get at it only through a menu) that shows you which characters in a font you can get simply by pressing certain key combinations. Keyboard Viewer presents an image of your keyboard, with each key showing what character lurks beneath it, ready to appear when you hit that key. You can select from its Font menu the typeface you want to investigate.

When you open Keyboard Viewer, you see the characters you get when you type without holding down ⎇Shift⎇. Holding down ⎇Shift⎇ causes Keyboard Viewer to show what characters you get when you type with ⎇Shift⎇ held down. The same goes for holding down ⎇Option⎇ and for the combination of ⎇Shift⎇ and ⎇Option⎇. This means that every key on your Mac keyboard can deliver up to four different characters.

In Key Caps, each character you "typed" there appeared in a window from which you could cut and paste them into your document, where they would appear at the insertion point. That window is gone in Keyboard Viewer, but a click on any character displayed will do the same thing. You can, in effect, type with your mouse.

Compound keystrokes for accented characters

Keyboard Viewer also clues you in to some more elaborate keyboard commands, although the clues are a bit abstruse.

When you hold down ⎇Option⎇, you'll see that certain keys are highlighted. You use these keys to get a range of accented characters, such as *é, Ö,* and *î.* When you press one of these key combinations—say, pressing Option U for a dieresis (or *umlaut*)—you see the diacritical mark appear onscreen. Your next keystroke selects the letter over which you want the diacritical mark to appear. So for an Ö, you would press Option U and then Shift O (for uppercase O). This technique works for the following diacritical marks: acute accent (´), grave accent (`), circumflex (^), dieresis (¨), and tilde (˜).

You can place the first four of these accents over upper- and lowercase vowels, and sometimes *y*. The tilde can be placed over *n, N, a, A, o,* and *O*.

Language-specific keyboard layouts

Most of the time you'll use the Input menu to switch keyboard layouts, which makes it easier for touch typists to work in other languages. Note that in Mac OS X 10.2 and later, font-specific keyboard layouts (such as those in earlier versions of Mac OS X for fonts, including Symbol and Dingbats) no longer exist.

When you switch keyboard layouts, Keyboard Viewer adjusts its display accordingly. If you're using a non-English keyboard layout with an English-language keyboard, you'll probably want to keep Keyboard Viewer open at all times to help you find the characters you need.

Keyboard Layouts and System Preferences

When you're creating or editing multilingual documents that use several different font encodings (say, English and Cyrillic), switching from one keyboard layout to another can become a confusing hassle. To make things somewhat easier, Mac OS X allows you to coordinate fonts and keyboard layouts, so that when you click in a bit of text that was formatted using a specific font encoding, your keyboard layout switches accordingly. Click in the Cyrillic text, and your keyboard layout switches automatically to Cyrillic. Click back in the English text, and the keyboard layout switches back to English. Slick.

To allow this automatic switching to happen, click the Input Menu tab in System Preferences' International pane, and then click Options. One of the options you'll find there is "Try to match keyboard with text." Check the box next to it to put this synchronization into effect. (In Mac OS X 10.2 and earlier, this feature is called "Font and keyboard synchronization.")

Some applications allow you to do the same thing in their own preferences. In Microsoft Word X, for example, check the box next to "Match font with keyboard" in the Preferences window's Edit pane. If you set up automatic keyboard switching in Mac OS X, it will work in all your applications. If you set it up in only one application, it will work only in that specific application.

Selecting and Using Fonts (JF)

It's always been my contention that the Font menu in a program should really be called the Typeface menu. Because although in theory you're selecting a font that your Mac will use to image your type, what you're really doing is selecting a typeface that will define how your type looks. Besides, there are many fonts—Arial, for example—that contain the images of several different typefaces, such as regular, bold, italic, and bold italic. But this is a semantic battle I'm not going to win, so I'll descend from my soapbox.

Mac OS X provides a standard way for all applications to allow you to select a typeface: the Font panel (**Figure 15.15**). That said, many programs don't use it, including Microsoft Word and most leading desktop-publishing applications, such as Adobe InDesign. If your application supports it, you'll find it in one of the applications' font or formatting menus. (For example, TextEdit does use the Font panel; select Format > Font > Show Fonts to access it.) There's a good reason why many applications do not support the Font panel—it is an awkward, horsey thing.

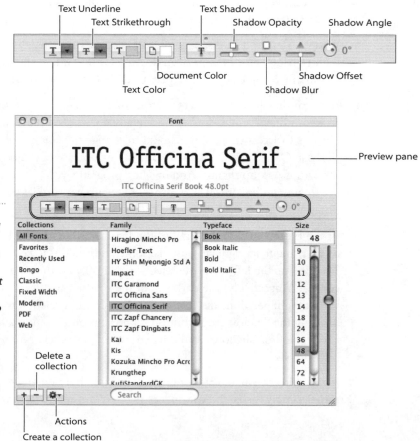

Figure 15.15

The main problem with the Font panel is its size. It's intended to replace a program's Font menu, but you don't always want a whole dialog just to change a typeface. With all the panel's columns, making it small enough to be unobtrusive also makes it even more of a hassle to use.

Using the Font Panel

The Font panel is handy if you don't know—or can't remember—what your typefaces look like. Otherwise, using it feels like going the long way around to get a simple thing done, which is to select a different typeface or type size. Whatever changes you make here are instantly reflected in your document.

The Font panel is divided into four columns: Collections, listing collections of fonts (see "Font collections," below); Family, listing font families (groups of fonts representing several versions of typefaces bearing the same name, such as Times, Times Italic, Times Bold, and Times Bold Italic in the Times group); Typeface, listing the members of a selected family; and Size, a list of arbitrary type sizes, measured in points (see the sidebar "The Measure of Type," later in this chapter). You can type in any point size you like for a custom view, or add new sizes to the list.

When you select a font family and a specific family member by clicking them, their name appears in that typeface in a resizable pane across the top of the panel. Clicking a type size changes the size of the display. (If the pane isn't displayed, you can click the little dot under the panel's title bar and drag it down to reveal the pane.)

Whatever typeface and size you select become the active typeface and size at the insertion point in your open document. If you have text selected in your document, it will take on the typeface and size that you choose in the Font panel.

Beneath the preview pane are buttons that allow you to add underscore and strikeout lines (single, double, and in any color; click the triangles next to the buttons to access these options) and to change the color of any selected type (in Mac OS X 10.2, these color controls are accessed by choosing Color from the Extras pop-up menu). And in some programs you can control the color of the document background (a great way to run your inkjet printer dry in no time flat).

In the button area, to the right of the first four buttons on the left is a vertical divider, and to its right are buttons, some with sliders, to control drop shadows. The one on the left turns the effect on and off, and the ones to the right of it control (respectively) the darkness of the shadow, the degree of its blurriness, its left-right position, and its rotational position in relation to the source type. Turning the Shadow Angle button with the mouse pointer allows you to rotate the drop shadow around its character. Very slick. Not terribly useful, but very slick.

 If you don't see all of the options we mention here when you open the Font panel, simply resize the window to make it larger and they will all appear.

Font collections

To reduce the number of font names listed in the Font panel, you can choose to organize your font library into *collections*. One font can be in any number of collections, and you choose which collection you want to display by clicking its name in the Collections column at the left of the panel.

To create a new collection, click the plus sign (+) in the lower left of the panel. To add fonts to a collection (new or old), open the All Fonts collection and drag your choices onto the name of the collection you'd like them to be a part of.

To delete a collection (which doesn't delete any fonts—don't worry), select it and click the minus sign in the lower left of the panel.

In Mac OS X 10.2, access these functions by choosing Edit Collections from the Extras pop-up menu.

 If you can't find the font you're after in a large collection, you can use the Search field at the bottom of the panel.

 Take advantage of the collection titled Recently Used, which contains a small number of the fonts you've just been using. Going here to find your fonts can save you a lot of scrolling through lists representing larger collections.

High-end typography with the Font panel

With version 10.3, Mac OS X introduces some typographical capabilities usually seen only in high-end desktop-publishing programs, and often not even there. These are lurking in the menu you get by clicking the Actions button (with the little gear icon) at the bottom left of the Font panel or by clicking the Text Color button in the Font panel.

- The Color option opens the Colors palette (found by choosing Color in the Extras menu in Mac OS X 10.2), which gives you five ways of applying color to type. You can choose the standard color wheel; sets of sliders (for grayscale, RGB [red/green/blue, as used onscreen], CMYK [cyan/magenta/yellow/black, as used for specifying printing inks]; HSB [hue/saturation/brightness]); and, for the rest of us, a box of preset colors in the image of a box of crayons. You can also use the Image option to pick up a color from a digital image that you import. It's overkill, but it's marvelous.

- Selecting the Characters option opens the Character Palette (see "The Character Palette," earlier in this chapter).

- The Typography option is where things get interesting for type lovers. Here you can opt to have Mac OS X do such things as automatically insert ligatures (see "Ligatures," later in this chapter), small capitals, and old-style numerals. You can also use sliders to add space before or after characters and to control their elevation relative to the baseline (the invisible line on which most characters appear to sit). Unfortunately, these sliders have no units or even numbers associated with them, so you can't exercise precise

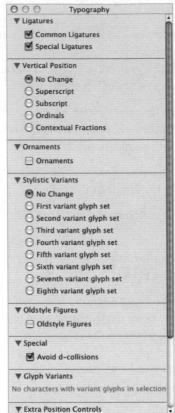

Figure 15.16

The options available in the Font panel's Typography dialog (accessible from the Actions pop-up menu) depend on which font you've selected. The myriad options here belong to Zapfino, a calligraphic font with huge numbers and alternative glyphs that can be inserted automatically as context demands.

control. But it's a start, and it adds some fine typographic tools to every program that uses the Font panel.

The options available to you in the Typography dialog vary according to the capabilities built into the font. Even a generic old PostScript font benefits from a few basic controls, but advanced TrueType and OpenType fonts such as Zapfino offer you much more, especially regarding substitution of alternate characters (**Figure 15.16**).

Font panel miscellany

Most of the other controls in the Font panel's Actions menu are more or less self-explanatory. (In Mac OS X 10.2, their equivalents are found in the Extras pop-up menu.) Add to Favorites, for example, adds a selected font to the collection named Favorites. Hide Preview and Hide Effects reduce the size of the Font panel by hiding these features. Using Edit Sizes, you can add or delete type sizes from the list in the right-hand column.

Selecting Managing Fonts sends you to another of Mac OS X 10.3's powerful new type features: Font Book, which is covered in "Font Book: A Built-In Font Manager," below.

The problem with the Font panel

The Font panel's main problem is its size. You can scale it down to make it less obtrusive, but it's still underfoot all the time. Unless you need to make an aesthetic decision about a typeface choice, a simple pull-down menu of installed fonts (as used by Word and many other programs) is much more efficient. Many programs (including Word) allow you to display their Font menus in preview mode, so typeface names are displayed using their own fonts.

The issue is that there's just too much going on here, too many controls that you use only occasionally in a place that you need to run to all the time. The Font panel could stay the way it is if there were some other, more efficient way to do the simple, oft-performed task of simply changing a typeface.

Managing Your Fonts (JF)

One of the biggest changes in Mac OS X 10.3 is the power it gives you to manage your font library. Fonts multiply like bunnies, even if you're buying them legitimately (you *are* buying them, aren't you?), which can make the simple job of selecting a typeface a chore by clogging Font menus with scores of choices. Font Book to the rescue!

But before you bid adieu to your current font-management program, keep in mind that Font Book is pretty basic in what it can do, and specialized font-management programs still have a place in the lives of heavy-duty type users. The current contenders are described in "Specialized Font-Management Programs," below.

Font Book: A Built-In Font Manager

Font Book is a program in its own right, so you'll find it in the Applications folder (**Figure 15.17**). You can also open it through the Manage Fonts option in the Font panel's Actions menu.

Figure 15.17

Font Book allows you to decide which individual fonts or collections of fonts will appear in your Font menu and be available to your programs. Here we just added Comic Sans to our Fun collection of fonts.

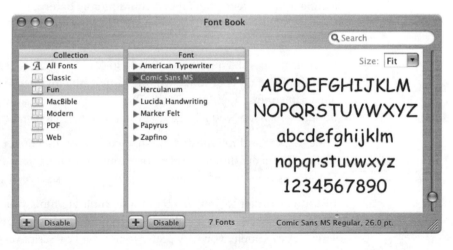

You can use Font Book to install new fonts (as described in "Installing and Enabling Fonts," earlier in this chapter). The main purpose of Font Book, though, is to make large libraries of fonts easier to cope with.

In Mac OS X there's no longer any limit to the number of fonts that a Fonts folder can contain, and no limit to the number of fonts the Mac OS can support. But that doesn't mean you have to scroll through 700 fonts to find your way down to Zapf Dingbats. Font Book allows you to select which fonts will be listed in your Font menu or Font panel. It does this in two ways.

First, you can gather your fonts into collections and then choose which collection(s) you want to appear in your Font menus. These can be organized thematically (Handwriting Fonts), for example, or historically (Venetians), or stylistically (Decorative), or however you please (Ugly, Squat, Annual Report Fonts, OpenType Fonts, and so on). One font can be in any number of collections. If you're working on a specific project, you can make a collection containing only the fonts it needs and then enable that one collection.

Second, Font Book allows you to disable selected fonts within a particular collection.

The technique for accomplishing either goal is the same: Select the collection of fonts and click Disable. A dialog appears, asking if you're sure you want to disable the selected fonts. After you click Disable in the dialog, the word *Off* appears to the right of the selection and the selection is displayed in light gray. To enable the collection or font, select it and click Enable. Again, you're asked if you're sure that you want to enable the font; click Enable.

 You can remove fonts from your system by selecting them from the Font list and using the File > Remove Font command. This doesn't just take the font out of circulation—it also puts it in the Trash, so be careful. When you remove a collection, however, the fonts it contains stay behind.

Weeding out duplicate fonts with Font Book

With all the possible places for fonts to lurk in Mac OS X, it's easy to end up with duplicate fonts or fonts with the same name installed at the same time. This can confuse applications, the OS, and you, too, because none of you can be sure which font you'll be getting when you select a name from a Font menu.

Font Book flags duplicate and like-named fonts with a bullet (•) next to their names. To fix the situation, select the troubled font name and choose Resolve Duplicates from the Edit menu. Mac OS X will take care of the rest.

But it may matter to you which of those duplicate fonts you use, so you won't want to let the Mac OS decide which font will be disabled and which left active. For example, you may prefer to use the PostScript version of Helvetica instead of the TrueType version. In this case, click the triangle next to the font's name to see a list of the duplicate fonts, and select them one by one. With Show Font Info selected in the Preview menu, Font Book reveals the details of each of the fonts, including format and manufacturer. You can then choose to disable the duplicates of your choice.

If you're unsure about where a certain font lives, you can select it and choose Show Font File from the File menu. This opens up a Finder window and highlights the font in question in the folder in which it resides.

Seeing inside a font

Font Book's Preview menu lets you decide what will appear in the program's preview window. The default view (called Sample) is a basic collection of upper- and lowercase letters, plus numerals and a few symbols off the keyboard. Choosing Repertoire reveals the entire character set of a font, which is a good way to see if a particular font has the specific characters you need (**Figure 15.18**).

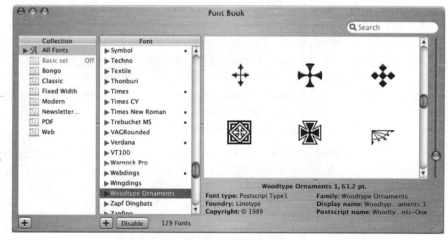

Figure 15.18

Font Book's Repertoire preview lets you pore over a font's character set. Often your selection of a font may hinge on what characters it includes, making this a handy tool indeed.

The Custom preview option looks at first like the Sample preview, but everything in the window is editable. You can create your own preview by selecting and over-typing just as you would in a word processor.

No matter which preview you choose, you can control the size of the type using the outer slider at the right (the inner one is for scrolling).

Specialized Font-Management Programs

There's more to font management than just controlling which fonts are listed in your Font menus. Specialized font-management programs can, for example, automatically activate all the fonts needed for a document you open. They can also search for and often repair damaged font files. In short, they have a whole bag of tricks that can come in very handy when you're an intensive font user. Here's a rundown on the leading contenders.

Suitcase

Extensis's **Suitcase** ($99.95; www.extensis.com) is actually a suite of programs. Suitcase itself manages font collections and allows you to control the activation and deactivation of fonts. FontDoctor looks for damaged fonts (which can cause crashes and printing problems) and fixes them when it can.

Lemke Soft's FontBook (which is included with Extensis Suitcase) is dedicated to printing elaborate sample pages, either for your own font catalogue or for client approvals.

Suitcase gathers fonts in batches that you can enable or disable easily from an icon located in the Dock. It can also recycle font sets from the defunct Adobe ATM Deluxe and convert them into Suitcase sets. A particularly useful feature is its preview pane, which lets you display several fonts simultaneously, making comparisons much easier.

Suitcase can auto-activate fonts in both Mac OS X and Classic modes. When you open a document, Suitcase listens in while your application asks the Mac for the fonts it needs. If those fonts aren't currently enabled, Suitcase enables them. This doesn't work with all Mac applications, but it does with most of the usual suspects, including the biggies from Microsoft, FileMaker, and Macromedia. Suitcase auto-activation plug-ins are available for Adobe InDesign and Illustrator as well as for QuarkXPress.

There's also a workgroup version—Suitcase Server—which manages a fonts database so that all users have up-to-the-minute access to all fonts available on the network.

MasterJuggler

Alsoft's **MasterJuggler** ($89.95; www.alsoft.com) is an easy-to-use font manager with particularly good previewing tools. Its Font Guardian scans fonts for all kinds of possible problems, including minute technical ones that will make a difference only to real type experts. Because there are so many ways for a font to be "nonconforming," Font Guardian does not try to "repair" fonts, since their shortcoming may well not be a functional flaw, just a nonstandard feature.

MasterJuggler's font sets can be nested one inside another, and its font-management tools are easily accessible from the Dock. Its Glyph Map offers an excellent view of the contents of a font, especially complex Unicode fonts. Importantly (especially for Asian languages), it shows glyph variants that share a single Unicode ID number, as well as related glyphs with different numbers.

The program also offers excellent control over custom type samples, which makes it easy to create type catalogues and to compare typefaces in the settings of your choice.

Font Reserve

Extensis's **Font Reserve** ($99.95; www.fontreserve.com) works by creating a secure "vault" in which your fonts are stored. From there, they're served up in such a way that they're protected from the damage that often afflicts font files. As they're being put into that vault, they're scanned to make sure they're in tip-top condition and that all their screen fonts are accounted for (if they're needed).

The contents of the vault are organized into a sort of database, a catalogue from which you do your managing. Here you can organize your fonts into sets or categories for easy searching and handling en masse. The program has a host of helpful sorting options. A series of filters allows you to search for fonts with particular characteristics.

Font Reserve can automatically activate the fonts needed for a particular document, and it can activate fonts temporarily, so that they won't be reactivated when you restart your Mac—they stay enabled only during the current work session. Font Reserve also has a networked version for managing large font collections for an entire workgroup.

Just before *The Macintosh Bible* went to press, DiamondSoft was bought by Extensis, makers of its competitor, Suitcase. No plans have yet been announced for how the two programs will coexist or how they might be merged. Expect some announcement in the middle of 2004.

Type Onscreen (JF)

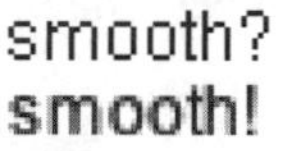

**smooth?
smooth!**

Figure 15.19

Font smoothing works by using both gray and black pixels to render type onscreen. At a magnification of 300 percent, this technique becomes apparent, but at normal text sizes, smoothed type (bottom) looks more like printed text than unsmoothed type.

Generally, the higher the resolution of your monitor, the more what you see onscreen will look like what you print. To make type look better onscreen, the Mac uses a technique called *smoothing,* or *anti-aliasing* (an alias, in tech terms, is an artifact—an inaccuracy in display—usually caused by mediocre resolution). The basic problem is that the dots used to create your screen type are just too big, so small type looks as if it were made out of tiny bricks, and jagged edges abound. To create a more realistic appearance, smoothing uses an aura of gray pixels around characters in addition to the black ones that form the core of each character image. The gray pixels partially fill in the *jaggies.* The resulting type is blurrier (and hence harder on the eyes), but it gives the impression of type more resembling that on the printed page (**Figure 15.19**).

Controlling Type Smoothing

Type smoothing is governed in System Preferences' Appearance pane. You have four choices for how smoothing will be carried out. Standard works best for CRT monitors—the big, TV-like models (*CRT* stands for "cathode ray tube"). The Light, Medium, and Strong settings use a different technology and work best for LCD monitors.

Because smoothed type at small sizes can be very hard to read (the blurry aura tends to overwhelm those little letters), Mac OS X allows you to set the minimum size at which you want smoothing to take place. Oddly, you get only six choices: 4, 6, 8, 9, 10, and 12 point in Mac OS X 10.3. You have no option to turn it off altogether. These restrictions are arbitrary and dumb.

In Mac OS X 10.2 and earlier, type smoothing is even more limited. It is governed in the System Preferences' General pane, and you can choose only the minimum size at which you want smoothing to take place. In addition, you only have four choices within that: 8, 9, 10, and 12 point.

Fonts for Documents on the Move (JF)

All documents except for plain-vanilla text files (those with a .txt filename extension) include calls for the use of specific fonts ("Century Old Style, here, please!"). If someone tries to open a file on a computer that doesn't have the necessary fonts installed, the operating system of that computer substitutes some other font(s). It might first ask which substitutes are preferred, but in any case the document won't look like the one you created.

In a simple word-processed document consisting of nothing but running text, this may not be a big problem. But for documents with complicated layouts—a newsletter, for example—font substitutions can wreck everything. This is because different typefaces take up different amounts of space on the page, so when fonts are changed, so are line endings, and blocks of type can become much longer or shorter. Layouts go kerblooey.

Font substitution is not just an aesthetic issue, so you have to take some measures to make sure that electronic documents you send out into the world will maintain the good looks that you worked so hard to build into them.

Cross-Platform Font Compatibility

A file can travel from a Mac to a PC (or vice versa) and appear exactly the same when it gets there only if identical versions of the fonts used to create it are present in the file's new home. Even if a font with the same filename exists on the new host machine, success is not guaranteed—the fonts on both machines have to be in the same format and from the same vendor.

 If the documents you send are mainly for reading (as opposed to editing), consider sending them as PDF (Portable Document Format) files. PDF files created by the Mac OS automatically include all the fonts you used to create them, so they're guaranteed to be spitting images of the originals, no matter what kind of computer you send them to. If that computer's not a Mac with Mac OS X, though, the recipient will need Adobe Reader or some other PDF-reader software to open the file.

Core fonts

In the infant days of desktop publishing, Adobe decided to equip every user of a PostScript printer with a core set of fonts. This ensured that anyone anywhere creating a document for PostScript output would have a common—if small—font library. These were Times Roman, Helvetica, and Courier (each in regular, italic, bold, and bold italic), plus Symbol (a *pi font* consisting of miscellaneous, well, symbols).

Microsoft, meanwhile, developed its own core set of fonts for Windows, but for legal reasons it couldn't use all the same fonts as Adobe's and Apple's. (This would have been logical but far too easy for users, and we can't have that!) Instead, Microsoft, partnering with Monotype, developed a set of core typefaces that looked much like those on the Mac but were subtly different and had different names (**Figure 15.20**). (Actually, Monotype's Times is the original version of that popular face.)

Figure 15.20

The fonts for the typefaces on the left used to be exclusively Macintosh; their Windows equivalents are shown on the right.

Times Roman — Times New Roman
Helvetica — Arial
Courier — Courier New
Symbol (δ♥∴∞×) — Symbol (δ♥∴∞×)

Realizing that on some fronts, at least, cooperation is better than competition, Apple now includes versions of the Windows core fonts with every version of the Mac OS it sells, so you can be sure that you have at least a base library of fonts in common with your PC-using colleagues. If you want to be absolutely sure that the pages you create look the way you want them to when they are opened on a Windows PC, use these fonts, which include Arial, Times New Roman, Courier New, Symbol, and Wingdings.

Font embedding

Core fonts solved the problem of document mobility, but at the cost of limiting your choice of typefaces. In a world of more than 30,000 typefaces, though, this clearly wasn't ideal and didn't suit the needs of designers. So applications soon began to *embed* the fonts a document needed right into the file itself. Instead of the document's traveling stark naked to its new home and hoping for appropriate clothes there, it packed a bag and brought its wardrobe along with it.

This is still a common and successful solution, but it has two problems. One is that it makes files much larger, as a single font can be 40 KBytes and up. Second, some font vendors don't like the idea of font embedding because at the very least it cuts into font sales, and at the worst it allows people to steal their fonts (because it's quite easy to un-embed a font and use it without authorization).

 TrueType and OpenType fonts contain a switch that font designers can flip to prevent their fonts from being embedded in a file. If your efforts at font embedding fail, this may well be the reason.

To get around the problem of file-size increases, programs that can embed fonts usually allow you to embed only a subset of the font (**Figure 15.21**). In other words, your file will contain only part of the font, with information for only the characters that appear in its pages. In fonts with huge character sets, this can make a big difference in file size, as most of what you type will consist only of alphabetic characters, numerals, and a dash of punctuation.

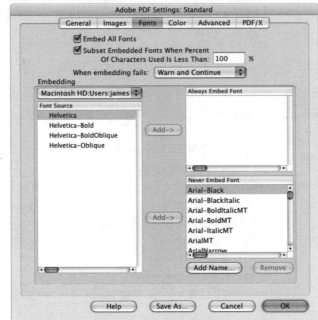

Figure 15.21

Adobe Acrobat Distiller has a typical set of font-embedding controls for use in creating PDF files. You can choose to embed only subsets of fonts (consisting of only the characters that actually appear in the document), as well as selecting specific fonts to embed or not embed. There's probably no sense, for example, in embedding fonts such as Arial that exist on virtually every personal computer.

When someone receives a document from you that contains embedded fonts, it will appear just as you created it, regardless of whether the required fonts are on the user's machine. The programs simply pull the fonts they need out of the file itself.

Practice Good Typography (JZ)

Today, most of us who use words for a living are expected to put our documents together ourselves with little or no training in typography. For help and guidance, people look to their coworkers or to the publications, signage, and screen displays all around them. The problem with this approach is that bad typesetting, like bad grammar, is ubiquitous, and much of what we see around the office, on the street, and on the Web has been created by people who have never learned the basics of typography.

If most people are comfortable with this self-taught approach, why waste your time learning about typography and grooming your documents according to old standards? Because typography is not about rules, it's about creating documents that are inviting and user-friendly, easy to read and a pleasure to look at. A nicely typeset document gets attention and conveys information quickly and with style.

The Measure of Type (JF)

Type has its own measuring units that are appropriate to the fine scale of the work at hand. The basic units of measure—akin to feet and inches—are *picas* and *points*. Their definitions have varied over the ages, but a point is now popularly defined as $1/72$ inch. There are 12 points to a pica, hence 6 picas to the inch. The size of type is usually expressed in points, as is the distance between lines of type, called *leading* (after the lead once used to cast type) or *line spacing*. Picas are usually used to express widths of pages, columns, and other elements.

Picas and points are absolute measurements, but type also uses relative measurements. The basic relative measurement is an *em,* which is equal to the size of the type in use. In 12-point type, an em is equal to 12 points. (Contrary to popular myth, it doesn't relate to the width of an *M.*) An *en,* in turn, is equal to half an em, and—you guessed it—has nothing to do with the width of an *N.*

Relative units are handy because they work equally well when the type they're used with changes size. A paragraph indent expressed in ems retains its proportional relationship to the type even if the type size is altered. Likewise, tiny corrections to the spacing between characters—called *kerning*—are measured in fractions of an em. When kerned type is resized, the kerning adjustments remain proportionally correct, which would be impossible if the spacing adjustments were made in absolute measurements.

Preparing the Raw Text (JZ)

Before you can begin formatting your text (also known as *copy*), you must strip it clean of the baggage of bad typography. You'll want to use all the correct characters and spacing so that as you format, you're getting an accurate view of how the final text will look. You don't want to finish all your formatting and *then* go back and replace double hyphens with em dashes, double word spaces with single ones, and so on, since these types of changes will cause your text to reflow, possibly disrupting your carefully constructed page layouts. Here are some tips for preparing perfect raw text (**Table 15.1** lists keyboard shortcuts for common typographical elements).

Table 15.1 Font-Related Keyboard Commands

Command	Result
Option [	Creates opening quotation marks
Shift Option [	Creates closing quotation marks
Option]	Creates single opening quotation marks
Shift Option]	Creates single closing quotation marks
Option –	Creates an en dash
Shift Option –	Creates an em dash
Option ;	Creates a one-character ellipsis
Option Spacebar	Creates a nonbreaking space between ellipsis points
Shift Option 5	Creates the fi ligature
Shift Option 6	Creates the fl ligature
Shift Option 1	Creates a fraction bar (/)

One space, please

The convention of using two spaces after a period is a holdover from the days of typewriters. Typewriters produced monospaced type, which uses the same amount of space for an *i* as it does for an *m* and creates an overall feeling of slack spacing. An additional space after periods opened a more effective gap between sentences. Most typefaces, though, are proportionally spaced—the characters have varied and natural proportions—so the extra space is not needed (**Figure 15.22**).

`This is Magda Clean Mono. It is a monospaced typeface.`

This is Magda Clean. It is a proportionally spaced typeface.

Figure 15.22

In monospaced typefaces (top line), every character takes up the same amount of horizontal space on the page. In proportionally spaced faces (bottom line), the widths of the characters reflect their natural proportions.

Use typographer's quotes

A common mistake is using straight quotation marks instead of typographer's, or *curly,* quotes. Straight quotes appear when you type by simply using the quotation-marks key. Many programs now have a setting for *smart quotes,* which automatically converts straight quotes to typographer's quotes. If your program can't do this, replace straight quotes with typographic quotes by using find and replace with the following keystrokes: Use [Option][[] for opening quotes (") and [Shift][Option][[] for closing quotes ("). For single quotation marks, press [Option][]] for opening quotes (') and [Shift][Option][]] for closing quotes (') and apostrophes.

Use real dashes

Many people use single and double hyphens instead of *en* and *em* dashes. Using the proper dashes makes your text much more elegant and readable.

Use an en dash to replace the word *through,* as in dates (1999–2004) or a series (G–P). Although it's not strictly legit, you can also use an en dash as a minus sign, as it is easier than hunting down a true minus sign, such as the one in Symbol (by pressing a hyphen) and other specialty fonts. Type an en dash by pressing [Option][-] (hyphen).

An em dash is used to separate two or more related phrases when commas or a colon aren't quite right. Em dashes can also be used like parentheses to set off phrases within a sentence. Type an em dash by pressing [Shift][Option][-](hyphen).

Never add spaces around your dashes. If you must adjust the spacing, kern slightly between the characters and the dashes so that they are evenly and tightly spaced but not touching.

Set proper ellipsis points

Ellipsis points are usually used to represent omitted text in a quotation: "Astonishing . . . original, daring, brilliant." They are also used to represent a pause or trailing off of a thought. There is no consensus on the best way to present ellipses. Some prefer to use the one-character ellipsis ([Option][;]). This way, the dots will always stay together. But the one-character ellipsis is very tightly spaced, and there is no way to adjust the spacing. Many typographers prefer to use three periods in a row. To prevent the dots from ending up on different lines, use a nonbreaking space (Option Spacebar) between the periods. You may have to tighten the spacing with kerning.

Say no to all-cap words

If you have words within your body copy that are typed in ALL CAPS for emphasis, change them to upper- and lowercase. Give words emphasis by setting them using bold and/or italic versions of your typeface. This rule does not apply to acronyms (such as JPEG), trademarked names (such as IBM), headings, or other text destined to be styled in all caps.

SETTING LONG PASSAGES OF TEXT IN ALL CAPS MAKES IT HARD TO READ. IT ALSO TENDS TO VISUALLY OVERPOWER OTHER AREAS OF TEXT ON THE PAGE. UNLESS YOU ARE SETTING A GOVERNMENT WARNING LABEL AND HAVE NO CHOICE, AVOID USING ALL CAPS FOR BLOCKS OF TEXT.

Choosing Your Typefaces

Once you have cleaned up your text, you are ready for some fun. But remember not to have too much fun—one of the most common errors made in formatting text is using too many typefaces. One of my first jobs was in a design studio where the creative director insisted that anything could be designed using Helvetica Neue and Helvetica Neue Condensed. I'm not advocating such a severe approach (it was no fun at all), but one or two typefaces *per project* is all you really need.

The right face for the job

If your project has a large amount of text, you should choose a serif face (a typeface that includes little adornments at the end of the letters' main strokes; *The Macintosh Bible* uses a serif face for the text). Serif faces are easier to read because the serifs give the eye additional clues to quick letter recognition. This speeds the reader along with little effort. Try Bembo, Caslon, Fairfield, Galliard, Garamond, Janson, Minion, or Palatino.

For a small amount of text, such as a title, heading, caption, sidebar, or ad copy, you could branch out to sans serif faces. Sans serif faces look modern and clean and offer a nice contrast to serif body copy. Franklin Gothic, Frutiger, Futura, Gill, Meta, Myriad, Ocean, and Univers are versatile choices.

Script faces are beautiful but difficult to read. Use them for logos, titles, and as accents, such as display caps or short headings. Never set large amounts of text in a script face unless it is for a formal invitation or a declaration of independence.

If you are producing a document that is destined exclusively for an electronic kiosk or the Web, look into typefaces that have been designed specifically for screen display. One such is Verdana. Designed by Matthew Carter (one of the mostly highly regarded type designers in the world), it is installed along with many of Microsoft's products. Many foundries have also developed versions of popular faces that have been optimized for the Web.

Use display faces sparingly. They should be used only for logo design, titles, product identity, CD covers, billboards, posters, and the like. Hence the name *display*. Think of them as condiments, not food.

Play to the audience

Typeface design is as much about form as it is about function. For the most influential presentation, choose a typeface that will resonate with your audience. Your typeface choice for an invitation to a charity fund-raiser benefiting a children's hospital will be very different from your typeface choice for a flyer announcing a hip-hop CD-release party.

The logos in **Figure 15.23** were designed to appeal to youths in two different age groups.

Figure 15.23

The logo on the left was designed for young children using a friendly tortoise and Adobe Tekton, an equally friendly typeface. The logo on the right was designed for teenagers. It features a coyote paw print and P22 Mayflower, a rugged-looking face fit for any explorer.

Matchmaking

To avoid getting into trouble when you choose more than one typeface for a project, try the following approaches:

- Choose serif and sans serif versions from the same families (groups of typefaces with the same name). Such typeface families include Legacy, Lucida, Goudy, Officina, Penumbra, Rotis, Scala, and Stone.

- To find two typefaces that work together, choose one first then find a mate that shares some of its characteristics. For instance, a square geometric sans serif with a large *x height* (the height of its lowercase letters) like Eurostile pairs well with Melior, a similarly drawn serif face. Some other examples of sans serif and serif pairs that harmonize are shown in **Figure 15.24**.

Eurostile Demi abcdefghijklmnopqrstuvwxyz

Melior Medium abcdefghijklmnopqrstuvwxyz

Franklin Gothic Demi abcdefghijklmnopqrstuvwxyz

Caslon Book abcdefghijklmnopqrstuvwxyz

Cronos MM abcdefghijklmnopqrstuvwxyz

Chaparral MM abcdefghijklmnopqrstuvwxyz

Gill Sans Bold abcdefghijklmnopqrstuvwxyz

Legacy Serif Book abcdefghijklmnopqrstuvwxyz

Figure 15.24

When searching for a headline typeface to pair with your body copy, look for design similarities that create visual harmony, as shown in these examples.

Finding a text typeface to coordinate with a display face is more difficult. Again, look for similarities in letterform and proportion. Some successful examples are shown in **Figure 15.25**.

Dogma Script Bold

Tarzana Wide abcdefghijklmnopqrstuvwxyz

Diskus Bold

Trebuchet abcdefghijklmnopqrstuvwxyz

Pompeia Inline

Skia abcdefghijklmnopqrstuvwxyz

Mason Regular

Bembo abcdefghijklmnopqrstuvwxyz

Figure 15.25

Assertive display type must be paired with a more subtle typeface for body copy that is easy to read.

All in the typeface family

If you are working on a large project such as a book, magazine, annual report, or corporate identity, choose a typeface that is part of a large family. These families contain versions that vary by weight—light, regular, book, medium, demi, bold, heavy, black, super, and poster—and have corresponding italic versions. They may even have condensed (narrow) and expanded (wide) versions. These variations are helpful when you need to design several coordinating type treatments or to keep a consistent look for collateral spanning many media. Larger type families may also contain expert-set fonts, which include alternate characters such as decorative initial capitals and ornaments—these all make setting type easier and more fun.

Final Type Touches

Many typefaces come with extensive character sets. Because many of these characters seem strange and mysterious, many people shy away from using them. This is a mistake, because in return for a small amount of effort, they greatly enhance the readability and beauty of your documents.

Ligatures

Have you ever noticed that some letter pairs, such as *f* and *l,* bump into each other? You could kern them so that they don't touch, but this creates too wide a gap between them. The better solution is to replace them with a *ligature,* a single character that combines two or three letters (**Figure 15.26**).

Figure 15.26

Ligatures (such as the fi and fl used in the top line) solve the problem of letters' bumping into each other (bottom line); they improve spacing and make your type tidier and more attractive.

You will find that Baskerville is fit to flatter text.

You will find that Baskerville is fit to flatter text.

The ligatures *fi* (Shift Option 5) and *fl* (Shift Option 6) are available in most fonts. For an expanded set of ligatures, use a typeface that includes an *expert set* (which may or may not be in a separate font). To locate these ligatures in an expert-set font, use Keyboard Viewer. In a font with many ligatures included, use the Character Palette.

To easily convert your letter pairs to ligatures, use your program's auto-ligature setting or find and replace. Unless your applications are OpenType-savvy, they will probably not be able to properly hyphenate words that contain ligatures. This is because most programs see ligatures as exotic symbols, not representations of several characters. Spelling checkers may likewise fail to recognize the meanings of ligatures.

Fractions

There are two ways to set fractions properly. Many expert fonts and large-character-set OpenType and TrueType fonts have a good selection of common fractions. To access these fractions, look them up in Keyboard Viewer or the Character Palette.

Alternatively, you can build fractions yourself. It is important to use the *fraction bar* (/), which you get with Shift Option 1. Don't use the slash (/), also called a *virgule*. A true fraction bar sits on the baseline, is more steeply angled, and is designed to space properly with the numerator and denominator. To style the numerator and denominator, use your program's settings for superscript and subscript. You may have to adjust these settings in your application preferences to produce numbers of the proper size and position (**Figure 15.27**).

Alternatively, you can adjust the numerator and denominator by reducing their type size and using baseline shift.

Figure 15.27

$$2^9/_{32}$$

$$2^9/_{32}$$

The upper fraction is set with a virgule (slash), which sits at an incorrect angle and extends below the baseline. The lower fraction is set properly using a fraction bar. Neither example has had its spacing manually adjusted (kerned)—the fraction bar is designed to space correctly automatically.

 If you work on projects that contain more math than the occasional fraction, save yourself hours of labor by investing in a mathematical font. Mathematical fonts allow you to easily build your equations within body copy.

Small caps

Small caps are smaller versions of uppercase letters that are designed to blend in with other text. They are sometimes used for abbreviations such as AM, PM, BCE, and AD. They also work well for author attribution at the end of an article.

Some programs offer small caps as an option in the Style or Font menu, but this produces incorrect small caps that are simply scaled-down versions of the font's capitals. They appear lighter and thinner than the regular text. True small caps are specially designed for their smaller size, which maintains a balanced line weight. To access them, choose the expert set in your typeface. Many OpenType and TrueType fonts contain large character sets with true small caps as well as old-style numbers and other alternate glyphs.

Old-style numbers

Maybe if old-style numbers had a new name, they would receive the attention they deserve. Far from being fuddy-duddy or old-fashioned, they are marvels of good design. Varied in size and baseline placement, old-style numbers have the visual impact of upper- and lowercase text. They blend into body copy and addresses rather than sticking out awkwardly. **Figure 15.28** shows an example set in Hoefler Text, a font that comes with Mac OS X.

A 24-bit color gamut is capable of 16 million colors but an offset printing press may only be capable of 5,000 colors.

Figure 15.28

Numerals set as old-style numbers (sometimes called lowercase numerals) visually blend with body copy and are easier to read than full-size, lining numerals.

A warning about using style options

Once you have chosen your typeface, please respect it. Many programs offer horizontal scaling as a substitute for using condensed or expanded fonts. This distorts the characters in the typeface, making the horizontal strokes thinner or fatter than the vertical strokes; the effect is obvious and ugly, especially when pushed to extremes. If you need a condensed or expanded typeface, use one designed for that purpose. If you do find yourself using this feature, use it minimally and apply it consistently to all similar copy, not just to a paragraph you're trying to squeeze into a tight space.

Other style options you should stay away from are Underline, Shadow, Outline, Emboss, and Engrave, unless, of course, you particularly *want* to be known for your bad taste.

Designing Your Layout (JZ)

There is more to typography than the form of the letters. Every block of text needs attention to type size, leading, justification, kerning, and tracking (the overall spacing of characters in a passage of text). These decisions have to be made in a way that creates a balance between type and the blank "canvas" surrounding the type.

Well-designed type is inviting and easy to read. The key to achieving this is using the right amount of leading for your type size. Too little leading in body copy makes focusing on one line at a time a chore. Too much leading makes it difficult for the eye to jump from the end of one line to the beginning of the next. The length of each line influences the amount of leading you need. Shorter lines of text need less leading than longer lines of text.

 If you set ten different typefaces at the same size, they will appear to be different sizes. This is because the x-height of typefaces—the height of their lowercase letters—varies in relation to their ascending and descending characters. Typefaces with small x-heights and long ascenders and descenders need to be set at a larger size and allowed more leading than typefaces with large x-heights.

Books, magazines, newsletters, brochures, and similar publications are generally set at anywhere from 8-point text on 10 points of leading to 10-point text on 13 points of leading. With larger point sizes, the line length can go up to 30 picas (about 5 inches). With smaller point sizes, the column width can be as small as 12 picas (2 inches). Anything smaller is annoyingly jumpy to read. Exceptions to these guidelines are publications for young children and seniors that need larger type and more leading.

Text in the wide single columns that are the convention for letters is generally set in 11- or 12-point type on 13 to 14 points of leading. Keeping the page margins wide and adding space between paragraphs increases readability.

Misplaced Graphics

Placing a graphic under type is very popular. The idea is that too much type is boring and an image behind it enhances the page. In my opinion, this creates two problems: a graphic that cannot be seen for the type covering it, and type that cannot be read because of the busy background.

Another common design problem is when a graphic cuts so far into a column of type that only one or two words can fit on each line. Wrapping type around images needs lots of care and attention to pull off successfully. It helps to keep the shortest line of type no shorter than 12 picas (2 inches) wide.

Take Care with Alignments

Most Mac software allows you to align your type in several ways. Text that is left-aligned (like this paragraph) is usually more attractive and easier to read than text that is justified (where all lines are forced to be the same length). Left-aligned (or *flush-left*) text maintains consistent spacing between words, while justified text forces words to be squeezed or stretched in order for the lines to align with both edges of the column.

Justified text can be beautiful, but it takes a good amount of work to get it right. You'll also need software that allows you to adjust its *hyphenation and justification* (H&J) settings. These H&J settings define the spacing within and between words and also define hyphenation rules. The goal is to produce columns of type without gaps or pinches in the word spacing while maintaining a uniform shade of gray. Gaps that plunge down many lines of type are referred to as *rivers*. Pages that have tight paragraphs in one area (in both word and letter spacing) and loose paragraphs in another are said to have *uneven color.*

Once you have decided on your alignment, it's best to use the same alignment for all the text in your document. However, if you feel adventurous, you might use a different alignment for titles, heads, captions, and sidebars.

Right alignment is handy for *folios* (page numbers) and other headers and footers. I have seen it used successfully for artistic purposes in text and for captions, pull quotes (quotations from the text that are set in larger type and treated as a graphic), and other elements, but I don't recommend setting large amounts of copy with right alignment.

Center alignment can be used for titles, headlines, subheads, letterhead, mastheads, film credits, invitations, cards, and poetry. It is not very useful for body copy.

Tweaking the Spacing

Kerning is used to adjust letter pairs whose spacing is not consistent with that of the surrounding text. Titles, heads, and other display type in particular need special kerning attention, because at large point sizes, irregular spacing is more obvious. "Tight, not touching" is the convention, but letterspacing in display type does not have to be tight as long as it is consistent.

Tracking adjusts the spacing for whole passages of text at a time. Tracking is used to adjust spacing for text at different point sizes—larger text usually needs tighter spacing. It can also be used with restraint to eliminate *widows* (short last lines of paragraphs) and *orphans* (last lines of paragraphs that appear at the top of a page or column). Some people like to "track out" text as a style or to "fill" areas of white space. This is not a style or a solution; it is a major typographic faux pas.

Font-Editing Programs (JZ)

No matter how many fonts you have, you will inevitably run into a need for a custom font. Perhaps you want to set a sidebar in a demi weight of your text typeface, but it doesn't exist, or you crave an oblique version of a typeface that was never made by its creator. Or you may simply want to add a logo or everyday symbol to one of your text fonts. That's when you need the help of a font-editing program.

BitFonter. FontLab's full-fledged bitmap font editor ($499; www.fontlab.com) inputs, outputs, and edits virtually every bitmap format, including Palm, HP (used by many Hewlett-Packard printers), and BDF. (BDFs, or binary distribution fonts, are commonly used where royalty-free or compact font distribution is desired, as in Java applets. They're most commonly used in Unix environments.)

DTL FontMaster. Dutch Type Library's **DTL FontMaster** (about $1,650 at press time; www.fontmaster.nl/english/index.html) is a set of high-end utilities for professional font production. It includes modules for designing and editing letters in Bézier formats; interpolating fonts; testing and correcting contours; generating and converting font formats; editing Ikarus-format fonts (fonts created in the native format of URW's Ikarus font-editing software, which is used by most commercial vendors); generating and editing kerning pairs; and scanning and auto-tracing letters and logos. These tools are available à la carte or as a bundle.

FontLab. FontLab's professional font editor ($549) bridges the gap between the aging Macromedia Fontographer and high-end commercial systems such as URW's venerable Ikarus system. Create your own type masterpiece with a large palette of drawing tools, extensive glyph-editing options, a professional metrics and kerning editor, and full support for Unicode and OpenType.

Macromedia Fontographer. Fontographer ($349; www.macromedia.com) lets you create an entire typeface from scratch or add characters to existing fonts in PostScript and TrueType formats. Beware: This innovative program seems to be falling by the wayside; Fontographer does not run under Mac OS X, but only under Mac OS 9.2.2 and earlier.

ScanFont. FontLab's picture and font converter ($99) will let you turn practically anything that fits on your scanner bed into a typeface. Practical applications include converting obsolete-format fonts to contemporary formats, adding your signature to a font, making custom handwriting fonts, and converting company logos into fonts, among other great uses. Just remember to use your powers for typographic good, not evil.

TransType. So you've found the perfect typeface but there's only one problem: it's in a PC format! Don't curse the bitter reality of Windows hegemony—get this little utility from FontLab ($97). TransType does only one thing, but it does it well: it converts between Mac and PC, TrueType and PostScript Type 1, Multiple Master in multiple ways, whatever direction you need—the choice is yours.

TypeTool. FontLab's lite version of its FontLab program ($99) is a basic font editor that contains much of the drawing and editing functionality of its sibling software, minus some of the more advanced features. People who want to alter their existing fonts should get TypeTool; those who want to create fonts from scratch should get FontLab.

Typeface-Identification Tools

Met a great typeface but don't know its name? Here are two Web sites we recommend that can help you identify that mysterious font.

WhatTheFont (www.myfonts.com/WhatThefont). MyFonts.com's Web-based font-recognition system analyzes uploaded image files and then finds the closest match. Images can be color or black-and-white. They don't even have to be very high quality (although that helps).

Identifont (www.identifont.com). Another useful Web-based font identifier, this site asks users to answer a detailed set of questions on such telling type details as serif heights and tail characteristics. Identifont includes information about fonts from most major type libraries.

Building a Font Library (JZ)

Mac OS X now ships with more than 70 fonts. This starter library is quite useful, but you may want to think about ways to round it out to better suit your needs. When investing in typefaces, it is smart to buy a complete typeface family, not just one or two fonts. This gives you more design options, as well as access to the characters you will need for good typography. (See "Where to Get More Fonts," below, for a list of font vendors.)

Serif Faces

It is always nice to have a versatile serif typeface of your own choice. Look for one that has a large character set. The style you choose is highly personal. A favorite of mine is **Mrs Eaves**, by Zuzana Licko, from Emigré. Mrs Eaves comes with an extended set of beautifully drawn characters and is designed to suggest letterpress printing. It is available in OpenType format.

Mrs Eaves is an historical revival based on the design of Baskerville. In translating this classic to today's digital font technology, Zuzana Licko focused on capturing the

Bembo is a classic serif face that looks distinctive at display sizes yet is a very readable text face. Stanley Morison supervised the design of Bembo for the Monotype Corporation in 1929. It is also available from Adobe in OpenType format.

Bembo was modeled on typefaces cut by Francesco Griffo for Aldus Manutius' printing of *De Aetna* in 1495 in Venice, a book by classicist Pietro Bembo about his visit to Mount

Sans Serif Faces

With Mac OS X you already have a good assortment of sans serif faces, so you may want to hold off on new purchases for a while. That said, I would recommend **Meta,** by Erik Spiekermann. Meta, part of the FontFont library, is available in as many weights as you could possibly need. I don't think I'm wrong in stating that it is the new Helvetica. It is subtly distinctive and undeniably now. I have seen it used for just about everything, including high-tech logos, museum signage, and advertisements everywhere. Buy it and you will be instantly cool.

Meta was originally conceived in 1985 as a typeface for use in small point sizes. It very quickly became one of the most popular typefaces of the computer era, and

Serif and Sans Serif Pairs

Scala and **Scala Sans,** by Martin Majoor (also part of the FontFont library), are a stunning modern duo with many weights and full character sets. I use them whenever I'm in doubt.

In 1988, Martin Majoor started working as a graphic designer for the Vredenburg Music Centre in Utrecht. He designed the typeface Scala for use in their printed

Scala and Scala Sans follow the same principle of form but are two distinct designs. The second largest newspaper in Holland uses both for text and headlines

Display

There are so many different styles of display faces available that you may want to put off purchasing a display face until you have a specific need. Two that I find particularly handsome and versatile are **Cochin,** by Matthew Carter (Linotype, also available in Open Type format from Adobe), and **Parkinson,** by Jim Parkinson (Font Bureau).

Cochin, named for the nineteenth-century printer Nicolas Cochin, has a small x-height with long ascenders and several unusual letter shapes,

Parkinson is a display family originally designed during the mid-seventies by Jim Parkinson for Roger Black. Jim describes it as "a sort of Nicholas Jenson on

Script

Matthew Carter's **Shelley** typeface (Linotype) captures the sublime beauty so important to its Romantic poet namesake, without the threat of death and decay. The Shelley family includes three variations (Andante, Allegro, and—shown here—Volante) on one inspired theme.

The Shelley family is comprised of Allegro, Andante, and Volante. The three script faces have identical lowercase letters, with design variations in the capitals. It is a formal script that brings

Handwriting

Tekton, by David Siegel (Adobe Original), was conceived as a font for architects. In practice, it is a casual, friendly typeface used by just about everyone. It's available in OpenType format.

Tekton is based on the hand-lettering of Seattle-based architect and author Francis D.K. Ching. Although Tekton was initially designed with architects in mind, it quickly

Calligraphic

Brioso, by Robert Slimbach, is a newly released Adobe Original typeface designed in the calligraphic tradition of elegant lettering. Named after the Italian word for "lively," it is also stately, majestic, and readable. Available in OpenType format.

Brioso is an energetic type family modeled on formal roman and italic script. In the modern calligrapher's repertoire of lettering styles, roman script is the hand that most closely

Decorative

Some typefaces of historical significance, such as **Bauhaus,** by Ed Benguiat and Vic Caruso (ITC), become decorative faces over the passage of time. Others are created to capture a historic moment or the style of the moment. A recent eye-catcher is **Aragon,** part of the Sherwood Type Collection, by Ted Staunton (P22), which is based on rounded Lombardic medieval forms.

Herbert Bayer of the Bauhaus School in Germany, designed the inspiration for Bauhaus, known as the Universal typeface, while he was teaching there in

Aragon is a whimsical face with robust curlicues designed for display lines on show programs, posters, print ads, etc. It is part of the Sherwood collection of 28 historically based fonts named

Where to Get More Fonts (JZ)

People do not go into the business of designing type to make money. They are drawn to it as to any art form. Some do end up making a good living, but even for these people, designing type is a labor of love. They live on the usually meager royalties from the sales of the fonts they design. On the road to acquiring more fonts, it is important that you honor the work of type designers by paying for the fonts you use.

Foundries are eager to help you find the right fonts for your projects and are happy to provide printed samples, catalogues, and incomplete digital fonts to help you decide. Most have Web sites for searching their libraries, downloading or previewing free samples, and purchasing online. Many offer a rotating collection of free downloadable fonts. There are scores of font vendors; here we list the major vendors plus a few of our favorite small vendors.

Adobe Systems (www.adobe.com). The Adobe Type Library now features more than 3600 typefaces from internationally renowned foundries, as well as exclusive Adobe Originals. Adobe has converted its entire library to OpenType.

Agfa Monotype (www.agfamonotype.com). Acquired by Agfa in 1998, Monotype has been a leading font supplier for over 100 years. Its library of more than 1300 fonts includes the world-renowned Times New Roman, Gill Sans, and Arial.

Berthold (www.bertholdtypes.com). This highly regarded European foundry has been around for over a century, offering such classics as Akzidenz Grotesk, Berthold Garamond, Berthold Caslon, and Berthold Bodoni.

Bitstream (www.bitstream.com). Bitstream's latest collection of 1450 fonts features new fonts from 36 contributors, including 22 new typeface designers.

Carter & Cone Type (www.carterandcone.com). Matthew Carter, one of the most highly regarded type designers in the world, began his career 40 years ago creating hand-cut punches for Linotype. His designs include ITC Galliard and Snell Roundhand, as well as fonts for Apple and Microsoft.

Elsner+Flake (www.elsner-flake.com). Founded 15 years ago by Veronika Elsner and Günther Flake, this German foundry is committed to preserving the highest standards of typographic quality in the digital age.

Emigre (www.emigre.com). For many, Emigre practically defines modern digital design. In addition to creating some of today's best-known typefaces (including Template Gothic and Mrs Eaves), husband-and-wife team Zuzana Licko and Rudy VanderLans publish the ultra-cool *Emigre* magazine.

Font Bureau (www.fontbureau.com). Headed by type luminary David Berlow and noted media designer Roger Black, the Font Bureau has a retail library consisting mostly of original designs and featuring more than 500 typefaces.

FontFont (www.fontfont.com). All FontFont designs are juried by noted aestheticians Erik Spiekermann, Neville Brody, and Erik van Blokland on such criteria as originality and ability to reflect the current zeitgeist. With up to 300 new fonts each year, the FontFont library is one of the largest and most exciting collections available.

Hoefler Type Foundry (www.typography.com). Jonathan Hoefler was named one of the 40 most influential designers in America by *I.D.* magazine; his publishing work includes award-winning original typeface designs for *Rolling Stone, Harper's Bazaar, The New York Times Magazine, Sports Illustrated,* and *Esquire.*

House Industries (www.houseind.com). House's style may be funky, fresh, and firmly rooted in pop culture, but frivolous hipster fluff it is not. For example, House's latest typeface, Neutraface, is an extensive typeface collection inspired by the work of the noted modern architect Richard J. Neutra.

International Typeface Corporation (ITC) (www.itcfonts.com). ITC has been a leader in typeface design for over 25 years. While known for classic designs, ITC is aggressively expanding its scope to include more contemporary designs. ITC develops and releases more than 100 new typefaces each year.

Linotype Library (www.fontexplorer.com). What can you expect from a company that helped invent the typesetting machine? How about almost 4000 fonts and more than a century of experience? Visit the Web site and explore the company's expert FontIdentifier application or take a typographic break at the Font Lounge.

P22 type foundry (www.p22.com). Take a tour through art history with the fonts from P22. Inspired by significant individuals and movements in art and history, each font set is packaged with information related to its source and inspiration.

Plazm (www.plazm.com). Since 1991 designer Joshua Berger, master fontician Pete McCracken, and the rest of the Plazm Media collective have steadily put out slyly subversive type as an outgrowth of *Plazm* magazine, a quarterly publication that serves as the collective's printed laboratory for graphic exploration.

Stone Type Foundry (www.stonetypefoundry.com). Sumner Stone, principal and founder of Stone Type Foundry, is the designer of the ITC Stone, Stone Print, Silica, Cycles, and Arepo typeface families. Stone serves on the board of directors of the Association Typographique Internationale and is the editor of *Type: A Journal of the Association Typographique Internationale.*

Treacyfaces/Headliners (www.treacyfaces.com). Treacyfaces/Headliners is a collection of 400 high-quality fonts, all with extensive kerning (1700 to 5000 kerning pairs per font).

URW++ (www.urwpp.de/english/home.htm). URW++ sells fonts from the world's leading type foundries, along with its own group of exclusives, which are styled at the company's design studio in Hamburg, Germany.

Resellers

In addition to font vendors, there's a slew of companies that sell a variety of fonts from various vendors and independent designers. Here's where to go.

Fonts.com (www.fonts.com). A division of Agfa Monotype, Fonts.com allows you to preview, purchase, and immediately download fonts.

FontHaus (www.fonthaus.com). If you're looking for a new typeface, a special dingbat, an unusual picture, or just a bargain, check out FontHaus. With more than 35,000 fonts in its ever-growing collection, FontHaus serves as one of the type industry's largest resources.

FontShop (www.fontshop.com). FontShop carries more than 25,000 fonts from more than 50 international type foundries, large and small, from Adobe to X-Space, with many now available online. FontShop also publishes *Fuse,* an award-winning experimental typographic publication, and the FontBook, a comprehensive reference book on digital typefaces.

MyFonts.com (www.myfonts.com). Founded by Bitstream, this is an online source for finding, trying, and buying fonts. With over 28,000 fonts to choose from, you may be able to find the one you're looking for.

Phil's Fonts (www.philsfonts.com). As the state of typography changes in the digital era, Phil's Fonts continues its love affair with beautiful faces, making fine typography available to artists and communicators around the world.

Precision Type (www.precisiontype.com). One of the first independent font-software distributors to the professional graphic arts market, Precision Type represents more than 70 different font foundries from around the world, offering over 13,000 typefaces.

Where to Read More About Fonts and Type

Just in case you haven't had your fill of fonts by now, you can always look to these sources for more information. Resources range from publications that focus on design issues to those that profile some of the best font designers today.

Periodicals

Communication Arts (www.commarts.com). One of the preeminent design magazines in the world, *Communication Arts* showcases the top work in graphic design, advertising, illustration, photography, and interactive design. In addition to inspiring galleries and interviews with leading professionals, the magazine offers practical columns on legal affairs, freelancing, and relevant design issues.

Graphis (www.graphis.com). First published in Switzerland in 1944, *Graphis* magazine is a premier chronicler of contemporary design, featuring extensive showcases of the world's best designers that are gorgeously laid out with first-class production values. *Graphis* also publishes annual and biannual books displaying international innovations in advertising, design, photography, and corporate identity.

Books

The Complete Manual of Typography, by James Felici (Adobe Press, 2002; www.adobepress.com). This is the only book that teaches you how to set type like a professional; it covers topics from font formats and character selections to hyphenation and justification, setting tables, kerning, tracking, and exacting type refinement. From a founding father of *Macworld* and *Publish* magazines.

The Elements of Typographic Style, Second Edition, by Robert Bringhurst (Hartley & Marks, 2002; www.hartleyandmarks.com). A definitive reference, this popular book explores the history of typography and uses that history to explain why the rules of typography exist. The book briefly mentions digital typography but otherwise ignores it, focusing instead on general typography and issues of page and type design.

FontBook: Digital Typeface Compendium, 2nd Edition, by Mai-Linh Thi Truong, Jürgen Siebert, and Erik Spiekermann (FontShop International, 1998; www.fontshop.com or 800/333-6687). In this second edition of *FontBook,* the previous two volumes have been combined into one monstrous hardcover book, boasting a collection of 4850 type families and packages.

Stop Stealing Sheep & Find Out How Type Works, by Erik Spiekermann and E. M. Ginger (Adobe Press, 2002; www.adobepress.com). An exploration of good typographic practices, this classic work is lushly illustrated and explains typography in layman's terms. The latest edition includes explanations of good Web typography.

Type: Hot Designers Make Cool Fonts, by Allan Haley (Rockport Publishers, 1998; www.rockpub.com). Features the tools and working methods of 15 successful designers, including David Berlow, Matthew Carter, Tobias Frere-Jones, Jonathan Hoefler, Jim Parkinson, Sumner Stone, and Carol Twombly. Includes a type timeline and a short directory of foundries.

Interview: Jeff Harbers

Though not well known to most Macintosh users, Jeff Harbers holds an important place in the Mac's history because he championed the Mac at Microsoft and led the development of the first Mac applications there. After graduating from college with a degree in mechanical engineering, Harbers ran a research station in Antarctica, then ran a computerized scheduling system in Prudhoe Bay, Alaska. He got into software development while working for an electronic scale maker and subsequently became interested in word processing when hired as head of software at a Redmond, Washington-based research subsidiary of Atex, at the time a leading maker of dedicated publishing systems.

> We were completely convinced that the Mac was going to shatter the world. We were total Mac converts. It was everything that we saw as the future of computing.
>
> —*Jeff Harbers, on the Microsoft App group's vision of the Macintosh*

In 1981 Harbers tried to recruit Charles Simonyi, who had created Bravo, a pioneering graphical-interface word processor, at Xerox PARC. Simonyi, however, had already decided to move to Microsoft, and Harbers ended up joining him in the company's fledgling applications group in June 1981. When Microsoft began developing for the Mac later that year, Harbers became deputy director of applications development and technical lead for Macintosh products—a role he kept through the release of three early applications (Multiplan, Chart, and File), Word, and finally Excel in 1985. Harbers went on to become Microsoft's director of applications development for both Windows and Macintosh in 1985. Since 1993, although classified as an "internal consultant" at Microsoft, he has devoted most of his attention to other interests, including aviation and raising registered Black Angus cattle on his ranch in Montana. —Henry Norr

When did you first find out about the Mac?

Jobs came up in October 1981, and we went out to the Seattle Tennis Club, where he told us about what they were doing. He didn't have a machine to show, but he talked about the Lisa and work they were doing on GUI interfaces, and this idea that this machine was going to cost $1,000 and have a bitmapped display and GUI interface and such.

What was your reaction to all that?

We were totally lovestruck. I mean, he was talking about the perfect computer, the computer we'd always dreamed about and had always wanted and would love to write software for. Everybody in Apps [the then-new Microsoft applications group] would have wanted to work on this machine. And [Bill] Gates was totally behind it, because he, and certainly everyone on the apps side, was totally focused on GUI—we saw that as the power of the future.

Did you immediately start planning to implement the apps for the Mac?

Bill and Steve worked out a deal where we were going to develop software and sell it to Apple to distribute. At that time it was Multiplan, Chart, and File—those were the three apps Apple wanted to buy. Because we knew word processing was a key component of our entire office-productivity strategy, we were also doing Word for the Macintosh, but we weren't doing that for Apple. Steve didn't want to buy a word processor, because Apple was doing their own.

What was your personal role in developing the Mac apps?

I became the technical lead for Macintosh products at Microsoft, so I was in charge of all the Mac applications from the very beginning. I was the liaison—I was the guy who would go down to Apple and bring our suggestions and problems and bring back the new information and hardware. At the beginning there were just four or five of us in the [Mac] group, and we were sworn to secrecy. We couldn't talk about the Mac to anybody.

Was that at Apple's insistence?

I'm sure it was, and we were glad to do it. It made sense, because by then clearly we were Apple's worst enemy, in that we supported their biggest enemy, which was IBM at that time—the IBM PC had just taken the heart out of the Apple II and the Apple III.

We went down [to Apple] for a visit. Andy Hertzfeld showed us a breadboard [circuit board designed for prototyping] with a screen with Pepsi cans or balls or something bouncing on it. When we saw the machine, we were again just even more in love with it. We brought back a breadboard, a display, and an Apple II drive. We carried it on the plane in our secret bag and guarded it with our lives.

When we got back to Microsoft, we had this windowless room, like a big closet, near the lobby. I coined a name for the project—the Sand project. Sand stood for "Steve's amazing new device," and it also stood for a story Steve had told us about this vision he had, where you would bring sand to one end of a factory, and out the other end would come these Macintoshes. Because we called it the Sand machine, when people were going off to work on it, they'd say, "I'm going to the beach."

In fact, we enjoyed the secrecy. We were completely convinced that the Macintosh was going to shatter the world. We were total Mac converts. It was everything that we saw as the future of computing, so we didn't want to ruin the surprise. I was completely convinced that they were going to sell a million Macs.

What did you think of the Apple people? Did you get along well with them?

The Mac group was an incredible group of people. Andy [Hertzfeld] and Susan Kare, Bill Atkinson, the whole team—they're very smart and very creative. They did an amazing job, and to interact with them and be part of a team was just a terrific thing. Relations were good. My group wasn't a "creative" group. We were much more of an engineering team working to adhere to and extend the Apple GUI. Because of that, I think they viewed us like we were kind of boring, geeky guys.

continues on next page

When the Mac finally came out, were you still as high on it?

Yeah, we were very excited about it. But the problem was, we were starting to learn about the real world at that point. The problem with the Mac, especially the 128K Mac, was that in terms of getting something done, it was just way behind what you could do with a PC at that time. It was slow, and it didn't have a hard drive. In offices people were calling it a toy. The guy with his IBM PC and Lotus 1-2-3 could do things you just couldn't do on a Mac. So we were starting to feel a little beaten up and wanting to see more hardware, more power coming out of Apple.

We had already started a project to compete head-to-head against 1-2-3—that's what became Excel. We were really targeting the speed of 1-2-3, and we were going to have more features. It was originally going to be for the PC, but I remember lobbying very hard to move it to the Mac. My feeling was that we at Microsoft had a leg up over Lotus on the Mac—we'd been working with it a lot longer—and basically I thought we weren't going to win head-to-head on the PC. I thought if we could change where we were focused and have a different platform, we might have a chance.

Turned out to be a smart move.

Well, it turned out to be the way that we won against 1-2-3, because we did it on the Mac first, then went to Windows, and we took them apart that way. With that project we basically said, "Look, raw speed is the key," and we started hand-coding all the places where we were slow because all we wanted was blazing speed. We also started hacking into the Mac OS, which the Apple guys didn't appreciate, but we were just fanatics. Our approach was speed and power—that's what people wanted on the Mac, that was our Holy Grail.

In the meantime, Lotus was thinking, "Ah, what people want is real ease of use. Jazz will be this wonderful ease-of-use-type application." They were doing what we did with our first version of [Microsoft's earlier] Mac apps, and when Excel came out, we kicked their butt. It was a chance for all those guys who had been abused by their IBM PC friends for two years to step up and say, "Well, you want to see what my 'toy' can do now?" I think because of that, even though Excel had bugs, people never complained about them. Excel could do no wrong. The press loved it, Apple loved it, the users loved it. It was the right app at the right time to satisfy everybody's deep need for being able to say the Mac was a real machine.

16

Web Design and HTML

Tara Marchand and Joanna Pearlstein are the chapter editors and authors.

Gene Steinberg was the chapter editor and author for the 8th edition of **The Macintosh Bible,** *from which portions of this chapter are taken.*

Now that surfing the Web has been a global pastime for years, everyone from retired eBay sellers to young students is creating Web sites. The days when you could create a Web page only by laboriously typing out bits of *HTML (Hypertext Markup Language)* code are, thankfully, long gone. Today there are a bevy of tools that make creating Web pages as easy as writing a letter in your word-processing program. Now, instead of hoping the code you develop looks half-decent in a Web browser, you can rely on *WYSIWYG* (say "wiz-ee-wig"; it stands for "What you see is what you get") editors to speed your work.

In this chapter we offer a tour of the most popular Mac Web design tools and provide some design tips. We'll discuss the new phenomenon of Web logs, or *blogs,* which allow quick Web publishing without the need to touch raw code or upload files. We'll also run through the basics of HTML. While the availability of WYSIWYG editors is great news for would-be Web publishers, coding directly in HTML is still de rigueur for many. And for users who want to fine-tune their work or develop sophisticated sites, HTML is still important to know. For those reasons, we'll talk about programs that can help you work hands-on with the code. Finally, we'll talk about how to include graphics in your pages, and we'll introduce you to the nuts and bolts of incorporating animation, sound, and video into your Web pages.

In This Chapter

Web Hosting Basics

Before you build a Web site, you'll need a place to put it. If you have an Internet service provider (ISP), your account may come with storage space for Web pages and graphics. Some service providers, such as EarthLink, not only provide Web hosting space but also offer premade page designs and other tools that can help you set up a site quickly. If your ISP doesn't provide hosting space, you might want to investigate sites like Yahoo GeoCities (http://geocities.yahoo.com), Tripod (www.tripod.lycos.com), and Angelfire (www.angelfire.com), which offer free Web hosting space to consumers; however, they are likely to sprinkle your pages with pop-up windows and banner advertisements. Of course, Apple's own Internet service, Mac.com ($99.95 per year; www.apple.com), provides Web hosting space (along with email and many other services), including templates for easily creating attractive pages.

 Since companies hosting your pages could be held liable for any material you publish, they may insist on holding the copyrights to your content or they may assign responsibility to you for anything you post that's illegal. It's a good idea to read the fine print when agreeing to a site's terms and conditions.

While the days of selling domain names for hundreds of thousands of dollars are—we hope—a phenomenon of the past, having the URL *YourName*.com can be handy. If you run a small business, want to create a Web site for your family, or just prefer to have a unique Web-site name that's under your control, you can buy a domain name through a domain-name registrar like Network Solutions (www.networksolutions.com). Registrars are authorized to hand out domain names and ensure that multiple people don't snap up the same ones. Normally, you pay a registration and handling fee to a registrar, and you also need to pay to host your domain somewhere. Many of these companies offer both registration and hosting services for an annual or monthly fee, as do many ISPs. Alternately, you can register your domain name and then use an ISP such as the ones mentioned above to host your Web site.

 Be careful when registering a domain name that is someone else's trademark, such as Target or Virgin: many a lawsuit has been fought and won by large companies trying to protect their brand names.

 You can register a domain name and park it on an ISP until you're ready to create your Web site. For example, EarthLink lets you do this for $4.95 a month.

Once you know the site's destination, it's time to draw up a project plan: What is your site going to be used for? How many sections or pages does it need? What kind of navigation system do you want? What do you want it to look like? Your site will undoubtedly be better organized and designed if you develop a strategy before you begin to create your first Web page. Even if you're just making a single page, think about its content and design before getting started.

The Lowdown on Blogs

In the past few years, the cachet enjoyed by tech geeks who had personal Internet domains and dot-com riches has now been afforded to normal folks who set up simple, low-budget Web logs, or *blogs,* as they're more commonly called. Blogs let people publish content online without learning the innards of HTML and JavaScript. People use blogs to publish personal diaries, record their dog's behavior, track developments in fields like educational technology, publish photographs, or add links to other Web sites. You name it, there's probably a blog for it—think of blogs as an ever-growing subset of the Web, just as diverse as the Web itself.

So how do you create a blog? If you're just getting started, you can sign up for a free account with a service that offers a Web interface for designing templates and posting new content. In most cases, you'll need to find a place to host the content you're publishing, since not all Web-log services offer their own hosting. One place to try is Blogspot (www.blogspot.com), which provides free hosting with some restrictions and advertising requirements.

To create a blog, check out the popular service Blogger (www.blogger.com), run by Pyra Labs, which was bought by Google in 2003. With Blogger's basic service, which is free, you can choose from a library of templates and modify them as you please, or use your own design (**Figure 16.1**). Blogger also offers Web hosting. Many blogs are updated frequently, and because of that, entries are often preceded by a date or time stamp. In addition, since multiple people can contribute to blogs, the contributor's name also appears. You can usually set the parameters of these features in your blog's setup.

continues on next page

Figure 16.1

If you want to set up a Web site quickly, you may want to check out Blogger. The site offers free tools to set up simple blogs; you can post to your blog by filling out a Web form.

The Lowdown on Blogs   *continued*

Once you've perfected your design, you can post to your blog simply by going to a Web page, entering your content into a form, and clicking a button. Some systems let you post content through a client-side application. Either way, you're usually given the opportunity to review your contribution before publishing it officially to the Web. Blogs can have "comments" links next to entries that allow readers to contribute their own thoughts (**Figure 16.2**). This is another feature that's typically specified during the blog's setup.

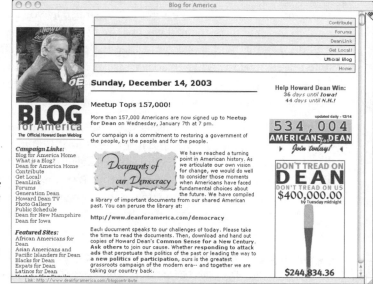

Figure 16.2

Democratic presidential candidate Howard Dean made headlines for his use of blogs to build community. His site lets any registered user post comments about Dean's candidacy.

While there are a few free blogging tools out there, you can also find a number of paid services and software packages, ranging from Six Apart's **Movable Type** (free for personal use, $150 commercial; www.movabletype.org) to UserLand Software's **Radio UserLand** ($39.95 per year includes a blog-hosting option; www.userland.com). But while you could theoretically create a blog with a product like Macromedia Dreamweaver or Adobe GoLive, we wouldn't really recommend it: setting up a blog through one of the aforementioned services is so easy that we'd hate to see you reinvent the wheel. Another cool feature of blogs is the ability to syndicate content from them through an XML format called *RSS* (for *RDF Site Summary* or *Rich Site Summary*). An RSS feed contains a summary of postings to a blog in a format that RSS-enabled programs such as Ranchero Software's NetNewsWire Lite (free; www.ranchero.com) can read. News organizations publish RSS feeds, as do many blogs. Yahoo has a directory for this category; search on "RSS news aggregators" to find it.

One relative of the blog is something called a *wiki*. A wiki is a Web site that many people work on. The concept is somewhat similar to that of open-source software: users can make changes to content posted by other contributors. Blogs, on the other hand, typically allow visitors to post only comments. One popular example of a wiki is Wikipedia, a free encyclopedia project (www.wikipedia.org).

Web Authoring Basics

HTML has evolved through many versions and has been enhanced as the Web has matured. At its most basic, however, HTML tells a Web browser how to render the content of a page. HTML tags, demarcated by angle brackets (< and >), indicate how type should be displayed, what colors should appear where, how graphics are contained in pages, and how to display hyperlinks to Web and email addresses. Beyond those tasks, HTML pages can contain other commands, like *Cascading Style Sheets (CSS),* which let you embed style sheets for Web pages in the same manner you apply style sheets in word-processing or desktop-publishing applications. (See the sidebar "The Dirt on Cascading Style Sheets," below). HTML code can also contain *JavaScript,* a language for scripting the Web that, confusingly, is unrelated to Sun Microsystems' Java programming language, which is also used on the Web.

Desktop-publishing applications let you insert images directly within documents, but with HTML, all content that isn't text is referenced. Essentially, the HTML code says, this is the image to display, this is where it's located, and this is how to display it. Because of this, if you're including any images at all, it's a good idea to determine where they'll be physically located. As you'll see later, putting all your images in the same folder that contains your HTML files will save you time when creating your Web page.

 If you want an in-depth tutorial on HTML, we recommend *HTML for the World Wide Web with XHTML and CSS: Visual QuickStart Guide,* **Fifth Edition, by Elizabeth Castro (Peachpit Press, 2002).**

HTML is platform-independent, which means that a file created with HTML isn't restricted to a specific operating system, and only needs an HTML-aware browser application to be viewed. That's also the shortcoming of the language and the source of great headaches for Web designers. Different browsers or different versions of the same browser may vary, sometimes extensively, in the way they interpret the contents of a Web page.

The Dirt on Cascading Style Sheets

Cascading Style Sheets (CSS) allow users to create sophisticated text styling and layouts not easily achieved with the HTML of yore. With CSS, you can define style sheets as you would in a word-processing or page-layout program. You can link style sheets to multiple Web pages, so that once you've changed something in a style sheet, those changes will be implemented on all pages that use that style sheet.

Style sheets can define typography formats, such as fonts, font sizes, and font colors, and they can specify how elements like headers and footers appear. You can also use style sheets to position elements on a page—a technique that's a bit more complex and advanced than using invisible HTML tables to create layouts. You can apply more than one style sheet to a page or Web site.

Adobe GoLive CS and Macromedia Dreamweaver MX, along with other programs, help users create and implement style sheets. Although most modern browsers support CSS, they do so in different ways, and each has its own quirks in how it implements CSS. For more information, visit the Web site of the World Wide Web Consortium (W3C), which oversees Web-oriented standards including CSS (www.w3.org/Style/CSS).

A Very Short Course in HTML

If you've ever been exposed to old-fashioned text-based word processors or traditional typesetting, you'll see a passing resemblance between the way that HTML and the coding used for those documents work. For example, HTML consists of an opening tag that appears before the material you're formatting and a closing, or end, tag that appears at the end of the material.

To separate HTML from regular text, you place the commands within angle brackets, beginning with the less-than sign (<) and concluding with the greater-than sign (>). For example, one basic tag, <i>, specifies italicized text. Everything following that simple command is in italics. To switch back to roman text, you simply close the tag with a slash, like this: </i>. Of course, this command structure can get quite involved when you expand your HTML arsenal to specify the attributes of linked Web sites or graphics.

Another, more complicated command is this one, which tells a browser not only what image to display, but also how text should wrap around it:

```
<img src="images/doghouse.gif" height="100" width="75" align="left">
```

This tidbit tells the browser to look in the images directory for a file called doghouse.gif. The browser is then instructed to show the image at a height of 100 pixels and a width of 75 pixels, and to align the image on the left. That means text will wrap around it to the right.

To create a link to a Web site or email address, you use the <a> tag, followed by the HREF command's *attribute*. HREF is the command used to specify a page's location; an attribute provides special instructions for the command to use—in this case the attribute is the URL for the page you want to link to. To make a link, you need two things: first, the address to which you're linking, and second, the text you want people to click on to activate the link (in other words, the text that often appears in blue underline). For example:

```
<a href="http://www.dynamitedogwalkers.com">Try our dog-walking
services!</a>
```

In this code bit, the browser will display "Try our dog-walking services!" in blue underline (or whatever style you've chosen to display links in—you can specify settings like the color of hyperlinks). When users click that text, they'll be sent to the site www.dynamitedogwalkers.com (which didn't exist at this writing). You can use the same code to link an image to a URL—so that clicking the image takes you to a specific page—and you can modify the code so that it directs the user's email program to address a new message to a specific email address.

Basic HTML Tags

We won't pretend to offer a complete course in HTML, but we will cover the basics. Once you get the hang of it, some practice and regular reference to a book will do wonders to increase your knowledge and abilities.

The beginning of a Web site

First things first: every Web document must have some basic tags that identify it to your browser, and you must enter additional tags in a specific order. To start your page, enter the <HTML> tag. You'll close your page with an </HTML> tag at the bottom. The latter, like all end tags, contains the telltale slash that indicates a closing command. Once you've established at the beginning of the page what kind of page you're building, you then need to separate the head from the body copy. Here's the way you'd set up your basic page:

```
<HTML> <HEAD> <TITLE>Dynamite Dog Walkers</TITLE> <BODY>
```

Use the area following the <BODY> tag for the main text of your document. Of course, the process doesn't end there. Your code will include tags that specify the text style, graphics, and links to other sites. You'll use special tags to add tables, frames (multiple pages within a single page), JavaScripts, and animation.

Your Web page concludes with this:

```
</BODY>
</HEAD>
</HTML>
```

You can use the tags in **Table 16.1** to build a simple page with text and headlines from scratch using just your word processor or text editor. Now we will move on to some of the more, sophisticated tags.

 While most commands require opening and closing tags, not all of them do. For example, image references begin but never end.

Table 16.1 *Common Web Tags*

Tag	Purpose
<H1> and </H1>	Opens and closes a first-level heading. There are six levels of headings in regular HTML, with number 1 being the largest. For a smaller head, you could use <H3> and </H3>.
<B> and </B>	Makes the text that follows it bold, and then changes the bold text back to light.
<P> and </P>	Specifies the beginning and end of a paragraph in your body copy. Browsers usually display an extra return between paragraphs on a Web page for easy reading.
 	This tag—one that begins but doesn't end—tells the browser to insert a single line break. It's handy for positioning images and text exactly as you want them, especially when you don't want the extra carriage return that the <P> tag inserts.
<HR>	Another tag without an end point: it creates a horizontal rule.
<UL> and </UL>	Starts and ends an unordered or bulleted list.
<OL> and </OL>	Starts and ends an ordered list (for example, a list of items preceded by numbers or letters).
<LI> and </LI>	Formats the text that follows a bullet or number so that it's indented within the bullet or number, depending on whether you have an unordered or ordered list.

The next level

Once you get past the basic formatting instructions, you'll start adding *attributes*—elements that provide special instructions describing the command's use. You can, for example, specify a background color for your Web page. Otherwise, your users will see a drab gray background (depending on the browser).

One of the simplest colors to use is plain white. We'll show you the code and then deconstruct it to explain how it's set up:

```
<body bgcolor="white">
```

That's an easy one. The attribute—in this case, the background color—appears after the equals sign (=), enclosed in quotes (""). You can specify basic colors such as red or blue by name alone or in hexadecimal format (a base-16 numbering system, which uses the digits 0 through 9 plus the letters A through F). Many of the major programs used to create Web sites, such as Adobe Photoshop and Macromedia Dreamweaver, will translate the color you choose into hexadecimal format. Here's an example for specifying a background color:

```
<BODY BGCOLOR="#FFFFFF">
```

Complex shades always use a value rather than a name.

To insert a picture, you'd use an *image tag,* which is simply a reference to the picture and its location—as we demonstrated earlier in this section. This is similar to how a page-layout program such as QuarkXPress handles pictures behind the scenes, which is by storing a *reference* to the file rather than inserting the file itself.

HTML commands aren't case sensitive, so it won't matter if you write an italics tag with <I> or <i>. However, when you refer to files or directories, you should presume that your Web server is case sensitive and refer to locations exactly as they are named.

To create a Web site, you have several options. First, you can write code in a text editor like TextEdit, which comes with Mac OS X. You can also use your word-processing program, such as Microsoft Word or AppleWorks, to develop Web pages. More-sophisticated options include the WYSIWYG programs Adobe GoLive and Macromedia Dreamweaver, both of which offer exhaustive sets of HTML editing tools. And Bare Bones Software's BBEdit is a popular text-based editing program that includes built-in shortcuts and code-writing tips for those who want to work directly in HTML.

An Overview of HTML Editors: the Key Players

It is possible to write all your HTML code yourself in text form, even in Mac OS X's TextEdit. But it takes time and dedication to master HTML's nuts and bolts. You probably want a program that can both write tight HTML code and display a fully formatted document that closely resembles what visitors to your Web site will see.

In the following pages we'll provide an overview of several major HTML editing programs. We'll show you where they might suit your purposes and where they might fall down on the job. If a company has a demo version, you'd do best to give it a test run before ordering a copy. That way, you can see if it really meets your needs.

Microsoft Word does a decent job of converting documents to HTML. If you have a few simple pages and don't care much about design, using Word as an HTML editor works reasonably well. However, if you're a purist in any way, know that Word tends to insert lots of extra code to make the Web page mirror its appearance in Word as closely as possible. This might not bother you, but if you want streamlined HTML, you may want to examine the product of Word's conversion. Macromedia Dreamweaver MX actually has a command specifically for cleaning up Word's less-than-pristine HTML code.

Macromedia Dreamweaver

For many professional Web designers, **Macromedia Dreamweaver** ($399; www.macromedia.com) is the program to beat—it's handy for everything from single Web pages to complex Web sites. Dreamweaver MX 2004 is part of a suite of Web design tools from Macromedia that includes Macromedia Fireworks MX 2004, which is a graphics editing tool, Macromedia Flash MX 2004, which is animation software, Macromedia FreeHand MX, which is a vector-based drawing program, and Macromedia ColdFusion, which is an Internet application development tool. (You can purchase Dreamweaver MX 2004 separately or as part of a bundle called Studio MX Professional, which also includes the other programs and costs $999.)

Dreamweaver features three display options: WYSIWYG only (for those who don't want to see the code), HTML source code in a split screen above the WYSIWYG display, or source code only (**Figure 16.3**). Using these different views, you can fine-tune your site as you create or edit it without having to close one window and open another.

Figure 16.3

Macromedia Dreamweaver MX includes a collection of reference tools from O'Reilly for commonly used Web technologies. It also provides three options for viewing your Web content; here is a combo of source code and WYSIWYG screen display.

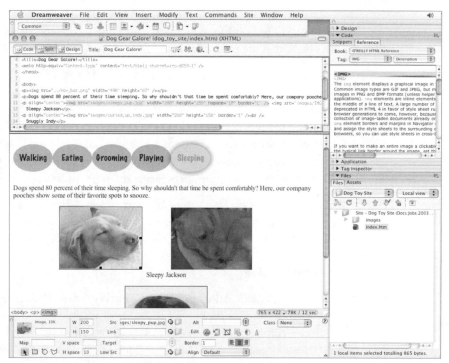

If you can use a word processor, you can probably create a simple Web page in Dreamweaver without much trauma. Dreamweaver lets you easily create tables, forms, frames, links, image maps, anchors, and bulleted and numbered lists; format text; insert images or other multimedia files; and set pages' background and default text colors.

One of the program's more-advanced content-editing features is its templates function. If you've decided on a basic design for your site, you can create a template file that includes navigation bars, images, background colors, text, and other standard elements to be used throughout your site. You use that template to create individual pages, and if you later change an element of the template, those changes will be reflected in each page based on that template. Library items are another handy feature: they're like templates, only they consist of smaller elements instead of entire pages. For example, you might store a table or a set of images as a library element. Another variation on this is Dreamweaver's code snippets feature, which stores bits of code, like HTML and JavaScript, for quick and easy reuse.

When you can't remember how to do something in HTML, Dreamweaver helps you out. It includes references for HTML, CSS, JavaScript, and Advanced Server Pages. At this writing, Macromedia had just released Dreamweaver MX 2004, which the company said includes better support for CSS. The new version also contains a basic graphics editor, which is based on technology taken from Macromedia's standalone Web graphics editor, Fireworks MX 2004 (see "Macromedia Fireworks," later in the chapter). Dreamweaver will also tidy up its own HTML and let you tailor your code to the versions of HTML and browsers that are most important to you.

On the server side of things, Dreamweaver lets you manage whole Web sites, and it can synchronize files between your local hard drive and your Web server. It can also FTP files to your server (through regular or secure FTP), eliminating the need to launch a separate FTP client. Dreamweaver includes database connectivity features, so you can link common database types directly to your site. The company's ColdFusion MX application, which is a development tool for creating Web applications, provides a fuller set of database connectivity tools.

Finally, Macromedia's custody of programs like Fireworks and Flash means that such programs integrate easily with Dreamweaver, making it easy to edit files and move between applications relatively seamlessly.

Adobe GoLive

In the fall of 2003, Adobe released **Creative Suite Premium** ($1,229; www.adobe.com), a package of the company's design applications that includes Adobe Photoshop CS, Adobe Illustrator CS, InDesign CS, Acrobat 6.0 Professional, Version Cue, and Adobe GoLive CS, the new version of Adobe's Web authoring software. The suite is meant to help you integrate your workflows so that you can be more efficient.

For example, with the suite you can insert graphic files directly into GoLive and then edit those images in their native applications by double-clicking them. GoLive will also convert those graphics to Web formats. In addition, applications in the suite share a common user interface and set of tools; for instance, the cropping tool in GoLive CS mirrors the one found in Photoshop CS. The programs also use a common technology called Color Engine, which ensures color consistency between media and applications.

Creators of print and Web publications can use the suite to move documents from one medium to another; for example, images created in RGB format for the Web can be converted to CMYK format for print. Part of this functionality comes from what Adobe calls Smart Objects, a technology that identifies elements that can be edited by Adobe applications. When you open GoLive files that include Smart Objects, the application checks to see if those files have changed since the document was last edited and updates the files accordingly.

But if you don't need the whole shebang, you can still buy GoLive CS on its own for $399. Since the last version, GoLive 6, GoLive has added expanded support for PDF files—you can now view PDF files, edit links to PDF files, and export Web pages as PDF files. The program now lets you assign rollover states to native Photoshop documents so, for example, you could create a Web page in Photoshop and then assign various actions to occur when a user rolls a pointer over certain spots. And if you are tired of squinting at your computer monitor, you will appreciate GoLive CS's zooming capabilities: you can enlarge the view of documents up to a huge 1600 percent. GoLive also lets you customize your editing environment so that you can choose to see all or part of the source-code editor, an outline view, or a layout view.

Taking a cue from Macromedia's Contribute application (a program designed for use by teams of Web authors), Adobe has introduced Co-Author, a collaboration feature, in GoLive. You can create templates that contain editable text, image, and hyperlink areas, and collaborators can insert their own content without altering the underlying template. Groups that want to contribute content with Co-Author will need to purchase copies of Adobe GoLive CS Co-Author Editor for $89 each.

The new version of GoLive contains expanded support for XML (see "What's XML" below) and CSS, providing a visual environment for creating CSS Levels 1 and 2. Its code-completion feature automatically closes HTML tags when you hand-code. The program also now offers a feature that helps creators of content for mobile phones, including NTT DoCoMo phones. The upgrade lets you open, edit, and export a variety of video formats, including QuickTime, AVI, and MPEG-4 (for more on these formats see Chapter 17).

What's XML?

XML, short for *Extensible Markup Language,* is a slimmed-down version of yet another markup language, called *SGML,* for *Standard Generalized Markup Language.* Designed for Web documents, XML is a *meta language* that lets designers create and use their own customized tags. XML tags are typically tailored to the content they define, and as such there's no underlying common set of tags for XML, but XML has a definite structure and rule set.

For example, XML can define not only how a document is formatted, but also just what kind of content that document contains. It's popularly used to display and format data from enterprise systems like corporate databases. Often XML has a data hierarchy—for example, a company tag could contain elements of a product tag, which could include tags for color, cost, location, and size.

BBEdit

Bare Bones Software's **BBEdit** ($179; www.barebones.com) isn't your typical HTML editor—in fact, it didn't enter the world destined for use in Web design at all. The program is a rich text editor long favored by programmers. Before WYSIWYG Web authoring existed, text editors like BBEdit were Web designers' sole option. Today, even with the plethora of tools available, some developers prefer to live primarily in BBEdit. Others use the tool to spot-check code generated by programs like GoLive and Dreamweaver.

The Mac-only program offers extensive search options, colored HTML tags, site-management features, sophisticated copy and paste functions, customizable palettes and command keys, and integrated FTP support. It handles files in a variety of formats, from DOS to Unix to QuickTime, and includes a built-in spelling checker. BBEdit also supports DHTML (Dynamic HTML, which lets you make your Web pages more interactive), CSS, JavaScript, Perl (the language used to write small Web scripts called Common Gateway Interfaces, or CGIs), PHP (a general-purpose scripting language that can be embedded into HTML), and XML. Those familiar with the Windows authoring tool HomeSite, from Macromedia (formerly sold by Allaire, which Macromedia acquired), will find BBEdit a familiar environment.

In the past, Bare Bones offered a slimmed-down version of BBEdit called BBEdit Lite. The product has been discontinued, and the company now directs customers to its product **TextWrangler** ($49), which offers some text-editing capabilities but isn't particularly Web focused.

PageSpinner

If you're overwhelmed by the heft of Macromedia's and Adobe's products but aren't prepared to delve into BBEdit, consider Optima System's **PageSpinner** ($29.95; www.optima-system.com). At less than $30, you can't go wrong with this text-based authoring program. PageSpinner offers color-coded tags, table creation, and search-and-replace features; editor modes for CSS, JavaScript, and PHP; and built-in FTP support. The popular author and Web designer Jeffrey Zeldman (www.zeldman.com) uses PageSpinner, and if it's good enough for him, it might be adequate for you, too.

Macromedia Contribute

A relative newcomer to the Mac Web design scene is **Macromedia Contribute 2** ($99). Designed for use by teams, the program is a content-management system that combines limited Web authoring features with workflow tools. It's designed primarily for nontechnical people who need to contribute content to a Web site—hence the name. An administrator sets access privileges to ensure that contributors aren't mucking with fonts or page layouts inappropriately, or aren't updating the wrong department's content. To publish new information, users check files out of the system and then check them in when they're finished; Contribute keeps tabs on who's editing what. The application handles Microsoft Word files and comes with a system for setting up PayPal e-commerce capabilities. If you manage a workgroup that publishes Web content, Contribute may be worth a look, but it's not really suited to individual Web authors.

Other Tools of the Trade

Unless your Web site is made up only of text (which might make it a bit drab), you're likely to want to invest in tools that can help you create and edit digital images and multimedia files. In this section we'll review the basic graphics and animation formats as well as tour the main programs for creating these kinds of files.

Graphics Formats 101

Image files on the Web come primarily in two formats: GIF and JPEG. Any Web browser will display these images, and most programs that create images for the Web will generate either format. But what exactly is the difference between them? And you may have heard vague rumblings about "PNG" and "SVG"—what do these acronyms mean?

GIF

GIF (which stands for *graphics interchange format* and is pronounced either "jiff" or "giff" with a hard *g*) was the subject of a patent dispute in the 1990s and might be thought of as the original Web image format. It's best used for buttons, banners, graphical text, and line art. GIFs can contain only 256 colors and are often smaller than JPEG files.

GIFs can be transparent, which is handy if your site's background color is something other than white. You can adjust transparency settings in image-editing tools so that your green triangle button won't have a white background on your peach-colored Web page.

GIFs can also be animated. Simple GIF animations are composed of multiple frames—think of them as digital flip books. You have to create GIF animations frame by frame, without much help from your image-editing application. An animated GIF is a single file, just like a standard GIF.

JPEG

This slightly more robust image format (JPEG is pronounced "jay-peg" and stands for Joint Photographic Experts Group, the group that created the format) is best used for full-color or grayscale images such as photographs. JPEGs tend to be larger than GIFs and are recommended for images with many colors or details. JPEGs aren't as well suited to text and line-art images; use the GIF format for those files.

PNG

PNG (say "ping"), short for *Portable Network Graphics,* is a newer graphics format that was in some ways intended to replace the GIF standard, but it's never managed to do so entirely. PNG's compression and color handling are considered superior to GIF's. Not every browser reads PNG, however, so it may not be the best choice for your site's graphics. PNG is Macromedia Fireworks' native file format, but as we'll see in "Macromedia Fireworks," below, the program can convert those files to other formats.

SVG

SVG (short for *Scalable Vector Graphics)* is a system for describing two-dimensional graphics in XML (see "What's XML?" above). Championed in part by Adobe Systems, SVG is an emerging standard that's designed to connect to back-end databases so that data-based graphics such as revenue charts can be created on the fly.

Web Graphics Jargon 101

Once you move beyond the basics of Web development, you may start to wonder about the more-advanced techniques for using Web graphics in your pages. Here's a summary of some common options.

- **Slicing**—This technique, available in programs such as Adobe Photoshop and ImageReady and Macromedia Fireworks, is the practice of dividing an image into multiple parts so that it loads more quickly or can have different functions, such as rollovers, assigned to different regions. You might slice a large photo or image into parts to speed page delivery, or slice a navigation bar into parts to create different buttons that perform different actions.

- **Rollovers**—Surely you've seen these on Web pages: you glide your pointer over text that says "Soda," and a glass of ice appears. Creating a rollover requires you to create multiple "states" for a single image: you might tell a program to swap in a different image when a user clicks, moves over, moves up, or moves off a given image. Rollovers are written in JavaScript, a scripting language for the Internet.

- **Image maps**—Let's say you have a picture of five products, each of which has its own Web page. With an image map, you can select an area of an image and indicate a URL to load when that area is clicked. You can create image maps in Web authoring and graphics tools. Unlike rollovers, image maps don't require JavaScript—they use basic HTML to execute commands.

- **Anti-aliasing**—This setting in Web graphics programs helps eliminate jagged edges on text images and other graphics. To do this, software programs add soft grays or colors to the edges of images to make them appear smoother. This has the net effect of making images appear slightly fuzzier, but anti-aliased images generally look better than jaggedy ones.

- **Transparency**—All GIFs are rectangular, even if the images within them are not. For example, if you have a portrait of a person with no set background, the image file that you save will be a rectangle, not a cutout. In order to ensure that the background of your portrait isn't a different color than your Web page's background, you'll need to set the GIF's background to be the same color as your Web page, and then make it transparent. (The first step—setting the image's background to be the same as the Web page's—is particularly important when your image has a drop shadow or fuzzy borders.)

Graphics Editors

For creating and editing images, your choices range from $30 shareware programs like Lemke Software's GraphicConverter to the granddaddy of all image-editing programs, the $649 Adobe Photoshop. If you're creating a large site and have a substantial number of images to manage, you're an artist, or you plan to create sophisticated graphics, you might opt for a heavyweight application like Photoshop. On the other hand, if you have only a handful of images and a handful of cash, you might prefer to stick with a more-modest program like GraphicConverter.

GraphicConverter

GraphicConverter ($30 shareware; www.lemkesoft.com) is valuable because of its versatility. It's capable of handling a wide variety of file formats—about 175 at this writing—which means that if your Uncle Milton has sent you a family photo in an obscure Windows graphics format, GraphicConverter can probably help (**Figure 16.4**). GraphicConverter can display a group of images in a browser view, optimize them for the Web, and batch-convert them to another format.

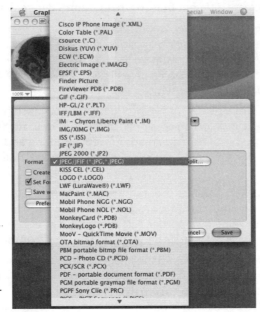

Figure 16.4

Lemke Software's GraphicConverter can convert nearly any image type you encounter to a Web-friendly format.

Adobe Photoshop and ImageReady

Crucial for graphic designers, **Adobe Photoshop** ($649; www.adobe.com) has also become indispensable for many Web developers. The latest version, Photoshop CS, now includes ImageReady, Adobe's Web-oriented image-editing program.

If you're familiar with Photoshop, you might want to stick with using it and ImageReady for your Web graphics needs. Photoshop's sophisticated image-manipulation functions—such as filters, batch processing, effects, and layers—make it a robust tool for Web designers. You can save images for the Web through a simple dialog; the program allows you to preview and optimize images and, through its 2-up and 4-up settings, compare the results of different image-optimization settings. Photoshop's file browser is useful for anyone managing multiple images, and the program also has a simple system for automatically creating Web photo galleries.

ImageReady's interface will be familiar to anyone used to working in Photoshop. The program builds on Photoshop's Web editing features to offer tools for GIF animation, page layout, rollovers, and basic drawing and editing. One handy feature: if you design an entire Web page in ImageReady, the program can save it as HTML. The latest version of ImageReady, included with Photoshop CS, exports files to Macromedia Flash, has a spiffed-up interface, and imports data from spreadsheets and databases.

While Photoshop's image-editing capabilities for print are unmatched, unfortunately you can't get ImageReady's handy features without paying for Photoshop's girth. If you need Photoshop, the choice is easy, but if you want to spend less than $649 for a full-fledged image editor, try Macromedia Fireworks MX 2004.

Macromedia Fireworks

If you have to pick one graphics tool for your Web arsenal, consider **Macromedia Fireworks** ($299; www.macromedia.com). While we wouldn't part with Photoshop for print tasks, we prefer Fireworks' more intuitive approach to image handling for Web tasks. Plus, it's $350 less than Photoshop.

Fireworks MX 2004 offers the basics—image rotation, button creation, text and bitmap editing, optimization, GIF animations, and previews (**Figure 16.5**). It can also create rollovers (including ones that are more-sophisticated than those that Photoshop generates), make Web photo galleries, use XML to generate data-oriented graphics, integrate with Macromedia Flash MX 2004, and assist with Web-site navigation design.

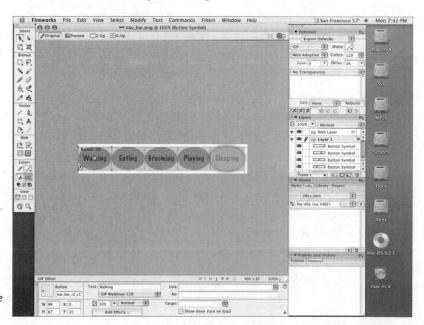

Figure 16.5

In Macromedia Fireworks MX, you can create buttons for navigation to apply throughout your Web site and assign URLs to those buttons.

Another one of Fireworks' selling points is its integration with Dreamweaver. If Macromedia's Web authoring tool is your application of choice, Fireworks is a good bet for Web graphics. The company likes to tout its so-called round-trip editing features, which let users work on Web pages and graphics in multiple applications and move between those programs easily.

Clip Art and Photography

Fortunately for the less artistic among us, there's a wealth of images available, freely or inexpensively, online. One way to find images easily is to borrow them from other sources: for example, if you needed a picture of a doghouse, you could use Google's image-search function to find line art or photographs of one. While this may be a common practice on the Web, it also introduces potentially serious copyright issues. The bottom line: don't borrow an image unless you're sure you have permission to use it.

A better way to find images is to use free clip-art sites, or sites that catalog art that's in the public domain, such as #1 Clip Art (www.1Clipart.com) or Clipart Connection (www.clipartconnection.com). The next option is to use a service such as ClipArt.com (www.clipart.com), a subscription-based site that costs $99.95 for a six-month subscription or $9.95 for a one-week subscription. Members can download photos, line art, bitmap images, fonts, and sounds in a variety of formats. Since a one-week subscription is only $9.95, it's a great option for someone looking to find a handful of images quickly. Also, even if you don't love the inexpensive images you might find at Clipart.com, you can use them as a starting point while you create your own images.

Professional clip-art services, like Corbis and Getty Images, provide high-quality images—both photographs and illustrations—that often carry a higher price. You can choose to purchase a Web or print version of an image, which has different resolutions, file sizes, and costs.

With sales of digital cameras surpassing those of film cameras in the United States, it's easier than ever to add your own photographs on your Web site. In many cases, the best image you'll find may be your own.

Working with Other Types of Content

When you are first starting out, you'll probably be satisfied creating an easily navigable, informative site with basic text and graphics. But at some point you may decide you want more—more interactivity, more drama, more pizzazz. That's when you might want to consider adding animation, audio, or video to your site. Here's what you need to know to start down that path.

Macromedia Flash

Macromedia's Flash technology has become the de facto standard for Web animation. Flash can be used for everything from animating a single button to creating complex movies, from making small animations to making entire Web sites. Unlike HTML files, Flash animations require the use of a separate piece of software—a browser plug-in—on the user's end to be viewed. These days, most browsers include the Flash Player plug-in, but it's always possible that visitors to your site won't have the requisite software. Therefore, if you use Flash, you should be prepared to point your visitors to the download site (www.macromedia.com) and, perhaps, provide a non-Flash version of your site for the Flash-impaired. (As with JavaScript, you can write code asking the browser to detect the presence or absence of Flash and display the appropriate content.)

Despite their complexity, Flash animations can be relatively small, which has helped drive the format's popularity. Since the graphics it creates are vector-based, they can be resized easily. You can also incorporate audio and video files within Flash, and build interactive games with the technology.

Source files that are created in Flash are saved with the .fla extension, while files that go on the Web are saved with the .swf extension. Similarly, Photoshop-native files have the .psd extension, but you convert them to GIFs and JPEGs to put them up on the Web. To make Flash content, you use Macromedia's **Flash** ($499; www.macromedia.com). Both the Flash technology and the Flash MX 2004 program have fairly steep learning curves that can be challenging unless you have a background in video or audio editing or in animation. The user interface of Flash MX 2004 can take some getting used to. Because of Flash's complexity, we recommend that you consider taking a class or checking out Katherine Ulrich's *Macromedia Flash MX for Windows and Macintosh: Visual QuickStart Guide* (Peachpit Press, 2002).

Audio and video for the Web

If you want to include audio or video in your Web site, you'll have several decisions to make. First, what format is your audio or video content in currently? Unless it's already in a Web-friendly format, you'll probably need to convert the files. For tips on that process, see Chapter 17.

For the most part, Web browsers can't play audio and video files on their own: they need to use player plug-ins or applications such as RealNetworks' RealOne Player, Microsoft's Windows Media Player, or Apple's QuickTime Player. QuickTime Player, for example, can play back MPEG-4 video and ACC audio files. You may be able to assume that most visitors to your Web site have at least one of the aforementioned products installed. To be on the safe side, however, you can always make a note about the requirements on your Web page and create links to a download area for each of these applications.

Let's take a look at the ways you can provide audio or video to your audience.

- If you have individual audio or video files that you want users to experience as they choose, you can upload the files to your Web server and add links to those files in your Web pages. Users can then download the files at their leisure. One caveat: audio and video files tend to be large, so make sure you have ample room on your Web site before getting started.

- You can also opt to *embed* the content within a page. For example, when a QuickTime video is embedded within a page, the QuickTime Player's controls appear within that page when it's downloaded, and users can view the video without leaving their browsers.

- If you have more-substantial content—say, a long training video or an audio broadcast—you may want to consider using streaming technology. With streaming, audio or video content is broadcast to a user's computer in small bursts, which are then viewed in real time. This way, large files aren't stored on the end user's hard drive. However, streaming content requires a streaming server such as Microsoft's Windows Media Services or RealNetworks' Helix Universal Server.

Finally, a small plea from Web surfers in offices everywhere: if you choose to embed audio or video in your Web page, please, oh please, be sure to set up your code so that an off switch is readily available. There's nothing worse than loading a loud Web page in an office setting with no way to turn down the sound.

Tips for Creating Good Web Sites

Before you begin creating your Web site, think about sites you visit frequently: what do you like and dislike about them? Are there sites you avoid because of the way they work? Are there sites where you spend more time, in part because of the way they're organized and implemented? Since the Web is such a flexible medium, there are dozens of ways you can design your site. But just because you can create a site with a bright green background and yellow text doesn't meant you should.

A growing school of thought, led by Web design guru Jakob Nielsen, believes that Web sites should be usable—easy to learn, searchable, readily navigable, logically organized, and reliant on consistent presentation and controls. If you're interested in learning more about this topic, check out Nielsen's site, useit.com (www.useit.com).

Web Design Basics

While we can't cover every single point regarding great Web design, we can at least give you some of the most-important guidelines. If you follow these, chances are you'll end up with a Web site that's as clean and functional as some of those created by the real pros (**Figure 16.6**). Here are some basics to consider when you begin your Web authoring journey:

Figure 16.6

It's no surprise that Apple's Web site is easy on the eyes. The site provides lots of links in a relatively small amount of space, but it never feels crowded or busy.

See how others do it

There's no secret as to how your favorite Web site is designed. You can easily view the source code whenever you want. Just bring up the site in a Web browser and then use the browser's source-viewing feature to display the information. In Apple's Safari browser, for example, go to the View menu and select View Source, or [Control]-click or right-click in the browser window to bring up the contextual menu and select View Source. By looking at the code of pages you like, you can easily learn the secrets of the top Web designers. You can then adopt some of those tags on your own site and see how they work. This is also a great way to learn about and borrow JavaScripts and style sheets.

Although examining source code is a great way to learn your craft, just remember not to attempt to copy and publish copyrighted content, such as text or pictures, because that could easily run you afoul of the author's intellectual-property rights.

Come up with a plan

Before you create your first HTML file, think about how you want your site to operate and how you want it to be organized. Think about the different sections of your site: How will they be structured, how will users get to them, and what will they be called? How much content, including text and images, do you have now, and what might you want to add later? When designing your site's structure and navigation, think about whether you'll want to add entire sections down the line. Storyboard your site: try sketching out the home page and other key sections. You're likely to find that a bit of planning at the outset will save you some headaches later on.

A Web site is like a puzzle that you want to make easy to solve. Wherever a visitor goes, he or she should be able to get back to the starting point without any difficulty. If moving to different areas of your site requires a number of steps, try to create direct paths instead. Each page should have links for all related pages (don't forget that home-page link). Put the links in visible places, with large, clear buttons. If you use a title for a link, clearly label what it points to. For a large site, consider adding a search engine (this isn't as hard as it seems) or creating a *site map*—basically, an index listing all the links at your site, organized by topic or alphabetically. Also, do you want new links to open in the same browser window or a new one? You can set links to open in a new browser window by using the `target` attribute of the <a> tag; most HTML programs will guide you through the setup. You can also use JavaScript to have links open in small pop-up windows.

Make it simple

There are so many Web design options available that it's tempting to try each one in your site. Don't! Clutter can make your site confusing, and including all those extra commands, pictures, and animations can slow the loading of your site to a crawl. Remember that not everyone has a cable modem or DSL; the vast majority of users still connect to the Internet via analog modems, and not all of these are the latest 56 Kbps designs (which, in fact, seldom approach the maximum connection speed). It's common for folks to just pass by a site that takes forever to generate its content. If your site is devoted to a top-grossing movie, perhaps your visitors will be willing to endure the wait. Otherwise, they'll go elsewhere. The best thing to do is test the page with a Web browser at every step of your development process and see what content takes longest to appear. Scale down graphics as much as possible; your graphics software's optimizing tools can make them smaller. Use animation only when you really need it. Your visitors will thank you for your efforts by staying around to check out your site.

Consider Google (www.google.com). Its search results make it wildly popular, but check out its home page; at this writing, it had one graphic, it looked great in different browsers on many operating-system platforms, the page adapted well when a browser window was resized, and it had just a dozen links (**Figure 16.7**). Yahoo.com used to have an almost comically simple design. That's not the case today, but the site's simplicity of yore probably helped lead to the company's success today.

Figure 16.7

You can't beat Google's site for its simplicity. In these days of sites bursting with links, ads, and pop-up menus, Google is refreshingly plain.

Know your audience and medium

For the most part, people visiting Web sites don't expect to read the full text of *War and Peace*. Keep your text short, use lots of "bite-sized" paragraphs, and use headlines and subheads to break up content into easily digestible chunks. Keep this rule in mind: the most important stuff should be at the top, and users shouldn't have to page through much more than two screens' worth of text.

Try to reach the masses—don't create a site that's set up for unusually small or large screen resolutions. Currently, a resolution of 800 by 600 pixels is a good lowest common denominator to use in your design.

Another consideration is your audience's monitor sizes. You may want to avoid designing your site so that it requires a large number of pixels for the whole width of your site to fit comfortably on your audience's screens. HTML allows you to specify either actual pixel dimensions or percentages for things like tables and table cells. If you choose percentages, then items will scale to fit the individual's browser and monitor.

Design kindly

Heed the cry of far-sighted people everywhere and stay away from minuscule type. Select a readily available and easy-to-read font for most text. For example, your Mac may have that cool Da Vinci font installed, but you can't assume that most people's computers will. And even if they do, reading large blocks of text in something that mimics 15th-century handwriting may not be much fun. For that reason, stick with the most common and readable fonts. There are lists of fonts that come with Windows and Mac operating systems or that are installed with some Web browsers: your HTML editor can help you see what fonts are commonly available by listing them in a menu, and some programs can even write code that will look for fonts in a certain order and display text in whichever font is available.

 Keep in mind that fonts often appear larger on Windows machines than they do on Macs.

Mind your tones and hues

Some computer monitors are set to display only 256 colors. (In truth, nowadays most people's computers will display thousands or even millions of colors, but you may want to be conservative when choosing colors to reach the widest possible audience.) This means that the hours you spend picking out a precise shade of vermilion could be in vain. Most Web authoring and graphics programs will help you select colors from a Web-safe color palette.

In addition, Mac and Windows computers don't see the world the same way; because of the OS's different video settings, colors often appear darker on PCs. For simplicity's sake, and to support older displays, Web designers use the old 8-bit (256-color) browser-safe standard, which goes right back to the days of the earliest color Macs. The problem is that the 256 colors a Mac displays are not quite the same as those you see on a PC. This doesn't mean that red becomes blue on that other platform; in fact, both do support 216 of the same colors, which form the core of the browser-safe palette. It is from these colors that Web designers make their selections.

Fortunately, you don't have to figure out which of those 216 colors you can use. Just about all graphics programs and WYSIWYG Web tools support the Web-safe color palette. A simple selection from a pop-up menu should get you a listing of the correct hues.

Set your table

HTML tables have two basic functions: the first is to lay out content that you want to appear in a table format, as it might in Microsoft Excel, and the second is to organize your entire page. Some of the most innovative Web designers are now turning to CSS to lay out their pages instead of using tables. In ordinary contexts, however, tables are an excellent way to organize groups of information. First you access the table feature, and then you specify the rows and columns and perhaps the table's overall dimensions. After that, it's generally a matter of inserting various text and picture elements into each cell, making a little adjustment here and there, and presto—you have a table! You can also finesse your table by setting its border size and color, cell padding, individual cell colors, and text alignment. Some HTML programs, such as GoLive and Dreamweaver, can even import tabbed text directly from a spreadsheet program, such as Excel, and format it into a table for you.

Percentages are your friend

HTML tables have been a designer's friend when it comes to page layouts: tables help position page elements more precisely than plain paragraph and indentation tags can do. (We mean tables that contain an entire page's content, not a single table that might, for example, show a price listing for a handful of products.) For some, CSS layouts have taken the place of tables, but tables still suffice for most novices. When you do use a table for page layouts, you'll need to specify the table's width. And here comes the hard part: visitors to your site will inevitably have different monitor and browser configurations that will make a one-size-fits-all approach less than ideal. This is where percentages come in. Instead of specifying a pixel width for your table, you can tell the HTML authoring tool to set the table's pixel width at 100 percent. This means that the table will fill the browser properly whatever its settings, and the table will even resize if the user expands or shrinks the Web browser's window. Most Web authoring tools will let you specify this when creating tables. You can also use percentages for elements like horizontal rules.

Be an equal-opportunity Web designer

You may be designing your site on a Macintosh, but it's pretty unlikely that everyone in your audience will be viewing it on Macs. For that reason, it's always a good idea to view your site not only in multiple browsers and browser versions, but also on multiple platforms, if possible. Older Web browsers may not implement newer technologies like CSS properly. If you're using more-advanced Web design techniques, you may want to determine a minimum standard for which you want to design.

 One handy tool in the arsenal of a Web designer who doesn't have a Windows computer around is a Windows emulator—Microsoft's Virtual PC for Mac ($129–$249, depending on which OS you need; www.microsoft.com/mac). An emulator is nowhere near as fast as the real thing, but you aren't playing 3D games with it—you just want to view your site in Windows to make sure it looks right.

To frame, or not to frame?

HTML frames—which break one browser window into multiple parts, or *frames,* with different pages appearing in each—are less popular than they used to be. One criticism of frames is that users can find it difficult to bookmark a specific section of your Web site if they use frames to get there. Make sure you know what you're doing before using frames.

A spelling check is smart business

 Just as you wouldn't want a typo in your company's brochure, your Web site should be free of spelling and grammatical errors. Ask a detail-oriented friend to proofread your site if you don't trust yourself to catch errors.

Pick a background

The default background on an HTML page is drab gray. Black text on a white background is probably easiest to read, but if you want to spice things up, try another muted color, like a light yellow or blue, for the background. Keep in mind that your text's readability is directly related to the background on which it appears, so white text on a light yellow background is not a good call. In general, very bright background colors aren't likely to be the most user-friendly. You can pick an image for your background, but we aren't fans of this approach unless the image is very subtle. In general, a high contrast between your text and page background is desirable.

Anchors aweigh!

Anchors help users navigate to a particular point on a page. Most Web author-ing programs will help you create anchors. To set anchors, you use the `<a>` tag with the `name` attribute. For example, if you wanted to send a user to a page called Gear and an area of that page called "leashes," you might name the anchor `leashes`, as in `<a name="leashes"></a>`. Then you would write your HTML link as follows:

```
<a href="http://www.dynamitedogwalkers.com/gear.html#leashes">
Check out our leashes!</a>
```

Interview: David Bunnell

By the time Apple authorized David Bunnell to start Macworld *magazine in 1983, he already had a long list of computer publications to his credit, including a newsletter launched in 1975, the first computer magazine (*Personal Computing*) in 1977, and both* PC Magazine *and* PC World *in the early 1980s.*

In 1984, just the idea that you could change the fonts and make the screen look like the final printed product would look—that was a big deal.

—David Bunnell on the original Mac

He had come to technology publishing, however, by an unusual route. In the early 1970s he worked as a school teacher in inner-city Chicago, then on the Pine Ridge Reservation in South Dakota, until he was fired because of his support for the militant American Indian Movement. Bunnell moved to Albuquerque, New Mexico, and got a technical writing job at MITS, a small manufacturer that was then developing what's generally considered the first personal computer, the Altair 8800. Sold by mail order in the form of a kit that buyers had to assemble, the Altair 80 became a sensation among electronics enthusiasts when it was featured on the cover of Popular Electronics *magazine in January 1975. Inspired by the story, Bill Gates and Paul Allen dropped out of Harvard and came to Albuquerque to write software for the Altair. When they set up their own company—Microsoft—Bunnell designed its original logo and letterhead and created ads and promotional materials for it; in exchange, Gates and Allen wrote columns for* Personal Computing. *After working at* Macworld *until 1989—as publisher and then editor in chief—Bunnell went on to found ten more magazines. As of late 2003, Bunnell was focusing most of his energy on a startup called the Long Life Club, a Web site designed to help people learn how to live a longer, healthier life (www.longlifeclub.com).*

When did you first hear about the Mac?

I heard about it from Bill Gates in late 1982, when I was interviewing him for the first issue of *PC World*. He said Apple was coming out with this new computer, and that it was a computer that his mother could use, and that he was very excited about it, and that it was going to do very well. Then I just started pursuing it, and eventually I got a meeting set up with Steve and Mike Murray, the number two guy in the Mac division. It turned out that Steve really liked *PC World* magazine—that was the key—so he thought we could do the best Mac magazine.

Did they give you a Mac to play with?

Yeah, they gave me one in maybe the spring or summer of '83. I took it home and started to learn to use it. Just the idea that you could change the fonts and make the screen look like the final printed product would look—that was a big deal. The bitmapped screen and the mouse—it's kind of amazing to think back that those things were so novel!

continues on next page

Apple helped pay for the magazine in some form, didn't it?

Yeah, I was in the middle between Pat McGovern [founder and chairman of *PC World*'s parent, IDG] and Jobs, which was a very interesting situation. At first McGovern was skeptical because of the Lisa, so he wanted me to figure out a way to get Apple to help pay for the magazine. I thought "Oh, my god, how am I going to do that? I'm just lucky Apple's letting me do the magazine." But I came up with this idea involving the warranty card. I found out that Apple got a fairly low percentage of people to fill out the warranty cards on the Apple II, and it was in their best interest to capture a higher percentage. So the idea was, if you fill out the warranty card, you get six free issues of *Macworld* magazine. That would increase the response to the warranty card, and then Apple would pay us $1 an issue for those issues. It seemed like that was going to work, but then McGovern said, "Well, what if they don't sell very many Macs, and we're going to still have to make this investment in this magazine?" So we had to get a guaranteed payment. Of course Steve balked at that.

The whole thing just seemed to be unraveling, but Mike Murray and some of us kind of conspired. We just kept working on the magazine as the launch was getting closer and closer, until everything was ready to go to the printer. When it reached that point, I got McGovern to go down to Apple with me and meet with Steve. Pat was very impressed, because Steve had just a little cubicle—his office was very minimal. McGovern liked that because he's [pause] cheap. So we finally came to an agreement. [Apple] ended up guaranteeing a lot less than we wanted, but it was basically the same deal. We were able to publish the first issue of *Macworld,* and we passed it out during the announcement of the original Mac.

Did Apple have anything to say about the content of the magazine?

None. To their credit, they definitely did not want to create that impression, or have any say.

Did you expect the Mac to be a serious challenge to the PC?

Oh yeah, I thought it would just kind of take over, because it was so much easier to use. I had learned to hate DOS, and I thought, "I'll never have to use DOS again!"

For *Macworld*, did you try to come up with a style that would be suitable for the Mac market?

Yes, we did an oversize design and we gave it a lot cleaner look, more graphic and artsy-looking than with *PC World*. And we were one of the first magazines, if not the first, to use a matte paper stock like they use in books—it wasn't glossy. It had a beautiful look. You could see right away that the Mac would appeal to the graphic-arts crowd and creative people, so we tried to play off that.

Were you disappointed that sales of the Mac didn't do better?

Oh, I thought it was great the first year. Then it kind of leveled off. What happened was that Apple was very slow in getting a hard drive. Sculley actually told me that the Mac team was so burned out, the way Steve drove them to meet that original deadline, that they were practically worthless for the next year or so—they just didn't get things done very fast. There was also starting to be a lot of conflict over the direction of the company, and the bad feelings with the other [non-Mac] Apple people probably made it hard to get things done there.

Did you become a Mac user yourself?

I actually used the Mac exclusively for ten years, until 1994, when I decided I needed to be familiar with both platforms. It wasn't until Windows 98, though, that I really abandoned the Mac. I use Windows XP now—I wouldn't even think about [a Mac].

Did you have fun with the Mac?

I loved it. Even though it was sometimes frustrating dealing with Apple, it was just really great fun. And the people in the whole surrounding development community were way more creative and interesting, really, than the PC types. It was like being an artist—if you were into the Mac, you got to be an artist, a musician, a real creative genius-type person and not just a number cruncher.

17

Digital Lifestyle

Michael E. Cohen is the chapter editor and author.

Welcome to the chapter formerly known as "Multimedia."

For many of you, the subjects we discuss in this chapter are what made you buy a Mac in the first place. The digital lifestyle is about music. It's about pictures. It's about movies.

It's about how that iBook that you write your term papers on is also the coolest jukebox ever. It's about how that PowerBook that you run your sales projections on is also a slide-show theater that exhibits your entire collection of nature photos, complete with musical accompaniment by Norah Jones and Stan Getz. It's about how that flat-screen iMac you use to send email to your daughter in college is also the bass player in your garage band and the studio where you produced your band's first rock video.

It's about what the Mac has really *always* been about, from that day in 1984 when the first Mac was rolled out onstage and said "Hello" to the audience. It's about the fun stuff.

In This Chapter

The Chapter Formerly Known as Multimedia

Over the years, the multimedia chapter in each edition of *The Macintosh Bible* has grown bigger and bigger, as the Mac, like a mutant straight out of *X-Men*, has developed ever more amazing super powers. Lately, Apple has finally told us what's up with this extreme evolution: it's not just multimedia we're talking about here, kids, but a whole lifestyle—a "digital lifestyle," centered around a "digital hub" (your Mac, of course) connected to all sorts of digital devices (we call them "cool toys"). And to help you live that digital lifestyle, Apple graciously (and for a *very* low price) provides a portfolio of programs that it collectively calls iLife: iTunes, iPhoto, iMovie, iDVD, and GarageBand.

It's not too much to say that the Mac has been reborn (yet again) in the past few years as a marvel of multimedia magic, sporting optical drives that not only read but also write DVDs, flat panel displays that present crystal-clear digital video, high-quality speakers that play sharp digital sound, and high-speed FireWire ports that connect to anything that needs to push a lot of data around really, really quickly, like a video camera or an iPod. And, of course, there's a shiny new operating system, Mac OS X, that's tuned to handle all the media devices and data you can throw at it.

Digital media loves an operating system that understands its needs. The classic Mac OS has always been an understanding operating system, and, like its predecessors, the new, gleaming, Aqua-fresh Mac OS X continues the tradition: while other computers often require special driver software to play digital media, every Mac comes knowing how to play them … and, even more important, how to combine them.

Not that every model Mac is an ideal media machine: some current models may lack certain amenities, like DVD burning or analog audio inputs, and some cannot be expanded with the specialized hardware components that professional digital-media producers require. But all current Macs can play digital media just fine, and you can inexpensively outfit just about any Mac model to handle all but the most demanding media-production tasks.

Living the iLife

Apple now conceives of the Mac as a digital hub that enables you to live your digital lifestyle. This is certainly an effective marketing concept, judging by the number of other computer manufacturers who began to claim the same thing for their machines mere days after Steve Jobs first publicly mentioned it back in 2000. But what, exactly, is a digital hub?

Quite simply, it is the concept of the Mac as a device designed to connect to all the other digital devices you may own and to bring together all the information that those devices create and use. Plug in, say, a portable MP3 player—it doesn't even have to be a spiffy white Apple iPod—and up pops iTunes (one of Apple's five iLife programs), ready to synchronize the player's song collection. Plug in a digital camera and up pops iPhoto (another of Apple's iLife programs), ready to import your photos, to help you organize and print them, and even to build slide shows and screensavers. Plug in a digital camcorder and up pops iMovie (yet another of Apple's iLife programs), ready to help you edit your video into a professional-looking award-worthy masterpiece. Then plug in a USB music keyboard, fire up GarageBand (the newest iLife program), and compose your video's award-winning score. It doesn't stop there: after you've got your music, photos, and video footage gathered in your digital hub, there's iDVD (yep, it's an iLife program, as well) to let you put it all together, burn it onto a DVD, and play it on your wide-screen plasma display TV (which, courtesy of Apple's new Rendezvous networking software, will probably be able to talk directly to your Mac by the time this reaches print, meaning that your Mac could act like a TiVo unit to communicate with a networked plasma display TV by means of IP addressing to transmit picture data or to display controls).

 You may also hear iTunes, iMovie, iPhoto, GarageBand, and iDVD referred to as iApps. This is what Apple nicknamed these applications before it came up with the iLife concept to reflect a lifestyle centered around a Mac as a digital hub.

 If you don't have the iLife programs, you can download iTunes for free from Apple's Web site (www.apple.com). You cannot, however, download the other iLife programs from the site. To get them, you will need to purchase the iLife package from Apple for $49, which includes all five programs (that's less than $10 a program). Or you can buy a new Mac and get them for free (minus the cost of the Mac, of course).

Apple has not only created and distributed the iLife programs to help make all this possible, but it has also built the necessary software underpinnings into the Mac OS X operating system so that other developers can quickly create the specialized programs that the techno-jolly folks living their digital lifestyles crave. What's more, deep in the inner recesses of Mac OS X live things like HAL (not the evil computer from *2001* but the developer-friendly Hardware Abstraction Layer, which protects the Mac from many driver-related crashes) and Core Audio (which enables developers to build sophisticated and powerful audio applications much more easily) and Quartz (not a shiny rock but powerful software that can handle sophisticated graphics processing with great speed and clarity). And then there's QuickTime.

You're going to hear lots more about QuickTime in this chapter.

In short, the digital hub represents an enormously powerful and sophisticated integration of hardware and software designed for one purpose: to make your Mac the place to go when you want to play with all your other cool toys.

10-der Is the Mac—a Few Words About Mac OS X

Around the turn of the century, Apple introduced its next-generation operating system, Mac OS X. And suddenly, every single program written for the Mac was instantly obsolete.

No, Macs didn't immediately all stop working, the earth didn't spin out of its orbit, and Pauly Shore didn't become an award-winning thespian. But the world did change.

Although the shiny new face of Mac OS X does look a lot like the Mac of old (yes, we know, it doesn't *exactly* look like previous systems … work with us here, people—we're trying to make a point), the software underpinnings have been radically revamped. These changes make the Mac far more stable than it has ever been (crashes that require a reboot are as rare as fur coats at a PETA convention) and let the Mac do far more at one time than it ever could before (you can compress a QuickTime movie while downloading a file while printing a report while listening to a CD). But those changes work only for programs written to work with Mac OS X.

Apple does provide Classic, which is just Mac OS 9 running in a software bubble inside of Mac OS X, and nearly all the pre–Mac OS X software can run in it—but for the digital-media world, the problem is that phrase, "nearly all." What doesn't work in Classic under Mac OS X are all those programs that need to get up close and personal with the Mac hardware itself—programs that talk to things like scanners, audio cards, graphics tablets, and MIDI interfaces. That is, digital-media creation and editing programs.

Fortunately, between the last edition of *The Macintosh Bible* and this one, Mac OS X has become far more media savvy, and both software and hardware developers have been polishing up their Mac OS X wares with a vengeance. If you are planning to work with digital media, there are fewer and fewer reasons to stick with Mac OS 9 and more and more reasons to move to Mac OS X.

The biggest reason, of course, is that Classic is the past and Mac OS X is the future. Apple will continue to fix bugs in Classic, but it won't be advancing the state of the art—all its digital-media attention is squarely focused on Mac OS X. Third-party developers are going to be less and less apt to release new programs for Mac OS 9 as time goes by, too, and even bug fixes may be fewer and farther between.

In short, if you want to work with digital media on the Mac (and if you are reading this, we're willing to bet some pretty good money that you do), the time to think about moving to Mac OS X is today. In this chapter we're pretty much going to assume that Mac OS X is your operating system of choice—if something relevant to Classic comes up, of course we're going to mention it, but Mac OS X is where digital media's happening on the Mac.

And we couldn't be happier.

QuickTime beneath

QuickTime has been a part of the Macintosh experience since December 1991, back in the halcyon days of System 7. At first it was merely an interesting add-on technology that could play grainy video the size of a postage stamp (which, a dozen years ago, was *incredible*). But as the Mac evolved, QuickTime evolved with it. Now, QuickTime has become an essential, inseparable part of the Macintosh operating system. Although you can start up Mac OS 9 and earlier systems with QuickTime disabled, you probably won't enjoy the experience because very few programs will work properly without it. And QuickTime is even more essential to Mac OS X than it is to Mac OS 9—you don't even have the option to turn off QuickTime in Mac OS X. In fact, there's very little you can do with digital media on the Mac today that doesn't involve the use of QuickTime at some level.

The latest version of QuickTime for Mac OS 9 and earlier systems is QuickTime 6.0.3, and Apple has made it clear that the Mac OS 9 flavor of QuickTime won't be updated further beyond occasional bug fixes. The handwriting on the wall is clear: for QuickTime, and for the Mac itself, Mac OS X is the future. If you plan to work with digital media at all seriously (or even playfully), you really do want to move up to Mac OS X if your Mac supports it.

Most people confuse QuickTime with the QuickTime Plug-in (a bit of code that lets you view movies embedded in Web pages) or the QuickTime Player (a powerful little media-playing application that shows up as a big blue Q in Mac OS X's Dock [**Figure 17.1**]). That's a bit like confusing a cat's meow with the cat itself.

Figure 17.1

The Big Blue QuickTime Q is the icon for the QuickTime Player, which is just one part of QuickTime itself. (And yes, we know the Q looks gray here ... trust us, it's blue.)

QuickTime is much more than a media player—it is a set of services and features that make an astonishing variety of digital-media experiences possible. And not just on the Mac: QuickTime for Windows provides almost exactly the same high-quality digital-media services for the humble but aspiring Windows family of operating systems as it does for the Mac.

In short, QuickTime is the Mac's digital-media architecture.

If you haven't yet done so, download and install the full version of QuickTime (www.apple.com/quicktime). Then whip out your credit card and give Apple $29.99 for a QuickTime Pro registration. Don't argue—it's worth it. QuickTime Pro, among other things, lets you edit QuickTime movies, display them full screen, export them to different formats, and save unprotected QuickTime movies that are embedded in Web pages. It also does away with the "nag" screen that periodically asks if you want to get QuickTime Pro.

There's Something About QuickTime

QuickTime provides its digital-media services both to programs running on the Mac and to the Macintosh operating system itself. These services include digital-media conversion (such as converting a JPEG image to a standard Macintosh PICT file), media playback (such as being able to see previews of movies in the Finder), and media import (such as capturing digital video from a DV camcorder). Any program written for the Macintosh can take advantage of QuickTime's services, and a great many do. (Did you know that you can embed and play QuickTime movies in a Word document? Well, you can.)

One of the most important and fundamental services that QuickTime provides is, as QuickTime's very name suggests, timing. Remember, much digital media—like sound, video, and animation—exists in and because of time. QuickTime provides a "master clock" that can be used to synchronize various time-based media: for example, it is QuickTime's clock that keeps a movie's sound track synchronized with its picture. This service sounds trivial, but, as any programmer who has ever had to work with time-based media will tell you, in media programming as in stand-up comedy, timing is everything.

QuickTime also manages a variety of digital-media components and formats developed by companies other than Apple, and it makes sure that all these pieces work together by providing the programming hooks, or *application programming interfaces* (APIs), that connect and coordinate these disparate pieces of code. As of QuickTime version 6.5 (the current version as of this writing, and probably already out-of-date by the time you read this), any program using QuickTime has access to the following:

- 25 video compressors
- 14 audio compressors
- 52 file importers
- 26 file exporters
- 18 built-in video effects

In addition, QuickTime provides a file structure so versatile that it has been adopted by the International Organization for Standardization (ISO) as the file structure for MPEG-4, the latest cross-platform digital-media standard, designed to play on anything from a high-definition TV to a cell phone screen.

Without the raft of services provided by QuickTime, the folks who write digital-media software for the Mac would have a much harder job, the programs they developed would be both far fewer and far more expensive than they are, and digital-media programs that were able to exchange information with other media programs would be the exception rather than the rule. And, of course, the Mac would be a lot less fun to use.

Audio Media

When Steve Jobs unveiled the original Macintosh in 1984, the astonishing little machine actually said "Hello" to its audience. Macintosh audio has come a long, long way since then—in fact, many professional musicians use Macs as the centerpieces of their production studios. Here's what you need to know about playing and making music or other sounds on your Mac.

Fundamental Tones— Understanding Digital Audio

You don't have to be a knob-spinning audio engineer to work with sound on the Mac, but it helps to understand some of the basic concepts and learn a few of the basic terms.

To begin, sound is just quivering air—the faster the quiver, the higher the sound; the more violent the quiver, the louder the sound. Sound *pitch* (the speed of the quivering air), or *frequency,* is measured in units called *hertz* (abbreviated as Hz), and a thousand of those units are called a *kilohertz* (abbreviated as kHz). The best human ears can hear frequencies ranging from a low, throbbing 20 Hz to a squealing 20 kHz. Sound intensity (the violence of the quivering air) is often measured in *decibels,* and the range from the softest sound to the loudest in any given recording is called the *dynamic range.*

Audio data stored on the Mac (or any other computer) usually contains the information needed to re-create both the frequency and the intensity of the sound in any given instance. Most simply, this means measuring the intensity of the sound at regular intervals (usually thousands of times a second) and recording the intensity as a number. Given the rate of measurements (the *sampling rate*) and the measurements themselves, your Mac can easily re-create the sound waves.

The quality of any digital sound on your Mac ultimately depends on two factors: how many measurements you take per second (the more measurements, the higher the frequency you can reproduce) and how precise each of those measurements is (the more precise, the smoother the sound). But the more measurements you take and the more information you store in each measurement, the more disk space or memory is required. With sound (and, as we'll see later, with video), you often find yourself making tradeoffs between quality and storage.

To get a sense of the numbers involved, let's look at the standard audio CD. It stores two channels of sound. Each channel consists of 44,100 samples per second, and each sample takes up 16 bits (2 bytes) of storage. This means that *each second* of CD-quality sound requires more than 176 Kbytes of disk space, and a single minute takes up 10 MB.

When you face numbers like these, you can well understand why audio compression was invented. Some common sampling rates and sizes for a single channel of uncompressed audio appear in **Table 17.1.**

Table 17.1 *Sampling Rates and Sizes for Uncompressed Audio*

Sample Rate	Sample Size	Storage for 1 Minute of Sound
11.025 kHz	8 bit	645 Kbytes
22.050 kHz	8 bit	1.26 MB
44.100 kHz	8 bit	2.52 MB
11.050 kHz	16 bit	1.26 MB
22.050 kHz	16 bit	2.52 MB
44.100 kHz	16 bit	5.04 MB

The Lowdown on Sound—About Audio Formats and Compression

Sound comes packaged in all sorts of ways on the Mac, and if you've never looked at sound before, you can find yourself so blinded by the deafening array of audio-related terminologies and acronyms that you'll collapse into a twitching jumble of mixed metaphors. Ahem.

Part of the confusion arises from the historical proliferation of file formats for storing uncompressed sound, and it's then compounded by the seemingly endless proliferation of methods for compressing sound. Both file formats and compression formats are plentiful, and combining the two can create such monsters as a "128 Kbps AAC VBR 3GPP-compliant MPEG-4" file.

So let's divide and conquer and see if we can make things a bit simpler. We'll look at uncompressed sound first.

Uncompressed audio

As we saw earlier in "Fundamental Tones—Understanding Digital Audio," an audio file needs to store nothing more than a bunch of audio samples. It's the audio file's *format* that specifies *how* the samples are stored. For example, are the samples for stereo recordings stored *interleaved* (one sample for the left channel, one sample for right, and so on) or some other way (say, 1 second's worth of samples for the left, followed by a second's worth of samples for the right)? Where is the information stored that tells a player program how big each audio sample is? How many samples make up a second's worth of sound?

Because different audio file formats were developed to meet specific technical needs (and sometimes just to compete with a format developed by a business competitor), even something as seemingly simple as uncompressed audio comes in a number of standard formats. Here are a few common ones you might encounter on the Mac:

AIFF. A basic cross-platform format developed by Apple, AIFF can support samples of various sizes at all common sampling rates. Just about every program for digital-audio editing on the Mac can handle AIFF sound. In Mac OS X, your alert sounds are stored in AIFF files.

SND. This is the original Macintosh sound file format. In Mac OS 9 and earlier, system alert sounds are stored in SND format, and it is *the* format you'll use if you need to store a sound in a file's resource fork (if you don't know what a resource fork is, don't worry—they're becoming less and less common in the Mac OS X world). This was once the dominant audio format on the Mac, but most applications now use other (usually cross-platform) formats.

QuickTime. QuickTime can store uncompressed audio data in its QuickTime movie file format. The audio data becomes a track in the QuickTime movie and can be played, as well as exported into a number of other formats, with QuickTime Pro. Many audio applications on both the Mac and Windows can read QuickTime audio files.

WAV. This is the most common Windows audio file format. Though using WAV files on a Mac originally meant that you first had to convert them to AIFF or SND with a special-purpose utility, that's not been true for some time: QuickTime Player, for example, can handle this format with ease.

Compressed audio

Uncompressed audio can eat up a lot of disk space quickly, and although today even the humblest iMac ships with many gigabytes of storage, that space isn't infinite. If you want to keep a lot of audio on your hard disk, you need to make it as small as possible … and if you're planning to pass it along over the Internet, you *really* need to make it as small as possible (some of us still have modems!). That's where compression comes in.

Audio tends to resist compression: the data is complicated and varies constantly, and there's usually not much in the way of redundant information to eliminate. Consequently, most audio-compression schemes are designed to throw away nonredundant data (this is called *lossy* compression). But once enough of the data is gone, you start to notice its absence. The best audio compressors work hard to find just the right chunks of data to eliminate or to represent in a simpler form, without degrading the sound too severely. A number of them, such as the MP3 format, which lately seems to have become the bête noire of the commercial music industry, use something called *psychoacoustic compression* to discard sound data that would not ordinarily be perceived.

Many people think that *MP3* stands for "MPEG-3," but that's incorrect: it actually refers to the MPEG-1, Layer 3 audio format.

Once the audio is compressed, it must be *decompressed* to be played: the more sophisticated the compression, the more processing is required to decompress the audio. However, the harder a decompressor has to work your Mac's processor, the less processor time the Mac has available to *play* the decompressed sound while keeping on doing whatever else it was doing. The latest generation of audio compressors and decompressors (when paired, they're called *codecs*) require a fast processor in order to work effectively in a multitasking environment like Mac OS X. Once upon a time, the computing power required to decompress files in some of the most advanced compression formats could tax a desktop computer even if it wasn't doing much else. Today, however, even the least powerful Mac in Apple's lineup has more than enough processing power to handle the chore of decompressing and playing audio without even blinking, which means that you can feel free to crank up iTunes and rock out while you browse the Web and write the report that was due yesterday.

A bestiary of audio formats

Ever since the Internet exploded into mass public awareness, stuffing high-quality audio into tiny packages has become a top priority for the digital technology and entertainment industries. Many (often proprietary) audio codecs have made their way to market over the last decade, although not all of them have had staying power.

The latest audio-compression schemes available on the Mac generally fall into three categories: those for which QuickTime has a codec (**Figure 17.2**); those formats that QuickTime can decompress but not compress; and third-party proprietary formats that haven't been licensed (or reverse engineered) for QuickTime at all, meaning that QuickTime cannot compress *or* decompress them. Following is a list of the current formats, with brief descriptions of their purposes. Which one you choose for a particular project will depend on a variety of factors, such as the performance capabilities of your (and your users') Mac, the codec's compression rate, and what type of audio (voice, music, and so on) you plan to use.

Figure 17.2

The QuickTime Audio Export Options menu lists the various audio formats that QuickTime can compress.

You can choose to do a full, partial, or basic installation of QuickTime, and each includes various combinations of codecs. Also note that while some codecs are free, you may have to buy others, either from Apple or from third-party developers.

AAC (QuickTime has a codec). Advanced Audio Coding first reared its head in the MPEG-2 standard (that's the media standard used for most commercial DVDs) in 1997, and it has made its way into the recent MPEG-4 standard. AAC is the default codec used for importing music in iTunes 4, and it provides sound of a quality equivalent to MP3's but at a lower *data rate* (the amount of data transferred per second).

AMR Narrowband (QuickTime has a codec). The Adaptive Multi-Rate speech encoder was designed for digital telecommunication (think cell phones) and was adopted as an international standard by the European Telecommunications Standards Institute (ETSI) in 1999. As of this writing, it can be added to QuickTime by installing Apple's 3GPP Component (available from www.apple.com/downloads/macosx/apple/quicktime3gppcomponent.html). It works best with human speech. (3GPP, by the way, is an international standard for multimedia playback on cell phones and other communication devices that use high-speed wireless networks—it is related to, but not part of, the MPEG-4 standard.)

AU (QuickTime has a codec). This format—common on Unix systems—comes in two standard variants, A-Law and μLaw. AU stores data in 8-bit chunks, but in a logarithmic format roughly equal to 14 bits of ordinary sample data. It compresses the audio only by half and is not very useful for high-quality sound because it sounds muffled and is generally of low quality (not surprising, since it was originally developed for voice data on the telephone).

IMA 4:1 (QuickTime has a codec). Developed by the International Multimedia Association, this format reduces audio to about a quarter of its uncompressed size. The format is relatively simple, so the processor doesn't have to work very hard (which is good if you own an older Mac). Unfortunately, this also means that audio files compressed using this format will probably still be too big to put on the Web. IMA 4:1 offers pretty good quality—to most people, it sounds about as good as an FM broadcast—as long as you're not a raging audiophile (if you are, you probably don't even like *uncompressed* CD audio).

IMA ADPCM 4:1 (QuickTime has a codec). This version of the Adaptive Differential Pulse Code Modulation audio codec can be played natively on most Windows systems. Now, via QuickTime, Mac folks can play it and produce it as well. Like IMA 4:1, it doesn't tax the processor much, nor does it produce very small files, but it supplies good-enough quality.

MACE (QuickTime has a codec). Don't go there, sister—this one's obsolete.

MP3 (QuickTime has a decompressor). This is the codec that gives the Recording Industry Association of America (RIAA) nightmares. It performs best when compressing audio to a rate of about 16 Kbytes per second (KBps) of sound—not nearly small enough for modem-speed streaming but quite acceptable for swapping audio files over the Internet; hence the RIAA's fear and loathing. Although you can stream MP3 over the Internet to users with fast connections, the arrangement of the data in an MP3 file is not very friendly to the streaming process: you'll really notice any data drop-outs. It seems odd that Apple doesn't provide an MP3 encoder with QuickTime, especially given that the company *does* provide a dandy one with iTunes, but sometimes Apple is just *so* inscrutable.

Ogg Vorbis (QuickTime has a codec). A popular codec among the Linux crowd, Ogg Vorbis provides quality and compression similar to MP3 and AAC. Unlike those codecs, however, it is nonproprietary, open source, and patent-free. Ogg Vorbis is not included in Apple's QuickTime Installer, but you can download a free component for QuickTime, in both Mac OS 9 and Mac OS X versions, from the Web at http://qtcomponents.sourceforge.net.

QDesign Music (QuickTime has a codec). Developed by QDesign Corp. (www.qdesign.com), this codec uses a proprietary psychoacoustic method to compress recorded music. The compression method is slower than MP3 and AAC by a considerable margin, and the decompressor requires at least a 100 MHz PowerPC (but if you are using a machine this slow and want to work with digital media, we suggest you move up to something faster—a 100 MHz PowerPC is *so* last century!). QDesign can reduce audio files to a hundredth of their uncompressed size (considerably smaller than MP3 or AAC) and still deliver acceptable quality. If you plan to use this codec frequently, you should consider getting the professional version at $399—it provides many more compression settings and is optimized to work with the PowerPC G4's and G5's Velocity Engine.

Qualcomm PureVoice (QuickTime has a codec). From the digital-phone folks, the PureVoice codec works best with, well, pure voice: it reproduces human speech very nicely, and reproduces music and sound effects not so nicely. PureVoice can compress voice data in real time to less than 60 Kbytes for a full minute and still deliver telephone quality, perfect for that marathon reading of *Harry Potter and the Order of the Phoenix* that you want to email to all your friends.

 With *streaming,* instead of your first having to download an audio or video file to your Mac in order to play it, the data is played as it is received: it stays on the streaming server except for the little bit being transmitted at any given instant.

RealAudio (unavailable to QuickTime). This proprietary format is designed for streaming audio from a remote server, although Real's Real Player (free; www.real.com) will let you play RealAudio files stored on your hard disk as well as play streaming audio from the Web. The player is free, though Real will try hard to persuade you to pay $9.95 a month for a SuperPass to its subscription-only media services. The format is extremely common on the Web; RealAudio is still the most widely used streaming format. Its compression is quite good, and at some data rates the quality slightly exceeds the best that any currently available QuickTime codec can provide.

However, the format does not integrate well with other applications: your choices are pretty much either the Real Player application itself or the Web browser plug-in that comes with it. If you want to extract the sound from a RealAudio file and convert it to some other format, forget it. The RealAudio format is like a Roach Motel—sounds go in but they don't come out. Finally, if you happen to have a server and want to stream Real Audio files, prepare to get a Windows machine or a non-Mac Unix system (Real's Helix Universal Server software doesn't run on Macs). The server software price is high (there is a free version, but it can serve only to a few people at a time) and goes up as you increase the number of users you want to serve.

Windows Media (unavailable to QuickTime). This is Microsoft's answer to both QuickTime and RealAudio. The current Mac OS X version of the Windows Media Player (often referred to as WMP; free; available at www.microsoft.com/mac) supports five audio codecs comparable in quality to the ones QuickTime and Real provide. The Mac OS 9–compatible version of WMP supports a slightly older set of audio codecs, and Microsoft is no longer developing it. The format is very common in the Windows-using world and on the Internet because Microsoft is backing it strongly—very strongly. The company has targeted customers who are concerned about protecting intellectual-property rights. The format features both Microsoft's Digital Rights Manager and its Windows Media Rights Manager, technologies designed to protect the content creators' rights. WMP on the Mac lets you play the format, but if you want to develop multimedia for it or serve WMP files, Microsoft offers no Mac options: the folks in Redmond very much want you both to develop your multimedia on Windows and to serve it from Windows. (All right, stop laughing … they're *serious*!)

Playing Audio

"The player's the thing," wrote Shakespeare (before he realized he'd made a typo). And when it comes to audio, there are plenty of players for the Mac—even for Mac OS X now.

Mac OS 9 and earlier has long been rather beloved by the professional digital-audio crowd, so over the years a rich set of tools, including audio players, has been developed. But when Mac OS X came out, its audio terrain was bleak and desolate; not only had developers had little lead time to build things for it, but the first versions of Mac OS X had an unfinished set of core APIs for audio (an API is an *application program interface,* and it is what developers use to make their programs talk to, and through, the operating system). That is no longer true: Mac OS X 10.2 (Jaguar) brought us an audio API known as Core Audio; Mac OS X 10.3 (Panther) improved the API significantly, and it is now a feverish hotbed of audio development. In fact, from the looks of the popular download sites (such as VersionTracker, at www.versiontracker.com), it seems as though every developer and her Aunt Sadie is writing an audio application for it.

At the head of that list of developers is Apple itself.

iTunes, you tunes, we all tunes for iTunes

Once upon a time (just after the turn of the century), it seemed that the MP3 revolution was going to pass the Mac by. Though the audio pros loved and used the Mac for making professional-grade recordings, all the kewl warez (the various hacks for copying and compressing MP3 audio, some of which are legal, some not, and some shady but not yet determined to be illegal) seemed to be popping up on that other platform (you know the one we mean). And forget about burning CDs: at Apple, DVD-ROM was the golden child and Macs just didn't ship with CD writers. While you could get a third-party CD burner and Roxio's Toast software for burning CDs, the fact that Macs did not ship ready-to-burn meant that not many Mac users had the appropriate hardware and software. As a result, very few developers were creating nonprofessional music applications for the Mac. Something had to change.

It did.

Apple began bundling CD-R drives into Macs, but the company didn't stop there. It hired the author of one of the few, and best, MP3 players on the Mac (SoundJam from Casady & Greene), crafted its own offering to the digital music gods, and called it iTunes. And it was good. And it was free.

And it still is. You can download the current version of iTunes from Apple (www.apple.com/itunes) if you're running Mac OS X 10.2 or later. Mac OS 9 users will have to be satisfied with the last version developed for the classic Mac OS, version 2.0.4 (http://docs.info.apple.com/article.html?artnum=120073). iTunes is also part of Apple's iLife bundle, which you can get from Apple on CD and DVD for $49 (www.apple.com/ilife).

It plays. iTunes is a CD player with a brain the size of a planet (**Figure 17.3**). Stick an audio CD into your Mac, and iTunes opens; it checks the Internet to get the name of the album and its songs so that it can display this information in its window, and then it starts playing. That is, it will do this if you are running

Mac OS X 10.2 or later and haven't changed the CDs & DVDs System Preferences (**Figure 17.4**). If you aren't connected to the Internet when you pop in a CD, iTunes will simply display the songs on the CD as Track 01, Track 02, and so on. You'll need to click the Play button to get the music rolling.

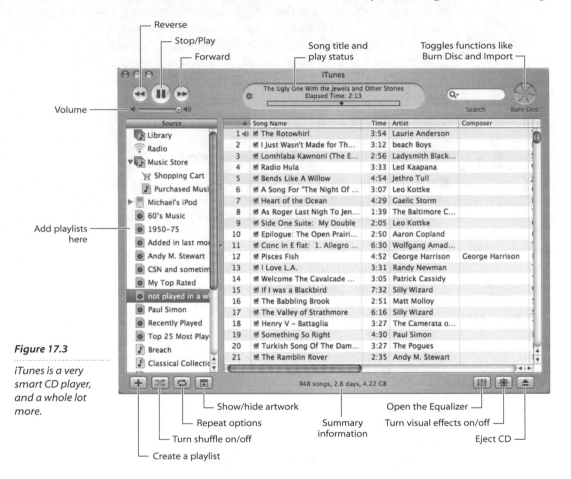

Figure 17.3

iTunes is a very smart CD player, and a whole lot more.

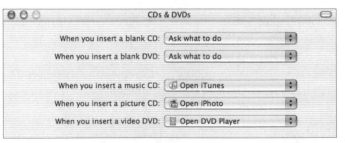

Figure 17.4

The CDs & DVDs System Preferences pane lets you choose what you want your Mac to do when you insert a CD or DVD.

Like any self-respecting CD player, iTunes can control the volume, shuffle the tracks, let you pick just the tracks you want to play, scan forward and backward, and repeat. As it plays CDs, iTunes shows you the name of the currently playing track, and its elapsed time, remaining time, or total time, which you select by clicking the display to cycle through the options. It also provides a sound-enhancement setting to make the music sound tolerable through tiny laptop speakers, gives you a cross-fade setting to let one track play seamlessly into the next, and offers a graphic equalizer so that you can fine-tune the audio of each track and even save the settings with the song for the next time you play it (**Figure 17.5**).

Figure 17.5

The iTunes graphic equalizer lets you fine-tune the audio for individual tracks.

Nor is iTunes limited to playing audio CDs; it can play just about any sound file that QuickTime can understand. Toss it an MP3, MP4, SND, AIFF, or WAV file and iTunes will play it.

It rips. iTunes can also *rip* CDs—that is, import the audio data so that the songs on the CD are copied into iTunes' library, which by default lives in your Music folder in your home directory in Mac OS X (**Figure 17.6**).

Figure 17.6

iTunes offers one-click CD ripping. When you insert an audio CD into your Mac, you'll see this Import button in the upper-right corner of iTunes. Click it to copy the songs on the CD to your Mac.

You can rip songs as WAV or AIFF files, and they will be almost identical copies of the data on the CD—and correspondingly as big: a 3-minute file in either of those formats will run to about 30 MB. Or you can rip them as MP3 or AAC files, which will end up being about a tenth the size of the originals and sound almost as good. (And by "almost as good" we mean that you can probably hear the difference if you play them through a really good hi-fi system and pay close attention, but almost certainly not if you play them through your car stereo while tooling down U.S. 101—but, as always, your mileage may vary.)

Mac the Ripper

By the way: the term *rip* does not derive from the slang expression *rip-off*, meaning *to steal*, but from the word *rip*, as in to *rip a sheet from a pad of paper*. Ripping a CD is not stealing. Ripping and sharing the data with a few hundred of your closest friends *is* stealing—or, to be precise, it is *copyright infringement* and constitutes a violation of federal law for which you can be both fined and sued.

Don't steal music. We mean it.

It organizes. Even the least expensive Mac in Apple's current lineup has a pretty spacious hard disk: the smallest hard drive we could find in our recent (5 minutes ago) visit to the Apple Store was 30 GB, and by the time you get your hands on this book, disks so small doubtlessly will be a quaint memory. Thirty GB is a *lot* of room for music; even if you load a disk that size with useless stuff like software and documents, you're likely to have enough room left for a few thousand songs in MP3 or AAC format.

A collection of music that large can become an organizational nightmare, but iTunes is more than capable of helping you sort it out. The program lets you search for any item in its library, and the search is fast: the moment you type a single letter in iTunes' search pane, it winnows its list of songs to just those with that letter in the title or in the name of the performer or album, so with just a few keystrokes you can quickly find any tune you want. Or you can browse your music collection by album, genre, or artist. Or you can sort your entire song list, or any portion of it, by title, artist, composer, album, time, date imported, date last played, playing length, genre, file format ... or even by the rating you gave the songs yourself. With iTunes' vast organizational powers, it becomes hard *not* to find the song you want.

 With iTunes' Export Song List command in the File menu, you can export text files containing information about all the songs in iTunes' library or in any selected playlist. You can then import these lists into a database program, for example, or edit them and use them to create labels for CDs that you burn with iTunes.

You can also use iTunes to arrange your songs into individual playlists, giving you the almost-godlike power to build the ultimate Weird Al Yankovic mix just by dragging and dropping songs around your screen. Or, if dragging songs to a playlist is just too much physical effort for you, you can have iTunes build a Smart Playlist: you can tell it, for example, to make a playlist of 20 songs that are longer than 3 minutes, were recorded before 1996, and have the word *love* in the title, and iTunes will build it for you almost before your finger finishes clicking the mouse button (**Figure 17.7**).

Figure 17.7

Tired of creating playlists manually? Use this dialog to make a Smart Playlist in iTunes.

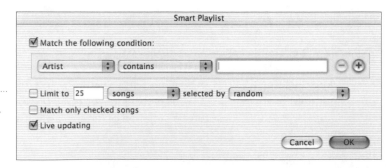

ID3 for You and Me

When iTunes rips a song, it checks the Internet to get information about the song such as its name and the name of the album and stores that information along with the song's audio data in something called an *ID3 tag*. (Note that you'll need to be connected to the Internet the first time you play the CD in iTunes in order for it to automatically get information about the song; otherwise, you'll need to use the Get CD Track Names command in the Advanced menu to manually get the information when you are online.) This data about data, called *metadata* by information technology wonks, can contain all sorts of stuff: title, composer, performer, date of recording, beats per minute, original release year, volume adjustment, equalization, and even a picture of the album cover. The ID3 information becomes part of the song file itself: copy the song to another Mac or an iPod, and the ID3 tag goes along for the ride.

iTunes lets you edit much of this information with its Get Info command (access this from iTunes' File menu or by pressing ⌘ I), just in case the Internet database that clued iTunes in to the song's information got it wrong (mistakes *can* happen) (**Figure 17.8**).

You can find out more about ID3 tags at the ID3v2 Web site (www.id3.org).

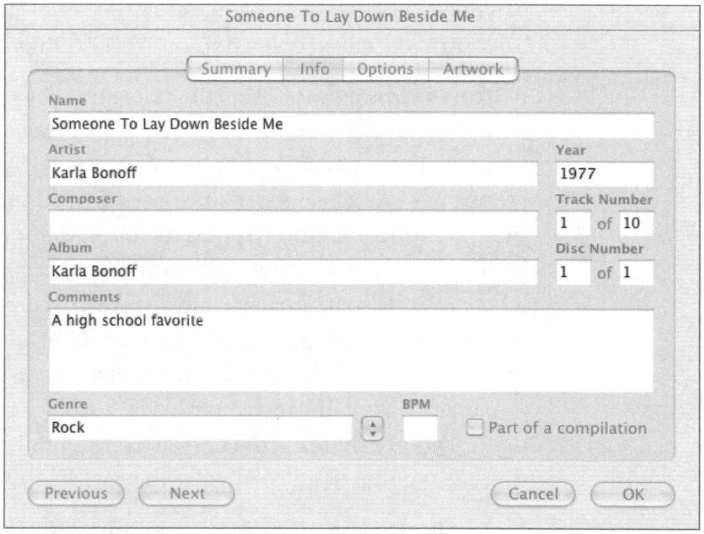

Figure 17.8

iTunes will automatically download information about songs from the Internet, but you can edit this information using the program's Get Info command.

It streams. You want to listen to Internet radio? iTunes comes with a radio button that will bring up a list of hundreds of Internet audio streams to which you can listen. Modem users need not feel left out: a large number of the streams that iTunes offers are perfectly suited even to slower modems. Note that iTunes plays only MP3 audio streams; the Real Player described in "A bestiary of audio formats," earlier in the chapter, above can play MP3 audio streams as well as RealAudio streams.

If you have a home or office network, iTunes will let you stream your own music collection to your family, friends, and coworkers. The most recent version of iTunes lets you share your entire collection, or selected playlists, over a local network to as many as five listeners at a time (granted, with a potential mass audience of five people and with being limited to a local network, you won't find yourself competing on a level playing field with Clear Channel's more than 1200 radio stations, but you've got to start somewhere).

It burns. You can't run iTunes in your car (well, you could do it on a laptop, but if we catch you playing with a laptop while you're driving, we'll give you such a smack!), and you probably don't have your Mac in the family room next to the stereo, but that doesn't mean you can't play your music in these places: iTunes can burn a playlist to a CD with just a few clicks (as long as your Mac has a CD recorder). Almost any CD player can play the discs that iTunes burns, so with the cost of blank recordable CDs being well under a dollar, and with almost every current Mac sporting a CD-R drive or better, there's no excuse for not being able to take the songs you like anywhere you like. If your CD player is capable of playing MP3 CDs (some modern CD players can), you can fit as many as 100 songs on a single disc. iTunes can also back up your music collection onto a DVD if your Mac has a SuperDrive.

It glows. Missed the 1960s the last time they came around? Not to worry—with iTunes' visualizer you can see a light show, synchronized to whatever is playing, that is groovy enough to make the *White Rabbit* keep on *Truckin'*. iTunes has had a visualizer since version 1.0, and not only does it show no sign of fading away, but Apple has released a software developers' kit (called an SDK by those fun-loving acronym-embracing developers) that lets anyone who can craft some gnarly code build a visualizer plug-in for iTunes. The built-in one is a tough act to follow, though, and provides enough in the way of hidden controls to satisfy most geeky Easter-egg hunters: press ? when the visualizer is running and you can see a few of the hidden keyboard commands that let you customize it. There are more hidden under the hood as well, but we're not going to tell you what they are—why spoil the fun?

 To find Easter eggs, simply try pressing different keys on the keyboard. Or put a cat on the keyboard while the visualizer is running: something interesting is bound to happen!

It pods. Apple's handheld digital music player, the iPod, and iTunes were made for each other. Literally. iTunes knows all about the iPod and can keep it automatically synchronized with your music library every time you plug that delightful little bundle of metal and white plastic into your Mac.

iTunes can also work with a variety of other portable MP3 players. In fact, the first version of iTunes, released in the long-long ago before the iPod emerged, was one of the best programs going when it came to working with portable

MP3 players, and it still provides fine support for third-party devices. You can find a partial list of the players that iTunes supports at http://docs.info.apple.com/article.html?artnum=75451. On the other hand, we can't see any reason not go with the iPod if you can afford it: the iPod rocks (www.apple.com/ipod).

It vends. New in iTunes 4 is the highly publicized and already widely imitated iTunes Music Store. The Music Store appears directly inside the iTunes window and provides one-click shopping for digital music. Apple swung a deal with the five largest recording companies (the same ones that are busy putting all their fingers in the great leaking dike that is Internet-based file-swapping) to sell music at 99 cents a track, or $9.99 an album. You can listen to a high-quality 30-second sample of any track, and you can download your purchases immediately to your iTunes library. Impulse shoppers beware: the store is highly addictive (**Figure 17.9**), though you can put an allowance on a Music Store account to help control binge shopping sprees.

Figure 17.9

Better hang on to your wallet if you spend any time in the iTunes Music Store: it's addictive.

In order to placate the record industry, Apple has made its first major foray into digital rights management (DRM) with the iTunes Music Store. Each track is protected, so it can play, at least initially, only on the Mac on which it was purchased or on any iPod that connects to that Mac. Apple makes it possible for you to authorize two additional Macs at a time to play the purchased music as well, and you can burn any music you purchase to an audio CD within limits: you can burn the same playlist only ten times if it has purchased music in it; after that, you have to modify the playlist, so you can't mass-produce CDs this way. If you purchase a new Mac, you can use iTunes to deauthorize your old Mac and to authorize your new Mac to play songs purchased from your account. Then just copy your music files from your old Mac to your new one. The name that Apple has given this DRM system is FairPlay, and, though the system *is* somewhat limiting, it shouldn't inconvenience most fair-minded music fans.

The store opened in April 2003 with roughly 200,000 tracks of audio available for purchase, and the catalog is continually growing; it more than doubled in size by the end of the year. Independent music companies have also been invited to join the fun. The catalog *is* spotty in some pretty major places, though, largely because of complicated rights issues and the reluctance of some artists to trust their works to the digital bazaar of the Internet. Apple dedicates every Tuesday to unveiling the newest additions of the week—the only reason we can finish writing this chapter is because it's Saturday right now.

Other audio players and aids

With iTunes clearly the 800-ton gorilla ("Have you ever heard of ... *Kong*?") in the Mac audio-player world, you'd think that no developers would be interested in exploring that particular application niche. Fortunately, you'd be wrong. Below is a list of programs (and one useful device) that tread some of the same ground that iTunes does, and others that hike up a different hillside.

The **Amazing Slow Downer X** ($39.95; www.ronimusic.com), from Roni Music, performs a neat trick. As the name suggests, this program slows down music (or any other type of audio) without changing its pitch. It can speed it up, too. Why would you want to do this? If you ever need to add musical accompaniment to an iMovie, but the music you want is just a bit too short or too long to fit the visuals, then you'll appreciate this program.

iTunes' Visualizer can show you abstract pictures that dance to the music as it plays, but **AudioXplorer** ($15; www.curvuspro.ch/audioxplorer), from Curvus Pro, can give you pretty pictures that actually *mean* something. This real-time audio analyzer shows sonograms and audio spectra as music plays, as well as letting you statically examine a sound's characteristics. It's also an Apple Audio Units host, meaning that third-party audio digital-signal-processing plug-ins designed according to Apple's new Audio Units standard for Mac OS X will work with it.

AudioFinder ($35; www.mysticalsun.com or www.versiontracker.com), from Mystical Sun, will help you find all the music and sound on your hard disk and play it. It has a Finder-like interface and playlist capabilities, and it will even let you find drum-loop files based on their tempos.

Panic's **Audion** ($29.95; www.panic.com) claims to be a single program that handles all your audio needs (**Figure 17.10**). Overarching statements aside (after all, we can have rather esoteric audio needs), this one does give iTunes a pretty good run for its money and passes it in a few places: it can save MP3 streams to disk, lets you edit ID3 tags right in the playlist, lets you edit MP3 audio files, provides speed control, lets you record from any input, and will even wake you up in the morning.

Figure 17.10

Panic's Audion MP3 player gives iTunes some real competition.

If you're staging a school play and you need to cue up a bunch of sound effects to play in a particular sequence, **Beeper Pro** (free; http://homepage.mac. com/a_logan/PWS), from Paperweight Software, will organize and play them for you. The company also provides a $20 Studio version, which includes full screen mode, and sells sound-effects packages for $15 each.

Dave Ahmed's **Blues Music** (free; http://homepage.mac.com/davidahmed/ bluesMusic.html) doesn't play anything unless you do. It provides a bunch of blues guitar riffs for three different songs, accompanied by drums and bass, with which you can unleash your inner blues master. The program also provides a graphical accompaniment to your blues.

Your Mac has a speaker. And headphone jacks. And maybe an Apple Pro Speakers jack. And USB ports that can connect to other audio output devices. Rogue Amoeba's **Detour** ($12; www.rogueamoeba.com/detour) can send the audio output from different programs to different output devices: it can route your iTunes music to your gnarly powered speakers, divert annoying system beeps to the internal speaker, and silence the annoying sound-enhanced ads in your browser that seem to be all the rage on the Web these days.

Emu Music Player (free; http://homepages.tig.com.au/~cthulhu/modern/ emu/app.html) is a tiny player that harnesses the awesome power of QuickTime to play music files of various formats. It can play all the files in a folder, including files inside folders inside the chosen folder. Recursion, anyone?

The globular, crystalline, Harman Kardon-designed 18-watt Apple Pro Speakers that come with the flat-panel iMacs have a special connector (the Apple Pro Speaker jack) that makes them incompatible with any other computer. No more, though: the hardware hackers at Griffin Technology have cobbled up the **iFire** ($39.99; www.griffintechnology.com) to allow you to use those speakers with any computer that has a FireWire port and a normal stereo minijack. With the iFire you can even use your round shiny Apple Pro Speakers with an iPod.

Party on with **MacDJ** ($9.95; www.danicsoft.com), a real-time audio-mixing program from Danicsoft that lets you assemble a playlist with custom cross-fades and volume adjustments. Simple, and it provides just a bit more control than iTunes' playlists offer.

David Ahmed has more than the blues on his mind; his **MakingMusic** (free; http://homepage.mac.com/davidahmed/makingmusic.html) is a full-bore online musical-instrument encyclopedia. The program, the client part of an ongoing freeware project, connects to a constantly growing online database of musical instruments that supplies pictures, descriptions, and sound samples for each instrument.

MusicPlayer X (free; www.xnation.net), from Xnation, plays movie files as well as music files, can create playlists, can add live effects, and can perform a neat trick that iTunes deliberately won't, in order to ease the concerns of the recording industry (our Good Friends at the RIAA): it can import music from an iPod.

Apple has released what was once a part of its Final Cut Pro package as **Soundtrack** ($299; www.apple.com/soundtrack). The program contains a royalty-free library of thousands of professionally recorded sound loops and effects that you can mix, match, and assemble into musical tracks for a media project.

Whamb (free; www.whamb.com), from the eponymous French Whamb team, is a player for MP3 files and streams, Ogg Vorbis files, and audio CDs. The player is skinnable (meaning that you can add new looks to the player's interface), and it can share music over a local network using Apple's Rendezvous technology. Low-impact processor use, a nice Dock menu, and hierarchical playlists complete the tale.

P2P sharing and streaming music

P2P file sharing is a phrase that causes the executives of the major entertainment industry companies to reach for their heartburn and blood pressure drugs. The peer-to-peer sharing of files and the network protocols (such as the very popular Gnutella) that support it have real, honest, legitimate uses, however, and should not be considered a synonym for copyright infringement. It is true that when you start sharing files with the world, and you don't own the copyright of some of those files, you could end up on the defendant side of a nasty and expensive lawsuit. But if you take some reasonable care and remember to listen to the good cartoon angel sitting on your shoulder, you can use file sharing to enrich your Mac musical experience.

Streams are the Internet equivalent of radio: instead of downloading an audio file to your Mac in order to play it, you play the data as it is being received. The data stays on the server except for the little bit being transmitted at any given instant. But you needn't be just a listener; as we saw with iTunes in "iTunes, you tunes, we all tunes for iTunes," earlier in the chapter, you, too, can be a streamer.

Here are some of the more Mac-friendly Internet services that engage in legitimate and legal file sharing and streaming, and some programs (and a device) that help you do the same.

You can turn your Mac into a streaming server with Scott Matthews's **Andromeda** ($35; www.turnstyle.com/andromeda) package, from Turnstyle. Relying on Mac OS X's built-in Apache Web server and its ability to run scripts written in PHP, Andromeda lets you drag and drop audio files into a folder to publish them instantly for streaming on the Web. You can even use Andromeda to stream your iTunes library beyond the bounds of your local area network. Note, though, that you'll need a reasonably fast Internet connection and a static IP number if you want to establish a true online presence.

The problem with listening to streaming audio is that you need to have an Internet connection active to hear it. With Rogue Amoeba's **Audio Hijack Pro** ($30; www.rogueamoeba.com/audiohijackpro), though, you can connect, record the stream, and then listen to it later when you're disconnected—perfect for the laptop user on the go. Audio Hijack Pro can record the audio output of any application, too, so you can capture the thrilling sound track of the last 6 hours you spent playing Master of Orion III.

Most of the action in the P2P world seems to be on the other platform, but the Mac is not totally bereft of options. **Drumbeat** ($34.95; www.drumbeat.info) connects to OpenNap servers to find individual users on the Internet who are sharing files and lets you download from them. The program features what it calls IntelliSearch Technology to quickly find the file you want. Unlike many other P2P programs for the Mac, Drumbeat conforms to the Mac OS look and feel.

Need to jam to some indie music? The **IUMA** (Internet Underground Music Archive; www.iuma.com) provides a place for independent musicians and composers to post their music. You can listen to their MP3s in your browser or you can download them; it also streams some material in RealAudio format.

LimeWire (free; www.limewire.com) is a client program for sharing files over the peer-to-peer Gnutella network. Written in Java, the program has a look and feel that is a weird blend of Mac OS X Aqua and Windows conventions. The program assumes that you want to share your files as well as download those that others are sharing, and the installer creates a sharing folder for you, as well as littering the application's own folder with tons of separate data files. Nonetheless, it is a stable client for traipsing around in Gnutella-land if that's where you want to traipse.

If you've got files in LimeWire's shared folder, you are implicitly opting to share them with others on the Internet. If you do this, make sure that you own the copyright to those files, or you could be engaged in illegal file sharing.

Live365 (free; www.live365.com) is the source of many of iTunes' radio stations, but you can browse all its offerings on the Web as well. Playing material from the site requires that you register with it, though. Mac users can share their files on Live365 by uploading files to Live365's server; make sure you read its Terms of Service for what you can and can't do.

Apple says that its **QuickTime Streaming Server** (free; www.apple.com/quicktime/products/qtss) is for Mac OS X Server, but it runs quite nicely on the consumer version of Mac OS X as well. The streaming server, which you configure and control through your Web browser, can stream QuickTime movies, MPEG-4, 3GPP, and MP3 playlists. You must remember to open the appropriate network ports if you have a firewall, and, as is true for most Internet servers, it helps if you have a static IP number or have made friends with a nearby DNS. QTSS (as the QuickTime crowd calls it) is an industrial-grade product, supporting as many as 4000 simultaneous streams if you have the CPU horsepower and the bandwidth (anyone for a rack of Xserves?).

The Griffin Technology hardware folks have made TiVo for radio—broadcast or Internet. **RadioSHARK** ($69.99; www.griffintechnology.com) is a USB device (due in 2004), with a built-in antenna, that can record AM or FM radio broadcasts as well as Internet radio streams from almost any application. The device looks like a shark's dorsal fin—hence, the name.

Radiostorm.com (free; www.radiostorm.com) is a streaming Internet radio station with six channels of rock, alternative, and hip-hop. Its streams come in the form of .pls playlist files that your browser downloads and opens with iTunes. You don't have to register to listen, but you will hear ads from time to time.

SHOUTcast (free; www.shoutcast.com) is the home of thousands of Internet broadcasters. It's hosted by the makers of WinAmp (a popular MP3/Windows Media player that is similar in some ways to iTunes), but don't let that put you off: it works just fine with iTunes or Panic 's Audion player/encoder program (see the previous section). SHOUTcast offers a wide selection of MP3 streams as .pls playlist files, and its search functions provide effective help when you explore their extensive broadcaster community.

Radio@Netscape Plus (free; http://music.netscape.com/) an Internet broadcast service (formerly called Spinner.com), presents hundreds of streams of various types of music. The site uses Real's RealAudio plug-in in a small browser pop-up window to play the chosen stream. The player window displays the song name, artist, and album and gives you the opportunity to buy the currently playing CD. Marketing synergy, folks; it's what's for breakfast.

Ambrosia Software, which has developed many Mac games and more than a few utilities through the years, has a new utility, **WireTap** (free; www.ambrosiasw.com/utilities/freebies), that uses a tape-recorder-like interface to let you capture any sound playing on your Mac in a variety of formats (AIFF is the most common). The capture quality is only as good as the input.

Making Audio

So you've listened to everyone else's music or audio files and you're thinking you'd like to create some of your own. Creating audio on a Mac can be as simple or as complicated as you'd like it to be. Whether simple or complicated, though, you'll need to capture the audio, possibly edit it, and then save it on a CD or another medium. Here's what you need to know.

Rip-a-dee-doo-dah—capturing audio

Sound (like love) is all around us; the trick with sound is to get it inside your Mac and keep it there (what you do with love is your business). The process of getting sound into your Mac is variously called *capturing, digitizing,* or *ripping,* depending on what technique is used. Sound sources come in a lot of forms, so it shouldn't be surprising that there are a lot of different ways to capture sound.

Capturing CD audio. If you have iTunes and a CD drive, capturing audio couldn't be simpler. Put in the CD. iTunes opens. Click the CD in iTunes' source list, and click the big friendly Import button in the upper right corner of iTunes' window. The tracks are imported into your iTunes library using iTunes' current import settings (usually MPEG-4 AAC format). If you want an uncompressed format (best if you plan to tinker with the sound), you can set iTunes' import settings for AIFF or WAV before you import, but expect each minute of audio in those formats to devour 10 MB.

 Capture raw, cook it later: because audio compression blithely discards information, you should delay compressing your audio data for as long as possible. Instead, bite the bullet and capture the best raw (that is, uncompressed) sound your system can handle. When you finish editing and otherwise manipulating your audio, that's when you want to compress it.

Capturing analog audio. Unlike CD audio, which is digital from the git-go, analog audio (such as the output of a cassette deck) must first be converted into digital form before you can save it on your Mac. Luckily, if you have one of the Macs equipped with an audio line-in or microphone jack, you already have an analog-to-digital converter compatible with most consumer audio equipment—one that provides good-enough quality for many digital-media projects. Apple supplies a program in Mac OS X 10.2 and later called Audio MIDI Setup, which you may need if you are capturing audio. The program (found in the Utilities folder inside the main Applications folder) lets you examine all the current audio input and output devices that your Mac recognizes, and lets you control them (**Figure 17.11**).

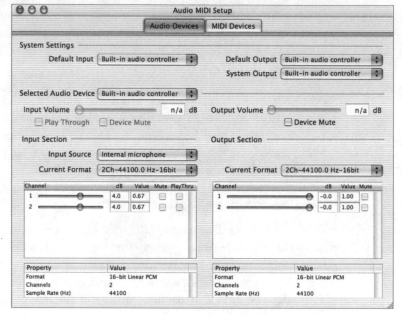

Figure 17.11

Apple's Audio MIDI Setup utility lets you see which audio devices your Mac is currently using.

 If your Mac does not include an audio input jack, you still have some inexpensive options. Third-party products that provide audio input via the standard USB connectors on Macs are easy to come by. Griffin Technology's surprisingly inexpensive **iMic** add-on ($35; www.griffintechnology.com) provides cleaner sound input via its miniplug than the typical Mac's analog input and doesn't require any special driver software. Griffin's **PowerWave** ($99.99) gives you RCA line inputs and outputs, as well as an amplifier and a jack for connecting external speakers to it.

Also playing in the USB audio-capture arena is Edirol Corp. Its **Edirol UA-1X** ($95; www.edirol.com) provides RCA audio inputs and outputs and even S/PDIF optical output (S/PDIF is the Sony/Philips Digital Interface, a common professional standard digital-audio connector). If you need a bit more flexibility, take a look at the company's **Edirol UA-20** ($179). This little box provides RCA line level, ¼-inch guitar, mic, and S/PDIF optical inputs; MIDI input and output; and a big, authoritative black input-level knob.

You can kill two birds with one stone if you want both basic audio-capture capability and full-bore home-theater 7.1-channel surround-sound output: M-Audio's **Sonica Theater** ($119.95; www.m-audio.net) has outputs galore, though its input is limited to a stereo miniplug. Sonica's **Revolution 7.1** PCI card (also $119.95) provides the same home theater output capabilities but offers both line-in and mic inputs.

Demanding audio professionals will want to outfit their Macs with a dedicated capture system that's compatible with high-end studio equipment (you're one of those people if you can't bear to live in a world without S/PDIF, ADAT optical, and MIDI I/O). Digidesign (www.digidesign.com) is one of the product leaders in this area (it's owned by Avid, which also makes professional Mac-based video-editing systems). If you want to set up a small home recording studio, the USB-based **Mbox** ($495) capture system, which comes with Digidesign's Pro Tools LE, will get you started. On the other hand, if you're a professional audio engineer (or an *extreme* audiophile), and money (at least, $13,995 of it) is no object, you may want to go all the way to the Digidesign's top-of-the-line **Pro Tools|HD 3 Accel** three-card 24-bit digital-audio pro-duction system, which requires at least an AGP Graphics–equipped Power Mac G4.

Once you have the hardware figured out, you'll still need software to handle the actual capturing. The high-end capture systems usually come with their own software for this, but at the lower end you'll have to look around for suitable applications. You needn't look very far, since several shareware and freeware solutions are readily available.

If you have a Griffin iMic or PowerWave, you can download the company's **Final Vinyl** software (free; www.griffintechnology.com/software/software_imic.html), which gives you a simple interface for capturing audio. It also includes RIAA equalization settings so that you can record directly from a turntable without having to go through an analog preamp.

Spark LE Plus ($49; www.tcelectronic.com/SparkLE), from TC Electronic, is a digitizing and audio editing tool that is surprisingly full featured for a piece of inexpensive software. It can handle all major audio formats, supports VST plug-ins (Virtual Studio Technology is an audio software plug-in standard developed by Steinberg that is used in many audio editing packages), provides accurate waveform editing, and includes a playlist feature for creating CD projects.

At the low-priced-but-not-free end of the spectrum is Realmac Software's **AudioX** ($19.95; www.realmacsoftware.com). This application, which sports windows with a metal finish like those in Mac OS X 10.3, can record sound from any audio input source your Mac recognizes. It has a note-taking feature and provides a speed control for playback. It also converts sound files to several formats.

HairerSoft's **Amadeus II** ($25; www.hairersoft.com), developed by physicist Martin Hairer, can capture, edit, filter, and analyze your sound files; it also provides built-in support for Ogg Vorbis and MP3 formats (**Figure 17.12**).

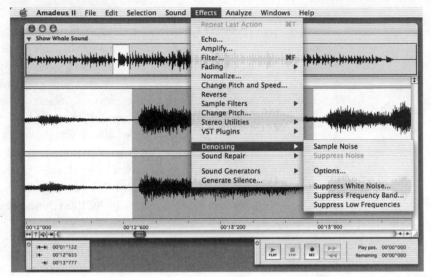

Figure 17.12

Mozart might have used Amadeus if he'd had a Mac and the shareware fee.

Sound Studio ($59.95; www.felttip.com/products/soundstudio) from Felt Tip Software captures audio, and it also provides good basic sound-editing capabilities, audio filters, and pitch shifting (here's your opportunity to transform the late, great Barry White into a tenor!).

CD burning beyond iTunes

iTunes is all you really need if you just want to burn an occasional audio CD without too much fuss or bother. But if you want to make something a little more complex, such as a hybrid CD containing both audio tracks and data, you'll need something more feature rich.

Discribe ($69.95; www.charismac.com), from long-time Mac developer Charismac Engineering, supports a wide variety of CD burners and can create CDs in most of the popular formats, including the CD Extra, or Blue Book, format, used for commercial audio CDs that include extra multimedia content. It also converts audio formats on the fly when you create audio CDs. It even lets you drag and drop QuickTime movie files, extracting the sound and adding it as an audio track, which is handy for creating an audio CD containing the sound tracks of QuickTime movies.

NewTech Infosystems' **Dragon Burn** ($45.95; www.ntidragonburn.com) can burn multiple CDs at once if you have multiple CD burners attached to your Mac (how many of you out there have multiple CD burners?). Aside from that, it offers support for a wide variety of standard CD formats, including CD-Text on audio CDs, which provides a way to include text such as lyrics or liner notes on an audio CD in a manner that won't interfere with playing the CD on standard audio CD players.

Probably one of the most popular CD-burning applications, Roxio's **Toast Titanium** ($99.95; www.roxio.com), supports all the CD formats you might possibly want, can write to the higher-capacity 700 MB CD-R discs, and will perform file optimization for faster reading. Roxio bundles a number of other applications with it: iView Media, for dealing with photos; Audion, for playing CDs; Magic Mouse Discus, for printing CD labels and case inserts; and CD Spin Doctor, for creating audio CDs from any analog source (can you say "vinyl LP"?). The package's big brother, **Toast with JAM** ($189.95), is designed for audio professionals, and it allows for between-track cross-fades, gain controls for both channels of each track, and track-trimming tools. It also bundles BIAS Peak LE VST to let you perform audio editing and enhancing.

MIDI ditty

Anyone who plays electronic instruments probably knows more about this standard than we can cover here, but for the rest of us, *MIDI* stands for *Musical Instrument Digital Interface* and is a long-established standard way to interconnect electronic music devices so that they can exchange information. As the name indicates, this information is digital, so it's not surprising that your Mac can understand and manipulate MIDI data. The data is not digitized sound but, rather, information about a musical performance: which keys the player pressed, for how long, and so on. You can store such data very compactly and manipulate it very easily—a MIDI file representing ten separate instruments playing, say, a minute-long piece typically takes up just a few kilobytes on disk.

MIDI files contain *sequences,* and a sequence can contain one or more *channels,* where each channel represents the performance of a single instrument and each instrument has a corresponding *program* number. In the electronic music world, MIDI data usually goes to a synthesizer, which plays the sequence using its own sounds (these can be either hardware generated or predigitized sound samples).

Although the basic MIDI standard lets a musician assign any instrument to a MIDI program number, another standard, called General MIDI, helps musicians work together by assigning specific instruments to specific program numbers. For example, in General MIDI, 0 is always a piano sound and 12 is a vibraphone. Using this specification, musicians can exchange MIDI files and get reasonably comparable results on their different playback systems.

Macs can both play and produce MIDI. Among QuickTime's many other features, it provides MIDI playback support, allowing Apple's QuickTime Player to open any standard MIDI file and play it back using QuickTime's built-in Roland GS samples, which adhere to the General MIDI specification. QuickTime Pro even lets you change the instruments assigned to each channel (**Figure 17.13**).

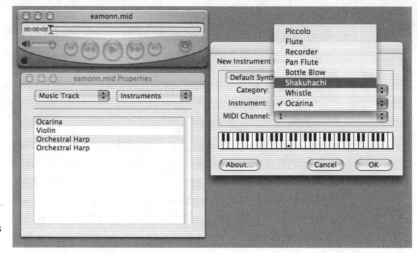

Figure 17.13

QuickTime Pro unlocks QuickTime's MIDI capabilities.

MIDI and the modern Mac. Hooking up a MIDI instrument (such as a keyboard) to your Mac used to be simple, then it got complicated, and now it's getting simple again. On older Macs with serial ports, you could hook up an inexpensive MIDI interface device to one of the Mac's two serial ports (each port could support 16 MIDI channels). However, modern Macs don't have serial ports—but they do have USB ports, and though there were a couple of years of confusion and frustration when USB MIDI interfaces were hard to find and problematic to use, they are now quite common and well supported.

Similarly, the Mac transition to Mac OS X created much uncertainty and not a little teeth-clenching in the musical world because of the early versions' very incomplete audio underpinnings. Fortunately, the situation has improved mightily. Mac OS X 10.2 and higher has a complete Core MIDI component that eliminates the need for software like Free MIDI or OMS (ad hoc standards for connecting MIDI devices to the Mac) to provide the Mac with MIDI support (not surprisingly, Core MIDI was developed by one of OMS's developers).

 For those running Mac OS X 10.2 or later, Apple's Audio MIDI Setup utility (look in the Utilities folder inside your Applications folder) can show you the MIDI devices attached to your Mac and let you add new devices. If you use MIDI, you need to know about this application.

Interfaces. M-Audio (www.m-audio.net) provides a range of USB-based MIDI interfaces, from the single audio in/audio out **Midisport Uno** model ($49.95) to the eight audio in/audio out **USB MIDISport 8x8/s** ($399.95). Mark of the Unicorn (www.markoftheunicorn.com), a long-time player in the MIDI world, also sells a variety of USB MIDI interfaces, starting with its low-end 2x2 **FastLane** ($79) and going up to its 8x8 **MIDI Timepiece AV** ($595).

Sequencers. MIDI files consist of sequences, and the programs used to write them are *sequencers*. Generally, you have to know a good deal about music to use them, and even the simplest sequencers provide much music-making power. Prices range from rather low to very high. Five12 has a modular MIDI performance sequencer called **Numerology** ($50; www.five12.com). Intuem has a sequencer called, not surprisingly, **Intuem** ($79; www.intuem.com). Sagan Technology's **Metro SE** ($69.99; www.sagantech.biz) will suit some beginning users, but its bigger and more expensive sibling **Metro** ($319.99) will probably appeal to those with more than basic needs. Germany's Ableton offers **Live** ($399; www.ableton.com), which it describes as "the audio sequencer you can play like an instrument"; like many of the higher-end sequencers, it also imports, edits, and mixes analog audio.

One widely used high-end MIDI sequencer is Steinberg's **Cubase SX** ($799; www.steinberg.net); another is Mark of the Unicorn's **Digital Performer** ($795; www.markoftheunicorn.com). If you want to stay close to the Cupertino mother ship, Apple-owned Emagic will be happy to sell you its **Logic Platinum** ($699; www.emagic.de), which sequences, mixes, and scores. Many others are available as well, and musical pros apparently never tire of discussing the features and quirks of the sequencer du jour.

Creating scores. MIDI can also take the drudgery out of transcribing music. The MIDI data contains the notes played, the duration of those notes, and the volume … and that's just what a musical score is all about. After all, why labor to write down your music when you can just play it and have your Mac lay out the score? The top-of-the-line product for such interactive music notation is MakeMusic! Inc.'s **Finale 2004** ($600; www.finalemusic.com), which provides unlimited staves, professional notation, and seemingly endless features (with the concomitant seemingly endless learning curve). **NoteAbilityPro,** from Opus1Music ($225; www.opusonemusic.net), can also generate scores from MIDI input, as can **Overture,** from GenieSoft ($349; www.geniesoft.com). A less complex (and less expensive) notation program that understands MIDI is Ars Nova's **SongWorks II** ($125; www.ars-nova.com); an even less expensive one is the shareware **Melody Assistant,** from Myriad Software ($15; www.myriad-online.com).

MIDI potpourri. Developers have been churning out all sorts of hybrid products that employ MIDI as aids to musicians. Yow has **Girl** ($99; http:// girl.yowstar.com), which lets you do your interactive dub mixing under MIDI sequencer control. Chris Reed has built a virtual MIDI keyboard in **MidiKeys** ($15; www.manyetas.com/creed/midikeys.html). You can generate chords and arpeggios automatically with the MIDI performance assistant **ReMIDI** ($14.95; www.amplitude.demon.nl/remidi.html). And you can contemplate the sound of geeks and musicians colliding with **Symbolic Composer** ($395; www.mracpublishing.com), which the publisher describes as the "most powerful music molecular language available for computers" and which lets you write programs to "generate fractal and chaos music with an extensive set of functions." We find that a toddler with a keyboard can do the same.

MIDI uses. Aside from its obvious uses for musicians and composers, MIDI fits right into many multimedia projects. Games often use MIDI tracks to provide background music, Web sites occasionally play background MIDI sequences (and we really wish they wouldn't, as they are usually extremely annoying), and, because QuickTime can easily play MIDI, interactive QuickTime projects often use MIDI samples for button-click sounds and other effects.

MIDI has other, nonmusical uses as well—technicians have even used it to control the lighting during stage shows … you know, *analog* multimedia.

GarageBand: A Studio for the Rest of Us

Apple's GarageBand (**Figure 17.14**), the latest iLife application, brings both MIDI and analog audio recording and audio mixing capabilities to newer Macs.

continues on next page

Figure 17.14

GarageBand lets you rock out at a price even a starving musician can afford.

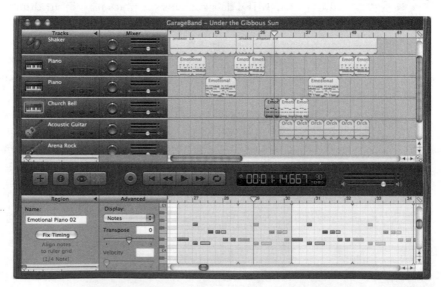

GarageBand: A Studio for the Rest of Us   *continued*

Did you ever blow out your parents' eardrums (or, at least, your home's circuit breakers) in your attempt to be the next 14-year-old rock star? Did you suffer through years of piano lessons and wonder why? If so, this program is for you.

Designed to work with the advanced audio capabilities lurking inside Mac OS X and the newer Macs, GarageBand lets you plug in microphones, electric guitars (Apple sells a Monster Instrument Adaptor cable for them for $19.95), MIDI keyboards (Apple sells an M-Audio Keystation 49-key USB keyboard, too, for $99), and other electronic musical instruments (yes, the Apple Store also sells a $199 Edirol PCR-30 MIDI keyboard controller) into your Mac, record your own musical tracks, and mix them together. GarageBand includes 50 different software instruments that you can play from your MIDI keyboard (or even, if you are really strapped for funds, GarageBand's onscreen keyboard). Plus, the package provides 200 audio effects you can apply to your recordings, including guitar amplifier settings that can make your guitar sound as though it is playing through anything from a small practice amp to a huge arena sound system.

This virtual studio comes with more than 1000 "loops"—prerecorded MIDI and analog audio musical snippets that you can add to your musical composition for backing or rhythm. The MIDI loops (called *software instrument loops)* can even be transposed to any key you need. And Apple will sell you additional loops and instrument effects in its **GarageBand Jam Pack** ($99). You can even edit the software instrument loops after you put them into a track, adding notes, deleting them, or adjusting their timing and volume. And you can edit your own MIDI recordings as well: no more bad notes!

Once you've laid down your tracks, refined them, and mixed them (GarageBand lets you tweak the audio levels and speaker placements of each track), you can export a completed version of your song directly into iTunes, where it is ready to be put on your iPod or added to the soundtrack of an iMovie video, an iPhoto slide show, or an iDVD disc.

Of course, it's up to you to add the talent.

Audio editors

If you plan to use digital audio in a media project, chances are you'll need to edit the sound at some point.

For those of you who just need to trim a sound file or splice two sounds together, all you really need is **QuickTime Pro** ($29; www.apple.com/quicktime). The editing commands are similar to what you'll find in a word processor. Position the slider where you want to start (or end), ⇧Shift-click to select a range, and then choose Cut, Copy, or Clear from the Edit menu. You can paste a sound from one file to another by simply cutting or copying it from the source, selecting the location in the destination file, and choosing Paste from the Edit menu.

QuickTime files can point to other files. That is, when you copy media from one file to another in QuickTime Pro, all you are really copying is a reference to the sound's location in the first file. You'll need to have both files on your disk to play the edited piece. (This is actually very useful while you are working on a project because it saves a lot of disk space and processing time while you experiment with different versions.) If you want your edited sound to end up in one file, save the file as self-contained: from the File menu, choose Save As and click the "Save as self-contained" button in the file dialog.

QuickTime Pro doesn't have the editing chops for detailed work, so you'll want to use a more full-featured audio editor if your project requires much fine-tuned audio editing. A good audio editor will let you mix multiple tracks, filter sounds, add audio effects, and edit sounds with fraction-of-a-second precision. Two previously mentioned shareware products—Sound Studio and Amadeus II (see "Rip-a-dee-doo-dah—capturing audio," earlier in the chapter)—are creditable audio editors that can take you quite a bit further than QuickTime Pro for very little cost.

The tools that professional sound editors use usually come in a complete package that includes audio hardware, such as Digidesign's previously discussed suite of products in "Rip-a-dee-doo-dah—capturing audio." If you want to experience Digidesign's audio editing approach and are running Mac OS 9, try a reduced version of its **Pro Tools** editing software (free; www.digidesign.com/ptfree), which can handle eight separate audio tracks (as well as 48 MIDI tracks). For a professional-quality editor that falls between the shareware and freeware offerings and the really big-ticket suites, you might consider Bias's **BIAS Peak** ($499; www.bias-inc.com) full-featured audio editor, or the more-powerful sibling of the low-cost Spark ME, TC Electronic's **Spark XL** ($599; www.tcelectronic.com/SparkXL).

Graphics

The Mac and graphics are inextricably bound, and have been for the two decades since the original beige box debuted. After all, the very first Mac featured a graphical user interface in a world of text-only displays, and it included one of the very first of an eventual tsunami of digital painting programs (ah, MacPaint, with your 1-bit graphical goodness—shall we ever see your like again?). Over the years, many a company built its reputation on the graphical back of the Macintosh. Macs and graphics: they go together like Stilton and pears.

Chapter 13 thoroughly covers graphics on the Mac, so we'll concentrate here on what you need to know about graphics in the context of other digital media.

Understanding Pictures

Digital pictures can be made in two ways. They can be defined as either a bunch of *pixels* (short for *picture element*)—that is, a collection of dots, usually 72 to 96 of them per inch—or a bunch of instructions for drawing the lines and colors that compose them. The first sort, the dot sort, are commonly called *bitmap* graphics; the second sort are usually called *vector* graphics.

The untidy real world, the kind that you can photograph or paint, tends to be best represented with bitmap graphics. The world of human artifice—the world of architectural plans, logos, and typefaces—tends to be best represented with vector graphics.

Vector graphics can be easily *scaled*—made bigger or smaller—without a loss of resolution. Bitmap graphics tend to look more blurry, or ragged, as they are made larger. The more complicated the vector graphics are, the more processing power is needed to display them. The more complicated the bitmap graphics are, the more memory is needed to display them.

 When it comes to bitmap graphics, the more dots per inch (dpi), the finer the resolution. Bitmap graphics that are meant to be printed tend to have a lot of dots per inch (300–600), which makes for some pretty big files. Bitmap graphics for the screen can, and should, have much lower resolution—somewhere in the 72–96 dpi range.

All this, of course, seriously oversimplifies a complex and subtle field of digital endeavor. But it should be enough to get you started. Besides, there's always Chapter 14 to help you with some of the finer distinctions.

The color dilemma

Color is complicated—just ask any prepress specialist. There are two basic ways of defining color: color that's meant for the screen and color that's meant for the printed page. On the screen, every color you see is a combination of red, green, and blue dots: turn all the dots really bright and you get white; make some brighter than others and you get various hues; turn them all off and you get black. On paper, unless you are using special *spot color* inks, the colors you see are a combination of cyan, magenta, yellow, and black inks. Two acronyms encapsulate the distinction: RGB (for red, green, blue) and CMYK (for cyan, magenta, yellow, and black).

 Most digital-media projects tend to live in an RGB world, since most digital-media projects are designed for the screen.

A format affair

Digital image formats are many and varied, but only a few of them matter to those folks (like you) who are interested in building digital-media projects. The JPEG (Joint Photographic Experts Group) format may be the most common one you'll encounter: it is an open standard for storing compressed color bitmap images, like photographs, and is ubiquitous on the Web. JPEG compression is *lossy*; the more the image is compressed, the more data is lost, and the fuzzier the picture looks. TIFF (tagged image file format) is the most common high-resolution storage and exchange format. In many cases, you may want to store your high-resolution images as TIFFs and make lower-resolution JPEG copies for use in your projects. PDF (Adobe's Portable Document Format) is a common exchange format for both vector graphic images and bitmaps; Mac OS X employs it extensively. SVG (Scalable Vector Graphics) is another open-standard exchange format for vector-based artwork. Exclusive to the Mac is Apple's own PICT format, which can represent both bitmap and vector graphics.

Focus on iPhoto

Just a few years ago, Apple tried to kick-start the nascent consumer market for digital cameras with the introduction of its QuickTake camera. As with many of Apple's pioneering endeavors, it succeeded in popularizing the concept while failing as a product: the QuickTake is no longer among the living, but digital cameras today rival film cameras in popularity. Their advantage? Cost-free instant "developing"—just transfer your camera's photos to your computer and they're ready for viewing. Their drawback? The "just transfer your camera's photos to your computer" part, which could (and for non-Mac users often still does) involve installing drivers and other special less-than-intuitive software.

Apple's iPhoto shrinks that drawback to gnatlike proportions. Designed to work with most digital camera models, iPhoto makes the transfer of pictures to your Mac comfortingly simple. Managing, retouching, organizing, and printing your photos are also comfortingly simple. Chapter 13 explores iPhoto's graphics manipulation and printing features in detail; here we'll look at how iPhoto works in the context of digital-media production. iPhoto is included with every new Mac, or you can purchase the $49 iLife bundle, which includes iPhoto, iTunes, iMovie, iDVD, and GarageBand.

It organizes. When Steve Jobs introduced iPhoto in January 2002, he referred to it as a "digital shoebox" for photos. It's one clever shoebox. iPhoto maintains a database of the photos it contains, creates and stores thumbnails of the photos, and lets you arrange your photos in multiple albums.

You can see your photos organized by *roll*, a roll being any group of photos that were imported at the same time (**Figure 17.15**). iPhoto can also arrange your photos by date or by name. You can change the name and date of any photo to suit your needs or whim; iPhoto, however, does retain—and displays—the EXIF data (see the sidebar "EXIF to Your Right," below) that most digital photos contain, so you can always find out a picture's original name and date. You can also assign keywords to photos and search your picture collection for all photos that match a set of keywords. Or you can search by name and by comment (yes, iPhoto allows you to attach a textual comment to any picture). You can give your photos ratings, too, and sort them into "smart albums" based upon several different criteria.

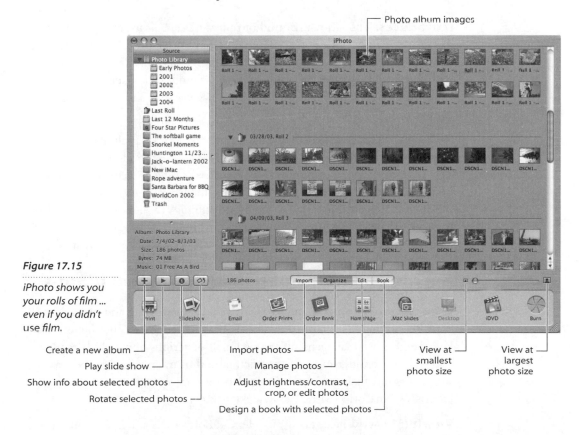

Photo album images

Figure 17.15

iPhoto shows you your rolls of film ... even if you didn't use film.

Create a new album
Play slide show
Show info about selected photos
Rotate selected photos
Import photos
Manage photos
Adjust brightness/contrast, crop, or edit photos
Design a book with selected photos
View at smallest photo size
View at largest photo size

iPhoto provides archiving capabilities as well: you can burn selected albums or individual photos directly to CD or DVD, and when you insert the disc in your Mac, iPhoto shows it in its list of photo libraries and albums.

As a tool for managing and retrieving still images to be used in a digital-media project, iPhoto is certainly worth considering, especially given that it isn't just limited to photos: iPhoto can handle any image format that QuickTime can read.

EXIF to Your Right

EXIF is the Exchangeable Image File format, developed by the former Japan Electronic Industry Development Association (JEIDA merged in 2000 with the Electronic Industries Association of Japan to form JEITA) for storing metadata (information about information) in image files, usually files created by digital cameras. Think of it as being like an ID3 tag for digital photos.

EXIF tags can contain (among many other things) the name of the camera model, the camera orientation, the image's resolution, the date and time the picture was digitized, the shutter speed used when the picture was taken, the camera's f-stop setting when the picture was taken, and a thumbnail of the image.

It produces. Though many of iPhoto's features are aimed at creating actual physical prints of your photos, iPhoto does have some digital-media creation savvy as well. You can export any iPhoto album as a QuickTime slide show with transitions between pictures and with a sound track taken from your iTunes music library. iPhoto can create screen-saver slide shows, too, and even turn your Mac Desktop into a slide show.

It shares. iPhoto is designed to work with the other iLife applications. As we've seen, it uses the iTunes music library for its slide show sound tracks, but it also works with iMovie and iDVD. iMovie has complete access to the iPhoto library, so you can use your pictures in your movies, and iDVD can use your iPhoto pictures for title menu art or for creating DVD slide shows. And if you have a local area network, you can share your iPhoto albums over the network with Rendezvous, just as you can with your iTunes songs and playlists.

Seeing and Managing Images Beyond iPhoto

iPhoto is certainly an easy and inexpensive tool for viewing and managing your images, but it's not the only one. Following are some other options for lower-end image management. Professionals or serious photographers may also want to consider more feature-rich (and thus more complex and expensive) programs such as Canto's **Cumulus** ($69.95; www.canto.com) or Extensis's **Portfolio** ($199.95; www.extensis.com).

ViewIt ($19; www.hexcat.com) by HexCat Software is a drag-and-drop image viewer that is small, quick, and useful. Like iPhoto, it can import pictures from a camera and create slide shows; unlike iPhoto, it can sort selected pictures into various folders on your disk via programmable function keys.

ToThePoint Software's **Photologist** ($19; www.ttpsoftware.com) supplies a Folder Manager to help you sort your photos, a Gallery Window so that you can see all of a folder's photos at once, and a number of photo-editing tools. It also lets you stamp text onto selected photos.

Aside from providing many of iPhoto's niceties, such as slide shows, picture viewing and printing, and Web-page creation, iView Multimedia's **iView** ($29.95; www.iview-multimedia.com) has extensive image-management features, including custom annotation types, catalog creation, color labeling, and drag and drop between it and other applications.

Finally, if you've never outgrown the need to pass secret messages in class, you'll like Big Green Software's **PictureSpy** (free; http://homepage.mac.com/ biggreen). It uses a technique called *steganography* to encode messages invisibly into pictures, which you can then email to your coconspirat ... uh ... colleagues and friends, who can decode them. (My name is Bond ... Ansel Bond.)

Making Pictures

What are you looking here for? See Chapter 13; it's all *about* making pictures.

Video

Sit down and get comfortable, folks—watching video may require nothing more than a couch, a remote control, a TV, and a bag of chips (optional), but understanding how video works, especially in our new, happy fun-time digital world, is a tad more intellectually *involving*. Learning how video works can also be much more enjoyable and satisfying than merely watching the stuff, and you can still munch your chips on the couch as you read and learn.

Video by the Numbers

As you probably know already, movies don't really move; they're simply sequences of still pictures that go by so fast that they fool your brain into thinking it's seeing motion. This is true whether you're sitting in your neighborhood cineplex watching the latest summer blockbuster, at home watching the latest survivor get booted off the island, or in front of your Mac, watching the latest movie trailers on Apple's QuickTime Web site.

You probably know, too, that everything you see on your Mac's screen is made up of pixels. Just as a quick succession of still pictures can fool the brain into perceiving motion, an array of small, closely spaced dots can fool it into perceiving a seamless picture.

The quality of a video experience depends on the *frame rate* (how many still images are displayed each second), the *bit depth* of each image (how many bits of storage each pixel takes up, which dictates the range of colors each pixel can display), and the *frame size* (the number of pixels, horizontally and vertically, that make up each image). The faster the frame rate, the smoother the motion; and the larger the frame size, the better looking the video. However, as video quality increases, the more storage is required and the harder your Mac's processor and other components must work to display the video.

Let's look at some numbers. Suppose we want to display video that's roughly equivalent in quality to American television. The picture will be 640 pixels wide and 480 pixels tall, each pixel will require 3 bytes (24 bits) of storage to provide a full range of color, and the frame rate will match the TV standard of 30 frames per second (fps). (Broadcast professionals may call for 720 by 480 pixels to account for digital video's rectangular pixels, 32 bits of color to provide an alpha channel, and a frame rate of 29.97 fps, which is what American TV standards dictate—but let's not quibble.) This means that each image will require 900 Kbytes, and a single second of video will consume a walloping 26 MB.

Processing that's enough to get a G5 Mac's nine fans really whirling.

Fortunately, they usually don't have to. Many technical compromises are made to deliver an analog TV signal to you, and even so-called uncompressed digital video can take advantage of these compromises to lower the data rate to a somewhat more manageable 3 MBps. You can easily handle that on an iBook. Still, most video usually needs to be compressed for use in digital-media projects, which leads us to ...

Big and Small—Video Compression Tips

Even at the dawn of a new millennium, video compression remains an art and not a science: the right way to do it varies from video to video and depends very much upon the intended use. Here are some tips and guidelines.

Know your audience. The compressor you choose for your video (see "A Catalog of Video-Compression Formats," below) depends as much on its special virtues as it does on the end user. For example, Sorenson Video *can* look great at 100 KBps, but if your audience consists of elementary school teachers running five-year-old Macs, they simply won't have the CPU power to handle it. In many cases you'll want to make separate versions of your video and compress each using different settings—or even different codecs—to create versions that the entire spectrum of your intended audience can use. This is especially true for Web-based delivery (many people out there are still using modems).

Experiment. Even if you think you have *the* ultimate recipe for compressing video, do yourself a favor—extract a minute or two of your video and compress it several different ways, using different data rates, compression options, and even codecs. Sometimes the settings that worked perfectly for one video don't suit another. You should look especially hard at action sequences and video effects (such as dissolves and wipes), because that's where compressors often have the most trouble producing good results.

You don't need 30 frames per second. Just because your TV gives you 30 fps (well, 29.97) doesn't mean you must use that frame rate. You can save a lot of space by simply choosing a lower frame rate when you compress. You can drop down to around 10 fps before the motion looks obviously jerky, and even that rate (or lower ones) may be acceptable for some materials. If you drop frames, choose a frame rate that lets you drop them evenly (that is, choose a final frame rate that evenly divides into the source frame rate). For example, if your source material is at 30 fps, choosing 15 fps when you compress lets you drop every other frame.

Shrink and crop. Full-screen video is not always necessary or even desirable, and it can easily eat up disk space and processing power. For most digital-media projects (including Web-based projects), something smaller than a 640-by-480-pixel frame size is usually practical, and even when it isn't, you can often cut the frame dimensions in half when you compress and then double the frame size for playback. You might also consider cropping the source video before compressing it; most TV producers use a *safe area*, well inset from the edges of the frame, simply because many TVs are not properly adjusted and chop off some of the picture's top, bottom, or sides. If your source material was originally intended for broadcast, a little judicious cropping can save storage space. (Note that many codecs work best when the frame dimensions are even multiples of 4 or 16, so you should crop or shrink the frame with your codec in mind.)

Use high-quality source material. All things being equal, the better your source video, the more efficient (and better-looking) the final compressed version. A codec will compress everything, including distortion and static, and because most codecs tend to look for areas of uniform appearance to compress (either within a frame or within adjacent frames), static makes the codec work harder. If you must capture and compress from VHS tape, don't use long or extended play speeds, since these settings sacrifice more of the picture quality. Compressing from original digital source material is always preferable. And don't even think about recompressing video already compressed for delivery (for example, with Sorenson or MPEG-1). It will take a long time and almost always produces unattractive results.

Trade money for time. For occasional compression tasks on the Mac, QuickTime Pro or RealSystem Producer, from Real (this latter works in Mac OS 9 and Classic only), can often meet your needs. But if you have to do a lot of compression and you don't want to become a dedicated expert, a few strategic investments will save time and effort, and provide better-quality results. "Little big movie—compression programs," later in the chapter, discusses some of the compression programs available.

Compressing Time and Space

Video exists in time (the duration of the video) and space (the size of the frame). Most video-compression schemes therefore work with both time and space when crunching video down to a practical size.

Spatial compressors try to reduce the size of individual frames, using a variety of means (usually lossy)—for example, removing redundant information or combining areas of similar color.

Temporal compressors examine nearby frames and store only the differences between frames. They usually use a *key frame* (which contains a complete image), followed by a sequence of *difference frames* (which contain only data that differs from the key frame); eventually the differences are big enough to warrant the creation of a new key frame.

Most video codecs use both spatial and temporal compression (and a host of other tricks, too).

A Catalog of Video-Compression Formats

As with audio, digital video on the Mac tends to fall into three categories: video for which the QuickTime architecture has a codec (**Figure 17.16**); video that QuickTime can play (decompress) but not create (compress); and third-party proprietary codecs that haven't been licensed (or reverse engineered) for QuickTime at all, which means that QuickTime cannot either decompress or compress them. The formats listed below are the main ones currently available; your particular installation of QuickTime may or may not include them. To get other codecs, either access Apple's Web site through the QuickTime System Preferences or go to the individual developers' Web sites.

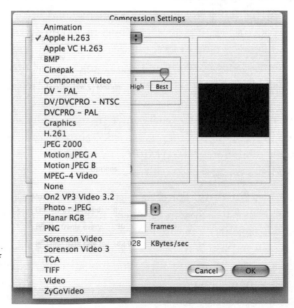

Figure 17.16

Here's a sampling of some of QuickTime Pro's video export choices.

ACT-L (QuickTime has a codec). Designed for high-bandwidth network streaming, Streambox's codecs (there's ACT-L2 and ACT-L3) are an optional QuickTime component: if you open a QuickTime file in one of these formats, QuickTime fetches the codec for you over the Internet. Streambox offers a live ACT-L2 encoder for Apple's QuickTime Broadcaster, which is an application that performs real-time video compression and delivers it to Apple's QuickTime Streaming Server in order to create live broadcasts.

Apple Animation (QuickTime has a codec). Use this for animated materials (especially images with unvarying colored areas and with small differences between frames). The compressor provides several quality settings, and at a 100 percent quality setting it is lossless but can still cut down on size. You'll probably use this as an intermediate format and apply a different compressor to your final product.

Apple None (QuickTime has a codec). Not a codec at all, this provides no compression and creates huge files, but it's good if you need to archive perfect-quality video or apply various filters and effects to it. You want a very fast Mac with a boatload of storage when you work with this one.

Apple Video (QuickTime has a codec). Apple Video was the first QuickTime codec. It compresses quickly and doesn't require much processor power, making it good for tests and quick mock-ups. It compresses at a ratio of about 7:1. You might sometimes hear it referred to by the nickname "Road Pizza" because although it squishes video flat, it isn't very pretty.

Cinepak (QuickTime has a codec). In the early 1990s, this was the leading codec for QuickTime video, providing 10:1 compression ratios. You may not want to use this on new videos because the video quality does not match up with that of more modern codecs (which also produce much smaller files), but it's good to have around for older materials.

DivX (QuickTime has a codec). Not to be confused with the abortive time-limited DVD format, DivX is a free, open-source codec based on MPEG-4 and is very popular among video file-swappers. Movies are usually created in the Windows AVI format, which can be played back by the Windows Media Player on Windows or the QuickTime Player (or any other QuickTime-enabled application) on the Mac, if the DivX codec is installed.

DV (QuickTime has a codec). Digital camcorders use this format, which compresses during filming. The data rate is a fixed 3 MBps, and the format allows you to transfer data between the Mac and the camera via a FireWire connection with no data loss. Apple's iMovie and other video-editing programs use this format, so you can shoot video, edit it on the Mac, transfer it back to the camera, and then show it on your TV. For digital-media projects, you'll usually recompress DV with a tighter codec when you finish editing your video.

H.261 (QuickTime has a codec). H.263's predecessor, it is outdated but still in use by some.

H.263 (QuickTime has a codec). Designed for videoconferencing applications (iChat AV, Apple's videoconferencing software, uses it), this codec compresses quickly and relatively efficiently. It supports only a few discrete frame sizes, and it's best for talking-head material and other video with relatively little change between frames.

Indeo (QuickTime has some codecs for Mac OS 9 or earlier only). First pop-ularized on Windows, Indeo began as a codec for Microsoft's AVI video format. Indeo 3, 4, and 5 are successive versions of the codec but are not inter-changeable; 3 is the oldest and is roughly comparable to Cinepak; 4 and 5 are more-recent developments and are designed to work with a later Microsoft video architecture, DirectShow. Indeo 5 (as one might expect from a codec designed by Intel) takes advantage of the MMX processing available on Pentium CPUs and does not work as smoothly on the Mac (there's no reason why it can't, but if you were Intel, would you go to all that trouble?). The Indeo 3 and 4 codecs are both built into QuickTime for Mac OS 9; an Indeo 5 codec for Mac OS 9 is available separately from Apple. You'll probably want an Indeo codec only if you have a file you want to play that was compressed using it.

M-JPEG (also known as Motion JPEG) (QuickTime has a codec). Not to be confused with MPEG, M-JPEG is a JPEG-based codec, good for capturing, editing, and storing high-quality material. It does only spatial, not temporal, compression, and isn't suited for delivery purposes because the files are quite large compared with those in other formats, and playback consumes lots of processing power and disk throughput. Some *offline* digital editing systems (which are used to create draft videos) use M-JPEG for editing work, though the final cut usually is made from the original uncompressed video in order to achieve the highest quality available.

 Because video consists of a sequence of pictures, it is possible to use any image codec (even those designed for still images) to store video data. QuickTime is especially flexible in this regard: if you want to, QuickTime can store your video as a sequence of Windows bitmapped (BMP format) images! You may not ordinarily need to do something this weird, but it's nice to know you can.

MPEG-1 (QuickTime has a decompressor). The Moving Picture Experts Group developed this standard for both audio and video compression (that's where MP3 came from). It was designed to play high-quality video and audio at data rates around 150 KBps but requires a good deal of processing power to decompress; it originally required additional hardware on an add-in card. Today's fast processors have no problem with its computational requirements, and it is a popular cross-platform format for delivering video but almost useless as an editing format for reasons having to do with the way the video is stored.

MPEG-2 (QuickTime has a decompressor). A successor to MPEG-1, this is the DVD and digital broadcast video/audio format. It uses a higher data rate than its predecessor (between 300 KBps and 1 MBps) and requires even more computational power to decode. Most DVD players and drives have special MPEG-2 decoding hardware to handle the load, although most of today's Macs are powerful enough to decode it entirely in software. Apple's iDVD and DVD Studio Pro packages can produce MPEG-2 files (and even burn them to DVD), and you can purchase an MPEG-2 decoder from Apple for $19.99 (it doesn't come with the standard QuickTime installation).

 The terms *encoding* and *decoding* are not necessarily interchangeable with the terms *compressing* and *decompressing,* respectively. For example, the MPEG-2 standard includes encryption, so compressing/decompressing is only part of the whole process. The terms *encoding* and *decoding* encompass all the various steps.

MPEG-4 (QuickTime has a codec). There are two main versions of the MPEG-4 codec: the legitimate one finalized by the Moving Picture Experts Group (and that both Apple and Real support), and a codec that Microsoft developed, based on an early draft of the standard. Microsoft has since renamed its codec Windows Media Video, but the company achieved its objective: many people now think MPEG-4 is a Microsoft technology. MPEG-4 is actually designed to support audio, video, and interactivity (the MPEG-4 file format, in fact, is based upon the QuickTime architecture). Apple is increasingly using and promoting MPEG-4. Its quality is roughly comparable to that of Sorenson at similar data rates. QuickTime Pro can export both QuickTime movies using the MPEG-4 video codecs, and MPEG-4 files, which can be played by any MPEG-4–capable player, such as Real Player (free; www.real.com) or QuickTime Player. Because MPEG-4 is an evolving standard, however, some players may not be able to display all the various profiles that MPEG-4 can create.

On2 VP3 (QuickTime has a codec). An optional QuickTime component, On2 VP3 (free; www.vp3.com) was formerly a proprietary codec but is now open source. It compresses video well at low bandwidths and is a reasonable choice for Web and broadband uses if you don't mind your users' having to download the codec first.

RealVideo (unavailable to QuickTime). Like RealAudio, this codec is designed for the RealOne player, and it primarily distributes streaming video. The video codec, based on Intel's Indeo Video Interactive codec, is quite scalable: Real's HelixServer can selectively drop information from the Real video stream to accommodate narrow bandwidths or network congestion, giving good results at a wide range of connection speeds. On the Mac (but only in Classic), RealSystem Producer (free; www.realnetworks.com), an authoring package for creating Real audio and video presentations, converts QuickTime (or other) video files to Real video format. The package is no longer supported and may be hard to find on Real's site, but it is still available as we go to press.

Sorenson (QuickTime has codecs). Sorenson 3 provides very tight compression and is particularly good at low data rates; you can get very respectable results at rates as low as 10 KBps. Conversely, at data rates higher than 100 KBps, the codec begins to impose a considerable load on the processor, especially compared with the quality of results you get in return. Sorenson takes a lot more time to compress than to decompress, and compressing can be slow even on a dual-processor G4 (we haven't seen it on a G5 yet). It is still the current standard QuickTime video codec for Web delivery and streaming video. A $299 Pro version is available from Sorenson Media (www.sorenson.com); it compresses faster, takes advantage of the G4 and G5 Velocity Engines, and provides a wealth of compression options. Version 2 of Sorenson Video came with QuickTime 4, and QuickTime 5 added Sorenson Video 3, a more-advanced compression format that provides substantially better performance. Both codecs are still included in QuickTime 6.

Windows Media (unavailable to QuickTime). Microsoft's Windows Media Player for the Mac can play some, but not all, of the Windows Media family of codecs. If you really want to use this in your digital-media projects, you may be reading the wrong book.

ZyGoVideo (QuickTime has a codec). An optional free QuickTime component, ZyGoVideo uses wavelet transformations (a mathematical technique) to compress video. Results are roughly comparable to those of MPEG-4; it works especially well for video that contains text or sharp edges. You can download ZyGoVideo for free from Apple's Web site using the QuickTime System Preferences.

Playing Video

Each of the three major desktop-video architectures (QuickTime, Real, and Windows Media) comes with its own free player.

Real Player. Real's player provides access to RealVideo streaming content. It claims superior video performance; it offers more-sophisticated audio- and video-playback controls than earlier versions; and it can, like QuickTime Player, show MPEG-4 video natively (**Figure 17.17**).

Figure 17.17

The RealOne Player is free, but we'd want it even if it weren't.

Windows Media Player. Microsoft's player provides basic playing capabilities for various Microsoft formats not otherwise available on the Mac. The player can also handle old-style QuickTime video (before version 3).

QuickTime Player. As the name implies, this will play your QuickTime files, and it plays many other formats as well. Upgrading to QuickTime Pro (as the player will occasionally annoy you about doing) costs $29.99, though the price buys you little above the free player's capabilities when it comes to playing video (the Pro version *does* let you choose a full-screen presentation mode). What the money buys beyond that is access to editing features, format conversion, compression … in other words, a complete basic tool kit for QuickTime editing and multimedia construction.

Because QuickTime is a system-level architecture, a fair number of developers have put together QuickTime-enabled movie players.

Ambroise Confetti's **Cellulo** (free; www.cellulo.info) presents an iTunes-like interface where you can play any file for which QuickTime has a codec (**Figure 17.18**).

Figure 17.18

Ambroise Confetti's Cellulo looks like iTunes but it plays back video.

From Germany, Monkeybread Software brings you **Desktop Movie Player** and **Full Screen Movie Player** (free; www.monkeybreadsoftware.de). The latter lets you play QuickTime movies full screen, even without QuickTime Pro; the former will play a movie on your Desktop behind the Finder's icons and window (though we are not sure why that's a good thing).

Based on the Linux MPlayer movie player, the open-source **MPlayer OS X** (free; http://sourceforge.net/projects/mplayerosx) is able to play almost any movie file type, including Real media and Windows ASF format (Advanced Streaming Format, Microsoft's proprietary answer to the open-standard real-time streaming protocol—RTSP—used by QuickTime and Real).

BitPlayer (free; www.tanjero.com) can catalog, create playlists, and perform batch exports of movies using QuickTime.

For playing video from live sources like Webcams or video cameras, look at **Video Viewer** ($9; www.schubert-it.com). It can also capture still frames and present video in a floating window, in the Dock, or as the Desktop picture.

Trailerpark QT ($12.50; http://home.bluemarble.net/~anarchoi/trailerparkqt) lets you drag and drop folders to build playlists of QuickTime and other media files, which it can then play in a floating window.

Lap Theater

For those who have a DVD-ROM drive or a SuperDrive in their Macs, Apple's DVD Player can turn even an unassuming iBook into a high-quality DVD player. The software provides all the basic DVD Player functions: slow motion, step, chapter navigation, and subtitles. The controller is easy to use and goes away when you don't want it cluttering up the screen. DVD Player can be controlled and enhanced by AppleScripts to give you extra features. You can also play movies full screen, which on a 17-inch PowerBook can be a breathtaking experience.

Making Video

Now that you've learned all about video compression and video formats, it's time to have some fun and make your own video. Apple provides iMovie to help you, but there are also a batch of other video editors available as well. Here's how to capture, edit, and share your videos.

Making video with iMovie

iMovie is to digital video cameras what iPhoto is to digital still cameras: the easiest way to use your high-tech toy with your Mac. It comes as one of the programs in the $49 iLife package from Apple or free with your new Mac. The price is definitely right, but you may need to save your money to buy additional hard-disk space: iMovie only edits DV-format video, and 5 minutes of DV can eat up more than a gigabyte of storage.

It connects. Plug a FireWire-equipped digital video camera into your Mac and iMovie takes over from there, sucking the video down the cable right to your Mac's hard disk and breaking it up into individual clips, based upon when you paused the camera as you shot your video. When you finish editing, slap a fresh tape in your camera and iMovie sends your finished production out to tape. The program's onscreen controls let you operate the camera's transport mechanism with a few clicks.

It arranges. Editing in iMovie is simple: just drag your clips into the order in which you want them (**Figure 17.19**). If you need to trim a clip, you just drag the playhead to where you want to trim, split the clip into two clips, and throw away the piece you don't want. iMovie also has a more traditional time-line editor view that gives you finer control over your editing and allows you to add sound tracks. You can also separate the sound track from the video, edit it, and manipulate its volume.

It enhances. iMovie comes with a rich assortment of transitions that you can drag between your clips—fades, dissolves, wipes, and warps, among others— and each one comes with a set of custom controls. There's also a nice collection of visual effects, including fog, rain, aged film, and fairy dust (**Figure 17.20**). And there are sound effects, too: iMovie has an eclectic assortment from Skywalker Sound as well as some old standards from previous versions of iMovie. Several vendors offer additional visual and audio effects and transitions for iMovie—see www.apple.com/imovie for links to some of them. You can also record your own voice-overs directly into iMovie if you have a microphone, or your own talking-head image with your iSight camera, and you can superimpose titles in various layouts over the video. iMovie isn't a full-blown postproduction suite, but it sure offers a lot of value for the price.

Video-clip library

Figure 17.19

In iMovie you simply drag and drop your clips in the order in which you want to view them.

Toggle for editing video
Toggle for capturing video
Adjust audio and video timing
Add and arrange clips

Movie sequence

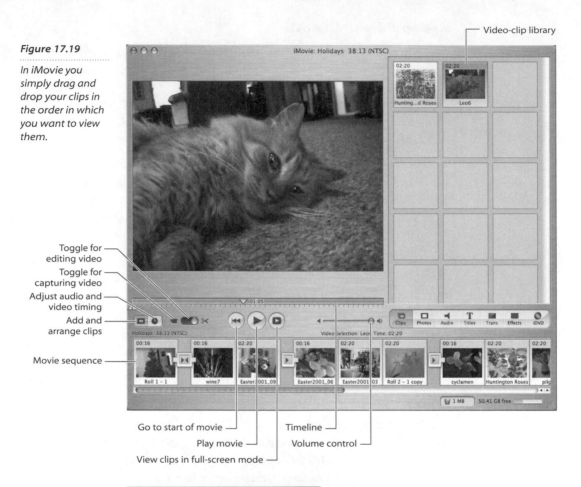

Go to start of movie
Play movie
View clips in full-screen mode
Timeline
Volume control

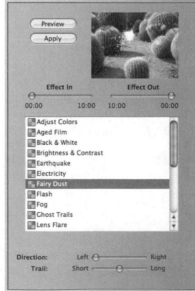

Figure 17.20

iMovie can sprinkle fairy dust on your videos.

It shares. As you would expect from a program that's part of the iLife suite, iMovie is well aware of its digital-media brethren. You can listen to any song from your iTunes library (including songs you've exported from GarageBand) and add it as background music to your video. Similarly, you can see and add any photo from your iPhoto library. What's more, iMovie provides the *Ken Burns effect* for still images, so you, just like the documentary filmmaker for whom it is named, can artfully pan and zoom over your snapshots. iMovie shares with iDVD, too, allowing you to quickly send off your masterpiece to be burned to a DVD-ROM for the delectation of your family, friends, and Hollywood agent.

Grabbing at light—capturing video

With FireWire as a standard Mac accoutrement, Apple has made video capture much easier. Between iMovie and FireWire, the Mac has sparked a desktop-video revolution that may rival the desktop-publishing revolution.

Setting up for capture. Today's Macs have fast processors and large, speedy hard disks, but video capture can tax even those. It is still prudent to take a few steps to ensure a flawless capture.

- Quit CPU-intensive applications and network connections (in Mac OS 9, disable all unnecessary extensions, too). Some programs (and extensions) work continually in the background, taking small chunks of processing time away from the capture process. For example, if you have AppleTalk turned on, the Mac will be checking the network periodically, and while it's doing that, it won't be working on your video.

- Capture your video at the final frame *size* you wish to use. If you're planning to show your video in a 180-by-120-pixel window, it doesn't make sense to capture it at a larger size; this will merely consume extra disk space and processing time. Worse, if you plan to show your video in, say, a 360-by-240 window and you capture it at 180 by 120, it will look terrible scaled up.

- Capture your video at the final frame *rate* you wish to use. You should capture video at some even divisor of the TV standard—30 fps—for the best playback. Usually 15 fps is a good choice. Otherwise, you may encounter jerky motion, dropped frames, and other oddities.

Capturing digital video with FireWire. Here's the simplest way: Connect your DV camera and your Mac with a FireWire cable. Click iMovie's Import button. There's no step three.

But iMovie may not be everyone's cup of tea. Although it's simple, that simplicity comes at the price of eliminating many useful capture options. If you'd like a bit more control over your captures, download Apple's free **HackTV** (http://developer.apple.com). Written as an example for developers who want to learn how to do QuickTime programming, this unassuming application provides enough basic capture options to suit the casual user's needs: frame size, frame rate, audio-capturing format, and more.

Capturing analog video. Capturing video from a non-FireWire device usually requires a capture card to digitize the video; if your Mac has slots, you may want to look into getting one of them. These days, most capture cards are aimed at high-end professional users and tend to be rather pricey; expect to pay $500 or more for the lower-end cards, with the price (and capability) rising swiftly from there.

But there is an analog capture solution for those with FireWire Macs who aren't members of the professional video fraternity or who don't have a Mac with slots: a FireWire analog-to-digital converter. Among others, Canopus makes the **ADVC100** ($299; www.canopus.us), and Formac sells the **Studio DV** ($199; www.formac.com).

Finally, if you have a FireWire Mac and a DV camera that accepts analog input (and many do), you're in business: just dub your analog video onto a DV tape in your camera and transfer that video to the Mac. Once again, there's no step three.

Hollywood, here I come!—video editors

Editing can involve anything from simply trimming the ends of captured videos to overlaying multiple images, adding floating captions, adding complex dissolves and wipes, mixing sound tracks—in short, full-on professional work. The Mac has editing tools that span the range.

The Versatile QuickTime Player

Among QuickTime Pro's many capabilities are its media-integration and editing tools. The QuickTime Player lets you cut and paste tracks and track sections; adjust their placement, orientation, and size; and modify their time scale. QuickTime Pro also offers extensive support for AppleScripts, making it possible to automate the building of complex multimedia projects. A description of all of QuickTime Pro's features could fill a book, and in fact it has: *QuickTime 6 for Macintosh and Windows: Visual QuickStart Guide,* by Judith Stern and Robert Lettieri (Peachpit Press).

At the low end are a number of shareware and low-cost commercial products. **BTV Pro** ($40; www.bensoftware.com) can both capture and edit video, and it provides stop-action animation tools. Mien Network produces **Media Edit Pro** ($79.99; www.miennetwork.com), which both edits video and lets you paint directly on it. For a limited time, video-editing powerhouse Avid is giving away its **Avid Free DV** (free; www.avid.com) video editor; the deal may still be in place by the time you read this. **Montage,** from Arboretum ($149; www.arboretum.com), edits video and audio, provides effects and titling tools, and can even do time stretching.

Slightly more expensive is U&I Software's **VTrack** eight-track video editor and sequencer ($249; www.uisoftware.com); Apple has a slightly scaled-back version of its Final Cut package, **Final Cut Express** ($299; www.apple.com/finalcutexpress), designed for the digital video–editing prosumer. (*Prosumer* is a term used by many technology companies to describe a user who has higher-end needs than the casual consumer but fewer needs than the true professional.)

Climbing up the price mountain, we find Avid's **Avid Xpress DV** ($695; www.avid.com) package, which offers full editing capabilities, color correction, real-time effects, and Avid's own DV codec.

Apple has its own entry in the professional arena: **Final Cut Pro 4** ($999; www.apple.com/finalcutpro). This program builds upon QuickTime to add real production value, including media-management tools, real-time compositing and effects (by way of supported PCI cards), support for Adobe After Effects filters, built-in compression tools, and Soundtrack, a music-composition tool. And of course it has all the capabilities of its competitors in this price range.

As we step up to a higher price plateau, we find **Media 100**'s set of professional editing packages (www.media100.com). The hardware-and-software packages in the Media 100 i product line range in price from $1,995 to $4,995. For the money you get the ability to edit almost any format of video, produce interactive streaming output, and generally work in the big leagues.

Finally, Avid's line of digital video–editing products is still the Hollywood standard, with Hollywood-style prices. Its **Media Composer** products, commonly used in commercial broadcast production, cost around $12,000 for a basic system for offline work, but prices, and options, go up quickly from there.

Little big movie—compression programs

Video wants to be big. But it needs to be small, if it is to fit on Web pages or even DVDs. That's why there are so many codecs for video. If you work with video a lot, you'll find yourself compressing it a lot. Here are some packages to help you with that process.

Totally Hip (and we just *love* that name) produces **HipFlics** ($49.95; www.totallyhip.com), which uses QuickTime's built-in codecs for compressing. It provides batch processing, custom presets, and cropping, and you can even use multiple codecs in a single movie.

Compressing with QuickTime Pro

If you pay Apple the $29.99 fee to upgrade QuickTime Player to the Pro version, you get access to the File menu's Export command, your gateway to QuickTime's compression features.

To use these features, open an audio or video file and export it. In the Save File dialog, you'll see two pop-up menus. The first, Export, lets you save the file in a variety of file formats (including some popular Windows formats). The second, Use, offers a list of prepackaged settings for compression and export. The available presets change depending on the export format you choose; the QuickTime movie settings provide several useful presets for streaming movies (**Figure 17.21**).

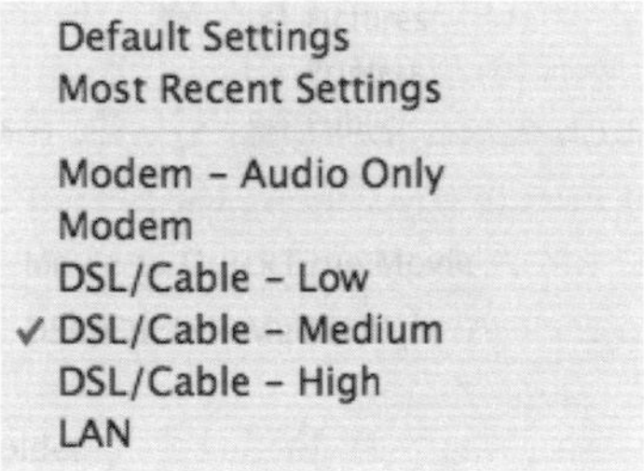

Figure 17.21

QuickTime Pro provides prepackaged settings for compressing files. These are your options for streaming movies.

```
Default Settings
Most Recent Settings

Modem – Audio Only
Modem
DSL/Cable – Low
✓ DSL/Cable – Medium
DSL/Cable – High
LAN
```

And if that isn't enough control for you, click the Options button in the Save File dialog. This brings up a dialog where you can specify exact settings for video and audio compression, as well as set detailed streaming options. If you're a pro on a limited budget, you shouldn't do without QuickTime Pro.

Sorenson, the company that made the Sorenson codecs for QuickTime, sells a compression package called the **Sorenson Squeeze Compression Suite** ($449; www.sorenson.com). It can do variable bit-rate compression (the number of bits used to encode each second of video varies depending on the complexity of the video being compressed, which can often produce superior results but takes longer when compressing), produces high-quality MPEG-4 as well as Sorenson output, and offers a number of filters for both audio and video. It even compresses video for use in Macromedia's Flash MX 2004 (see "Animation," later in the chapter). **Cleaner 6**, from Discreet ($549; www.discreet.com), is a sound investment: this product *knows* compression inside and out, providing a wide variety of built-in settings and wizards to get the best results possible. It can create QuickTime files; MPEG-1, -2, and -4 files; and even Kinoma files for video on handheld devices. If you run it in Classic, you can also compress to Real format and Windows Media. Cleaner handles batch processing, so you can sleep the sleep of the just while your Mac toils all night long compressing files.

Sharing Video

What's the point of making a great video if no one sees it (aside from juicing up your karma a smidgeon)? Here's some help dealing with video distribution—technically, that is; the economics of it are, thankfully, none of our concern.

Gently down the stream—delivering video on the Internet

First, unless you've been specifically asked, *do not email video*! Video is big, mailboxes are small, connection speeds can be slow, and your recipients will not thank you for it. If you put your video on a Web site, you can email a URL and your recipients can view the video whenever they like.

There are two main ways in which video is delivered via the Web: *streaming* and *downloading*.

Streaming video requires a special server, like Apple's QuickTime Streaming Server. The server establishes a connection with the client (such as a Web browser with the QuickTime plug-in or QuickTime Player itself) and then feeds the video to the client just as fast, but no faster, than the client can receive it (**Figure 17.22**). A streaming file must not send more data each second than the client can receive, which means that for a typical DSL connection, the file's data rate can't go much above 50 KBps (for a modem connection, it can't go higher than 5 KBps). If it does, the video gets choppy, frames are dropped, and the audience utters a great big "Yecchh!" The big advantage of streaming: the file never ends up on the user's machine in its entirety, which helps to protect against copyright infringement.

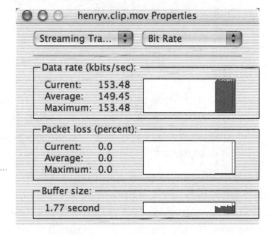

Figure 17.22

QuickTime Pro can show you a variety of streaming statistics.

Downloading means that the entire file is sent to the user. In the case of downloadable files viewed in a Web browser, the files are usually hidden somewhere in the browser's cache and are automatically discarded after they are viewed, but they are still, at some point, entirely on the user's machine. The big advantage to downloading is that the file's data rate is not restricted by the connection speed: even if you have a modem connection, you can view a file that plays at 100 KBps—you'll just have to wait a while before it starts playing. QuickTime employs a feature called *progressive download*, which means that the file starts playing as soon as enough of it has arrived for it to play through to the end without pausing. For example, a 30-second file that plays at a rate twice as fast as the connection speed will start playing after 15 seconds even though the whole file hasn't yet arrived; it will have arrived by the time the end is reached. This is how Apple presents movie trailers on its site (www.apple.com/trailers).

Apple has a fine set of tutorials at www.apple.com/quicktime/tools_tips that go into the various ways you can deliver QuickTime video over the Web. It's well worth a visit. If you need to deliver video in another format, you'll have to look elsewhere, though ... but why would you want to? QuickTime *rocks!*

One-Eyed Macs Are Wild—iChat AV

Apple has made it possible for you to stream live video over the Internet right from your Mac—to an audience of one. The program is iChat AV (www.apple.com/ichat), an enhancement to Apple's instant-messaging program that provides the ability to engage in audio and video chat sessions with other iChat AV users. All you need is the software (free with Mac OS X 10.3 and $29 for Mac OS X 10.2 users) and a FireWire camera to provide the video.

Apple will even sell you the camera: it has released a tiny, lightweight $149 camera called the iSight, which mounts on your computer and plugs into the FireWire port. There is nothing else to set up. Plug in the camera, launch iChat AV, and start talking. Just remember to put on some clothes and comb your hair first.

Putting video on disc

Probably the best way to distribute high-quality versions of the videos you make is to put them on optical media, like CDs or DVDs. (If you want to put your videos on tape, you can connect a VCR to one of the analog-to-digital converters mentioned in "Grabbing at light—capturing video," earlier in the chapter.)

Putting video on an ordinary CD is extraordinarily simple if you have a Mac with a CD burner (and, these days, they almost all have one). Simply put a CD-R in the drive, drag your video files over to the disc, and burn it using the Burn Disc command in the Finder's File menu. The disc will be compatible with both Macs and Windows computers.

You will need to use commercial disc-burning software if you wish to produce a Video CD (VCD) or Super Video CD (SVCD). These formats are popular with hobbyists and are common in Asia; many commercial DVD players can play them. A VCD uses video in MPEG-1 format, while SVCD uses MPEG-2. Both formats use an ordinary CD-R, rather than a more-expensive DVD-R. Roxio's **Toast Titanium** ($99.95; www.roxio.com) will burn VCDs and SVCDs.

If you want to burn a DVD but have a DVD burner other than Apple's SuperDrive in your Mac, you won't be able to use Apple's iDVD (see below). You can, however, burn video DVDs with Toast Titanium. Charismac's **Discribe** ($69.95; www.charismac.com) also can burn video DVDs.

iDVD (an iLife application). iDVD comes with every Mac that has a built-in SuperDrive, as well as being included in the iLife package, and it's all you need to burn a video DVD—or even a data DVD, for that matter. The program integrates with iMovie, iPhoto, and iTunes to let you build DVDs that contain movies, photo slide shows, and data files. It comes with a multitude of beautiful and dramatic templates for interactive DVD menus, which you can modify and enhance (**Figure 17.23**). There's not much more to it than that—iDVD is meant to be as simple as its results are impressive.

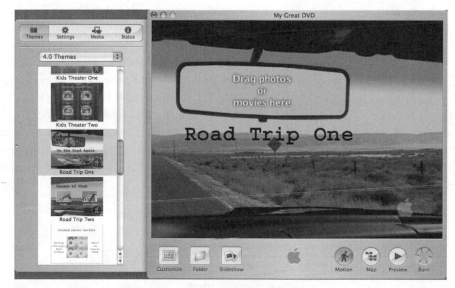

Figure 17.23

iDVD can build a good-looking DVD menu, which lets you select which video, or portion of a movie, you want to view.

If you need a more full-featured DVD authoring solution, check out Apple's professional-grade **DVD Studio Pro** ($499; www.apple.com). It can handle 99 video tracks, eight audio streams, and multiple language tracks, and can support projects up to 9 GB in size.

Other Visual Media

Besides audio, video, and digital photos, your Mac can play host to a variety of other types of digital media—for example, animation, 3D graphics, and virtual reality panoramas. Here's what you need to know about each of these.

Animation

Animation involves drawing pictures—lots of them—and then assembling them in the right order and showing them rapidly enough to fool the eye into seeing motion. Much of what you see on your Mac's screen is animation: the bouncing Dock icons, the genie effect of minimizing windows, the floating pointer, and the spinning wait pointer (the rainbow-colored spinning ball). In this case it is the Mac OS that draws the pictures, assembles them, and shows them, and this highlights an important point: the Mac is a natural home to animation.

Digital Termite Terrace—understanding animation

"Termite Terrace" was the nickname that the Warner Bros. cartoon artists of the mid-20th century used for their less-than-palatial offices on the studio lot. There you could find animators, in-betweeners, inkers, painters, and background artists plying their crafts: animators drew their characters and other moving objects in key positions using pencil and paper; in-betweeners (often apprentice animators) drew the frames in between each key position; inkers and painters copied these pencil drawings to transparent sheets of celluloid (called *cels*) and colored them in; background artists painted backgrounds upon which the cels were placed one by one and photographed; and voilà— soon another 7½-minute masterpiece was playing in theaters around America.

All these tasks can now be performed digitally, and many of them can be automated, but animation still involves drawing key positions, in-betweening, coloring, and layering images over a background. All that's missing are the termites.

Flash dance—playing animation

Many animations are converted into other forms, such as QuickTime, RealVideo, or Windows Media videos, so you will need the correct player to view these animations. Other animations are presented as *animated GIFs*, a variation on the graphic GIF format that allows multiple frames to be included in a GIF file and to be played back when presented in a Web browser or other GIF-compatible player (such as QuickTime Player); many Web advertisements use animated GIFs.

However, two media formats designed for presenting animations, both developed by Macromedia (www.macromedia.com), are very common: ShockWave and Flash. The **ShockWave Player** (free; http://sdc.shockwave.com) plays Macromedia Director files that have been *shocked*—that is, designed for Web delivery; the player is actually a Web-browser plug-in. Similarly, Macromedia's **Flash Player** (free; http://sdc.schockwave.com) is a browser plug-in that plays files in the extremely popular Flash format; after animated GIFs, Flash is the most widely available animation format on the Web.

 Macromedia has made the Flash file format available to other developers, allowing QuickTime Player, for example, to play Flash files directly. Third-party Flash players such as QuickTime Player, though, can seldom play files in Macromedia's most recent version of Flash, since the developers of these players cannot begin to work on supporting the latest version of Flash until well after Macromedia has released it. When in doubt, install the most recent Flash plug-in.

Adobe offers a competitor to the Flash format: SVG. Based on an open XML standard, SVG has yet to achieve anything approaching the ubiquity of Flash. Nonetheless, if you are interested in viewing Web animation, you'll want to add the **SVG Viewer** (free; www.adobe.com/svg) to your plug-in collection.

Tween wolf—making animation

You will want at least one good drawing program if you plan to do any serious animation work, and you can find recommendations for a bunch of those in Chapter 13. But you'll also need a program to help you assemble the drawings you make into animations.

Jeremy Wood, a student at the University of Tulsa, describes his **Flipmovie** ($20; www.personal.utulsa.edu/~jeremy-wood/software) as "a modest tool to combine still frames into animations." It also provides cropping, titles, and layering capabilities.

iStopMotion (free; www.istopmotion.com), from Boinx Software, works with uncompressed images in order to maintain high quality. It has features that let you examine and tune your 'toon, such as onion-skin (a faint view of a drawing that you can trace over) and blink (swiftly alternating between two images, such as two consecutive frames of animation, so that you can see their similarities and differences). iStopMotion can also link to external graphics editors. The program can control a digital camera for stop-motion work and comes with an interesting licensing scheme: it's free for small animations (320 by 240 pixels) but costs $39.95 for a DV-quality version.

Loud Inc. offers **Loud Animation Studio** ($129; www.loudinc.com), which is aimed at digital animators and art students. It can control a digital video camera for stop-action work, does onion-skinning and flicker previews (which are the same as blink), and can show audio waveforms to help with synchronizing sound to video.

From Toon Boom Technologies comes **Toon Boom Studio** ($374, $144 for students; www.toonboom.com) and **Toon Boom Studio Express** ($144). The full Toon Boom Studio comes with built-in vector drawing tools, sound-clip editing tools, lip-synch tools, and 3D scene-layout tools that scale and position drawings. It can output finished work to Flash and QuickTime formats. The Express package has many of the same tools but is designed for short animations (fewer than 1000 frames) and can output to either Flash or iMovie.

Although **Macromedia Flash** ($499; www.macromedia.com) is the most popular animation-development package for creating Web-based interactive-media presentations, it is also widely used just for its animation-creation power. The latest version, Flash MX 2004, has extensive drawing tools (**Figure 17.24**), a powerful timeline view, tweening capabilities, layering, anti-aliased text support, and media object libraries. It can incorporate digital video, audio, and a variety of image formats in addition to its own vector artwork.

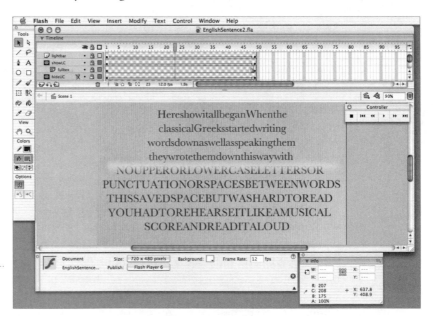

Figure 17.24

Flash has its own extensive set of drawing tools.

Macromedia Director ($1,199) is designed for creating "heavier" interactive media for CD, DVD, and intranet delivery, but it, too, has a rich assortment of animation capabilities. Director MX 2004 has vector drawing tools, precise sound controls, support for more than 40 media types, and a whole lot (a *whole whole lot*) more.

Adobe After Effects ($699), now in version 6, is the must-have professional tool for creating motion graphics (that's animation, kids) that will be incorporated into video. Text animation, visual effects, and lighting tools are its particular strong points, and its vector drawing tools, as well as tight integration with Adobe's other graphics creation products, only make it stronger.

Space Media—3D and VR

Virtual reality and 3D modeling both attempt to break the boundaries of the two-dimensional display to create an illusion of depth and space. Though just a few years ago the Mac was something of an afterthought in the 3D world, Mac OS X's OpenGL 3D graphics engine, along with advances in the Mac's hardware, have made it a player to be reckoned with.

Understanding 3D and VR

Three-D modeling software uses the magic of mathematics—lots of mathematics—to create images that can be viewed from various angles and can be animated. Artists construct their models using *primitive* shapes (spheres, cylinders, cubes, cones, and the like) and *polygons* (multisided shapes that are mathematically defined). These shapes are then altered, reshaped, and *rendered*—that is, colored, dressed with textures, and lit using complex algorithms with names like *phong shading* and *ray tracing*, a process that requires a great deal of computation. The finished models can be viewed from a number of angles. If you've played any computer games in the last decade or so, you've seen more than a few 3D models.

Take video and turn it inside out, and you have *virtual reality:* a bunch of pictures viewed all at once, forming a complete environment. Often called VR, especially by those who have gotten tired of having to say something as ungainly as "virtual reality" all the time, this medium usually begins as a series of still images— drawn or photographed—that are *stitched* together to form a complete environment that you can view and seemingly move through by means of a viewing program that is (surprise!) capable of viewing such things. VR often makes use of 3D models to create a virtual space through which you can navigate. QuickTime's ability to store a sequence of pictures that can be randomly accessed, which is so useful for presenting video and animation, can also be used to create virtual spaces; QuickTime VR provides both a user interface and an underlying file structure to implement such spaces. There are other VR technologies on the Mac, but QuickTime VR is the most common. To learn more about QuickTime VR, visit Apple's Web site at www.apple.com/quicktime/qtvr.

Viewing 3D and VR

There are dozens of 3D file formats running around in the wild, and it would be inconvenient and frustrating if you needed separate players to view each type.

Fortunately, in most cases you don't need a special player to view 3D models, since the models tend to be animated and used in the context of video presentations or, most commonly, in games where the 3D model viewer is an integral part of the game itself.

At one time Apple had its own 3D technology—QuickDraw 3D—which had its own file format, called *3DMF.* If you run across a 3DMF file (and it is possible, since developers other than Apple adopted the format), you can view it with **3DMF Viewer** ($10; http://alphaomega.software.free.fr) from AlphaOmega Software. **Geo3D** (free; www.topoi.ch) also displays 3DMF files for Mac OS 9 or Classic users. You can view *DXF* files (DXF is another 3D file format used by programs such as AutoCAD) with White Box's **SMViewer** (free; http://s.sudre.free.fr).

VR on the Mac usually comes in the form of QuickTime VR files (**Figure 17.25**), which can be viewed on the Mac with QuickTime Player or the QuickTime Plug-in, which is automatically installed when you install QuickTime. Another VR format you may run across is *VRML* (Virtual Reality Modeling Language); **Cortona VRML Client for Mac OS X** (contact for price; www.parallelgraphics.com) is a browser plug-in viewer for VRML files.

Figure 17.25

A QuickTime VR panorama lets you move around in a landscape as though you are actually there.

Making 3D and VR

We won't kid you—it's not easy to create 3D objects or VR landscapes. If you want to create 3D images, there are several packages available that vary widely in cost and complexity. Unfortunately, you have very few choices when it comes to VR software.

3D modeling. Applications for 3D modeling and animating on the Mac range in cost from completely free all the way up to a sell-a-spare-kidney buy-in.

Peter Eastman's **Art of Illusion** (free; http://aoi.sourceforge.net) is an open-source Java package that offers 3D modeling and rendering. Its features include multiple cameras (so that you can view the model from different positions), primitives, multiple lights, and textures. As a Java application, it's not the speediest tortoise in the race, and, being open source, it is constantly under development, but the price is right if you want to get your toes wet in the 3D sea.

Amphorium, from Electric Image ($149; www.electricimage.com), provides 3D modeling and animating abilities and can output to QuickTime and Flash. The interface for creating models has been described as being tactile and rather like sculpting with clay.

Eovia's **Carrara Studio** ($399; www.eovia.com) provides both photo-realistic and non-photo-realistic modeling. The interface is divided into *rooms* (Modeling, Assembling, Texture, Animation, and Rendering) to help simplify the creative process.

Ashlar Vellum (www.ashlar-vellum.com) produces a variety of 3D applications, ranging from **Neon** ($595), for basic 3D creation and editing intended for Web and publishing uses, all the way up to its high-end **Cobalt** ($3,995), for those who need 3D models for product design and engineering purposes.

NewTek's **LightWave 3D** ($1,595; www.newtek.com) offers a real-time subdivision surface modeler and a motion mixer; its renderer features lighting effects such as caustics and radiosity, HyperVoxels (a sort of 3D pixel for creating complex surfaces like smoke or fire), and hair and fur rendering.

Alias's **Maya Complete** ($1,999; www.alias.com) provides polygons, NURBS (*Non-Uniform Rational B-Splines,* a mathematical representation of a three-dimensional object), and subdivision surface tools; its character-animation tools include forward and reverse kinematics, skinning, and deformers. If you are already a 3D fan, you'll probably know what these features are. But if you just want to try out the program, you can get Alias's **Maya Personal Learning Edition** for free—it provides most of Maya Complete's features but adds watermarks to all the program's output.

VR creation. The number of VR-creation tools on the Mac is rather small, even though QuickTime VR presentations are becoming ever more common. Apple does not seem to have much confidence in its own technology: its **QuickTime VR Authoring Studio** ($395; www.apple.com/quicktime/qtvr), which provides panorama stitching and object-making tools, works only in Mac OS 9 or Classic.

If you want a native Mac OS X QuickTime VR solution, you'll have to look to a third-party developer, VR Toolbox. Its **VR Worx** ($299; www.vrtoolbox.com) features drag-and-drop panorama building and distortion correction, and is cheaper than Apple's own offering.

Click Here Design (www.clickheredesign.com.au) sells two utilities that you can use once you've made a QuickTime VR. **CubicConverter** ($69) converts cylindrical panoramas into cubic VRs (which provide 360 degrees of viewing vertically as well as horizontally), and **CubicConnector** ($79) creates multi-node VRs (which have hot spots you click to move to a different place in the VR space) from a set of cubic VRs.

Interactive Media

As a certain chef puts it, let's kick it up a notch. Making music, making movies, making animations (either 2D or 3D) … all that's fun, but when you get to combine them into something you or your audience can *actively* enjoy, well, that's even more fun.

Interactive media is about two things: putting different media together and making something with them that the audience can control. A simple Web page is a form of interactive media: text and pictures are combined into a single document, and the user can click links to go to other pages.

A Web page, though, is just one of many ways to combine media and give the audience a way to control them. Creative developers, artists, and authors come up with new ways all the time. However, most of those ways are built upon metaphors that fall into a few general categories:

- **The slide show.** Slide shows typically consist of one frame of text and/or graphics (maybe including a visual effect and some sound) followed by another. For example, in many business meetings *<click>* or product briefings you can find *<click>* the interactive slide-show technique *<click>* used to make a series of points. The presenter, of course, is the only one with control here, though slide-show presentations can be distributed so that each member of the audience gets a copy and thus becomes both the audience and the presenter.

- **The book (or stack of cards).** Interactive books arrange their content in a series of virtual pages, which are usually designed to fit the screen (that is, without scroll bars); users can read through them, going from one page to the next, or leaf randomly through them. Booklike interactive media usually provide interactive tables of contents that let readers go to specific sections, and they tend to be used when there are large amounts of information that need to be arranged and presented—as in a book.

- **The movie.** These are collections of time-based media. The audience plays them, but not passively. Interactive movies often offer the audience ways to select and play the various media they contain. Computer action games, in a sense, can be considered extremely elaborate examples of interactive movies.

- **The web of objects.** A web of objects combines several of the various other interactive-media metaphors. A click can take you to a slide show, which, when it concludes, can take you to an interactive movie that might pause and give you the opportunity to read an interactive booklet on some related topic, and so on.

Tracking Your Tracks

There's one digital-media problem that doesn't get enough attention: how to keep track of all your various image, sound, and video files. This problem is sometimes called *digital asset management*. (Now you know why the problem doesn't get enough attention: with a name like that, it sounds like a boring keep-your-sock-drawer-organized kind of problem.) If you are willing to do just a little work and maybe spend just a little money, investigate the programs that can help you track all your digital assets—your clippings, sound files, pictures, drawings, movies, and such. (Apple's iTunes and iPhoto, for example, can help you track sound and picture assets.) But without spending any money, and armed with nothing more than what comes with your Mac, some common sense, and a soupçon of foresight, you can make the task of managing your media assets easier.

Take advantage of what Mac OS X's own filing system does for you (Mac OS 9 users, feel free to play along; you can pretty much imitate this by creating a few folders). Inside your home directory you'll find a Documents folder. That's a really good place to keep folders containing text files, project notes, and some media projects—but not all your media. That's because there are a few other folders that many of Apple's programs, as well as third-party programs, also tend to use as holding bins for some of the files the application needs to run. The Movies folder is a perfect place to put movie project folders (just ask iMovie). The Pictures folder is a great hangout for folders that hold artwork files (it's good enough for iPhoto). And the Music folder is not a bad place for collections of sound files—at least iTunes seems to think so. Keeping your media sorted out among these folders will help you to find things as your media collection grows. And grow it will.

Name things sensibly and consistently. When you name your media files, try to use one to three short, *specific* descriptive words to describe the content ("wedding breakfast," "slow guitar solo" are sensible; "vacation picture," "second movie" are less so)—long filenames are harder to see in Open and Save dialogs and they can be a pain to search. Using a number or a date in the filename as well as a short descriptive phrase can help you find things in alphabetical lists ("02 wedding breakfast," "blues jam 6-24-2003"), which is how Mac OS X's column-view windows like to show things.

Don't fight the system. If iTunes, iPhoto, or some other program likes to keep its things organized on your disk in a certain way, let it. If you need to move a file somewhere else for a particular project, try making an alias of the file instead and put *that* where you want it. That usually works just fine (and if a media program can't deal with something as basic as an alias, it's probably got bigger problems than that).

Playing Interactive Media

Most interactive media comes ready to play these days. If it comes on a CD or DVD, the player is almost always included. If it's delivered over the Web, it probably uses plug-ins that you already have installed in your browser. Flash, QuickTime, and Shockwave are the most common plug-ins used for Web-based interactive media, and usually your browser will offer to fetch you the appropriate plug-ins if you don't already have them.

All you'll ordinarily need, then, is a machine that is fast enough and that has enough memory to handle the interactive media. How much is enough? The most precise answer we can offer is, it depends. Interactive-media authors like to use the latest, coolest technologies, which usually require higher-end machines, but the authors' business partners like to reach the widest audience possible and therefore tend to keep the system requirements down to a sane level.

In other words, if you have a relatively recent Mac with more than the minimum amount of RAM installed that's needed to run the Mac OS, you're likely to have a suitable machine. And if not, there's always the Apple Store.

How to Drive Yourself Completely Insane ... and Have a Fabulous Time Doing It—Making Interactive Media

You don't need to become a jack-of-all-media to make engaging and useful interactive media. On the other hand, it couldn't hurt.

Constructing interactive-media projects requires you to keep track of all the *digital assets* you plan to use (the pictures, audio, video, text, and animation you've made or acquired), to develop a scheme for presenting those assets in some sort of structure or order that your audience can comprehend, to conceive of a navigational scheme that your audience can use to move around in that structure you've devised, and to present it all in an aesthetically pleasing way. It's enough to make your brain pack its bags and head off to Kaimbu Island for a few months. Unless you like that sort of thing—happily, we do. A lot.

If you're up for Extreme Media Mania, here are some tools you might use.

Slide shows

Apple's rather neglected stealth office suite, **AppleWorks** ($79, free with new iMacs and iBooks; www.apple.com/appleworks), has a slide-show module that lets you incorporate text, movies, graphics, sound, and visual transition effects into a linear presentation. The program also has word-processing, painting, and drawing modules, so you can use it to prepare the media assets you want to use in your slide shows; it comes with templates and clip art as well.

You can use AppleWorks' spreadsheet and database modules to keep track of your media assets, even if you don't use it for media creation.

Microsoft PowerPoint (www.microsoft.com/mac) is the predominant slide-show presentation program in the Windows world, and—courtesy of Microsoft's Macintosh Business Unit—it is available on the Mac, too. You can get it either bundled as part of Microsoft Office v. X ($399) or as a separate purchase ($229). PowerPoint X provides tools to manage the slides you make, including a Slide Finder. It offers a rich library of clips and templates to assist you, and it lets you view your presentation as an outline, making navigation easy. The program supports standard image formats for the Web (including animated GIFs) and QuickTime. You can save your PowerPoint presentation as a QuickTime movie, either self-contained or along with a set of assets for later editing, or you can publish your presentation to the Web, which converts the presentation's outline into a home page with links to all the slides.

Built to the exacting (albeit idiosyncratic) requirements of Apple's CEO, Steve Jobs, **Keynote** ($99; www.apple.com/keynote) builds visually stunning slide-show presentations, employing Mac OS X's underlying graphics capabilities to their full advantage. Relying, as does PowerPoint, on a text outline to provide a presentation's structure, Keynote provides a large assortment of profession-ally designed templates, along with a set of 3D transition effects (**Figure 17.26**). It can import (and export) PowerPoint files, as well as import files in a range of media types, such as QuickTime, PDF, MP3, Flash, and Adobe Photoshop.

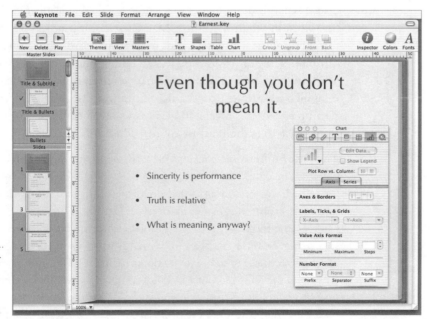

Figure 17.26

Apple's Keynote pre-sentation software has attractive, professionally designed templates.

Books and stacks

Though now on life support, Apple's interactive-media classic, **HyperCard** ($99; www.apple.com), is still popular in education for quickly creating multimedia on the Mac. Built on the metaphor of a stack of cards, the program by itself supports text (including sophisticated search capabilities), black-and-white graphics, visual transitions, and interactivity. Add-on features provided by Apple in the HyperCard package let you add color and QuickTime support to HyperCard stacks, and you can add almost any functionality via external commands (called XCMDs) and external functions (called XFCNs). The program includes a simple but powerful scripting language, called HyperTalk, that lets you do anything from creating simple flip-book animations to developing complex commercial applications. Unfortunately, HyperCard runs only in Classic or Mac OS 9, and it seems unlikely to enter the world of Mac OS X.

SuperCard ($179; www.supercard.us) began as a third-party attempt to remedy HyperCard's limitations by integrating color, better drawing tools, and multiple windows, and it has had a difficult journey through life, including ownership by a succession of companies—the latest is Solutions Etcetera. SuperCard provides many of the same features as HyperCard and some additions, including a more-powerful programming interface and a drag-and-drop converter for HyperCard stacks. Best of all, it runs in Mac OS X, providing a migration path for the legions of HyperCard users.

From Edinburgh's Revolution Ltd. (www.runrev.com), **Runtime Revolution** takes HyperCard-like stacks to a whole new, cross-platform level. With versions that work in Windows, Linux, Mac Classic and Mac OS X, among other platforms, Runtime Revolution adds to its HyperCard-ish features database-access capabilities, regular-expression text searching (think of this as wild-card searches on steroids), vector graphics, and native interface appearance for the platforms on which it runs. Its license price varies from free for a 30-day evaluation version up to $999 for a version that works on all supported platforms (and there are at least 16 of them at last count); educational pricing is available.

The **Adobe Acrobat** package ($449 Professional, $299 Standard; www.adobe.com) has developed from a program designed solely to exactly reproduce the look of a printed document into something rich and strange. Today's Acrobat files can contain hypertext links, interactive forms, and QuickTime media—yet they still look like printed documents. This is hardly surprising, because Acrobat, now in version 6, uses Adobe's sophisticated printing technology to create its documents in PDF. Acrobat allows you to embed all the fonts in your PDF files so that they will look exactly as they should on both Macs and Windows computers. The free Adobe Reader can open and read PDF files (the Preview program in Mac OS X can also read PDF files, though Preview may not have access to all of Acrobat's special features, such as PDF annotations). Acrobat PDFs are one of the most popular ways to distribute electronic books, and Adobe has built an entire e-commerce system to support its publishers.

Night Kitchen's TK3, developed by some of the people who pioneered the electronic book at the Voyager Company in the early '90s, is designed to create sophisticated and elegant interactive multimedia books. Like Adobe, Night Kitchen (www.nightkitchen.com) provides a free reader, called the TK3 Reader, to go with the authoring tool, **TK3 Author** ($149). TK3 Author lets you *flow* a main text (in HTML or Microsoft's RTF format) into the book and then adorn that text with annotations, which can either pop up in separate windows or stick to the page. Books have automatically generated tables of contents, are extensively searchable, and offer useful (and customizable) navigation tools. The current version runs only in the Classic Mac OS as of this writing, but a Mac OS X version reportedly is in development.

Movies

We've already looked at Macromedia Flash as an animation tool (see "Tween wolf—making animation," earlier in the chapter), but that's less than the half of it. Flash has extraordinary interactive capabilities powered by its ActionScript development environment and augmented by its ability to use XML in conjunction with external database servers. The latest version of Flash can even incorporate short video segments in its presentations.

We also considered Macromedia Director as an animation tool (again, see "Tween wolf—making animation"), and, as with Flash, that's just scratching the surface. No one could have predicted more than a decade ago that VideoWorks, a simple animation program, would become the digital-media powerhouse that is today's Director, but after acquiring a scripting language called Lingo (based on HyperCard's HyperTalk) and a plethora of interactive-media authoring features, the ugly duckling grew up to become … well, a really big, *strong* ugly duck. Director uses a timeline and stage metaphor, with various multimedia objects (sprites, graphics, sounds, and videos) serving as cast members that enter and leave the stage at various points on the timeline. You can attach scripts to each cast member, controlling its behavior and the behavior of others, and you can attach scripts to individual frames on the timeline; these scripts run when you reach that point in the movie. Director calls its assemblages of cast members and scripts *movies,* which can be confusing when you realize that one kind of cast member in a Director movie is a QuickTime movie (the program supports dozens of media types). In fact, a *lot* about Director may confuse the beginning interactive-media author, but you'll find much arcane Director lore readily available on Macromedia's Web site (www.macromedia.com), and active Director user groups can also help the initiate.

LiveStage Pro is a totally hip product—literally: Totally Hip's LiveStage Pro ($449.95; www.totallyhip.com) is the QuickTime developer's coolest friend. The program was designed to take advantage of nearly all the features that Apple built into QuickTime but never bothered to provide tools to access. Did you know that QuickTime can do math? That you can script it? That it can handle tweening? That it understands XML and can talk to remote servers? It can do all this and a lot more, and LiveStage makes these features available. Like Director, LiveStage has a scripting language (QScript), a stage, sprites (graphic characters that can move onstage and respond to user actions), and a timeline (**Figure 17.27**). But unlike Director, LiveStage produces QuickTime movies that any QuickTime-compatible program can play. LiveStage lets you assemble any QuickTime-supported media (including Flash) into interactive-media presentations; visit Totally Hip's Web site to see just how hip QuickTime can be.

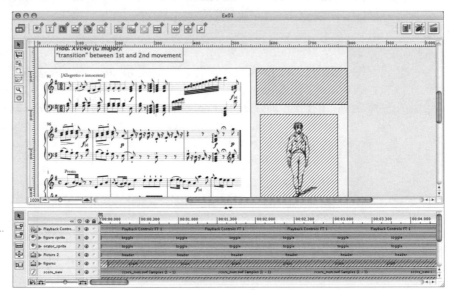

Figure 17.27

LiveStage Pro lets you assemble complex QuickTime creations.

Webs of objects

eZedia (www.ezedia.com) produces two packages: **eZedia QTI** ($99), for lightweight Web-based interactive media, and **eZedia MX** ($169), for CD-based interactive media. Both products allow you to drag and drop media elements into a frame, which you can then link to any other frame just by drawing arrows. eZedia QTI produces QuickTime movies that can be embedded in any Web page, while eZedia MX files require the free, cross-platform eZedia Player to be viewed. You can build some powerful nonlinear media presentations for a low price with either package, and do it all without scripting.

A highly evolved descendant of Apple's old Apple Media Tool, Tribeworks' **iShell** (www.tribeworks.com) handles the multiple personalities of multiple media types by letting you arrange them in containers (called *shells*) and then put these containers into other containers. You can control your containers by scripting them to handle events such as mouse clicks. The interface is drag and drop: you drop both media and event handlers on containers. iShell supports both CD-based and Web-based projects, and it can handle many media types, relying upon QuickTime extensively to do so. It can also extend its capabilities with add-on modules, available from Tribeworks when you become a Tribe member. iShell is free to try out; a single-platform version with limited support with free upgrades costs $495. In addition, the company offers yearly subscriptions at various levels and costs. A Silver Membership costs $895 for the first year and gets you tech support, manuals, and a run-time license. A $2,995 Gold Membership gets you a software-development kit, unlimited run-time licenses, and much more extensive technical support. Educational memberships are also available; call for pricing.

And then, of course, there's the ultimate media platform, the World Wide Web; see Chapter 19 for more about that.

Interview: Jeff Raikes

Jeff Raikes is best known for his role at Microsoft, where he has worked since 1981, but he got his start in high tech at Apple. Even after he turned down a job on the Mac team and instead joined Microsoft, he played a role in Mac history—partly because he led the development of Microsoft's applications business, including its Mac apps, and partly because he wrote a celebrated strategic memo to Apple's then-CEO, John Sculley, in 1985.

I wrote a memo to Bill [Gates] about the importance of the Mac gaining critical mass. My primary recommendation was that we should help Apple license the Macintosh operating system.

—Jeff Raikes, on his controversial memo to Apple

Raised on a cattle ranch in Nebraska, Raikes has done well by his commitment to Microsoft: in a 2003 profile Forbes estimated his net worth at $490 million. As group vice president of productivity and business services, he runs Microsoft's lucrative applications business, as well as its licensing programs for business customers. He's generally ranked third, behind only Bill Gates and Steve Ballmer, in the company's executive hierarchy, and Forbes said, " Among Microsoft's 55,000 employees, Raikes stands alone in his ability to challenge Gates' brilliance and Ballmer's bluster." —Henry Norr

When were you at Apple, and what did you do?

I worked for Apple in 1980 and '81 as VisiCalc program engineering manager. My primary job was to help Software Arts get VisiCalc [the first electronic spreadsheet] onto the Apple III, and then also to write spreadsheet models.

So you were a programmer?

Sort of. I would not have qualified as a programmer at Microsoft, but I could at Apple [he laughs].

Did you know about the Mac project when you were at Apple?

Yeah, I knew some. In fact, Jobs had offered me an opportunity to work on the Mac. I think I would have been about the seventh or eighth person on the team.

How did you come to move to Microsoft?

When the Apple III was introduced in the spring of 1981, the product marketing people wanted me to go out and demonstrate VisiCalc. They felt that I did a good job of articulating what VisiCalc was and how people could use it. At that time there wasn't a lot of understanding of what an electronic spreadsheet was. My job was to attend some trade shows and present VisiCalc. There were some Microsoft people at one of the trade shows. I didn't know it at the time, but they were starting an applications business and they approached me. Then Steve Ballmer called me up and asked me to have dinner with him, and one thing led to another.

Were you working on DOS applications at that point?

My first job was to be the Multiplan product manager. Multiplan was Microsoft's first spreadsheet, and it was on a wide range of personal-computer architectures. [A Mac version, released in 1984, was Microsoft's first product for the Mac.]

When did Apple show prototypes of the Mac to Microsoft?

I think it was either December of 1981 or January of 1982.

Was there debate about doing Mac applications?

The minute that Bill saw the Mac, there was no question that he wanted to do Microsoft BASIC as well as our applications for the Mac.

Was there a plan for Excel at that point?

No, Excel came up later. We had a retreat in October of 1983 to brainstorm how we could do a spreadsheet that would be competitive with Lotus 1-2-3. The first plan for Excel was to do a character-interface spreadsheet on the PC; it wasn't until the spring of 1984 that Bill and I concluded that we really needed to redirect Excel to first ship on the Macintosh with a graphic interface. That was very controversial. My conclusion was the way to win big was not to take on Lotus 1-2-3 on its home turf, but instead to make the bet on the graphic user interface, first on the Mac and then on Windows. A lot of people were pretty disappointed, because they were anxious to take on Lotus 1-2-3 on its own turf. We made that decision probably in April of '84, and we released in September of '85 on the Mac. I think it was the fall of '87, maybe '88, when we came out with the Windows version.

When did Microsoft start developing Windows itself?

I think it was in the fall of 1981, at Comdex, that Xerox demoed the Xerox Star, and it was around that time that Microsoft had started a project called Interface Manager, and that was what became Microsoft Windows. I think we demoed Interface Manager to Wang Computer about January or February of 1983.

But it was definitely before you guys had a Mac?

Absolutely. I mean, just like Steve Jobs was very cognizant of the Xerox Star, we were as well. In fact, one of the chief architects of our applications, Charles Simonyi, came from Xerox PARC and had done the first graphic-user-interface word processor. My first year at Microsoft, we got a Xerox Star and installed it at the company.

continues on next page

How did your memo concerning licensing the Mac OS come about?

By May of 1985 I was quite concerned about the poor sales of the Mac. As an applications vendor, the computers are the sockets you sell into, so if a company's not selling very many sockets, you've got a problem. So I wrote a memo to Bill about the importance of the Mac gaining critical mass. My primary recommendation was that we should help Apple license the Macintosh operating system. Bill liked the idea, so we sent the memo off to John Sculley— Jobs had just been booted out.

Somehow the memo and, I think, the idea got painted as a Machiavellian plot. My intent was just to make the Mac be more successful, and I basically said, "Look, the Mac is just not gaining critical mass to encourage a broad range of software and hardware peripheral development. The way to do that is to selectively license the architecture to a few manufacturers."

Too bad Sculley didn't listen.

Well, you know, it's ironic. What was it, seven, eight years later, I think it was Michael Spindler [CEO of Apple 1993–1996] who decided that was what they should do, and then they decided not to do that. In the end, part of the irony is the fact that because they didn't take my suggestion, it actually helped Microsoft and Windows.

Have you kept up with the Mac?

Not really. By 1993 I'd pretty much fully switched over to using Windows PCs.

18

Fun!

Bart G. Farkas (BF) is the chapter editor.

Lucian Fong (LF), Greg Kramer (GK), Mike Phillips (MP), and Corey Tamas (CT) are the chapter coauthors.

Sure, many of us have come to rely on our Macs as the backbone of our businesses. The Mac is an indispensable tool for creating our best materials while cruising the Internet for the latest news. But all work and no play makes Mac a dull computer.

The continual technological leaps the Mac has taken have greatly increased our favorite machine's ability to play the hottest games on the market without sacrificing quality or speed. Fast processors and specialized graphics boards make it possible for games to sport stunning real-life effects such as natural lighting and 3D worlds while still keeping the action moving at a fast clip. And as more and more people get fast Internet access, playing games online with anyone anywhere in the world is becoming a reality.

Now sit back and let us do the hard work for you so that you can get on to the more-important tasks of unraveling mysteries and raiding enemy camps. We'll give you the lowdown on where to buy games, how to buy them, and what you'll need to play. In addition, we'll tell you all about the different types of games available, from action games to puzzle games to role-playing games and more. You'll get a preview of the best games on the Mac market today—the classics as well as what's up and coming—in every imaginable category. And finally, we'll survey the hardware that can help you take advantage of all that your Mac has to offer in the realm of games.

In This Chapter

About Mac Gaming

If there's any doubt that the Mac is capable of reaching the loftiest entertainment heights, you need only look at the recent advances in the Mac's processing ability and the cutting-edge video cards now available (see "Video Cards," later in this chapter) to see its true gaming power.

That said, if you are a hard-core gamer, you might want to supplement your Mac's gaming power with a standalone gaming machine such as the PlayStation 2 or Xbox. That way, you can play enthralling games on your Mac anywhere, as well as play cutting-edge games on another system at home. Besides, playing games on a dedicated system frees up your Mac for other fun pastimes like video editing.

Buying a Game (CT)

Buying a game may seem simple enough, but there are a few things you can do to save some time searching for them and also avoid wasting money on the wrong title.

System requirements

Take a moment to examine the system requirements listed on the box of any game you're considering buying to make sure that you've got the right hardware to run it. You can also check the publisher's Web site or peruse magazine and online reviews for this information. (Often reviews will let you know if the minimum system requirements for running a game are realistic; many leading-edge games run poorly on a system equipped with the manufacturer's base configuration.) Also, don't assume that just because you have the latest Mac, it's automatically configured for every game on the market; check System Profiler (inside the /Applications/Utilities folder) and compare your computer's specifications with the game's requirements.

Internet connection

Increasingly, games are designed to be played over the Internet; your connection speed might be a factor with such games. Few games can function on a connection of 33.6 Kbps or slower, though Internet-playable card or board games often fare quite well with even the slowest connections. Strategy games can struggle along on a 56K dial-up–modem speed, but most players prefer a high-speed connection. If you are going to play any game that depends on your reflexes over the Internet, you'll need a broadband connection, such as cable modem or DSL. Wireless or satellite Internet connections can be fast but often suffer from high latency (a short delay before data is transferred), which makes action games difficult to play.

Demos

While it seems to be something of a dying art these days, some publishers still release a demo of a game in order to whet your appetite. Generally speaking, demos include only one or two missions from the full game or restrict some of the features. You can find demos online at popular Web sites such as MacGamer (www.macgamer.com), Mac Game Files (www.macgamefiles.com), or even Apple's own Demos gaming page (www.apple.com/games/demos). Also, .Mac subscribers can explore their iDisks for game demos, as Apple often makes them available in the Software/Mac OS X Software/What's New folder. If you don't want to go to the trouble of downloading a demo (or can't because of a slow connection), check Mac magazines such as *Macworld* (www.macworld.com) and *MacAddict* (www.macaddict.com), which often come with game demos on their CDs.

Reviews

There's no need to guess whether or not a game is going to be to your liking; the world is full of high-quality Mac game reviews and commentary. Every month, *Macworld, MacAddict, macHOME* (www.machome.com), and other magazines provide in-depth reviews of Mac games and detail the information that matters most, such as performance, price, and simply how fun a game is to play. If you want up-to-the-second game news and reviews, head for the Web, where quality Mac gaming sites abound. MacGamer, Inside Mac Games (www.insidemacgames.com), IGN.com (http://mac.ign.com), and Apple's Games site (www.apple.com/games) all give information about which games are good and how to get the most out of them.

Where Can You Get Game?

There's more than one place to get your games, and each has its pros and cons.

Retail

What's easier and faster than getting the games you want from the local retailer? Thanks to the increasing popularity of the Mac in the last ten years, it's more and more common to find Mac games in stores that have been inclined to carry only PC or console games. Policies among large retailers about carrying Mac games can change unpredictably and frequently: one day they may have a section dedicated to Mac games; the next month it's gone; six months later it's back again. Electronics Boutique, Target, and CompUSA have all changed their strategies on carrying Mac games more than once, so make sure to check back if you don't find any Mac software on a particular day. If your local retailer carries the Mac games you want, give it your business.

continues on next page

Where Can You Get Game? continued

Online

For convenience, buying online is the way to go; order by credit card over the Internet and get home delivery. More and more options for buying games online have opened up in recent years. One of the best places to find Mac games is none other than the Apple Store (www.apple.com/store). It carries the latest games and has a name you can trust. If you're looking for a broader selection, GoGamer (www.gogamer.com) is an excellent option; its selection is broad and its prices are reasonable (you can often preorder games). Most game publishers, like Aspyr Media (www.aspyr.com) and MacSoft (www.macsoftgames.com), sell their games right off their Web sites. And some publishers, like Ambrosia Software (www.ambrosiasw.com), sell online exclusively.

Secondhand

Computer games don't have a "best before" date; as long as the media a game is shipped on is intact, a game never ages. This fact makes purchasing secondhand games a viable alternative to getting games new at a much higher price. eBay (www.ebay.com) is a mecca for used goods of all sorts and, despite urban legends to the contrary, is actually a safe and reliable place to buy and sell secondhand games (make sure you read eBay's guidelines thoroughly so that you know how its system works). It's not hard to find gamers trying to unload some old games through Web-based forums or Usenet, but make sure that your transactions have a paper trail (for example, use a money order or cashier's check instead of cash) in case you're not happy with the outcome. One resource that gamers in the Internet age often forget is the local Mac users group; almost every community has one, and they provide a great venue through which to trade and sell secondhand games. Check your local phone book as well as Apple's Web site and Google (www.google.com) to find a Mac users group near you.

News About Mac Gaming (CT)

The world of Mac gaming is moving forward at breakneck speed. Players expect a lot from their games: better graphics, better performance, and revolutionary ideas. Now, more than ever, the Mac is equipped to keep up with the changing gaming scene and the community around it. Let's look at a few of the coming trends and evolutions in gaming.

Doom 3, forthcoming from id Software (www.idsoftware.com), promises to take game graphics to an entirely new level. The extensive use of per-pixel lighting and shading makes the environments and monsters very lifelike; shadows move as lights flash, reflections ripple over textured surfaces, and liquids look and behave like real liquids. Though no firm release date was set at the time of this writing, Doom 3 is Mac-bound and runs under Mac OS X.

Graphics aren't the only emerging development in the Mac gaming world: more and more games are using the Internet to build and take advantage of virtual communities. Where once gamers would log in to Quake servers to play a deathmatch against one another, they now log in to *persistent world servers*—servers that keep the world running and things happening no matter whether you are playing or not, just like in real life. In this scenario, players around the world form guilds and squads, and work in teams over days, weeks, and sometimes months to attain goals and complete missions. Sony pioneered this mode of play, often referred to as *massively multiplayer online* gaming, with the online game **EverQuest** ($49.99; http://everquest.station.sony.com). This type of gaming has since become the form and function of countless other titles (see "Online Gaming," later in this chapter for examples). The writing appears to be on the wall: the future of gaming is about building virtual communities and creating immersive worlds that can evolve.

In the summer of 2003, one of the most important developments in the history of Mac gaming went virtually unnoticed by the public: Apple announced Xcode (www.apple.com/macosx/panther/xcode.html). This humble, free tool is intended to assist developers in programming more quickly and easily on the Macintosh, and it will most certainly have a direct impact on the state of Mac gaming. Creating Mac games and porting PC and console games to the Mac cost developers a lot of time and money. As those obstacles are removed, more developers and programmers will come to the Macintosh to create and port games because it will be just plain easier and faster. This, of course, is great news.

Emulation

What happens when you're so voraciously hungry for great games that even the wide assortment of titles available on the Macintosh isn't enough to satiate you? One answer is to turn to game emulation—a technology that allows your Mac to mimic other kinds of gaming machines. You can find a wide variety of either free or inexpensive options for opening up new worlds of gaming.

A word of caution about the legality of emulation: emulation on the Mac is something of an ethical gray area. A lot of illegal ROM files (software-only versions of games that originally came on cartridges) of popular games are circulated on the Internet without the permission of the people who own the intellectual property. If you didn't pay for a game, it's not legal to own and play it. Remember: every game you play is thanks to the developers' hard work, so don't cheat them out of the compensation they're due.

continues on next page

Emulation *continued*

If you're looking to effectively emulate games on the Mac, there are several excellent choices. Possibly the best option for effective emulation of older games, such as those from Atari, is **MacMAME** (free; www.macmame.org); *MAME* stands for *Multi-Arcade Machine Emulator*. This is a well-developed program that works with Mac OS X and runs a plethora of emulated games; it even allows for cheating, saving replays, and supporting controllers. Few people need more in a game emulator than MacMAME offers.

 You might be tempted to buy Microsoft's Virtual PC for Mac ($129–$249; www.microsoft.com/mac) to run PC games on your Mac, since the program allows you to create a PC environment on your Mac in which you can install Windows, Linux, or any other PC-based operating system. Unfortunately, most games won't run under Virtual PC. Virtual PC does not allow full use of the DirectX technology, which Windows uses for 3D gaming, sound, and controller input. In short, no amount of powerful Mac hardware will give Virtual PC what it needs to run most PC games.

If you're a fan of Nintendo's Game Boy Advance, the best way to emulate it on your Macintosh is to use **BoycottAdvance** (donationware; http://boycottadvance.emuunlim.com). This easy-to-use emulator lets you play Game Boy ROM files with ease and offers features that go beyond the original Game Boy, such as controller support and resolution switching. There are other great emulators out there as well, such as the shareware program **sixtyforce** ($15; www.sixtyforce.com), which emulates the Nintendo 64. Programming an emulator is something of a black art, however, so there's no guarantee that these constantly-in-development programs will work the way you want them to. But if you've got the urge for some old-school gaming, it's worth giving them a try.

Game Titles

Whether you're looking for a little mental stimulation via a nice game of chess or you want to get your pulse racing with an action game, Mac game makers probably have what you're looking for. Here's an overview of the types of games that are available.

Action Games (CT)

Action. Is there any word that better typifies what gaming is about? From the earliest days of computer gaming, when Atari's Pong was being played in bars and rec centers all over America, to the present day, when international computer-gaming competitions are backed with hundreds of thousands of dollars in corporate sponsorship, gaming has always typified the enduring quality of action—and lots of it. There are more action games than ever, from old-school arcade-style shooters to deathmatches.

Action games generally come in *first-person* or *third-person* perspectives. In first-person-perspective games, your view is that of the person involved in the action. For example in a shooter game, you would view the action just as though you were the person behind the gun in real life. In third-person-perspective games, generally the camera is in a fixed location in each scene and you see the action from the perspective of the camera.

Nearly all action games these days also have both *single-player* and *multiplayer* modes. In multiplayer mode, you can generally play the game either over a network or over the Internet. To play over the Internet, most companies require that each player have a copy of the game with its own unique code in order to prevent multiple players from being able to use just one copy of the game.

First- and third-person shooters

Here are some of the top shooter games around as of early 2004.

For many years Bungie Software was a Mac-only development house that churned out such classics as Pathways into Darkness and the Marathon Series. Now, however, it has teamed up with Microsoft to work on its Xbox titles. Fortunately for us, it still hasn't forgotten its Macintosh roots, and Aspyr Media has released the best-selling **Halo: Combat Evolved** for the Mac ($49; www.aspyr.com). Halo is a groundbreaking third-person/first-person shooter with a complex story that pits humans against an alien race in the distant future. Arguably the best game of 2002, Halo still stands up with incredible action and visuals.

Aspyr Media's **Medal of Honor: Allied Assault** ($49) is a first-person shooter that immerses you in World War II front-line combat with a gripping, tense single-player mode and a challenging Internet or network multiplayer mode. If you ever wanted to live *Saving Private Ryan,* this Quake III–engine title is the game for you. Medal of Honor's expansion pack, titled Spearhead, is also available for the Macintosh.

 Often you'll see games claiming to be based on the Quake III or Unreal Tournament engine. The *engine* refers to the software behind the mechanics of a game; engines can be very time-consuming, costly, and complex for developers to create. So once a good engine is developed, the creators will license it to other companies. Quake III, for example, was a groundbreaking first-person game that let you walk through a 3D room smoothly and realistically. Developers who use the Quake III engine provide their users with that same experience. Unreal Tournament offered developers a way to provide their user base with tournament play.

An adult game that combines gothic horror with erotically suggestive themes, Aspyr Media's **BloodRayne** ($29) casts the player as a half-human, half-vampire heroine who fights foes from the swamps of Louisiana and Hitler's

Third Reich. The third-person vantage point gives away the game's roots as a console game. BloodRayne is single-player only, and definitely not for the squeamish.

The Force is with you in another great action game from Aspyr Media: **Jedi Knight II: Jedi Outcast** ($49.99). This *Star Wars*–based action game has you using firepower, Jedi Force skills, and, of course, a lightsaber to pursue a villain through space while eliminating remnants of the now-fallen Empire. Viewed in first- or third-person mode, this Quake III–engine game offers a lot of gameplay in single-player mode, but it also lets you test your saber-swinging skills against others' in network or Internet multiplayer gaming as well.

MacPlay's **No One Lives Forever 2: A Spy in H.A.R.M.'s Way** ($49.99; www.macplay.com) is a first-person spy shooter that puts you in the role of Cate Archer, aka the Operative, and takes you through late '60s Europe and the Middle East to dismantle a criminal cabal known as H.A.R.M. (**Figure 18.1**). Peppered with lots of interesting puzzles as well as flat-out action, No One Lives Forever is a witty and original variation on the standard action game. Players can enjoy the solo mission as well as a full-featured multiplayer game over a network or the Internet.

Figure 18.1

In No One Lives Forever you take on the first-person perspective of Cate Archer, an operative whose goal is to dismantle a criminal cabal.

Soldier of Fortune II: Double Helix ($49.99), also from MacPlay, casts you in the role of weapons specialist and military consultant John Mullins. You pit your military-antiterrorist expertise against a covert organization that wants to release a deadly virus upon the world in this Quake III–engine game of brutal violence and tactical know-how. A wide variety of weapons and other assault devices come into play in both the single and multiplayer versions. But the multiplayer (network or Internet) game is particularly noteworthy for its random scenario generator, which keeps the action fresh.

Aspyr Media's **Tom Clancy's Ghost Recon with Desert Siege** ($39.99) is another chapter in the series inspired by Clancy's Rainbow Six stories. Ghost Recon allows you to command teams of soldiers charged with infiltrating terrorist ranks and eliminating hostile agents. Superrealistic first-person gameplay makes every shot count, and both solo and multiplayer options over a network or the Internet are available.

For those who enjoy a gritty reality game that's on the edge, MacSoft's **Max Payne** ($19.99; www.macsoftgames.com) is the game for you. Set in the seedy underbelly of New York, Max Payne is the story of a cop who suffers the loss of his family and is being framed for the murder of his partner. As you push forth in this ultraviolent 3D third-person shooter, pieces of the puzzle are revealed until Max finally confronts the foes who ruined his life. Great graphics and gameplay, but its depiction of drug- and violence-riddled New York is definitely not for kids.

If you're a fan of Clive Barker, then **Undying** ($9.99), from Aspyr Media, will certainly satisfy. Playing Undying, which was conceived by author Barker, is like living in a horror movie. In this first-person Unreal Tournament–engine game you play the role of Patrick Galloway, coming to the aid of an old friend who fears that his ancestral estate has become the home of evil supernatural forces. As you prowl the creepy hallways and parlors of the haunted mansion, surprises will make you leap from your seat.

In Aspyr Media's **Return to Castle Wolfenstein** ($39.99) you're U.S. Army soldier B. J. Blazkowicz, sent behind enemy lines to investigate a Nazi plot to bring legions of the undead into service. Based on the Quake III engine, this first-person shooter takes you on an action-packed journey in which you have to contend with Nazi storm troopers, elite ninjalike soldiers, and, of course, the undead. Once you've finished the solo game, try out the squad-based multiplayer game on a network or the Internet.

Graphsim Entertainment's **Red Faction** ($19.95; www.graphsim.com) is another fabulous shooter game. Imagine yourself caught in a furious uprising within a vast Martian mining colony, where corporate greed makes slaves of workers and a mysterious virus is wiping out the population. This first-person shooter is best known for its GeoMod engine, which allows you to destroy the environment you're in with your heavy weaponry—blow holes in walls, knock guard towers down, drill for an escape route. You'll find lots of action in the single-player game and a lot more in the network or Internet multiplayer mode.

Leap into the world of B movies and alien invasions with Pangea Software's **Otto Matic** ($34.95; www.pangeasoft.net), a 3D third-person game about a little robot that seeks to save humanity (**Figure 18.2**). From the same company that made Bugdom, Otto Matic is a light-hearted and often funny action game that's suitable for children as well as adults.

Figure 18.2

In the third person action game Otto Matic, you see Otto's world from a fixed camera perspective.

In MacSoft's **Unreal Tournament 2003** ($49), gladiators on a killing rampage meet in a closed futuristic environment for fierce combat with heavy weaponry. This game excels at multiplayer action in a first-person shooter. Players can take on each other (or computer-controlled *bots*) in regular kill-or-be-killed deathmatches or can play any one of several variations on the theme, including Capture the Flag and Bombing Run (sort of a futuristic rugby). Unreal Tournament 2003 is too violent for many gamers, but it's a prime example of what first-person shooters are all about.

Harry Potter and the Sorcerer's Stone ($19.99) and **Harry Potter and the Chamber of Secrets** ($39.99), from Aspyr Media, are the two Harry Potter games that have been released since the stories took to the big screen. These 3D third-person action games are based on the Unreal Tournament engine. Harry solves puzzles, leaps his way through difficult passages, and vanquishes ill-wishers with his magic wand. The two games play nearly identically, and each is well suited to gamers between the ages of about 10 and 12, especially those who have fallen in love with the books or movies. With the franchise still going strong, you can bet there will be more installments in the Harry Potter game series to come.

Arcade games (CT)

Arcade games are often called *twitch* games because you need to have ultrafast reactions to play them well. Most of these games are reminiscent of old arcade games that you may remember from childhood.

Pangea Software's **Bugdom 2** ($34.95; www.pangeasoft.net) is the sequel to one of the most popular Mac-first games ever made. It puts you in the role of Skip the grasshopper, who has had his bag stolen by a kleptomaniac bumblebee. Off he goes on a great adventure, running free in suburban gardens, surfing down eave troughs, and bombing ants with a balsa-wood airplane. This game is a little young for hard-core gamers, but there's a lot of great third-person gameplay here for younger kids (there's even a mode in which enemies will not attack).

A variation on the classic Breakout arcade game, Ambrosia Software's **pop-pop** ($25; www.ambrosiasw.com) gives you a paddle with which to bounce a ball into a wall of bricks, knocking out a few with each strike. The problem? Every brick you knock down is added to your opponent's wall, and vice versa. If someone's wall collects enough bricks to put him over the line of destiny, he's out of commission.

Strange Flavour's shareware game **Airburst** ($9.95; www.strangeflavour.com) is a nifty variation on the old paddle-and-ball-style arcade game. This variation puts you high in the air atop a raft of balloons, along with three other players (either computerized or human). A spinning ball of blades floats between all the players, threatening to pop balloons from under you if you don't whack it away from yourself (and toward others). It's a simple but engaging top-down action game with lots of gameplay variation and power-ups to keep things interesting.

21-6 Productions' **Orbz** ($19.95; www.21-6.com) is a colorful 3D arcade game in which the player scores points by shooting orbs at targets. Single and multiplayer (network or Internet) modes give this game more longevity, and bright, nonviolent gameplay makes it great for younger kids. On the other hand, BraveTree Productions' **ThinkTanks** ($19.95; www.bravetree.com) is a cartoonlike 3D ride in a puttering tank, blasting away at other tanks within range. Great single and multiplayer (network or Internet) action gives this game its value. The overall cutesy look is a selling point as well.

Freeverse Software's **Wingnuts: Temporal Navigator** ($29; www.freeverse.com) pits you as a fighter pilot against the wicked Baron Von Schtopwatch, chasing him through the entirety of the flying age and beyond. You must survive as his planes, ground turrets, and gunboats open fire. If you make it to the end of the round in this top-down, arcade-style shooter, you go face-to-face with Schtopwatch's own gigantic flying fortress. Peppered with Freeverse's characteristic sense of humor, Wingnuts is reminiscent of '80s-era arcade games but has a more modern, polished feel.

KewlBox (www.kewlbox.com) makes a variety of free games. While most of the games are not very challenging in gameplay (which is great for kids or game-playing novices), they are charming, imaginative, and just plain fun. Among the favorites is **Adventure Elf,** in which Frank and his penguin pals invade Santa's sleigh, and Oliver the Elf (that's you) must return the gifts to Santa (**Figure 18.3**). **Sketchy Snow Sledding** has you guiding smart-mouthed snow-sledders past various obstacles—and hearing their pains when you mess up.

Figure 18.3

Adventure Elf is an arcade adventure game reminiscent of Super Mario Brothers.

Online Gaming (MP)

Most games today offer both single-player and multiplayer capabilities. Blizzard Entertainment's Warcraft III, for instance, features a single-player campaign with the option to lead armies into combat on the Internet. (You log in to the Blizzard server to play online.) Confusingly enough, however, there are other types of online games. These can range in complexity from games that you play by opening your browser and going to a Web site where you play with other people (typically, these are card or board games on sites such as Yahoo or Electronic Arts' Pogo [www.pogo.com]) to massively multiplayer online persistent worlds (see "News About Mac Gaming," earlier in this chapter). Online games tend to give users the most bang for their proverbial buck, as the games are updated often and have potentially endless replay value. In fact, most browser-based games are free of charge. You can't beat a free game that never ends!

Thanks to Mac OS X, the folks at GameHouse (www.gamehouse.com) have opened their doors to us Mac gamers. At GameHouse, players have a myriad of browser-based games from which to choose (most of which are free), with genres ranging from puzzle to casino. For example, those who enjoy the thrill of Las Vegas but don't want their wallets cleaned out can play roulette or poker right in their Web browsers. Wordsmiths can try their mouse in a number of word games, including crossword puzzles and an interesting title called **Super TextTwist!** ($19.95). In Super TextTwist!, players form as many words as possible from scrambled letters (**Figure 18.4**). There are also plenty of puzzle games to tease one's brain. So fire up Safari and drop by GameHouse.

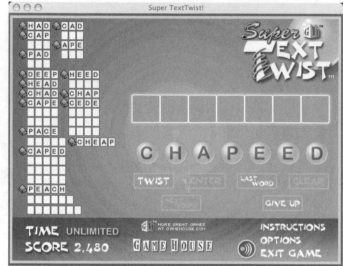

Figure 18.4

SuperText Twist! is just one example of an online game that you can play right from within your Web browser.

A great title for card pros and hustlers alike is **Masque Online Poker** (free; www.masque.com). In order to access Masque Publishing's virtual poker tables, players simply visit the Web site, register a free account, and download a small client application. No fuss, no muss. Once installed, the Masque Online Poker client puts every popular poker variation at your fingertips, including 5-Card Draw, 7-Card Stud, and Texas Hold'em. Once in a game, players can chat with (or taunt) their opponents, all while praying for pocket aces or bluffing a straight flush.

For something completely different, there's TQworld's **Tranquility** (free or full membership for $10; www.tqworld.com), a game for aspiring Zen masters. Tranquility is best described as a 3D online game of hide-and-seek that is a visual and aural feast. Players first download a client application from TQworld, which they use to connect to the Tranquility game server (**Figure 18.5**). The game is unique because it rewards subtle mouse movement, patience, and a keen eye. From within a first-person view, players float in a sea of brightly colored geometrical shapes, trying to carefully bounce from platform to platform in an attempt to catch the Spinner. The game changes with every login and is never the same twice.

Figure 18.5

Massively multi player games such as Tranquility require you to download a client application in order to access the game's server. Here you and other players attempt to catch the Spinner.

Playnet.com's **World War II Online** ($19.99, plus $12.99 monthly subscription; www.playnet.com) is a massively multiplayer online game in which thousands of players battle it out in an intense simulation of World War II. Gamers can play every role from front-line infantryman to a high-flying fighter pilot, with every kill helping to shape the tide of war. That's right—in this simulation the Germans could achieve victory or the French could repel an invasion. Furthermore, with each mission, players can potentially gain in rank from lowly private to high-ranking general. World War II Online features historically accurate weapons and vehicles. New models are added as the war progresses; thus gameplay constantly evolves. The only caveat is for those who wish to control vehicles: a joystick is required.

Future Pastimes' **Cosmic Encounter Online** ($8.50 monthly subscription; www.cosmicencounter.com) is a unique online browser game that requires the Macromedia Shockwave plug-in, a quick wit, and a thirst for galactic domination. In order to play, you simply warp on over to the Web site and register. There's a free demo version of Cosmic Encounter Online, but fully registered users gain access to the game's 75 alien races, the ability to invite nonmembers into full games, and participation in organized tournaments. Once you select an alien race and the game begins, players try to capture four planets outside of their territory while protecting their own. When attacking, you send out up to four ships and an Encounter pod; Encounter pods are numbered discs that determine attack strength. If you have more ships, including the Encounter pod, than the defender, then you are the victor. You can play a session of Cosmic Encounter Online over a lunch break—it's a perfect quick diversion.

Ubi Soft's **Shadowbane** ($29.99 plus $10.95 monthly subscription; www.ubi.com) is a major massively multiplayer online role-playing game (MMORPG). Unlike MMORPGs like EverQuest, in which players work together to kill monsters and gain levels in an endless loop, Shadowbane offers a player-versus-player experience. After creating a character from one of four types (Fighter, Healer, Mage, or Rogue), players begin life on an island called Tyranth Minor. On this island, players cannot kill each other and are encouraged to work together to smite various beasts and gain levels. After ten levels, players choose from one of many professions, each with dozens of skills and powers. For instance, Bards use magic to aid those around them, whereas Assassins slink about in the shadows, looking for a quiet kill. As players gain strength, they must move to Tyranth Major, where death can come from beast or fellow player. It's at this point that Shadowbane distinguishes itself from the rest of its kind; players can actually form guilds, build cities, and lay siege to enemy cities, thus shaping the game world. Once-prospering cities can fall under the might of an enemy army. All this action does come at a price. Macs equipped with anything less than a G3 processor need not apply; the visual splendor of large-scale combat is crippling to those machines.

Role-Playing Games (MP)

There's nothing better than a good book with an enthralling story and intriguing characters that evolve throughout their adventure. It's satisfying to follow a character's journey from obscurity to greatness, whether such greatness is welcome or not. For many people, role-playing games (RPGs) are akin to books, as they tend to focus on story progression and character development rather than enduring action. In an RPG, a hardworking farmer can become a noble paladin or powerful mage, but not before having a few arduous adventures. Role-playing games also feature rich stories set in lush fantasy or even sci-fi worlds. One could perhaps say that an RPG is like an interactive work of literature. These games can be single-player and multiplayer.

For those old-school Dungeons & Dragons players, there's MacSoft's **Neverwinter Nights** ($49.99; www.macsoft.com), a game that's based on the Advanced Dungeons & Dragons 3rd Edition rule set. In Neverwinter Nights, you take on the role of a heretofore-unknown student at a prestigious training academy in the city of Neverwinter (**Figure 18.6**). A tale of epic scale quickly unfolds, placing you in a desperate race to stop a deadly plague from decimating the populace. Neverwinter Nights lets gamers create dozens of different character types, allowing for a completely customized experience. For example, creating a Human Paladin entails using heavy armor, brute force, and noble deeds to succeed, whereas a Half-Elf Sorcerer requires cunning and arcane magic. The game also contains a combat system that allows players to pause the action and issue attack commands. Players can band together and play the entire game online, as well as download player-created adventures. Finally, Neverwinter Nights makes use of dazzling 3D graphics and visual effects.

Figure 18.6

Beautiful 3D graphics and visual effects are the hallmark of popular role-playing games like Neverwinter Nights, in which you take on the role of the hero.

If action is what you demand, MacSoft's **Dungeon Siege** ($49.99) is the way to go. To appease hard-core RPG traditionalists and those who prefer Blizzard's Diablo II–esque hack-and-slash adventuring, Dungeon Siege combines an engaging story, a unique character-advancement system, and combat that's full of action. You begin as a simple farmer but must quickly take up arms and band together with others in order to thwart an evil that threatens to engulf all of humanity. Character development is based upon whatever skills you use most. For example, using a sword in combat raises sword skill, thus creating a perfect fighter. The stunning 3D world in Dungeon Siege is seamless and requires no level loading, making for smoother gameplay.

RPG fans looking for something completely different need look no further than MacPlay's **Freedom Force** ($29.99; www.macplay.com). Instead of featuring the usual dragons and wizards, Freedom Force is an RPG that is reminiscent of a silver-age comic book (the classics dating from 1947 to 1983). A strange alien substance called Energy X has landed on Earth, imbuing both good and evil people with super powers. Thus, two factions arise and conflict ensues. As in other RPGs, characters gain levels, upgrade their skills, and add members to their groups, but Freedom Force offers twists that others do not. For example, characters with super strength can rip lampposts straight from the pavement and hurl them at enemies. Characters who harness laser beams can blast incoming debris from the sky. You must do battle with a vast array of dastardly foes, including ten vile bosses, various alien minions, and even a Greek god. Freedom Force is the perfect choice for RPG fans who long to be superheroes.

In the arena of classic RPGs, there's the **MacPlay Adventure Pack** ($29.95). The Adventure Pack consists of two groundbreaking role-playing games, **Icewind Dale** and **Baldur's Gate II: Shadows of Amn**, both of which are based on the Advanced Dungeons & Dragons 2nd Edition rule set. Icewind Dale is the tale of the journey of a group of adventurers into the treacherous Spine of the World Mountains in order to thwart an unknown ancient evil. The game features an intriguing story, dozens of graphically rich locations, a plethora of weapon and armor types, a multitude of powerful priest and wizard spells, 150 monster types (including Giants), intense combat situations, and snow, lots of snow. Players also have the ability to create their entire adventuring party. Icewind Dale is centered on melee combat, so hack-and-slash fans will be quite pleased.

Baldur's Gate II: Shadows of Amn tells the story of one of the children of Bhall, a god known as the Lord of Murder. Being the child of one of the world's most infamous gods, it's hard to avoid those who wish to tap such power and use it to their own ends. Thus, at the game's opening a dark sorcerer kidnaps and experiments on you. Baldur's Gate II is a game of massive scope and detail that spans five CDs. This game features lushly detailed 2D graphics coupled with 3D spell effects, a multifaceted story with hours of side quests, and a multitude of monsters, weapons, and spell types. Unlike Icewind Dale, in which melee combat rules the day, Baldur's Gate II requires the player to keenly grasp the art of arcane spell-crafting. If an enemy casts a magic shield, you must quickly dispel that shield and deliver a death blow. For adventurers who are partial to magic, this game is a fine choice.

Board, Card, and Puzzle Games (MP)

If you find today's leading-edge games to be too frenetic, complex, and edgy, there are more than enough other games that cater to you. Indeed, the Mac hosts a cornucopia of the finest board, card, and puzzle games available on any platform. These games can provide hours of single-player and multiplayer excitement without bringing about a stress-induced aneurism.

Board games

For classic board games on the Mac, turn to the **Freeverse Deluxe Board Games** ($19.95; www.freeverse.com)—a suite of eight board games (**4 in a Row, 7th Fleet, Checkers, Chess, Go, Mancala, Reversi,** and **Tic Tac Toe**). Each game is both single- and multiplayer-ready (except Go, which is multiplayer only), and replete with zany Freeverse charm. In single-player mode, gamers battle it out against bots of varying skill levels, and thus the game is accessible to players of all ages and levels of expertise. Freeverse's GameSmith match and ranking service handles multiplayer mode for online gaming. You can also opt for multiplayer games over a network.

If you enjoy playing the role of military strategist, check out Freeverse Software's **Solace** ($19.95), a unique game that's loosely based on the Axis & Allies board game. In Solace you take control of the armies of either the Red Mountain Onslaught or the Jintar Alliance in an epic struggle for domination. Like many board games of its genre, Solace gives you control of armies that attempt to capture every country on the map, one turn at a time. Game pieces include Archers, Cavalry, and even Transport Ships for sea invasions. Thanks to a step-by-step tutorial, you'll never feel overwhelmed. You can play Solace in multiplayer mode over the Internet or a network. Solace even offers a unique play-by-email feature. The game also boasts nicely rendered graphics, making it pleasing to the eye as well.

Card games

Freeverse Software's **Classic Cribbage** ($19.95; www.freeverse.com) is a witty card game. Originating in England, traditional cribbage is an addictive card game with just a hint of board game sprinkled on top. The object of this game is to be the first to move your peg to the end of the cribbage board by playing combinations of cards that add up to 15 or 31. You can play Classic Cribbage in a two- or three-player free-for-all mode or four-player (two against two) team mode. The game features computer-controlled bots so that you can play by yourself, as well as online multiplayer support via Freeverse's GameSmith matching service. Classic Cribbage is also pleasing to the eye, with its whimsical Roaring '20s motif.

Another great card game, also from Freeverse Software, is **3D Hearts Deluxe** ($24.95). Four players battle it out in an attempt to score as few points as possible, which is, of course, easier said than done. Each player lays down one card at a time, and the one with the highest card takes the bunch. The trick is that if you receive any hearts, they count against you by one point each. Capturing the queen of spades will set you back another 13 points. But in yet another twist, if you manage to capture *all* of the hearts *and* the queen of spades, each of your opponents gets 26 points against him or her. Unlike most computer card games, in which computer-controlled bots are dull and lifeless, 3D Hearts Deluxe features animated bots with delightful (or evil) personalities. Like all other Freeverse card games, 3D Hearts Deluxe offers GameSmith support for multiplayer excitement online, as well as network gaming.

For those who need a little "me" time, there is the ever-wacky **Burning Monkey Solitaire 3** ($24.95) from, you guessed it, Freeverse Software. Quite often, solitaire can amount to the height of tedium, but that's not the case with this version of the game. It has 26 types of solitaire, amusing sound effects, colorful graphics, statistic tracking, bad puns, and many monkeys to taunt and heckle you. You can also look forward to numerous jokes and secret tricks. For instance, try typing out the Japanese title of a creepy movie about an infinite loop (aka

"The Ring") and watch what the monkeys do; it's not pretty. All in all, Burning Monkey Solitaire 3 is a completely new and hilarious twist on a usually dull card game. As for why they call it "Burning," just buy it and see.

Puzzle games (MP)

Those who seek a digital addiction might want to check out MacPlay's **Bejeweled & Alchemy** ($19.99; www.macplay.com), two of the Mac's most addictive games. In Bejeweled, players swap brightly colored jewels on a game board in an attempt to align jewels of the same color into rows of three. When three jewels of the same color line up, they vanish and more fall from above. When no more matches are possible, the game is over. You can play Bejeweled for points or against the clock. In the game Alchemy, players place colored runes on bricks of lead to make gold. This is simple enough, except that you can't place runes of different colors and shapes next to each other.

Another great puzzler is MacPlay's **Enigmo** ($24.99). Players must divert free-flowing liquids (water, oil, and lava) into their appropriate containers by placing and manipulating various mechanical devices in their paths (**Figure 18.7**). To add to the challenge, there's a time limit. Enigmo features 70 levels plus a built-in level editor that allows players to create and trade levels to their hearts' content. Visually, Enigmo is unlike any game of its kind. It offers lush 3D graphics and particle effects; water has never sprayed or flowed more realistically in any puzzle game.

Figure 18.7

Quite the conundrum, Enigmo forces you to divert free-flowing liquids by placing various mechanical devices appropriately before the liquids overrun you.

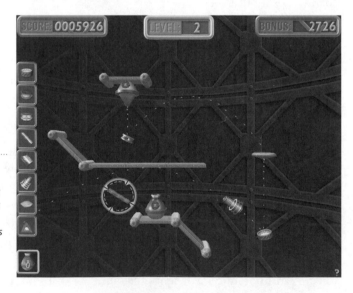

Real-Time Strategy Games (BF)

Real-time strategy (RTS) games are a special breed. To be successful you must be able to manage miniature armies in real time (rather than turn by turn) against both human and computer opponents. Real-time strategy games allow the gamer to manage the economic, military, and infrastructure aspects of a race of beings in an attempt to conquer the realm. What makes an RTS game special is the fact that there is no way to pause the game—you must think on the fly and manage under the same time constraints as the other players in the game.

The Mac doesn't have as broad a selection in this game genre as other platforms, but the titles that are available are the top games of all time in the category. Thanks are due especially to Blizzard Entertainment, which faithfully develops its titles concurrently for the Mac and PC so that both versions are released on the same day.

Blizzard's **Warcraft III: Reign of Chaos** ($39.95; www.blizzard.com) and **Warcraft III: Frozen Throne** ($29.95) are arguably the two best RTS games available (although there are some Starcraft and Command & Conquer aficionados who would disagree). Blizzard has taken key elements of its Diablo II game, such as hero items, stashes, and character building, and combined them into a fantastic real-time strategy experience in both of these games.

Microsoft's **Age of Empires II: The Age of Kings** ($19.99; www.microsoft.com) is another of the big-daddy RTS games that have dominated this niche. While Age of Empires has many RTS elements, there are also simulation- and civilization-related elements woven into the gameplay for a truly immersive (and time-consuming) experience.

The new kid on the block is Feral Interactive's **Warrior Kings** ($50; www.feral.co.uk). Warrior Kings is an RTS game that takes place in an era of knights and demons, and it lets you build up a powerful kingdom with which you can completely abuse your newfound power. The 3D world allows you to move around the maps freely to see the action from any angle.

Simulation Games (GK)

Simulation games (aka *god games*) empower you to take control of the workings of a world (a city, a banana republic, and so on) and make decisions that will shape the evolution of that world. Think of these complex and open-ended games as extremely detailed ant farms.

The current king of the simulator hill is Aspyr Media's **The Sims** ($49.99; www.aspyrmedia.com). Described as a digital dollhouse, the Sims puts you in charge of a household (or several of them) and the people in it (**Figure 18.8**). Your goal is to maximize their happiness by providing for their needs, usually in the form of increasingly powerful and expensive possessions. The happier they are, the more friends they accumulate, the more successful they are in their careers, and the more money they make. Money, in turn, buys more possessions.

Figure 18.8

The king of all simulation games, The Sims puts you in charge of a household and the people that populate it. It's up to you to make them happy.

The basic game of the Sims is extremely satisfying and absorbing, but there's so much more. Publisher Aspyr Media has also released six expansion packs that can be added to the original game: **Livin' Large**, **House Party**, **Hot Date**, **Vacation**, **Unleashed**, and **Makin' Magic** ($29.99 each). Each expands the world with new objects and locations, and builds in entirely new elements (such as pets, dating, parties, and holidays).

If just being *like* a god isn't enough for you, how about actually *being* a god? If this sounds tantalizing, try Feral Interactive's **Black & White** ($40; www.feral.co.uk). In this staggeringly original game, you're the god of a land. The goal: take over the world by making people believe in you. The beauty of this game is that you can play as either a good, nurturing god who takes care of his followers, or an evil god for whom believers are nothing more than fuel for the sacrificial fire. At your side in this quest is your earthly incarnation: a beast of tremendous size that's yours to train and grow. Creatures can likewise be good or evil.

Many game fans found the original Black & White's real-time strategy elements a bit monotonous, preferring instead the intricate and rewarding creature training.

The **Black & White: Creature Isle** expansion pack ($45) lets you focus exclusively on this element and permits your creature to train his own creature and even mate. You can purchase both titles together in the **Black & White Platinum Pack** ($60).

The most famous simulation franchise is Aspyr Media's SimCity, where you must run and maintain a thriving city and all the various (and often competing) elements within it. In the latest version, **SimCity 4** ($49.95), all the elements of past SimCity games have been enhanced and reimagined. In addition to the beautiful new 3D graphics, the game features unprecedented detail in the gameplay. You can also import your characters from the Sims to live in your city and have them report on what they like and don't like about the city.

The other major simulation classic is MacSoft's **Civilization III** ($39.99; www.macsoft.com). Though it's a bit long in the tooth, since after ten years on the market the concept is a bit dated, it delivers all the nation-building intricacy and challenge of its predecessors.

As if these weren't enough almighty choices for you, you can also manage other worlds. MacSoft's **Tropico: Mucho Macho Edition** ($19.99) puts you in charge of a burgeoning banana republic. Aspyr Media's **Zoo Tycoon** ($49.99) enables you to design and run your own menagerie.

Sports Games (BF)

One area where the Mac is not exactly bursting at the seams with titles is in the realm of sports games. The big-time titles like Madden Football, FIFA Soccer, and NHL 2004 are not available on our beloved platform (although Madden 2000 is available through Aspyr Media), and auto racing and flight sim titles are few and far between. Still, there are a few fantastic sports games out there.

The Tony Hawk series has been a best seller for years on consoles such as the PlayStation 2, and the Mac version does the series proud. Aspyr Media's **Tony Hawk's Pro Skater 4** ($39.99; www.aspyr.com) for the Mac allows the gamer to take on the role of Tony Hawk himself (and 13 other athletes) as they skate through multiple levels of skateboarding heaven. With 190 increasingly difficult goals and many of the greatest skateboarding stunts ever conceived, Tony Hawk's Pro Skater 4 is sure to make your heart soar.

Aspyr Media's **Tiger Woods PGA Tour 2003** ($49.99) is an incredible golf game that raises golfing to new levels on the Mac. The world is completely 3D, and there are eight world-class courses to choose from. The Career mode will immerse you in the drama of the PGA tour.

If car racing is your bag, then check out **NASCAR Racing Season 2002** ($39.95) from Aspyr. While not among the best racing simulators ever created, NASCAR successfully captures the excitement of nail-biting races by producing jaw-dropping graphics and equally impressive sounds. The result of this experience is that you feel like you're behind the wheel of a serious speed demon. By the time you read this, NASCAR 2003 should be available, and it promises to produce even better heart-pounding NASCAR action.

The golden age of flight simulations on the Macintosh is over, but fortunately the golden boy of flight simulators is still available for our beloved machine. Billed as the most comprehensive, powerful flight simulator for personal computers, Laminar Research's **X-Plane** ($39; www.laminarresearch.com) is, indeed, arguably the best flight simulator made for *any* platform. As a former Cessna 172 Pilot myself, I can tell you that this claim is true. With both subsonic and supersonic flight dynamics, X-Plane comes with the Bell 206 Jet-Ranger helicopter, the Cessna 172, and even the Concorde, among many other aircraft. Every aspect of flight, from wind shear to gravity, can be adjusted; there's even a Mars module that allows you to fly over the red planet!

Hardware (LF)

The selection of hardware for Mac users has grown significantly over the past few years, due in part to the resurgence of Mac gaming. Games like Tony Hawk's Pro Skater series and NASCAR Racing are much more enjoyable if you play them with the right devices, such as gamepads and racing wheels. Logitech and Microsoft, two of the most popular PC-peripheral makers, have responded by marketing their products to Mac users. You can also use a wide variety of multichannel speaker systems (previously inaccessible), thanks to M-Audio's consumer sound cards. These products represent only a small portion of what's available. There are a myriad of audio devices and USB controllers labeled PC-only, but if you check the specifications on the box or on the manufacturer's Web site carefully, you may discover that they are Mac-compatible, too.

Video Cards

The complexity and power requirements of the latest *video cards* (also called *graphics processing units,* or *GPUs*) exceed even the fastest desktop computer processors. The major video-card vendor in the Mac market is ATI, and while the company's products debut on the Mac six to nine months after the PC release, the products' raw power isn't any less. The impressive graphical effects being used in modern games demand high-end video cards, making them the object of every Mac gamer's desire.

ATI offers a few retail products to satiate the upgrade market. Its biggest and baddest video card is the **Radeon 9800 Pro** ($399; www.ati.com), a 3D accelerator so powerful that only when it's plugged into the 8x AGP Pro slot of Apple's fastest Power Mac G5 does it realize its full potential. The graphics chip is clocked at 380 MHz and has eight pixel pipelines, resulting in a massive fill rate of 3 gigapixels per second. It is fed data at a rate of 21.7 GBps from the 128 MB of double-data-rate memory, through a 256-bit-wide bus. With a pool of onboard memory so large and so fast, frame rates will still be buttery smooth when you increase the resolution and texture details in games.

Besides uncompromising performance, the Radeon 9800 Pro has features that enhance image quality. For instance, ATI's SmartShader is largely responsible for some of the realistic lighting, shadow, and texture effects you see in id Software's Doom 3 and Bungie's Halo. That's because SmartShader lets developers program these effects into games without a Herculean effort. Another feature that comes with this card, SmoothVision, detects and removes *aliasing artifacts* (jagged edges) in 3D games. The result is a sharper, more natural-looking image. While anti-aliasing may sound trivial, the effect is apparent. Once you play a game with SmoothVision turned on, you'll never want to leave it off again.

Casual gamers who don't need the incredible fill rates and memory bandwidth of the Radeon 9800 Pro can opt for ATI's **Radeon 9000 Pro** ($129). Based on ATI's previous-generation graphics chip, the Radeon 9000 Pro can push pixels at a rate of 1.1 gigapixels per second, which is enough to run many 3D games smoothly. Graphics professionals will appreciate the dual display capabilities that the card provides via the ADC and DVI connectors, and crisp 2D image quality. Topping off the Radeon 9000 Pro's feature list is SmartShader and SmoothVision support.

Audio

Our sense of sound is attuned to noises that please our ears, which is why we bounce our heads to music and cringe when fingernails scrape across a chalkboard, and why audiophiles debate endlessly over which brand of speaker cable transmits the cleanest signal. Audio quality can be highly subjective, especially when components costing thousands of dollars are involved. But most people can tell which speakers sound "better" to a reasonable degree of accuracy, even if they are not able to articulate the aural differences. In general, a more-expensive speaker system made by an established company will be more capable, in terms of accurately reproducing audio. There are, however, a few exceptions.

Sound cards

Mac users clamored for a capable yet inexpensive consumer sound card after Creative Labs' abortive attempt to enter the Mac market. We finally got what we were looking for: M-Audio's **Revolution 7.1** ($99; www.m-audio.com), a product that is indeed revolutionary for Mac users.

Revolution 7.1 is a PCI sound card that features four analog outputs (for up to eight discrete channels of sound), one coaxial digital output, a microphone input, and a line input. It's not necessary to own a multichannel speaker system to take advantage of Revolution's features, though. M-Audio uses high-quality components, which improves audio fidelity over the Mac's built-in audio. Also, you can get a surround-sound effect from a two-speaker setup or headphones, thanks to TruSurround XT technology from SRS Labs, which this card supports.

Owners of 4.1, 5.1, 6.1, and 7.1 speaker systems (see the sidebar "Audio Terminology," below) will benefit from SRS Labs' Circle Surround II, which creates multichannel surround sound from a stereo source, such as an MP3 or an audio CD. This feature is particularly useful for simulating positional audio in games and DVDs. Macs running Mac OS X 10.3 (Panther) and equipped with Apple's DVD Player are capable of playing back six discrete channels of sound, so you can experience true surround sound if you have multiple speakers. You will, however, need a decoder to direct the Mac's sound channels to the speakers. Some speakers have a decoder built in; otherwise, you'll need to purchase a separate decoder box. Decoders are available from most of the major stereo component manufacturers, such as Sony and Panasonic; the cost of these ranges from $150 right up to $500.

Of course, not all Macs have PCI slots, so M-Audio developed a USB solution. **Sonica Theater** ($119.95) is an external device with capabilities similar to those of Revolution 7.1, the only notable omission being the microphone input. Audio quality will also be slightly lower if you are connecting Sonica Theater to a USB 1.1 port, due to the bandwidth limitations.

Audio Terminology

Computer speakers are available in many different configurations; the most common is stereo, which is usually referred to as *2.1*. The first number refers to the number of satellite speakers, and the second represents the *LFE* (low-frequency-effects) channel, or *subwoofer*. The 4.1 and 5.1 configurations are becoming increasingly popular with gamers and mini-home-theater enthusiasts. Creative Labs offers a few 6.1 speaker systems, but they are still uncommon. A 7.1 setup is usually reserved for high-end home-theater systems. There are currently no companies that sell such a package to consumers (to get them you'll need to have a professional installer purchase and install them for you), but you can assemble your own system from less-expensive speakers. For the most consistent sound quality, you should use speakers of the same brand and specifications.

Speakers

Unless you enjoy the wonderful world of mono sound, one of the first accessories you should purchase for your Mac is a set of external speakers. Just the product for the budget-minded Mac user is Logitech's **Z-340** ($79.95; www.logitech.com). It's a 2.1 system that has a total power output of only 33 watts *RMS (root-mean-square)*—6.5 watts RMS per satellite, 20 watts RMS subwoofer—but packs a surprising amount of punch in its diminutive package. The midrange and high-end tones are fairly clear and crisp across most of the volume range. However, the subwoofer muffles some of the detail and refuses to perform at times. Despite this flaw, the Z-340 is an excellent value.

Altec Lansing's **621** ($149.95; www.alteclansing.com) not only has impressive specifications (45 watts RMS per satellite, 53 watts RMS subwoofer), but it also sounds better than many speaker systems in its class. Powering each speaker is a 3-inch full-range driver and 1-inch tweeter, which are capable of faithfully reproducing the audio in music, movies, and games. The subwoofer bangs out tight, accurate bass lines without being overwhelming. To match its elegant sound, Altec Lansing dressed the 621's satellite and subwoofer drivers in a gray cloth grill trimmed with silver accents.

In the arena of 5.1 audio, speaker systems are generally more powerful, more feature-filled, and of course more expensive. Cambridge SoundWorks (www.cambridgesoundworks.com), now a subsidiary of Creative Labs, has created an affordable yet capable 5.1 package. The **MegaWorks THX 550** ($280) includes five satellites, each rated at 70 watts RMS; a massive subwoofer that pumps out 150 watts RMS; and a THX certification to ensure that you experience George Lucas's movies as they were meant to be. Even more important than the 500 watts of total system power is the MegaWorks 550's ability to play back all types of audio with pleasurable results. Classical music pieces are sharp and colorful, games are immersive with Circle Surround II enabled, and movies sound amazing in Dolby Digital. Your head will whip around when bullets whiz by and ricochet off walls, and explosions will literally shake the windows. The MegaWorks 550's only weakness is the center channel, which is sometimes drowned out by the front satellites.

MidiLand doesn't have the recognition that Logitech, Altec Lansing, and Creative Labs have, but the **S4 MidiLand 8200 v2.0** ($399.95; www.midiland.com) has caught the eyes and ears of many gamers. The S4 MidiLand 8200 v2.0 isn't as powerful as other systems (200 watts RMS; 20 watts RMS per speaker, 100 watts RMS subwoofer), but it can submerge a bedroom in sound. The 3-inch drivers, encased in a sturdy wooden enclosure, produce warm, clean sound in concert with the 6.5-inch subwoofer. There's a barely noticeable hiss and the midrange is flat, but that can be fixed by using high-quality speaker wire such as that made by Monster Cable. The most compelling accessory included with the S4 MidiLand 8200 v2.0 is the **ADS 4000** Dolby Digital/DTS/ProLogic decoder and receiver (you can buy it separately for $159.95). It has two digital coaxial inputs, one S/PDIF input, and two analog inputs, so you can have several audio sources connected. Three sets of RCA outputs allow you to pair nearly any six-channel speaker system with the ADS 4000.

(For additional speaker recommendations, see Chapter 7.)

Controllers (BF)

Game controllers are designed to make gaming more immersive by providing a comfortable interface that simulates real-world mechanics and controls (**Figure 18.9**). Ask those who have flown in a dogfight with a joystick or driven a sports car with a racing wheel about their experience, and they'll tell you how natural and engrossing it was. For first-person shooters and real-time strategy games, you should have a mouse that is accurate and smooth if you want to come out on top. Now that Mac OS X fully supports *force feedback* devices, which provide realistic sensations, including tension and vibration, Mac gamers can experience a whole new level of realism.

While some games need only a keyboard and mouse, many require a special controller for you to have complete mastery over the gameplay. There are many kinds of controllers, most of which are useful depending on the game they are associated with. For example, platform games require a gamepad-style controller that mimics the controllers of dedicated gaming consoles, while flight simulators are best enjoyed with a joystick or flight yoke system. When choosing a controller, it's best to consider comfort, ease of use, and compatibility with your favorite games before plopping down your hard-earned money.

Figure 18.9

Gamepads, joysticks, and racing wheels can all make gaming a much more enjoyable experience.

Immersion Corporation developed TouchSense, the technology that gives us force feedback. The company has certified numerous joysticks, gamepads, and driving wheels for use with the Mac, including those from companies such as Gravis (www.gravis.com), Logitech (www.logitech.com), Macally (www.macally.com), Saitek (www.saitekusa.com), and Thrustmaster (www.thrustmaster.com). Any USB controller that uses TouchSense technology should be recognized by your Mac and force feedback–enabled games.

Gamepads

Gamepads mimic the controllers that come with dedicated video game systems such as the PlayStation 2 and the Nintendo GameCube. These controllers are held with two hands and usually offer a bevy of buttons that allow the user to control every aspect of gameplay without having to let go of the device. When choosing a gamepad, it's best to look for one that has all the standard controls (analog sticks, directional pad, left and right triggers, etc.) and feels good in your hands. Remember, you'll be gripping these for many hours, so comfort is important. Logitech's **Dual Action Gamepad** ($35; www.logitech.com) and Saitek's **P880** ($40; www.saitek.com) are good examples of standard gamepads. If you want to take a walk on the wild side, check out Belkin's **Nostromo SpeedPad n52** ($50; www.belkin.com) for perhaps the best of the gamepads (certainly the best-looking).

Joysticks

Most people think of joysticks mainly in relation to flight simulators. Indeed, flight-simulator fanatics swear by their *HOTAS (Hands-On Throttle and Stick)* systems, which are modeled after controls in real fighter planes. Still joysticks can be used with many other types of games and don't need to conform to fighter plane controls. Joysticks are a catch-all group of controllers that can be used successfully for platform games and even first-person shooters; it's all a matter of preference. If a cordless experience is important, check out Logitech's **Freedom 2.4** ($60; www.logitech.com). As the name implies, the Freedom 2.4 is cordless and works on a 2.4 GHz wireless system, which is handy if the seating is far from the screen.

Racing wheels

Trying to use the arrow keys to navigate a sports car through a series of twists and turns at high speeds can be a frustrating experience. A steering wheel (and pedals) not only is a more-intuitive control scheme, but it also allows precise maneuvers not possible with a keyboard. Perhaps the best wheel on the market is Logitech's **MOMO Racing Wheel** ($90; www.logitech.com). This is a wheel and shifter in one package that delivers precise racing action for the

Mac. ACT Labs also makes the **GPL USB Shifter** ($59.99; www.act-labs.com), which is handy for hard-core racers who want to track the rpm of their car to maximize shifting performance. Unfortunately, these days there are very few good auto-racing games available for the Mac.

Other controllers (LF)

A few peripherals belong in their own categories because of their unique appeal. XGaming's **X-Arcade** ($149.95; www.xgaming.com) is one such game controller. It's a replica of a two-player arcade joystick that is without a doubt on the wish list of every MAME junkie. The entire unit—from the buttons and switches to the sturdy wooden enclosure—is constructed from arcade cabinet parts, which gives it an extremely authentic feel. Each joystick has a complement of eight buttons, not including the one- and two-player buttons and paddle controls on each side of the X-Arcade.

X-Arcade Solo ($99.95), also from XGaming, is a more-compact and portable version of X-Arcade. As the name suggests, there is only one set of controls, so you won't be bumping elbows with anyone. Both the X-Arcade and X-Arcade Solo are compatible with the most popular consoles and any Mac or PC. XGaming sells adapters for Dreamcast, GameCube, PlayStation, PlayStation 2, and Xbox.

Interview: Donn Denman

"The whole user-programming challenge—how do users configure and customize their machines—has been my focus in my career," says Donn Denman. Mac veterans whose memories stretch back to System 6 may remember him as the author of MacroMaker, an Apple utility that made it possible to automate many repetitive operations just by recording the steps. In the early 1990s he was instrumental in the development of AppleScript, a technology that has played a big part in the Mac's success—especially in the professional publishing world—ever since. But to Apple old-timers and Mac history buffs, Denman is probably best known for a contribution that never saw the light of day: MacBASIC, a much-anticipated programming environment that Apple killed before its release at the behest of Bill Gates. Denman left Apple in 1993. Since then he has worked for game-maker 3D, for PowerTV, and as a contractor for several other companies, including Apple and TiVo.—Henry Norr

> *I think for me, and maybe for other people, that was where we saw how Microsoft could be really predatory— I think that was an eye-opener.*
>
> *—Donn Denman, on Microsoft's negotiations to kill MacBASIC*

When did you start working at Apple?

I landed at Apple in early 1979. I went back to get my bachelor's degree from Antioch College that spring, then returned to Apple as a full-time employee around July.

Were you doing language stuff from the beginning?

That's right. I started out on an update to AppleSoft BASIC that never really worked out. [AppleSoft BASIC was a version of the BASIC language that shipped with the Apple II+ and later. It was based on code licensed from Microsoft in 1977.] When I came back as a full-time employee, the Apple III was just starting up, so I worked for the next year or two on what they called BASIC III for the Apple III, which was an AppleSoft derivative. I was proud to get that done and have it come out on time. Then in 1982 they recruited me into the Mac group, and I started working on MacBASIC.

Was the idea that it would be bundled, Apple II-style, with the Mac?

Yes. At that time a machine couldn't really be released without BASIC, and because of my experience I was sort of the man to do it. I thought it was a wonderful opportunity to redo it from scratch and do a more modern implementation. I think I succeeded, but didn't succeed in doing it in time.

Was there some special problem?

It was a combination of not being experienced enough to know how to manage the project, not knowing how to say no to new features, not understanding how long it was going to take. And then I got sidetracked because when it got close to the shipping time for the computer, it became clear that the BASIC wasn't going to be ready in time, so I was recruited to do the Alarm Clock and NotePad desk accessories and to test the final product to get it out.

continues on next page

After the launch you went back to the BASIC?

Yeah, and I worked on it for the next year, and it was in beta and getting very close to being ready to ship, and the news came down that it had been canceled because of a deal with Microsoft.

Explain that, if you would, because I've heard several versions of the story.

I was never given an official version of what happened, but here's my understanding: AppleSoft BASIC, which was in ROM on every Apple II then, had an eight-year license that was about to expire. That license needed to be renewed—otherwise, we couldn't ship our bread-and-butter product. So Steve Jobs cut a deal with Bill Gates, and part of what Gates required was for us to stop developing MacBASIC.

Was the motive just purely financial—just to protect sales of their BASIC?

I think the finance was part of it, but you know Bill Gates got started with BASIC—that's how he started Microsoft—so that was sort of vital to his self-image. I think he found it quite threatening that my BASIC was substantially better. And people did believe that it was sub-stantially better, because it was a new technology. It wasn't strictly interpretive.

I always thought BASIC by definition was interpreted?

Yeah, but the technology I built was very much like Java is today. It compiled into a pseudo-code that is designed to be quickly interpreted, to get better performance. And the better performance I think was just one of the things that made my BASIC superior. It was a full, integrated development environment that was quite deluxe. It had direct text editing. As you edited, it would compile immediately, so you would see whether a line you had just typed was syntactically correct or not, and then it would bold the keywords—that sort of thing. That was really the problem that caused it to be late; we kept putting in new features.

How did you feel when it was killed?

I was really angry. I felt like it was my two-year-old baby that had been taken away from me. I immediately went out and rode my motorcycle in a crazy way and wrecked it. After that I took a leave of absence from Apple. Looking back, I think for me, and maybe for other people, that was where we saw how Microsoft could be really predatory—I think that was an eye-opener.

What computers do you use now?

I use Mac OS X primarily, but I also use Windows, and then at TiVo I learned to use Linux, so I'm pretty multicomputer. I've really enjoyed the development of Mac OS X. It keeps bringing me new things that I can't do any other way, at least not easily, like the iTunes Music Store—I really love that—and iChat AV.

Do you have any urge to go back to Apple?

I really love being independent now, but if Apple were to do a next-generation user interface, that would be really exciting. I'd love to be part of that. I still see Apple as sort of my first love.

Part 4

Extending
Your Reach

19

The Internet

Jonathan A. Oski (JO) is the chapter editor and coauthor.

Joseph O. Holmes (JH) edited earlier editions of **The Macintosh Bible,** *from which portions of this chapter are taken.*

Since the inception of the Internet, many of its underpinnings—both servers and network protocols—have come from the same Unix operating system that serves as the foundation for Mac OS X. This new foundation for the Macintosh makes your computer comparable to many of the servers that make up the World Wide Web. Ever since the release of Mac OS X, the Internet has become even more interwoven with the Macintosh computing experience. If you have recently upgraded to Mac OS X or set up a new Macintosh, you'll recall that your Internet-access and email settings were the few pieces of information you were asked to provide.

In this chapter you'll learn how to get your Mac connected to the Internet: how to make sure you have the right hardware and software, choose an Internet service provider (ISP), and pick the right plan. You will learn how to pick the browser that best suits your needs and how to tune your browser preferences for maximum functionality and performance. Choosing an electronic-mail (email) application or service is another important step in maximizing your Internet experience; we'll go over the nuances of the popular email applications to help you ferret out the package that works best for you, as well as show you how to avoid spam and filter your messages.

The Mac OS and Apple's Web site offer many great services. Sherlock makes searching the Internet part of the Macintosh experience. Apple's .Mac offers a suite of features to Mac users, such as virus protection, backup, shared disk space, and Web-site hosting. We round things out with a discussion of instant messaging, Web logs, newsreaders, content filtering, and the Mac's video-telephone capabilities.

Read on to get started using your Mac on the Internet and making the most of your Internet experience.

In This Chapter

Getting Connected

With Mac OS X, connecting your Mac to the Internet has never been easier. The first time you start up Mac OS X—whether you've upgraded, done a fresh installation, or bought a new Mac—the Mac OS X Setup Assistant guides you through the initial configuration of your Mac, including most necessary Internet settings. And since all new Macs come equipped to connect to the Internet with no additional software or hardware, all you will need to get connected is a phone line. (Even if you've purchased a new Macintosh—desktop, iMac, or PowerBook—within the last few years, chances are you have all that you need to get connected.)

Once Setup Assistant has gathered your registration and account information, it collects the information needed to configure your Internet connection. The information you'll be asked to provide varies according to the connection method you choose (**Figure 19.1**).

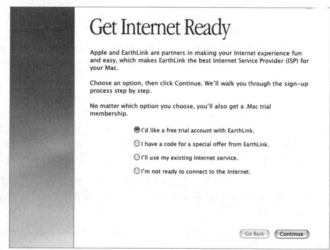

Figure 19.1

Internet Setup Assistant walks you through the process of getting your Mac connected to the Internet, regardless of the method or service provider you choose.

One nice thing about Setup Assistant is that you can run it at any time. If you aren't ready to configure your Internet connection when you start running the assistant, you can run the program later. You'll find Setup Assistant in /System/Library/CoreServices (you can access the CoreServices folder quickly from the Finder by choosing Go > Go to Folder and typing /System/Library/CoreServices).

If you don't already have an account with an Internet service provider (ISP), you'll need to consider your options and decide which is best for you. (See the sidebar "Choosing a Connection Method," below.) Setup Assistant first asks whether you want to create a new account or use one you already have.

Choosing a Connection Method

Dial-up or *broadband* (cable or DSL)—which is the best for you? With all the high-bandwidth content, such as music, streaming video, and games, on the Internet, you would presume that people would be flocking to broadband access. To the contrary, dial-up is still the most prevalent method for connecting to the Internet. Granted, broadband is more expensive and still is not available in many areas, but even in areas where cable or DSL access is available, fewer than 20 percent of the homes served subscribe to broadband access.

Though there is some variability in pricing, unlimited dial-up Internet accounts with leading national providers such as EarthLink, MSN, AOL, and AT&T typically cost close to $20 per month. (There are some lower-cost options available from second-tier providers like NetZero and Juno, but these are often riddled with advertisements on the interface.) The typical fees for a broadband account (cable or DSL) are much higher and usually run between $45 and $70 per month. Before you choose what looks like the least expensive service, consider the following points:

- **How much time do you spend online?** If you plan to use the Internet for a few hours a day and have only one phone line, you'll be tying up your line and won't be able to accept calls while you're searching, surfing, and reading your email. If you add the cost of a second phone line (about $20–$25 per month), then your total cost for dial-up is comparable to what you'd pay for broadband, and broadband performance is significantly better. Also, if you subscribe to more than one service from a broadband provider—such as phone or cable TV, you can often get a discount for the bundled services that makes broadband an even more compelling choice.

- **Do you have more than one personal computer in your home (or business)?** If you want to access the Internet from more than one computer and rely on dial-up Internet access, you can try to share the slow dial-up connection or add phone lines for each computer. Broadband connections can be shared easily using an inexpensive router, a wireless access point, or a Mac acting as a router. (See "Sharing a Connection," later in this chapter.)

- **Are you concerned about the security of your computer when you're connected to the Internet?** With broadband Internet access, it is easy to install a firewall or router to protect your computer(s) from intrusion.

- **Do you travel or need to access the Internet when you're away from your home or office?** Most broadband providers do not include dial-up as an alternative access method (EarthLink is one exception). If you choose a broadband connection and need access to the Internet while traveling, you may also need to subscribe to a dial-up service. (You can probably subscribe for close to $10 per month if you don't need unlimited access.) Most broadband providers let you read your email using a Web browser, so any Internet connection (dial-up or at an Internet café) should suffice for accessing your email.

If you're upgrading from Mac OS 9, Setup Assistant copies your current settings so that you don't need to reenter them.

Apple offers a free trial of EarthLink's dial-up Internet service; you can also sign up for a new account using the assistant. If you are going to be using an existing account, you should have the following information handy to complete the setup process:

- User name (for dial-up or a high-speed PPPoE connection)
- Password (for dial-up or a high-speed PPPoE connection)
- A local Internet access number (dial-up only)
- Internet IP address (cable, DSL, or LAN if your ISP doesn't use DHCP—but most do)

Your ISP can provide an access number and Internet IP address information if you do not already know these.

In addition to collecting information about your Internet connection, Setup Assistant can set up your .Mac account. Apple's .Mac (pronounced "dot Mac") service should not be confused with the connectivity services offered by ISPs. .Mac is a collection of Internet-based services that extend your Macintosh-based digital life to the Internet. If you are on the fence about whether .Mac is something you need, Setup Assistant offers you a free 60-day trial membership so that you can experiment before paying the $99 annual subscription fee. You can also go to www.mac.com to get more information on .Mac and a trial membership. (See ".Mac," later in this chapter, for more information on all that's included with the service.)

When you are done with Setup Assistant, your Internet-connection settings should be complete. Should you prefer to configure your service manually, or view or change these settings, you can use the Network System Preferences pane and, if you use a dial-up connection, the Internet Connect application. (See "What's Your Preference?" below).

What's Your Preference?

You'll use the Network pane in System Preferences to manage most of your Internet-related network settings (**Figure 19.2**). How you set these preferences depends largely on the type of Internet connection you have. You can also use the Network pane to create custom Internet settings that you can switch between, depending on where you plan to access the Internet (see the sidebar "Using Location Manager," below).

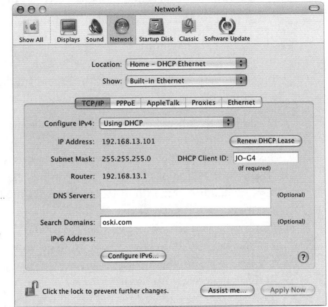

Figure 19.2

Since your TCP/IP address is vitally important to getting your Internet connection working, you need to pay careful attention to the information in the Network pane. In most cases, DHCP will automatically perform the setup for you.

Dial-up connections

To configure your dial-up settings, open the Network preferences pane and then make sure that your modem is selected in the Show pop-up menu. (If your modem doesn't appear in this list, you need to make sure that Internal Modem is checked in the Network Port Configurations pane, which is accessible from the Show pop-up menu.) The tabs in the Network pane are used to control the settings for PPP, TCP/IP, Proxies, and Modem. If you're not using America Online (AOL) as your ISP, you can set the TCP/IP tab's Configure pop-up menu to Using PPP and then go to the PPP tab.

The PPP tab is where you enter the account information and access numbers for your ISP (**Figure 19.3**). The Service Provider field is optional, but you might find it useful if you have more than one ISP. The important fields are Account Name, Password, and Telephone Number—all of which should have been provided to you by your ISP.

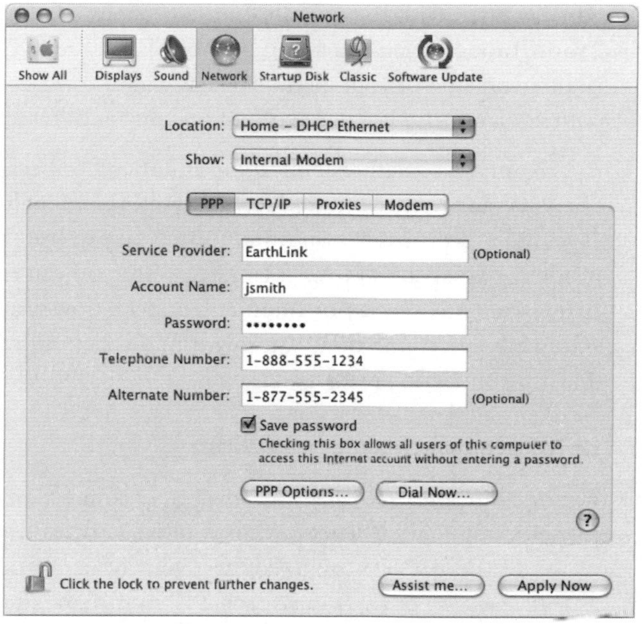

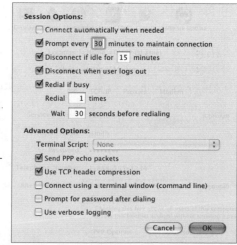

Figure 19.3

Point-to-Point Protocol (PPP) is the lingo your Mac uses to communicate with a dial-up ISP. If you used Internet Setup Assistant, these fields will be populated for you—but if you want to add numbers for connecting (say, if you travel), this is the place to make these changes.

Clicking the PPP Options button reveals some additional settings that you may find useful for managing your dial-up connection (**Figure 19.4**). You can probably leave these all with the default settings unless you find that your connection doesn't behave the way you want it to (or your ISP tells you to make changes). For example, the default setting is to disconnect if your Mac is idle for 10 minutes. You might prefer to stay connected until you explicitly disconnect, in which case you should uncheck this option. Though the "Connect automatically when needed" setting may sound appealing, you'll probably find your Mac dialing up more often than you want. This is because any attempt to access an Internet-based service (email or Web browsing, for example) will initiate a connection.

Figure 19.4

Several PPP options control the way your connections are made and maintained. You should not change any in the Advanced Options section unless instructed to do so by your ISP.

You can stick with the defaults on the Modem tab, but make sure that the "Show modem status in menu bar" box is checked. This puts an icon on the right-hand side of your menu bar that makes it very easy to connect and disconnect from the Internet without opening another application.

Apple provides another application, Internet Connect, to handle dial-up connections (and Virtual Private Network [VPN] and built-in Ethernet connections as well). You probably won't find it necessary to use this if you've added the modem status icon to your menu bar, since you can connect directly from there. One nice feature of Internet Connect, however, is that it displays the status of your connection. You might find it helpful when troubleshooting a dial-up connection that's gone awry.

Local area network connections

For our purposes, *local area network (LAN)* connections to the Internet are those that use an Ethernet port in your Mac. Broadband, both cable and DSL, uses an Ethernet network to connect your Mac to a device (often referred to as a *cable modem* or *DSL modem*) that is, in turn, connected to your ISP's network. Likewise, if you have a dedicated high-bandwidth connection from your home or business to an ISP using a T1 line (or something similar), you'll connect to your home/office LAN using Ethernet. In these cases, a router shuttles network packets between your network and the Internet.

Regardless of the type of broadband connection you may have, you use the Network preferences pane to manage your settings. In most cases your network settings will be provided via *Dynamic Host Configuration Protocol (DHCP)*. The nice thing about DHCP is that it frees you from managing any of your TCP/IP settings. The settings are "leased" to you for a set period of time, and your Mac renews this lease automatically for you. If you use your Mac on a regular basis or leave it powered on most of the time, your TCP/IP address information won't change that often since your lease is renewed before it expires.

Digital Subscriber Line (DSL) is a form of broadband that operates at high speeds over the same network as your telephone. DSL connections typically use *Point-to-Point Protocol over Ethernet (PPPoE)* and require authentication similar to dial-up. These settings are entered on the PPPoE tab of the Network preferences pane (**Figure 19.5**).

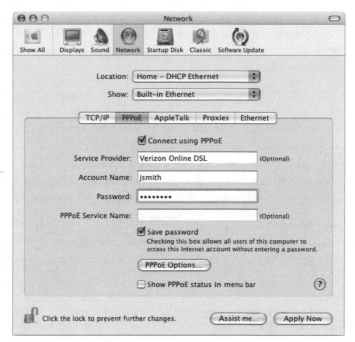

Figure 19.5

PPPoE is typically used for DSL connections. These mimic dial-up connections over Ethernet, and hence you must supply a user name and password before your ISP will let you send and receive data.

 What's a *proxy*? Proxy servers are often used to control traffic flow or add security. Think of the server as another device on the network that acts on your behalf. For example, when you are using a Web (http) proxy, your requests for Internet content are sent to the proxy server. It can look in its cache to see if what you're looking for is already stored on the server, and if not, it will retrieve it and then forward it to you. The caching Web proxy conserves Internet bandwidth by storing frequently accessed information locally. Most home and small business users can ignore the Proxies tab in the Network preferences pane. You should ask your ISP before specifying any proxy settings.

Email and Web preferences

Mac OS X 10.2 and earlier included an Internet preferences pane that provided a convenient way to manage your primary Internet-related settings in one location. You could specify .Mac, iDisk, email, and Web settings there. With Mac OS X 10.3 (Panther), however, the Internet preferences pane was replaced by the .Mac preferences pane, which pertains solely to .Mac accounts (see ".Mac," later in this chapter, for more on these settings). To set email and Web-browser preferences under Mac OS X 10.3, you need to use your application's preferences settings.

Whether or not you plan to use Apple's Mail client, you will need to open the application to specify some of your email preferences. For example, you will need to use the General tab in Apple Mail to specify your default email-reader application. Your account and mail-server information is now specified only in the application and cannot be shared across several applications as it was in versions prior to Mac OS X 10.3 (and in Mac OS 9). You should refer to the Accounts section of the mail program you'll be using—once you've decided which one to use.

Likewise, you'll need to open Safari, Apple's Internet browser, to specify your default Web-browser application. This is done in the General pane of Safari Preferences, where the browsers installed on your system should appear in the Default Web Browser pop-up menu. As is the case with email, though, other settings (like your default home page and location for downloaded files) should be made in the browser application of your choice, since they can no longer be shared among several applications as they could in Mac OS 9.

 You might consider placing your downloads in an easy-to-find folder on the root level of your disk so that you can easily get to them. (You can also create an alias to this folder in the Dock to make navigation easier.)

Using Location Manager

The Location pop-up menu in the Network preferences pane provides a handy way to store different network settings. This feature is probably most applicable to iBook and PowerBook users who change locations often or use a combination of wired and wireless connections. The Automatic option will attempt to find the right location settings for you based on network activity on each of the ports on your system. A great thing about the Location feature is that you can change your location any time you want using the Location item in the Apple menu (**Figure 19.6**).

Figure 19.6

If you connect to several different networks, then saving your location-specific network settings is a real time-saver. You can create snapshots of your network settings from the Network preferences pane and then switch between them simply by picking a location from the Location submenu under the Apple menu.

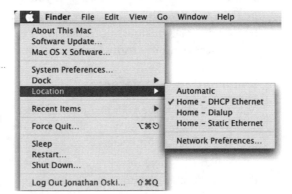

Sharing a Connection

A broadband cable router gives you some very good protection from intrusion at a very low cost. This is because it provides access via *network address translation (NAT),* and you use private IP addresses on the network that sits "behind" the router. These private addresses cannot be accessed easily from outside your home or business. The cable router connects your private network to the one managed by your ISP. Its main function is to funnel all the traffic from your private network to the Internet using the single address that is provided to you by your ISP. Since the addresses you use on your private network cannot be reached from the Internet, they're safe from hackers if you use the default configuration for your router.

There are some configuration mistakes to avoid with a cable router unless you are an advanced user and know what you are exposing by changing the default configuration suggested by your router's manufacturer. For example, don't allow your router to be managed from outside your home. Be careful about specifying any virtual hosts on your router unless you need to make an IP-based service available to folks on the Internet. (Since there are several inexpensive alternatives to hosting your site at home, you should consider using .Mac or Web space provided by your ISP as a safer way to go.)

A variety of easy-to-install cable routers for sharing an Internet connection are available from vendors like Linksys (www.linksys.com), Netgear (www.netgear.com), and D-Link (www.dlink.com) for $30–$70. The instructions are usually geared for Windows users, but the devices typically can be configured using a Web browser, and most have a wizard that guides you through the few steps you need to take before you can share a connection. Apple's AirPort, though more expensive, is also well suited to sharing a single Internet connection among both wired and wireless computers in your home or small office. (See **Figure 19.7** for a basic depiction of a shared Internet connection.)

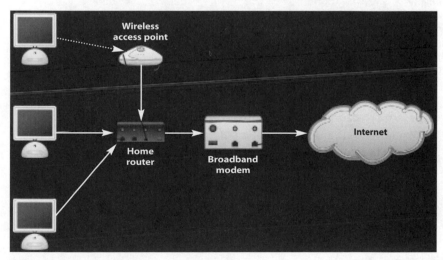

Figure 19.7

This diagram depicts a simplistic view of a home or small-office network where several computers share a single broadband Internet connection. You can now buy a wireless router to share your Internet connection and protect your computers from intrusion for less than $100.

Software-based router options for sharing your Internet connection are also available. Go to the Sharing preferences pane and click the Internet tab (**Figure 19.8**). Then check the box for the port where the computers you want to share your connection with are attached, such as your Ethernet port. This option allows you to share a single dial-up connection with other computers in your home or business. Sustainable Softworks' **IPNetRouterX** ($100; www.sustworks.com) and Vicomsoft's **SurfDoubler** ($49; www.vicomsoft.com) offer more-advanced features than those built into Mac OS X. These include DHCP, port filtering, port forwarding, and more.

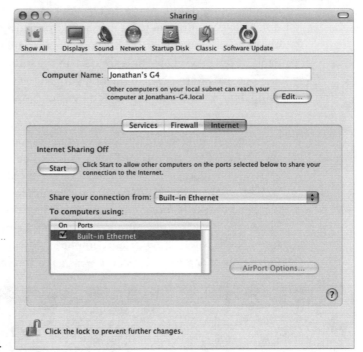

Figure 19.8

A Mac running Mac OS X can share its dial-up or broadband Internet connection with any other Macs on its network. Though there is some risk doing this—since your Mac is usually exposed to the Internet—it is easy to set up and costs nothing.

 Using a Mac to share an Internet connection can be risky unless you take some extra precautions to protect the computer that is acting as a router. Installation and careful configuration of firewall software on the router Mac is necessary to protect it from being hacked. Since hardware-based routers are so inexpensive these days, they provide a cheaper and safer way to share your Internet connection.

Do I Need My Own Domain?

Why have some nondescript email or home-page address when you can be master of your own domain? Have you ever changed ISPs (voluntarily or not) and been forced to send out change-of-address messages to everyone in your address book? Phone-number portability is now widely available, but you can't easily keep your favorite email address when your ISP (or cable company) is sold. The great news is that owning your own domain is not strictly reserved for geeks any longer. With the services offered by many of the domain registrars, you can cheaply and easily have your own domain for as little as $30 a year. Try the following registrars:

- VeriSign (www.verisign.com)
- Domain Registry of America (www.droa.com)
- eNom, Inc. (www.enom.com)

You'll first need to find a clever domain name that is available, and all these sites will help you search for one. Once you have registered a domain, you can use Web and email forwarding features provided by the registrar to have messages sent to *YourName@YourCleverDomain.com* forwarded to the in-box of your choosing (for example, the one given to you by your ISP).

Choosing and Using a Browser

Exploring the World Wide Web (aka *the Web* or *the Net*) is what people do with their Internet connection. The exploration, sometimes referred to as *surfing,* is done with an Internet browser. Browser applications read the source text from a Web site, encoded using a markup language like *HTML (Hypertext Markup Language),* and display it as a combination of text and graphics.

Microsoft's Internet Explorer has been the default browser on the Mac OS ever since Steve Jobs' historic deal with Bill Gates and crew back in the '90s to ensure Microsoft's continued development of applications for the Mac. Internet Explorer was ported to Mac OS X and until very recently remained the default browser for the Mac. This is apt to change, though, as Microsoft recently announced that it was suspending development of Internet Explorer for the Mac and passing the baton to Apple's newly released Safari browser. Unfortunately, you can't let go of Internet Explorer just yet, as there are still many sites that won't work properly without it. (There are also some sites that won't work on a Mac, no matter what browser you use.)

Internet Explorer remains largely unchanged from the Mac OS 9 version, with the exception of some updates to the user interface. Safari, Mozilla, and a handful of other browsers for Mac OS X offer the Mac user several additional options for a browser. Read on for a quick discussion of some of these alternatives.

How to Read a URL (JH)

Before you dig any deeper into this chapter, you'll need to learn a little about Internet addresses, known as *URLs,* for *Uniform Resource Locators.* Most people pronounce URL "you are ell," though some folks pronounce it "earl" (which is why otherwise literate people may sometimes write "an URL"). Every accessible resource on the Internet has its own unique URL, and you can learn about what a URL points to by reading it piece by piece (**Figure 19.9**).

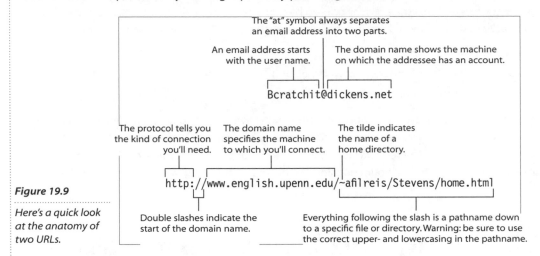

Figure 19.9

Here's a quick look at the anatomy of two URLs.

URLs are divided into three parts. First comes the *protocol,* a few letters that specify both the resource at the address and the tool that will reach it (such as *http*). After a separator—either two forward slashes (//) or the "at" symbol (@)—comes the domain name, which spells out the host computer or network on which the resource is located. Finally, beginning with a slash, you'll find the file path through the host's hierarchy of directories all the way down to the resource itself.

Email—look for the @. If the separator is an @, it's an email address.

Every Internet email address begins with the addressee's *user name,* the unique name assigned at the service or company. For example, Bob Cratchit may have picked his own user name, *bcratchit,* through his Internet service provider, Dickens Internet Services. On the other hand, his office network at Scrooge, Inc., may have assigned him the user name *bobc.*

The portion following the @ separator, known as the *domain name,* is the host on which that user has an email account. The domain name breaks down into subdomains, specifying first the organization or company, then typically the machine, and then a final three-letter domain type: *com* indicates a commercial organization; *net,* an Internet service provider; *gov,* a U.S. government site; *edu,* an educational institution, such as a college; *org,* a nonprofit organization; and *mil,* the military. (You can find a guide to country codes at www.iana.org/cctld/cctld-whois.htm.) Thus Tiny Tim's email address at Oxford University might be ttim@oxford.edu.

continues on next page

How to Read a URL continued

Domains aren't just picked willy-nilly—a host must purchase and register a domain name with an organization known as InterNIC (www.internic.net). If you'd just love to have ebeneezer@scrooge.com as your email address, don't print up your business cards just yet. Someone else may already have registered the domain name Scrooge.

You can email someone from anywhere in the online universe by addressing a message to *username@service.xxx*. Thus you'd write to Bob Cratchit at bcratchit@dickens.net or bobc@scrooge.com. You must know Cratchit's exact user name and the exact name of his service. One little typo and your message will bounce back to you undelivered or disappear into the ether forever. Your friend Tiny Tim may have an account on America Online, but simply guessing at his email address, with ttim@aol.com, will probably miss the mark.

Now let's say that, by coincidence, someone else also picked the user name *bobc*. That creates no confusion as long as he's on a different service, because his email address remains unique: If Bob's provider is Heaven Connections, his address is the unique bobc@heavens.net. No service will allow two users to pick identical user names.

Two notes: You needn't worry about uppercase and lowercase in email addresses. BCratchit@scrooge.com and bcratchit@Scrooge.COM are considered identical email addresses. And a space in a user name in an online service (*bob cratchit* on America Online) is simply dropped for Internet purposes *(bobcratchit)*.

Other Internet URLs—look for the //. If the first part of the URL is followed by a double slash (//), then the leading protocol tells you what sort of address it is: *http* indicates a World Wide Web page; *ftp* is an FTP site from which you can download a file (see the "FTP" section, later in the chapter); *gopher* is a gopher site, and *wais* is a searchable text database called *WAIS*, for *Wide Area Information Services*. Gopher and WAIS are tools that preceded the World Wide Web and were useful for finding information using a menu-based approach (gopher) or searching through indexed material (WAIS). Web-site domains usually begin with *www*, as in http://www.peachpit.com. Similarly, FTP sites usually begin with *ftp*. Many Web browsers will understand a URL that is missing the protocol *ftp://* or *http://* as long as the domain name begins with *ftp* or *www*. As with email addresses, a single typo in a URL and you're nowhere.

Finally, slashes after the domain name are used to show the path through various directories (as with the Mac's folders) to the file's location. Thus if you go to the address ftp://mirrors.aol.com/pub/info-mac, you'll see a list of all the files that reside inside the info-mac directory, which is in the pub (for *public*) directory at the AOL Mirrors FTP site. When you see a tilde (~) at the beginning of a Web URL path, you've spotted the Unix identifier for the home directory of the account. While most of the URL isn't case sensitive, upper- and lowercasing does matter in the pathname. That's the first thing to examine when you get a "404 Not Found" error in your Web browser.

Safari

Steve Jobs introduced Apple's Safari Web browser in January 2003 Macworld Expo in San Francisco. This marked a bold entry by Apple into a market that theretofore had been dominated by Microsoft. Billing Safari now as the default Web browser for Mac OS X, Apple claims, "It loads pages more quickly than any other Mac Web browser." Safari is fast, but whether it is truly the fastest is hard to determine since there are so many other variables that control speed at any given time. At any rate, you should experience a noticeable difference between Safari and any Mac OS 9 browser you may be accustomed to. If you don't have Safari, or you need to upgrade to the latest version, go to www.apple.com/safari/download or use Software Update.

 Safari requires Mac OS X 10.2.3 or later.

Safari is a great product with a number of new and innovative features that make Web browsing more fun and efficient. Some of the most notable of these features are Google integration, tabbed browsing with AutoTab support, SnapBack, AppleScript support, pop-up window suppression, and iSync support.

Safari preferences

To enable some of these great features, you'll first need to make some changes to the default preferences. Launch Safari and choose Preferences from the Safari menu (or use the shortcut ⌘,) and look at the General settings. If you've set your default browser and home page in the Internet preferences pane in Mac OS X 10.2, you should see those settings reflected here (**Figure 19.10**). Other General settings to consider: how you want new windows to open (with your home page, a list of bookmarks, a copy of the current page, or blank) and how you want links from other applications to open. It is often annoying to click a link in another application and lose your place in your browser, so you should consider checking "in a new window."

The Tabs settings (**Figure 19.11**) are where you can control Safari's tabbed-browsing feature—which improves greatly on Internet Explorer's multiwindow approach (see "Tabbed browsing," below). Your best bet is to check all the boxes in this settings page and take note of the shortcuts that appear in this window. Once you've started using tabbed browsing, you'll wonder how you ever lived without it.

Finally, review the Security settings to make sure that Safari will adequately protect you from intruders (**Figure 19.12**). You can opt to block annoying pop-up windows here (or choose Block Pop-Up Menus from the Safari menu). You probably want to accept cookies only from sites you navigate to, and if you want to review and/or remove any of the cookies in your system, you can click the Show Cookies button in this window. Also, you should make sure that Safari gets confirmation from you before sending data on a nonsecure page. Make sure to check the box at the bottom of the page to enable this feature.

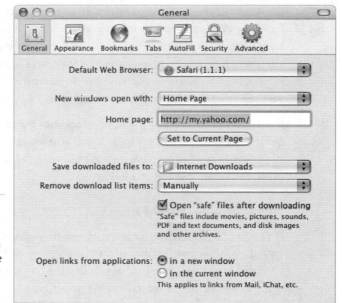

Figure 19.10

Safari's General preferences have some of the elements formerly found on the Web tab of the Internet preferences pane in Mac OS X 10.2 and earlier. These settings control some of Safari's behavior when you are following links and downloading files.

Figure 19.11

Tabbed browsing is one of the best new browser features in some time. With tabs, you can easily open and jump between several pages without needing to open a new browser window. One of the best secrets is that you can quickly open a few pages by ⌘-clicking a folder in your links bar or favorites window.

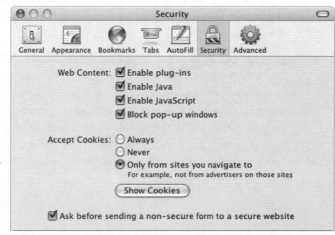

Figure 19.12

Check Safari's Security preferences to block annoying pop-up windows, limit the cookies you'll accept, and—if you prefer—disable Java and plug-ins.

Cookies are small pieces of information that are downloaded to your Mac from the Web sites you visit. They're generally used by the site's author to help keep track of where you are within the site, whether you've been to the site before, and any preferences you may have for the site. There can be malicious uses for cookies—such as storing personal information—so it's best if you tell your browser to accept cookies only from the site you're visiting.

 If you don't see some of the familiar toolbar buttons or the status bar, use Safari's View menu to check the items you want to see. The status bar shows the URL for any link you pause your mouse over, and it gives an indication of progress when you select a link.

Quick Google searches

If you are familiar with the Internet search engine Google (www.google.com), you are probably well aware of its elegance, speed, and accuracy. With Safari's Google integration, you can save yourself a trip to the Google site when you want to use this great search engine. Just type your query into the rounded rectangle in the upper-right corner of Safari's toolbar and press Return to perform your search (**Figure 19.13**).

Figure 19.13

Type any Google query in the search rectangle in the upper-right corner of Safari's window to do a Google search without having to go to the Google portal site. You can also recall prior searches quickly by clicking the magnifying glass.

If you perform the same searches on a frequent basis or want to recall a search that you performed previously, you can click the magnifying glass button in the Google search box to have it reveal any of the recent searches via a pop-up menu.

This is a good time to bring up Safari's SnapBack feature. If you have ever gone to a site and then navigated away by clicking a series of links, finding your way back to where you started can be a painful process. Click the SnapBack button (a small round orange button with a white arrow), which appears at the right end of the address bar or Google search box after you've left your original location, and you'll be instantly teleported back to the place where you started. For Google searches, you will be returned to the original results page, so you can easily try another of the hits on your search.

Tabbed browsing

Tabbed browsing, a feature introduced a few years ago in the Netscape/Mozilla browser, is one feature of Safari you'll especially grow to love (**Figure 19.14**). If you like to have several sites open concurrently, such as Yahoo (for news and information), MacInTouch (to stay up-to-date on the latest Mac news), and Apple Support (to search through the Knowledge Base or newsgroup postings), Safari lets you open these all in one window! The sites appear as different tabs below the toolbar, and you can quickly switch back and forth between different sites by clicking their tabs (or using the keyboard shortcuts ⌘ Shift → and ⌘ Shift ←).

Figure 19.14

Press ⌘ T to open a new tab in Safari without navigating away from where you started. When you ⌘ Option -click a link in your current page, you create a new tab for that link.

If there are groups of sites you visit frequently, Safari lets you open all of them at the same time. Simply create a folder in Safari's bookmark manager by choosing Add Bookmark Folder from the Bookmarks menu and then copying links to all the sites you want to open concurrently into the new folder. Finally, drag the folder to the bookmarks bar and then ⌘-click the folder to tell Safari to open all the links in the folder as separate tabs in the current window.

 Using tabs does not preclude you from having several Safari browser windows open concurrently—you can have multiple windows with several tabs open at the same time, which allows you to do real Web multitasking if you need to.

Microsoft Internet Explorer

Though largely unchanged from the Mac OS 9 version and no longer under development at Microsoft for the Mac, Internet Explorer (IE) (www.microsoft.com/mac) remains a must-have for Mac users simply because there are still many sites that won't work properly (if at all) with anything other than Internet Explorer. These tend to be sites for financial institutions, but you might also find that Web-based management of certain devices, like home firewalls, routers, and wireless access points, only works with IE. Try using Safari first, and then if you encounter a problem, use IE.

Some other reasons to keep IE around are handy features that are not yet available in Safari or other popular browsers. One such feature is IE's offline-viewing capability. IE's Scrapbook feature allows you to save pages on your computer so that you can view the site's content when you are not connected to the Internet. An even more intriguing feature of IE is its ability to save a *Web archive*. A Web archive is a single file that can include all links up to five levels deep for a site. This offers an even more comprehensive means of viewing a site when you are offline (**Figure 19.15**).

Figure 19.15

One of the great features of Internet Explorer that hasn't yet made it to Safari is the ability to save Web archives. Choose Save As from Internet Explorer's File menu to save the current site with several depths of links (and images) so that you can view the site when you are not connected to the Internet.

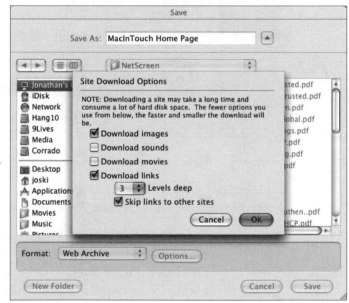

Mozilla/Netscape

Mozilla (www.mozilla.org) and its cousin Netscape X (www.netscape.com) are the stalwart browser applications of this time. Their heritage dates back to the very beginning of the Web, and they clearly served as the platform on which many of the innovations we now take as routine were introduced.

Figure 19.16

Both the Mozilla and Netscape X browsers have a unique sidebar feature that lets you quickly access a variety of functions without leaving the current site in your browser. The MapQuest tab, for example, lets you quickly get a map to any location.

They are also two of the few browser alternatives that are available on virtually every platform (including Mac OS 9, Mac OS X, Windows, Linux, Solaris, HP-UX, AIX, and several other Unix variants). Mozilla and Netscape X are built from the same code base and generally have feature parity. Mozilla is open source, while Netscape is more "commercial."

Mozilla and Netscape are unlike other applications in the way they both offer functionality that extends beyond simple browsing. In addition to being a great alternative to Safari and IE, they can serve as an email client, an address book manager, a Usenet newsreader, and a Web-page-creation tool. Their strengths lie in some of the extensions they've made to the browser concept. Mozilla/Netscape was the first application to pioneer the concept of tabbed-browsing that Apple has implemented so elegantly in Safari. Another innovation is the sidebar—a selection of tabbed sections on the left-hand side of the browser window that allow you to quickly see related sites, bookmarks, and your address book; perform searches; and much more (**Figure 19.16**). With the available library of add-on tabs for the sidebar, such as MapQuest, Mozilla/Netscape can become almost Sherlock-like in its categorized-search functionality.

Others (Camino, iCab, OmniWeb)

If you've tried Safari, Internet Explorer, and Mozilla/Netscape and are still looking for an application that better suits your Internet surfing style, there are more options.

Camino. The first of these is **Camino** (www.mozilla.org/projects/camino). Camino is a project under development by the same folks who created Mozilla and the current Netscape browsers. Formerly known as Chimera, Camino is a Web browser for Mac OS X that is simple, small, and fast. Camino is still in the beta stage of its development but is stable enough to use day-to-day.

iCab. iCab (www.icab.de/index.html) is another browser for the Mac that is still under development. It has a number of appealing features that you won't find in some other browsers, such as the ability to be configured to run in kiosk mode (when you'd like the browser to be the only application available) and the ability to save portable archives (compressed Web pages that include all image and text content and can be used on any system). It also has very granular cookie controls that let you select very specifically which cookies to accept and which to reject. The developers plan to charge $29 for a pro version once they're ready to release the product.

OmniWeb. **OmniWeb** (www.omnigroup.com/applications/omniweb) from the Omni Group is another commercial browser for Mac OS X that has some unique features. At $29.95 it is not too expensive, but it's not free like the other very good alternatives discussed earlier. You can download a trial version and see if the options it provides you, such as the ability to search your history, control the browser with voice commands, and block all sorts of pop-ups, are compelling enough to justify the fee.

Managing Bookmarks

When you visit a site that you want to be able to return to with ease, you typically bookmark it using the Bookmarks or Favorites menu in your browser. However, when you want to be able to go to the same site with a different browser or from a different computer, you need a different way to manage your bookmarks outside of your browser. Several applications provide this functionality. One popular example is Alco Blom's **URL Manager Pro** ($25; www.url-manager.com). This utility gives you systemwide access to your bookmarks through a menu that is available all the time (**Figure 19.17**).

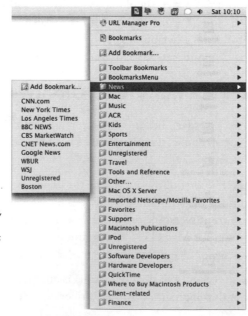

Figure 19.17

With URL Manager Pro you can quickly go to any URL (Web site, FTP server, email message, and so on) by clicking the program's icon in your toolbar and selecting the Web site. This great utility lets you manage a single collection of bookmarks across several browsers, too.

Another unique way to manage bookmarks without URL Manager Pro is via Internet location files. By dragging a URL to your Desktop from the address bar in your browser, you can create a file that can be double-clicked (or opened) from the Finder and that will launch your default browser and open the site referenced in the file. Using this approach, you can easily copy these shortcuts from one workstation to another.

Searching the Net

Thanks to Mac OS X's built-in searching tool (Sherlock) and the continued improvements of Internet-based search engines (like Google and Yahoo), finding the needle in the haystack continues to get easier. Apple was first to pioneer the integration of Internet searching with the operating system with Sherlock back in Mac OS 8.5. One thing that made the tool so great was its ability to search across multiple sites with one query. Another key benefit was its extensibility. Apple published an *API (application programming interface)* that allowed anyone to write a plug-in to allow Sherlock to search for content on any site.

Today's Sherlock is considerably more mature and is joined by other tools that help you search the Internet without launching your browser. These tools don't necessarily replace the searching capabilities offered on the Web, or the integration with Google that's in Safari. What they're great at is category-based searching—for example, searching only within categories like movies, telephone numbers, and stocks.

Sherlock

Version 3 of Sherlock is included in Mac OS X 10.2 and later and marks a change in direction for this Apple product. When Sherlock first appeared, it became the standard search tool for the Mac OS—whether you were searching for something on your local system or on the Internet. Version 3 is just for searching Internet content.

Sherlock performs searches based on categories, or *channels*. The default channels are Internet, Pictures, Stocks, Movies, Yellow Pages, eBay, Flights, Dictionary, Translation, and AppleCare, although you can add your own. The content sources for each channel vary depending on the channel file you're using and are displayed at the bottom of the page (**Figure 19.18**).

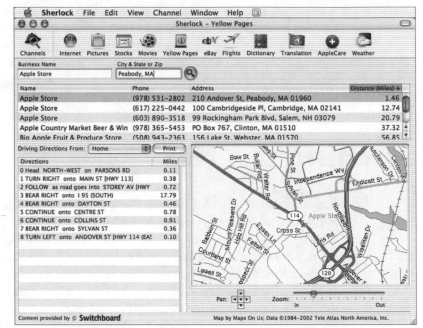

Figure 19.18

Tell Sherlock what you are looking for, and it not only tells you where you can find it, but it also shows you how to get there from a variety of locations.

Personalizing Sherlock

One of the first things you should do before using Sherlock is set your preferences (**Figure 19.19**). Preferences give Sherlock information about your location for channels that provide results relevant to where you are, like Movies and Yellow Pages. Adding multiple locations makes it easier to narrow your searches when you are away from home.

Figure 19.19

Since Sherlock factors proximity into many of its searches, such as when you are looking for Movies or Maps, take the time to enter all the addresses you search from—such as your home and office—and it will give you more relevant results.

You can also add channels to extend Sherlock's searching capabilities beyond those included by Apple. There are several sites to visit to get Sherlock channels, including Clan Mac's Sherlock Channels Web site (http://Sherlock.clanmac.com).

Watson

Karelia Software's **Watson** ($29; www.karelia.com), widely considered superior to Sherlock, is another Mac OS X application for searching the Internet. At first glance you're apt to think you're using Sherlock, and many have criticized Apple for copying Watson when it revamped the Sherlock interface in version 2. One big difference between Watson and Sherlock is that Watson is not free. You can use it for a limited time before paying $29 for a license, and many have found this program worth the small fee. (There is also a household license available that allows you to use Watson throughout your home for a flat fee of $39.)

When you first launch Watson, you will quickly notice its similarity to Sherlock—with quite a few more channels (**Figure 19.20**)! As with Sherlock, you can customize the toolbar to show the channels you want. (You'll want to do this, as Watson ships with twice as many channels as Sherlock, so that you can access the tools you use frequently with just a click.

Figure 19.20

Watson looks virtually identical to Apple's Sherlock but costs $29. You'll find the money well spent after you've used some of its unique features, such as reverse phone book lookup.

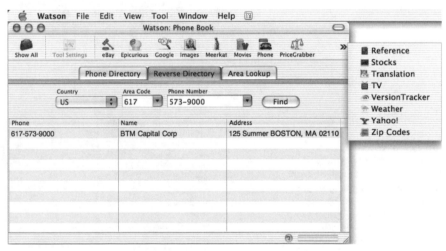

Dig deep into Watson, look at all the channels and the configuration options available for each one, and you'll quickly see what the buzz is about. Here are just a few of Watson's great features:

- You can do reverse phone lookups with the Phone Book channel, where you enter the phone number and Watson finds the company or person and the address.
- You can buy movie tickets using the Movie channel.
- You can find recipes that are formatted for printing.
- You can view Doppler radar and infrared satellite images using the Weather channel.

Other Search Tools

If you're looking for a different variation on searching tools, there are several general-purpose applications geared for quick submissions to your favorite Internet search engine. Like Sherlock and Watson, these tools can do their magic for you without a browser—saving you the time it would take to launch your browser, go to a site, and enter your query.

One nice general-purpose search utility is Ranchero Software's **Huevos** (free; www.ranchero.com). Huevos comes preconfigured for 15 popular search engines, and you can add others. One way to use Huevos is to leave it lurking in the background all the time. When you want to perform a search, simply activate its small application window using a user-selected hot-key combination (such as Control Esc), enter your search word or phrase, and then pick the search engine you want to use (**Figure 19.21**). Huevos will then display your search results in a new browser window. Unfortunately, Huevos doesn't remember your searches like the Google bar in Safari.

Figure 19.21

Huevos is a configurable search utility that you can use to quickly search in a variety of sources. Pick the place you want to search or search engine you want to use from the pop-up menu and enter your query, and your default browser displays the results—it's that simple.

Two similar utilities are the Google-focused Pomm'soft's **SearchBar** (free; www.pommsoft.com) and NetsoWork's **GooSearch** (free; www.geocities.com/netso1415/nw), which only searches Google databases. However, unlike the built-in Google search bar in Safari, these utilities allow you to search Google Images, Groups, Directory, News, and "special search areas" like Apple Macintosh, Microsoft, Linux, and the U.S. government. SearchBar is similar to Huevos in that you can specify any of a long list of databases to search. It can be extended using plug-ins or user-defined search sites.

Getting More from Google

Most people know that you can type a word or phrase into a Google search box (on the Google site or in Safari) and quickly get a list of results from the vast Google Web database. But did you know that you can also use Google to look up phone numbers, addresses, maps, stock quotes, and definitions? By prefacing your search with the keyword for the search you want to perform, you can direct Google to do a specific search for you. For example, if you type phonebook:smith, Boston, MA, you'll get a phone book listing of all the people in Boston with the last name Smith. (To restrict your search to residential listings, use *rphonebook* instead of *phonebook.*) Similarly, type stocks:AAPL INTC to get quotes and stock-performance information for Apple Computer and Intel from Yahoo Finance. (You'll also get quick links to other financial information sites, like the Motley Fool and MSN Money.)

If you want to limit your search to a specific site or top-level domain, you can use the *site:* directive in your Google search. For example, if you want to search the *New York Times* site for a particular story (without going to www.nytimes.com), enter a search phrase like "Macworld Expo" site:nytimes.com. Likewise, if you want to search just .edu sites for certain information, put site:edu in your search phrase.

These examples just scratch the surface of what you can do with Google. Look on the Google site (www.google.com/options/index.html) for more information about what you can do with the search engine. Armed with this information, you can make the Google search box in Safari do a lot more for you.

.Mac

First off, Apple's .Mac service is not a Web site per se, but rather a collection of Internet-based services integrated with Mac OS X and some of the iLife applications. Apple's .Mac service replaced the free iTools service when Mac OS X 10.2 was released in 2002. Apple's about-face from a free collection of services to a subscription service ($99 per year) drew much criticism from those who claimed that Steve Jobs reneged on his promise of a free Internet service for Mac users. To combat this criticism, Apple improved the level of integration and expanded the number of services that are included.

It's not .Mac's long list of features that makes it compelling—it's .Mac's ease of use and integration with Mac OS X applications. Here is what you get when you subscribe:

- An email account (*yourname*@mac.com)
- 100 MB of iDisk storage
- Virus protection (McAfee Virex)
- Backup software
- A personal Web site
- iSync support for your address book, calendar, and bookmarks

Mail and iSync

.Mac email isn't wholly different from what you can get free from a variety of Web-based email providers. iSync support and integration with the Apple Mail application, however, helps .Mac email stand out in this crowded field.

Unlike many other Web-mail services that are accessible only via a Web browser, .Mac lets you use Apple's Mail application to access your .Mac account. This allows you to read and compose mail while offline, and manage your mail using the additional features in the Mail application. (See "Apple Mail," later in this chapter.)

Using iSync, you can synchronize your Desktop address book with your .Mac one. You can also use this to keep address books on separate Macs—your PowerBook and desktop Mac, for example—synchronized (**Figure 19.22**). Synchronization technology is commonly used to maintain parity between your Mac and PDA calendar and address book. Launch iSync and you'll notice that .Mac is the first icon in your toolbar. We mentioned Address Book earlier, but iSync and .Mac can also be used to synchronize your iCal calendars and Safari bookmarks between several Macs (such as your PowerBook and desktop Macs at home and work). You can synchronize on a schedule so that you don't even have to remember to run iSync—it just works.

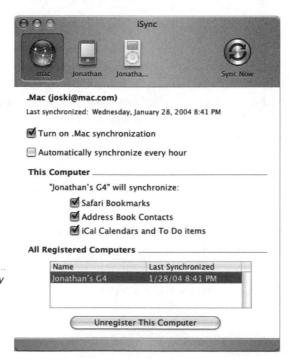

Figure 19.22

Mac users can easily synchronize their address books, calendars, and bookmarks on several Macs using iSync.

iDisk

.Mac's iDisk service starts with 100 MB of storage that you can access from both Macs and PCs. It is an ideal solution for anyone who has a broadband Internet connection, uses more than one computer (at home and work), and needs to be able to access some documents from both locations. (iDisk will work over a dial-up connection, but you'll spend a lot of time waiting if you try to move anything but small files over a slow link.) You can certainly use portable drives, USB drive key fobs, or removable media to have access to files at multiple locations, but iDisk frees you from having to carry something around with you. You can also download Apple software updates and selected freeware, shareware, and trialware. (The space consumed by these items doesn't count toward your quota.)

The .Mac Backup solution can be configured to back up selected files to your iDisk as well. While it's no substitute for more-robust backup applications like Dantz Development's Retrospect, .Mac Backup to iDisk instantly gives you an off-site backup solution for a limited number of files. Backup is preconfigured to back up various files you probably don't want to lose. These include your Address Book, Stickies notes, iCal calendars, Safari bookmarks, and keychains, but you can easily add more files and folders to the list of items to be backed up. (Just keep in mind that you start with only 100 MB of space on your iDisk—although you can purchase more space—and backing up over your Internet connection won't happen very fast.) You can also use Backup to back up to any other writable removable media that are attached to your Mac (**Figure 19.23**).

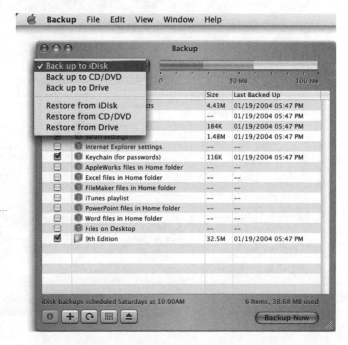

Figure 19.23

With the Backup utility that's included with a .Mac subscription, you can program your backups and never have to worry about changing media, since selected data is copied to your iDisk on the schedule you specify.

You're a Webmaster

One of the most ingenious features of .Mac is the creation tool for Web sites and home pages. It is so easy to use—and tied to iLife applications such as iPhoto—that you can literally publish a photo album with just a few clicks. If you've been pestered by family members and friends asking for copies of pictures before you've had a chance to print them, you can send your family and friends the URL for your .Mac home page and let 'em print the ones they want on their own.

.Mac's HomePage creator is chock full of themes to fit a wide variety of topics. These include photo albums, file directories, home movies, writing, résumés, invitations, and more. The process of creating a page or site with .Mac's HomePage tool is as simple as selecting the theme, clicking the Edit button for the page, and then adding your content (**Figure 19.24**). In Edit mode you specify the title for the page, choose the images or QuickTime movies you want to include on the page, and type (or paste) the text you want to include. You can also add a counter that displays the number of times the page has been visited, as well as a link that visitors can use to send you email. When you're satisfied with what you've built, click the Publish button and you're done. You can announce your site just as easily, using .Mac's iCard feature. It lets you build an electronic postcard that you can email to anyone you want to notify about your new site.

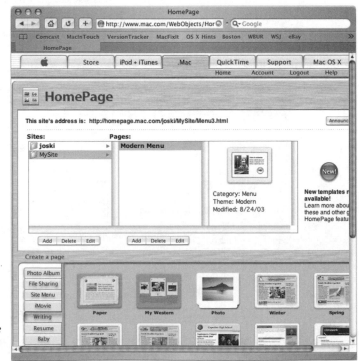

Figure 19.24

With .Mac it's easy to create a home page for your photos, movies, and files; you can choose from several themes and site templates.

If you are so inclined, the HomePage tool also lets you upload your own HTML files. There is no need to fuss with FTP or quirky means of uploading your files to the server. You can just copy them to your iDisk and then publish that folder.

There are some things to keep in mind before you get carried away with your .Mac home page. First, .Mac is not designed for high-bandwidth sites. If Apple detects that traffic on your site is too high, it will temporarily suspend access to the site. This won't affect most users, but it is designed to make sure that the Apple servers are capable of serving all .Mac members equally. Also, .Mac is not intended for commercial purposes, so you shouldn't plan to use it to host a high-volume Web store. These limitations are all spelled out in the membership agreement. Simply put, you won't find an easier solution than .Mac's HomePage tool for sharing your iLife with your family and friends.

More .Mac Perks

A .Mac account includes several other benefits to help justify its annual fee. If you don't already own an antivirus program (see Chapter 8), you can protect your Mac from viruses by downloading the copy of Virex that is included with your annual subscription. Free training courses, games, and discounts on a variety of Macintosh items are also included. The list of free perks varies from time to time, but you can get many of your .Mac questions answered on the .Mac FAQ list at www.mac.com/1/mac_faq.html.

Email

It's hard to imagine not having at least one email account these days. The explosive use of the Internet has brought email to the masses. You might have an account on your company's email system that's connected to the Internet, a home account through your ISP, an account with a free Web-based email provider, or all of the above. In just a few short years, email has become as widely used and accepted as the telephone—a task that, for the latter, took much, much longer.

Virtually every new computer sold today ships with some form of email program, and the Mac is no exception. We'll consider a few of the most popular email clients for the Mac today. You will learn how to configure these products, personalize your messages by adding a signature, manage your mail using folders and rules, avoid spam, and more.

This section assumes that you have already obtained an email account with your ISP. (If you have Web access but are unsure as to whether you have an email account, you should check with your ISP. Most ISPs bundle at least one email mailbox with Internet access services.)

What to Ask Your ISP

All the email clients discussed in this section require some basic information for initial setup. This information is the same for all the clients, and most of it comes from your ISP. You should ask your ISP the following questions:

1. **What type of mail server will I connect to?** While a large majority of ISPs provide access via Post Office Protocol (POP), some now offer Internet Message Access Protocol (IMAP) as an alternative.

2. **What are my account name and password?** Most ISPs will let you select these yourself and give you the means to change your password later. Your account name is usually used as part of your email address.

 Some ISPs offer the option of having several mail accounts for the same sub-scriber. If several family members share your Internet connection, check with your ISP to see if this option is available so that family members can have their own email accounts/addresses.

3. **What is my email address?** This address is usually in the format of *accountname@ispname*.com or .net.

4. **What is the address of the POP or IMAP server or host?** You need this address to retrieve your mail from your ISP, and it is usually in the format of *POP.ispname*.com or .net.

5. **What is the address of the SMTP server or host?** You need this to send email that you compose; it is usually in the format of *SMTP.ispname*.com or .net.

Setting Up Your Mail

Once you have the five pieces of information listed above, you can use this to set up your preferred email application. Every email client application has its own setup nuances, but the information you will need to supply is always the same. You need to find the place where you specify your account information and enter it there. For example, if you plan to use Apple's built-in Mail application, open Preferences from the Mail menu and then click the Accounts tab to enter your account type, address, login name, password, and server information. For other applications, Preferences is the best place to start looking for where to enter your account and server information.

Adding your John Hancock

Once you've got your account properly set up and you are able to send and receive mail, there are a few other things you might want to configure before using the email application. First, you can include all your relevant contact information in every message you send by creating a *signature.* Most applications will automatically append a default signature to every message you create (regardless of whether you are originating the message or replying to someone else's). A signature should be brief and to the point so that you do not add a lot of unnecessary "weight" to every message you send. Standard signatures begin with a line consisting of two dashes followed by a space and then a carriage return—after this, you can add anything you like. (Adhering to this standard convention allows applications to easily recognize where the content portion of a message ends and the signature begins.)

Some of the things you could include in your signature are your full name, street address, phone number(s), fax number, favorite quotations, and so on. You should avoid things like images, even scanned signatures, since these can make your signature larger than the message you are sending.

Avoiding clutter

If you receive a high volume of messages, you'll quickly find it inefficient to scroll through a long list of messages in your in-box when trying to find a specific message. Most mail applications let you search through your messages by limited attributes, such as sender or subject, and some even let you search for words or phrases in the body of the message. However, if you want to organize your messages by grouping them based on variable attributes—such as messages from your family members—you are better off creating folders in which to organize your email. Folders are also good for storing copies of messages you receive on a periodic basis. For example, newsletters or threads from newsgroups you subscribe to are well suited to storage in a folder hierarchy.

You can make this even easier on yourself by using rules that automatically file messages that meet certain criteria (**Figure 19.25**). Most email applications support some type of rules-based processing for your messages, and it's quite simple to set up. The easiest place to begin is to examine the characteristics of the messages you want filed by a rule. If you'd like to have all your messages for a particular newsletter you subscribe to automatically filed in the same folder when they're received, look first in the messages' From field or Subject field to see if they have something in common. Then choose the folder where you'd like the messages filed when you get them.

Figure 19.25

Creating rules to manage your mail is simple. This example shows how you specify the conditions and actions to be taken on any message that meets your criteria. You'll find that this Apple Mail example translates easily to other popular mail applications.

Choosing and Using an Email Client

Apple includes a very capable email client with Mac OS X, simply called Mail. It has gradually improved since the initial release of Mac OS X and has continued to improve with the release of Mac OS X 10.3. So you may ask yourself, "If Apple includes a good email application, why should I look further?" There are several reasons, so choosing the one that is right for you may take some experimentation. Apple Mail, Microsoft Entourage, Qualcomm's Eudora, and Bare Bones Software's Mailsmith are popular options, but if you search VersionTracker (www.versiontracker.com) or MacUpdate (www.macupdate.com) for email clients, you'll find several more to try out.

Apple Mail

The version of Mail in Mac OS X is equal to some of the best alternatives available. It does a good job of filtering spam, can be used with POP3 and IMAP servers, allows you to view HTML messages, and lets you access your .Mac email. Unlike most other programs, Mail does not include an address book. Instead, it integrates with the Address Book program that also comes with Mac OS X.

The key to getting the most out of Mail—and most other mail applications— is setting your preferences. You use Mail's Account preferences to enter the information about your account and ISP that was discussed earlier in this section. The Special tab lets you specify how you want some of the special folders, like Sent, Junk, and Trash, handled. If you want a permanent record of the messages you've sent, you should tell Mail to never delete your sent messages.

This gives you the most flexibility, since you can manually delete them from your Sent messages folder any time you like. Your Junk and Trash folders are obviously different. If you want to give yourself some time to ensure that you don't delete anything too hastily, you might consider having your Junk and Trash folders emptied automatically on a weekly or monthly basis (**Figure 19.26**).

Figure 19.26

You can tell Apple Mail how often you want routine house-keeping tasks performed on the Special Mailboxes tab of the Accounts pane in Mail's preferences.

Mail is quite good at filtering junk mail, especially once you've spent the time to train it properly. When you first start using Mail, you should tell it to mark your junk mail but not move it to the Junk folder. Once you're happy with the way junk mail is being identified, you can turn on automatic filtering, and Mail will automatically move junk messages to your Junk mailbox (**Figure 19.27**). You can easily classify any message you receive as Junk, and then Mail will know how to handle messages from the sender in the future. Customizing your toolbar in Mail by adding the Identify as Junk button lets you quickly mark Junk messages in your in-box—and they'll then get moved promptly to your Junk mailbox.

Mail in Mac OS X 10.3 added a great new feature that allows you to quickly identify messages that are part of a thread (for example, messages that are part of a send-and-reply or reply-to-a-reply discourse). In the Viewing preferences, check the "Highlight related messages using color" option to be able to quickly find messages that are like the one that is currently selected (**Figure 19.28**).

Figure 19.27

Apple Mail's Junk Mail filter, which is based on the Bayesian algorithm, does a great job of limiting the amount of spam in your in-box, once you've spent a few days training it.

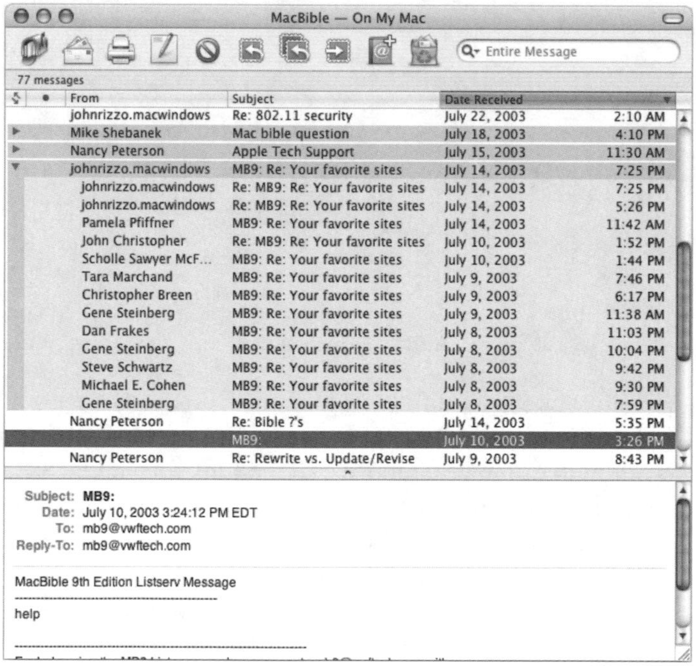

Figure 19.28

Apple Mail's organize-by-thread option lets you quickly see all messages related to a single topic or from the same sender.

You should also consider the format you choose for your messages. While more and more mail applications can display messages in rich text (or HTML format), plain text is still the best format to ensure that your messages will appear to the receiver the same way they appear on your screen. You can set this preference in the Composing pane of Mail preferences.

Finally, the Rules section of Mail's preferences is the key to managing your incoming messages, as described in "Avoiding clutter," above. Clicking the Add Rule button on the Rules pane summons a dialog that guides you through the process of creating a rule to handle messages that meet specified criteria.

Microsoft Entourage

Microsoft Entourage X ($99 standalone; www.microsoft.com/mac) is the successor to Outlook Express, Microsoft's free email application for Mac OS 9. Available as part of the Microsoft Office v. X for Mac suite or separately, Entourage is much more than a mail client—and herein lies the biggest difference between it and Apple Mail. Entourage is a comprehensive personal information manager that includes a calendar, address book, to-do list manager, Usenet newsreader, and email application. Though there are tools to synchronize your Entourage address book with Mac OS X's built-in Address Book, you should decide whether you prefer the à la carte approach offered by Apple's Mail, iCal, and Address Book or the all-in-one personal information manager approach embodied by Entourage.

 If you have a Hotmail account that you use in addition to (or instead of) a traditional POP account, it is worth noting that Entourage can retrieve and send messages via your Hotmail account too. (It is the only Mac mail client that offers this functionality.)

Entourage X remains largely unchanged from the Mac OS 9 version that accompanied Microsoft Office 2001. Its integration with the other Office programs makes it easier to send Word, Excel, and PowerPoint documents directly from these applications. If you spend a lot of time using these applications, you might find the integration a compelling reason to use Entourage as your mail client and personal information manager.

Web-based alternatives

If you travel a lot or don't have a Mac that you can call your own, you might want to consider a free or fee-based Web-mail alternative. Many of the leading portal sites, such as Yahoo, Netscape, and MSN-Hotmail, offer free Web-based email. These accounts are accessible via a browser virtually anywhere, so they're perfect for use in Internet cafés when you are away from your computer. Unless you are willing to pay a nominal annual fee, you are usually limited in the amount of mail you can store on their servers. The biggest drawback to these free services is that you tend to get a lot of spam with them.

 A relative newcomer to the Web-mail game is **Mailblocks** (www.mailblocks.com). It is offered as a tiered service that begins with a small mailbox for free and scales up to 100 MB for $25 per year. You can access it with most popular browsers, and you can use it to make the mail you receive virtually spam-free, through a tool called Challenge/Response, which helps ensure that an actual person instead of an automated program sent you a message. You can then pull down your Mailblocks mail using your favorite IMAP client—such as Apple Mail, Eudora, MailSmith, or Entourage.

Instant Messaging

We have been able to talk to one another using telephones for some time now, so why are so many people, especially teenagers, using instant-messaging systems to converse? (My kids can carry on several concurrent private chat conversations with their buddies—something that is close to impossible with a telephone.)

In addition to email and Web browsing, instant messaging has become a mainstream Internet application. Popularized by America Online's AOL Instant Messenger, or AIM, instant messaging now has a crowded field of clients including Apple's iChat, Microsoft's MSN Messenger, Yahoo's Messenger, and a bevy of applications that work with many different instant-messaging systems. All of the clients come in Mac and PC versions. Also, many cellular phone services now include Short Message Service (SMS), and some can be used interactively with popular instant-messaging systems.

Two issues germane to instant messaging that have yet to be resolved are the lack of a universal standard and messaging-system interoperability. Probably the largest instant-messaging system belongs to AOL, with AIM. For some time there has been a cat-and-mouse game between developers of instant-messaging clients and competing service providers, and AOL. Software developers and service providers periodically figure out how to interoperate successfully with AIM, and then AOL makes a change that cripples the alternative systems so that non-AIM clients cannot exchange messages with AIM users. Once a universal instant-messaging standard is available, the ability to send messages between different instant-messaging systems should improve, so you'll be able to pick the client and system that suits you best. For now, if you want to be able to IM with the biggest crowd, your best bet is to get a free account using AIM.

Apple iChat AV

Apple chose wisely when it chose AOL as the instant-messaging system to work with its **iChat and iChat AV** client (free; www.apple.com/ichat) since AOL's system is so popular with both Mac and PC users. At first glance, iChat AV looks like a dumbed-down version of AOL's AIM client. It is strictly for one-on-one interaction (typing back and forth) and lacks the news and portal-oriented add-ons that AOL includes with AIM. But hook up a microphone and FireWire camera (such as Apple's iSight) to your Mac, and you're ready for some space-age videoconferencing with full-duplex audio (both people can talk at the same time without clipping). One of the most attractive things about this alternative to the telephone is that there are no long-distance charges, and you don't need a lot of bandwidth to have a high-fidelity conversation (**Figure 19.29**).

Figure 19.29

Apple's free iChat AV application, coupled with a digital video camera and micro-phone, can instantly transform the phone calls to your child while you are away from home to a face-to-face encounter.

Conferencing is all based on buddy lists. Since iChat connects to the AIM service, your AIM buddy list is instantly available to you when using iChat. You can also use it to connect to others with .Mac accounts. If none of your "buddies" have AV-capable setups (they have no microphone or camera), you can find buddies online at public registry sites like iChatFinder.com, MyiSight.com, and iSighting (www.isighting.com).

 Since you can hook up any FireWire video source to your Mac and use it with iChat, you can broadcast (stream) your own videos to family members over the Internet.

AOL Instant Messenger

America Online's **AIM** client (free; www.aim.com) has been available for Mac OS X for some time now. It has not changed a great deal from prior versions—nor is it wholly different from the version available for Windows clients. AIM provides a wide array of information such as news, weather, stock quotes, and more while you are using it—iChat and MSN Messenger don't have anything similar. After you've downloaded and installed the client, the real fun begins.

You can group messaging buddies in folders and store them on your buddy list. When they are online, their names will appear in the Online portion of the list. You can even configure the software to alert you when one of your buddies appears online so that you can pounce on him or her with a greeting.

To start a chat session using AOL Instant Messenger, you select someone on your buddy list who is online and then click the IM button. A window appears for your conversation, where you can type whatever you like; you then press [Enter] or click Send to send the message. You can change the appearance and emphasis of your messages using the same character formatting (such as fonts, bold, underline, italics) that you use in word-processing and other Macintosh applications. To display emotions in your message text, you can pick from a good collection of icons. Another way to embellish your messages is to include "images." These can be short movie clips, recorded sounds, or still images.

This is not the free-for-all you might expect. If there are people you do not wish to chat with, you can send them warnings or block them entirely (**Figure 19.30**).

Figure 19.30

America Online's Instant Messenger lets you create buddy lists; AIM will let you know when your friends are online. You can also block people you do not wish to chat with.

Beyond Browsing and Email

While surfing the Web and sending email are the most popular uses for the Internet, there are other things you can do with it as well. Here's a sampling.

Web Logs

Web logs (also known as *blogs*) have been a bit of a rage for the past couple of years. You may have read about them in your favorite newspaper or magazine—they're that much of a hit. A blog is a personal journal that is available on the Web. Anyone who has something to say or publish can now do so quite easily and make it available for everyone to see on the Web. Most blogs are listed in reverse chronological order—so the most recent entries are at the top of the list. The easiest way to find and learn more about blogs is to type blog into the Google search bar in Safari.

FTP

Not surprisingly, the Internet offers the universe's largest collection of software, available for download by a process known as *FTP* (for *File Transfer Protocol,* a set of rules dating back to the early days of the Internet). You can use FTP to download (and upload) files from thousands of sites all around the Internet, many of them at universities, that make software libraries available to the general public.

You can access public FTP sites on which you have no account by means of *anonymous FTP*—give *anonymous* as your user name and your email address as your password. Then just supply the URL—the host name and the path to the file you're seeking. If you're not allowed in, try this trick: use *anonymous* for your user name and the @ symbol for your email address.

There was a time when you needed special software to connect to FTP servers. Since Mac OS X has its own built-in server and client, it is no longer necessary. There are several ways to connect to FTP servers with your Mac. You can use the Connect to Server option in the Go menu in the Finder (⌘K) and then put in the full URL for the FTP server you want to connect to (**Figure 19.31**). For example, you would use the URL ftp://jsmith:passwd@ftp.apple.com to connect to the server named ftp.apple.com with an account named *jsmith* and a password of *passwd*. Once you've connected, you'll see the server mounted on your Desktop just like any other fixed or removable volume on your system. You can also enter the same URL into your favorite browser and get similar results. Once the volume is mounted on your Desktop, you can copy files to and from the server using familiar drag-and-drop actions. (Of course, you need to have the right privileges to view, add, or change files on the server.)

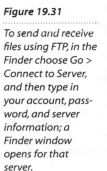

Figure 19.31

To send and receive files using FTP, in the Finder choose Go > Connect to Server, and then type in your account, password, and server information; a Finder window opens for that server.

If you prefer to use a more-sophisticated FTP client application, you won't find a more-mature product than **Fetch** ($25; www.fetchworks.com), from Fetch Softworks. This gem of an application has been around from the very early days of the Mac and TCP/IP networking. Fetch allows you to save all the information you need to connect to frequently accessed sites. It also allows you to pause and resume uploads and downloads, and it transmits and receives files very quickly.

Newsreaders

Usenet is the largest bulletin board system on the Internet. It operates on distributed servers that replicate content from one to another so that postings on one server quickly appear throughout the world on other servers that carry that list. Most ISPs provide news-server access as part of your subscription. If information about your ISP's news server was not included with your subscription package, go to its Web site or ask it for the name of its news server so that you can set up your newsreader application.

There are several dozen newsreader clients to choose from, but three solid choices are MT-NewsWatcher, Microsoft Entourage, and Netscape X/Mozilla (**Figure 19.32**). You can find all these at VersionTracker (www.versiontracker.com) or MacUpdate (www.macupdate.com).

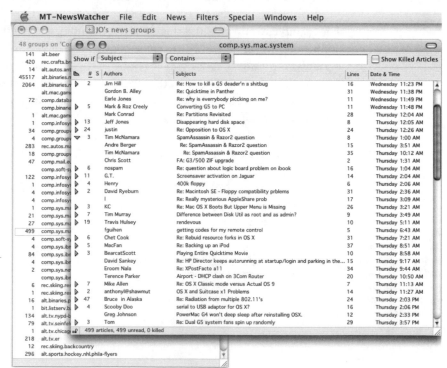

Figure 19.32

The Usenet newsreader application MT-NewsWatcher lets you manage lists of subscriptions and neatly organizes messages into threads.

Being a vast network of message boards, Usenet is widely considered the original network for online discussion and sharing of rich media (such as photos and graphics). Today, Usenet is becoming more easily accessible and searchable through friendly Web-based connections. Before services like these came along, Usenet's text-intensive interface made access and participation difficult, espccially for nontechnical people.

 If you don't feel like fussing with another client application, check out Google's popular Web-based alternative for searching and reading Usenet content, at http://groups.google.com. It is a comprehensive Usenet archive you can search without a newsreader client.

Once you've familiarized yourself with the type of content that is posted on a particular newsgroup and you find topics that interest you, you'll be able to quickly tap into a vast amount of knowledge on a specific topic. Newsgroups can come in very handy when you're trying to troubleshoot a problem on your computer, in your home—or in your car, when *Car Talk* isn't on NPR!

RSS

RSS (short for *RDF Site Summary*) newsreaders provide another relatively new means of accessing information on the Internet. An RSS reader, such as Ranchero Software's popular **NetNewsWire** ($39.95; www.ranchero.com) and **NetNewsWire Lite** (free), lets you quickly peruse the headlines on your favorite news sites. (That is, those sites that summarize their news properly so that an RSS newsreader can see it.) Using NetNewsWire's three-paned window, you can easily select a site, see the list of headlines on it, and then get a quick summary of a selected story (**Figure 19.33**). Then, when you want to dive deeper into the story and read it in its entirety, simply click the link in the window and the site will appear in your default browser window.

Figure 19.33

NetNewsWire Lite lets you quickly browse the summarized headlines on all your favorite news sites. Click a site name to display the headlines and then drill down if you want to read the full story.

Content Filtering

If you want to limit the Internet content that is available on your Mac—for example, if you have young children—you should consider a content filter. These utilities limit access to certain Web sites and Internet applications. You can grant or revoke access to categories of content such as violence, sex, adult material, and shopping. This is typically done in conjunction with a subscription-based update mechanism that properly classifies new sites so that access can be restricted. These applications sit between your browser and the Internet and act as a proxy for all your Internet surfing. When you try to go to a Web site that is blocked by the application, a message typically pops up informing you that you are trying to go to a restricted site.

Two excellent content-filtering options for the Mac are MAKI Enterprise's **Kids GoGoGo OSX** ($30; www.makienterprise.com) and Intego's **ContentBarrier** ($59.95; www.intego.com) (**Figure 19.34**). In addition to filtering incoming content, these applications can be used to restrict or limit the time your child can use the Internet. They can also detect and disable spyware and limit the types of information your child can provide to others.

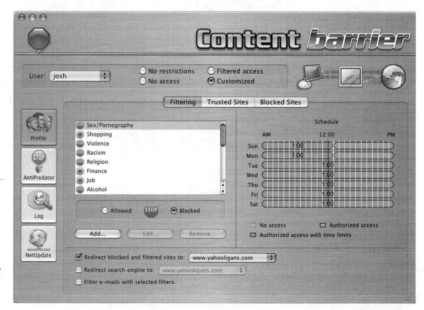

Figure 19.34

Content-filtering applications like Intego's ContentBarrier also let you limit the use of Internet-based services (like instant messaging, mail, and browsing).

These approaches to content filtering are by no means foolproof. They generally rely upon people to categorize sites with potentially objectionable material. With new sites appearing all the time, it is hard for those responsible for maintaining these lists to stay ahead of some sites that may contain material you would rather your child not view. In the end, there is no substitute for supervised browsing to prevent the presentation of unwanted content.

Interview: Steve Capps

Born in 1955—like Steve Jobs and Bill Gates, among others—Steve Capps started working at the Xerox Corp. while still a computer science student at the Rochester Institute of Technology. In 1981 he joined Apple, originally to work on the Lisa project, and in late 1982 he joined Bruce Horn in developing the Macintosh Finder. Capps left Apple in 1985 to travel and relax. In 1986 he wrote three groundbreaking music programs for the Mac: Jam Session, Super Studio Session, and SoundEdit (still marketed, now by Macromedia). Returning to Apple the following year, he became chief software architect for the Newton and was awarded the prestigious title of Apple Fellow. From 1996 to 2001 he was a user-interface architect at Microsoft, where he contributed to Internet Explorer and led the development of MSN Explorer, an Internet "dashboard" for subscribers to the Microsoft network. As of late 2003, Capps was the named inventor on 53 granted patents, with numerous others still pending. He is currently chief executive officer and chief technical officer at OneDotO, a small Silicon Valley startup he founded. —Henry Norr

> *Neither of those experiences I would trade for anything—working on the Mac and working on the Newton.*
>
> *—Steve Capps, on his time at Apple*

What did you do before you joined Apple?

I started at Xerox in 1977. I discovered an Alto [the world's first computer with a graphical user interface, developed by Xerox for internal research purposes in the early 1970s] sitting in a closet. "This is cool," [I thought]. I had a full-page display on the Alto at first, and just before I joined Apple, I got a two-page display—literally, it could show two typewritten pages. Then I came to Apple, I looked at the Lisa, I go, "Geez, that screen is small." And then I go over to the Mac and I go, "Geez!!"

Did you join the Mac group immediately?

No, I worked on Lisa. I wrote a game, Alice, one Christmas. [The game pitted Alice against the Queen of Hearts and other Wonderland characters on a 3D chessboard. Published in 1984 under the name Through the Looking Glass, it was the first commercial Mac software title, and the only Macintosh game Apple ever published.] Unbeknownst to me, Steve [Jobs] at that point started saying they were going to steal me [for the Mac project]. Finally, at one point I run into Jobs in Los Gatos, and he goes, "We're going to nab you!" And I go, "Uh, OK."

When did you go over to the Mac team, and what did you do?

It must have been December 1982. I always said I was a designated hitter. I showed up, and there was no text-editing package. They said, "If you can write one that fits in 2000 bytes, that's great." So I did that. And then I did StandardFile—you know that little dialog that comes up when you pick a file from an application?

continues on next page

You were also listed in the original Finder as coauthor, along with Bruce Horn.

Yeah, I went to work on that because a lot of people were convinced we weren't going to get it done on time. I went to Bill [Atkinson]'s house one time, after we had shipped, and there was this big hole in the wall. He sheepishly admitted he was so convinced we were going to tank the introduction that he picked up a mouse and threw it through the wall.

When did you start working on the Newton?

In 1987. I did that until 1996.

A long time!

Yeah, and neither of those experiences I would trade for anything—working on the Mac and working on the Newton.

When the Newton died, you went to Microsoft. What did you do there?

Basically, I was hired to be kind of an intellectual gadfly. We were going to do a handheld Internet thing, but when I got up there, I said, "But the browser is so much more interesting," so I just started putting stuff into the browser.

The browser for that device, or …

No, Internet Explorer. I did this document, where I say, "It's all in the details, you guys. You've got to get your brain around this, you can't just ship out crap like this." And I go, "I can come up with 101 things to fix in the user interface." And somebody said, "Well, do it." I got to about 80 pretty quickly; the last 20 were tough.

What was funny was that people there just didn't get things that were in our culture at Apple, like if you have a menu that has a, b, and c in that order in one place, and you have an almost identical menu somewhere else, then don't do it in c-b-a [order]. Nobody there got that.

Then I basically proposed what ultimately became MSN Explorer. That was the biggest product I did there.

Do you have any thoughts about what Apple should do?

You know, I don't understand the business. I don't understand what the goal is. Overall, I'm kind of bored with desktop computers, either Windows or Mac. We're stuck with this double-click, iconic view of the world, and the user base is just so big I don't know if we're ever going to change that. I think both [Mac and Windows] suck, but it's like swearing at the cable company at this point. So that's why I'm much more excited about a different space, which is cell phones.

Is that what you are doing at OneDotO?

Not a cell phone, a communications device. I have a metaview that handhelds and cellular phones are like computers were in the early '80s—too many random standards that don't make any sense, and they're no good, basically. Somebody needs to do the Mac of cell phones.

Can you say anything about what it's going to be like?

It's kind of a radical and different project. My philosophy for the last four or five years is what I call "people-centricity." I keep saying that a file-centric worldview is wrong: you should have a people-centric view, and it's all about communication. File organization, the whole concept of apps—it just doesn't scale to communication, which is very ephemeral. We don't record our phone conversations; you don't record your IM [instant messaging] conversations. Or pictures. Now people basically take pictures and send them. So that's what's been driving me. Just say I'm designing a UI around communications, use of photos, music playing.

Have you heard Steve Jobs' rap about Panther? I think "user-centric" is the word he uses.

His strategy, which I think is pretty good, is to downplay the Finder with the iApps. But still when you get a Mac, fresh out of the box, the first thing you have to worry about is file organization, and I think that's just wrong. I'm so dismayed by the lack of innovation with either Windows or Mac. If you look at the pace of innovation in 1982–1984 versus 1984–2003, it's embarrassing.

What computer do you use now?

I've run Windows regularly for years now.

20

Networking

John Rizzo is the chapter editor and author.

Before the rise of the Internet, before email, before the Web, you could network Macs. In the mid-1980s—at a time when most PC users were considering whether to switch from command-line DOS to this new Windows thing—Mac users were forming networks so that they could exchange files and share printers. These days, networking consists of much more than mere file exchanges and printer sharing—there's sending email, doing file sharing and group scheduling, sharing Internet access among a group of Macs, and more.

The Mac's networking success has always been due to built-in networking operating-system software that Apple designed specifically to control the hardware. Mac OS X gives you networking features such as file sharing, email, and Web-browsing software, which you can use over cables or through the air in a wireless network. You can use these features with other Macs, or with Windows and Unix machines on a network.

With each new version of Mac OS X, Apple adds new network capabilities and changes the configuration settings slightly. With Mac OS X 10.3 (Panther), Apple even changed the way networking works. If you haven't done Mac networking since Mac OS 9, you have some new things to learn.

There's a lot you can do with networks, and there are a lot of ways to do it— which is why entire books are written on networking. In this chapter, you'll get a foundation in network basics and learn how to set up your Mac for most common networking tasks.

This chapter starts with a high-level description of some of the components of a network. After that, I describe how to get your network up and running. (For specifics on connecting to the Internet, see Chapter 19.)

In This Chapter

Networking Macs: A Primer

A *local network* is the computer network in your room, building, or campus. Local networks are also called *local area networks*. The *area* seems to have been included to make the acronym *LAN* pronounceable. But since networking has enough unavoidable acronyms, I'll just stick to the term *local network* in this chapter.

You can think of the Internet as a connection of lots of local networks all around the world. Your local network has a lot of similarities to the Internet. It uses some of the same network protocols (see "Network Foundation: Protocols," below), and you can use some of the same network services, such as a Web server or email, locally or globally via the Internet. On local networks, Mac users often use file sharing to move files between computers. On the Internet, FTP servers are more commonly used for file sharing. However, Mac OS X includes FTP services that can also be used locally.

Most of the Mac's networking infrastructure—the built-in hardware and system software—is used for local networks as well as for the Internet. Getting your Mac ready for the Internet is similar to getting it ready for a local network. In some cases, one configuration works for both.

 While Mac OS X 10.3 does do a few network tricks not found in Mac OS X 10.2, it also inexplicably takes away some features, notably in file sharing. If you're happy with Mac OS X 10.2's networking features, you may want to hold on to it for now.

Network Foundation: Protocols

You can think of a network as a discussion between computers using one or more network *protocols* as the common language. The discussion takes place over the network medium, which is usually the Ethernet cables—or the air, in the case of AirPort, Apple's wireless networking technology (see "Wired or Wireless," below, for more on these two methods of connecting). Your Mac is a native speaker of two network protocols, *TCP/IP (Transmission Control Protocol/Internet Protocol)* and *AppleTalk*. Both can run at the same time over the same wires.

These days, networking is focused on the TCP/IP protocol. AppleTalk is on its way out because it isn't as efficient and is mostly used only by Macs. Both TCP/IP and AppleTalk are able to handle network software communication such as file sharing and print sharing. However, Internet software runs only on TCP/IP.

You don't need to configure AppleTalk beyond turning it on and off. TCP/IP is not as user friendly and does need to be set up before it will work.

Configuring TCP/IP is the first thing you do after plugging into your network (or connecting wirelessly). We'll show you how to configure both of these protocols in "Setting Up TCP/IP and AppleTalk," later in this chapter.

Turning on AppleTalk or configuring TCP/IP is an enabling step, but it doesn't allow you to actually do anything yet. Next, you'll need to set up your *network services*—the tools that let you perform network tasks. We'll cover all this later in the chapter.

Network Services: Servers and Clients

Network services are the functional features that let you work. For instance, file service lets you see files on other computers and move files around. Email is a network service, as is whichever group-calendar program you may use.

Network services require two parts to work—the *server* software and the *client* software—which communicate with each other. The server software provides the service to all the computers on the network. It can run on a dedicated server computer that is not doing double duty as a user's workstation. Server software can also run on your Mac, providing a service (such as the ability to access your files) for other users. Dedicated servers are faster than servers running on a user's Mac and can handle more simultaneous connections to other computers (the clients).

The client software is what you, the user, typically work with. For instance, Apple's Mail application is an email client. It communicates with an email server, either on your local network or on the Internet. Sometimes client software is invisible to you. For example, Mac OS X's Software Update application can run behind the scenes to check Apple servers for new versions of your system software. You see it only if it finds something.

Mac OS X comes with both client and server software for various tasks. For instance, there's a file-sharing client that lets you access other computers. You don't see an application that is a file-sharing client because the functionality is integrated into Mac OS X. You also don't have an application for Mac OS X's integrated file-sharing server. When you turn on file sharing to allow other users to access your Mac, your Mac is acting as a server.

Table 20.1 lists the basic network services that are integrated into various versions of Mac OS X. (It doesn't list the email client, Web browsers, or other network software applications that come with your Mac—these aren't integrated services.) You can see from the table that Mac OS X has several more network services than Mac OS 9. It has clients for accessing Windows file-sharing servers and for accessing Unix *NFS (Network File System)* servers and has a server for allowing other computers to access files on your Mac using FTP.

We'll look at the configuration and use of all these built-in, integrated network services. But first, we're going to go back to the beginning of the network story and discuss the network media, over which communication occurs.

Table 20.1 Integrated Network Services in the Mac OS

Feature	Mac OS 9	Mac OS X 10.2	Mac OS X 10.3
File sharing over AppleTalk (client and server)	yes	yes	yes
File sharing over TCP/IP (client and server)	yes	yes	yes
Windows file-sharing client	no	yes	yes
Printing over AppleTalk	yes	yes	yes
Printing over TCP/IP	yes	yes	yes
Printing to Windows printers	no	no	yes
Web server/sharing	yes	yes	yes
FTP server	no	yes	yes
Unix NFS file-sharing client	no	yes	yes
Virtual Private Network client	no	yes (PPTP)	yes (PPTP and IPsec)

Wired or Wireless?

This used to be the point in *The Macintosh Bible* where we'd start talking about how to plug in your Macs. Since the appearance of AirPort on the networking scene a few years ago, you no longer need to "plug in" to get connected, as wireless networking is an attractive alternative to using your Mac's built-in Ethernet port. You can also create a network of mixed media, wireless and wired. Regardless of the media, any network software that works on one network medium will work on the other.

 Mac OS X is more advanced than Mac OS 9 and earlier when it comes to the network media. Mac OS X supports *multihoming,* a feature that allows it to connect over multiple network media types at the same time. Mac OS 9 and earlier can connect over only one type of medium at a time.

When you begin planning a network, you should seriously think about whether you want to go with an Ethernet network, a wireless network, or some combination of the two. Ethernet networks are still simpler to set up than wireless AirPort networks, and they don't require users to log in to the network. Wireless networks can be more convenient, especially with iBooks and PowerBooks that are used in different locations or aren't located next to a wall socket. For instance, some schools are putting their computer labs on carts. A teacher wheels a cart full of iBooks into an AirPort-equipped classroom and unloads the iBooks, and soon the students are all cruising the Internet.

The comparative cost of each type of network medium varies. If you're just stringing cables across the floor, Ethernet is less expensive than AirPort. However, if you need to route wires through walls or between floors, the labor costs can easily exceed the cost of the AirPort hardware.

Ethernet is also faster. AirPort Extreme is limited to 54 megabits per second (Mbps). This is fast enough for Internet connection and simple network tasks, but if you are transferring mass quantities of files or have a lot of computers on the same local network, you might need the 100 Mbps or Gigabit Ethernet that today's Macs can now handle.

Ethernet

Ethernet is like a public highway. You can run any protocol on it using any software on any computer running any operating system. Macs have supported Ethernet since the late 1980s. So, most likely your Mac has a built-in Ethernet port with a standard connector (see the sidebar "Extinct Ethernet" below for what to do if your Mac predates Ethernet). Ethernet comes in various compatible flavors that differ in the bandwidth they can support.

Ethernet Bandwidth

The total *bandwidth* of a network is the maximum amount of traffic it can carry at one time. Bandwidth is related to speed but is not the same thing. The more Macs you have on a network, the more traffic is on the network and the more bandwidth is taken up. The more bandwidth is used, the slower the performance for each user.

You can think of bandwidth as the width of a hallway in a popular train station. At rush hour, hallway number one, which is 10 feet wide, can allow 100 people per minute to pass through it. Hallway number two, which is 20 feet wide, can allow 200 people per minute to pass through. You might say that hallway two is "faster," because you don't have to wait as long to get through, but really it's just wider, or has more bandwidth.

So it is with Ethernet. Another reason why bandwidth is not equivalent to speed is network overhead. At 100 Mbps, if you move a file that is 100 Mb in size, it won't reach its destination in 1 second. This is partly because about a third of network bandwidth is used for carrying data and commands that keep communication organized and identified. Additionally, you never actually get 100 percent use of the bandwidth because of something called *packet collisions*—signals representing pieces of data bumping into each other as on a crowded freeway.

Apple uses three Ethernet bandwidths in various Mac models:

- **10Base-T,** providing 10 Mbps (found in older Macs)
- **100Base-T,** providing 100 Mbps (also called Fast Ethernet)
- **1000Base-T,** providing 1 Gbps (commonly known as Gigabit Ethernet)

The Mac's Ethernet port can sense the bandwidth at which the network is operating and will choose the appropriate speed to send and receive data. There is no setup or configuration required. However, you do need to make sure to buy an Ethernet hub (see "Hubs," below) that supports the bandwidths at which you want to run.

 If you want to increase the Ethernet bandwidth of an older Mac and it has an expansion slot, you can add an Ethernet *network interface card* (sometimes called a *NIC*). For instance, you can add a Gigabit Ethernet card to the first Power Mac G4 models, which support only 10/100Base-T. Older Power Macs, such as the Power Mac 7600 and the 8500, came only with built-in 10Base-T. You can upgrade these with a NIC as well. Just make sure the card comes with driver software for the version of the Mac OS you are running.

Cables and Connectors

All Macs produced since the mid-1990s have an Ethernet port that consists of some networking electronics on the motherboard and an RJ-45 connector. An RJ-45 plug on an Ethernet cable looks like a slightly fatter telephone connector, usually made of clear plastic.

The typical cable used in Ethernet networks is known as *Category 5* cable (or just *Cat 5*). A Cat 5 cable is required to run 100Base-T. If you are running only 10Base-T Ethernet, then you can use a lower-quality Category 3 cable. The category designation is usually on the cable.

You can connect two Macs directly with an Ethernet cable to create a small network of two computers. This can be handy for a temporary network, where you need to move files from one computer to another. For this purpose, all Macs can use a special Ethernet cable known as a *crossover cable* (a cable that "crosses over" or reverses its pin contacts on each end). However, most Ethernet cables you see in stores are not crossover cables—they are *patch cables* (which keep the pins the same on each end). For this reason, Apple's newer Macs don't need crossover cables to connect two Macs directly to each other—they can also use standard Ethernet patch cables.

 To find out which Mac models require an Ethernet crossover cable for a one-to-one connection, check out the Apple Knowledge Base article at http://docs.info.apple.com/article.html?artnum=42717.

Hubs

To network more than two Macs, you need an *Ethernet hub* (**Figure 20.1**). This is a box that all the computers on the network plug into using Ethernet patch cables. Prices vary depending on the number of ports and the speed.

Figure 20.1

You'll need an Ethernet hub if you want to network more than two Macs.

You can mix 10Base-T, 100Base-T, and Gigabit Ethernet connections as long as the hub supports these bandwidths. If you buy a 10Base-T hub, you will be limited to 10 Mbps bandwidth, even though your Macs most likely support 100 Mbps or more. There is no such thing as a "Mac hub"—there are only Ethernet hubs. Thus, you can buy hubs from any vendor without worrying about Mac compatibility. Some vendors, such as Asanté (www.asante.com) and 3Com (www.3com.com), however, offer a good variety of hubs as well as solid Macintosh support, should you run into a problem.

Some hubs are called *switched hubs*, or *switches*, because they have an active switching mechanism between ports. Switched hubs are commonly used in office networks, because they can handle a greater amount of network traffic.

Extinct Ethernet

If you have a decade-old Mac sitting around, you may have an *AAUI (Apple Attachment Unit Interface)* connector instead of a standard RJ-45 Ethernet connector. The AAUI connectors are compatible with your hub-based Ethernet network, if you have a small AAUI–to–RJ-45 transceiver box. These can be hard to find; try We Love Macs (www.welovemacs.com) or eBay. A lot of old Macs have both an RJ-45 port and an AAUI port. In this case, just ignore the AAUI port.

Older types of Ethernet that predate 10Base-T may not be at all compatible. One was called *thick Ethernet*, and the other was called *thin Ethernet* (also called *Thinnet* or *10Base-2*, which really wasn't all that thin). These used coaxial cables, similar to cable TV cable. The cable was strung from one computer to the other, which was much less convenient than using hubs.

LocalTalk

Macs developed before the iMac and laser printers both have another type of networking hardware called *LocalTalk*. The LocalTalk port was the same as the printer port—the port did double duty. Apple dropped LocalTalk when it introduced the iMac because LocalTalk had many drawbacks. It was slow (240 Kbps), could not handle many Macs (32 maximum), and could not run TCP/IP—it could only run AppleTalk. (This is why the LocalTalk ports on older network laser printers were sometimes called AppleTalk ports.) You can get an older LocalTalk device, such as a faithful LaserWriter printer, on Ethernet with a LocalTalk-to-Ethernet bridge such as Asanté's **AsantéTalk** ($130; www.asante.com).

Networking Without Wires: AirPort

Mac support of wireless networking began with the first iBook model. Today, every iMac, iBook, eMac, PowerBook, and Power Mac has a slot for an AirPort card and a built-in antenna for sending and receiving data. You can also buy a preinstalled AirPort card when you order a new Mac. Networking software and protocols that work over Ethernet will work over AirPort wireless networks.

AirPort implements an industry standard called *IEEE 802.11 Direct Sequence Spread Spectrum (DSSS)*. The standard uses low-power radio frequencies that can travel a short distance through walls, although large structures such as brick walls can block the signal.

 AirPort is called AirMac in Japan.

There are two types of AirPort (or IEEE 802.11) that Macs can use. Apple's current AirPort Extreme has a maximum bandwidth of 54 Mbps. AirPort Extreme is known to the rest of the (non-Mac) world as IEEE 802.11g. The original AirPort (IEEE 802.11b) has a maximum bandwidth of 11 Mbps. AirPort Extreme is backward compatible with the original AirPort, so a newer Mac can communicate with an older Mac wirelessly. There are also third-party IEEE 802.11b and IEEE 802.11g cards that will work in Macs.

 Although AirPort Extreme can communicate with the original AirPort, the two types of cards are different, which means you can't put an AirPort Extreme card in a Mac with the original AirPort slot.

AirPort uses encryption to prevent someone with an iBook outside your window from eavesdropping on your network traffic. This means that users have to log in to an AirPort network. You can do this from the AirPort menu.

AirPort networks use an encryption standard called *Wired Equivalent Privacy* (or *WEP*). Data being transmitted through the air between a Mac and an access point, such as the AirPort Base Station, is encrypted using an encryption key that both the Mac and the Base Station have. This is why you use a password to join a wireless network—the password tells the Base Station to send your Mac an encryption key. WEP is just used locally over the air and not over the Internet. You can turn WEP encryption off in the Base Station using AirPort Admin Utility from a Mac. You might want to turn WEP encryption off if you are having trouble communicating with Windows PCs over the wireless network.

AirPort Network Configurations

Most wireless networks require a wireless access point such as Apple's AirPort Extreme Base Station, a kind of wireless hub and Internet gateway rolled into one. However, you can also run an AirPort network without an access point. In either case, each Mac that you plan to connect to the network needs an AirPort card. You have three basic ways to configure an AirPort network:

- Two Macs (maybe more) without an AirPort Base Station (computer to computer)

- As many as 50 Macs and PCs with an AirPort Extreme Base Station (or up to 10 computers with the original AirPort Base Station)

- As many as 10 Macs *without* an AirPort Base Station, using one Mac as a base station and Internet connection

 PowerBook and iBook users can maximize battery life by turning off power to the AirPort card: select Turn AirPort Off from the AirPort menu, which is located on the right side of the Finder's menu bar.

Let's take a look at these scenarios.

Setting Up a Two-Mac AirPort Network

Just as you can use an Ethernet cable to connect two Macs directly without a hub, you can connect a few AirPort-equipped Macs directly without any other hardware. This is called a *computer-to-computer network*. This can save you the cost of an AirPort Base Station and enable you to create a spontaneous network if, say, you and a friend happen to meet with your iBooks on the subway.

Apple recommends that you use computer-to-computer mode for only two Macs, but you should be able to get more than two Macs communicating if they are close together. The drawback to having more than two Macs on this type of network is that performance may suffer. Apple says the two computers need to be within 150 feet of each other.

You use the AirPort menu on both computers to create and join a computer-to-computer network. You can also use it to switch from using the AirPort Base Station to using direct computer-to-computer communications.

To establish a computer-to-computer AirPort network, one Mac creates the network and the other joins it. To create a new network, go to the AirPort menu and select Create Network. The Computer to Computer dialog appears, with your Mac's name filled in (**Figure 20.2**). You can change the name to anything you like. Click OK.

Figure 20.2

You can set up an AirPort network for just two Macs, with no base station, simply by selecting Create Network in the AirPort menu.

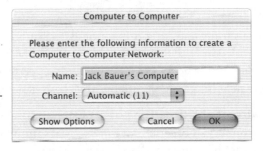

To join this newly created network on the other Mac, go to the AirPort menu. You'll see the name of the network you just created listed (**Figure 20.3**). Select it and log in.

Figure 20.3

Another Mac can join your newly created network simply by your selecting it from the AirPort menu.

 Notice that you won't be asked for a password to join the network. This is because AirPort doesn't use WEP encryption in computer-to-computer mode. This could be a problem in a public setting, as someone across the room with an iBook and an AirPort card could join your network and access your Public folder. If you are doing file sharing in computer-to-computer mode in a public place, you may want to make sure that there isn't anything in your Public folder that you want to keep secret.

Of course, you need to have TCP/IP or AppleTalk or both turned on and configured for AirPort (see "Setting Up an AirPort Base Station," below).

About the AirPort Base Station

The AirPort Extreme Base Station used for most AirPort networks is a multi-functional device. It's a wireless hub, it's an Internet gateway, it's an Ethernet bridge, and it comes with a set of Ginsu knives! (Well, no, it doesn't actually come with Ginsu knives, but you get the idea.) You can use other IEEE 802.11b or 802.11g access points with your AirPort network, but many don't have all the functions of the AirPort Base Station, which are as follows:

Wireless access point. The simplest function of the Base Station is to act as a wireless hub: when it receives a signal from your computer, it broadcasts the signal to the other computers. This is called a *wireless access point.*

Apple recommends using one AirPort Extreme Base Station for every 50 users. (The older AirPort Base Stations could support only 10 users). The drawback to having a lot of active users, though, is that performance can suffer. For bigger networks, you can use multiple base stations.

Ethernet-to-wireless bridge. The AirPort Extreme Base Station can also act as a *bridge* to connect an Ethernet network to Macs running AirPort. When you plug an Ethernet hub into the Base Station's Ethernet port, you enable the computers on the wired network to communicate with those on the wireless network.

Internet gateway. The Base Station uses a standard technique called *Network Address Translation (NAT)* to act as an Internet gateway. With NAT, you need only one IP address that is visible to the Internet. All the Macs on the network get an IP address from the *Dynamic Host Configuration Protocol (DHCP)* server in the AirPort Base Station (see "Dynamic Addressing and Self-Configuration," later in the chapter). NAT passes traffic from the Internet to the Macs and sends the traffic from the Macs to the Internet. A NAT gateway provides security, in that the Internet can't directly see the Macs on your network. It is less expensive than leasing multiple Internet IP addresses for all your Macs from your Internet service provider.

You can also use the Base Station's Ethernet port to connect to a high-speed Internet connection, such as a cable modem or DSL modem. The more expensive of the AirPort Extreme Base Stations also has a built-in modem to connect to the Internet using a dial-up account.

DHCP server. The DHCP server in the Base Station assigns IP addresses to Macs automatically over the network. Using AirPort Admin Utility, you can set a base station to act as a DHCP server by clicking the "Distribute IP addresses" check box.

Setting Up an AirPort Base Station

You can set up the Base Station using AirPort Admin Utility or AirPort Setup Assistant (/Applications/Utilities). AirPort Setup Assistant is a more-automated tool than AirPort Admin Utility and is useful when setting up the Base Station for the first time. For instance, the assistant can transfer your Mac's Internet settings to the AirPort Base Station.

AirPort Admin Utility is better for making changes to base station settings. You can also use it to configure multiple AirPort Base Stations at the same time. (If you want to set up an AirPort Base Station from Mac OS X, you'll need at least version 10.1.)

To get your Base Station up and running in Mac OS X 10.1 or later, do the following:

1. Plug in the AirPort Base Station power cord. This will turn it on.

2. Plug your Internet connection into the AirPort Base Station (either a phone line to the modem port or a high-speed line to the Ethernet port).

3. Start with your Mac set up to connect to the Internet, but don't switch it to use AirPort. Setup Assistant will do this for you.

4. Launch the AirPort Setup Assistant (/Applications/Utilities).

5. If you already have AirPort running on other Macs or have a base station turned on, you'll see a dialog (**Figure 20.4**). If this is the case, choose "Set up an AirPort Base Station" and click the Continue button. If you don't see this dialog, you haven't turned on the Base Station (that is, you've skipped step 1). Once you get past this dialog, follow AirPort Setup Assistant's instructions.

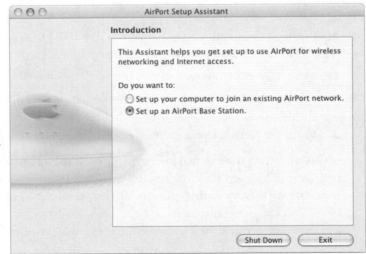

Figure 20.4

Here's the first step in setting up a base station using the AirPort Setup Assistant. If you don't see this dialog, your base station may be turned off.

After you finish, you'll notice that AirPort Setup Assistant has created a new configuration called AirPort in the Network pane of System Preferences. The new TCP/IP configuration will be set to get its IP address from the Base Station's DHCP server.

Joining AirPort Networks

In order to begin communicating with the Base Station, each Mac must join the AirPort network. For Macs that have never connected to the Base Station before, open AirPort Setup Assistant on each Mac and select "Set up your computer to join an existing AirPort network." Fortunately, you don't have to run the assistant every time you want to join the AirPort network. You can go to the AirPort menu and select the Base Station. You'll be prompted for a password (**Figure 20.5**). If you have a high-speed Internet connection such as DSL or cable modem, you'll be able to access the Internet right after you click OK in the Enter Password dialog. If the Base Station is using a modem connection, you'll have to tell it to dial in.

Figure 20.5

Enter the password for the AirPort network you want to join, and you're in!

Another way to join an AirPort network is to use the Internet Connect utility (located in the /Applications/Utilities folder).

1. Open Internet Connect.

2. Click the AirPort icon. From the Configuration pop-up menu, choose AirPort.

3. From the Network pop-up menu that appears, choose your network.

If you are having trouble making an AirPort connection, there may be some interference between you and the Base Station or Mac you are trying to communicate with. Devices that generate signals near the 2.4 Hz frequency used by AirPort can cause interference. These include some cordless telephones and microwave ovens. Nearby power lines can also generate interference. Some building materials may cause problems. Metal (as in steel beams) can cause the most interference. Concrete can also be a problem, and brick walls can weaken signals. Wood-and-plaster walls don't pose much of an interference threat.

Using a Mac as a Base Station

You can designate one of the Macs to function as an access point using software running on the Mac. You'll need a Mac with an AirPort card and with AirPort configured and turned on.

In Mac OS X 10.2 or later, you do this by turning on Internet Sharing:

1. Connect the Mac to the Internet using whatever means you normally would.
2. Open the Sharing pane in System Preferences.
3. Click the Internet tab.
4. Click the Start button to turn on Internet sharing.
5. Create a new AirPort network using the Create Network option in the AirPort menu on the right-hand side of the Mac's menu bar.

Other Macs can now join the AirPort network. This Mac will act as the wireless hub and as the connection to the Internet. The software access point works with a dial-up modem as well as high-speed connections.

Mac OS 9 doesn't have an Internet Sharing feature, but you can use AirPort Setup Assistant. In the first screen, choose "Set up an AirPort Base Station." (If the software doesn't detect a base station, this will be the only choice.) Then follow the directions. If your Mac is already using AirPort, you can also use AirPort Admin Utility. When AirPort opens, click the Software Base Station button. A new window opens. You can give your network a name and enable WEP encryption (as you can with a hardware base station).

A Rendezvous with Rendezvous

You may have seen the term *Rendezvous* in Printer Utility or the AirPort menu. Rendezvous is Apple's name for a protocol standard called *ZeroConf*. Its purpose is to enable devices and applications to "find themselves" over an IP network. Apple uses it in a variety of ways: in file sharing, in iTunes music broadcasting, and in iChat AV. It's used in some printers, cell phones, and other peripherals. You don't actively "use" ZeroConf any more than you actively use the Mac OS X kernel. It's an enabling technology that's just there.

Although Apple marketing describes Rendezvous as "revolutionary," what ZeroConf does has been around for a long time. Mac OS 8.6 could self-configure an IP address on a Mac, and the AppleTalk protocols (including the Apple File Protocol and the Printer Access Protocol) of the mid-1980s were self-discovery mechanisms that did what ZeroConf does on IP networks. Apple switched to ZeroConf from its own proprietary technologies, just as the company switched from Open Transport to Unix standard networking.

Unless you are a software developer, you don't need to worry about Rendezvous any more than you need to worry about the lines of code that make up the Mac OS.

Setting Up TCP/IP and AppleTalk

Whether you use Ethernet or AirPort to network your Macs, you will need TCP/IP or AppleTalk to actually *do* anything on your network. These are the network transport protocols that enable your Mac to talk to other network devices and to the Internet. Other, more specific protocols work "on top" of these transport protocols. For instance, there are protocols for printing, file sharing, using email, and the various other tasks you might do on a network. But these specific protocols are mostly invisible to the user. You need to configure TCP/IP; with AppleTalk, you merely turn it on.

 Don't confuse AppleTalk with AppleShare. These are two different things and not necessarily tied together. AppleTalk is a network transport protocol, as is TCP/IP. AppleShare is a network service and is what Apple calls *file sharing over the network*. AppleShare can occur over AppleTalk or over TCP/IP. (See "Enabling Others to Access Your Files," later in the chapter.)

To a user, it's not always clear when AppleTalk is being used and when TCP/IP is being used, but you can always find out from the Network pane of System Preferences. Select Built-in Ethernet from the Show pop-up menu and then click the TCP/IP and AppleTalk tabs to see the status.

A Note on Sharing Printers

Since 1985, Macs have had the ability to share laser printers. In fact, sharing laser printers was the first reason why people created Mac networks. Not all laser printers are network printers, but those that are—such as some of the trusty old Apple LaserWriters and Hewlett-Packard LaserJets—can plug into a network directly and don't need to be connected to a Mac or a server. Many older network laser printers use AppleTalk, but most newer models use TCP/IP.

You can also share USB inkjet printers via a Mac OS X feature called Printer Sharing, which uses TCP/IP. Mac OS X, particularly Mac OS X 10.3, lets you do more networked printer sharing than ever. For instance, with a printer connected to your Mac, you can do the following:

- Share your printer with other Mac users via Rendezvous. This is easy—just check the Printer Sharing box in the Sharing pane of System Preferences.

- Share your printer with Unix users via LDD/LPR. Mac OS X will make your printers automatically available to Unix users who are using the Common Unix Printing System (CUPS). These users must know your IP address and must send the print job as PostScript, even if your printer is not a PostScript printer.

- Share your printer with Windows users via SMB. In order to do this, both the Windows Sharing and Printer Sharing items in the Sharing pane of System Preferences must be selected.

You can also print to laser printers on the network and to USB printers connected to Macs and Unix machines. If you have Mac OS X 10.3, you can print to shared SMB printers connected to PCs.

The Lowdown on AppleTalk

At one time, AppleTalk *was* Macintosh networking. There were cables and printers named after it; Mac networks were AppleTalk networks. Later, Apple added TCP/IP support to enable Macs to access the Internet. But this support was incomplete, and the performance wasn't good. In 1995, Apple rewrote the Mac OS's networking software, calling it Open Transport. Open Transport made TCP/IP a core protocol equal to AppleTalk. Mac OS X makes even more use of TCP/IP with additional IP-based network services. Today, AppleTalk isn't the necessity it once was.

Pros and cons of AppleTalk

For the past few years, Apple has been adding more TCP/IP-based services, while moving away from AppleTalk. It carried out this plan in the first versions of Mac OS X (10.0 through 10.0.4), which do not do file sharing over AppleTalk—only printing. This was actually the same level of AppleTalk support as found in Windows NT and 2000 Workstation. However, the outcry from users was such that Apple restored file sharing over AppleTalk in Mac OS X 10.1.

Apple's shift toward TCP/IP was part of the company's move to adopting industry standards in its operating-system software. The Internet has made TCP/IP the industry standard for a network transport protocol. Additionally, AppleTalk is inferior in some ways. For one, AppleTalk is slower than TCP/IP. It sends data in smaller packets than TCP/IP can and thus takes longer to transmit. TCP/IP can stream data continuously, something AppleTalk cannot do. And while TCP/IP is ubiquitous, AppleTalk is rarely found on Windows or Unix PCs.

The main benefit of AppleTalk is that it is easier to set up than TCP/IP and is the first choice for home and small-office networks of Macs running Mac OS 9 and earlier. AppleTalk is also still preferable to TCP/IP for printing to many network laser printers.

AppleTalk zones

Zones are probably the most misunderstood aspect of AppleTalk. The concept of AppleTalk zones is tied to AppleTalk *routers*—devices or software running on servers that connect network segments. Routers are used in large networks, such as those in corporations. Some routers for TCP/IP also support AppleTalk, and Microsoft included software AppleTalk routers with Windows NT Server and Windows 2000 Server.

So how are routers and zones linked? When a network administrator configures an AppleTalk router, he or she can also choose to create AppleTalk zones. For example, one router may be configured to have zones for, say, the marketing and production departments. If you see zones when browsing for file servers and printers, your Mac is connected to the network via an AppleTalk router.

 If you want to check for AppleTalk zones on your network, open Network Utility (/Applications/Utilities), click the AppleTalk button, and click "Display all AppleTalk zones on the network."

If you are setting up an AppleTalk router, use the following guidelines to help you decide whether you need AppleTalk zones:

- If you don't have a large network, you don't need AppleTalk zones.
- Zones only appear with AppleTalk and are not used with TCP/IP.
- An AppleTalk zone is a logical creation, not a physical one.

This last point goes to the heart of the issue. An AppleTalk zone does not correspond to a network segment but rather is a logical grouping of servers and shared network printers, regardless of physical location. The purpose of a zone is only to organize large numbers of servers, Macs with file sharing turned on, and printers into several lists of AppleTalk network resources. These lists are presented to the user when they log on to the network. For instance, a network administrator might put all of the printers for the marketing department in a "marketing" zone.

Each Mac will find a default zone to belong to (depending on how the routers are set up). You can change the default zone for each Mac in its Network pane in System Preferences by clicking the AppleTalk tab (make sure you have selected Built-in Ethernet from the Show pop-up menu) and then selecting the zone you want from the AppleTalk Zone pop-up menu. The zone you specify is the one your Mac will use for file sharing. That is, if you have file sharing turned on, then your Mac will appear in the list of servers for that zone.

Setting Up AppleTalk

You use the Network pane of System Preferences to turn on AppleTalk in Mac OS X. You'll first choose a network medium: Ethernet, AirPort, or Modem. Mac OS X calls this a *port*. You then turn on AppleTalk.

Open System Preferences and click the Network icon. Mac OS X 10.3 and later will show you a Network Status pane (**Figure 20.6**). This pane lists the network configurations on the "network ports" (the network media) on your Mac: Internal Modem, Built-in Ethernet, and AirPort if you have an AirPort card installed. If you have a Power Mac with a third-party Ethernet card installed, it could appear here as well. If the lock icon in the lower-left corner is closed, you will need to click it to open it and thus be able to make changes.

You can now choose where you want to turn on AppleTalk. You can do it for both Ethernet and AirPort if you wish, but you have to configure them one at a time. To turn on AppleTalk on Ethernet, double-click Built-in Ethernet and click the AppleTalk tab. (You can also choose the network media from the Show pop-up menu. In fact, if you have Mac OS X 10.2.8 or earlier, you must use the Show pop-up menu.)

The AppleTalk tab of Built-in Ethernet and AirPort is the same (**Figure 20.7**). Click the Make AppleTalk Active check box. Then click the Apply Now button.

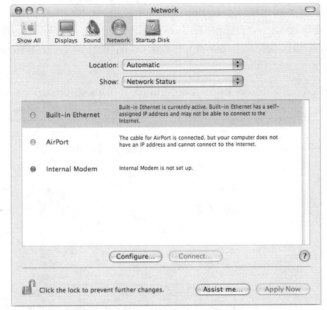

Figure 20.6

The Network Status view of the Network pane in System Preferences gives you a summary of your network configurations.

Figure 20.7

Click the AppleTalk tab to turn on AppleTalk for Ethernet, AirPort, or a modem.

If you have zones configured on an AppleTalk router, you can choose a default zone in the AppleTalk Zone pop-up menu. The Configure pop-up menu lets you select Manually for setting AppleTalk addressing—handy for troubleshooting.

AppleTalk with PPPoE

There is one exception to the above procedure: If you have *PPPoE (Point-to-Point Protocol over Ethernet)* turned on for a DSL Internet connection, you won't be able to turn on AppleTalk using the Built-in Ethernet setting. Instead, you'll have to either use AppleTalk on AirPort or create a new network configuration over Ethernet.

You create a new network configuration in the Network pane of System Preferences:

1. Click the Show pop-up menu near the top of the Network pane and choose Network Port Configurations (**Figure 20.8**).

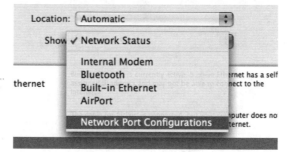

Figure 20.8

Choose Network Port Configurations from the Show pop-up menu on the Network pane of System Preferences to begin creating a new network configuration.

2. Click the New button in the resulting pane.

3. A dialog opens, asking you to name your new configuration and choose a port. Name your configuration something recognizable, such as Ethernet with AppleTalk, and then select Built-in Ethernet from the Port pop-up menu.

4. Click OK. The dialog rolls away and you see your new configuration listed in the Port Configurations box.

5. Click Apply Now.

6. Click the Show menu again. Your new configuration (Ethernet with AppleTalk) now shows up in the list as a choice.

7. Select your new configuration. You can now make AppleTalk active in the AppleTalk tab.

Mac OS X will run both your new AppleTalk port setup and your PPPoE-configured port at the same time.

The Lowdown on TCP/IP

Many users new to TCP/IP networking want a simple answer to the question, "How do I set up my Mac for IP networking?" Unfortunately, there is no simple answer that works for everyone. How you configure TCP/IP depends on the type of network you have, how it is set up, and how you are connected to the Internet.

Your TCP/IP setup is based on an *IP address,* an identifying number that each computer has. You can either designate the IP address yourself or set your Mac to get an address from one of several other sources. Depending on which you choose, you may have to specify several other related items.

Every Mac needs an IP address to identify itself on the network. Getting an IP address for your Mac is the key to setting up TCP/IP. This issue applies equally to Mac OS X and to Mac OS 9 and earlier. However, while Mac OS 9 can have only a single IP address, Mac OS X can have multiple IP addresses running simultaneously; this feature is called *multihoming.* You might want multiple IP addresses if, for example, you are using your Mac as an Internet gateway. One IP address would be used on the Internet, and the other would be used to communicate with the local Macs.

A Mac can get an IP address in several ways. It can get an address from a DHCP server (such as the AirPort Base Station) or a PPP server, or it can give itself an IP address. All these methods are called *dynamic addressing* because the IP can change whenever the Mac starts up. The IP address can also change several times during the course of a day.

Static addressing is when the IP address doesn't change. Static addressing is manual addressing—you have to type an IP address and other information. This is more difficult, because you need to know the rules of IP addressing for the network to work.

We'll first look at the easy method, dynamic addressing, and then move on to static addressing.

Dynamic Addressing and Self-Configuration

The easiest way to configure TCP/IP is to use DHCP, which works with or without a DHCP server. A DHCP server is software that gives IP addresses to computers on a network. These addresses can change every few hours or stay the same. DHCP servers can run on network servers such as Windows 2000 or XP Server, or in Internet gateway software and hardware such as the AirPort Base Station. If there is no DHCP server, the Mac will pick its own IP address, consistent with all the rules of IP addressing. This is similar to the way AppleTalk works. However, DHCP may not be the method you need to configure TCP/IP.

Another common dynamic-addressing scheme you can choose is PPP. Your Mac gets an IP address from an Internet service provider's PPP server or PPPoE server (in the case of a DSL connection). You normally don't use PPP to get an IP address on a local network.

Yet another choice for dynamic IP addressing is BootP, which behaves similarly to DHCP but is an older standard. If you don't have a BootP server, you can ignore this settings choice.

Along with the IP address, dynamic addressing also sets other data, such as the subnet mask. You may still have to enter certain information, such as the *Domain Name Server (DNS)* address.

Setting up DHCP, PPP, and other dynamic addressing

Since DHCP is the default setting, you won't need to set it yourself in many cases. However, if you want to switch to DHCP from something else, or set addressing to PPP, you will need to do the following:

1. Open the Network pane in System Preferences.
2. In the Show pop-up menu, select your network medium (Built-in Ethernet, AirPort, Internal Modem, and so on).
3. Make sure the TCP/IP tab is selected.
4. In the Configure pop-up menu in the TCP/IP pane select the method of getting an IP address. You'll have a choice of PPP, DHCP, BootP, and possibly other methods. (The exact list changes with different network media and some of your other settings.)
5. Click Apply Now.

    Keep in mind that PPPoE (used for a DSL connection) is not the same as PPP (used for a dial-up modem connection). To enable PPPoE, go to the PPPoE tab and check the box for "Connect using PPPoE."

If you have "Connect using PPPoE" checked on the PPPoE tab, you won't be able to choose DHCP. You'll have to create another configuration (see "Creating and Using Multiple Configurations," later in the chapter).

You also can't use DHCP with the Bluetooth port configuration. This configuration is meant for Internet connectivity through a Bluetooth-enabled mobile phone.

Static Addressing

The opposite of dynamic addressing is static addressing—setting IP addresses manually. Macs that are being used for servers on the Internet often need to have static IP addresses set. If you need to set IP addresses manually, read on.

Setting a static IP address can be tricky, as you need to follow a lot of rules. I'll mention some of them here. First, you need to know that an IP address takes the form of four numbers from 0 to 255, separated by periods. For example, this is a valid IP address:

169.254.2.192

Within the range of 000.000.000.000–255.255.255.255, there are ranges of addresses that are used for specific purposes. Every computer *directly* connected to the Internet must have a unique IP address—no other computer anywhere on the planet that is directly connected to the Internet can have the same IP address. Because this would be difficult to manage, and because being directly connected to the Internet opens up some security problems, many networks use some sort of Internet gateway. The Internet sees only the IP address of the gateway. The computers on the network use IP addresses from one of several *private* address ranges. (A private IP address is one that isn't used directly on the Internet but is reserved for local networks.)

There are several private-address ranges. One is the range that Macs give themselves when you set them to use DHCP (described in the previous section), which makes them a good choice for static addressing. These are IP addresses that start with 169.254. Here is the range:

169.254.0.0 to 169.254.254.255

Note that the last number can be 255, but the one before it can only go as high as 254.

Two other private ranges:

10.0.0.1 through 10.255.255.254

192.168.0.1 through 192.168.0.254

If you manually configure the IP addresses of your Mac for a local network, you can use IP addresses from any of these ranges as long as all the Macs on the network are in the same range. Also, no two computers on your network can have the same IP address. Again, you cannot use these addresses to connect directly to the Internet, but you can use them to connect indirectly to the Internet through a gateway (such as an AirPort Base Station).

If you are configuring a server for the Internet, you will use an IP address given to you by your service provider. In this case, the IP address is not "private" but is in a range that can be seen on the Internet. (There are rules for these nonprivate addresses as well.)

When you enter an IP address, you may also have to give the Mac a *subnet mask number,* depending on your other settings. (If the Subnet Mask field appears, you need to enter the number yourself.) A subnet mask number is part of the addressing scheme that helps identify your Mac on a TCP/IP network. *All Macs on the same network segment must have the same subnet mask.* For a small local network, the subnet is usually this:

255.255.0.0 or 255.255.255.0

The next few sections cover setting up static addressing.

Setting up a static IP address

To configure static IP addresses in Mac OS X, do the following:

1. Open the Network pane in System Preferences.
2. Choose Built-in Ethernet from the Show pop-up menu (**Figure 20.9**).

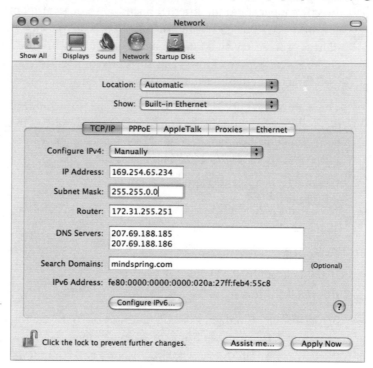

Figure 20.9

To set up a static IP address, you'll need to enter information manually.

3. On the TCP/IP tab, select Manually from the Configure pop-up menu.
4. Type an IP address.
5. Type a subnet mask number.
6. Fill in any other required fields (see "Other IP Settings," below).
7. Click Apply Now, and quit System Preferences.

Static IPv6 Addressing in Mac OS X 10.3

Mac OS X 10.3 and later supports a new version of the Internet protocol called *IP version 6,* or *IPv6.* It's not in wide use yet, but if your institution is using it, Mac OS X 10.3 can use it. IPv6's main advance is that it uses IP addresses that are bigger (128 bits versus the standard 32 bits), which gives the world a big increase in the number of IP addresses available for use.

Mac OS X sets IPv6 addresses automatically, but if you need to manually set them, you can:

1. Open the Network pane of System Preferences.

2. Choose the network medium you want to use with IPv6 (such as Built-in Ethernet or AirPort).

3. Click the Configure IPv6 button.

4. Choose Manually from the Configure IPv6 pop-up menu.

5. Fill in the IPv6 Address, Router, and Prefix Length fields (**Figure 20.10**). You can get these numbers from your network administrator or Internet service provider. IPv6 has its own rules for addressing that are different from those previously described.

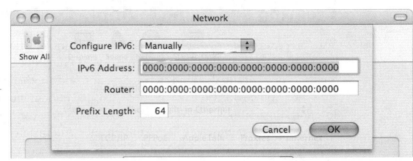

Figure 20.10

Manually setting an IPv6 address is an advanced feature, but it's there if you need it.

Other IP Settings

Getting an IP address isn't the end of the story. Whether you are configuring your IP address dynamically (PPP, DHCP, BootP) or statically, you may need to fill in some other fields. In Mac OS X, these settings are located on the TCP/IP tab of the Network pane of System Preferences. (In Mac OS 9, these settings are on the TCP/IP control panel.)

Domain Name Server (DNS) in Mac OS X. The DNS associates IP addresses with IP domain names (such as apple.com). You will need to fill in the DNS Servers field if you are configuring a direct Internet connection or your local network has a DNS. You can leave this field blank if you are configuring a Mac for a small local network.

"Name server addr." in Mac OS 9 or earlier. *Name server* here refers to the DNS. Here is where you type the IP address of your DNS. This field is always shown, but you may not need to fill it in, as described in the previous section.

Router in Mac OS X ("Router address" in Mac OS 9). This appears only when you select Manually in the Configure menu and is used on large networks that have IP routers (not AppleTalk routers). It will be the router's IP address. If you have been given a static IP address from an Internet service provider, you will need to enter this here. If you have a small local network, you can leave this field blank.

Search Domains. This field typically contains the domain name of your ISP (such as mindspring.com). If your Mac is part of a large local network, you may have one or more domain names to enter. As with the other fields, you'll have to get these names from your network administrator.

Creating and Using Multiple Configurations

You can create and save multiple TCP/IP configurations for different purposes. For instance, you might want one for a DSL (PPPoE) Internet account, another for a backup dial-up Internet account, and another for AirPort or Ethernet. You could also have multiple dial-up configurations for different locations on an iBook or PowerBook. To create a new configuration, simply follow the steps outlined earlier in this chapter. Alternately, you can set up a configuration in the Network pane of System Preferences and then choose New Location from the Location pop-up menu. A dialog rolls down, where you can name your new configuration (for example, "New York office" or "Parents' house").

 If you use the New Location option to create a new configuration, everyone who uses your Mac will be able to choose that configuration from the Apple menu without entering a password.

In Mac OS X, it is possible to run multiple configurations simultaneously. In Mac OS 9, you can run only one configuration at a time.

However, you may not necessarily want to run multiple configurations at once. For example, your PowerBook may have multiple configurations that you use depending on where you are working. You can turn port configurations off by selecting Network Port Configurations in the Show pop-up menu of the Network pane and clicking the On check box next to a configuration's name (**Figure 20.11**). When you turn a configuration off, the check box is no longer checked and the Show menu no longer lists the configuration.

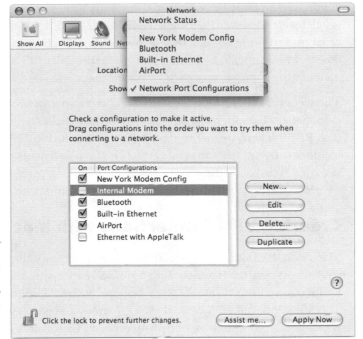

Figure 20.11

Figure 20.11

Your new configuration shows up along with the other network media choices; you can temporarily turn some of them off.

 You can change the order of the port configurations by dragging the configuration names up or down in the Port Configurations box. Why do this? Because it determines the order in which they appear in the Internet Connect application. It can be handy to have the configuration you use most at the top of the list, as it becomes the default in the Internet Connect application's Configuration pop-up menu.

Virtual Private Networks

Mac OS X 10.2 and higher allows you to create a *virtual private network (VPN)* link, which is a secure method of connecting to a local network or server through the Internet. Over a VPN link you can do anything that you can do while on a private network, including share files and access other types of network services.

For you to create a VPN link, your Mac must connect to a VPN server or gateway. This VPN service can be running on a Windows server or on a stand-alone gateway or router, such as those from Cisco Systems, Check Point, Netopia, and others.

There are two basic VPN protocols that your VPN software can use. The first is Microsoft's *Point-to-Point Tunneling Protocol (PPTP),* which is what you'll often find running on Windows servers. Using PPTP is easier than using other VPN protocols, but it isn't quite as secure. Mac OS X 10.2 and later includes the ability to create PPTP connections.

The second basic VPN protocol is *IPsec (Internet Protocol Security),* which provides better encryption and stronger security, as well as better performance, than PPTP. There are different ways to implement IPsec. Mac OS X 10.3 includes software that can create an *L2TP (Level 2 Tunneling Protocol)* over an IPsec VPN link. Other types are possible using third-party software. Before we get to third-party options, let's look at what comes with Mac OS X.

Creating VPN Connections with Mac OS X

Mac OS X 10.2 and higher uses the Internet Connect utility to create a VPN connection over the Internet. With Mac OS X 10.2, you can create only a PPTP connection. Mac OS X 10.3 supports both PPTP and L2TP over IPsec. This VPN link will work over whatever Internet connection you have, whether it's via DSL, cable modem, or dial-up modem. However, VPN connections over dial-up modems can be very slow.

To set up a VPN connection in Mac OS X 10.3, open the Internet Connect utility and click the VPN icon in the toolbar. When you do, a dialog appears, asking you to choose a connection type (**Figure 20.12**). Choose either PPTP or L2TP over IPsec, depending on what is being used by the VPN server you are trying to connect to. Click Continue.

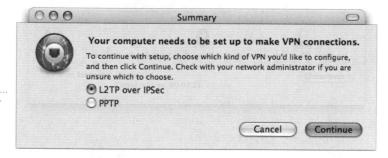

Figure 20.12

In Internet Connect choose the type of VPN account you want to create.

In the next dialog that appears, fill in the IP "Server address," Account Name, and Password fields for the VPN server you want to connect to (**Figure 20.13**). You are now ready to create a VPN link by clicking Connect. When you quit Internet Connect, you're asked to name your VPN configuration. This name will appear in the Configuration pop-up menu.

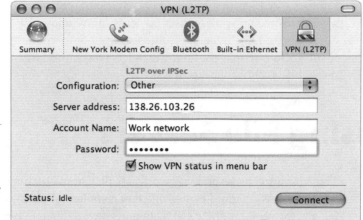

Figure 20.13

You'll need to know several facts about the VPN server you want to connect to in order to configure it correctly in Internet Connect.

If you need to connect to more than one VPN server, you can create multiple VPN configurations using the Internet Connect utility. Just go to the File menu and select New VPN Connection. Follow the steps as before.

Your VPN connections will appear in the Network pane of System Preferences when you choose Network Status from the Show pop-up menu, along with your Ethernet, AirPort, or modem configurations. If you need to delete a VPN connection, you can do so from the Network pane of System Preferences. To do this, select Network Port Configurations from the Show pop-up menu, highlight the VPN connection you want to delete, and click Delete.

Third-Party VPN Clients

If the built-in VPN client in Mac OS X doesn't work with your organization's VPN hardware, there are third-party products that provide other types of IPsec, and other types of authentication that the Mac OS X built-in VPN client doesn't support. You can also use a third-party VPN client to access IPsec VPNs with Mac OS X 10.2.

One of the most versatile VPN clients is Equinux's **VPN Tracker** ($89.90 Personal Edition, $199.90 Professional Edition; www.equinux.com), an IPsec client tuned to work with a variety of VPN concentrators and gateways. It works with Mac OS X 10.2 and later. VPN Tracker can connect you to several dozen VPN servers and concentrators, including those from Check Point, Netgear, Netopia, PGPNet, SonicWALL, Windows servers, and FreeS/WAN running on a Linux server. The Professional Edition also lets you use your Mac to connect two networks together over a VPN link, as well as secure AirPort networks.

Another PPTP client for Mac OS X, Gracion Software's **DigiTunnel** ($58; www.gracion.com/vpn), focuses on accessing Windows VPN servers and Mac OS X Server. DigiTunnel has some features not found in Mac OS X's built-in client, including split-routing, which lets you connect directly to any Internet sites while a VPN connection is active.

Accessing File Servers

The Mac provides several ways to access files stored on other networked computers. As described earlier, different computer platforms can use different file-sharing protocols. Mac OS X supports several different types of file-sharing protocols that you can use for logging in:

- **AFP (AppleTalk Filing Protocol)**—This is traditional Mac AppleShare-compatible file sharing, and it is still the most stable and trouble-free of Mac OS X's file-sharing methods. Computers that support AFP file service over TCP/IP include Macs with Mac OS 9 or later, Apple's Mac OS X Server and AppleShare IP, Windows 2000 Server and Windows Server 2003 with Services for Macintosh installed, and Linux servers with Netatalk installed.

- **SMB/CIFS (Server Message Block/Common Internet File System)**—SMB is the main method of Windows file sharing. Mac OS X doesn't support it quite as well as Windows PCs or Thursby's DAVE. SMB is also used on Linux servers running Samba, a suite of Unix applications that support the SMB protocol. Mac OS X was the first Mac OS to include support for logging in to SMB servers.

- **FTP (File Transfer Protocol)**—FTP is the old Internet standard. The Finder has a built-in FTP client.

- **NFS (Network File System)**—An old Sun Unix standard, NFS is also used with Linux.

- **WebDAV (Web-Based Distributed Authoring and Versioning)**—WebDAV uses Web protocols. Apple's iDisk (from the .Mac Service) uses WebDAV.

 In early versions of Mac OS, AFP only ran over AppleTalk. In Mac OS 9, AFP file sharing can run over both AppleTalk and TCP/IP. In Mac OS X 10.0–10.0.4, AFP file sharing ran only over TCP/IP. Apple restored AFP over AppleTalk with version 10.1 of Mac OS X.

Browsing vs. URL Access

Mac OS X gives you two methods of logging in to a file server: browsing for a server or typing in a URL to open it. To use the browsing method, you bring up a window that displays a list of servers or shared computers on the network. In the other method, you type in some sort of address to log in to a networked computer.

With Mac OS X 10.2, both of these procedures are fairly simple and straight-forward, and they occur in the same place: the Connect to Server dialog, which you access from the Finder's Go menu.

With Mac OS X 10.3, Apple made logging in to a file server more complicated (some would say needlessly) and confusing if you don't know what to expect. That's because there are two different methods of logging in, and each yields different results. Here are the main oddball behaviors you should know about:

- You type in a URL to log in to servers in a place that is *different* from where you browse to log in. You browse for servers using Mac OS X 10.3's Network icon in the sidebar of Finder windows. You type in a URL in the Server Address field in the Connect to Server dialog (which you access from the Finder's Go menu). Note that there's a Browse button in Mac OS X 10.3's Connect to Server dialog—clicking it takes you to the Finder's Network window.

- Accessing servers from the different places gives you different results— that is, the server behaves differently, depending on whether you browsed for it or typed in a URL. (Oddly, logging in with a typed URL gives you the more Mac-like behavior.)

- You can log in to the *same* file server *twice*, using *both* methods. It's strange, but it gives you the best of both worlds—the full behaviors of both.

So what are these two radically different behaviors? If you go to the Connect to Server dialog in the Go menu to log in by typing a URL, the server will behave as it always has since Macintosh file sharing began around 1986: the server will act like a drive, mounting on the Desktop and becoming available through the Open and Save dialogs. Dragging the server to the Trash logs it out.

However, the behavior is completely different (and un-Mac-like) if you browse for an AFP, SMB, or NFS volume in the Network window. To start with, a different login screen appears, with no obvious way to add the pass-word to the Mac OS X Keychain. When you double-click a server, it will not act like a drive, but rather as a folder at this location:

/private/var/automount/Network/ServerName/ShareName

And there's more. Mac OS X 10.3 won't mount servers on the Desktop if you log on by browsing for them, and they don't appear at the hard-drive level in Open and Save dialogs. To access servers from an Open or Save dialog, you have to click through the directory structure (through AppleTalk Zones if you have them).

In fact, if you log in by browsing, Mac OS X 10.3 gives no real indication that you are connected to the server other than the fact that you can see folders on the server—a problem if you're using a PowerBook and aren't continually connected to a network, as disconnecting can result in long periods of watching the spinning rainbow disc. The one feature you do get with this method is that you can log in directly from the Open and Save dialogs.

The only way to get the best of both worlds is to use *both* of these login methods to log in to the same server twice.

 In a perfect world, it would seem most natural to have both methods of logging in give you the full set of behaviors—both a Desktop mounting option and login access from the Open and Save dialogs, using the same dialog and supporting keychain access. Apple says that Mac OS X 10.3's schizophrenic file-sharing behavior is a feature, not a bug, but the dichotomy is clearly confusing to most of us mere mortals.

Now, on to the specifics of how to log in.

Log in to servers by browsing

In Mac OS X 10.2 and higher, you can browse for AFP, SMB, and NFS servers. (To log in to FTP or WebDAV servers, you need to type a URL.)

Browsing for SMB servers is limited to servers located on the same *subnet,* or network segment, as your Mac. Servers on other subnets will not appear. For those servers, you'll need to type in a URL to log in, or use Thursby's **DAVE** ($119; www.thursby.com) to browse for the server. On Windows networks that have successfully integrated Macs with Microsoft's Active Directory, you will be able to see Windows SMB servers located on other subnets.

 As of this writing, Mac OS X 10.3 browsing had problems with SMB servers not appearing even when on the same subnet. You may be able to fix this by opening the Directory Access utility in the Utilities folder. Click the Services, and make sure that SMB is enabled and selected. Now click Configure, and then click your workgroup name (or Windows domain name) in the Workgroup field.

On networks with Microsoft Active Directory running, there is another step you may need to do. Enable Active Directory, select the Active Directory, and click Configure. Enter your Active Directory domain name in the Active Directory Domain field and click OK. Then click Apply. For more on this problem, see the MacWindows Mac OS X 10.3 (Panther) Cross-Platform Report (www.macwindows.com/panther.html).

The file-server browsing procedure is very different for the two versions of Mac OS X. Mac OS X 10.3 uses the Finder's Network icon; Mac OS X 10.2 uses the Connect to Server dialog.

Log in by browsing in Mac OS X 10.3

In Mac OS X 10.3, start browsing your local network by opening any Finder Window to access the sidebar (**Figure 20.14**). Click the Network icon in the sidebar and then the Servers icon. You'll then see folders representing other users' computers where file sharing is enabled, and you may see folders representing Windows workgroups, AppleTalk zones, or other network grouping. You can open these to look for servers or computers to log in to. You may also see a folder called Local that contains servers on your local network segment. The Server icon can also include servers.

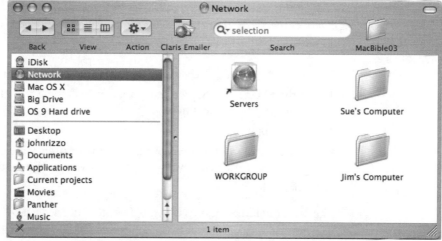

Figure 20.14

The Network icon is where you start when you want to browse for available servers.

To log in to a computer or file server, double-click the folder or icon that represents it. This brings up a login dialog, where you type in a name and password. When you're connected, the contents of the server volume appear in the Finder window. The server does *not* appear on the Desktop, however.

During login, you can add your name and password to the Mac OS X Keychain for future automatic entry of these items. You do this by clicking the Options button in the login window.

Log in by browsing in Mac OS X 10.2

To browse local networks for file servers in Mac OS X 10.2, you use the Connect to Server command in the Finder's Go menu. Here you may see a list of individual users' computers and AppleTalk zones, and you'll find a Local icon that lists servers when doubled-clicked.

The Connect to Server dialog also lists the computers you've accessed recently in a pop-up menu. You can choose a server from this list.

To log in to a computer or file server, double-click it and enter a password. Click the Add to Keychain box to have the password added to the Mac OS X Keychain.

 In Mac OS X 10.2 you can't use the Network icon in the Finder to access AFP and NFS servers. Only files on Unix NetInfo networks will appear here.

Log In by Typing a URL

In a URL that you use to access a Web site, the first part, *http://,* tells the browser that you are looking for a Web site. On Macs running Mac OS 8.6 and later, URLs can also be used to log into AFP, SMB, NFS, FTP, and WebDAV file servers. These addresses begin with *afp://, smb://, nfs://, ftp://,* and *http://,* respectively. This beginning can be followed by words or an IP address.

To log in this way in Mac OS X, do the following:

1. Select the Connect to Server command in the Finder's Go menu.
2. In the Connect to Server dialog that appears, type a URL for the server in the Server Address field.
3. Click Connect.
4. In the login window that appears, type your user name and password and the name of the Windows workgroup, if you have one, on your network.
5. Click OK.

The server volume mounts on your Desktop, in Mac OS X 10.2 and higher. You can add a server to the Favorite Servers list by clicking the plus button. The next time you log in, you can just choose it from the Recent Servers pop-up menu (**Figure 20.15**).

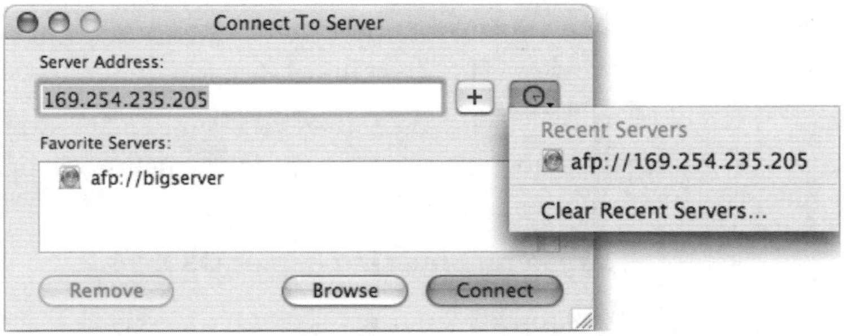

Figure 20.15

The Connect to Server dialog lets you access a server directly by typing in its URL. You can add servers to your favorites list by clicking the plus button; then you can always choose them from the Recent Servers pop-up menu.

The Browse button in Mac OS X 10.3's Connect to Server dialog takes you to the Finder's Network icon.

The forms of the URLs vary with the type of server. With some types of servers you can include a name and password, or other types of information. For any type of server, you can always use the server's IP address. (For more on IP addresses, see "Static Addressing," earlier in this chapter.) Here are the specifics:

AFP. AFP servers have URLs that take one of these forms:

afp://*ComputerName* or, on bigger networks, afp://*ComputerName.CompanyName*

SMB. SMB servers have the following basic URL:

smb://workgroup;*ServerName*/*ShareName*

The workgroup and semicolon aren't always necessary, and you may not need them on a smaller network. The server name can be the computer name or the DNS name. The share name is the name of the shared folder you are trying to access. You can also add your user name to the URL, like this:

smb://workgroup;*UserName*@*ServerName*/*ShareName*

This sometimes works when you're having trouble otherwise.

FTP. To log in to an FTP site (either locally or on the Internet), use one of the following URLs:

ftp://*DNSname* (such as ftp://acme.com) or, including the user name, ftp://*user*@*DNSname*

You can specify both your user name and password using this form:

ftp://*user:password*@*DNSname* (such as ftp://bob:bellweather@acme.com)

NFS. NFS URLs are similar to FTP URLs:

nfs://*ServerName*/*pathname* where *pathname* is the name of the directory or directories.

If you have a .Mac account, you can log in to your iDisk in various ways. However, you can connect to other WebDAV servers using this URL:

http://*DNSname*/*pathname*

Enabling Others to Access Your Files

Just as you can access file servers of different types, your Mac lets you share your files using different file-sharing protocols, so that different types of computers can access them. Here are the file-sharing protocols the Mac supports.

AFP-based file sharing. This enables users to access files on your Mac using traditional Mac file sharing.

SMB/CIFS. This lets Windows and Linux-based PCs access your Mac.

FTP. Mac OS X has a built-in FTP server. All you have to do is turn it on, and users can access it using a Web browser or FTP client such as **Captain FTP** ($25; http://captainftp.xdsnet.de).

Personal Web Sharing. This starts the Web server that is built in to Mac OS X. You can use it to display Web pages you've created and let other users download files from your Mac.

You enable all these types of services from the Sharing pane of System preferences.

Turn on File Sharing

The procedure for enabling access to your computer by AFP, SMB, FTP, and Web sharing is similar. First, make sure that TCP/IP is correctly configured. You can have both TCP/IP and AppleTalk enabled. If file sharing is on, turn it off before you turn on AppleTalk.

To turn on file sharing:

1. Open the Sharing pane in System Preferences.
2. Make sure the Computer Name field is filled in.
3. Click the Services tab.
4. Select the type of file sharing you'd like to start with. In the Service list, AFP file sharing is called Personal File Sharing, SMB file sharing is called Windows Sharing, and the FTP service is called FTP Access.
5. To start, either click the Start button or click the check box next to the service you want to start.

After the file-sharing service starts, the Sharing Preferences pane displays a URL for the selected service at the bottom (**Figure 20.16**). This is the URL that someone else would use to access your Mac.

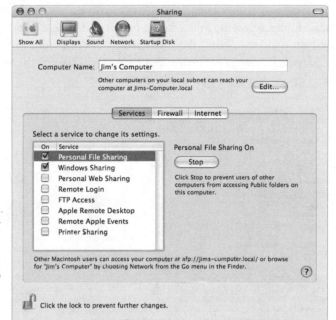

Figure 20.16

After you start a file-sharing service, the Sharing Preferences pane shows you the URL that people can use to access that service from other computers.

Now you need to decide what password users will need. You have three choices:

- **No password**—Users will be able to log in to the Public folder in your home folder without a password. If you want to share files this way, you need to put them in the Public folder.

  (This is not an option for FTP, as Mac OS X doesn't permit guest access, which is called *anonymous user* access in FTP-speak. To access your Mac's files via FTP, you must set up a user account in System Preferences' Accounts pane.)

- **Use your administrator's password** (the password you use to log in to your Mac)—This gives you (or whomever you give the password to) access to the entire Mac, not just the Public folder. This is the way to go for your Macs at home.

- **Require a password to access your Public folder**—To do this, create a new user account in the Accounts pane of System Preferences by clicking the plus button in the bottom-left corner. Set a user name and password. You can then give this password to everyone you'd like to allow to access your Mac over the network. You could also create an account for each user, using different passwords. However, this would create home folders on your Mac for each of these users.

 In Mac OS X 10.2, if you want Windows users to be able to access your Mac, you must check the box for Enable Windows Users to Access in the account you are creating. This is *not* necessary in Mac OS X 10.3.

If you want to change how other users can access a particular folder in your Public folder, select the folder in the Finder and choose File > Get Info. In the Get Info window, expand the Ownership & Permissions section and expand the Details subsection (**Figure 20.17**). You will change the selection in the Others pop-up menu. You have four choices:

Figure 20.17

You can use the Get Info window to change the access privileges that other users will have to folders in your Public folder.

- **Read & Write**—Users can copy files both to and from your Mac.
- **Read only**—Users can only copy files from your Mac to their computers. This is the default setting.
- **Write only (Drop Box)**—Users can copy files into the folder but can't open the folder to see what's in it.
- **No Access**—This prevents others from making changes to the folder.

Interview: Mitch Kapor

Back in the 1980s Mitch Kapor was one of the best-known names in high tech. He started programming in 1965, at the age of 15, and graduated from Yale in 1971 with an interdisciplinary major in cybernetics. After stints as a disc jockey, a teacher of Transcendental Meditation, and a mental-health counselor, he bought an Apple II in 1978 and began programming it. Shortly afterwards he went to work as a product manager for Personal Software, Inc., the publisher of VisiCalc for the Apple II, the world's first electronic spreadsheet.

> The whole user experience has always been better on the Mac. I defy anybody to make a case to the contrary.
>
> —*Mitch Kapor, on switching back to the Mac from the PC*

In 1982, the year after the release of the first IBM PC, he founded Lotus Development Corp. and designed Lotus 1-2-3, the spreadsheet that helped propel the PC into the corporate mainstream. In 1983, Lotus's first year of operations, the company achieved revenues of $53,000,000 and had a successful public offering, and the following year its revenues nearly tripled.

Kapor resigned as chairman of Lotus in 1986. He then founded ON Technology, which developed, among other products, cross-platform scheduling software called Meeting Maker. In 1990, together with former cattle rancher and Grateful Dead lyricist John Perry Barlow, he cofounded the Electronic Frontier Foundation, a nonprofit organization that fights for individual rights and liberties in the technology domain.

He has also been an active investor in high-tech startups. He currently leads the Open Source Applications Foundation (www.osafoundation.org), which is developing an open-source email and personal information program that will run on the Mac, Linux and Windows. —Henry Norr

When did you first see a Mac?

We heard about it six months before it shipped, so in mid-1983, but I don't think we actually saw one until 1984. We wanted to port 1-2-3, and Apple did not want us to do that, for reasons we failed to understand [at the time], but it was because Microsoft had negotiated a spreadsheet exclusive. They [Apple] wanted us to do a personal finance program, and we weren't interested in that, so we really had to wait until the machine came out to start developing anything.

What did you think when you saw it?

You know, the introduction of the Mac is probably still the defining event of my career, in terms of the single most important thing, for long-term impact.

continues on next page

That's surprising, since your name is usually associated with the PC. Why was the Mac so important to you?

Well, because it was just so cool. It had a new height of cool [he laughs]. It was a radical departure in terms of personal computers. The Lisa was this $5,000 business machine that was slow and clunky, and the Mac—it was inexpensive and small and light, and it was just so elegant. It had so many new ideas, and [Apple] did such a good job integrating what was in that original Mac. It's really a testament to what they did right, considering everything that was not in the original Mac—there was no hard drive, there was no network, there was no letter-quality printer, it had this extreme memory limitation, and of course no slots. Basically, it was a toy, but it was the world's coolest toy.

Did you think it would sell in high volume?

You know, I think I was not thinking clearly then—that just did not seem to be a terribly relevant question [he laughs]. And then it became apparent by the time Jazz came out that the Mac was going nowhere as a product. In fact, they had to do a series of things, including the 512K Mac and the laser printer and AppleTalk, and then the Mac II [before the platform really took off].

So did you hesitate about whether to do a product, given the limitations?

Oh no, we absolutely wanted to do a product. But we made a bad choice strategically. We did Lotus Jazz, which was kind of Symphony for the Mac. [Symphony for the PC was a much-anticipated but ultimately unsuccessful integrated "AppleWorks-style" program for DOS.] We would have been much better off just doing a straight version of 1-2-3, of course.

Which you eventually did in 1991.

Yeah, but it was too little, too late—it was post-Excel, and it wasn't as good as Excel.

What's your analysis of why Jazz failed?

Jazz was a brave and ambitious product; it just wasn't crisp and fast and bug-less.

Were you personally involved in the development?

Lotus had gotten big—it was 1984, 1985, and we'd gone from zero to $200 million—so I was not very involved in the product definition. I got very involved at the end, because they were having trouble getting it finished. I actually was in the daily bug triage.

The stupidest, the single most expensive mistake I made was approving a $7 million TV ad budget for Jazz. We didn't know what we were doing. Of course, it was absurd. We could have just had a bonfire of $100 bills on the roof of the building and barbecued some steaks—then at least we would have been fed.

Because those ads didn't really bring in any customers?

No! I mean, it wasn't a mass-market product.

I remember it took quite a bit longer than planned—was there any particular reason?

Development in those days was a b—. You had to use the Lisa development environment, and the tools weren't good, and there was just a huge amount of overhead in it. And, you know, the Mac was a very limited machine.

Do you think there's anything you could have done that would have made Jazz a success?

Yeah! I guess the first thing would have been to look at what we'd done and say, "The important thing is the spreadsheet." Simplicity would have been the right product strategy. And stick to it—keep working on it until you get it right. Microsoft had the right strategy for applications—just the simple basic product categories, strong functionality, and stick with it.

What computer do you use today?

I am in the process of switching back to the Macintosh full time. I've been hung up on the fact that I have a shared calendar that other people can see, based on an Exchange server. And I just finally decided to go and use iCal and publish it. It's going to make more work for my assistant—she's going to have to have two machines on her desk. But for six months I've been figuring out how I'm going to move my entire environment, application by application, and all the data—make sure everything works. I'm done with the research phase, and so literally an hour and a half ago I placed the order …

A big high-end G5, I suppose?

No, a 15-inch PowerBook. I have a 12 [-inch PowerBook], which I like, so my assistant's going to get that.

Why are you moving to the Mac now?

The whole user experience has always been better on the Mac. I defy anybody to make a case to the contrary. The reason not to be on the Mac, for quite a while, was that the necessary breadth of software just wasn't there, and the compatibility with the PC world just wasn't there. But they've obviously fixed that, in stages, since Steve came back. And they didn't have a modern operating system. But now you look at it—I can do everything I need to do, one way or another, and the user experience is just so much better, and it's simpler. And now there are all these cool utilities people are doing. Plus you get a Unix box underneath if you really want to geek out.

And you know, the Mac is more fun. I'm trying to remember when I switched to the Mac, probably the mid '80s, when I was still at Lotus. And I was on the Mac for many, many, many years, until like the late '90s. And then I went to a PC, just because the Mac was at this real low point. So probably, if you look at it, I've spent half my career on Macintoshes, and it's time to go back.

21

Working Across Platforms

John Rizzo is the chapter editor and author.

Don't worry, they said. Go ahead and buy a Mac—it can do everything a PC can and more. Now you're having trouble working collaboratively with your Windows-using colleagues. You can't open a file someone sent you, or you can't run a program someone wants you to, or you can't connect to a network.

This may sound like blasphemy in *The Macintosh Bible,* but here goes: the Mac has limitations. The cruel fact is, Windows PCs can share files and otherwise communicate better with other Windows PCs than they can with Macs. Let's face it—it's a Windows world, and it's up to you to deal with it.

The good news is that you *can* deal with it. Each new version of Mac OS X has added more tools designed for PC compatibility. With some know-how and a few extra utilities, you can join the Windows world without leaving the comfort of the Mac. Sometimes the solutions are simple; other times they're not. But there *are* solutions for most cross-platform problems.

Most Mac-PC compatibility issues have to do with using PC files and creating files your Windows colleagues can use. This chapter describes the differences between Mac and PC files and their most common cross-platform problems.

Another major area of cross-platform problems is networking—a technical area that can be difficult to get a handle on. Mac OS X 10.2 (Jaguar) and Mac OS X 10.3 (Panther) each added some tools to your Mac to get it talking Windows.

Some of the problems I describe in this chapter also apply to dealing with Linux and Unix users, and I point it out when they do. Mac OS X tends to have fewer problems with Linux and Unix, since it has Unix built into its core.

In This Chapter

Working with Files

Files are the items that hold your work. And files are where many of your cross-platform problems lie. Most people don't realize that a lot of the problems with files downloaded from the Internet are actually cross-platform file problems.

Some of the file incompatibilities you may run into have to do with the fact that Mac files are intrinsically different from Windows and Linux files. This section first deals with some basic differences between Mac files and files created on other computers, and it describes how these differences cause cross-platform problems. Then we look at specific problems with using files that PC users send you and problems with files you send to PC users.

 Most PCs do Windows, but many Intel-based PCs are running Linux. When I refer to *PCs*, the statement can apply to PCs running either the Windows or Linux operating systems. I use the term *Windows* to refer to issues specific to that operating system.

What's in a Mac File

Macintosh files are a bit more complex than Windows files. Mac files have some invisible components that Windows, Unix, and Linux files don't have and consequently don't support. (Mac OS X is one flavor of Unix that *does* support these Mac file attributes.) Special server software designed to support Mac clients can handle these Macintosh file components, even if the servers are running Windows or Linux. However, non-Mac desktop machines don't support Mac file attributes, and neither do many servers for Internet email, Web, FTP, and other services. These operating systems simply ignore and lose the Mac file attributes. This can have various results, from the loss of a file's icon to the destruction of the file.

So what are these mysterious, unseen file attributes? There are several, but the most important is the resource fork, which holds code. Then there are the type and creator codes, which help the Mac identify a file.

File forks

Figure 21.1

A generic file icon can indicate a missing resource fork as well as missing type and creator codes.

Traditional Mac files consist of two *forks:* a *data fork* and a *resource fork.* The data fork contains the data contents of a file—the text, formatting, graphics, and sound you created. The resource fork contains programming code and file resources, such as the file's icon.

If you move a file from a Mac to a PC and then back to a Mac, the file loses its icon—the icon becomes generic (**Figure 21.1**). The same is true if you move a Mac file to Unix, Linux, or many Internet servers and back. This is because the file has lost its resource fork.

The loss of an icon in a document file is not fatal—you can still open the file from the Open dialog box of an application that supports the file format. But if an *application* loses its resource fork, the program won't work. That's because the resource fork is where the application keeps the executable programming code that makes the application run.

Self-expanding archives (denoted with three-letter extensions such as .hqx) and self-mounting disk-image files also contain code (small programs) in their resource forks. This code decompresses the archive or mounts the disk image on the Desktop. If the resource fork of these types of files is lost, the embedded program is lost, and the file won't open.

This means that merely moving these types of files to PCs and back to Macs can destroy them. To prevent this, some application software creates files that combine the resource and data forks. These types of files are said to be *flat*. All Windows files are flat. Some Mac software can create flat files. QuickTime files, for instance, are flat and can run across platforms on Macs and PCs.

Apple encourages Mac OS X developers to enable their new applications to create flat files. That is, the applications will put the resources in the data fork of new document files you create. This makes the files more portable and able to move around the Internet and to Windows PCs without problems. Mac OS X can also use files with file forks (separate resource and data forks), like the ones Mac OS 9 requires.

As time goes on, we may see the use of file forks diminish and eventually fade away. However, at this time you will find that many files created in Mac OS X do have data and resource forks, as do all files created in Mac OS 9 and earlier.

Type and creator codes

The type and creator codes are Macintosh file attributes that PCs lose along with the resource fork. A file's *creator code* tells the Mac OS which application to launch when you double-click the file. The *type code* identifies the file format, such as JPEG, plain text, or Microsoft Word 2001. Together, a file's type and creator codes determine a file's icon and what application will launch when you double-click the file.

If you know the type and creator codes, you can add them back in if they've disappeared (see the sidebar "Using Sherlock 2 to View and Edit Type and Creator Codes," below). **Table 21.1** shows a few common type and creator codes. Note that type and creator codes are case sensitive.

Table 21.1 Codes and Their Descriptions

Type Code	Description
APPL	Application
CWSS	AppleWorks spreadsheet
CWWP	AppleWorks word-processing file
PDF	PDF file
TEXT	Text (generic) file
W8BN	Microsoft Word file
XLS8	Microsoft Excel file

Creator Code	Description
8BIM	Adobe Photoshop
BOBO	AppleWorks 6
CARO	Adobe Reader
MOSS	Netscape Communicator
MSWD	Microsoft Word
XCEL	Microsoft Excel

Mac OS X–native files don't always need type and creator codes—new Mac OS X–native software can create files without them. Mac OS X can use type and creator codes or use the filename extensions to assign icons. At this point, even Apple doesn't have consistent behavior for its Mac OS X–native applications. Some of Apple's applications, such as Keynote, don't use type and creator codes. But Apple still uses them in other applications, such as iDVD.

If you have a problem opening a file when you double-click it, you can use the file's Get Info window to tell Mac OS X which application to use to open the file (see "The wrong (or no) app opens when the file is double-clicked," later in the chapter).

Using Sherlock 2 to View and Edit Type and Creator Codes

In Mac OS 9 and earlier, you can use Sherlock to read the type and creator codes of a file. Unfortunately, Mac OS X's Find command never picked up this trick. However, if you have an older dual-boot Mac (a Mac that can start up with Mac OS X or Mac OS 9 or earlier), then you have a copy of the old Sherlock that you can run in Mac OS X Classic mode. Here's how to use it to view a file's codes:

1. Open the Applications (Mac OS 9) folder and double-click Sherlock 2. You'll get a warning message telling you that this version of Sherlock is not optimized and that you should use Mac OS X's Sherlock instead. Ignore it by clicking Cancel.

2. In Sherlock 2 click Edit.

3. Drag the file you are interested in from the Finder to Sherlock's More Search Options window.

4. Look under Advanced Options. The "file type" and "creator" fields will display the codes for the file. If these fields are blank, then the file does not have the codes. A file created on a PC might show random characters or question marks in the "file type" and "creator" fields.

5. To change the type and creator codes, simply click the check box next to each option to make it active. Then enter the type and creator codes you want the file to have.

If a PC-created file is giving you trouble, you can change the file's type and creator codes with other tools, such as DataViz's MacLinkPlus Deluxe (see the next section). Go to the MacLinkPlus File menu and select Set Type and Creator. A new box appears, where you can edit the codes.

Sending and Receiving Email Attachments

Sending files by email is one of the most common ways in which people move files. Unfortunately, moving email attachments between Macs and PCs can cause some problems. The good news is that once you know what's going on, these problems are easy to prevent and to solve.

We'll first look at opening attachments from PC users and then move on to sending attachments so that Windows users will be able to read them.

Opening email attachments from PC and Mac users

You know something's wrong when you double-click an attached file and it just won't open. Or maybe you can open it, only to be greeted by garbled, random characters. You ask the PC user to resend the file, and the same problem occurs.

The problem is that the PC user's email software is using either encoding or compressing standards that your email software doesn't understand. Unrecognizable encoding or compression can also be a problem when downloading files from the Internet.

Compression is the easier problem to diagnose and fix, so let's consider it first. Compression is used to make the file smaller to speed the time of transfer over the Internet. Macs usually compress files in the .sit format, appending .sit to the ends of the filenames. However, compressed files from Windows users are usually in the Zip format, with filenames ending in .zip. Compressed files from Linux or Unix users can be in a variety of formats, including .gz (also called .gzip), .bzip, and .tar.

Unlike compression, encoding does not make a file smaller. In fact, encoding often slightly increases the size of a file.

Mac OS X comes with Aladdin Systems' StuffIt Expander application, which can decompress files in .sit, Zip, gz, tar, bzip, and other formats. If a file doesn't decompress automatically, try dropping the file on top of the StuffIt Expander icon. It's in the /Applications/Utilities folder. If you have a file that is compressed in a format not supported by StuffIt Expander, you'll have to get another decompression utility. There are plenty to choose from, including Aladdin Systems' **StuffIt Standard Edition** and **StuffIt Deluxe** ($49.99 and $79.99, respectively; www.stuffit.com), and many freeware and shareware utilities. For a list of cross-platform compression utilities for the Mac, see the MacWindows Web site (www.macwindows.com/compress.html).

One type of compression format created by PC software is the self-expanding Windows archive, sometimes called an EXE archive; StuffIt Deluxe can decompress EXE archives and extract the files inside. However, all Windows applications also end in .exe—just because a file has the .exe extension doesn't mean it's an archive.

Email attachments you receive may be both compressed and encoded, in that order. If that's the case, you have to decode first, and then decompress. Decoding can sometimes be trickier than decompressing, as more can go wrong.

StuffIt Expander (and some of the other decompression programs as well) can decode as well as decompress files. Drag your problem file on top of the StuffIt Expander icon in the Utilities folder. This sometimes works when double-clicking the file doesn't. However, sometimes StuffIt Expander just can't recognize the file, particularly if the email message headers have gotten mixed in with the encoded file.

You can try cleaning up the file manually:

1. Open it with a text editor (Word, AppleWorks, or SimpleText will work).

   If you see the line "Content-Type: text/plain," the file is a MIME/Base64-encoded file. Delete everything above this line. (MIME/Base 64 is the most common type of encoding used on the PC.)

If you see a line that begins with the phrase "begin 644," it's a field encoded with the uuencode format. (Uuencode is a Unix encoding standard that is also sometimes used by Windows.) Delete everything before this line.

2. Now use the Save As command to save the file as a text-only file (and not a Word or AppleWorks file if you are using one of those programs).

3. Drag the file onto StuffIt Expander.

 StuffIt Expander for Mac OS X does a better job with Unix encoding and compression standards than StuffIt Expander for Mac OS 9. Unfortunately, double-clicking a compressed or encoded file in Mac OS X often launches the Mac OS 9 version of StuffIt Expander, which causes Classic to launch. To prevent this, don't double-click the file. Instead, drop it on top of the Mac OS X version of StuffIt Expander.

DataViz's **MacLinkPlus Deluxe** ($79.95; www.dataviz.com) tends to do a better job of recognizing encoded files, stripping out email headers, and recognizing and decoding the encoding format, all automatically. You don't have to open the file and manually strip out anything.

You decode and decompress with MacLinkPlus in the same way you would translate a file (see "Applications can't open the file," later in the chapter):

1. Drop the file on top of the MacLinkPlus Deluxe utility icon (or drag it into the utility's window if it's open).

2. Select the file and click Decompress. (This works for decoding as well, in which case the button will say Decode.)

Decoding Winmail.dat files

Have you ever received an attached file called Winmail.dat? Or you might get a file with the type designation of application/ms-tnef. You can't open it and your decoding utilities can't handle it. This is a special type of decoding problem sometimes seen with email coming from Microsoft Outlook for Windows under certain circumstances. The causes are fairly technical, but the upshot is that the Microsoft Exchange Server will encode the file using a Microsoft-specific encoding style.

The best fix is a free program called **TNEF's Enough** (http://homepage.mac.com/joshjacob/macdev/tnef). It can decode the Winmail.dat file and extract an attached file. If the utility is having trouble, try StuffIt Expander first, and then TNEF's Enough. The TNEF file might also have been encoded with Base64 or another format.

Sending email attachments to PC users

The same compression and encoding issues come up when you send a file to a PC user. You have to make sure to use encoding that the PC email software will be able to decode. Otherwise, your file will look like a garbled mess.

To guarantee that a Windows user can decode your email attachment, use the MIME/Base64 encoding format. If you are sending a file to a mixture of Mac and PC users, you can try the AppleDouble format. (This is what the Mail program uses.) Uuencode is good for Linux and Unix users; some Windows users might be able to handle uuencode as well. When in doubt, use MIME/Base64 for Windows users.

Some Mac users may also be able to handle MIME/Base64 and uuencode, but these formats won't retain a file's Mac icon or resource fork. The best bet for sending enclosures to Mac users is to use BinHex encoding.

Unfortunately, the Mail program that comes with Mac OS X is not very good about letting you change the encoding used for attachments. In fact, in versions of Mail before Mac OS X 10.3, you could not change the AppleDouble encoding at all. With Mac OS X 10.3, the Mail application added an option for MIME/Base64 that Mail calls Windows Friendly Attachments. You get the option when you click the Attachments button in an outgoing mail message. A file browser window appears with an option called Send Windows Friendly Attachments (**Figure 21.2**). However, once you've opted for this setting, Mail doesn't let you see your setting or change it.

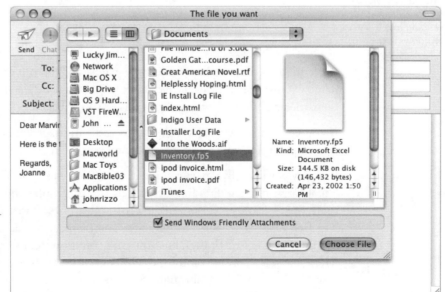

Figure 21.2

Mail gives you this Windows Friendly Attachments option when enclosing a file, but you can't change it later.

Microsoft Entourage has an easier and more flexible way to set encoding. You do it in the new-message window itself. Here's how:

1. Click the triangle next to Attachments to open the Attachments list. This should display your attachment and its size.

2. Click the "Encode for" bar below the Attachments list. A dialog pops up, listing encoding formats (**Figure 21.3**).

3. Under "Encode for," choose your encoding format—Windows (MIME/Base64) is the best choice for Windows users.

4. Under Compression select None.

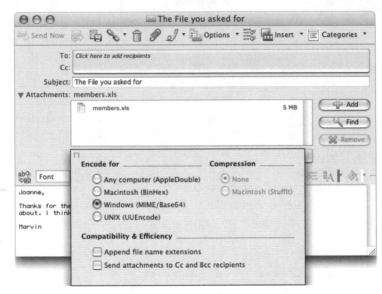

Figure 21.3

In Microsoft Entourage, you can easily set the attachment encoding for a file you're sending to a Windows user.

If the filename doesn't have a filename extension, you can check "Append file name extensions." However, the file shown in Figure 21.3 already has the .xls filename extension, so we can leave this box unchecked.

If you've already attached a file and closed the message window and now want to change the encoding, just go back and open the message window.

You may wonder why we set compression to None in step 4. That's because Mac email software, including Entourage, defaults to compressing files using StuffIt (with the filename extension .sit), a format most PC software doesn't recognize. The free versions of StuffIt for Windows and Linux (www.aladdinsystems.com) can decompress StuffIt files, but you can't count on PC users' having a copy. These days, file compression isn't as important as it was when everyone's Internet connection was through 28.8K modems.

If the file you are sending is large and you think it should be compressed, then compress it first in Zip format using a separate compression utility. (Email attachments are always compressed first and then encoded as your email software sends them). You can compress in Zip format with Tom Brown's **ZipIt** utility ($20; www.maczipit.com), as well as with StuffIt Deluxe. Just make sure that MacBinary is turned off in the ZipIt Preferences settings (**Figure 21.4**). If you can't Zip it, then turn compression off in your email software.

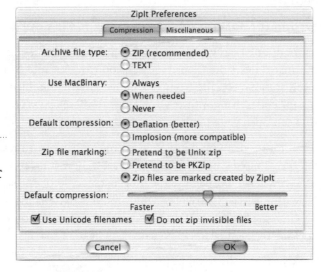

Figure 21.4

ZipIt lets you compress files before sending them to PC users. Just make sure to turn off MacBinary in the ZipIt Preferences settings before compressing.

Using Files from Windows

One of the most annoying things about living in a PC world is not being able to open a file that a PC user sent you. As we saw in the previous sections, the process of sending a file via email can mess up a file going from PC to Mac. However, you can also have problems not related to email, even with files you receive from a local network or a CD-ROM. There isn't a single cause of this problem, but there are some likely suspects.

This section describes problems with PC files coming to your Mac. We'll talk about sending Mac files to PC users in the next section, "How to Create Files for a PC."

File corruption

Occasionally, a file can be damaged during the process of moving it between a Mac and a PC. There were well-known file-corruption problems with certain versions of Mac OS X 10.2 when files were placed on a Windows server using the Mac's SMB/CIFS file-sharing feature (described in Chapter 20). In this case, operating-system updates from Apple eventually fixed the problem. *Repeatability* was the key to determining that it was a bug that caused the problem—that is, the problem occurred on multiple Macs with different types and sizes of files.

File corruption also occurs in files transmitted across the Internet, but this is rare, and it's usually caused by some fluke, not a bug. If you ask a Windows user to resend the file and the same problem occurs, the repeatability indicates some other cause, such as encoding, described earlier, or one of the problems described next.

The wrong (or no) app opens when the file is double-clicked

As was mentioned earlier, Windows doesn't use type and creator codes with files but instead uses the filename extension (for example, .doc for Word files). However, sometimes a file from a Windows user has garbled, nonsense type and creator codes that confuse Mac OS X. In these cases, you have an application that can open your file, but your Mac doesn't know it.

One symptom is that you double-click a file and an error message tells you that the file cannot be opened. In other cases, the wrong application may launch and will fail to open the file. For instance, someone sends you a file created with FileMaker Pro 5 for Windows, but Excel launches when you double-click the file. Or you might see a Classic application even though you have a perfectly good Mac OS X–native application that can open the file.

You can usually fix this kind of problem by specifying the application that you want to use to open the file in the file's Get Info window:

1. Click once to select a file you're having problems with.

2. Press ⌘I (or select Get Info from the File menu).

3. Click the triangle next to "Open with" to expand the dialog (**Figure 21.5**).

4. Click the pop-up menu under "Open with." **Figure 21.6** shows some Mac OS X and Classic applications listed in the menu. If you have another drive or partition with an older version of Mac OS X on it, applications on that partition may also appear here.

5. If you don't see the correct application in the list, select Other at the bottom of the pop-up menu.

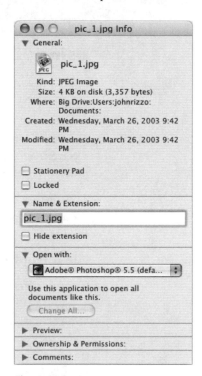

Figure 21.5

Expand the "Open with" area of the Get Info window to specify the application that will open a particular file.

6. Select your application.

   If you want all applications of this file type to open with the application you just selected, click the Change All button. Otherwise, just close the window.

Now, when you double-click this file, it will open with the application you specified.

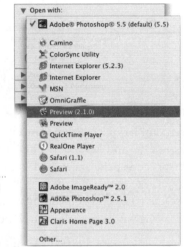

Figure 21.6

The "Open with" pop-up menu in the file's Get Info window gives you a selection of Mac OS X and Classic applications that might open your file. If you don't see the right application listed here, select Other.

Applications can't open the file

If you get a file and none of your applications can open that type of file, you may have to convert the file into a format that your applications *can* read. This kind of problem isn't really related to differences between the Mac and Windows. If someone sends you a Word file and you don't have Word, it doesn't much matter whether it was created on a PC or on a Mac—the result is the same. You can't open it.

You might also run into the same type of problem if you have an older version of an application. For instance, if you have AppleWorks 5 and someone gives you a file created with AppleWorks 6, you won't be able to open it.

The tool you need in these cases is a file translator—software that reads the file you can't open and creates a new file in a format your computer can read. Some file translators are separate utilities. Others are files that work with applications such as AppleWorks.

IcWord , icExcel. icWord and **icExcel** ($19.95 each, $29.95 for both; www.panergy-software.com) are great tools for people who don't have Microsoft Office. Both utilities let you view and convert Office files to AppleWorks, RTF (rich text format), and text formats. icWord can also read PowerPoint presentations.

To convert a file, you first open it in icWord or icExcel by dragging and dropping the file on the utility's icon. Use the Save As command in the file menu, and a dialog appears, giving you a list of file formats to convert to (**Figure 21.7**).

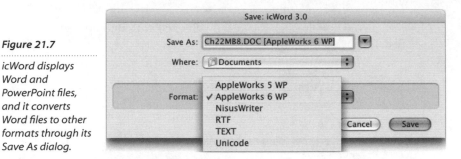

Figure 21.7

icWord displays Word and PowerPoint files, and it converts Word files to other formats through its Save As dialog.

MacLinkPlus Deluxe. DataViz's **MacLinkPlus Deluxe** ($79.95; www.dataviz.com) has been around since the 1980s and can translate the widest variety of PC and Mac files. This includes files created with old or new word processors and spreadsheets and some database formats. MacLinkPlus Deluxe can translate between various versions of AppleWorks and Microsoft Office. It also translates between common graphics formats, including GIF, JPEG, TIFF, BMP, WMF, and Mac and Windows EPS.

MacLinkPlus Deluxe translates PC files into Mac formats and Mac files into PC formats. It translates file details such as text formatting, footnotes, page numbering, tables, hyperlinks, margins, columns, and embedded graphics. Its translation ability is limited by the features your application supports. For instance, since AppleWorks spreadsheets don't support pivot tables, MacLinkPlus Deluxe translates Excel pivot tables into ordinary tables.

MacLinkPlus Deluxe can also decode email attachments and decompress compressed archives from PC users. (For more about email attachments, see "Sending and Receiving Email Attachments," earlier in this chapter.) You can use MacLinkPlus Deluxe in several ways to translate a file. The fastest way is to [Control]-click a file from within the Finder to bring up the contextual menu. From the contextual menu, you select MacLinkPlus, choose Translate to > Mac Format, and select the Mac file format you want the new file to use.

For the full range of options, use the MacLinkPlus Deluxe application as opposed to just using the contextual menu. By keeping MacLinkPlus Deluxe in the Dock (or as an alias on your Desktop in Mac OS 9 or earlier), you can drag any file—or a folder full of files—onto the icon to launch MacLinkPlus Deluxe. The utility will try to identify the file and let you peek inside.

To look at the contents of the file without translating it, select the file in the MacLinkPlus Deluxe window and click View. A new window opens, displaying the unformatted text (or graphic) inside the file. (This doesn't work too well with spreadsheets, however, as all the cells and formulas get jumbled together.)

If you decide to translate the file or folder full of files, click Translate. In the window that appears, select the file format for the new file from one of the pop-up menus. Type a name for the new file, and click Translate.

AppleWorks. If you have AppleWorks 6.1 or later for Mac OS 8, Mac OS 9, or Mac OS X, you have translators for Word and Excel files. (Some earlier versions of AppleWorks and ClarisWorks included file translators, but version 6.0 does not.) In fact, these AppleWorks translators are MacLinkPlus translators. You don't get *all* of the MacLinkPlus translators or the MacLinkPlus Deluxe application, but you do get the ability to open and save in Word for Macintosh 6 and Word for Macintosh 98; Word for Windows 6/95 and Word for Windows 97/2000; Excel for Macintosh 5 and Excel for Macintosh 98; and Excel for Windows 5 and Excel for Windows 97/2000. The translators also let you save AppleWorks files in HTML and RTF.

AppleWorks enables you to use the MacLinkPlus translators directly from its Open and Save dialogs. Here's how to open a Word or Excel file in AppleWorks 6.1 or later:

1. Choose Open from the File menu.

2. Choose "Word processor" or "Spreadsheet" from the Document Type pop-up menu.

3. Click the File Format pop-up menu, and select the application (**Figure 21.8**).

4. Select the PC file you want to translate.

5. Click Open.

The translator creates a new AppleWorks version of the PC file, keeping the original intact.

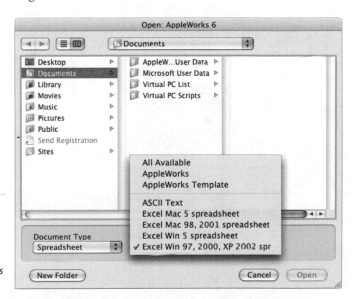

Figure 21.8

The AppleWorks 6 Open dialog lets you open files generated on both PCs and Macs; here Excel for Windows is selected.

To save an AppleWorks document as a Word or Excel file, choose Save As from the File menu. In the Save As dialog, click the File Format pop-up menu and select the desired format. Click Save, and a new file is created.

QuickTime multimedia translators. Mac OS 8, Mac OS 9, and Mac OS X come with a set of QuickTime file translators that can translate a variety of PC and Mac graphics and sound formats. There isn't a translation utility, but you can access the translators from several locations, such as QuickTime Player.

The QuickTime translators also show up in the AppleWorks 6 Open and Save dialogs. In the AppleWorks Open dialog, when you choose Painting or Drawing from the Document Type pop-up menu, the File Format pop-up menu lists dozens of multimedia file formats followed by "[QT]" to indicate that QuickTime translators will convert the file (**Figure 21.9**).

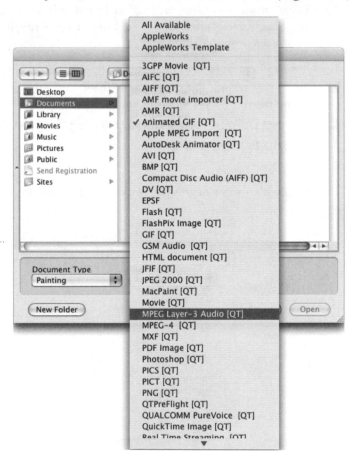

Figure 21.9

You can access QuickTime's graphics and sound file translators from within AppleWorks' Open dialog.

You can also use QuickTime Player to access these QuickTime translators, but only if you've upgraded to QuickTime Pro ($29.99; www.quicktime.com). With QuickTime Pro, the Edit menu of QuickTime Player gains Import and Export commands. You can use the Export command to save a file in a number of Mac and PC formats (**Figure 21.10**). The translators are always there—QuickTime Pro "unlocks" them in QuickTime Player.

Figure 21.10

When you upgrade to QuickTime Pro, QuickTime Player can import and export in a number of Mac and PC file formats.

GraphicConverter. An inexpensive shareware file-translation utility from Lemke Software, **GraphicConverter** ($30; www.lemkesoft.de) picks up with graphics formats where MacLinkPlus Deluxe leaves off. It can translate dozens of PC, Mac, and Unix graphics formats.

GraphicConverter also adds some graphics-editing tools—features that MacLinkPlus Deluxe and QuickTime don't have. Editing tools are often needed for translating graphics files, which don't always translate exactly. GraphicConverter is not a Photoshop replacement, but it has some handy selection and draw and paint tools, as well as effects such as dithering, gamma correction, and other color manipulations.

To convert a file, open it from the GraphicConverter dialog or drag the file onto the GraphicConverter icon in the Finder. Choose Save As from the File menu, and in the Save dialog select the type of file from the Format pop-up menu. GraphicConverter creates a new file in the specified file format.

Fonts and translation

File translators don't translate fonts that are specified in a document you are converting. Instead, they try to match fonts, specifying a font similar to the original. The results can vary. If you want to see the same fonts on both a Mac and a PC, make sure that both machines have Mac and Windows versions of the same font. For instance, if both PC and Mac users are working with Microsoft Office, ensure that the PC document is specifying the fonts that come with Office. Another way to ensure that documents look exactly the same on both platforms is to purchase font families that come in both Macintosh and Windows versions, and install those fonts on all of your machines.

Ordinarily, fonts themselves are not cross-platform—you need Mac and Windows versions installed on each platform. However, Mac OS X has the ability to use certain Windows TrueType fonts, those ending in the .ttf filename extension, and font families ending in the .ttc filename extension. OpenType fonts are designed to be cross-platform and can run in both Mac OS X and Windows. PostScript Type 1 fonts are not at all cross-platform. (For more on these font formats, see Chapter 15.)

Some utilities can translate between Mac and Windows font families. These utilities translate the font files themselves, not the fonts specified within files. The idea is to translate a font and then install it on each computer. Then you can pass around files that specify the fonts.

TransType, from FontLab ($97; www.fontlab.com/html/transtype.html), is a universal font-translation utility that converts between Mac and PC TrueType fonts or Mac and PC PostScript Type 1 fonts. TransType can even convert between TrueType and Type 1 fonts. You can convert one font at a time or do batch conversions of libraries of fonts.

Another font translator is the shareware utility **TTConverter** ($10). It converts between Mac and PC TrueType fonts. It doesn't handle Type 1 fonts. As of this writing, TTConverter didn't have its own Web site, but you can download it at ftp.visi.com/users/thornley/TTConverter1.5.sit.hqx. You can also find TTConverter by searching for it at www.versiontracker.com.

Moving software (applications) from PC to Mac

Here's another common problem: You have a PC at work with a fast Internet connection and a Mac at home with a slow modem Internet link. To take advantage of your office's fast link, you want to download Mac software on the PC and move it to your Mac on a Zip disk. But when you get the software to your Mac, the computer doesn't recognize it.

Notice that we are now talking about executable Mac software rather than data files. This cause of this problem goes back to the resource fork that Mac files have (see "File forks," earlier in this chapter). Windows will ignore the application file's resource fork—where the programming code is kept—and send only the data fork on to the Mac. Half an application just won't run on a Mac.

The solution is to *not* decode or decompress the application in Windows. Keep the file in its compressed archive, move it to the Mac, and then decode it or decompress it (or both) on the Mac. Disabling decoding and decompression may require you to muck about in the Properties dialogs of your Windows Web browser or email client.

 Windows software does not run on a Mac unless you are running Windows on your Mac with an emulator such as Microsoft's VIrtual PC. Filenames for Windows applications end in .exe.

How to Create Files for a PC

When sending a file to a PC user, you can use some of the same techniques described earlier for opening PC files, only in reverse. However, there is a difference: you are in control. You have to choose file formats and encoding and compression standards. You also have a new issue to deal with: naming your files so that PCs will be able to read them.

Translating Mac files to PC formats

The techniques for translating Mac files into PC formats are the same as for translating PC files into Mac formats. (Refer to "Using Files from Windows," earlier in the chapter, on using file-translation tools, such as those that come with AppleWorks, MacLinkPlus Deluxe, and icWord and icExcel.) If you are using Microsoft Office, PC users will be able to read and edit the files you create.

You do have an alternative to translating a file into a specific PC-application file format: turn it into a PDF file. Just about everyone has the free Adobe Reader, which reads PDF files. This is one of the best ways to send a file to Windows users or to a group of mixed Mac and Windows users—as long as the file doesn't need to be editable. The file will look just the way you want it to when opened on the PC, including any fancy layouts or embedded graphics.

In Mac OS X, you can save any file as a PDF file using the Print dialog (**Figure 21.11**):

1. With the document open, choose Print from the File menu (or press ⌘P).

2. Click the Save As PDF button.

    The Save to File dialog appears, asking you to name the file.

3. Name the file, making sure to include the .pdf extension on it, and click Save.

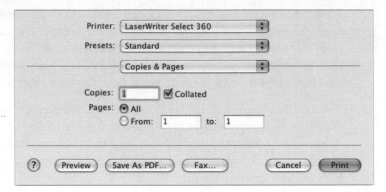

Figure 21.11

In Mac OS X, you can save any file as a PDF document using the Print dialog.

Another cross-platform format you can use is RTF. The benefit is that an RTF document is editable; the drawback is that the format supports only basic formatting and is for text-based files. AppleWorks and Word can save files as RTF files, and both Mac and PC versions of these programs can read RTF.

PC filenames

When naming files that will run on a PC, you need to observe certain rules. Otherwise, the file may not open on the PC. In some cases, if you incorrectly name a file, it can disappear from the view of PC users when posted to a local file server.

Here are the rules:

Don't use "illegal" characters. These include slashes (/ and \); most punctuation, including the question mark (?), colon (:), semicolon (;), quotation marks (" and "), and comma (,); square brackets ([and]) and angle brackets (< and >); and plus and equals signs (+ and =). Underscores and hyphens are OK to use.

Don't use more than one period (dot) in a filename. Use a dot only before a filename extension.

Don't use spaces in names. Filenames that begin or end with a space are particularly problematic.

Always end a filename with the appropriate extension. Some examples are .doc, .txt, and .jpg. These are always three characters long in Windows.

You can make this last item easier by having Mac OS X always display the filename extension. If you have the filename's extension hidden, you might forget that it's there and add a second extension, as in myfile.doc.doc, which will confuse Windows.

To set Mac OS X to always display the filename extensions, go to the Finder, click the Finder menu, and select Preferences. In Mac OS X 10.3, click the Advanced button and click the "Show all file extensions" check box (**Figure 21.12**). In Mac OS X 10.2 and earlier, click the "Always show file extensions" check box.

Figure 21.12

Setting Finder Preferences to always display file-name extensions can prevent problems with naming files for PC users.

Sharing Disks

With the rise of the Internet, email, and cross-platform local networks, sharing disks with PC users just isn't as important as when the floppy disk was the main method of moving files. But it is still handy to move CDs, Zip cartridges, and other media between Macs and PCs. You can even move hard drives between the two platforms.

Disk Formats

The main issue with sharing disks between Macs and PCs is that of *disk format,* the method used to lay down information on disk storage devices. It shouldn't come as a surprise that Macs and PCs use different disk formats for many storage types.

The standard disk format used in Mac hard drives is *Mac OS Extended,* also known as *HFS+ (Hierarchical File System Plus).* Mac OS X also supports hard disks formatted in *UFS (Unix File System).* You can create a Mac OS X startup disk formatted with either HFS+ or UFS. You would use UFS if you wanted to use the Mac for Unix-type tasks, such as running a Web server or developing Unix software.

 You will often see the Unix file format UFS confused with UDF (Universal Disc Format), the format used for DVDs. These are not the same format. Unfortunately, the confusion is common, even on reputable computer Web sites and in print.

PC hard disks running Windows 95, 98, or Me or Linux use the *FAT (File Allocation Table)* format. FAT has been around for a while and is available in several versions, such as FAT16 and FAT32. Linux running on Intel-based hardware also uses FAT-formatted hard drives.

Windows NT, 2000, and XP can also use a newer disk format known as *NTFS (NT File System)*. NTFS is mostly used for hard drives. If you have a Zip disk or other removable media from a PC, it is probably formatted as a FAT volume.

 If you see references to "DOS-formatted" disks in the Mac help system and elsewhere, be aware that this is Apple's term for FAT. Yes, this is confusing, since most PCs run Windows, not DOS, which is why I stick to the standard use of FAT.

Optical media can be formatted with HFS+ or FAT, but they are more likely to be formatted with optical standards—ISO 9660 for CDs and UDF for DVDs. Mac OS X supports these optical-disc formats.

Now that you know what the various formats are, here's what you need to know about getting them to work with your Mac.

Reading PC Magnetic Disks

The Mac OS has had the ability to read FAT-formatted magnetic disks for many years. The disk can be a FireWire drive, a USB drive, an internal ATA drive, or an internal or external SCSI drive (on a Power Mac equipped with a SCSI card). To use a FAT-formatted hard drive, just plug it in and it mounts on the Desktop. For removable storage such as a Zip or Jaz cartridge, insert the FAT-formatted media and it also mounts on the Desktop.

If the disk isn't mounting, you can use System Profiler (in the /Applications/ Utilities folder) to force the Mac to look for the drive. System Profiler's user interface changed drastically in Mac OS X 10.3 (**Figure 21.13**). In the Contents pane on the left, you can now select the driver interface (FireWire, ATA, and so forth) under Hardware. The right pane displays the devices connected to that interface. If you don't see your driver, choose Refresh from the View menu. (You may need to do this two or three times.) This should force your PC drive to show up.

Mac OS X cannot read NTFS-formatted drives. However, there is a free utility called *NT Filesystem for Mac OS X* (https://sourceforge.net/projects/ntfsosx), created by Brian Bergstrand. At publishing time, this utility was read-only— that is, you could copy files from an NTFS drive connected to your Mac, but you could not copy files to the NTFS drive. Before NT Filesystem for Mac OS X was developed, there was no support for NTFS on the Mac.

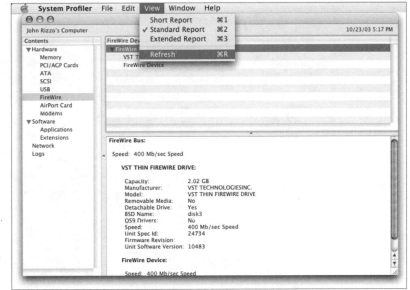

Figure 21.13

System Profiler's Refresh command can help you mount a FAT-formatted drive.

Preparing a Magnetic Disk for Use on a PC

If you want to create a disk that someone with a PC will be able to use, you should format it as a FAT disk. You can do this with Mac OS X's Disk Utility, located in the /Applications/Utilities folder. Apple doesn't use the term *FAT*, however. It refers to the format as MS-DOS (or sometimes MS-DOS File System).

Formatting erases a disk, so be sure you've copied everything you need from the disk before you start. After you connect the drive to your Mac, do the following:

1. Open Disk Utility and click the disk you want to format (**Figure 21.14**).

2. Click the Erase button near the top of the window.

3. Go to the Volume Format Pop-up menu and select MS-DOS File System.

4. Name the disk.

5. Click the Erase button at the bottom-right of the window.

 An alternative to giving FAT disks to PC users is to enable Windows to read and format Mac disks by adding HFS+ support to the PC. You can do this with several products, including MediaFour's **MacDrive** ($49.95; www.mediafour.com) and DataViz's **MacOpener** ($49.95; www.dataviz.com). Both support a wide range of disk types and integrate with the Windows interface.

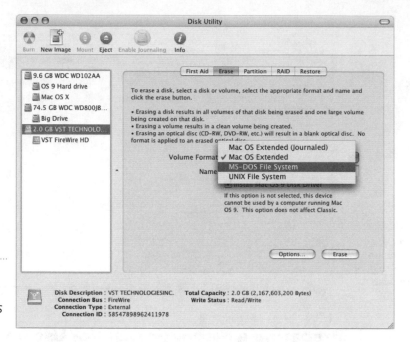

Figure 21.14

You can use Disk Utility to format disks as FAT, which Apple calls MS-DOS File System.

In Mac OS 9 and earlier, you can format a disk as FAT from the Finder. (This can be a floppy disk or a hard disk.) Select the disk in the Finder and choose Erase Disk from the Special menu. In the Format pop-up menu, select DOS. Give the drive a name that is 11 characters or less. Click Erase, and you now have a FAT-formatted drive.

Blank Zip cartridges usually come formatted as FAT disks. If you do need to format a Zip or Jaz cartridge, use the Iomega Tools utility located in the Iomega folder you may have installed with your drive.

Reading Optical Media: CDs and DVDs

Mac OS X can read CDs formatted as FAT or as ISO 9660, and DVDs formatted as UDF. (Optical discs can also be formatted in Mac-only HFS+.)

However, CDs from some Windows users can be problematic. You should be able to use the CDs, but the filenames may be truncated if the discs are formatted using Joliet. Joliet is a Microsoft expansion of the ISO 9660 standard that supports filenames longer than 8.3 (eight characters plus the three-character extension). Joliet supports filenames up to 64 characters long and allows spaces in them. The Mac OS doesn't support all versions of Joliet and displays filenames on some Joliet discs in truncated 8.3 without spaces. You might also have trouble accessing files on Joliet CDs.

You many have similar problems with CDs formatted using the Rockridge standard. The Rockridge standard takes the ISO standard and expands the maximum length of filenames to 128 characters.

 If you have an older Mac running Mac OS 9 and earlier, you can make it Joliet-aware and Rockridge-aware by using Joliet Volume Access, by Thomas Tempelmann ($15; www.tempel.org/joliet). With this shareware extension file installed, the Finder will display filenames up to 31 characters. For file-names longer than 31 characters, the full name is viewable in the file's Get Info window.

Writing Optical Media for PC Users

You can use third-party tools, such as Roxio's **Toast** ($100; www.roxio.com), to create CDs and DVDs in different PC file formats, including Joliet. A lower-priced tool useful for burning PC discs is **DiscBlaze,** from RadicalBreeze ($19; www.radicalbreeze.com). If you are sending optical discs to PC users on a regular basis, you should have a utility such as Toast or DiscBlaze.

You can also burn an optical disc in the Finder. Mac OS X doesn't give you a choice of formats but instead burns a disc as a hybrid, in multiple formats that Windows PCs can read. This includes HFS+ (which Windows can't normally read), ISO 9660 with Rockridge, and Joliet with Rockridge.

Networking Macs and PCs

You can do quite a lot with Macs and PCs on the same network. Sometimes you need to add some software to accomplish your goals; other times you can use features built into your computers.

When creating a cross-platform network, you should start by asking yourself what it is you want to do. The reply "Connect my Mac and PC" won't help you find the right answer—it's too vague and has no real meaning. You need to get specific as to what you want to accomplish—access a virtual private net-work, share files, or go wireless, for instance. Each is a different problem with a different solution. Sometimes the fix is in hardware; sometimes it's in software.

These days, the network hardware is the easy part. It's mostly cross-platform—or rather, platform independent. Often, software will solve your Mac-PC networking problem. This section begins with hardware issues and then moves on to software solutions.

Cross-platform networking is a large subject area, worthy of a book the size of the one you are reading. In this section I cover the basics and point you in the right direction for locating answers to cross-platform networking problems. First you might want to review Chapter 20 to see how Mac networking works. You can find more help on cross-platform networking at my Web site, MacWindows (www.macwindows.com). Finally, this chapter assumes that you know how to set up your PC for networking. After all, this is *The Macintosh Bible*—we don't do Windows.

Connecting Network Hardware

The hardware that moves the bits along the cables or through the air is inherently cross-platform. There's no such thing as "Mac-compatible Ethernet" or a "PC-compatible hub." As with peripherals such as printers, both Macs and PCs use the same hardware—it's the software driver that's different. If a driver is required, it has to be specific to the operating system.

Remember, connecting the hardware is just the first step. After this, you'll have to consider the software you need to use.

Ethernet

Ethernet is the main means of connecting Macs and PCs. The same rules described in Chapter 20 apply to cross-platform networks. Most PC makers don't build Ethernet into their machines as Apple does with Macs, but you can get an Ethernet card for the price of inexpensive shareware.

You connect Macs and PCs to the same Ethernet hub, or you can directly connect one Mac to one PC. When you do, take care to use the right cable. There are two types:

Patch cable. This is the cable to use if you have an Ethernet hub. If you have a Mac made in the past few years, you can use a standard patch cable to directly connect the Mac to the PC.

Crossover cable. Use this type if you are directly connecting an older Mac to one PC. To see which models require a crossover cable, see this page on the Apple Web site: http://docs.info.apple.com/article.html?artnum=42717.

The only difference between the patch and crossover cables is that the wires are reversed in the crossover cable. Most cables you see in stores are patch cables. If you want a crossover cable, you may have to ask for it.

Wireless networks

AirPort is Apple's implementation of the IEEE 802.11b Direct Sequence Spread Spectrum (DSSS) wireless networking standard. The newer AirPort Extreme is Apple's implementation of the faster IEEE 802.11g standard. Both are cross-platform by nature, like Ethernet. PCs can be on the same wireless network using 802.11 cards from Lucent, 3Com, Dell, and other companies.

PCs can connect to your AirPort Base Station to connect to the Internet or to Macs using AirPort. Some people also use the AirPort Base Station to connect a wireless Mac network with PCs on an Ethernet network.

The AirPort Base Station is not the only 802.11 wireless access point. You can use others, such as those from Lucent and NetGear. Some of these products provide a larger wireless range and better performance than the AirPort Base Station. But many of them lack AirPort's bridging function, which is the ability to connect multiple base stations wirelessly to extend the network. And not all of them include Internet connectivity. Apple's entry level Base Station is still one of the least expensive (and easiest to use) wireless access points. It's for these reasons that I recommend it highly.

The best way to proceed is to get your AirPort Base Station set up and running from a Mac using Apple's AirPort Admin Utility. When configuring the wireless settings on the PC, you may need the name of the network that you've given for the AirPort Base Station.

 Apple doesn't ship PC configuration software with the AirPort Base Station, but you can find programs that work from a PC. One program, FreeBase (http://freebase.sourceforge.net), written by Rop Gonggrijp, is a free Windows utility that can do the job. Another is Jonathan Sevy's free AirPort Base Station Configurator, written in Java (http://edge.mcs.drexel.edu/GICL/ people/sevy/airport).

Once the Macs and PCs are connected to the wireless network, any cross-platform network software that runs on Ethernet will run on the wireless network.

If your PC isn't communicating wirelessly, it could be having trouble with WEP (Wireless Encryption Protocol). To see if this is the case, turn WEP off on the Mac and the AirPort Base Station. If WEP is not the problem, you don't have to leave it turned off in order for the PCs to be part of the wireless network. Check the PC's authentication method in Windows—it should be set to Shared, not Open.

Network Protocols

Protocols are where you start getting into the acronym soup of networking: TCP/IP, AFP, SMB, and so forth. You can think of network protocols as working in layers. At the bottom are basic transport protocols, such as TCP/IP and AppleTalk. On top of these are protocols that perform certain functions, such as file sharing, browsing, or connecting to various types of servers. We won't get too deep here, but it is important to know a little about protocols when trying to understand how Macs and PCs can communicate.

Transport protocols

TCP/IP is the main transport protocol for connecting Macs with PCs. The Mac OS, Windows, and Linux all come with TCP/IP. Mac OS 9 and Mac OS X also come with AppleTalk, which is an alternative. Although Windows and Linux don't come with AppleTalk support, you can get software that helps Windows communicate via AppleTalk—most notably Miramar Systems' **PC MacLAN** ($189; www.miramar.com). However, with Apple moving away from AppleTalk, the software vendors, including Miramar, have added TCP/IP support.

Another transport protocol is IPX, which at one time was the basis of older Novell NetWare networks. It supported Macs with software called MacIPX. Novell has since moved on to TCP/IP. However, you still occasionally run into IPX on multiplayer network games, which will provide a copy of MacIPX. This is rarer with each passing year.

Using TCP/IP in cross-platform networks

The biggest drawback to TCP/IP is that each computer needs a unique IP address (see Chapter 20). Large networks usually have a DHCP server to assign IP addresses. Some Internet gateway hardware (devices that allow you to share an Internet connection with a network of computers) includes a DHCP server.

For a small network without any servers, you can set the Mac OS and Windows operating systems to get IP addresses using DHCP. When they don't find a server, the computers will give themselves IP addresses. I cover this procedure for the Mac in Chapter 20. In Windows this is done through the Network control panel.

File-sharing protocols

Apple and Microsoft developed two different file-sharing protocols. More-recent versions of Mac OS X support both. Macs have long used file sharing via the *Apple File Protocol (AFP);* Windows machines use the *Server Message Block/Common Internet File System (SMB/CIFS)*. AFP can run over a variety of transport protocols (such as TCP/IP, AppleTalk, and IPX), although TCP/IP is the most common. However, you need to be aware of both the transport protocol and the file-sharing protocol when doing cross-platform networking.

For instance, Windows NT Server can support Mac file sharing using AFP, but only over AppleTalk. Mac OS X before version 10.1 can connect to AFP file servers, but only over TCP/IP. Therefore, Mac OS X before version 10.1 cannot access files on Windows NT Servers. Today's servers, such as Windows 2000 Server and Windows Server 2003, support AFP over TCP/IP or AppleTalk.

We'll look at some of the solutions for cross-platform file sharing in the next section.

Cross-Platform Network File Sharing

File sharing with Windows PCs basically comes down to a choice of using Apple's file-sharing protocol, AFP, or Microsoft's protocol, SMB. Both can run on TCP/IP and AppleTalk, though TCP/IP is far more common today.

To access both types of servers in Mac OS X 10.3 and later, you use the Network icon, which is found in the sidebar of any Finder window (**Figure 21.15**). However, SMB has some limitations.

Figure 21.15

You can see file servers and client computers that use AFP and SMB by clicking the Network icon in Mac OS X 10.3 and later.

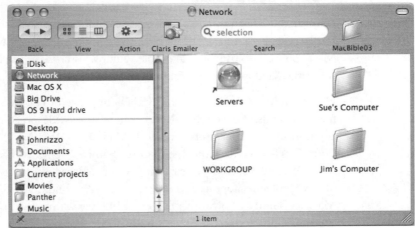

File sharing with AFP

The Apple File Protocol is what the Mac uses when you turn on Personal File Sharing in the Sharing pane of System Preferences. AppleShare-compatible servers also use it. Windows servers can become AppleShare-compatible with special software that provides the AFP service to Macs. Microsoft's Services for Macintosh is an AFP service that comes with every Windows server CD, although it isn't installed by default. Although Network administrators must choose to install it to support Macs, there are some advantages to AFP over SMB. For one, it tends to have fewer problems than SMB.

You can also replace Services for Macintosh with third-party TCP/IP-based AFP server software running on the Windows server. Group Logic's **ExtremeZ-IP** ($675; www.grouplogic.com) offers numerous improvements over Microsoft's AFP server, including better performance and two-way printer sharing (which allows Macs to use PC printers and vice versa). ExtremeZ-IP also runs on workstation versions of Windows—something that Services for Macintosh won't do.

If you have just a few PCs in your Mac environment and you don't want a server, you can use a product that installs AFP on Windows on a peer-to-peer basis, such as PC MacLAN. This enables the Windows PC to do file sharing with all the Macs, and lets all the Macs access the PC.

 Another free method of file sharing is to use the FTP server built into every copy of Mac OS X. PC users can download files from the Mac using a Web browser or FTP client software. See Chapter 20 for a description of how to enable the FTP file-sharing feature of Mac OS X.

File sharing with SMB

Administrators of Windows networks like you to use SMB to access Windows files servers because they don't have to do anything different to support your Mac. You can also use SMB to enable Windows users to access files on your Mac, selecting Windows File Sharing in the Sharing pane of System Preferences.

However, Mac OS X's built-in SMB client proved to be troublesome with many versions of Mac OS X 10.2.x. There were widespread reports of file corruption and other problems. With Mac OS X 10.3, Apple used a new version of its SMB client, the open-source Samba 3. Unfortunately, although Mac OS X 10.3 solved some of the SMB problems of earlier versions, a host of new problems appeared. If you want a really solid SMB client on your Mac, try Thursby Software's **DAVE** ($149; www.thursby.com). It's never had any of the problems that Apple's built-in SMB clients did.

As with AFP servers, SMB file servers should show up in the Network icon's window in Mac OS X 10.3 or later. Windows PCs with file sharing turned on should also appear there. However, there is one limitation: you'll be able to see only the SMB servers that are on the same local subnet, or network segment, as your Mac. On big networks there are ways to overcome this, using Microsoft's Active Directory server. The details go beyond the scope of this book, but we can say that Mac OS X 10.3 makes it even easier for network administrators to integrate Macs with Active Directory. However, the best tool for Active Directory integration is Thursby Software's **ADmitMac** ($149; www.thursby.com). It gives the Mac complete integration and installs entirely on the Mac—no changes are required for the Windows server.

Even if your Mac isn't integrated with Active Directory, however, there is still a way to access Windows SMB file servers that are not showing up in your Network icon's window. In the Finder select the Go menu and choose Connect to Server. A dialog appears (**Figure 21.16**). In the Server Address field you can type in a URL in this format: smb://*workgroup;ServerName/ShareName*.

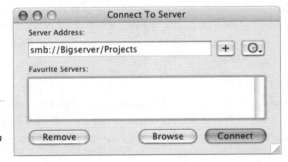

Figure 21.16

The Connect To Server dialog lets you access Windows servers that don't appear when you click the Network icon.

The workgroup name isn't always necessary, and you may not need it on a smaller network. The share name is the name of the shared folder you are trying to access. You can also add your user name to the URL: smb://*workgroup;UserName@ServerName/ShareName*.

This sometimes works when you're having trouble without it.

Running Windows on Your Mac

When all else fails, you can run Windows itself on your Mac—provided you install an *emulator*. A PC emulator is a complex application that tricks Windows or x86-based Linux into thinking it is running on a real PC. An emulator is not a replacement for a real PC running Windows—it's not as fast or as compatible—but it does give you access to Windows applications on your Mac. An emulator can run most business applications and various other types of Windows software but does not run games.

Today, there are only two PC emulators available for Macs. The main one is **Virtual PC for Mac** ($129 to $249, depending on the Windows operating system bundled; www.microsoft.com/mac), which Microsoft purchased from Connectix in 2003. The other is **Blue Label PowerEmulator,** from Lismore Systems ($35; www.lismoresystems.com). One of the reasons why Blue Label PowerEmulator costs so much less than Virtual PC is that is does not come with a preinstalled version of Windows. You'll have to supply and install your own copy. However, at publishing time, there was still no Mac OS X version of Blue Label PowerEmulator available, and version 1.8 does not run in the Classic environment. Therefore, we'll focus the rest of this section on Virtual PC.

Running Windows Apps without Emulation

Another way to run Windows applications on your Mac is with Microsoft's free **Remote Desktop Connection Client for Mac,** or RDC (www.microsoft.com/mac). RDC isn't an emulator, but rather it is a type of networking client that connects to Windows machines running Remote Desktop Services. This can be a user's Windows XP machine, or a Windows NT Terminal Server, Windows 2000 Server, or Windows Server 2003. The Windows application is actually running on the PC—the user interface for the program is sent to your Mac, where you can control it. RDC works well if you have a network environment and is a great solution if you don't want to pay money to put Windows directly on your Mac.

Other, similar solutions are available. Citrix Systems' Citrix MetaFrame Server is an application server that runs Windows software for users over a network. If your organization has a Citrix server, you can download a free **Citrix ICA Client for Mac OS X** (www.citrix.com; check the Downloads area).

Finally, if you have your own PC that isn't running Windows XP, and you like to control the applications from your Mac, check out **Timbuktu Pro,** from Netopia ($94.95 for single user download version; www.netopia.com). You install a copy on the PC and another on your Mac. Not only can you control the Windows applications from your Mac, but the PC user can also control your Mac applications, if you desire.

Virtual PC

You can buy Virtual PC with Windows 2000 or Windows XP preinstalled. If you have your own copy of Windows (including Windows 95, 98, or NT), you can buy Virtual PC with DOS and save a substantial sum on the purchase price. If you are using your own copy of Windows, be sure you launch Windows and install the Virtual PC Additions from Windows. (You'll find Virtual PC Additions on one of the CDs.)

 Virtual PC can run certain versions of Linux, but the Linux success rate varies with each version of Virtual PC and of Linux, so it's not an officially supported operating system for Virtual PC.

Virtual PC lets you have multiple versions of Windows operating systems installed—a very handy trick if you need to access different versions of Windows. You can even have multiple versions booted at the same time and switch between them using the Virtual PC List (**Figure 21.17**).

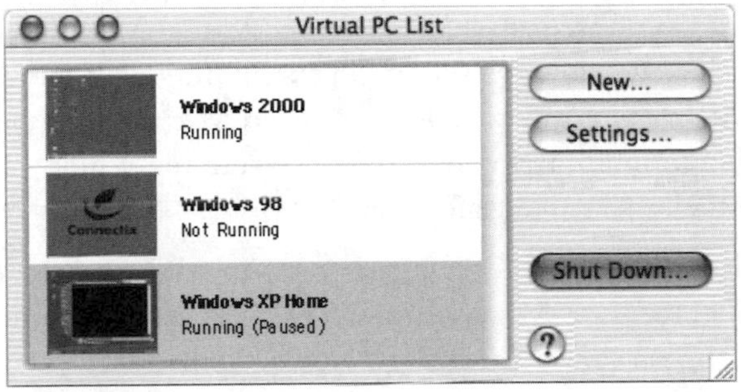

Figure 21.17

With Virtual PC, you can have multiple versions of Windows booted at once and switch between them.

Virtual PC is designed to run Windows business software, such as databases, communications, and office suites. It doesn't do well with games, which will run very slowly or poorly, or won't run at all. That's because business software tends to stick to Windows programming conventions. Software that bypasses Windows to make direct calls to hardware will be problematic or incompatible with emulators. Business software also doesn't make a lot of demands on hardware the way game software does. Virtual PC does not support hardware graphics acceleration, which most games depend on. If you want to run Windows games, a better choice is to buy the games when they are ported to the Mac. Or buy a PC or a dedicated gaming machine.

On the positive side, a Mac running Virtual PC can participate on Windows networks using a variety of Windows networking software. The other PCs and servers see a Mac that's running Virtual PC as just another PC. Because Virtual PC uses so much RAM and hard-disk space, it's best to seek a native Macintosh networking solution first. But if you can't find one, or if you need to run some specialized Windows software in conjunction with a network, Virtual PC will serve your needs.

Virtual PC supports some standard PC peripherals, such as printers, scanners, and storage devices. However, it can have problems recognizing more specialized USB devices. USB is not supported in Windows 95 or Windows NT.

Burning discs from Windows? Not on your Mac. Virtual PC does not support burning CD-Rs, CD-RWs, DVDs, or DVD-ROMs from Windows.

What You Need

Got RAM? You'll need lots of it to run an emulator. That's because you're running two operating systems at the same time, so you'll need enough memory for both. Just how much RAM depends on what versions of Windows and the Mac OS you are running. You'll need less RAM with older operating systems, such as Windows 95 and 98. The minimum with these operating systems is 128 MB. With Windows 2000 or XP and Mac OS X, consider 256 MB the absolute minimum. If you're going to be running Windows a lot, consider stuffing the Mac with a gigibyte of RAM.

You'll also need some processing power. Virtual PC needs at least a PowerPC G3 or G4 processor. Microsoft says 500 MHz is the minimum, but Virtual PC will run on slower processors. However, the faster your Mac, the faster that Windows will run. Best is 1 GHz and beyond.

At publishing time, Virtual PC 6.1 was not compatible with the PowerMac G5. It is likely that a later version of Virtual PC will be compatible.

You will also need enough free hard-disk space to support Windows and your Windows applications. With Windows 98, this is about a gigabyte. You'll need more for Windows Me, 2000, or XP.

Tips for Emulation

The main goal when running an emulator is to maximize performance. Here are some tips that can help you get the greatest possible speed out of your emulated PC.

Use Windows 2000. Windows 2000 is the fastest Windows operating system to run in Virtual PC. Windows 98 and Windows Me have some 16-bit code that slows down the emulator. Windows XP is loaded with graphics gizmos that use a lot of processing power. Windows 2000 strikes the optimum balance, as a 100 percent 32-bit operating system with lean graphics requirements.

Set CPU Usage to High. This is a Virtual PC setting that will use more of your Mac's processing power. In the Virtual PC menu, select Preferences. Now click the CPU Usage button in Virtual PC's Preferences window. You'll see two sliders. Move the slider labeled "CPU usage when Virtual PC is in the foreground" all the way to the right to the High setting. The other slider is labeled "CPU usage when Virtual PC is in background." If you want Windows to continue working at full strength while you check your email or use another Mac application, move this slider to the High setting as well.

Leave enough memory free for your emulator. If necessary, quit other applications before launching the emulator.

Allocate as much RAM as possible to Windows. This is another setting that is specific to each copy of Windows you have installed.

1. When you first start up Virtual PC, you'll see the Virtual PC List dialog. Select the Windows installation you want to configure.

2. Click the Settings button.

3. In the Settings dialog click PC Memory in the Current Settings menu (**Figure 21.18**).

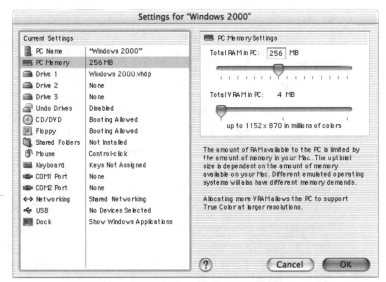

Figure 21.18

Boosting this PC Memory setting in Virtual PC can improve Windows' performance on your Mac.

4. Move the top slider to the right to allocate more RAM to Virtual PC. The Total RAM in PC field will tell you how much RAM you've allocated. Don't allocate more RAM than is physically available, however.

5. Click OK if Windows isn't running. If Windows is running, you'll see a Restart button, which you will click instead.

Defragment your Mac hard disk. Use a utility like Symantec's **Norton Utilities for Macintosh** ($99.95; www.Symantec.com). This is important. An emulator will install a large disk image of a PC boot drive. This file can be a gigabyte or more—a large file by any standard. If this file is fragmented, performance in your Windows or Linux environment will suffer.

Defragment your PC virtual C drive from within Windows. Use the Windows defragging tool. You can do this periodically to tune up performance.

Leave some free space in your PC C drive. Windows will slow down if the C drive is nearly full.

Set the processor to maximum in PowerBooks, iBooks, and Power Mac G5s. PowerBooks, iBooks, and Power Mac G5s have an energy-saving (or battery-conservation) method that can slow down the processor. Most applications aren't affected, but the performance of processor-intensive applications (such as audio and video editing apps and PC emulation) can suffer. You can change this setting to give you better Virtual PC performance using the Energy Saver preferences:

1. Open System Preferences and click the Energy Saver icon.
2. In the Energy Saver Preferences in Mac OS X 10.3, click the Options tab (if you don't see this tab, click Show Details).
3. Open the Processor Performance pop-up menu and choose Highest.

This setting will use more battery power in notebook Macs.

This is an issue only in PowerBooks, iBooks, and Power Mac G5s. With other Macs, you won't see the Processor Performance pop-up menu.

Try not to tax the "Pentium processor." Of course, there *is* no Pentium processor with an emulator, which is the point. Don't run multiple Windows tasks at the same time or use unnecessary multimedia settings. Taxing the PC "hardware" will slow performance much more than it would on a real PC.

Turn off Windows sound. Sound takes processing power, which you might rather have running your Windows applications instead of making beeps and blips. You can do this in Virtual PC's Preferences dialog. Click Sound and check the "Mute sound in background" check box.

Start up from Mac OS 9 in dual-boot Macs. Older Macs have the ability to start up from Mac OS 9 as well as from Mac OS X (from the Startup Disk pane in System Preferences). Virtual PC runs faster in Mac OS 9 than in Mac OS X.

Interview: Randy Wigginton

Hired at Apple at age 15 while still a student at Bellarmine High School in San Jose, California, Randy Wigginton was a key contributor to both the Apple II and the Macintosh. For Mac old-timers, he's best known as the author of MacWrite, the groundbreaking word processor that, along with MacPaint, set the original standard for graphical-interface applications. For the last several years Wigginton has been employed at eBay, where he's a member of what's called the SWAT team—a group whose role is to respond to urgent technical problems on the sprawling auction site. —Henry Norr

We thought we were so far ahead, no one else would be able to do what we had done.

> —*Randy Wigginton, on anticipating Microsoft's foray into graphical interfaces*

Where did you get the skills to get a job at Apple while still in high school?

I just picked it up all by myself. Computer technology seemed like the coolest thing around. Of course, in those days computers weren't all around, so we had to find a way to learn about them. I wanted to build my own, so I started to attend the Homebrew Computer Club [a group of early personal-computer enthusiasts who met at Stanford University in the mid-1970s]. But I wasn't old enough to drive, so I had to catch a ride. This really nice guy down the street volunteered. His name was Steve Wozniak.

How did you go from catching a ride with Woz to working at Apple?

When Apple started, it just seemed like the most natural thing in the world, because I loved working with him—he's a great guy.

What did you do at Apple?

I was mainly a software guy. I helped with the Apple I, then I did a lot of the original Apple II ROM, with Woz. Then I did AppleSoft [BASIC], taking Bill Gates' foundation and adding a lot of extensions to it. [Though Woz had written his own implementation of the BASIC language, Apple also licensed Microsoft's version, extended it, and, beginning with the Apple II+, included it with every machine under the name AppleSoft BASIC.]

When did you move on to the Mac?

When the group started—well, depending on how you define that—let's just say early on. I started off doing the file system in, like, 1981. Then we needed someone to do the word processor, so Steve [Jobs] chose me to write the word processor.

All by yourself?

Well, I hired a couple of friends to help me write it.

continues on next page

Was the idea from the beginning to bundle it with the machine?

Yeah. The idea Steve always had at the beginning was to make the Mac like an appliance—you just turn it on and start using it. Like your toaster—you never go out and get extra things for it. He wanted it to be useful right out of the box.

What about including a spreadsheet? Was that considered?

It was considered, but we just didn't have the ability to do it. We hired Microsoft to do Multiplan, and that was supposed to be ready right when the Mac launched, and it wasn't.

Apple paid money for that?

No, we didn't pay money for it, but we sure helped them a lot.

Did you think that the Mac was a historic breakthrough?

Yeah, Steve convinced all of us that it was. You know, we were changing the universe.

In what respect?

Around the ease of use. He was right. It was so hard to use an Apple II. There were people using it for all kinds of stuff, and we saw the way people would flounder around and not be able to use the Apple II for just doing things like writing a letter. So that was sort of why the idea of the Macintosh crystallized in Steve's mind. [We] wanted something that everyday people could use. And that wasn't horribly expensive, because at that time we were also selling the Lisa, and people were saying, "This is interesting, but boy, it's big; boy, it's slow; boy, it's expensive."

Did you anticipate that others would try to copy what you were doing?

We thought we were so far ahead, no one else would be able to do what we had done. We were more than a little bit arrogant. But we sort of expected that there would be copies.

Were you thinking of Microsoft as a possibility?

No [he laughs], we didn't. That was a big mistake. When IBM entered the market [with the launch of the IBM PC, running an operating system from Microsoft, in August 1981], we were actually up at Microsoft, trying to recruit them to write software for the Mac. And I remember Jobs getting the paper and showing us the big ad, you know, "Welcome, IBM—seriously." I mean, talk about irony!

How would you compare the actual impact the Mac has had with what you expected?

Speaking on a global level, I think it's had a larger impact, because it's influenced so many things and brought so much potential to the world. Looking at it from the Apple perspective, I think it has been far, far, far below our expectations.

Because you thought it would put the company on top of the world?

Yeah. We thought we were on the way to world domination. And, you know, it was a great idea, and I think it really did bring about a graphical user interface several years before it would have [emerged otherwise]. Who knows what we'd be working on now without it? So from that aspect, I'm extremely happy. From how much it helped Apple, ehh, it's pretty sad.

What computers do you use now?

I use a couple of Windows boxes, and I still use a Mac for a lot of my work. At home I just have a Power Mac, and here I use a PowerBook G4. My wife has an iMac and an iBook; my son, who's 14, has a Cube, and my daughter doesn't have one of her own yet—she's 7.

Are you using Mac OS X?

Oh yes. I love it. The classic Mac interface was much easier, but you couldn't do nearly the same amount.

If they put you in charge of Mac OS X, what would you do with it?

Wow. I just think Steve is doing an awesome job of running it right now. I think that orienting it towards online services, like the iTunes Store, is absolutely the way to go. The only thing I would do is probably make it so that it ran on top of Intel architecture, so that we could start selling it into the Windows world. I guess I still have this fantasy of the Mac taking over the world.

What do you use for a word processor now, and how would you compare it with MacWrite?

Uh, Word. It has so much crap in there that I can't figure out how to do basic stuff. It's so frustrating—they've just added features every single year, and they've never removed anything. It'll do anything you can possibly think of, but getting it to do it is really hard. They've really overcluttered it. It's like driving a car with the cockpit of a jet engine.

Any urge to go back to Apple?

Well, sometimes. I've talked to them a little bit, but I'm pretty happy at eBay. And, you know, things change. I'd rather remember the happy times. But I don't know—if Steve called me in and said he was going to try and change the world again, I'd probably join him.

Right now, eBay in its own way is kind of on top of the world.

Yeah, well, we'll see if we make the same mistakes—getting, you know, arrogant.

Appendix

Switching to the Mac from Windows

John Rizzo is the appendix editor and author.

If you've just bought your first Macintosh after years of being a Windows user, welcome. This appendix is for you.

After 1000 or so pages of detailed information about Macs, we're ending *The Macintosh Bible* by going back to basics, but from a different point of view. This chapter explains differences in Mac and Windows terminology and describes what you'll need to know to make your transition a smooth one. We even offer tips that will make the Mac a bit more familiar to a Windows user.

We start with Mac OS X's user interface, which represents the biggest change in your computing experience. You'll find some items that look familiar and others that don't, and you'll wonder where yet other items might be lurking. Don't worry—everything you need is there. The middle of the chapter is devoted to the Mac itself—the hardware and peripherals. Here is where we explain the differences between the Mac and PC keyboards and mice. We end with a section of tips on making the move itself—bringing over your files and other information from your old PC to your new Mac.

In This Appendix

Mac OS X for Windows Users

Mac OS X has some great features, many of which you may have been using in Windows. Trouble is, you don't know how to access those features on a Mac. This section gives you a tour through Mac OS X from a Windows user's point of view. Mainly, we'll point out the differences.

Lets start with some of the high-level differences that you'll probably notice right away.

No Start menu. There is no single equivalent of the Windows Start menu in Mac OS X. The items found in the Windows Start menu are spread around in different places in Mac OS X (see "Make the Dock act like the Windows Start button," later in this appendix).

Pervasive menu bar. In Mac OS X a menu bar is always present at the top of the screen; it never appears on Mac OS X windows. This changes the way you work when you have multiple windows open (see "The menu bar," later in this appendix).

No right mouse button. Don't panic. Mac OS X actually does support a two-button mouse. Apple doesn't think you need one, but you can plug a "normal" mouse into your Mac. (See "PC-style mice," later in this appendix.)

Terminology differences. Think about the New Yorker who is visiting London and follows a sign pointing to a "subway" but can't find any trains. That's because in London, a *subway* is a passageway under a roadway. A New Yorker's *subway* is a Londoner's *underground*.

If you want to fully comprehend the previous 1000 pages of this book as well as Mac OS X's Help system, you'll need to learn what I call "Mac-speak." Apple uses different terminology from Microsoft's. For instance, you will never hear the term *drop-down menu*. In Mac-speak, this type of menu is called a *pop-up menu* when it's in a dialog or window and a *pull-down menu* when it's in the menu bar at the top of the computer screen. (User-interface wonks will point out that the behaviors of drop-down and pop-up menus are different. To the average user, though, these differences are trivial.) Knowing Mac-speak is essential when searching for information on a feature in the Mac Help system.

Equivalents, or lack thereof. New converts to the Mac are always looking for equivalents. OK, they say, there's no Start button, but what is the closest thing? In this case, the answer is nothing, but some equivalents do exist. For instance, Alt is Control on the Mac, and the Recycling Bin is the Trash icon in the Dock. Other equivalents are not so clear-cut. The taskbar is *sort of* like the Dock. But the Dock also does things the taskbar doesn't, and vice versa.

OK, let's dive into the starting place for Mac OS X, the Finder.

The Finder vs. Windows Explorer

When you first boot up (or *start up,* in Mac-speak), the Finder appears. The Finder gives you the Desktop (the Mac's main working area) and the windows and menus that you use to access disks and files. The Finder has a Find command, as well as several other tricks up its sleeve.

Figure A.1

The Dock's Finder icon puts its best face forward.

The Finder performs the functions of Windows Explorer—you use it to browse through the hierarchical directory structure of folders and disks. If another application is in front and you need to get to the Finder, just click the Desktop or the Finder's smiley-face icon in the Dock (**Figure A.1**). The Finder and Trash icons are the only ones you can't remove from the Dock.

You can bring up a new Finder window by double-clicking a drive icon on the Desktop, pressing ⌘N, or choosing New Finder Window from the Finder's File menu. (For more on the Mac's command keys, see "The Mac Keyboard and Mouse," later in this appendix.) The left portion of a Finder window is called the *sidebar,* and it displays your drives and important folders. The sidebar is new with Mac OS X 10.3 (Panther). It doesn't have a hierarchical (multilevel) view as in Microsoft Windows Explorer. You can, however, get a hierarchical view on the right side of a Finder window: just go to the Finder's View menu and choose "as List" (**Figure A.2**). The Mac's *disclosure triangles* act like the + (plus) and – (minus) signs in Windows Explorer. A triangle pointing to the right means the folder is closed, indicated by the + in Windows Explorer. A down-pointing triangle means the folder is open, which the – indicates in Windows Explorer. As in Windows Explorer, when you drag files around, your pointer in the Finder has a plus sign when you are copying a file. If no plus sign is visible, you are moving the file.

Figure A.2

The windows of the Finder (left) and of Windows Explorer (right) have some things in common, including the ability to display folders in a hierarchical list view; however, the sidebar at the left of the Finder window is only found on the Mac.

Typing and viewing folder paths

Like Windows Explorer, the Finder lets you type in a pathname to go directly to a particular directory (which is called a *folder* in Mac lingo.) The Finder doesn't have the Address toolbar of Windows XP. Instead, you use the Go to Folder command in the Go menu (or press ⌘ Shift G) (**Figure A.3**). If you don't see a Go menu, click the Desktop or the Finder icon in the Dock to bring the Finder to the front.

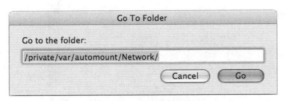

Figure A.3

The Go to Folder dialog lets you type a pathname to access a folder.

You have to type the pathname exactly right. Don't add an underscore or spaces if the folder name doesn't have one.

To separate folder names in Mac OS X pathnames, always use the forward slash (/), as in Web addresses—not back slashes (\), as in Windows. For example:

/Users/Jim/Library/Preferences/Microsoft/

Mac OS X uses Unix conventions for its pathnames. This means you always start a path with a slash (/), or, to signify the home folder, a tilde and a slash (~/). Starting with the tilde, the pathname we just mentioned would be shortened to:

~/Library/Preferences/Microsoft/

 Using the Go to Folder dialog enables the Finder to display folders that ordinarily don't appear in the Finder. These are the Unix directories of Mac OS X (which are all lowercase), including /bin, /etc, /usr, and /var. If you don't have a Unix background and don't know what these directories are, it's best to leave them alone.

In Windows, the Address toolbar provides a place to type a URL, and it also offers a handy way to see where you are in the directory structure. The Finder gives you a different way to see where you are in the directory structure. Simply press ⌘ while you click the name of the window. A pop-up menu shows you the path (**Figure A.4**).

Figure A.4

The Finder shows
you the path of any
folder if you ⌘-click
the window title.

Storage media in the Finder

The above discussion on pathnames hints that the Finder treats drives differently than does Windows. While Windows paths start with a hard-drive letter, such as C:\, pathnames in Mac OS X start with a slash (/), which is the top-level root directory, or your home directory (~/). In Mac OS X paths, no hard drive is specified when the directories are all on the boot drive (the drive that Mac OS X uses to start up.)

If you are typing the pathname of a folder that is on another hard drive, you can type its name as it appears on the Desktop. For instance:

/External FireWire HD/My Important Folder/

Although you may not need to type the name of a hard drive often, this does illustrate an important point: Mac drives don't have letters. There is no such thing as drive mapping in Mac OS X, so you'll never have to worry about it. The Finder identifies hard drives, CDs, and network drives with names.

Another significant difference from Windows is that removable-media drives (such as optical or Zip drives) don't appear in the Finder—only the *media* does. So if your CD/DVD drive doesn't have a disc in it, it won't appear in the Finder. When you eject a CD, its icon disappears from the Finder.

Minimizing, the Dock, and the Windows taskbar

There is a lot of information about the Dock in Chapter 1, but a comparison with the Windows taskbar can shed some light on how it works. The Dock is more than just a Mac version of the taskbar, but the two have in common the ability to act as the resting place for minimized windows, and as a place to switch between programs that are running.

The Windows taskbar differentiates between permanent items—the Quick Launch application icons you can add to the left side—and items that are open, which reside in rectangles in the taskbar. In contrast, the Dock gives everything an icon of the same size, whether it's running or not (**Figure A.5**). Adding your own "quick launch" applications to the Dock is easy—just drag an icon from the Applications folder to the Dock.

Figure A.5

The Mac OS X Dock (bottom) uses same-size icons to represent both open items and "quick launch" items. The Windows taskbar (top) separates out the Quick Launch items on the left.

Another difference between the Dock and the taskbar is the way they treat open folders: the Windows taskbar includes them, but the Dock does not display open folders unless they are minimized. You can, however, use the Dock to switch between open folders. Click the Finder icon and hold it for a few seconds. A menu listing all the open folders appears. Select one to bring it forward. (You can also select an open folder from the Finder's Window menu at the top of the screen.)

Although minimizing a window in Mac OS X is just a matter of clicking a button in the top corner of a window, PC users may find the method a bit disorienting. Here, it's helpful to think opposites. Mac OS X not only puts the close, minimize, and zoom (the Mac version of maximizing) buttons on the opposite side of the window (the left side), but it also changes the order of the three buttons (**Figure A.6**). Only the close button is colored the same—red—on both operating systems. From left to right:

- **Mac OS X:** Close (X, red), minimize (–, yellow), and zoom (+, green)
- **Windows XP:** Minimize (blue), maximize (blue), close (x, red)

On Mac OS X, the symbols (X for close, – for minimize, and + for zoom/maximize) appear only when you move the mouse near the buttons.

Figure A.6

The close, minimize, and zoom/maximize buttons on the Mac (left) and in Windows (right) are on opposite sides of the window and in a different order.

The zoom/maximize function works a bit differently in the two operating systems. In Mac OS X it doesn't make a window fill the screen the way it does in Windows, but merely *enlarges* a window. With some applications, the zoom button also does some other things. For instance, with iTunes, it shrinks the main iTunes window down to a dialog that displays the current song title and has play and volume-level controls.

Make the Dock act like the Windows Start button

I mentioned earlier that the functionality of the Windows Start button is spread out in Mac OS X: some functions are in the menu bar, some are in the sidebar of the Finder windows, and some are in the Dock. However, you can easily use a feature called *Dock menus* to give the Dock and all of its icons the functionality of a Start menu. Every Dock icon has a menu that you bring up by clicking the icon and holding it for a few seconds. The Dock menus of some applications let you perform functions without going to the program's window. For instance, you can control most of iTunes' music-playing abilities from its Dock menu. If you've placed a folder in the Dock, its Dock menu displays the contents of the folder.

So here's how you get Start-button functionality in the Dock. Drag your home folder and your Applications folder to the Dock, to the area next to the Trash. From the Dock menus of these two icons you'll be able to access just about anything you need without opening a window—as with the Windows Start button. The menus are hierarchical (**Figure A.7**), so you can dig into subfolders. (You can also drag a hard-drive icon to the Dock, but it unnecessarily adds levels of directories that you'll have to browse through.)

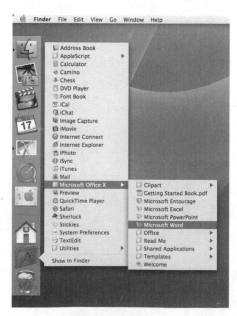

Figure A.7

Dragging your home folder and your Applications folder to the Dock gives you functionality similar to that of the Windows Start button.

The home and Applications icons will be on the right side of the Dock near the Trash. If you want to keep them in the more-familiar lower-left corner of the screen, move the Dock to the left side of the screen. (To do this, go to the Apple menu, choose Dock, and then choose Position on Left).

Aliases vs. shortcuts

Windows file shortcuts are handy for opening files from the Desktop, even when the files are nested deeply in many layers of folders. In Mac OS X, file shortcuts are called *aliases*. Double-click an alias, and it opens the original file, folder, or hard drive. You create an alias by selecting an icon in a Finder window and then choosing Make Alias from the File menu or pressing ⌘L.

Aliases have some advantages over Windows shortcuts. You can rename the alias to anything you like, and you can move it around to different folders. The alias still opens the original file when you double-click it. If you move the original file to a new location, Mac OS X 10.3 is usually smart enough to keep track of the move so that the alias will still work. Every once in a while, however, Mac OS X 10.3 gets confused (Mac OS X 10.2 and earlier did not keep the associations between an alias and the original file.) In that case, when you double-click the alias, a message pops up asking you where the original file is. Selecting the original file "fixes" the alias, so that it will work perfectly the next time you use it.

Running Software in Mac OS X

Once you are using a familiar program, such as Microsoft Word or Internet Explorer, or Adobe Photoshop, you generally won't find many major differences from using the same program in Windows. However, there are a few differences that an ex-Windows user may need to know about.

First, don't bother looking for a Run command in Mac OS X—it doesn't exist. To launch a program, double-click its icon or the icon of a file that belongs to it. This applies to running an application and to installing new software.

The next few sections cover some of the other differences. After that, we'll take a quick look at Microsoft's Virtual PC, which can help smooth your transition to the Mac.

The menu bar

Unlike Windows, Mac OS X always has a menu bar, and it stays at the top of the screen—menu bars are not attached to windows, as they are in Microsoft Windows. So how do you know which window the menu bar applies to if you have multiple files open simultaneously? Commands in the menu bar act only upon the window that is in front—the *active* window. The menu bar changes when you bring a new application to the front.

Generally, the menus in the menu bar are presented, from left to right, in order of increasing specificity. The far-left menu in the menu bar, the Apple menu, is always present. It provides commands for the entire Mac, such as Shut Down and Force Quit.

The next menu is generically referred to as the Application menu, and it always takes the name of the application (such as Safari, Excel, or iMovie). This menu has commands that apply only to this application and to all of the application's documents. Here you'll find the Preferences and Quit commands. The third menu from the left, File, contains commands that pertain to a single file, including Open and Save. The next two menus are often Edit and View, but these are not universal. Toward the right, there are usually Window and Help menus. On the far right are menus represented by icons instead of words. These are optional menus, such as Volume, AirPort, and Bluetooth, which are present no matter what application is running. You can choose to display these by selecting the appropriate options in corresponding areas within System Preferences.

Force Quit

Occasionally, you many need to force-quit an application that isn't responding. Mac OS X has an equivalent to the Windows force-quit command, Ctrl Alt Delete ; in Mac OS X it's ⌘ Option Esc . This brings up a dialog letting you choose an application to force-quit. (You can relaunch the Finder, but you can't quit it.)

Installing and removing software

In Mac OS X there are no setup.exe files for installing software (actually, no Mac file ends in .exe). Instead, installer programs are named Installer. Sometimes these programs launch automatically (like setup.exe in Windows). Other times, you have to double-click the installer icon to get started.

Some software, including Microsoft Office, has no installer program. You just drag a folder or file from the CD to your Applications folder. With software that you download, you often drag a folder from a *disk image*—a compressed file that acts like a hard drive. Double-click the disk image, and a fake hard drive appears on your Desktop. Double-click this to open it, and then drag the software inside to your Applications folder.

Application programs in Mac OS X are not as spread around as in Windows— that is, there aren't nearly as many files in different locations on the hard disk. Because removing software is not as complex as in Windows, Mac OS X does not have an equivalent of the Add or Remove Program item in the Windows Control Panel. With a lot of software, you can remove the application using the installer program you used to install it. If you use the installer program to remove an application, you would use an option called Uninstall, which is usually available in a pop-up menu (its location varies from application to application.) With other software, you can simply delete the file or folder from the Applications folder. Some software manufacturers provide a list of files to delete for complete removal of the application. Mac software does not often change lines of code in configuration files the way Windows software installations do, so you don't have to worry about opening up text files and deleting the right line of text.

Running Windows software with Virtual PC

The best software to run on a Mac is Mac software. Native Mac software runs the fastest, is the most stable, and has the best compatibility.

Still, there are occasions when a recent convert may need or want to run Windows software on a Mac. You can do this with Microsoft's **Virtual PC for Mac** ($129–$249, depending on which version of Windows you need; www.microsoft.com/mac), which actually runs Windows on your Mac. Virtual PC emulates PC hardware, tricking Windows and Windows software into thinking they are running on PC hardware.

 If you are planning to purchase a copy of Microsoft Office v. X for Mac anyway, the most economical way to buy Virtual PC is to purchase the Professional Edition of Office v. X for Mac ($499) because it includes Virtual PC for Mac.

For PC users switching to the Mac, Virtual PC can be a useful transition tool, particularly if you have a library of Windows software that would set you back a few thousand dollars to replace. Virtual PC is also useful if you can't find a Mac version of an application that you absolutely must use. Virtual PC runs most business software, and it can even run Windows networking software.

You should be aware, however, that Virtual PC is not a panacea. It has real drawbacks.

- First, because Virtual PC is an emulated environment (not a real PC), it will never be fast, and can be slow. In fact, it can be downright poky. The faster your Mac, the faster Virtual PC will run. But you can't expect it to have the power of actual PC hardware.

- Second, Virtual PC is not a solution for playing PC games. Many games will not run at all, and those that do run often run too slowly to be enjoyable. If you're a gamer, look for native Mac OS X games or for other gaming hardware.

- Third, although most business software does run just fine, there is the occasional Windows program that is incompatible. These are usually programs from smaller companies.

For more on Virtual PC, including tips on how to get it to run as fast as possible, see Chapter 21.

The Mac Command Line

Like Windows, Mac OS X has a command-line interface that power users can access. However, you won't be able to use your DOS expertise, since the Mac command line does not use DOS commands or syntax. That's because it is a Unix shell, which is very different from DOS. If you know your way around Linux or BSD, you'll be in good shape here.

To access the command line, go to the Applications folder, open the Utilities folder, and launch the Terminal utility. A window opens with the Unix prompt, awaiting your command.

For more information on Terminal, see Chapter 2. If you care to learn Unix, there are also plenty of good books available, including Matisse Enzer's *Unix for Mac OS X: Visual QuickPro Guide* (Peachpit Press, 2002).

Right-button menus

Although the standard Mac mouse doesn't have a right button, Mac OS X does have a right-button shortcut menu (**Figure A.8**). Apple calls it a *contextual menu*, and you bring it up by holding down (Control) while you click something. As in Windows, this works within applications and on the Desktop; the menu changes depending on what you're (Control)-clicking.

Figure A.8

A right-button menu on a Mac is called a contextual menu.

If right-clicking is just too much to give up, relax—you don't have to give it up. You can buy a two-button mouse from other vendors. The right button usually will act the same as a (Control)-click. Mice with scroll wheels are also common. For more on mice that work like your PC mouse, see "PC-style mice," later in this appendix.

Settings

Just about every Mac OS X application has a dialog called Preferences that lets you set choices for how the application works. You access the Preferences dialog from the Application menu (the menu that has the name of the application you are running).

Mac OS X has its own place for choosing systemwide settings, an application called System Preferences (**Figure A.9**). You access System Preferences from the Apple menu or the Dock. System Preferences is the Mac OS X equivalent of the Control Panel in Windows. Unlike Windows, Mac OS X doesn't make you restart the computer when you change system preferences. The changes take effect when you either click an Apply button or quit System Preferences.

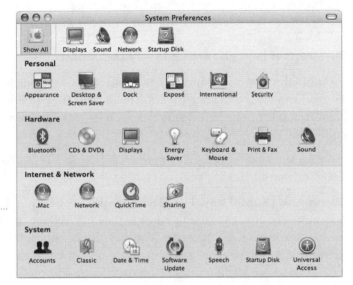

Figure A.9

System Preferences is the Mac OS X equivalent of the Control Panel in Windows.

System Preferences arranges items in categories. You can also choose items from the System Preferences View menu. However, you can change the look of System Preferences to make it more like the "Classic" view in the Windows XP Control Panel—a straight alphabetical arrangement of icons, without the categories. Just go to the View menu and select Organize Alphabetically.

Hardware Issues

Mac OS X doesn't have an equivalent to Windows' My Computer, so accessing and managing peripherals is different than on PCs. But this is just a superficial difference. Inside and out, Macs use a lot of the same hardware as PCs. In fact, Apple Macs and Dell PCs have more interchangeable parts than Fords and Chevys. This also means that you can bring over many of your PC peripherals and plug them into your Mac.

Lets start with the most frequently used peripherals—the keyboard and mouse.

The Mac Keyboard and Mouse

You won't have to learn a new way of typing when you move to a Mac keyboard, but you will need to become accustomed to the fact that certain keys behave differently. In fact, you'll see some new keys that aren't on your PC's keyboard, and you'll also notice that a few of the keys on your PC keyboard are missing from your Mac keyboard. Likewise, the standard-issue Apple mouse has only one button, although you can replace it with a multibutton mouse.

Differences in keyboards and key commands

Probably the most confusing keyboard difference is the one between the PC Ctrl key and the Mac Control key—these keys work differently on the two platforms. There's also no Windows key on the Mac keyboard, and no real equivalent, either.

Here are the Mac keys that either are not found on a PC keyboard or behave differently on a Mac.

Command (Apple) key. The ⌘ (Command) key has an Apple and a cloverleaf on it. The ⌘ key is the equivalent of the PC's Ctrl key. Some of the commands you would issue using the Windows Ctrl key under Windows are the same as those you issue on a Mac using the ⌘ key. For instance, Open, Save, and Undo are ⌘O, ⌘S, and ⌘Z on the Mac instead of Ctrl O, Ctrl S, and Ctrl Z on Windows.

However, if you plug a PC keyboard into your Mac's USB port (as described in "Using a PC keyboard on the Mac," below), the Windows key (not the Ctrl key) sometimes acts as the Mac ⌘ key.

Option key. The Option key on the Mac is the equivalent of the Alt key on Intel-based PCs. (In fact, many Mac keyboards also label Option with "alt" in smaller letters.) Some Alt key commands from Windows work on the Mac, but many don't. For instance, to exit an application in Windows you would issue the Alt F4 key command, but that won't work on the Mac. (⌘Q, however, always works to quit an application on the Mac.)

You also can't automatically use the Option key to navigate menus, as you can in Windows. To access menus from the keyboard, you'll have to go to the Keyboard & Mouse pane of System Preferences, click the Keyboard Shortcuts tab, and then click the check box next to "Turn on full keyboard access."

On the Mac, Option also produces special characters when you hold it down while typing any letter or number. To see what these special characters are without simply experimenting by pressing Option and a letter or number, you'll need to enable Keyboard Viewer in Mac OS X 10.3 (see Chapter 15) or use the Key Caps utility in the Applications > Utility folder in Mac OS X 10.2 and earlier.

Control key. This is not the equivalent of the PC Ctrl key. (That designation goes to the Mac's ⌘ key, described above.) The Control key is uniquely Mac, used mostly as the equivalent of the PC's right mouse button when held down while clicking. (That is, it brings up the shortcut, or contextual, menu.) It's also used for accessing menus with the keyboard when keyboard access is turned on.

Delete key. This is the Mac equivalent of the Backspace key on your PC keyboard.

Forward delete. This key works as it does on a PC keyboard. On a Mac keyboard, it is the key directly under the Help key and includes a forward arrow with an "x" inside it.

Return and Enter. These keys behave slightly differently on PCs and Macs, particularly in dialogs with multiple fields for entering text. On a Mac, Return and Enter do the same thing in fields. In Windows, you often need to press Enter (and not Return) in a field, because Return will add a return character *in the field*. This doesn't happen when you use the Return key under the Mac OS. Instead, it will usually move the pointer to the next field.

On the Mac, pressing either Return or Enter selects the default (colored) button in a dialog, such as Save or OK.

Eject key. This key displays a triangle with a bar below it (**Figure A.10**). Pressing and holding the Eject key for about a second opens the CD tray or, in slot-loading optical drives, ejects a disc. (If your Mac keyboard doesn't have an Eject key, pressing F12 will give you the same result.)

Speaker keys. These are the three keys with speaker icons in the upper right of the keyboard (**Figure A.10**). They control the Mac's internal speaker, and they stand for softer, louder, and off.

Figure A.10

In the upper right of the Mac keyboard are the speaker-volume controls (from left, softer, louder, and mute) and the Eject key.

Using a PC keyboard on the Mac

For some people, keyboards are like favorite pillows—difficult to part with, especially if it means getting used to a new one. If your favorite keyboard has a USB connector, you can plug it directly into the USB port on your new Mac. If it's a PS/2 or other serial keyboard, you can get a PS/2-to-USB converter or a box called a KVM switch, but you might end up spending less money just buying a new USB keyboard.

On a Mac, many of the PC-only keys will behave as if they were their Mac equivalents. For instance, the [Alt] key of your PC keyboard will act as the Mac [Option] key. Usually, the Windows key (not the [Ctrl] key) will act like the Apple/Command ([⌘]) key when the PC keyboard is plugged into the Mac. You'll be able to use all of the Mac commands on your PC keyboard, although some of the actual keystrokes may be different than, say, what a Mac manual may tell you.

To make sure the keyboard works as best it can, check to see if the keyboard manufacturer has a Macintosh driver. For instance, Microsoft offers the free IntelliType Pro driver (www.microsoft.com/mac), which works with most Microsoft keyboards. The Microsoft driver even lets you customize the keyboard.

PC-style mice

If you've become an expert at using your mouse's right button and scroll wheel, the standard Apple one-button mouse can be quite a disappointment. While you can bring up a contextual menu (the Mac version of a shortcut menu) with a [Control]-click, you may still be more comfortable with a two-button mouse. There are plenty of two- and three-button USB mice, many with scroll wheels, marketed for the Mac. Macally (www.macally.com) and Logitech (www.logitech.com) both offer a good selection of full-featured, Mac-friendly mice. Mac OS X is smart enough to recognize the right mouse button.

Mice from Microsoft also work with Mac OS X. You can download Microsoft's Mac mouse drivers at www.microsoft.com/mac.

Using PC Peripherals with Your Mac

Switching to a Mac doesn't mean you have to run out and replace all of your peripheral hardware. Most should work with your new Mac. It's easier to get newer PC peripherals to work with Macs, but you can even connect such technological artifacts as dot-matrix printers to your Mac.

USB vs. FireWire

All Macs made during the past several years have both USB and FireWire ports. On earlier Mac models, USB served as the low-speed port, and the 400 Mbps FireWire was the Mac's port for high-speed peripherals like digital camcorders.

 In Mac-speak, FireWire is the exact same thing as the IEEE 1394 standard.

Then the PC industry updated USB to USB 2, which runs at 480 Mbps, and for a while there was a Mac-PC platform battle between USB 2 and FireWire. Apple and digital camcorder manufacturers had adopted FireWire, while Intel was pushing USB 2 for adoption in PCs. The fight is now over. Both are here to stay.

USB ports in many newer Mac models are the new, faster USB 2 variety. Some higher-end Mac models also have 800 Mbps IEEE 1394b ports, which Apple calls FireWire 800. Both USB 2 and FireWire 800 are backward compatible with older peripherals.

If you have USB 2 peripherals from your PC, be sure to choose a Mac model that has a built-in USB 2 port. If your Mac has both USB 2 and FireWire 800 ports, you should choose FireWire 800 over USB 2 for the interface when shopping for a new peripheral. That's because FireWire has a few advantages over USB 2. FireWire can deliver more power to devices that charge directly from the computer. FireWire 800 can also run over longer distances of cable than USB 2, which is one reason why it is being rapidly adopted by professional digital audio equipment manufacturers.

Cameras

If you have a still digital camera that connects to your PC via USB, chances are it will work with your Mac without your having to install any software. Mac OS X can recognize most still cameras.

The Mac can also recognize a large number of digital video cameras that connect via FireWire. (Sony's implementation of FireWire, called iLink, works just fine on Macs.) However, there are a few camera models that don't work with the Mac—check the specifications on the box or on the manufacturer's Web site to find out if the model you want is compatible with the Mac. You may also find occasionally that certain features won't work with the Mac, such as those that require you to install Windows software. In many cases, however, these are features that are already built into Mac OS X, so they aren't needed.

Printers

There's a good chance you have one or more perfectly good printers that you'd like to use with your new Mac. Fortunately, today's Macs can print to more types of printers than ever before. And printing in Mac OS X is dependable and high quality. You can even expect fewer printing hassles than with Windows.

The interface for setting up printers and managing print jobs has changed with new versions of Mac OS X. In Mac OS X 10.3 the Print & Fax pane in System Preferences handles print and fax management, and the Printer Setup Utility in the Applications > Utilities folder is where you configure printers. In Mac OS X 10.2 the Print Center utility takes care of both these functions.

There are two issues you'll need to consider when moving your printer to your new Mac:

- **Printer drivers**—software that enables the Mac and the printer to communicate
- **Connection methods**—the cables and connectors

Printer drivers are not much of a problem anymore. Mac OS X 10.3 can print to more types of printers than previous versions of the Mac OS because it comes with a lot of printer drivers. It also includes some Unix system software called Gimp-Print, which lets your Mac recognize hundreds of new and old PC printers of various types.

If you have Mac OS X 10.2, you can download **Gimp-Print** for free at http://gimp-print.sourceforge.net. (You can't use Gimp-Print with older versions of the Mac OS, however.)

Physically connecting a PC printer to a Mac can be trickier. Connecting a USB printer is not a problem as long as your Mac has a USB port. If you have a parallel-port printer, you'll need to connect it to your Mac using an inexpensive (under $75) print server box with one or more parallel ports. You then connect your Mac to the print server via Ethernet. One good choice is D-Link's **DP-101P+ Pocket Ethernet Print Server** ($59; www.d-link.com), which has one parallel port and one Ethernet port.

For more on Mac printing, see Chapter 6.

Expanding and Upgrading Mac Hardware

There are two big myths about the Mac's expansion capability that are so pervasive, I've even heard IT professionals profess them. Since they are myths, let's debunk them right away.

Myth number one: the Mac is not expandable

Yes, you can expand your Mac's capabilities. And not just if you have the big Power Mac—you can expand the capabilities of iMacs, eMacs, PowerBooks, and iBooks. You can add memory (RAM) to any Mac model yourself, and it's usually easier than adding memory to a PC. Replacing an internal hard drive with a bigger one is not as easy, but it's definitely possible.

You'll even find that there are internal processor upgrades for the so-called nonexpandable models, such as iMacs. Chances are, if you have a brand-spanking-new Mac, you won't find a processor upgrade for it. But if you look at the Web sites of the processor-upgrade manufacturers, you will find upgrades for three-year-old and older Mac models. Makers of Mac processor upgrades include Giga Designs (www.gigadesigns.com), PowerLogix (www.powerlogix.com), and Sonnet (www.sonnettech.com).

It is true, however, that Power Macs are the most expandable Macs. Like PCs, they are easy to open up so that you can pull hardware out of them and plug things into them. PowerBooks have PC Card slots you can use to add new or improved functionality.

You can also open up Macs that Apple doesn't want you to open up. Often the upgrade manufacturer provides instructions with photos. Note, however, that you'll void Apple's one-year warranty (or three-year warranty, if you've purchased AppleCare) by opening up any Mac but a Power Mac to get at the hard drive, graphics card, or processor. If you are nervous about opening up your Mac, you can pay someone to do the upgrade for you, although even having an Apple authorized dealer perform the upgrade will still void the warranty if you have any model other than a Power Mac.

Finally, many expansion hardware options that used to be available only as add-in cards are now available as external USB or FireWire boxes. For example, if you want to beef up your Mac's audio capabilities, you don't have to install a sound card—you can use external USB hardware. You can also install a TV tuner as an external box, and boost your Mac's video input and output with external devices.

Myth number two: you need special Mac hardware to expand your Mac

For the most part, there is *no such thing* as Macintosh-only expansion hardware. Macs generally use the same expansion hardware components as PCs. The memory, graphics cards, hard drives, and optical drives found in your Mac are also found in PCs. This is not to say that every model of upgrade hardware is compatible with your Mac. It depends on the kind of upgrade you're considering. Most hard drives are compatible with your Mac, but the operating system is fussier about what graphics cards and optical drives you put inside it. It's best to check with the manufacturer or an outfit that sells to Mac users to verify Mac compatibility.

Power Macs have PCI slots, the same expansion slots found in PCs, and PowerBooks have the same PC Card slot found in Windows notebooks. You may need to install drivers in order to get some cards to work on your Mac.

The big exception to all this, of course, is processor upgrades. Macs don't use Intel or AMD processors—they use PowerPC processors. This helps to make Mac processor upgrades more expensive than processor upgrades on PCs.

Storage Drives

Since storage drives are the same on Macs and PCs, the only real issue to be aware of is the format of the drive or disk, which is the method used to lay down the data. Mac OS X recognizes PC drives formatted in File Allocation Table (FAT) format. It does not recognize Windows NT File System (NTFS)–formatted drives, however. CDs that you burn with your Mac will work in Windows PCs, although the opposite is not always true. Chapter 21 has information on using drives and storage media created in PC formats on your Mac, and vice versa.

What to do with floppy disks

Apple did away with floppy drives in Macs long ago. If you have a large collection of floppies that you need to access, or you still have people sending you files on floppy disks, you can plug a USB floppy drive into your Mac. You can find many different brands of inexpensive USB floppy drives, including the **Imation USB Floppy Drive** ($49.99; www.imation.com), LaCie's **USB Pocket Floppy Disk Drive** ($35; www.lacie.com), and the Macally **USB Floppy Disk Drive** ($69; www.macally.com). The Mac reads PC floppy disks just fine. Plug the drive into a USB port, insert the disk, and the icon appears on your Desktop. (Unlike Windows, Mac OS X does *not* display a floppy drive if it doesn't have a disk in it.)

Making the Move

Switching from Windows to the Mac is a lot like moving from one house to another. You usually don't leave all of your belongings behind when moving to new digs. Likewise, you can grab some of your old digital belongings from your PC and move them into their new home on your Mac.

Chapter 21 describes the various methods of moving files from a PC to a Mac, including using a network, CDs or hard disks, and even Bluetooth, so we won't cover that here. In this section we'll look at the content that you'll want to move and where to put it. This section also describes which files you will be able to use. There's no point in simply copying all the files from your PC's hard disk to your new Mac. You'll want to move what is useful. There are several types of files in your PC:

Document files. These are the files that you work with or use directly—such as word-processor files or MP3 music files. Most of these will be useful on the Mac. Some may need to be converted to a format that your Mac will recognize (see "Moving Document Files to a Mac," below).

Email messages. Email is not easy to move between platforms, but it can be done with the right tools (see "Moving Email to a Mac," below).

Web data. Web data mostly consists of your favorites from Internet Explorer. This is something you'll want to bring over if you have a lot of favorites (see "Moving Web Data to a Mac," later in this chapter).

Application programs. These are files that you generally don't want to move from your PC's hard disk. For one thing, your Mac can't normally make use of Windows software, unless you are running Virtual PC. However, even with the emulator, you need to install your Windows software from the installation CDs in order to have it function properly.

Configuration files. These have no value on your Mac. You may want to open up some of your settings dialogs, such those that show your network and email settings, and jot down the configurations so that you can more easily get up and running on your Mac.

The next few sections look at moving document files, email messages, and Web data from your PC to your Mac.

Moving Document Files to a Mac

As much as you might hear about the differences between Macs and PCs, the plain fact is that you will be able to use most of the document files you created with Windows programs on your Mac. If there is a version of your PC software installed on your Mac, then you will be able to use the files you created with that application on your Mac. You'll also be able to use files that have been saved in standard file formats, such as those for music and images. Chapter 21 describes some tools and techniques you can use to convert even those files that your Mac software doesn't understand. Among the many types of document files that you can use on your Mac, two categories—Microsoft Office files and multimedia files—are worth mentioning here because these are the two most commonly used types of files.

Microsoft Office files

If you have Office v. X for Mac installed, you will be able to use your Windows-generated Word, Excel, and PowerPoint files. Just move them to your Mac and double-click to open them. (If you don't have Office v. X for Mac, Chapter 21 describes other methods of using your Office for Windows files.)

Microsoft does not make a Mac version of Microsoft Access, however, so you'll have to use a Mac database program such as FileMaker Pro to work with these files (see Chapter 11 for more on databases for the Mac). If you have Access database files you want to use on your Mac, you'll need to export them in a simple format, such as tab delimited, which will allow you to import them into your new Mac database program. You'll need to perform the export within Windows before you move the files onto the Mac. (Again, if you have Virtual PC on the Mac, you can run Microsoft Access.)

Multimedia files

You can also use the multimedia files you've created on your PC: MP3 and WAV music files, JPEG photos (as well as photos in other standard formats such as GIF or TIFF), and movie files. Mac OS X has folders that are the equivalents of similar-sounding folders in Windows XP:

My Pictures. Mac OS X has a folder called Pictures in the home folder. You can put your images there, or you can drag them into Apple's iPhoto application (see Chapter 17). iPhoto places the files in its own folder structure inside the Pictures folder.

My Music. The Mac equivalent is the Music folder inside the home folder. iTunes keeps its music files there, in its own folder structure. You can drag your music files directly into iTunes, which copies the files from your disk or mounted network drive into this folder structure. (See Chapter 17 for more on iTunes.)

My Videos. The Mac equivalent is the Movies folder. Unlike other iLife programs, however, iMovie is not used to organize files. And unlike iTunes and iPhoto, iMovie isn't required to use your files. When you double-click a movie, QuickTime Player will usually launch to play it.

 While it is a good idea to keep all of your document files in the home folder, you don't have to put them in the Documents folder. A lot of application software keeps related files in the Documents folder, which just gives you more to search through. For my work files, I like to set up a folder called Current Projects in my home folder, thereby separating the wheat from the chaff.

Moving Email to a Mac

It's likely that you'll want to migrate your stored email messages and your email address book. These items are stored deep inside special data files; moving them is not a simple matter of dragging and dropping.

Microsoft Outlook is the most popular email program on Windows. Fortunately, thanks to a little utility, it is easy to move Outlook email to a Mac.

Moving Outlook email, contacts, and calendars

If you are using Outlook for Windows, there's an easy way to move your data files using an inexpensive program from Little Machines called **Outlook2Mac** ($10; www.littlemachines.com). This little utility can save you hours of painstaking work and give you better results than if you attempted it yourself. (In fact, moving email is such an impediment to switching that if I were an Apple bigwig, I'd bundle Outlook2Mac with every Mac to entice Windows users over.)

Outlook2Mac extracts messages, attachments, the address book, and even calendar entries from Outlook 97, 98, 2000, and 2003 and moves them into a single folder that you then move to your Mac. Once you are in Mac OS X, Outlook2Mac's help files tell you exactly how to import the data into the top Mac OS X email clients, including Apple's Mail (which comes with Mac OS X), Microsoft Entourage (which comes with Office v. X), Bare Bones

Software's excellent **Mailsmith** ($99; www.barebones.com), Qualcomm's **Eudora** ($49.95; www.qualcomm.com), and CTM Development's **PowerMail** ($49; www.ctmdev.com). Outlook2Mac takes Outlook's calendar events and moves them into Mac OS X's iCal. (You can also move them into Entourage with a little effort.)

If this were all that Outlook2Mac did, it would be worth two or three times the ten bucks that Little Machines asks for it. In a series of wizard panes, Outlook2Mac also gives you a range of options for denoting exactly what data you'd like to move. You can choose which stored-mail folders to move (**Figure A.11**) and specify a range of dates for email or calendar items to export (**Figure A.12**). You exclude Windows-only attachments (such as .bat and .exe files) and attachments larger than a certain size.

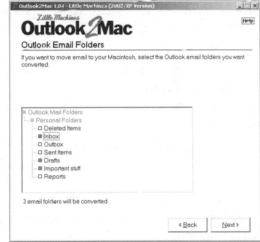

Figure A.11

While running on Windows, Outlook2Mac lets you choose which email data to export to your Mac.

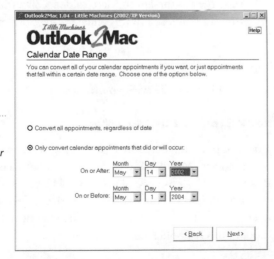

Figure A.12

Outlook2Mac lets you select a range of email or calendar dates to export. Here you see the calendar dates selected; you select the date range for emails in another screen.

Unfortunately, Outlook2Mac works only with Outlook on the PC. If you use other email programs, your options are more limited.

Moving Eudora email to a Mac

If you are using Eudora on your PC, it is not that difficult to move your email to a Mac, provided that you will be using Eudora for Mac. All you need to do is locate and move several files on your PC:

- in.mbx
- out.mbx
- trash.mbx

These files, which handle the content of your In, Out, and Trash mailboxes, are located in the Eudora directory inside the Application Data directory, which is located in different areas in different versions of Windows. You can do a search for it if you can't find it. Move the files to your Mac and delete the .mbx filename extension.

Next, you'll have to open each of the three files listed above and replace the hard returns with line breaks. Fortunately, there's an easy way to do this with a word processor. You can use Microsoft Word for this—drag and drop the file on top of the Word icon to open the file with Word.

In Word's Edit menu, select Replace. Click the triangle at the bottom left to expand the dialog. Click in the "Find what" field at the top of the dialog, and then go to the Special pop-up menu at the bottom of the dialog; choose Paragraph Mark. Now click in the "Replace with" field and choose Manual Line Break from the Special pop-up menu. Click the Replace All button. Save the resulting files as plain text.

Now you can drop the files in the appropriate folder. Click the Desktop to make the Finder active and choose Go to Folder in the Go menu. Type the following path:

~/Documents/Eudora/Mail Folder/

Replace the In, Out, and Trash files with your newly edited files, and you're set.

Moving Outlook Express email to a Mac

If you're still a user of the old Microsoft Outlook Express, your best bet is to use Detto Technologies' **Move2Mac** ($49.95; www.detto.com). It's a bit overpriced and isn't as slick or as versatile as Little Machines' Outlook2Mac. But if you have Outlook Express on your PC, it is the easiest way to get your email and contacts over to the Mac. Move2Mac also handles the standard version of Outlook, but Outlook2Mac does a better job for Outlook at one-fifth the price.

Moving Web Data to a Mac

Mac OS X comes with two Web browsers, Internet Explorer and Safari. You can move your Internet Explorer favorites to either browser. You can also move your favorites to other Mac Web browsers, such as the open-source Camino.

 On many Mac browsers, favorites are known as *bookmarks*.

Moving Internet Explorer favorites from Windows to the Mac

To move your Internet Explorer favorites from Windows to Internet Explorer for the Mac, do the following:

1. In Windows, launch Internet Explorer.
2. Go to the File menu and select Import and Export. This brings up the Wizard window.
3. Click Next, and then Export Favorites.
4. After several screens, you'll be asked to choose a location for the exported favorites file, which is called bookmark.html. Choose a folder and click through the rest of the wizard screens.
5. Move the bookmark.html file to the Mac.
6. Rename the file Favorites.html.
7. In Mac OS X, choose Go to Folder from the Go menu. Type this pathname:

   `~/Library/Preferences/Explorer/`

   This opens the Explorer folder.
8. Now drag the Favorites.html file into the Explorer folder. The Mac asks you if you want to replace an existing favorites file. Click Yes.

The favorites from Windows will now appear in the Favorites menu of Internet Explorer on your Mac. If you'd like Internet Explorer to be your default Web browser, you have to set it, as described in "Making Internet Explorer the default browser," below. If you want to move your favorites into Safari or Camino, read on.

Moving Internet Explorer favorites from Windows into Safari on the Mac

Safari doesn't have an import function for bookmarks, so you'll have to move your favorites in manually. Do the following:

1. Drag the Favorites.html file you created in the previous section onto the Safari icon in the Dock. Safari opens, displaying your Internet Explorer favorites.
2. Go to Safari's File menu and select New Window.

   With the new window on top, go to the Bookmarks menu and select Show All Bookmarks.

3. Click the icon called Bookmarks Menu in the sidebar to the left.

4   Go to the Window menu and choose Favorites (this selects the Favorites.html file window).

5. Select the links and drag them from the Favorites.html window to the Bookmarks window.

Moving Internet Explorer favorites from Windows into Camino on the Mac

If you haven't heard of Camino, try it out by downloading it for free at the Camino Home Page (www.mozilla.org/projects/camino/homepage.html). Unlike the importing process for Safari, importing bookmarks into Camino is a snap. Go to the Camino menu (in Mac-speak, that's the Application menu) and select Import Bookmarks. A small dialog slides down from the title bar. It has one drop-down menu, which is called a *pop-up* menu on the Mac. If you already moved your bookmarks into Internet Explorer on the Mac, simply choose Internet Explorer from the pop-up menu and click the Import button. That's it.

If you haven't moved your bookmarks into Internet Explorer, choose Select a File from the pop-up menu and browse for the Favorites.html file you created earlier.

Making Internet Explorer the default browser

Safari is the default Web browser in Mac OS X. If you'd rather have Internet Explorer (or Camino) launch from your email or other programs, you can change this. There is good reason for you, as a former Windows user, to make Internet Explorer your default Web browser. Not only will using Internet Explorer for Mac make your Web-browsing experience more like your Web-browsing experience on your old PC, but IE can render more types of Web pages than Safari and can run more scripts. In Mac OS X 10.2 and earlier, you set your default browser using the Internet settings pane of System Preferences. With Mac OS X 10.3, Apple made switching default browsers more difficult by eliminating this setting. You still can change your default browser, however—you have to use Safari to do it:

1. Launch Safari.

2. Select Preferences from the Safari menu.

3. In the dialog that opens, click the General icon.

4. In the Default Web Browser pop-up menu, choose Internet Explorer or any other browser installed on your Mac (**Figure A.13**).

5. Quit Safari.

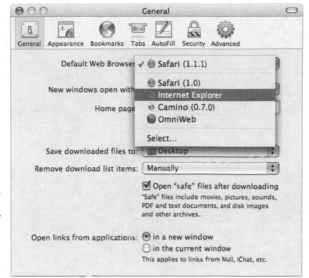

Figure A.13

Changing the default Web browser in Mac OS X 10.3 and later requires that you go to Safari Preferences.

To change your default email client, you use a similar procedure in Apple's Mail program.

Glossary

3D (three-dimensional) Normal graphics use two dimensions—height and width (x- and y-axes)—while 3D graphics add depth (z-axis) to the original dimensions.

A

access point A hardware device or software that serves as a link to connect wireless users to a wired local area network (LAN) that already has a router. Apple's AirPort Base Station is a type of access point.

active window The topmost window; the window that is currently receiving mouse and keyboard input.

ADB See *Apple Desktop Bus*.

AGP (Accelerated Graphics Port) The slot for a video card on newer Macs. You'll see specifications for this slot listed as 2x, 4x, and 8x. The higher the number, the greater the graphics speed.

AIFF (Audio Interchange File Format) The standard sound format on the Mac.

AirPort Apple's wireless networking technology. There are AirPort cards, which fit into Macs, and AirPort Base Stations, which communicate with the cards. The original AirPort uses the IEEE 802.11b Wi-Fi technology, which runs at 11 megabits per second (Mbps).

AirPort Extreme The latest wireless networking technology, based on the IEEE 802.11g standard. Apple includes it on all currently shipping Macs. It's about five times faster than the original AirPort, running at 54 Mbps.

alias A file that points to another item, such as a file, folder, or application. When you double-click an alias, the item it points to is opened. In Mac OS X, an alias is distinguished by a small arrow in its icon.

all-in-one An adjective describing a desktop computer system in which the monitor and CPU are housed in one unit. All iMacs are all-in-one Macs. Although portable computers such as the PowerBook have the monitor, keyboard, and CPU contained in one unit, they are not considered all-in-one machines. Why? Maybe the same reason that *flammable* and *inflammable* mean the same thing.

AltiVec See *Velocity Engine*.

anti-aliasing The blurring of certain pixels to smooth out an image. Usually used to make screen fonts easier to read.

API (application programming interface) The interface by which an application program accesses the operating system and other services. Operating-system developers such as Apple create APIs to help software developers create programs.

Apple Desktop Bus A low-speed serial bus that connects peripherals such as keyboards and mice to first-generation Macs. This has been supplanted by USB on the modern Macs. See also *Universal Serial Bus*.

Apple menu In Mac OS X, a menu for accessing systemwide commands (such as Shut Down and Log Out), preferences, and recent documents and applications.

AppleScript A simple scripting language, included with the Mac OS, that you can use to automate many of your Mac's functions. Well, simple compared with other languages, like C++.

AppleShare IP Apple's commercial server software.

applet A small Java application that is usually downloaded and run via a Web browser. Many online puzzle games are applets.

AppleTalk Apple's local area network architecture. Macs can use it to communicate with each other and with network peripherals.

application A program designed for end users (meaning normal, everyday people). Example: Microsoft Word.

Application menu In Mac OS X, the menu to the right of the Apple menu; its name is the name of the currently active application, and it gives users access to preferences for the application.

Aqua The name of the interface in Mac OS X, so called because of its translucent blue highlights.

ASCII (American Standard Code for Information Interchange) A code for designating characters in which each letter or symbol is assigned a number. Thus, ASCII files are text only, with no added styles like bold or italic.

B

bandwidth The amount of data that a system can deliver over a set period of time. High bandwidth is good.

base station The part of a wireless system that is responsible for sending and receiving radio signals.

BinHex Short for *binary-to-hexadecimal*. BinHex is a process for converting Mac OS files into ASCII files. It's mostly used for transferring files via email or FTP.

bit Short for *binary digit*. A bit is the smallest unit of information on a computer. A single bit can hold only one of two values: 0 or 1, which represents on or off.

bitmap A representation of a graphic image, consisting of rows and columns of dots. The density of the dots, or resolution, determines how sharply the image is represented. This is often expressed in dots per inch (dpi). Bitmapped graphics are often referred to as *raster graphics*. See also *vector graphics*.

blog Short for *Web log*. A blog is a Web site that is a kind of public diary, usually containing the author's personal thoughts along with links to things he or she finds interesting.

Bluetooth A short-range wireless communications protocol for connecting PDAs (personal digital assistants), computers, mobile phones, and accessories without cables. Bluetooth's range is slightly more than 30 feet, and data is transmitted at 1 Mbps. Bluetooth includes device-registration and security capabilities that, for example, make sure your wireless headset works with your phone only, even if other Bluetooth phones are close by.

bookmark A Web-browser term for a saved reference to an Internet address. Same thing as a *favorite*. The term varies depending on what browser you are using.

boot To load and initialize the operating system on the Mac.

broadband An adjective used to describe a high-speed Internet connection, such as cable or DSL. Sometimes used by itself to denote such service. For example, "I just got broadband, and it's great! I downloaded a bunch of movie trailers last night!"

browser An application for accessing and displaying pages on the World Wide Web. Safari and Microsoft Internet Explorer are browsers.

BSD (Berkeley Software Distribution) Mac OS X uses BSD, the version of the Unix operating system developed at the University of California, Berkeley. BSD runs on top of the Mach kernel. See also *Mach*.

bug A programming glitch. (If someone finds a productive use for the glitch, the company responsible for the bug might call it a feature.)

burn To write data to a CD or DVD.

bus A connection that transmits data between the CPU (central processing unit) and internal components, such as drives and video cards. Current Macs use several different bus technologies.

byte A unit of storage capable of holding one character, which is 8 bits.

C

cable modem   A modem enabling you to connect to the Internet via the same lines used by cable television. It is much, much faster than a telephone modem and in many cases faster than a DSL connection.

cache   A storage mechanism used to speed up computing. There are disk caches and memory caches. A disk cache stores recently used data in a memory buffer, speeding up its retrieval. A memory cache stores often-used instructions in high-speed static RAM instead of slower dynamic RAM.

Carbonized   A Carbonized application has been rewritten by its developer using the Carbon set of APIs, which allows it to run on most Mac OS 8 and 9 systems and on Mac OS X systems. See also *Classic* and *Cocoa*.

CD-R (compact disc–recordable)   Discs you can write to only once.

CD-ROM (compact disc–read-only memory)   The discs on which most programs and music are available. You can't write to these.

CD-RW (compact disc–rewritable)   Discs you can write to multiple times.

Classic   A Classic application is one written for Mac OS 9 or earlier but not rewritten for Mac OS X. (More technically, the developer has not used Apple's Carbon APIs to rewrite the application.) Classic applications run in the Classic environment of Mac OS X and on Mac OS 9 and earlier.

Classic environment   In Mac OS X, the Classic environment lets you run most of your old Mac OS 9 applications. When you launch a program written for Mac OS 9 or earlier, Mac OS X starts up a copy of Mac OS 9 and then runs that program inside the virtual operating system.

client   A Mac program that connects to a server. For example, email programs are clients, as they connect to mail servers to send and receive messages.

clip art   Generic images used to illustrate documents. Many programs, such as AppleWorks, come with collections of royalty-free clip art.

Clipboard   A special section of memory dedicated to items you cut and paste. When you use the Cut command, the selection is placed in the Clipboard. Paste places what is in the Clipboard at the insertion point.

close button   The first button on the left in Mac OS X windows, colored red. Clicking the close button closes the window. See also *window buttons*.

Cocoa   In Mac OS X, a development environment for writing Mac OS X applications. A Cocoa application can easily take advantage of Mac OS X's built-in services, such as the Font Panel. A Cocoa application, however, can't run on Mac OS 9 and earlier systems. See also *Carbonized* and *Classic*.

contextual menu   Provides access to commands associated with an item. When the user presses Control while clicking an item, a contextual menu appears next to the item.

CPU (central processing unit)   The brains of the computer. In current Macs, the CPU is a PowerPC processor.

crash   An incident that causes a program or computer to cease functioning. The cause can be faulty software coding or a hardware malfunction.

cross-platform   An adjective describing something compatible with more than one type of computer system. For example, Microsoft Word files are cross-platform because they can be used on Macintosh or Windows computers.

CRT   Short for *cathode ray tube,* a type of monitor. These are the old-style monitors, which are similar to television sets.

cursor   A graphic symbol that indicates where a user-initiated action will take place and what kind of action it will be. On the Mac, the cursor usually takes the shape of an arrow, called a *pointer.*

D

Darwin　The open-source component of Mac OS X.

database　A software program for storing, retrieving, and manipulating multiple pieces of information.

default　A setting that is chosen if a user does not specify another. For example, the default home page for some Web browsers is the developing company's site.

Desktop　The main area of the Mac OS interface; the part that contains icons for drives, files, and folders.

DHCP　(Dynamic Host Configuration Protocol) A method for automatically assigning the unique IP addresses required for every computer on a TCP/IP network, such as the public Internet.

dialog box　An alert that asks for user input. In Mac OS X, abbreviated as dialog.

digital hub　Apple marketing-speak when referring to the Macintosh. The idea is that the Mac can help you manage all your digital devices—cameras, music players, DVD players—from a central place.

disc, disk　When you're talking about a CD, a DVD, or other optical media, it is a *disc*. When referring to magnetic media such as those used in hard drives or Zip drives, it's a *disk*.

disclosure button　The triangle that reveals more options or contents when you click it. Also called a *disclosure triangle*.

display　Shorthand for *display screen*. A monitor.

DNS　See *Domain Name System*.

Dock　In Mac OS X, the Dock is a strip of icons representing running applications, frequently used items, and the Trash.

domain name　A name that identifies one or more IP addresses. Domain names are used in URLs to identify specific Web pages. For example, in the URL www.peachpit.com, *peachpit* is the domain name.

Domain Name System (DNS)　An Internet service that translates domain names into IP addresses. For example, the domain name www.example.com might translate to 198.105.232.4. If one DNS server doesn't know how to translate a particular domain name, it asks another one, and so on, until the correct IP address is returned.

double-click　A sequence of two quick consecutive clicks.

download　To retrieve a file from another computer over the Internet.

driver　A piece of software that facilitates communication between a piece of hardware and the operating system.

DSL　(Digital Subscriber Line) A high-speed way to connect to the Internet over phone lines.

DVD　(digital video disc) A type of CD-ROM that can hold nearly 5 GB of data per disc, enough for a feature-length movie.

DVD-R　(digital video disc–recordable) Discs you can write to once.

DVD-RAM　(digital video disc–random-access memory) An early precursor to DVD-RW technology. DVD-RAM discs are used in some home DVD/DVD-RAM recorders, but are mostly incompatible with Apple's DVD SuperDrive.

DVD-RW　(digital video disc–rewritable) Discs you can write to multiple times.

dynamic RAM　RAM that needs to be constantly refreshed to retain its contents. Slower than static RAM. See also *RAM*.

E

eMac　An all-in-one Mac model. It's built along the lines of the original iMac, which has morphed into something more futuristic.

email　Electronic mail, the transmission of messages over a network.

emulation Mimicking another program or hardware device in software. For example, Microsoft's Virtual PC emulates the Windows environment, allowing you to run Windows programs on the Mac. See also *native software.*

encryption The encoding of data so that it is unintelligible to unauthorized parties.

Ethernet The most common LAN technology. Ethernet connects devices using coaxial cable and currently comes in three speeds: 10Base-T, which offers data speeds of up to 10 Mbps; 100Base-T, which offers data speeds up to 100 Mbps; and 1000Base-T (or Gigabit Ethernet), which offers data speeds up to 1000 Mbps.

Exposé A fancy name for a window-control feature in Mac OS X 10.3. Pressing certain function keys tiles, sorts, or hides open windows.

F

FAQ (frequently asked questions) A FAQ is a list of frequently asked questions with answers about a specific subject. It is a time-saving device so that folks in the know, be they technical-support staff or newsgroup veterans, don't keep answering the same basic questions.

favorite A Web-browser term for a saved reference to an Internet address. Same thing as a *bookmark.*

Favorites A folder in Mac OS X that holds often-used items. The Mac OS builds in quick access to this particular folder: it's always found in the Finder's Go menu.

file A discrete collection of data that has a unique name.

file server A storage device on a network dedicated to holding files.

File Transfer Protocol A means of moving files from one computer to another over the Internet. The common abbreviation is *FTP.*

FileVault A security feature of Mac OS X 10.3. It encrypts and decrypts the contents of your home directory on the fly using the Advanced Encryption Standard, provides for secure deletion of files, and allows automatic sign-ins.

Finder The main application of the Mac OS. The Finder manages the Mac's files and folders.

FireWire A communications standard developed by Apple. It transmits data, video, audio, and power over a single line. There are now two versions of FireWire: FireWire 400, which can transfer data as fast as 400 Mbps, and FireWire 800, which can transfer data as fast as 800 Mbps. FireWire's high transfer speeds make it a popular choice for digital audio and video professionals. How popular? In 2001, Apple won an Emmy Award for FireWire's impact on the TV industry. Sony calls it iLink, and others refer to it as IEEE 1394.

Flash A Macromedia technology that is commonly used for animation and interactive pages on the Web. Macromedia also makes the Flash program, which is an application for creating Web animations using the Flash technology.

flat panel A type of monitor, usually LCD. A flat panel is generally much smaller physically than a CRT with the same size viewing area.

FTP See *File Transfer Protocol.*

G

G3, G4, G5 Different iterations of the PowerPC processor used in Apple computers. G5 is the latest and greatest, introducing 64-bit architecture to personal computing. Don't worry about what that means—just know that it makes Macs go real fast.

GarageBand Apple's software package that lets you create music on your Mac. Part of the iLife bundle.

gigabyte A gigabyte (abbreviated as *GB*) is 1,073,741,824 bytes, not a jillion.

gigahertz A measure of electromagnetic wave frequency equal to 1 billion (1,000,000,000) hertz (abbreviated as *GHz*), used to specify the operating speed of computer processors. The bigger the number, the faster the processor.

GUI (graphical user interface) An interface that takes advantage of a computer's graphical capabilities to make the computer easier to use. A GUI usually features menus and icons representing disks and files. Commands are sent to the computer via mouse clicks. The antithesis of a GUI is a command-line interface, where the user types in commands after a prompt. DOS and Unix use a command-line interface.

H

hard disk A magnetic storage medium for computer data. Also called a *hard drive.* The word *hard* is used to differentiate it from floppy disks. In common usage, a hard disk is the big disk inside your Mac.

hardware The physical elements of the computer—for example, the processor, the printer, the disks, and the monitor.

HFS See *Hierarchical File System.*

HFS+ (Hierarchical File System Plus) Officially called Mac OS Extended, this updated version of HFS makes much more efficient use of the space on high-capacity hard disks than does the older Hierarchical File System.

Hierarchical File System Usually referred to as *HFS*, this was the standard file format for the Macintosh. Apple now officially calls it the Mac OS X Standard Format. HFS Plus is the newest version.

home folder In Mac OS X, each user of the system gets a home folder to store documents, music, pictures, and other files. You don't actually see something called a Home folder because the system names it after the user: Marty, for example.

hotspot Common name given to a location that offers wireless Internet access, such as an Internet cafe or an airport mobile office.

HTML (Hypertext Markup Language) The language used to create Web pages.

I

iBook Apple's consumer-oriented portable computer.

iCal A free calendaring application from Apple. Works only with Mac OS X 10.2 or later.

iCards A feature of the .Mac service that lets you send greeting cards to your friends, relatives, lovers, and enemies.

iChat Mac OS X's instant-messaging feature. It "leverages" AOL Instant Messenger, which really means that you can use it to chat on AOL.

icon Apple's free convicted-felon software ... no, wait—an icon is a graphic representation of a file, application, or folder; it can also act like a button.

iDisk The storage and file-sharing component of the .Mac service.

iDVD Apple software for editing and producing DVD discs. Part of the iLife bundle.

iLife A collection of digital entertainment software, including iDVD, iTunes, iPhoto, iMovie, and GarageBand.

iMac The all-in-one consumer Macintosh. It used to come in several cheery colors, but now it's a futuristic-looking dome with a flat screen on a stick.

IMAP (Internet Message Access Protocol) The main email alternative to POP. With IMAP, messages remain on a central server and can be accessed from different machines without having to be downloaded. It's handy for business travelers or for those who work in more than one location.

iMovie Apple's basic moviemaking software. Part of the iLife bundle.

insertion point The location where items are placed in a document when you type or paste. It's usually represented by a blinking vertical bar.

installer A special program made to place a program on your Macintosh. Installers usually put several files in specific locations, saving the user a lot of hassle.

instant messaging An Internet technology that allows you to receive from and send messages to another person online in real time. When comparing instant messaging with email, it may be helpful to think of instant messaging as a telephone to email's, um, mail. Two instant-messaging applications are AOL Instant Messenger and MSN Messenger.

interface The means by which a user communicates with the computer. The Mac uses a graphical user interface. See also *GUI*.

Internet A global network that connects millions of computers.

IP (Internet Protocol) A low-level communications standard that is usually paired with a higher-level standard such as TCP, which establishes a virtual connection between a source and a destination.

IP address An identifier for a computer or device on a TCP/IP network. Networks using the TCP/IP protocol route messages based on the IP address of the destination. The format of an IP address is a 32-bit numeric address written as four numbers separated by periods. Each number can be zero to 255. For example, 1.180.10.240 could be an IP address.

iPhoto Apple's basic photo organization and editing software. Part of the iLife bundle.

iPod A portable MP3 music player from Apple.

ISDN (integrated services digital network) A way to send data over phone lines. ISDN supports speeds of 64–128 Kbps; faster than your standard 56 Kbps modem but slower than DSL or a cable modem.

iSight Apple's Webcam designed for use with iChat instant messaging.

ISP (Internet service provider) A company that sells access to the Internet. America Online is a big ISP, as is EarthLink.

iSync Synchronization software from Apple that coordinates data on your PDA, cell phone, or iPod with data on your Mac.

iTunes Apple's free music recording, cataloging, and playback program. It also lends its name to the iTunes Music Store, where Apple sells downloadable music. Part of the iLife bundle.

J

Jaguar The nickname of Mac OS X 10.2.

Java A cross-platform programming language developed by Sun Microsystems. The theory is that a developer could write a program in Java and have it work on Windows machines and Macs without altering it.

Jobs, Steve Apple interim CEO (or iCEO) and then CEO, 1997 to the present. One of the fathers of the Mac.

K

Keynote Apple's presentation software.

kilobyte A kilobyte is 1,024 bytes, not exactly 1,000 as would seem logical (although there is a movement afoot to change the numbering scheme). Abbreviated as *Kbyte*.

L

LAN (local area network) A collection of computers and devices sharing a communications link within a small geographic area, such as an office building.

Linux An alternative, open-source operating system.

M

.Mac Apple Computer's paid Internet service, which provides online storage space, email, antivirus protection, Web publishing, and file backup, among other things.

Mac OS The official name of the Macintosh operating system.

Mac OS X The *X* is the Roman numeral ten and pronounced "ten." A complete departure from earlier Macintosh operating systems, Mac OS X was written from the ground up based on the BSD version of the Unix operating system.

Mach Mac OS X uses the Mach kernel, originally created at Carnegie Mellon University. The kernel handles such tasks as memory allocation and scheduling which tasks the computer is doing. See also *BSD*.

macro A sequence of commands activated by a single command. A shortcut. A macro in Microsoft Word, for example, might open a new document and put your name and address at the top.

megabyte A megabyte is 1,048,576 bytes, not 1 million. Abbreviated as *MB*.

megahertz A frequency measurement equaling 1 million cycles per second. The speed of microprocessors is expressed in megahertz. Abbreviated as *MHz*.

menu A list of commands from which the user can choose.

microprocessor A chip that contains a central processing unit (CPU). The PowerPC, the heart of the Macintosh line, is a microprocessor. But if you call it a *processor* or a *CPU,* people will know that you mean microprocessor.

minimize button The second button from the left in Mac OS X, colored yellow. Clicking the minimize button places the file or folder in the Dock. See also *window buttons*.

modem A device that allows computers to communicate over phone lines. The name is short for *modulation-demodulation.*

monitor A video display for a computer. These days you have either a flat-screen (LCD) or a CRT monitor.

motherboard The main circuit board of a computer. It holds the CPU and slots for expansion.

mouse The Mac's pointing device, a peripheral that controls the movement of the pointer on the screen.

MP3 Short for *MPEG 1, Layer 3* (*MPEG* itself is short for *Moving Picture Experts Group*), a scheme for compressing audio. It has quickly become the standard for digital audio.

multimedia Content that uses more than one medium for communication, as in video and audio.

multiprocessing Using more than one processor to complete a task. Some high-end Macs have two CPUs; special programming can take advantage of the extra processing power.

N

native software Software designed to run on a particular microprocessor. Apple designed Mac OS X to run specifically on PowerPC G3, G4, and G5 processors, and Mac OS X's Mail application is designed to run specifically on Mac OS X: both are native software for the PowerPC G3, G4, and G5 processors. Through emulation software, an application designed to run on one processor can be tricked into thinking it is running on another one. See also *emulation*.

network A collection of interconnected computers and devices.

newsgroup A collection of messages about a specific topic redistributed throughout Usenet, a network of such groups. Just about any topic you can imagine—and some you'd rather not imagine—has its own newsgroup.

O

online To be connected to the Internet or a local network.

OpenGL An API and software library for 3D graphics. If you don't know what those terms mean, no short explanation here will help you. What's really important about OpenGL is that it allows developers to make cool games for the Mac.

open source Descriptive term for software whose underlying code has been made available by its developer for modification. Parts of Mac OS X and all of Linux are open source.

operating system Software that controls the functions of a computer. An operating system tracks input from a keyboard and mouse, sends output to display devices, negotiates resources among running programs, monitors files and folders, and controls peripherals, among other things. Abbreviated as *OS*.

OS See *operating system*.

P

pane An area in a dialog or other window. The contents of a pane can change when you click a tab or a button or choose an item from a pop-up menu.

Panther The nickname of Mac OS X 10.3.

parallel port An interface that transmits several bits of data simultaneously. Compare with *serial port*.

parameter RAM Persistent memory that holds system-configuration data, such as date, time, and desktop settings. Also known as *PRAM*. Unlike regular memory, which forgets everything the moment the power is cut, PRAM is powered by a separate battery so that it remembers its contents—well, at least until the battery dies, although, fortunately, that can take years to happen.

PCI (Peripheral Component Interconnect) An expansion bus. Macs have PCI expansion slots for things like video cards and SCSI cards.

PDA (personal digital assistant) A PDA is usually a handheld device that helps you organize your schedule and contacts.

PDF (Portable Document Format) This is an Adobe technology that is built into Mac OS X. PDF files can be viewed on almost any platform using the free Adobe Reader application. You don't need to have the application that created the file to view it; thus PDF is a very, well, portable file format.

pixel A single point in an electronic image.

plug-in An extra piece of software that adds functions to another program. For example, plug-ins in Adobe Photoshop add ways for users to manipulate images.

pointer See *cursor*.

POP (Post Office Protocol) The method most email programs use to retrieve messages from a server.

pop-up menu In a dialog, a menu that presents a list of choices when the triangle button is clicked. The menu disappears when an action is selected.

PowerBook Apple's line of professional portable computers. Oddly enough, these were called PowerBooks even before the advent of the PowerPC chip, so there are non-PowerPC PowerBooks.

Power Macintosh A desktop Mac that usually has a PowerPC processor. Note that *Power Macintosh* is two words, unlike *PowerPC* and *PowerBook*. Older models of the Power Macintosh (often shortened to *Power Mac*) may or may not have a PowerPC processor. Yes, it's confusing.

PowerPC The name of the processor used in the Power Macintosh line and manufactured by both Motorola and IBM.

PRAM See *parameter RAM*.

Print Center In Mac OS X, you use this to select printers.

protected memory A memory scheme that sets aside unique space for each application so that if one program crashes, it will not affect the others. This is a feature of Mac OS X.

protocol A standardized format for transmitting data between devices.

P2P Short for *peer-to-peer,* an adjective usually used in describing a network connection. These days the most common use of the term is in reference to Internet file-sharing services like Kazaa. There isn't one central server holding all the files that users on the network access. Rather, the files are on individual computers, so when you download a file, you make a direct connection to the computer that is hosting the file.

Q

Quartz The graphical underpinnings of Mac OS X. It has a 2D drawing engine and takes care of windowing in the interface. Quartz Extreme, which was introduced in Mac OS X 10.3, takes things a step further, promising to speed up overall system performance by letting the graphics card, rather than the CPU, draw windows on the screen.

QuickTime Apple's software for playing audio and video on a computer. It's actually more complicated than that; it's also a media-authoring platform and a file format. But for most of us—regular old computer users—it's just a media player.

R

RAM (random-access memory) Allows any byte in memory to be accessed randomly. Well, isn't that self-referential? The more RAM your Mac has, the more easily (and quickly) it can perform tasks.

read-me file A document that contains important information for the user, usually about the pitfalls of installing software.

Rendezvous Apple's latest networking technology. It lets computers and devices automatically detect what services are available on the network, making connections less of a headache.

resolution A measurement of the clarity of an image. Resolutions are given for monitor displays (how many pixels are on the screen), printer output (dots per inch), and image files (number of pixels).

RIAA (Recording Industry Association of America) You may wonder why these folks are mentioned in a book about Macintoshes. Well, ever since people have been trading, buying, and selling music via MP3s, the RIAA has taken a legal interest in the phenomenon. If you use iTunes, it might be a good idea to keep an eye on what the RIAA is doing.

rip To convert audio files (like a song or a whole CD) to MP3 format for playback on a computer or portable music player.

S

Safari Apple's Web browser.

screensaver An application that displays images, animation, or other information when the computer has been idle for a specified amount of time. Mac OS X has one built in.

scroll bar The bar on the side or bottom of a window that controls what part of a document is displayed.

SCSI (Small Computer System Interface) A parallel interface standard for connecting peripherals. Pronounced "skuzzy." SCSI has mostly been replaced these days by USB and FireWire interfaces for consumer peripherals.

serial port An interface that transmits data one bit at a time. Compare with *parallel port*.

server A computer on a network that manages network resources.

shareware Free-distribution software that users pay for only if they decide to continue using it. Most shareware is written by smaller developers.

Sherlock Apple's Internet-searching utility. It originally was a disk-search utility, but over time it has morphed into a tool for finding information on the Internet, such as stock prices, news, and movie info.

sleep A low-power mode in which the Mac's monitor and drives are powered down.

SMTP (Simple Mail Transfer Protocol) The method most email servers use to deliver messages.

software Computer code or data. If it can be stored electronically, it is definitely software. If you can copy it, it is probably software.

spam Unsolicited bulk email. It's usually considered a bad thing. On some message boards or newsgroups, off-topic posts are considered spam as well. Very loosely, some folks consider that anything they aren't interested in takes up bandwidth and is thus spam.

startup disk The disk used to start up a computer, or a disk capable of starting up a computer. You can designate which disk is used in the Startup Disk pane in System Preferences in Mac OS X.

static RAM RAM that does not need to be refreshed to keep its contents. Faster and more reliable than dynamic RAM, but more expensive.

StuffIt A compression utility from Aladdin Systems that is pretty much the default standard for Mac users.

SuperDrive Catchy name for Apple's drive that can burn CDs and DVDs.

System The folder that holds files crucial to the running of Mac OS X.

T

T1, T3 Transmission systems commonly used in the Internet. T1 provides a continuous, dedicated transmission rate of up to 1.5 Mbps; T3, 44.7 Mbps. T1 and T3 lines are expensive and generally for business and science use, not consumer use.

TCP/IP (Transmission Control Protocol/Internet Protocol) Used to make connections on the Internet.

Terminal An application that lets you use Mac OS X's command-line interface.

Titanium A type of PowerBook, so named because of the metal used in its case.

title bar The top border of a window, which contains its name.

trackball A pointing device that consists of a ball held in a stationary base.

trackpad A pointing device. The user moves the pointer by dragging a finger across the surface of the trackpad. Used in PowerBooks and iBooks.

Trash The holding area for items you want to delete from your computer.

U

undo A command that takes back the previous command, "undoing" it. For example, if you delete a word from a sentence, Undo puts it back. The shortcut for Undo is usually ⌘Z.

Universal Serial Bus *USB* for short. USB is a technology for connecting peripherals—such as pointing devices and printers—to your computer. Apple has standardized on USB, which is much faster than Apple's older Apple Desktop Bus (ADB) standard and much faster than traditional serial ports. Currently there are two versions of USB: the older 1.1 version, which runs at 12 Mbps; and the newer 2.0 version, which runs nearly 40 times faster, at 480 Mbps, and thus challenges FireWire.

Unix An operating system. Mac OS X is based on a version of Unix. See also *BSD*.

upload To transfer a file to another computer over the Internet.

URL (Uniform Resource Locator) A URL is the address of a specific spot on the Internet. For example, the URL for Apple Computer's home page is www.apple.com.

utility A program that performs a specific task (such as an extensions manager) or supplements the functions of other programs (such as an add-on spelling checker).

V

vector graphics With vector graphics, images are represented as mathematical formulas that define all the shapes in the image. Unlike bitmapped graphics, vector graphics look the same even when you scale them to different sizes. In contrast, bitmapped graphics become ragged when you enlarge them. See also *bitmap*.

Velocity Engine An addition to the PowerPC processor architecture, implemented on the G4 chip. It is built to speed up tasks such as graphics processing, and developers have to write special code to take advantage of it. Also known as *AltiVec*.

virus A malicious program that attaches itself to or replaces another program to reproduce itself, generally without the knowledge of the target computer's user.

W

Web Short for *World Wide Web*.

Wi-Fi Short for *wireless fidelity* and used generically when referring to any IEEE 802.11 network.

window A rectangular, movable display box in a graphical user interface (GUI). Windows can hold documents, folder contents, and applications, among other things.

window buttons The buttons in the top-left corner of a Mac OS X window. The left button (red) is the close button. The middle button (yellow) is the minimize button, which places the file or folder in the Dock. The right button (green) is the zoom button, which makes the window expand to the size of the whole screen (or a reasonable facsimile) or return to its original size.

wizard A help program that guides a user step-by-step through a task, such as the creation of a document or the setting of Internet preferences.

World Wide Web A collection of interconnected servers on the Internet that use the Hypertext Transfer Protocol (HTTP). This allows documents written in Hypertext Markup Language (HTML) to link to other documents and files, so that the viewer can quickly jump from one to another using a browser.

X

Xserve Apple's line of servers.

Z

zoom button The third button from the left in Mac OS X windows, colored green. Clicking the zoom button makes the window expand to the size of the whole screen (or a reasonable facsimile) or return to its original size. See also *window buttons*.

Index

F

X

Z